THE BLACKWELL ENCYCLOPEDIA OF THE
American Revolution

Edited by Jack P. Greene and J.R. Pole

BLACKWELL
Reference

Copyright © Basil Blackwell Ltd 1991, 1994
Editorial organization © Jack P. Greene and J. R. Pole 1991, 1994

First published 1991
First published in paperback 1994
Reprinted in paperback 1994

Blackwell Publishers, the publishing imprint of Basil Blackwell Inc.
238 Main Street
Cambridge, Massachusetts 02142, USA

Basil Blackwell Ltd
108 Cowley Road, Oxford OX4 1JF, UK

Library of Congress Cataloging-in-Publication Data
The Blackwell encyclopedia of the American Revolution / edited by Jack
P. Greene and J. R. Pole.
    p.   cm.
Includes bibliographical references and index.
ISBN 1-55786-244-3
ISBN 1-55786-547-7 (Pbk)
    1. United States—History—Revolution, 1775-1783—Encyclopedias.
I. Greene, Jack P.   II. Pole, J. R. (Jack Richon)
E208.B635   1991
973.3'03—dc20   91-3190
                                                                            CIP

British Library Cataloguing in Publication Data
A CIP catalogue record for this book is available from the British Library.

Typeset in 10 on 11½ pt Photina
Printed in Great Britain by
T. J. Press (Padstow) Ltd, Padstow, Cornwall.

This book is printed on acid-free paper

Contents

CONTENTS

Part 3: Themes and events, from 1776

iv

Part 4: External effects of the Revolution

Part 5: Internal developments after the Revolution

Part 6: Concepts

Part 7: Biographies A–Z

Preface

THE American Revolution was an event of the first importance in the creation of the modern world. The first large-scale anti-colonial revolt in modern history and the first political revolution animated by the concept of progress, it provided the occasion for the creation of the United States and the most extensive and ambitious experiment in republican government up to that time. As students of this event, the editors have long thought that a comprehensive, authoritative, and accessible encyclopedia devoted to that subject would be valuable for the student and the general reader alike. This volume is intended to meet that goal. The seventy-five substantive articles cover all of the major topics related to the Revolution, including its central events, the context in which it occurred, its causes, its effects, and the principal concepts associated with it. Each written by a recognized specialist on the subject, these articles are all informed by the latest scholarship. The volume is rounded out by brief biographies of the more important actors involved in the Revolution and by an extended chronological table.

The editors wish to thank the authors of the articles and biographies and to acknowledge the significant role of the editorial staff in the Reference Department at Blackwell Publishers. The enthusiasm, high competence, and high standards of the staff, most especially, Richard Beatty, the senior desk editor in charge of the project, and Caroline Richmond, the copy editor, have contributed enormously to its timely completion. The editors also wish to thank Professor Ian R. Christie for checking British surnames and titles.

Jack P. Greene
Irvine, California

J. R. Pole
Oxford, UK

18 April 1991

Illustration acknowledgments

The illustrations in this book are reproduced by courtesy of the following: Abby Aldridge Rockefeller Folk Art Center, figure 51; American Philosophical Society Library, figure 23; Arquivo Nacional, Brazil, figure 44; Boston Athenaeum, figure 19c; Bowdoin College Museum of Art, Brunswick, Maine, figure 69; British Library, figure 42; Chase Manhattan Archives, figures 29 and 30c; Chicago Historical Society, figure 32; Clements Library, University of Michigan, Ann Arbor, figure 7; Dover Publications, Inc., New York, figures 11 (from John Grafton, "The American Revolution") and 53 (from "The American Eagle in Art and Design"); Easton Area Public Library, Easton, Pennsylvania, figure 54; Fitzwilliam Museum, Cambridge, figure 21; The Fogg Art Museum, Harvard University, Cambridge, Massachusetts, Louise E. Bettens Fund, figure 37b; Copyright The Frick Collection, New York, figure 59; Guildhall Art Gallery, Corporation of London, figure 60; Historical Pictures, Chicago, figure 20; The Historical Society of Pennsylvania, figure 47b; © 1990 Indianapolis Museum of Art, James E. Roberts Fund, figure 63; The Library Company of Philadelphia, figures 16, 46, 50 and 61; Library of Congress, Washington DC, figures 2, 9, 10, 15, 17, 18, 22, 25, 26, 27, 28, 31, 36, 37a, 39, 40, 45, 52, 66, 67, 71 and 75; Maryland Historical Society, Baltimore, figure 57; Massachusetts Historical Society, figures 1b, 1c, 19d and 34; Museum of Fine Arts, Boston, figures 64 (Bequest of Robert C. Winthrop, Acc. no. 94.167) and 65 (Deposited by the City of Boston, Acc. no. 30.76d); National Archives of Canada, figure 41; National Gallery of Canada, Ottawa. Transfer from the Canadian War Memorials, 1921, figure 58; National Portrait Gallery, London, figures 8 and 43; The New York Historical Society, N.Y.C., figures 13, 19b and 72; The New York Public Library, Astor, Lenox and Tilden Foundations, figures 3, 38 (Rare Books and Manuscripts Division), 30a (Thomas Addis Emmet Collection, Rare Books and Manuscripts Division) and 35 (I.N. Phelps Stokes Collection, Miriam & Ira D. Wallach Division of Art, Prints and Photographs); New York State Historical Association, Cooperstown, figure 56; The Pennsylvania Academy of the Fine Arts, Philadelphia, figures 70 (Bequest of Richard Ashhurst) and 73 (Gift of Mrs Sarah Harrison. The Joseph Harrison, Jr. Collection); Private Collection/photo Scottish National Portrait Gallery, Edinburgh, figure 1a; The Rhode Island Historical Society, figures 14 and 30b; from Albert E. Van Dusen, "Connecticut", Random House, New York, 1961, figure 47a; Virginia Museum of Fine Arts, Richmond, Gift of David K.E. Bruce, figure 24; Washington/Custis/Lee Collection, Washington and Lee University, Lexington, Virginia, figure 74; Winterthur Museum, figures 49 (Gift of Mrs Julia B. Henry) and 62; Yale University Art Gallery, figures 48 and 68; Yale University Library, Harold Wickliffe Rose Papers, Manuscripts and Archives, figures 5a and 5b.

Picture research by Helen Ottaway

Every effort has been made by the publishers to trace the copyright holders of all illustrations in this publication. However, if copyright has been infringed, we will be pleased, on being satisfied as to the owner's title, to make proper acknowledgment in future editions.

Cover illustration: *Washington and his generals at Yorktown* (*c.* 1781], by Charles Willson Peale (1741–1827). The Marquis de La Fayette stands to Washington's right, and the Comte de Rochambeau to his immediate left. (Collection of the Maryland Historical Society).

Maps and map acknowledgments

Note: A contemporary map of the West Indies is reproduced as figure 42 (page 509).

The editors are grateful to the contributors for their help in preparing the maps. In addition, they would like to acknowledge the following sources for permission to adapt copyright material, as follows:

Map 1: Redrawn from page 41 of Lester J. Cappon (ed.) *Atlas of Early American History: The Revolutionary Era 1760–1790* (Copyright © Princeton University Press, 1976); Maps 3–6: Redrawn from Don Higginbotham *The War of American Independence* (copyright © Macmillan Publishing Company, New York, 1971), with additions and modifications; Map 7: Modified from Peter S. Onuf *Origins of the Federal Republic* (Philadelphia, 1983), based upon pages 16, 17 and 62 of *Atlas of American History: The Revolutionary Era 1760–1790*.

Contributors

John Algeo
University of Georgia

David L. Ammerman
Florida State University

Joyce Appleby
University of California, Los Angeles

Robert A. Becker
Louisiana State University

Richard R. Beeman
University of Pennsylvania

Ruth H. Bloch
University of California, Los Angeles

Colin Bonwick
University of Keele

R. Arthur Bowler
State University of New York at Buffalo

Maurice J. Bric
University College Dublin

Stuart Bruchey
Columbia University

Robert M. Calhoon
University of North Carolina at Greensboro

E. Wayne Carp
Pacific Lutheran University

Selwyn H. H. Carrington
University of the West Indies, St. Augustine, Trinidad

Robert J. Chaffin
University of Wisconsin, Oshkosh

Ian R. Christie
University College London

Thomas Cole
Hollins College, Roanoke, Virginia

Stephen A. Conrad
Indiana University, Bloomington

David W. Conroy
Alliance of Independent Scholars

Edward Countryman
University of Warwick

Murray Dry
Middlebury College, Vermont

Jonathan R. Dull
The Papers of Benjamin Franklin, Yale University Library

Clyde R. Ferguson
Kansas State University

E. James Ferguson
Queens College, Flushing, New York

Mary E. Fissell
University of Manchester

Milton E. Flower
Carlisle, Pennsylvania

Alan Freeman
State University of New York at Buffalo

Sylvia R. Frey
Tulane University

Jack Fruchtman, Jr.
Towson State University

Edwin S. Gaustad
University of California, Riverside

David P. Geggus
University of Florida

Eliga H. Gould
Baltimore, Maryland

Norman S. Grabo
University of Tulsa

Jack P. Greene
University of California, Irvine

Ira D. Gruber
Rice University

Ronald Hamowy
University of Alberta

Don Higginbotham
University of North Carolina at Chapel Hill

Ronald Hoffman
University of Maryland at College Park

Herbert A. Johnson
University of South Carolina

Mark D. Kaplanoff
Pembroke College, Cambridge

Lee Kennett
University of Georgia

Craig Evan Klafter
University of Manchester

James T. Kloppenberg
Brandeis University

Isaac Kramnick
Cornell University

Douglas Edward Leach
Vanderbilt University

J. A. Leo Lemay
University of Delaware

Jan Lewis
Rutgers University, Newark

Donald S. Lutz
University of Houston

Grant E. Mabie
Oseola, Indiana

Elizabeth P. McCaughey
Center for the Study of the Presidency

Katherine M. J. McKenna
Queen's University, Kingston, Canada

x

Bruce H. Mann
University of Pennsylvania

Elise Marienstras
Institute Charles V, Université de Paris VII

Peter Marshall
University of Manchester

Clonna Matthews
Stanford University

Kenneth Maxwell
Camões Center, Columbia University

Elizabeth Mensch
State University of New York at Buffalo

James H. Merrell
Vassar College, Poughkeepsie, New York

Frederick V. Mills Sr.
LaGrange College, Georgia

Kurt W. Nagel
Baltimore, Maryland

James H. O'Donnell III
Marietta College, Ohio

Alison G. Olson
University of Maryland at College Park

Peter S. Onuf
University of Virginia

William Pencak
Pennsylvania State University, Ogontz

Edwin J. Perkins
University of Southern California

J. R. Pole
St Catherine's College, Oxford

Jim Potter
Institute of United States Studies, London

Jack N. Rakove
Stanford University

G. A. Rawlyk
Queen's University, Kingston, Canada

John P. Reid
New York University

Hans Rogger
University of California, Los Angeles

Michal J. Rozbicki
American Studies Center, Warsaw University

Robert A. Rutland
University of Tulsa

Steven J. Sarson
Baltimore, Maryland

Jan Willem Schulte Nordholt
University of Leiden

Robert E. Shalhope
University of Oklahoma

Peter Shaw
New York, NY

Richard K. Showman
Rhode Island Historical Society

R. C. Simmons
University of Birmingham

W. A. Speck
University of Leeds

Rebecca Starr
Cheltenham and Gloucester College of Higher Education

Ian K. Steele
University of Western Ontario

Peter D. G. Thomas
University College of Wales, Aberystwyth

J. Mark Thompson
Chapel Hill, North Carolina

Alan Tully
University of British Columbia

Mary Gwaltney Vaz
Cincinnati, Ohio

Maurice J. C. Vile
Canterbury, Kent

Robert V. Wells
Union College, Schenectady, New York

Franklin B. Wickwire
University of Massachusetts, Amherst

Betty Wood
Girton College, Cambridge

Melvyn Yazawa
University of New Mexico

Stephen A. Young
Baltimore, Maryland

Rosemarie Zagarri
Catholic University of America

Introduction

JACK P. GREENE AND J. R. POLE

THE American Revolution was many different events. It not only looked different, but was differently experienced, from the points of view of a wide variety of active participants on both sides of the Atlantic; it presented sudden opportunities – of business profits, political and legal office, and military promotions – to the more enterprising, public spirited, or opportunistic; but its anguish and travail represented experiences of a different kind for innumerable passive participants who were caught up in and affected, more or less willingly, by its passage. In planning this *Encyclopedia* we have tried to do justice to these varieties, which are as much conceptual as experiential, and which therefore involve an ordering of concepts as well as an account of events.

CONTEXT

The political framework in which Britain's North American and Caribbean colonies developed with such rapidity in the eighteenth century was itself a crucial ingredient of the problem. We therefore begin with the structure of British politics and pass to the administration of the colonies from the point of view of the metropolitan authorities. The policies pursued by these British governments, looking at the colonies as integral but subordinate parts of a vast and scattered empire, were determined by certain preconceptions, in which British interests undoubtedly played a dominant part; and in the course of time, and of colonial economic, geographical and demographic development, they came into conflict with an increasingly aroused colonial consciousness of increasingly distinct colonial interests.

These interests, however, were so widely dispersed and so various in kind that they had very little natural inclination to see themselves as a unity. Articles on the economic and strategic importance of the colonies to the empire itself – an importance which controlled imperial policy but was of no small significance to the colonies themselves – on colonial political and demographic development, on the varieties of religious experience and on the growth of a colonial culture, are designed to give explanations of all these aspects of American development within the overall imperial framework. It was this framwork that provided the colonies with their own basic unities, enabled them to identify their problems in a common language of rights and resistance and eventually to form a common cause. But we do not wish to convey an impression that we use words like "framework" or "context" in an unimaginatively rigid sense. In all history, "context" must itself be understood as a developmental concept; and in the period of the American Revolution we are dealing with a constantly changing context, made all the more complicated by the fact that one or another of the ingredients often changes faster than or in different directions from others.

CHRONOLOGY

From this frame of reference we pass to the chronology of events, under which heading we begin with the detailed workings of British policies and colonial reactions. On both sides of the rising dispute, on opposite sides of the Atlantic, the situation was complicated by differences of opinion and interest, in turn reflected in widely differing perceptions of the meaning of events. This was nowhere more apparent than in the motives people on different sides attributed to each other. American colonists accused the British authorities of tyranny; the British bitterly resented what they regarded as American ingratitude. But in Britain itself, a new wave of radicals saw their own cause represented by American resistance, while some colonial spokesmen identified themselves with the interests of British radicals. But there were also influential and experienced elements in colonial politics, often in historic positions of authority, who felt threatened by the rise of a revolutionary movement in their own provinces and sought to contain the protest within the bounds of formal political discourse. American interests were also complicated by their latent hostility to the indigenous population, whom the British were more inclined to regard as objects of imperial protection.

We have divided the chronological sections at the Declaration of Independence. From that point onwards the revolt becomes a revolution and the course of American events passes definitively into American hands. There was much for the new authorities to attend to, on many different fronts: there was, in the first instance, an army to maintain, and a war to fight; but fighting included finance and every form of economic mobilization; the responsibilities of the Continental Congress included the opening up of a new field of European diplomacy requiring the care and attention of men with no such experience, and who in most cases had never been further from home than Philadelphia. But most of the responsibility for domestic government fell to the states, which asserted their sovereignty in the loose code of continental government which, after years of foot-dragging, was established in 1781 in the Articles of Confederation. Essays under the appropriate headings deal extensively with developments in the states, from constitution-making to social attitudes and policies affecting church and state, education, poverty and crime, legal reform and slavery. Much of the wealth of the American colonies rested on the labor of slaves, already an intricate institution sustained by laws and codes of conduct. It would be a grievous error to suppose that the concept of republican government depends on a necessary basis of slave labor; but the prosperity which sustained the practice of republican government in the Chesapeake and southern colonies did rest on slave labor, as contemporaries well knew, whether they lived in those colonies or further north. The paradox occupied many minds in that generation. Both the institution of slavery and the rise of anti-slavery find their place in the pages that follow.

The Confederation achieved more than it has sometimes been given credit for, but in the opinion of many well-placed observers it was unequal to the manifold problems of continental government. The rise of the movement that led to the Constitutional Convention, the making of the Constitution and the subsequent passage of the Bill of Rights by the first Congress of the United States complete the chronological sections.

EXTERNAL EFFECTS

No one made the mistake of imagining that an event as politically and ideologically repercussive as the American Revolution could be contained within American shores. Independence had depended vitally on French naval and military intervention as well as on French and Dutch finance. French soldiers and a number of their ecclesiastical and intellectual contemporaries had seen republican government in action and they took that experience home with them. But the external effects of the Revolution can be understood only in the context of the circumstances and histories of the different countries it affected. There could be no worse mistake than to generalize these effects into a crudely Americanized view of the domestic future of the world beyond America. The consequences were felt in spheres as diverse as the Spanish and Portuguese empires, the British slave holding colonies in the West Indies, in Ireland, Canada and in the nations of continental Europe; and often the effects within any one of these spheres were themselves diverse. We have sought to cover all these areas with appropriate geographical breadth while doing justice to the intricacy of the local scene in each case. We have represented the world-wide consequences of the Revolution but have not sought to interpret them in any immediate sense as world-wide revolutionary consequences.

INTERNAL DEVELOPMENTS

The different societies of the colonies were not only in states of development, but in many cases, of differing types of development, in the generation before they were overtaken by the War of Independence. When the breach with Britain seemed inevitable, no one could be sure what it would mean for the colonies themselves. This uncertainty was a cause of profound apprehension in some circles, of equally exalted hope in others. The questions associated with the internal consequences of Independence are among the most complex and difficult in the study of the period; they can only be explained in connection with developments that were already taking place in colonial society, but it is inherently difficult to separate these from the precipitating effects of war, economic and military mobilization, and the need for new governments – to mention only a few of the issues. The effects of Independence ranged through such diverse themes as the heightened level of American national consciousness, and medical, technical, educational and legal advances, arising from immediate needs as well as from an invigorated republican ideology; they also extended to the gradually evolving concept of the new role required of women in a republic, and, after the failure of the Articles of Confederation to provide adequate governmental power, eventuated (if indirectly) in the creation of a new national Constitution. In assigning topics which encompass all these and other themes, we have sought to recognize both their diversity and their tendency to overlap one another. This section, more than any other, provides the materials and the arguments for the debate on the essence of the Revolution and what kind of revolution it was. In its own time it certainly looked revolutionary to many who were involved or who observed it. The historical perspective was shifted when it was soon overtaken by the French Revolution, which dramatically changed the whole concept. Yet that earth-shaking event may itself be considered, in no small part, as an *external* effect of the American Revolution.

CONCEPTS

As historians have sought to create in their own and their readers' minds a framework for the understanding of the American Revolution, which was very much the greatest event of its kind of which people at that time had any knowledge, they have had to recapture a conceptual world which has passed into the distance of history. This way of arranging the past itself reflects the fact that the Revolution was in large measure created by systems of thought. Men – for it was men who made these events – had developed sets of ideas associated with their forms of law and government, religion and property. For the most part, although these ideas can be generalized at a speculative level, they were rooted in very familiar ways of life. The liberties men valued were the liberties they were accustomed to, and the same was true of their institutions, such as those of political representation.

These concepts, of Liberty, Equality, Property, the Rule of Law and others, make an important contribution to our own attempt to understand the issues at stake for the Americans and for their British rivals because they played such important parts in the conceptual world of the period. It is only natural that many of them overlap with each other and often represent slightly different perspectives on similar principles, values and ideals. We have ascribed a separate essay to each of the main concepts, as we see them, and although each contributor has seen the subject in his or her own way, and we have made no attempt to impose a set of preconceived principles, we believe that these broad structures of ideas can best be understood within the context of the life of the institutions which embodied them in practice.

BIOGRAPHIES

The Revolution was made by people. They acted in ways that derived from their experiences, their circumstances and the conceptual framework of their world. And, of course, they acted collectively. But no encyclopedia would be complete without biographical information about the individuals whose personal decisions made the events of the time.

The more prominent actors select themselves. No explanation is needed for the inclusion of George Washington or Lord North in an *Encyclopedia of the American Revolution*. But the editors have sought to reach for more than a conventional history, or collection of histories, of the making of events. Revolutions and wars are usually supposed to be of some benefit to the common people, but the common people usually remain unnoticed in the background. We observed above that the Revolution was *experienced* by many people – a majority, if it comes to that – who did very little to contribute to it, and many of whom undoubtedly felt that they had little at stake. Some of these people survive in journals and relatively obscure records, while other more active participants survive in folk memories as well as in formal documents. Because this is particularly true of women, who not only experienced the Revolution in the passive sense, but whose work was indispensable to the man-made world of war and politics, we have tried to recapture this dimension in a large number of short biographical sketches of relatively obscure women.

It is relevant to the recreation of the social psychology of the period to observe that this dimension was not very adequately appreciated; nor did it find much of a place in political philosophy. It is not easy to reconstruct more than a few fragments of the detail of the lives of individual women, but much can be inferred from what we know of the household, and the churches; moreover, a surprisingly large number of small businesses were run by women, as advertisements in the mid-century colonial newspapers testify. If some of our entries are pathetically brief, they play their part as representing – in the best sense of the word – one half of the population, most of whom are buried from historical sight. We would also recall our comment about experience; men only too often made events which women experienced. That experience is itself a part of the history of the American Revolution, and we have tried in places to capture it here.

PART I
CONTEXT

I

The structure of British politics in the mid-eighteenth century

W. A. SPECK

THE American Revolutionaries found it hard to put their fingers on the causes of their discontents. Where was the responsibility to be placed for the policies which sought to make them pay taxes without representation in the British Parliament? At first they blamed factions, cliques of ministers from George Grenville's ministry to Lord North's, whom they accused of taking a leaf out of Lord Bute's book by seeking to impose their allegedly unconstitutional views on Parliament and the Crown. Appeals to the legislature and to the King were consequently made to open their eyes to the machinations of these ministers. When these failed then Parliament itself was held to be the culprit. A body composed of a decadent aristocracy and a corrupt and unrepresentative Commons had arrogated unwarranted powers to itself. Addresses were therefore sent to the King to act as honest broker between the Houses and the colonies. Finally, when these too were unavailing, the Declaration of Independence laid the blame squarely on the shoulders of George III himself. The ultimate appeal was to British public opinion, to the majority of George III's subjects who should have been sympathetic to a just cause. Since they refused to be convinced, then a virtuous republic was fully justified in breaking away from a vicious monarchy.

Such contemporary confusion about the location of power in mid-eighteenth-century Britain demonstrates the complexity of its political structure. For the bodies held accountable for American woes – the Crown, factions, Parliament, and public opinion – all played a role in the functioning of the system. The problem now, as then, is to ascertain their relative significance.

I. THE MONARCHY

Constitutionally, Britain was a monarchy. Moreover, its monarchs were required to rule as well as to reign. It was not until the nineteenth century that the Crown made the transition from being an efficient part to becoming merely a dignified element of the constitution. In theory the monarchs directed all the affairs of the state. The Hanoverians still enjoyed the most essential prerogatives of their Stuart predecessors. Thus they appointed and dismissed ministers, summoned and dissolved Parliament, and declared war and made peace. Even in theory, however, they did not enjoy these prerogatives unreservedly. They were not absolute monarchs. Rather, limited monarchy was held to have been established in the Revolution Settlement of 1689. Where absolute monarchs were responsible to God alone, limited monarchs were accountable to Parliament.

Mixed monarchy was theoretically a balanced constitution wherein the three estates

3

of Crown, Lords, and Commons were held in perfect equilibrium. Together they offset the tendency of each estate to arrogate more power to itself when it ruled singly. Thus the Lords and the Commons countered the Crown's aspirations towards tyranny; the Crown and the Commons countered the Lords' inclinations towards oligarchy; and the Crown and the Lords offset the Commons' tendency towards anarchy.

2. THE HOUSES OF PARLIAMENT

While the notion that the House of Lords represented the hereditary peerage was qualified by the presence there of 26 spiritual lords, the bishops of the Church of England, and, after the union with Scotland of 1707, the 16 Scottish peers elected by the noblemen of the northern kingdom, the regular summoning of about 160 titular peers of the realm – barons, viscounts, earls, marquises, and dukes – meant that the Upper House was largely a hereditary body. But the concept that the Lower House represented 'the Commons' strikes twentieth-century students as odd. The electoral system fell far short of enfranchising every adult male, let alone female. The highest estimate is that, about 1700, one in four men had the right to vote. Subsequently the growth of population and the actual erosion of the franchise in some constituencies reduced the proportion of enfranchised adults quite significantly, particularly by contrast with the American colonies, where between a half and four-fifths of white adult males could vote. Another development occurring during the first half of the eighteenth century which further qualified the claims of the Lower House to represent the Commons in general was the growth of oligarchy. The process whereby many small boroughs became progressively subject to the influence of patrons led to an increase in the number of members who were nominated by magnates rather than chosen by electors. As early as the general election of 1734 it became clear that the electorate as such enjoyed a genuine choice only in the minority of constituencies – counties and cities – with more than 500 voters, where the extension of influence could be resisted.

3. RELATIONS BETWEEN PARLIAMENT AND THE CROWN

In practice, parliamentary limitations on the Crown were not usually irksome. There were statutory restrictions on the powers of appointment and the dissolution of Parliament. For example, judges could only be appointed on good behavior and not at the pleasure of the Crown, so that they could not be dismissed arbitrarily. Again, the maximum interval between general elections was limited in 1694 to three years, which restricted the prerogative of dissolution. However, in 1716 the interval was lengthened to seven years, which greatly eased the restriction. Besides Acts of Parliament, conventions developed after the Revolution which made the monarchy more dependent upon Parliament. Thus the practice of laying treaties before the Houses for their approval was established. Annual sessions also date from 1689. No legislation necessitated these practices. It was the absolute necessity to have Parliament meet in order to vote supplies to sustain the unprecedented burden of war finance incurred in the conflict with Louis XIV which led to their adoption. It also became a convention, after the last use of the power by Queen Anne in 1708, that the monarch should not veto bills passed by both Houses.

Yet the Hanoverians did not allow the veto to lapse out of constitutional necessity. It atrophied because they found they did not need to use it. Their ability to influence the outcome of proceedings in Parliament was considerable, making resort to the vetoing of legislation unnecessary.

The Lords Over the Lords, the Crown had virtual control throughout the early Hanoverian era. Although the first two Georges had in reserve the power to create peers for political purposes, unlike Queen Anne they did not exercise it, largely because they wished to preserve the elite status of the peerage, but partly because they were under no pressure to do so. The 16 elected Scottish peers were almost always those whom the government backed in the elections. The appeal of court patronage was a strong inducement to the impoverished nobility of Scotland to vote for the side which buttered their bread. Again, the 26 bishops who sat in the Upper House had all, by 1750, been preferred by George II or his father. These 42 spiritual and Scottish peers gave the Crown a sizable bloc vote in a House which numbered little more than 200 all told. Moreover most of the key ministerial posts went to peers, creating more dependents in the Upper House. Any nobleman ambitious to progress up the ladder of the aristocracy from baron to duke would think twice about risking his family's future by opposing the wishes of the Crown.

Not that the Upper House was puppet theater, with the strings manipulated by the kings. The Scottish contingent could refuse to cooperate if they thought that the interests of Scotland were threatened. Likewise the bishops could prove difficult if they felt the Church to be in danger. Individual lords could be the most independent of politicians. The journals of the House of Lords bear frequent testimony to the occasions when a minority in a division used their right to enter a protest in the official record. Moreover, the practice of proxy voting meant that it did not require a large attendance to mobilize opposition to the court. The Crown had therefore to tread carefully to avoid ruffling the prejudices of the peers. It could not treat the Upper Chamber as a rubber stamp. Nevertheless its influence over the House of Lords was sufficient to make problems of parliamentary management less formidable there than in the Commons. Often measures were allowed to pass the Lower House so that they could be stifled in the Upper, to avoid an embarrassing defeat in the elected Chamber.

The Commons Even over the Lower House the Crown had formidable influence. Many members of Parliament were offered, and accepted, posts in the administration. Some were major offices of state, such as the chancellorship of the exchequer or the attorney generalship, while others were sinecures. The numbers of MPs who were "placemen," as the occupants of such posts were called, varied, growing from about a quarter to over a third of the House during the early eighteenth century. To these might be added those members chosen with the help of the government in their boroughs. The court had considerable influence over the 45 tiny constituencies in Scotland, most of whose members supported the ministry in Parliament. Several small English boroughs also returned members with the assistance of the government, for example Harwich, where the Post Office employed many voters in its packet boat service to the Continent, or Queensborough and Rochester in Kent, where nearby military and naval installations gave the Admiralty and the War Office major interests.

Contemporary critics claimed that the systematic exploitation of its patronage, amounting to corruption, created for the court a built-in majority in the Commons. The promotion of MPs to places procured a well-drilled army of members ready to obey orders from the ministers, while the exploitation of the government's interest in elections reduced many boroughs with under 500 voters, which comprised over half the constituencies, to returning representatives of the court rather than of the Commons. Thus although opposition candidates trounced government supporters in the counties and cities, where electors numbered thousands, they were offset by those returned for the corrupt boroughs.

Such critics overstated their case. Not all MPs who accepted places became automatic lobby fodder, nor did their numbers ever amount to an overall majority. As for bribing voters, the government's direct electoral interest was restricted to a handful of boroughs. It was the court's cultivation of borough patrons which procured it a majority of seats in the smaller constituencies. Many noblemen and country gentlemen maintained electoral interests in local boroughs. The relationship between these patrons and the burgesses was sustained by a variety of means. In some it was merely a crude use of power, whereby landlords would turn out tenants who polled against candidates whom they had recommended, or refuse to deal with tradesmen who did likewise. But this was exceptional. The normal pattern was one of deference to the wishes of a social superior, provided he solicited the favor and did not demand it. Such deference sprang from a deeply hierarchical view of society. It was not just a duty owed by social inferiors to their superiors but required reciprocal duties too, being upheld by a subtle interdependence. The country house on the outskirts of a parliamentary borough engendered myriad social and economic links between the two communities. One was that the owner of the house would procure advantages for his neighbors as well as requiring obligations. Employment in the large households of peers or country gentlemen for the sons and daughters of neighboring burgesses was one way in which the relationship could be cemented. And Crown patronage was another. Local positions of all kinds were in the gift of the Crown, from deputy lieutenancies in the county militias and places on the commissions of the peace, which usually were bestowed on gentlemen, to posts in the revenue administration, such as gaugers in the excise. The judicious disposal of such places of status or of profit to the clients of noblemen and gentry in the localities could clinch their interests in parliamentary boroughs on the side of the government. In order to retain control of the Commons, therefore, ministers had to appeal to members other than the placemen or representatives of government boroughs. Traditionally they had done so since the accession of George I by forging a link with the Whig Party. The Whigs had upheld the Protestant succession in the House of Hanover against Tories, whom they accused of supporting the exiled House of Stuart. However much truth there might have been in the charge that the Tories were Jacobites, by 1750 there was really very little if any substance left in it. After the suppression of the Jacobite rebellion of 1745 it could be assumed that almost all active politicians were pro-Hanoverian. Although the terms Whig and Tory were still in use, neither side concerted their activities any more in a united party. The religious issues which had polarized them under Queen Anne were no longer as divisive. Under Queen Anne the Tories were known as the Church party because of their championing of the Church of England against Protestant dissenting sects such as the Presbyterians and the Independents. The Whigs, by contrast, upheld the claims of dissent against the Established Church. While most dissenters continued to support the Whigs under the early Hanoverians, time and time-serving caused many Anglicans to transfer their allegiance from the Tories to their rivals. Certainly by 1760 the Tory Party was not the Church party of the closing years of Anne's reign. Where on her death the incoming monarch had been in a position to choose between two parties, on the demise of George II his grandson George III cannot be said to have been in a comparable situation.

4. POLITICAL FACTIONS AROUND 1750

At one level the state of affairs in the 1750s and 1760s can be seen as a choice between a number of connections. These were groups of politicians held together by kinship ties and electoral interests. For example, the Bedford connection, led by the fourth Duke of Bedford, included Lord Gower, to whom he was related, and MPs returned from constituencies such as Bedford, Lichfield, and Tavistock, where the two lords had family interests. Those associated with such interests tended to dominate debates in both Houses of Parliament. All told, they composed a small coterie of peers and politicians well known to each other. Their world was a small one, dominated by an aristocratic oligarchy. Politics at this level was a game between a small number of players; the kings, who were participants and not referees, much less spectators; the heads of connections which were in office; and the leaders of those who were struggling to get in.

Yet to see the political system as one confined to the "outs" against the "ins" is to take too narrow a view of politics. This was the mistake which the American colonists made when they brought themselves to believe that factions were at the root of their troubles. They soon learned that the parameters of the problem extended beyond the interplay of factions to Parliament itself. Alongside the placemen and the political connections was an amorphous mass of members who were independent in the sense that they owed neither a post to the government nor their seats to patrons. These included knights of the shires and the members for cities and large boroughs. Usually they were prepared to uphold the government of the day, since opposition was still regarded as disloyal. Opposition politicians had their work cut out to convince them to oppose the court. Conventional ploys were to try to persuade them that the ministry was intent on subverting fundamental liberties, either through corruption or the growth of a standing army. Occasionally they were presented with issues which could be turned to the government's disadvantage. The excise crisis of 1733, wherein Walpole miscalculated that he could persuade the Commons to replace the customs duties on tobacco and wine by inland duties, was the most celebrated of such episodes before the Stamp Act crisis of 1765–6. Since many independents represented large constituencies, pressure could be brought to bear upon them from their constituents. Thus addresses against the Excise Bill and the Stamp Act were organized to persuade these members to oppose these measures. In each case outside pressure was instrumental in obtaining the withdrawal of parliamentary support for them. By the middle of the eighteenth century the techniques of organizing constituency campaigns to pressurize the independent members of Parliament were quite advanced. Since the final lapsing of the state censorship in 1695 the press had developed a nationwide network of communications which politicians were able to exploit. London boasted a number of newspapers – daily, tri-weekly, and weekly. Provincial towns also printed their own papers, some carrying two or even three. The main centers for these organs were precisely the kind of large parliamentary constituency whose representatives were sensitive to electoral pressure, such as Bristol, Newcastle-upon-Tyne, Norwich, and York. The first politician effectively to mobilize this network on behalf of a political campaign was John Wilkes.

By the accession of George III, therefore, there were two political structures in Britain. One was the restricted society of aristocratic connections, based for the most part on electoral interests in small boroughs, which made eighteenth-century politics appear so oligarchic. The other was the community of counties and large cities opened up by the development of the press and of turnpike roads, which was responsive to political campaigns such as that orchestrated by the Wilkites. The American colonists were to appeal first to the traditional political structure, then to the alternative to it which had emerged by the reign of George III. Apart from the successful campaign to repeal the Stamp Act, their appeals to both were to be in vain until after the battle of Yorktown.

FURTHER READING

Brewer, J.: *Party Ideology and Popular Politics at the Accession of George III* (Cambridge: Cambridge University Press, 1976).

Clark, J. C. D.: *The Dynamics of Change: the Crisis of the 1750s and English Party Systems* (Cambridge: Cambridge University Press, 1982).

Colley, L.: *In Defiance of Oligarchy: the Tory Party, 1714–1760* (Cambridge: Cambridge University Press, 1982).

Cruickshanks, E.: *Political Untouchables: the Tories and the 'Forty-five* (London: Duckworth, 1979).

Namier, L. B.: *The Structure of Politics at the Accession of George III* (London: Macmillan, 1957).

O'Gorman, F.: *Voters, Patrons and Parties: the Unreformed Electorate of Hanoverian England, 1734–1832* (Oxford: Clarendon Press, 1989).

Rogers, N.: *Whigs and Cities: Popular Politics in the Age of Walpole and Pitt* (Oxford: Clarendon Press, 1989).

Speck, W. A.: *The Butcher: the Duke of Cumberland and the Suppression of the 'Forty-five* (Oxford: Blackwell, 1981).

2

Metropolitan administration of the colonies, 1696–1775

IAN K. STEELE

T HE structure of British imperial administration altered little during the 80 years between 1696 and 1775, but political developments changed policies as well as office-holders and altered the relative importance of the various offices involved in colonial affairs. Basic assumptions, to protect metropolitan power in the colonies and to encourage colonial trades through England, were established long before 1700 and remained intact, but specific controls and their enforcement varied considerably. The Board of Trade brought thoroughness and creativity to colonial administration for a brief period after its foundation in 1696, but initiative subsequently passed to the Secretaries of State, who had many other responsibilities. The Duke of Newcastle held this post for 25 years, focusing on patronage rather than policy, and establishing colonial expectations of delegated power that would later be challenged. The change to a more vigorous British governance of the empire began before the Seven Years' War. The increasing role of the British Treasury and Parliament in governing the colonies after 1760, presaged in the Molasses Act, affected policy in ways that were central to the coming of the American Revolution.

Government of the colonies remained formally the King's business during these 80 years, though his executive power was delegated to royal officials and compromised by the increasing role of Parliament and colonial assemblies. The metropolitan administration of the empire included several departments, headed by major officers of state, who also had power in the Privy Council and the Cabinet. These departments had some direct colonial responsibilities, and developed a growing number of patronage positions in England and the colonies that became networks of influence. Routines, traditions, and precedents developed within the departments, enhancing the power of departmental secretaries, under-secretaries, and clerks, while masking the ignorance or inattention of some political appointees whom they served.

I. THE PRIVY COUNCIL

The monarch appointed and replaced governors of royal colonies, issued royal proclamations, assented to legislation of Parliament affecting the empire, and heard petitions from myriad groups and individuals. These functions were performed by the King's Privy Council, after receiving political, administrative, legal, or strategic advice from within the government. Although it had lost executive power to the great officers of state, the royal Privy Council remained the official registry of decisions, called Orders-in-Council, on many imperial questions. Revival of a standing Privy Council committee on colonial affairs in 1714 was an initiative which added another stage of deliberation in many disputes. The Privy Council remained the final court of legal appeal for substantial colonial cases throughout the colonial period.

2. THE BOARD OF TRADE

The Lords Commissioners of Trade and Plantations, usually called the Board of Trade, was the center of routine colonial administration from its founding in 1696. This office inherited the functions, but not the power, of a standing Privy Council committee of similar name, and reported to the Privy Council through the Secretary of State.

The Board of Trade prepared the commissions and instructions for royal governors, which evolved quickly and then ossified as formal and increasingly outdated assertions of royal prerogative. It corresponded with governors regularly and received additional information from royal officials, colonial councils, and assemblies, as well as petitioners and lobbyists. It encouraged colonial governments to appoint official agents to expedite their affairs in Whitehall, and it became a forum for agents and conflicting interests seeking government support or protection. While much of its work became reactive and routine, the Board did initiate policies, such as its early wars on piracy and proprietary government, and the later control of appointments under the Earl of Halifax.

3. THE SECRETARY OF STATE

The Secretaries of State were a decisive influence on the personnel and policies of colonial administration in the first half of the eighteenth century. In addition to wide-ranging diplomatic and military responsibilities, the Secretary of State for the Southern Department was the senior royal executive officer who reported to the Cabinet and the Privy Council concerning the colonies and issued resulting orders in the monarch's name. The Duke of Newcastle's long term of office (1724–48) demonstrated a pre-occupation with patronage rather than policy in colonial administration. William Pitt the elder used that same office between 1756 and 1761 to dominate the government and direct the military conduct of the Seven Years' War.

A separate Secretary of State for the Colonies was established in 1768, giving cabinet rank to the Earl of Hillsborough, who also continued as President of the Board of Trade. In both capacities he advocated rigorous enforcement of legal controls over the colonies (see HILL, WILLS). His successor, the Earl of Dartmouth (1772–5), was more flexible but less diligent, leaving many of the details of policy preparation and enforcement to his under-secretaries, John Pownall and William Knox, (see LEGGE, WILLIAM, GERMAIN, LORD GEORGE, and KNOX, WILLIAM).

4. THE ADMIRALTY

The Admiralty Board, chaired by its "First Lord," provided convoys for the colonial trades and royal navy "guardships" on colonial station to protect the colonies against enemies and pirates and to enforce the Acts of Trade. The permanent squadron at Jamaica (1695) and the naval bases at Antigua (1731) and Halifax (1749) expanded the regular naval strength available in America. The institution of vice-admiralty courts in the colonies created expeditious but arbitrary courts which decided whether ships captured from enemies were legal prize. These courts, without juries, also settled disputes between ship masters and crewmen and tried violations of the Acts of Trade.

The Admiralty issued letters of marque to legalize privateers and Mediterranean passes to protect colonial merchant ships from Barbary corsairs, and provided the final court of appeal in maritime cases – the High Court of Admiralty. The Admiralty and its subsidiary Navy Board also encouraged subsidies for colonial pitch, tar, and turpentine, as well as more contentious measures to reserve colonial trees suitable as masts for the Royal Navy, and to force British and colonial merchant seamen to serve in naval vessels.

5. THE TREASURY

The Treasury collected English and colonial customs duties, postal revenues, and royal dues. Its Board of Customs Commissioners supervised collectors and comptrollers of customs in English and colonial ports, as well as overseeing the oddly titled "naval officers" who became bonded recorders of ship movements in colonial ports. Customs officers in America were supervised directly by two traveling Surveyors General of Colonial Customs. The General Post Office was also under the Treasury, though significant revenues were never received from the colonial Postmasters-General. However, the Post Office built a self-funding service in British America that improved communications within the empire. Royal revenues collected from the colonies were examined by another agent of the Treasury, the Surveyor and Auditor General of Plantations Revenues.

The greatest power of the Treasury was control over government payments, including salaries and contract purchases. This often equalled an effective veto of projects already apparently approved; the minister who controlled the Treasury was usually the Prime Minister. The Seven Years' War (1756–63) brought massive British expenditures in the colonies and increasing Treasury scrutiny of colonial currency laws and wartime expenses of colonial governments, a portion of which the British Government agreed to repay. The Treasury's role in colonial policy increased markedly thereafter, focusing on colonial taxation.

6. PARLIAMENT

Parliament's vital role in colonial administration was exemplified in the last of the Navigation Acts, passed in 1696. These acts, initially passed between 1651 and 1673, had evolved to exclude foreign shipping from the colonial trades and to ensure that major colonial products, led by sugar and tobacco, would be initially exported to England, where these had a monopoly but were subject to revenue-generating import duties. These duties, ultimately paid by English consumers of colonial luxuries, were by far the largest "colonial revenues." Parliament protected this imperial trade system, but was usually resistant to other administrative efforts to tighten imperial control before 1763. Parliament's own rise to power at the expense of the Crown in the seventeenth century became a model for the rise of colonial assemblies against their governors in the eighteenth century. The Seven Years' War transformed the role of Parliament, which thereafter legitimized Treasury initiatives to raise revenues in the colonies.

7. OFFICERS IN THE COLONIES

The Governor was the civil and military head of a colonial government throughout this period, though his freedom of action was gradually eroded both by the colonial assemblies and by London administrators. The Governor was both the royal representative and the civil and military head of local government (*see* figure 1). Other royal officers appointed from London included the Lieutenant-Governor, Secretary, Attorney-General, Deputy Auditor, Naval Officer, and Customs Collector. The appointed Council in royal colonies, usually manned by a dozen prominent colonists, served as a legislative upper house, the highest court in the colony, and executive advisory group to the Governor. Appointments to the Council rested with the British Privy Council, with the Governor usually nominating and the Board of Trade scrutinizing.

8. DEVELOPMENT, 1696–1720

The Board of Trade was established by the Crown in 1696 to ward off a similar initiative by Parliament and to help execute the last of the Navigation Acts. During a generation of war and trade disruptions (1689–97, 1702–13) the defense of a self-sufficient empire was an administrative preoccupation. During an interlude of peace (1697–1701) the Board of Trade completed the vice-admiralty court system, inspired an effective campaign against piracy, and attempted to gain control over proprietary and chartered colonies. Regular scrutiny of colonial legislation, from all colonies except Connecticut, Maryland, and Rhode Island, required the regular assistance of the Attorney-General and the Solicitor-General until the Board acquired a legal officer in 1718. To tighten control of colonial legislation, after 1706 the Board began requiring suspending clauses which postponed implementation of specified types of colonial laws until these were confirmed by the Crown. The categories of law subject to this restriction expanded to create a significant colonial grievance. Intensifying British political partisanship in the decade after 1706 weakened the Board's expertise, thus expanding the imperial responsibilities of the Secretary of State.

9. ACCOMMODATION, 1721–48

Colonial policies gave way to pragmatic politics in the generation named for Robert Walpole and the style of imperial administration associated with the Duke of Newcastle as Secretary of State and Martin Bladen at the Board of Trade (1717–46). The triumph of patronage politics meant that administrative appointments, colonial and otherwise, were used to control a majority in Parliament. Peace and the complete victory of Whig politicians allowed the decentralization of political initiative. When there were military threats to the empire, in 1721 and 1739, the inclination was to encourage inter-colonial cooperation rather than British expense, even at the risk of fostering colonial independence. Colonial elites were able to consolidate their local positions by using British connections. This accommodative generation was marked by the continuing rise of the colonial assemblies and by fewer policy initiatives from the Board of Trade, the Secretary of State, or the colonial governors. Royal governors were not particularly inept, but their management of colonial councils and assemblies was further weakened by loss of control over minor local appointments to London.

The most explosive political battle of a comparatively stable period was linked to the excise crisis, which shook Walpole's administration between 1727 and the Molasses Act of 1733 (*see also* Chapter 1, §4, and Chapter 16, §2). Powerful interest groups raised public opinion against his plan to convert the import duties on wine and tobacco into excise taxes. In mustering the political support of interest groups,

(a)

(b)

(c)

FIGURE I (a): John Murray, Earl of Dunmore, Royal Governor of Virginia, 1770–6: portrait by Sir Joshua Reynolds (1765); (b): Thomas Hutchinson, Royal Governor of Massachusetts, 1771–4: portrait by Edward Truman (1741); (c): Thomas Pownall, Royal Governor of Massachusetts, 1757–9: painting by Henry Cheever Pratt (1861) after the engraving made in 1777 by Richard Earlom taken from the original painting by Francis Cotes (c. 1763)

Walpole made numerous concessions that affected the empire. The powerful Irish lobby gained direct import of some colonial products in 1731. English hatters won the Hat Act of 1732, prohibiting the colonial export of hats. A well-organized philanthropic lobby gained a charter and government grants to establish Georgia. More significant was the lobbying of the West Indian sugar interest to restrict trade between

13

the French islands and British North America. Inexpensive French colonial molasses had become central to the burgeoning American rum industry, as well as being widely used as a sweetener. The West Indians won a clear political victory with the passing of the Molasses Act, which allowed the legal importation of French West Indian sugar and molasses into British colonies, but levied a higher duty on these than on products of the British islands. This differential duty was a new approach to channeling imperial trade; complete prohibitions had previously been customary. Although the Molasses Act was not primarily a revenue measure, it levied a substantial tax on imports into the colonies. Imperial centralists would later cite this Act as a precedent for taxing the colonies without their consent. American patriots would look back on the resulting smuggling as the beginning of the protest which undermined the legitimacy of imperial control in America.

Colonial administration in the Walpole era made another contribution to the coming of the American Revolution. Many colonials came to regard the accommodation of interests achieved in this period as the working of the true imperial constitution. "Salutary neglect" of a Whig-dominated British administration allowed colonial legislators and colonial agents considerable power. British imperial reformers and centralists looked back on the Walpole era as one of negligence and patronage-driven decisions which sacrificed the well-established prerogative powers of the Crown and undermined the right of Parliament to legislate for the empire.

Walpole was driven from office in 1742, early in a decade of renewed war against Spain (1739–42) and France (1744–8), but the Duke of Newcastle continued the same policies and practices as Secretary of State for the Southern Department for another six years in a government now headed by his brother, Henry Pelham. British commitment of resources to war in America was limited, avoiding serious challenge to the duke's style of colonial administration.

10. TRANSITION, 1748–60

British political expediency, rather than a reappraisal of colonial administration, prevoked change. To bolster its parliamentary support, the Pelham ministry was forced to accept a new approach when the Duke of Bedford was brought into the Cabinet as Secretary of State for the Southern Department in 1748, soon followed by the able and ambitious Earl of Halifax as President of the strengthened Board of Trade (see DUNK, GEORGE MONTAGU). The Board gained unprecedented control of all significant colonial appointments for a decade (1751–61) and oversaw the government-sponsored settlement of Halifax, Nova Scotia. It also became involved in schemes to control the upper Ohio valley and supported measures that led to Anglo–French confrontation there. Parliamentary grants for the colonies of Georgia and Nova Scotia and agreement of the British Government to pay the salary of the governor of North Carolina were new fiscal investments in empire made before the Seven Years' War, and these new costs brought new levels of parliamentary scrutiny.

A significant contest over colonial policy was emerging. Newcastle and his supporters favored continuing delegation of power and responsibility to the colonial assemblies. Halifax and the Dukes of Bedford and Cumberland led those favoring stronger measures against France in America, more commitment of British resources to the colonies, and assertion of imperial control. Some thought of the royal prerogative as the vehicle for this, but others, including Charles Townshend of the Board of Trade, saw constitutional as well as practical reasons why initiatives should be through

Parliament (see TOWNSHEND, CHARLES). The unprecedented commitment of British men and money to the successful Seven Years' War in America greatly strengthened the argument of those holding these views.

II. RESURGENCE, 1760-75

The accession of George III and the victory over France in North America altered the contest over British colonial policy. George III pursued government by "King-in-Parliament," and this closer identification of the prerogative with Parliament made lobbying more expensive and complicated for colonial agents. The King's determination to manage his own ministries brought political instability, the unrestrained clash of interest groups, and more initiative for senior departmental bureaucrats committed to imperial control.

The costs of victory had been high, and the concern about revenues came to dominate colonial administration after the Peace of Paris (1763). The Treasury's search for American revenues was not to help repay Britain's war costs, but to offset the peacetime costs of administering and defending the enlarged North American empire (see Chapters 11 to 13). The fiscal preoccupation of senior colonial administrators was also evident from the increased use of the Royal Navy for customs enforcement, from the establishment of an American Board of Customs Commissioners based in Boston (1767), and from the revitalization of the vice-admiralty courts (1768). These measures provoked continuing friction with the colonial mercantile community, highlighted by the Boston Massacre (1770) and the *Gaspée* incident (1772).

Although customs confrontations continued in America, Lord North's administration of the Treasury (1770-82) refrained from new initiatives. Nonetheless, colonial agents and their London supporters were becoming more isolated from British policy makers and more distracted by constitutional issues. The Tea Act of 1773 was not a revenue measure, but the sharp colonial reaction indicated that the contest had developed beyond a dispute about parliamentary right to tax the colonies. Administrative initiative shifted to the American Department, where Lord Dartmouth was Secretary of State, but the real authority rested with his under-secretaries, John Pownall and William Knox. Pownall, Secretary of the Board of Trade under Halifax and Under-Secretary in the American Department from its inception until 1776, was instrumental in the strong administrative and legislative response to the Boston Tea Party.

Before 1763 colonial assemblies had found that Parliament's Whiggish principles protected their expanding power against reassertions of royal prerogative. Growing fiscal initiatives of the ministry and Parliament encountered American resistance thereafter. By 1775 inter-colonial congresses were urging the King to use his prerogative to save them from Parliament, and the King refused. Although the resulting struggle was political, constitutional, and eventually military, the administrative shift of imperial power had affected and reflected contentious revivals and innovations in colonial policy.

FURTHER READING

Clarke, D. M.: *The Rise of the British Treasury* (Hamden, Conn.: Archon Press, 1960).
Henretta, James A.: *"Salutary Neglect": Colonial Administration under the Duke of Newcastle* (Princeton, NJ: Princeton University Press, 1972).

Kammen, M. J.: *Empire and Interest* (New York: Lippincott, 1970).
Steele, I. K.: *Politics of Colonial Policy* (Oxford: Clarendon Press, 1968).
Wickwire, F. B.: *British Subministers and Colonial America, 1763–1783* (Princeton, NJ: Princeton University Press, 1966).

3

The changing socio-economic and strategic importance of the colonies to the empire

ALISON G. OLSON

I. THE WARS FOR SUPREMACY IN EUROPE

FROM 1689 to 1713, with a five-year break after the treaty of Ryswick in 1697, England and France were at war to determine the balance of power in Europe. In the first of the two wars William III of England, who was also Stadtholder of Holland, allied the English with Holland, Sweden, Spain, and the Holy Roman Empire against France. In the second the same countries were at war again, only this time the French king claimed the throne of Spain for his grandson and the Spanish were allied with the French. The war ended in 1713 with a British/Dutch triumph recognized in the Treaty of Utrecht.

In neither war were the tiny English colonies on the continent of mainland America important. They were small, isolated, economically insignificant except for tobacco, and lacked political clout in the councils of Europe. In the last decade of the seventeenth century English colonists, estimated to be 220,000 to 250,000 in number (compared with more than five million in the mother country), were settled thinly along the east coast of North America in a band stretching from eastern Maine to the northern border of the Carolinas, then again farther south in a ring around Charles Town. Farthest south of all were the English Caribbean islands, most notably Barbados, the Leeward Islands, and Jamaica. Rarely did the continental population extend more than 50 miles inland, and since the colonists were constantly moving west their frontiers were marked by small civilian settlements rather than forts.

At no point did the English colonists run up immediately against settlements of Spanish or French. The 25,000 Frenchmen in North America were located in 15 or 20 fur trading centers along the Mississippi, the Ohio, the Great Lakes and the St. Lawrence River, and in Acadia, and the 2,000 Spaniards in Florida were mainly at St. Augustine. A far greater danger came from the Indian tribes that existed in between the English settlements and the French and Spanish. Many of the Indians had been seriously weakened in a related series of tribal wars with the English in the late 1670s, but the French and Spanish urged others to make periodic raids on the exposed English settlements; the French were particularly effective in provoking the Abenaki in Northern Maine and the Spanish encouraged the Creeks, Yamasees, and Tuscaroras against the Carolinas. It was with these, rather than with other European settlers, that the colonists were most concerned.

2. TRADE IN 1700

In 1700 the mainland colonies were still one of the least significant parts of the British Empire, and far less important to the British economy than continental Europe. They were required by a series of regulatory Navigation Acts passed between 1651 and 1673 to export most of their produce directly to England in English or colonial vessels and to pay duties in colonial ports for a few enumerated items allowed to be exported elsewhere. European products could be sent to the colonies only in English ships or those of the country where they originated, and they had to be brought to England for re-export. Nevertheless, the colonies' commerce was less than 6 per cent of the value of total English commerce, and less than one-sixth that of Northern Europe; it was not quite two-thirds that of the West Indies and was less even than that of the East Indian trading stations. Only tobacco, at times taxed at more than 100 per cent its worth, proved very profitable to the mother country. Tobacco from the Chesapeake averaged in value £200,000 per annum, and total Chesapeake trade with England (imports as well as exports, £490,000 per annum) accounted for two-thirds the value of all the mainland trade taken together. The other colonies were still of little economic consequence. The total value of New England's trade was only £133,000 (18 per cent) per annum, of the middle colonies (wheat mainly from New York and Pennsylvania) only £66,000 (12 per cent) per annum, and the Carolinas (rice) only £25,000 (3 per cent) per annum. Only New England and Pennsylvania fitted the mercantilist ideal of importing more from the mother country than they exported to her.

3. MILITARY CONSIDERATIONS

Finally, the seaboard mainland colonies at the end of the seventeenth century had little effective way of appealing for military support from the home government, since they had weaker political organization in London than had any other part of the empire. The colonial trade was best handled by mercantile firms of two or three partners at the most, and the firms, with the exception of tobacco merchants, still found it hard to exert coordinated pressure on the government. The Atlantic seaboard trade did not lend itself to direction by a large and potentially powerful company (as did Hudson's Bay or India) and it was not in the hands of a combination of wealthy merchants and well-connected absentee land-owners (as were the West Indies). Land in the colonies was not yet particularly valuable – and hence not worth defending – and neither, in English thinking, were the settlers, who had a reputation for instability and lack of cooperation.

Not surprisingly the English put their military priorities elsewhere. The colonies were mentioned only as after-thoughts in the declarations of war, and for most of the fighting the inhabitants were left to carry on for themselves with the limited help of the British regiments that were there before the combat started. The colonists received no imperial help in defending themselves against French-inspired Indian raids on frontier villages in the Carolinas, New York, and Massachusetts. On three notable occasions they took the initiative themselves, once in each war when Massachusetts men captured Fort Royal in Acadia, and on another occasion, at the beginning of war in 1702, when Carolinians destroyed the town (though not the Fort) of St. Augustine. The English government generally confined its efforts to dispatching convoys to protect the tobacco fleets and appointing governors of New York with instructions to rally inter-colonial support against the French in Canada. Only in 1710 did the British send any appreciable forces – 70 ships and 10,000 men to take Quebec – and that expedition, having sailed up the St. Lawrence, backed off without firing a shot. At the war's end, very little territory had changed hands.

The lack of American importance was further made clear by the provisions of the Treaty of Utrecht which ended the War of the Spanish Succession in 1713. In it Great Britain obtained, in addition to the asienta (the exclusive monopoly of supplying slaves to the Spanish colonies), Newfoundland, Nova Scotia, Hudson's Bay, Nevis, and the island of St. Kitt's. But all the mainland boundaries – the bounds of anything, in fact, that was not an island – were either left vague or entrusted to commissions to settle; the fate of the French who already lived in Newfoundland or Nova Scotia was undetermined; and the question of the French strengthening their trade routes along the Mississippi and the Great Lakes was not addressed. France renounced special trading privileges in Spanish and Portuguese America; Spain promised never to give any of her American territories to France, but for the time the European balance of power was more important than the American: the thrones of France and Spain were eternally to remain separate.

4. EUROPEAN IMMIGRATION

After the war the British Government aggressively encouraged immigration to the colonies, hoping particularly that settlers of non-English stock would take up residence in the areas left undefined by the Treaty. Such settlement was in line with current mercantilist thinking. Non-English immigrants (or English convicts, 17,000 of whom were shipped directly to the colonies) would not subtract from England's supply of labour at home, while they would produce raw materials that could be processed in England for domestic use or re-export; they also created new markets for English manufacturers, and, when settled on the frontier, they constituted something of a buffer against the French and Spanish. "For every thousand who will be transported thither," it was argued, "[England] will raise the means for employing four thousand more at home."

After several batches of continental refugees arrived in England the British began actively assisting non-English to leave their homelands, not always an easy job when foreign princes were reluctant to lose manpower from their own territories or to lose money from fines levied on emigrants from other territories passing through. British agents were located in every major city of Holland and the empire to negotiate permission for would-be emigrants to leave home and pass toll-free through various principalities, to arrange transportation, food, and housing at local stopovers, to give security that emigrants passing through towns would depart by an agreed-upon time, and to leave the emigrants money. The Board of Trade often negotiated directly with ship captains to transport the settlers. With their encouragement, nearly 100,000 Germans and nearly a quarter of a million Scots Irish went to the colonies, in addition to thousands of Scots, Irish, Huguenots, and Swiss.

Once the settlers arrived in the colonies the Board of Trade worked with governors to get them land and then exemptions from paying taxes on it for seven to ten years. In 1740 Parliament passed a Naturalization Act authorizing governors by themselves to naturalize foreign Protestants who had lived in the colonies for seven years, and in 1747 Moravians in the colonies were allowed to become naturalized without having to take oaths. In 1732 Parliament voted the first of a series of annual grants to the newly chartered province of Georgia, created as a haven for continental emigrants as well as English debtors and as a buffer for the Carolina rice growers against Spanish Florida.

Such British encouragement of non-English immigration was regarded as a mixed blessing by the established colonists, though the merchants generally supported it. It gave promise of buffer areas against the French, Spanish, and Indians, provided field labor for farmers of particular crops and domestic labor that gave non-English families a satisfying chance to keep ties with the old country, and produced wheat for export markets and purchasers for local goods. But it also drained seaboard resources by requiring colonial governments to provide institutions and defence for the new settlers at the very time many of the immigrants were not yet paying taxes. In the eyes of many colonists it also diluted the very Englishness of colonial culture, and there was a good deal of resentment of the British Government for encouraging it all.

5. EXPANSION OF TRADE

With nearly a fivefold expansion in population over half a century, resulting from a combination of immigration and native increase, the mainland colonies became the fastest-growing part of the British Empire before 1750. (Britain itself had only a 25 per cent population increase in the same period.) The value to Britain of mainland and West Indian trade (imports and exports combined with re-exports) increased more than 225 per cent, from £1,855,000 per annum at the beginning of the century to £4,105,000 per annum at mid-century, making these colonies second only to Northern Europe in the total value of their trade. British trade with Northern Europe was growing much more slowly; in the same period it had increased from £4,500,000 per annum to £5,300,000 per annum, less than 20 per cent. Trade with India was more than doubling, from £800,000 per annum in 1700 to £1,700,000 per annum in 1750, but even this growth was not as rapid as that of the American colonies. The increase in American trade value was accounted for by the mainland colonies: they contributed 10 per cent of the value of British trade at mid-century compared with less than 6 per cent a half century before. The value of West Indian trade grew from £1,121,000 per annum in 1700 to £2,073,000 per annum 50 years later, but while in 1700 it had been half as great again as the mainland colonies, in the later period it was only slightly greater.

As British trade with the mainland colonies grew, the number of Englishmen interested in the colonies increased accordingly. Englishmen smoked American tobacco, ate American sugar, grain, and fish, dressed in clothes colored with American dye, and sailed in ships with American masts. The number of occupations associated with American trade expanded, from the processing of American raw materials such as tobacco and sugar, to the textile manufacturing using American dyes, to the insuring of American ships and the warehousemen who supplied American merchants to the merchants themselves.

Ever-growing numbers of merchants were trading with the mainland colonies. Unlike the East Indian nabobs, many of whom levied in the East for several years before returning home with substantial fortunes, or the absentee West Indian planters living handsomely in England off the profits of their Caribbean estates, the English merchants trading with Americans were active men of business, generally among the middling ranks of the mercantile community.

6. THE INFLUENCE OF ENGLISH MERCHANTS ON COLONIAL GOVERNMENT

Increasingly over the first half of the century, the merchants trading to mainland America, so weakly organized at the beginning of the century, came to influence imperial decisions about the colonies. Gathered in coffee houses and clubs, they organized effective lobbies to influence the Board of Trade, ministers, and Parliament. Individual mercantile leaders became important consultants to ministers on colonial policy. They testified before Parliament and the Board of Trade, addressed Prime Ministers almost at will, and several of them as a group called on William Pitt, Prime Minister during the Seven Years' War; one of them was actually a leading candidate for head of the Board of Trade. Possessing first-hand information about American trade that the government needed, the merchants were instrumental in shaping the government's decisions about America.

In general the English merchants supported the demands of their American correspondents – planters and merchants wealthy enough to be interested in colonial politics and/or interested in developing political connections in England – and most of these wanted the British Government to back colonial expansion and protect colonial trade. So in local American encounters with the French or Spanish or their Indian allies, the Board of Trade tended to support the aggressive activities of individual colonial governors even though the Prime Minister from 1721 to 1742, Sir Robert Walpole, was working to prevent a recurrence of war. Since the Treaty of Utrecht had left a number of boundaries undetermined and trade arrangements unexplored, governors had a good deal of opportunity to encourage activities of the settlers that might lead to conflict. Indeed, the most capable governors at the time of the Treaty, men such as Robert Hunter of New York, anticipated that conflicts would soon enough escalate into a struggle for control of the entire North American continent. They urged that more soldiers and settlers be sent to the colonies, more forts be built, and more efforts made to cultivate the friendship of the Indians, and as a general rule the British Government followed their recommendations.

7. DEFENSE OF COLONIAL FRONTIERS

The Board of Trade stressed anew making frontier areas safe for certain settlement, and to this end they sent out governors with instructions to get the colonial assemblies to provide adequate defense and carefully reviewed the assemblies' legislation on defense. They backed the New Englanders in driving the French-inspired Abenakis out of Maine and in 1729 made a treaty with them in which the Abenakis recognized English authority. They took the government of the Carolinas away from proprietors who had provided no help in the colonists' war against the Yamassee Indians in 1715 and they appointed as governor Francis Nicholson, a military commander with extensive experience.

The British continued to rely on forts far less than the French, who concentrated on strengthening strategic defensible positions, building additional forts from the mouth of the Mississippi to the St. Louis area, then to the Great Lakes area and the enormous fort at Louisburg on Cape Breton Island at the mouth of the St. Lawrence, the only large island left to them after Utrecht. The British were aware of the French objective of encircling them with a string of forts, but they themselves centered into fort-building almost half-heartedly. The government supported New York's Governor

William Burnet in building Fort Oswego on the south of Lake Erie to protect the fur trade, even though the Great Lakes were assumed to be under French, not English, occupation. They also backed Governor James Oglethorpe in his attempt to erect fortifications at the mouth of the St. Johns River against the Spanish, even though the Savannah River, considerably to the north, was assumed by the Spanish to be their natural border. Much later George Washington was sent out to build British forts along the Ohio River, but backed down when the French arrived there first.

8. RELATIONS BETWEEN THE COLONIES AND THE WEST INDIES

The Board of Trade also encouraged colonists from the middle and northern mainland provinces to expand their trade with the French West Indies, though this was not strictly in accord with mercantilist doctrine. As early as the 1720s northern colonies were already seeking to export wheat to the French West Indies in return for sugar which the New Englanders would distill into rum. Governors of British West Indian colonies protested against such attempts, but in 1724 the Board, having begun an investigation into the trade a year before, recommended that the government give the French trade open support. In 1733 the West India interest in England, having obtained very little from the Board of Trade, pushed through Parliament the Molasses Act, placing prohibitive duties on French sugars, but the Act was never enforced and there was scarcely a New England merchant by mid-century who did not engage in some French West Indian trade in violation of the law. The Molasses Act was the result of jockeying for influence between mainland and West India interests, with the West India interests able to do better with Parliament and the mainland interests better able to influence the Board of Trade, in good measure because they knew what laws could and could not be enforced among the colonists with whom they dealt. In the three and a half decades after Utrecht the British Government, urged on by the merchants trading with America, was thus encouraging the growth of new world settlement and trade.

The only relatively declining areas in North America were the West Indian islands: they were losing more of their lead with every year. Their amount of trade was going down because of a decline both in their own productivity and in the European market. By early in the eighteenth century, land in the smaller islands was losing fertility because of long use and lax management. It took increasing numbers of slaves to produce the same amount of sugar. The French islands, by contrast, more recently cultivated and better managed because their owners were not absentee, were increasingly productive, and over the first half of the eighteenth century French sugar captured the European market. The British consumption of sugar per capita doubled in the period, but whereas 40 per cent of West Indian sugar in 1700 was re-exported from Britain, only 4 per cent was re-exported by the 1730s. The British ended up paying considerably more for the domestic consumption of sugar. Nor were the islands improving as a market for British exports, since the non-slave populations of the islands remained stationary.

9. RESULTS OF POPULATION GROWTH

Among the mainland colonies, the wealthiest were the middle colonies and the Chesapeake, which had large population increases in the generation after Utrecht. The Chesapeake colonies simply expanded the amount of their tobacco production

FIGURE 2 A cartouche from the map of Virginia and Maryland by Joshua Fry and Peter Jefferson (1775) showing a trading scene: on the left is a slave, in the centre is a book-keeper checking off the cargo, and on the right is a cooper tightening the end of a tobacco hogshead; the loading crane and the ship appear in the background.

(*see* figure 2) as the population moved west: by 1751 their share of the total value of mainland trade with Britain had fallen to 39 per cent, but their absolute trade had continued to expand from £490,000 per annum to £803,000 per annum, almost £300,000 per annum more than even the middle colonies. So rapidly was Chesapeake population growing that, by the 1740s, speculators, admittedly thinking of wheat rather than tobacco, were already looking to lands in the Ohio Valley. By the late 1740s agents of Virginia land companies, such as Christopher Gist and Dr. Thomas Walker, were sent to reconnoiter grants to the Ohio Company and the Loyal Company respectively. (They represented companies formed in 1747 and 1748 with large land grants from the King in the case of the Ohio Company and the Virginia Council in the case of the Loyal Company.)

The growth of the middle colonies was both faster (from 12 per cent of mainland trade with Britain in 1700 to 25 per cent in 1751, with an absolute increase from £88,000 to £506,000) and more complex. It was based on a combination of wheat, furs, and the carrying trade, and population growth was reflected not only in agriculture but also in the expansion of the largest ports, New York and Philadelphia. Indian tribes had begun moving into the Ohio area from both the east and the west to pursue the fur trade, the easterners because, with the overkill of the beavers in New England and eastern Canada, the remaining animals were moving west, and the westerners from Illinois in order to capitalize on the extension of European, and particularly British, trade connections. In the late 1740s fur traders such as William Johnson of New York and George Croghan and Conrad Weiser of Pennsylvania joined land speculators from Virginia in the Ohio Valley; Weiser represented the colony of Pennsylvania in negotiating at Logstown, on the Ohio, a treaty in which the Indians agreed to do business with Pennsylvania traders.

10. MILITARY ACTION, 1740–58

Despite the rapid growth of the mainland colonies (and the wealth of the middle and Chesapeake colonies in particular), and despite the Board of Trade's positive response to colonial pressure for expansion, transmitted by the merchants, the British Government was slow to recognize their military importance when war broke out with the French again in 1740. The War of the Austrian Succession (1740–8) was, as its title suggests, prompted by European politics. The only important fighting on the American mainland occurred in 1745, when an exclusively American effort took the French fort of Louisburg. Massachusetts supplied the manpower and New York, New Jersey, and Pennsylvania the equipment. And, much to the colonists' disgust, all conquered territories including Louisburg were returned to their prewar status by the Treaty of Aix-la-Chapelle in 1748.

After the war the French, with some Indian allies, defeated the British and their Indian supporters at Pickawillany and began to erect a series of forts between the Ohio River and Lake Erie. The Governor of Virginia sent out troops but they proved powerless to stop the French. Even now, however, the British ministry still saw British interests as being primarily on the European continent, and when it was clear by 1754 that fighting was going to resume on the North American continent they simply planned a series of piecemeal attacks on the French, all of which came to failure. The first phase, in which troops starting from Virginia were to attack Fort Duquesne on the Ohio, and troops from New York and New England were to take forts on Lake George and Fort Niagara between Lakes Ontario and Erie, was headed for failure almost before it started, when General Braddock with a combination of British and American troops was defeated on his way to Fort Duquesne in 1755. From then until William Pitt became Prime Minister of Great Britain, three years later, the British suffered one defeat after another.

11. PITT'S MINISTRY

With Pitt's accession to power in 1758, the fortunes of the British on the North American continent turned around. Pitt's strategy and abilities have both been questioned, and it is recognized that American conquest was only part of his plan, which also included subsidizing the King of Prussia to fight the French on the European continent, blockading French continental ports so their navy could not get out, and sending troops to India.

Nevertheless his administration was important for the American Empire in several indisputable ways. For one thing, his administration brought stability to a government that had endured one cabinet reshuffle after another from 1754 to 1757; for another, Pitt had close political ties with the very groups of middling merchants in London who had long urged an aggressive imperial policy, and his appointment showed clearly a shift in the balance of power in the ministry away from supporters of a continental and towards supporters of an imperial emphasis in the war. Pitt also favored extensive use of Americans in the war (many of his cabinet colleagues had doubts) and, though his initial overall plan was simply the traditional one of attacking the French up the Hudson River on the west and down the St. Lawrence from the east, he now added another prong up the Ohio and Allegheny, and he entrusted the campaigns to able generals such as James Wolfe.

Whatever the influence of Pitt, it is clear that four decades of colonial growth had greatly increased the number of British people with occupations related to America, the amount of coverage of American events in the British newspapers, the number of pamphlets devoted to American issues, the number of American books reviewed in British journals, the number of American products consumed, even (well before Pitt came to power) popular interests in the relationship between colonial and metropolitan society. British authors were contrasting the ruggedness of Americans with the effeminacy of Continentals – a far cry from their emphasis on the instability of the colonists in the seventeenth century – and some were even suggesting that America might sooner or later provide a model for social change in Britain. The debate over whether America or Europe should constitute Britain's first military priority was by no means confined to factions within the government.

12. MILITARY ACTION, 1759–62

The campaign of 1759, the "Annus Mirabilis" of British military action in North America, was an extension of the plans begun the year before, combining attacks on Montreal and Quebec from the Great Lakes in the west, Lake George to the south, and the St. Lawrence entrance to the east. With larger armies than they had fielded in America before, better generals, and the support of Americans delighted with Pitt's promise of postwar reimbursement, and convinced by the press and the evangelists that the war was to determine for all time whether the North American continent was to be Protestant or Catholic, the Anglo-American forces succeeded in all their major campaigns, and in September 1759 took Quebec. Montreal was not captured until the following year, but in American thinking the war wound down with the fall of Quebec.

In the Caribbean and Southern Europe the fighting did not end until 1762, mainly because the belated Spanish entrance into the war delayed its conclusion for ten months. In the Treaty of Paris signed the next year the British were clearly the heavy gainers, getting from the French all of Canada except Miquelon and St. Pierre (two tiny fishing islands), all the land east of the Mississippi River except New Orleans, and former French possessions in Africa and India. From Spain the British received Florida. The various Caribbean islands retained their prewar allegiances.

13. ECONOMIC RESULTS OF WAR

For the mainland colonies the immediately visible result of the settlement was that they were no longer surrounded by a chain of Spanish and French forts. The long-run results of the war were less clear.

On the one hand, the colonies continued, after a brief postwar collapse, a spurt of economic growth that actually accompanied the mid-century conflicts. By 1772 the mainland colonial trade comprised 17 per cent of the value of total British trade (though the mainland now included Canada), an increase of 7 per cent in 20 years. Even the value of West Indian trade had increased an astonishing 5 per cent, to 15 per cent of the value of all British trade. The standard of colonial living climbed after 1740. Chesapeake exports expanded in value from £165,000 to £476,000 per annum, but the shift in the Chesapeake economy was revealed by the fact that per capita income from tobacco increased by only 17 per cent, while that from grain exports went up by 300 per cent. Chesapeake exports continued to be the most valuable among those of the mainland colonies, but per capita income and the accumulation of portable wealth were growing far faster in the North, where shipping and ship-building were expanding rapidly in the third quarter of the eighteenth century. By the 1760s all American coastal trade and three-quarters of all direct trade between the northern colonies and Great Britain was in colonial hands; one-third of the British merchant marine was built in the middle or northern colonies.

The productivity of the colonies and their value to the empire, therefore, continued to increase, along with the colonial standard of living, during and after the mid-century wars. But as the value of their trade with Great Britain went up, their influence on the economic decisions of the mother country went down. After winning a "territorial" empire in North America the British Government seemed to decide it had wanted a mercantile one all along. The Board of Trade, which had encouraged the expansion of colonial settlement as well as trade, abruptly lost power in successive shifts of the British Government.

With the British domination of Canada, the older mainland colonies found them-selves competing for influence with a formidable new lobby of British merchants, whose interests were often competitive. The shifting influence was revealed in part through the Quebec Act of 1774, among other things assigning lands to Canada between the Ohio River and the Great Lakes, from which the New Englanders had been exporting furs. Even though the British now had undisputed title to lands east of the Mississippi, they immediately attempted to restrict colonial expansion into lands between the Appalachians and the Mississippi (by the Proclamation Line of 1763), and they withdrew support from the very land companies that had been awarded tracts of land in the late 1740s. Though the declining importance of the West Indian islands was shown by British disinterest in claiming more of them, Parliament passed, and this time seriously attempted to enforce, the Sugar Act, levying prohibitive duties on sugar from the French islands. Finally, the very importance of the North American lands, new and old, prompted Parliament to consider regulatory laws for the continent as a whole, leaving the colonies, used to lobbying on a regional basis, without influence.

The immediate results of the wars were thus mixed, more so for the Americans than the British, and so also were the long-term results of the American membership in the British Empire. The results for the mainland colonies have long been debated, partly on the basis of a counterfactual question – what would the American per capita income have been if they had not been required to handle the bulk of their trade through the British Isles? Historians stressing restrictions on commodities the colonists could manufacture, the overseas markets with which they could exchange goods, and the added charges when colonial produce was re-exported to other markets through Britain conclude that British economic policy was harmful to the colonists, enough so even to be a grievance promoting the American Revolution. Historians impressed with the bounties the British offered on certain American products such as indigo, with British knowledge of world markets the colonists lacked, with British provision for colonial defense, and overlooking the colonial smuggling of the important French West Indian sugar, point out that the colonists did not seem to think the economic restrictions a hardship and never complained of them until their effect was com-pounded by new laws in the decade before the Revolution. With counterfactual arguments now virtually exhausted, historians are concluding that the Navigation Acts cost the colonists approximately 1.8 per cent of their income from exports and added .25 to 1 per cent to the cost of imports, not a particularly onerous burden.

14. ADVANTAGES AND DISADVANTAGES OF THE COLONIES TO BRITAIN

The arguments about British benefits from the American Empire, however, have not yet stabilized, some historians assuming that the British profited "handsomely" from their American trade and others going back to Adam Smith in calling the colonies "mere loss instead of profit." Contemporaries assumed that the colonies profited Britain because they provided a market for her manufacturers and with it jobs and profits for those in industry. Colonial consumption increased from 10 per cent of England's exports in 1701 to 37 per cent in 1772. Contemporaries also thought that raw materials imported from the colonies provided inexpensive consumer goods for the British public, or jobs and profits for people who processed them for re-export, and colonial trade stimulated the growth of British shipping. Recent historians have been doubtful of all these assumptions, suggesting mainly that the patterns of trade would have been essentially the same whether the colonies were in or out of the empire. They also argue that while the average British per capita income was rising in the first part of the eighteenth century, while food prices were falling, the change could be explained in good part simply by the growth of English manufacturing.

Some economic historians further argue that the British might have been better off without American ties: they could have consumed more of their own manufactures more cheaply if they had not exported them to the Americans. Re-export profits were deceptive because once the per capita consumption of tobacco peaked and the consumption of sugar began profiting the French West Indian islands at the expense of the British, the continent began declining as a re-export market for colonial produce. The British would have done better to use their own manufacturers to cultivate trade with the more developed nations of continental Europe. Finally, the British emerged from the Seven Years' War financially exhausted, in part because of the heavy burden of defending the American colonies. Questions about the value of the first British Empire remained long after its demise with the American Revolution.

FURTHER READING

Deane, Phyllis, and Cole, W. A.: *British Economic Growth, 1688 to 1959* (Cambridge: Cambridge University Press, 1962).

Floud, Roderick, and McClosky, Donald: *The Economic History of Britain Since 1700*, vol. I: *1700 to 1860* (Cambridge: Cambridge University Press, 1981).

Greene, Jack P., and Pole, J. R. (eds.): *Colonial British America* (Baltimore: Johns Hopkins Press, 1984).

Henretta, James: *The Evolution of American Society, 1700 to 1815* (London: D. C. Heath, 1973).

McCusker, John J., and Menard, Russell: *The Economy of British North America, 1607–1789* (Chapel Hill: University of North Carolina Press, 1985).

Mitchell, B. R., and Deane, Phyllis: *Abstract of British Historical Statistics* (Cambridge: Cambridge University Press, 1962).

Savelle, Max: *The Origins of American Diplomacy: the International History of Anglo-America, 1492 to 1763* (New York: Macmillan, 1967).

Schumpter, Elizabeth Boody: *English Overseas Trade Statistics, 1697 to 1808* (Oxford: Oxford University Press, 1960).

Shepherd, James F., and Walton, Gary M.: *Shipping, Maritime Trade, and the Economic Development of Colonial North America* (Cambridge and New York: Cambridge University Press, 1972).

United States Bureau of the Census: *Historical Statistics of the United States, Colonial Times to 1957* (Washington, DC: Government Printing Office, 1960).

4

The political development of the colonies after the Glorious Revolution

ALAN TULLY

DURING the last decade of the seventeenth century and the first three-quarters of the eighteenth, Britain's North American colonies went through a remarkable political evolution. At the time of the Glorious Revolution in 1689, they were a variegated collection of small, faction-ridden societies sharing little in common; by 1775 the colonies were capable of joining together to seek political independence by challenging the most powerful country in Europe. What gave them the political confidence to strike out on their own was their evolution into competent societies in their own right. The main political elements of that metamorphosis were the rise to power of the colonial assemblies, the appearance of politically able colonial elites, and the development of widespread public support for provincial political leaders. These developments took place in a political environment distinguished by strong institutions of local government, a comparatively broad colonial franchise, a largely unrestricted press, and freedom for most white males to associate for political purposes. All of these were important underpinnings of the kind of stable and deferential politics necessary to produce a coherent resistance to British authority, yet they were also shaded with enough ambiguity to foreshadow some of the political fragmentation that occurred under the stress of revolution.

I. THE COLONIES AT THE TIME OF THE GLORIOUS REVOLUTION

Just as it was in Great Britain, the Glorious Revolution was an important turning-point in the political development of the British American colonies. The early to mid-seventeenth century had seen the establishment of various institutions of representative government at the local and provincial levels in the Chesapeake and New England colonies. But the restoration of the Stuart monarchy in 1660 brought ambivalent policies to the English colonies. One one hand, the Crown granted colonizing rights to proprietors who, in the case of Pennsylvania, New Jersey, and the Carolinas, promised varying degrees of representative government as an inducement to immigration. On the other, the Stuart monarchs were determined to reduce the autonomy that the New England colonies frequently claimed as their right. The Crown accomplished that end in 1686 by establishing the Dominion of New England, a governmental unit running from New Jersey to Maine, which abolished the colonial assemblies and centralized colonial power in the hands of one governor and council. When the Glorious Revolution in Great Britain handed the North American colonists the opportunity to rid themselves of regimes associated with Stuart tyranny, they quickly did so. In Massachusetts, New York, and Maryland, popular uprisings overthrew colonial officials, who were tainted with the Stuart brush of autocracy and Catholicism. The new *ad hoc* governments attracted the support of colonists by claiming that they championed traditional English rights, rights that included a considerable measure of representative government.

Faced with the collapse of the Stuart experiment in colonial reorganization, the pragmatic William of Orange and his successors in England opted for new policies. They made no effort to consolidate the various colonies, and they accepted the claims that English colonies had a right to assemblies and local representative institutions. But they attempted to make the colonies more amenable to British direction by establishing the Board of Trade as a supervisory body, and by reorganizing some of the charter and proprietary colonies as royal governments. By the early 1720s only five colonies had escaped royalization (Connecticut and Rhode Island remained charter colonies, Pennsylvania, Delaware, and Maryland proprietary ones), and the governors of both charter and proprietary colonies were subject to many of the same laws and regulations that guided royal governors. The governors were intended to be the locus of power. As a representative of the monarch, the governor possessed vice-regal status and power. He symbolized the sovereignty of the Crown, exercised such prerogative powers as a veto over colonial legislation, and was responsible for the administration of both British regulations and provincial laws. His chief source of political support in each colony was the legislative and executive council, a body composed of approximately a dozen eminent appointees who were to take the lead in generating political support for Crown policies. Acting in concert, the governor and council were expected to dominate colonial politics, keeping the elected assemblies in a subordinate role.

2. THE RISE OF COLONIAL ASSEMBLIES

In the decades following the Glorious Revolution, the most important strand of political development was the emergence of the lower houses of assembly as the dominant force in provincial politics rather than the governor and his council. British hopes that the governor and council would be the focal point of governmental power were unrealistic, if not naive. The assemblies of various colonies had haphazardly and unevenly extended their powers in the seventeenth century, despite the autocratic forces arrayed against them. The Glorious Revolution, with its emphasis on the protection of English rights, encouraged the elected politicians in the lower houses of assembly to push for powers consistent with the great importance they assigned to representative institutions as the chief protector of traditional liberties. The early eighteenth century saw the assemblies of four major colonies (Massachusetts, New York, Pennsylvania, and South Carolina) consolidate their power to the point where at worst they could battle the governor, council, and British Government to a stand, and at best they could control much of the provincial political agenda. In Massachusetts the constraints of a new royal charter, imposed in 1691, did little to curb the assertion of popular powers grounded in a half century of Puritan corporate autonomy. In New York, where James II's personal control had prevented the establishment of an assembly, the Glorious Revolution inaugurated a short period of speedy change. Once in existence, the New York Assembly moved quickly against a handful of corrupt governors to strip them of a number of their prerogatives and thus enhance popular powers. In the proprietary colonies of Pennsylvania and South Carolina the assemblies preyed on proprietary weakness. In 1701 Pennsylvania pried from William Penn a Charter of Privileges that quickly established its assembly as the most powerful in all the colonies; South Carolinians' continuous battles with their proprietors provided the assembly with incremental gains that they consolidated and expanded in the 1720s during the colony's conversion to royal government. The assemblies of other colonies, even of such long-established ones as Virginia and Maryland, did not stake out their ground with the same rapidity as the aforementioned quartet, but, as the eighteenth century wore on, all the lower houses of assembly were successful in expanding their areas of activity and influence.

The assemblies achieved their prominence by consolidating their power in a number of areas. Of first importance was their determination to control as much of the raising and distribution of tax money as they could. Initially they claimed the sole right to frame and amend money bills, and then they pushed for additional powers: the right to audit accounts, to control expenditures by specific appropriations, to appoint commissioners to oversee expenditures, to name local officers responsible for collecting provincial taxes, to keep royal officials on the short rein of annual salary grants, and to regulate administrative fees. Simultaneously, the assemblies tried to insulate themselves from executive influence. They claimed the right to control the ordering of their business and procedures, to oversee the conditions under which elections were held and resolve election disputes, to appoint their own officers, to regulate the release of governmental news to the press, and to direct agents responsible for conducting colonial business in London. Cumulatively, it was a formidable list.

The most common rationale leading assemblymen offered for their quest for power was an analogy to the British House of Commons. The structure of colonial government was close enough to the British model that apologists could liken the assemblies to the House of Commons and urge comparable powers for comparable bodies. This type of thinking was most explicit in the late seventeenth and early eighteenth centuries, when even royal governors occasionally accepted the analogy in order to help clarify the confusing relationship that often soured executive–legislative dealings. But that tendency fell out of favor as time wore on. Increasingly, governors tried to deflate assembly pretensions by reminding them that they were subordinate corporate bodies unlike those that composed Parliament. Assemblymen, meanwhile, recognized that as the lower houses gained powers beyond those of the British House of Commons, the analogy could be turned back on them.

What prompted the assembly politicians to assert their institutional power with such vigor were a number of circumstances, including an intense colonial awareness of English constitutional rights. Like many of their counterparts who remained at home in the British Isles, immigrants to North America were frequently well-versed in the conflicts over constitutional rights that wracked Stuart England. In the seventeenth century and for the first quarter of the eighteenth century, this consciousness was reflected in various attempts by colonial assemblies to secure explicit statutory guarantees of the colonists' rights to the laws of England, an effort that subsequently lost force with the customary, if selective, application of the common law by colonial judges throughout the late colonial period. The Glorious Revolution enhanced this rights consciousness, as did the writings of English radical Whigs who, throughout the eighteenth century, urged Englishmen to be ever vigilant of their liberties and freedoms. The belief that valued rights could be safeguarded only by an alert and powerful representative body accompanied that awareness. Moreover, many colonists believed that the corporate rights of the assemblies were synonymous with the rights of the people, and thus assembly rights were to be defended, clarified, and asserted without qualification.

Moreover, the exaggerated prerogative powers of the colonial governors underlined the apparent need for assembly vigilance. In theory, at least, colonial governors retained many prerogative powers that the Crown had lost in the wake of the Glorious Revolution in England. Not only did royal and proprietary governors have the authority to veto legislation, but, should the Crown's representative prove lax in his use of this power, the Privy Council had the right to disallow colonial acts upon their review in London (see Chapter 2, §1). In addition, executive authority included the appointment of all judicial officers at pleasure, the right to set up chancery courts, and, in the case of most royal colonies, an unfettered power to prorogue, dissolve, and indefinitely extend the life of any assembly. The sweep of these powers seemed so extensive that colonial politicians felt popular liberties were constantly under siege. Responding to the perceived threat, they augmented the institutional power of the assemblies at every opportunity, much as they perceived Parliament had done in the face of Stuart tyranny in seventeenth-century England.

The assemblies' growing strength was, by and large, the result of a spontaneous political opportunism that developed unevenly among the various colonies. Yet popular politicians in all of the colonies shared common approaches and convictions: a consciousness of the importance of English rights and of the principal role the assembly should play in protecting them; a determination to duplicate, consolidate, and in some instances extend traditional English rights in the colonies; a conviction that the royal prerogative was a constant danger to colonial liberty; and a historical perspective that encouraged them to confine such power. Shared assumptions, along with the attention the assembly leaders paid to the experiences of neighboring colonies, meant that by the Seven Years' War many of the lower houses of assembly had reached a stage of maturity that inspired colonial self-confidence. They had become formidable political institutions strong enough to confront Parliament.

Powerful as the provincial assemblies became, it is important to keep in mind that gubernatorial influence was not completely emasculated. Where they had them, the governors retained their powers of prorogation and dissolution. They retained strong control over the judiciary, and they continued to wield the veto power. More importantly, a few governors were able to use what limited patronage they had to build court parties within the assemblies. In New Hampshire, Massachusetts, and Maryland, court factions, supportive of the prerogative, took some of the initiative away from the most outspoken advocates of assembly power. In other colonies, such as New York and Pennsylvania, political compromises were reached which forced the assemblies to back away from their most extreme claims. In colonies such as Virginia and New York, where the governors' councils retained prestige and maintained a voice on such issues as land policy, the influence of the governor and the Crown could softly seep into the political groundwater of public opinion. In other areas, where proprietary property rights were growing more valuable as they grew older, a political conservatism appeared that expressed some partiality for royal power and prerogative rights. All of these developments were important qualifications on popular power.

3. THE APPEARANCE OF COLONIAL ELITES

The second important feature of eighteenth-century colonial political development (a feature intimately connected with the growth of assembly powers) was the appearance of colonial elites who sought political power commensurate with their emerging socio-economic prominence. By the late seventeenth century the older provinces had begun to produce a wealthy precocious group of men who closely identified their own and their families' fortunes with the success of their colony. Among the new colonies, such as New Jersey, Pennsylvania, and the Carolinas, rapid growth and attendant prosperity tended to enhance the process of elite development, so that they, too, produced a recognizable group of social and economic leaders by the early eighteenth century. As time progressed, these elites tended to strengthen themselves by involving new men who rose to prominence in their midst, at the same time as they stressed the importance of inherited wealth and social position and the reputation of their forbears as requirements for colonial leadership. Whether immigrant or creole, elites were concerned about entrenching themselves behind upper-class barriers and passing on their status to their children. As a result, many turned to politics, hoping through political activity to perpetuate a socio-political climate protective of the advantages they associated with colonial residence.

Too numerous to be absorbed into the governors' councils, and without the political leverage necessary to procure imperial appointments, many prominent colonials gravitated towards the assembly. Analogous in a general way to the British House of Commons, the assembly was the ideal vehicle for giving expression to their desire for the consolidation of local political power and for expanding areas of colonial autonomy. Although many of those who became involved in assembly politics remained back benchers for all of their political life, there appeared within all of the colonies a succession of politicians who dominated assembly committees, mastered assembly procedures, and led attacks against gubernatorial pretension. These pre-modern versions of the professional politician, along with a sprinkling of others who were more polemicists than strategists, were instrumental in crystallizing public opinion behind efforts to restructure the royal prerogative and consolidate assembly powers.

As the early immigrant elites were replaced by creole sons, and as initial political gains were followed up by further successes, colonial political leaders became convinced of their own competence and of the soundness of their political judgment. Ironically, this development was prompted by a sense of inferiority that provincials often felt towards metropolitan centers. Aware of their rustic surroundings, prominent people in all of the colonies paid an obeisance to London by imitating the English in everything from style of dress to standards of professionalization. As the eighteenth century wore on, transatlantic shipping ties grew stronger and facilitated the Anglicization of colonial elites. That process strengthened political leadership in two ways. As the colonists selectively adapted a variety of English cultural norms, they became adept at turning standards of English political conduct back on the British – that is, in defending local autonomy on the grounds of British liberty. It also created a common cultural language among the various provincial elites, which helped to create a larger sense of colonial community. Inspired by the self-confidence that Anglicization and a primitivist sense of provincial rectitude bred, politically active provincials pushed their interests to the point where they could see the British imperial connection only from their blatantly colonial perspective. The power of the assemblies and their vigorous assertion of popular liberties during the mid-eighteenth century simply reflected the self-confidence of the colonial elites who manned the provincial legislatures.

Of course, there was no simple correlation between the longevity of the elites and the power of the colonial assemblies. Virginia had one of the oldest creole elites, but the Virginia assembly was relatively slow in its movement towards governmental dominance. Pennsylvania's case was very different. There, first-generation Quaker immigrants drove the assembly to a level of power never eclipsed by any other colony.

But despite the variations that occurred from colony to colony, the overall tendency was the same: self-conscious colonial elites used the assemblies to legitimize their search for political power, and, whatever their degree of political autonomy, they felt their position consistent with their loyalty to the British Empire.

It is important to recognize, however, that, no matter how closely colonial political elites were bound by social and economic interests, they were frequently fractured by factional disputes. In most colonies, the late seventeenth and early eighteenth centuries were distinguished by intra-elite conflicts that accompanied efforts to augment assembly power. Rarely were governor and council bereft of all support, and colonials warred among themselves over which faction should be the leading champion of assembly rights. As the eighteenth century wore on, the character of factional behavior varied from colony to colony. In Massachusetts a pro-governor court faction appeared in opposition to an assembly-based country faction. In the proprietary colonies of Maryland and Pennsylvania popular and proprietary parties imparted structure to intra-elite conflict. Virginia and New York were opposites: faction virtually disappeared in Virginia, while it split New York's elite at various junctures. While provincial elites shared a general interest in augmenting this sphere of colonial autonomy, that did not prevent periodic disagreements about who should take the lead, or at what point reconciliation with imperial demands should take place.

4. LOCAL GOVERNMENT INSTITUTIONS

One of the major reasons why the colonial assemblies and the political elites who directed them were able to consolidate their power so effectively in eighteenth-century America was that political activity was so broadly based. Levels of local government underlay the assemblies, a broad franchise included many citizens as voters, a comparatively open press provided opportunities for politicization and mobilization, and there were few impediments to open public expression of popular discontent. Local representative institutions were ubiquitous in the colonies, and they frequently served both as a proving ground for potential provincial leaders and as a vehicle for politicizing the population. Of course, most local governmental institutions originated in the seventeenth century during the first years of each colony's life; but, no matter how the nature of local government changed over the decades, most maintained their vitality during the eighteenth century. Moreover, as most colonies expanded, they replicated and frequently elaborated their older institutions of local government. In New England town government marched with new settlers into vacant lands and bred in each settlement a sense of political competence. In the mid-Atlantic, county government intersected with provincial government at numerous junctures. In the Chesapeake country, small planters participated in a great variety of local offices. Such widespread experience with local government built up feelings of self-reliance that in turn enhanced the confidence of politicians who would go on to become provincial leaders.

5. POLITICAL AWARENESS AND THE FRANCHISE

One of the most distinctive features of the American colonies in the eighteenth century was the broad franchise that brought to many the opportunity to vote in provincial elections. Franchise requirements varied from colony to colony, but the level of property ownership, the rental value of real estate, or the amount of personalty they required in all cases was relatively low. While voting eligibility depended on the economic structure of different towns or townships, in most cases the majority of adult males had sufficient resources to qualify for the vote. The growing stratification of wealth in colonial cities may have decreased the percentage of eligible voters in such urban centers as Boston or New York City, but it is not clear that such trends were sufficiently widespread to reduce the percentage of voters who turned out for closely contested elections in the later colonial decades. Although provincial politicians occasionally voiced ambiguous feelings about the desirability of a broad and active electorate, frequent victories at the polls confirmed their right to govern and convinced them that in doing so they were speaking on their neighbors' behalf. Because colonists put considerable emphasis on the existence of tangible ties between community and representative, widespread electoral support legitimized political leadership. But so, too, did electoral apathy. When voter participation dropped to very low levels, as it frequently did in the absence of contending personalities or contentious issues, political leaders argued that a *pro forma* ratification of their incumbency demonstrated the community's trust. In either case, the fact of a broad electorate encouraged confidence among members of the political elite.

As colonial populations increased during the eighteenth century, one of the most important means of politicizing and mobilizing the electorate was through the press. Newspapers began to appear in the colonies in the early eighteenth century, and their numbers gradually multiplied. Printers were generally prepared to publish any pamphlet that brought them a profit. Politicians quickly recognized that polemics could be used to persuade voters to support assembly battles against prerogative claims, or to strengthen their factional position over such issues as currency management, defense appropriations, or the conflicts of personality and advantage that from time to time divided them. There is no question that the informational infrastructure which the press represented did produce some notable instances of politicization and mobilization during the late colonial decades. In absolute terms, the numbers of colonial residents who occasionally responded to political appeals by voting in elections increased during the eighteenth century. In some areas, they increased in relative terms as well. In Boston, for example, the percentage of adult males who voted in provincial elections rose by approximately 10 per cent between the 1720s and the early 1760s. But the trends were not always so clear. Despite the growing number of voters who turned out to support Philadelphia's politicians, in relative terms the percentage of voters was greater before 1750 than it was during the 25 years before the Revolution. While an active press could convince popular politicians that the community stood behind them, such signs of politicization did not always presage the willingness of voters to go to the polls in great numbers. Apparent politicization did not signify a predictable electoral mobilization.

A political environment in which the franchise was broad and the habits of local government weighted towards inclusion, and where an open press encouraged politicization, would seem to invite a robust articulation of community opinion anytime neighbors felt so inclined. In fact, colonial mobs did appear from time to time – to enforce community standards which elected or appointed officials ignored; to disrupt traditional electoral proceedings; to exert pressure on behalf of a particular governmental policy; or to express some social- or economic-based outrage at current conditions. Given the speed with which citizens could transform themselves into mobs, and the absence of a coercive force capable of containing the crowd (militia men were frequently mob participants), members of the colonial political elites were at times uneasy with what they perceived as their precarious perch atop the existing social order. Mitigating this sense of unease were the many instances in which established political leaders emerged unscathed from local crises. On some occasions they faced down mobs; on others, they either tacitly encouraged or passively accepted crowd activities in order to consolidate their claims to popular support. Such successes, and the absence of any major socio-political upheaval in any of the colonies in the eighteenth century, built up confidence among colonial leaders that they had the ability to withstand challenges and to control local affairs.

6. STABILITY AND DEFERENCE

The political strength that the various colonial societies had developed by the mid-eighteenth century is best described by reference to the ways in which stability and deference characterized colonial politics. Two of the three most striking features of eighteenth-century politics were the rise to power of the assembly and the con-solidation of colonial elites. Both tended to bring stability to colonial affairs. Insti-tutionally, most assemblies quickly became strong enough to control a considerable portion of the provincial political agenda, and thus they were able to prevent sudden changes in the relationship between colonists and imperial authorities – provided, of course, the British did not bring Parliament or the military into the equation. At the same time, tenacious colonial elites, distinguished by wealth, education, close kinship connections with other provincial politicians, and a gentry style of life, tightened their grasp on assembly seats. As they did so, the turnover rate of politicians dropped, suggesting fewer contested elections and growing electoral advantages for incumbents. Factional splits lost the quick-changing, life-threatening intensity that had dis-tinguished them in the late seventeenth century, and evolved into what became familiar structural or ideological differences. Of course, there were occasional realign-ment crises in most colonies, but rarely did these upheavals produce much of a departure in the substance of politics, and never did they alter the status of those who occupied assembly seats.

When we add to these observations the third salient characteristic of eighteenth-century colonial political development – that colonists enjoyed an open political environment with a strong tradition of participatory government – it is clear how the notion of deference has come to play such an important part in explaining the stability of colonial politics. Time after time in the colonies, voters of middling and lower social rank elected the rich and the well-connected to represent them. Ordinary citizens deferred to gentlemen whose upper-class friends touted them as men of capacity, well fit to defend liberty on behalf of their fellow citizens. By voting as they did, and refusing to challenge the leadership of the provincial elites, the bulk of the politically active colonial population lent legitimacy and stability to regimes that in socio-economic terms were relatively narrow and exclusive. At the same time, the deference that middling and lower-class colonists ostensibly paid to their political leaders was of considerable importance in putting those leaders at ease. Without serious electoral challenges from the lower classes, members of the colonial elite frequently felt free to compete openly among themselves, and in the process to encourage political mobi-lization among members of the larger community. Encouraged by their long and tight control of elected offices, and confident of their abilities to continue leading the electorate, many members of the colonial elite were prepared to challenge British plans for reorganizing the empire during the late colonial years.

7. THE CHALLENGE TO BRITISH RULE

Looking at the eighteenth-century political development of the British North American colonies from the perspective of the American Revolution, we must recognize the double-edged nature of that development. As the assemblies rose to power, the colonists focused their loyalty for British imperial government increasingly on the lower houses. The assemblies gained a *de facto* legitimacy that allowed them to challenge Great Britain on behalf of their respective communities during the late 1760s and early 1770s. At the same time, however, the assemblies remained integral to the imperial structure of government, and led the way to various accommodations with the Crown and with Parliament. During the crisis of independence, for example, the Pennsylvania Assembly simply refused to repudiate British authority, and ultimately was swept away by the upheaval of revolution.

The elites who peopled the colonial assemblies were subject to the same problem of competing loyalties. Throughout the early and mid-eighteenth century, colonial elites consolidated their power, and were near unanimity in pushing for enlarged spheres of colonial autonomy. The confidence they gained in achieving that end, along with the experience they acquired in government, encouraged them to oppose British authority when imperial policy changed during the third quarter of the century. Yet, as in the case of the assemblies, there were members of the colonial elite who took the lead in accommodation with the British, and who saw themselves as quintessential Anglo-Americans. Many of these individuals were unwilling to jump into the void of independence. In some colonies, too, rivalries were so strong among the leaders of competing factions that the espousal of political radicalism by one group meant that others backed away from political risks they might otherwise have taken. Factionalism among the colonial elites fostered division in the revolutionary years.

A similar mixed legacy flowed from the colonial experience with vital institutions of local government, a broad electorate, an open press, and a tradition of legitimate community activism. The prevalence of widespread participation in local government reinforced the view that representative provincial institutions with a wide area of competency were essential for political legitimacy. However, just as a vital localism could contribute immensely to provincial strength, so could it undermine that power. In the contest over independence, and during the war that accompanied it, communities could withdraw into local non-involvement, or inter-act with provincial authorities in the most pragmatic and selective fashion. The broad franchise, of course, generated confidence among colonial leaders that they had the backing of the people. But either a sizable electoral vote or a low voter turnout did not always signify the kind of community support that provincial politicians chose to infer. A large turnout frequently meant a divided electorate, and a low voter count could mean apathy, quiet antipathy, or passive compliance rather than endorsement. As for the press and its power to politicize and mobilize, the record is mixed. Frequently provincial spokesmen were successful in mobilizing public opinion in support of their demands for colonial liberties, but the press could alienate as well as attract, and popular perspectives viewed from various social vantage points could extend beyond the horizons of political leaders. Politicization did not always mean mobilization in the way that established politicians intended. That was most evident in the case of community mobilization in public meetings, or in mobs. Although pre-revolutionary public demonstrations throughout most of the eighteenth century were tame affairs with limited objectives which rarely threatened popular political leaders, the potential

36

was always there for more radical political action. As the points of tension between Great Britain and the colonies multiplied, existing popular leaders frequently found themselves unwilling and unable to speak for various social and economic elements in the community who demanded that public policy respond to their concerns.

In considering the deference and stability that permeated eighteenth-century colonial politics, we must also bear in mind some caveats. Both deference and the stability which accompanied it may have been increasing in some of the southern colonies; deferential attitudes may also have been growing stronger among some social groups in the mid-Atlantic and New England colonies. But towards the end of the colonial period, there were indications that the old regimes had ossified and were showing signs of structural weakness. The mid-Atlantic colonies and South Carolina were slow to extend representation to their burgeoning back country, and a number of political demands were thus excluded from the assembly forums. Periodic tensions, born of economic and occupational stratification in the major colonial cities, may have fostered lower- and middle-class discontent with their political leaders. The consent of the governed may have come to rest less on deference than on performance in New England, on the tangible benefits of Quaker government in Pennsylvania, and on the interplay between power and clientage in New York. The competitive bidding for electoral support by competing political factions may have had a cumulative politicizing effect that encouraged lower social groups to speak out on their own behalf during the pre-revolutionary crises of authority. Finally, the professionalization of colonial politics may have brought some weakness as well as strength. Preoccupation with the processes of politics could lead to important political gains, but it could also blind provincial leaders to the larger concerns of those who composed colonial communities.

Unquestionably, the colonies did develop stable political regimes that were supported by deferential attitudes. But the kind of dynamic economic social and political adjustments that the colonies were undergoing in the third quarter of the eighteenth century meant that future periods of relative political stability would have to rest on a variety of new and different social bases. The political characteristics that distinguished the eighteenth-century colonies and made independence a possibility would not go through an era of revolution without some profound alterations.

FURTHER READING

Bailyn, Bernard: *The Origins of American Politics* (New York: Alfred A. Knopf, 1968).
Dinkin, Robert J.: *Voting in Provincial America: a Study of Elections in the Thirteen Colonies, 1689–1776* (Westport, Conn.: Greenwood Press, 1977).
Greene, Jack P.: *The Quest for Power: the Lower Houses of Assembly in the Southern Royal Colonies, 1689–1776* (Chapel Hill: University of North Carolina Press, 1963).
——: "Political mimesis: a consideration of the historical and cultural roots of legislative behavior in the British Colonies in the eighteenth century," *American Historical Review, 75* (1969), 337–60.
——: *Peripheries and Center: Constitutional Development in the Extended Politics of the British Empire and the United States, 1607–1788* (Athens and London: University of Georgia Press, 1986).
Jordan, David W.: *Foundations of Representative Government in Maryland, 1632–1715* (New York: Cambridge University Press, 1987).
Labaree, Leonard W.: *Royal Government in America: a Study of the British Colonial System before 1783* (New Haven, Conn.: Yale University Press, 1930).

Murrin, John M.: "Political development," *Colonial British America: Essays in the New History of the Early Modern Era*, ed. Jack P. Greene and J. R. Pole (Baltimore: Johns Hopkins University Press, 1984), 408–56.

Nash, Gary B.: *The Urban Crucible: Social Change, Political Consciousness, and the Origins of the American Revolution* (Cambridge, Mass.: Harvard University Press, 1979).

Pole, J. R.: "Historians and the problem of early American democracy," *American Historical Review*, 67 (1962), 626–46.

——: *Political Representation in England and the Origins of the American Republic* (New York and London, 1966); repr. (Berkeley and Los Angeles: University of California Press, 1971).

5

Population and family in early America

ROBERT V. WELLS

THE American Revolution was clearly a political and constitutional event. Nonetheless, in order to comprehend the social and economic context within which the Revolution occurred, it is necessary to understand the nature of the American population. The rapid growth of the population by 1775 made it possible for Americans to consider physical resistance to British rule, an option that would not have been possible a generation earlier. Because growth had occurred not only through natural increase (the excess of births over deaths), but also through immigration, only half the American people could claim English ancestry by 1775, and many of them had distant ties at best. Other characteristics of the population, such as age distribution, sex ratio, racial mix, and the presence of unfree people, gave life in the colonies a tone quite different from that in Britain, and even the various parts of America were sufficiently distinct from each other so that union was not an inevitable outcome. The importance of demography in the era of the Revolution becomes clearer when patterns on the continent are compared with those of Britain's island colonies.

Demographic structures are of interest not only for broad social and economic reasons, but also because they shape and are shaped by families. Families in early America were more important in the affairs of every individual than they are today, so we will examine how they were organized and what they did to and for their members. Finally, demographic patterns limited the choices that were available to American leaders during and after the Revolution. If nothing else, political structures had to be found that could govern a heterogenous people, spread thinly over a vast territory, with a history of rapid expansion and independent action.

Before discussing the actual patterns of the population, some mention of the sources for our information is necessary. Nothing in the colonial period compares with the censuses of the twentieth century. The British Government did manage to get censuses taken in some of the colonies, especially after 1700. Their success was limited, however, for colonies such as New York and Rhode Island have a long series of counts, but Virginia has nothing resembling a census after 1703, and Pennsylvania, the second largest colony by 1775, never counted its people. The first comprehensive survey of all the American people occurred only with the first federal census in 1790. In spite of the gaps in the censuses, estimates of the population have been made, making use of tax and militia lists to fill the holes. These estimates outline the basic trends in the decades before the Revolution. In addition, scholars have painstakingly pieced together significant details of life in a number of communities from New England to the Chesapeake. From these studies, patterns of birth, death, and marriage have become clearer, and their effects on family life have been described. Such details can be used to reinforce and elaborate on the information from the early censuses.

I. SIZE, GROWTH, AND DISTRIBUTION

From tentative beginnings in Jamestown, Virginia, in 1607, the population of the colonies grew to about two and a half million in 1775. The early years of settlement, however, were anything but impressive. For example, the population of Jamestown was about 500 in October 1609, but by the time winter was over only 60 people were left alive. Between 1618 and 1624 the Virginia Company, which owned the colony, sent approximately 6,000 settlers to America to join those already there. The mortality of these people was so high that a census taken in 1624, after an Indian attack and years of mismanagement, showed fewer than 1,300 residents. The first winter for the Pilgrims in Plymouth colony on Cape Cod was almost as bad, as about half the initial 100 settlers died and often no more than six or seven colonists were healthy at any one time. Later immigrants also went through a period of high mortality, known as seasoning, but by 1700 the colonies were clearly going to succeed.

Several features of Britain's colonies on the North American continent set them apart demographically from European colonies elsewhere in America or the rest of the world. When Europeans assumed control over new territory, their intent was to rule the conquered people for purposes of trade and extracting wealth. To these ends, the Portuguese and Spanish, for example, sent small garrisons of soldiers to rule the more numerous natives who did the work. By the time the English began to seek territories of their own, all the heavily populated parts of America were already claimed. They had to be satisfied with a few thinly settled islands in the Caribbean, which the Spanish no longer wanted, and the coast of North America, where there were few people and less gold to attract Britain's rivals. Within the first ten years of settlement, the companies and proprietors, who sponsored colonies for profit, realized that in order to make money they would have to recruit English men and women to work in the fields and provide markets for English goods. In 1618 the Virginia Company offered to potential settlers incentives that gave special shape to the future of American society. Anyone who moved to the new world received 50 acres of land for every passage paid. Thus, a man who brought his wife and two children to Virginia was granted 200 acres. The company also recognized that control over the colony from Britain was difficult, given uncertain transportation, and so provided for an assembly of local citizens to aid in government. Other colonies offered similar inducements, and added religious freedom. Thus, Americans quickly came to expect land, self-government, and religious toleration as part of living in the colonies.

Although the numbers were small at first, population began to grow rapidly by the middle of the seventeenth century, and continued to do so, through the era of the Revolution, down to the Civil War. This was one of the world's first great population explosions, with growth rates equaling or exceeding those in rapidly growing areas in the twentieth century. Table 1 provides details on this phenomenon, and shows figures for the population of the colonies that eventually became the United States. Two estimates of the population are given. The first, in column A, was made in 1909; the second was done in 1957. Although the numbers in column B are given to the last digit, they remain estimates and no more. Starting in 1790, the figures were derived from the census required by the Constitution of 1787. The two estimates, while in general agreement about the rapid growth of the population, differ over details. As is evident from the third column, which shows the ratio of the first estimate to the second, the figures produced in 1909 are almost always higher than the later

Table 1   Size and growth of the population in the colonies, 1610–1820

Year	A	B	Ratio A/B	Growth in decade ending in year given A	B	% black B
1610	210	350	.60			
1620	2,499	2,302	1.09	1090.0	557.7	
1630	5,700	4,646	1.23	128.1	101.8	1.3
1640	24,947	26,634	.94	390.3	473.3	2.2
1650	51,700	50,368	1.03	85.0	89.1	3.2
1660	84,800	75,058	1.13	64.0	49.0	3.9
1670	114,500	111,935	1.02	35.0	49.1	4.1
1680	155,600	151,507	1.03	35.9	35.4	4.6
1690	213,500	210,372	1.02	37.2	38.9	8.0
1700	275,000	250,888	1.10	28.8	19.3	11.1
1710	357,500	331,711	1.08	30.0	32.2	13.5
1720	474,388	466,185	1.02	32.7	40.5	14.8
1730	654,950	629,445	1.04	38.1	35.0	14.5
1740	889,000	905,563	.98	35.7	43.9	16.6
1750	1,207,000	1,107,676	1.09	35.8	22.3	20.2
1760	1,610,000	1,593,625	1.01	33.4	43.9	20.4
1770	2,205,000	2,148,076	1.03	37.0	34.8	21.4
1780	2,781,000	2,780,368	1.00	26.1	29.4	20.7
1790	3,929,625	3,929,625	1.00	41.3	41.3	19.3
1800	5,308,483	5,308,483	1.00	35.1	35.1	18.9
1820	9,638,453	9,638,453	1.00			18.4

Sources: US Bureau of the Census: *A Century of Population Growth* (Washington, DC, 1909), 9–10 [A]; and US Bureau of the Census: *Historical Statistics of the United States* (Washington, DC, 1960), Z 1–19 [B].

estimates. Even more interesting are the differences in the growth rates for the various decades, as the first estimate shows a much more stable pattern of growth after 1670. Until the decade of the 1780s, growth, according to the first study, ranged between 28.8 per cent and 38.1 per cent. In the second set of estimates, the range was from 19.3 per cent in the 1690s to 43.9 per cent in the 1750s, as growth exceeded 40 per cent four times in the eighteenth century and was under 30 per cent twice. Neither study provides a sufficient explanation of how the estimates were made to explain the difference, but the second set of figures appears to allow for more variation in the flow of immigrants in peace and war. It also may reflect the fact that the slave trade was uneven over the decades. Because the set of figures in column B tried to estimate the number of black Americans, they have been used to calculate the proportion of the population that was black.

The important aspects about the population are the same, whichever set of figures is used. From about 50,000 in 1650, the number of people reached 250,000 or more in 1700. This meant that the early fears about the colonies' survival no longer concerned either the English or the Americans. This fivefold increase was not matched in the next half century, but growth was still impressive, as the totals exceeded a million by a comfortable margin in 1750. By the outbreak of hostilities in 1775 the colonies counted about two and a half million inhabitants. Almost four million people were noted in the first census under the new government, and by 1820, when the revolutionary generation had given way to a new set of leaders, the country had almost ten million inhabitants. Between 1700 and 1800 the population increased almost 20 times. Both the English and Americans were aware of this growth and drew lessons from it that influenced their attitudes during the Revolution.

Ironically, the year in which representative government first made its appearance in Virginia (1619) was also the year in which the first black colonists were sold into bondage. The last column in table 1 traces the increase of the black part of the population, a change that has had lasting effects. The legal definition of slavery had evolved out of a system of unfree labor, affecting many different colonists, to focus almost exclusively on Blacks by 1660, when they comprised only a small part of the population. Following upheavals among white servants in Virginia in 1676, the opening up of the slave trade to free market operation after 1690, and a decline in the number of immigrants from England, white land-owners increasingly sought to purchase slaves to work for them. By 1700 one of every ten colonists was black. Heavy importations of slaves between 1730 and 1750 doubled the percentage of Blacks, so that at the time of the Revolution just over one of every five Americans was a slave. The end of major slave purchases lowered that proportion slightly by 1820, just before major influxes of Europeans reduced the percentage of Blacks in 1900 to the level of 1700.

Important sectional differences underlie the overall totals. New England, the middle colonies, and the South were distinguished by their demographic characteristics as much as by agriculture, culture, and climate. Table 2 illustrates several important points. In 1650 New England and the South were about equal in numbers, with just a scattering of Dutch and Swedes in the Hudson and Delaware valleys. By 1700 the South was slightly larger than New England, while New York, New Jersey, and Pennsylvania had started the growth that would take them past New England at the

Table 2 Regional differences in population, 1700–90

	1700	1750	1770	1790
New England				
Local population	92,763	360,011	581,038	1,009,206
% of all	37.0	30.8	27.0	25.7
% white	98.2	96.9	97.3	98.3
% black	1.8	3.1	2.7	1.7
Middle colonies				
Local population	54,464	296,459	555,904	1,017,087
% of all	21.7	25.3	25.9	25.9
% white	93.3	93.0	93.7	93.8
% black	6.7	7.0	6.3	6.2
South				
Local population	104,588	514,290	1,011,134	1,903,332
% all	41.7	43.9	47.1	48.4
% white	78.5	60.2	59.5	64.4
% black	21.5	39.8	40.5	35.6
Total population	250,888	1,170,760	2,148,076	3,929,625

Source: US Bureau of the Census: Historical Statistics of the United States (Washington, DC, 1960), Z 1–19.

end of the century. By the time of the Revolution almost half of all Americans lived in the South, with the remainder divided equally between the other two sections.

One of the most pronounced differences among the sections was the presence or absence of slaves. In New England the proportion of Blacks never exceeded 3.1 per cent. The corresponding figure for the middle colonies was 7 per cent. In the South, Blacks accounted for 21.5 per cent of the people in 1700 and 40.5 per cent in 1770. Even these figures cover up more local differences. For example, in 1750 the proportion of Blacks in Rhode Island was 10.1 per cent, about five times that of New Hampshire. In New York, 14.4 per cent of the people in 1750 were black, compared with only 2.4 per cent in Pennsylvania. South Carolina may have been the only mainland colony to have a black majority, but Virginia was not far behind. North Carolina, however, had a population that was only 27.1 per cent black. A look at Britain's island colonies places these figures in an interesting perspective. By 1774 Blacks accounted for 93.9 per cent of Jamaica's population and 78.2 per cent of Barbados's. Only Bermuda, with 45.1 per cent black in 1774, was like even the most heavily slave-oriented continental colonies. Other demographic patterns also varied by region, but none so pronounced as race.

2. DEMOGRAPHIC COMPOSITION

The composition of a population is as interesting as its size, and is often more important in determining the number of people available to work, run the government, or support social institutions such as churches or schools. As already mentioned, race was an important element in the population of the colonies, but so too were age, sex, ethnicity, and rural/urban residence.

In the early seventeenth century, colonies often had very unusual population because of selective migration. Lists of passengers for Virginia in 1634 and 1635 record six men for every one woman going to the colony; only 5 per cent of the migrants were under the age of 16. In contrast, New England received four women for every six men and many children in the years between 1620 and 1638. By the time of the Revolution, however, patterns had become more settled and similar among the mainland colonies.

Patterns for a select group of colonies are presented in table 3. Maryland is the only

Table 3 Age and sex composition (Whites, selected colonies)

Colony and year	Total population	% white	% age under 10	under 16	60 up	Number of men per 100 women
Connecticut (1774)	197,842	97.6	32.0	—	2.2[a]	98
Rhode Island (1774)	59,607	91.5	—	46.0	—	91
New York (1737)	60,437	85.2	32.6	—	—	99
New York (1771)	168,007	88.2	—	46.2	5.6[b]	109
Maryland (1755)	153,505	70.5	—	49.3	—	113
Bermuda (1774)	11,155	55.0	—	37.1	—	93
Barbados (1773)	88,164	21.8	—	38.0	—	72

[a] Over 70
[b] Males only

Source: Wells, Robert V.: *The Population of the British Colonies before 1776: a Survey of Census Data* (Princeton, NJ, 1975).

43

southern colony for which there is information after about 1700. Barbados, in 1773, and Bermuda, in 1774, provide interesting contrasts. The six colonies included in the table differed noticeably in size. Bermuda, with just over 11,000 inhabitants in 1774, was one of Britain's smaller colonies. Connecticut, New York, and Maryland were 15 to 20 times larger, and they in turn were eclipsed by Massachusetts, Pennsylvania, and Virginia. Of the latter, only Massachusetts counted her people after 1700, and that census was in 1764. One of the most obvious points of difference is in the proportion of Whites. Connecticut, with 97.6 per cent white, was much like the rest of New England, with the exception of Rhode Island, where 91.5 per cent were white. In New York, black slaves were more common, accounting for 14.8 per cent of the population in 1737 and 11.8 per cent in 1771. By 1755, the last year for which there is a census in the colonial period, Maryland's Whites made up only 70.5 per cent of the people. In the islands the proportion of Whites was lower still. Bermuda, with 55 per cent white in 1774, may have been a lot like South Carolina at the time. Barbados, on the other hand, was overwhelmingly committed to slavery, as fully 78.2 per cent of her people were black, and that island had more Whites than most of the Caribbean colonies.

The age composition of a population is important to study because the proportion of children affects the ratio of workers to consumers, the numbers in need of schooling, and the number of people old enough to assume political responsibility and military duty. In colonial America, 16 was the age at which young men were considered old enough to be taxed and serve in the militia. Attaining the age of 60 exempted one from these duties. Thus, many early censuses used 16 and sometimes 60 as ages for grouping the population. Women were also grouped in the same way, even though they did not pay taxes or serve in the militia. In general just under half of the population in the continental colonies was under 16 by the end of the eighteenth century, as is evident from the figures for Rhode Island, New York, and Maryland. Both Bermuda and Barbados had significantly fewer children. For some reason the Connecticut census of 1774 and the New York count of 1737 divided the population differently. In both cases, about one-third of the people were less than ten years old. This is normal in a population with about half under 16. The Connecticut census also recorded 2.2 per cent over 70, while 5.6 per cent of the males in New York in 1771 were 60 or older.

Since women were limited in their economic and political options in the eighteenth century, the ratio of men to women could also affect economic and political affairs. The main point illustrated by table 3 in this regard is that there were distinct regional differences among the colonies. By the outbreak of the Revolution, much of New England had a slight majority of females, at least among adults. As recently as 1755 Rhode Island's sex ratio had been 103 men for every 100 women. In Connecticut the ratio of men to women among those aged 20 to 70 was 98 to 100. There was a male surplus in the younger ages but an even more pronounced female majority over 70. South of New England, males generally predominated. The New York sex ratio for 1771 of 109 is much more in keeping with the full set of figures for that colony than is the ratio for 1737. New Jersey also had about 110 men for every 100 women from 1726 to 1772. The Maryland sex ratio reflects the presence of a number of white indentured servants, who were more likely to be male. In 1704, when servants had not yet given way to slaves in that colony, the sex ratio was 154 men to 100 women. The sex ratio in both Bermuda and Barbados shows a definite female majority. This was not always the case in the islands, for males were in the majority in most of the

Leeward Islands in 1756. The island of Tobago, which had recently been acquired from the French, had a most unusual population in 1775. All the Whites listed were adult males; among the Blacks, who accounted for 95.7 per cent of the total, 89.1 per cent were adult, and there were 151 men for every 100 women. This last figure was down from 212 men to 100 women in 1771. The 1775 sex ratio for Tobago is similar to those of slave populations on the mainland in the eighteenth century. There were more black children on the continent, but they were not as prevalent as the white young.

By 1775 the population of Britain's colonies was increasingly not English. One out of every five Americans traced his or her roots to Africa, not Europe. But even among the Whites, English ties were growing rarer. In the late seventeenth century the population in England ceased to grow and may even have declined briefly. As a result the colonies, which had once been seen as an outlet for excess people, were now viewed as a threat to the English population. Although a few non-English had come to the colonies before 1700, after that year Germans, Irish, Scots, and Welsh all began to move to America. The traditional estimate was that about 30 per cent of the total population were Whites from other than England. In the eighteenth century, Scots and Welsh, as well as Germans (*see* figure 3), were quite different from the English, and were proudly conscious of that fact. Recently, a new estimate of the ethnic composition of the United States in 1790 (which should reflect the situation in 1775) has suggested that there were more non-English than previously thought. In addition

FIGURE 3 Among the first Germans to arrive in America in search of freedom and security (they settled in Georgia) were the Salzburg Lutherans, a Protestant group whose members had been driven from their homes during the many religious wars (from "Die freundliche Bewillkommung der Salzburgischen," broadside, 1732).

Table 4   Major centers of urban population, 1700–90 (estimates and counts)

City	1700	1750	1770	1790
Boston	13,000	15,731	15,520	18,038
Newport	4,640	6,600	9,200	6,716
New York	8,600	13,300	21,800	33,131
Philadelphia	8,500	13,400	28,000	42,444
Charles Town	n.a.	<8,000	10,863	16,359
Baltimore	n.a.	n.a.	n.a.	13,503
Salem, Mass.	n.a.	n.a.	4,500	7,921
Providence	3,916	3,400	4,320	6,371
Total	38,656	60,431	94,203	144,483
% of total population	6.1	5.5	4.4	3.7

Source: US Bureau of the Census: *A Century of Population Growth* (Washington, DC, 1909), 11, 163.

the unequal distribution of these people enhanced sectional differences. For example, Scots may have accounted for only 8.7 per cent of Connecticut's population, compared with the 81 per cent who were of English ancestry. In contrast, 32.9 per cent of South Carolinians may have been Scots, and only 36.7 per cent of the Whites were English. The estimates for Pennsylvania include 19.5 per cent English, 33.3 per cent German, and 42.8 per cent Celtic (Welsh, Scots, and Irish). Overall, the white population of New England was about 75 per cent English, but, from New York on south, non-English were in the majority. Of course this was also where the vast majority of Blacks lived.

Although the vast majority of Americans were farmers, a significant number lived in towns. Urban residents were significant beyond their numbers because they were most directly linked to the British Empire and were most immediately affected by changes in colonial policy. Because colonial governments were located in the colonial towns, the residents there were generally better informed about and more active in politics. Table 4 indicates the size of the most prominent colonial towns in the eighteenth century. Boston, which was the largest town in 1700, grew until about 1740, but then war and environmental problems brought on by too many people in too little space brought a half-century halt to its growth. In contrast, both Philadelphia and New York prospered during the century, with Philadelphia gaining a temporary edge after 1750. Newport experienced moderate growth until 1770, but was damaged severely during the Revolution and was eventually overtaken by its rival, Providence. Charles Town, South Carolina, was the single major town in the South until the rapid emergence of Baltimore after 1750. The most important southern city in the nineteenth century, New Orleans, was under French and Spanish control until 1804. Although these towns grew rapidly from 1700 to 1790, they did not keep pace with the rest of the colonies, with the result that their proportion of the colonial total fell from 6.1 per cent to 3.7 per cent.

3. CAUSES OF GROWTH AND CHANGE

Three factors determine the size and composition of all populations: fertility (births), mortality (deaths), and migration. The exact balance of these forces has not yet been determined, but it is possible to indicate the general relationship among these factors within each of the major divisions of the colonies. In New England the major determinant of the population quickly became the balance of births and deaths. After 1650 immigration was minimal. Although New England was eventually outstripped by the other sections, growth was still rapid because of high fertility and mortality levels that were probably as favorable as any in the world before 1800. The middle colonies shared in the rapid natural increase caused by high birth rates and low death rates. There, however, migration had a more significant impact. After 1700, Germans, Scots, Irish, and Welsh moved in to help swell the population. This immigration was uneven both in its impact on the individual colonies and over the course of the century. Some slaves were also imported, but not to the same extent as in the South.

Patterns in the South contrast sharply with those farther north. It is also necessary to distinguish the seventeenth from the eighteenth century. Migration to the South was higher throughout the entire colonial period. It did, however, undergo some marked changes, when English immigrants of the seventeenth century gave way to Blacks in the eighteenth along the coastal regions. In the middle of the eighteenth century, Scots and Germans moved into the western hill country. Mortality in the South was much higher in the seventeenth century than in the other sections, and although life expectancy improved after 1700 the climate continued to be favorable for diseases such as malaria. The birth rate was low in the early years because of the scarcity of women and high death rates. As the sex ratio came into better balance and mortality improved, family sizes in the South compared favorably with those elsewhere. The most distinct region in America was the Caribbean islands. They were almost the exact opposite of New England. Life was short for both Blacks and Whites, childbearing was low, and a steady stream of black slaves meant society was more New Africa than New England.

Migration Migration deserves first detailed comment, if only because it was so influential in differentiating the sections. Estimates of the total number of immigrants to the mainland vary because records are scattered and uneven in quality. Recent work has, however, made it clear that immigrants were a major force in colonial life. Equally important, many of them came involuntarily. About 350,000 slaves were imported in the eighteenth century alone. No less than 65,000 Germans arrived in Philadelphia between 1727 and 1776. Perhaps as many as 100,000 Scots and Irish came to America in the decade before Independence, joining the 17,500 convicts who were shipped to the colonies between 1718 and 1772. In the period between the Boston Tea Party and the end of the first year of actual fighting, 5,196 English and 3,872 Scots came to the increasingly rebellious colonies. In all, a million people may have moved to the colonies between 1607 and 1776.

Who were these people? The answer depends on the time and place. The differences in the early migrants to New England and Virginia have already been noted. Perhaps half to two-thirds of the Whites came as indentured servants. A study of 20,657 servants recorded in English registers at various years from 1655 to 1775 shows 81.6 per cent were male and 75 per cent were aged 16 to 25. The tendency for servants to be young males was more pronounced after 1700 than before. Interestingly, servants claimed skilled occupations 85 per cent of the time in the 1770s, compared with 30 to 35 per cent in the 1680s. Of the total, 55 per cent of the women and 52 per cent of the men went to the Chesapeake. Pennsylvania received 6 per cent of the men and fewer women. Only 2 per cent of both men and women went to the other mainland colonies. Barbados was the primary destination of servants in the 1650s, and Jamaica dominated from 1730 to 1749. Together, however, they attracted only 28 per cent of the men and 26 per cent of the women over the entire period. After 1750 almost all servants went to the Chesapeake, with a few heading to Pennsylvania.

The 9,364 migrants who arrived just as the imperial conflict was escalating can be described in detail. In general, two different groups moved to America. Single laborers from London and the immediate vicinity went to Maryland, Pennsylvania, and Virginia. Families left economic hardships in Scotland and the north of England for new farms in New York and North Carolina. As might be expected, children were more common among the Scots than the English. Only 3.4 per cent of the latter were under ten, compared with 15.1 per cent of the former (see table 3). Almost no older people went. Of the English, 83.8 per cent were male, compared with 59.9 per cent among the Scots. About two-thirds of the migrants went alone, as the proportion moving with their families was 18.2 per cent for the English and 41.7 per cent for the Scots. Artisans were the most common occupational group in both streams. The English, however, were much more likely to be indentured. About a quarter of the migrants indicated why they were moving. Most of the English saw the move as a new opportunity, while the majority of the Scots were fleeing a harsh life. Poverty was mentioned by 307 Scots as a reason to move; no English made this claim.

Fertility and mortality   Fertility and mortality also shaped the colonial population. Of these, fertility was the most important because it contributed to the high proportion under the age of 16. In general, families in the colonies averaged six to eight children during the eighteenth century. The corresponding figure for England was nearer four. One reason for the large family size was early marriage on the part of women, brought on by the number of men seeking wives. Once married, couples lived together for 25 to 30 years and so were able to have numerous children. Children arrived once every two years, much as in England, but they arrived over a longer period. The South did not achieve this level of childbearing until the death rates declined after 1700. But by 1750 most colonists had large families.

Death rates were subject to greater variation. The terrible mortality of the early years lasted well into the seventeenth century in the South. In contrast, New Englanders quickly achieved remarkably long lives. Precise figures are rare because adequate records are missing. When illness and death were common, however, life expectancy may not have exceeded 25 years at birth. At best, life expectancy reached 45 or even a little higher. (At the end of the twentieth century it is over 70.) A life expectancy of 25 means that more than 300 out of every 1,000 babies will not see their first birthday. Under half will reach marriageable age, and only 170 will attain 60. With life expectancy at 45, 850 of the 1,000 infants will live to the age of one, 716 will survive to marry, and 430 will celebrate 60. Today, however, a higher proportion live to 60 than made it to one even under the best of colonial conditions. Smallpox, malaria, and tuberculosis were some of the more important killers the colonists faced. On the other hand, Americans may have been as well fed, housed, and clothed as any people in the world once the hardships of the early years passed.

4. FAMILY AND POPULATION

The demographic patterns examined so far were both shaped by and in turn influenced families. Birth, death, and marriage were obviously closely linked to families. Single migrants sought to establish families as soon as possible when they were free to do so. The term "family" can be defined in a number of different ways. Perhaps the most common use of the word in the eighteenth century was to refer to a domestic unit of parents, children, and servants, all of whom were engaged in common economic activity under the control of a single head. Kin were also part of the family and could be called on to help in time of trouble, or to assist in family business.

Demography had a greater impact on three other aspects of the family: children born, households, and the life course. Once a man and woman married, they could expect to have between six and eight children if their marriage was not broken by an early death. This was the result of early marriages for women and good health for all. Because both fertility and mortality were unpredictable, individual experience varied considerably from the average. For example, both large and small families were common among one group of women, who averaged 7.4 children. Women who had ten or more children accounted for 24.3 per cent of all wives. Another 10.9 per cent had no more than three children. From the children's perspective, large families were relatively common, if only because one family with ten children had as many offspring as five couples with two each. Thus, 50.7 per cent of the children lived in families with nine or more children. Where mortality remained high, or immigration created an imbalanced sex ratio, family life was more uncertain and children scarcer.

The household is another way to look at families. In this case, the perspective is on how many people lived together at any given moment, as births added new members, and marriages, deaths, and migration subtracted old. In the eighteenth century, white households on the continent contained an average of 5.5 to 7 persons. Once again, averages are deceiving. In Rhode Island in 1774, the average for all households was 6.3. Only 1.4 per cent of the households were people living alone; 15.8 per cent had at least ten members; 51.2 per cent of the households had five to nine members. Since colonial houses were relatively small, crowding was common and the ability to get along was critical.

Several factors account for the variations in household size. As the age of the head of the family increased, so too did the number of people under his or her control. The longer a couple was married, the more children would be living at home until the head reached the age of 45 or 50. In addition, older householders often had enough money to be able to buy servants or slaves. When the family head was a woman, the household was generally smaller both because of the absence of a husband and because women were not as wealthy. Wealth also affected the size of households among men, with rich families being larger than poor. Generally, racial or ethnic minorities had households that were smaller than their neighbours'. Some of these factors are related, but at present the ties among age, race, and wealth cannot be separated. Perhaps a major source of variation among households was the presence or absence of servants or slaves. In 1790, for example, the average household size for Whites was 5.7. In South Carolina, households averaged 9.5 members when slaves are included. The average modern American household has under three people. As might be expected, households in the Caribbean colonies were quite different from those on the mainland. They were much larger, had many more slaves, and fewer children.

When a young man and woman married, prevailing demographic patterns provided some expectations about what course their lives might follow. The following, based on the experience of some Quakers in the middle colonies, is representative of the northern colonies in the latter half of the eighteenth century. The family was formed when marriage occurred, at about 25 for men and 20.5 for women. Children arrived quickly, and kept arriving every two and a half years for most of the next two decades. Once a woman reached 40 she was not likely to have more children, but the youngest would probably not marry for another 20 years. By this time, either the husband or wife would have been dead almost ten years. In contrast, childbearing at the end of the twentieth century seldom lasts even ten years, and couples can anticipate a long life together after their children have left home.

Probably no institution in colonial America was as important to the well-being of both individuals and society as the family. Families were the center of economic activity in an agricultural society. Both production and consumption occurred at home as parents, children, and servants worked at various tasks around the farm. In the absence of any welfare system, families took care of the sick, elderly, and orphaned. Even single people were placed in a family when they needed help. Government depended on families for taxes, voters (the head of the family only), militia, and control of subordinates. At a time when police were unheard of outside the towns, parents, and especially fathers, were expected to control their families. Although there were a few schools in the colonies, families provided much of the education, both to their own children and to apprentices. Churches taught obedience to women, children, and servants, and in exchange won members from the next generations. Paternal authority was the norm, and was enforced by custom, teaching, civil authority, and economics. In a world where age, sex, and race automatically disqualified a person from power both at home and in public, democracy was not yet widespread.

As the eighteenth century brought better life chances and a more even sex ratio to slaves, family life became a stabilizing force on plantations with numerous slaves. In the end, however, slave marriages were never recognized as legally binding by the masters, who felt free to separate families by sale or transfer to a new plantation.

The Revolution brought modest changes to family life by 1800. Divorce, which had been almost impossible in the colonial period, was made somewhat easier. Women experienced moderate gains in economic opportunities. Many reformers urged that the future mothers of the republic's citizens needed to be educated in order to raise their children properly. Children gave some evidence of resisting parental authority, both by insisting on more say in whom they would marry, and by starting their families before they were married. Although the connection is not clear, at least one group of Americans began consciously to limit the size of their families as the Revolution broke out. At the time few noticed these changes, but they became an increasingly important part of American society after 1800.

5. POPULATION AND THE REVOLUTION

Direct connections between demography and the resistance to Britain are hard to demonstrate. But population patterns did influence the course of events from 1760 to 1820. The most obvious link is between the growth of the colonies and their ability to fight. In 1700 military resistance to Britain would have been unthinkable; it was a possibility by 1775. Here, the contrast to the Caribbean is instructive. The island colonies agreed with many of the objections their northern counterparts raised about continued British control. In the end, however, they remained loyal, partly because they were small and isolated, and partly because the Whites who ruled were unwilling to give up British protection against the vast majority of slaves. Only Jamaica, with

209,000 people in 1774, rivaled the mainland colonies in size, but the critical point was that almost 197,000 of the inhabitants were slaves.

The growth of the colonial population had a psychological effect in both America and Britain. By 1763, the English were well aware of the rapid growth that the censuses were recording. As the Seven Years' War came to a close and the royal officials began to consider how to restructure the empire, they debated what to do with the colonial population. One suggestion was to encourage the colonists to spread out so they would be unable to aid each other. The counter-proposal was to restrict the settlers east of the Alleghenies, where they would be accessible to British merchants and soldiers. In spite of efforts to enforce the latter policy, British governors were complaining in the 1770s about their inability to control the restless and independent pioneers.

Americans, too, were aware of growth, but they drew quite different conclusions. In one way or another, prominent Americans such as Benjamin Franklin; Ezra Stiles, President of Yale; and Edward Wigglesworth, a Harvard professor, all pointed with pride to the rapid increase. They saw this as a sign of American virtue (an important idea in republican thought), and told readers on both sides of the Atlantic that Americans would soon outnumber the English. This was an important conclusion in an age that believed that population meant wealth and wealth meant power.

After the war the creation of a union was rendered difficult by population patterns. The preferred form of government was a republic, but, according to theory, republics should be small and homogeneous. The new states were anything but that. A population of three and a half million was thinly scattered over the seacoast from what is now Maine to Georgia. In addition, immigration in the eighteenth century had produced a complex array of cultures, which had already led to political clashes before 1775. Slavery was another point that divided many Americans who were beginning to take seriously their rhetoric of freedom and equality. Thus, the debate in the Constitutional Convention over representation was serious not only in an abstract sense, but also because of the realities of population. The establishment of a regular census and the 3/5ths Compromise (which determined that five slaves would be counted as three free persons for purposes of taxation and representation) are two of the more obvious effects population had on the formation of the government. James Madison made an important contribution to overcoming the fears over an over-large republic when he suggested, in *Federalist*, No. 10, that republics might be safer with a large, complex population that could not agree on anything than in a small country where a tyrannizing majority might easily grab power.

The nineteenth century saw demographic revolutions that rivaled the political one of the previous century. Between 1800 and 1920, Americans swept over the continent to the Pacific, became an urban people, received 30 million immigrants, cut the size of their families in half, and improved their health and life expectancy. The world of Woodrow Wilson was no longer that of Washington or Jefferson. Just as Americans determined their political fate in 1776, they began to assert control over matters of life and death, and so transformed their existence in ways never before seen.

FURTHER READING

Bailyn, Bernard: *Voyagers to the West: a Passage in the Peopling of America on the Eve of the Revolution* (New York: Alfred A. Knopf, 1986).
Demos, John: *A Little Commonwealth: Family Life in Plymouth Colony* (New York: Oxford University Press, 1970).

McDonald, Forrest, and McDonald, Ellen Shapiro: "The ethnic origins of the American people, 1790," *William and Mary Quarterly*, 37 (1980), 179–99.

Potter, James: "The growth of population in America, 1700–1860," in *Population in History*, ed. D. V. Glass and D. E. C. Eversley (London: Edward Arnold, 1965), 631–88.

Tate, Thaddeus W., and Ammerman, David L. (eds.): *The Chesapeake in the Seventeenth Century: Essays on Anglo-American Society* (Chapel Hill: University of North Carolina Press, 1979).

United States Bureau of the Census: *A Century of Population Growth: From the First Census of the United States to the Twelfth, 1790–1900* (Washington, DC: Government Printing Office, 1909).

Wells, Robert V.: *The Population of the British Colonies in America Before 1776: a Survey of Census Data* (Princeton, NJ: Princeton University Press, 1975).

——: *Revolutions in Americans' Lives: a Demographic Perspective on the History of Americans, Their Families, and Their Society* (Westport, Conn.: Greenwood Press, 1982).

6

Socio-economic development of the colonies

EDWIN J. PERKINS

T HE economy of the North American colonies developed in very independent fashion in the seventeenth and eighteenth centuries. The economic events precipitating the independence movement began in the mid-1760s when Parliament tried to readjust the overall character of its political and economic relationship with the colonies by bringing them more within the administrative and fiscal sway of the home government. A large standing army was permanently stationed in North America to protect these highly valued overseas colonies from uncertain, ill-defined threats, and the British Exchequer sought tax revenues from the prime beneficiaries of this military protection to offset at least a small portion of defense costs. But the Americans resisted, claiming the new taxes violated their rights and liberties. Parliament insisted on demonstrating the superiority of its position, and the irreconcilable debate over the issue of sovereignty led to an armed rebellion and total independence. For an entire half century, from 1765 until 1815, economic interaction between Great Britain and the 13 political units in North America, which in tandem possessed the highest living standards around the globe, were periodically and often drastically interrupted, with the result that neither party in this prolonged conflict fully enjoyed all the mutual advantages accruing from the transatlantic exchange of goods and services.

The aggregate output of goods and services in the 13 colonies grew at a very rapid pace over the course of the seventeenth and eighteenth centuries. Fueled by burgeoning population growth and gradual but nonetheless steady increases in the productivity of workers, the size of the colonial economy expanded at a rate three or four times faster than that of Great Britain over the three-quarters of a century before American independence. Starting from a very low base, colonial production in 1650 was minuscule on a comparative basis; by 1700 output was rising, but it remained less than 5 per cent of the mother country's. By 1775, however, the future United States had developed a robust economy nearly two-fifths the size of Great Britain's. It was no longer a mere colonial outpost on a distant continent. Moreover, per capita incomes, or median living standards, for members of free, white households in British North America were higher than those in England and probably the very highest that the world had ever witnessed for a region with a population of over two million.

On the eve of their declaration of political independence, the rebellious colonies possessed a strong and vibrant economy, and they bitterly resented the persistent efforts of parliamentary leaders to consider them in an unequal, subservient light. Benjamin Franklin had projected, on the basis of prevailing rates of economic expansion, that North America would likely surpass Great Britain within two more generations – and his estimates were not far off the mark. Indeed, the most thriving economy under British rule was situated along the eastern shore of the North Atlantic.

But British leaders in the 1770s insisted on taking a static rather than a dynamic view of political and economic developments within the empire. Their outlook was shortsighted and unrealistic since, by the third quarter of the eighteenth century, the underlying value of a close connection with North America was not within the realm of political control but linked instead to the steadily increasing opportunities for mutually advantageous trade in raw materials, manufactured goods, and shipping services.

1. POPULATION GROWTH AND THE ECONOMY

Demographics and economics were closely linked in colonial America. Population growth, stemming from immigration and natural increase, drove the economy forward at expansion rates as high as 40 per cent or more per decade (*see also* Chapter 5, §1). Birth rates were high as a result of early marriage, while death rates for both infants and adults were relatively low in comparison with those in Europe. American women married in their early twenties, several years sooner than in Europe. Most wives who survived to age 40 typically gave birth to six or seven children, of which four or five survived to adulthood. Because of the mild climate, hearty diets, and inexpensive wood for household heating, persons who survived childhood diseases generally lived into their late fifties and sixties.

The voluntary immigration of young people from Britain and northern Europe, who were responding to reports of unprecedented opportunities for upward mobility in North America, also contributed to the rapid climb in population. After 1670 the forced immigration of enslaved Africans had a demographic impact as well; by independence, Blacks accounted for over 20 per cent of the total population. In the southern colonies, where slavery reigned, Blacks comprised more than two-fifths of the workforce. In 1775 the size of colonial population, at 2.6 million – including 2.1 million Whites, 540,000 Blacks, plus perhaps 50,000 Native Americans – was ten times greater than at the start of the century. Taking into account improvements in productivity as well, the aggregate economy was about 14 times larger when Thomas Jefferson penned the Declaration of Independence than in 1700.

2. SUPPLY OF LAND

Three vital economic factors had a profound effect on population growth and the structure of the economy: the colonies had a surplus of fertile land and other natural resources but shortages of the labor and capital required for development. The ownership of land was the main goal of most pre-industrial peoples, and in North America that goal was within the reach of almost every free citizen. The availability of thousands of acres of undeveloped land stimulated immigration and likewise encouraged the formation of large family units because parents were confident that their many children would be adequately fed in youth and that, upon marriage, a couple could always earn an adequate living by farming. Except in certain areas of New England, population pressure did not hold down the median size of farms for succeeding generations. Farmers, who comprised about three-quarters of the colonial workforce, typically lived on properties containing 60 to 100 acres, a huge farm by European standards.

Only about one-third of farm property was planted in crops. The additional land was a combination of pasture and forest. The main food crops were maize (Indian corn), wheat, rye, and rice. Maize was an indigenous food source raised by Native American tribes from Maine to Georgia. The European settlers quickly adopted this food staple, for it complemented other agricultural crops ranging from grains to tobacco. Rye was planted extensively in New England, while wheat was important in the middle colonies and, after 1730, in the Chesapeake region. Rice was eaten in South Carolina and Georgia. Farmers also raised barley for brewing beer, apples for cider, and oats and hay for livestock. Vegetable gardens were planted in season. Ample forests provided wood for cooking and household heating.

The high incomes of farmers by contemporary world standards was revealed most clearly in their heavy consumption of meat and dairy products. Total meat consumption was around 200 pounds annually for adult males, with lesser amounts for women and children; the high protein content of diets translated into the achievement of near modern heights for the general population. Americans were on average about two inches taller than their English counterparts. Colonial farms kept a varied livestock. The typical farmer in Connecticut in the mid-eighteenth century, for example, owned 10 cattle, 16 sheep, 6 pigs, 2 horses, and a team of oxen. Cows produced milk, cheese, and butter, chickens laid eggs, while sheep provided the wool for warm clothing. Virtually every farm household was self-sufficient in terms of food production. Except for the first few decades after the settlement of Virginia in 1607, starvation was not a serious threat in British North America.

In addition to producing enough food to provide a hearty diet for every member of the household, the family farm also generated surpluses available for sale in markets at home and abroad. Depending on the climate and fertility of the soil, households had the opportunity to divert up to two-fifths of total output to the market-place. Some families chose to divert extra grain into building their livestock herds, while others sold surpluses for cash or credit and purchased a variety of products and services from either neighbors, local towns, or overseas suppliers. By the mid-eighteenth century, roughly one-quarter of all goods exchanged in local markets had been transported across provincial borders. A substantial share of the discretionary income of colonial farmers was spent on imported English goods.

British credit to colonial merchants The American market loomed ever greater in British foreign trade over the course of the century, and London merchants extended huge amounts of credit to colonial merchants and southern planters to finance that trade. The debts accumulated by colonial buyers were incurred because of the optimism of both English creditors and colonial creditors about the future prospects of the economy. The offering of credit was an inducement to increase sales, and colonial households with rising incomes responded accordingly. The old argument, sometimes advanced by earlier generations of historians, that linked American rebelliousness to the burden of indebtedness has been grossly exaggerated. Large plantation owners in the Chesapeake were prone to complain in private about mounting debts and even expressed resentment about the tone of business relations with English merchants, but they kept buying and adding to their outstanding balances because of their overriding desire to maintain the material component of their high life styles. At no point in colonial history were Americans dependent upon the good will of English creditors for their well-being and prosperity. Credit was voluntarily extended and voluntarily accepted, with all parties, or the vast majority, obtaining the benefits bargained for and anticipated.

55

Land prices   Land prices were very low in the colonies compared with those in Europe. Indeed, the very existence of substantial tracts of land for sale in an impersonal market made the new world vastly different from the old. Even youths who failed to inherit substantial property were usually able to earn enough money from various labors to raise the down-payment to acquire a small farm. Unlike the situation in Great Britain, most tenant farmers did not remain landless over the course of their lives. Eventually the tenant household purchased the farm it occupied from the landlord, or the family pulled up stakes and moved into unsettled areas where land prices were very low.

The majority of farm households were independent units. Owners made their own decisions about crop selection and farm management, and they reaped the profits from the steady rise of land prices as local population increased. Since most married white males held title to sufficient property to meet requirements for voting, they were eligible to vote for all elected officials. The continuous availability of inexpensive, affordable land in every province was the major factor which led to the creation of a relatively highly participatory society in North America.

Distribution of wealth   In addition to its political impact, the large supply of salable land led to a surprisingly wide distribution of property. The majority of households had at least a modest stake in society, and they favored laws protecting property rights in land and in other bonded human beings, namely servants and slaves. The extremes of wealth and poverty so common in Europe were not as evident in the 13 colonies. Few Americans remained members of indigent households throughout their lives. Although up to one-third of all adult males held title to little tangible property, a careful analysis of the age distribution of wealth-holders reveals that most of the propertyless were unmarried persons under 30 years old. Over the course of the normal life-cycle, a person who survived to the age of 40 could anticipate living in a household of middling wealth and income. Only 3 to 5 per cent of middle-aged white males were genuinely poor and dependent on charity; a higher percentage of older widows fell into poverty, however. Slaves and indentured servants held no property, yet the living conditions provided by owners were generally adequate to maintain good health. No occupational group in the colonies had reason to fear the possibility of starvation or long-term deprivation.

A few privileged colonial households did control a disproportionate share of the aggregate wealth. Families which arrived in a given locale when it was undergoing initial settlement and then proceeded to save and expand their land holdings over several generations formed the core of an American counterpart to the English gentry. Since primogeniture and entail were legal principles less vigorously applied in North America, and particularly in the northern colonies, the patterns of land-ownership rarely led to great extremes of wealth. Even the very richest Americans were persons of only modest wealth by English standards. The colonies had no inherited nobility, and no large land holdings controlled by religious orders. Large estates in the South relied upon slave labor rather than white tenant families.

By the 1770s, the top 10 per cent of wealth-holders held somewhat over one-half of the region's net worth (assets minus liabilities) – a measurement that includes the ownership of indentured servants and slaves. The lower half of all wealth-holders laid claim to less than 5 per cent of colonial net worth. The middle colonies – New York, New Jersey, Pennsylvania, and Delaware – had the least skewed distribution of property, with the wealthiest 10 per cent holding only about two-fifths of net worth. The 13 colonies were certainly not a classless society. Differences in wealth and income were clearly evident in North America, but the rigid divisions so prevalent in European societies were modulated in the colonies. Equally important, movement upward from poor to middling status in one lifetime and then up to moderate wealth within several generations was a genuine possibility for white family units, given hard work and good fortune. Again, the primary economic factor promoting a relatively wide distribution of property among the upper half of wealth-holders was ready access to vast stretches of undeveloped land in the interior at prices which thousands of potential buyers could reasonably afford.

3. SUPPLY OF LABOR

The shortage of labor in the colonies likewise had major consequences, some positive and others highly negative. On the plus side, artisans were in such demand that incomes typically exceeded the earnings of their counterparts across the Atlantic Ocean. As a result, artisans did not need to form guilds in an effort to hold up wages by placing restrictions on the entry of newcomers into labor markets. Few apprentices and journeymen remained dependent employees much beyond their mid-twenties; master artisans usually found substantial work at good wages in both urban and rural areas. The property qualifications for voting were applied in such a manner that most middle-aged artisans held the franchise, and some were elected to public office at the town and county levels.

The favorable market for labor also meant that unskilled youths seeking work opportunities prior to marriage were generally able to find at least part-time employment in the fields and shops of neighbors. In an agricultural economy based largely on the labor resources of the family unit, there were numerous times throughout the year when households sought to hire extra hands to plow fields, plant seeds, and harvest crops. In wheat-growing areas, the maturing crop had to be harvested quickly or left to rot in the fields. Households with numerous children but few males over the age of 12 invariably sought to employ unmarried youths living on neighboring farms to assist in the spring planting and fall harvesting. In households with many small children, parents often hired teenage girls from nearby farms to help with domestic work. Since employment opportunities came up regularly in any given locality, able-bodied children over the age of 12 were rarely an economic burden.

The shortage of labor had less fortunate consequences as well. In the southern colonies, where tobacco and later rice became plantation crops, land-owners could not recruit enough free labor to take full advantage of profit opportunities in exporting to European markets. Their solution was bonded labor. In the Chesapeake colonies of Virginia and Maryland, a market in white indentured servants quickly emerged in the seventeenth century. Adventuresome persons in England without the money to finance the ocean voyage essentially bartered a four to seven year claim on their labor services in return for transatlantic transportation, routine maintenance (food, shelter, clothing), plus modest freedom dues upon the expiration of their legal contract. Between one-half and three-quarters of all Chesapeake arrivals in the seventeenth century came as indentured servants. In total, over the whole colonial period perhaps as many as 500,000 northern Europeans, some in complete family units, sailed to North America with an obligation to provide labor services under indenture contracts.

From the use of bonded white labor under contract for a fixed period of years, it was just another short step to the adoption of the pernicious system of black slavery.

Slavery was a labor system based strictly on race in North America; only Africans and their children – and all future generations – were subject to permanent enslavement. Black slavery had been common in the Caribbean and South American colonies of European states since the sixteenth century, but it did not migrate to the Chesapeake tobacco colonies in full force until after 1670.

The shift from white indentured servants to black slaves occurred primarily because of movements in relative prices for bonded labor. Because of improving economic conditions in Great Britain, the number of servants willing to emigrate declined and the prices of indenture contracts rose. Meanwhile the number of slaves available for purchase along the coast of Africa rose steadily and the cost of transporting them across the Atlantic fell because of improvements in shipping services. Beginning in the 1670s the prices for slaves, after adjustment for the expected length of service, were competitive with servant contracts, and tobacco growers responded accordingly. The southern colonies embraced slavery because the system was compatible with the cultivation of their major exportable crops – tobacco, rice, and indigo – and it provided the most convenient and immediately profitable solution to the problem of short supplies of human labor for the development of abundant natural resources (*see* figure 4).

Occupations   The occupation profile of the colonial workforce reveals that about 80 per cent of all free males were involved primarily in agricultural pursuits. Artisans, both in rural and more urban areas, constituted from 10 to 15 per cent of the male workforce, depending on location and date. Merchants, professionals, and storekeepers

FIGURE 4 Negro slaves processing indigo (from Pierre Pomet's "A Compleat History of Druggs," 1725): Eliza Lucas Pinckney was the first to make indigo a profitable crop in South Carolina, by perfecting a new production process and making use of slave labor.

comprised perhaps 5 per cent of the population. Occupational overlapping was fairly common as well: most artisans kept some livestock and farmed a few acres for household consumption; few rural storekeepers could earn a livelihood on the profits of trade alone; and farmers were involved in some form of non-agricultural economic activity during the off-season. Male slaves were mainly field hands, but perhaps one-fifth did labor service as trained artisans or house servants.

White women performed domestic service – including child care, cooking, and cleaning – and they normally undertook related tasks such as tending livestock, churning butter, spinning thread, and sewing clothes. Except during the harvest season, free women did not routinely engage in field work. Many black women in the southern colonies, however, did perform double duty – working in the fields during the day for the owner and returning home at night to perform domestic services for their own family units.

4. SUPPLY OF CAPITAL

The shortage of capital was likewise a handicap to economic development. Financial and credit markets were much less organized than those in England and Scotland. The colonies were unable to attract substantial amounts of capital from overseas to finance the direct development of natural resources. The largest volume of foreign capital entered the economy through the credit lines extended to American merchants and planters by numerous British firms involved in colonial trade. These sums climbed steadily throughout the eighteenth century, and by the mid-1760s the amount outstanding was on the order of £5 million annually.

The bulk of the capital for the conversion of raw land into productive farmland arose from the savings and investments of the colonists themselves. Most of the savings were not pecuniary, since no banks existed, but arose as a result of foregoing leisure and diverting the potential rewards of labor away from consumption and into clearing forests, constructing barns and fences, building livestock herds, and, in the South, enlarging the bonded workforce. By Independence, the colonists had amassed total physical assets valued at approximately £110 million, or nearly $500 million, with just under one-fifth of the total accounted for by investments in bonded labor.

Monetary system The monetary system of the colonies was based on the use of Spanish coins from mines in Latin America, since Parliament had refused to allow the export of English coins or the establishment of a colonial mint. The colonies supplemented the coinage with paper monies which the 13 assemblies issued independently at various times through two different mechanisms. In the first instance, they issued currency to pay pressing government debts. These sums were scheduled for retirement in future years through taxation. In a second instance, the assemblies created loan offices which advanced currency to borrowers who offered as collateral their equity in real-estate properties; the retirement of these currency issues was linked to the repayment of loans by private parties. In both instances, a given emission of paper money was scheduled to remain in general circulation for 10 to 20 years.

When assemblies failed to collect the scheduled taxes or private borrowers failed to repay their loans, colonial currencies depreciated heavily. Depreciation was a constant threat in New England in the first half of the eighteenth century, and Parliament forbade the issuance of any additional paper monies in those provinces after 1751. South Carolina was banned from increasing the volume of paper currency after 1731.

The remaining colonies, however, collected the necessary taxes and insisted on the repayment of private loans, and their respective currencies retained their value relative to gold and silver.

Thus, it came as a profound shock when Parliament tried to suppress the remaining paper money in North America in 1764. The colonies which had acted responsibly for decades in managing their monetary affairs protested vehemently and unceasingly, and after much controversy Parliament finally agreed in 1773 to let them resume the issuance of currency under slightly revised legal tender terms. Thereafter, British creditors received ironclad protection from any losses associated with the depreciation of colonial currencies.

In their handling of financial affairs, the middle and southern colonies ranked among the most innovative societies in the early modern period for their persistent use of monies created from paper rather than metals. Because paper money was printed in a wide range of denominations, high and low, the ease and convenience of making routine exchange transactions was much greater in the 13 colonies than in most of Europe or elsewhere. The large infusions of paper money into some colonies at certain dates may have also served to stimulate their economies and pull them out of business and trade recessions.

Taxation   The level of taxation was very low in the colonies compared with the rates prevailing in the mother country. Local governments financed a large portion of their limited services through user fees – in particular, the court system. Farmers frequently accepted work assignments on roadways leading to local markets to meet their obligations to towns and counties. Since much of the population lived reasonably close to the Atlantic coastline or near the banks of navigable rivers, provincial governments invested little monies in developing an internal transportation system. Goods and persons destined for intermediate and longer distances usually traveled by water. Salaries for the governor and a small administrative staff were often the only major peacetime appropriations of the 13 assemblies. Several provincial governments collected sufficient interest revenues from the operations of their loan offices to cover all their normal annual expenditures. New Jersey and Pennsylvania collected no direct taxes at all from citizens for several decades.

Tax rates were minimal in large part because the governmental bureaucracy was small and defense costs were low. The British Navy patrolled the North Atlantic to protect ships engaged in trade within the empire, and, beginning with the Seven Years' War, Parliament reimbursed the colonies for a portion of the monies they had expended in that contest. Low taxes were among the factors which left the typical colonial household so much disposable income and allowed it to maintain the highest standard of living in the world by the mid-eighteenth century. Parliamentary efforts in the 1760s to raise imperial taxes and thereby shift at least a small portion of the tax burden for North American defense to the colonies themselves led instead to an unanticipated rebellion (*see* Chapter 12). The initial controversy over Parliament's attempt to impose a modest level of imperial taxation soon escalated in a full-blown debate over political rights and principles. During the trade boycotts organized to protest against imperial taxation, British merchants lost the opportunity to earn thousands of pounds in profits on foregone colonial sales. The lost private profits added up to a much greater sum than Parliament had ever hoped to raise in imperial taxes, which explains why representatives of the mercantile sector in London finally convinced the King's ministers to rescind all the controversial American taxes except

60

the duty on tea. The tea tax remained as a symbol of the power and authority of Parliament, and its continued existence sparked an incident in Boston harbor in 1773 that put the two countries on the road to war (*see* Chapter 20, §2).

5. FOREIGN TRADE

Throughout the era, the economies of the 13 colonies received stimulation from both external and internal forces, with the impact varying by time and geography. The export sector was critical in the settlement and development of the three wealthiest southern colonies. The European demand for tobacco led to the expansion of Virginia and Maryland, while rice, and later indigo, produced the bulk of the wealth in South Carolina. By the mid-eighteenth century, the export of wheat and other foodstuffs from the middle colonies contributed greatly to the vitality of that region's economy. Indeed, foodstuffs combined, including all grain and livestock products, were more important to colonial foreign trade than tobacco. By the third quarter of the eighteenth century, the foreign trade sector was linked to the generation of roughly one-fifth of aggregate colonial income.

In typical mercantilist fashion, Parliament applied trade restrictions, a series of so-called Navigation Acts, on colonial trade beginning in the 1650s. The goal was to make certain that all trade reverberated to the benefit of the mother country and fostered its economic strength *vis-à-vis* competitive European powers. A few specific products were enumerated, meaning that they had to be shipped directly to British ports. Foremost in the enumerated category was tobacco. The negative effect of this policy was that colonial shippers were prohibited from seeking out buyers in other nations who might be willing to pay higher prices than British merchants. Another regulation required all trade within the empire to travel across the oceans in British vessels. This second rule became a boon to American interests. Because of the lower cost of raw materials, primarily wood, colonial shipbuilders received numerous construction contracts. Meanwhile, merchants in the New England and middle colonies garnered substantial earnings from the provision of shipping services. On balance, the Navigation Acts had a mildly negative effect on the American economy. Trade restrictions were once cited as one of the main grievances promoting the rebellion, but economic historians have reassessed the evidence and downgraded their importance in fomenting discontent.

Although foreign trade was crucial to the development of certain colonies, the volume of production destined for local consumption and internal markets was vastly greater. Some economic historians believe the expansion of domestic markets was by far the most dynamic factor in propelling the economy forward so rapidly. American producers specialized in growing certain crops for exports because of comparative advantages linked to soil and climate, yet if foreign demand for those products had dwindled, the colonists possessed the flexibility and capacity to shift into other productive activities. The colonies imported increasingly large quantities of finished and manufactured goods from English suppliers by choice; if necessary, however, the colonists were fully capable of producing reasonably close substitutes, as they proved in convincing fashion during the organized boycotts of English goods in the 1760s and 1770s.

In addition to fertile land, the colonies had in abundance the natural resources necessary for the production of iron. The most advanced technology of the era still relied on wood as the primary fuel in smelting. England had undergone much deforestation by the eighteenth century and most of its iron ore was far removed from large stands of trees. In North America, however, wood was plentiful everywhere. The colonies were smelting more iron ore than Great Britain by 1750. Pig iron became the fourth most valuable export in the bilateral trade with Great Britain, trailing only tobacco, rice, and indigo. Although American iron production lapsed after the war for independence, the economy had demonstrated its capacity for manufacturing and the promotion of industrial ventures.

6. PATTERNS OF SETTLEMENT

In terms of the mix of the rural versus urban population, the colonies revealed differing patterns over the decades. Because so many settlers initially hovered along the Atlantic Coast, the residents of towns and villages constituted a larger percentage of the total population in the seventeenth than in the eighteenth century. Although the size of port cities continued to expand, the number of settlers in outlying areas and along the frontier climbed at an even faster pace. Except for the port of Charles Town in South Carolina, the southern provinces had few large towns throughout most of the colonial era, although Baltimore and Norfolk were on the upswing after 1750. In the northern colonies the five largest cities by 1775 were Philadelphia, New York, Boston, Newport, and Providence – all thriving ports. With roughly 30,000 residents, Philadelphia was the largest colonial city by the 1770s, and indeed after London it ranked, along with Manchester, among the most populous and economically developed urban areas in all of Great Britain and North America.

The merchants in the larger ports were not only successful in accumulating wealth, but, unlike their counterparts in the mother country, many were also very active in political affairs. In the northern colonies, merchants often aligned themselves with provincial governors and thereby received numerous appointments to the upper chambers of their respective legislatures. Because of their direct involvement in government, they were able to sponsor laws that created a favorable environment for the promotion of trade and private initiatives of all varieties. The business orientation of American society – so prominent and so obvious to foreign critics and admirers in later centuries – had its roots deep in the nation's colonial heritage. When Adam Smith published *The Wealth of Nations* in 1776, he cited the British colonies in North America as the prime example of an economy which had profited from the application of his universal principles – namely the absence of monopolies and the existence of free markets in every sector from land to labor.

FURTHER READING

Brock, Leslie: *The Currency System of the American Colonies, 1704–1784* (New York: Arno Press, 1975).
Clemens, Paul: *The Atlantic Economy and Maryland's Eastern Shore: From Tobacco to Grain* (Ithaca, NY: Cornell University Press, 1980).
Doerflinger, Thomas: *A Vigorous Spirit of Enterprise: Merchants and Economic Development in Revolutionary Philadelphia* (Chapel Hill: University of North Carolina Press, 1986).
Galenson, David: *White Servitude in Colonial America: an Economic Analysis* (Cambridge and New York: Cambridge University Press, 1981).
Jones, Alice Hanson: *The Wealth of a Nation to Be: the American Colonies on the Eve of the Revolution* (New York: Columbia University Press, 1980).

Innes, Stephen: *Labor in a New Land: Economy and Society in Seventeenh-Century Springfield* (Princeton, NJ: Princeton University Press, 1983).

Lemon, James: *The Best Poor Man's Country: a Geographical Study of Early Southeastern Pennsylvania* (Baltimore: Johns Hopkins University Press, 1972).

McCusker, John J., and Menard, Russell: *The Economy of British North America, 1607–1789* (Chapel Hill: University of North Carolina Press, 1985).

Main, Jackson Turner: *Society and Economy in Colonial Connecticut* (Princeton, NJ: Princeton University Press, 1985).

Perkins, Edwin J.: *The Economy of Colonial America*, 2nd rev. edn. (New York: Columbia University Press, 1988).

Schweitzer, Mary M.: *Custom and Contract: Household, Government and the Economy in Colonial Pennsylvania* (New York: Columbia University Press, 1987).

Shepherd, James F., and Walton, Gary M.: *Shipping, Maritime Trade, and the Economic Development of Colonial North America* (Cambridge and New York: Cambridge University Press, 1972).

Walton, Gary M., and Shepherd, James: *The Economic Rise of Early America* (Cambridge and New York: Cambridge University Press, 1979).

7

Religion before the Revolution

EDWIN S. GAUSTAD

I. COLONIAL RELIGION, 1700

By the beginning of the eighteenth century, religion in Britain's 12 mainland colonies had assumed the following shape. The two largest denominations, without any genuinely close competitors, were first, Congregationalism (a phenomenon almost exclusively of New England), and second, Anglicanism (strongest in the South but with significant presence elsewhere). Followers of other denominations also visible by this date included the Baptists, Quakers, Dutch Reformed, Presbyterians, Roman Catholics, and Lutherans. But the number of churches in all these latter groups, even added together, scarcely matched the Congregationalists in number of meeting-houses.

Congregationalism represented the one truly effective establishment of religion in colonial America, though such establishment was limited to three colonies: Massachusetts, Connecticut, and New Hampshire. Here the close cooperation between ecclesiastical and civil authority resulted in a homogeneity that was as impressive as it was jealously preserved. Dissenters were discouraged by a variety of means: fining, jailing, exiling, hanging. As a consequence, it was possible to mold a "New England way" or "Puritan mind" that had influence far beyond the revolutionary era and far beyond the borders of these three colonies. The New England town was dominated by the meeting-house in more than a merely architectural sense, as politics, education, family life, and social organization all took on a Puritan hue. When later in the eighteenth century an Anglican missionary organization began to send its agents into New England, the Congregationalists could properly protest that no part of all America was as well-churched, as thoroughly "gospelized," as this corner of the country.

Rhode Island, however, was an irritating exception to the unchallenged dominance of Congregationalism in New England. Founded by a Massachusetts exile in 1636, this colony early became a haven for religious dissenters of all types: first Baptists, then Quakers, then sectaries of many sorts and dispositions. Its bubbling religious variety led the Puritan Cotton Mather early in the eighteenth century to observe with scorn that Rhode Island seemed to have just about everything within its tiny confines: "Antinomians, Familists, Anabaptists, Antisabbatarians, Arminians, Socinians, Quakers, Ranters – everything in the world but Roman Catholics and real Christians" (Mather, 1702, vol. 2, pp. 495–6).

The Church of England had an even earlier start as the official and established church of Virginia, but by 1700 it was clear that Virginia would have great difficulty re-creating the national Church of England on new world soil. Virginia had no towns, the clergy had no bishops, the government had little force or wealth or will with which to bring about a full-fledged establishment. Dissent had made no meaningful

(a)   (b)

FIGURE 5 The interior (a) of Aquia Church, Stafford County, Virginia (dated 1757), and (b) of Mill Creek (Mauck's) Baptist Meeting House, Virginia (dating from colonial times), showing the contrast between the elegance and ornamentation to be found in the established Church and the simplicity and denial of all worldly pretension expressed in nonconformist buildings.

penetration by 1700, but the implacable forces of economy and geography had certainly made themselves felt. Nonetheless, Anglicanism was stronger in Virginia than anywhere else in the colonies, with dozens of parishes duly laid out and even with its own Anglican college, William & Mary, second only to the Congregationalists' Harvard in point of time.

The neighbor with whom Virginia shared the closest economic ties, Maryland, followed a strikingly different path of religious development. Founded by English Roman Catholics in 1634, Maryland served as haven for those who experienced the heavy hand of government often raised against them. Nevertheless, by the end of that first century of its history, Maryland began to resemble its near neighbor religiously no less than economically. When in 1692 the proprietary colony became yet another royal colony, the Church of England lost little time in moving legislators at home and patrons abroad to support its position as the official church. Catholicism did not disappear and Quakers on the scene did not vanish, but Anglicanism in Maryland soon moved into a position of strength second only to that in Virginia.

South Carolina, a half-century or more behind Virginia and Maryland in origin, was likewise receptive to the Church of England, especially in and around the South's one real city, Charles Town. North Carolina (not a wholly separate entity until 1729) proved more hospitable to dissenters than to churchmen, with Quakers in particular making their presence felt. Later to be settled than either Virginia or South Carolina, North Carolina enjoyed no flattering reputation; in fact, scorn and ridicule were heaped upon what was regarded as an inhospitable wilderness, known (in the words of one early missionary) for its "damp Colds in Winter, and muschatoes in Summer" (Gaustad, 1976, p. 3).

Recognizing that the Church of England was not nearly as strong in England's own colonies as it ought to be, some churchmen (notably Thomas Bray) decided that private philanthropy promised more than governmental initiative for rectifying the situation. Founding both the Society for Promoting Christian Knowledge (1699) and the Society for the Propagation of the Gospel (1701), Bray did help Anglicanism to have a voice if not a commanding presence in all the colonies. Particularly in New York, New Jersey, and Pennsylvania, the strength of Anglicanism in the eighteenth century owed much to the efforts of these private societies that worked closely with sympathetic bishops back in England. Even with such help, however, Anglicanism never attained the kind of effective, pervasive, enduring establishment that Congregationalism enjoyed in New England.

Apart from these two "power churches," the other denominational entities were either regional in scope or minimal in number. The Dutch early claimed as their own much of the area around the mouth of the Hudson River. Despite the English conquest in 1664, Dutch religion and culture continued to have significant presence in New York and East Jersey. William Penn's Quaker connection had great implications for the ecclesiastical history of Pennsylvania from the 1680s on, as did his dedication to the principle and (more importantly) practice of religious liberty. Penn's colony quickly became a haven for dissenters of many stripes: Mennonites, Moravians, Brethren (Dunkers), Scottish Presbyterians of varying loyalties, Welsh Baptists, German Catholics, and more beside. Presbyterians grew to major strength in the middle colonies, that strength augmented by a close cooperation with New England's Congregationalism. Lutheranism first appeared in Swedish garb along the Delaware River, but in the eighteenth century German Lutheranism, first in New York, then more vigorously in Pennsylvania, constituted Lutheranism's principal ethnic strain.

2. THE GREAT AWAKENING

At the beginning of the century, then, national churches or colonial establishments dominated the American scene, a religious scene that was American only in a geographical sense, remaining European in virtually every other way. But this situation was soon to change radically, as by mid-century all the colonies experienced the tumult and tumble of waves of revivalism. Collectively known as the Great Awakening, these broadly based religious agitations permanently altered the religious landscape, creating a new and more characteristically American emphasis in denominational life: vigorously evangelical, slightly anticlerical, scornful of parish boundaries and liturgical niceties. Religion derived from and shaped by the Awakening would henceforth be the ally not so much of law and order as of individual experience and spiritual striving. The only message that counted was a biblical one: "Behold, I make all things new" (Revelation 21:5).

The Awakening traveled on the wings of Calvinism, the broadest theological tradition in the colonies at this time. Congregationalists, Presbyterians, Dutch and German Reformed stood solidly in the Calvinist tradition, as did Baptists after the Awakening and as did some Anglicans, notably George Whitefield, a regular visitor to America's shores. But like all revivalism, the Awakening tended to play down denominational differences and accentuate instead the necessity of conversion. "So many persons come to me under convictions," reported Whitefield, "that I have scarce time to eat bread. Wonderful things are doing here" (Whitefield, 28 September 1740, as quoted in Gaustad, 1957, p. 27). From Georgia to Maine, hundreds crowded to hear this mesmerizing orator as well as many other itinerants who moved freely, boldly wherever invited and even wherever not. Colonial boundaries counted for as little as denominational ones as a new and important inter-colonial community of like-minded evangelicals was created. The sweep of the movement was impressive: across lines of class, race, and gender. And the resulting realignments had long-lasting implications for politics and education, for theology and ecclesiastical order.

Of course, not all groups heartily joined in a movement that, to some, appeared little more than emotionalism run wild and obscurantism unleashed. The Church of England, Whitefield notwithstanding, held itself aloof from the raging storm, a quiet refuge for those seeking above all else decency and order. Quakers, Lutherans, and Catholics had little to do with this palpably Calvinist display. But members of the other denominations, even incipient Methodists, found themselves or made themselves part of this surge of religious passion. Both Congregationalists and Presbyterians were greatly affected and deeply divided by the Awakening, the former separating in the Old Lights (anti-Awakening) and New Lights (pro-Awakening), the latter in Old Side and New Side. While inevitably weakened by a bitter schism, both groups nonetheless acquired new blood and new energies that resulted in a revived theological and institutional life. Jonathan Edwards among others led in Congregationalism's intellectual rebirth, while Jonathan Dickinson was one of those who played a similar role among the Presbyterians.

Baptists, a relatively small denomination before the Awakening, took on a dramatically different character as a consequence of that movement. Now earnestly evangelical and possessing a gospel message preached in simplicity and accepted with gratitude, the Baptists (many of whom had separated from the Congregational establishment) moved from such early centers as Rhode Island and eastern Pennsylvania into all the colonies. Their proclamations seemed equally suitable for Blacks and Whites, for farmers and merchants, for rich or poor. Methodism, though not officially a separate denomination until 1784, had its chapels and lay preachers firmly in place long before the organizational structure caught up. For this Wesleyan pietistic movement within the Church of England, the Awakening was regarded as heaven-sent, drawing attention to the very kind of personal, experiential religion that Methodists in Britain no less than in America had been trying to promote. These two denominations, destined to become the largest in American Protestantism, did much to give colonial religion a distinctly American cast. Their imitators as well as their own unruly progeny (schisms abounding) made that new direction irreversible.

3. THE EVE OF REVOLUTION

By 1775, therefore, the tone and direction of American religion differed sharply from that which had prevailed at the beginning of the century. National churches, having little appeal beyond their own ethnic enclaves, were engaged for the most part in a kind of holding action. The strongest national church of all, the Church of England, could not even do that, as revolutionary sentiment caused the populace to turn against all things English – its Church as well as its Parliament and its King. The campaign of some Anglican clergy to bring to America a bishop of their very own backfired badly (*see* Chapter 18, §1). Lutheranism seemed mired in its Germanness, Dutch Reformed in its loyalty to Amsterdam, Catholicism in its obedience to Vatican direction.

Those groups governed at home and, fired by revivalistic zeal, enjoyed enormous advantages which they played to the hilt.

The Congregational establishment, immune to the Anglophobia that so damaged the other establishment (the Church of England), did manage to hold its own, this despite the divisions provoked by the Awakening and despite the growing theological chasm that would later result in the Unitarian separation. Two factors helped Congregationalism to maintain its cultural force. First, Congregationalism was clearly a case of home rule (at times almost too much rule) – not subject to foreign control, not swayed by foreign influence. Second, Congregationalists (especially the New Lights) worked closely with the middle colony Presbyterians (especially New Side) to help break out of their New England confinement. Congregationalists and Presbyterians together had by far the largest number of churches and the largest degree of cultural dominance on the eve of the Revolution. The comment of King George III that the American Revolution was nothing more than a "Presbyterian rebellion" has more merit if one understands "Presbyterian" to include the Congregational forces as well. For the two groups were in fact theologically united, the thin line of separation being confined largely to their different notions of ecclesiastical governance and to their different areas of colonial settlement.

The Revolution, of course, was far more than a Presbyterian rebellion, however broadly that modifying term is understood. Persons of many other religions and of none joined in the revolt on the patriot side. Baptists and Methodists (the latter going against John Wesley's clear sentiments) enlisted heavily, with Dutch and Germans finding war against England no great crisis of conscience. America's first Roman Catholic bishop, John Carroll of Baltimore, was part of an important diplomatic mission to Canada seeking help there, or failing that at least neutrality. Lutheranism's Henry Muhlenberg and his family form part of the mythology of the Revolution's clerical regiment. So the support for the American cause enjoyed a broad religious base.

Nor did loyalism follow clear religious lines. The closest thing to a regular pattern may be discerned in the missionaries sent out by the Society for the Propagation of the Gospel. With family and friends and employer back in England, it is no surprise that many sought an early opportunity to return to their homeland. Others were prompted to do so by a populace outraged by the prayers read for the King or by the mere failure to speak out in favor of this "most causeless, unprovoked and unnatural [rebellion] that ever disgraced any country," to quote the New York City Anglican Charles Inglis (Gaustad, 1982, p. 244). Yet, the patriotism of southern Anglicans, lay and clerical alike, was as evident as it was essential to the revolutionary cause. Anglicanism in the South had by 1775 become greatly Americanized, sufficiently distant from London's oversight as to see no need for a bishop in America, certainly not in Virginia. Middle colony and New England Anglicanism, on the other hand, dismayed by its minority status or even in some cases its extra-legal status, tied its cause much more closely to England's destiny.

In Pennsylvania many Quakers remembered that the King had been their benefactor and protector when so many others seemed determined to obliterate their struggling sect. Without Charles II, moreover, their colony might never have come into being. It was one thing to rail against Parliament, quite another to throw off or condemn the King. But Pennsylvania had a problem larger than pockets of Anglican or Quaker loyalism: namely, pacifism. Not only Quakers but Moravians and Mennonites and others made the revolutionary cause in that colony difficult, even problematic. Benjamin Franklin, the conciliator here as in so many other instances, persuaded many of

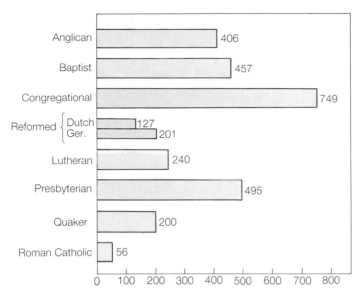

FIGURE 6 The number of churches in the American colonies in
1780 (by separate denomination)

the pacifists at least to serve as a kind of civil defense force, aiding the wounded and
ill, assisting persons to find safety far from battle, acting as a fire brigade when
necessary, and in general serving as a second line of defense behind the troops engaged
in battle. In the Revolution as in every American war, however, pacifism aroused
strong resentment outside those fellowships of faith, and sometimes even within the
households themselves.

One final question about religion on the eve of the Revolution is frequently raised:
how significant a factor was religion anyway? Was it a major cultural force or only
a minor one? Here church membership data are often trotted out to make the point
that only a minority of Americans were church members in 1775. While the data are
far from solid (no census figures on religious membership are available for this period
or for decades thereafter), it is almost certainly true that the majority of Americans
were not members of any church or synagogue (only five synagogues are known to
have existed at this time). But with equal certainty, one can indicate the vital role of
the church as a social, cultural, and political force of unrivaled power. All pulpits
tended to be "bully pulpits" in 1775 and all meeting-houses served as information
centers and propaganda disseminators. Membership was selective and restrictive;
congregational attendance and participation was neither. The church, standing virtually alone as a community and cultural gathering place, therefore reached (and
often persuaded) an "auditory" of far greater breadth than scanty membership figures
can possibly suggest (*see* figure 6).

FURTHER READING

Bonomi, Patricia U.: *Under the Cope of Heaven* (New York: Oxford University Press, 1986).
Gaustad, Edwin S.: *The Great Awakening in New England* (New York: Harper & Brothers, 1957).
———: *Historical Atlas of Religion in America*, rev. edn. (New York: Harper & Row, 1976).

Gaustad, Edwin S.: *Documentary History of Religion in America* (Grand Rapids, Mich.: William B. Eerdmans Publishing Co., 1982).

Goen, C. C. (ed.): *The Works of Jonathan Edwards*, vol. 4: *The Great Awakening* (New Haven, Conn.: Yale University Press, 1972).

Henry, Stuart C.: *George Whitefield, Wayfaring Witness* (New York: Abingdon Press, 1957).

Mather, Cotton: *Ecclesiastical History of New England* (1702) (New York: Russell and Russell, 1967).

8

The cultural development of the colonies

MICHAL J. ROZBICKI

D ID the British colonies in America develop a culture of their own? Did it evolve distinct, original features or was it merely imitative of the distant metropolis? Was it homogeneous or a mosaic of several cultures? What main periods in its development can be distinguished? What sort of yardsticks should be used to judge it: those of the high culture of the cultivated elites, or those of the vernacular, popular culture of the common people? These are some of the fundamental questions that we must ask when attempting to gain a comprehensive synthetic overview of American colonial culture.

To explain colonial America we need a rather broad understanding of the concept of culture, one that brings whole regions of experience into simultaneous focus. Such synthetic history makes it possible to correlate the particular facts and expressions of social life which together make up a culture. Culture may thus be defined as the framework of socially established and inherited practices, meanings, values, and norms shared by members of a society. These patterns can be abstracted from its behavior and from its symbolic products, such as language, artifacts, and institutions, but they can also be formulated explicitly. Culture gives meaning to social reality; one of its main functions is to make sense of life – a vital need of all people.

The cultural history of colonial America may be divided into several periods. The early stage, from the founding of Jamestown in 1607 to the 1680s, was characterized by a high degree of fluidity, fragmentation, and disorientation. The death rate, especially in the southern areas, was so high, and the ratio of men to women so unbalanced, that more permanent patterns of interaction, except in the tiny New England settlements, were slow to evolve (*see also* Chapter 5, §1). By the last decades of the seventeenth century the societies of the older colonies had become more stable, native-born elites were emerging, and the economy was becoming more diversified. With the second decade of the eighteenth century we observe a crystallization of social hierarchies and the entrenchment of creole elites which had concentrated much wealth and power. A certain standardization of genteel tastes was taking place, enhanced by similar political and legal patterns as well as by the extensive commerce. Finally, the years from 1763 to the Revolution brought a gradual increase in awareness of America's differences from Britain and a noticeable growth of American cultural identity. The Seven Years' War mobilized the colonists towards greater, even if still relatively weak, inter-colonial cooperation and educated American military and political leaders who would play a central role in the Revolution, while the new, more aggressive imperial policy of London forced many colonists to reassess the status of America against Britain not only politically, but also in cultural terms. The latter process was slow and continued long after Independence.

I. TWO STREAMS OF CULTURE

Those who would identify culture only with its high version, an attribute of the educated minority, may even dismiss colonial culture as practically non-existent. Such an approach would be as restrictive as that which assumes that American culture was an attribute only of the white population, or that which claims that it was merely a copy taken from the British matrix. In colonial America, as in any society, culture did not exist as one, homogeneous set of patterns shared by all. There was social and, consequently, cultural stratification between the narrow, literate elite and the majority, many of whom could not read or write. For instance, even in the late seventeenth century, Maryland governors complained that too many colonists occupying official positions as justices and sheriffs could not even sign their names. It is therefore necessary to distinguish, especially with regard to the eighteenth century, two major traditions in early American culture: a high culture of the elites, and the low culture of the non-learned. The two traditions were by no means hermetic, separate worlds; there were many similarities and a constant interactive relationship between them. Common folk acquired certain tastes from the elites. In the mid-seventeenth century the Massachusetts magistrates felt obliged to pass a law in which they lashed out against men and women of "mean condition" who wore gold, silver, silk scarves, and other attributes of genteel dress. Similarly, the cultivated gentlemen of Virginia were far from separated from the popular culture, as they had to deal with the unadorned and prosaic reality of business and the daily running of their plantations. A good example of the osmosis between the high and low traditions were the witch trials of 1692 in Salem, Massachusetts, when 20 people were executed for being possessed by evil spirits, and over 200 more were accused. The persecutions became possible when distinguished theologians and learned men, such as, for instance, Cotton Mather, leader of the Massachusetts church and state, elaborated formal theories of witchcraft based on ideas borrowed from old and widespread folk beliefs; these ideas then returned to the wide public with the sanction of high authority.

The American colonists, as all societies, had certain aesthetic needs, a receptivity to symbolic expressions of their fears and desires, a need for leisure time, a need for information. Economic and educational opportunities differentiated the ways these needs were realized; these varying opportunities can be seen in different cultural tastes reflecting the status of their publics. Such stratification had political implications; cultural values which were durably internalized in the process of education and socialization tended to reproduce behavior, including the social order. This explains why the dominant groups in society insisted on control over certain cultural meanings. The genteel-style silk scarves worn by commoners and criticized by the Massachusetts magistrates belonged to such a class of symbolic meanings, which mediated status and power relations between social groups. One of the functions of elite life styles was to set elite groups apart from the common folk; that is why their exclusiveness was closely guarded. Consequently, open questioning of these styles was perceived as an attack on the status of the elite. The simple life styles of the Virginia Baptists in the eighteenth century contrasted sharply with the conspicuous "high" style of the local, wealthy gentry; the latter group aggressively asserted their style and persecuted the Baptists for ostentatiously rejecting some of its elements, such as pleasure, gaming, dancing, and physical aggression.

2. REGIONAL CULTURES

In the past, the "exceptionalist" approach, emphasizing new and homogeneous features of colonial America, not only minimized the British cultural inheritance but also, in order to create the origins of a uniform American culture, neglected local, regional differences among the colonists. Today, we are better aware of the strength of regional cultures. Until Independence, the colonists identified themselves mainly with the localities – they considered themselves Virginians and Pennsylvanians rather than Americans. The very difficulty in organizing collective public action during and after the Revolution is evidence of such regional orientations. These differences were present not so much in the sphere of high culture, which tended to be more homogeneous, but in the popular life styles, the quality of everyday life, the local social and economic patterns and values.

The region of New England was conspicuous in that it was relatively stable almost from the beginning, its organization based on the family unit and town covenants, its ideals made cohesive by the religious domination of Puritanism, law, and rhetoric. In the second half of the seventeenth century the orthodox Puritan ethos was confronted by the growing secularism and individualism of wealthy merchants and entrepreneurs, creating many spiritual and political tensions. It has for long been a popular assumption that colonial New England, as a more stable, cohesive, and literate society, represented the prototypical American community, and that its cultural patterns radiated as norms across the rest of British America. More recently, it has been pointed out that the New England society, except for the earliest decades, was not monolithic but mobile, differentiated, urbanized, rapidly becoming more commercialized and individualistic, especially after 1660. Therefore the model of colonial New England "declining" from the original integrity is not particularly useful for analysing cultural change in the region, and even less so in the colonies to the south. New York and Pennsylvania were from their beginnings more pluralistic, multi-ethnic, cosmopolitan, and tolerant. The early plantation society that developed in the Chesapeake region was distinct in a very different way: highly mobile, demographically unbalanced, vastly more atomized and secular, with weak social ties and authority, settlements widely dispersed, and an exploitative economy producing for export markets. New England successfully tried to remain traditionally English as long as possible, while the tobacco colonies were giving rise to a more original, dynamic, and individualistic society. Individualism and attitudes oriented towards economic achievement were destined to become the dominant values of American culture, and in this sense early New England was an exception rather than the rule.

3. THE EFFECT OF ALIEN ETHNIC GROUPS

One common element of the American scene that profoundly affected the colonial culture was the presence of ethnic groups alien to the British: Indians and Africans. Close contact with them, the acceptance and resistance to the results of such confrontations on the part of each of the three races, were among the major forces modifying colonial culture. The Indians not only supplied certain technical skills, traded goods, and fought against common enemies; the Africans not only labored on the plantations; but also, through the very existence of these two races, the Europeans were able to reassert their identity in terms of "civilization" as opposed to "savagery," that is in categories of superiority. Since the arriving colonists did not possess culturally established patterns of reacting to such alien cultures, these confrontations were among the first aspects of colonial life modifying local culture in relation to Britain. The colonists had to build the Indian, and later the African, into their notions of world order. In both cases it resulted in the emergence of separatist and exclusionist attitudes towards non-Europeans. The English, unlike the Spaniards, never incorporated the Indians into their society and culture. The emergence of the class of black slaves facilitated white solidarity and muted tensions by creating the assumption that poor Whites had general interests similar to those of the wealthy elite. The presence of Indians and Africans also contributed to a faster assimilation of other European immigrants, such as Germans, Scots, Scots-Irish, Swedes, and Dutch, into English culture.

4. COLONIAL ARCHITECTURE

The development of colonial architecture illustrates well the cultural processes taking place in British America. The first phase involved simple continuity and transplantation. The early English colonists in Massachusetts reproduced typical English wooden-frame cottages with mud and plaster walls and thatched roofs. Since they soon found that these constructions had to be changed in order to resist a climate much harsher than that in England, the traditional pattern was modified by the second half of the seventeenth century, and the frames as well as roofs were covered with shingles or clapboards. A version of this house, characteristic for New England, was the so-called salt-box, where the roof was contained down on the rear side to cover an additional storey and a half. The plans of New England towns usually reflected English traditions; each had a town common where a rather large meeting house was placed centrally, indicating the role of religion in the life of these Puritan communities. Since the meeting house served for political and other gatherings as well, it may also be seen as a symbol of the close social cohesion within the settlements in this area. The first Dutch colonists in New Amsterdam also reconstructed the familiar, as they built Flemish-style urban brick houses with crow-stepped gables or, in the countryside, Walloon-style farmhouses with low roofs and two chimneys on both sides. Similarly, the Swedes who settled around Fort Christina transplanted their ethnic styles, building stone houses with high gambrel roofs. The Chesapeake area was different; in contrast to New England, the plantation system and individual access to numerous waterways created a dispersed settlement system which gave a distinct character to southern culture. Although English architecture was also reconstructed, often with a typical lack of adjustment to the hot and humid climate, there were more attempts to transplant "high" style. The wealthier owners of plantation residences often aspired to imitate the English country houses of the gentry. They were not built by gentle-born colonists but mostly by those who came to America as indentured servants and made their fortunes on tobacco. Such was the case of Adam Thoroughood, whose house in Norfolk, Virginia (1636–40), displays brick masonry and traces of Elizabethan and Jacobean styles in its proportions, all surmounted by a large, medieval chimney. The proportions of another Virginia residence, the 1655 Arthur Allen house, known as Bacon's Castle, with its projected towers in front and rear, massive chimney stacks and Flemish gables, were far from harmonious but displayed a typical early southern example of amateur design struggling to express European taste.

Urbanization   The progress of urbanization, begun in the second half of the seventeenth century and much accelerated in the eighteenth century, brought about the founding of new cities and a rapid development of some of the old ones on the Atlantic seacoast, making them prominent centers of trade and culture. Plans for newly established cities often reflected rationalist ideas of harmony and a strong desire to create a well-ordered society. Symmetrical squares and rectangles, and the regularity of space division, were characteristic of such diverse projects as New Haven, said to have been planned by John Davenport according to the layout of the New Jerusalem in the Revelation of St. John; Philadelphia, founded in 1682 and designed by William Penn on a grid pattern which was divided into four quadrants by Broad and Market Streets, with a large square for public buildings at their intersection, a central square in each of the quadrants as a public center, and individual buildings within all blocks spaced by gardens; and the only major city founded in eighteenth-century colonial British America, Savannah in Georgia, established in 1733 on a pattern designed by Robert Castell, with broad, straight streets, divided at regular intervals by squares and parks. In Williamsburg, which was laid out in 1699 as the new capital of Virginia, the central axis of the town was formed by a 99-feet broad boulevard, closed at one end by a square with a capitol and at the other by the building of the College of William & Mary. The boulevard was intersected by a perpendicular street leading to the Governor's Palace surrounded by formal gardens. The plan was so precise that it even defined the size of the houses and their distance from the street axis.

The Colonial Georgian style   The eighteenth century, which brought an increase in wealth, better education of the well-to-do classes, and more frequent contacts with the metropolis, also created pressures to model styles more closely on England's current fashions. More impressive residences were needed to establish a more refined environment for an emergent genteel class and to emphasize social domination. In architecture this period witnessed the rise of the Colonial Georgian style. Because it was based on sets of abstract, normative principles, information about which was gained mostly from standard British books and manuals, it displayed much more uniformity across the colonies than had been the case in the preceding century. The style was distinguishable in buildings constructed from Maine, through New Hampshire, Massachusetts, and Pennsylvania, to the Chesapeake colonies: Ionic or Corinthian pilasters, richly decorated entrances, quoins at the corners, high ceilings allowing for more space, and ornamentation indoors. In the first half of the eighteenth century the colonial style was influenced mostly by the concepts of Inigo Jones and Christopher Wren, and in the second by the ideas of James Gibbs, whose *Book of Architecture* (1728) was at this time the most popular of its kind in the colonies.

An early example of the Colonial Georgian style, typical of the buildings designed by Christopher Wren constructed in England, is the Governor's Palace in Williamsburg. Its shape is rectangular, it is symmetrical in plan and facade, harmoniously divided into horizontal ranges by means of balustrades, roofs, cornices, and string courses, while the articulation of details, such as windows and edges, is enhanced by classical ornaments. The neighboring College of William & Mary (1695–1702), built in similar style, on an axial plan with a rear court, a forward central pavilion covered with a steep gable, and a prominent cupola on a hipped roof, provided a model for other college halls, such as Harvard and Yale. Many churches were built in the style of Wren in the first decades of the eighteenth century, but after 1730 chiefly after Gibbs's work. The most often copied model was his St. Martin-in-the-Fields in London;

its imitations include the red brick Christ Church (1727–54) in Philadelphia and the wooden-frame First Baptist Meetinghouse (1774–5) in Providence, both designed by amateurs using Gibbs's plates.

The southern mansions, usually standing alone on large tracts of land and often set in landscaped gardens, are well exemplified by Westover, the residence of William Byrd II in Charles County, Virginia. Designed by the owner himself, it was built in red brick, externally symmetrical, with a steep roof, string courses between floors, an ornamented main door, and extensions on both sides of the main building. Since southern residences were usually centers of large plantations, the various dependent buildings, housing kitchens and other service facilities, were often connected by covered passageways with the main building. Some residences also boasted of sophisticated interior design, including paneled walls with pilasters and entablatures, and grand staircases. Mansions comparable in size and style, ornamented with classical pilasters and pedimented doorways, were built for wealthy New England merchants in Salem, Newport, or Marblehead, as well as in New York and Philadelphia, but they more often resembled English town houses than country seats. Most of the great Colonial Georgian houses were not designed by professional architects, who were rarely available, but by gentlemen-amateurs who took their models from books. A prominent case was Peter Harrison (1716–75) of Newport, Rhode Island, who designed several sophisticated Georgian buildings, including the Touro synagogue, the first of its kind in America, and the Palladian-style Redwood Library, both in Newport.

The lack of architects meant that a significant role in the final outcome of these endeavors was played by trained carpenters and builders, who often had to solve practically, with the help of handbooks, many problems concerning details and ornamentations. A high degree of competence was also achieved by other artisans, especially those producing furniture to equip the newly spacious residences and public buildings. Philadelphia especially, which in the second half of the eighteenth century grew into the most urbane of American cities, became known for its artisans turning out elegant furniture in the style of Thomas Chippendale. Locally made high chests with rococo ornamentation could easily compete with their imported British counterparts. Furniture of high quality was also made in Newport by John Goddard and John and Edmund Townsend.

5. FINE ART

While applied art made rapid advances as wealth increased in the colonies, fine art was scarce and aesthetic theory almost non-existent. Painting, in the noble sense of creating ideal forms, was not classified as virtuous activity. Journeyman painters produced portraits of the more substantial citizens, but their skills, except for Dutch painters in New Amsterdam, where traditions of painting were stronger, were not outstanding. The wealthiest commissioned portraits in England. Much of other painting was based on imitating or copying from engravings imported from England; in this process forms were usually made simpler and plainer. As with architecture and furniture, much depended on the availability of imported books with appropriate models. The two truly outstanding painters, John Singleton Copley and Benjamin West, both decided, despite, or perhaps because of, early success, to leave America and settle in England – the first in 1774, the second in 1760. They both hoped for an audience different from the colonial one, which treated painting as just another useful trade and not as a noble art. (For examples of portraits by these artists, *see* figures 60, 62, and 65.)

6. LITERATURE

Just as in other spheres of culture, for the writers in colonial America the spiritual home was England. If literature is treated in terms of *belles-lettres*, as one of the forms of high culture, then in the American colonies it was mostly trying to be a copy of its English counterpart, and did not draw much on the realities of local life. In this sense we cannot speak of a distinctly American literature before the Revolution or even for several decades after it. England was not only a source of forms and style for American writers but in many cases also of a reading public, since the circles of cultivated readers of polite letters in the colonies were extremely narrow. But, just as culture, in the sense of a style of life and of the meaning that a society gives to its common experience, is not restricted to the sophisticated, intellectual rendering of this experience by small elites, so literature, understoood broadly, and not only in terms of *belles-lettres*, always reflects the realities of life in the country in which it is created, and America was no exception. Its colonial literature was taking on native, local qualities even if somewhat in spite of itself.

Puritan writers Most of seventeenth-century writing originated in New England, where the society was incomparably more literate than in other areas and where the first printing presses in British America were established. The Puritan mission as well as the early wealth of Massachusetts attracted several prominent and erudite ministers and theologians, such as Thomas Hooker and John Cotton. Messianic and millennial sentiments were a powerful stimulus for publications in which New England affairs were inseparably linked with those of the Church, and local history was presented as a series of God's interventions. It is worth noting that the writings of the Puritans were not only often printed in London but also aimed at the English public. Even in these mostly theologically oriented texts, one can observe certain American peculiarities. The lack of opposition made the colonial writings noticeably more dogmatic in content and the pietist fervor put an emphasis on didacticism in style. The theological poem by Michael Wigglesworth, *Day of Doom*, published in Cambridge in 1662, had a very practical aim: to popularize Puritan theology in easy ballad meter. The morbid verse seldom approached the poetic but, because of its appealing and simple style, it became immensely popular and was reprinted many times. Another case in point is the wilderness baroque of Cotton Mather, whose attempts to give a heroic, epic dimension to New England Puritanism in his huge compendium *Magnalia Christi Americana* (1702) resulted in a didactic, grandiloquent style, full of digressions, anecdotes, puns and anagrams, and overstuffed with erudition. Even if incompatible with belletristic standards, Mather's writings reveal a characteristically American amalgam, later to be visible in Whitman, of an enthusiastic vision of a new man combined with an exaggerated style. In marked contrast to such writing was Robert Beverley's *The History and Present State of Virginia*, published in London in 1705: the author, in a typically Virginian fashion, had little interest in ecclesiastical problems or providential history, wrote in simple language, and demonstrated strong local patriotism towards his native region. New England had to wait until 1764 for a more secular history than Mather's: it was only then that Thomas Hutchinson's *History of the Colony of Massachusetts Bay* appeared in London. Notable for its objectivity, and its solid foundation in manuscript sources, it was the most sophisticated and thorough work of colonial historical writing, exemplifying an Enlightenment mind and a considerable literary talent.

The anti-aestheticism and didactic orientation had a negative effect on literature; only a few Puritan writings, such as, for instance, the fine verse of the pastor of Westfield, Massachusetts, Edward Taylor (c. 1644–1729), a follower of the English metaphysical poets, carry great aesthetic value. Nevertheless, the influence of colonial Puritanism on American literature has been durable. The sense of mission echoed in American writing for a long time, just as did the inclination to analyse the soul, to see the world in symbolic and allegorical terms, and to refer to Biblical motifs. The tendency to explain the world rationally while holding feelings suspect has also been attributed to the Puritan world view and its belief that aesthetic experience was superfluous and vain; the conspicuous lack of love scenes in American literature until the first decades of the twentieth century may be partly explainable by that heritage. The Puritan culture of New England expressed itself particularly well in the prosaic and polemic form of the pamphlet, widely used to explain and justify its church government. The years preceding the Revolution witnessed the greatest boom for this genre, with such famous examples as Thomas Paine's *Common Sense*, and *The Federalist* articles.

The literature of fact Not only Puritan but colonial writing as a whole was dominated by the literature of fact: diaries, histories, relations, pamphlets, travel, and promotional tracts. Most of the authors did not aim to create works of literature; they wrote mostly for practical purposes: to record events, describe the country and its people, promote religion, or educate. Captain John Smith, member of the Jamestown expedition, wrote his *General History of Virginia* (1624), after he had returned to England, to refute his enemies and to promote colonization. William Bradford, governor of the Plymouth colony for three decades, wrote *Of Plymouth Plantation* (1620–48) not for publication but as a record and monument to the glory of the founders of the new society. John Winthrop, leader and several times governor of the Massachusetts Bay colony, kept a detailed journal of events, mostly perceived as a record of God's providence, from 1630 to 1649; it was published in full only in the mid-nineteenth century. Smith's style is, in a typically Elizabethan way, colorful and dramatic, at times consciously creating legends. Bradford's is plain, simple, and direct, while Winthrop's is dry; both have the stamp of Puritan seriousness. A diametrically different approach to life is seen in the writings of William Byrd II, the Virginian gentleman and planter. His *History of the Dividing Line Run in the Year 1728*, a journal of his journey to the frontier between Virginia and North Carolina, is a witty, observant narrative, full of lively comment and biting humor, conspicuously secular and pragmatic. A similarly worldly and graceful style is present in his extensive diary. Not intended for publication, it was deciphered and published only in the twentieth century and remains one of the best sources on the nature of the planter aristocracy. The contrast between Bradford's and Byrd's diaries reveals not only a basic division between the culture of New England and the South, but also between the more egalitarian approach of the former, earlier author and the upper-class perspective of the latter. Social polarization and the emergence of the gentry's identity in Byrd's times is visible in his description of the North Carolina frontiersman's life; taking a businesslike, utilitarian position, he deplored the primitive subsistence economy of the squatters whom, because they were unable to cultivate land effectively, he regarded as useless to society.

Only the last decades of the eighteenth century brought literary works idealizing the frontiersman and consciously rejecting an aristocratic view of society. Such was John Filson's *Kentucke* (1784), with its famous passage on the adventures of Daniel Boone, the now legendary pioneer, presented as a person free from the corruption and artificiality of civilization, living a simple but noble life based on the good rules of Nature. This motif was often to reappear later in American literature in the works of James Fenimore Cooper, Mark Twain, and Walt Whitman. Perhaps the most persuasive arguments for such a concept were given by Michel Guillaume St. Jean de Crèvecoeur in his *Letters from an American Farmer*, published in London in 1782, where he used it to define the newly emergent American culture. Aware that the multi-ethnic, immigrant society of America had one basic, common element of identity – the fact that they almost all came from Europe in search of economic opportunity – he had turned this quality into a central value and made it the distinctive feature of the new society. Opportunities for economic advancement implied, in his view, a freeing from the old, European society with its hierarchic dependences; the new American man had new opportunities for education, self-reliance, and independence from the inherited system. Crèvecoeur juxtaposed European high culture, which was accompanied by wars, poverty, and disease, with the harmonious, dignified life of an American farmer. His image may be a Rousseauistic idealization but it is also an early articulation of the concept that American culture grew out of new, anti-aristocratic principles.

The Franklinians and the genteel tradition　　Two parallel and at times conflicting currents emerged in eighteenth-century American culture: the practical, middle-class trend, best exemplified in the prose of Benjamin Franklin, and the genteel, modeled on the styles of the English landed gentry and even aristocracy. Franklin, pragmatically oriented, free of ambition to achieve classical elegance, saw the written word mainly as an effective tool for educating society. His *Poor Richard's Almanack* (1733–58), which made him widely popular, had the usual form of a calendar supplemented by a compilation of various kinds of useful information, humor, maxims, proverbs, and illustrations, all with the secular purpose of instilling frugality and virtue as well as promoting self-education. As for Daniel Defoe, trade was for Franklin a most noble way of life. A distrust for purely theoretical learning, and an emphasis on practical results, marks a typical trait of the Franklinian current. The American Philosophical Society he founded in 1743 had "useful knowledge" in its full title. This intellectual climate was conducive to such scientific undertakings as those of the naturalists John Bartram, Cadwallader Colden, Alexander Garden, or the instrument maker and astronomer David Rittenhouse. The Franklinians sharply criticized idleness, often ridiculing the gentleman whose well-born status did not allow him to work with his hands.

The genteel current involved the idea of cultivation, accomplishment, and elegance, often accompanied by conspicuous consumption, so abhorred by the Puritans. By the mid-eighteenth century such a life style further integrated the elites which already held political and economic power; a polite gentleman was expected to represent similar qualities in any colony. The genteel tradition looked for its norms and tastes to London. News about the fashions, manners, and style of the court, supplied in the colonial press, would be closely followed and displayed in church and court, during elections and fairs, or at races. It must be noted that with increasing prosperity, growing supply of consumer goods, and more leisure time the genteel life style was becoming somewhat democratized and less exclusive. Besides, the American gentleman, who was mostly self-made, with his wealth a result of entrepreneurship, has rarely held the standpoint of the English aristocracy or old gentry that commercial activities were "beneath their quality"; on the contrary, materialist ambitions and commercial occupations were not seen as antagonistic to the idea of polite status. Books in the colonial gentlemen's libraries were usually dominated by works of a utilitarian nature, useful for self-improvement and practical affairs.

7. THE THEATER

Cultural imports from England at times met with strong popular opposition from some circles and enthusiastic support from others. Such was the case with the theater, welcome in the polite company of Annapolis and Charles Town but opposed in Philadelphia and Boston. The long debate on whether theater should be allowed reveals some of the local cultural forces at work in America, especially the contrast between the tastes of the leisured elite and those of the middle class. In the 1760s the American Company, a dynamic group of professional English actors touring the colonies, producing the latest drama, and stimulating the construction of theaters, attracted much publicity by stirring deep controversy between its supporters and opponents. Attempts to erect a theater in Philadelphia brought angry petitions of the citizens to the government, demanding an end to such practices. Theater was perceived by many, especially Puritans and Quakers, as a form of extravagance equivalent to such excesses as drinking and gambling, and as such deserved condemnation. Religious arguments that theater demoralized and corrupted were paraded. It was opposed by merchants and tradesmen on the economic grounds that it not only pulled people away from industry and spoiled a healthy business mentality by making leisure a virtue, but also took scarce money out of circulation. Despite such reactions, the existence of a wealthy leisure class, and the more secular world views, especially in the South, allowed for the development of theater in the early eighteenth century; the first theater was built in 1716–18 in Williamsburg, and was followed by another in 1752. Plays were also staged in Charles Town in the Court House in the 1730s, and in a permanent theater from 1736. By the mid-eighteenth century drama by English authors such as William Shakespeare, John Dryden, Joseph Addison, or William Congreve was performed by students or professional, itinerant actors, such as the troupe led by Thomas Kean and Walter Murray, who produced several plays in Philadelphia and New York at this time, or the company headed by Lewis Hallam who performed in Charles Town, Annapolis, Williamsburg, New York, and Philadelphia. Almost all drama performed was English. The earliest play written by a native-born American was *The Prince of Parthia*, a romantic, blank-verse tragedy imitative of various contemporary and Elizabethan English authors, written by the Philadelphia poet Thomas Godfrey and produced in 1767.

8. MUSIC

The beginnings of American musical history are associated with the eighteenth-century New England music of worship, particularly psalmody, practiced both at religious gatherings and at home. The so-called *Bay Psalm Book* (1640) was so popular it went through at least nine editions in the seventeenth century. The concern of ministers to improve church music led to the publication of instruction books

FIGURE 7 The frontispiece to William Billings's "New-England Psalm-Singer" (1770) showing singers seated around a table performing his "Canon of 6 in One with a Ground" (engraving by Paul Revere).

("tunebooks") and then to the establishment of the singing-school movement, a unique system of musical education that paved the way for American composers. The singing-school became an important musical and social institution in British America: native-born itinerant singing-masters offered instruction not only in New England but also in the middle and southern colonies. The most distinctive and stylistically homogeneous group of composers was the New England school which emerged in the 1770s and included such popular authors of music as William Billings (*see* figure 7), Daniel Read, Jacob French, Jacob Kimball, Samuel Holyoke, and Oliver Holden. Characteristic for their Yankee musical style was the "fuging tune"; it typically began with a choral hymn with the principal air in the tenor voice, which then gave way to entrances by each of the voice-parts, and was led to a full close, followed by the repetition of the "fuge."

9. THE SHAPING OF AN AMERICAN CULTURAL IDENTITY

From the 1760s America underwent accelerated cultural evolution. It is this period that saw the first native epic poetry, novels and musical compositions, the establishment of the first permanent theater, the first professional staging of an American play (in Providence in 1761), and the major paintings of West and Copley. The Revolution stimulated an outburst of nationalism and, consequently, more frequent articulations of a new concept of American cultural identity, emphasizing common education over inheritance and common sense in place of traditional English patterns. Noah Webster, a fervent Federalist, designed his famous *Spelling Book* (1782) to meet American needs and help standardize American orthography that differed from the English; in his essays he argued against foreign education for Americans, and advised them to obtain a better knowledge of their own country. All this should not be interpreted as a break in cultural continuity. Many calls for cultural autonomy were really only political tools of the Revolution. The education of such revolutionary leaders as Samuel Adams, Thomas Jefferson, or James Madison may have been American, but it also unmistakably derived from British culture and its intellectual, political, and legal traditions. The movement for political independence did not imply a cultural separation; the criteria of culture remained British. For instance, long after the Revolution, the literary ambitions of the new nation were often expressed in efforts to meet the standards of English *belles-lettres*. Such were the products of the Connecticut Wits, a literary group based in Hartford, who, driven by ambition to celebrate native society and history, wrote poetry entirely modeled upon current English styles; their striving for the perfect imitation brought excessive hyperboles and grandiose sentimentality, spiced with local, orthodox Calvinism, and Federalist social conservatism.

The basic facts underlying the shaping of the cultural identity in British America were that the colonists were exiles and that their lives were played out in the situation of the frontier. All had to come to terms with these two factors. America could not be a simple extension of England, a microcosm of English society and culture. The immigrants were a socially selective group and there was a lack of many institutions present in Britain, such as the king, courts, bishops, or aristocracy. Frontier life brought a confrontation with alien cultures. When the inhabitants of one country abandon the culture area with which they are associated and find themselves in a new and basically different environment they do not, and, in fact, are not, able to abandon their past and traditions. At the same time the new environment and the distance from the mother country place them on the periphery of the old culture. The necessity of adjusting to their new, often disordered, experience brought a typical reaction by the colonists of strongly asserting their Englishness. Such self-assertion was a shield against both the instability of their new environment and contempt from the English, who often treated the colonists with disdain as inferior citizens. It would be misleading to label colonial culture as imitative; certainly some aspects of English high styles, such as artistic or literary forms, were simply imitated, but continuity rather than imitation more appropriately describes the whole of colonial culture, both high and vernacular. English culture was broadly reproduced, mostly in a natural, non-conscious way, even if reconstructing some of its patterns in the new circumstances required much conscious effort. Cultural conservatism was strengthened by the fact that Americans were relatively isolated from the deep changes taking place in contemporary Britain, by the original motivation of many immigrants to escape from some of these developments, and by the consciousness of being in many ways deficient, provincial. Hence the intensity of efforts to re-create English material and spiritual patterns and life styles. Most British Americans felt English throughout the colonial period. After all, the Revolution against London, undertaken to win the same rights as those enjoyed by Englishmen in Britain, was itself an indicator of such feelings; the drive for political self-determination did not imply a separate cultural identity; it was Independence that stimulated such separateness.

Although no new, entirely separate American culture had yet evolved, British colonial culture was being in many ways modified by the need to adjust to local conditions. The new country was not a blank space to be filled by imported cultural forms; its native populations, climate, and landscape were powerful formative influences on colonial life, just as were the new, colonial forms of economic organization. This combination brought to the forefront such features as intense individualism, practicality, and orientation towards economic achievement, which clearly emerged in the colonial period as the central values of British-American culture.

FURTHER READING

Allen, D. G.: *In English Ways: the Movement of Societies and the Transferal of English Local Law and Custom to Massachusetts Bay in the Seventeenth Century* (New York: W. W. Norton, 1982).

Canny, N. and Pagden, N. (eds.): *Colonial Identity in the Atlantic World, 1500–1800* (Princeton, NJ: Princeton University Press, 1987).

Fischer, D. H.: *Albion's Seed: Four British Folkways in America* (New York: Oxford University Press, 1989).

Greene, J. P.: *Pursuits of Happiness: the Social Development of Early Modern British Colonies and the Formation of American Culture* (Chapel Hill and London: University of North Carolina Press, 1988).

Greene, J. P., and Pole, J. R. (eds.): *Colonial British America: Essays in the New History of the Early Modern Era* (Baltimore and London: Johns Hopkins University Press, 1984).

Nash, G. B.: *Red, White, and Black: the Peoples of Early America* (Englewood Cliffs, NJ: Prentice-Hall, 1974).

Rozbicki, M. J.: *The Transformation of the English Cultural Ethos in Colonial America: Maryland, 1634–1720* (Lanham, New York, and London: University Press of America, 1988).

Wright, L. B.: *The Cultural Life of the American Colonies, 1607–1763* (New York: Harper & Brothers, 1957).

9

Ideological background

ISAAC KRAMNICK

HE political, economic, and social confrontation between the colonies and Great Britain was filtered through the lens of political ideas. Available to the parties on both sides of the Atlantic was a varied set of intellectual perspectives that served both to explain events and to inform positions. In their pamphlets, sermons, broadsides, and editorials, colonial polemicists could call upon a large number of available political and intellectual traditions. Present-day scholars may disagree about which of these traditions played the larger or more seminal role, but most agree that at least six ideological perspectives were available to the revolutionary mind: liberalism, Protestantism, juridical rights, republicanism, the Enlightenment, and the Scottish school.

I. LOCKEAN LIBERALISM

Especially evident in the rhetoric of the revolutionary period was the language of Lockean liberalism. James Otis's *Rights of the British Colonies Asserted and Proved* (1764), Richard Bland's *An Inquiry into the Rights of the British Colonies* (1766), Samuel Adams's *A State of the Rights of the Colonists* (1772), and, of course, Thomas Jefferson's *Declaration of Independence* (1776) are all grounded in the writings of the Englishman John Locke (*see* figure 8), whose *Second Treatise of Government*, written in the early 1680s, proved extremely useful to opponents of Britain's new colonial policy. Government for the Lockean liberal was a voluntary creation of self-interested individuals who consent to be governed in order to protect their personal rights to life, liberty, and property. Originally equals in a natural society without government, men entered into a contractual relationship of trust with a government which serves at their will as a common umpire protecting individuals from other individuals who would interfere with their natural rights. Should the agent-government not protect the rights of the individuals who have consented to its creation, or should that government itself invade individual rights, then Locke allows for the dissolution of that government and its replacement with another.

At the heart of Lockean liberalism is individualism. Neither God, tradition, divine right, nor conquest is the source of political obligation. Self-regarding individuals intent on protecting their individual private rights provide legitimacy to government by their individual acts of consenting to be governed. That government is then a servant granted only the very limited task of safeguarding individual rights to life, liberty, and property. In so privileging individualism and individual freedom, liberalism symbolized the new social ideals challenging the older vision of a static hierarchical politics which had individuals subordinate to larger corporate entities, as well as assigned or ascribed to specific social ranks.

84

FIGURE 8 A portrait of John
Locke by Sylvester
Brounower
(c. 1685)

A particularly important source of Lockean liberal ideas on individual freedom in politics, religion, and the economy for revolutionary America was its articulation by a group of English Protestant dissenters in the 1760s and 1770s, whose writings were well known to fellow non-Anglicans in the colonies. Writers such as Richard Price, Joseph Priestley, James Burgh, and Thomas Paine gave Locke's political ideals a social as well as political relevance for the highly individualistic culture emerging in colonial America.

Locke's suggestion in Chapter V of his *Second Treatise of Government* that unlimited acquisition of money and wealth was neither unjust nor morally wrong was a move absolutely essential for a liberal agenda of competitive individualism and equal opportunity. Locke's very Protestant God commands men to work the earth, and in turn the hard-working and industrious have the right to possess what they work. Since God had given "different degrees of industry" to men, some have more talent and work harder than others. It is just and ethical, then, for them to have as many possessions as they want. This is crucial to the emerging ideology. If individuals are to define themselves in terms of what they achieve in the race of life, and if this sense of achievement is seen increasingly in terms of work and victory in a market society where talent and industry have their play, then the traditional Christian and moral economy barriers to unlimited accumulation have to fall. How else can achievement and sense of self be known if not by economic success?

An utterly new understanding of the individual and society emerges in the liberal world-view. Ascription, the assignment to some preordained rank in life, came more

85

and more to be replaced by achievement as the major definer of personal identity. Individuals increasingly came to define themselves as active subjects. They no longer tended to see their place in life as part of some natural, inevitable, and eternal plan. Their own enterprise and ability mattered; they possessed the opportunity (a key word) to determine their place through their own voluntary actions in this life and in this world.

The political implications of these liberal social ideals are clear. Governments could tax property, the fruit of virtuous labor, only with the individual's consent, and more profoundly even, ruling classes of idle nobility and useless monarchy would be challenged everywhere by the assertive hard-working men and women of real ability and individual talent.

2 . PROTESTANTISM

Closely allied to Lockean liberalism is another intellectual tradition available to colonial Americans, Protestantism and the Protestant ethic. Many Americans knew work-ethic Protestantism derived from Richard Baxter, John Bunyan, and the literature of the calling and of "industry." In the later decades of the eighteenth century it was this discourse that monopolized the texts of the English dissenters whose writings were so influential in the founding generation.

Central in work-ethic Protestantism was the vision of a cosmic struggle between the forces of industry and idleness. Its texts vibrate with the dialectic of productive hard-working energy, on the one hand, and idle unproductive sloth, on the other. Work was a test of self-sufficiency and self-reliance, a battleground for personal salvation. All men were "called" to serve God by busying themselves in useful productive work that served both society and the individual. Daily labor was sanctified and thus was both a specific obligation and a positive moral value. The doctrine of the calling gave each man a sense of his unique self; work appropriate to each individual was imposed by God. After being called to a particular occupation, it was a man's duty to labor diligently and to avoid idleness and sloth. Virtuous man is a solitary and private man on his own, realizing himself and his talents through labor and achievement; corrupt man is unproductive, indolent, and in the devil's camp. He fails the test of individual responsibility.

The American response to English taxation centered on a dual policy of self-denial and commitment to industry. Richard Henry Lee, as early as 1764, when hearing of the Sugar Act, assumed it would "introduce a virtuous industry." The subsequent non-consumption and non-importation policy of colonial protestors led many a moralist to applaud parliamentary taxation as a blessing in disguise, recalling America to simplicity and frugality. As Edmund Morgan notes (1967), the boycott movements were seen by many as not simply negative and reactive. "They were also a positive end in themselves, a way of reaffirming and rehabilitating the virtues of the Puritan Ethic."

Early Puritan settlers had seen themselves as a chosen people who with God's help were building a city on a hill for all the world to imitate. Although this conception of the New England experiment rarely penetrated south of the Hudson River and lost force even in New England during the eighteenth century, a secular variant that saw the colonies as the home of liberty everywhere was apparent. The Quaker Thomas Paine could tap that tradition in his plea in *Common Sense* that Americans, like Old Testament prophets, reject monarchy. Their calling was to provide an asylum for freedom so recently evicted from Europe by its useless kings.

3. JURIDICAL RIGHTS

Paradoxically, one of the secular signs of their special covenant with God was the colonists' unshakable commitment to the rights of Englishmen. If their pamphlets and sermons spoke often of universal, transcendent, and abstract natural rights and natural law, they just as often were grounded in discussions of historical and contingent rights, the positive rights of Englishmen. Sam Adams, for example, used the conventional formula familiar to all colonial pamphleteers which depicted the English common law and statutory Acts of the British Parliament as sources of "the absolute rights of Englishmen," or "the Rights, Liberties and Privileges of Subjects born in Great Britain." In their political formulation these legal rights focused on the supremacy of the legislature, the rule of law as opposed to arbitrary decree, and the illegality of government seizure of property without the subject's consent "in person, or by his representative."

This tradition of juridical rights was of profound importance to the colonists and the ideal of law as a restraint on the Crown informed much of the rhetoric of colonial protest. Statutory as well as common law, the intricate set of legal precedents and customs, which had evolved over time, guaranteed the sanctity of an Englishman's life, liberty, and property, as well as the rights of trial by jury, representative government, and habeas corpus. In the hands of seventeenth-century jurists such as Sir Edward Coke (1552–1634) the juridical rights tradition emerged as a major constraint on Stuart monarchical pretensions as well as the principal defender of an "Ancient Constitution" which protected the liberty and property of Englishmen against the claims of royal prerogative. Older even than the common law, this "Ancient Constitution" was assumed to have roots in Saxon England and to have been reaffirmed, in the wake of Norman assaults, through great charters such as the Magna Carta.

According to the juristic notion of the "Ancient Constitution," Parliament was an age-old institution, by no means created by or dependent on the will of monarchs. English liberties and freedom of the subject were born in the forests of the tribal past and survived the attack of the "Norman Yoke" only through the assiduous care of lawyers and parliamentary statesmen. No matter that many historians faulted the historical assumptions of the "Ancient Constitution," its political success in the constitutional struggles of seventeenth-century England ensured its appeal to colonial Americans.

For many in the colonies the particular figure in the juridical school cited over and over again in the late eighteenth century was Sir William Blackstone, whose *Commentaries on the Law of England* (1765–9) was regarded as the definitive statement on the British Constitution. Blackstone, it was assumed, codified the ideal of the "Ancient Constitution" as the source of the unique British tradition of parliamentary government and the common law as constitutional alternatives to arbitrary rule.

4. REPUBLICANISM

To this point we have looked at the ideological background of the Revolution very much in British terms: Lockean liberalism, Puritanism, and the British Constitution. The set of traditions available to the colonists was by no means so provincial. Indeed, in recent decades a good deal of attention has been given to an intellectual influence on the revolutionary era that has roots far broader than merely Britain. Chroniclers of this republican or civic-humanist tradition see it, in fact, as much more influential than Lockean liberalism.

Part Aristotle, part Cicero, part Machiavelli, civic humanism conceives of man as a political being whose realization of self occurs only through participation in public life, through active citizenship in a republic. The virtuous man is concerned primarily with the public good, *res publica*, or commonweal, not with private or selfish ends. Seventeenth-century writers such as James Harrington and Algernon Sidney adapted this tradition, especially under the influence of Machiavelli (according to J. G. A. Pocock), to a specifically English context. This significantly English variant of civic humanism, "neo-Machiavellianism" or "neo-Harringtonianism," became, through the writings of early eighteenth-century English Augustans such as Davenant, Trenchard, Gordon, and especially Henry St. John, Viscount Bolingbroke, the ideological core of the "country" ideology that confronted Walpole and his "court" faction. Bolingbroke provided a crucial link in this intellectual chain by associating corruption with social and political themes, a critical concept in the language of eighteenth-century politics. Much richer than simple venality or fraud, the concept is enveloped by the Machiavellian image of historical change: corruption is the absence of civic virtue. Corrupt man is preoccupied with self and oblivious to the public good. Such failures of moral personality, such degeneration from the fundamental commitment to public life, fuel the decline of states and can be remedied only through periodic revitalization by returning to the original and pristine commitment to civic virtue. Calls for such renewals, for *ridurre ai principii* (Machiavelli's phrase), form the response to corruption.

Bolingbroke's achievement was to appropriate this republican and Machiavellian language for the social and economic tensions developing in Augustan England over the rise of government credit, public debt, and central banking as well as for political issues, such as Walpole's control of Parliament through patronage or concern over standing armies. Themes of independence and dependence, so critical to the republican tradition (the former essential to any commitment to the public good), were deployed by Bolingbroke into a social map of independent country proprietors opposing placemen and stock jobbers and a political map of a free Parliament opposing a despotic court. In addition, Bolingbroke stamped this eighteenth-century republican-country tradition with its socially conservative and nostalgic quality, in terms of not only its anti-commercialism but also its anti-egalitarianism.

To a great extent, the innovative scholarship of J. G. A. Pocock has shaped this new way of looking at English political thought. His writings on Harrington and his magisterial *The Machiavellian Moment* (1975) have made the concept of civic humanism and republicanism a strikingly useful tool with which to understand the political mind of late seventeenth- and early eighteenth-century England. However, in the hands of Pocock and others, this insightful reading of early eighteenth-century politics through Bolingbroke's dichotomy of virtuous country and corrupt court does not stop with Augustan England. It becomes the organizing paradigm for the language of political thought in England as well as America throughout the entire century.

Locke and possessive individualism in this scheme have had to go. A chorus of distinguished scholars has joined in de-emphasizing the importance of Locke throughout eighteenth-century Anglo-American thought. "Eighteenth century English political thought," according to Gordon Wood (1972), "perhaps owed more to Machiavelli and Montesquieu than it did to Locke." Indeed, Bernard Bailyn has persuasively argued (1967) that "the effective triggering convictions that lay behind the [American] Revolution were derived not from common Lockean generalities but from the specific fears and formulations of the radical publicists and opposition politicians of early eighteenth century England."

Pocock has applied this revisionist verdict about Locke to an alternative reading of America and its founding. American political culture, according to Pocock, has been haunted by myths, the most mistaken of which is the role of Locke as "the patron saint of American values." The proper interpretation "stresses Machiavelli at the expense of Locke." The Revolution was, in Pocock's reading, "the last great act of the Renaissance ... emerging from a line of thought which staked everything on a positive and civic concept of the individual's virtue." The Revolution was a Machiavellian *rinnovazione* in a new world, "a republican commitment to the renovation of virtue." America was born in a "dread of modernity," according to Pocock.

Americans could come to republican ideas directly, as well as through the mediation of Renaissance Italy or English Commonwealth or Country Ideology. Greek and Roman authors were well known to the colonial mind. From Cicero, Aristotle, and Polybius, all widely read in America, notions of a higher law as well as constitutional arguments for mixed and separate powers in a stable government could be found. Perhaps the most influential text from antiquity in eighteenth-century America was Plutarch's *Lives of the Noble Greeks and Romans*. In it the greatest historical glory is reserved for the "law giver" as "the founder of commonwealths." This classical celebration of those who serve the common good is found in Hamilton's republican aspirations. In a pamphlet written in 1777 attacking congressmen for not better realizing the potential of their position, Hamilton had written of true greatness and fame. He signed the pamphlet with the pseudonym "Publius," a fabled figure in Plutarch's *Lives* and the name later used by him and his fellow authors of *The Federalist*. Hamilton's vision transcended the walls of Congress in the infant nation and spoke to the historic discourse of republicanism.

> The station of a member of C .... ss, is the most illustrious and important of any I am able to conceive. He is to be regarded not only as a legislator, but as the founder of an empire. A man of virtue and ability, dignified with so precious a trust, would rejoice that fortune had given him birth at a time, and placed him in circumstances so favorable for promoting human happiness. He would esteem it not more the duty, than the privilege and ornament of his office, to do good to mankind.

5. THE ENLIGHTENMENT

Another primarily non-British source of political ideas and ideals for the colonists was the Enlightenment, which, to a great extent, took the secular wisdom of classical antiquity as a source for its crusade against both Christianity and the *Ancien Régime*. The writings of Jefferson, Franklin, and John Adams reveal deep understanding and familiarity with the ideas of the French *philosophes*, and their European connections as well as correspondents were often leading figures in the Enlightenment. From them they acquired a rational skepticism about supernatural religion as well as a passionate commitment to ameliorative and practical science and technology as engines of progress and reform. The French Enlightenment with its rejection of original sin and pessimism directed energy to this world and spoke to the ease of reforming outdated social institutions. Jefferson's transformation of Locke's sacred triad of life, liberty, and property to life, liberty, and happiness bears the stamp of the this-worldly, more hedonistic orientation of the French Enlightenment.

The generally secular and liberalizing tone of the Enlightenment pervaded the educated revolutionary mind. In addition to Jefferson, Franklin, and Adams, America's own *philosophes*, ordinary pamphleteers were familiar with and cited Montesquieu on the influence of climate, or the intricacies of the separation of powers. The Italian legal reformer Beccaria was a frequent source, as were other Enlightenment luminaries such as Rousseau, Pufendorf, Grotius, Vattel, and Burlamaqui.

6. THE SCOTTISH SCHOOL

The final component of the ideological background of revolutionary America requires a return to Great Britain, but not to England, for a powerful influence on the eighteenth-century colonial mind was the Scottish Enlightenment. Much the most interesting group of writers and thinkers in Britain during the eighteenth century were the Scottish intellectuals from Glasgow, Edinburgh, and St. Andrews. They offered a conception of human nature and a reading of history quite different from those offered by Lockean liberalism or neo-classical republicanism. Francis Hutcheson as well as David Hume and Adam Smith depicted men as neither asocial nor autonomous as liberalism did. Men, they wrote, were moved to community by a common "moral sense" which produced sociability and benevolence. Nor was the quest for a moral life the product of a disinterested and rational perception of the common good; it was informed by sentiment and affection. A "moral sense" was innate in all mankind, giving them an intuitive knowledge of what is right and wrong. In a fundamental sense, then, all people were seen as equal by the moral sense school, since all people had the moral capacity for sociability and benevolence.

If the thrust of the Scottish school's views on human nature runs counter to liberal views, then its attitude to history runs directly contrary to much of the republican tradition. Scottish writers such as Hume, Smith, Adam Ferguson, and Lord Kames did not see history as a repetitive cycle of corruption and virtuous revitalization. Nor did they see economic modernity as a morally inferior era of luxury and selfishness. They depicted history as evolving in terms of developmental stages characterized principally by the mode of production. Societies moved through four such stages, the ages of hunting, herding, agriculture, and commerce. Commerce produced economic abundance and a freer, more civilized social order. For David Hume and for Adam Smith, modern market society not the classical or Saxon past produced freedom and happiness.

The Scots differed among themselves, to be sure. Thomas Reid, for example, shared few of his countrymen's historical concerns. His "Common Sense" philosophy, however, had a great deal of influence on American thought in the revolutionary generation.

Americans, in turn, differed in their evaluations of Scottish thinkers. David Hume, a particularly influential member of the Scottish school, is a case in point. His writings on politics with their emphasis on factionalism, his conviction that politics could be reduced to a science, and his widely read historical judgments made him an often cited writer in the revolutionary generation. Yet, Jefferson disapproved of Hume because of the allegedly Tory sentiments of his *History*. Madison, on the other hand, was very much influenced by Hume in crafting his social and political world-views. Whether he turned to Hume more often than to Locke or republicanism is, alas, another, perhaps unanswerable, question.

FURTHER READING

Bailyn, B.: *The Ideological Origins of the American Revolution* (Cambridge, Mass.: Harvard University Press, 1967).

Greene, J. P.: *The Intellectual Heritage of the Constitutional Era* (Philadelphia: Library Company of Philadelphia, 1986).

Kramnick, I.: *Republicanism and Bourgeois Radicalism: Political Ideology in Late Eighteenth-Century England and America* (Ithaca, NY: Cornell University Press, 1990).

McDonald, F.: *Novus Ordo Seculorum: the Intellectual Origins of the Constitution* (Lawrence: University Press of Kansas, 1985).

Morgan, E.: "The Puritan ethic and the American Revolution," *William and Mary Quarterly,* 24 (1967), 3–43.

Pocock, J. G. A.: *The Machiavellian Moment: Florentine Political Thought and the Atlantic Republican Tradition* (Princeton, NJ.: Princeton University Press, 1975).

Pole, J. R.: "Enlightenment and the Politics of American Nature," *The Enlightenment in National Context,* ed. Roy Porter and Niklaus Teich (Cambridge: Cambridge University Press, 1982).

Wills, G.: *Inventing America* (New York: Vintage Books, 1979).

Wood, G.: *The Creation of the American Republic* (New York: W. W. Norton, 1972).

PART 2
THEMES AND EVENTS, TO 1776

10

The origins of the new colonial policy, 1748–1763

JACK P. GREENE

IN THE decades following World War II, most historians have come to agree that, by the mid-eighteenth century, Britain's North American colonies were well socialized to the British imperial system and that they were driven to resistance and rebellion primarily by changes in metropolitan colonial policy that occurred after the conclusion of the Seven Years' War in 1763, changes that gradually over the next dozen years led to the alienation of colonial affections from Britain and eventually in 1775–6 to the emergence of broad support for independence. More recently, however, it has been shown that British officials developed this "new" British colonial policy not during the early 1760s but more than a decade earlier, during the late 1740s. As early as 1748, the metropolitan government began to abandon its long-standing posture of accommodation and conciliation towards the colonies for a policy of strict supervision and control, a policy that in both tone and content strongly resembled that usually associated primarily with the post-1763 era.

I. REASONS FOR THE CHANGE

The explanation for this change is to be found in four separate conditions. Far and away the most important was the phenomenal growth of the colonies in the decades following the Peace of Utrecht in 1713. Between 1710 and 1750, the extent of settled territory, the size of the population, the volume of immigrants, the number of African slaves, the volume of commodity production, the amount of foreign trade, and the size of major urban centers all increased at an extraordinarily rapid rate (*see* Chapters 5 and 6). Demographic growth was unparalleled. The free population rose by 160 per cent between 1710 and 1740 and by 125 per cent between 1740 and 1770, while the slave population grew by 235 per cent during the former period and 200 per cent during the latter.

Territorial and demographic growth in turn made it possible for the colonists both to send to Britain increasing quantities of raw materials, many of which were subsequently profitably re-exported by British middlemen, and to purchase ever larger quantities of British manufactures, thereby providing an important stimulus to the development of British industry. During the eighteenth century, in fact, the colonial trade became the most rapidly growing section and accounted for a significant proportion of the total volume of British overseas trade. Imports from the colonies (both continental and West Indian) accounted for 20 per cent of the total volume of English imports in 1700–1 and 36 per cent in 1772–3, while exports to the colonies rose from 10 per cent of the total volume of English exports during the former year to 37 per cent during the latter. The colonial trade was thus a critical segment of the British economy and was becoming more important with every decade.

For the British political nation, the extraordinary growth of the colonies was, however, a source not only of celebration for the vast power and profits it brought but also of acute anxiety, which manifested itself through the middle decades of the eighteenth century in the frequent expression of two related ideas. The first was that the colonies were of crucial importance to the economic and strategic welfare of Britain. The second was that the colonists secretly lusted after and might possibly be on the verge of trying to achieve their independence from Britain.

At least since the closing decades of the seventeenth century, metropolitan officials and traders had intermittently voiced the fear that the colonies might eventually seek independence, set up their own manufactures, and become economic rivals rather than subordinate and complementary partners with Britain. By lending increasing plausibility to this fear, the extraordinary growth of the colonies, along with the concomitant increase in their economic and strategic worth to Britain, contributed to a significant rise during the late 1740s and the 1750s in the frequency and urgency of explicit expressions of anxieties within metropolitan circles over the possible loss of the colonies. Such expressions were everywhere manifest in Britain: in official reports prepared by the Board of Trade, in correspondence between metropolitan officials and royal governors, in parliamentary debates, and in a proliferating number of tracts, both published and unpublished, on the state of the colonies and the need for reforms in their administration. So consequential had the burgeoning colonies become to Britain that, as Horace Walpole put it, any "Apprehension of their being lost" could "easily ... create a consternation."[1]

If the long-term rapid and substantial growth of the colonies, along with the corresponding increase in their importance to Britain, was the single most important precondition behind the shift in British policy beginning during the late 1740s, a second, closely related, medium-term precondition was the threat of French or perhaps even Spanish conquest of such valuable possessions. The Treaty of Aix-la-Chapelle, signed in October 1748 at the conclusion of the third inter-colonial war, was widely understood as offering only a temporary respite from the decade of conflict between Britain and the Latin powers that had begun in 1739 with the War of Jenkins's Ear. The stakes in the prospective conflict were widely recognized to be no less than supremacy over the entire western, and even some of the eastern, world.

With so much at risk, there could be no question of allowing the colonies to be lost, and British officials were particularly concerned following the peace of 1748 to strengthen colonial defenses in preparation for a renewal of hostilities. The areas of greatest vulnerability seemed to be the two ends of the chain of colonies stretching along the east coast of North America from the Altamaha River in the South to the Strait of Canso in the North. At the northern end, Nova Scotia relied for its defense almost entirely upon a small British military establishment that lived in perpetual fear of rebellion by the numerically dominant "neutral" French in the Annapolis Valley or of attack from the superior French military force at Louisburg on nearby Cape Breton Island. Despite more than 15 years of government support, including major expenditures from parliamentary revenues, Georgia, at the southern end, was in an obvious state of decay, perhaps even an easy prey for the small Spanish garrison at nearby St. Augustine. Fear of colonial independence and French or Spanish conquest combined to stimulate still a third fear: that strong and rebellious colonies might sell their favors to the highest bidder among Britain's European rivals.

96

The actual timing of the change in British colonial policy can be accounted for by the temporary cessation of hostilities in 1748 and two additional short-run circumstances. First was the end of the domestic political turmoil that had begun with the outbreak of war in 1739 and was intensified by the vigorous competition for power through the mid-1740s following the fall of Sir Robert Walpole in 1742. Having already won the confidence of George II and wooed many opposition leaders to the side of government, Henry Pelham finally managed to establish his administration on a sound basis as a result of the government's overwhelming victory in the elections of 1747. For the next seven years, until Pelham's death in 1754, the government enjoyed a new freedom from domestic distractions that enabled its leaders to devote significant attention to the colonies for the first time since the mid-1730s.

A second, and even more important, short-run condition that determined the timing of the shift in colonial policy was the apparent breakdown of metropolitan authority in many colonies during the late 1740s. For the previous 30 years, metropolitan officials had held the colonial reins loosely. Preoccupied with domestic concerns and relations with continental European powers, they rarely gave close attention to colonial problems unless they were perceived as threatening to powerful economic interests within the home island. There were two important results of what Edmund Burke later called this "wise and salutary neglect." One was the relaxation of tensions that had characterized relations between metropolis and colonies for much of the period between 1660 and 1720. The second was the emergence of a functional balance between metropolitan authority and local power based upon the existence of undefined and unacknowledged ambiguities in the nature of the metropolitan–colonial relationship. These ambiguities permitted local leaders to achieve a large measure of *de facto* control over the internal governance of the colonies without calling into question long-standing assumptions within Britain about the supremacy of the metropolis over all aspects of colonial life.

But a number of corollary developments between 1720 and 1750 rendered this balance extremely precarious by making it increasingly difficult for metropolitan authorities to retain even an illusion that they had the colonies under any kind of firm control. With the administration showing so little interest in the details of colonial matters, metropolitan institutions charged with overseeing the colonies atrophied. The Board of Trade, the only body for which the colonies were a primary concern, gradually became little more than a housekeeping organization, and a very sloppy one at that. Moreover, the colonial bureaucracy became increasingly politicized during these years, as the ministry expropriated administrative resources for political purposes, and patronage, not expertise or competence, became the main criterion for appointments. These developments helped to break the spirit of governors and other royal officials in the colonies. In all but a few settlements, governors found themselves with insufficient resources to resist strident demands for power from the colonial lower houses and in many instances simply capitulated to local interests. By 1750, more and more of the governors had become thus creolized.

By the late 1740s, these several developments seemed from the perspective of London to have produced a much more ominous one: the breakdown of metropolitan political control in many of the colonies. From the dispatches and papers that had accumulated in the colonial office, especially after 1745, the situation in America appeared to be truly alarming. Metropolitan merchants complained that the legislatures of several colonies, in direct violation of metropolitan prohibitions, had issued large sums of paper money during the war and were subsequently refusing to enact measures to protect British debts against its rapid depreciation. At the same time, West Indian sugar planters and metropolitan customs officials in the colonies charged that merchants from the continental colonies were violating the Molasses Act of 1733 at will, to the severe economic detriment of the sugar producers. In both instances, colonial behavior showed a blatant disregard for metropolitan authority.

A review of conditions in individual colonies seemed to reveal even greater cause for concern. The situation was most serious in New Jersey, where the inability of the royal administration to restrain widespread rioting against the East Jersey proprietors after 1745 had produced what Lord Chancellor Hardwicke described as "disorders and confusions" that had been "carried almost to the height of revolution."[2] In New Hampshire and North Carolina, legislative activity had been brought to a halt and civil government rendered tenuous as a result of the desperate efforts of the governors to enhance royal power by altering the apportionment of representatives to the lower houses. The same result had been produced in Bermuda by Governor William Popple's vituperative altercation with the assembly over a number of issues. In New York, where Governor George Clinton had engaged in violent quarrels with the lower house over the extensive financial powers it had wrested from him and his predecessor during the early years of the Spanish and French war, the situation was marginally better but only because opposition leaders had not yet, in contrast to their counterparts in New Hampshire, North Carolina, and Bermuda, become so enraged with the governor as to cut off all further business with him. In Jamaica, a powerful faction was challenging Governor Edward Trelawny's right to remove judges, while Barbados had only just been rescued from a distracted political state by the prudent behavior of its new governor, Henry Grenville.

From all these colonies and others – from all of the royal colonies except Virginia, Massachusetts, and the Leeward Islands – governors complained frequently, and in agonized tones, that they were powerless to carry out metropolitan directives against the opposition of local interests. They charged that the elected assemblies had far too much power and called for the remodeling of the constitutions of the colonies. A growing number of governors thought that the situation could only be corrected through the intervention of Parliament.

In the face of so many such complaints, no wonder that to authorities at a distance in London the whole American empire from Barbados to Nova Scotia seemed to be on the verge of disintegration. At the precise moment at which the economic and strategic worth of the colonies was becoming apparent to all and the French seemed to be preparing themselves to challenge British hegemony over them, there thus seemed to be a grave – and general – crisis of metropolitan control over the American Empire. This crisis of control in turn helped to generate a serious crisis of confidence. Colonial officials in Britain responded to the peace of 1748 not with exaltation but with strong feelings of unease and anxious fears about the impending loss of the colonies and the consequent decline of Britain itself. Such fears underlay and provided the primary impetus for the shift in colonial policy that would eventually lead to the rebellion of the colonies a little more than a quarter of a century later.

2. BEGINNINGS OF THE NEW POLICY, 1748–56

As early as 1745, the Board of Trade responded to the apparent breakdown of metropolitan authority in the colonies by showing signs of a vigor it had not demonstrated since the early decades of the century. But it received little support from the administration during the war. Not until November 1748, when the ambitious and energetic GEORGE MONTAGU DUNK, Earl of Halifax, was appointed as the new president of the Board, did the systematic and sustained attention called for by the situation begin to be accorded to colonial affairs. For the next eight years, from 1748 until the revival of hostilities with France in 1756, metropolitan officials engaged in a vigorous effort to deal effectively with the many outstanding problems relating to the colonies. This effort fell into two distinct periods.

The first lasted from the fall of 1748 through the winter of 1751-2 and was a period of activity and frustration. Inspired and driven by Halifax, the members of the Board worked with diligence in an effort to define the problems facing it and to work out a system of priorities for dealing with them. The Board gave top priority to the problem of strengthening the defenses of the northern colonies against French Canada by making Nova Scotia into a fully-fledged British colony. In a series of detailed memoranda and reports emphasizing the colony's strategic importance for the security of the North American Empire, the Board provided the justification that enabled the administration to secure an annual parliamentary grant for Nova Scotia similar to one extended to Georgia for the previous 15 years and sufficient to support the subsidized settlement of the colony with British and New England colonists which began in earnest in 1749. At the same time, the Board was less successful in its efforts to respond to the clamors of British merchants against colonial paper currencies. Its bill, introduced into Parliament in March 1749, to restrain the further issuance of paper money in the colonies and to prevent those already in existence from being legal tender, was not enacted.

If Halifax and his colleagues gave highest priority to the settlement of Nova Scotia and the restraint of colonial paper money, they were by no means neglectful of the many problems relating to the internal governance of the colonies. Initially, the Board's approach to these problems was almost entirely piecemeal and *ad hoc*, as it sought to find an appropriate solution for the particular difficulties of each colony. But its actions all tended in the same general direction: towards much closer supervision over and more intimate involvement with colonial affairs. Demonstrating an impressive attention to detail, the Board read the dispatches and papers transmitted from the colonies with far greater alacrity and care than it had in the past and made increased use of its legal counsel, Matthew Lamb, and the Attorney-General and Solicitor-General to scrutinize colonial laws to determine if they were suitable for confirmation.

In the colonies themselves, the Board insisted that royal governors adhere as strictly as possible to their instructions from the Crown and was quick to censure those who assented to laws in violation of those instructions. Indeed, the Board tried to give those instructions legal standing by including in its 1749 Currency Bill a clause declaring any colonial legislative enactments contrary to those instructions null and void. But this clause provoked such an outburst of opposition from several colonial agents that the administration agreed to reserve it for future consideration.

In the meantime, the almost invariable refusal of all colonial assemblies to comply with the instructions meant that the only effects of the Board's careful scrutiny of colonial legislation and gubernatorial conduct was to deepen discord in the colonies by intimidating governors into taking unyielding stands that were unacceptable to local interests. After 1748, governors had to contend not only with recalcitrant legislatures and other powerful leaders in the colonies but also with a group of metropolitan officials who, given the conditions that had developed over the previous

30 years, were demanding a standard of conduct that was wholly unrealistic. Henceforth, governors had to keep one eye on their adversaries in the colonies and the other closely on their superiors in London.

The positions of the governors in each of the major trouble spots – Bermuda, New Hampshire, North Carolina, New York, and New Jersey – was rendered even more difficult by the Board's inability to secure prompt action upon their several problems. Overwhelmed by a tremendous volume of business, the Board either put the governors of those provinces off or altogether ignored their plaintive letters. During these early years, the Board managed to produce long reports on the two colonies with the most serious problems, New Jersey and New York, recommending sending troops to quiet the riots in the former and the passage by Parliament of a declaratory bill to restrain the extensive authority of the legislature in the latter. But the Board had no authority to enforce its recommendations. Although the Privy Council followed its suggestions for the disallowance of many colonial laws and the ministry in 1751 guided through Parliament a bill to prohibit further issuance of legal tender paper money in the four New England colonies, neither of the reports on New Jersey and New York received ministerial support sufficient to secure its implementation.

Rumors circulated on both sides of the Atlantic that the delays in dealing with the problems of these and other colonies were the result of the ministry's determination "to settle a general plan for establishing the King[']s Authority in all the plantations" before dealing with any of them in particular.[3] In anticipation of such an event, several favor seekers and aspiring imperial statesmen, including James Abercromby, Henry McCulloh, Robert Hunter Morris, and THOMAS POWNALL, submitted elaborate plans for the overhaul of both metropolitan administration and the colonial constitutions. But no such plan ever received serious ministerial attention. However desperate the colonial situation might appear to Halifax and others who were well informed about it, the ministry exhibited no inclination to undertake comprehensive reform.

Except for the Nova Scotia settlement, the Currency Act of 1751, and a desk full of unheeded reports, Halifax and his colleagues at the Board had little to show for three years of diligent application. Not a single one of the convulsed situations Halifax had inherited when he assumed office had been resolved. To make matters worse, the Board's aggressive behavior towards the governors was even then in the process of escalating relatively minor problems in South Carolina, Jamaica, and the Leeward Islands into major ones. If anything, metropolitan control over the colonies must have seemed to be even more tenuous at the beginning of 1752 than it had four years earlier.

The result was wholesale frustration in both the colonies and the Colonial Office. Colonial governors still had no more than vague promises from a body that, it was becoming increasingly clear, was unable to deliver on them. The endless delays, punctuated only at infrequent intervals by perfunctory and evasive letters from the Board, drove governors to distraction and despair. That matters of such importance had been so long delayed in resolution was equally dispiriting to Halifax, who pushed hard, beginning in the summer of 1750, to have himself appointed as a separate Secretary of State with broad jurisdiction over and full responsibility for the colonies. Although he failed in this effort because of opposition from George II and the two existing Secretaries of State, he finally succeeded in early 1752 in securing enlarged powers for the Board of Trade. An order in council of March 11 gave the Board exclusive authority over the appointment of all governors, councilors, attorneys-general, and secretaries in the colonies and made those officers directly responsible to the Board.

The enlargement of the Board's powers marked the beginning of a second phase in the metropolitan effort to come to grips with the apparently declining authority of the parent state in the colonies. This period, lasting until the outbreak of the Seven Years' War in 1756, was one of renewed activity – and failure. Armed with its new powers and building upon its experiences over the previous four years, the Board embarked upon an even more vigorous campaign to bring the colonies under closer metropolitan control. It immediately moved to secure more up-to date information on the colonies by insisting that governors provide new answers to the formal queries hitherto required only irregularly and send home all public papers promptly, and in 1755 it sought to establish more regular communications with the colonies by setting up a packet boat system. The Board also moved to strengthen the defenses of the continental colonies, continuing to promote the settlement of Nova Scotia and converting Georgia into a royal colony in 1754.

Halifax also seems to have sought more effective personnel for appointments both to the Board and to colonial offices. At least in part because he was unable to resist the patronage of his superiors, the caliber of his initial appointees to colonial governorships was not very high. Sir Danvers Osborne of New York committed suicide shortly after his arrival, while Charles Knowles of Jamaica, John Reynolds of Georgia, and William Denny of Pennsylvania proved to be such maladroit politicians that each was either encouraged to resign or cashiered after a stormy tenure in office. Robert Dinwiddie of Virginia, Charles Lawrence of Nova Scotia, Robert Hunter Morris of Pennsylvania, and Arthur Dobbs of North Carolina all performed significantly less well than Sir William Gooch of Virginia and William Shirley of Massachusetts, the most successful of the previous generation of governors. Following these initial mistakes, however, Halifax and his colleagues do seem to have done consistently better during the last half of the 1750s. Most of their appointees served capably, managing to walk the narrow line between the competing demands of their metropolitan superiors and the local political establishment without giving major offense to either.

The standards to which the governors were expected to adhere had been mostly worked out over the previous four years and revolved around the Board's dictum that only in the most extreme circumstances should they ever deviate from their instructions. The Board's insistence upon this point was only a general policy designed to achieve several more specific goals the Board had come to regard as essential for the retention of the colonies as viable parts of the empire. One of the most important of those goals was to check the power of the lower houses of assembly. The Board never seems to have entertained any thought of governing the colonies without assemblies. In both the new royal colonies of Nova Scotia and Georgia, it insisted upon the establishment of representative government, in the former case even against the opposition of the governor on the spot. But the Board did hope to reduce the power of the assemblies in the older colonies by depriving them of many powers they had long enjoyed, including the right to establish new constituencies, apportion representatives, determine their own tenures, settle accounts, appoint local officers, and exercise a wide variety of other privileges and powers.

To that end, the Board continued to review colonial legislation carefully, to secure disallowance of objectionable statutes, and to insist strenuously, and with few exceptions, upon the inclusion of a clause suspending operation until metropolitan approval had been accorded in an ever-wider variety of colonial laws. It also recommended, though unsuccessfully, that the legislatures of all the colonies follow the example of the Virginia Assembly in reducing all earlier statutes into a clear and well-digested body of laws that (as had happened in the Virginia case) could carefully be pruned of improper statutes by metropolitan authorities. To decrease the extraordinary financial powers of the lower houses, the Board urged the governors to secure laws creating a permanent revenue that would support the entire civil list independent of further legislative appropriations.

In addition to striking at the power of the colonial assemblies, the Board pursued several other policies aimed at securing the same general objectives. After 1752 it sought, whenever the opportunity arose, to rationalize the court systems of individual colonies and to alter the ordinary terms of judicial tenure from good behavior to royal pleasure. It also endeavored to prevent the emission of any further legal-tender paper currency by adamantly insisting that the colonies south of New England comply with the terms of the Currency Act of 1751, even though it did not actually apply to them, and made preliminary investigations aimed at checking the further engrossment of land by large owners, especially in Virginia, New York, and Jamaica. It also sought to extend its jurisdiction over the private colonies, demanding that the corporate colonies of Rhode Island and Connecticut transmit their laws to the Board for information, and seeking to force the proprietors of Pennsylvania and Maryland to follow the example of the Board in attempting to curtail the authority of the lower houses in those colonies. In the case of Pennsylvania, the Board actually managed to gain a major voice in the selection of governors. Finally, in response to continued complaints from West Indian interests about violations of the Molasses Act by traders from the northern colonies, the Board toyed with the idea of recommending that Parliament revise that act in such a way as to produce a revenue.

The outbreak of hostilities between the Virginians and the French Canadians along the Ohio River in 1754–5 provided an opportunity for Halifax to try to achieve still another of his ideas for augmenting metropolitan colonial authority. The Board had proposed to send troops to quell the riots in New Jersey as early as January 1749. Immediately upon securing enlarged powers for the Board in 1752, Halifax pressed for the appointment of a governor-general for North America who, also acting as governor of New York and New Jersey, would preside over a military force to restore some semblance of metropolitan control in those two colonies. Halifax conceived of this proposal as a major step in the creation of a continental military union that might help the colonies to put forth a concerted effort in the event of a war with French Canada.

This plan got nowhere in 1752 for want of ministerial backing. But the proposal for a unified military command gained steady support in 1754–5 following Braddock's defeat and the Albany Congress. As part of the decision to send more metropolitan troops to the colonies to fight the French, the government appointed a commander-in-chief with full military authority over all the colonies. The appointment of two royal commissioners of Indian affairs in 1754 was a slightly earlier and similar move to shift responsibility for Indian diplomacy from individual colonial governments to officials directly responsible to Whitehall. The main purpose of this concentration of authority over military and Indian affairs was to produce a more effective military effort against the French. But several writers pointed out that the large contingent of British troops being sent to America might also be used to force the colonists to comply with metropolitan measures.

Few people in Britain in 1756 were yet persuaded of the necessity for such draconian measures, but the results of the accelerated effort to tighten metropolitan control over the colonies after 1752 had done little to allay the fears that lay behind such proposals – fears, as one writer put it, that without the "Colonys in America" Britain would lose the "greatest part of" its "Riches and Glory" and become, once again, "a small state not more respectable than Denmark, Sweden, [or] Switzerland."[4] Almost everywhere, in fact, metropolitan initiatives ran into stiff opposition, as the lower houses and other powerful local interests in the colonies refused to accede to them. In one colony after another, the assembly denounced every effort to diminish its authority or enhance metropolitan power as an attack upon their established constitutions and a violation of the traditional and long-standing relationship as it had been gradually worked out over the previous century. Even with its increased power and its new assertiveness, the Board of Trade could not effectively cope with such opposition. It could intimidate its governors into a faithful observance of their instructions. But that only reduced their room for maneuver when, in the absence of effective support from London, they needed all the latitude possible to accomplish the difficult assignments demanded of them.

Not that the metropolitan campaign did not achieve some limited successes. By taking extraordinary pains, the Board of Trade managed in the new civil polities of Georgia and Nova Scotia to make them the models of colony government that, it hoped, would eventually be emulated by the older colonies. In addition, by 1756 political conditions in North Carolina, New Hampshire, New Jersey, and Bermuda were much improved from the chaotic circumstances of the late 1740s. With the possible exception of North Carolina, however, these results owed more to local developments than to metropolitan initiatives. Indeed, the Board's jealous defense of the prerogative and its zealous attacks on the powers of the assemblies had contributed significantly to the development of new problems in the Leeward Islands, Virginia, South Carolina, Pennsylvania, Georgia, and Massachusetts and had been in major part responsible for throwing Jamaica into total civil chaos. No less than their predecessors a decade earlier, new governors who went to the colonies in the mid-1750s still, despite vigorous metropolitan efforts after 1748, complained that their powers were reduced within narrow limits.

By the beginning of the Seven Years' War in 1756, Halifax and his colleagues were painfully aware that their campaign to amplify metropolitan authority in the colonies was a failure. Especially in the older colonies, both on the continent and on the islands, metropolitan control was not significantly greater in 1756 than it had been eight years earlier when the whole campaign had begun. Unable to accomplish its objectives with the prerogative powers at its command, the Board of Trade from the late 1740s on had been increasingly driven to threaten the intervention of Parliament. Except in the case of the Currency Act of 1751, however, the ministry had proven reluctant to involve Parliament in its reform efforts. But in 1757, the House of Commons, acting with the full approval of the Colonial Office, actually did intervene in the purely domestic affairs of a colony for the first time since 1733. It thereby created an important precedent when it censured the Jamaican Assembly for making extravagant constitutional claims while resisting instructions from London. That metropolitan authorities were quite willing to take similar actions against other colonies was clearly indicated by the pains they took to inform all the colonies of the Commons' action in the Jamaica case.

The metropolitan program of reform between 1748 and 1756 engendered among the colonists considerable, if mostly only temporary, individual, group, and local dissatisfaction with specific metropolitan actions. But it did not produce either the sort of generalized discontent that might have brought the colonists to rebellion or a significant predisposition towards revolution among them. The impact of most of its components was too local to invite collective opposition, and the program as a whole was sufficiently diffuse and contingent as to conceal from those not at or near the center of metropolitan administration its general thrust and implications. Not until the Stamp Act had brought representatives from several colonies together and put earlier metropolitan actions in a new perspective did colonial leaders begin to perceive that, as Christopher Gadsden wrote from South Carolina in December 1765 following his return from the Stamp Act Congress, the "late attacks on different parts of the Constitution in different places" carried "the appearance of design" and were "very alarming."[5]

The result was that the whole program could be interpreted by the colonists as nothing more than some additional episodes in the ongoing efforts of metropolitan administrators to enhance the prerogative in the colonies. By the 1750s such efforts may even have come to seem less threatening than they had been 50 or 100 years earlier when the colonists had had less experience in coping with them. Yet, despite the fact that colonial leaders in most instances had effectively frustrated metropolitan designs between 1748 and 1756, the new aggressiveness in metropolitan behavior clearly exacerbated traditional colonial fears that metropolitan officials were intent upon establishing some extraordinary power over the colonies. By the mid-1750s, some were beginning to worry that the conclusion of the war would bring renewed efforts to strengthen prerogative power in the colonies, while others, disturbed by the rising volume of threats of parliamentary intervention into colonial affairs, were anxious lest Parliament might lend its support to such efforts. Still others predicted that the troops sent to the colonies might eventually be used to keep them in subjection.

However exaggerated such rumors might have been, the efforts of Halifax and his colleagues between 1748 and 1756 clearly constituted a major transformation in metropolitan behavior towards the colonies, the general thrust of which involved a dramatic shift from an essentially permissive to a fundamentally restrictive philosophy of colonial administration. The deep fear that Britain might lose the colonies resulted in the widespread conviction that the colonies had too many privileges and that those privileges ought to be reduced. In pursuit of such goals, metropolitan authorities between 1748 and 1756 attempted to implement a wide range of measures, many of them the very ones colonials found so objectionable between 1764 and 1776, which seemed to threaten or actually to violate fundamental aspects of the traditional relationship between Britain and the colonies as the colonists had come to perceive that relationship over the previous century.

Yet, the causal significance of this shift in metropolitan posture and policy for the American Revolution lies much less in the relatively localized and transitory pockets of discontent it created in the colonies than in its almost total failure to achieve any of the objectives for which it had been undertaken. For this failure served both to intensify metropolitan fears that the colonies would sooner or later get completely out of hand and to increase metropolitan determination to secure tighter control over the colonies.

3. THE SEVEN YEARS' WAR AND THE NEW COLONIAL POLICY, 1756–63

The need for a concerted effort against the French during the Seven Years' War forced the suspension of the metropolitan reform effort starting in 1756. But experience during the war exposed the weakness of British colonial authority more fully than ever before and thereby intensified the reform impulses in London. Throughout the war, aggressive lower houses openly used the government's need for defense funds to pry still more authority away from the governors; many colonial traders flagrantly violated the Navigation Acts, in many cases with the implicit connivance of the colonial governments and even of imperial customs officials; and many colonial legislatures failed to comply with metropolitan requisitions for men and money for the war effort – even with the promise of reimbursement. By the concluding years of the war, the question was no longer whether imperial administration would be reformed but how.

Not surprisingly, as soon as the British and colonial armies had defeated the French in Canada in 1759 and 1760 and colonial support for the war was no longer so essential, metropolitan officials undertook a variety of new restrictive measures calculated to restrict the colonists' scope for economic and political activity. Between 1759 and 1764, they both revived most of the measures they had pursued unsuccessfully between 1748 and 1756 and inaugurated several new ones in an attempt to diminish the inflated privileges of the colonial assemblies and to resolve problems that had come to the fore during the war, including especially the lax enforcement of the Navigation Acts.

In these new efforts, metropolitan authorities had the benefit of two important lessons they had learned from their earlier failures. The first was that only a sweeping reformation of the government and trade of all the colonies would be effective. The kinds of *ad hoc* and local solutions attempted between 1748 and 1756 obviously had not worked. The second was that any such comprehensive reconstruction would have to be undertaken by Parliament. Whether even the authority of Parliament would be accepted in the colonies seems not to have been doubted in London. The issue had never been put to the test, and, in the absence of colonial resistance to parliamentary authority, metropolitan officials could comfortably assume that Parliament had jurisdiction over colonial affairs and that its regulations would effectively be obeyed.

4. LESSONS AND SIGNIFICANCE

The conclusions drawn from the experience by the metropolitan political nation, not the many specific and local and largely unconnected grievances they generated among the colonists, are thus the primary reason why the reforms of 1748–56 must be assigned a central place in the causal pattern of the American Revolution. It need not be argued that revolution was logically inevitable thereafter or that, in response to different empirical conditions, metropolitan officials might not have reverted to their earlier policy of salutary neglect. But, by contributing to build sentiment for still more restrictive and, the officials hoped, more effective measures when a favorable opportunity presented itself, metropolitan experiences between 1748 and 1756 helped to stiffen the determination to put colonial affairs on a more rational – and more controllable – footing. That determination would continue powerfully to inform metropolitan behavior between 1759 and 1776 and would ultimately constitute the primary animating force in driving large and strategic segments of the colonial population to resistance, rebellion, and independence.

REFERENCES

1. Walpole to Duke of Newcastle, 18 June 1754, Newcastle Papers, British Library, London.
2. Hardwicke to Jonathan Belcher, 31 August 1751, in *The Life and Correspondence of Philip Yorke, Earl of Hardwicke*, ed. Philip C. Yorke (Cambridge: Cambridge University Press, 1913), II, 27–9.
3. Cadwallader Colden to George Clinton, 12 February 1750, Clinton Papers, Box 10, William L. Clements Library, Ann Arbor, Michigan.
4. W. M. to William Pitt, 16 November 1756, Chatham Papers, PRO 30/8/95, Pt. 1, ff. 194–5, Public Record Office, London.
5. Gadsden to Charles Garth, 2 December 1765, in *The Writings of Christopher Gadsden, 1746–1805*, ed. Richard Walsh (Columbia: University of South Carolina Press, 1966), 67.

FURTHER READING

Basye, Arthur H.: *The Lords Commissioners of Trade and Plantations* (New Haven, Conn.: Yale University Press, 1925).
Bumsted, John: "'Things in the womb of time': ideas of American independence, 1633 to 1763," *William and Mary Quarterly*, 31 (1974), 533–64.
Dean, Phyllis, and Cole, W. A.: *British Economic Growth, 1688–1959: Trends and Structure* (Cambridge, Mass.: Harvard University Press, 1962).
Ernst, Joseph A.: *Money and Politics in America, 1755–1775* (Chapel Hill: University of North Carolina Press, 1973).
Greene, Jack P.: "An uneasy connection: an analysis of the preconditions of the American Revolution," in *Essays on the American Revolution*, ed. Stephen G. Kurtz and James H. Hutson (Chapel Hill: University of North Carolina Press, 1973), 65–80.
——: *The Quest for Power: the Lower Houses of Assembly in the Southern Royal Colonies, 1689–1776* (Chapel Hill: University of North Carolina Press, 1963).
Greene, Jack P., and McLoughlin, William G.: *Preachers & Politicians: Two Essays on the Origins of the American Revolution* (Worcester, Mass.: American Antiquarian Society, 1977).
Henretta, James A.: *"Salutary Neglect": Colonial Administration under the Duke of Newcastle* (Princeton, NJ: Princeton University Press, 1972).
Knollenberg, Bernhard: *Origin of the American Revolution: 1759–1766* (New York: Macmillan, 1960).
Rogers, Alan, *Empire and Liberty: American Resistance to British Authority, 1755–1763* (Berkeley: University of California Press, 1974).

11

The Grenville program, 1763–1765

PETER D. G. THOMAS

THE Stamp Act of 1765 is conventionally taken as the commencement of the sequence of events immediately comprising the American Revolution. But it was only the most famous of the series of policy decisions concerning the colonies enacted by George Grenville's ministry of 1763–5. For by 1763, after a generation of war and a century of neglect, the British Government had turned its attention to America. The measures enacted during the next two years forced the colonies to face up to the implications of imperial rule.

The key decisions for new colonial expenditure and for consequential taxation of America had already been made when Grenville became Prime Minister in April 1763. There always had been an army in America. The change in 1763 was that this would be much larger than before in peacetime. The reason given to Parliament on 4 March 1763 by the Bute ministry was France's decision to maintain 20,000 soldiers in its West Indian colonies. This potential menace from Britain's traditional enemy, and the need to control the new subjects of Canada, then estimated at 90,000, meant that the army would be garrisoned for the most part outside the 13 old colonies – in Canada, the Floridas, and the wilderness of the Mississippi and Ohio valleys. It is a long-exploded myth that the British Army was in America to maintain military control over the settlement colonies. Nor was it to be the size of 10,000 men customarily stated. That was the establishment only for the transitional year of 1764. Thereafter it was 7,500 until further reductions took place from 1770.

The Bute ministry assumed that the cost burden of this army would be unacceptable to Parliament. Estimated in 1763 at only £225,000, the average annual cost between 1763 and 1775 was to be £384,000. The announcement of the decision about a large American army was therefore coupled with a promise that after the first year the colonies themselves would pay for the American army.

These were not the only policies inherited by the Grenville ministry. Lord Egremont, the minister responsible for the colonies as Southern Secretary, already had a scheme ready to fix a western boundary for the existing colonies. New settlements in Indian territory had been discouraged since 1761. There was to be military occupation only of the western lands, and regulation of trade with the Indian tribes. The policy was recommended by Egremont to the Board of Trade on 5 May 1763 and, after news of the Pontiac Rising, enacted by the Proclamation of 7 October. New colonies were created in Quebec, East Florida, and West Florida, with the area west of the mountain watershed left as an Indian reservation (*see* Chapter 15).

More central to Grenville's colonial policy, and certainly closer to his heart, was the detailed investigation during 1763 into American evasion of the trade laws: the Customs Board estimated the average annual revenue from the American customs to be a mere £1,800. This state of affairs was found intolerable by a Prime Minister whose guiding principles were strict adherence to legality and financial solvency. Attempts to enforce the existing trade regulations, as by incentives to naval officers and customs officials, preceded their alteration by Parliament in the American Duties Act of 1764. That comprised numerous alterations in the trade laws and new methods of enforcement. The most controversial was the creation of a new vice-admiralty court for the trial of smuggling cases at Halifax, Nova Scotia, a location remote from local pressures and a mode of procedure where judges sat without juries (*see* Chapter 16, §2).

1. THE MOLASSES ACT

But the most famous provision of this measure, which has often given it the name of the Sugar Act, was the alteration of the molasses duty so as to convert it into a source of revenue as well as a trade regulation. This was the first deliberate attempt to tax the colonies and to fulfil the promise of 1763: for the money was to be used towards the cost of the army in America. The Molasses Act of 1733 had imposed what was intended as a prohibitive 100 per cent duty of 6d a gallon on the import of foreign molasses, used to make rum. This was evaded by smuggling and by collusion with the customs officers, who charged about 10 per cent of the duty. The revenue had been around £700 a year, instead of the £200,000 to be expected from a trade estimated at eight million gallons. Grenville's Treasury Board dropped the idea of prohibition, accepting that the trade was vital to the economy of New England, which bought the molasses with its fish and lumber. The rate of duty that would produce the highest revenue became the Treasury's sole concern. At the end of 1763 this was calculated to be 3d a gallon, which would reduce molasses imports by two-ninths but yield £78,000. On 27 February 1764 the Treasury Board confirmed this decision by rejecting a memorial from colonial agents asking for a duty of only 2d.

The proposal was introduced to Parliament as part of Grenville's Budget on 9 March. He justified the decision by reminding MPs of Britain's vast expenditure on behalf of America during the recent war; and explained that the molasses duty had the twofold aim of producing a revenue and maintaining imperial preference, since there would still be no duty on molasses from the British West Indies. There was little criticism, for the idea of a colonial tax was popular with independent opinion in the Commons. The right of Parliament to raise such taxation was generally assumed, and no MP publicly challenged it. The Duke of Newcastle, head of the main opposition party, was under pressure from the West Indies interest not to delay the Bill. The only important debate arose over the rate of duty, when an amendment at the Committee stage on 22 March for a reduction to 2d was defeated by 147 votes to 55.

2. THE CURRENCY ACT

There was also parliamentary legislation in 1764 on the status of colonial paper money as legal tender. The assemblies issued paper bills of credit for a specified number of years, and they served as legal local currency. The Currency Act of 1764 applied only to the nine colonies south of New England, which had had a similar act since 1751. Only two colonies, Virginia and North Carolina, had a suspect currency, but the British Government thought a general regulation preferable to a discriminatory measure. The problem centered on the use of depreciated Virginia currency for the payment of debts due from that colony to British creditors. Early in 1763 the Board of Trade, during the Bute ministry, had warned the Virginia Assembly to mend its ways, but without effect. The Board thereupon took up the matter at the end of the year, and on 9 February 1764 its President Lord Hillsborough sent to the Privy Council a report condemning the practice of legal-tender paper money as fraudulent and unjust. It recommended a ban both on all future issues and on extending the time-limit of current paper money when it expired. The Grenville ministry, however, showed no inclination to enact the proposal that session, and it might have lapsed but for the initiative of Anthony Bacon, an MP concerned in trade to North Carolina. On 4 April he moved for a Bill to prohibit immediately all colonial paper money as legal tender, and met a favorable reception for this idea. Colonial agents and parliamentary friends of America thereupon at once agreed to accept the Board of Trade report, since that would not cancel existing monetary issues. That was the basis of the Currency Act, which therefore had little immediate effect and did not incur sustained colonial criticism until after the Stamp Act crisis.

3. THE STAMP ACT

That the American colonies should, like Britain, pay stamp duties was an idea often proposed before 1763, when such a suggestion from the London merchant Henry McCulloh found favor with Grenville, then seeking a colonial revenue. On 8 September the Treasury instructed McCulloh to consult with Thomas Cruwys, Solicitor to the Stamp Office, about drafting appropriate legislation. Preparation of the Bill continued until 9 March 1764 in the expectation that it would form part of Grenville's financial plans. In his Budget speech that day Grenville spoke of the stamp duty as a measure intended for that year, and moved a resolution accordingly. He then changed his mind during the debate, accepting the argument of John Huske, a native American, that due notice of such an important step ought to be sent to the colonies, and it was postponed until 1765.

Since various colonial agents formed conflicting impressions of Grenville's intention, they had a meeting with the Prime Minister on 17 May to clarify the point. Grenville explained his determination to introduce a Stamp Duties Bill in 1765, but he would listen to any colonial suggestions on the subject: one agent, Charles Garth, even thought he was willing to accept an alternative parliamentary tax. What Grenville made clear was that he would not agree to the 26 colonies in North America and the West Indies each taxing themselves instead. There is no substance in the contemporary and historical allegation that Grenville on 9 March said that he would allow this, and then later withdrew the offer. Grenville agreed to meet the agents again early in 1765 before any legislation was enacted, in order to learn the view of the colonists. He apparently envisaged the colonial role as combining general consent to the proposed taxation, which might establish a valuable precedent for prior consultation, with the opportunity to suggest detailed modifications.

Grenville, however, failed to send his proposal through the proper channel of an official letter to colonial governors. It is not known whether every colony was even informed by its agent. Certainly no suggestions about either the stamp duties or alternative parliamentary taxes were received by the British Government. Instead colonial agents were instructed to oppose the Stamp Bill, and a delegation met Grenville on 2 February 1765 to suggest the adoption of the traditional method of requisitions, whereby the Crown asked each individual colony for money. Grenville believed that this procedure had not worked satisfactorily even in wartime, and rejected the idea.

The postponement of the Stamp Bill was for political reasons, and there is little evidence to substantiate the idea that lack of detailed information was a motive; for during the summer of 1764 the ministry did little more than obtain precise details of legal documents used in the colonies. Thomas Whately, Treasury Secretary, was the politician in charge of the Bill, and on 6 December he explained the principles to the Treasury Board. The duties were to be lower than the equivalent ones in Britain, but they would be widespread for fairness, more than 50 altogether. Only nine, all non-recurrent, were over £1, and those likely to be paid often were nearly all 1/- or less. The final draft of the Bill stipulated that stamped paper would have to be used for newspapers, many legal documents, and ships' clearance documents, so the tax would be paid regularly by printers, lawyers or their clients, and merchants. A whole range of other items would also be taxed, such as liquor licenses, land grants, press advertisements, pamphlets, playing cards, dice, and calendars. Very few colonists would escape altogether.

By the time the Stamp Bill was introduced into Parliament the chief motive of the Grenville ministry had changed from the collection of revenue to the assertion of sovereignty. News of colonial protests during 1764 against Parliament's intention to tax America (*see* Chapter 12, §1) caused Whately to write to an American correspondent on 9 February 1765 of "the important point it establishes, the right of Parliament to lay an internal tax on the colonies. We wonder here that it was ever doubted. There is not a single member of Parliament that will dispute it" (Thomas, 1975, p. 86). The Grenville ministry did not proceed with the Stamp Act in ignorance of colonial opinion, but thought the measure would be accepted under protest.

The main parliamentary debate took place on 6 February, when Grenville introduced the stamp tax resolutions. He used the argument of virtual representation as the basis of Parliament's right to tax America, and said that in Britain fewer than 5 per cent were directly represented. Nor had any colony been granted exemption, by charter or otherwise. The defence of America was expensive, and the burden of the colonists' own internal taxation very light. The revenue from stamp duties would increase as the colonies prospered, and the tax would be largely self-enforcing through the nullity of unstamped documents. Colonial objections were to all taxation, not to this particular method. If Parliament backed down now, he said, America would never be taxed. Although a dozen MPs during the subsequent debate opposed imposition of the tax, none challenged Parliament's right to do so, not even ISAAC BARRÉ, who on this occasion made his famous reference to Americans as "Sons of Liberty," whose ancestors had fled from tyranny in Britain. The West Indies planter and City radical William Beckford, a follower of the absent William Pitt, put a procedural motion to postpone a decision, but it was defeated by 245 to 49. That was the only parliamentary vote on the stamp tax in 1765. This test of opinion deterred critics of the Bill subsequently from more than desultory sniping. During its passage, however, the ministry shifted its ground from Grenville's initial contention of virtual representation to the claim of the right of Parliament to tax and pass laws for the colonies as the supreme legislature of the British Empire. On 21 February a clause was added to enforce the measure by vice-admiralty courts; but to meet complaints about the remoteness of Halifax, three more would be created at Boston, Philadelphia, and Charles Town. There was no debate in the House of Lords on the Stamp Bill, which received the royal assent on 22 March.

Great care had been taken to make the Stamp Act acceptable to the colonies. The total tax envisaged was small. The wide range of duties, which averaged only about

70 per cent of their equivalent in Britain, had been devised to provide an equitable distribution of the burden. All money raised by both this tax and the 1764 molasses duty would be handed over to army paymasters in the colonies. There was never any foundation for the contemporary and historical myth that Britain would drain money from America. The two revenue measures would cover only one-third of the annual army cost in the colonies, now being estimated at £350,000, and Britain would have to cover the balance. The Stamp Act, moreover, was to be administered by leading resident colonists, not by officials sent out from Britain. This decision was implemented as soon as the legislation had passed. The key post was that of Stamp Distributor, one for each colony. It would provide income, power, and prestige, and was bestowed as patronage; for colonial resistance was not anticipated in London at the time, even by men, such as Benjamin Franklin, recently arrived from America.

4. THE QUARTERING ACT

Before the Stamp Act was passed the Grenville ministry unexpectedly found itself called upon to initiate what would be another controversial colonial measure, the Mutiny Act, also known as the Quartering Act. On 1 March there arrived a letter from General Thomas Gage, army Commander-in-Chief in America, complaining of difficulties over the quartering of soldiers and other problems caused by colonial obstruction. The Secretary at War Welbore Ellis informed Lord Halifax, now Southern Secretary, that Britain's Mutiny Act did not apply to the colonies, and was directed to prepare one. His first draft authorized the billeting of soldiers in private houses when necessary, and was altered by Grenville to a vague phrase endorsing previous practice. This was still liable to the same political objection, billeting being an infringement of personal liberty, and was fiercely attacked in the Commons on 1 April for that reason. The ministry faced a parliamentary storm over the Bill, and used the Easter recess to consult colonial agents and other experts. The solution was a clause authorizing the billeting of soldiers on uninhabited buildings if no barracks or ale-houses were available. A further new clause stipulated that in such cases the colony concerned should provide the soldiers, free of charge, with heat and light, bedding and cooking utensils, and beer or cider. This provisions clause was to be the controversial part of the Mutiny Bill, but in 1765 no complaint was anticipated about a measure deliberately altered to meet colonial objections as understood in London.

5. GRENVILLE'S INFLUENCE

The notion of a "Grenville program" for America is too modern a concept. That Grenville's ministry gave so much attention to the colonies was due not to any positive ideological approach, but to the need to solve problems, old and new (*see* figure 9). The phrase also implies a coherence that did not exist, for the colonial measures sprang from diverse antecedents. The Proclamation of 1763 was for the most part based on earlier wartime decisions. The policy of maintaining a large army in America, and the crucial public commitment to finance it by a colonial tax, were both legacies of the Bute ministry. The initiative for the Currency Act came from an independent MP. The Mutiny Act was prompted by a request of General Gage. Yet there are two circumstances that do give the phrase "Grenville program" some validity. Grenville's American measures can be seen as part of a wider British attempt in the 1760s and 1770s at a reconstruction of the empire that involved tighter control over not only

FIGURE 9 "The Great Financier, or British Economy for the Years 1763, 1764, 1765": a contemporary cartoon showing George Grenville and William Pitt (center) trying to balance the budget, aided by a figure representing economy. An American Indian wears a yoke with the words "Taxed without Representation" and kneels before the ministers with a sack of dollars.

America but also India and Ireland, while there can be no doubt that the conscientious and industrious Grenville left his personal mark on American policy. A great deal was done in a short time. Grenville, a financier with a legal background, was shocked at the disorder and defiance of authority revealed in the American scene. Hence the comment of an anonymous contemporary, "Mr. Grenville lost America because he read the American despatches, which his predecessors had never done" (Thomas, 1975, p. 113). The Stamp Act was introduced to restore Britain's authority as much as to raise money.

FURTHER READING

Bullion, J. L.: *A Great and Necessary Measure: George Grenville and the Genesis of the Stamp Act, 1763–1765* (Princeton, NJ: Princeton University Press, 1982).
Ernst, J. A.: "Genesis of the Currency Act of 1764: Virginia paper money and protection of British investments," *William and Mary Quarterly*, 22 (1965), 33–74.
Lawson, P.: *George Grenville: a Political Life* (Oxford: Clarendon Press, 1984).
Morgan, E. S.: "The postponement of the Stamp Act," *William and Mary Quarterly*, 7 (1950), 353–92.
Thomas, P. D. G.: *British Politics and the Stamp Act Crisis: the First Phase of the American Revolution, 1763–1767* (Oxford: Clarendon Press, 1975).

The Stamp Act crisis and its repercussions, including the Quartering Act controversy

PETER D. G. THOMAS

THE Stamp Act crisis was the first phase of the American Revolution. It raised the basic issue of Britain's sovereignty over her settlement colonies. The measures of Grenville's ministry, and especially the passage of the Stamp Act, were based on British assumptions that Parliament had complete legislative authority over the empire. It was a sovereignty that had never hitherto been exercised in this positive manner. While British opinion could see no distinction between taxation and other modes of legislation, the American colonists certainly did. Although the first colonial challenge concerned only taxation, the implications embraced the whole of Parliament's sovereignty, as Grenville pointed out when on 6 February 1765 he introduced the Stamp Act resolutions. "The objection of the colonies is from the general right of mankind not to be taxed but by their representatives. This goes to all laws in general" (Thomas, 1975, p. 89). He was referring then to the protests of 1764. After the passage of the Stamp Act in 1765 the colonists did more than complain. They nullified the operation of that measure, and adopted retaliatory devices to compel a change of British policy. This was achieved in 1766, but not as the Americans either believed or would have wished.

I. THE COLONIES COMPLAIN IN 1764

In 1764 the American colonies were confronted with the news of the Sugar Act and of the prospective stamp duties. They were already suffering from a postwar economic depression. News of the actual and intended taxes, on top of what seemed a bleak future, prompted alarm. It was natural for the colonists to question the constitutional right of Parliament so to alter their lives. But while there could be no doubt over the ominous significance of the proposed stamp duties, the Sugar Act was the adaptation of trade regulations to an additional purpose of revenue. The wording of the act showed the molasses duty was intended as a tax (*see* Chapter 11, §1), but the traditional method employed led to a confused response. It was also one limited geographically, since that duty would directly affect only a few colonies. The Massachusetts politician James Otis did challenge the Sugar Act as a tax in his pamphlet *Rights of the British Colonies Asserted and Proved*. But his stand was not a typical response.

Massachusetts, Rhode Island, and New York had already protested about the Sugar Act before its passage, though their complaints had arrived too late. They were the colonies most likely to suffer from it. Of the 127 rum distilleries listed for North America in 1763 which used molasses as their raw material, 64 were in Massachusetts and 40 in Rhode Island and Connecticut; none were south of Pennsylvania. Aware of the potential damage to their trade and industry, Massachusetts and Rhode Island complained about the Sugar Act only on economic grounds, but the New York Assembly protested about this exploitation of a trade duty to extract revenue. "All impositions, whether they be internal taxes, or duties paid for what we consume, equally diminish the estates upon which they are charged: what avails it to any people, by which of them they are impoverished" (Morgan and Morgan, 1963, p. 56). But North Carolina was the only other colony to complain about the Sugar Act as a tax.

The prospect of a universal stamp tax provoked a wider response. Massachusetts sent a petition to the Commons asking for a continuation of the "privilege" of internal taxation, evidently with the proposed stamp duties in mind. Altogether the assemblies of at least eight colonies protested against the proposed Stamp Act, the others being Rhode Island, Connecticut, New York, Pennsylvania, Virginia, North Carolina, and South Carolina. The evidence may be incomplete, for South Carolina's agent told his colony that all the agents had been instructed to oppose the measure. No colony took up Grenville's offer to consider modifications of the stamp duties or suggested alternative parliamentary taxation. To do so would have been an acknowledgment of Parliament's right. It was this invariable and possibly unanimous response of the colonies that Grenville perceived as a challenge to parliamentary sovereignty over America, and made him determined to proceed with the Stamp Act.

2. THE COLONIES PROTEST IN 1765

News of the passage of the Stamp Act reached the American colonies during April 1765. The initial response was not indignation, but resignation. William Smith, an author of the 1764 New York protest, commented that "this single stroke has lost Great Britain the affection of all her colonies" (Morgan and Morgan, 1963, p. 121), but he did not envisage any riposte. Still less did Lieutenant-Governor Thomas Hutchinson of Massachusetts, who on 4 June wrote from Boston that "the Stamp Act is received among us with as much decency as could be expected. We shall execute it" (Gipson, 1961, p. 291). None of the assemblies still in session made any response until 29 May. The Virginia House of Burgesses was only one-third full when the young lawyer Patrick Henry, a nine-day member, rose to win instant fame. The legend that he defied shouts of treason has long been exploded. But he did carry five resolutions asserting the doctrine of no taxation without representation. The evidence as to precisely what happened is unsatisfactory, but it would appear that his boldest resolution, claiming for the assembly the exclusive right of taxation, was carried by only one vote and expunged the next day. The opposition to Henry came from men who had put forward similar doctrines in the 1764 petition, and merely reflected personal animosity. The significance of the Virginia Resolves was the publicity afforded them in the colonial press, and the more so in that it was misleading. Henry had drafted seven resolutions, and one of the others was a declaration to disobey parliamentary taxation. The Virginia Assembly had discussed the question of resisting the Stamp Act, but had decided not to endorse such a stand. But the American newspapers conveyed the opposite impression by printing all of Henry's resolutions as if they had been voted by the assembly.

The Virginia Resolves changed the mood of America. This was demonstrated when assemblies met again later in the year. In September that of Rhode Island, which had made no complaint in May, voted all that Virginia was thought to have done. Other assemblies, perhaps better informed on that point, did not go so far; but Pennsylvania and Maryland also voted declaratory resolutions that month, and by the end of the year Connecticut, Massachusetts, South Carolina, New Jersey, and New York had also done so. In June even Massachusetts had merely decided to send respectful petitions to King and Parliament; but it had also proposed, on the suggestion of James Otis, a meeting in New York of delegates from the various colonies to frame a joint petition. That proved the crucial step. Nine colonies were to send a total of 27 delegates to what has since become known as the Stamp Act Congress when it met in October. New Hampshire declined, but later approved what was decided. Virginia, North Carolina, and Georgia were prevented from attending by the refusal of their governors to summon assemblies; but Delaware and New Jersey overcame the same obstacle by unofficial choice of delegates.

The issue that concerned the Congress was not the financial burden of the Stamp Act but the belief that it was unconstitutional. The delegates were agreed on that point, but it took about a fortnight's discussion before 14 resolutions were devised. These set out the colonial view of the imperial relationship. Allegiance to the Crown and subordination to Parliament were acknowledged. But the colonists, who claimed the rights of British subjects, were not and could not be represented in Parliament, only in their assemblies, which therefore alone had the power to tax them. The Stamp Act and other revenue measures were condemned for "a manifest tendency to subvert the rights and liberties of the colonists." This was a distinction between taxation and legislation, which would not be acceptable at Westminster. The additional argument was then put that since the colonies were obliged to purchase Britain's manufactures they indirectly contributed to the taxation levied there. The final resolution was a decision to petition King, Lords, and Commons for repeal of the taxes, and these petitions were drafted before the Congress broke up on 25 October.

The chief argument within the Congress had been whether to balance the denial of Parliament's right to tax the colonies with an acknowledgment of its right to regulate trade. Those who argued for this statement believed that it was necessary to make such an offer to persuade Britain to give up the right of internal taxation, but they failed to get their way. Since the Sugar Act had shown how trade duties could be used to raise revenue, the majority of delegates would not risk any admission. The declaration merely made a vague statement of the "due" subordination of the colonies to Parliament, without mention of any specific legislation such as the trade laws.

Historians have differed in opinion as to the precise nature of the colonial objection to Parliament's right of taxation. The traditional interpretation, as championed by Gipson (Gipson, 1961), is that the Americans objected only to "internal taxes," such as the Stamp Act, and not to "external taxes," revenues deliberately raised from customs duties. This was generally understood to be so in Britain, and that is why CHARLES TOWNSHEND chose such duties as his mode of taxation in 1767. When the Americans thereupon denied altogether any parliamentary right of taxation, they were then and have often subsequently been held to have changed their ground. Morgan argues that this was not the case, and that they had objected from the first to all taxation (Morgan, 1948; Morgan and Morgan, 1963). Both interpretations can be supported by selective evidence, but it would seem that the colonists had the Stamp Act in mind, whether they spoke of "taxes" or "internal taxes." Americans may not have specifically denied Parliament all powers of taxation; but neither did they make any positive acknowledgment of Parliament's right to raise money from the colonies –

hence the cautious refusal of the Stamp Act Congress to admit even a right to regulate colonial trade, since that might be used to produce revenue.

3. COLONIAL RESISTANCE TO THE STAMP ACT

Words of protest were accompanied by deeds of resistance. This took three forms. Firstly, the Stamp Act was prevented from coming into operation on its due date, 1 November. Secondly, the colonists then continued most of the relevant activities, for to refrain from doing so would have been a tacit admission of that Act's validity. Thirdly, methods of retaliation were devised to bring pressure on Britain for its repeal. This resistance was often characterized by caution and initial hesitation. The colonists were aware of the enormity of the challenge they were making to Britain, but they also knew there was no constitutional way to change parliamentary decisions, and

FIGURE 10 "The Bostonian's Paying the Excise-man, or Tarring & Feathering": a hostile but not inaccurate English cartoon showing five Bostonians pouring tea down the throat of a tarred and feathered excise man in front of a liberty tree, on which a sign reading "stamp act" hangs upside down (probably by Philip Dawe, 1774).

MPs had seemed deaf to their earlier pleas. Physical resistance appeared to be the only method to alter Parliament's attitude. The achilles heel of the Stamp Act was the appointment of local men as the Stamp Distributors who were to supervise its operation in each colony. If they could be prevented from doing so the whole taxation measure would be nullified.

Boston was to show the way (*see* figure 10). The initiative there did not come from the Massachusetts political leaders such as James Otis and Samuel Adams. But they may well have directed the artisans and shopkeepers who comprised the small ginger group called the Loyal Nine, later expanded into the Sons of Liberty, who instructed the mob that first erupted on 14 August (*see* Chapter 19, §2). Andrew Oliver, rumored to be the Massachusetts Stamp Distributor, was then hanged in effigy and had his house wrecked after he had fled for his life; next day he promised to resign. The ostensible object had been achieved. Yet on 26 August the Boston mob again went on the rampage, attacking the homes of several officials, notably that of Lieutenant-Governor Thomas Hutchinson. Although Hutchinson had attempted to stop the attack on Oliver and was deemed a supporter of the Stamp Act, such other motives as personal enmities and the destruction of customs and legal records better explain this second riot.

News of the first Boston riot led to a similar disturbance in Newport, Rhode Island, from 27 to 29 August, which caused the resignation of the Stamp Distributor Augustus Johnston. After these events the mere threat of violence usually sufficed to secure the resignation of Stamp Distributors elsewhere. In New York James McEvers resigned as early as 22 August, stating that he had a warehouse containing £20,000 worth of goods at risk. The notorious New York City mob was not, however, deprived of its riot, for a clash with the military and civil authorities occurred on 1 November, when that port, like many others in America, went into public mourning to mark the formal commencement of the Stamp Act. By that date the Act had been effectively nullified by the resignation of all the other Stamp Distributors. On 2 September William Coxe in New Jersey resigned before any threat, and the same day Zachariah Hood in Maryland fled after having his house wrecked. Two others who had, like Hood, obtained the appointment for themselves in Britain, resigned immediately on arrival back in America, George Meserve for New Hampshire on 11 September and George Mercer in Virginia on 31 October. A fourth who had done so, Jared Ingersoll in Connecticut, resisted mob pressure for some weeks before resigning on 19 September. John Hughes, appointed at Benjamin Franklin's request for Pennsylvania and Delaware, also resisted pressure until 7 October, when he promised not to act. Caleb Lloyd of South Carolina gave the same undertaking on 28 October. No news of the appointment of Stamp Distributors for North Carolina and Georgia had even arrived by 1 November, when there was not one willing to act in the 13 colonies. In any case the stamped paper was unobtainable: some had been destroyed, some had not arrived, and most had been stored for safe-keeping in forts or on navy ships. North Carolina's Stamp Distributor was to resign when his appointment was notified on 16 November; but in Georgia the only non-American, George Angus, did officiate for a fortnight after his arrival on 4 January 1766, before discretion prevailed.

Governors outside Massachusetts blamed Boston for this sequence of events. But the resolutions of Virginia and other colonies, and of the Stamp Act Congress, logically implied some action; and the speed and unanimity of the colonial response shows that Boston was merely a convenient scapegoat. The Sons of Liberty became a general phenomenon as resistance crystallized in each colony.

Boston took the lead only in violence. Other colonies opened their ports first. Everywhere in America as many ships as possible had sailed before 1 November, but this apparent reluctance to break the law was soon overcome by commercial pressures, as customs officials were coerced into acting without stamped papers. Philadelphia never really closed, by the device of issuing clearance papers before 1 November to ships not yet loaded. Virginia reopened after one day, on 2 November, Rhode Island on 25 November, and Pennsylvania, New York, and New Jersey early in December, but Boston not until 17 December. Connecticut and New Hampshire opened by the end of December, Maryland in January 1766, and the two Carolinas and Georgia in February. Ports in all 13 colonies were open before news of the prospective repeal of the Stamp Act.

Opening the law courts was another matter. Lawyers faced the problem that decisions on unstamped papers would be invalid. Delays of several months were customary in legal proceedings, and many people, such as debtors, were happy to see the courts closed. Judges and lawyers sometimes changed their minds, and often found it easier to resort to adjournments until news came from Britain; the impending repeal relieved the pressure for awkward decisions. There is therefore no consistent pattern, nor even any clear picture of the colonial response, for the evidence is incomplete. It would seem that only in Rhode Island did the courts never close, and that they might not have opened in such colonies as New York or Virginia, but that in most there was a gradual trend towards resuming normal legal business.

The printers, together with the merchants and lawyers, formed the third main occupational group whose livelihood was directly affected by the Stamp Act. The colonial press in 1765 played a key role in American resistance both by deliberate propaganda and by simply reporting words and deeds of defiance. The newspaper printers had no intention of paying the stamp duties, but most adopted the cautious response of suspending publication from 1 November. Of the 23 colonial newspapers then in existence, it would seem that only eight continued publication without a break, and some then by altering titles or appearing anonymously. During the ensuing weeks, though it was sometimes months, there was a gradual resumption of publication by the others, either under local pressure or from fear of losing their customers, for four new papers were founded to exploit market gaps that had arisen. Most newspapers were defying the law long before news of repeal arrived.

Refusal to pay the stamp duties, and ignoring the Stamp Act by the resumption of taxable activities, produced only a stalemate. What America wanted was repeal of the Stamp Act, and, while this was requested in petitions, direct pressure on Britain was deemed necessary. There was talk both of refusal to pay debts to British creditors and of armed resistance, but these ideas were not seriously canvassed, although awareness of them in Britain helped to swing opinion there in 1766. The method that was adopted was the economic pressure of a refusal to purchase British goods. This was instigated by individual ports, for the Stamp Act Congress had confined itself to verbal remonstrances. New York City took the initiative on 31 October, when two hundred merchants there signed an agreement to stop ordering British goods until the Stamp Act was repealed. Four hundred Philadelphia merchants did the same on 14 November and two hundred Boston merchants on 9 December. Elsewhere, as in Rhode Island, merchants usually suspended British orders without formal agreements. The propaganda impact of this boycott was enhanced by a publicized campaign for the colonial manufacture of clothing and other goods customarily bought from Britain. It was the threat implied by the boycott that was to be of significance in resolving the

Stamp Act crisis, rather than its actual effect. For this must necessarily have been limited in the time-scale involved: and in any case Britain's trade to America amounted only to about one-eighth of her total exports. But the confusion of the boycott threat with the commercial and industrial recession already in existence was to produce an exaggerated effect on British opinion.

4. THE BRITISH DECISION ON POLICY

In July 1765 Grenville's ministry was replaced by one headed by the 35-year-old Marquis of Rockingham, who earlier in that year had succeeded Newcastle as head of the political group that liked to regard itself as the Whig Party. Young and inexperienced, the new administration was faced by the hostility of Grenville, while Pitt and his followers acted as a neutral third party who might support or oppose the ministry. The reasons for this change were unconnected with America: Grenville had given personal offence to George III. But it was important that at the time of the Stamp Act crisis there should have come to office an administration not responsible for the measures that had aroused discontent in the colonies. A change of policy was not inevitable, for the men of the new ministry had made little resistance to Grenville's legislation, but they would be more likely to consider conciliation of some kind.

News of the colonial resistance to the Stamp Act gradually reached Britain during the second half of 1765. In August the new ministry thought the Virginia Resolves did not truly represent American opinion, and did not anticipate much difficulty in enforcing the Stamp Act. But by October America was on the political agenda. News had come of the Boston and Newport riots, and of various protests and resistance elsewhere. The ministry played for time by sending formal orders, through Southern Secretary Conway on 24 October, that the law should be upheld, but the governors had no military force or other means to obey this instruction. The ministry tacitly postponed any policy decision on whether or not to enforce the Stamp Act until the end of the year, awaiting more information. There was still hope that opposition was not widespread, that the crisis would resolve itself. The administration meanwhile came under pressure for suspension or repeal of the Stamp Act, from Benjamin Franklin and other agents, and from British merchants concerned about the threat to trade; one of them, Barlow Trecothick, instigated a national campaign to petition Parliament by circulating 30 towns on 6 December. Rockingham himself approved this letter. He foresaw that British complaints about the American trade slump would assist any move to persuade Parliament to make concessions over the Stamp Act. This was the first sign the Prime Minister had decided on conciliation.

The decline in colonial trade and the economic depression in Britain had begun before the Stamp Act crisis. The evidence that was to be presented to Parliament in February 1766 depicted an industrial recession in Britain that had already lasted for some time. But the colonial boycotts of imports did not begin until 31 October 1765, and news of them did not reach Britain until mid-December. The Rockingham ministry, in assuming that the economic recession in Britain was caused by the colonial trade embargo, misunderstood the situation.

By December 1765 the Rockingham ministry could no longer hope that the Stamp Act would come into operation after colonial disturbances had ceased. The apparent choice was between military coercion and some form of concession, which might be modification, suspension, or complete repeal of the Act. But ministers knew that it would be impossible to assemble the army needed to enforce the taxation in the face of such overwhelming colonial hostility: they had been told so by General Gage, Commander-in-chief for North America. Conciliation was therefore the only possible short-term solution. But simple repeal would be unacceptable to British political opinion, as too obvious a surrender to mob violence. The administration faced up to reality, and, after numerous consultations and private discussions, on 27 December produced a preliminary policy decision. There would be a Declaratory Act to assert the supremacy of Parliament over the colonies, and a subsequent offer of "relief" to America, ostensibly on economic grounds. Members of the government held different opinions as to what this should be. The ministry had not only to agree on a policy but devise one acceptable to King and Parliament. George III had no firm opinion, and would as usual accept his ministry's decision, albeit with reluctance. The key to Parliament was the attitude of William Pitt. While both public rumor and the behavior of his followers pointed to his support of conciliation, he rebuffed a ministerial enquiry about his opinion, stating that he would give it only to Parliament, which was to meet on 14 January 1766. No final policy decision was therefore taken before then, and the King's Speech to Parliament reflected this ministerial predicament. Ostensibly a statement of policy, its vague wording left open a wide possible choice of options.

The debate on the Address resolved the situation. Pitt attended the Commons after a two-year absence, and spoke in favor of complete repeal. Adopting what was generally thought in Britain to be the colonial view, he denied that Parliament had any right to levy internal taxation on America, since the colonies were not represented there. His speech made it possible for Rockingham to convince his colleagues that repeal was both the inevitable course of action and one that Parliament would accept, with Pitt's advocacy, if there was the palliative of a Declaratory Act to allay uneasiness about the implications of such a turnabout. For Pitt's denial of the right of taxation had offended many independent MPs, who would not want repeal to be seen as an endorsement of this view.

On 19 January the Rockingham ministry came to a final decision on American policy. This would comprise a Declaratory Act that would avoid mention of taxation so as not to offend Pitt; it would be followed by the complete repeal of the Stamp Act, on the alleged grounds of its inherent faults and the detrimental effect it had had on the British economy. The Declaratory Act would assert the right of Parliament to legislate for the American colonies "in all cases whatsoever." This formal statement was an expression of political faith, and was to be an integral part of future Rockinghamite attitudes to America. But there was also the motive of tactical expediency, based on the realization that King, Lords, and Commons would all be unwilling to accept any surrender to colonial defiance.

5. THE REPEAL OF THE STAMP ACT

The ministry faced opposition to their policy on two flanks. Grenville would obviously resist repeal, while Pitt's denial of the right of taxation would cause him to challenge the Declaratory Bill. The campaign was therefore carefully planned. Parliament was kept fully informed about the gravity of the colonial crisis; but this tactic may have been counter-productive, for there is evidence of parliamentary resentment against America. A less subtle attempt to influence parliamentary opinion was the battery of petitions organized by Trecothick with ministerial blessing. In January 1766, 24 petitions from British ports and manufacturing towns were submitted to the House of Commons.

The case for the Declaratory Act was established first. The Lords and Commons both read through the American papers, and examined witnesses on the colonial resistance. On 3 February both Houses debated the declaratory resolution. Pitt's followers, led by Camden, forced a vote in the Lords, losing 125 to 5, but there was none in the Commons, even though Pitt spoke against the right of internal taxation. Government lawyers in both Houses deployed a wealth of precedents and arguments to deny that representation was necessary for taxation, or that there was any distinction between internal and external taxation or between taxation and legislation. The most important result of the debates was to clarify the point that the phrase "in all cases whatsoever" did include taxation.

The ministry took a buffeting in Parliament during the next few days. There were defeats in the Lords over opposition amendments to government motions, while in the Commons Grenville seized the initiative with resolutions of his own about compensation for riot victims and an indemnity for any offenders now willing to pay the taxes. He then announced that on 7 February he would move to enforce the Stamp Act. That would be the crucial test of parliamentary opinion. Rockingham therefore obtained permission from George III to make public the King's support of repeal. This news, a warning by Pitt that bloodshed would be the consequence, and another by Conway that Britain's European enemies might intervene in any conflict, combined to produce a majority of 274 to 134 against Grenville.

Even yet the success of the ministerial policy was not assured. George III let it be known that his personal preference would have been for modification rather than complete repeal, had that been a viable option, and customary government supporters then felt free to vote against repeal without offending their sovereign. Opinion in the Commons was still volatile over what was to many the unpalatable choice of complete repeal, and there was also the hurdle of the House of Lords.

Emphasis on Britain's economic distress was the chief ministerial tactic in securing the consent of the House of Commons to repeal. All the government witnesses examined in February, bar two, were merchants and manufacturers concerned with British trade to America. They had been carefully selected, and some were rehearsed beforehand. All, even under cross-examination, gave repeal as the only satisfactory solution. Trecothick, on behalf of the London merchants, was the most important witness, on 11 February: his evidence included the calculation that colonial debts to British merchants amounted to £4,450,000, with the obvious implication that much of this was at risk. The tale of economic woe throughout Britain by the procession of witnesses succeeded in alarming independent MPs. They were already aware of hunger riots in Britain, and feared more general disorder. While ministers sought to arouse such fears of disturbances in Britain, they played down the deliberate violence and constitutional claims of the colonists. They were portrayed respectively as spontaneous mob riots and as a challenge to Parliament only over internal taxation; the most famous witness, Benjamin Franklin, told MPs so on 13 February.

The great debate on repeal took place on 21 February. It was significant for the public formulation of British attitudes on America. Conway explained ministerial policy when he affirmed Parliament's right of taxation but said it was a right that ought not to be exercised. A tax revenue of £60,000 was not worth the sacrifice of British trade to America. Those who favored amendment were told that modification gave up the substance while keeping the shadow, a shadow that would frighten the Americans. Pitt put what was to be his characteristic view of the colonial relationship: that it was unfair both to tax America and to control its economy. Grenville argued vainly that the colonies were well able to pay all his taxes. The resolution for repeal was carried by 275 votes to 167. The key to this ministerial success had been the effort to win over independent opinion, for many customary government supporters had deserted.

On 4 March Pitt challenged the passage of the Declaratory Bill by moving to omit the words "in all cases whatsoever," but did not force a vote; the Commons passed the repeal the same day by 250 to 122. The ministry was nevertheless apprehensive about the House of Lords. Independent peers were few in number, and Rockingham did not deploy witnesses on the economic situation. He relied instead on royal pressure on important peers. This strategy proved successful in the only Lords vote over repeal, on 11 March. The ministerial majority was 73 to 61, increased by proxies to 105 to 71. Both bills received the royal assent on 18 March.

Repeal required practical implementation. The scanty revenue was secured, surviving stamped paper returned to Britain, and the accounts of officials settled. The gross revenue was £3,292, but with costs incurred of £6,863. An Indemnity Act was passed in May, to wipe the slate clean. Compensation for riot victims was recommended to the relevant assemblies, but Rhode Island proved evasive, New York did not vote enough, and Massachusetts refused to comply. This recalcitrance aroused indignation in Britain, and in December the Massachusetts Assembly, warned by its agent that the new Chatham ministry was adamant on the subject, voted to pay compensation to Thomas Hutchinson and other victims. But the same measure also pardoned all offenders in the Boston riots, the British indemnity having covered disobedience and not violence. This usurpation of the royal power of pardon infuriated both administration and opposition to Parliament. In 1767 they argued only as to the best method of nullifying it, before on 13 May the Privy Council declared the whole measure void.

6. THE AMERICAN TRADE ACT OF 1766

The Stamp Act was not the only American legislation of the Grenville ministry with whose consequences the Rockingham administration had to grapple. The other revenue measure, the alteration of the duty on foreign molasses to 3d a gallon in 1764, had also been a failure. The ministerial argument then had been that the planters in the French West Indies would reduce their price to keep the market, and the stability of the molasses price in North America seemed initial confirmation of this view. But that the continuance of widespread smuggling was the true reason was revealed by the failure of the 3d duty to produce the anticipated revenue of £78,000; it yielded only £5,200 in 1764 and £4,090 in 1765.

Consideration of that question formed part of the general review of the trade laws in 1766. While the ministry was concerned with the parliamentary contest over the Stamp Act, the North America and West Indies merchants agreed on 10 March that the duty on foreign molasses imported into America should be reduced to a realistic 1d a gallon. Rockingham accepted this idea, and witnesses told the Commons on 27 March how desirable such a change would be. America needed profits from the West Indies trade to purchase British goods. Repeal of the Stamp Act might restore the will of the colonists to trade with Britain, but such changes were needed to enable them to do so. West Indies planters, however, refused to endorse the 1d duty agreed by the merchants; as the planter William Beckford had the support of his mentor William

Pitt, and Grenville also criticized the change, political opposition threatened to wreck the plan.

The Chancellor of the Exchequer William Dowdeswell nevertheless proposed the 1d duty to the Commons on 30 April. It was criticized by Beckford as harmful to the British West Indies and by Grenville as a surrender to colonial smugglers. The ministry resolved the problem by direct negotiations with the West Indies lobby, offering concessions concerning inter-island trade in return for the remarkable new concession that molasses from the British, as well as foreign, islands would pay the 1d duty. The advantage would be the elimination of fraud: hitherto foreign molasses had often been passed off as British. But the change meant that the molasses duty was now simply a tax, and it was to be the only effective one devised by British politicians in the revolutionary period. This agreement, made on 8 May, was confirmed by the Commons the same day and enacted without debate as part of another American Duties Act by 6 June.

The Rockingham ministry, sympathetic to growing colonial complaints about the scarcity of legal-tender money, also considered alteration or repeal of the 1764 Currency Act, but the dismissal of the administration in July prevented enactment of any measure on that subject. This came about because George III had ascertained that Pitt was willing to form a ministry in disregard of what the King detested as "faction"; such an administration had been George III's aim since his accession. Royal disapproval of the Rockingham ministry's American policy was not the reason for its removal: it was only afterwards that the King came to see repeal of the Stamp Act as the measure fatal to Anglo-American union.

7. THE SIGNIFICANCE OF THE STAMP ACT CRISIS

Although the Stamp Act crisis was concerned ostensibly with the issue of taxation, it had raised the wider question of Britain's sovereignty over the colonies, and had consequences on both sides of the Atlantic. British opinion would not be satisfied with the formal claim of the Declaratory Act after such a rebuff, and would especially seek a colonial revenue. Within Britain politicians were now categorized according to their attitudes on America, even though these had largely been shaped by the chance of who was in administration or opposition when decisions were being made. Henceforth Grenville and his friends were hardliners or "Stamp men"; the Rockinghamite party would be pragmatic in approach, championing sovereignty in theory but not its exercise in practice. Those sympathetic to America were few in number – Pitt and his followers, a handful of radicals, and some Rockinghamites and independents. In America the colonists would now be suspicious of any British government policy, while in some individual colonies the Stamp Act crisis had considerable impact on local power structures. Those politicians identified with support of Britain, such as the Hutchinson–Oliver party in Massachusetts and Jared Ingersoll in Connecticut, had their influence weakened or destroyed. Conversely, championship of America had brought new men to power, notably Patrick Henry, or given established politicians victory over their rivals. Neither in general nor in detail would the Anglo-American relationship return to what it had been before the Stamp Act crisis.

8. THE QUARTERING ACT CONTROVERSY

The American Mutiny Act of 1765, known to colonists as the Quartering Act (see Chapter 11, §4), was soon found to be defective by both the army and the colonies.

The army had to accept that billeting on private houses, which had occasionally been the practice in the past, was now implicitly illegal, while the new dependence on assemblies for barrack supplies made the vote of army provisions a political weapon by which displeasure with the British Government or local governors could be manifested. The colonists had a double grievance. The provisions clause was regarded as a new tax; and it was one whose incidence was accidental and uneven, and therefore unfair. Postings were irregular and rarely permanent, and some colonies, such as Virginia, escaped a military presence almost altogether.

New York, containing the main port for the arrival and departure of soldiers, was the colony likely to bear the heaviest burden. At the end of 1765 its assembly refused to comply with the request of General Gage, army Commandier-in-Chief in North America, for provisions under the Quartering Act. Gage tried again, in May 1766, and in June the assembly did agree to supply firewood and candles, bedding, and utensils, but not the alcohol stipulated. The assembly also passed resolutions stating that the total number of soldiers for whom provision might have to be made was unknown, implying that the colony faced an unlimited demand on its resources, but that New York was willing to pay a proportionate share of the total American expense. New York had a real grievance, but such defiance of an Act of Parliament could not be allowed to pass without reprimand by any British government. The Chatham Cabinet on 5 August therefore decided that Southern Secretary Shelburne should write to the Governor stating that it was expected there should be "all due obedience" to parliamentary statutes; he did so on 9 August. The response of the assembly in December was a unanimous decision not to vote any supplies at all, and a complaint that the burden on New York would be greater than that on any other colony. The New Jersey Assembly in December voted only what New York had done in June, and declared that the Quartering Act was as much a tax as the Stamp Act, and more unfair, as soldiers were stationed in few colonies. Resistance to the Quartering Act was not universal. Pennsylvania fully complied with the Act up to 1774, the only colony to do so. Connecticut and even Massachusetts at this time supplied casual detachments of soldiers. That Georgia was defying the act in 1767 remained as yet unknown in Britain. It seemed that only New York was being obstructive.

The British ministry was determined to enforce the Quartering Act on that colony. The absent Chatham ruled that the matter should be referred to Parliament, and on 12 March 1767 the Cabinet met to decide what proposal to put to the House of Commons. Southern Secretary Shelburne's solution was the coercive billeting of soldiers on private houses. Northern Secretary Conway suggested a direct levy on New York by additional trade duties. Both proposals were rejected in favor of an idea of the Chancellor of the Exchequer Charles Townshend, that the New York Assembly should be prohibited from exercising its legislative function until it fully obeyed the Quartering Act. Not until 13 May did Townshend put this proposal to the Commons. It was more moderate than the alternatives preferred by the opposition parties. The Rockinghamite solution was to quarter soldiers on private houses, the same as Shelburne's idea in cabinet. Grenville suggested a direct order to the colony's treasury. The debate reflected almost universal agreement about the policy of coercing New York into submission. In that sense the majority for Townshend's motion, of 180 against 98, was a victory for moderation; and there is evidence that many MPs did not think New York would risk further defiance.

That proved to be the outcome. Early in June, before Parliament had passed the New York Restraining Act, the colony's assembly voted a sum sufficient to pay for all items stipulated in the Quartering Act, but without formal reference to that measure. The Governor reported this as compliance with it, and Shelburne agreed that the Restraining Act, due to go into operation on 1 October, had been rendered unnecessary. The matter was ended as far as the ministry was concerned, but the Quartering Act continued to be an intermittent colonial grievance during the next few years. The Massachusetts Circular Letter of February 1768 complained of the financial burden, and later that year Gage met obstruction in Boston that caused him to request a revision of the Act. This was accomplished in 1769, after both the Grafton Cabinet and the Commons had rejected the idea of billeting on private houses; it was proposed respectively by the American Secretary Lord Hillsborough and the Secretary at War Lord Barrington, and killed by Lord North. During a routine renewal of the Quartering Act the former Massachusetts governor Thomas Pownall carried an amendment giving army officers and civil magistrates discretion to make mutually satisfactory arrangements. Another amendment even allowed colonies to opt out of the Quartering Act if they passed their own legislation for the same purpose. The Cabinet rejected this suggestion from Hillsborough, but the Commons adopted the Pownall amendment to that end. No colony took advantage of this choice, but Hillsborough devised a pragmatic solution to the problem in 1771. Since 1767, colonies with army detachments had made provision for them with little protest except in the heated atmosphere of 1769 during the Townshend Duties crisis, but New Jersey refused to pay in 1771. Hillsborough's answer to the problem was the withdrawal of army units from disobedient colonies, rather than coerce New Jersey, as had been the case with New York in 1767. This would prompt realization that the economic and military benefits of an army presence outweighed the financial burden. A regiment might spend £6,000 a year in pay, quite apart from its maintenance costs, while soldiers could sometimes be useful to maintain order. The removal of New Jersey's regiment in 1771 aroused alarm that all the middle colonies were going to be evacuated. New York and Philadelphia voted their contributions promptly, and so did New Jersey when regiments later returned. Apart from the special case of Massachusetts, the problem of the Quartering Act had virtually been resolved.

FURTHER READING

Gipson, L. H.: *The British Empire before the American Revolution*, Vol. X: *The Triumphant Empire: Thunder-Clouds Gather in the West, 1763–1766* (New York: Alfred A. Knopf, 1961).

Knollenberg, B: *Origin of the American Revolution, 1759–1766* (1960), 2nd edn. (New York: Collier Books, 1961).

Langford, P.: *The First Rockingham Administration, 1765–1766* (Oxford: Oxford University Press, 1973).

Morgan, E. S.: "Colonial ideas of parliamentary power, 1764–1766," *William and Mary Quarterly*, 5 (1948), 311–41.

——: *Prologue to Revolution: Sources and Documents on the Stamp Act Crisis, 1764–1766* (Chapel Hill: University of North Carolina Press, 1959).

Morgan, E. S. and Morgan, H. M.: *The Stamp Act Crisis: Prologue to Revolution* (1953), 2nd edn. (New York: Collier Books, 1963).

Schlesinger, A. M.: *Prelude to Independence: the Newspaper War on Britain, 1764–1776* (1957), 2nd edn. (New York: Vintage Books, 1965).

Shy, J.: *Towards Lexington: the Role of the British Army in the Coming of the American Revolution* (Princeton, NJ: Princeton University Press, 1965).

Thomas, P. D. G.: *British Politics and the Stamp Act Crisis: the First Phase of the American Revolution, 1763–1767* (Oxford: Clarendon Press, 1975).

13

The Townshend Acts crisis, 1767–1770

ROBERT J. CHAFFIN

THE Townshend Acts of 1767 consisted of a series of taxes on goods imported into the American colonies, a reorganized Board of Customs Commissioners stationed in Boston to collect the taxes and enforce other revenue measures, and the New York Restraining Act. Reasons for passing these measures included a symbolic gesture to show the colonies that the mother country had the right to tax the colonies, raise a revenue to support some governors and justices, and punish New York for refusing to abide by the Mutiny Act (also known as the Quartering Act). As a consequence of these measures, relations between Britain and its provinces deterioriated. The crisis did momentarily pass with minor alterations of the tax measures in 1770, but not before the Boston Massacre had taken place. Additional changes in the tea tax three years later, however, led to the Boston Tea Party, setting the two sides on the road to war.

1. BRITAIN'S NEED FOR REVENUE FROM THE COLONIES

Shortly after assuming office in 1766, the Chatham ministry concluded that the colonies should contribute additional revenue to the Treasury. Augustus Henry Fitzroy, third Duke of Grafton, led the Treasury Board. With the assistance of Charles Townshend, Chancellor of the Exchequer, Grafton directed his staff to transmit a report on colonial quitrents.[1] He wanted to know how quitrents were collected, how much was received, and the provincial legislation relative to it. He also sought each colony's sources of income, expenditures, and taxes. The inference was that once the Board obtained a complete report of colonial accounts, it could devise new tax measures.

The Chancellor of the Exchequer simultaneously gathered data for his system of colonial revenue. Ambitious and opportunistic, the 41-year-old Townshend was the most experienced member of the Chatham Cabinet. Not even Pitt, the once "Great Commoner," could boast of such a varied background. During his two decades in Parliament, Townshend had served under George Montagu Dunk, Earl of Halifax, at the Board of Trade, where he had received a thorough education in colonial affairs. Later he held such posts as Secretary at War, President of the Board of Trade, First Lord of the Admiralty, and Paymaster of the Army, all of which dealt directly or indirectly with the colonies.[2]

In October 1766 William Dowdeswell, Townshend's predecessor at the Exchequer, wrote that "a rebate of part of the customs on teas imported to America" would be "a very good thing" if the English market could be effectively supplied and American smuggling controlled.[3] The heart of Dowdeswell's suggestions – an amply supplied

English market and the control of smuggling – offers a clue to one aspect of Townshend's schemes. In negotiations with the East India Company in the spring of 1767, the government agreed to lower the inland duty on teas going to Ireland and America. In return for these concessions, the company agreed to pay the government £400,000 annually. The settlement caused the price of tea to drop, increased exports to the colonies, and placed the company in a stronger position against smugglers and its continental competitors.[4] Townshend also considered placing a 6d per pound duty upon tea imported into the colonies, but finally reduced it to 3d in the Committee of Ways and Means, presumably because the higher rate would have increased the price of tea.[5]

Aware that the previous administration had considered permitting colonies to import wines and assorted fruits directly from Spain and Portugal without first stopping in England, Townshend incorporated that scheme into his tax program.[6] Besides tea, wines, and fruits, other items attracted Townshend's attention. From the London Customs House he learned that the value of china exported annually amounted to more than £51,000. Because the china carried a tax rebate when exported to the provinces, it provided an attractive taxable item. He dropped the rebate in his revenue acts. Salt also held enticing tax possibilities. He considered placing upon it a duty of five to ten pence, depending upon quality, and granting a bounty upon salted fish exported from the colonies. He never introduced the salt tax, however, because colonial agents persuaded him enforcement would prove difficult.[7]

In drawing up his tax plans, Townshend showed himself a skillful innovator rather than a creative genius. The idea of laying import duties upon unimportant items had its origins in 1710, when the government considered laying an import tax upon all goods imported into New York. As Townshend said in 1754, he thought it unwise to encumber with duties important British manufactured products going to America. For this reason, then, he chose articles of little consequence upon which to place his taxes: wine, fruits, white and green glass, red and white lead, painters' colors, and paper and pasteboards. Unfortunately, no evidence exists to suggest why Townshend chose those particular items. Several possibilities are apparent, however. The plan to lay duties upon fruits and wines was taken from the Rockingham administration, as already noted. Articles such as glass, paper products, lead, and painters' colors were unimportant in the total amount of American trade, and taxes on those items would leave established patterns of trade undisturbed. Moreover, England monopolized trade in those articles, for colonies were prohibited from purchasing them elsewhere. While conceding that Britain had the right to lay duties upon colonial imports, Benjamin Franklin had admitted during his House of Commons interrogation in February that colonies might begin to produce their own manufactures if such an event occurred. Perhaps for this reason Townshend chose items difficult to manufacture. Glass, for instance, took a degree of technical sophistication almost unknown in the provinces. Quality paper, paper boards, and painters' colors likewise were not produced in America. And except for wine, none of the articles was suitable for smuggling. His calculations showed that he could obtain £43,420, exclusive of the tea duty – not a large amount, but new tax measures often are small and increase only after the taxpayer has grown accustomed to paying them. Moreover, the duties were sufficient for their immediate purpose, which was to provide independent salaries for some governors and magistrates.

In the House of Commons, on 26 January 1767, Townshend promised to lay a new set of duties upon America without first obtaining the Cabinet's permission. William

Wildman, Lord Barrington, Secretary at War, moved for £405,607 for the army in the colonies. George Grenville, father of the Stamp Act, immediately proposed an amendment calling for the troops to be supported by the colonies.[8] Townshend quickly rose in opposition; nonetheless, he spoke "warmly for making America bear her share of the expense." In his pocket diary, Sir Roger Newdigate recorded in his minute scrawl that Townshend "pledgd. himself that something shd. be done this session . . . towards creating a revenue in the colonies."[9] When pressed to explain himself more fully, Townshend replied that he did not mean to create a revenue immediately adequate to meet all colonial expenses, but would do everything "to form a revenue in time to bear the whole," that he would "plan by degrees" and use "great delicacy." Clearly Townshend intended to begin his program with small levies, gradually increasing them until the income was sufficient to relieve England of all colonial expenses. Impressed with Townshend's plans, the House voted down Grenville's motion.

2. DIFFICULTIES WITH THE NEW YORK ASSEMBLY

Townshend's promise to lay fresh taxes on the colonies was only one of the problems the ministry faced. A second was a petition from New York merchants. With remarkably poor timing they had petitioned Parliament, complaining that their trade was severely restricted by certain Navigation Acts passed in 1764 and 1766.[10] William Petty, second Earl of Shelburne, Secretary of State for the Southern Department, thought the petition ill-advised, especially since the New York Assembly had refused to abide by the Mutiny Act and provide fully for the troops stationed in the colony.[11]

Already perturbed because of the petition, both the Cabinet and Parliament were prepared to deal harshly with New York because of its refusal to abide by the Mutiny Act. Fearful that unqualified support of the British Army would set a precedent for a new tax act, the New York Assembly had carefully restricted its grants. This action not only violated the Mutiny Act, but it also implicitly repudiated the Declaratory Act, which stated that Parliament had the right to legislate for the colonies. Britain's answer to this challenge to its authority was the New York Restraining Act, officially a part of the Townshend Acts.

In April Shelburne offered a plan to Chatham, one that would have strengthened the Declaratory Act. The general consensus in the Cabinet, he said, was to pass an act reiterating the Declaratory Act and "to recite the new effect of that law in the instance of the Mutiny Act."[12] Because colonists had failed to see the significance of the Declaratory Act, Shelburne believed the government should grant a general pardon for all past violations. But after three months he wanted it declared "*High Treason* to refuse to *obey* or *execute* any laws or statutes made by the King with the advice of Parliament under the pretence that the King and Parliament hath not sufficient authority to make laws and statutes to bind his American Colonies." Moreover, anyone who questioned the Declaratory Act by writing, preaching, or speaking against it should be tried for misprision of treason.

Spurred on by pressure from the opposition, the ministry finally reached a decision on 26 April.[13] Shelburne probably did not offer his harsh corollary to the Declaratory Act. A second plan, offered by Henry Conway, Secretary of State for the Northern Department, was to place a "local extraordinary port duty" on New York. Townshend earnestly objected to Conway's tax proposal because it would have obstructed trade between the West Indies and England, increased smuggling, and failed to achieve the principle they were seeking – colonial recognition of Parliament's supremacy.

Townshend suggested "addressing the Crown to assent to no law whatever, till the Mutiny Act was fully obeyed."[14] The attractive feature of this plan was its simplicity. Merely by refusing to sign any legislation, the governor could compel obedience to the Mutiny Act. Townshend recognized, of course, that the ministry might have to provide the governor's salary if the Assembly refused to bend. The Lord President of the Council, Robert Henley, Lord Northington, immediately disapproved, partly because the address applied only to one colony, and partly because an address carried little weight. Agreeing that an act was preferable to an address, the Cabinet ordered Townshend to write what later became a part of his Acts.

Townshend confronted the Cabinet with the question of army extraordinaries on 12 March. He threatened to resign, Grafton reported to the ill and absent Chatham, unless "the reduction of them was not determined before the closing of the Committee of Supply, by drawing the troops nearer the great towns, laying the Indian charges upon the provinces, and by laying a tax on American ports,"[15] the same system, in short, that he and Grenville had earlier agreed upon in debate. He had committed himself to colonial taxes in the House, he continued, upon what had been discussed in the Cabinet, implying that cabinet discussions had led him to believe the ministry favored American taxation.[16]

Townshend in the meantime, continued to work on the budget, drawing up duties, regulations, and savings. Shelburne and Grafton apparently had agreed with Townshend that a civil list free from colonial control was desirable. They wanted it funded with quitrents, however.[17] Townshend was not opposed to a colonial revenue fund based upon quitrents, a favorite scheme of Shelburne's. He asked Grafton for permission to introduce the plan, which would "be of infinite consequence tomorrow and of little use afterwards."[18] He also urged Grafton to obtain the King's permission to allow him to introduce his own tax schemes when he opened the budget. No evidence shows that Grafton answered Townshend or approached the King. The Chancellor of the Exchequer never mentioned quitrents when he introduced his budget.

After a two-day postponement because of illness, Townshend presented his budget to the House of Commons. Townshend noted that he had collected more than £469,000 out of the savings of office and cash dormant in the Exchequer. The House approved the budget without a division, and the next day it adjourned for the Easter holidays.[19]

3. PLANS FOR A CUSTOMS COMMISSION

During the adjournment, Townshend's plans to create a customs commission in America reached maturity. Who first suggested the commission is uncertain, though Charles Paxton, the Boston customs official who had also advised Townshend on his duties plans, might have been responsible. Shelburne informed Chatham on 1 February that the Chancellor of the Exchequer had a "plan for establishing a Board of Customs in America."[20]

In one of two reports to Townshend in January 1767, the British Board of Customs explained the problems it faced in America.[21] It noted that the great distance between the colonies and Britain, lack of supervision of colonial customs officers, and the hardships under which they worked posed onerous problems. Moreover, colonists started prosecutions against revenue men upon the slightest pretense, the report complained, the result of which was that several officers had "lately been fined and imprisoned for obeying their instructions." To remedy the situation in America, the report proposed that "seven commissioners be appointed, three of whom to constitute a Board, and to reside at Philadelphia, for managing the said American duties." The Customs Board estimated the commissioners, their secretaries, and assistants would cost £5,540 in salaries; savings resulting from the dissolution of old offices would amount to £3,071. The new system would, consequently, incur about £2,469 in additional expenses. But because the new Board would result in a more efficient collection, it would soon compensate for the increased costs. Without such a system, the report warned, American duties would soon have to be abandoned because they would fail even to "yield sufficient income ... to defray the salaries of the officers."

Attached to the first report was a list of customs officers the Customs Board wished to see provided for.[22] Henry Hulton, a plantation clerk, was named one of the seven commissioners, as were the four colonial Surveyors General – John Temple, Charles Steuart, Peter Randolph, and Thomas Gibbs. The report called for two more commissioners, but made no effort to name them. Only two on this list, Hulton and Temple, actually became members of the American Board of Customs. John Robinson, who suffered much in the Stamp Act riots, became a third; William Burch, about whom nothing is known, was named a fourth; and Charles Paxton, Townshend's tax advisor, was appointed to the fifth post.

Though the Treasury Board accepted the proposal, not until the following August, two months after the Bill became law, was the number of American commissioners finally agreed upon as five and their permanent residence fixed at Boston. Why the number was reduced from seven to five remains unexplained. Each commissioner was to receive £500 annually. Perhaps the prospect of saving £1,000 enticed the Treasury Board to name only five commissioners. Because Paxton, Robinson, and Temple were residents of New England, the shift from Philadelphia to Boston may have been made simply on grounds of convenience to the new commissioners.

4. TOWNSHEND'S PROGRAM

Plans to punish New York and establish an American Board of Customs were agreed to by the end of April, and Shelburne and Grafton had accepted the idea of an independent civil list for America. But the First Lord of the Treasury still proved reluctant to grant Townshend authority to present his tax schemes to the House. On 13 May, the New York Restraining Bill was considered by the Committee of the Whole House. Though some colonies had abided by the Mutiny Act, Townshend noted, New Jersey had complied evasively and New York had "boldly and insolently" defied it and the authority of Parliament. Because New York had been the most refractory, he thought it should receive "an adequate punishment to deter others."[23] Moving on to the subject of taxes, he cautioned that they should be moderate and prudent. With all the characteristics of a compromise between himself and Grafton, he next proposed to "mention some tax not as Chancellor of the Exchequer but as a private man for the future opinion of the House in the committee of Ways and Means."[24]

Speaking as a private man he thus dissociated himself from the ministry. Later, he said, he would recommend levies on fruit, oil, and wine from Spain and Portugal imported directly to the colonies and taking off all or part of the tax rebate on articles such as china, glass, red and white lead for painting, and colored papers for furniture.[25] The new duties would, in his estimation, amount to between 30 and 40 thousand pounds yearly, a sum sufficient to pay some colonial governors and magistrates their salaries. And to assure the collection of the duties, he called for the creation of an American Board of Customs. He realized, he concluded, that his plans might exacerbate relations between Britain and the colonies, but the "quarrel must soon come to an issue. The superiority of the mother country can at no time be better exerted than now."[26] With that, he moved his resolutions that "New York had been disobedient to the acts of the legislature of Great Britain," that the colony's act for providing for troops was "void and derogatory to the honor of the King and legislature," and that "instructions be sent to the Governor to give no assent to any acts of assembly till a compleat and entire submission to an execution of the Billeting Act" was accomplished.[27]

In proposing his program, Townshend urged moderation and prudence, punishment for New York, an independent civil list, and a Board of Customs to ensure the collection of duties. He had shrewdly side-stepped Grafton's roadblock when introducing his tax plan for future consideration by declaring himself a private man. In spite of his bluster and threats, it is doubtful that he would have attempted even that maneuver without prior consultation with Grafton.

At one o'clock in the morning – after eight hours of debate – the vote was taken. The first two propositions, that New York had become disobedient and that its Provisioning Act was null and void, were passed unanimously. The House divided over the New York restraining resolution after Grenville proposed an amendment to enforce the Mutiny Act. The question whether Townshend's proposal should stand as first offered was carried by a comfortable majority, 188 to 98.[28] Upon the committee report on 15 May, the opposition offered new propositions. But by majorities of three to one Townshend carried the day. It was his personal triumph.[29]

A fortnight later, on 1 June, Townshend proposed his duties plan to the Committee of Ways and Means. He gave up his proposal for direct trade between Spain, Portugal, and the colonies because, as Franklin reported, the British merchants trading to those countries made such a clamor. By dropping the duties on fruit, he lost some £12,000 from his original estimates. But he compensated for this reduction with his proposal for a 3d per pound duty on tea payable in the colonies, which would bring an estimated £20,000. By dropping the rebate on china and placing small duties on glass, various kinds of paper, pasteboards, red and white lead, and painters' colors, the government could obtain an additional revenue. Townshend estimated that china earthenware would bring £8,000; glass, £5,000; paper and pasteboard products, £9,000; and lead and painters' colors, £3,000. The purpose of the duties was, as the preamble of the Acts showed, "for making a more certain and adequate provision for the charge of the administration of justice, and the support of the civil government, and defraying the expense of defending, protecting and securing the said colonies."[30]

The committee presented the Duties Bill, along with the measure for creating the American Board of Customs, on 10 June. Several amendments were offered by the opposition, but the Bills survived substantially the same as Townshend had first presented them. Receiving the Bills on 15 June, the House of Lords returned them unchanged at the end of the month.[31]

After signing the bills on 2 July 1767, the King prorogued Parliament. George III observed in his speech (written by his ministers) that it was not "expected that all the great commercial interests should be completely adjusted and regulated in the course of this session." Yet he was persuaded "that by the progress you have made, a solid foundation is laid for securing the most considerable and essential benefits to this nation."[32] Obviously the King and authors of the speech believed the Townshend Acts would provide gains that would strengthen Great Britain.

5. REACTIONS TO THE TOWNSHEND ACTS

Both were wrong. The Acts aggravated an already tense situation in the colonies. The provinces responded to Townshend's measures in three ways: philosophically, politically, and economically. Each activity, often interwoven with the others, confirmed the colonists in the righteousness of their cause – resistance to perceived British encroachments on their rights.

John Dickinson's Letters   Many colonists reacted to the Townshend Acts in newspapers and pamphlets. None, however, was as influential as the 12 *Letters from a Farmer in Pennsylvania* by JOHN DICKINSON. The *Letters* were first published in the *Pennsylvania Chronicle and Universal Advertiser*, beginning with the issue for 2 December 1767, and their popularity and circulation surpassed that of all other publications in the revolutionary war period save Thomas Paine's *Common Sense*. They were reproduced in 19 of the 23 English-language colonial newspapers; at least seven pamphlet editions were printed, as were two editions in Europe.

Joseph Harrison, a Boston customs collector, thought the *Letters* were "dangerous and alarming," and "the principal means of spreading ... general disaffection among the people."[33] Georgia's Governor James Wright was convinced they had "sown the seeds of sedition," which had been "scattered in very fertile soil."[34] They received a mixed review in England. The conservative *Critical Review* considered them seditious and superficial, while the liberal *Monthly Review* thought they presented a full enquiry into the rights of Parliament that would be difficult to refute.[35]

Offering nothing new or profound, the *Letters* documented and dignified radical ideas already held by many colonists. The author utilized such popular Whig themes as the executive's threat to the liberties of assemblies, the loss of power to tax themselves, the proliferation of offices, the danger of standing armies, and worse tax measures to follow if colonists allowed the Acts to set precedents.[36] Dickinson admitted that Britain could regulate trade for the benefit of the empire. But he also argued that the mother country could levy no taxes on the colonies, because they had no representatives in Parliament. Fidelity to the monarch, mutually beneficial trade, traditional affection – these were the tenuous ties that bound the two together. Always the reluctant rebel, Dickinson suggested few methods of redress. Besides petitions to the King, he advised boycotting British goods until colonial grievances were rectified. In that way, he said, colonists could achieve their goals, disappoint their enemies, and elate their friends.

Adams's Circular Letter, Massachusetts Assembly   The Massachusetts Assembly followed Dickinson's advice. Called into session on 30 December 1767, it devoted the next 18 days preparing remonstrances against the Acts. Among those remonstrances was the Circular Letter. Mainly the work of SAMUEL ADAMS, Clerk of the Lower House, the Letter urged other colonies to resist the Acts, and argued that no people could enjoy full freedom if the monarch had the right to pay salaries of, as well as appoint, colonial officials.[37] The Letter went on to note that Parliament had no legal right to tax the colonies for the sole purpose of raising a revenue, a position put forth most vigorously by the Pennsylvania farmer.

The British Government's response to the Assembly's activities heightened tensions even further. Wills Hill, first Earl of Hillsborough, had recently become Secretary of State for the new American Department. In a circular of 21 April, he ordered all governors to prorogue or dissolve their assemblies rather than allow them to countenance Massachusetts' Circular Letter.[38] In addition, Hillsborough ordered the Massachusetts Governor FRANCIS BERNARD to require the Assembly to rescind the Letter and resolutions and declare its dissent from those measures.[39] Aware that his directive might lead to trouble, Hillsborough also alerted General Thomas Gage at New York to prepare his troops in case they were needed in Boston.[40]

Dissolving assemblies in wholesale fashion to oblige obedience to the British ministry was at the very least an extraordinary step for the Cabinet to take. It was a dangerous experiment that could only result in arousing a spirit of unity Britain wished to avoid. In contrast to the New York restraining measure, debated upon at length in the House of Commons and applying only to one colony, Hillsborough's actions were indicative of the ministry's determination to gain colonial recognition of Britain's sovereignty as spelled out in the Declaratory Act. Except for deepening the Townshend Acts crisis, the policy failed.

The conflict between Bernard and the Assembly grew even more acute in the spring session of 1769. Troops had arrived in Boston in October 1768 at the instigation of the Governor and customs commissioners. The town was torn by turmoil as the Governor attempted to find suitable housing for the soldiers. Actions by the British Government added to these tensions. Meeting in December 1768, Parliament had confirmed the ministry's use of troops in Boston and proposed that Boston ringleaders be brought to trial under the 35th Henry VIII. This obsolete law, entitled "An Act for the Trial of Treason Committed out of the King's Dominion," would have enabled the ministry to bring to England any colonist accused of treason.

Bernard was chagrined but not surprised to find that, of the 17 members who had voted to follow Hillsborough's commands to rescind the Circular Letter in 1768, only five had been re-elected and only two of those were courageous enough to attend. Out of a House of 120 members, no more than ten could be counted on as firm supporters of the government.[41] With the radical character of the House so apparent, Bernard braced for battle. It was not long in coming. At the first meeting, the House sent the Governor a message filled with "insolent terms." After choosing their speaker, members of the House elected councilors for the Upper House, declaring openly that "they would clear the Council of tories." Accordingly, they turned out four of those who had in the past shown an inclination to support the government. Bernard retaliated by vetoing six radical choices before a council was agreed upon by both sides. For the first fortnight the House's attention was dominated by the question of troops in Boston. No other business was conducted until the Virginia Resolves arrived (see Chapter 12, §2). Similar to resolutions already passed by Massachusetts, the House readily agreed with them. This was too much for Bernard; he prorogued the House and recalled it at Cambridge, hoping thereby to modify the legislature's high spirits. It was a futile gesture.

As impertinent as the House appeared, Bernard was unprepared for the resolves it passed in the first week of July. To Commodore Samuel Hood, rarely given to exaggeration, the resolves were "of a more extraordinary nature than any that have yet passed an American assembly." Governor Bernard – "whom fear acts upon very powerfully," Hood caustically observed – viewed the House's actions as the opening of a revolt. Aware that General Gage intended to reduce the number of troops at

Boston, the Governor felt that the resolves' tendency "was such that it seemed rather to require a reinforcement" of troops, not a reduction.[42]

Largely the work of Samuel Adams, the resolves declared that "no man can be justly taxed by, or bound in conscience to obey, any law to which he has not given his consent in person, or by his representative." Formerly the House, like most colonial assemblies, had agreed it could not be taxed without representation. Now it went to the next logical step and maintained it need not abide by any legislation in which it had not participated. The resolves also accused Bernard of giving "a false and highly injurious representation of the conduct" of the Council, magistrates, and inhabitants of Boston so that he could "introduce a military government into the province; and to mislead both Houses of Parliament into such severe resolutions." Furthermore, establishment of a standing army in the province in peacetime without the Assembly's consent was an invasion of the people's natural rights, the Magna Carta, and the Bill of Rights, as well as the charter of the colony. Finally, the resolves declared that instituting the 35th Henry VIII was "highly derogatory of the rights of the British subjects," because it denied them the privilege of being "tried by a jury from the vicinage, as well as the liberty of summoning and producing witnesses on such trial."[43]

After 46 days of frustrating and acrimonious disputes between the Governor and Assembly, Bernard prorogued the House until the following January. Rarely had the House sat so long; never had it accomplished so little. With justification, Bernard complained that the Assembly had devoted most of its time "in denying the power of the Parliament, arraigning and condemning its acts, abusing the king's ministers at home and his principal officers in America." Members of the House had implied "in plain if not direct terms their right and intention to separate themselves from" the British Government.[44]

The Assembly thus displayed increasing – almost hysterical – hostility towards Governor Bernard and Great Britain. At first according Parliament control over trade, the House had moved by 1769 to the point where it denied that legislature any power over Massachusetts. Few other assembles were prepared to go as far in denying the mother country's control. Yet few others had endured as much as Massachusetts. The home government had arbitrarily dismissed the Assembly because it had refused to rescind the Circular Letter and had stationed troops in Boston. Customs commissioners, rigidly interpreting the Navigation Acts, were attempting to enforce all the revenue laws; the Governor had become almost paranoid, sending exaggerated reports to the ministry; Parliament had violently condemned the colony and threatened to have arrested and sent to England for trial anyone suspected of treason. No other colony had to contend with such factors. But this was the price the province had to pay for leading resistance to the Townshend Acts.

The effects of the New York Restraining Act　Citizens of New York understandably showed less immediate concern for the Townshend Duties Act than for the Restraining Act directed at their colony. In 1766 the Assembly had refused to fulfill all requirements of the Mutiny Act because it was considered an unconstitutional tax, and because the measure placed no limit upon the number of troops a colony could be required to support. Faced with the prospect of having none of its legislation become law as a result of the Restraining Act, the Assembly responded in 1767 with more generous support of the army. But even the threat of a restraining measure failed to force the legislators to recognize Parliament's right to impose such acts upon them.

Ignoring the Mutiny Act by name, the Assembly passed a bill appropriating £3,000, a sum thought adequate to provide all items called for by the Act.[45]

At the end of the year a Committee of the Whole House drew up a set of constitutional resolves that asserted the rights of the colony's citizens – a bill of colonial rights. Besides a list of privileges, the resolution noted that the legislature in which both king and citizen were represented could not constitutionally be suspended by Parliament. Only the Crown had such authority, it argued. The resolution also declared firmly in answer to Hillsborough's instructions that the Assembly had the right to correspond with any of its neighboring assemblies or any part of the dominion.[46]

Disturbed at the Assembly's surprising behavior, Governor Moore attempted to explain and justify it to Hillsborough. The Restraining Act had never gone into effect, he observed, troop maintenance had been settled, and merchants and traders had paid the Townshend Duties for almost a year with little complaint. Why, then, the angry memorials and resolves? He believed that a small faction in the House supported by Sons of Liberty in the city had intimidated other members. An equally important reason for the Assembly's actions was that "a rash and intemperate measure approved" in one colony "will be adopted in others." To have done less would impugn the patriotism of the colony.[47]

Regardless of its reasons, New York made clear its attitude towards the Townshend Acts. Unlike their frequent complaints about the Navigation Acts, the legislators viewed the Townshend measures as violating fundamental constitutional principles. Repudiating the Declaratory Act, they held that a mere Act of Parliament could not abridge such venerable documents as the Magna Carta and Bill of Rights. The British constitution, as Samuel Adams had already observed, was an unchanging instrument.

South Carolina's response to the Townshend Acts   Slow to respond to the Townshend Acts, South Carolina became by 1770 one of their most uncompromising opponents. In April 1768 the House directed its Committee of Correspondence to order the South Carolina agent in London, Charles Garth, to work for the repeal of the Acts and to prevent the clause for billeting troops in the colonies from being inserted in the next Mutiny Act. The Commons House had begun to look upon continued support of His Majesty's troops as an unnecessary burden. Before it received the Massachusetts Letter, the House was prorogued. But the speaker, Peter Manigault, assured Speaker Thomas Cushing of the Massachusetts Assembly that he would lay the Circular before the House at the first opportunity.[48]

That opportunity was long in coming. With the triennial term approaching its end, the extreme heat, and the absence of the ill Governor Montagu, the opening of the new session was postponed until November 1768. Lieutenant-Governor William Bull hoped the delay would prevent "the forming of precipitate and disagreeable resolutions" which were "more easily prevented than rescinded." He was aware, however, that many remained "fixed in the opinions adopted and encouraged from the north."[49]

The new Commons House opened on schedule in November and closed less than a fortnight later. With the doors barred, the legislators considered the Massachusetts and Virginia Circular Letters, resolved they were founded on constitutional privileges, and agreed to petition the monarch for relief from the Townshend Acts. The Committee of Correspondence was directed to keep Garth informed of the House's resolutions and advise him to continue to work for the repeal of the Townshend Acts. Because of

Hillsboroughs's directive, Governor Montagu was left with little choice. He dissolved the House.[50]

A new Commons House met in June 1769, but, from the Governor's point of view, it was no improvement over the legislature he had dismissed some seven months before. It affirmed the Virginia Resolutions on 19 August and declared it lawful and expedient to join with other colonies in circulars that supported the "violated rights of America." In answer to the threat of the 35th Henry VIII, the House believed that Parliament had misconstrued the Act in "an arbitrary and cruel" way. Since the colony had adequate laws to handle felonies, treason and misprision of treason, the House saw no need to transport suspects to England to stand trial. Aroused by what they perceived as a threat to keep colonies cowed, members of the House agreed to petition their sovereign "to quiet the minds of his loyal subjects ... and to avert from them those dangers and miseries" which would "ensue from the seizing and carrying beyond [the] sea any person residing in America suspected of any crime whatsoever." As they interpreted the ministry's intentions, not only those suspected of treasonous activities, but those accused of any kind of crime, could be transported to the mother country to stand trial.[51]

Fear and hostility were similarly evident in the House's response to Governor Montagu's request of 17 August to provide supplies for British troops in transit through the colony. Destined for St. Augustine, the troops were ordered to wait in South Carolina until sufficient barracks could be built in Florida. Many members of the House had already declared publicly that they would grant no further supplies to the army. They confirmed that promise on 19 August.[52] The legislators reasoned that South Carolina was not bound to support troops even if the colony had applied for them. After all, they argued, the Townshend Acts were passed expressly for "protecting, defending and securing his Majesty's dominions." Let the government use these "illegal" revenues to pay for the troops' expenses. Indeed, the Commons House firmly declared that "under the circumstances ... we are constrained to refuse making the desired provision during the existence of those acts – acts which strike at the very root of our constitution, by taking our property without our consent, and depriving us of the liberty of giving to our sovereign." Furthermore, the Governor had acted unjustly and improperly by requesting support for the troops while the Townshend Acts were in force. The House promised to maintain this stern posture until the acts were repealed.[53]

By using the Townshend Acts as an excuse to withhold supplies from the army, the House had presented a remarkable rebuttal which, if assumed by other colonies, could have had dangerous repercussions for Britain. Why other provinces never vigorously pursued a similar policy after South Carolina initiated it is difficult to understand. Hillsborough candidly admitted to Gage that the Commons House position had "a face of plausibility." He was convinced that Parliament would have to alter the Mutiny Act to counter arguments that South Carolina offered against it. Bull made no effort to refute the House's contentions and, rather than dissolve the Assembly, he quietly prorogued it after signing ten bills.[54]

6. THE COLONIES BOYCOTT BRITISH GOODS

Besides their political reactions to the Townshend measures, colonies also responded with boycotts of British goods. Boston's radicals quickly developed boycott plans that found a welcome in other Massachusetts communities. By the middle of January

1768, at least 24 towns had voted to abide by an agreement. Encouraged by the response, a Boston town meeting in December 1767 unanimously decided to instruct its representatives in the General Court to recommend bounties on domestic manufactures and to petition Parliament to repeal the Townshend Acts.[55]

The Assembly responded by passing a resolution in February 1768 calling for economy. With the tacit approval of the Assembly, the boycott gained momentum. Ninety-eight merchants meeting on 1 March voted to give consideration to non-importation. As Bernard observed, "This may be said to be the first movement of the merchants against the acts of Parliament." Concerned over the growing unfavorable balance of trade, the merchants claimed that restricting British imports under certain conditions would help correct the deficiency. On 4 March they concluded that the Townshend Acts had increased the specie shortage, slowed trade, caused further indebtedness among the traders, and threatened the constitution. Accordingly, they resolved not to import for one year any goods save necessities, such as fish hooks, wire, and lead, and would invite other trading towns in Massachusetts, New York, New Jersey, and Pennsylvania to cooperate with them. They also agreed to encourage manufacturing, inform British merchants why they were withholding orders, and appoint a committee to correspond with other colonial merchants.[56]

New York's merchants stirred themselves to action in April 1768. Already unhappy over the hostile reception their petition of December 1766 had received, distressed over declining trade, and encouraged by Boston's example, the merchants of the city signed a non-importation agreement even more restrictive than that of their New England neighbors. Meeting on 28 April, the traders agreed to rescind all orders sent to Britain after 15 August and stop further importation after 1 November. Subscribers who violated the agreement would be considered "enemies of their country." By September the association of merchants widened its restrictions with the threat to withhold its patronage from those traders who refused to abide by the agreement. Other towns fell in line behind the city. Albany concurred with the merchants' plan, though some of its traders wanted to continue importation of Indian trade goods.

South Carolina also joined the boycott, but not without controversy. Some individuals had the "integrity and resolution to withstand" intimidation and "flattering arguments," Lieutenant Governor Bull wrote, because the agreement was "contrary to their opinion and conscience." To make an example of these recusants and simultaneously show how few their numbers were, the general committee of merchants ordered circulated throughout the colony handbills on which 31 names were listed. The handbills, the standard colonial weapon with which to beat those who refused to cooperate, sparked the controversy between those who opposed and supported non-importation.[57]

William Wragg, planter, trader, and leader in the Commons House for a decade before 1768, saw his name on the list as an "honourable certificate." It proved to him that he was one of those who refused to violate his judgment by "swimming with the stream." The constitution and common law alike indicated to him that he had the right to withhold his assent to propositions he disapproved. Believing non-importation would be "destructive of the end proposed," he saw neither reason, justice, nor charity in forcing one to forego British goods. He would, he said, endure anything "rather than have the freedom of my will or understanding limited or directed by the humours or capricious proscriptions of men not having authority."[58]

The second response to the handbills came from William Henry Drayton, nephew of Lieutenant-Governor Bull. Born to wealth and educated at Oxford, the 26-year-old

137

Drayton was firmly fixed in the ethereal regions of Charles Town society. Under the name "Freeman," he had attacked non-importation in August 1769. "That Harlequin Medley Committee," he wrote, in its efforts to stigmatize him, had only given public testimony of his "resolution and integrity to persist in acting agreeably to the dictates" of his reason. He abhorred "the laying illegal restraints upon the free wills of free men, who had an undoubted right to think and act for themselves." He was, he thought, at least as capable of thinking for himself as those "gentry" were for themselves.[59]

Their angry rhetoric aside, Wragg and Drayton touched upon a fundamental dilemma for all non-importation associations. In their haste to protect the traditional freedom of representation and taxation, subscribers to associations violated an equally important freedom – liberty of conscience. Though good tactics, printing names of those who refused to accept the agreement was more insidious than mere physical abuse which some suffered in some communities. For the handbills attacked the individual's reputation and character, two delicate elements that were quick to wound and slow to heal.

Boycotts began to fail by 1770. While complex, the causes for their ultimate breakdown began in New York, where many issues were at work. A keen distrust of Boston, an acute currency shortage, and growing unemployment were all factors that influenced the merchants to renew importation. Even in the face of New York's desertion, many colonists were determined to carry on the fight. They believed that the ministry offered them no great concessions, and that the critical question of parliamentary sovereignty remained unanswered. Yet their protests were muffled by merchants who thought they had sacrificed enough and who refused to cooperate further. As non-importation began slowly to break apart, trade was resumed, and normalcy returned to all colonies by the beginning of 1771.

Non-importation failed as an instrument of protest in 1770, but colonists learned their lessons well. All the associations "were drawn up in a hurry and formed upon erroneous principles," the Virginian George Mason wrote in December. Differences between the various schemes adopted in different provinces caused increasing frustration. To correct weaknesses in non-importation, he felt that all colonies had to agree to one general plan of non-importation "exactly the same for all the colonies." Only in that way could inter-colonial suspicions and jealousies be removed. "Such a plan as this is now in contemplation," Mason concluded; "God grant we have no cause to carry it into practice." Of course, the first Continental Congress carried just such a plan into operation when its members formed the Continental Association in October 1774[60] (*see* Chapter 20, §4, and Chapter 22, §5).

7 · REPEAL OF THE TOWNSHEND DUTIES

The British ministry had thrown out hints that if the Americans would behave, would stop boycotting British products, the government would consider altering the Townshend Acts. "Upon the whole, it was not a very lively debate," William Samuel Johnson said of the debate to alter the Townshend Duties Act on 5 March 1770.[61] London merchants presented their petition to the House, setting off the debate. After the petition was read, Lord North suggested that the interruption of trade about which merchants complained was the result of non-importation associations in America. Many people had attempted to persuade him to support repeal of the whole Act, North continued. But tea was not an article of English manufacture; it was a luxury item.

Of all taxable goods, it was the most proper to carry a tax. Furthermore, as a result of the agreement with the East India Company, the price of tea had actually fallen in the colonies, acting in effect as a bounty for Americans. In answer to those who claimed the tea duty produced only trifles, he made an observation that had generally been ignored. Without equivocation or qualification, he observed that the tea tax

> was one of the best of all port duties. When the revenue is well established, it will probably go a great way towards effecting the purpose for which it was laid, which was to give additional support to our government and judicatures in America.[62]

North and presumably others in the ministry thus looked upon the tea tax as the most effective way to make some colonial civil administrations independent of the people – the very purpose Charles Townshend had in mind when he first proposed his measures.

North pointed out that not only was the tea duty profitable, but colonial complaints towards it were really aimed at the preamble. Americans "had laid it down as a rule that England has no right to tax her for the purpose of raising a revenue; they therefore desire to have all these duties repealed." A total repeal would mean giving up the preamble, which stated that the duties were for the purpose of raising a revenue. England, North cautioned, should never give up its rights to raise levies in America. "If you are to draw a line, it is better to draw a line with this act." Yet he repeated the assurances given in a Hillsborough circular of the previous May that his ministry had no intention of further taxing Americans for revenue.

Other reasons convinced North that Parliament need repeal only part of the duties. Doubtless using information supplied by the Boston publisher John Mein and Robert Hallowell, a customs official, North noted that, by "the last letters from Boston," it appeared the people had already begun to feel the bad effects of non-importation. "Many of the chief promoters have indulged in little deviations from the line they struck out." Prices had risen as much as 100 per cent; a new subscription had ended with few names; some traders who had consented to hold their goods had begun to sell. Most important, in North's view, "many ships are gone full freighted from England to America, and there is every reason to expect that these associations will not long continue."

North's carefully prepared arguments were clear: those duties on British goods should be repealed to relieve the plight of English merchants, not to meet American demands. Parliament should retain the tea duty because it was the most profitable way to carry out Charles Townshend's goals, and because its retention would protect the government's right to tax the colonies. And because of the unmistakable evidence that non-importation agreements were breaking apart, there was no need to go further. With that, North moved "to bring in a bill to repeal so much of the said act as lays duties upon glass, red lead, white lead, painters'colours, paper, pasteboards, mill boards, and scaleboards."

Although the opposition urged the repeal of all the taxes, neither North nor any of his colleagues attempted to refute their arguments. There was no need to do so, for when the vote for an amendment to include the tea duty in the repeal was put, it was defeated by 204 to 142. The main question, the repeal of the lesser items, was carried without a division. The fight to repeal all the Townshend Duties was nearly at an end.

The opposition made one last effort to include the tea duty in the repeal on 9 April, when one of its members moved to bring in a bill for that purpose. He reminded the House of the value of American trade, the monopoly Britain held over it, and the absurdity of raising a revenue in the colonies. Members of the ministry quickly disputed the propriety of the motion, arguing that it violated a well-known House rule that any motion which had once received a negative could not be introduced again in the same session. Rejecting the motion, the House voted by 80 to 52 in the negative. This vote moved William Samuel Johnson to observe that "it is now absolutely and finally determined not to repeal the duty on tea in this session."[63]

It would be inaccurate to claim that a major part of the Townshend Acts had been repealed. The revenue-producing tea levy, the American Board of Customs and, most important, the principle of making governors and magistrates independent all remained. In fact, the modification of the Townshend Duties Act was scarcely any change at all. Charles Townshend had always been fearful lest the colonies become infected with the bacillus of independence; his antidote had been to buttress the executive and judicial branches of colonial administration. The North ministry agreed with that position and put it into effect. In Massachusetts, the Governor and Lieutenant-Governor, along with the jurists on the Superior Court, received their salaries from revenue collected from the tea duty. By 1772 the tea duty supported almost every important civil office in Massachusetts. Similarly, New York's governors obtained their salaries from those funds, as did the Chief Justice of New Jersey.[64]

The major concession Britain made had nothing to do – at least directly – with the Townshend Acts. That concession was the pledge never to raise another tax for revenue in the colonies. The Grafton ministry first made it, and North repeated it in the repeal debates. Admittedly, the administration could not bind future ministries to that promise, but once given up it would be difficult to re-establish. It was manifest why the ministry felt it could be magnanimous on the question of future taxation: it planned to strengthen the power of colonial officials. Little wonder that Lord North fought vigorously to retain the duty on tea. But if the struggle to end the Townshend Acts was finished in England, the battle continued in the colonies, especially in Massachusetts.

8. THE BOSTON MASSACRE

"The madness of mobs or the insolence of soldiers, or both, should, when too near each other occasion some mischief difficult to be prevented or repaired," Franklin observed upon learning that the government had ordered troops for Boston in 1768. Franklin's fears proved tragically reliable, for resentful citizens and hostile soldiers made a volatile brew. But the explosion did not occur until the spring of 1770. In the meantime, radical tactics exacerbated a situation already made serious by ministerial blunders.[65]

Like many March evenings in New England, it was clear but cold and crisp that night of the 5th. Snow and ice clung stubbornly to the shaded and protected cobblestones, the last evidence of a hard winter. With disquieting suddenness the meeting house bells began to ring, bringing the curious into the streets. Standing in King Street with their backs pressed against the customs house, Captain Thomas Preston and a small contingent of soldiers faced a milling, taunting crowd. "Fire, damn you! Fire!" someone shouted. Those in the rear pressed the front of the mob towards the pointed bayonets. A stick flew out of the darkness, striking the gun barrel of Private Hugh Montgomery. He stepped back, or slipped on the icy street, and fired his weapon. Knocked to the ground, he screamed to the other soldiers, "Fire! Fire!" Panicked by now, the troopers followed Montgomery's example and shot point-blank into the mass of bodies (*see* figure 11). The solid mass flew apart as the mob shoved

FIGURE 11 "The Bloody Massacre perpetrated in King Street Boston on
March 5th. 1770 by a party of the 29th. Regt." (engraving by Paul Revere,
1770): one of the victims, Crispus Attucks, was black, a fact that Revere
appears to have suppressed.

and pushed and trampled to escape the line of fire. One soldier was seen to take careful
aim at the back of a fleeing youngster, but his shot missed. Within seconds King Street
was deserted except for the soldiers, the wounded, and the dead. Three were killed
outright, two lay mortally wounded, and six others were less seriously wounded. The
meeting house bells continued to chime and were soon supported by the staccato
drum beat of the call to arms. Originally rung by a member of the mob, the bells could
now more properly be tolled for the dead.[66]

The streets quickly filled with angry, armed citizens. Expresses were sent to neighboring towns requesting support against the army. Only after receiving assurances
from Acting Governor Thomas Hutchinson that those soldiers responsible would
receive proper punishment did the crowds sullenly disperse. Before dawn the next
morning Captain Preston and eight soldiers were remanded to jail and ordered to
stand trial for the murder of one Crispus Attucks, a runaway slave from Framingham,
Massachusetts.

The evidence seems to suggest that this affray was the tragic and final product of
an accumulation of small, hostile acts between soldiers and citizens, with each event
growing more serious, making the social fabric more flammable. Only a spark was
needed to ignite it; that came in the form of an insult. On Friday 2 March, Samuel
Gray, a rope-maker at John Hancock's wharf, and later one of the massacre victims,
asked a passing trooper of the 29th Regiment if he wanted a job. When the underpaid

soldier nodded in the affirmative, the rope-maker laughingly told him to clean out his privy. The trooper took the remark as an insult and attacked Gray. Soon other dock workers and soldiers joined in the battle with clubs, sticks, and cutlasses. Both sides came away badly bloodied, though there were no deaths. Fighting continued the following day, but eased somewhat on the Sabbath.

On Monday 5 March, fighting again broke out. At first isolated frays occurred. Corporal John Eustace and one Mr. Pierpoint met as Eustace walked from his post at the Neck guard house. Words were exchanged and a fight ensued. Other fights continued that evening, and intensified when several soldiers attacked and beat two boys, one 11 years old and the other 14. A crowd gathered and in a frenzy attempted to charge into the main barracks after the soldiers. Several officers held off the mob with their swords. Frustrated and hearing the noise of another group not far away, the mob departed. Shortly thereafter several of its members broke into the meeting house and began to ring its bell, the signal for fire, bringing hundreds of people into the streets.[67]

Captain Preston, the 40-year-old officer of the day, was informed that the ringing bell signified that inhabitants were assembling to attack the troops. As he made his way to the main guard house, the gang which had assaulted the barracks passed by, heading towards the customs house. There it joined a group of youths who were already taunting the lone sentry. A townsman informed Preston, he later claimed, that the mob intended to kidnap and possibly murder the sentry. Preston immediately sent off a non-commissioned officer and six soldiers to protect both the guard and the King's revenue. He soon followed the troops because he feared the non-commissioned "officer and soldiers by insults and provocations of the rioters, should be thrown off their guard and commit some rash act." Why he sent only a handful of soldiers – fewer than a dozen – to face a howling mob, he left unexplained. This body of men was large enough to feed the mob's anger, but too small to do anything more than barely defend itself.[68]

The "rash act" – the massacre – resulted in the removal of all soldiers from Boston to Castle William in Boston harbor at the insistence of the inhabitants. This was a prudent decision, for, had the troops remained, it was a "moral certainty" – as Hutchinson put it – "that the people . . . would have taken to their arms and that the neighbouring towns would have joined them."[69]

The key issue in Preston's long trial, which began on 24 October 1770, was whether he had actually ordered his men to fire upon the mob. As the evidence unfolded, it became apparent that Private Montgomery, not Preston, had yelled out the order. During the trial, Justice Peter Oliver observed that it "appears quite plain to me that he must be acquitted; that the person who gave the orders to fire was not the captain, and indeed if it had been he, it at present appears justifiable." Within three hours after retiring, the jury had decided upon an acquittal for the officer.

Begun on 27 November, the trial of the eight soldiers lasted more than seven days. The basic facts were that, though there were eight defendants, only six or seven shots were fired. It was shown convincingly that Private Montgomery shot Crispus Attucks and that Private Matthew Kilroy shot Samuel Gray. But much doubt remained over which of the other troopers fired into the mob. At least one of them did not fire at all. Led by John Adams and Josiah Quincy, the defense pointed out that a reasonable doubt existed over who fired their weapons. Adams went on to say the soldiers were under an extraordinary provocation by a "motley rabble of saucy boys, negroes and mulattoes, Irish teagues, and outlandish jack tarrs" – that is, outside agitators. Placing the blame of the assault on the soldiers to outsiders was a shrewd tactic, for it offered the jurors a way to bring in an acquittal without impugning the town's reputation. Six of the eight soldiers were found innocent, but Montgomery and Kilroy were found guilty of manslaughter, a capital crime. Both later pleaded benefit of clergy, were branded on the thumb, and released.[70]

Undoubtedly the Townshend Acts accelerated the deterioration in relations between the mother country and her colonies. By sending troops to Boston to assist in enforcing those measures, the ministry implicitly admitted it could control Massachusetts only with an army. For a nation rightfully proud of its benign rule, this was a terrible confession. Unfortunately, the troops' presence exacerbated a situation already made volatile by radicals, Bernard, and the customs commissioners. Had the ministry declared martial law instead of carefully abiding by legal and constitutional restrictions, perhaps it could have brought a semblance of peace to the colony. As it was, the small army became the ugly symbol of an oppressive regime attempting to enslave a free people. With few restrictions on their behavior, skirting the law at will, radicals made life miserable for the soldiers. The troops responded with predictable pugnacity.

The British Government ignored the lesson of the massacre – that the madness of mobs and insolence of soldiers made an explosive setting. After the Tea Party in 1773, the North ministry again sent troops to Boston. Shortly thereafter the Revolution began. And it must surely rank as the supreme irony of the pre-revolutionary decade that the massacre occurred on 5 March, the same day that Parliament moved to temper the measures which had occasioned it.

REFERENCES

1. Treasury Minutes, 23 Sept 1766, Class 29, Pieces 38–41, Public Records Office, London.
2. Namier, Lewis, and Brooke, John: *Charles Townshend* (New York, 1964).
3. Dowdeswell Papers, post 25 Oct, William L. Clements Library, Ann Arbor, Michigan.
4. Labaree, Benjamin W.: *The Boston Tea Party* (New York, 1964), 13–14.
5. Whately to Grenville, 20 Oct 1766, in *The Grenville Papers*, ed. William J. Smith, 4 vols. (London: John Murray, 1852–3), III, 332–6.
6. "Proposals for Regulating the Plantation Trade," 14 March 1766, Rockingham Papers, Wentworth-Woodhouse Collection, Sheffield City Library, England.
7. Sosin, Jack: *Agents and Merchants* (Lincoln: University of Nebraska Press, 1965), 104–5.
8. Conway to George III, 26 Jan 1767, in *Correspondence of King George III*, ed. Sir John Fortescue, 6 vols. (London: Macmillan, 1927–8), I, 451.
9. Newdegate Papers, Box B26, B2548/3, Warwick County Public Record Office, Warwick, England [NB The spelling of Newdigate was changed by his descendants].
10. 9 Dec 1766, Colonial Office Papers, Series 5/1137, 8–10.
11. Shelburne to Chatham, [16 Feb 1767], in *Correspondence of William Pitt, Earl of Chatham*, ed. W. S. Taylor and J. H. Pringle (London, 1838, 1840), III, 206–9.
12. Shelburne to Chatham, 26 April 1767, Chatham Papers, 30/8, LVI, 86–90, Public Record Office, London.
13. ibid.
14. Townshend Papers, Buccleuch MSS, VIII/31, Dalkeith, Midlothian, Scotland.
15. Lord Charlemont to Henry Flood, 13 March 1767, *Correspondence of William Pitt*, III, 231–2.
16. Shelburne to Chatham, 13 March 1767, ibid.
17. 12 April ?1767, Grafton Papers, Public Records Office, Bury St. Edmunds, England.
18. ibid.
19. Sackville to Irwin, 20 April 1767, in Historical Manuscripts Commission: *Manuscripts of Mrs. Stopford-Sackville*, 2 vols. (London: Eyre and Spotiswoode, 1905), I, 123.

20. Shelburne to Chatham, 1 Feb 1767, *Correspondence of William Pitt*, III, 105.
21. 6 Jan 1767, Townshend Papers, Buccleuch MSS, VIII/31.
22. ibid.
23. West to Newcastle, 13 May 1767, Newcastle Papers, Add. MSS 32891, 323, British Museum.
24. ibid.; Ryder shorthand notes, 13 May 1767, Doc. 46, Harrowby MSS, Sandon Hall, England.
25. Charles Garth to Committee of Correspondence, 17 May 1767, *South Carolina Historical and Genealogical Magazine*, XXIX (1928), 228–9.
26. Ryder shorthand notes, 13 May 1767, Doc. 46, Harrowby MSS.
27. ibid.
28. Cobbett, William (ed.): *Parliamentary History of England* (London, 1806–20), XVI, 331.
29. Bradshaw to Grafton, 16 May 1767, in *Autobiography and Political Correspondence of Augustus Henry, Third Duke of Grafton* (London: John Murray, 1898), 179–81.
30. Garth to Committee of Correspondence, 6 June 1767, *South Carolina Historical and Genealogical Magazine*, XXIX (1928), 295–305; *London Magazine*, XXXVII (1767), 179.
31. *London Magazine*, XXXVII (1767), 177; Newcastle Papers, Add. MSS 33037, 65–173.
32. *Boston Gazette* (14 Sept 1767).
33. Rockingham Papers, RII, 63.
34. To Hillsborough, 23 May 1768, Colonial Office Papers, Series 5/678, 48.
35. *The Critical Review*, XXVI (London, 1768), 16; *The Monthly Review*, LIX (London, 1768), 18.
36. Halsey, R. T. H. (ed.): *Letters from a Farmer in Pennsylvania* (New York, 1903).
37. Commager, Henry Steele (ed.): *Documents of American History*, 6th edn. (New York: Appleton Century Crofts 1958), 66–7.
38. Shelburne Papers, LXXXV, 182–3, Clements Library, Ann Arbor, Michigan.
39. 23 April 1768, Colonial Office Papers, Series 5/757, pt. 1, 113–17.
40. Gage Papers, Colonial Office Papers, Series 5/86, 109.
41. Bernard to Hillsborough, 23 Jan, 29 April, 1–17 June 1769, Colonial Office Papers, Series 5/758, 95–7, 227–8, 255–65.
42. Hood to Philip Stevens, 11 July 1769, and Bernard to Hillsborough, 7 July 1769, ibid., 334–42, 309–14.
43. *Boston Post-Boy and Advertiser* (3 July 1769).
44. Bernard to Hillsborough, 17 July 1769, Colonial Office Papers, Series 5/758, 349/54.
45. Assembly address to Moore, 3 June 1767, Colonial Office Papers, Series 5/1098, 657.
46. Assembly Journal, 1–31 Dec 1768, Colonial Office Papers, Series 5/1100, 5–54; Gerlach, Don R.: *Philip Schuyler and the American Revolution in New York, 1733–1777* (Lincoln: University of Nebraska Press, 1964), 149–70.
47. Moore to Hillsborough, 4 Jan, 30 March 1769, Colonial Office Papers, Series 5/1100, 37–43, 265–6.
48. *South Carolina Gazette* (6 Sept 1768); Montague to Hillsborough, 25 Nov 1768, Colonial Office Papers, Series 5/409, 57.
49. Bull to Hillsborough, 23 Oct 1768, Colonial Office Papers, Series 5/409, 55–6.
50. Resolutions of the Commons House, 19 Nov 1768, Colonial Office Papers, Series 5/391, 155–8; Montagu to Hillsborough, 25 Nov 1768, Series 5/409, 57.
51. Resolutions of the Commons House, 17–19 Aug 1769, Colonial Office Papers, Series 5/379, 71–2.
52. Resolutions of the Commons House, 23 Aug 1769, Colonial Office Papers, Series 5/392, 93–4; Montagu to Hillsborough, 30 June 1769, Series 5/409, 63.
53. Resolutions of the Commons House, 23 Aug 1769, Colonial Office Papers, Series 5/392, 93–4.
54. Hillsborough to Gage, 9 Dec 1769, Colonial Office Papers, Series 5/87, 367/8; Bull to Hillsborough, 28–9 Aug 1769, Series 5/409, 67–70.
55. Bernard to Shelburne, 14 Sept, 14 Nov 1767, Colonial Office Papers, Series 5/756, 243–5, 295–6; *Boston Post-Boy and Advertiser* (28 Dec 1767).

56. Bernard to Hillsborough, 21 March, 9 Aug 1768, Colonial Office Papers, Series 5/757, pt. 1, 151–7, pt. 3, 749–50; Diary, 1, 4, 9 March 1768, in *Letters and Diary of John Rowe, Boston Merchant*, ed. Anne Cunningham (Cambridge, Mass.: W. B. Clarke, 1912), 152–3.
57. Bull to Hillsborough, 25 Sept 1769, Colonial Office Papers, Series 5/409, 72–3.
58. *South Carolina Gazette* (25 Sept 1769).
59. Dabney, William, and Dargan, Marion: *William Henry Drayton and the American Revolution* (Albuquerque: University of New Mexico Press, 1962), 25–39; *South Carolina Gazette* (3–17 Aug 1769).
60. Mason to unknown correspondent, 6 Dec 1770, in Kate M. Rowland: *Life and Correspondence of George Mason*, 2 vols. (New York, 1892), I, 148–51.
61. Johnson to Trumbull, 6 March 1770, Massachusetts Historical Society Collections: *Trumbull Papers* (Boston, 1885), IX, 421–6; Cavendish shorthand notes, Egerton MSS, 221, foll. 4–53, British Museum, London.
62. Cavendish shorthand notes, Egerton MSS, 4–53.
63. Johnson to Trumbull, 14 April 1770, Massachusetts Historical Society Collections: *Trumbull Papers* (Boston, 1885), IX, 430–2.
64. Dickerson, Oliver M.: "Use Made of the Revenue from the Tax on Tea," *New England Quarterly*, XXXI (1958), 240.
65. Franklin to Cooper, 24 Feb 1769, Franklin Papers, Clements Library, Ann Arbor, Michigan.
65. Wroth, L. Kinvin, and Zobel, Hiller B. (eds.): *Legal Papers of John Adams*, 3 vols. (Cambridge, Mass.: Harvard University Press, 1965), III, *passim*; Zobel, Hiller B.: *The Boston Massacre* (New York: W. W. Norton, 1970), *passim*.
67. Depositions of John Eustace, 24 July 1770, Alexander Mall, 12 Aug 1770, Henry Malone, 24 July 1770, Jeremiah French, 25 July 1770, Hugh Broughton, 24 July 1770, Colonial Office Papers, Series 5/88, 521, 425–?, 431, 519, 451–?.
68. Deposition of Capt. Thomas Preston, no date, Colonial Office Papers, Series 5/759, 247–53.
69. Hutchinson to Hillsborough, 12 March 1770, ibid., 119–22.
70. Wroth, L. Kinvin, and Zobel, Hiller B. (eds.): *Legal Papers of John Adams*, 3 vols. (Cambridge, Mass., 1965), III, esp. 1–34, 67, 77, 115, 118–19, 314.

FURTHER READING

Barrow, Thomas: *Trade and Empire: the British Customs Service in Colonial America, 1660–1775* (Cambridge, Mass.: Harvard University Press, 1967).
Brooke, John: *The Chatham Administration, 1766–1768* (London: Macmillan, 1956).
Bullion, John L.: *A Great and Necessary Measure: George Grenville and the Genesis of the Stamp Act, 1763–1765* (Columbia: University of Missouri Press, 1982).
Christie, I. R.: *Crisis of Empire: Great Britain and the American Colonies, 1754–1783* (New York: W. W. Norton, 1966).
Donoughue, Bernard: *British Politics and the American Revolution, 1773–1775* (London: Macmillan, 1964).
Flower, Milton: *John Dickinson, Conservative Revolutionary* (Charlottesville: University of Virginia Press, 1983).
Greene, Jack: *The Quest for Power: the Lower Houses of Assembly in the Southern Royal Colonies, 1689–1776* (New York: W. W. Norton, 1972).
Labaree, Benjamin W.: *The Boston Tea Party* (New York: Oxford University Press, 1964).
Langford, Peter: *The First Rockingham Administration* (New York, 1973).
Namier, Sir Lewis, and Brooke, John: *Charles Townshend* (New York: St. Martin's Press, 1964).
Ritcheson, Charles R.: *British Politics and the American Revolution* (Norman: University of Oklahoma Press, 1954).
Thomas, P. D. G.: *British Politics and the Stamp Act Crisis: the First Phase of the American Revolution, 1763–1767* (Oxford: Clarendon Press, 1975).

14

The British Army in America, before 1775

DOUGLAS EDWARD LEACH

URING the latter part of the seventeenth century the need for regular troops in the North American colonies was only occasional, but in the eighteenth century, with the growth of international rivalries and civil challenges to British authority, the army's involvement and responsibilities increased significantly. Gradually the enlarged garrison force, owing allegiance directly to the monarch, became closely linked with British imperial administration, being based in particular colonies under the command of provincial governors, many of whom were themselves professional military officers. In its simplest form the army's assignment was twofold: to defend imperial territory against Indians or European foes, and to aid local authority in repressing any civil insurrection. From time to time, depending on circumstances, one or the other of these two missions was dominant. Given the well-known conditions of colonial development, with growing conflict between American and British interests as well as mutually antipathetic attitudes, it is not surprising to discover considerable and sometimes intense friction between regulars and colonists. Thus the military presence is properly recognized as a contributing factor in the coming of the American Revolution.

I. THE SEVENTEENTH CENTURY: ACTION AND COMMUNICATIONS

The first large-scale use of regulars occurred in 1677, when more than 1,000 soldiers landed in Virginia to stamp out Bacon's Rebellion, only to find that the royal governor had already done the job for them. At Boston in 1689 and New York in 1691, during the colonial version of the Glorious Revolution, regular troops again played a repressive role (although in Boston it was the redcoats, not the citizenry, who were disarmed). These seventeenth-century episodes did much to plant in the American mind the idea that the regulars were essentially a police power.

The British Army in the colonies operated under heavy handicaps. Consider, for example, the great length of its line of communication from London in the era of sail. Royal governors and military commanders alike often had to choose between inaction while awaiting instructions and action that might later be censured. Even when specific orders did arrive they were not always helpful, for the ministry at home usually had a clouded view of American conditions, including geography. Officers posted to North America found themselves in an unfamiliar environment amidst a diverse and sometimes perverse people. Each colony had its peculiarities, including currency. There was a great variety of ethnic and religious groups. One heard foreign tongues as well as strange accents. There were thousands of Africans, nearly all held in slavery. And there were numerous Indians, to many officers an enigma and to many soldiers a terror. Towns were few and widely scattered, interconnected only by water routes or primitive roads that would have been scorned by Roman legions. Moving troops and supplies over such long distances across wilderness territory often proved extremely difficult. The very attitude of many colonists was hampering. Farmers and merchants alike profiteered at the army's expense, while taxpayers in general made clear to their representatives in the assemblies that taxes should not be increased just to aid the army in its mission. Usually the colonists backed the army when it was furthering their own interests, but then might shift into stubborn opposition if the troops seemed troublesome. Commanders soon realized that they had to be diplomats as well as soldiers.

Service in America had an adverse effect on the army in many ways. Commanders and other officers were frequently frustrated by what they viewed as provincial hostility. Among the officers there was a fairly high level of absenteeism, some officers, especially colonels of regiments, lingering long in Britain before rejoining their units. The enlisted men were often accommodated in badly deteriorating barracks or make-shift quarters, subject to rampant disease, scorned by the local community as immoral or vicious. Soldiers who tried to supplement their meager pay by working for hire during off-duty hours were accused of competing with local labor. Many seized an opportunity to desert, sometimes aided by colonists, which in turn angered the officers who were struggling to fill vacancies in the ranks. Altogether it makes for a picture of a garrison force far from home, discouraged, unappreciated, neglected, deteriorating.

2. ACTION, 1702–48

These severe difficulties should be kept firmly in mind while examining the army's role in North America during the first three-quarters of the eighteenth century. Queen Anne's War (1702–13) brought additional troops into the colonies. This was especially true in 1711, when about 4,300 redcoats used Boston as a base in preparation for a joint army–provincial expedition against Quebec. By accident this large and expensive venture came to grief in the treacherous currents of the St. Lawrence River, adding little to the reputation of army or navy.

During the long interlude following the Peace of Utrecht (1713) the colonists saw little of the regular army excepting the few independent companies permanently stationed in South Carolina and New York. Such companies were unaffiliated with any regiment, being specially constituted and maintained for garrison duty in certain locations. These small units typically remained for many years where assigned, suffering greatly from imperial neglect, with the result that their aging members lost both military polish and pride, becoming objects of local contempt. At best they remained as visible symbols of imperial authority, weak props for royal government amidst a growing and expanding colonial populace.

Increasing friction between Britain and Spain culminated in the War of Jenkins's Ear (1739–48), again bringing the British Army to the fore. One regiment had already been sent to the defense of the recently founded colony of Georgia under the overall command of General James Oglethorpe, participating in both the futile expedition against St. Augustine in 1740 and the successful defense of Georgia two years later. Then France entered the war in 1744, thereby providing New England with an opportunity to strike at the menacing French fortress of Louisburg on Cape Breton Island. After a motley New England army aided by the Royal Navy had besieged and forced the surrender of Louisburg in 1745, the victorious provincials were relieved

FIGURE 12 "The morning of the Battle of the Plains of Abraham, Quebec," 13 September 1759 (painting by Frederic Remington from "Harper's Monthly," vol. 103, June 1901): the British line is awaiting the arrival of the French.

by a substantial garrison of redcoats, who remained there until the area reverted to France at the Peace of Aix-la-Chapelle (1748).

3. CHARACTER AND ORGANIZATION

Here we may pause briefly to examine the character and organization of the mid-eighteenth-century British Army. Most of the commissioned officers were career soldiers drawn from the lower ranks of the British aristocracy and the upper middle class. Their commissions had been purchased rather than earned by merit, although some officers were highly experienced and competent. The enlisted men, by contrast, had been enticed into the army from their places in the lower levels of British society, mostly by the lure of guaranteed maintenance and security plus the prospect of adventure. Some but not all had been at odds with the law.

Having clutched the King's shilling, the new recruit was outfitted with a uniform consisting of tricornered hat; shirt and stock; waistcoat; tight white breeches; gaiters; shoes; and (most distinctive of all) a red outer coat with brass buttons, facing, and tails. He was also issued a .75 caliber Brown Bess musket with attachable bayonet. This muzzle-loading flintlock gun was deadly at close range, but quite ineffective beyond about a hundred yards.

The army was a fully professional fighting organization equipped and trained in accordance with the prevalent military concepts of the day, featuring exacting parade-ground drill and harsh discipline. Approximately 80 per cent of the personnel were infantry, most of the remainder being mounted troops not used in America before the

Revolution. Engineers and artillerymen were specialists ordinarily outside the normal line of military command until temporarily attached for a particular mission.

In speaking of infantry organization there is danger in being too precise, for numbers changed with changing circumstances. A company of foot soldiers usually numbered about 40 men under the command of a captain or other superior officer, who was assisted by a lieutenant, an ensign, and several non-commissioned officers. Nine or more companies comprised a battalion or regiment (in America the two terms were virtually interchangeable, although some regiments in the army did include more than one battalion). Thus a typical regiment, identified by the name of its colonel or, more frequently, its assigned number, consisted of about 400 officers and men. Headed by a colonel who owed his office to royal favor, the regimental staff also included a lieutenant colonel, a major, a quartermaster, and a surgeon.

Tactics were traditionally and officially linear, the units of infantry confronting the enemy while standing erect in drill-perfect lines at short range. The troops were intensively trained to load, fire, and reload their muskets simultaneously by units at the words of command, the objective being to deliver one or more devastating volleys, followed, if necessary, by a bayonet charge to clear the field. It is incorrect, however, to assume that the British Army was totally ignorant of any other style of fighting, including guerrilla warfare; nevertheless, most officers were more thoroughly versed in the traditional tactics and felt most comfortable employing them.

4. THE GREAT WAR FOR THE EMPIRE

In the opening phase of the Great War for the Empire (1754–63) the disastrous defeat of General Edward Braddock's 44th and 48th regiments shocked the British world, and planted in the American mind a notion that redcoats were vulnerable to irregulars. As the British suffered further defeats in 1756–7, American respect for the regulars was further eroded, while colonial self-interest worked to shift more and more of the burden of the war onto the imperial government. Determined to win despite the inadequacy of American support, the ministry dispatched many more regiments to North America, also shouldering more of the cost, a policy that produced major victories in 1758–60 and the eventual defeat of France (*see* figure 12). The British Army emerged from the war with considerable glory and increased contempt for the provincial troops with whom they had shared the field; many colonists who had experienced British arrogance and insensitivity reciprocated.

5. THE AMERICANS' RESISTANCE TO BRITISH TAXATION

Conquered territory in the West needed careful guarding, so London decided to retain 15 regiments in North America, the bulk of these troops to be stationed in a string of frontier posts stretching from the St. Lawrence through the Great Lakes, down the Mississippi Valley, to the Gulf of Mexico and Florida. Their main mission was to keep the various Indian tribes pacified by preventing British colonists from abusing them in the fur trade and encroaching on tribal lands. The government intended to defray at least part of the heavy cost by colonial taxation, but neglected to clarify for the Americans the nature of the army's mission. Americans would resist the taxation while suspecting the army's motives. Pontiac's Uprising of 1763 revealed the army's unreadiness, and, although the regulars did eventually prevail, they simply were not capable of fulfilling the ministry's expectations (*see* PONTIAC).

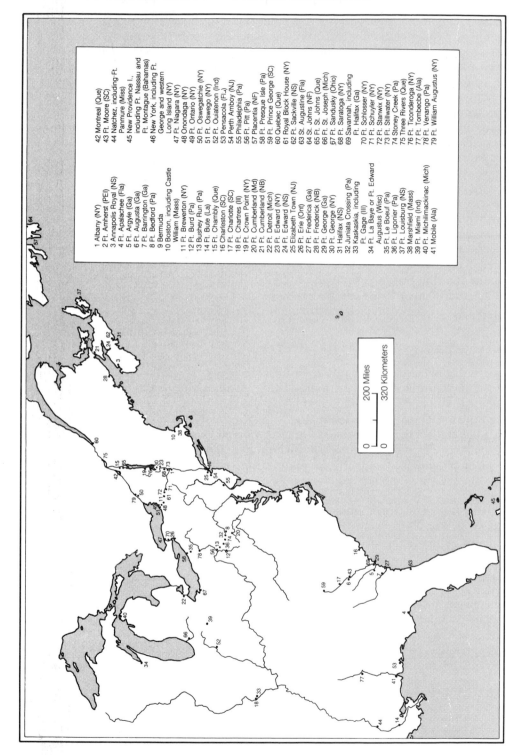

1 Albany (NY)
2 Ft. Amherst (PEI)
3 Annapolis Royal (NS)
4 Ft. Apalachee (Fla)
5 Ft. Argyle (Ga)
6 Ft. Augusta (Ga)
7 Ft. Barrington (Ga)
8 Ft. Bedford (Pa)
9 Bermuda
10 Boston, including Castle
   William (Mass)
11 Ft. Brewerton (NY)
12 Ft. Burd (Pa)
13 Bushey Run (Pa)
14 Ft. Bute (La)
15 Ft. Chambly (Que)
16 Ft. Charleston (SC)
17 Ft. Charlotte (SC)
18 Ft. Chartres (Ill)
19 Ft. Crown Point (NY)
20 Ft. Cumberland (Md)
21 Ft. Cumberland (NB)
22 Ft. Detroit (Mich)
23 Ft. Edward (NY)
24 Ft. Edward (NS)
25 Elizabeth Town (NJ)
26 Ft. Erie (Ont)
27 Ft. Frederica (Ga)
28 Ft. Frederick (NB)
29 Ft. George (Ga)
30 Ft. George (NY)
31 Halifax (NS)
32 Juniata Crossing (Pa)
33 Kaskaskia, including
   Ft. Gage (Ill)
34 Ft. La Baye or Ft. Edward
   Augustus (Wisc)
35 Ft. Le Boeuf (Pa)
36 Ft. Ligonier (Pa)
37 Ft. Louisburg (NS)
38 Ft. Marshfield (Mass)
39 Ft. Miami (Ind)
40 Ft. Michilimackinac (Mich)
41 Mobile (Ala)

42 Montreal (Que)
43 Ft. Moore (SC)
44 Natchez, including Ft.
   Panmure (Miss)
45 New Providence I.,
   including Ft. Nassau and
   Ft. Montague (Bahamas)
46 New York, including Ft.
   George and western
   Long Island (NY)
47 Ft. Niagara (NY)
48 Onondaga (NY)
49 Ft. Ontario (NY)
50 Ft. Oswegatchie (NY)
51 Ft. Oswego (NY)
52 Ft. Ouiatenon (Ind)
53 Pensacola (Fla)
54 Perth Amboy (NJ)
55 Philadelphia (Pa)
56 Ft. Pitt (Pa)
57 Placentia (NF)
58 Ft. Presque Isle (Pa)
59 Ft. Prince George (SC)
60 Quebec (Que)
61 Royal Block House (NY)
62 Ft. Sackville (NS)
63 St. Augustine (Fla)
64 St. Johns (NF)
65 Ft. St. Johns (Que)
66 Ft. St. Joseph (Mich)
67 Ft. Sandusky (Ohio)
68 Ft. Saratoga (NY)
69 Savannah, including
   Ft. Halifax (Ga)
70 Ft. Schlosser (NY)
71 Ft. Schuyler (NY)
72 Ft. Stanwix (NY)
73 Ft. Stillwater (NY)
74 Stoney Creek (Pa)
75 Three Rivers (Que)
76 Ft. Ticonderoga (NY)
77 Ft. Tombecbe (Ala)
78 Ft. Venango (Pa)
79 Ft. William Augustus (NY)

MAP 1 Forts and posts occupied by the British Army up to 1775

The Quartering Act of 1765 By 1768 the imperial government had recognized the failure, while feeling intensified concern over American insubordination, causing a shifting of major troop strength from the West to the populated coastal area, with concentrations at Halifax, New York, Philadelphia, and St. Augustine. The troops were housed in barracks where available, otherwise in taverns and other non-domestic buildings. There was doubt as to whether or not the British constitution permitted forced quartering in occupied dwellings; nearly all Americans were certain it did not, and except under emergency conditions British commanders avoided forcing the issue. The Quartering Act of 1765, even though it did not authorize domestic quartering, had imposed a form of taxation and raised American ire (*see* Chapter 11, §4, and Chapter 12, §8). One should be aware that under the British constitution the army had no free hand. Troops could not be employed against rioters until summoned by a civil magistrate. A governor would be foolish to make such a request without the support of his council whose members, in turn, were reluctant to offend their fellow colonists. Although the army was expected to act decisively, it often could not.

Further complicating the situation was the military office of commander-in-chief, the unfortunate Braddock having been first in a succession that included Governor William Shirley of Massachusetts, the Earl of Loudoun, General James Abercromby, General Jeffrey Amherst, and, from 1763, General Thomas Gage. Army headquarters were in the town of New York. The office tended to blur the authority of the provincial governors, who traditionally had control of all military forces within their respective jurisdictions. Most governors after 1754 tended to defer to a strong commander-in-chief.

The Boston Massacre The seaport of Boston was in the forefront of American resistance to British taxes and the customs service, yet no garrison force had been sent there. In 1768 the ministry ordered Gage to remedy that deficiency. Before this could be accomplished the Liberty Riot occurred as a blatant affront to royal authority, causing London to dispatch a sizable force. The first units began landing on 1 October 1768, covered by the menacing guns of several warships. By the end of the year the garrison consisted of the 14th, 29th, 64th, and 65th regiments plus part of the 59th. These were sufficient to prevent all but petty harassment by the sullen inhabitants, who viewed the soldiers as the arm of ministerial oppression. After the situation had stabilized, Gage eventually withdrew most of the troops, leaving only about 600 men to shiver through the winter of 1769–70 under the taunt of "lobsterback" and even less flattering epithets hurled by Boston's gamins.

That same winter saw violence in New York, where the Sons of Liberty had erected a liberty pole as a symbol of defiance. After redcoats of the town garrison cut down the pole, rioting patriots brawled with the troops on Golden Hill, fortunately without loss of life on either side. Elsewhere in the colonies, wherever redcoats and patriots were in proximity there was likely to be tension if not open violence, as tempers on both sides grew shorter. This was especially true in Boston, where the townsfolk made every effort to discomfort the soldiery.

The culmination was the Boston Massacre of 5 March 1770 (for illustration, *see* figure 11, p. 141). On that tragic evening an ugly-spirited mob so harassed and frightened a small party of troops on guard duty that first one and then others of the soldiers discharged their muskets into the crowd, killing five. Later brought to trial and defended by John Adams, all but two of the soldiers were acquitted and none was hanged. Local radicals seized upon the "massacre" as proof of British bestiality, emitting whole volleys of skillful propaganda excoriating the garrison. To ease the situation, the troops were withdrawn to Castle Island in the harbor.

The Boston Tea Party and the Coercive Acts   Boston again showed its determination not be coerced when its Sons of Liberty organized and hosted the now-famous Tea Party of 16 December 1773, efficiently destroying 90,000 pounds of dutiable tea in less than three hours (*see* Chapter 20, §2). It is noteworthy that, although both the navy and the army were within call, neither took preventive action. Outraged by the defiant destruction, Parliament passed the Coercive Acts, two of which in particular affected the army. A new Quartering Act required the colonies to provide quarters for troops *wherever needed*, but still failed to endorse forced billeting in private homes. The Administration of Justice Act (applying only to Massachusetts) was intended to secure a fair trial for any royal official or soldier accused of killing a colonist in the line of duty by permitting the case to be transferred to another colony or even to England. Radicals charged that the new law gave soldiers a license to murder. Also, in the spring of 1774 Massachusetts acquired a new royal governor – none other than General Gage – who now moved from New York to Boston, combining civil authority and military command in one person.

The authority of the new governor was supported by large numbers of additional troops. By the beginning of 1775 the offending town was garrisoned by nine regiments plus portions of two others, which meant one redcoat for every five inhabitants, surely enough to keep the lid firmly clamped down on the Boston teapot. It should have been clear to everyone, even the most radical patriot, that Parliament and the Crown meant business.

FURTHER READING

Frey, S. R.: *The British Soldier in America: a Social History of Military Life in the Revolutionary Period* (Austin: University of Texas Press, 1981).

Higginbotham, D.: *The War of American Independence: Military Attitudes, Policies, and Practice, 1763–1789* (New York: Macmillan, 1971).

Leach, D. E.: *Arms for Empire: a Military History of the British Colonies in North America, 1607–1763* (New York: Macmillan, 1973).

——: *Roots of Conflict: British Armed Forces and Colonial Americans, 1677–1763* (Chapel Hill: University of North Carolina Press, 1986).

Shy, J.: *Toward Lexington: the Role of the British Army in the Coming of the American Revolution* (Princeton, NJ: Princeton University Press, 1965).

15

The West and the Indians, 1756–1776

PETER MARSHALL

THE 20 years preceding Independence were accompanied by constant conflict and change in the West. If the reduction of the French empire in North America and the acquisition of Spanish colonies had demonstrated the extent of British ascendancy, the period proved to be even more clearly marked by the victor's inability to establish effective control over an immense territory in which Indians, settlers, speculators, colonial governors, and imperial officials found themselves continually opposed. The events of these years indicate that western expansion had contributed significantly not to the strength but rather to the bankruptcy of imperial policy. It had given rise to military humiliation during the Seven Years' War and the Conspiracy of Pontiac, to administrative failure to organize the regulation of Indian affairs, and to ministerial incapacity to control western settlement or establish new colonies. Victory in war was followed, in the West, by seemingly insuperable problems.

To all those colonists engaged in Indian trade, western land purchase, and frontier settlement, the formal declaration by Britain of war with France in May 1756 was an event of no great significance; far more relevant to their condition were episodes such as Washington's surrender at Fort Necessity in July 1754, and in the following year the expulsion of the Acadians from Nova Scotia and Braddock's defeat and death on the Monongahela. A European war served to draw attention to an American conflict long sustained by imperial rivalry, colonial settlement and speculation, and Indian concerns. If neither colonists nor Indians held each other in trust or esteem while the acquisition of land and the conduct of trade lacked any element of imperial control, by 1756 both groups had needs which could only be satisfied by trade and treaty. Self-sufficiency had long been abandoned by Indians. As JOHN STUART, Superintendent of Indian Affairs south of the Ohio, reported to London in 1764:

> The original great tie between the Indians and Europeans was mutual conveniency. This alone could at first have induced the Indians to receive white people differing so much from themselves into their country.... A modern Indian cannot subsist without Europeans; and would handle a flint ax or any other rude utensil used by his ancestors very awkwardly: so what was only conveniency at first is now become necessity and the original tie strengthened. (De Vorsey, 1966, p. 12.)

While it generated continual conflict and dispute, trade bound Indians and colonists together. For the Indians it afforded essential recourse to arms, ammunition, tools, strouds, and rum; the colonists might obtain furs, deerskins and, with increasing frequency during the third quarter of the century, land grants of uncertain extent and validity.

1. THE NEED FOR A COORDINATED INDIAN POLICY

In the early 1750s the region where the consequences of these encounters were most evident comprised the western districts of Virginia and the Carolinas. A number of factors assured turbulence. Expansion from the north had brought, from the 1730s, Scots-Irish and Germans to settle close to Indian lands and had also stimulated Pennsylvanian and Virginian territorial claims. The organization in 1747 of the Ohio Company and in 1749 of the Loyal Company, two Virginian enterprises whose immediate lack of success would neither extinguish their claims to land nor deter subsequent speculative ventures, marked the beginning of corporate land ventures in a location where geographical access and Indian numbers did not debar settlement. The proximity of New York to New France and an exaggerated respect for Iroquois fighting strength focused attention on threats developing north of the Ohio. The Albany Congress of 1754 had testified to colonial concern for the establishment of a coordinated Indian policy, an aim apparently further advanced in the following year by the appointment of an imperial Indian Superintendent for the Northern District. The post could be bestowed on an obvious candidate: WILLIAM JOHNSON was unsurpassed for his understanding of and influence among the Iroquois. The powers conferred upon this new office remained uncertain. Although, when Loudoun became Commander-in-Chief in 1756, Johnson's new commission was accompanied by a letter that declared "the whole management of this branch of the service will be left entirely to your discretion," the superintendents remained permanently dependent on military funds. If Johnson's standing and influence was such as to secure him a certain freedom of action, or at least room for financial argument, the appointment in 1756 of Edmond Atkin as Superintendent for the Southern District carried no such advantages. Before his death in 1761 Atkin had demonstrated merely that capacity to write at some length on Indian history and Indian policy did not insure ability to transact Indian affairs. His successor John Stuart would, in the years before the Revolution, exercise an altogether more effective control in an extent of territory and circumstances that were such as to invite failure.

2. THE INDIAN POPULATION AND THEIR RELATIONS WITH THE COLONISTS

The number of Indians in contact with colonial expansion can only be roughly calculated, particularly since estimates emanated from those whose interests seemed more personal than scientific. Figures were offered in terms of warriors, and needed to be multiplied by four or five to calculate the total population. In 1763 Johnson asserted that his district contained some 8,020 warriors: the Iroquois and their dependents accounted for 2,230; Canadian Indians allied to them, 630; the Indians of the Ohio Valley 1,100; while the remainder, for whom accurate figures could not be given, lived round the Great Lakes. Stuart's figures, provided in the following year, indicated a somewhat greater and even more widely dispersed body of southern Indians. The Cherokees, located at the southern end of the Appalachians, and the nation most in contact with the colonists, were estimated to comprise 2,750 warriors; the Creeks, to their south and west, possessed 3,600; and on lands located in the present State of Mississippi were to be found 5,000 Choctaw and 450 Chickasaw warriors. From these conservative figures, the Indian population in the South

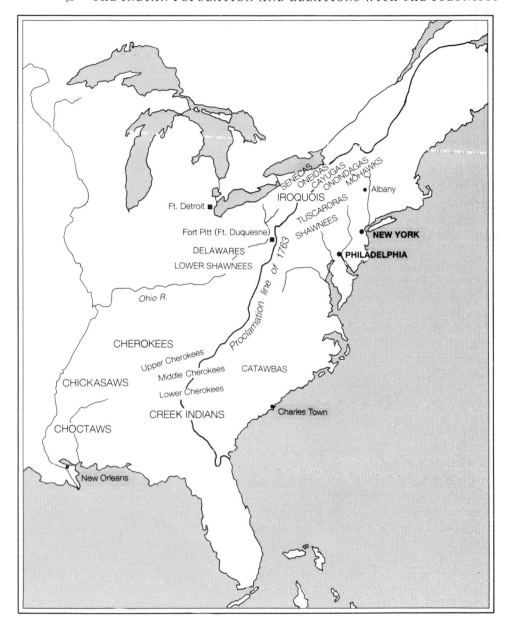

MAP 2 The location of some major Indian nations in the years leading up to the Revolution

amounted to some 60,000, and the superintendents could claim responsibility for relations with more than 100,000 Native Americans.

During the Seven Years' War, and in its aftermath, colonists and Indian officials could not rely on the maintenance of peace and friendship. In the North only Johnson's

155

adopted Mohawks, in the South only the Chickasaws, could be considered faithful. Proof of Indian duplicity and capacity to wipe out frontier posts and settlers did not need recall from a distant past: until the summer of 1758 French regiments and Indian raiders inflicted death and devastation, while the Cherokee war of 1760 brought much slaughter and little military glory to South Carolina. If the events of 1759 saw a dramatic and, as it proved, conclusive end to French power in North America, the Conspiracy of Pontiac of 1763 (*see* PONTIAC) demonstrated a continued Indian capacity to attack. French regiments might have departed, but the tribes remained and could still command fear and respect.

3. RESULTS OF THE PROCLAMATION OF 1763

The establishment of supremacy over other European powers in North America had involved Britain in unprecedented costs and commitments. Three colonial governments had to be created. The province of Quebec, as delimited in 1763, saw New France reduced in extent, both in the Gulf of the St. Lawrence and, much more significantly, west of the Ottawa river, so excluding the entire Great Lakes region from any form of civil rule; while in the far south Spanish Florida became the colonies of East and West Florida. The Proclamation of 7 October 1763, which had detailed these arrangements, also sought to protect Indian lands. Governors, both of the new and of the other North American colonies, were forbidden to acquire areas reserved for the tribes within settled limits, or "beyond the heads or sources of any of the rivers which fall into the Atlantic Ocean from the west or north-west ..." The withdrawal was ordered of any colonists already settled beyond this line. The purchase of Indian lands within the colonies would be undertaken only by governors. Indian trade was to be "free and open," but conducted under license and regulations which, if breached, would involve a cancelation of permit and forfeit of security payment. The Proclamation had been issued before news of the attacks on the western posts reached London. Intended as an interim, not a permanent, measure, it left undrawn the line that divided settled from Indian lands. The task of repairing this omission would, until the Revolution, occupy much of the superintendents' attention.

Between 1763 and 1774 the problems of western expansion and of Indian relations appeared indistinguishable. They existed in a situation far more complex than one composed of tribes and settlers. Imperial authority had to be imposed, defined, and paid for; conflicting colonial claims had to be resolved; innumerable land schemes, pursued by individuals, syndicates, or companies, testified to ambitions of territorial gain extending seamlessly from Nova Scotia to Florida. The process of settlement created continual change, challenging and disturbing a variety of interests that ranged from those of imperial order to those of Indian custom. Ambition, rather than achievement, had the upper hand.

4. IMPERIAL CONTROL OF TRADE WITH THE INDIANS

Amherst's refusal, as Commander-in-Chief, to accept that the Indians still posed any military threat after the French had surrendered had been totally invalidated by the events of 1763. The overwhelming of so many military posts might seem to have proved Johnson's point that it was essential to maintain good Indian relations. Official recognition of his views reached a high point with the circulation by the Board of Trade on 10 July 1764 of an elaborate plan for the future management of Indian

FIGURE 13 A testimonial certificate engraved by Henry
Dawkins for Sir William Johnson (1770): this was for
distribution to friendly Indians in order to allow them to
pass British military lines and to protect them from white
persecution and random violence.

affairs. Its proposals, 43 in number, seemed to proclaim Johnson's preferences. Indian
trade, placed under imperial control, would be confined to the posts in the North and
the Indian towns in the South, each being provided with a commissary, an interpreter,
and a smith. The superintendents would assume sole responsibility for Indian relations
and diplomacy, remain independent of military commanders, and negotiate all treaties
and land grants for the colonies. The commissaries would fix the places and rates of
trade for those licensed to conduct it. Liquor, swan shot, and rifled guns were not to
be supplied, and a precise and exact Indian boundary would be established. The
scheme was estimated to cost about £20,000 a year, a sum to be found either by a
duty on the trade or by traders' payments.

The raising of revenue required legislation and the listing of places where trade
would be conducted and the tariffs which might be imposed. The Board of Trade,
having circulated the plan, awaited comments from the colonies. Two years to the
day later, the Board was writing to Johnson to explain that "it has been impossible
for us, amidst the other pressing business that has occur'd, so to prepare our thoughts
& opinion upon this important subject, as to be able as yet to lay them before His
Majesty . . ." Ministerial changes, the Stamp Act crisis, conflicting colonial responses,
had prevented progress. Though lacking formal authority, Thomas Gage, now
Commander-in-Chief, reluctantly acquiesced in an unofficial and partial implementation of the plan. This involved the General in financial outlays which he feared
would never be approved or recovered. The superintendents continued to perform
duties without legislative support; imperial control of Indian affairs remained, accordingly, dependent on individuals, not on statute.

The superintendents' uncertain standing encouraged a tendency to merge personal with official concerns. Johnson was particularly open to this approach. He sought to reconcile the responsibilities of office, his commitment to the Mohawk, his standing with the Iroquois, his landed interests, and his political ambitions (*see* figure 13). This was not always possible, especially in respect of expansion in New York. It encouraged Johnson to divert attention further south and direct settlement and speculation towards the western extents of Pennsylvania and Virginia. There, the territory might seem more accessible, a more widespread demand might be satisfied, and Indian claims were less significant. The lands of the Delawares and Shawnees in this region could be held disposable by the Iroquois on behalf of their "nephews." Johnson believed that this would serve to lessen pressure on "his" Indians, enable land profits to accrue to himself, and maintain peace on the frontier. The Iroquois would not lose by relinquishing claims to lands they could no longer control – a solution also adopted by Stuart in respect of the Cherokee. Persistent demand for land in conditions that lacked formal means of regulation or transfer resulted inevitably in temporary outcomes that guaranteed permanent problems.

Boundary negotiations   The superintendents had devoted much attention to the establishment of a boundary line. Building upon the Congress of Augusta, held in November 1763, Stuart concluded eight treaties between 1763 and 1768. Johnson entered into 11 treaties between 1764 and 1766. Boundary negotiations proved easier in the South, where the Cherokee were principally concerned. Stuart reached an agreement with them in October 1768 at the Treaty of Hard Labor. This completed the process and established a line which, in the Carolinas, ran well to the east of the 1763 Proclamation Divide. In the North the boundary was not confirmed until Johnson had concluded the Treaty of Fort Stanwix in November 1768, and afterwards the line north of the Mohawk river remained unfinished.

5. THE RETURN OF INDIAN AFFAIRS TO COLONIAL CONTROL

In any event, by the end of 1768 the completion of the boundary line had lost its purpose. The authority to finalize it, which had been received by Johnson in February, was undermined in July with the receipt of the Board of Trade's report of March on American affairs. The proposals of the plan of 1764 were now set aside. Imperial regulation of Indian trade was to be abandoned and, as far as possible, the army was to withdraw from western posts. Although the boundary line was still to be run, the superintendents would, in future, be restricted to diplomatic, not administrative, duties. This return of Indian affairs to colonial control proved a signal for disorder: local arrangements were quite inadequate and attempts to initiate inter-colonial cooperation were quashed by the ministry. With the steady removal of garrisons from the western posts – 24 had been abandoned by the beginning of 1773 – imperial management of the interior had been almost totally relinquished. This did not mean, however, that the Indians would remain undisturbed.

It is almost certain that even wholehearted imperial intervention in Indian affairs would have failed to keep order and control in the West, an area far too extensive to permit control of trade, provide military protection, or prevent further settlement. Acquisition of land exercised a particular attraction, whether expressed by individual occupation or by the establishment of companies aiming to secure large tracts. So by 1766, much of the Monongahela Valley in western Pennsylvania had been peopled without official consent or even Indian purchase. The Ohio Company of Virginia, though lacking in vigor, still maintained an interest in the region of Pittsburgh, while the Mississippi Company, formed in June 1763, represented a further attempt to secure two and a half million acres further down the Ohio. In the East, however, Pennsylvanians faced a challenge from the Susquehannah Company, organized in Connecticut in 1753 and revived and redeveloped after the war, claiming land under its colony's sea-to-sea charter. If, in the new colonies, attempts to attract British migrants to Quebec proved largely unsuccessful, applications for land grants in the Floridas demonstrated an altogether more lively interest. Although in a large majority of cases receipt of grant was not a prelude to successful settlement, the disturbances engendered by land projects can hardly be overestimated.

Extending the boundaries The most serious attempt at communal land acquisition had its origins in the bid to secure compensation for losses suffered by traders at the hands of the French and Indians, both in 1754 and also in 1763. In consequence there emerged in 1765 a group backed by the Philadelphia trading enterprise of Baynton, Wharton, and Morgan, which included Johnson's assistant, George Croghan, and which had obtained the Superintendent's support for claims in respect of the 1763 losses. In May 1765 the Six Nations and Delawares offered the "suffering traders," at Johnson's insistence, a grant of land between the Ohio and the Alleghenies, to be called Indiana. By the following year Johnson, while continuing to urge approval of this grant, was also pressing the Board of Trade to permit the establishment of the Illinois Company, which would petition for the grant of 1,200,000 acres on the Mississippi near Fort Chartres. Half the shares of the company were owned by Baynton, Wharton, and Morgan, and a quarter were divided unobtrusively between Johnson and Governor William Franklin. The London advocate of this project was, as might be expected, Benjamin Franklin. By the summer of 1767 the ministry, lacking leadership and beset by conflict between the Chancellor of the Exchequer, Townshend, requiring a reduction in American expenses, and Shelburne, the Secretary of State, responsible for American policy but submerged in detail and uncertainty, had considered but not confirmed the Secretary's proposal that new colonies be established at the Illinois and Detroit.

The Board of Trade report of March 1768 considered at length and rejected the case for inland colonies. This, however, did not prove a major obstacle to the speculators, who soon derived great encouragement from the cessions obtained by Johnson at the Treaty of Fort Stanwix in November. Although Hillsborough, now Secretary of State for America, saw no merit in the Superintendent's achievement, others moved to profit from it. In return for meeting the costs of the Fort Stanwix treaty (calculated to be £10,460 7s 3d), a group of Philadelphia traders, headed by Samuel Wharton and expanded after Wharton's arrival in England to include the politician and banker Thomas Walpole, Benjamin Franklin and other Post Office officials, and additional figures of influence, sought from 1769 to obtain the cession of 2,400,000 acres. The Grand Ohio Company, as it became known, attempted to establish a proprietary colony south of the Ohio. The proposal was quite unacceptable to Hillsborough, who resisted its acceptance until a hearing of the case before the Committee of Privy Council, from which Wharton emerged much the superior, and which concluded with a report favoring the application; in August 1772 Hillsborough resigned from office. By 1773 the establishment of the first inland colony, now named Vandalia as a supposed compliment to the Queen, appeared imminent.

6. COLLAPSE OF IMPERIAL AUTHORITY

A situation which had for so long told against Wharton was not, however, as altered as he may have thought. Conditions on the Ohio were out of control: the competing interests of Virginians, Pennsylvanians, and would-be Vandalians had plunged the region into chaos, a condition even more evident in the summer of 1774 when Lord Dunmore, as Governor of Virginia, made war on the Shawnee. By that time the disintegration of imperial control was a far more significant issue than the creation of another colony. When action was taken, in the summer of 1774, it assumed the form of a revision of the boundaries of Quebec. The new Act not only extended the province to the Ohio but followed the river to the Mississippi, then turned north to meet the territories of the Hudson's Bay Company: the entire Great Lakes region was thus reunited and restored to its previous limits. Imperial authority had been bestowed upon one new colony.

The opposition aroused by this despairing attempt to impose some measure of control upon the territories and peoples of the West formed part of the grounds on which, less than a year later, hostilities would begin. It is impossible to calculate with any accuracy the number of settlers who had entered Indian country by the time of the Revolution: it must have amounted to some thousands, only a minority of whom remained loyal to the Crown. The collapse of imperial authority was obvious and confirmed by the departure of garrisons and the death of Johnson in 1774. In these circumstances it was not surprising that most of the Indian tribes proved unwilling to opt for either side. In the South, where Stuart remained as Superintendent, only the Cherokees moved, in the summer of 1776, against the Carolinas. Prompt and effective counter-attacks devastated their lands and towns and cowed other tribes. In the North the new Superintendent, Sir William's nephew Guy Johnson, was unable to launch the Six Nations against the rebels. Twenty years of constant endeavor to link imperial and Indian interests could be seen, as war broke out, to have resulted in little of benefit to British efforts to retain control of the North American colonies. Whatever the Declaration of Independence may have claimed, "the merciless Indian savages" were not to take a decisive part in the Revolution.

FURTHER READING

Abernethy, Thomas Perkins: *Western Lands and the American Revolution* (New York: Russell & Russell, 1959).

Alden, John Richard: *John Stuart and the Southern Colonial Frontier* (Ann Arbor: University of Michigan Press, 1944).

De Vorsey, Jr., Louis: *The Indian Boundary in the Southern Colonies, 1763–1775* (Chapel Hill: University of North Carolina Press, 1966).

Jones, Dorothy V.: *License for Empire* (Chicago: University of Chicago Press, 1982).

Sosin, Jack M.: *The Revolutionary Frontier, 1763–1783* (New York: Holt, Rinehart and Winston, 1967).

16

Trade legislation and its enforcement, 1748–1776

R. C. SIMMONS

I. TRADE AND POWER

SOME discussions of the Revolution have stressed British trade legislation and the measures taken to enforce it as fundamental colonial grievances. For important planting and merchant interests, especially after 1763, the disadvantages of the commercial (including currency and credit) system seemed increasingly to outweigh its advantages. Other discussions have accepted contemporary denials of any wish to end traditional commercial subordination. Discontent arose because of new legislation seeking less to regulate trade than to raise revenue. Most American evasions of duties and attacks on customs officials, even if fueled by resistance to the Stamp Act, were not part of any principled opposition to the Trade Acts. About Great Britain, however, there is general agreement. Fears that Americans might try "to get loose from the Acts of Navigation" led to substantial support for firm action, support fostered by the belief in the inter-dependence of the parts of the British commercial empire. George III shared these fears, prophesying the West Indies following the Americans "not [into] independence but must for its own interest be dependent on North America: Ireland would soon follow the same plan ... then this Island would be reduced to itself, and soon would be a poor Island indeed, for reduced in Her Trade Merchants would retire with their Wealth to Climates more to their Advantage, and Shoals of Manufacturers would leave this country for the New Empire" (Fortescue, 1927–8, IV: p. 351).

The essence of British commercial thought was that colonies had value only in so far as they benefited the mother country economically. Trade legislation and its enforcement had been laid down in the seventeenth century, as the importance of overseas commerce and colonies grew together. Governments had learned to enjoy revenues that could be obtained relatively easily from taxes on imports. They now began to appreciate that commerce could be aided by the possession of colonies producing valuable staples. These, if re-exported, particularly in manufactured form, contributed to a favorable balance of trade, to wealth and employment in the mother country, and to a satisfactory maritime sector. Colonies might also become large markets for metropolitan goods. Commerce more than agriculture was the foundation of national wealth, power, and happiness. It sometimes needed fostering and always needed regulating. All European economic thought in this period was strongly protectionist, emphasizing competition between states as the natural order of things. Despite literary and philosophical effusions about the civilizing effects and cultural benefits of commerce, war was seen as a proper extension of commercial rivalry.

These ideas were not seriously challenged until after the publication in 1776 of Adam Smith's *Inquiry into the Nature and Causes of the Wealth of Nations* (which included an analysis of American commercial relations with Great Britain and a statement that, although the denial to Americans of complete economic freedom broached "the most sacred rights of mankind," it had not hurt them or prevented them from becoming wealthy). Edmund Burke, despite his pro-American sympathies, believed the old commercial system to have been a triumphant success needing little change. So did William Pitt, architect of British colonial supremacy over France. In his epitaph for Pitt (who died in 1778), Burke praised him for "raising his nation to a high pitch of prosperity and glory," for uniting commerce with and making it "flourish by war." Few persons of his generation would have seen any reason to question this judgment.

2. LAWS AND INSTITUTIONS

The commercial system in 1748 and until 1776 rested on seventeenth-century legislation. Early laws had been aimed at the Dutch in an attempt to prevent them from engrossing colonial commodities and the carrying trade. Basic legislation (1651, 1660, 1661) prohibited non-English owned and manned ships from carrying goods to and from England's overseas possessions. But – and this was important – the colonies and colonial settlers were here counted as English. The law also prohibited the colonial export of enumerated commodities (indigo, sugar, tobacco, ginger, cotton, and some dyestuffs) unless these went directly to England, for use there or for re-export, or to other English colonies. Additions to these enumerated commodities continued: rice and molasses (1704; although rice was later allowed to be sent directly to European destinations south of Cape Finisterre), naval stores (1704, 1725), copper (1721), beaver and other furs (1721), and iron (1764). In 1663 a complementary Act forbade the colonial import (with some few exceptions) of European goods that had not passed through the mother country.

Enforcement of this legislation was parceled out to a variety of agencies. Colonial governors were charged with enforcing Acts of Trade and Navigation, including the taking of bonds and the keeping of records, and in theory were liable to financial penalties and dismissal for failure. Some governors appointed their own officials ("naval officers") to carry out these duties. By an Act of 1673, ships's masters without appropriate English documentation had to pay a duty at the colonial port of clearance and to deposit a bond promising that any enumerated goods not carried to another English colony would be taken to England. The English Customs Commissioners were to "order and manage" the levying and collection of rates and duties within the colonies. A process of appointing colonial customs officers (begun in 1671) followed. By the 1680s this was complete for the Americas, and the customs officials were empowered to use the navy to seize offenders. Indeed, three sets of officials – gubernatorial, customs, and naval – were as often rivals as colleagues. An Act of Trade of 1696 also dealt with enforcement, placing further obligations on colonial governors, subordinating naval officers to customs officials (whose powers of search were also enlarged), and extending vice-admiralty courts to America. Unlike in the mother country, vice-admiralty courts could be used for dealing with trade offenses, though there was also provision for such offenses to be tried by ordinary courts with juries. In the same year (1696) the government created the Board of Trade, whose special responsibilities included oversight of the colonies and of commerce.

With some amendments, the legislative structure just outlined lasted to 1776. Other more or less significant developments also took place by the middle of the eighteenth century. Restrictions were placed on some forms of colonial manufacturing that might have competed with that of Britain, mainly by forbidding exports of any manufactured goods across colonial boundaries: woollens (1699), hats (1732), iron (1750). This policy complemented British prohibitions on the emigration of skilled workmen and on the export of certain machines and tools. However, shipbuilding, a major and profitable colonial industry, and certain types of iron manufacturing were never forbidden. Encouragement was also given to commodity production useful to the mother country, notably naval stores and Indigo, by paying bounties on them as they entered Britain.

A striking piece of new legislation resulted in part from lobbying by sugar traders and illustrates the clash of interests within the system. British West Indian sugar had a virtual monopoly in the home market since, although heavily taxed, foreign sugar was taxed even more. A sugar lobby also sought a trade monopoly with the North American colonies, where distilleries used great quantities of non-British sugar products. The Molasses Act (1733) set a high duty on the import of foreign sugar, rum, and molasses into British North America. North Americans were also the main suppliers of provisions and timber products to the West Indian slave societies. If the French (and to a lesser extent the Dutch) could no longer sell the continentals sugar, they could also not pay for these vital goods, which might lead to a glut, forcing down their price to the British islands. The position was complex, since the imports and profits from the foreign West Indian trade and from the northern colonies' exports of rum helped pay for their British imports. This Act seemed to attempt to raise a revenue in North American ports, whereas most trade legislation did so at British ones. But another interpretation is that the high duties were meant to exclude or regulate rather than to raise revenue and, in fact, the British Government made little effort to enforce the Act. Widespread evasion continued even in times of war.

The operation of the commercial system has been viewed from several angles. One portrays it as working satisfactorily and to the advantage at least of Great Britain and the mainland colonies, whose commerce rapidly expanded. The most important North American commodity, tobacco, had a semi-protected market and found successful re-export destinations; by the 1750s the Chesapeake had begun to diversify, with wheat exports becoming important money-earners. The northern and middle colonies developed a considerable shipping sector, good export markets, and substantial craft and proto-manufacturing sectors in shipbuilding and iron; British restrictions on other forms of manufacturing had marginal impact, since capital was lacking and skilled labor expensive. Moreover, North Americans were able to import large and growing amounts of relatively cheap British manufactured goods, and their trade, shipping, and territory received the protection of the British military and the credit and insurance benefits of an expanding empire. Although enforcement was lax and smuggling occurred, the majority of officials were competent (in eighteenth-century terms) and the majority of transactions were legal. A differing interpretation emphasizes the prevalence of evasion (by collusion, fraud, and smuggling) and the looseness of enforcement. Therefore, ultimately market factors – supply and demand – not commercial legislation, formed the channels of trade.

One aspect of legislation which affected trade and which has received recent attention is the place of paper money and of credit. British and some colonial merchants certainly lobbied for restrictions on the issue in the colonies of paper money and bills, mainly to protect themselves against the depreciation of such instruments. Private banks were forbidden by law in 1741; in 1751 a Currency Act set certain restrictions on the issue of paper bills by the New England governments (*see* Chapter 6, §4). Later this and new legislation, together with the growing feeling that American trade was too closely tied to British credit and its sometimes frightening fluctuations, as well as the growth of Chesapeake planter indebtedness, provided a context for growing disillusionment with the workings of the commercial system.

The year 1748 saw the appointment of George Montagu Dunk, Earl of Halifax, as a strong reforming President of the Board of Trade. It was apparent that the Peace of Aix-la-Chapelle was only a temporary measure and that North America and the West Indies would have a central place in the coming struggle between France and Britain. Halifax's main concerns were therefore strategic rather than commercial, although ways of tightening up the enforcement of legislation and of increasing state revenues were also under active consideration. During the war years (1754–63), cooperation with the colonies rather than reform was obviously a paramount consideration, but sustained complaints about colonial trade with the French and Spanish in the West Indies, often carried out under special licences or flags of truce but seen as treasonable by many in the mother country, stimulated investigations and suggestions for action during the 1750s. After British victory these evasions, together with a huge budget deficit created by the war, provided conditions in which reform seemed crucial. Its main implementation was during George Grenville's premiership (*see* Chapter 11).

The bedrock of reform as it affected trade legislation was a drive for adequate enforcement in order to improve revenue collection. Executive threats of dismissal for absentee customs officers and other measures aimed at efficiency were followed by an Act (April 1763) for "the improvement of His Majesty's revenue of customs," which provided for the inspection of ships below 50 tons burden in coastal waters and sought to ensure cooperation between naval ships and customs officials in the prevention of smuggling. The government over the next two years also moved in response to long-standing reports of deficiencies in the Customs Service to increase the numbers of customs officials and provide for staffing by persons from Britain rather than local men who, experience seemed to show, were unwilling or unable to act forcefully. A Customs Fees Act, which tried to guarantee payments to colonial customs officers, became law in 1765 but created problems of enforcement.

Major parliamentary legislation also sought strict enforcement of the Acts of Trade. A complex "Bill for granting certain Duties in the British Colonies ..." became law in April 1764 and is now generally (perhaps misleadingly) known as the Sugar Act. It incorporated the permanent continuation of the Molasses Act of 1733 but with the duty lowered from 6d to 3d per gallon; a total prohibition of the import of foreign rum and spirits into the colonies; a requirement for increased documentation to be held by ships' captains in a wide variety of cases, including intercolonial trading; the extension of the list of enumerated products to cover pimento, coffee, cocoanuts, whalefins, raw silk, hides, and skins; a requirement that all duties and fines be paid in sterling; a stipulation that the burden of proof in the event of seizures for non-payment of duties should rest with the defendant; and a provision that the prosecutor or informant be allowed to choose the court, including vice-admiralty courts, in which he wished to have trade cases tried. The Act also made reference to a new vice-admiralty court, to which any case could be sent, and which was established in the autumn of 1764 at Halifax, Nova Scotia. In 1764 the government further legislated to extend the provisions of the Currency Act of 1751 to colonies from New York south, prohibiting paper bills of credit, hereafter to be issued, in any of His Majesty's colonies or plantations in America, from being declared to be a legal tender in payments of money; and to prevent the legal tender of such bills as are now subsisting from being prolonged beyond the Periods limited for calling in and sinking the same.

This Act was in fact aimed at preventing English and Scottish merchants in the Chesapeake tobacco trade from being paid in depreciated colonial paper.

To what extent the Stamp Act of 1765 may be viewed as trade rather than fiscal legislation is arguable; it certainly sought to raise money by duties on many commercial transactions, but some of its provisions (i.e., that stamps to the value of 4d be applied to bills of lading) were, perhaps, aimed at preventing fraud rather than obtaining revenue. It also gave the Halifax vice-admiralty court appellate jurisdiction and allowed all the vice-admiralty courts to hear cases arising from offenses against its provisions. But some Americans, notably Franklin, and some Englishmen argued that there was a difference between legislation to raise "internal" and "external" (i.e., customs or port duties) "taxes," and that the latter aspect of the old commercial system had been acceptable while the Stamp Act was not. Others joined to this or advanced separately the argument that the "old" commercial system had not sought to raise revenue, except as a kind of incidental method of enforcement, but only to regulate trade and manufacturing. The new system (i.e., 1764 and after) – "our newly adopted system of colonial policy," Burke called it – with its fiscal objectives, therefore broke a kind of original compact with the colonies. If Americans "share your taxes," will they not "claim the right of manufactures, of free trade, of every other privilege of the mother country?" (Simmons and Thomas, 1982–7, II: p. 83). But Grenville, his followers, and successors vigorously maintained that "the distinction between internal taxes and commercial regulation was a distinction without a difference. Paying duties upon imports was paying internal taxes ..." (Simmons and Thomas, 1982–7, II: p. 610), and that the Acts of Trade and Navigation had always included a substantial revenue component as well as regulatory purposes.

Certainly the Stamp Act created an opposition which forced all these questions into the public arena. Other Acts of the Grenville administration in 1765 were conciliatory, exempting undecked boats of under 20 tons used in the American coastal trade from the need to carry detailed documentation and allowing the direct export of colonial iron and lumber to Ireland. While repealing the Stamp Act in 1766, however, the Rockingham ministry did not uphold any idea that the Acts of Trade in their American context should be used only to shape and regulate commerce and not to raise a revenue. It reduced the duty on foreign molasses imported into North America to 1d per gallon but established the same tax for imports from the British islands and allowed the importation of foreign sugar into North America on payment of a duty of 5s per cwt. It also created two freeports in the Caribbean, a radical departure from precedent, but extended the requirements of earlier statutes that ships give bond not to land cargoes in Europe north of Cape Finisterre, except in Great Britain. The ministry's measures were conciliatory in that no further action was taken to tighten up customs or vice-admiralty jurisdiction, and it adopted a sympathetic attitude to the problems of American currency.

Rockingham's government had also contemplated but did not undertake a method of raising revenue by allowing the direct importation of certain specified European commodities into America on payment of duties at the port of entry – another break with the "old" system. Under the subsequent Pitt–Grafton administration the same idea formed the basis of the Townshend Duties Act of 1767. Townshend claimed to base his policy "upon laying taxes upon America, but not internal taxes, because though he did not acknowledge the distinction it was accepted by many Americans and this was sufficient" (Simmons and Thomas, 1982–7, II: p. 464). He also believed in adequate enforcement, and the Townshend Act allowed the issue at will of writs of assistance by the supreme or superior court in each colony. This was accompanied by legislation placing the management of the customs service in America under a new American Board of Commissioners in Boston. In March 1768 another Act created three new superior vice-admiralty courts (Boston, Philadelphia, Charles Town) to add to that at Halifax. The creation of an American Civil List was also expected to improve enforcement by reducing the dependence of colonial officials on popular assemblies.

Lord North's government did not materially add to these measures and, of course, repealed all the Townshend Duties except that on tea (*see* Chapter 13, §7). In fact North sought conciliation. He refused to contemplate further reforms in the Act of Trade, since it was obvious that the government was powerless properly to enforce them, and legislated in 1773 to allow some relief from the Currency Act. Colonies would be able to establish loan offices issuing legal tender bills for public obligations. North's government in addition legislated on an annual basis to allow certain concessions to American exports; the famous Tea Act did not alter the duty levied on tea imports into America and was meant to lower the actual price of tea to Americans.

3. COMMERCE AND REVOLUTION

Much of the legislation discussed above represented responses to reports of the difficulties of enforcement and administration in the colonies. The Sugar Act sought to take account of years of complaints about deficiencies in the Acts of Trade and Navigation, the Townshend Acts in part to correct deficiencies arising from the operation of the Grenville legislation. However, there was no coherent or at least no successful overall administrative review, and the operation of the Acts of Trade remained subject to technical and administrative problems. Characteristic of the 1760s were continual bickerings among governors, customs officials, and naval commanders – the three main agents of enforcement – who were, in fact, rivals for the rewards of successful searches and seizures, since some payments based on the values of the cargoes were made to them. Enforcement came also to rely more and more on the navy, whose presence in North American waters was considerably increased. Admiral Lord Colvill, the naval Commander-in-Chief from 1763 to 1766, reputedly hoped to make his fortune from customs seizures and tended to treat colonial governors like midshipmen. His and other officers' brusque attitudes led contemporaries to ask "Are the gentlemen of the navy judges of the nature of commerce and the liberty of the subject?" Later, the patriotic historian George Bancroft wrote of "A curiously devised system, which bribed the whole navy of England to make war on colonial trade." When the British Government sent regiments to Boston in 1768, it also seemed that the army was being brought in to do on land what the navy did at sea, particularly to support the American Board of Customs Commissioners.

One famous early struggle, preceding Grenville's reforms, involved writs of assistance and a legal argument in Boston in 1760–1 over the rights of customs officials to search for suspected goods under their authority. The Superior Court, after a reference back to London, eventually found in favor of the officials, though even in the future these writs were used only with difficulty and were challenged in the colonial courts. Here the argument over the enforcement of trade laws, linked to the politics of the day, eventually led on to a general statement by James Otis that certain forms of parliamentary legislation attacking liberty and property were void. The Boston merchant community (perhaps jealous of the non-enforcement of customs legislation in neighboring Rhode Island) and the Boston press joined in the condemnations of the "rats" gnawing at the subject's property. On 4 January 1762 the *Boston Gazette* appealed to the rights of Englishmen against "the great *patrons* of this writ." Governor Bernard believed that Thomas Hutchinson's connection with "the Admiralty and Customs House," through his granting writs of assistance, made his house the target of the Boston mob during the Stamp Act disturbances. Later the Townshend Act's amendments to writs of assistance were themselves poorly drafted, and it is not clear how often they were successfully used after 1767. What is clear is that, in the New England colonies, the writs entered popular and political rhetoric as despotic instruments that allowed brutal customs officers to raid the homes of innocent families, and were seen as similar to the general warrants used in London against John Wilkes, friend of America and another victim of oppression and corruption. General warrants were condemned as illegal in Britain both by the Court of Common Pleas and by parliamentary resolution. The use in America of writs of assistance, which so closely resembled them, added to colonial grievances, to the sense of unequal treatment.

The other instruments and agencies for operating the revitalized commercial system were also condemned with similar language and charges. The vice-admiralty courts, unlike the revenue courts which tried trade offenses in England, were juryless. Their judges were often Englishmen appointed in England. Their officials had an interest in the fees they could collect. Cases were often brought before them as a result of information laid by persons who would also gain financially from conviction. Similar charges were brought against active customs officials. In the political climate that prevailed in many colonies after 1765 these facts were used to bewail the inequality of American and British rights and the alleged cavalier disregard of British ministries for American liberty and property. The colonial courts became involved both in writs of assistance and in vice-admiralty cases, demonstrating the general problem of trade enforcement, since it was commonplace for them not only to find against customs officers but to admit counter-claims for false arrest and the like and award substantial damages against them, even to imprison them. Governors, even if well disposed, could not provide protection or redress. Sometimes customs agents could find no lawyers willing to act for them and were forced to appeal to or return to England for assistance. It is also obvious that crowd or group action was another obstacle to enforcement and that the threat of violence shadowed customs and naval personnel.

In number the cases of mob or crowd action were in fact few (and, unlike such affrays in eighteenth-century Britain, involved no deaths), but they were widely reported and helped to shape public opinion in America and government actions in the mother country. In Charles Town, South Carolina, in May 1767 Captain James Hawker was attacked by a mob led by gentlemen, who (he claimed) insulted the King, Parliament, and the British flag. In Norfolk, Virginia, in September 1767 the people, headed by the mayor, attacked Captain Morgan and his men, who had come ashore looking for deserters. Considerable parliamentary attention was given to the seizure in June 1768 of the *Liberty*, owned by John Hancock of Boston, which led to threats to the American Customs Commissioners and their flight from the city. Two years later, a New Jersey collector was severely beaten and his son beaten, tarred, and

FIGURE 14 "The burning of the Gaspée" near Providence, Rhode Island, on the night of 9 June 1772 (painting by Charles DeWolf Brownell, 1892)

feathered. In 1772 the burning of the royal navy schooner *Gaspée* and the wounding of her commanding officer caused outrage in British Government circles (*see* figure 14).

Such incidents, although sometimes involving attacks on ships' captains who were known or believed to be customs racketeers, were seen by the home authorities with other forms of colonial resistance as evidence of the need for severe responses. Among Americans (and they were widely reported in the press) they were incorporated into the prevailing political rhetoric and ideology. Novel and oppressive legislation enforced by brutal and corrupt agents was part of the attack on liberty. Such beliefs came to be held by otherwise conservative merchants such as Henry Laurens of South Carolina, whose experiences with the customs service led him to radical pamphleteering and ultimately to revolution.

Yet there is some debate as to how far colonial opinion was ready to deny the Acts of Trade and call for free trade. The most common patriot point of view from about 1765 onwards seems to have been to deny that the raising of revenue was a legitimate part of the Acts but to assert that the colonists accepted an obligation to

> carry the chief of their produce there [Great Britain] and to take off her manufactures in return; and as they must conform to her price in both buying and selling, one would think the advantage she reaps by their trade sufficient.

There was a strength of feeling in the northern and middle colonies for freer intercourse with the West Indies, expressed, for example, in an outspoken New York merchants' petition presented to Parliament in 1767 and some (largely ineffectual) attempts at encouraging home manufactures in order to lessen dependence on British imports during and after the Stamp Act crisis. By the 1770s protests at British restrictions on manufacturing were appearing in petitions to the mother country. There was also disquiet about a British credit crisis in 1772–3, which had severe American effects, particularly in the Chesapeake, and may have further increased doubts about the real benefits of the colonies' place in the existing system. But if statements were made or positions taken that seemed to look beyond the Acts of Trade and Navigation to the rise of America as an independent economy with a developing manufacturing sector and a profitable export trade of great agricultural surpluses to the rest of the world, it is doubtful if these had much general circulation before 1776 or were important in the causes of the Revolution.

On the British side no politician failed to defend the Acts of Trade and Navigation. Indeed Chatham in January 1775

> observed that if ... the views of America were ultimately pointed to defeating the act of navigation, and the other regulatory acts, so wisely framed and calculated for that reciprocity of interests, so essentially necessary to the grandeur and prosperity of the whole empire ... there was no person present, however zealous, would be readier than himself to resist and crush any attempt of that nature in the first instance. (Simmons and Thomas, 1982–7, V: p. 273)

Burke, Barré, and other friends of the American and the merchant community tended to take the line that the evident and increasing opposition to British rule, including British commercial legislation, was due to mistaken British policy after 1763 – not only the introduction of the Stamp Act but the attempt to collect substantial revenues by the Sugar Act and the Rockingham legislation of 1766. A return to the status quo before the Sugar Act was advisable, presumably including a return to the lax enforcement of legislation. Their argument rested on an almost religious belief in the importance of North America's commerce to Britain and other parts of the empire. Its loss would mean ruin. "You have not a loom nor an anvil but what is stamped with America," Barré told the House of Commons in March 1774, and Shelburne, in December 1775, reminded the House of Lords of "the great Palladium of our Commerce, that great source of all the advantages that we now happily enjoy."

Lord North and his ministers countered with the arguments that Americans indeed wished to destroy British commerce, since they were aiming at the dismantling of the Acts of Trade, and anyway, when the "clearest rights" of the legislative power of Britain were invaded and denied and when in consequence the people so denying were in "actual and open rebellion," that then there were points of greater importance to be settled than those of "commerce and manufacture..."

Before 1776 the struggle between America and Britain was largely fought out in terms of attacks on each other's commerce, with trade boycotts on the American side after the Stamp Act and the Townshend Duties and with movements to greater American self-sufficiency. Some of the bitterness of the conflict was undoubtedly due to the economic recession following the Seven Years' War. Yet from about 1770 to 1774 British–American trade was possibly never greater and customs revenues never higher. In 1774 and 1775 British retaliation against colonial actions was directed first against Boston as a commercial center, then against the trade of all 13 colonies. On the American side independence meant throwing open American ports to all comers. During the war, trade questions were obscured. After it they once more became central, stimulating the move towards federal union, and causing many Americans to protest as vigorously against their exclusion from the British commercial system as they had before 1776 at its enforcement.

FURTHER READING

Andrews, C. M.: *The Colonial Period of American History*, vol. IV, *England's Colonial and Commercial Policy* (New Haven, Conn.: 1938; repr. New Haven and London: Yale University Press, 1964).

Barrow, T. C.: *Trade and Empire: the British Customs Service in Colonial America, 1660–1775* (Cambridge, Mass.: Harvard University Press, 1967).

Dickerson, O. M.: *The Navigation Acts and the American Revolution* (Philadelphia, 1951; repr. New York: A. S. Barnes and Co., 1963).

Ernst, Joseph A.: *Money and Politics in America, 1755–1775* (Chapel Hill: University of North Carolina Press, 1973).

McCusker, J. J., and Menard, R. M.: *The Economy of British America, 1607–1789* (Chapel Hill and London: University of North Carolina Press, 1985).

Simmons, R. C., and Thomas, P. D. G.: *Proceedings and Debates of the British Parliaments Respecting North America, 1754–1783*, vols. I–VI (White Plains, NY: Kraus-Thomson, 1982–7).

Tucker, R. W., and Henderson, D. C.: *The Fall of the First British Empire: Origins of the War of American Independence* (Baltimore and London: Johns Hopkins University Press, 1982).

Ubbelohde, Carl: *The Vice-Admiralty Courts and the American Revolution* (Chapel Hill: University of North Carolina Press, 1960).

17

Ongoing disputes over the prerogative, 1763–1776

JACK P. GREENE

HISTORIANS have traditionally stressed the centrality of the issue of parliamentary authority in the constitutional debates that preceded the American Revolution, and they have been correct to do so. Beginning with the Stamp Act crisis in 1764–6, the long-standing conflicts over the relative balance between prerogative power and colonial rights, conflicts that had been an endemic feature of metropolitan–colonial relations ever since the middle of the seventeenth century, had been subordinated to the new and more pressing debate over the extent of Parliament's colonial authority, over the respective jurisdictions of Parliament and the several legislatures in the American colonies. Yet, the older conflict over the boundaries of metropolitan executive authority in the colonies remained alive. Manifest in a variety of important incidents and controversies, it continued throughout the era from 1763 to 1776 to function as a major irritant in constitutional and political relations between metropolis and colonies.

1. 1763–6

Indeed, not since the late 1740s had there been so many serious controversies between metropolitan authorities and local legislatures as there were in the years just before and during the Stamp Act crisis. During the early 1760s, there were several serious confrontations over the extent of the King's prerogative in the colonies. Though they were often intensely fought, most of these, such as the altercation that occurred in Massachusetts in the fall of 1762 over Governor Francis Bernard's attempts to expend public funds without prior legislative authorization, elicited a sudden burst of protest but were soon resolved and rarely involved authorities in London.

In a few instances, however, these disputes lasted for years and seriously disrupted provincial political life. Such had been the case in Virginia, where the so-called Two Penny Act Controversy persisted for the better part of six years between 1758 and 1764. Involving the Crown's insistence by royal instruction that, no matter what the apparent exigencies of the situation, the Virginia legislature could pass no law that modified a measure already confirmed by the Crown without a clause suspending its operation until it had been reviewed and approved in London, this dispute elicited widespread denunciation among Virginians of the Crown's attempt to use its prerogative powers to reduce the scope of legislative authority in the colonies.

At roughly the same time, New York was the scene of an even more debilitating battle between metropolitan prerogative and colonial privileges. Throughout the early 1760s, a running dispute raged between Lieutenant Governor Cadwallader Colden and local leaders over two related issues: the tenure of the colony's superior court judges and the authority of the Governor and the Council to overrule jury decisions on appeal from the defendant.

Since the Revolution Settlement in 1688–1701 the Crown's judges in Britain had held office during good behavior, which meant, in effect, for life. But metropolitan officials had always resisted the extension of this practice to the colonies, where, they argued, it would be "subversive of that Policy by which alone Colonies can be kept in a just dependance upon the Government of the Mother Country."[1] Instead, they insisted that colonial judges, like English judges before the Glorious Revolution, should hold their commissions only during the Crown's pleasure. Such a tenure made colonial judges, also like English judges under the Stuarts, subject to removal whenever they decided a case contrary to metropolitan orthodoxy, thereby depriving them of that celebrated independence enjoyed by judges in Britain.

Notwithstanding metropolitan attitudes on this subject, however, New York judges had enjoyed tenure during good behavior since the mid-1740s, a privilege that had been wrested for them from a weak executive. When, upon the death of Chief Justice James De Lancey in 1760, metropolitan authorities refused to grant similar terms to his successor, New York leaders, unsurprisingly, regarded that ruling as an attack upon an established constitutional right. The ensuing fight over this question between the Assembly and Colden persisted for two years, during which the first Crown appointee resigned in frustration and the Board of Trade responded by issuing a categorical general instruction prohibiting governors of all colonies from appointing judges during good behavior and thereby setting the stage for similar altercations in New Jersey, South Carolina, and North Carolina during the following decade. In all these colonies, the local political establishments lost the battle for colonial judicial independence. Deeply resented, this defeat was attributed by colonial leaders to an aggressive prerogative that was bent upon depriving colonists of constitutional protections routinely enjoyed by Britons in the home islands.

The second issue in New York arose out of Colden's decision in 1764 to hear an appeal from Waddel Cunningham in a case in which a jury had convicted him of assaulting Thomas Forsey and awarded Forsey damages of £1,500. Local leaders regarded Colden's actions as a judicial innovation that struck at the sanctity of the jury system by enabling a governor to subvert the Englishman's traditional right to trial by jury. The decision of the British Privy Council in 1765, at the height of the Stamp Act crisis, to back Colden and order him to hear the appeal raised the specter of still another unwarranted exertion of prerogative by Crown officials in the colonies and called forth condemnation not just by New York leaders but by the Stamp Act Congress. When it met in New York in October 1765, that body pointedly endorsed trial by jury as the right of all British subjects, whether in the colonies or in England. Unlike the controversy over judicial tenure, however, this dispute was settled in favor of New York when the Board of Trade, in consultation with the Crown's chief law officers in London, ruled against Colden's hearing such appeals.

Similarly prolonged and even more intense disputes left both South Carolina and Jamaica without an operative legislature for long periods and were resolved only by the resignation or removal of the royal governors. In South Carolina, beginning in September 1762, legislative government came to a virtual halt when the Commons House of Assembly, despite some minor irregularities in a by-election held the previous March, voted to admit the Charleston merchant CHRISTOPHER GADSDEN as representative from St. Paul's Parish. Endeavoring to force the Commons House to pass a new election law conformable to metropolitan stipulations, Governor Thomas Boone seized this occasion to illustrate the looseness of the existing law. Refusing to administer the oath of office to Gadsden, he charged the Commons House with acting contrary to the existing election law, precipitately dissolved that body, and called for new elections.

When the new legislature met in the fall, it denounced Boone's behavior as a blatant violation of its exclusive constitutional right to judge the legitimacy of the elections of its own members, a right that had been long enjoyed by the British House of Commons and had not been disputed in South Carolina for nearly 40 years. Accordingly, the Commons House voted to do no further business with Boone until he had apologized for his actions. Boone's refusal to apologize resulted in a complete stoppage of legislative business for the next 19 months. Despite the urgent need at one point for legislative action to defend the back country against attacks by Creek Indians, the Commons House stubbornly refused to resume legislative intercourse with the Crown's executive until May 1764, after Boone, in despair, had left for England to seek support from metropolitan authorities.

In Jamaica, Governor William Henry Lyttelton was reluctantly drawn into a controversy in which he took measures that also could be seen as an effort to restrict the customary parliamentary privileges of the local legislature. Members of the Jamaica House of Assembly had long enjoyed exemption from suits at law during legislative sessions, and when, in late 1764, court officials seized the coach and horses of representative John Olyphant in partial fulfillment of a judgment against Olyphant, the Jamaica House took into custody and charged with contempt both the two judicial officers who had carried out the seizure and the plaintiff in the suit.

These events set the stage for a long and bitter impasse between the Assembly and the Governor. Unable to resolve the matter by informal persuasion, Lyttelton, in response to a petition from the jailed men, issued a writ of habeas corpus to free them, whereupon the Assembly passed a series of resolutions denouncing this action as an unwarranted and unconstitutional violation of its privileges, and refused to do any further business with Lyttelton until he had made reparation. The London authorities took Lyttelton's side in this controversy, and over the following year Lyttelton thrice dissolved the Assembly and called new elections. But the Assembly remained adamant and did not again transact business with the royal Governor until after Lyttelton had been recalled in the summer of 1766, more than 18 months after the onset of the dispute.

With the exception of the Two Penny Act Controversy and the quarrel over judicial tenure in New York, all of these incidents arose out of maladroit or unavoidable actions by Crown governors in the colonies and were not immediately provoked by directives from London. In both the South Carolina and Jamaica cases, metropolitan officials eventually found that effective government could not be restored unless they catered to local opinion by removing the offending governors, and they actually condemned Boone for his rash behavior in stimulating and perpetuating discord in South Carolina. In every case, however, the actions of the governors had been to some considerable measure conditioned by the growing insistence by metropolitan authorities that governors strictly observe their instructions from the Crown and resist efforts by the assemblies to increase the scope of their authority. In the Jamaican case, moreover, metropolitan officials strongly backed Lyttelton until after it had become clear that he had lost all political credibility within the colony.

Underlining the persistence of the long-standing tensions between metropolitan authorities in London and local legislatures in the colonies, these battles all revolved around the familiar issues of the previous century: whether the royal prerogative in the colonies should be placed under the same restraints to which it had been subjected in Britain in the wake of the Glorious Revolution, whether royal instructions had constitutional standing, whether the rights of British people in the colonies were equal to the rights of those who continued to reside in the home islands, whether colonial legislatures were entitled to the same privileges and powers enjoyed by the metropolitan House of Commons, and whether custom had the same constitutional authority in the colonies as it had traditionally had in Britain itself. Underlying these battles, moreover, were the same old fears. While metropolitan authorities worried that the continual grasping after power by these distant colonial legislatures would eventually erode all control from the center, colonial leaders were anxious lest the Crown's continuing efforts to extend the "prerogative beyond all bounds"[2] should sooner or later cheat the colonists "out of their liberties" and thereby actually degrade them "from the rank of Englishmen" to "a condition of slavery."[3]

2. 1767–76

Throughout the last half of the 1760s, during the crisis over the Townshend Acts, this ancient contest between prerogative and liberty was superseded or at least pushed into the background by the debate over Parliament's relationship to the colonies. Coincident with the repeal of most of the Townshend Duties, however, a new series of quarrels developed over the scope of the Crown's colonial authority, quarrels that punctuated the so-called period of quiet during the early 1770s and revealed that the debate over the limits of the Crown's prerogative was still a live and profoundly significant issue between metropolis and colonies.

Major controversies developed in several colonies. In Georgia during the spring of 1771, Governor James Wright, acting on directions from Lord Hillsborough, Secretary of State for the Colonies in London, rejected the Georgia Commons' nominee as speaker, and thereby initiated a dispute over the Governor's right to negative the legislature's choice of speaker that agitated Georgia politics for nearly 21 months. In proprietary Maryland in late 1770, following the failure of the two houses of the legislature to agree on a bill for that purpose, Governor Robert Eden's proclamation setting the scale of officers' fees instigated a three-year controversy over the Governor's authority by virtue of proprietary prerogative to set the fees of public officers without legislative consent. In North Carolina in late 1773, the Assembly devised a new superior court law that pointedly ignored a recent royal instruction forbidding colonial governors to assent to any laws providing for the attachment of the property of non-residents in suits for debts. The ensuing dispute seriously disrupted legislative affairs in the colony and left it without superior courts for the last three years before the Declaration of Independence.

Even more serious were conflicts in two other colonies, Massachusetts and South Carolina. In the former, Crown officials led by Hillsborough sought by instruction in the summer of 1768 to punish Boston for its leading role in opposing the Townshend Acts by encouraging Governor Francis Bernard to call the Massachusetts General Court to meet in Cambridge or Salem instead of in Boston, the capital and customary meeting-place of the legislature. When Bernard in June 1769 and his successor Thomas Hutchinson in March 1770 acted on this instruction by removing the sessions to Cambridge, they set off a constitutional crisis of major proportions.

At issue was the question of whether the Crown by virtue of its prerogative powers could legally employ the royal instructions to alter or violate established customary constitutional practices in the colony. With metropolitan authorities standing firmly behind him, Hutchinson argued that he was bound to obey his instructions, while a series of General Courts insisted that instructions could not supersede the colony's basic rights as manifest in provincial laws and customs, railed against the use of ministerial mandates to overturn the settled constitution of the colony, and charged the Crown officials with trying to incapacitate the legislature so that it would be less able to resist efforts by both Parliament and prerogative to subvert colonial liberty. Only after a protracted struggle of more than two years was this controversy ended, in June 1772, with an inconclusive compromise.

The more prolonged Wilkes fund controversy in South Carolina was never resolved. For several decades, the South Carolina Commons House had assumed authority to issue money from the public treasury without the consent of the Governor and Council, a practice the British House of Commons had never been bold enough to attempt. The existence of this peculiar constitutional tradition first came to the attention of London officials following the Commons House vote in December 1769 of a gift of £1,500 sterling to the Society of the Gentlemen Supporters of the Bill of Rights, a London organization formed to pay the debts of John Wilkes, who over the previous few years had successfully set himself up as the chief symbol of resistance to arbitrary ministerial authority in the metropolis. London officials responded to this audacious act by issuing an instruction on 14 April 1770 that threatened both the royal Governor and the Treasurer with severe penalties if they permitted any money, including the sum voted to Wilkes, to be issued from the South Carolina treasury without executive approval.

Regarding this instruction as an attack upon a constitutional custom it had long enjoyed, the South Carolina Commons House refused to act in accordance with its stipulations. For the next five years, the instruction was the central issue in South Carolina politics. The normal processes of legislative government were entirely suspended. No annual tax bill was passed in the colony after 1769 and no legislation at all after February 1771, and local leaders became increasingly resentful of what they regarded as an unconstitutional effort by metropolitan authorities to deprive the Commons House of its customary legal rights through the use of what they denounced as ministerial mandates. Only the outbreak of the War for Independence and the assumption of legislative authority by a provincial congress in 1775 brought this bitter altercation to an end.

3. SIGNIFICANCE

With the exception of the Maryland controversy, all of these disputes revolved around metropolitan efforts to use royal instructions to curb the power of local assemblies. In one sense, they were merely the latest rounds in the ongoing contest in the extended polity of the British Empire between central prerogative power and local colonial rights as championed by the several provincial assemblies. From the 1670s on, and more systematically since the late 1740s, the "Governing of Colonies by Instructions," as Franklin observed in January 1772, had "long been a favourite Point with Ministers" in London.[4] Ministers, they believed, had made so many "daring and injurious attempt[s] to raise and establish a despotic power over them"[5] that, as the Maryland lawyer Charles Carroll of Carrollton remarked during the fee controversy in Maryland in May 1773, it had long since become "a common observation confirmed by general experience" that any "claim in the colony-governments of an extraordinary power as ... part of the prerogative" was "sure to meet with the encouragement and support of the ministry in Great-Britain."[6]

From the perspective of the crisis over the Stamp and Townshend Acts and the debate over Parliament's new pretensions to authority over the internal affairs of the colonies, however, these old questions about the Crown's relationship to the colonies acquired a new and heightened urgency. If, as an impressive number of colonial spokesmen had begun to argue during the late 1760s, sovereignty within the empire rested not in the Crown-in-Parliament but in the Crown alone, then it became especially important for the colonists to establish the boundaries not just of parliamentary but also of royal authority in the colonies. For that reason, colonial defenders in all of the battles of the early 1770s revealed a pronounced tendency to build upon their own particular local constitutional heritages to argue, as their predecessors in earlier generations had often done, that, no less than in Britain itself, the Crown's authority – the freedom of its "will" – in the colonies had been effectively limited over the previous century by specific idiosyncratic constitutional developments in each of the colonies. Again just as in Britain, these developments had led, colonial leaders believed, irreversibly in the direction of increasing authority in the hands of the local legislatures and greater restrictions on the prerogatives of the Crown. By this process, they argued, the rights of the inhabitants in the colonies had gradually been secured against the power of the metropolis.

As refined and elaborated during the contests of the early 1770s, this view of colonial constitutional history powerfully helped to reinforce traditional views of the colonial legislatures as both the primary guardians of the local rights of the corporate entities over which they presided and, like Parliament itself in Britain, the dynamic forces in shaping the colonial constitutions. Insofar as the constitution of the empire was concerned, this emphasis upon the peculiarity and integrity of the several colonial constitutions comprised a vigorous assertion of what one recent scholar has referred to as constitutional multiplicity that had profound implications for the new, post-1764 debate over the nature and location of sovereignty within the empire.

For, together with the emerging conviction that Parliament had no authority over the colonies, the renewed contention that the Crown's colonial authority was also limited by local constitutions as they had emerged out of not just the colonists' inherited rights as Englishmen and their charters but also local usage and custom pushed the colonists towards a wholly new conception of sovereignty in an extended polity like that of the early modern British Empire. That conception implied that ultimate constitutional authority – sovereignty – lay not in any institution or collection of institutions at the center of the empire but in the separate constitutions of each of the many separate political entities of which the empire was composed.

That by no means all of the constitutional grievances that drove the 13 colonies to revolt could be laid at the door of Parliament was dramatically revealed in the Declaration of Independence (*see* chapter 27). Although Parliament was certainly responsible for those grievances the colonists found most objectionable, especially the effort to tax them without their consent, 17 of the 18 counts of unconstitutional behavior by the metropolitan government listed in that document referred to actions or policies undertaken not by the Crown-in-Parliament but by the Crown and its officers acting in their executive capacities. The content of this list made clear that the Crown's ancient claim for more extensive prerogative powers in the colonies than it enjoyed in Britain continued to be an important source of unease throughout the constitutional struggles that preceded the American Revolution. Indeed, the many continuing contests between prerogative and liberty during the years between 1763 and 1776 only gave added force to the conviction, explicitly articulated in the Declaration, that a connection with Britain of the kind advocated by many colonial leaders from the late 1760s through mid-1776 – that is, one through the Crown independent of Parliament – would not provide a safe foundation for the security of colonial rights.

REFERENCES

1. Board of Trade Report, 11 November 1761, in *Documents Relative to the Colonial History of the State of New York*, ed. E. B. O'Callaghan (Albany: Weed, Parsons, 1853–87), vol. 7, 473–5.
2. James Otis: *A Vindication of the Conduct of the House of Representatives of the Province of Massachusetts-Bay* (Boston: Edes & Gill, 1762), 51.
3. [Nicholas Bourke]: *The Privileges of the Island of Jamaica Vindicated* (London: J. Williams, 1766), 47, 64.
4. Benjamin Franklin to James Bowdoin, 13 January 1772, in *The Papers of Benjamin Franklin*, ed. Leonard W. Labaree et al., 26 vols. to date (New Haven, Conn.: Yale University Press, 1959–), vol. 19, 11.
5. William Bollan: *The Free Britons Memorial* (London: J. Williams, 1769), 15.
6. First Citizen's Third Letter, 6 May 1773, in *Maryland and the Empire, 1773: The Antilon-First Citizen Letters*, ed. Peter S. Onuf (Baltimore: Johns Hopkins University Press, 1974), 149.

FURTHER READING

Greene, Jack P.: *The Nature of Colony Constitutions: Two Pamphlets on the Wilkes Fund Controversy by Sir Egerton Leigh and Arthur Lee* (Columbia: University of South Carolina Press, 1970).
——: *Peripheries and Center: Constitutional Development in the Extended Polities of the British Empire and the United States, 1607–1788* (Athens: University of Georgia Press, 1986).
——: *The Quest for Power: the Lower Houses of Assembly in the Southern Royal Colonies, 1689–1776* (Chapel Hill: University of North Carolina Press, 1963).
Klein, Milton M.: "Prelude to Revolution in New York: Jury Trials and Judicial Tenure," *William and Mary Quarterly*, 17 (1960), 439–62.
Knollenberg, Bernhard, *Origin of the American Revolution, 1759–1766* (New York: Macmillan 1960).
Lord, Donald C., and Calhoon, Robert M.: "The Removal of the Massachusetts General Court from Boston, 1769–1772," *Journal of American History*, 55 (1969), 735–55.
Metcalf, George: *Royal Government and Political Conflict in Jamaica, 1729–1783* (London: University of London Press, 1965).
Peter S. Onuf (ed.): *Maryland and the Empire, 1773: the Antillon-First Citizen Letters* (Baltimore: Johns Hopkins University Press, 1974).

18

Bishops and other ecclesiastical issues, to 1776

FREDERICK V. MILLS, SR.

THE Treaty of Paris ended the Seven Years' War in Europe and the French and Indian War in America. By this treaty Great Britain gained French Canada, the Spanish Floridas, all North America to the Mississippi, much of the West Indies, and India. The military success of the British meant that the freshly acquired territory in the New World would be organized according to the directions of King and Parliament. Then, too, colonial policy as it related to the previously developed colonies was subject to review. Between 1763 and 1776 the development, revision, and implementation of policy for British America was the focal point of activity within the empire. The governance of Canada by royal proclamation until the enactment of the Quebec Act in 1774 and the announcement of the Proclamation Line in 1763 foreshadowed the coming of a new era. This shift in policy from "salutary neglect" in the pre-1750s to one of imperial direction was a change of major importance.

1. ARCHBISHOP SECKER'S INITIATIVE

The structuring of imperial policy provided an opportunity for advocates of the Church of England to press their case to King George III and his ministers for support in extending the Church as a Christianizing and culturalizing agent in British America. To churchmen the advancement of the Anglican Communion spread the Christian gospel but had the added benefit of promoting loyalty to the British Constitution and hence stabilizing society. The Archbishop of Canterbury, Thomas Secker, took charge of the effort to extend the Church into the newly acquired territories and to strengthen it where it already existed in America. He confided to a long-time promoter of the colonial church, Dr. Samuel Johnson, President of King's College, New York City, "Probably our ministry will be concerting schemes this summer, against the next session of Parliament, for the settlement of His Majesty's dominions; and then we must try our utmost for bishops" (Mills, 1978, p. 29).

It was the office of bishop, of all the features of the Anglican Communion, that provoked controversy between churchmen and dissenters on both sides of the Atlantic. To churchmen a bishop was a third order of the clergy, consecrated and essential to the existence of the Church in addition to his royal appointment. Dissenters, those who opposed the Church of England and rejected communion with it, viewed bishops as royal officials subsidized by Parliament and ecclesiastically unnecessary for a church. The possibility that such a royal ecclesiastical person might be sent to a colony or region where dissenters were dominant, e.g., Massachusetts or New England, was regarded as a threat to the internal colonial constitution. Indeed, it was primarily the constitutional-political implications of Anglican episcopacy that caused the issue

FIGURE 15 American colonists chase an Anglican bishop onto a ship named the "Hilsborough": a hostile American cartoon representing the Whig and Congregationalist point of view of what might have happened had Archbishop Secker's plan, supported by the Secretary of State for the Colonies Lord Hillsborough, to send a bishop to North America been implemented.

of a colonial episcopate to become intertwined with the mounting tensions between Whitehall and the colonies between 1763 and 1776.

The Church of England in British America in 1763 was the established church in the five colonies from Maryland to Georgia and in the counties surrounding New York City. In the dozen years before the outbreak of the War for Independence, Anglicanism experienced remarkable growth from New England to Georgia. The Society for the Promotion of Christian Knowledge and the Society for the Propagation of the Gospel in Foreign Parts were major contributors to this advance. But a persistent problem was the absence of a bishop to perform ordination, confirmation, and the consecration of churches. Royal governors acted as ordinaries of the Bishop of London, in whose diocese the colonies were located, but they were hardly a substitute for a bishop. Nor were commissaries, licensed by the Bishop of London, although they could convene, examine, and reprove the clergy; but they could not ordain, and their decisions were subject to appeal to the Bishop of London.

Archbishop Thomas Secker, assisted by the Archbishop of York, Robert Hay Drummond, petitioned King and ministry in 1764 to procure bishops for British America, including the British West Indies. Their approach was low-keyed and highly confidential. Secker, as a member of the Privy Council, naturally would be consulted on ecclesiastical matters. But, unexpectedly, the Reverend East Apthorp, SPG missionary in Cambridge, Massachusetts, published in 1763 *Considerations on the Institution and Conduct of the SPG*. Apthorp intended to vindicate the SPG, but the inclusion of the subject of episcopacy in his treatise ignited a controversy. Jonathan Mayhew, a Congregational minister from Boston, challenged Apthorp's assessment of the SPG and charged that a plot, including an episcopate, was afoot "to root out all New England churches" (Bridenbaugh, 1972, pp. 224–9) (*see* figure 15). Mayhew's counter-blast in his *Observations on the Charter* was so severe that Archbishop Secker, writing anonymously, supplied the rebuttal in *An Answer to Dr. Mayhew's Observations on the Character and Conduct of the SPG*. On the matter of an episcopate, Secker stated that the bishop would not reside in New England but only visit there and instead reside in a colony that invited him. No tax support would be sought, no political influence exerted. In past clashes between dissenters and churchmen, their disagreements ranged over many issues, but after the Apthorp–Mayhew encounter the other issues became secondary to the subject of a colonial episcopate.

In correspondence with Dr. Samuel Johnson in May 1764, Archbishop Secker expressed guarded optimism about the episcopal plan but cautioned that it might depend on "various circumstances." What had happened was that two ministries in four years had fallen and a third was likely to be changed. After a dispute over war policy, William Pitt resigned in October 1761. Lord Bute, his successor, did not last two years in office. The Duke of Newcastle, after a disagreement with George Grenville over the conduct of the Treasury, left office. At the time Secker wrote he could not know that in 1765, Grenville, whose ministry gave the episcopal plan "a hearing," would fall from power even before the repeal of the Stamp Act. Understandably the Archbishop advised his American friend, "I beg you attempt nothing without the advice of the Society, or of the bishops" (Mills, 1978, pp. 28–34). The problem of ministerial instability continued until Lord North came to power in 1770, but his ministry, like those of his predecessors, was reluctant to introduce intentionally measures that would generate controversy as the episcopal issue had.

2. THE CAMPAIGN OF DRS. JOHNSON AND CHANDLER

In spite of these conditions Thomas B. Chandler, supported by Dr. Johnson, called a voluntary convention of Anglican clergy to meet in Elizabeth Town, New Jersey, in October 1766. The convention's sole purpose was "to use their joint influence and endeavors *to obtain the happiness of bishops*" (Mills, 1978, p. 48). Nineteen clergy were present, from Connecticut, New York, New Jersey, and Pennsylvania. Dr. Johnson, Dr. Chandler, Samuel Seabury, Charles Inglis, Myles Cooper, Jeremiah Leaming, Abraham Jarves, and Bela Hubbard were there. Richard Peters (rector of Christ and St. Peter's churches in Philadelphia) and his assistant, William Sturgeon, attended. Two prominent clergy, Provost William Smith of the College of Philadelphia and Henry Caner from Boston, were absent. Zeal for their church, which in most cases was their adopted faith, was the moving force behind their High Church view on episcopacy. The completion of their historic and apostolic tradition was at stake, and no substitute for bishops was acceptable. To this end petitions were sent to the Archbishop of Canterbury, the Bishop of London, and the Bishop of Oxford. Agents were authorized and sent to the governors of Maryland and Virginia in the hope of securing support from the major colonies where Anglicanism was established.

The idea of an American episcopate had been raised earlier, during the tenure of Henry Compton as Bishop of London (1675–1713), and it came close to realization before the death of Queen Anne in 1714 ended it. The Bishop of London in 1748, Thomas Sherlock, revived the idea of suffragan bishops for America, but he too failed. At the conclusion of the French and Indian War, a pamphlet written by the Dean of Gloucester, Josiah Tucker, again promoted the idea of a suffragan bishop, but this time for Canada. Richard Peters presented to the Archbishops of Canterbury and York a treatise entitled *Thoughts on the Present State of the Church of England in America*, in 1764, which favored the appointment of four suffragan bishops by the King, without recourse to Parliament, within the archdiocese of Canterbury for service in America. When this same Peters in the Elizabeth Town convention in 1766 offered an alternative plan, prepared by Provost Smith, which called for the appointment of commissaries, the other delegates were shocked. The only difference between previous commissaries and the new ones was an enlargement of their respective jurisdictions from one to two colonies.

This Smith–Peters plan met defeat at the Elizabeth Town convention. Hostility to the idea of commissaries was expressed in letters to the Bishop of London and the SPG. Commissaries simply could not ordain, confirm, and consecrate. This counter-proposal, which might have won acceptance in England and avoided controversy in the colonies, was rejected. But the paradoxical conduct of Richard Peters from 1764 to 1766 actually reflected the changed reality in Pennsylvania. At the end of the war Great Britain was hugely admired, but the new imperial policy expressed especially in the Stamp Act of 1765 generated hostility towards the British Government. Moreover, Peters and Smith were aware that the Pennsylvania proprietors, Sir Thomas and Richard Penn, were opposed to any possible extension of royal authority in America and particularly in Pennsylvania. In this colony a considerable political faction was seeking to have the home government convert Pennsylvania into a royal colony. The creation of a colonial bishop, no matter how defined or wherever located, would have the appearance of extending royal authority. Smith and Peters were prepared to put the local interest of the Church ahead of a particular ecclesiastical issue, even episcopacy, to preserve what the Church had already achieved and to avoid involving it in unnecessary controversy.

In the fall of 1767, New Jersey Anglicans hosted another inter-colonial convention under Chandler's leadership, and this time the delegates urged him to prepare a pamphlet setting forth the episcopal cause. *An Appeal to the Public on Behalf of the Church of England* was the result. It was believed that a rational approach to the subject of bishops would allay dissenter fears and rally indifferent and passively resistant Anglicans to the cause. The *Appeal* stressed that only "a purely spiritual episcopate" was sought for America: one with no temporal power, no special relations with the state, no state functions, and no exclusive civil privileges as the bishops had in England. The fury of independent opposition to the *Appeal* found expression in Charles Chauncy's response. Chauncy, the most influential clergyman in New England, was minister of First Church, Boston. His tract, *An Appeal to the Public Answered*, was the initial blast in pamphlet and newspaper intended to refute totally the position stated in Chandler's *Appeal*. In time, the pamphlet contest included *The Appeal Defended* by Chandler; this was answered by Chauncy, *A Reply to Dr. Chandler's "Appeal Defended." The Appeal Farther Defended* was answered by *A Compleat View of Episcopacy*.

The second phase of the controversy exploded with a series of newspaper articles entitled "The American Whig," which appeared in Parker's *New York Gazette* in March of 1768 and ran for 57 issues. Behind the series were three Presbyterian laymen: WILLIAM LIVINGSTON, WILLIAM SMITH, JR., and John Morin Scott. Their objective was to explode the idea that Anglicans wanted a primitive bishop. The episcopal plan was described as a veiled attempt to secure a benign episcopate and later endow it with full prelatical powers. Although SAMUEL SEABURY, Charles Inglis, and Myles Cooper contributed a series of articles entitled "Whip for the American Whig," which appeared in Gaine's *New York Mercury*, they had a difficult time handling their opponents' arguments. "The American Whig" series also appeared in the *Boston Gazette* and the *Pennsylvania Journal*. In Philadelphia, Francis Alison, John Dickinson, and George Bryan, all Presbyterians, articulated their opposition to the *Appeal* in a series entitled "Centinel," which was countered by Provost Smith in a series labelled "Anatomist."

The rancorous rhetoric used by both sides in the episcopal controversy served to emphasize the essential constitutional problem and caused many churchmen, especially in the colonies where the Church of England was established, to downgrade the importance of episcopacy and resist the Johnson–Chandler plan. When three clergy in Maryland tried to advance the scheme, Hugh Hamersley, secretary to Lord Baltimore, wrote, "His Lordship by no means wishes to see an episcopal palace rise in America," and this virtually foreclosed the subject. On 4 June 1771, when 12 clergy out of more than 90 in Virginia met in convention, the subject was raised. Four of the clergy present openly opposed the scheme. Press coverage of the event extended from 30 May 1771 to 5 March 1772 and included some 23 letters for and against episcopacy, with the opposing side making the most forceful and effective case. William Nelson, President of the Virginia Council, stated succinctly, "We do not want bishops" (Mills, 1978, p. 85). No record exists of an attempt in North and South Carolina or Georgia to raise the issue. But the harsh treatment the Johnson–Chandler plan received in the two colonies where the Church of England was strongest was a major setback. In Maryland, the scheme was viewed as an encroachment upon the proprietor's prerogative; in Virginia it was perceived as a threat to their local ecclesiastical arrangements.

3. OTHER ECCLESIASTICAL ISSUES

In the period 1763–76 the Church of England in America was in a paradoxical position. At the very time when colonial resentment over the Proclamation Line, Revenue Act, Stamp Act, and Townshend Duties reached fever pitch, the Anglican Communion was experiencing remarkable growth. It was not until zealous churchmen cooperated with and then initiated an episcopal plan that grave difficulties were encountered. As long as the Church itself was perceived to be under local control it did not become an object of abuse, as did stamp agents, revenue commissioners, and admiralty judges. The suspicion, however, that the zealous advocates of episcopacy were also desirous of an extension of British authority proved correct. In the 1775–6 period, Thomas B. Chandler wrote at least three pamphlets supportive of Great Britain's policies and critical of America's actions. Myles Cooper and Charles Inglis did likewise, but Samuel Seabury, in his *Letters of a Westchester Farmer*, became the most noted loyalist of the group.

Tensions between Anglicans and Congregationalist-Presbyterians flared up over related ecclesiastical matters in at least three northern colonies. In 1763, the Privy Council disallowed a Massachusetts law creating an Indian Mission under Congregational auspices, and Archbishop Secker was suspected of playing a role in the defeat. Then, too, Anglicans in Massachussetts were unable to win Assembly approval for a proposed college to be located in the Berkshires. Churchmen in both Massachusetts and Connecticut frequently complained to British authorities that they were denied tax money whenever their parishes were without a minister. But it was in New York that the episcopal controversy became so deeply involved in local issues that the labels "Anglican" and "Presbyterian" were used to identify political factions. Livingston, Smith, and Scott, with other Presbyterians, fought against Anglican domination of King's College and endeavored to have the Ministry Act of 1693, which provided tax support for Anglicans, repealed. The acrimony and emotion expressed over these issues in local contexts simply added another dimension to the larger episcopal controversy.

It is worthy of note that in spite of repeated assurances from dissenters and churchmen alike, similar to what Thomas Hollis wrote in 1763, "You are in no real danger at present, in respect to the creation of Bishops in America if I am rightly informed," the episcopal controversy continued throughout the decade (Mills, 1978, p. 149). Why was this so? The need for resident ecclesiastical oversight of the American part of the Anglican Communion was real, and the sincerity of the proponents was compelling. On the other hand, dissenter fears of episcopacy, though based largely on accounts of seventeenth-century prelacy, were real. The inter-relatedness of Church and State under the British Constitution clearly made bishops officials of the State as well as of the Church. This meant that a bishop, even a suffragan one, resident in the colonies would represent, at the very least symbolically, an extension of British authority over the internal affairs of the colonies. This idea posed a potential threat to the evolving colonial constitution to which dissenters and large numbers of churchmen subscribed. To have acquiesced in the settlement of a resident bishop between 1763 and 1776 would have been a contradiction to the argument used by the colonists to oppose the emerging imperial policy.

FURTHER READING

Bridenbaugh, Carl: *Mitre and Sceptre: Transatlantic Faiths, Ideas, Personalities, and Politics, 1689–1775* (New York: Oxford, 1962).

Cross, Arthur L.: *The Anglican Episcopate and the American Colonies* (New York: Longmans, Green and Co., 1902).

Mills, Frederick V., Sr.: *Bishops by Ballot: an Eighteenth Century Ecclesiastical Revolution* (New York: Oxford, 1978).

Overton, J. H., and Relton, F.: *The English Church from the Accession of George I to the End of the Eighteenth Century* (London: Macmillan, 1906).

Sykes, Norman: *Church and State in England in the Eighteenth Century* (Cambridge: Cambridge University Press, 1934).

19

Social protest and the revolutionary movement, 1765–1776

EDWARD COUNTRYMAN

"MOBS, a sort of them at least, are constitutional" (Maier, 1982, p. 24). The year of the statement was 1768. Its author was Thomas Hutchinson, the Lieutenant-Governor of Massachusetts. Three years earlier Hutchinson had seen his own house virtually demolished by one of the most destructive mobs of the era. Thanks to Pauline Maier we know that even after that ordeal he still believed that popular uprisings could be legitimate. Thanks to her and to many others we now have a well-developed understanding of how ordinary people took part in the American Revolution, including its riots, of the difference they made to the Revolution's course, and of the difference that taking part made to them.

The phrase "social protest" is too simple to describe what took place. The "progressive" historians of the early twentieth century, who first posited the idea that there was an internal American Revolution, put their arguments in terms of flat, hard confrontation. In Carl Becker's words, the Revolution was a struggle for "the democratization of American politics and society" as well as for "home-rule." To him the history of pre-independence political parties fed directly into "the history of the Federalist and Anti-Federalist parties under the confederation" (Becker, 1909, pp. 5, 276). Three-quarters of a century later the questions that Becker and his contemporaries raised remain valid, but we reject most of their precise formulations. Instead of flat confrontation, historians of the Revolution's internal dimensions and conflicts now see process, change, and development. This is so at every level from individual consciousness to the grand coalitions of resistance, of revolution, and of national construction.

Popular upheaval was central to the revolutionary process. Among the major events were the Stamp Act risings of 1765 and 1766 (Boston, New York, Newport, and Albany, among other places), the *Liberty* riot (Boston, 1768), the Battle of Golden Hill (New York, 1770), the King Street Riot (or "Boston Massacre," 1770), the destruction of the British revenue vessel *Gaspée* (Providence, 1772), the Boston Tea Party (1773), the popular response to the Coercive Acts (especially in rural Massachusetts, 1774) and to the news of war (1775), and the destruction of the Pennsylvania provincial government (1776).

In addition were movements in many parts of the countryside. In the crisis decade itself came the Regulator uprisings in the two Carolinas, the Hudson Valley tenant insurrection of 1766, and the guerrilla warfare against New York authority that resulted in the birth of Vermont in 1777. Reaching backwards, we might also cite the New Jersey land riots of the late 1740s, Hudson Valley tenant unrest throughout the 1750s, and the Paxton Boys' march on Philadelphia in 1763. Reaching forwards, the list includes militant popular loyalism during the war in the Deep South, in Maryland, and in New York, Shays's Rebellion in Massachusetts in 1786, and the Whiskey Rebellion in Pennsylvania in 1792.

Nor were these outright uprisings the only form of protest. Virginia was the only province/state that did not experience explicitly political internal upheaval. But the emergence within it of militant evangelical churches – Baptists and Methodists – came close to the same thing (see Isaac, 1982). In large part (though not entirely) the direct risings were the work of white males. However disadvantaged some of these may have been, all of them were members of both the ruling race and the ruling gender. But during the Revolution both Blacks and women began to find voices of their own and to act together to change their situations.

I. THE NATURE OF POPULAR UPHEAVAL IN THE COLONIES

The upheavals of the Revolution emerged from the social fabric and the culture of colonial America and, by extension, of the European world of their time. Thomas Hutchinson's observation that crowd risings could be "constitutional" reflects their ubiquity in the world he knew. In part, as Maier notes, risings were so frequent because colonial society had no other way to defend itself. The posse, the volunteer fire company, the militia unit: these were simply crowds that had received official sanction and leadership. A crowd that drove away smallpox victims to prevent contagion or that closed down a house of prostitution was doing much the same work as they. Rioters of this sort might cover the entire social spectrum from wealthy merchants, often clad in working mens' costume, to journeymen and apprentices. Women did join some of these "constitutional" mobs, and there were occasions when men rioted in female disguise. "A rabble of negroes and boys" was the standard phrase to describe a mob that did not have official approval. But the phrase appears so often in the sources that we may be sure Blacks and youths rioted as well.

"Mixed" crowds acted to defend a community when there was no other way; these were the sort of which a man like Hutchinson might approve. But even these had a distinctly plebeian flavor, and there were other times when uprisings grew out of the experience of class rather than of community. In Boston and New York, and perhaps elsewhere, lower-class crowds celebrated "Pope's Day" each 5 November with parades, bonfires, and sometimes a brawl. This popular ritual commemorated the discovery of the "Popish Plot" to blow up the House of Commons early in the seventeenth century; the day is still celebrated in England. Pope's Day created a brief moment of "misrule," when the social order could be inverted. It also kept alive the most radical traditions of English Protestantism. Among those traditions were the memories of Oliver Cromwell, of Cornet George Joyce, the reputed captor of Charles I during the English Civil War, and of the regicides who found shelter in New England after the Stuart restoration in 1660. All of those memories came forcefully to the surface during the American Revolution.

Lower-class crowds had more mundane concerns as well. Among the most important was the long-standing tradition that society's rulers bore the duty to control the market-place so that poor and middling people could get basic necessities at affordable prices. If they failed, direct action became legitimate, either to remedy the problem itself or to convey its seriousness to society's rulers. The French called this *taxation populaire*; Edward Thompson has described its English variant as the "moral economy of the crowd" (Thompson, 1971); students of early America have referred to it as "corporatism." We know that this tradition of social responsibility crossed the Atlantic; it figures prominently in the social thought of New England Puritanism. We know as well that in eighteenth-century America its salience increased as urban development created wealth, poverty, and greater dependence on the complexities of the market place. This tradition, too, fed into popular revolutionary militance.

If Hutchinson had been pressed, he would probably have agreed that urban crowds were more likely to be "constitutional" than rural ones. Both in Britain and in America the same authorities who tolerated risings by townsfolk over bread or smallpox used all the force they could muster to put down risings by country people. Parliament showed the way with its response to the Scottish insurrections of 1715 and 1745 and with the "Black Act" of 1723 against illicit hunting. The colonial and state legislatures of South and North Carolina, Maryland, New York, and Massachusetts and the United States Congress all found reason to follow its example. The reason may have been that an urban riot was an event, growing from a specific issue, but a rural rising was a movement, directed against the larger pattern of authority and social relations.

Popular upheaval may be central to the process of the great revolutions, but by itself it is not necessarily revolutionary. The very fact that Hutchinson and men like him could regard rioting with equanimity suggests that far from posing a danger to the world they controlled it was a functioning part of that world. The deep *ancien régime* background that historians have uncovered on both sides of the Atlantic explains why and how popular upheaval appeared in revolutionary America. But by itself it does not explain why American crowds became revolutionary.

2. THE SONS OF LIBERTY

For that, we must turn to the Sons of Liberty, who made themselves into the Revolution's popular leadership. The term was coined not in America but by a sympathetic Member of Parliament, Colonel ISAAC BARRÉ, during the debates on the Stamp Act. The Americans adopted it quickly, both as a general description for people committed to resistance and as a name for the organized radical leadership.

The first group to emerge was the "Loyal Nine," who planned the Stamp Act resistance in Boston. Other groups took shape from Charles Town, South Carolina, to Portsmouth, New Hampshire. As a formally constituted network the Sons existed only for the duration of the Stamp Act crisis in 1765 and 1766. But for practical purposes they never disbanded at all. Their members remained active in local, provincial, and eventually continental radical politics (*see* Chapter 22, §1, and Chapter 23, §1).

The social make-up of the Sons varied widely. According to John Adams, the members of the Loyal Nine in January 1766 were "John Avery Distiller or Merchant, ... John Smith the Brazier, Thomas Crafts the Painter, [Benjamin] Edes the Printer, Stephen Cleverly the Brazier, [Thomas] Chase the Distiller, Joseph Field Master of a Vessell, Henry Bass [merchant]" and "George Trott Jeweller" (Maier, 1972, p. 307). Charles Town's Sons were mostly master artisans. In New York the Sons were led by small merchants such as Isaac Sears and Alexander McDougall, but they had a strong artisan following. There were gentlemen of the first order among the Sons in Maryland and in Virginia.

To these must be added the Revolution's radical intellectuals. The most important, perhaps, was SAMUEL ADAMS, a Harvard graduate who was driven by a vision of turning Boston into a Christian Sparta where pious, virtuous men would put the public good ahead of their own. But Adams found he could work closely with a man as unlike himself as Dr. THOMAS YOUNG. Young was a self-taught physician and a man of startlingly unorthodox belief about the nature of God and the universe. He loathed the landlord-ridden society of his native province of New York as much as he scorned conventional religion. A wanderer, he helped found the Sons of Liberty in Albany – his name comes first on a list of their members made in 1766 – before moving to Boston and eventually to Newport and Philadelphia. He also involved himself at a distance with the Green Mountain insurrection that created Vermont.

What the groups of Sons shared was not specific social characteristics but rather commitment to determined action in the face of the British crisis. They were as much a coalition of different sorts and groups as the revolutionary movement they created and led. Their tactics varied as well, as the contrast between their revolutionary journalism in Boston and in New York City shows. In the former town, Benjamin Edes's *Boston Gazette* confined its politics solely to the British issue. In the latter, John Holt's *New York Journal* published article after article on New Yorkers' own "distressed situation."

Whether or not their press gave prominence to local issues, however, the Sons understood two cardinal rules of revolutionary politics. One was to establish discipline among the people they led; inchoate rage and uncontrolled violence had no place in their movement. Perhaps the best example was provided in February 1770 by the Boston radical William Molyneux. An angry crowd had attempted to confront a known customs informer named Ebenezer Richardson, and anger turned to outrage when a panic-stricken Richardson opened fire, killing an 11-year-old boy, Christopher Sneider. But through Molyneux had been active in organizing the confrontation, he personally saved Richardson from the crowd's vengeance for the boy's murder.

But for all their insistence on discipline, their other great principle was militance, and they understood that militance required making the British issue come alive in terms of people's lives. The Loyal Nine provided a fine example in the way they generated the first American resistance to the Stamp Act.

Boston's resistance to the Stamp Act   The action happened on 14 August 1765. By then the Virginia House of Burgesses had given a stirring lead, condemning the Act itself and (depending on the published version of their resolves) seeming to call for outright resistance. The Loyal Nine set out to dramatize the effect of the Act on everyday life, and they set up a mock stamp office on Boston Neck, the narrow spit that connected Boston to the mainland. They carried out their business beneath America's first Liberty Tree, in which they had placed effigies of Stamp Distributor Andrew Oliver and the Devil peeping out of an old boot. The boot's sole was green and vile with corruption. The effigy represented a double pun, on both the name of the Earl of Bute, the hated Scot who had been George III's first Prime Minister, and that of George Grenville, Bute's successor and the prime mover of the Stamp Act. But the two effigies were also strongly reminiscent of the effigies of the Pope, the Devil, and Guy Fawkes with which lower-class Bostonians paraded each 5 November. The Loyal Nine may have shunned any appeal to outright class resentment. But they appealed directly to lower-class culture.

When night began to fall, a crowd gathered, as the Loyal Nine had anticipated. The Nine had already recruited Ebenezer Macintosh, a shoemaker who was leader of one of the two traditional Pope's Day crowds, and he led a parade with the Liberty Tree effigies. When the crowd reached the waterfront it leveled a brick building that Andrew Oliver had under construction. Then it advanced on Oliver's house, where it did minor damage before dispersing. Oliver immediately resigned his office, which meant that there was no one in Boston legally capable of distributing the stamps. Crowds elsewhere followed Boston's widely reported example (for illustration, *see* figure 10, p. 116), and by 1 November, when the Act was due to take effect, it was virtually unenforceable.

To the Loyal Nine, and to others like them, that was all that was necessary. But their "followers" went further. On 26 August, 12 days after the Liberty Tree demonstration, another crowd gathered in Boston and marched on another great man's house. The intended victim was Thomas Hutchinson, who was Oliver's brother-in-law and who was simultaneously Lieutenant-Governor, Chief Justice, and holder of several other high offices. He opposed the Stamp Act as unwise, but he believed in British authority. A native Bostonian, Hutchinson had long been unpopular; when his house caught fire in 1749 by-standers had cried, "Let it burn." By 1765 that house was also an island of opulence in a Boston that was suffering from long-term economic stagnation and from the general trading depression that followed the end of the Seven Years' War. Oliver had escaped with minor damage; Hutchinson saw his property utterly devastated.

Other cities follow Boston's example Nor was Hutchinson's house the only victim of such destruction. On 31 October it happened to carriages and sleighs in New York that belonged to Lieutenant-Governor Cadwallader Colden and to a house in the same city that had been rented by Major Thomas James of the British Army. In Newport it happened to the houses of Martin Howard and Dr. Thomas Moffatt. The following May a New York City crowd poured into a newly opened theater, disrupting the performance and then destroying the building. There was discipline in the American movement, but there was also genuine anger.

In some of these instances the crowd's motivation seems obvious. Major James had been directly responsible for putting Fort George, at the foot of Manhattan Island, in a state of preparedness, which included training its guns on New York City itself. Hutchinson, Colden, Howard, and Moffatt were all outspoken supporters of British authority. The Loyal Nine repudiated the sacking of Hutchinson's house and together with the town fathers they took strong steps to bring Boston under control. But the New York radical leadership made no objection to what happened to Colden's property and to James's rented house. They actually led the crowd that sacked the Chapel Street theater, and the crowd's members shouted "Liberty! Liberty!" as they paraded with the wreckage. It would seem that more was involved than the British issue by itself.

3. IMPERIAL ISSUES VERSUS DOMESTIC DISTRESS

Underlying this urban rioting was a combination of sharp distress, stemming from the mid-1760s depression, and the "corporatist" tradition of political economy. Hutchinson's house and Colden's carriages and sleighs were symbols of opulence and privilege, and they were resented for their own sake as well as for the politics of their owners. In the case of the New York theater the imperial issue did not count directly at all. The events that took place early in 1770 in New York and in Boston help to show how imperial issues and domestic distress meshed and balanced.

In both places, British soldiers and American working men came to blows. New York City saw a week of civilian–soldier rioting in January. In Boston five Americans died when troops who were guarding the customs house opened fire on a crowd on the evening of 5 March. One reason for the violence lay in the Whig political language of the era, which taught that any standing military force betokened imminent tyranny. Benjamin Edes never stopped making that point to his Boston readers and the troops who were stationed in his town seemed determined to drive it home. Their mission was to protect the American Board of Customs Commissioners from the townspeople's hostility, while the commissioners presided over an outright despoliation of the American maritime economy by their minions. The soldiers took over Boston Common for a camp ground and a number of public buildings for barracks. They paraded on Sunday mornings, disrupting church services with their racket. To stop desertion, they established guardposts, including one at Boston Neck. Bostonians who remembered the mock stamp office of 14 August 1765 must have remembered the Loyal Nine's predictions each time they had to stop for a sentry's challenge. In New York ALEXANDER MCDOUGALL pressed the same point, that troops portended tyranny, in his impassioned address "to the betrayed inhabitants." The "betrayal" was by politicians who had given in to British demands that the city's garrison be supplied from provincial funds.

But other themes appeared as well. While McDougall was writing of betrayal, "Brutus" was telling New Yorkers that off-duty soldiers were taking employment away from people who needed it: themselves. Seeking part-time work was the soldiers' customary right, and it made the difference between lives of misery and lives with any comfort or enjoyment. Heretofore it had caused little distress, for New York's garrison had always been small and Boston had had none at all. But now each city contained several regiments, and the times were hard. In these maritime towns, with economies that were suffering both from British "customs racketeering" and from a severe trading slump, the soldiers' customary right turned into explosive provocation.

The Boston Massacre   The Boston events are particularly revealing. Only a few days before the riot, an off-duty soldier from the 29th Regiment approached a ropewalk seeking work. One of the rope-workers offered the soldier a job cleaning his "necessary house," and the soldier took the offence that the rope-worker intended. He gathered comrades from his barracks and a brawl broke out. Boston leaders and British officers joined to break up the brawl. But the town was already seething because of the death of Christopher Sneider, and feelings remained high. Soldiers from the same regiment were guarding the Customs House on the night of 5 March, and a crowd began pelting them with snowballs. Thinking they had received an order, the soldiers fired, killing five members of the crowd (for illustration, *see* figure 11, p. 141). What the Boston crowd did in those late weeks of winter makes sense only against the background of its whole situation. In 1770, as in 1765, the town's Sons of Liberty strove hard to maintain control, and by and large they succeeded. But the sustained revolutionary militance that people like those rope-workers were developing grew from the problems they faced in their daily lives as well as from the great dispute with Britain. Had there been no British crisis, the domestic problems would not have led to revolution. But had there been no domestic problems, the response to the British issue would have been muted rather than militant.

4. THE INVOLVEMENT OF COUNTRY PEOPLE

Though the great port towns were the Revolution's "urban crucible" (Nash, 1979), their people comprised less than a twentieth of the whole American population. The movement could not have become a genuine revolution without the massive involvement of the countryside. The land riots in New Jersey and New York, the Regulator movements in the Carolinas, and the Paxton Boys' march in Pennsylvania (*see* figure 16) show that the back country was as ridden with turmoil as the port towns. But these were parallel to the direct movement against Britain rather than part of it. When the New York City radical John Morin Scott joined in suppressing the Hudson Valley rising of 1766, one British army officer quipped that the Sons of Liberty were "of opinion that no one is entitled to Riot but themselves" (Countryman, 1981, p. 67). How, then, and why did country people become involved in the main movement?

Massachusetts provides the clearest picture. In 1772 the Boston Town Meeting established a committee of correspondence and gave it the job of rousing the interior. From then until the aftermath of the Boston Tea Party the committee strove to raise rural consciousness. Its extensive papers show that towns all over the province agreed with its analysis of the situation America faced. This analysis held that a major plot against American liberty had been hatched in London and that it had to be resisted. But as in the case of townsfolk, it took more than political language to generate a movement of resistance and then to turn it into a movement of revolution.

At first the farmers confined their commitment to words. Even in 1773 and early 1774, some were so removed from the great political issues that they feared the whole movement stemmed from a plot among Boston merchants to sell off their excess goods.

FIGURE 16 Philadelphia prepares to repel the Paxton Boys' march (engraving by Henry Dawkins, 1764): the Paxton episode arose out of conflicts of interest between the Western settlers of Scots-Irish descent, who felt unprotected and underrepresented, and the merchant grandees of Philadelphia. After murdering a number of inoffensive Indians the Paxton men marched menacingly to Philadelphia, where residents had to overcome Quaker scruples about taking up arms in order to defend the city.

Fears and doubts dropped away, however, when the news arrived of Britain's response to the Boston Tea Party. Boston's port was closed; the royal charter of Massachusetts was altered; Crown officials accused of misdeeds in Massachusetts could now be tried far away; troops could be billeted on the people. The response was strong: all across the interior town meetings decided not simply to protest against Parliament's new laws but to nullify them.

The result was that when the judges of the county courts assembled for their new session late in the summer of 1774 they found themselves unable to open for business. The court houses were surrounded by armed men, drawn up in their militia units and insisting that the judges resign. The judges were the immediate representatives of British authority, for they held their commissions under the reformed Massachusetts charter. Through them the farmers were confronting the whole structure of British power, because closing the courts meant closing down the government. The farmers knew it: they would not accept the judges' private resignations. Instead they insisted that they humble themselves by doffing their ceremonial wigs and robes and walking through the ranks of the crowds as they read their resignations aloud. Resistance was becoming revolution, and by the autumn of 1774 the royal governor, General Thomas Gage, found that his authority extended only where his troops could march.

On the surface it would seem that the issues were purely constitutional, and that social protest had nothing to do with the farmers' rising. The leaders of Massachusetts certainly insisted that was the case. According to their official explanation, what was happening was not a revolution against British authority. It was a restoration of legitimate authority in place of illegitimate. The Massachusetts Government Act was a nullity; the old charter was still in effect; the provincial assembly, meeting in Salem, was administering it. The governorship and the judiciary were vacant, but the province would do without them until the Act was formally repealed and they could be restored.

But, as in the port towns, more was at stake than simple constitutionality. As Richard Bushman has shown, the farmers' uprising sprang from problems that were rooted deep in their society and their historical memory as well as from the immediate issue of relations with Britain (Bushman, 1976). From the beginning, rural New England had been trying to maintain a precarious balance between the medieval world and the modern. On the one hand, it completely repudiated feudal forms of land-holding and its people loathed the whole idea of lordship and vassalage. On the other, its village way of life was in many ways pre-commercial and even communal (see Berthoff and Murrin, 1973). By the time of the Revolution, demographic change and economic development were bringing the New England way under ever-greater pressure. But the vision of living together, in harmony and without overlords, retained its power.

The land question   The key issue was land. By 1774 the experiments with open-field farming of the early years were a distant memory. Freehold farmers took pride that each of them could sit "under his own vine and fig-tree." But they also understood that their tenure could be precarious. They knew that late in the seventeenth century their ancestors had faced down another British attempt to change the terms of their government and to challenge their hold on their property. Perhaps the worst of it had been that Sir Edmund Andros, whom James II had named to rule them, had regarded their land as open to seizure for the benefit of his henchmen and himself. They had been quick to clap Andros in jail when the news arrived that his royal master had been overthrown in England's Glorious Revolution of 1688.

Now it seemed the nightmare had returned. Governor Thomas Gage was no Edmund Andros, but he was still a British general on active duty, commanding all the troops in North America as well as governing the province. His task was to enforce Parliament's will. Parliament had shown clearly enough that its will was to impose taxes the farmers could not pay. Failure to pay could lead to court proceedings that would end in the seizure of a person's land. Land that was so condemned could easily be bought up by someone with money to spend, and such a person might readily make himself lord of a new estate, worked by tenants who had once been the land's owners. The logical candidates for the new role of landlord were men of the sort that had risen to positions on the bench of the county courts. They were Massachusetts men, not Englishmen, but they held their commissions by the Governor's favor, and they had attracted his favor because they were already possessed of prominence and wealth.

By closing the courts the farmers were not just confronting Britain's latest assertion of its claim to rule them; they were also confronting their strongest memories and fears, and asserting their sense of what their world should be like. As they reached into the past they found models to emulate as well as bogeys to fear. Alfred Young has noted the importance to them of the memory of revolutionary England (Young, 1984). New Englanders took pride that after the Stuart Restoration in 1660 the surviving regicides, who had executed Charles I, found refuge among them. Oliver Cromwell, who had led the Puritan Revolution, was a figure of evil to the orthodox English Whig tradition, but to these people he remained a hero. A Massachusetts farmer named Asa Douglass addressed Washington himself as "Great Cromwell" in 1776, and new-born boys all over the region were being christened Oliver in Cromwell's honor. As Young puts it, a New Englander then would have spoken Cromwell's name with the same respect that an African-American would speak of "Malcolm" or "Martin" now.

Was this social protest? Perhaps not, if we are looking for outraged peasants attacking the castle. But the rising of the New England farmers drew on their whole social experience. It opened the possibility of remaking their political world so that it would suit their sense of what society should be like. By 1776, when it had become clear that Parliament would not back down and the old charter would never be restored, the farmers were looking to the future they would make themselves rather than to the past their ancestors had bequeathed to them (see Chapter 34, §4).

Moreover, their rising had much in common with rural protest elsewhere in the colonies. The Hudson Valley had been in turmoil since mid-century as New England migrants crossed the Berkshires and joined New York tenants in confronting New York's manorial land system. The Green Mountains were claimed by New York, which intended to create a society of landlords and tenants there as well. But they were being settled by New Englanders who wanted to re-create the village world they knew. The landlord–tenant issue underlay the mid-century rioting in New Jersey as well, and it figured in the North Carolina Regulator movement. Not all of these issues fed directly into the movement against Britain. In some places, including the Hudson Valley, Maryland's eastern shore, and the Carolina interior, protest led to loyalism rather than to revolutionary patriotism, as discontented farmers found that their own opponents were among the Revolution's leaders. But whatever the precise course politics took, social discontent and social protest ran through rural experience during the era.

5. REVOLUTION AND RADICALISM IN PHILADELPHIA

As the independence movement gained strength, social protest and political experience began combining to create new public identities. The case of Philadelphia shows the process particularly well. Pennsylvania's capital took little part in the great uprisings of the Stamp Act period; its stamp distributor resigned with little ado and there was virtually no rioting. But by the end of the 1760s relations within the city were growing tense. The issue was the non-importation movement with which the colonies had responded to Parliament's Townshend Duties of 1767. These were an attempt to meet the supposed colonial objection to "internal" taxes, such as the Stamp Tax, by imposing "external" duties on colonial imports. The colonials had long accepted Parliament's right to impose duties in order to control their behavior, such as the Molasses Act of 1733. By and large they were even paying the duties imposed by the Sugar Act of 1764. It seemed to the British that they had made the external–internal distinction themselves. On all counts, it looked as if Parliament had found a way of taxing the colonials that the colonials would accept.

They did not accept it. Instead, they agreed to boycott British commerce until the taxes were repealed. To the merchants of the great ports it was a disagreeable necessity: they would not accept Parliament's right to tax them, but transatlantic commerce was their life. But to Philadelphia's artisans it was another matter. Like New Yorkers and Bostonians, Philadelphians were enduring the depression that had settled on the colonies at the end of the Seven Years' War. It seemed to the artisans that non-importation offered a chance to bring prosperity back. Without British imports there would be more of a market for their own goods. But when Parliament repealed four of the five Townshend Duties in 1770, leaving only the duty on tea in place, non-importation began to collapse.

To the merchants the issue was simple: they were the traders and they had the right to decide whether to import or not. But to one Philadelphia "tradesman" the "consent of the majority of the tradesmen, farmers and other freemen . . . should have been obtained." A "lover of liberty and a mechanic's friend" wrote that a "good mechanic" was "one of the most serviceable, one of the most valuable members of society" but that merchants were only "weak and babbling boys – clerks of yesterday." "Brother Chip" asked Philadelphia artisans whether they did not have "an equal right of electing or being elected. . . . Are there no . . . men well acquainted with the constitution and laws of their country among the tradesmen and mechanics?" (Countryman, 1990).

The issue was one of social and political consciousness more than it was one of overt social conflict. The Philadelphia artisans wanted an equal voice in the making of their community's major decisions. But in their self-assertion they were also redefining the terms of their membership in the community. In the colonial period they may have accepted that their political position and their social rank were inferior. Now they were casting such beliefs aside and developing instead the ideology of equal rights which would become dominant in American political culture.

The involvement of artisans   From its slow start in 1765, Philadelphia went on to become the most radical urban center in revolutionary America. Politically the culmination came in June 1776, when the old provincial government was forcibly overthrown. One element in the coalition that overthrew it was the militant members of the Continental Congress, who were determined to have independence and who recognized that the Pennsylvania Assembly formed the last major obstacle to it. But they were joined by Pennsylvanians whose vision of America demanded transformation as well as independence. Many of them were master artisans, the people who had asserted their right to an equal political voice in 1770. But now they were joined by lesser men, most notably the journeymen and laborers who formed the bulk of the city's revolutionary militia. The artisans had found the means to express themselves in the city's committee of safety. Like similar committees elsewhere this had begun to take shape in the aftermath of the Boston Tea Party, and by 1776 its voice was dominant in the city's popular politics. The emergence and triumph of such committees was the surest possible sign that a full political revolution was underway. The spread of their membership to include men who would never have had such a voice in running the old order was as sure a sign that the Revolution had a profound social dimension (see Ryerson, 1978, and Countryman, 1981).

But Philadelphians took it further. They met the final crisis as a bitterly divided people. For reasons of both religion and self-interest the city's old elite of Quaker and Anglican merchants were rejecting the revolution. The non-Quaker patriot elite, typified by the lawyer and pamphleteer JOHN DICKINSON, proved unwilling to accept the consequences of what they had helped to begin. In 1768 Dickinson's own *Letters from a Farmer in Pennsylvania* had been enormously influential in rousing opposition to the Townshend Duties and his "Liberty Song" had been sung from New Hampshire to Georgia. In it he had urged, "Come join hand in hand, brave Americans all, and rouse your bold hearts at fair Liberty's call," but now his own heart was timid and he held back from joining his own hand to the cause of independence. It was Dickinson and his like, not open loyalists, who were using the old provincial assembly to put the moment of independence off, and it was their power that dissolved when the popular committee and the Continental Congress joined their own hands to bring the assembly down.

The militia   Meanwhile another group had also taken on shape and consciousness: the privates of the city's militia. Philadelphia's Quaker pacifist heritage meant that it had no military tradition, which meant that there were no established lines of military authority. When a militia became necessary its officers were drawn from the better and middling sorts, and the privates came from the city's journeymen, apprentices, laborers, and servants. But the terms of the militia law were lenient, and a man who had conscientious objections could easily avoid service. To the city's Quakers it was a matter of religious belief. But to the militiamen liability to military service became a matter of political principle.

The consequence was that the militiamen established their own committee and formulated their own program for the Revolution. Equal liability to service was only one of the points they put forward. They scorned the paternalistic willingness of some of their officers to equip the troops they commanded; instead they wanted officers and men alike to be uniformed in simple hunting shirts. They wanted to elect their officers themselves, rather than serve under men appointed by higher authority (see Rosswurm, 1987). Their demands found echoes elsewhere. Hunting shirts became the costume of revolutionary commitment in Virginia. A committee of artisans took shape in New York City, and in May 1776 it issued a strident set of demands to the "elected delegates" in the province's provincial congress. One of those demands was that under the new order the system of popular committees that had taken power during the final crisis be able to reconstitute itself whenever the people might choose.

Thomas Paine's "Common Sense" The need for governmental simplicity and responsiveness became one of the dominant themes in popular political discourse. No one put the point more clearly than the pamphleteer THOMAS PAINE. His first great piece in a long career of radical political writing was *Common Sense*, published in Philadelphia in January 1776 (*see* Chapter 26). Paine was a former corset-maker and British customs official, and he had migrated from England only in 1774. He had known Benjamin Franklin there, and through the famous former printer he found an entrée to the artisan community just at the point when it was awakening to political consciousness.

Paine set himself three distinct projects in *Common Sense*. One, after nine inconclusive months of war, was to convince Americans that reconciliation was impossible. Full independence was the only course worth following: "the weeping voice of nature cries 'tis time to part." The second was to argue the case for simple republicanism: "let the assemblies be annual, with a president only." The third was to put his case in a political language that would be sophisticated but also simple. Paine's predecessors in the Revolution's pamphlet literature had been gentlemen and they had written for other gentlemen. Paine's own roots were plebeian, and he wrote for people like himself (see Foner, 1976).

His impact was enormous. *Common Sense* sold some 150,000 copies and was read and discussed from one end of the 13 provinces to the other. People had been waiting for an unequivocal call for independence. Artisans and farmers were ready for a major piece of political writing that was neither beyond them nor condescending to them. Paine had made himself the voice of these people. The power with which he spoke for them was a measure of their own importance to the revolutionary movement. It was also a measure of how much their consciousness and situation had changed over the decade since the crisis first began. His call for republican institutions of the simplest sort, directly responsive, open to anyone's participation, devoid of the complications and balances of the old order, expressed the conclusions that the people who devoured *Common Sense* were drawing from their experience in the revolutionary movement.

6. LATER DEVELOPMENTS

The fullest measure of social protest in revolutionary America came after 1776, and it is beyond the main scope of this article. Independence brought the collapse of existing political institutions, and the collapse provided opportunity for many sorts of Americans to try to change their situations. Paine's people – white working men – pressed for institutional settlements of the sort he sketched in *Common Sense*. Their fullest opportunity came in Pennsylvania itself, where the patriot wing of the old elite gave way to panic and lost control. The result was the state's radical constitution of 1776, and its provisions found echoes elsewhere. It was copied directly in the Green Mountains, where the New England settlers seized the moment and cut themselves free of New York. Their choice of the Pennsylvania model suggests the political mentality of revolutionary rural America. So does the equally simple New England proposal called *The People the Best Governors*. Following Paine, the Pennsylvanians repudiated the whole idea of a governorship, appointing a "president only" to see to public business. The title bore none of the quasi-regal meaning it would later take on in American political culture, and others proposed it as well: South Carolina, Delaware, and New Hampshire in their first constitutions and New York in a constitutional proposal of 1776.

All of these changes took place among white men. Mary Beth Norton, Linda Kerber, and Ira Berlin have pointed the way for understanding the terms on which women and African-Americans confronted the Revolution, entered it, and tried to take advantage of the possibilities it presented (Norton, 1980; Kerber, 1980; Berlin and Hoffman, 1983). (Both groups receive full treatment elsewhere in this volume.) Enough here to make four points. The first is that they started from situations far less privileged than those of any white males. The second, springing from the first, is that neither women nor Blacks found themselves in a position to claim full political equality or direct political power. The third is that members of each group were to at least some extent actors in the main events between 1765 and 1776. The most notable case is that of Crispus Attucks, who was black and who was one of the five Bostonians slain in the King Street Riot in 1770. The fourth is that some members of both groups did make the most they could of the political and the ideological opportunities that the Revolution presented.

The American Revolution does not, perhaps, fit a mechanistic model of a social revolution. But that is not to say that the Revolution did not have a profound social dimension, both in its origins, to which this article has referred, and in its short-term and long-term consequences. One starting point for the people who made the Revolution was their common membership in a dependent, colonial yet British society. The other was their many different situations within that society and their relations with one another. During the political crisis with Britain they found themselves confronting their own social situations and relationships as well as the large imperial issues. The process and the great transformations of the Revolution grew from its domestic and social aspects as well as from its imperial and political ones.

FURTHER READING

Becker, Carl Lotus: *The History of Political Parties in the Province of New York, 1765–1776* (Madison: University of Wisconsin Press, 1909).
Berlin, Ira, and Hoffman, Ronald (eds.): *Slavery and Freedom in the Age of the American Revolution* (Charlottesville: University Press of Virginia, 1983).
Berthoff, Rowland, and Murrin, John M.: "Feudalism, communalism and the yeoman freeholder: the American Revolution considered as a social accident," in *Essays on the American Revolution*, ed. Stephen G. Kurtz and James H. Hutson (New York: W. W. Norton, 1973).
Bushman, Richard L.: "Massachusetts farmers and the Revolution," in *Society, Freedom and Conscience: the American Revolution in Virginia, Massachusetts and New York*, ed. Richard M. Jellison (New York: W. W. Norton, 1976).
Countryman, Edward: *A People in Revolution: the American Revolution and Political Society in New York, 1760–1790* (Baltimore: Johns Hopkins University Press, 1981).
——: " 'To Secure the Blessings of Liberty': Language, the Revolution and American Capitalism," in *Beyond the American Revolution: Further Explorations in the History of American Radicalism*, ed. Alfred F. Young (Dekalb: Northern Illinois University Press, 1990).
Foner, Eric: *Tom Paine and Revolutionary America* (New York: Oxford University Press, 1976).
Isaac, Rhys: *The Transformation of Virginia, 1740–1790* (Chapel Hill: University of North Carolina Press, 1982).
Kerber, Linda K.: *Women of the Republic: Intellect and Ideology in Revolutionary America* (Chapel Hill: University of North Carolina Press, 1980).
Maier, Pauline: *From Resistance to Revolution: Colonial Radicals and the Development of American Opposition to Britain, 1765–1776* (New York: Alfred A. Knopf, 1972).
Nash, Gary B.: *The Urban Crucible: Social Change, Political Consciousness and the Origins of the American Revolution* (Cambridge, Mass.: Harvard University Press, 1979).

Norton, Mary Beth: *Liberty's Daughters: the Revolutionary Experience of American Women, 1750–1800* (Boston: Little, Brown, 1980).

Rosswurm, Steven: *Arms, Country and Class: the Philadelphia Militia and the "Lower Sort" During the American Revolution* (New Brunswick, NJ: Rutgers University Press, 1987).

Ryerson, Richard A.: *The Revolution Is Now Begun: the Radical Committees of Philadelphia, 1765–1776* (Philadelphia: University of Pennsylvania Press, 1978).

Thompson, E. P.: "The moral economy of the English crowd in the eighteenth century," *Past & Present*, 50 (February 1971), 76–136.

Young, Alfred F.. "English plebeian culture and eighteenth-century American radicalism," in *The Origins of Anglo-American Radicalism*, ed. Margaret Jacob and James Jacob (London: Allen & Unwin, 1984).

20

The tea crisis and its consequences, through 1775

DAVID L. AMMERMAN

THE Boston Tea Party initiated a series of events which led directly to the American Revolution. On 16 December 1773, a group of Bostonians, disguised as Indians, boarded three vessels and threw the cargo of tea into the harbor. The party ended three weeks of negotiation between the town and Governor Thomas Hutchinson. The citizens did not want the tea landed because they feared that paying taxes on it would establish a precedent. The Governor was determined to land the tea, in part because of his conviction that any failure to enforce the law would encourage disregard for British authority.

In response to the destruction of the tea, the British Government adopted four Acts. These Acts, known in the colonies as the Coercive or Intolerable Acts, closed the port of Boston, redesigned the government of Massachusetts Bay to increase British authority, provided for moving trials of British officials to another colony or to England when local opinion was inflamed, and permitted the housing of British troops in unused buildings. The British considered the Acts essential for the effective governing of the colonies; the Americans viewed them as an unwarranted exercise of arbitrary power.

A fifth Act, the Quebec Act, was not adopted in response to the Boston Tea Party, but was unpopular in the colonies and was included – by the Americans – with the Coercive Acts because it seemed to favor the Catholic church in Canada, provided for a government without an elected assembly, and – perhaps most importantly – transferred large areas of western lands to the Canadian colony, thus threatening land speculators.

News of the Coercive Acts aroused widespread dissatisfaction in the colonies and led to the calling of the First Continental Congress. This body adopted an embargo of British goods and called for the repeal of the Coercive Acts as well as all legislation levying taxes or altering traditional rights of trial by jury. Congress authorized the election of Committees of Inspection in local communities throughout the colonies as a means of enforcing the embargo. It also provided for non-exportation to begin in the fall of 1775 if Great Britain did not agree to its demands.

The British ministry, faced with the demands of Congress as well as the impossibility of enforcing its will in Massachusetts, decided on an armed response. The Colonial Secretary, Lord Dartmouth, acting on instructions from the Cabinet, ordered General Thomas Gage (the recently appointed Governor of Massachusetts Bay) to march into the countryside either to arrest leaders of the resistance or to confiscate arms being stored at Concord. The resulting skirmishes at Lexington and Concord touched off the American Revolution.

I. THE TEA ACT OF 1773

It is unusual, perhaps unprecedented, for a revolution to begin over lowered commodity prices. Yet that was the case with the American Revolution. It has been a continuing source of puzzlement to historians that the Boston Tea Party – and subsequent events leading to the American Revolution – occurred in response to a British measure which reduced the price of tea throughout the colonies.

By 1773 the East India Company was on the verge of bankruptcy and the government undertook to save the company – and the nation – from such a fate. One aspect of this effort involved helping the company to sell the large quantities of tea stored in its warehouses. The company had had difficulty selling tea since 1767 when the American colonies had adopted a boycott of all products, including tea, taxed by the Townshend Duties. When the other duties were repealed in 1770, the government had maintained the tax on tea and the colonies had continued their boycott. By 1773 it seemed that one way to help the East India Company increase its profits would be to lower the price of tea in America and thus increase sales.

The simplest way to reduce the price of tea would have been to repeal the 3d tax levied in the colonies. That was unacceptable to the ministry. When the government repealed the Townshend Duties, it had kept the tax on tea as a means of demonstrating to the colonists that Parliament had the right to levy taxes. The same considerations proved determinative in 1773. England kept the colonial tax, but still managed to lower the price of the commodity in America. The means adopted to achieve this goal were to prove lethal to the empire, but the method was simple. Since all tea had to be imported to England before being sent on to the colonies, and since a tax was charged when the cargo arrived in the mother country, a rebate was arranged. Merchants who exported tea from England to the colonies were refunded the original tax. Thus the price was lowered and the colonial tax was maintained.

One other provision of the Tea Act would arouse the ire of colonial merchants. It gave the East India Company the right to select certain merchants in America and consign shipments of tea to each. Thus, in effect, the company decided who could sell tea in the colonies, and the resulting monopoly naturally irritated those to whom consignments were not made.

Colonial objections came from three different groups. Professional patriots charged that lowering the price of tea while maintaining the colonial tax constituted another attempt by the British Government to trick them into accepting taxation. Merchants, as noted above, were upset over the implications of permitting the East India Company to select its own factors. This constituted a monopoly of tea sales, they said, and might well lay the groundwork for similar measures in the future. Finally, smugglers were irritated over the prospect of lowered prices on legal tea. It seemed not unlikely that the prospect of buying legal tea at prices lower than smuggled tea would lure away their customers. This combination (professional patriots, merchants, and smugglers) provided formidable opposition.

2. THE BOSTON TEA PARTY

In the summer of 1773 the East India Company dispatched shipments of tea to the four major ports in the colonies: Charles Town, Philadelphia, New York, and Boston. The effort proved unsuccessful. In New York and Philadelphia the colonists refused

FIGURE 17 The Boston Tea Party (engraving, 1789); there are no contemporary depictions of the incident.

to allow the cargo to be unloaded and the vessels simply left the harbor. In Charles Town the situation was more complicated, but in the end the tea was unloaded and stored without paying the tax. Only in Boston did the situation lead to violence.

To say that Thomas Hutchinson, acting Governor of Massachusetts Bay, was a man of conviction, would not be an overstatement. And one of his convictions held that the common people of Massachusetts Bay – if not all America – had gotten out of hand. If government is to govern, Hutchinson believed, it must do precisely that. Compromise and submission only encouraged mob rule, and the time had come to put an end to such encouragement which had already caused problems in Massachusetts Bay. Hutchinson believed that the shipment of tea to Boston provided a unique opportunity to restore order and authority. Once the ships had entered the harbor, British law forbade their leaving until all taxes had been paid. Fortuitously, from the acting Governor's point of view, the guns of Castle William controlled egress from the harbor and permitted Hutchinson to stop the ships from leaving Boston.

Captain Rotch, the commander of the three vessels which brought the tea to Boston, is one of those historical figures caught in the flow of events. Hoping only to extricate himself from a difficult situation, he traveled back and forth between the town meeting – which repeatedly refused to allow his ships to unload – and the acting Governor – who repeatedly insisted that the ships remain in port.

Hutchinson apparently believed that he had the citizens of Boston in a bind. Authorized by law to unload a cargo which waited in port for three weeks without paying the required taxes, the acting Governor apparently intended to do just that. He would then presumably be able to use military force to unload the cargo and see that it was disposed of according to the provisions of the law. A commercial transaction would, in effect, become a governmental transaction. Thomas Hutchinson's thoughtful preparations failed. As the ships bobbed in Boston harbor and the frantic captain ran between the town meeting and the Governor trying to avert disaster, colonial leaders planned a fateful step. Samuel Adams, serving as moderator of a massive town meeting in Old South Meeting Hall, listened to Rotch explain Hutchinson's final refusal to permit the ships to leave. Then, according to tradition, he banged his gavel three times and declared that since "*this* meeting" could do no more to protect the rights of America it stood adjourned. Subsequently, a group disguised as Indians swooped down on the harbor and tossed the tea into the salty water (*see* figure 17). Boston must have been deceptively quiet that night as the colonists celebrated their apparent victory behind closed doors and shuttered windows.

3. THE REACTION OF THE BRITISH GOVERNMENT

What makes the Boston Tea Party so significant was not the event itself but the response of the British Government. Crowd action, as historians have repeatedly demonstrated, was not unusual in the eighteenth century and the Boston Tea Party was a classic example of this phenomenon. The decision of the North ministry, however, to use the event as a justification for closing the port of Boston, restructuring the government of Massachusetts Bay, and ordering changes in the system of justice was unprecedented.

It seems clear, in retrospect, that the British Government saw the Boston Tea Party as an opportunity to restore its authority in the American colonies. Ever since the repeal of the Stamp Act, there had been a growing belief in England that – as General Gage would later put it – the colonists would be lions "whilst we are Lambs." The clear implication of such an attitude was that at some point the British Government must take a stand and maintain it at all costs. The Tea Party appeared to present a perfect opportunity for decisive action.

In the first place the actions of the Boston mob were almost universally condemned in England. Few, even among the supporters of the colonists, could justify the destruction of private property and the flouting of established law, especially when that law had resulted in reducing the price of tea. Even many colonists believed that the Bostonians had taken events to the extreme. George Washington and Benjamin Franklin were among those prominent Americans who expressed reservations about the events of 16 December. Moreover, Massachusetts Bay seemed to stand alone. Although New York, Philadelphia, and Charles Town had refused the tea, none of these cities had gone to the extreme of destroying it. Consequently it was possible to single out Boston and Massachusetts Bay for punishment and, since this city and province were thought to be the center of colonial resistance, bringing them to order would presumably entail a lesson for all America. No one seems to have considered the inherent contradictions in a policy which sought to isolate a group as a means of teaching a lesson to other groups.

The Coercive Acts   Parliament adopted four specific Acts in direct response to the Boston Tea Party: the Boston Port Act, the Massachusetts Government Act, the Justice Act, and the Quartering Act. A fifth Act, usually lumped together with these four, termed the Coercive or Intolerable Acts in the colonies, was the Quebec Act, which was not attributable to the events in Boston Harbor.

The Boston Port Act closed the port of Boston. Declaring shipping to be unsafe in that area, Parliament forbade ships to enter or leave the port until compensation had been made for the tea. Even then, commerce would not be restored until the King determined that it was safe.

The Massachusetts Government Act altered by parliamentary fiat, as the colonists saw it, the basic structure of colonial government. It provided that the upper house, or council, should henceforth be appointed by the King rather than selected by the governor from a list nominated by the lower house. It also brought local administration more directly under the control of the governor. Towns were allowed to hold their cherished meetings only once a year and were forbidden to concern themselves with other than local matters. The thrust and intent of the law was to limit the "democratic" features of New England government.

The Justice Act was intended to protect British officials in their efforts to enforce the law. It provided that in capital cases government officials, or those working under their direction, be protected from vindictive local juries. If the governor determined that a fair trial could not be had, he might order a change of venue either to another colony or even to Great Britain itself.

The Quartering Act altered existing legislation in an effort to provide more effectively for British troops. It stipulated that when the colony offered quarters which were unacceptable, the governor could take over unoccupied public buildings for the use of the troops. It did not, as generations of American school children were taught, permit the housing of troops in private homes.

Because of its timing and provisions, the Quebec Act was also considered by the colonists to be a part of this punitive legislation. In fact the Act was an enlightened effort on the part of the British Government to organize the recently acquired colony of Quebec. It allowed the Catholic Church to continue at least a quasi-established position in the colony and also continued French civil law – a system which did not guarantee trial by jury. It set up a government without an elected assembly and, perhaps most galling to the English colonists, it added the Old Northwest Territory – where many of the original 13 colonies had land claims – to Quebec. To the colonists the Act favored Catholics, established a government without representation, interfered with their land claims, and limited trial by jury.

4. THE FIRST CONTINENTAL CONGRESS

Perhaps the major miscalculation of the North ministry in adopting these measures was the assumed isolation of Massachusetts Bay. Although many of the other colonies were reluctant to rush precipitously into a trade boycott – as Boston asked – they clearly rejected the Coercive Acts as an unwarranted intrusion into colonial affairs. During the late spring and early summer of 1774, leaders in every colony except Georgia had arranged for the election of delegates to attend a "Grand Congress" in Philadelphia. Moreover, virtually all of those colonies had committed themselves to some sort of trade boycott and some – such as Virginia – had already adopted measures directed at that objective.

The First Continental Congress met in Philadelphia in September 1774 and immediately set itself three objectives. The delegates proposed to draw up a clear statement of colonial rights, list the Acts of Parliament which violated those rights, and propose measures to secure the repeal of that legislation. It is notable that the first of these objectives proved impossible, the second was accomplished with some clever sleight of hand, and only the last – the decision which led to revolution – was achieved with little debate and adopted by acclamation.

In drawing up a statement of rights, Congress rejected outright Parliament's right to tax, to interfere with traditional rights of trial by jury, or to adopt the Coercive Acts. All of these were beyond the authority of the British Government in the American colonies. The divisive issue concerned Parliament's right to regulate trade. Five colonies wanted to approve that right, five wanted to deny it, and two – including Massachusetts Bay – found themselves split on the question. In the end the delegates adopted an ambiguous document wrapped around such statements as "the necessity of the case" which said little and guaranteed nothing.

Turning to its list of grievances, Congress once again stumbled on the issue of trade regulation. Should the delegates complain of the Acts of Trade and Navigation? What about the Hat Act or the Woolens Act? In the end they adopted a clever, if devious, solution. Deciding that a conspiracy to deprive Americans of their rights had been hatched about the year 1763, they concluded that legislation passed before that year could be passed over for the time being. It is significant that Congress did not legitimatize such legislation but simply decided to limit its debates to Acts passed after the agreed-upon date.

It must have been with some relief that the delegates turned to that issue upon which they were virtually unanimous – the means by which the colonists should secure repeal of grievances. Without apparent dissent, the delegates invoked non-importation to begin in December 1774 and followed that with a resolution to begin non-exportation the following fall if Parliament had not rescinded the objectionable legislation. A number of delegates wanted to begin non-exportation immediately but apparently submitted to the representatives of Virginia, who adamantly refused a measure which would prevent them from marketing tobacco that was already in the ground.

The Continental Association   In pursuing these objectives Congress endorsed a document known as the Continental Association. That document listed the Acts that Parliament was to repeal and endorsed non-importation and delayed non-exportation as a means of securing that repeal. It also called upon towns and counties throughout the colonies to establish Committees of Inspection, each of which would take responsibility for enforcing the trade boycott. In establishing local committees for the purpose of enforcing what might easily be viewed as a piece of legislation, Congress took an enormously important step in the development of a quasi-legal governmental structure. One of the problems facing a revolutionary movement is the maintenance of order. These committees, in effect, would become the means by which both the Provincial and the Continental Congresses would provide local government as the revolution progressed.

Another aspect of the Association merits mention. In an effort to encourage the colonists to develop an economic independence from Great Britain – and, perhaps, not incidentally, to demonstrate their determination to the government – the delegates approved a number of resolutions designed to promote self-sufficiency. Americans were asked to protect sheep in order to encourage the production of woolen cloth. They were warned to avoid the exchange of expensive (and imported) gifts at funerals and to develop domestic manufacturing in order to lessen their dependence on Great Britain. In brief, Congress asked all Americans to adopt a frugal and independent life style which would not only promote economic self-sufficiency, but would also demonstrate to the mother country their determination and willingness to sacrifice.

Galloway's Plan of Union Despite the unanimity with which Congress adopted its trade embargo with England, a number of delegates remained dissatisfied with the ambiguous Statement of Rights. They argued that Congress had been instructed not just to secure repeal of colonial grievances, but also to establish a firm basis on which the connection with England could be maintained. Individuals such as JAMES DUANE and JOSEPH GALLOWAY believed that the failure of Congress to recognize Parliament's right to regulate colonial trade was unacceptable. The matter, in the opinion of such delegates, remained unsettled.

It was in this context that Galloway introduced his now famous Plan of Union. Although often touted as a conservative alternative to the trade embargo, it was nothing of the sort. Galloway's proposal came after Congress had endorsed non-importation and non-exportation and it was, in fact, an attempt to deal with the question of the imperial relationship rather than immediate problems. The Galloway Plan of Union was one of the most radical proposals put forth in Congress. It envisioned a reorganization of the empire, with an American Congress sharing power with the British Parliament. Had it been endorsed by the Congress it would almost certainly have been rejected by the British Government.

The plan was rejected by Congress. When first proposed by Galloway the delegates voted, by the margin of a single colony, to lay it on the table. Historians have occasionally suggested that the plan was rejected by a single vote, but that was not the case. Those colonies which voted to table it simply indicated a willingness to consider it at a later time. When it was brought up for resolution, near the end of the meetings, it was rejected, but by what margin was not recorded. New York voted for the plan, but there is no evidence that any other colony did, and it is even possible that Pennsylvania, whose delegation had been altered by the addition of John Dickinson, did not support the proposal in the final vote.

Resolutions adopted by Congress Before adjourning, Congress adopted two resolutions which had far-reaching effect. Fearing that Massachusetts Bay – which was widely regarded as more radical than other colonies – might initiate conflict with the troops stationed in Boston, Congress sought to avoid that possibility. The delegates asked Massachusetts to avoid taking aggressive measures and promised that if the Bay Colony was attacked it would be supported by the other colonies acting in concert.

The delegates further agreed to call a second meeting of Congress in the spring, allowing enough time for Great Britain to respond to their measures. Their timing, as it turned out, would be propitious, since news of the conflict at Lexington and Concord reached many of the delegates as they set out for the May meeting of the Second Continental Congress.

5. SUPPORT FOR CONGRESS IN THE COLONIES

As the delegates left Philadelphia they were almost certainly divided in their expectations. More militant members such as Sam Adams and Richard Henry Lee were certain that the efforts of Congress would not change British policy. They had argued, unsuccessfully, that Congress should instruct the colonists to prepare for war. Others – James Duane and John Dickinson are notable examples – hoped that the decisions of Congress would persuade the British that the colonists were united and determined and thus lead to a modification of government policy.

The work of Congress was widely acclaimed and supported throughout the colonies.

From the point of view of most Americans, the delegates had adopted a moderate but determined stand. They had rejected all proposals for military preparation, had petitioned the government in respectful terms, and had invoked an embargo policy which had, apparently, proved ineffective in previous crises provoked by the Stamp Act and the Townshend Duties. Consequently a substantial majority of colonists determined to show their support for Congress by adopting and enforcing its resolutions. In town, county, and provincial meetings throughout the continent they approved the program adopted by the Congress, appointed committees to see to its enforcement, and took steps to ensure their economic independence from the mother country.

Committees of Inspection   One of the most important gauges of support for the Continental Association was the swift appointment of committees. In New England the response was almost unanimous. Hundreds of committees were appointed, even in the smallest and most remote of communities. The sincerity of these community efforts is perhaps best demonstrated by the town of Sutton, Massachusetts. Noting that the punishment for violating the resolutions of Congress was social ostracization, citizens discussed the exact meaning of that term. They concluded that those who spoke to offenders might be forgiven if they had done so inadvertently, to convince the offender of his or her error in ignoring the resolutions of Congress in a situation which involved a threat to their lives or the lives of their domestic animals, or for purposes involving religion and the state of the offender's soul.

It is somewhat more difficult to assess support for Congress in the middle colonies. Certainly the embargo was effective in the major port cities of New York and Philadelphia, and committees actively enforced the dictates of Congress in both. Records in smaller towns and counties are fragmented, but where they exist they show general approval. New York was the only colony – excepting Georgia, which sent no delegation to Congress – in which the Assembly failed to ratify the Continental Association.

In the southern colonies there was generally enthusiastic support for Congress and the appointment of committees seems to have been the rule. Virginia, of course, led the way. The Virginia *Gazette* reported the formation of nearly 50 county committees to enforce the Association. In South Carolina the Provincial Congress appointed committees, and while it is difficult to assess local support the committees apparently operated effectively. Counties in Maryland appointed quite large committees, each of which seems to have divided into smaller groups to provide effective local surveillance.

It would be difficult to overemphasize the significance of these committees in the development of revolutionary government in the colonies. Literally thousands of citizens were brought into the movement through their activities as committeemen. This included not only the pre-crisis leaders (Governor Dunmore reported from Virginia that local Justices of the Peace were active *only* as committee members) but others who had not previously been active in government. In Maryland, for example, members were constantly added to the committees, which suggests a conscious effort to broaden the basis of support for the patriot program.

The activities of these Committees of Inspection were nearly as varied as the localities in which they were appointed. In major port cities a large proportion of time was spent enforcing the embargo through the inspection of incoming vessels, merchant inventories, etc. In other communities the committees went from house to house collecting signatures on copies of the Continental Association or calling citizens before them to explain reports that they had drunk a cup of tea. Newspapers reported a number of incidents in which individuals were forced to recant before local committees for having cast aspersions on various members or on the committee itself. As the crisis deepened, the Committees of Inspection gradually evolved into Committees of Safety and took upon themselves responsibility for such governmental policies as collecting taxes for the revolutionary governments and recruiting soldiers.

Significantly, these committees acted not under the authority of the Provincial Assemblies or even the Provincial Congresses, but considered themselves enforcement agencies of the Continental Congress. In New York, for example, where the Provincial Assembly did not specifically endorse the work of Congress or call on local communities to enforce its resolutions, many communities appointed committees anyway. In nearly every colony Committees of Inspection were appointed before any provincial body had met or acted on the decisions of Congress. Even many conservative colonists supported local committees because they were rapidly becoming the only bulwark between order and chaos. As provincial and local government ceased to function under the authority of King and Parliament, it was essential that some form of authority step into the void. That authority was most often the local Committee of Inspection.

6. REACTION IN BRITAIN TO THE CONGRESS

In Great Britain the response to the resolutions of the Continental Congress was, at first, confused. By the time word of the events in Philadelphia arrived in England the government was, for the most part, dispersed and already engaged in the general inactivity which characterized the Christmas holidays. Rumors circulated in the colonies that the ministry had been favorably impressed with the work of the Congress and that the King and Parliament would respond in a conciliatory fashion. Nothing could have been further from the truth, but the state of communications in the eighteenth century and the inactivity of government during the holidays prevented the contradiction of those reports for several months.

The British Government faced a situation which virtually demanded vigorous action. Massachusetts Bay was clearly in rebellion and the regular government had ceased to function outside the city of Boston. Governor (General) Thomas Gage had dissolved the General Court of the colony in June 1774 when he learned that the delegates were appointing representatives to the Continental Congress. When he ordered new elections under the provisions of the Massachusetts Government Act, which had established an appointive Council, the deputies simply refused to meet with the so-called mandamus councilors. Instead, they gathered in Concord and invited the previous Council – organized under the provisions of the Charter granted by William and Mary – to meet with them. They also invited Governor Gage to participate but he, not surprisingly, refused.

Even in Boston Gage found it hard to govern. The Massachusetts Government Act had decreed that town meetings should be held only once a year, a provision that the Boston Town Meeting had rendered ineffective by simply adjourning from week to week. So difficult had Gage's position become that he wrote to the Cabinet proposing that the Coercive Acts be "suspended" until Great Britain was in a position to see them enforced. Before leaving England the Governor had believed that the colonists could be brought to heel by a show of force and determination. On the spot in Boston he discovered that opposition in Massachusetts Bay was not confined to the "rabble" and a few radical leaders, but, rather, had infected the entire province.

206

The government could not avoid taking action. According to the Declaratory Act of 1766 the King and Parliament had the right to legislate for the colonies "in all cases whatsoever," and in adopting the Massachusetts Government Act they had done so. Massachusetts had simply refused to abide by the terms of that legislation, and the duly appointed governor of the Bay Colony now sat impotently in Boston while the province proceeded to flout British law. The only possible means of avoiding a confrontation with the colonists would have been for the government to adopt a conciliatory position towards the resolutions of Congress and begin negotiations based on the assumption that the Coercive Acts would be repealed. That was not possible. Even Gage's suggestion that the acts be "suspended" was scoffed at by the Cabinet and by Dartmouth, who wrote that he was not aware of any provision in British law for "suspending" Acts of Parliament.

Ignoring the resolutions of Congress, the evidence from a number of British officials in the colonies that the Americans were united in their determination to resist the Coercive Acts, and the insistence of Gage that his forces were inadequate to enforce the law, the government continued to believe that the crisis could be ended through a show of force. Perhaps the fatal flaw in British policy at this time was the failure of the government to acknowledge the extent of colonial resistance. It was conventional knowledge among the ministry that opposition in the colonies was the work of a few radical leaders who had inflamed the rabble. If only the government would take a stand, show that they were determined to enforce it, and send the royal standard out into the countryside, the vast majority of the colonists would rally to the cause. Cabinet members even suggested, privately, that Gage's about-face since his arrival in Massachusetts Bay was evidence of cowardice on his part.

As events stood in January 1775, conflict was virtually inevitable. Both sides had made up their minds that a show of determination and force was needed. Many colonists were convinced that British policy reflected a failure on the part of the King and Parliament to recognize colonial unity. If the government could be persuaded, they believed, that the American colonies stood united, then concessions would follow. Similarly with the members of the British government: failure in the past, they concluded, had resulted from a perception in the colonies that the government did not have the will to enforce its legislation. Failure to enforce the Stamp Act and then the Townshend Duties had, the British leadership believed, contributed to a lack of respect for order in the colonies. Now was their chance to correct that perception. The laws would be enforced and, when the colonists realized that the mother country meant business, resistance would fall apart.

litary action   In the early part of 1775 the Cabinet began to consider measures to deal with the crisis in America. After considering and rejecting a number of possibilities the ministers decided to follow through on their assumptions about the weakness of the opposition and take action in Massachusetts Bay. Lord Dartmouth was instructed to draft a letter to Governor Gage instructing him to use the forces he had at hand to make a show of force in the countryside outside Boston.

The Cabinet's instructions to Gage left little room for interpretation. Gage was informed that his observations about the extent of resistance in the province had been considered and rejected. He was ordered to take action. The Cabinet would have preferred that he march into the countryside and arrest certain presumed leaders of the resistance movement, but admitted that since he was on the scene he would have to be the judge of that. Nevertheless, he was to do something. If he decided that it was impossible to make such arrests he was to confiscate military stores or in some manner indicate that the time for concession was past.

Dartmouth reported the Cabinet's overwhelming belief that, despite Gage's assertions to the contrary, the resistance would collapse once British troops showed a determination to enforce British law. He acknowledged Gage's conclusions that military action would precipitate civil war but informed the General that the Cabinet disagreed. Even if Gage were correct, the Cabinet had determined that if war were inevitable it would be better to begin the conflict immediately rather than allow the colonists to become better prepared for military conflict. These lengthy instructions reflect the contempt of the British Government, not only for colonial unity but for colonial military prowess. It was apparently inconceivable to the Cabinet that the Americans had either the will or the ability to resist the British military.

Meanwhile in Massachusetts Bay, Samuel Adams, among others, awaited the conflict which he knew was coming. The Provincial Congress, meeting in Concord without the mandamus councilors or the Governor, proceeded to conduct business, collect taxes, and govern the province outside Boston. Although the delegates avoided precipitating armed conflict with the British – perhaps because they remembered the promise of Congress to come to their assistance provided that they were the aggrieved party – they were preparing for an expected attack. If men like James Duane in New York and John Dickinson in Pennsylvania still held out hope for overtures of peace, most of the Massachusetts leadership knew better. They even provided for patrols on the roads leading out of Boston in order to alert the countryside when the British finally decided to march. Paul Revere, William Wadsworth Longfellow aside, did not just happen to be in place on the "18th of April in seventy-five." Similar patrols had been active for some time.

The British march on Lexington and Concord is too well known to be detailed here. Gage, following specific orders, determined that his best chance was to send a force to Concord to destroy or confiscate military stores collected there. In the early hours of the morning of 18 April 1775 British regulars approached Lexington Green, where they were confronted by a small force of militiamen who had been alerted of their approach. As the Americans began to disperse, having made a show of resistance, a shot rang out, and before the British officers could stop the firing a number of colonists had been injured or killed.

Continuing on to Concord the British did, indeed, seize and destroy some of the military stores collected there. Even as they marched, however, militia from throughout Massachusetts and Connecticut were marching towards the temporary colonial capital. By the time the regulars began their retreat to Boston they found themselves harassed by increasing numbers of colonials who fired from behind barns, hedges, and stone walls. The remnants of the expedition straggled back into Boston demoralized and defeated. It appeared, as a minor British governmental official would later comment, that the colonists had been more determined than anticipated.

News of Lexington and Concord was electric throughout the colonies. In New York thousands signed the Association and turned out in support of the upcoming Congress. Reports of the battle reached Patrick Henry in Virginia, who responded with his now famous "Give me Liberty or Give me Death" speech. Perhaps more important, reports of the conflict reached many of the delegates to the Second Continental Congress as they approached Philadelphia, and the news set the tone for the meeting. George Washington appeared on the scene in the uniform of his native Virginia and would soon accept the command of the American army offered by Congress. Meanwhile, thousands of militiamen headed towards Boston, where they surrounded the city and effectively bottled up the British troops, ultimately forcing them to withdraw.

7. SUMMARY

In retrospect it appears that the British Government did virtually everything wrong. In adopting the Coercive Acts they had seriously miscalculated the possibilities of isolating and punishing Boston as an example to the rest of the colonies. The Acts themselves touched on almost every sensitive point in the colonial mind, almost as if calculated to provoke resistance. The Massachusetts Government Act had altered a colonial charter by fiat, a move which threatened many colonists regardless of the alterations made. The Justice Act interfered with traditional British concepts of trial by jury, prompting even so conservative a colonist as George Washington to refer to it as the "Murder Act." The Boston Port Act appeared to many as a virtual declaration of war, with British naval vessels sent to blockade an American port. The Quebec Act managed to incite colonial Protestants by protecting the Catholic Church in Canada, and threatened land speculators through its transfer of territory to a distant – and "foreign" – jurisdiction. Nearly every colonial interest felt threatened by these Acts. Moreover, the Massachusetts Government Act, unlike the Port Act, the Quebec Act, or even the Justice Act, could be enforced only with provincial cooperation or through force. It was inconceivable that the British Government could permit its army to sit idle in Boston while the rest of the province ignored an Act of Parliament. By adopting this Act the ministry put itself in a position of either acknowledging its weakness or taking forceful action.

Having aroused almost universal opposition and having put its prestige on the line, the British Government proceeded to initiate conflict in such a manner as to allow Massachusetts to proclaim its innocence and its suffering "in the common cause." Since the First Continental Congress had promised to come to the assistance of Massachusetts in case of attack, the delegates had little choice but to follow through on that assurance. And, propitiously for the men from the Bay Colony, the attack was undertaken on the eve of the second meeting of the Congress.

Finally the British suffered a disastrous defeat, both in actuality and in the propaganda war. The vaunted reputation of the redcoats was in tatters and their casualties were far greater than those of the colonists. They had retreated in disarray. It appeared that regular troops were no match for the virtuous wrath of an aroused citizenry. The colonists stood aggrieved, attacked, and victorious, and the British Government was totally unprepared to subdue a continent. Before further activities could be undertaken by the ministry, troops would have to be raised, taxes collected, and plans for conquest formulated. And while the British undertook these preparations, the colonists had time to raise an army, organize an intercolonial government, embark on measures of wartime finance, and win the initial military successes of the war in New England.

FURTHER READING

Ammerman, David: *In the Common Cause: American Response to the Coercive Acts of 1774* (Charlottesville: University Press of Virginia, 1974).

Brown, Richard D.: *Revolutionary Politics in Massachusetts: the Boston Committee of Correspondence and the Towns, 1772–1774* (Cambridge, Mass.: Harvard University Press, 1970).

Countryman, Edward: *The American Revolution* (New York: Hill and Wang, 1985).

Donoughue, Bernard: *British Politics and the American Revolution: the Path to War, 1773–1775* (New York: St. Martin's Press, 1964).

Gross, Robert A.: *The Minutemen and their World* (New York: Hill and Wang, 1976).

Labaree, Benjamin Woods: *The Boston Tea Party* (New York: Oxford University Press, 1964).

Maier, Pauline: *The Old Revolutionaries: Political Lives in the Age of Samuel Adams* (New York: Knopf, 1980).

Marston, Jerrilyn Greene: *King and Congress: the Transfer of Political Legitimacy, 1774–1776* (Princeton, NJ: Princeton University Press, 1987).

Middlekauff, Robert: *The Glorious Cause: the American Revolution, 1763–1789* (New York: Oxford University Press, 1982).

Nash, Gary B.: *The Urban Crucible: Social Change, Political Consciousness, and the Origins of the American Revolution* (Cambridge, Mass.: Harvard University Press, 1979).

21

The crisis of Independence

DAVID L. AMMERMAN

FROM the Battle of Lexington and Concord in April 1775 until the Declaration of Independence in early July 1776, the American colonists engaged actively in warfare with Great Britain but did not declare independence. It is unusual in history for colonies to take up arms against the mother country while proclaiming that their only objective is reunification, and the refusal of the colonists to declare their independence hindered the war effort, thus making their situation even more remarkable. Delegates to the Second Continental Congress refused to open their ports to foreign nations because it violated British law, they held back on entering into negotiations for foreign military assistance because their objective was to return to the empire, they inventoried captured equipment and arms so that they could be returned to England after the conflict was over, and they toasted the health of the King and carried on business in his name until well into 1776.

A majority of Americans expected that their demands would ultimately be met by the British, which explains their behavior. They held on to the hope that George III and the opposition in Parliament would reverse the course of the ministry once it became clear that the colonists sought only to restore their rights as Englishmen and remain within the empire. These expectations proved unrealistic, yet they prevented a declaration of separation from Great Britain for over a year.

The actions of the British ministers and their colonial governors ultimately persuaded a majority of Americans that their only choice was between independence and submission. During the latter half of 1775 England declared them in rebellion, closed their ports, hired foreign mercenaries to carry on warfare against them, and made it clear that the government was determined to force them to accept the authority of Parliament. It became increasingly clear that the King himself supported these measures, and that the opposition in Parliament was ineffective. These events, and others like them, brought the colonists to accept the necessity for separation.

By February 1776 a majority in the Second Continental Congress supported independence. But even at that late date their majority was small. A number of colonies, including New Jersey, Delaware, New York, Pennsylvania, and Maryland, still opposed it. Indeed, Congress had to encourage a revolution in the government of Pennsylvania to win the support of that colony, and the New York delegates did not have instructions on how to vote when the issue came to the floor on 2 July. Not until February 1776 was independence even debated on the floor of Congress.

North Carolina, on 12 April 1776, became the first colony to instruct its delegates to agree, in concert with others, to independence. Two months later Richard Henry Lee, acting on the instruction of the Virginia Convention, proposed that the colonies "are, and of right ought to be, free and independent States." Several delegates threatened to leave Congress unless the vote was postponed, but their endeavors were only a delaying tactic. The vote was put off until early July, but the fact that a date had been set gave evidence of the approaching victory of those gathering support for independence. On 2 July 1776 Congress voted for independence, and two days later the document was embossed and signed. The decision to declare independence had been made. The effort necessary to win it remained.

I. DIVIDED OPINION IN CONGRESS

Armed conflict between the British and their American colonists broke out at Lexington and Concord on 18 April 1775, and news of that battle swept rapidly through the colonies. War had begun. And yet the delegates who assembled for the Second Continental Congress in May of that year were far from convinced that the empire was irrevocably shattered. It would, indeed, be more than a year before the Americans declared themselves independent, and during the intervening months many, if not most, of them continued to hope for reconciliation.

Certainly the colonists in North America did not look upon themselves as revolutionaries. In their determined insistence that they had been forced to arms in order to protect the traditional rights of Englishmen, they maintained the fiction that they were fighting not the King but only the machinations of wicked counselors. Until early 1776 Washington and his officers continued to toast the health of George III and to refer to their armed opponents as the "Ministerial Troops."

For many these protestations were propaganda and window-dressing. Leaders such as Samuel Adams not only expected independence but actively pursued it, and it seems unlikely that George Washington would have accepted command of the Continental Army had he expected the colonies to return to the British fold. For others, however – John Dickinson of Pennsylvania and James Duane of New York come immediately to mind – independence was virtually unthinkable. Such men were clearly "reluctant Revolutionaries" who accepted each step towards separation in the hope that it would be the last.

It did not take long for the divisions which separated the American colonists to make themselves felt in the Second Continental Congress. Three distinct groups rapidly emerged. The radicals, which included John and Samuel Adams, Thomas Jefferson, George Washington, and Benjamin Franklin, had little hope for reconciliation and were prepared for independence. Dickinson and Duane, along with John Jay of New York, provided leadership to a group on the other end of the spectrum. These conservatives, although determined to protect American rights, adopted military measures with great reluctance and hoped that petition and moderation would produce a change in British attitudes. No doubt the largest group in Congress stood between these extremes. The moderates, including Robert Morris of Pennsylvania, John Hancock and Thomas Cushing of Massachusetts, and the Rutledges of South Carolina, hoped for a return to the empire but had little faith that this could be accomplished by petition and moderation. They supported military measures as the only means of persuading the British to grant colonial demands. One of considerations that separated the three groups in Congress was their respective reading of political conditions in Great Britain. The radicals had no expectation that the British would moderate their demands. They were convinced that the ministry had the full support of George III and that neither petition nor armed resistance would result in reconciliation. The conservatives believed that there was strong opposition to British measures in Britain itself. They wanted, in so far as possible, to avoid armed conflict and relied on petition and remonstrance to convince the government, and particularly the King, that the Americans were loyal subjects whose grievances should be redressed. The moderates like the conservatives, hoped for reconciliation but, like the radicals, had little hope that this could be achieved through peaceful means. They were not ready to endorse independence, but they were prepared to support military resistance as the only hope of forcing Great Britain to meet colonial demands.

The radicals were correct. George III not only supported the ministry but in many cases pushed for more determined measures. Moreover, opposition in Parliament was small, divided, and demoralized. Anticipating the possibility of an extended contest with the Americans, Lord North had called for parliamentary elections and had won a resounding victory. Not until after the Battle of Yorktown in 1781 would the ministry face an effective opposition in Parliament. Throughout the American Revolution the government could count on comfortable margins in support of its measures.

In a very real sense, then, the months between the Battle of Lexington and Concord and the Declaration of Independence was a period of educating the moderates and conservatives in Congress to the realities of British politics. One by one the measures of the British Government brought new recruits to the radical block and ultimately to the acceptance of independence. Prohibiting trade with the colonies and declaring them in rebellion, encouraging opposition among the slaves and the Indians, hiring Hessians as combat troops were among the measures that gradually convinced the most reluctant of Revolutionaries that it was independence or submission.

2. THE AMERICAN MILITARY REACTION TO LEXINGTON AND CONCORD

There were a number of issues which Congress faced that influenced the question of independence. Perhaps the most immediate was what to do with the troops surrounding Boston. Incorporating the troops into a Continental Army and appointing officers were clearly the acts of a sovereign nation. Yet there seemed to be no alternative. The troops were there, and popular enthusiasm for fighting the British was at its height after Lexington and Concord. Moreover, Congress was more or less committed to such an action. Towards the end of the meeting of the First Continental Congress in October 1774 the delegates, in an effort to restrain the "radicalism" of Massachusetts, made a promise to the Bay Colony: if the Bostonians would avoid aggressive action and were attacked by British troops in spite of this moderation, all of America would come to their support. That was now the case.

The issue first arose when the New York Committee of 100 asked what to do if British troops arrived in New York City. Congress, determined to act on the defensive, told the committee to act only defensively. If the British committed hostile acts or attacked private property the New Yorkers could resist with force, but otherwise they should avoid conflict.

A few days later the delegates in Philadelphia learned that troops under the command of Ethan Allen and Benedict Arnold had captured Fort Ticonderoga on Lake Champlain and also Crown Point. While the Massachusetts Provincial Congress rejoiced, the Continental Congress worried about how to deal with this obvious act of colonial aggression against the mother country. In the end, the delegates ordered that a strict inventory of all arms and supplies be made so that they could be returned to England when the dispute was settled.

On 26 May Congress resolved that hostilities made it necessary to adopt a state of defense, and two weeks later the delegates committed themselves to raising troops and turned to the appointment of a commander-in-chief. George Washington, apparently the only member of Congress who appeared on the floor in military attire, was rumored to be available for the position. The Virginian was particularly acceptable because, as a member from one of the southern colonies, he would help solidify support for the New Englanders. His appointment on 15 June proved popular both in Congress and throughout the continent although, if John Adams is to be trusted on the issue, highly upsetting to John Hancock of Massachusetts, who had coveted the position himself. By instructing Washington "to command all the continental forces, raised, or to be raised, for the defence of American liberty," the Congress took a major step towards independence.

On 22 June the delegates made yet another advance. News of the Battle of Bunker (Breeds) Hill led to the election of eight brigadier generals and a vote to issue $2 million in paper money. Moreover it was decided to take command of the garrisons at Ticonderoga and Crown Point. These were clearly the acts of a sovereign power, although the letters and notes of the delegates indicate more concern with the politics of who would command the army than with the impact of the decision to create one.

Washington's acceptance of command is almost certainly indicative of his decision to pursue independence. It is almost inconceivable that he would have assumed this position had he expected reconciliation with the British Empire. Any outcome other than independence would have left the newly created general in a difficult position. Curtis Nettels, in his *George Washington and American Independence* (1951), has argued, persuasively if perhaps one-sidedly, that from the time of his appointment onwards the Virginian used every means within his power to advance the cause of independence. Certainly his push to create a navy, to define treason, and to insist that captured Americans be treated as prisoners of war and his numerous other activities helped commit the colonists to separation. The decision to invade Canada, coming some three weeks after Congress had resolved that no colonists should undertake or assist in such a venture, was further evidence of Washington's influence.

Was it not contradictory for the Congress to insist that it opposed independence and wanted to avoid conflict, even as it created an army, issued paper money, took command of the captured forts at Ticonderoga and Crown Point, and authorized an invasion of Canada. Certainly in many instances it was. John and Samuel Adams, Richard Henry Lee, and others clearly held neither a hope nor a desire of returning to the empire. For others, however, the position was not hypocritical. The Declaration of the Causes and Necessity of Taking up Arms, adopted on 6 July, fairly clearly – and no doubt honestly – expounded their position. They did not want armed conflict nor independence, and yet the presence of British troops and engagements such as those at Lexington, Concord, and Bunker Hill forced them to adopt measures to provide for their own defense.

3. BRITAIN'S RETALIATORY MEASURES

The apparently contradictory position of seeking reconciliation while adopting war measures is again a reflection of misinformation about the state of affairs in England. The Reconciliationists continued to hope that a change would be forthcoming in British policy. They clung to the belief that George III would heed their petitions and oust the evil ministers who had brought about this unwanted state of affairs. They

FIGURE 18 "The Olive Rejected, or the Yankees Revenge": Lord North, mounted on an ass, is being driven away by the Americans, even though he has an olive branch in his hat and the "Conciatory Bill" in his pocket.

continued to hope that the people of England – and the opposition in Parliament – would take control of the situation. None of those scenarios was even remotely possible. George III was, if anything, more committed to settling the issue with America than was his Cabinet. The opposition in Parliament was completely ineffective.

Slowly but purposely the British Government adopted measures which dashed the hopes of the Reconciliationists and forced them to the reluctant conclusion that there was no alternative to independence except submission. On 30 March 1775 the North ministry obtained passage of an Act restraining trade with New England, and on 13 April the measure was extended to Pennsylvania, New Jersey, Maryland, Virginia, and South Carolina. New York, Delaware, North Carolina, and Georgia were not at first included because the government hoped to drive a wedge between the colonies by offering a more conciliatory policy towards those that seemed less aggressive. North accompanied these Acts with a motion on reconciliation which proposed, in essence, that the colonies would not be taxed if they agreed to tax themselves. This so-called Olive Branch Resolution (see figure 18) was widely viewed in America as window-dressing, and so it was. North himself admitted in his correspondence with the King that he was more concerned with the opposition in England than with the possibilities of conciliation with America. Congress ultimately rejected the petition as having no substance.

4. LOCAL GOVERNMENT

Almost daily the delegates in Philadelphia faced problems that forced them to make decisions leading to independence. A major problem concerned the establishment of governments in the several colonies. Only a few legal governments were functioning, and it was imperative, if only to maintain order in the various provinces, that some sort of government be in place.

The First Continental Congress had, indeed, taken an important step in the direction of creating local governments when it authorized the appointment of committees of Inspection to enforce the Continental Association. That Association, which provided for non-importation of British goods, amounted to a national law adopted by a national Congress. This measure took on even more important implications because of its method of enforcement. Congress had authorized the establishment of town and county committees with power to inspect cargoes and punish those who failed to abide by the terms of the agreement. In doing so the delegates to the First Congress had bypassed provincial governments and thus established an embryonic national government with the committees acting as its agents. In time these committees raised taxes, enlisted soldiers, and took over most of the functions of local government. Although the First Continental Congress may have been unaware of the implications of this arrangement, the Association was a step in the direction of independence since it authorized the creation of local governments which in no way depended upon the support or the authority of the Crown or Parliament.

When Congress, during the second half of 1775, confronted the issue of entire provinces without government, the issue was more clearly tied to the question of independence. If Congress were to authorize the establishment of colonial governments acting in every way as sovereign powers but without the authority or approval of the British Government, would they not, in effect, be declaring independence colony by colony? Yet even the conservatives were forced to acknowledge that some such measure was necessary. John Adams recorded in his diary a conversation with a debtor who thanked him – and the Massachusetts Provincial Congress – for closing the courts since it was no longer necessary to pay debts. This had clearly not been one of Adams's objectives in leading the opposition to Great Britain, and it was certainly not an objective of more conservative colonists. If order was to be maintained, government must function, and in the absence of an established British-based authority, the Congress had to take responsibility for the creation of new, and non-imperial, governments.

The situation in Massachusetts is illustrative. With the failure of the British successfully to enforce the Massachusetts Government Act, the legal government had ceased to function. There had, in fact, been no royal government in the Bay Colony since Gage had dissolved the assembly as it was electing delegates to the First Continental Congress in June 1774. Council members appointed by the King had either been forced to resign or had fled to Boston. The assembly, meeting in Concord, invited the council elected before passage of the Government Act to meet with them and also issued an invitation to Gage to work with them until the crisis had passed. Gage, of course, had no intention of accepting that offer, and so government – outside of Boston – passed effectively to the lower house.

Conflicts among the patriots themselves brought the issue to the attention of the Continental Congress. The eastern towns and counties were, by and large, content simply to resume government under the terms of the charter granted them by William and Mary in 1691. The western portion of the colony, chafing under what it perceived to be under-representation in the government, agitated for a return to the original charter of 1629. On 9 June 1775 the Continental Congress resolved that the Assembly of Massachusetts Bay should elect a council, essentially as had been done under the charter of 1691, and that the legislature should then govern until such time as a royal governor would act according to the terms of the charter. In doing so, of course, the Congress endorsed the refusal of Massachusetts Bay to abide by the terms of the Massachusetts Government Act, and also put its weight and authority behind the creation of an independent government, albeit a temporary one.

Authorizing Massachusetts to resume government under the terms of a charter voided by Parliament and the King was a bold step, but still stopped short of actually instructing a colony to assume government based on the will of the people. On 18 October 1775 the New Hampshire Assembly asked Congress for instructions as to the creation of a new government for that colony. In responding to this request the delegates faced a more difficult decision than that taken with regard to Massachusetts Bay. In the end Congress recommended that New Hampshire assemble a "full and free representation of the people," and that if the representatives so decided they should establish a government as would "best produce the happiness of the people." In adopting this measure the Congress officially put itself in the position of authorizing provincial governments based on the will of the people rather than on the authority of England.

5. CONGRESS MOVES FROM RECONCILIATION TO SEPARATION

Nonetheless the majority in Congress continued to oppose independence and hope for reconciliation. Until early February 1776 those colonies favoring independence were in a minority even though the Reconciliationists were gradually forced to adopt measures characteristic of an independent nation. New York and Pennsylvania strongly opposed independence until at least June 1776, and even Maryland was not far behind. In November 1775 the New Jersey Assembly declared that reports of the colonies seeking separation from the British Empire were completely groundless, and on 11 January 1776 the Maryland Convention instructed its delegates not to consent to independence. Even the Massachusetts delegation, so long as it included Robert Treat Paine, Thomas Cushing, and John Hancock, was not committed to separation despite the fulminations of the two Adamses.

Events continued to strengthen the hands of the radicals. On 8 July Congress adopted its second petition to the King in which the delegates blamed the ministry for the present unrest in the empire, and explained the necessity of adopting "defensive" measures against those who sought to destroy the peace and harmony which had existed before their misdirected innovations. They begged the King to use his influence to end the armed conflict. Expectations of support from George III received a shattering blow when, in November, the news arrived that the King had refused even to receive the petition. Indeed, on 23 August 1775 a royal proclamation declared parts of America in open rebellion and threatened those in England who assisted the colonists with "condign" punishment. The punishment for treason at that time called not just for death but for dismemberment and other similarly drastic measures. It is doubtful that the ministry envisioned such punishment for William Pitt and Edmund Burke, but they clearly hoped to curtail the opposition in Parliament.

On 22 December 1775 Parliament passed the Prohibitory Act, putting a complete stop to American commerce. In effect, all American vessels and cargoes were declared forfeit to the Crown and the British Navy was legally entitled to seize them on the seas and in port. These two measures had enormous impact on sentiment in Congress and seriously weakened the arguments of those who continued to push for reconciliation. By declaring the colonies in open rebellion and refusing to hear the petition of

Congress, the King made clear his intention to force submission from America. Similarly, Parliament's Prohibitory Act, adopted by wide margins in both the Commons and the Lords, served as tangible evidence of the weakness of the opposition.

As if this were not enough the ministry proceeded to enlist foreign mercenaries to help fill the ranks of the army. Samuel Adams, who seems to have had an uncanny knack for predicting the actions of the British Government, had long argued that England would enlist German mercenaries to fight Englishmen in America. This step, which was objectionable to virtually every shade of opinion in America and to the opposition in England, had long been downplayed by those in Congress who sought reconciliation. In late January 1776 the ministry entered into treaties with several German states to provide nearly 20,000 mercenary troops. These troops were to be used not only for garrison duty in Europe but were to be sent to America to engage in combat with the colonists. That George III would permit the "slaughter" of his own subjects by mercenary troops unquestionably forced many opponents of independence to alter their stance.

But more than events in England served the cause of those seeking independence. British governors helped inflame colonial opinion. In July Governor Martin of North Carolina had called for a pardon for the Regulators and then fled to a British warship. Meanwhile in Virginia the efforts of the legislature to establish some sort of agreement with Governor Dunmore came to naught. In July and August 1775 the Virginia Convention – acting without the governor or any semblance of royal authority – levied taxes on the people, issued paper money for the purpose of conducting military resistance, and created two regiments. Governor Dunmore, also in residence on a British warship, probably ended all hope of a peaceful resolution of conflict in that colony when, in November, he offered freedom to all slaves who joined him in fighting their former masters. Few, if any, potential horrors loomed more menacing on the horizon in the southern colonies than the prospect of racial warfare, and the encouragement of such an event by a royal governor ended any influence he may have had. Less significant, but certainly objectionable to the Virginians, was the shelling of Norfolk, which destroyed much of the city on New Year's Day 1776. That much of the destruction was the result of actions by colonial troops had little impact on public opinion.

During the latter months of 1775 several other issues related to independence had come before Congress, but most of them had been left to lie on the table. On 21 July Benjamin Franklin had proposed a plan for union but, even though the union was to last only until the end of the conflict, such a step proved too much for those who feared separation from the empire. Clearly the establishment of an authorized continental government was not consistent with plans for reconciliation. The proposal was placed in a stack of unfinished business and left there. Similarly with proposals to open the ports of America to foreign trade and to negotiate with foreign nations. Both were advisable and both appeared increasingly necessary, but like the proposal for a union of the colonies such steps seemed too drastic for the more conservative members of the Congress, and no real progress was made until 1776. For example, Franklin and Richard Henry Lee had proposed in July that if the Acts restraining American commerce were not repealed the Congress should throw open all colonial ports to the ships of foreign nations, but, like the plan of union, these suggestions were tabled and ignored.

Changes took place during the first two months of 1776 which would put the supporters of independence in control. One important event took place in Massachusetts, where the assembly replaced Thomas Cushing with Elbridge Gerry, thus giving the radicals firm control of that delegation. Another important development was the publication of Thomas Paine's *Common Sense*, a pamphlet which unquestionably had an enormous impact not only on the public at large but upon the members of Congress. Within weeks more than 100,000 copies of the writing had been published and letters from the delegates in Philadelphia reveal that most, if not all of them, had been impressed with Paine's reasoning and style.

Two factors played a part in the importance of *Common Sense*. In the first place, Paine blamed the King directly for the misgovernment of America. He roundly condemned the entire system of monarchy and found the "royal brute" of England particularly culpable. The significance of this straightforward attack on George III assumes even greater significance when one notes that as late as mid-March the Continental Congress refused to adopt language blaming the King rather than the ministry for the war. Paine's persuasive prose was strong medicine for many who had been brought up to revere the monarchy.

Then, too, Washington began to speak more clearly in support of the need for independence. When he arrived in New York in April 1776 he found the citizens supplying the British with the apparent approval of the Provincial Congress. The General found this absolutely inexplicable given the fact that American ports had been closed, colonial trade destroyed, property seized, towns burnt, and citizens made prisoners. They must, Washington wrote, consider themselves "in a state of peace or war with Great Britain," and there was no doubt as to where his sympathies lay.

6. THE MOVE TO INDEPENDENCE

The first indication that the majority in Congress had been won over to independence came at the end of February 1776. The delegates, for the first time, considered the question of separation from Great Britain, and although no decision was reached the radicals apparently constituted a majority. The debate was ended because "five or six" delegations did not have the authority to agree to independence without consulting their respective provincial governments. Perhaps more significant was the decision, on 6 April, to open the ports of America to all nations except Great Britain and its dominions. That determination was certainly a declaration of economic, if not political, independence. North Carolina was to be the first colony actually to mention independence – from a positive point of view – in its instructions to its delegates. On 12 April 1776 the convention empowered its representatives in Congress to combine with the other colonies in separating from the empire. In May of the same year Rhode Island virtually declared its separate independence by refusing to continue the administration of oaths in the name of the king who had violated the compact of government. The colony then joined North Carolina in giving its congressional delegation the authority to join in a declaration of independence.

Still, no colony had actually instructed its delegates to call for independence, and an effort to achieve that result in Massachusetts Bay failed because of internal divisions in the colony. It was left to Virginia to initiate the move for independence. On 15 May 1776 the Virginia legislature, by roll-call vote, instructed its delegation in Congress to move for separation from the empire. North Carolina soon followed suit, and on 27 May the resolutions of these two colonies were laid before Congress.

On 7 June 1776 Richard Henry Lee rose in Congress to present three resolutions. The most important of these was that "these United Colonies are, and of right ought

219

to be, free and independent States." But the battle was far from over. By then the delegates generally agreed that independence was inevitable, but the debate concerned timing. A number of colonies wanted to delay as long as possible, and as late as early June several – including New York, New Jersey, Delaware, and Maryland – were unprepared to vote for independence. Threats to walk out of the Congress produced a compromise which, in the end, worked for those who favored independence. Congress agreed to delay a final vote on independence until 1 July.

In the meantime, an important political revolution had been engineered in Pennsylvania. Elections there on 1 May had given the opponents of independence a dramatic victory. The leaders of the independence movement in Congress recognized that they must have the support of that pivotal province. Consequently they successfully connived with the radical factions in Pennsylvania to bring down the provincial government and replace it with a more democratic system. In a desperate effort to avoid its demise the Pennsylvania Assembly rescinded its instructions against independence, but it could not protect itself. The assembly lost its power and Pennsylvania was removed from the list of opponents of independence.

Events now moved rapidly. Shortly after Congress voted to delay a decision on independence until 1 July, the new Pennsylvania Provincial Conference met and unanimously endorsed independence. On 15 June Connecticut called for separation from Great Britain, and Delaware followed suit on the same day. Maryland soon gave in, in part because of threats of internal disruption, and New York faced a similar situation. The New Yorkers moved so slowly that their delegates were not empowered to vote either yea or nay on 2 July 1776, but faced with a decision for independence by the other 12 colonies they also came around.

Resistance to independence did not dissolve in late June and early July. John Dickinson refused to sign the Declaration of Independence and the conservative party in Pennsylvania had clearly yielded to coercion. Many feared that independence would lead to the dissolution of government or, what was almost as bad, to the implementation of democracy. One is reluctant to quote again John Adams's comment about the difficulties of making 13 clocks strike as one, but the simile is apt. It had been a difficult battle and friction in Congress had been great. Nevertheless 13 colonies declared their independence on the same day.

7. THE PHILOSOPHY OF INDEPENDENCE

The Declaration of Independence is a statement of political philosophy which tells us a great deal about the struggle for separation from Great Britain. Interestingly enough the delegates did not directly mention Parliament in their explanation of declaring independence. Having spent well over a decade in conflict with Parliament, the colonists moved to the position that their only tie with the empire had been through the monarch. The major part of the Declaration is a list of ways in which George III had violated his contract of government with the colonies. Only one oblique reference is made to Parliament, when the delegates accused the King of having combined "with others" to deprive them of their liberties.

This statement of philosophy raises questions about the objectives of the colonists throughout the years of controversy following the end of the Seven Years' War in 1763. Certainly the Stamp Act Congress, which met in 1765, believed that the colonists were to some extent under the governance of Parliament. As late as 1774, when the First Continental Congress met to consider the Coercive Acts, the delegates were not prepared to reject entirely the authority of Parliament, although they left vague the exact boundaries of that authority. Were the colonists, as many in England believed, simply testing the boundaries of British authority? Were they, indeed, demanding independence all along but hoping to be able to obtain it without making a formal declaration?

The strength of the British position was consistency. Upon repeal of the Stamp Act in 1766, Parliament clearly stated that the government in England could legislate for the colonies "in all cases whatsoever." Not until late in the war did Parliament offer to back off from that position, and after the war was over George III claimed that his only error had been in agreeing to the repeal of the Stamp Act. Perhaps, as Ralph Waldo Emerson once put it, "a petty consistency is the hobgoblin of little minds."

The Americans were confronted with an unprecedented situation in 1764 when the Revenue Act for the first time imposed taxes for the purpose of raising money for the empire. Their halting steps in resisting that measure have led to accusations of hypocrisy but are more likely the result of confusion. Perhaps they were not initially clear in understanding exactly what they wanted, but, as Edmund Morgan has pointed out, they generally objected to revenue taxes while trying to construct a policy which would permit Parliament to continue its regulation of trade. By 1774 it was becoming increasingly clear that this was a distinction without a difference, at least in the hands of those who proposed to raise a revenue by whatever means came to hand. So the colonies moved slowly but surely towards independence, although that was almost certainly not their original objective.

The debates, letters, and diaries of the period between the Battle of Lexington and the Declaration of Independence suggest that the majority of American leaders opposed independence. Early on they did not understand that their definition of dependence was not compatible with the expectations of the British Government. In retrospect it is now clear that, with the adoption of the Continental Association in 1774, war was inevitable. While the British Government was adopting legislation to reconstruct the government of Massachusetts Bay, the delegates to the First Continental Congress were arguing about whether or not Parliament had the right to establish a Post Office in the colonies. Historians have often condemned the so-called radicals in the First Congress for rejecting Joseph Galloway's Plan of Union, but the simple fact is that such a plan would not have had a hearing in England. When all is said and done, the American colonists were determined to be governed a bit less, and the British were determined to govern a bit more.

The extent to which the "crisis of independence" was simply an issue of educating Americans to the reality of British politics is striking. Again and again the conservatives in Congress were encouraged by reports of commissioners being sent to negotiate a settlement, only to learn that the commissioners had no authority to make concessions. Again and again the conservatives persuaded Congress to make yet another "humble petition" to the King, only to be rebuffed by a monarch who believed that the time had come to settle the issue with the colonists. The correspondence of Samuel Adams is instructive on this issue. At least as early as 1774 he apparently understood that his independence – and he was certainly one American who had independence in mind at an early stage of the game – would be accomplished by the British. He repeatedly predicted that the British response to plea and petition would increase the ranks of those who supported independence. It was a knowledge of events in England that determined whether one was for or against independence after 1775, and the declaration of that independence took place when a majority in the Congress understood that their hopes for reconciliation, at least on the grounds they were willing to accept, were unrealistic.

FURTHER READING

Green, Jack P. (ed.): *The American Revolution: its Character and Limits* (New York: New York University Press, 1978).

Jensen, Merrill: *The Founding of a Nation: a History of the American Revolution, 1763–1776* (New York: Oxford University Press, 1968).

Maier, Pauline: *From Resistance to Revolution: Colonial Radicals and the Development of American Opposition to Britain, 1765–1776* (New York: Alfred A. Knopf, 1972).

Middlekauff, Robert: *The Glorious Cause: the American Revolution, 1763–1789* (New York: Oxford University Press, 1982). [Vol. II of the Oxford History of the United States].

Nash, Gary B.: *The Urban Crucible: Social Change, Political Consciousness, and the Origins of the American Revolution* (Cambridge, Mass.: Harvard University Press, 1979).

Nettels, Curtis: *George Washington and American Independence* (Boston: Little, Brown, 1951).

Rakove, Jack N.: *The Beginnings of National Politics: an Interpretative History of the Continental Congress* (New York: Alfred A. Knopf, 1979).

Ryserson, Richard Alan: *The Revolution is Now Begun: the Radical Committees of Philadelphia, 1765–1776* (Philadelphia: University of Pennsylvania Press, 1978).

Shy, John: *Toward Lexington: the Role of the British Army in the Coming of the American Revolution* (Princeton, NJ: Princeton University Press, 1965).

Young, Alfred F. (ed.): *The American Revolution: Explorations in the History of American Radicalism* (DeKalb: Northern Illinois University Press, 1976).

22

Development of a revolutionary organization, 1765–1775

DAVID W. CONROY

COLONISTS in North America initially organized in 1765 to protect what they conceived to be the traditional liberties of Englishmen in the British Empire, not to repudiate their connection with it. Indeed leaders of the Sons of Liberty all idealized the British Constitution as a model of political organization which staved off the twin evils of tyranny and anarchy. Thus when Parliament repealed the Stamp Act in 1766, the Sons dissolved their organizations amidst profuse professions of loyalty to a benevolent King. From the start, organization to resist new imperial policies possessed a dual purpose – to maintain order and discipline in resistance as much as to foment and execute it. The character and timing of activity received close attention. As late as 1774, leaders chose to organize non-importation associations – to demonstrate political virtue through collective sacrifice and austerity – as the primary means of resistance. Nevertheless Parliament's determination to reorganize colonial administration and extract new revenues gradually convinced colonial leaders of the existence of a conspiracy to abridge their liberties. By the 1770s, they even implicated the King. Extra-legal organization within the colonies became more extensive, communication between them more vital, and cooperation in a Continental Congress more imperative. Moreover the progressive experience of creating, leading, and following resistance organizations gradually transformed colonial political behavior by expanding the number of leaders, purging those reluctant from elected bodies, and making an informed and active citizenry the sovereign source of all political authority. As organizations of limited resistance gradually cast off traditional restraints governing political behavior, they became revolutionary harbingers of a new political order in which a King and all inherited privilege could have no place.

I. THE SONS OF LIBERTY

Passage of the Stamp Act provoked groups in all of the mainland colonies to organize to resist its enforcement during the summer months of 1765 (*see also* Chapter 19, §2). Leaders of the nascent Sons of Liberty sprang from the upper and middle ranks of colonial society. Several groups originated in urban voluntary associations such as the Loyal Nine, a social club in Boston, and the Charles Town Fire Company in South Carolina. In other colonies such as North Carolina, leaders of the Assembly took the initiative. The Sons of Liberty had ample precedents to draw upon in planning acts of resistance. Extra-legal crowd actions with specific, limited goals had long been an informal means of resolving public dilemmas, often with the tacit approval of constituted authorities. In this tradition, the Sons of Liberty organized street demonstrations in the major port towns and capitals, the hanging and parading of effigies, and acts of further intimidation to frighten Stamp Distributors to resign their commissions. This was accomplished in all of the colonies by 1 November except Georgia, where stamps were issued briefly.

To accomplish their goals, and justify their actions, steering committees recruited popular support and manpower. In Boston the Loyal Nine persuaded the North and South End gangs to put aside their traditional rivalry in order to unite in street protest. But when these aroused workmen later destroyed Lieutenant-Governor Hutchinson's house in an unplanned sacking of private property, leaders took steps to impress upon the rank and file of resistance the importance of restraint. The movement must not be discredited by the specter of anarchy and violence. A similar emphasis on discipline pervaded the organization of the Sons of Liberty in other colonies. In Maryland they formalized their organization in early November by the creation of the Society for the Maintenance of Order and Protection of American Liberty. These dual concerns also informed the rules that the Albany group wrote and published for itself in 1766, promising to discourage actions which slandered the character of individuals by disciplining its own membership. Local leaders insisted that they acted to uphold and defend established institutions, not overturn them. Thus the organization of the Sons of Liberty became as much an antidote to disorder as a weapon of resistance.

The strongest and most active groups organized in the major towns, but rural counties and towns emulated them to various degrees. As organizations multiplied within colonies to arouse the populace at large, prominent leaders of the Sons made efforts to establish ties between colonies to form an intra-colonial movement. In December 1765, representatives of the New York and Connecticut Sons met and subscribed to an agreement of mutual aid, the first of a series of pacts which linked groups from New Hampshire to Georgia. But organization receded or dissolved upon news of the repeal of the Stamp Act in 1766. The Sons were not revolutionaries. Nevertheless they had changed as well as defended the old order by creating organizations which mobilized ordinary colonists to participate in the resolution of issues of imperial import.

2. NON-IMPORTATION ORGANIZATIONS

Organization flowered anew in response to the Townshend Duties enacted in 1767. In some colonies such as New York and South Carolina, the Sons revived their organizations, but they now acted in assistance to a new layer of organized resistance: non-importation associations (*see* figure 19d). Such agreements had emerged during the Stamp Act crisis, but now became the primary means of resistance to duties considered to be thinly disguised taxation. Boston merchants formed progressively more strict associations to boycott English products in 1767 and 1768 providing that New York and Philadelphia merchants followed suit. New Yorkers responded swiftly, but Philadelphia merchants delayed until 1769. Still, by the end of 1769 all colonies but New Hampshire had associations pledged to either non-importation or non-consumption. Such associations perpetuated the spirit of vigorous but orderly resistance by adopting tactics which prescribed sacrifice and discipline. Everyone was enjoined to subscribe to or support associations which organized colonists into a collective demonstration of superior social and political virtue. Non-importation fused protest and self-imposed austerity together.

Like the Sons of Liberty, the instigators of non-importation acted in close harmony with their respective colonial assemblies, and did not seek to usurp constituted authority. In Maryland, 22 of the 43 signers of the association were delegates to the Assembly, and the Connecticut, New York, and New Jersey Assemblies all passed resolutions commending the associations. But these organizations also moved beyond their predecessors by assuming the authority to police enforcement. Association committees examined suspected cargoes, adjudicated violations, and punished infractions with alacrity. The association in Maryland published the proceedings of a committee appointed to investigate one shipment as a separate pamphlet and distributed it in all the counties, thus providing a model for extra-judicial proceedings. The movement also witnessed the emergence of artisans as a distinct voice in resistance organizations agitating for stricter enforcement. Artisans in Charles Town made sure that they be given equal representation to merchants and planters on the committee of enforcement. In Philadelphia, artisans challenged the right of merchants to dissolve the association when all of the duties except that on tea were repealed. They would later form their own "Patriotic Society," and help to elevate John Dickinson to the leadership of resistance over the objections of more conservative merchants. As the conviction arose that the Stamp Act and the Townshend Duties represented a concerted plan to curtail colonial autonomy, all members of elite governing groups came under scrutiny as to their devotion to the cause.

3. COMMITTEES OF CORRESPONDENCE

The associations disbanded in one colony after another when Parliament repealed all of the duties in 1770 except that on tea, which continued to be boycotted. Resistance leaders received fresh provocation, however, to develop new organizations between 1770 and 1773. Belief in a conspiracy hatched in Whitehall made it seem imperative to sustain and extend the networks of communication established in past years. When the Crown decided to use custom revenues to salary superior court justices in Massachusetts, SAMUEL ADAMS decided that the time was ripe to create a Boston Committee of Correspondence to elicit more formal and systematic expressions of support from the towns. This committee of 21 men, one-third of whom possessed degrees from Harvard, was formally created by the Boston Town Meeting. It sent plainly written explanations of the past and current state of imperial controversy to all of the towns in the colony, inviting them to elect their own committees and respond to the Boston leaders' concerns. More than half did reply, and the committee succeeded in encouraging participation in the controversy by the people at large on an unprecedented level. Continuing correspondence provided proof of the broad base of support for extra-legal actions against "unconstitutional" acts. Communication between the colonies was also raised to a more systematic level when the Virginia House of Burgesses wrote to all of the colonies requesting them to establish provincial committees of correspondence. Appointed by their assemblies, but able to act out of session, these committees strengthened ties between radical colonies and those less active or divided. They also reoriented communication away from England to intra-colonial networks at a time when faith in the efficacy of petitions and protests to the Crown was waning.

The Tea Act of March 1773, granting a monopoly of the sale of the still-dutied commodity, immediately stirred leaders to act. In the major ports they once again sought to involve and organize the people (*see* figure 19a, b, c), but cautiously and with every appearance of propriety. Mass meetings of the people became the vehicles

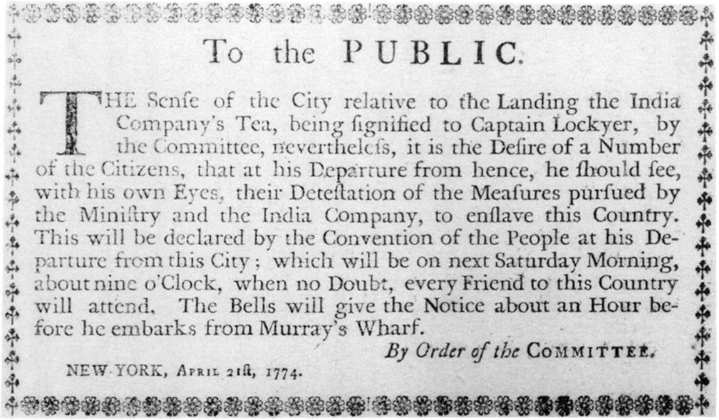

To the PUBLIC.

THE Senſe of the City relative to the Landing the India Company's Tea, being ſignified to Captain Lockyer, by the Committee, nevertheleſs, it is the Deſire of a Number of the Citizens, that at his Departure from hence, he ſhould ſee, with his own Eyes, their Deteſtation of the Meaſures purſued by the Miniſtry and the India Company, to enſlave this Country. This will be declared by the Convention of the People at his Departure from this City; which will be on next Saturday Morning, about nine o'Clock, when no Doubt, every Friend to this Country will attend. The Bells will give the Notice about an Hour before he embarks from Murray's Wharf.

By Order of the COMMITTEE.

NEW-YORK, APRIL 21ſt, 1774.

(a)

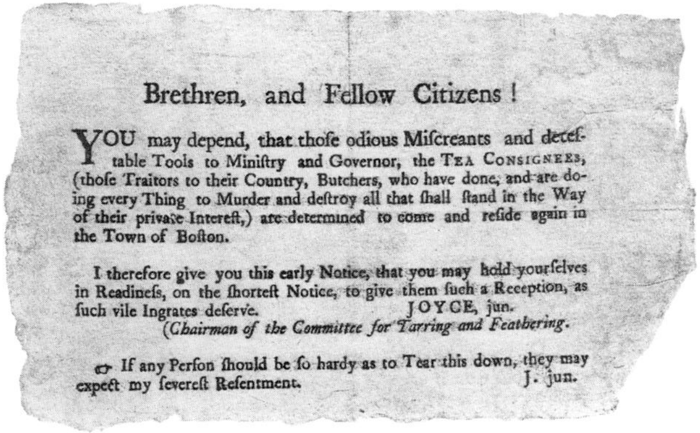

Brethren, and Fellow Citizens!

YOU may depend, that thoſe odious Miſcreants and deteſtable Tools to Miniſtry and Governor, the TEA CONSIGNEES, (thoſe Traitors to their Country, Butchers, who have done, and are doing every Thing to Murder and deſtroy all that ſhall ſtand in the Way of their private Intereſt,) are determined to come and reſide again in the Town of Boſton.

I therefore give you this early Notice, that you may hold yourſelves in Readineſs, on the ſhorteſt Notice, to give them ſuch a Reception, as ſuch vile Ingrates deſerve. JOYCE, jun.

(*Chairman of the Committee for Tarring and Feathering.*

☞ If any Perſon ſhould be ſo hardy as to Tear this down, they may expect my ſevereſt Reſentment. J. jun.

(b)

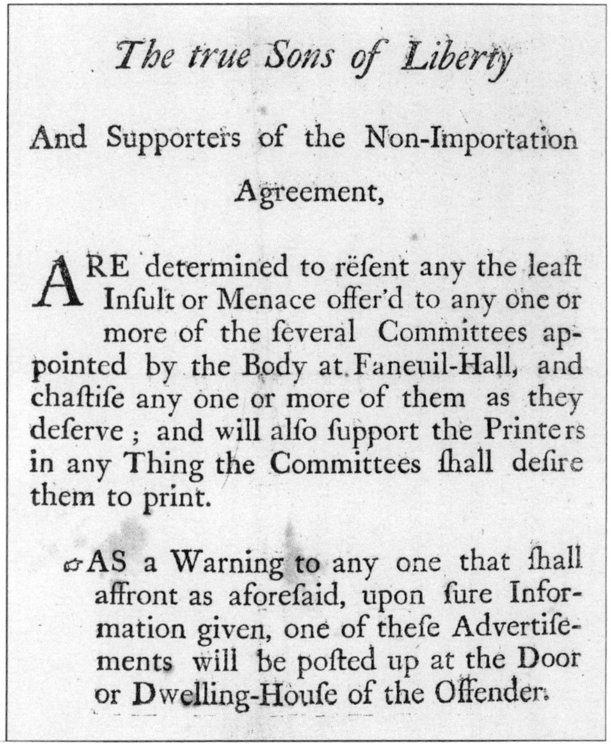

The true Sons of Liberty

And Supporters of the Non-Importation Agreement,

ARE determined to rëſent any the leaſt Inſult or Menace offer'd to any one or more of the ſeveral Committees appointed by the Body at Faneuil-Hall, and chaſtiſe any one or more of them as they deſerve; and will alſo ſupport the Printers in any Thing the Committees ſhall deſire them to print.

☞AS a Warning to any one that ſhall affront as aforeſaid, upon ſure Information given, one of theſe Advertiſements will be poſted up at the Door or Dwelling-Houſe of the Offender.

(c)

FIGURE 19 Three contemporary broadsides reflecting the escalating alarm of resistance leaders, their means of communicating this alarm to the public, and the general mechanics of the evolving resistance organizations:
(a) the New York committee plans to orchestrate a "convention of the people" to mark the departure of a tea ship;
(b) the Boston committee, in the florid hyperbole typical of the period, warns tea consignees to stay out of Boston;
(c) a bill illustrating the pressure brought to bear by the Sons of Liberty acting in assistance to the non-importation association.

to inform the populace, identify tea consignees, and pressure them to resign their commissions first in Philadelphia, then in New York, Boston, and Charles Town. Fall meetings in Philadelphia enlarged the committee of 12 to 24, as radicals pressured hesitant merchants to make a decisive response. In Charles Town, a mass-meeting in December demanded and received the resignation of all the tea consignees and appointed a steering committee to prepare for future meetings. Carefully orchestrated "Meetings of the People" in Boston resolved to prevent the tea from being landed. When Governor Hutchinson refused to allow reshipment, a disguised delegation from a December meeting dumped it in Boston Harbor. These self constituted mass-meetings were beyond the reach of the law and therefore could act free of the restraints which bound town and province government. At the same time, leaders such as Adams delayed taking any radical steps until every means of removing the tea legally had been formally explored. Publicly, "the People" had acted in Boston only after all other avenues of redress had been exhausted. Discipline in resistance was still paramount, especially when "the People" moved to destroy property.

4. THE FIRST CONTINENTAL CONGRESS

Reactions to the Boston Tea Party in the other colonies were mixed. But when news of the Port Act reached the colonies, followed by the other "Intolerable Acts," they united behind Boston. They became convinced, as suggested to them by a Boston Committee of Correspondence Circular, that Parliament planned similar punitive measures for all the colonies if they remained defiant. The previous establishment of regular communication between the colonies bore fruit as leaders in Providence, Philadelphia, and New York issued calls for an inter-colonial congress. Virginia Burgesses meeting unofficially in a Williamsburg tavern proposed going beyond the Stamp Act Congress of 1765 by making it the first of annual congresses. But royal governors attempted to prevent their colonies from electing delegates by dismissing their assemblies. This only stimulated the creation of a new layer of extra-legal organization. Seven colonies in the spring and summer of 1774 convened provincial conventions to choose delegates. South Carolina's convention elected a Committee of 99, which became virtually the temporary government of the colony. The still growing Committee of 43 in Philadelphia called a convention and developed a comprehensive committee system in the counties to coordinate resistance, all but overwhelming the voices of a conservative group of merchants. All of the colonies witnessed a new burst of extra-legal meetings and activities as the Intolerable Acts seemed to confirm beyond a doubt the sinister intentions of the British ministry. The Acts became the spark for the convening of the First Continental Congress on 5 September 1774 attended by representatives from all of the colonies except Georgia (see also Chapter 20, §4).

This Congress represents a milestone in the development of a revolutionary organization in the colonies. Heretofore, organization had developed most extensively and effectively at the colony level, and particularly in major ports. Massachusetts' more radical posture had sometimes threatened to isolate it in the past. With the organization of the Congress, however, the colonies now possessed a vehicle with which to speak with a united voice, and a potential means of integrating and consolidating the resistance organizations and conventions which had sprung up with renewed vigor in 1774, bringing several colonies close to the establishment of revolutionary governments.

5. THE CONTINENTAL ASSOCIATION

In formulating a pan-colonial policy, the Congress continued to adhere to principles clarified in 1765 counseling order and restraint in resistance. It adopted and recommended to the colonies the Continental Association as the principal means of forcing England to redress colonial grievances. Modeled on an association already drawn up by Virginia, the Continental Association prescribed comprehensive non-importation and non-exportation within a scheduled framework. Once again colonists were enjoined to unite self-sacrifice and discipline with vigorous opposition. Choice of such a tactic served to restrain the popular violence which threatened to weaken and divide the movement amidst the passions unleashed by Parliament's punishment of Boston. But it also served to encourage and extend organization in a uniform way in every colony by recommending the election of committees of inspection and observation in every town and county by all those qualified to vote for representatives in their respective colonies. Congress authorized these committees to become its local agents by policing the observation of the Association and punishing violators with public censure and ostracism. This program for organizing resistance was more elaborate and comprehensive than any previously adopted by a town or colony. The Congress proposed mass participation in resistance, but through mass organization to boycott trade with England.

Congress fell short of its goal of stimulating the election of committees in every locality, particularly in New York, whose delegates had refused to endorse the Association. But by April 1775, committees were in operation and the Association in effect to some extent in all the colonies. In Virginia, 51 of 61 counties elected committees, in Maryland 11 of 16 counties, and in Massachusetts at least 160 towns responded. The membership of these committees tended to be larger than that of their predecessors, ranging from an average of ten in Massachusetts to 100 in Maryland. By the spring of 1775, at least 7,000 persons had publicly identified themselves as leaders of a movement which the Crown had already condemned as rebellion. Local and colony organizations had brought the Congress into existence, but they now multiplied at the behest of Congress. The linking of so substantial a number of local leaders to an inter-colonial congress vertically integrated organized resistance to a new level of refinement, efficiency, and impact. Local committees often acted as engines of mobilization, as in Wilmington, North Carolina. Here the Committee pledged the entire town to sign the Association by sending a delegation to each household to secure signatures. The Committee proclaimed a boycott of those who refused, and within a few days they agreed to sign. In large sections of the colonies, organized resistance no longer existed apart from the political community, but became co-terminous with it. Many committees did not limit themselves to enforcement of the Association, but also began to set prices, promote manufactures, and regulate morals. They did not supplant existing institutions of local government, but they did assume authority for acting on issues of "continental" importance.

6. PROVINCIAL CONGRESSES

The erection of committees of inspection across the colonies during the winter of 1774 and 1775 not only invested resistance with new force and urgency, but also accelerated the transformation of traditional political values and behavior. Back in 1765, the Sons of Liberty had organized to preserve the rights of Englishmen in the colonies, professing their continuing reverence for King and British Constitution. By 1774, however, the proliferation of resistance organizations had multiplied the numbers of people holding positions of leadership, and encouraged the population at large to scrutinize carefully and regularly the beliefs and behavior of those leaders. In resistance organizations colonists had begun to act out what would only later be elevated to a revolutionary ideal: the sovereignty of the people over all branches of government, and the accountability of all elected officials to the people's will. The prestige of the hitherto idealized British Constitution with its much acclaimed balance between monarchy, aristocracy, and democracy faded as colonists began to construct alternative governments in 1774 entirely derived by direct or indirect vote of a politically aroused citizenry. Besides their local committees, voters elected provincial congresses and conventions far more democratic and representative than their assemblies had been at the outset of resistance. In both New Jersey and Maryland, the number of delegates in their provincial congresses was more than twice that of their previous regular assemblies. The South Carolina Congress had 180 members, triple the size of its Assembly. Substantial, educated men continued to dominate, but were joined by new faces elevated to authority by the movement. Philadelphia's leadership increasingly departed from the traditional model by being younger and more diverse in occupation, ethnic composition, and religious affiliation. Similar changes occurred in parts of New York, where large landowners had dominated local government. Resistance organizations thus became the seedbeds not just for a revolt against England, but for a repudiation of traditional models of government and political behavior. Magistrates could no longer expect deference from the small farmers and artisans now engaged in stripping royal government of what authority it could still muster.

7. THE CONTINENTAL ARMY

The final layer of organization which propelled the colonies towards revolution was once again sparked by events in Massachusetts. Although controversial, military preparations had begun in the New England colonies and in Maryland and Virginia by early 1775. Maryland's Provincial Congress had recommended to each county that they tax their inhabitants in order to purchase military provisions. By February 1775, the Massachusetts Congress had taken steps to prepare the colony for war. Already local minutemen companies drilled throughout the colony in anticipation of a foray by General Gage from Boston into the countryside to destroy munitions. After the Battle of Lexington and Concord in 19 April, the Massachusetts Congress ordered the mobilization of 13,600 soldiers. Thus when the Second Continental Congress convened on 10 May, it confronted the problem of addressing a state of war in Massachusetts.

The decision to organize a Continental Army commanded by Washington did not come easily. Heretofore, organization to resist imperial policy had been consciously designed to avoid violence and preserve every chance of reconciliation and restoration to a revered King. The Sons of Liberty had organized only to render the "unconstitutional" Stamp Act unenforceable. Non-importation associations had been formed only to force repeal of the equally loathed Townshend Duties. Committees of Correspondence had been created to expose the dark designs of a "corrupt" British ministry. The Intolerable Acts had been answered by a more comprehensive employment of tactics used previously. Each layer of new organization had been created and refined to counteract policies deemed violations of the British Constitution. But the cumulative experience of organized resistance had gradually eroded colonists' confidence in this Constitution of balance social orders. It now seemed an inadequate guarantor of traditional political liberties. Meanwhile the gradual, vertical integration of local committees, provincial congresses, and the Continental Congress had become an operating alternative in which the voting citizenry became the ultimate source of all layers of political authority. This refined state of organized resistance made the planning of military operations conceivable from a continental perspective. And now, after the battles of Lexington, Concord, and Bunker Hill, it seemed necessary if the carefully constructed unity of the colonies was to endure. Some members of the Second Continental Congress still hoped for reconciliation, as did numerous moderates and loyalists at the local level. But as Massachusetts had already demonstrated, the organization of an army was but a tiny step short of using it. Organization for resistance had become organization for revolution in 1775.

FURTHER READING

Ammerman, David: *In the Common Cause: American Response to the Coercive Acts of 1774* (New York: Norton, 1974).

Brown, Richard D.: *Revolutionary Politics in Massachusetts: the Boston Committee of Correspondence and the Towns, 1772–1774* (Cambridge, Mass.: Harvard University Press, 1970).

Maier, Pauline: *From Resistance to Revolution: Colonial Radicals and the Development of American Opposition to Britain, 1765–1776* (New York: Vintage Books, 1974).

Ryerson, Richard Alan: *The Revolution Is Now Begun: the Radical Committees of Philadelphia, 1765–1776* (Philadelphia: University of Pennsylvania Press, 1978).

Weir, Robert M.: *"A Most Important Epoch": The Coming of the Revolution in South Carolina* (Columbia: University of South Carolina Press, 1970).

23

Political mobilization, 1765–1776

REBECCA K. STARR

WHEN John Adams ventured the remark that one-third of all Americans were patriots, one-third were loyal to King George, and one-third were undecided, he was saying something about the success of radicals like himself in mobilizing public opinion for independence. Rhetorical claims to the contrary, political mobilization is an induced, not a spontaneous, process. It usually happens from the top down, led by a politically astute elite. But in a reasonably fluid society (such as was America in this period), it can also come from politically self-conscious minorities, such as artisans or women.

All mobilization, however, depends on some degree of organization. Because of its superior command of the channels of communication, the elite usually dominates the first step in the mobilization process – creation of organizations. But while a small leadership may supply the initiative required to formalize an association's structure, the organization's collective aims and ideals must encode ideas, values, attitudes, assumptions, and beliefs latent in the social practices and moral patterns already established in the society. At least in its early stages, political mobilization is the reification of values already present in the prevailing political culture. As mobilization progresses, however, not only is the way prepared for the reformulation of those values into new patterns of thought, but initiative for that change moves down through the hierarchy. Passing from the hands of a few official leaders, it spreads laterally into those of its constituency.

Political mobilization also requires an explicit message; hence an organization's first task is to provide a forum where generally shared ideas may be articulated, debated, refined, and agreed to in a consensus-making exercise. Its second purpose is to broadcast those ideas to the public. The broader the organization's basis, the wider the dissemination of its ideas.

But while a formal organizational structure supplies an umbrella for the already committed, mobilization of an unorganized and unconvinced public relies on tactics. Hence tactics are the true focus of the mobilization task. A successful tactical program will spread and increasingly intensify a shared body of ideas until a critical mass is reached. Then only some triggering event is needed to transform ideas into action. The first organization to evolve a set of tactics aimed at politicizing the public was the Sons of Liberty (on the organizational history of the Revolution, *see* Chapter 22). Although its purpose was specifically limited to achieving the repeal of the Stamp Act, the strategies and tactics developed by the Sons of Liberty set a pattern for subsequent public opinion mobilization right down to the Revolution.

One cannot talk about organizations and politics in this period without considering mobs and street action. Not truly organizations since they lacked formal structure, mobs still had an important, although unintended, impact on popular thought. Recent scholarship on crowd behavior has shown that mobs sometimes acted in the public welfare when civil authority failed, but most eighteenth-century men feared the anarchy of mob rule as much as they deplored a despotic monarch.

In political mobbing, if no law was broken or property destroyed, most leaders of the American opposition did not openly disapprove. A few individuals, such as Samuel Adams, might openly approve violence when all other legal means to secure redress had been exhausted, but most leaders simply refrained from commenting on actions like the Boston Tea Party.

But to say mob violence served no tactical purpose is to miss its most important, if unintended, consequence. Nameless, faceless, and without overt leadership, mob violence forced both the conservative public and established authority to look to a responsible opposition as an alternative to social instability. Mobs served to cast an aura of legitimacy on an opposition that insisted on practicing only constitutional tactics to secure redress.

I. THE STAMP ACT AND THE SONS OF LIBERTY, 1765–6

The Stamp Act of 1765 levied a tax on a seemingly endless list of items including newspapers, wills, deeds, contracts, diplomas, almanacs, playing cards, even dice. Because it affected nearly everyone, the Stamp Act set off a wave of resistance that cut across all divisions of rank, class, and interest. By the summer of 1765, Sons of Liberty groups were springing up almost spontaneously in most of the colonies. As Pauline Maier has written (1974), the organizing effort was intended not to create the Sons of Liberty, but to assemble them into formal structures. Some local groups went under other names. "The Respectable Populace" of Newport, Rhode Island, and the "Loyal Nine" of Boston are examples. But these groups soon changed their names or were subsumed into the Sons organizations. Others, such as the Charles Town [South Carolina] Fire Company, kept their name, but declared that they were the "brethren of the Sons of Liberty of America."

By late 1765, the idea of regularizing an inter-colonial movement against the Stamp Act surfaced in several of the colonies, but New York's early and intense organizational effort made it the unofficial hub of the movement. Its leadership culminated the following April when New York proposed a congress of the Sons of Liberty, but repeal rendered it unnecessary.

The central strategy of the Stamp Act resistance was unity. Hence the first priority of the Sons of Liberty, and of the later movements as well, consisted in winning a mass base by converting the populace at large into Sons of Liberty. Tactics included mass meetings, meant to draw in as many persons, and of as great an assortment in rank and condition, as possible. The mass meeting not only formed linkages across society, but imbued their proceedings and resolves with the authority of "The Body of the People."

Since mass appeal precludes secrecy, the Sons deliberately practiced openness, hoping to inform and engage the public politically as either activists or supporters. Newspapers (and their editors) were central to this strategy and became a forum for formulating an agreed-on public policy. In them, the Sons' leading committees published their sentiments and resolutions for public response and amendment.

At the same time, official committees of correspondence of local Sons organizations exchanged views among themselves at the township, county, and provincial levels, as in Maryland and New Jersey. Moving across provincial lines, Manhattan and Albany's organizations formed a correspondence circuit with Boston which soon enlarged to include several other Massachusetts towns, as well as centers in Portsmouth, New Hampshire, and Providence and Newport, Rhode Island. Charles Town's radicals established links with sympathetic Georgians in a pattern similar to New York's plan. Correspondence and circulars knit these networks together and helped to foster a uniform ideology at the top, which in turn encouraged a consistent, coordinated, and informed program for mobilization at the level of the public.

Potentially their most radical strategy lay in the military and police powers which the Sons assumed. There was always the possibility that the British might send soldiers to enforce the Stamp Act. If that happened, the Military Association of the Sons of Liberty declared that it could "assemble 50,000 fighting Men" in New Jersey and New York to resist.

At the same time the Sons took on a domestic peace-keeping role. The September Stamp Act riots in Boston and Newport which exploded before the Sons formally organized had proved politically counterproductive. Violence and property destruction alienated support and "hurt the good cause." Once they were organized, the Sons' brief was to uphold civil government in all its functions, only excepting the enforcement of the "unconstitutional" Stamp Act. That they must resist in order to save the constitution. To give credit to that claim, Sons of Liberty must strictly limit their resistance tactics to constitutional (lawful) means. (The Sons made a distinction between violence and coercion, such as was used to force Stamp Act distributors to resign.) This commitment to law and order also required that the Sons act to suppress popular anti-Stamp Act disorders. In Charles Town, it was the Sons of Liberty who dragged rioting sailors to jail in late 1765. And in New York, Providence, and Boston, Sons directly intervened in support of civil magistrates. In their readiness to protect the people from foreign invasion, and their commitment to curb domestic violence, the Sons of Liberty set themselves up as the defender of the public welfare, a stated object of government. This strategic but decisive step was the first in the shift of American resistance from a role of an opposition to that of a civil government.

But, as previously stated, the Sons made no claim to overturning established government. Upon news of the Stamp Act's repeal, they immediately dissolved their organizations in the belief that their task was done. But the business of learning tactical resistance had begun. Thus, when opposition resurfaced in 1767 upon the passage of the Townshend Acts, colonials had a body of methods to draw on that could mobilize the public behind a cause. With the Townshend legislation, Sons of Liberty across the colonies reorganized specifically to support non-importation, deemed the most effective of the tactics that had won the Stamp Act repeal. Building on previous methods of political mobilization not only lent an invaluable continuity, but partook of the lessons those methods embodied. To be legitimate, an opposition must involve the whole body of the people (an intimation of the doctrine of popular consent). It must rest on legal procedures, and it must have peaceful, not violent, enforcement measures.

2. TACTICAL ADVANCES AND THE TOWNSHEND ACTS, 1767–9

The Massachusetts circular letter With the passage of the Townshend Acts, Massachusetts radicals reactivated the tactic of the circular letter. This time, however, the letter expressing colonial concern was generated in the provincial legislature's committee of correspondence, and was not sent to the colony's agent in England as the committee's correspondence normally was. Instead, it was sent to the various colonial assemblies, and suggested a coordinated resistance. Royal government response in Massachusetts was to attempt to force the legislature to rescind the letter. Ninety-two members refused.

In South Carolina, the royal governor warned the newly elected Commons House of Assembly not to receive the Massachusetts letter. The moment a quorum assembled, however, the 28 members present voted unanimously to do so. Overnight, the "Ninety-Two Anti-rescinders" and the "Unanimous Twenty-Eight" achieved a rhetorical and symbolic power equal to that of number 45 in the Wilkes controversy. Ninety-two toasts were drunk to the Anti-rescinders and 28 to the unanimous Carolina assembly. Candles of these numbers were solemnly lighted at meetings and 92 and 28 cheers were shouted in street demonstrations. The mobilizing and unifying force of such rallying cries cannot be overlooked.

Another strategic development from the circular letter controversy in Massachusetts was the idea of a convention of towns. It was conceived originally as a protest against the dissolution of the House of Representatives after the Anti-rescinder victory, and against the proposed introduction of troops at Boston. When Governor Hutchinson refused to call a new assembly to consider the crisis, Samuel Adams and Thomas Cushing, Speaker of the Massachusetts House, called (in September 1768) for the election of delegates to a convention of towns. More than 100 of 250 towns sent representatives. The convention elected Thomas Cushing as chairman, and went on to adopt a petition to the King and an address to the governor. They ordered their proceedings published, then dissolved themselves without incident. Although the governor scorned the whole episode, "the people," wrote Andrew Elliot, "have, at present, great confidence in them [the delegates to the convention]." Thus radical leaders found a method of mobilizing local activism which bypassed regular political channels.

Non-importation associations   With the enactment of the Townshend legislation, the tactics of petition and non-importation immediately revived. The former remained unchanged, since it was an ancient procedure whose form was prescribed by law. But non-importation, an extra-constitutional method, made significant strides, especially in the matter of broadening its base. As a strategy, non-importation reached its most mature form in the South.

Merchants remained at the core of northern associations. Success depended largely on an unexceptional compliance by the importers. To protect themselves, merchants could boycott entire communities, as when New York, Philadelphia, and Boston imposed an absolute boycott on Newport and Providence, Rhode Island, when merchants there tried to withdraw from the agreements. Despite merchant dominance of the movement in the North, the popularity of non-importation with the public allowed political leaders to pull the base line of support within the constitutional framework. The Boston Town Meeting supported domestic manufacturing and proscribed violators. Provincial assemblies in New York, New Jersey, and Connecticut passed resolutions commending the movement to the people. These measures lent legitimacy to the *ad hoc* associations, even though the organizing impulse imposed non-importation from the top down.

In the South, however, the movement assembled at the level of the people. The Virginia Association took the form of a social compact among its subscribers, described as "his Majesty's most dutiful and loyal subjects." In Charles Town the association began with a "General Meeting of the INHABITANTS" which sought to be as inclusive as possible. In this way, its decisions might claim to represent the "Sense of the Whole Body [of the people]." After several plans foundered, the meeting adopted a compromise plan whose enforcement committee consisted of an exact balance between the colony's three main economic interests: planters, merchants, and artisans. Interest representation ensured concurrence among the three major economic and social subcommunities of Charles Town. The other southern agreements (in Maryland, Virginia, and North Carolina) also stipulated that membership of enforcement committees come from the community at large rather than merely from the trading community, but none attempted the internal balance of the South Carolina plan.

Less a policy of non-importation than of non-consumption, the southern plans shifted responsibility for success onto the willing cooperation of the entire population. Enforcement committees could only discover and publicize names of non-signers, but the economic boycotts, social ostracism, and shaming of offenders came from the consuming public. Moreover, non-consumption meant not only refraining from doing ordinary business with non-signers, but abstaining from the purchase of most luxuries from anyone. Emphasizing virtue and sacrifice, the non-importation leader Christopher Gadsden forbade the purchase of mourning for his wife's funeral. Patriotic austerity knit the community and mobilized participation and support in a way that enforcement from the top never could have done.

The general meeting and the committee structure proved a major advance in the art of political mobilization. Committees became institutional bridges for the will of the people as expressed in public meetings, such as Town Meetings (as in New England) and the general meetings of the inhabitants (as in the South), reflecting that will back through its implementation of policy. Committee resolutions resembled rules and its enforcement procedures were judgments. What the non-importation association as a grass-roots movement erected, as William H. Drayton of South Carolina recognized, was a new legislature.

But the committee could also serve as a mobilizing agent of nascent political forces, a method that reached its highest development in the Massachusetts Committees of Correspondence organized between 1772 and 1774.

3. COMMITTEES OF CORRESPONDENCE, 1772-4

Upon repeal of the Townshend Acts (except for the tax on tea), the non-importation associations disbanded. Expecting that Great Britain would eventually resume its policy of taxing the colonies, since she had not surrendered that right, Massachusetts opposition leaders used the relatively quiet period from 1772-3 to arouse the radicalism latent in the assumptions and habits of mind of townsmen. In September 1771 Samuel Adams proposed a network of corresponding societies to instruct and arouse the public.

The first of these was the Boston Committee of Correspondence. Created by the Boston Town Meeting, it partook of the people's unspoken acceptance of its town meeting's authority to create whatever committee it saw fit. The tactic of overlapping memberships in both the new committee and the General Assembly lent an additional official status to the group. Moreover, the committee met regularly, sitting even when the assembly was out of session.

In addition to the well-established methods of influencing the public through newspaper essays, pamphleteering, and publishing its proceedings, the Boston Committee of Correspondence carefully drafted individual replies to all correspondence sent from the 58 corresponding committees set up in other towns on the Boston model. These replies were read aloud in town meetings which all voters could attend. The Boston committee replies reinforced the beliefs and ideas expressed in the towns' letters, concentrating by reflecting them back to the writers. The committee flattered and approved, generally pointing to some passage or sentiment in the town's own proceedings, quoting it back with assurances that Boston agreed and joined in the sentiment. Gradually initiative passed from Boston to the towns themselves, as individuals in previously apolitical communities become politically activated. By the collapse of royal government in the summer of 1774, it was the towns that supplied a replacement political structure by creating *ad hoc* county conventions composed of two elected deputies.

The famous Suffolk Resolves adopted by the first Continental Congress grew out of a joint meeting of four county conventions, whose views were generally re-enacted by all nine of the Massachusetts county conventions. By that time public opinion was so thoroughly mobilized that the role of the Boston Committee of Correspondence in provincial politics had become superfluous.

The call by the Virginia House of Burgesses in March 1773 to form committees of correspondence in all the provinces made the movement inter-colonial. Provincial committees of correspondence met regularly, whether the elected assemblies were sitting or not. Thus they formed an alternative structure for mobilizing public opinion in the face of increasing official efforts to thwart such activity by dissolving the legislatures.

4. THE ASSOCIATION OF 1774

The British response to the Boston Tea Party was a series of acts popularly known as the Coercive Acts or the Intolerable Acts. Chief among these were the Boston Port Act, the Massachusetts Government Act, the Act for the Better Administration of Justice of Massachusetts Bay, and the Quebec Act. With a few pen strokes, Parliament altered the structure of Massachusetts's internal government, threatened its religious autonomy by establishing the Roman Catholic Church in nearby French Canada, interfered with jury trial procedures, and declared economic war on Boston by closing its port. These Acts were intended not merely to punish the Boston radicals, but to establish once and for all the principle of the British Parliament's supremacy over Massachusetts's internal affairs.

The Boston Committee of Correspondence countered with its only major tactical blunder. It tried to force the provincial towns to accept a plan for a commercial boycott of Great Britain before a general congress could meet to consider the crisis. As stated above, initiative for political decision-making in Massachusetts had already passed to the individual towns, most of which overwhelmingly rejected the Solemn League and Covenant (as the Boston plan was called) in favor of some concerted colonial action. Instead, a completely uniform, continental approach was to be the cure for all the tactical miscalculations of the earlier non-importations. Inconsistencies among the colonies in prohibited items, incongruities in timing, and the difference in scope between simple non-importation and non-exportation agreements and the broader-based non-consumption agreements were blamed for the incomplete success of the past.

In its emphasis on non-consumption, the Continental Association was a direct descendant of the southern pattern of non-importation agreements during the Townshend Acts. As a strategy for altering British policy, the association was a failure. But as a tactic for mobilizing those who were previously politically inert, either because they were geographically remote from the radical power centers in the seaports or major inland towns, or because of social or economic distance from the top in a hierarchical society, the association succeeded to an unexpected degree.

The association agreement that was hammered out by the delegates to the 1774 Continental Congress not only remedied all the mistakes of the past, it also supplied the final and crucial ingredient missing from previous agreements for a full political mobilization of ordinary Americans. It provided for committees of enforcement to be established not just in the major seaports, but in every township, county, and parish of every province. These committees recruited leaders for the American cause at the most parochial level.

David Ammerman (1974) has estimated that local committee elections brought some 7,000 Americans into local leadership positions. If the total colonial population stood at about three million, the association conservatively created one new leader for every 430 citizens, in addition to the elected, appointed, and voluntary leaders already in place. Once a saturation for local leadership had been achieved, the habit of deference did much to weld residual local opinion to that of its leaders. But other methods were dusted off and improved. Leaders in South Carolina, for example, realized that occupational and religious interest-groups were two additional handles by which the public's opinion-forming machine might be turned.

After the Continental Association plan granted an exemption to the non-exportation of rice, low-country indigo growers and up-country provisions exporters felt slighted, and the whole province was bitterly divided along both sectional and interest lines over the partiality shown to the rice planters. In response to the crisis, South Carolina's proponents of the association devised an elaborate scheme whereby these smaller producers could swap a portion of their crop for rice at a fixed ratio of value. In this way the burden of non-exportation would be shared by all, at the same time preventing the general economic collapse that would have followed a complete embargo on rice, the colony's premier cash crop. The plan was to be administered by special committees in each parish. Although never implemented, as a consciousness-raising exercise it brought the smaller planters and outlying farmers into the opposition movement in a more direct way than ever before.

An appeal to the largely apolitical but deeply evangelical back country was made on the religious interest. When the General Committee in Charles Town sent three emissaries to obtain support for the association from the violently opposed population of back-country producers, it sent two dissenting ministers, but only one Whig politician, to obtain signatures. Philadelphia radicals also played the religious card in declaring a "solemn pause" on 1 June, the date the Boston Port Act took effect. In its appeal to the Quaker disposition for silent worship, it strove to clothe a political cause in religious garb.

An additional tactic borrowed from America's dissenting religions was the powerful and informal language forms that emerged from religious revival movements, lending an evangelical strain to Whig ideology. It infused the egalitarian rhetoric of the classical Whiggery with ardor, and injected it with a meaning and imperatives it never originally possessed, thus empowering the dispossessed with a mobilizing impulse all their own. The rhetoric of Patrick Henry harks from this tradition (*see* figure 20). The

FIGURE 20 Patrick Henry addressing the Virginia Assembly

power of Thomas Paine's *Common Sense*, on the other hand, sprang from another non-classical rhetorical tradition whose touchstone was its unembellished, direct, and "plain" speech. It is not hard to imagine that it shared stylistic links with the striving for plainness among dissenting Calvinist faiths.

Religion and religious organizations also served as the natural route for mobilizing the political opinions and activities of women. Especially in New England, but in other colonies as well, groups of women dressed in homespun met at the home of their local minister. Here they spent the day spinning the cloth they no longer purchased from importers and discussing the issues that their labor supported. For refreshment they ate local produce and drank herbal tea. Occasionally they competed in a match format for the production of the greatest quantity and quality. These ladies, reported the *Boston Evening Post* on a Long Island spinning bee, "may vie with the men in contributing to the preservation and prosperity of their country, and equally share in the honor of it."

At least some of these "Liberty's Daughters," as several newspapers referred to them, may have been among those who saw in the struggle with Great Britain the ingredients for social reform. Certainly the ladies of Philadelphia had strong views on the political significance of their gender as well as their individual political identities. After canvassing for donations from house to house in a fund-raising effort organized and led entirely by women, the ladies objected to General Washington's suggestion that the money be spent on cloth for shirts for the soldiers. They felt the soldiers might consider this part of their normal entitlement from the public, and miss the point that women as women were promoting the war effort. When they were unable to dissuade the general from his views, the women complied, but pointedly signed the pocket of each shirt with their names, lest the wearer overlook their contribution as individuals as well as women.

Other groups belonged to the liberal wing of Whig ideology that fostered mobilization from the bottom up. We have already discussed the Sons of Liberty, whose rank-and-file members came from artisan classes. In some places it was the militia that became a school for political education, somewhat like Cromwell's New Model Army. In Philadelphia, the militia was by 1775 a center for intense debate. It organized its own committee of correspondence, and began putting pressure on conservative members of the legislature for a stronger stand on independence.

When in 1766 radical Whig politicians led by Samuel Adams moved the House of Representatives to build a public gallery, Thomas Young said it would turn the legislature into a "School for Political Learning," implying that enlightened elites would instruct the masses. But instruction worked both ways. Boston opinion was much more radical than that of the interior towns, and Adams's supporters from the city streets packed the galleries to exert pressure on the country members. The incident illustrates the complexity of the political mobilization movement, with its intermixed dynamics of inducement, argument, and coercion, all straining towards the goal of consent. It also re-emphasizes that mobilization flowed not only from the politically powerful at the top, but from the powerless at the bottom as well.

FURTHER READING

Ammerman, David: *In the Common Cause: American Response to the Coercive Acts of 1774* (Charlottesville: University of Virginia Press, 1974).

Brown, Richard D.: *Revolutionary Politics in Massachusetts: the Boston Committee of Correspondence and the Towns, 1772–1774* (Cambridge, Mass.: Harvard University Press, 1970).

Drayton, William Henry: *The Letters of Freeman, etc.: Essays on the Nonimportation Movement in South Carolina*, ed. with an Introduction and Notes by Robert M. Weir (Columbia: University of South Carolina Press, 1977).

Maier, Pauline: *From Resistance to Revolution: Colonial Radicals and the Development of American Opposition to Britain, 1765–1776* (New York: Vintage Books, 1974).

Marston, Jerrilyn Greene: *King and Congress: the Transfer of Political Legitimacy, 1774–1776* (Princeton, NJ: Princeton University Press, 1987).

Nash, Gary B.: *The Urban Crucible: Social Change, Political Consciousness, and the Origins of the American Revolution* (Cambridge, Mass.: Harvard University Press, 1979).

Norton, Mary Beth: *Liberty's Daughters: the Revolutionary Experience of American Women, 1750–1800* (Boston: Little, Brown, 1980).

Pole, J. R.: *The Gift of Government: Political Responsibility from the English Restoration to American Independence* (Athens: University of Georgia Press, 1983).

Rosswurm, Steven: *Arms, Country, and Class: the Philadelphia Militia and "Lower Sorts" During the American Revolution, 1775–1785* (New Brunswick, NJ: Rutgers University Press, 1987).

Ryerson, Richard Alan: *The Revolution is Now Begun: the Radical Committees of Philadelphia, 1765–1776* (Philadelphia: University of Pennsylvania Press, 1978).

Starr, Rebecca K.: "A School for Politics: Interest-group Strategies and the Development of South Carolina's Political Culture" (D.Phil. dissertation, Oxford University, 1989).

Stout, Harry S.: "Religion, Communications, and the Ideological Origins of the American Revolution," *William and Mary Quarterly*, 34 (1977), 519–41.

24

Opposition in Britain

COLIN BONWICK

OPPOSITION in and out of Parliament to the American policy of successive British governments grew slowly during the 1760s, reached a crescendo during the critical years of 1774–6 and continued throughout the war. Until the final crisis following General Cornwallis's surrender at Yorktown in 1781 it was always the stance of a minority. Within Parliament the critics included major statesmen such as William Pitt, his supporter and successor the Earl of Shelburne and their small group, the Marquis of Rockingham, his adviser Edmund Burke and their somewhat larger group, and Charles James Fox, who collaborated with Rockingham but retained political autonomy. Their failure to develop effective opposition was partly a consequence of Lord North's control of the House of Commons after 1770, but they could agree on only one principle: that the Anglo-American dispute should be – and could be – resolved within the framework of a continuing imperial connection. Their ability to form tactical alliances was seriously hindered by the fragmented nature of British parliamentary politics during the revolutionary era. Coherent parties in the modern sense were non-existent; in their place were shifting associations which centered on particular individuals and made sustained cohesion impossible. The problem was especially acute during the 1760s, when ministries changed frequently, but continued until well after the American war. Development of concerted opposition was also complicated before 1775 by the demands of issues such as Ireland, India, and the Falkland Islands overseas, and the Wilkes affair and Middlesex Election of 1768–9 at home, which frequently commanded greater attention.

I. THE GATHERING CRISIS, 1763–75

During the early years of the American dispute parliamentary opposition was limited in scope and largely pragmatic in character. All politicians applauded British success during the recently concluded Seven Years' or French and Indian War, and recognized that acquisition of Canada, Florida, and the lands east of the Mississippi River required systematic reorganization of the American empire, including provision for defence of the new territory and a revenue to finance it. George Grenville's Revenue or Sugar Act of 1764 was opposed only on matters of detail, and, apart from protests by General Conway, Isaac Barré, and a handful of others, the Stamp Act of 1765 passed with little opposition. Rockingham (*see* figure 21), Grenville's successor as Prime Minister, gained a reputation as sympathetic to America but repealed the Stamp Act in 1766 for political reasons rather than on grounds of principle. Moreover, his decision was influenced not by colonial resistance but the complaints of British merchants about the damage to their trade. Simultaneously Rockingham clarified his constitutional

FIGURE 21 Lord Rockingham with his secretary, Edmund Burke: an unfinished painting by Sir Joshua Reynolds (c. 1766–8); while Burke's attention is fixed on his employer, the Marquis looks out of the picture.

position in a Declaratory Act which stated that Parliament possessed authority to legislate for America "in all cases whatsoever," and revised the Sugar Act to improve the profitability of the revenue on American trade. He carefully evaded the question of whether parliamentary authority extended to taxation, but his general principle was simple: "I shall always consider that this country, as the parent, ought to be tender and just; and that the colonies, as the children, ought to be dutiful." Balancing this belief in parliamentary supremacy, however, was an appreciation of the strength of the colonies and an acceptance that policies should be adjusted to particular circumstances rather than directed by rigid adherence to constitutional principle. Outside government WILLIAM PITT, who enjoyed a great reputation in America, had demanded immediate repeal of the Stamp Act but attempted to distinguish between legislation and taxation. He applauded the colonists for defending their liberty but declared: "Let the sovereign authority of this country over the colonies be asserted in as strong terms as can be desired, and be made to extend to every point of legislation whatever. That we may bind their trade, confine their manufactures, and exercise

241

every power whatsoever, except that of taking their money out of their pockets without their consent." Revenue received from duties on trade was acceptable in his view, provided it was incidental to the regulation of commerce.

Even the Townshend Duties of 1767, which skirted American objections to the Stamp Act and would finance the salaries of colonial officials, failed to arouse opposition in England commensurate with protests in America. Ironically they had been imposed by a government nominally headed by Pitt (now Earl of Chatham). They were also compatible with Rockingham's previous policy and were not opposed by his group in the House of Commons. Nor was there any protest from British merchants, since improved trading conditions in Europe had made their American trade relatively less important. When Chatham collapsed the same year, an attempt was made to construct a coalition from his followers and the Rockingham group. Such a government might have been more conciliatory than the ministry formed by Lord North in 1770, but negotiations broke down for personal reasons. Thereafter the Rockinghamites remained out of office until 1782 and were joined by the Chathamite rump in 1770. While North consolidated his position, opponents of his American policy remained divided, partly because Chatham was fiercely independent in his views and personally erratic. They mustered 142 votes against retention of the tea tax in 1770 but were easily beaten, and Burke made a shallow speech in a debate on the Boston Massacre, but it merely demonstrated opposition weakness. In any case America virtually left the political agenda for a time.

2. THE CRITICAL YEARS, 1774–5

The Coercive or Intolerable Acts of 1774, introduced in response to the Boston Tea Party of the previous December, stimulated the beginnings of sustained opposition. No one condoned the destruction of property, and opposition to the Boston Port Act was negligible; only John Sawbridge, a London radical, denied Parliament's claim to tax the colonies. The other legislation aroused considerable opposition. EDMUND BURKE, adviser to the Marquis of Rockingham, insisted that imperial relations should be based on the principles of English liberty and warned of the dangerous consequences of using the army. Charles James Fox argued that Americans would only consider themselves attached to Britain if the right to taxation was abandoned. But opposition was ineffectual. The government's program passed through Parliament with exceptionally high majorities in both Houses. Later the same year a general election in which America was seldom an issue confirmed North's control of the Commons. Nevertheless, one difference of great significance emerged very clearly. Ministers were convinced that colonial resistance was the work of a small and malign minority of radicals. Their opponents were impressed by the evident maturity of American society and the colonists' willingness to defend their rights; they believed that resistance represented widespread American opinion.

Yet if the opposition's arguments are more congenial than those of the government, their constructive proposals contained serious weaknesses. They shared a common view that the foundations of the imperial connection must rest on mutual affection and common interests but beyond this could agree only on the necessity of some form of legislative supremacy. Chatham particularly feared the destruction of his achievements during the Seven Years' War. On 20 January 1775 he introduced a Conciliatory Bill in response to North's recent proposals. He reiterated the principles that the colonies were dependent on the Crown and subordinate to Parliament and

242

affirmed the Crown's right to deploy troops in America and Parliament's authority to regulate trade. But his Bill also recognized Congress as a permanent imperial institution, renounced the use of force against American liberties, abandoned claims to taxing power, acknowledged the sanctity of colonial charters and repealed or suspended all parliamentary legislation since 1764 against which there was protest. However, although he recognized the colonial legislatures' sole right to raise revenue, he envisaged authorization of a permanent revenue that would be placed at Parliament's disposal. Benjamin Franklin was impressed by the proposals, but they left crucial questions unanswered and had no prospect of acceptance.

A few weeks later, on 22 March, Edmund Burke spoke for the Rockingham group. He had been dismayed by the opposition's previous lack of energy, and presented a second alternative to North's coercive policy. As always his arguments were directed towards practicalities, but though he denied being a speculative philosopher they were grounded in philosophical ideas. He was convinced that the government ought to come to terms with circumstances and that since peace was the grand objective some form of reconciliation was necessary. Conciliation required concessions, and Britain could afford them. The real issue, he argued, was "not whether you have a right to render your people miserable; but whether it is not your interest to make them happy. It is not what a lawyer tells me I *may* do; but what humanity, reason and justice tell me I ought to do." Burke's proposals conceded almost everything demanded by the First Continental Congress. In particular they included repeal of all unacceptable legislation enacted since 1763 and the principle that financial contributions to imperial expenditure should be made voluntarily, as before that year. His speech was generous and even noble in spirit and his proposals were sufficiently flexible to allow for growth. Yet quite apart from their certain unacceptability to the government and probable unacceptability to the Americans his plan was flawed: he could not escape from the Rockinghamite commitment to the central principle of the Declaratory Act. All he could propose in a second speech on conciliation in November was that parliamentary supremacy should remain but by self-denying ordinance its powers should not be exercised. His first motion was defeated by 270 votes to 78, and his second by 210 to 105.

3. THE WAR YEARS

Efforts to construct a united opposition after the outbreak of war were unsuccessful. Chatham had annoyed the Rockingham group by failing to warn them of his proposals, and the summer of 1775 exposed their political weakness. An attempt to establish a chain of personal connections between the two groups failed during the following winter. Divisions were exacerbated by publication of Richard Price's *Observations on the Nature of Civil Liberty* early in 1776 (see PRICE, RICHARD). As a close friend and protégé, he commended Shelburne's Chathamite proposals for reconciliation with America but damaged relations with the Rockinghamites by launching a ferocious attack on the Declaratory Act: "I defy anyone," he said, "to express slavery in stronger language." But it was more their inability to influence government policy that demoralized the opposition, and in November 1776 the Rockinghamites formally seceded from Parliament in a futile gesture of protest.

General Burgoyne's surrender at Saratoga in October 1777 marked the beginning of a change of fortune. Nevertheless its effects were not felt immediately and it did nothing to unite the two groups. Chatham refused to modify his position and continued to insist that the connection with America must remain the basis for any peace settlement. Shelburne supported him in this view. Such a principle was now completely impractical and led to a final breach with the Rockingham group. Lord North attempted to exploit the breach by bringing him into the government but negotiations were abruptly halted by Chatham's death. Fox and some members of the Rockingham group naively hoped for some form of federal arrangement which they wishfully believed was compatible with independence. In contrast Rockingham drew the conclusion from Burgoyne's disaster that American independence would have to be conceded, and believed that it should be recognized immediately in the hope of averting war with France. Thereafter this new principle became the central plank in his policy, and in 1780 he refused to negotiate a coalition with North unless it was accepted as government policy.

News of the second British surrender, by General Cornwallis at Yorktown in October 1781, at last brought victory for the opposition. The attack on North's government began in earnest with a motion from Sir James Lowther, leader of a small independent group who had always opposed the war, which argued that operations against America should be terminated but implied that the war against France should continue. From January 1782 onwards the attack became relentless. Attendance in the House of Commons was extremely high, rising to about 500, and government support slowly drifted away. On 27 February General Conway's motion that offensive operations should be discontinued was passed by 19 votes. Privately North had already accepted that the war was lost, and on 20 March he resigned in order to avoid a motion of no confidence. The opposition had worked hard to achieve their victory, but the tide was turned by the disillusionment of independent members and the temporary defection of about 45 supporters of the government. Thereafter the two opposition groups formed an uneasy coalition government under Rockingham's leadership. Disagreement between the partners delayed negotiation of a peace treaty, for whereas Rockingham and Fox proposed immediate recognition of American independence, Shelburne still hankered after some form of connection. After Rockingham's death in July 1782 Shelburne became Prime Minister and concluded the treaty by recognizing American independence and offering generous terms as a means of encouraging reconciliation.

4. RADICALS AND DISSENTERS

Throughout the war Rockingham had stressed the importance of opposition outside Parliament. In general government policy was popular until the final crisis, but a small minority consistently supported the Americans and opposed coercion. The most prominent opponents were the "Commonwealthmen" or "Real Whigs" whose intellectual ancestry dated back to the radicalism of the seventeenth century, but whose numbers had fallen away in more recent years. Many were also religious dissenters or nonconformists, but some were members of the rationalist liberal wing of the Church of England. They included the dissenting ministers Richard Price and Joseph Priestley, both of whom were notorious radicals in orthodox eyes, Catharine Macaulay, author of the so-called republican *History of England*, and John Jebb, who had left the Church because he could no longer subscribe to its Articles of Religion. Other publicists included the parliamentary reformers John Cartwright and Granville Sharp, who campaigned for many reform causes but unusually was a devout Anglican. JOHN WILKES, who became the focus of radical activity in the 1760s and whose fate aroused much concern in the colonies, also supported the Americans after entering Parliament in 1774; whether he was entirely sincere remains open to question.

Radical opposition derived in part from a strong sense of the reality of transatlantic community. To a high degree Price and many others shared a common intellectual inheritance with the American Revolutionaries. They corresponded extensively with their American counterparts on matters such as theology, the anti-slavery campaign, and later the Anglo-American dispute, and read extensively in the literature of colonial protest, much of which was reprinted in Britain. Above all they enjoyed friendships with Americans living in London, particularly Benjamin Franklin. These associations encouraged a highly favorable view of colonial society, except for its tolerance of slavery, and made them receptive to colonial arguments. Moreover some Americans participated in reform politics; ARTHUR LEE of Virginia in particular was an active member of the Wilkite Society of Supporters of the Bill of Rights and frequently introduced American issues into its propaganda.

Opposition gathered pace slowly outside as well as within Parliament. During the 1760s dissenters among the radicals campaigned against Archbishop Thomas Secker's efforts to establish an American bishopric (see Chapter 18, §1); Thomas Hollis, who died in 1774, was especially active in distributing colonial tracts on the subject. Their objections lay in their fear that such an appointment would be accompanied by the apparatus of ecclesiastical authority and religious discrimination against which they had protested for decades in England. The coincidence of the bishopric campaign, the American legislation, and the Wilkes affair at home convinced the radicals that both parts of the empire faced a single crisis and that British ministers were attempting to suppress liberty on both sides of the Atlantic.

Attitudes crystallized as the crisis degenerated into war from 1774 on. Both London and Bristol were divided. Elsewhere the colonists' friends were widely scattered, though dissenters commonly were supportive. Sympathy for America was often a manifestation of long-running social divisions. Well-organized and vocal London supporters were mostly wholesale or retail shopkeepers and craftsmen, not great merchants. Outside the capital, sympathizers were usually men of middling social rank who were excluded from public authority and political patronage. After 1775 London critics were able to continue their orchestrated attacks on the government, but provincial opponents fell virtually silent since they lacked national organization and were largely unaware of each other's existence. Radical opposition to the government was directed towards finding a solution acceptable to both sides within the framework of a continuing empire. Dr John Fothergill used his connections as a physician to act as an intermediary between Franklin and the American Secretary Lord Dartmouth during the winter of 1774–5, but without success. More prominent was the radical contribution to public debate. Over one thousand pamphlets were printed on various aspects of the American crisis between 1764 and 1783, including many written by radicals. Several focused on the critical problem of representation and all rejected parliamentary supremacy. In 1774 John Cartwright published *American Independence the Interest and Glory of Great Britain*. Its title was misleading, for he proposed only legislative separation, not total independence, and argued that in practice Britain would become the dominant partner. Granville Sharp also argued in favor of local legislative autonomy coupled with continued loyalty to the Crown in his *Declaration of the People's Natural Right to a Share in the Legislature*, but it was Price's *Observations on the Nature of Civil Liberty* which caused the greatest outcry. In his view Britain should welcome the development of free states within the empire and should seek to bind them only by ties of affection and interest; it was absurd that a small group of men on one side of the Atlantic should control a vast continent on the other. His solution to the problem of government was a federal community within which each state would be self-governing and a senate representative of the general confederacy would balance the interests of individual members against the needs of the empire as a whole.

Those who opposed the government at first refused to accept the thrust of the Declaration of Independence. Cartwright and Sharp both insisted that Americans would accept parliamentary reform as a token of British good faith and would then negotiate a reconciliation. Only after Saratoga did they reluctantly come to recognize that the real alternatives were coercion or separation. Having done so they enthusiastically supported independence, in good measure because they regarded the United States as a model for political reform, and (a matter of great importance for dissenters) as an example of the practicality of religious liberty. During the closing years of the war the radical program of parliamentary reform at home and an end to hostilities against America attracted wider support, but only because the war had become unpopular.

Other than the Real Whigs there were few notable critics of government policy. Quakers had very strong connections with America and deplored the war but advised their members to remain true to the principles of pacifism and submission to lawful authority. At the other extreme *The Crisis*, a scurrulous newspaper published in 1775–6, attacked the King and made veiled threats of domestic revolution. Thomas Paine, the most notorious eighteenth-century radical, spent the Revolution in America, though *Common Sense* was reprinted several times in Britain, initially in an expurgated edition. The exception was Josiah Tucker. Far from being sympathetic to America he deplored its political culture and argued that the colonies had become a liability. He rejected mercantilist arguments and insisted that British as well as American trade would flourish if both economies were permitted to develop in freedom. Separation was in the British interest and independence should be welcomed.

FURTHER READING

Bonwick, Colin: *English Radicals and the American Revolution* (Chapel Hill: University of North Carolina Press, 1977).

Bradley, James E.: *Popular Politics and the American Revolution in England: Petitions, the Crown, and Public Opinion* (Macon, Ga.: Mercer University Press, 1986).

Derry, John: *English Politics and the American Revolution* (London: J. M. Dent, 1976).

Guttridge, G. H.: *English Whiggism and the American Revolution* (1942; Berkeley and Los Angeles: University of California Press, 1966).

O'Gorman, Frank: *The Rise of Party in England: The Rockingham Whigs, 1760–82* (London: George Allen & Unwin, 1975).

Sainsbury, John: *Disaffected Patriots: London Supporters of Revolutionary America, 1769–1782* (Kingston and Montreal: McGill-Queen's University Press; and Gloucester: Alan Sutton, 1987).

25

Loyalism and neutrality

ROBERT M. CALHOON

THE loyalists were colonists who by some overt action, such as signing addresses, bearing arms, doing business with the British Army, seeking military protection, or going into exile, supported the Crown during the American Revolution. Historians' best estimates put the proportion of adult white male loyalists somewhere between 15 and 20 per cent. Approximately half the colonists of European ancestry tried to avoid involvement in the struggle – some of them deliberate pacifists, others recent emigrants, and many more simple apolitical folk. The patriots received active support from perhaps 40 to 45 per cent of the white populace, and at most no more than a bare majority. Indians split into the same pro-British, pro-American, and neutralist alignments, with those tribes that British Indian Superintendents had courted since the 1740s proving most likely to support British arms. Eight hundred Virginia slaves fled their masters in response to the promise of freedom declared by the royal governor, Lord Dunmore, and hundreds of other Chesapeake Blacks knew of Dunmore's proclamation but were caught or placed under surveillance. Several thousand Blacks, many of them former slaves, worked in the garrison town of New York and fled to exile in Nova Scotia when the British evacuated the city in 1783.

Because the loyalists were a military asset and a political liability for the British, their history throws light on why the British lost the War for Independence and why the Americans had to expend more than six years of fighting, and secure French assistance, to win the struggle. Likewise, the loyalists articulated views of liberty and order at variance with those of the patriots and thereby deepened ideological struggle within the Revolution; as the patriots learned how to identify, isolate, discredit, conciliate, and ultimately reintegrate loyalists, they gained political capacity and maturity.

I. THE 1760S: ANTECEDENTS TO LOYALISM

While loyalism became a distinct phenomenon in late 1774 and 1775, there were important antecedents to loyalism during the pre-revolutionary decade. The Stamp Act crisis of 1765–6 exposed many Crown supporters to the rage of the populace. Lieutenant-Governor THOMAS HUTCHINSON of Massachusetts and his kinsman, stamp distributor Andrew Oliver, had their homes pillaged by mobs (*see* Chapter 19, §2). Lieutenant-Governor Cadwallader Colden of New York in vain tried to prevail on the British commander, Thomas Gage, to use military force against anti-stamp demonstrators in New York City demanding the surrender of tax stamps; Gage insisted that he could do so only on order from civil officials, placing the onus on Colden to issue such an order, which the Lieutenant-Governor declined to do. In South Carolina,

Attorney-General Egerton Leigh and former Councillor William Wragg, both future loyalists, and Henry Laurens, who would become a leader of the Revolution, all opposed boycotts and remonstrances against the Stamp Act and became public pariahs as a result. In Georgia, where James Wright alone among royal governors had personal command of British troops, stamps were protected and legally sold – the only province where the Act was enforced. Several future loyalists sought during the late 1760s and early 1770s to devise solutions to the disputes between Britain and the colonies. WILLIAM SMITH, JR., of New York, a member of the popular faction led by William Livingston, devised in 1767 a plan for imperial reorganization which he promoted so discreetly that almost no one knew its full terms until it was published in 1965. Also discreet and obscure was Hutchinson's contribution to reconciliation – an imagined dialogue between a knowledgeable British subject and a colonist about the merits of imperial policy and administration and colonial opposition. In contrast to Smith's and Hutchinson's penetrating private analyses, a group of high Anglican clergymen led by Thomas Bradbury Chandler, SAMUEL SEABURY, and Myles Cooper constructed and published searing attacks on colonial individualism, opposition politics, and dissenting religious practices, which they astutely and accurately blamed for the pre-revolutionary assault on British authority.

Seeking appropriate labels for themselves and their adversaries in the pre-revolutionary controversy, the advocates of colonial resistance called themselves "Whigs" and their enemies "Tories" – appropriating partisan labels from the politics of the reign of Queen Anne and before that the contending sides in the struggle in 1679–83 to exclude the Duke of York from succession to the English throne. English Whigs favored toleration of religious dissent, parliamentary supremacy, and an anti-French foreign policy, while Tories resisted each of those tendencies. After 1720 the terms lost much of their meaning as Tories became politically marginal and Whig factions multiplied and dominated English politics. Nor did the terms describe divergent colonial ideologies very aptly. Whigs and most Tories in America had so internalized John Locke's teachings about consent as to be predisposed to resist arbitrary governmental action; however, Tories – even those with a Lockean outlook – reacted with visceral anxiety to the idea of concerted, organized opposition against British authority. Thus, while Whig and Tory polemics from 1765 to 1775 were volleys which went past their respective targets, this nomenclature indicated where the dispute was heading and the libertarian Whig and prescriptive Tory assumptions underlying the controversy. Indeed, a case before the 1754 Privy Council – the "Pistole Fee dispute" over the power of the Virginia Assembly to regulate Anglican salaries – turned on the very question of whether colonial government depended in the final analysis on the "prescriptive" power of the parent state or on the "custom" of colonial autonomy built up by precedent. That distinction re-emerged on the eve of the Revolution as the crux of Whig–Tory disagreement (Greene, 1963, p. 163).

2. THE COERCIVE ACTS

When the British ministry decided in 1774 to impose the Coercive Acts and to use force to reimpose its authority in Massachusetts (*see* Chapter 20, §3), the pre-revolutionary debate had already aroused the supporters of the mother country – "the King's friends," or persons "inimical to the liberties of America," or "friends of government," as the earliest "loyalists" were variously called.

The text of the Coercive Acts, General Thomas Gage's governorship of Massachusetts, and substantial reinforcement of the British garrison in Boston all occurred during July and August 1774 (*see* GAGE, THOMAS). No one was more surprised by the abolition of the old elected Council and its replacement with a new appointed body than the 12 prominent Crown supporters named to the new Royal Council. After a short period of deceptive calm, crowds gathered in front of the homes of several of the new "mandamus" councilors and demanded their resignations and apologies. Those directly confronted complied, and all of the new appointees quietly slipped into Boston and repudiated resignations offered under duress. They soon discovered that Gage's authority did not extend beyond the Boston patrolled by British troops. By serving as a focus for outraged but largely non-violent demonstrations, the mandamus councilors unwittingly enabled popular leaders to seize control of the Massachusetts countryside by September 1774, the same month in which the last House of Representatives elected under royal rule converted itself into a Provincial Congress and began to oversee preparations for resistance.

Disastrously misreading the situation, the ministry in London dismissed Gage's request for 20,000 troops to restore order throughout Massachusetts and ordered him to march soldiers already under his command into the countryside to arrest the leaders of the insurrection. When Gage obeyed that order on 19 April 1775, he provoked a famous skirmish at the Lexington Green, heavy fighting at the Concord Bridge, and an outpouring of militiamen which forced the British troops to retreat ignominiously to Boston. Within days thousands of minutemen, volunteers from all parts of New England, surrounded Boston, effectively isolating Gage and British forces within the town. Gaining *de facto* control of the countryside by the autumn of 1774 and compelled to organize armed insurgency by the late spring of 1775, revolutionary leaders in New England focused their attention at this early stage on their potential opponents – prominent British supporters who had taken refuge in Boston and who went into exile when Britain evacuated the city in March 1776, as well as smaller fry who were neighbors and kinsmen hostile to colonial resistance and fit subjects for interrogation and surveillance by local committees of safety, correspondence, and inspection. Committee dealings with "persons inimical to the liberties of America," as these early loyalists were labelled, sought to define the community as a holistic and virtuous entity and Tories as offenders against the public good who acted out of ignorance, cupidity, or moral obtuseness. Encouraged by the committees to apologize in these terms, Tories were typically restored to good standing by their own candor and humility or ordered to post bond equal to the value of their property assuring their continued good behavior.

3. SOUTHERN BACK-COUNTRY LOYALISTS

North Carolina In a much more rudimentary, recently settled, and conflict-ridden setting such as the southern back country, loyalists posed a more serious threat to the Whig movement. In North Carolina a widely scattered and diverse population of Highland Scots, Scots-Irish, German-speaking, and English settlers had never coalesced into a unified political community. Opposition to British policy was strong but limited to pockets in the coastal lowlands, the Neuse and Roanoke river valleys in the east, and the two western counties of Rowan and Mecklenberg. The great influx of recent settlement lay in a broad, politically neutral belt in the upper Cape Fear river valley and central Piedmont region. With the aid of a Scottish officer in the British Army and a handful of his own agents, Governor Josiah Martin succeeded in encouraging back-country supporters – chiefly newly arrived Scottish settlers on whom he had lavished generous land grants – to prepare to fight against the rebels. Though forced to take refuge on a British warship, Martin received word on 3 January 1776 that a British expedition had been dispatched to the mouth of the Cape Fear River, the site of the town of Wilmington; and he called on the back-country loyalists to rise, march to the coast, and occupy Wilmington in advance of the arrival of British regulars. By 14 February 1776, 1,400 volunteers – two-thirds of them Highland Scots – assembled in the upper Cape Fear. At first successful in eluding a force of rebel militia, the loyalists headed south for Wilmington, but other patriot troops positioned themselves on wooded slopes on the bank of a creek in the path of the loyalists' line of march. Rashly trying to cross a partially dismantled bridge, which crossed Moore's Creek, the loyalists were completely routed by cannon fire. When General Henry Clinton, commanding the British expedition to the Carolinas, learned of the disaster, he canceled his plans to land troops at the mouth of the Cape Fear.

South Carolina In the South Carolina back country the loyalists had far better leadership than in North Carolina, and with almost no help from the royal governor they came very close to seizing control of the South Carolina–Georgia frontier in the summer and fall of 1775. The Whig leadership dominated the lowland aristocracy and the Charles Town merchant community; and in the first six months of 1775 the Whigs seized effective control of the lowlands, forcing the newly arrived governor, William Campbell, to seek refuge on a British warship in Charles Town harbor. The device that the South Carolina Whigs employed was an "Association," or oath, which all inhabitants were required to sign. When they tried to secure signatures in the back country, however, the new council of safety encountered stubborn resistance. The most powerful figure in the region, militia Colonel Thomas Fletchall, enormously overweight and vain, was irked at not receiving a more important position in the revolutionary movement, and he successfully blocked efforts to require all militiamen in the back country to sign the Association. Playing on Fletchall's vanity and influence, a number of committed loyalist leaders sensed an opportunity to make their region a bastion of British strength at the very moment imperial authority was rapidly eroding everywhere else. Not a single militiaman under Fletchall's command signed the Association; instead they adopted a counter-Association denying that the King had forfeited their allegiance or violated the British Constitution.

At this critical juncture, the Sons of Liberty in the Georgia back country seized and tortured Thomas Brown, an obstinate land-owner recently arrived from Great Britain, by jabbing burning splinters into the soles of his feet. The enraged Brown escaped, made his way to District Ninety-Six in the western portion of South Carolina, and became a fiery leader of the growing loyalist movement there. The council of safety sent one of its most politically adroit members, William Henry Drayton, to District Ninety-Six to counter the influence of the loyalist leadership. By skillful maneuver, Drayton managed to separate Fletchall from the loyalist leaders and negotiate in September 1775 a truce between Fletchall's militia and the Whig forces. The truce collapsed in late November, and more than 2,000 rallied to arms to fight for the Crown against a patriot force of 550. A blizzard occurred, which made marches and discipline extremely difficult, and after three days the fighting sputtered out and the loyalists dispersed. The loyalists had been waging a defensive campaign, most of them just wanting to be left alone. The Whigs had a more clearly defined aim: to discredit the leadership of the ambivalent Fletchall and the intransigent loyalists.

4. NORTHERN LOYALISTS

New Jersey   In northern New Jersey, the British enjoyed both military supremacy and a large pool of loyalist volunteers in arms. After his successful occupation of New York City, William Howe's holding of New Jersey thrust into view both the state's revolutionary leadership and its large loyalist population and initiated bloody internecine combat. In line with Howe's aim of expanding the area under British control, British troops occupied Burlington, Bordentown, and Trenton, on the Delaware River, as well as Princeton and New Brunswick. Howe sent Cornwallis in chase of Washington, but the cold wet weather of November 1776 was an inauspicious season for grim pursuit. Howe was briefly tempted in early December to catch his prey at Trenton, but again Washington responded quickly to Howe's movements and whisked his force across the river into Pennsylvania. Howe paused and issued another proclamation promising pardon to defectors from the rebel cause. He sought to multiply the psychological impact of these defections by holding frequent public drills of occupying British forces and by paying generous prices to loyalist farmers who brought goods to a procurement center at Bordentown. By spring, some 2,700 New Jersey residents had signed Howe's oath and received pardon. But as his forces moved across New Jersey they seized livestock and produce without ceremony and looted fine homes of silver plate, jewelry, clothing, and other household finery. British officers vied with each other to equip field headquarters with the fine mahogany furniture of the region. Uncomfortable in the New Jersey winter, troops appropriated all available firewood and destroyed farm buildings for more fuel. Numerous reports of rape and killing by British and Hessian troops appear to have been grossly exaggerated, but the offenses that did occur further fanned abhorrence of the British occupiers during the winter of 1776–7, when patriot morale was at its lowest ebb and the machinery of revolutionary government in New Jersey in near ruin. The combined effect of Washington's stunning victories against exposed British outposts at Trenton and Princeton plus resentment over the depredations of armed loyalist forces was to bring Howe's offensive in New Jersey to a halt.

New York   A more controlled environment for loyalist policing of British military control occurred in the garrison towns of New York, occupied from 1776 to 1783, and Philadelphia, held from September 1777 until the following June. The British commandant in New York, General James Robertson, struggled to reconcile the needs of the army and the interests of loyalist exiles who flocked to the city from patriot-held territory to the north and loyalist and neutralist inhabitants. He ended vandalizing and looting by British soldiers and protected loyalists from unauthorized seizure of their homes by British troops. Robertson located cramped quarters for British and Hessian troops and wives and children of British officers who had joined them in New York City – some 2,500 dependents by 1779. Warehouses were converted to handle British war supplies; churches were used as hospitals; and prisons had to be improvised in empty buildings and ships in the harbor. Housing for returning loyalists and refugees remained the most pressing problem in occupied New York City. Most rented rooms cost four times their prewar amounts. Not until 1780 did the army develop machinery to regulate and prevent abuses in its occupancy of private homes. Moreover, the army was supposed to pay loyalists for the use of their homes but regularly neglected these obligations. Loyalists in turn were not above falsely claiming ownership of buildings used by the British. In spite of General Robertson's tireless efforts to be fair, the shortage of accommodation and the absence of a court system to settle disputes over housing created persistent friction between loyalist inhabitants and the British Army.

General Howe appointed Andrew Elliot Superintendent of Exports and Imports for the port of New York. Elliot, the son of a Scottish official, had grown up in Philadelphia, married into wealth, established himself as a New York merchant, and held, from 1764 to 1776, the post of Receiver General and Collector for the port of New York. He also served as head of the Board of Police in occupied New York City. Elliot was the most important loyalist during the first half of British occupation of New York City. A civilian, he was responsible for the enforcement of detailed regulations and procedures preventing the illegal re-export of goods to other parts of the rebelling colonies. With his cronies, the former mayor David Mathews and the police magistrate Peter Dubois, Elliot monopolized political influence and authority in New York during the first half of the war. As prominent members of the Board of Police, the trio were responsible for a wide range of governmental functions: "suppression of vice and licentiousness," support of the poor, direction of the night watch, regulation of ferries, and maintenance of the "economy, peace, and good order of the city."

Philadelphia   The British occupation of Philadelphia in 1777–8 offered even more promising opportunities for loyalist allies of the Crown to help restore imperial administration of an American colonial community. JOSEPH GALLOWAY, an experienced Pennsylvania politician and advocate of compromise with Britain at the First Continental Congress in 1774, sought a position in occupied Philadelphia, analogous to Elliot's in New York, which he could expand into that of a powerful administrative overseer of British policy. He conceived of his role as Superintendent of Police more as that of a long-range constitutional theorist than that of a mere overseer of policy subordinate to the British commander. Galloway assumed the duties of political overlord of the Pennsylvania campaign as soon as the troops landed, on 25 August, at Head of Elk, at the northern end of Chespeake Bay. He hired intelligence agents, organized efforts at supply operations, and ordered Cornwallis to destroy a bridge the rebels had built across the Schuylkill River. Loyalists who helped prevent the burning of Philadelphia by retreating rebels received rewards for their courage from Galloway. He sought lucrative governmental positions for other conspicuous loyalists and forged his subordinates into an effective and adaptable administrative agency.

Galloway's personal corps of loyalist troops did conduct a wide range of irregular raids in Pennsylvania during the winter of 1777–8, seizing rebel provisions and supplies bound for Valley Forge, capturing many supporters of the Revolution within a 30-mile radius of Philadelphia, and collecting military intelligence. When Cornwallis had failed for six weeks to erect batteries on Mud Island in the Delaware River because tides kept washing over the foundations, Galloway organized and supervised a crew that built batteries there in less than a week, to the astonishment of the army's chief engineer. Galloway also conducted a census of the entire population of the city, designating the loyalty or disaffection of every inhabitant. He designed a campaign of newspaper proclamations urging voluntary restrictions on price increases, which prevented the kind of inflation rampant in occupied New York City. Events, however, frustrated Galloway's initially successful attempt to convert Philadelphia into a showplace of benevolent, vigorous, confident reimposition of royal authority. Howe, for example, vetoed his scheme to kidnap the revolutionary Governor and Council of New

Jersey. When news came that Philadelphia was to be abruptly abandoned to the Americans, the loyalist community asked permission to negotiate directly with General Washington for their safety. Habitually prone to overreaching himself, Galloway seemed to British officials in America as vain and undependable as he was loyal and efficient. Rebuffed, he went to London, where his testimony before a parliamentary inquiry discredited the cautious tactics of General William Howe and encouraged British legislators to believe that a vigorous military effort would tap vast reservoirs of loyalist support and crush the rebellion.

5. INDIANS SERVING THE LOYALIST CAUSE

The North   Through the work of Superintendents of Indian Affairs on the northern and southern frontiers from the late 1740s onwards, the British Government had built up a large reservoir of good will among Indian tribes which traded with the colonists and had fought with them against the French. Some Indians regarded themselves as allies of the British, acting from considerations of self-interest, while others concluded that British protection and support was a moral debt. The use of Indians as counter-revolutionaries was, however, fraught with difficulty. They made up about a third of an offensive strike force, commanded by Lieutenant Colonel Barry St. Leger, which marched from Oswego on Lake Ontario in late July 1777 in support of Burgoyne's offensive to rendezvous with Burgoyne near Albany, New York. Sir John Johnson, son and successor of Sir William Johnson – legendary Indian Superintendent from 1754 to 1774 – led a group of Indians and white loyalists as a part of the St. Leger offensive, which ambushed and destroyed a patriot force at the Battle of Oriskany and in the aftermath burned a neutral village of Oneida Indians, another Iroquois tribe. That act destroyed the delicate web of Iroquois unity and provoked vengeful attacks by patriots and Oneidas upon Mohawk settlements. This mutual destruction of villages and crops in turn wiped out the food supply of Indians on both sides of the conflict; these tribes had so widely adopted the white man's agricultural techniques to the neglect of hunting that, from 1777 onwards, famine and hunger became weapons of war that took a terrible toll. Deep divisions developed among white loyalists about the proper use of Indian warriors. Guy and John Johnson and their allies – JOSEPH BRANT, a brilliant Mohawk leader, and his sister MARY BRANT – wanted the Indians to operate as a disciplined, elite, and independent military force. But Governor Guy Carleton in Quebec wanted the Indians to serve a defensive and subordinate role, and he placed them under the command of the Johnsons' rival, Colonel John Butler, a wealthy western New York loyalist. Butler preferred to recruit braves by getting them drunk, and therefore most of the Indians he enlisted for the St. Leger offensive were so hungry and ill-clad that they did little fighting; when St. Leger's forces failed to capture Fort Stanwix and dispersed, the Indians robbed and assaulted retreating British and loyalist soldiers. With the surrender of Burgoyne at Saratoga, frontier New York ceased to be a strategic theater of the war, but it was nevertheless the scene of successive Mohawk and white loyalist terrorist attacks on patriot settlements and equally savage retaliation by patriots against Mohawk villages and crops.

The South   Similar divided counsel in the British offensives in the South from 1778 to 1781 prevented effective use of pro-British Indian tribes such as the Creeks and Cherokees. The Indian Superintendent in the South, John Stuart, realized that Indian fighting capacity was a highly expendable commodity, while headstrong loyalists such as Thomas Brown and the East Florida governor Patrick Tonyn wanted to use Indians to terrorize frontier patriots. Poorly supplied and with confusing lack of military direction, loyalist Indians in Georgia and the Carolina back country contributed little to the British conquest of the region in 1780. Indians sensed, with good reason, that a victorious independent American republic would be far less restrained than the British administration had been in dispossessing them of their land and extirpating their way of life.

6. RELIGIOUS GROUPS

Pietists A number of ethnic, religious, and social groups, sometimes labelled "cultural minorities" by historians of loyalism, had the same misgivings about American independence and stood aloof from the struggle for self-determination. The most visible were religious pacifists in Pennsylvania, both Quakers and German pietist. Of the latter, the most vulnerable were the Mennonites, who refused to sign a Test Oath prescribed by the Pennsylvania revolutionary government in 1777. The Mennonites were willing to sell grain to the Continental Army, to supply teamsters and wagons to the government on request, and to pay commutation fees in lieu of military service. But they refused to take the compulsory oath of allegiance to the state imposed in June 1777, and they refused to pay special war taxes. They objected not only because it was an oath – a mere affirmation would have satisfied the law – but also because it required renunciation of their allegiance to the King and affirmative endorsement of authorities in Philadelphia whom they had no reason to respect or support. Moreover, the oath implied their approbation of the warfare necessary for the establishment of the new government.

The Brethren, Dunkers, and Schwenkfelders suffered similar pressures. In 1776 the Ephrata community of Brethren simply declared their neutrality on the ground that they were subject to a higher magistrate "and consequently emancipated from the civil government." Though opposed to both military service and oaths of allegiance, the Brethren were far less strict in enforcing these prohibitions and ruled that the payment of fines in lieu of military service "would not be deemed so sinful" as actually bearing arms if it was done under "compulsion" and not "voluntarily." The Schwenkfelders adapted themselves to the conditions of war still more adroitly. The Church established a charitable fund to pay fines for non-participation in the militia. It was not military service but oaths or affirmations of allegiance that caused the greatest friction between pietist sects and the revolutionary government. One member of the sect refused on the ground that he had taken an oath of allegiance to the King when he was naturalized, and, second, the outcome of the war was still in doubt and it was not yet clear "upon what side God almighty would bestow the victory." As opportunistic and equivocal as the reasons appear, they represented an important pietist belief and one that distinguished these pacifists from the Quakers: the assurance that divine providence ultimately controlled the military struggle and that men could not alter oaths of allegiance until God had granted victory and spiritual legitimacy to one side or the other.

Quakers The most serious conflict between the government of Pennsylvania and pacifist citizens, of course, involved the Quakers. The Philadelphia Quakers were too wealthy and influential a group to be ignored by revolutionary leaders. Quaker aversion to any complicity with the war effort was both ingenious and scrupulous, but there were just enough wealthy Quakers who were outright British sympathizers to taint the neutrality of the whole sect. The Philadelphia Meeting for Sufferings called on Friends in the city "with Christian fortitude and firmness" to "withstand and refuse to submit to the arbitrary injunctions and ordinances of men who assume to themselves the power of compelling others ... to join in carrying on war by imposing tests not warranted by the precepts of Christ ... or the laws of the happy constitution under which [the Friends had] long enjoyed tranquillity and peace" – language that came perilously close to being non-neutral. Congress asked Pennsylvania officials to arrest 11 prominent Quakers – including James, Israel, and John Pemberton, Henry Drinker, Samuel Thomas Fisher, and Thomas Wharton – and to add to the list other names of persons "inimically disposed toward the American states," and recommended that Pennsylvania officials deport the prisoners to confinement in Virginia. The Council first ordered the militia to transport 20 unrepentant prisoners to Reading. A judge then ordered their release on a writ of habeas corpus, but a special *ex post facto* law denied the group the protection of habeas corpus. After a few days they were taken to Winchester, Virginia, arriving there in September 1777, just three days after the British had occupied Philadelphia. There they lived under lenient confinement until sympathy for the exiles persuaded the Supreme Executive Council to return them to Lancaster, Pennsylvania, and release them.

Quakers in New England were more vulnerable to harassment and more willing to seek an accommodation with revolutionary leaders as a demonstration of their peaceableness. Led by Moses Brown, the New England Friends sought to achieve a practical compromise between the demands of conscience and the actual exigencies of the time, between church government that imposed discipline on its members and one that responded to the concerns of its constituents. The first step was thoroughly conventional: the establishment of the New England Meeting for Sufferings, in June 1775, modeled on the Philadelphia Meeting for Sufferings, which had dealt with the legal and financial needs of pacifists and brought relief to other victims of war since 1756. Between December 1775 and January 1777, using funds contributed largely by Philadelphia Quakers, Brown and his co-workers assisted more than 5,000 destitute Boston-area residents whose incomes had been cut off by the commencement of hostilities.

Throughout the early years of the War for Independence, the New England Friends continued to seek a moderate means of practicing pacifism without appearing to be openly hostile to the revolutionary cause, and to maintain the unity of the fellowship without becoming narrowly exclusive. The New England Quakers agreed that they should not accept paper money issued by the Continental Congress or by revolutionary state governments because the issuance of this money was a means of financing the war. But, under Moses Brown's guidance, monthly and yearly meetings imposed no arbitrary prohibitions on transactions payable in the new currency and left the matter, instead, to the conscience of each individual. Open dissension arose over payment of taxes. Some purists wanted to refuse any tax payments to new state governments on the ground that support of a revolutionary regime was as evil as complicity in warfare, while a strong minority argued that Quakers had a responsibility to contribute to the costs of government even if by so doing they inadvertently contributed to the support of military activity as well. Trying to mediate between the two camps, Brown believed that on the issue of paying taxes members should be answerable only to their consciences and should be disciplined only for unauthorized public statements on

255

matters that weakened Quaker solidarity. The longer the war lasted, the stronger became the influence of doctrinaire Friends, and Brown only narrowly prevented the adoption in New England in 1780 of a rule making non-payment of taxes mandatory.

Methodists   Methodist preachers had just begun to arrive in the colonies in the early 1770s, preaching a message of assurance and grace which appealed to poor Whites and Blacks living on the fringes of polite society in the middle colonies and the Chesapeake. Their founder and leader, John Wesley, vociferously condemned the American Revolution, and this factor added to their reputation as outsiders and troublemakers. Methodist revivals on the Eastern Shore of Maryland and in adjoining portions of Delaware and Virginia therefore helped foment a kind of lower-class Tory populist revolt against the authority of patriot governments. Some Methodists were outright British sympathizers, while a larger number relegated politics to the level of worldly concerns, insignificant compared with the work of salvation. Dutch Reformed settlers in the Hackensack Valley of northern New Jersey split between a Tory faction aligned with church authorities in Holland and a patriot one bent on further Americanization of the Church; Dutch families around Albany, New York, with the greatest internal solidarity and distrust of English neighbors, were more prone to be loyalist than the families which had more varied social and business dealings; those prominent Dunkers in North Carolina, who were deeply involved in land speculation and estranged from humbler church members, saw General Charles Cornwallis as their savior and became avowed loyalists, while the bulk of the Dunker community simply feared disintegration of their communities under the pressures of war and fled North Carolina as soon as the conflict ended.

7. WAR IN THE SOUTH

The inability of the Continental Congress and Army to defeat the British in the middle Atlantic states between 1776 and 1778 and British failure to smash Washington's forces and induce a majority of the inhabitants of the region to return to affirm their allegiance to the Crown made loyalism and neutrality possible and also precarious; in the southern states from 1778 to 1781, a bold but poorly planned and executed British offensive also summoned loyalists to arms and encouraged the uncommitted to withhold their support from the revolutionary cause. But the war in the South also spread warfare beyond the battlefield and into the lives of non-combatants.

The southern offensive began auspiciously when forces sailing from the British base at St. Augustine, Florida, recaptured Savannah, Georgia, in February 1779 – enabling the British to re-establish civilian government in coastal Georgia and inland Augusta, the only instance during the war that regular British administration supplanted martial law in North America. Then in May 1780 General Henry Clinton brought an invading force from New York, landed near Charles Town, South Carolina, cut off supply lines to the city, and compelled the American defenders to surrender. Over the next eight weeks, resistance throughout South Carolina collapsed, and Clinton returned to New York leaving a portion of his forces under the command of General Charles Cornwallis to complete the pacification of Georgia and South Carolina, to occupy and pacify North Carolina, and then to march north into the Chesapeake.

The strategic weaknesses of the southern campaign became apparent as soon as Cornwallis tried to invade North Carolina in the early autumn of 1780. Clinton had saddled Cornwallis with two ungovernable subordinates, Major Patrick Ferguson and

Lieutenant Colonel Banastre Tarleton, both commanding loyalist troops and both brilliant, reckless officers. Ferguson allowed himself to be cut off from Cornwallis's army and trapped atop a spiney hogback ridge called Kings Mountain by a huge force of "over the mountain men" from what later became Tennessee. In savage hand-to-hand combat on 7 October 1780, the patriot frontiersmen annihilated the loyalists. Tarleton's defeat at Cowpens in January 1781 further eroded the offensive power of British arms. Most North Carolina loyalists abandoned any idea of rallying to the King's standard, and a few who did try to rendezvous with Cornwallis – when he occupied the state capital at Hillsborough – fell into an ambush set by Colonel Henry "Lighthorse Harry" Lee. Bereft of loyalist support and bogged down in a hostile wilderness, Cornwallis lost a quarter of his men to death and injury in an inconclusive battle at Guilford Courthouse in March 1781. He marched to the port of Wilmington to be resupplied and then decided to risk an invasion of the Chesapeake rather than fight on in North Carolina or return to Charles Town and adopt a defensive position in South Carolina. He was not convinced that the war could be won only if Britain transferred all of its available forces to the Chesapeake. And so he marched north into Virginia, where he occupied the town of Yorktown just before the French fleet entered Chesapeake Bay in force, severing British supply lines, communications, and means of reinforcement. Alerted of French naval plans, Washington and General Rochambeau moved their armies from New England, New York, and New Jersey to Virginia, beseiged Yorktown, and forced Cornwallis to surrender.

When the British departed from North Carolina in June 1781, they left behind a state exhausted from the struggle against the invader. Loyalists filled the vacuum. Major James Craig occupied Wilmington in January 1781 and in July appointed David Fanning commander of loyalist militia, already operating under Fanning's leadership. Craig and Fanning had finally learned how to fight irregular war in America successfully. Fanning devised a new guerrilla strategy based on what one authority calls "quickness, mobility, deception, and improvisation" (Watterson, 1971, p. 98). Fanning's raids concentrated on freeing Tory prisoners, capturing the most notorious persecutors of the loyalists, operating widely in eastern North Carolina under cover of darkness, "plundering and destroying our stock of cattle and robbing our houses of everything they can get." Fanning's men were disciplined and violence was carefully targeted against key officials. Throughout Cumberland, Bladen, Anson, and Duplin counties, pockets of dispirited loyalists felt emboldened by Fanning's exploits. General Nathanael Greene and Governor Thomas Burke sensed almost immediately what was happening. The only safe remedy was to hunker down and wait for events outside North Carolina to shift advantage away from the British irregulars. The use of retaliatory terror against known or suspected loyalists only played into Craig's and Fanning's hands, enabling them to present themselves as agents of justice for the oppressed and targets of barbarity. The Fanning–Burke duel in North Carolina in the summer of 1781 therefore pitted for the first time in the war adversaries who thoroughly understood the relationship between conventional and guerrilla warfare in the Revolution.

8. AFTER INDEPENDENCE: REINTEGRATION

Had the British kept sea lanes open between New York and the Chesapeake when Cornwallis encamped at Yorktown – or if the French fleet had not chosen to descend in force into the Bay in September 1781 – Cornwallis might well have savaged the

257

FIGURE 22 "Shelb--ns Sacrifice or the recommended Loyalists, a faithful representation of a Tragedy shortly to be performed on the Continent of America. Invented by Cruelty. Engraved by Dishonor": the British Prime Minister, Lord Shelburne, looks on approvingly while America, personified by Indians, slaughters loyalists who were not protected by the Treaty of Paris; a butcher weeps to see such bloodshed and Britannia attacks Shelburne in anger.

Virginia tidewater during the winter and spring of 1782 and then marched back into North Carolina to capitalize on Fanning's successful demoralization of the Whig regime in that state.

Instead, the surrender at Yorktown destroyed the political credibility of the ministry and forced the creation of a new government committed to peace even at the cost of conceding independence to the rebellious colonies. The treatment of the loyalists was the most difficult issue for British and American negotiators to resolve in 1782. The Crown insisted on the restoration of all confiscated property and amnesty from prosecution for all crimes allegedly committed by the loyalists in the course of the war. American negotiators were instructed to refuse any concessions in favor of the loyalists. Britain broke the impasse by abandoning its rigid defense of the loyalists' interests (*see* figure 22), and the Americans responded by agreeing that Congress would "earnestly recommend" to the states that loyalists who had not borne arms for the British could reclaim their property, and that those who had fought for the Crown or gone into exile would have one year to purchase back their confiscated estates from the new owners. The American Secretary for Foreign Affairs rightly called the loyalist clause of the peace treaty "a very slender provision ... inserted [by Britain more] to appease the clamors of these poor wretches than to satisfy their wants" (Norton, 1972, p. 180).

In 1783–4 most states ignored the provisions of the treaty protecting loyalists and British creditors. But in 1785 Alexander Hamilton in New York, Benjamin Rush in Pennsylvania, and Aedanus Burke in South Carolina each mounted public campaigns to restore property and political rights to most former loyalists. They argued that public vengeance was a self-inflicted wound on the American body politic, that a fragile republican polity would ill-afford the corrosive effects of such recriminations and retribution. By 1787 most states, needing the commercial skills of departed loyalist merchants, began repealing anti-Tory legislation.

Meanwhile 60,000 to 80,000 loyalists who departed with the British or fled to Canada or the West Indies after 1783 created new communities in the portions of British America which did not revolt (for illustration, *see* figure 41, p. 502). Half of the exiles settled in Quebec, New Brunswick, and Nova Scotia. Of these, about a thousand black loyalists were eventually resettled in Sierra Leone in West Africa. Seven thousand made their way to England. Disappointed by the ambiguous loyalist provisions in the peace treaty, the exiles in London redoubled their efforts to secure redress from the British Government. Parliament responded by creating a commission dealing with the losses and services of the American loyalists. Its investigation began in 1783 and lasted for six years. Hearings were held in London and also in Canada, at Halifax, St. Johns, and Montreal. The commission, which heard 3,225 claims for property and income lost on account of claimants' loyalty to the Crown during the Revolution, and which granted compensation to 2,291 claimants, did its work well. It eliminated fraudulent and inflated claims and required each claimant to produce witnesses from among other loyalist exiles and Crown officials who could testify to his character, devotion to the Crown during the Revolution, and the pre-revolutionary value of his estate or Crown office. The claimants did not recoup all of their losses, but the compensation of more than three million pounds amounted to 37 per cent of the successful claimants' estimates of their losses.

During the 1780s and 1790s, an assortment of loyalists with experience in mobilizing and leading pro-British Indians along the southern, Ohio valley, northwest, New York, and Vermont frontiers – notably Thomas Dalton and William Augustus Bowles – promoted the idea of systematic loyalist and Indian military activities in North America; during the War of 1812 loyalists played a key role in repulsing American incursions into Canada.

FURTHER READING

Brock, Peter: *Pacifism in the United States from the Colonial Era to the First World War* (Princeton, NJ: Princeton University Press, 1968).

Calhoon, Robert M.: *The Loyalists in Revolutionary America, 1760–1781* (New York: Harcourt, Brace, Jovanovich, 1973).

——: *The Loyalist Perception and Other Essays* (Columbia: South Carolina University Press, 1989).

Greene, Jack P.: *The Quest for Power* (Chapel Hill: University of North Carolina Press, 1963).

Nelson, William H.: *The American Tory* (Oxford: Oxford University Press, 1961).

Norton, Mary Beth: *The British-Americans: the Loyalist Exile in England, 1774–1789* (Boston: Little Brown and Co., 1972).

Watterson, John S. III: "The Ordeal of Governor Burke," *North Carolina Historical Review*, 48 (1971), 95–117.

26

Common Sense

JACK FRUCHTMAN, JR.

THE appearance of Thomas Paine's *Common Sense* (10 January 1776) was one of the most remarkable publishing events of the eighteenth century. Not only did it for the first time publicly present strong arguments for America's separation from England, but it also enjoyed phenomenal sales. Although exact figures are uncertain, scholars have estimated that well over 100,000 copies were sold in the first year of its publication. This does not consider sales after 1776 nor those of the French translation which appeared later. Paine turned all of his profits over to the American cause. More important than its sales history, the pamphlet became the conscience of the Revolution, providing "a summary of a large segment of the ideology of the American Revolution as well as a substantial contribution to that very ideology" (Aldridge, 1984, p. 17).

In early 1776, many Americans were still wavering about the idea of separation from Britain. Paine's pamphlet, first signed anonymously "By an Englishman," proved so popular that, in galvanizing opposition to the British Crown, it served as the final catalyst for those uncertain whether America should break with Great Britain. In so doing, it successfully shattered the residual American psychological resistance to independence, because Paine undertook a dual assault. First, he launched a frontal attack on the British monarchy in terms so graphically violent that only the most committed loyalist came away without a sense of hatred and loathing for Britain and its king. Second, he unequivocally showed, for the first time, how the relationship with Britain, should it continue, fatally threatened American republican virtue and simplicity. His goal was to awaken Americans to British ignorance and prejudice and thus teach them to reverence themselves. "Every thing that is right or natural pleads for separation," he wrote. "The blood of the slain, the weeping voice of nature cries, 'TIS TIME TO PART'' (Penguin edition, p. 87).

The pamphlet was accessible to many Americans for two reasons. First, because it cost but a shilling a copy, it was relatively cheap. Second, and perhaps more important, Paine's style attracted not only merchants and manufacturers, but also the artisans, tradesmen, and craftsmen (see §2 below).

1. AN OUTLINE OF THE WORK

Paine divided *Common Sense* into four principal sections. For the second edition, he enlarged it and included an appendix as well as a reply to the Quakers, who were distressed over the non-pacifist views Paine presented in the first edition. In the first part, Paine reviewed the history of man using Lockean themes of a state of nature and the social contract (*see* Chapter 9, §1). He told how man, at one time unconnected to his fellows by any form of government, at long last decided principally for security reasons to join others to form civil government. In this section, using the quotable turn of phrase for which he was so well known, he formulated one of his most famous remarks about the natural good of society and the corresponding evil of government: "society in every state is a blessing, but government even in its best state is but a necessary evil; in its worst state an intolerable one.... Government, like dress, is the badge of lost innocence" (p. 65). The British Constitution, with its divisions into King, Lords, and Commons, was not a republican form of government as its supporters claimed it was (*see* Chapter 70). For Paine, the House of Commons was the only republican element in British government.

This discussion led directly to the second part, which was a consideration of monarchy and hereditary succession. Here Paine inquired into the origins of kingship and the hereditary principle and gave long quotations from scripture. They described how the Bible condemned the ancient Hebrews, who were at one time free, as a sinful people because they wanted a monarchy when they had an opportunity to create a republic. For Paine, because human beings were created equal in the sight of God, it was an abomination for one family to set itself up in perpetuity over all others. England's problems grew out of its long history of monarchy and hereditary succession. These problems intensified because of William the Conqueror: "a French bastard landing with an armed banditti and establishing himself king of England against the consent of the natives is in plain terms a very paltry rascally original" (p. 78).

In his third section, Paine turned to the situation in America. His thoughts rested on nothing but the "simple facts, plain arguments, and common sense" (p. 81). Common sense told us that the relationship between America and Britain had become so bad that Americans had only one choice: they must stop negotiating a settlement with England and separate. "'TIS TIME TO PART" because America had entered "the seed-time of continental union, faith, and honor" (pp. 87, 82). America must become independent to ensure its protection and security from a Europe that was hopelessly corrupt. By separating from England, America would develop into a free port and enjoy a strong, lasting commerce. Its prosperity would be assured, its people happy, and the nation safe.

This would be realized when the Americans called a constitutional convention to draft a republican constitution with annual assemblies and a president who would be chosen each year from a different colony. Congress would be empowered to pass laws but only by a three-fifths majority. Unlike the rest of the world, America had the opportunity to be a free nation. All other countries had expelled freedom. It was time for America to "receive the fugitive, and prepare in time an asylum for mankind" (p. 100).

In the final part, Paine reviewed America's strengths, giving particular attention to her navy, and predicted that in a war with Britain America would be victorious. In the meantime, he recommended that America tell the world of her mistreatment by the British Government by means of a manifesto, somewhat like the Declaration of Independence of a few months later.

In the Appendix to the second edition, Paine briefly responded to some of the criticisms from those who wanted reconciliation, not independence. In his exploration of the consequences of separation, he made the remark most often quoted from this text:

we have every opportunity and every encouragement before us, to form the noblest, purest constitution on the face of the earth. We have it in our power to begin the world over again.... The birth-day of a new world is at hand (p. 120).

Paine concluded the work with an explanation of why war with Britain was necessary despite the arguments of the pacifist Quakers.

2. THE LANGUAGE AND STYLE OF *COMMON SENSE*

Paine's work has been acclaimed as masterfully capturing the essence of the argument for independence in a style accessible to his American audience. He wrote not in the learned style of an educated man but on a level that appealed to most Americans, no matter their station or class. The use Paine made of this style is controversial. For Foner, "Paine was the conscious pioneer of a new style of political writing, a rhetoric aimed at extending political discussion beyond narrow bounds to the eighteenth century's 'political nation'" (Foner, 1976, p. 83). For Wilson, however, "Paine's style is better understood as part of a wider 'revolution in rhetoric' that was taking place during the late eighteenth century" (Wilson, 1988, pp. xi–xii, 20–5). They agree that Paine's plain style was accessible to all his readers.

Beyond lucid writing, Paine also used exciting imagery to enhance his work. Although his formal education consisted only of attendance in grammar school, Paine developed a colorful, imaginative manner of presentation, perhaps the result of his participation in the tavern debates in Lewes and Philadelphia. He used powerful phrases and strong images that were richly graphic and engaging. Some examples will demonstrate how he captivated his audience.

First and foremost was his image of King George III. He mocked the King by dehumanizing him, saying he has "sunk himself beneath the rank of animals, and contemptibly crawl[s] through the world like a worm" (p. 114). Even worse, he compared the King to Saturn devouring his children, a favorite eighteenth-century theme: the father-king relished his children, the Americans, as his main meal. "Even brutes do not devour their young," he exclaimed. Still, the lovers of liberty have fled England to America in hopes of escaping "the cruelty of the monster" (p. 84; see Jordan, 1973). Meantime, aristocrats fared no better than kings. He called them the King's "parasites," who hold their station only because of hereditary right. They produced nothing by their own skills because they had no skills, and they "fed off the work and sweat of their subjects" (p. 84).

Paine also employed images from science and medicine, in particular health, disease, and youth, to distinguish the corruptions of monarchy from the virtues of the republic. He referred to "a thirst for absolute power" as "the natural disease of monarchy" (p. 69). Later he asked, "why is the constitution of England so sickly, but because monarchy hath poisoned the republic, the crown hath engrossed the commons?" (p. 81). In contrast to rotten England, the virtues and vigor of the republic would be fruitful. With great fanfare, he drew an image of how in America the law, as founded on true constitutional principles, would reign supreme. In contrast to the arbitrary laws of England, based only on the whim of the King and his ministers, American law would be protected by divine ordinance. God himself had ordained American separation.

[L]et a day be solemnly set apart for proclaiming the charter [the new constitution]; let it be brought forth placed on the divine law, the word of God; let a crown be placed thereon,

by which the world may know, that so far as we approve of monarchy, that in America
THE LAW IS KING. For as in absolute government the King is law, so in free countries
the law 'ought' to be King; and there ought to be no other. But lest any ill use should
afterwards arise, let the crown at the conclusion of the ceremony be demolished, and
scattered among the people whose right it is. (p. 98)

The smashing of the crown ended America's relationship with Britain forever.

3. THE IMPACT OF *COMMON SENSE*

The widespread distribution and huge readership of *Common Sense* had a multiple
impact. First, responses, pro and con, in the form of pamphlets, broadsides, and penny
numbers as well as newspaper articles, began to appear. All were devoted to the
controversial issue of separation, but Paine himself was always the central focus,
especially for the opposition. The most important of these were John Adams's *Thoughts
on Government* (*see* ADAMS, JOHN) and James Chalmers's *Plain Truth* (Aldridge, 1984,
pp. 158–215). Moreover, *Common Sense* convinced many Americans that a separation
was not only the inevitable but the only course for America. The pamphlet profoundly
transformed the debate over America's relationship with Britain and the meaning of
republican government (Foner, 1976, pp. 107–44).

Finally, *Common Sense* brought into the public arena many of the more radical
Philadelphia writers, such as Benjamin Rush and Timothy Matlock, Charles Willson
Peale and David Rittenhouse. Some of these men later assumed positions of leadership
in Philadelphia after America's break with Britain. Their participation in politics was
immediately made evident during the drafting of the Pennsylvania Constitution of
1776 shortly after the Declaration of Independence. With its unicameral legislature,
it was one of the most radical of the state constitutions of the time (*see* Chapter 29,
§4).

These factors all made *Common Sense* one of the most successful political pamphlets
ever written. It aroused public opinion in America in an unprecedented way and it
led ineluctably to the promulgation of the Declaration of Independence. Thomas
Paine's genius and style endowed the work with all that was necessary to stimulate
Americans to think seriously about their future, especially the end of their ties to
Britain.

FURTHER READING

Aldridge, A. O.: *Thomas Paine's American Ideology* (Newark: University of Delaware Press, 1984).
Foner, E.: *Tom Paine and Revolutionary America* (New York: Oxford University Press, 1976).
Greene, J. P.: "Paine, America, and the 'Modernization' of Political Consciousness," *Political
    Science Quarterly*, 93 (1978), 73–92.
Jordan, W. D.: "Familial politics: Thomas Paine and the killing of the king," *Journal of American
    History*, 60 (1973), 294–308.
Newman, S.: "A note on *Common Sense* and Christian eschatology," *Political Theory*, 6 (1978),
    101–8.
Paine, T.: *Common Sense* (Philadelphia: 1776); 2nd edn., repr., ed. I. Kramnick (Harmondsworth:
    Penguin, 1976).
Wilson, D. A.: *Paine and Cobbett: the Transatlantic Connection* (Kingston and Montreal: McGill–
    Queen's University Press, 1988).

27

The Declaration of Independence

RONALD HAMOWY

WHEN the Second Continental Congress convened in May 1775 few delegates supported complete independence from Great Britain. The events of the following eight months, however, were to make a reconciliation between the colonies and the mother country close to impossible. On 23 August the King proclaimed the colonies in "open and avowed rebellion" and in December Parliament enacted legislation declaring the colonies beyond the protection of the Crown and proscribing all trade with them. These responses to the colonists' petitions for a redress of their grievances and to the outbreak of hostilities at Lexington and Concord in April 1775 could only serve to strengthen the forces for separation. By early spring of 1776 the delegations of the two most populous colonies, Massachusetts and Virginia, were united in supporting independence, while the advocates of compromise in Congress, although still representative of a substantial portion of public opinion, found their task increasingly difficult.

The proponents of some accommodation with the Crown were dealt a decisive blow in January 1776 with the publication of Thomas Paine's *Common Sense (see* Chapter 26). In dramatic language, Paine argued the case for a complete break with Great Britain from whom, he concluded, the colonies derived no benefit or advantage. And in an electrifying passage, he called upon Americans to embrace their destiny to serve as an oasis of freedom and enlightenment in a world of oppression and darkness. Paine's pamphlet proved an astonishing success. Some estimates put the sales of *Common Sense* during the course of 1776 at approximately half a million, and newspapers throughout the colonies ran substantial excerpts from it. Its effect was almost immediate and the debate between the radicals and those supporting reconciliation which raged throughout the colonial press following its publication tipped decisively towards independence.

By May 1776 it was apparent to most that a complete separation between the colonies and Great Britain was inevitable. On 10 May the Continental Congress had enacted a resolution calling upon the various colonies to form their own governments, and five days later a far more radical preamble to this resolution, drafted by JOHN ADAMS, was adopted. Not only did the preamble recommend that the colonies assume full powers of government but also that all exercise of authority under the Crown be suppressed. While the Congress was thus committing itself to this militant position in Philadelphia, the Virginia Convention, meeting in Williamsburg, instructed its delegates to the Congress to propose that that body declare the colonies "free and independent states, absolved from all allegiance to, or dependence on, the Crown or Parliament of Great Britain." In compliance with the instructions received from Virginia, Richard Henry Lee, the colony's senior delegate, moved on 7 June "that these

United Colonies are, and of right ought to be, free and independent States, that they are absolved from all allegiance to the British Crown, and that all political connection between them and the State of Great Britain is, and ought to be, totally dissolved."

The pro-separatist forces, aware that so radical a measure would have far greater impact if supported by all the colonies, agreed to postpone consideration of Lee's resolution for three weeks, by which time, it was hoped, the Congress would be able to act unanimously. Inasmuch as the ultimate outcome of a vote was clear, however, the Congress on 11 June appointed a committee to draw up a preamble to the resolution, consisting of John Adams, Benjamin Franklin, Thomas Jefferson, Robert Livingston, and Roger Sherman. Jefferson, in turn, was selected by the committee to prepare a draft of the document which, as it was to turn out, was submitted to the Congress after only minor modifications.

In drafting the Declaration Jefferson set out not only to catalog the specific reasons which constrained the colonies to separate from Great Britain but also, and more importantly, to lay bear the ideological underpinnings upon which the Revolution rested. In doing so, he did not seek to offer an original theory of government, "not to find out new principles, or new arguments never before thought of," as he was later to put it, but to "place before mankind the common sense of the subject." The philosophical preamble of the Declaration attempts to set forth the ideological substance of American revolutionary thought, which was grounded in a theory of natural, inalienable rights and which reflected, Jefferson was later to write, "the harmonizing sentiments of the day, whether expressed in conversation or letters, printed essays, or in the elementary books of public right, as Aristotle, Cicero, Locke, Sidney, etc."

The principles of government expounded in the Declaration bear the unmistakable imprint of Whig revolutionary thought and particularly of its chief exponent, John Locke. The popularity of Locke's political views among the colonists, both directly through his works and through those writings heavily influenced by him, such as Trenchard and Gordon's *Cato's Letters*, was immense. Indeed, if any one work could be said to have captured "the harmonizing sentiments of the day" during the period immediately before the Revolution, it would be Locke's *Second Treatise of Government* (*see* Chapter 9, §1).

The principal argument of the *Second Treatise*, echoed in the Declaration's preamble, is easily understood. All men enter the world possessed of certain rights, which are theirs by virtue of their nature as human beings. These rights exist in advance of the establishment, and independent, of any civil authority and not as a consequence of the actions of that authority. The powers of the civil magistrate are founded on the consent of those who are governed and may be exercised solely in their interests. When any government violates this trust, it is the right of the people to abolish it and to create a new government more likely to effect those ends for which governments are established. Locke and the Declaration thus link a theory of natural rights to the notion that the authority of government rests on individual consent. That the Declaration articulates the principle that popular consent is the only legitimate basis of political authority should not, however, be taken to mean that governments may act in any manner consonant with popular approval. The Declaration is eminently clear on this point. While the authority of the magistrate rests on the consent of the people, that authority is by its nature severely limited.

Governments may act only insofar as they respect the inalienable rights with which all men are endowed. These rights are not the creatures of government but are rooted in man's very nature and, as such, are unconditional. Nor are they transferable by virtue of man's having entered into civil society. The purpose of government is the more efficient protection of these rights. The Declaration clearly affirms this when it asserts that all men "are endowed by their creator with certain unalienable rights, that among these are Life, Liberty, and the pursuit of Happiness" and "That to secure these rights, Governments are instituted among Men."

An analysis of the logical structure of the Declaration reveals that the rights to which Jefferson refers – and here he clearly follows Locke – are to be understood not as mandating individual or collective action of any kind but rather as restraining men from acting in certain ways. Or, put more simply, my right to something, say my liberty, entails only prohibitions on others and not positive commands. To the extent that I am free, I am "let alone" or "unhindered" by others. The only boundaries limiting the actions of other men are those prohibitions which extend around my liberty. There are no circumstances under which they are required to act but only a narrow set of instances where they are prevented from acting. When rights are thus negatively conceived it is apparent that there exist no conditions under which the liberty of one person can conflict with the liberty of another, for it is perfectly consistent with the liberty of each person that they be constrained not to act in any manner invasive of the liberty of another. It further follows from this reading that, since the transcendant function of political authority is to secure to each of us our inalienable rights (and since these require that we be prevented from acting in certain ways but never that we be forced into certain positive actions), the Declaration gives voice to a political philosophy of extremely limited government.

Of equal importance, Jefferson's claim that all men are created equal must be understood within the framework of this notion of rights. Men are equal in that all possess the same absolute rights, which others may not transgress under pain of violating the fundamental laws by which all men are governed. The equality to which the Declaration refers is not one of social or economic condition, nor does the Declaration make as one of the tests of government whether men become, in some sense, equal in attainments. We are equal only in that we are all invested with certain indefeasible rights, including the rights to our lives and our liberties and the right to pursue our happiness as we individually see fit, free from the intrusions of others, whether acting individually or collectively.

It is a tribute to Jefferson's stylistic abilities and to his skill in distilling the common political sensibilities of the day that his draft of the Declaration received only minor revision at the hands of the other members of the drafting committee. On 2 July the Congress adopted Lee's resolution, with 12 delegations voting in favor of independence and New York abstaining. Having thus declared the united colonies free states, independent of the British Crown, the Congress immediately turned its attention to a consideration of the Declaration, which offered a justification for the decision just reached.

While a number of alterations and deletions to Jefferson's draft were made by the Congress, at that point meeting in Committee of the Whole, it is significant that no attempt was made to tamper with the document's philosophical preamble. Nor is this particularly surprising; the American Revolutionaries had long embraced the legal and political principles expounded in the natural-law theories of Hugo Grotius and Samuel Pufendorf, through Locke and the other Whig radicals, and in the continental writers inspired by them, particularly Jean Jacques Burlamaqui. The central thrust of congressional revision was reserved for the main body of the Declaration, a list of specific charges against Great Britain. These charges were leveled not against the

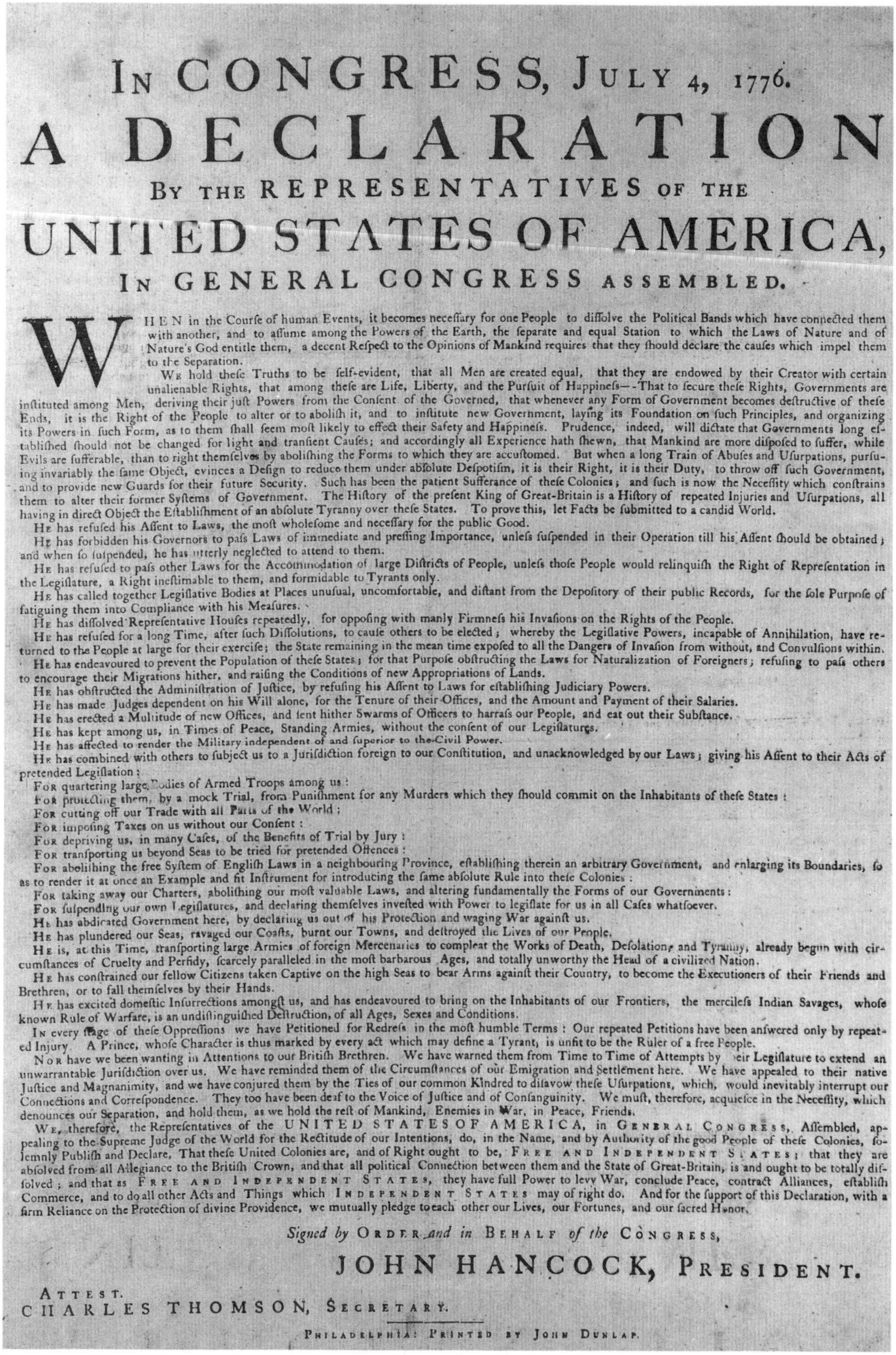

IN CONGRESS, JULY 4, 1776.

A DECLARATION

BY THE REPRESENTATIVES OF THE

UNITED STATES OF AMERICA,

IN GENERAL CONGRESS ASSEMBLED.

WHEN in the Course of human Events, it becomes necessary for one People to dissolve the Political Bands which have connected them with another, and to assume among the Powers of the Earth, the separate and equal Station to which the Laws of Nature and of Nature's God entitle them, a decent Respect to the Opinions of Mankind requires that they should declare the causes which impel them to the Separation.

We hold these Truths to be self-evident, that all Men are created equal, that they are endowed by their Creator with certain unalienable Rights, that among these are Life, Liberty, and the Pursuit of Happiness--That to secure these Rights, Governments are instituted among Men, deriving their just Powers from the Consent of the Governed, that whenever any Form of Government becomes destructive of these Ends, it is the Right of the People to alter or to abolish it, and to institute new Government, laying its Foundation on such Principles, and organizing its Powers in such Form, as to them shall seem most likely to effect their Safety and Happiness. Prudence, indeed, will dictate that Governments long established should not be changed for light and transient Causes; and accordingly all Experience hath shewn, that Mankind are more disposed to suffer, while Evils are sufferable, than to right themselves by abolishing the Forms to which they are accustomed. But when a long Train of Abuses and Usurpations, pursuing invariably the same Object, evinces a Design to reduce them under absolute Despotism, it is their Right, it is their Duty, to throw off such Government, and to provide new Guards for their future Security. Such has been the patient Sufferance of these Colonies; and such is now the Necessity which constrains them to alter their former Systems of Government. The History of the present King of Great-Britain is a History of repeated Injuries and Usurpations, all having in direct Object the Establishment of an absolute Tyranny over these States. To prove this, let Facts be submitted to a candid World.

HE has refused his Assent to Laws, the most wholesome and necessary for the public Good.

HE has forbidden his Governors to pass Laws of immediate and pressing Importance, unless suspended in their Operation till his Assent should be obtained; and when so suspended, he has utterly neglected to attend to them.

HE has refused to pass other Laws for the Accommodation of large Districts of People, unless those People would relinquish the Right of Representation in the Legislature, a Right inestimable to them, and formidable to Tyrants only.

HE has called together Legislative Bodies at Places unusual, uncomfortable, and distant from the Depository of their public Records, for the sole Purpose of fatiguing them into Compliance with his Measures.

HE has dissolved Representative Houses repeatedly, for opposing with manly Firmness his Invasions on the Rights of the People.

HE has refused for a long Time, after such Dissolutions, to cause others to be elected; whereby the Legislative Powers, incapable of Annihilation, have returned to the People at large for their exercise; the State remaining in the mean time exposed to all the Dangers of Invasion from without, and Convulsions within.

HE has endeavoured to prevent the Population of these States; for that Purpose obstructing the Laws for Naturalization of Foreigners; refusing to pass others to encourage their Migrations hither, and raising the Conditions of new Appropriations of Lands.

HE has obstructed the Administration of Justice, by refusing his Assent to Laws for establishing Judiciary Powers.

HE has made Judges dependent on his Will alone, for the Tenure of their Offices, and the Amount and Payment of their Salaries.

HE has erected a Multitude of new Offices, and sent hither Swarms of Officers to harrass our People, and eat out their Substance.

HE has kept among us, in Times of Peace, Standing Armies, without the consent of our Legislatures.

HE has affected to render the Military independent of and superior to the Civil Power.

HE has combined with others to subject us to a Jurisdiction foreign to our Constitution, and unacknowledged by our Laws; giving his Assent to their Acts of pretended Legislation:

FOR quartering large Bodies of Armed Troops among us:

FOR protecting them, by a mock Trial, from Punishment for any Murders which they should commit on the Inhabitants of these States:

FOR cutting off our Trade with all Parts of the World:

FOR imposing Taxes on us without our Consent:

FOR depriving us, in many Cases, of the Benefits of Trial by Jury:

FOR transporting us beyond Seas to be tried for pretended Offences:

FOR abolishing the free System of English Laws in a neighbouring Province, establishing therein an arbitrary Government, and enlarging its Boundaries, so as to render it at once an Example and fit Instrument for introducing the same absolute Rule into these Colonies:

FOR taking away our Charters, abolishing our most valuable Laws, and altering fundamentally the Forms of our Governments:

FOR suspending our own Legislatures, and declaring themselves invested with Power to legislate for us in all Cases whatsoever.

HE has abdicated Government here, by declaring us out of his Protection and waging War against us.

HE has plundered our Seas, ravaged our Coasts, burnt our Towns, and destroyed the Lives of our People.

HE is, at this Time, transporting large Armies of foreign Mercenaries to compleat the Works of Death, Desolation and Tyranny, already begun with circumstances of Cruelty and Perfidy, scarcely paralleled in the most barbarous Ages, and totally unworthy the Head of a civilized Nation.

HE has constrained our fellow Citizens taken Captive on the high Seas to bear Arms against their Country, to become the Executioners of their Friends and Brethren, or to fall themselves by their Hands.

HE has excited domestic Insurrections amongst us, and has endeavoured to bring on the Inhabitants of our Frontiers, the merciless Indian Savages, whose known Rule of Warfare, is an undistinguished Destruction, of all Ages, Sexes and Conditions.

IN every Stage of these Oppressions we have Petitioned for Redress in the most humble Terms: Our repeated Petitions have been answered only by repeated Injury. A Prince, whose Character is thus marked by every act which may define a Tyrant, is unfit to be the Ruler of a free People.

NOR have we been wanting in Attentions to our British Brethren. We have warned them from Time to Time of Attempts by their Legislature to extend an unwarrantable Jurisdiction over us. We have reminded them of the Circumstances of our Emigration and Settlement here. We have appealed to their native Justice and Magnanimity, and we have conjured them by the Ties of our common Kindred to disavow these Usurpations, which, would inevitably interrupt our Connections and Correspondence. They too have been deaf to the Voice of Justice and of Consanguinity. We must, therefore, acquiesce in the Necessity, which denounces our Separation, and hold them, as we hold the rest of Mankind, Enemies in War, in Peace, Friends.

WE, therefore, the Representatives of the UNITED STATES OF AMERICA, in GENERAL CONGRESS, Assembled, appealing to the Supreme Judge of the World for the Rectitude of our Intentions, do, in the Name, and by Authority of the good People of these Colonies, solemnly Publish and Declare, That these United Colonies are, and of Right ought to be, FREE AND INDEPENDENT STATES; that they are absolved from all Allegiance to the British Crown, and that all political Connection between them and the State of Great-Britain, is and ought to be totally dissolved; and that as FREE AND INDEPENDENT STATES, they have full Power to levy War, conclude Peace, contract Alliances, establish Commerce, and to do all other Acts and Things which INDEPENDENT STATES may of right do. And for the support of this Declaration, with a firm Reliance on the Protection of divine Providence, we mutually pledge to each other our Lives, our Fortunes, and our sacred Honor.

Signed by ORDER and in BEHALF of the CONGRESS,

JOHN HANCOCK, PRESIDENT.

ATTEST.

CHARLES THOMSON, SECRETARY.

PHILADELPHIA: PRINTED BY JOHN DUNLAP.

FIGURE 23 "A Declaration by the Representatives of the United States of Congress Assembled" (Philadelphia, 1776); John Dunlap was the printer who ran off the official copies of the Declaration on 5 July.

Parliament but against the Crown, in keeping with the colonists' conception of the constitutional status of the North American colonies. Americans regarded the colonies as linked to Great Britain only in that they acknowledged a common monarch. The Parliament of Great Britain, it was argued, had no more legal authority over the various colonies than did the legislature of one of the colonies have over its sister colonies or, indeed, over Great Britain itself. While the colonists conceded fealty to the British Crown, they did not regard themselves as British subjects and they predicated the right to rebel against tyrannical government not on the privileges granted them as British subjects but on the natural rights which they shared with all men.

It has been noted, with some justification, that the deletions and amendments made to the Declaration by Congress in almost all cases contribute to both its force and its elegance. It is particularly remarkable, as one eminent critic has observed, that a public body chose to reduce rather than increase the number of words in a document so political. Indeed, it is a reflection on how widely accepted were Jefferson's philosophical views by the delegates meeting in Philadelphia that the Declaration, with all its eloquent subtleties, is as brief as it is. There was one important exception, however. Jefferson included in his draft a fierce denunciation of the slave trade – for which he blamed George III. This was correctly regarded by delegates from southern states as an oblique attack on slavery itself, and to Jefferson's chagrin they insisted on striking it out.

The Committee of the Whole, having completed its revisions, reported the Declaration to the Congress on the evening of 4 July where it was duly approved without dissent. The document was then ordered authenticated and printed (*see* figure 23), at which point John Hancock signed the authenticated copy "by Order and in Behalf of the Congress." Five days later the New York provincial congress, meeting in White Plains, voted unanimously to ratify the Declaration, thus bringing New York into line with the other 12 colonies who had voted for independence on 2 July. As a consequence of New York's action, the Congress directed on 15 July that the word "unanimous" be added to the document's title "Declaration of the Thirteen United States of America," and that it be engrossed on parchment. Finally, on 2 August the engrossed copy was signed by the members of the Continental Congress sitting in Philadelphia. Copies of the Declaration were dispatched throughout the colonies immediately upon its passage in early July, where it was reprinted in all the newspapers and read before solemn assemblies of soldier-citizens, now more acutely aware that the struggle in which they were then engaged was energized by the highest principle.

FURTHER READING

Becker, Carl L.: *The Declaration of Independence: a Study in the History of Ideas* (New York: Alfred A. Knopf, 1942).

Boyd, Julian P.: *The Declaration of Independence: the Evolution of the Text* (Princeton, NJ: Princeton University Press, 1945).

Dumbauld, Edward: *The Declaration of Independence and What it Means Today* (Norman: University of Oklahoma Press, 1950).

Friedenwald, Herbert: *The Declaration of Independence: an Interpretation and Analysis* (New York: Macmillan, 1904).

White, Morton G.: *The Philosophy of the American Revolution* (New York: Oxford University Press, 1978).

PART 3
THEMES AND EVENTS, FROM 1776

28

Bills of rights and the first ten amendments to the Constitution

ROBERT A. RUTLAND

AMONG the many ironies created by the American Revolution was the colonists' insistence that they must fight the mother country in order to preserve their birthrights to English liberty under the law.

Five generations of American-born subjects had lived on the Atlantic seaboard (between Canada and Florida) and grown accustomed to exercising certain civil liberties when the break with Great Britain occurred. Proud emigrants from England spoke of their rights as Englishmen when they passed the Massachusetts Body of Liberties in 1641, giving solid form to their notions of a rule of law first embodied in the Magna Carta. Meanwhile, colonial charters in Maryland, Carolina, Pennsylvania, and New Jersey from 1639 onwards had encouraged English-American subjects to expect that the common law and certain personal rights were part of their heritage. These rights were sometimes called "natural," and in every-day practice they involved guarantees for jury trials, the rights of accused persons, and freedom of conscience, and provisions for peaceable assemblies, petitions to law-making bodies, and an exuberant (if often unbridled) press. The "not guilty" verdict that freed John Peter Zenger from a New York jail in 1735, after he was accused of printing sedition in his newspaper, was more than a legal landmark. Zenger's release indicated the unmistakable direction in which Americans were moving. Clearly there was more latitude for expressing ideas in America, but the colonists worshiped, assembled, and exercised other rights in the belief that their demonstrations were simply liberties conferred by the British Constitution. "We claim Nothing but the Liberty & Privileges of Englishmen, in the same Degree, as if we had still continued among our Brethren in Great Britain," the Virginian George Mason wrote during the Stamp Act aftermath of 1766 (Mason, 1970: 1, p. 71). Few American leaders would have disagreed.

I. THE FIRST CONTINENTAL CONGRESS

Parliamentary interference in domestic affairs ended the truce that followed the Stamp Act crisis. Punitive laws aimed at the citizens of Boston boomeranged to create unity in all the colonies. Amidst the tension exacerbated by the Boston Port Bill, delegates went to the First Continental Congress in Philadelphia to deliberate a course of action. Samuel Adams, the Boston firebrand who had labored overtime to bring on the crisis between Great Britain and her colonies, realized the importance of linking colonial grievances with time-honored British landmarks. "Should America hold up her own Importance to the Body of the Nation and at the same Time in one general Bill of Rights," Adams wrote to a Virginia delegate, "the Dispute might be settled on the

271

Principles of Equity and Harmony restored between Britain and the Colonies" (Rutland, 1983, p. 26). When the delegates concentrated on propaganda weapons to use in prying concessions from Parliament, Adams's brainchild was a declaration of rights couched in terms any British MP would understand and ranging from assurance for jury trials to the old bugbear of illegal "standing armies." The heart of the matter was the fifth resolution claiming that "the respective colonies are entitled to the common law of England," for had the mother country conceded this proposition there probably would have been no need for a Continental Congress, or a rebellion, or a bill of rights discussed beyond the pale of Westminster.

Before the Congress delegates adjourned they went a step further by sending a "Letter to the Inhabitants of Quebec," which may have been conceived as a propaganda ploy but still showed how the Americans were attached to the categorizing of rights. Congressmen admitted in the letter that French-speaking *Canadiens* might be ignorant of the "unspeakable worth" of an Englishman's rights, but since 1763 they had been George III's subjects and needed a lesson on their libertarian legacy. Rights similar to those in the Declaration passed two weeks earlier were listed and the delegates ordered this version of an Englishman's rights translated into French, published in pamphlet form, and dispersed where it would do the most good for their cause. The rights included jury trials and *habeas corpus* along with others that seemed to require a pedagogical tone. The importance of a free press, Congress insisted, involved "the advancement of truth." Did the Canadian subjects enjoy liberty of conscience? No, Congress answered, "God gave it to you," but Parliament denied the right by maintaining an established church in their midst (Rutland, 1983, p. 28).

If the American propaganda converted no Canadians, it reinforced local ideas on the right to resist perceived tyranny. Armed with the right of resistance, Washington took the time to write to English subjects in Bermuda for aid to his army besieging the British in Boston. "As Descendents of Freemen and Heirs with us of the same Glorious Inheritance," Washington told the Bermudians, "we flatter ourselves that tho' divided by our Situation, we are firmly united in Sentiment." Washington's plea was in vain, but the tone of his remarks was an echo of Jefferson's statement that he wanted Americans to move not forwards, but backwards, to claim their hallowed rights as transplanted Englishmen. Once the American leaders shared this view, when the time came to break all bonds with England the next logical step was to rewrite the British Constitution in American terms. To that end, the Virginia Convention of 1776 met in Williamsburg in May, committed to preparing a declaration of rights and constitution to replace the British laws and traditions that lost all their force on American soil after 4 July 1776.

2. THE VIRGINIA CONVENTION

Action by Virginia was expected, for her sons had been in the front ranks of the resistance movement from the start. Thus by mid-May 1776 the largest and most populous of the American colonies had (through her representatives) called on Congress "to declare the United Colonies free and independent states." A sister resolution from the Virginia Convention established a committee to prepare a declaration of rights and constitution for what would be the foremost of those free states. No time could be wasted. By late May a committee was busy with the details that independence required; and in this emergency George Mason (*see* figure 24), who had professed complete loyalty in 1766, showed he had undergone a change of heart and allegiance.

FIGURE 24 George Mason: a portrait by Dominic W. Boudet (1811)

"Things have gone such Lengths," Mason later recalled, "that it is a Matter of Moonshine to us, whether Independence was at first intended, or not" (Mason, 1970: 1, p. 435). What mattered was the business at hand, the drafting of an American bill of rights. "As Colo Mason seems to have the Ascendancy in the great work," a colleague noted, "I have Sanguine hopes it will be framed so as to Answer it's end, [which is] Prosperity for the Community and Security to Individuals" (Rutland, 1983, pp. 33–4).

Within days Mason's draft had been studied by the whole committee, slightly altered, and then sent to the full Convention. The opening resolution said that "all men are by nature equally free and independent," and they possessed immutable rights, "namely, the enjoyment of life and liberty, and the means of acquiring and possessing property, and pursuing and obtaining happiness and safety." Then came several general statements about the role of free government and the evils of hereditary office-holding, and praise for the separation-of-powers principle. Next came Mason's catalog of specific rights, enumerating the right of suffrage and a long list of limitations on governmental power. Free governments could not suspend laws, or deny accused persons their legal rights, or fine them excessively, or punish convicted criminals with

273

"cruel and unusual" means; and general warrants for searches and seizures were condemned as "grievous and oppressive." Mason's draft went on to laud the use of juries in civil law suits as an ancient right that "ought to be held sacred," called freedom of the press "one of the great bulwarks of liberty," praised the use of militiamen and condemned standing armies "in time of peace ... as dangerous to liberty," and insisted that "the military should be under strict subordination to, and governed by, the civil power." Two resolutions concerned the jurisdiction of the gigantic state of Virginia and the need for a government based on "frequent recurrence to fundamental principles." The last resolve aimed a blow for religious liberty, perhaps broader than Mason had intended when he first wrote in support of "the fullest toleration" for religious sects. James Madison, serving his first term in an elective body, suggested that the clause be altered to an all-encompassing statement that "all men are equally entitled to the free exercise of religion, according to the dictates of conscience." Mason consented, the delegates approved, and for the first time in recorded history a public body had taken a stand in favor of freedom of religion for "all men" (Mason, 1970; 1, p. 289). (To complete the business, a decade later Jefferson's "Statute for Religious Freedom" was passed to erect in Virginia an impregnable "wall of separation" between church and state.)

The message that Virginians had given a priority to human rights as they fashioned a new government was soon broadcast to the other erstwhile colonies. On 12 June 1776 the Virginia Convention approved the 16 resolutions in its Declaration of Rights, and it was soon printed in the Williamsburg newspaper, then reprinted in other journals along the Atlantic seaboard week by week until, by harvest time, leaders in every corner of the new republic knew its contents. "We all look up to Virginia for examples," John Adams remarked to Patrick Henry (Rutland, 1983, p. 37). Adams's flattering statement proved to be prescient, for the Virginia model was to be copied (sometimes verbatim) in seven other constitution-drafting states. When the wave of constitution-writing ended in 1784, 11 states had some form of a bill of rights, while Connecticut and Rhode Island operated under provisions of their colonial charters that carried substantial guarantees for personal rights.

3. THE FIRST TEN AMENDMENTS

The idea that a free government must operate within the limits imposed by a bill of rights, to which Americans had given a new twist by taking traditions and writing them into their laws, impressed Europeans already influenced by Enlightenment precepts from Montesquieu, Beccaria, and other writers. Thus a similar approach was followed by the French National Assembly when it adopted a Declaration of Rights in 1789. Three months before the French acted, James Madison had already fulfilled a pledge he made during the ratification struggle over the Constitution drafted in 1787. Madison introduced in the House of Representatives of the First Federal Congress a series of amendments for the Constitution that was ratified only after promises concerning a bill of rights had been extracted from the leading proponents of ratification. Eschewing originality, Madison relied on the Virginia Declaration of Rights for most of his proposed amendments. Pared by a committee from the preliminary list of 16 to 12 amendments, 10 were finally ratified in 1791, and these became the national Bill of Rights.

Fortuitously separated from the original Constitution, these ten amendments in time became the most admirable aspect of American law-making. The First Amendment, now considered the cornerstone of American civil liberty, prohibited congressional interference in religious matters and forbade federal curbs on freedom of speech, "or of the press; or the right of the people peaceably to assemble, and to petition . . . for a redress of grievances." The Second Amendment reflected an American preference for a home-grown militia instead of a detested standing army, and hence proclaimed "the right of the people to keep and bear Arms." Other amendments (Three, Four, and Five) prohibited the peacetime quartering of troops with civilians, general search warrants, and "unreasonable searches and seizures" by federal officers, and gave accused persons safeguards against self-incriminating testimony or the threat of a double-jeopardy prosecution, while providing that nobody could "be deprived of life, liberty, or property, without due process of law." A speedy jury trial in the vicinity of the offense was guaranteed to the accused by the Sixth Amendment, along with other legal safeguards for criminal trials, and the Seventh Amendment reinforced the American partiality for jury trials "in Suits at common law." Excessive bails and fines were forbidden in the Eighth Amendment, as were "cruel and unusual punishments"; the wording was familiar since it was borrowed verbatim from the 1689 English Bill of Rights. The Ninth and Tenth Amendments broadened the concept of the people's liberties but provided nothing specific (and thus never became useful in practice). These guarantees applied only to the federal government, and left to the states the practical matter of enforcing promises of unfettered liberties.

To gain acceptance of his list of amendments, Madison had been forced to browbeat reluctant colleagues into their passage and transmittal to the state legislature for ratification. That process proved to be cumbersome but effective, and by December 1791 the first ten amendments to the Constitution were in place. To many Americans on both sides of the dominant issues of the day, and to Madison and Jefferson in particular, these amendments proved that the spirit of freedom aroused by the American Revolution had been rekindled. Although their full enforcement was delayed until the twentieth century, the first ten amendments – the American Bill of Rights – provided a symbol for the new nation's commitment to liberty under the law.

FURTHER READING

Brant, Irving: *The Bill of Rights: its Origin and Meaning* (Indianapolis: Bobbs-Merrill, 1965).

Levy, Leonard W.: *Constitutional Opinions: Aspects of the Bill of Rights* (New York: Oxford University Press, 1986).

——: *Original Intent and the Framers' Constitution* (New York: Macmillan, 1988).

Mason, George: *The Papers of George Mason*, ed. R. A. Rutland, 3 vols. (Chapel Hill: University of North Carolina Press, 1970).

Rutland, Robert A.: *The Birth of the Bill of Rights, 1776–1791* (Boston: Northeastern University Press, 1983).

Schwartz, Bernard (ed.): *The Bill of Rights: a Documentary History*, 2 vols. (New York: Chelsea House, 1971).

29

State constitution-making, through 1781

DONALD S. LUTZ

THE early state constitutions stand as the fulcrum in American constitutional history. On the one hand they were the culmination of colonial political forms, and thus embodied and summarized that rich experience. On the other hand, they formed the ground upon which first the Articles of Confederation and then the United States Constitution was erected. Even the Declaration of Independence owed most of its contents to the state constitutions. Although each state maintained a basic continuity with its colonial institutions, and despite considerable innovation in some instances, the state constitutions written between 1775 and 1781 converged towards a common model characterized by a dominant bicameral legislature, a weak executive, and annual elections using a broad electorate. The standard model gradually evolved towards a more balanced executive–legislative relationship, and moved the power for adopting constitutions from the legislature to the people. This evolution achieved full expression in the 1780 Massachusetts Constitution, which became a model for later state constitutions, and, some feel, for the United States Constitution as well. The 1776 Pennsylvania Constitution represented a more radical alternative, and for a while was widely copied. However, the struggle in state constitution-making between those seeking a more radical, direct form of democracy and those inclined towards a government based on direct popular consent but structured by balanced institutions to become indirect in its actual operation was eventually won by the latter persuasion.

I. EARLY FORMS OF COLONIAL GOVERNMENT

In order to lay out the essentials of this process, it is necessary to begin with a discussion of colonial political institutions. Every American colony had started as an aggregation of communities, with each community having its own local government. In New England these local communities were towns, in the South they were counties, and in the middle colonies they were a blend of towns and counties. Thus, although colony-wide governments had important duties, most government remained at the local level. Elected colonial legislatures served as umbrella organizations for local communities in their relationship with Britain, which was usually represented by a governor appointed by the Crown. Local and colony-wide government rested upon an electorate that was much broader than it was in England at the time, and a popularly elected legislature was the centerpiece of colonial politics at all levels. When colonists began to organize politically to contend with what they considered to be British tyranny, the wellspring of organization was the same electorate and set of local institutions that had been used to run colonial government, and from these sources were derived, not surprisingly, the same basic institutions that had been erected earlier.

The move from colony to statehood was not a sudden one arising from a single act, but the result of a political process that took several years. The process actually began during the middle 1760s when, in reaction to Acts of Parliament such as the Stamp Act, the colonists in America developed experience in organizing for political resistance, an ideology to justify that resistance, and institutions for collective action independent of existing, legal ones. In many respects the Revolution began in 1765.

Events quickened in 1774, and the process that led explicitly to the writing of state constitutions began. Local committees of correspondence and safety began to spring up everywhere in early 1774 as a means of organizing for dealing with perceived threats from Britain. These committees were sometimes needed because royal governors failed to convene local or colony legislatures.

The committees of safety and correspondence successfully organized often took the lead in resisting Britain either by reconstituting their colonial legislature or replacing it with a parallel organization. The new or reconstructed legislature, now termed a convention or a provincial congress, constituted a political entity somewhere between a colony and an independent state. Typically, the congress appointed an executive committee to replace the recently departed governor, and these executive committees, frequently called committees of safety, ran provincial affairs when the congress was not sitting. The Continental Congress, composed of delegates from all the colonies, provided during these early years guidance to the several colonies.

The exceptions to this more or less spontaneous pattern that arose between 1774 and 1776 were Connecticut and Rhode Island, which had been virtually self-governing and had elected their own governors since the early 1660s. The Connecticut Charter of 1662 was essentially the same as the Fundamental Orders of Connecticut written and adopted by the colonists in 1639, while the Rhode Island Charter of 1663 preserved the government created by the colonists in the Acts and Orders of 1647. In both colonies, the governor was popularly elected, and the two charters functioned so effectively as constitutions that Connecticut and Rhode Island lived under them as fully constituted states well into the nineteenth century.

In the spring of 1776 John Adams introduced a resolution in the Continental Congress calling for all colonies that did not have a permanent constitution based upon the authority of the people to provide themselves with one. On 10 May 1776 the Continental Congress passed the resolution, and many considered this action equivalent to a declaration of independence. Still, it is difficult to point to one act as being decisive. Three of the 13 former colonies were already operating under state constitutions by the time Adams's proposal was approved, and most of the others were already at work on new documents. Every new state document adopted in 1776 and 1777 after approval of Adams's resolution, including the pre-Declaration constitutions of Virginia and New Jersey, was based upon a specific recommendation by the Continental Congress that a provincial congress write a constitution, and each individual recommendation by the Continental Congress was therefore, in effect, a declaration of independence. Indeed, the list of grievances that forms three-fourths of the official Declaration of Independence was essentially a compilation and summary of the lists of grievances found as preambles to the state constitutions adopted before 4 July 1776.

2. MASSACHUSETTS, NEW HAMPSHIRE, AND SOUTH CAROLINA

The first state constitution put into effect was that of Massachusetts. On 16 May 1775 the Provincial Congress of Massachusetts suggested that the Continental Congress write a model constitution for it and the other colonies. Afraid of alarming those who still hoped for reconciliation with Britain, the Continental Congress did not oblige. But on 2 June 1775 it did suggest that Massachusetts consider its charter of 1691 as still in force and the offices of governor and lieutenant-governor as temporarily vacated. It also recommended that new elections be held and a new governor's council be elected by the Provincial Congress. On 19 June 1775 the Massachusetts Congress elected a 28-member council that replaced the governor as executive. With this one alteration, the replacement of the governor with an executive council, the Massachusetts Charter of 1691 became the first state constitution. It was replaced in 1780 but in the meantime constituted, along with the Connecticut and Rhode Island charters, the most obvious link between colonial and statehood political institutions.

On 18 October 1775 New Hampshire put to the Continental Congress the same question that Massachusetts had asked the previous May. The intent of the request was to press the issue of independence, since a recommendation to frame a state constitution would be regarded by many as a declaration of independence. There was no functioning colonial charter which the Continental Congress could use to dodge the issue, so it advised the New Hampshire provincial congress to "establish such a government, as in their judgment will best produce the happiness of the people." The letter to the New Hampshire Provincial Congress added, however, that such reorganization should endure only until the conflict with Britain was over. In the face of this ambiguous recommendation, on 21 December 1775 the New Hampshire Provincial Congress met to draft a document. Prominent during these proceedings were Matthew Thornton, Meshech Weare, John Langdon, and John Sullivan. On 5 January 1776 New Hampshire became the first state to write a new constitition. As in Massachusetts, the major change from colonial practice was the election of a council by the House of Representatives. The council, the upper house in what was now a bicameral legislature, in turn elected a president who replaced the Crown-appointed governor.

South Carolina received the same recommendation from the Continental Congress on 4 November 1775. Prominent figures during the proceedings included JOHN RUTLEDGE, Christopher Gadsden, HENRY LAURENS, Charles Pinckney, and RAWLINS LOWNDES. As elsewhere, there was great hesitation to break openly with Britain, and the document approved on 26 March 1776 by the provincial congress of South Carolina amounted only minimally to a constitution. Designed to be in effect only until hostilities with Britain were over and passed as a normal piece of legislation by a legislature that underwent no special election to frame such a document, the "constitution" did not carry enormous authority and would be replaced in 1778. The indeterminate nature of the constitution reflected the position of the South Carolina Congress that wrote and adopted it. When it wrote the document, this body was simultaneously the old revolutionary legislature, the constitutional convention, and the new legislature created by the old legislature. During the morning of 25 March 1776, the men in this group acted in the first two capacities; in the afternoon of the same day they acted as an Assembly under the new government and elected the Council, which became the new upper house in the new bicameral legislature.

These first three state constitutions had a half-hearted quality to them. Rather short and incomplete as foundation documents, written and adopted by a sitting legislature in a manner indistinguishable from normal legislation, and bearing the marks of compromise between proponents for independence and supporters of reconciliation, they could in truth be viewed either as temporary expedients implying no significant alteration in colonial status or as manifestations of the intent to break with Britain. If the American Revolution had not been successful, perhaps history would have recorded them as the former. However, since the Revolution did conclude successfully and no other constitutional action was necessary for Massachusetts, New Hampshire, and South Carolina to assert their independence, we can view these three documents as being the constitutions of states establishing their independence. Still, their transitional status is clearly reflected in the fact that, by the time the United States Constitution was written in 1787, only these three states of the original 13 felt the need to write and adopt a second state constitution – South Carolina in 1778, Massachusetts in 1780, and New Hampshire in 1784.

3. VIRGINIA AND NEW JERSEY

There was no half-heartedness about the next constitution. The Virginia Provincial Congress had its share of reluctance about writing a state constitution, since such an action was viewed as equivalent to a declaration of independence. However, by 15 May 1776 the Virginia Congress had instructed its delegates at the Continental Congress to vote for independence. Thus, when Virginia turned to writing a declaration of rights and a state constitution, there was no doubt in the minds of the delegates about what they were doing. Although a committee of the provincial congress was charged with the task, GEORGE MASON was largely responsible for both the Declaration of Rights adopted on 27 May 1776 and the new constitution adopted unanimously on 29 June 1776. The similarity in wording between Virginia's Declaration of Rights and that found in the first two paragraphs of the Declaration of Independence can probably be accounted for by the close juxtaposition in time between the two documents, and Mason's close connections with his fellow Virginian Thomas Jefferson. Many of Virginia's most visible leaders were not available. George Washington was leading the army, and Jefferson was away serving in the Continental Congress, as were Richard Henry Lee and George Wythe. However, Virginia was blessed with a host of good minds, and among these Edmund Pendleton, Richard Bland, James Madison, Patrick Henry, Edmund Randolph, and Mason were in attendance and prominent in debates.

The New Jersey Provincial Congress barely missed beating Virginia. Although it did not start drafting a document until 21 June 1776, it was able to adopt a new constitution on 2 July 1776, only nine days after starting. The Virginia Congress had put in very long hours to write its document in 45 days, so one might conclude that the New Jersey Congress either worked around the clock, or, as is likely, was not scrupulously concerned about its new document. It is doubtful that such speed would have been possible in either Virginia's or New Jersey's case if there had not been a long colonial experience upon which to draw and an existing form of government successful enough to warrant close approximation. That New Jersey's hastily framed and adopted constitution lasted 44 years before being replaced is testimony to the utility of having an existing political system upon which to model a new constitution. Prominent in New Jersey's deliberations were the Reverend Jacob Greene, John Cleves Symmes, Lewis Ogden, Jonathan D. Sergeant, and Theophilus Elmer. Greene was the most influential and is reputed to have received considerable help from another cleric, the famous John Witherspoon.

4. PENNSYLVANIA AND DELAWARE

Thus, by the time the Declaration of Independence was adopted, seven fully constituted states were already in existence, counting Connecticut and Rhode Island. Almost three months elapsed before another group of state constitutions appeared, during late 1776. The brief hiatus allowed enough time for experience and evolving constitutional theory to support a number of innovations. The first of these was to use a specially elected rather than an already sitting legislature to write a constitution. Pennsylvania initiated the innovation, but Delaware, copying its neighbor, was the first to finish a constitution using the method.

Among proponents for independence there were two viewpoints concerning the method for writing new state constitutions. On the one hand were those who wished to emphasize the continuity between colonial and statehood institutions in service of the basic premise that Americans were breaking with Britain in order to preserve their constitutional tradition. The provincial congresses were the bearers of that continuity and thus were the bodies that should write constitutions. Also, during the colonial era constitution-like documents had occasionally been adopted by the legislature.

On the other hand, there were those who felt that the American commitment to popular sovereignty and the need to engage as many people as possible in support of the legitimacy of the new governments required both a distinction between constitutions and normal legislation and a more direct linkage with popular sentiment. Since masses of people could not directly write a constitution, the best alternative seemed to be a body elected specifically for the purpose. The second group gradually won its point as constitution-writing progressed. Americans would eventually move a step further and require that constitutions written by a special convention also be approved by the people at large in a referendum. As logical as this next step was, it was not taken until 1780, in the fifteenth state constitution adopted.

Delaware was slow in moving from a colonial assembly to a provincial congress, and did so only on 15 June 1776, when all public officials were requested to continue their power from that date forward in the name of the people of specific counties rather than in the name of the King. On 27 July 1776 elections were called for a legislature that was first to sit as a constitutional convention. This specially elected legislature convened on 2 September 1776 and adopted a declaration of rights nine days later. The process was speeded along by copying much of Pennsylvania's declaration. The convention adopted a constitution on 20 September 1776, with both George Read and Thomas McKean being mentioned as the document's primary authors. Despite the haste, the document would not be replaced for 39 years.

Pennsylvania's new state constitution was interesting for far more than its being written by a specially elected legislature sitting as a constitutional convention. More than any other state until that of Massachusetts in 1778–80, Pennsylvania worked at developing a constitution that would reflect the latest in constitutional theory. The result was the most radical document of the era, certainly the most innovative, and until the adoption of the 1780 Massachusetts document the primary contender as a model for future state constitutions. It was at least partially adopted by several states.

Like Delaware, Pennsylvania was slow to move to provincial status, and for the same reason – there were many who did not wish to replace the old government. The legal assembly proved unwilling to act, and the election of 1 May 1776 failed to alter significantly the make-up of the legislative assembly. The proponents for independence absented themselves from the legislature, thereby denying the assembly its quorum and rendering it impotent. Then a convention of county committees of inspection was called by the Philadelphia Committee of Inspection in an attempt to bypass the legal assembly. This convention met for a week in Philadelphia, and its 108 delegates in June scheduled an election for 8 July 1776. Ninety-six men were elected by an electorate that was potentially broader than usual, since the normal property requirements were waived, but was in fact narrower than usual, since it excluded from voting anyone who did not attest to their support for independence. These men became a legislature parallel to the legal one, but they first assembled as a constitutional convention and met across the street from the Continental Congress in Philadelphia.

The Pennsylvania Constitutional Convention was dominated by pro-independence men, and several of its more radically democratic members were prominent in writing the new constitution. Benjamin Franklin had a considerable impact on the document, but James Cannon, Timothy Matlack, and Cannon's good friend GEORGE BRYAN (who was not a delegate but worked closely with Cannon nonetheless) were the primary authors.

Pennsylvania's Declaration of Rights owed much to Virginia's, although Pennsylvania's was both longer and more far reaching. The resulting constitution, adopted along with the Declaration of Rights on 28 September 1776, was distinguished by creating a unicameral legislature, an extremely broad electorate, and a set of institutions designed to make the government as responsive to popular consent as possible. For example, in order to become a law a bill had to be passed in two consecutive sessions of the legislature. Since Pennsylvania had what became the standard American practice of annual elections, and bills approved the first time had to be published for public perusal, legislators were subject to explain their past and future votes between elections. Also, the constitution established a state-wide grand jury, called a Council of Censors, which was to be elected every seven years to review and evaluate all aspects of governmental action. Vermont would later copy most of this constitution, including its council of censors, and Georgia would emulate its unicameral legislature. Indeed, during the 1820s, 1830s, and 1840s the next generation of state constitutions would bring to widespread fruition many of the potentially highly democratic aspects of Pennsylvania's 1776 constitution.

5. MARYLAND, CONNECTICUT, RHODE ISLAND, NORTH CAROLINA, AND GEORGIA

On 3 July 1776 the Maryland Provincial Congress resolved that a new congress should be elected and that, in addition to acting as a legislature, it should write a new constitution. The electorate, defined by the same requirements as had chosen the current congress, was thus put on notice that they were selecting a constitutional convention as well as a legislature. Between 14 August 1776 and 8 November 1776 the body elected mixed constitutional matters with normal legislative concerns, although beginning in mid-October the congress focused on the constitution and deferred all but the most pressing legislative matters until a constitution had been approved. CHARLES CARROLL of Carrollton and SAMUEL CHASE were among the most energetic figures during the debates. A declaration of rights was approved on 3

November 1776, and the constitution itself was adopted and put into effect on 8 November 1776.

By this time state constitutions were taking on a standard pattern. Annual elections, a bicameral legislature (except in Pennsylvania and Georgia), and a weak executive were among the usual features of state constitutions. Maryland's was standard except for the striking innovation of using an electoral college to select the senate, an innovation that was used in the United States Constitution for electing the president. In one way or another, most of what is found in the national Constitution and its Bill of Rights can be traced back to one state constitution or another – usually several of the state documents.

Connecticut and Rhode Island had continued operating under their colonial charters as if they had been state constitutions all along. However, minor adjustments were made that amounted to recognition of complete independence. In October 1776, Connecticut's general assembly passed a law confirming that its 1662 charter was still in effect and functioning as its constitution. Rhode Island had passed a law in May of 1776 that the name of the king be stricken from all legal documents. These minor actions secured independence and ratified constitutional government under their respective colonial charters.

North Carolina followed a path that reflected its resolute commitment to independence and its participation in mainstream American constitutionalism. It had been among the earlier states to instruct its delegates to the Continental Congress to vote for independence (12 April 1776). In the letter of instruction to its delegates, the Provincial Congress claimed competence to frame and adopt a state constitution, and on 13 April 1776 it established a committee to write a temporary constitution. It approved a number of resolutions on 11 May 1776 as being a "temporary civil Constitution," but these resolutions did little more than create a council of safety for the entire colony. The result was so obviously interim, and the institutional structure so minimal, that it is not usually considered a true state constitution.

In August 1776 the 13-member North Carolina Committee of Safety called an election for 15 October 1776 and announced that the elected representatives would also write a state constitution in addition to their regular legislative duties. The new congress first met on 12 November 1776, and by borrowing copiously from the constitutions of Virginia, Maryland, and Pennsylvania had their own constitution ready in about a month. Prominent in the debate were Richard Caswell, Willie Jones, Thomas Person, and Abner Nash. The resulting document was mainstream in content and contained no notable innovation. The Provincial Congress adopted the constitution on 14 December 1776 and the Declaration of Rights three days later.

Georgia followed a pattern almost identical to that of North Carolina. Georgia's provincial congress on 15 April 1776 adopted a set of eight "rules and regulations" that amounted to a transitional "constitution," although the document was not called a constitution in its title and is usually not considered one. The eight laws essentially ratified the position of the provincial congress as the legislature and reflected the loss of its Crown-appointed governor by establishing a president, executive council, and court system. On 8 August 1776 the Provincial Committee of Safety scheduled an election for a new congress that would write a constitution as well as pass legislation. The new congress began meeting in October 1776, and on 24 January 1777 it appointed a committee to prepare a final draft of a constitution. The new constitution was approved by the congress on 4 February 1777.

Borrowing heavily from the constitutions of other states, as had North Carolina,

Georgia opted for Pennsylvania's unicameral legislature. This departure from what was becoming the standard format for state constitutions led to immediate and continued agitation in Georgia for a new constitution, as it did in Pennsylvania. In 1789 Georgia replaced its 1777 document with one establishing a bicameral legislature. (Pennsylvania replaced its 1776 constitution with one creating a bicameral legislature in 1790.)

6. NEW YORK

Discussions about a new constitution began in New York early in the spring of 1776, but differences of opinion as to whether the current provincial congress had the power to write one or whether a new congress had to be explicitly elected for that purpose clouded the issue and delayed action. By late May the provincial congress had decided to call for an election, and the new congress assembled on 9 July 1776. Significant opposition arose concerning this method, an opposition that had until now been scattered and inconsequential in other states. Some argued that no legislature, however elected, had the power to approve a constitution. Rather, by right, only the people could approve a constitution and put it into effect. This opposition was not nearly strong enough to carry the day, but it gave explicit expression to some of the logical implications of popular sovereignty for constitution-making in the American mode.

Constantly distracted by the presence of British troops in New York, the new congress several times had to move in order to avoid capture. The delay that resulted had one important consequence in that it gave members of the provincial congress time to reflect on what other states had been doing, and, rather than merely borrow the institutions of others, New York began an historically important alteration in the developing pattern of state constitutions.

During the colonial era politics had revolved around a competition for power between a popularly elected legislature and a governor who was in most cases appointed by the Crown. Gradually the legislatures had gained the upper hand, and with the coming of independence Americans were not eager to re-create strong executives which they associated with the abuse of power. Thus, except for the elected governors in Connecticut and Rhode Island, constitutions adopted before New York's generally had created an executive that was hardly worthy of the name. Appointed by the legislature, having few independent powers, carefully watched by a privy council drawn from the legislature, and sometimes simply replaced by a legislative committee, governors were no longer an important part of government in America.

New York began the process of defining an executive branch with sufficient independent powers to balance the legislature. Without such a balance the separation of powers as a constitutional strategy would have been impossible, and the United States Constitution might well have taken a radically different form. JOHN JAY is generally credited with having actually written the document, with considerable help from GOUVERNEUR MORRIS and ROBERT LIVINGSTON. Also prominent in the proceedings and influential on the outcome were James Duane, Robert Yates, and William Duer. The changes initiated in New York reached fruition in the 1780 Massachusetts Constitution, but one can see the New York document as a kind of half-way house. For example, the governor was made part of a council of revision which included the chancellor and supreme court judge as well. This council could veto acts of legislation, although the legislation could override the veto with a two-thirds vote. There was also a council of appointment composed of the governor and four senators which appointed the rest of the executive branch.

That such anemic powers can be considered a significant increase in executive strength is a measure of how debilitated the executive branch had become in the early state constitutions. In the 1780 Massachusetts constitution, written largely by John Adams, the governor alone would have a veto, subject to two-thirds override, and the power of appointment with senate approval. The United States Constitution would follow the Massachusetts example, but New York began pointing the way in the constitution adopted by the provincial congress on 20 April 1777. Another notable feature of the New York constitution was its use of reapportionment to produce equal representation by district in what amounted to a "one man, one vote" provision.

7. THE REVISIONS OF SOUTH CAROLINA AND MASSACHUSETTS

South Carolina, not satisfied with its "provisional constitution" from two years earlier, adopted a new one on 19 March 1778. The general assembly that began its session in January 1777 had been elected with the understanding that it would write a new state constitution. The assembly followed a highly deliberative process that included public hearings and on 5 March 1778 passed a new constitution as a piece of normal legislation. However, President John Rutledge (the chief executive in South Carolina was not at this time called governor) vetoed the bill on the technical grounds that since he had been sworn in to uphold the constitution of 1776 he could not legally approve its demise. Public sentiment was against him, he resigned, and on 19 March 1778 the new governor approved the legislation establishing the new state constitution.

On 16 June 1780 Massachusetts, after a lengthy process, adopted a constitution that replaced the 1691 charter. No constitution to this point had either been subjected to such a searching analysis or been the result of such careful process. The result was a state constitution that was to become the primary model for all later state constitutions as well as for the United States Constitution. Many believe that this document brought the design of state constitutions to its highest level during the eighteenth century.

The process began with an earlier constitutional proposal that was defeated. On 1 May 1776 the Massachusetts legislature, called the General Court, removed all references to the British Crown from the 1691 charter upon which it had based its legitimacy since 19 June 1775. It was clear that, despite claims to the contrary, Massachusetts government needed a more secure legal basis. There were desultory efforts during the summer of 1776 to draft a new constitution, but no document resulted. In September the General Court asked the towns to approve a method of adoption whereby the inhabitants would have an opportunity to examine the proposed constitution written by the General Court before the legislature also approved it. Seventy-four towns replied in the affirmative, which was a clear majority, but 23 towns said no with enough vigor to bring the process to a standstill.

There appeared to be strong sentiment, and cogent arguments, against the legislature writing and adopting a constitution that was supposed to limit the legislature. The minority opinion swayed the General Court to propose that the legislature write a constitution after voters had a chance to elect a new body and that the document be ratified by the electorate counted as individuals rather than as part of corporate units such as towns. Ratification would require two-thirds of all males free and over

21 years of age, which meant the property requirements were being waived in this constitutional referendum.

The House of Representatives (the lower house of the General Court), newly elected and authorized to write a constitution, met and began its work in June 1777. By February 1778 a new constitution had been drafted, and in March, for the first time in American history, a proposed constitution was submitted to a popular referendum. It was overwhelmingly defeated, 9,972 to 2,083. The arguments against the document were so diverse that some despaired of ever finding a majority in a referendum. However, many towns provided lengthy explanations for their opposition, and one in particular, the Essex Result written by THEOPHILUS PARSONS, clearly showed that more popular control rather than less would be required if the people were to be satisfied.

After mulling it over for a good while, the General Court asked the towns whether they would like to proceed with a new constitution if it were written by a constitutional convention instead of the legislature. By a margin of almost three to one the towns responded in the affirmative in April 1779. Elections were held for delegates to a constitutional convention, and the first such body in Western history, elected solely for the purpose of writing a constitution, convened on 1 September 1779. Samuel Adams, James Bowdoin, and especially John Adams were most prominent in the framing process. The final version was approved on 2 March 1780 and sent to the voters. The returns from the towns were very complex, and for a while no one could figure out how to count the votes. Finally, the convention simply declared that the draft had been accepted in its entirety by at least two-thirds of the voters, even when taking into account reservations about specific passages, and the constitution went into effect on 25 October 1780.

Massachusetts currently has the oldest functioning constitution in the world – in effect since 1780. The other early state constitutions, once Massachusetts, New Hampshire, and South Carolina adopted their second, permanent documents, would last, on average, more than half a century. The essential stability indicated by these figures resulted from the constitutions being built upon the secure base of a century and a half of colonial political experience.

8. POPULAR SOVEREIGNTY IN THE COLONIES

The notion of popular sovereignty had never taken hold in Britain. The sovereignty of the king had been replaced by parliamentary sovereignty after the Glorious Revolution of 1688, a constitutional alteration signified by the convention of "king in Parliament." In America, however, political institutions were effectively based upon popular sovereignty, even though they still technically rested upon the legal authority of the British sovereign. By 1776 Americans generally assumed that government in its formation and operation should rest upon popular consent, and this assumption was an important source of the controversy between Britain and America (see Chapter 71, §§1 and 2). Americans did not elect members of Parliament, were not represented there, and thus argued that Parliament could not pass laws directly affecting Americans without breaching the assumption of popular sovereignty. The British considered sovereignty to reside in Parliament and denied that popular consent was required either to create Parliament or to justify its acting. Parliament had not, after all, been created by an act of popular sovereignty. Americans, on the other hand, had for a century and a half been erecting their own legislatures on the basis of documents which they approved themselves.

Logic, therefore, would seem to dictate that new state constitutions should have a special status accorded them in keeping with the American practice of popular sovereignty. This did not at first occur. The initial constitutions were adopted by provincial and state legislatures rather than by constitutional conventions and were treated as pieces of legislation. Continuity between colonial political institutions was thereby assured, but the failure until 1780 to take the writing and approval of constitutions out of the hands of the legislature and thereby to distinguish between constitutions and normal legislation seemed implicitly to deny the basic American doctrine of popular sovereignty. The key to understanding this seemingly odd situation lay in how Americans viewed their legislatures.

During the colonial era the legislature was not generally viewed as distinct from the people. Rather, it was looked upon as a buffer between the people and the government (the Crown), with the majority of the legislature more or less automatically representing the interests of the community at large. The people could not all gather together to frame a constitution any more than they could gather to write legislation, so the body designed to embody the will of the people, the legislature, was the obvious instrument for both tasks. What made such a position plausible was the very close control maintained by the people over the legislature. A much more broadly defined electorate than that found in England used relatively frequent elections as the primary instrument of control. Furthermore, since the community was viewed as being an entity in which everyone's long-term interests were the same, the strong link between an electoral majority and a legislative majority made them appear indistinguishable.

Events during the Revolution led to an altered view of the legislature. Factions within the population undercut the notion of a community with common interests. Divisions within the legislature furthered this perception, and the fact that legislative factional divisions frequently did not match those within the population led to many rethinking the assumed identity of the people with its legislature. Among the many important political matters that increasingly divided Americans was the animosity and suspicion between the wealthier, more cosmopolitan cities and towns along the coast, and the smaller, more locally oriented towns and counties further inland. The legislatures represented these splits with varying accuracy. The outcome of bitter legislative debate was more likely to reflect the balance of forces within the legislature than the pattern of sentiment in the general population.

The response to the new perceptions was a logical and straightforward one. If the legislatures could not be trusted any longer automatically to reflect the interests of the community, then the community had to become more directly involved with matters of government, especially when it came to the writing of constitutions. Put another way, whereas before popular sovereignty was seen as being transmitted from the people through the legislature in the writing of constitutions, increasing doubt concerning the reliability of the legislature led many to wish the legislature removed as a link in the chain of constitutional design.

Perceptions changed faster than the ability to design new institutions. Like everything else during the founding era, political processes tended to evolve rather than break out in revolutionary new directions. The assumption of popular sovereignty led to a gradual move towards popularly elected constitutional conventions to write constitutions, coupled with popular approval of the document the convention produced. By 1780 the new institutional format for transmitting popular sovereignty was in place with the adoption of the Massachusetts Constitution.

9. THE COMMON POLITICAL CULTURE OF THE COLONIES

What is striking about the early state constitutions as a group is that, despite some institutional diversity, there were strong similarities among them that reflected a common political culture. That is, the political institutions developed in relative isolation by each colony converged over time, and during the revolutionary era the similarities became even stronger. To a certain extent this can be explained by the common practice of borrowing from other state constitutions, but it is doubtful that such borrowing would have been likely, or so successful, unless fundamental similarities had not already existed.

A general look at the 15 state constitutions adopted between 1775 and 1781 reveals the following patterns. All but two states used a bicameral legislature. Georgia went bicameral when it replaced its 1777 document in 1789, and Pennsylvania did so when it replaced its 1776 document in 1790. In all 15 constitutions the lower house was elected directly by the people. Although the percentage of white adult males enfranchised varied from state to state, on average the percentage was at least four times larger than it was in Britain.

Of the 13 constitutions creating bicameral legislatures, all but one had the upper house (senate) elected directly by the people, usually using the same electorate for both houses. Maryland, the one exception, used an electoral college to elect its senate. With only one exception, 1776 South Carolina, all constitutions provided for annual elections for the lower house. Of the 13 bicameral states, eight had annual elections for the senate, two had biennial elections, and three had staggered, multi-year elections.

In nine of the constitutions the executive was elected by the legislature, three used a popular election, and three used a popular election to identify the major candidates from among whom the legislature picked the governor. Eleven constitutions provided for annual elections of the governor, two for biennial elections, and two for triennial elections.

Twelve of the constitutions required voters to own property, usually about 50 acres or the equivalent, and three required voters to have paid taxes. Of the 13 bicameral legislatures, ten had the same property requirement to vote for the upper house as for the lower house. Of the nine states that involved the people in selecting the governor, eight used the same property requirement to vote for the governor as was required to vote for the lower house. All but one of the constitutions had property requirements to run for office, and nine for the 13 bicameral legislatures required more property to run for the upper house than for the lower house.

Ten of the early state constitutions included bills of rights. These bills of rights varied in length and detail, but generally had similar content. Virtually all rights later found in the United States Bill of Rights could be found in an earlier state constitution, usually in several.

Fourteen of the 15 constitutions were written and adopted by the respective state legislature, usually after an election where it was made clear that the new legislature would also write a new constitution.

Far from exhausting the similarities, the ones listed here indicate that, despite differences resulting from colonial experiences, regionalism, size, diversity, or degree of radicalism, there was a coherent shared political culture underlying the early state constitutions. Perhaps most obvious is the manner in which they produced political systems dominated by a bicameral legislature. The executive was invariably quite weak and a creature of the legislature. This was in keeping with both the colonial

287

tendency to focus upon the legislature as the embodiment of the people, and the colonial distrust of executives and executive privilege.

Typical provisions in state constitutions towards this end, in addition to having the legislature elect the executive, included the requirement that the legislature approve executive appointments, the creation of a small body drawn from the legislature to assist the governor in giving executive approval to legislation, granting pardons, or just generally telling him what to do. The extent to which separation of powers was actually found in state constitutions, aside from the 1780 Massachusetts document, it was limited to a prohibition on anyone holding simultaneously a position in the legislative and executive branches.

In this regard, the United States Constitution built upon and evolved out of state constitutionalism. The national executive was stronger than state executives, although only somewhat more so than the Massachusetts governor. The movement away from the radical model of direct, popular consent was also only a matter of degree with respect to the Massachusetts constitution. When taken together, some believe, the state constitutions and the political process that produced them shows the extent to which the national constitution was in most respects a logical development out of, or deflection from, what had come before rather than a radical departure or a conservative reaction. Regardless, the early state constitutions were the American laboratory for liberty, the base upon which the Continental Congress rested as it successfully prosecuted the war of independence and the first true written constitutions in world history. Even those who prefer to minimize the impact of these documents upon the United States Constitution admit the importance of the early state constitutions in these other respects.

FURTHER READING

Adams, Willi Paul: *The First American Constitutions: Republican Ideology and the Making of the State Constitutions in the Revolutionary Era* (Chapel Hill: University of North Carolina Press, 1980).

Dargo, George: *Roots of the Republic: a New Perspective on Early American Constitutionalism* (New York: Praeger, 1974).

Green, Fletcher M.: *Constitutional Development in the South Atlantic States* (Chapel Hill: University of North Carolina Press, 1930).

Lutz, Donald S.: *Popular Consent and Popular Control: Whig Political Theory in the Early Constitutions* (Baton Rouge: Louisiana State University Press, 1980).

——: *The Origins of American Constitutionalism* (Baton Rouge: Louisiana State University Press, 1988).

Main, Jackson Turner: *The Sovereign States, 1775–1783* (New York: New Viewpoints, 1973).

Nevins, Allan: *The American States During and After the Revolution, 1775–1789* (New York: Augustus M. Kelley, 1969).

Peters, Ronald M., Jr.: *The Massachusetts Constitution of 1780: a Social Compact* (Amherst: University of Massachusetts Press, 1978).

Selsam, J. Paul: *The Pennsylvania Constitution of 1776: a Study in Revolutionary Democracy* (New York: Octagon Books, 1971).

Thorpe, Francis N. (ed.): *The Federal and State Constitutions, Colonial Charters, and Other Organic Laws of the United States*, 7 vols. (Washington, DC: Government Printing Office, 1907).

Wood, Gordon S.: *The Creation of the American Republic, 1776–1787* (Chapel Hill: University of North Carolina Press, 1969).

30

The Articles of Confederation, 1775–1783

JACK N. RAKOVE

T HE Articles of Confederation established the first formal charter of national government for the 13 American states. Drafted by the Continental Congress in 1776 and 1777, the Articles were not formally ratified by all 13 states until February 1781. By then, many American leaders already sensed that Congress lacked effective authority to carry out even the tasks that the Articles had assigned to it. Efforts to amend the Articles began as early as 1781; ultimately they culminated in the Federal Convention of 1787, which proposed the new Constitution that replaced the Articles of Confederation in March 1789.

I. RESISTANCE AND CONFEDERATION

When resistance to the claims of parliamentary authority over America reached crisis proportions in the summer of 1774, 12 of the 13 colonies appointed delegates to the Continental Congress that met in Philadelphia in September and October (only distant Georgia went unrepresented). A Second Congress of all 13 colonies assembled in May 1775, after war had erupted in Massachusetts. Save for a short adjournment that summer, this unicameral body, which was formally known as the United States in Congress Assembled, served continuously as the effective national government of the new republic for the remainder of the war. The power Congress exercised ultimately rested on popular support and the success of the struggle against Britain. But by 1775 some delegates concluded that its authority should rest on a more solid foundation. Drafting formal articles of union would help to clarify the relations between Congress and the individual colonies (later states). Equally important, such a step would give Congress a credible basis for negotiating with potential allies in Europe.

Those delegates who believed that the British Government was intent on crushing the rebellion hoped that independence would be declared only after the creation both of a formal union and of legal governments in the individual states. By contrast, a number of delegates still hoped for reconciliation with Britain. In their view the act of confederating was tantamount to independence, and they accordingly opposed allowing Congress even to discuss the topic at all. Several rough drafts of a confederation had in fact been prepared by the winter of 1776. Benjamin Franklin presented the best known of these to Congress in August 1775; members of the Connecticut delegation prepared at least two others. But, in practice, the pressing need to maintain consensus within Congress favored the position of the moderate delegates well into 1776.

By early June, however, even they sensed that independence was imminent. On 7 June Richard Henry Lee of Virginia offered a set of resolutions calling for independence, the negotiation of foreign alliances, and the drafting of a confederation. Five days later Congress appointed a 13-member committee (one from each colony) to draft articles of confederation. Its leading member was JOHN DICKINSON of Pennsylvania, the celebrated author of *Letters from a Farmer in Pennsylvania*, a pamphlet that had played a crucial role in rousing resistance to the Townshend Duties of 1767. The most influential opponent of independence still sitting in Congress, Dickinson had long feared that separation from Britain would lead to endless conflict among the American colonies. Other members of the committee, such as SAMUEL ADAMS of Massachusetts and Roger Sherman of Connecticut, were far more militant.

2. DRAFTING THE ARTICLES

Although the committee kept no records of its deliberations, Dickinson evidently prepared the original set of articles: a first draft in his hand came to light only in the middle of the twentieth century. Dickinson envisioned a confederation that would restrain the autonomy of the states in significant ways. One notable article would have protected the freedom of religious exercise within the states while prohibiting the latter from making any further alteration in the existing structure of church–state relations, a recurring source of controversy throughout America. More important, Congress was to be vested with exclusive authority over peace and war, the conduct of foreign relations, the direction of the war, the resolution of disputes between states, and the disposition of the vast and unsettled western lands whose ownership was already the source of bitter conflict and rivalry among the states.

The committee met frequently during the second fortnight of June. Most of Dickinson's original plan survived its scrutiny (though the article on religion was rejected). A revised set of articles was reported to Congress on 12 July. By then Dickinson had left Congress, and, in his absence, none of the other members of the committee appears to have assumed the role he might have played as leading spokesman for their plan.

The draft articles were debated in a committee of the whole house from mid-July until 20 August 1776, when Congress ordered the printing of a revised report that would provide the basis for a final round of discussion. Some of the most important provisions the Dickinson committee had proposed were accepted with little if any dissent. Indeed, it is striking how little controversy arose over the task of dividing the basic functions of government between the union and the states. There was nearly unanimous agreement that Congress should retain exclusive control over the great affairs of war and foreign relations, while the states preserved full legal authority to regulate their "internal police" – that is, all the ordinary business of daily life. The states would retain the right to levy their own taxes and to determine how they would mobilize the other resources of men and materiel that the war would require. But, in both instances, the delegates expected that the states would faithfully execute whatever measures Congress asked of them.

On the whole, the surviving records of the deliberations of July–August 1776 do not suggest that the delegates were deeply concerned with the perplexing theoretical issues that are inherent in any system of federal government. There was no discussion, for example, of the whole question of the location of sovereignty – though that issue had been at the heart of the previous decade of constitutional debate with Britain. Instead, the framers of the Articles sought to divide major powers of government in a pragmatic way, creating two broad and largely exclusive spheres of authority for the union and the states, and trusting to patriotism and the imperatives of war to persuade these two levels of government to cooperate for the common good.

But if abstract questions of sovereignty and federalism did not figure prominently in the debates of 1776, other concerns of a different nature threatened to prevent either Congress or the states from agreeing upon any draft of confederation. The true sources of controversy centered on three other issues in which certain groups of states feared that their particular interests would be jeopardized.

The first of these involved the question of representation and voting in Congress. The drafting committee had followed the precedent set by the First Congress of 1774 of giving each state one vote in Congress, regardless of disparities in population and wealth. While delegates from the populous states of Pennsylvania, Virginia, and Massachusetts vigorously opposed the injustice of this measure, their colleagues from such small states as Rhode Island, Maryland, and Delaware argued just as vehemently that they deserved an equal vote because they were as fully committed to the revolutionary cause as their larger neighbors.

The problems posed by the two other controversial issues reflected the delegates' awareness that winning independence would not come cheaply. Northern and southern delegates disagreed whether the common expenses of the war should be apportioned among the states on the basis of total population (including slaves) or free population only. Similarly, a coalition of five states whose western boundaries were fixed by their colonial charters (Rhode Island, New Jersey, Delaware, Pennsylvania, and Maryland) argued that the vast territorial claims of the so-called landed states (of which Virginia was the most important) should be transferred to Congress in order to create a common stock of lands whose later sale could provide a relatively painless way to discharge the national debt. Only the united effort of all the states would bring the interior under American control, they argued; what would have to be gained at common expense should be used for the common benefit. On this issue the landed states were adamant, and they succeeded in striking every proposal designed to vest Congress with authority over western lands.

Continuing disagreement over these three issues of voting, expenses, and western lands helps to explain why Congress largely abandoned discussion of confederation after 20 August 1776. The tentative decisions the committee of the whole had taken on these points reflected neither compromise nor consensus. The objections of the dissenting minorities remained so strong that many members doubted whether the state legislatures could ever be brought to ratify the Articles. Moreover, the repeated defeats the American Army suffered in the summer and fall of 1776 left Congress with little time to continue its debate over the confederation.

3. COMPLETING THE CONFEDERATION

Not until April 1777 was Congress able to return to the Articles. Almost immediately, the delegates approved one amendment of major importance. THOMAS BURKE, a new delegate from North Carolina, proposed an article affirming that each state would retain "its sovereignty, freedom, and independence, and every power, jurisdiction, and right, which is not by this Confederation expressly delegated" to Congress.[1] After brief debate, this formula was approved by 11 of the 13 delegations. While it made no substantive changes in the actual allocation of power between the union and the states – one would have to look elsewhere in the Articles for that – it strongly implied that the ultimate power of sovereignty resided in the states. Yet this provision (Article

2 of the completed Confederation) had its ambiguities; even Burke later acknowledged that "the United States ought to be as One Sovereign with respect to foreign Powers, in all things that relate to War or where the States have one Common Interest."[2]

Once Congress adopted Burke's amendment, it soon found itself mired in the impasse over representation, expenses, and western land. By the summer of 1777 the subject of Confederation was again tabled. It was not resumed until October, when Congress (resettled at York, Pennsylvania, following the British occupation of Philadelphia) finally mustered the determination to complete the Confederation.

Two expedient calculations probably led to this decision. First, Congress was anxious to respond to the growing problem of inflation and the accompanying depreciation of its paper currency by submitting a comprehensive set of financial resolutions to the states. Second, Congress hoped that the dramatic American victory at Saratoga would at last persuade the French Government to conclude a treaty of alliance. In both cases, the delegates appear to have concluded that the completion of the Articles of Confederation would strengthen the hand of Congress *vis-à-vis* the states and its potential ally.

There were, however, no magical solutions to the problems that had delayed the completion of the Articles for more than a year. The speed with which Congress now dispatched these issues indicates that the delegates had decided to accept imperfect solutions in the interest of completing the Confederation. The issues of voting and western lands took only one day each to resolve. On 7 October Congress endorsed the one state, one vote precedent of 1774; on the 15th it rejected a final flurry of motions designed to give the union the power to set state boundaries and manage the land that would then lie beyond. The one issue that took time to resolve was the apportionment of expenses, which consumed five days of maneuvering before Congress narrowly accepted an unwieldy formula to base each state's share of the costs of national government on the value of its settled lands "and the buildings and improvements thereon."[3] By 15 November 1777 Congress had at last completed its work, and was prepared to submit the 13 Articles of Confederation to the states.[4]

The first three Articles gave the Confederation its title ("The United States of America"), recognized the principle of state sovereignty in the language of Thomas Burke's amendment, and declared the general purpose for which the states had united. Article 4 prohibited the states from discriminating against each others' citizens, provided for the extradition of fugitives, and obliged each state to give "full faith and credit" to the judicial determinations of other states. Article 5 defined the institutional character of Congress: it would meet annually; delegates could serve no more than three years out of every six, and were subject to recall by their states at any time; each state would have one vote.

The sixth Article demonstrated that the reserved sovereignty of the states was less than absolute by imposing a series of restrictions on their authority, especially in the general realm of external affairs. Article 7 dealt with the appointment of military officers, and Article 8 regulated the apportionment of common expenses among the states.

Article 9, enumerating the powers of Congress, was the most important. It gave Congress "the sole and exclusive right and power of determining on peace and war," conducting foreign relations, and "directing [the] operations" of military and naval forces. It established a detailed if cumbersome procedure for adjudicating disputes between states without allowing Congress itself to become a direct party to their resolution. Article 9 also gave Congress the authority to determine the expenses of the union and to appropriate the necessary funds; to emit bills of credit and borrow money; to set the size of the army and to require the states to raise the necessary numbers of men. In exercising all of these major powers, the consent of nine states would be necessary.

The concluding four Articles tied up a few loose ends. Article 10 prohibited the committee of the states – a body made up of one member from each state, which was to sit in the recess of Congress – from exercising any of the major powers that required the approval of nine states. Article 11 invited Canada to join the Confederation, but no other state was to be admitted without the consent of nine states. Article 12 extended the "public faith" to all debts contracted by the union before the formal completion of the Confederation. Finally, Article 13 obliged the states to "abide by the determinations" of Congress "on all questions which, by this confederation, are submitted to them." It also stipulated that the Articles must be ratified by all the states, with later amendments to be first proposed by Congress and then similarly approved by all the states.

The conditions under which the Articles of Confederation were framed had not encouraged the delegates to give sustained thought to the long-term nature of the union they hoped to consolidate. By 1777 their major concern was simply to complete a document that the states could quickly and unanimously approve. Had they proposed vesting Congress with authority to levy its own taxes or to coerce delinquent states into fulfilling their federal obligations, the prospects for ratification would have diminished. Rather than consider whether Congress would be able to command the continued allegiance of the states, the framers simply presumed that the states would have to do their duty.

FIGURE 25 A view of the state house in Chestnut Street, Philadelphia, described in a contemporary account as "a building which will, perhaps, become more interesting in the history of the world, than any of the celebrated fabrics of Greece or Rome"; the steeple was removed soon after the British evacuation of the city (engraving by James Trenchard after a painting by Charles Willson Peale, 1778).

4. RATIFICATION

The hope that the Confederation would be ratified quickly came to nought. By June 1778 it was known that ten of the state legislatures had either ratified or were preparing to ratify the Articles. With the first ambassador from France expected to arrive soon, Congress brushed aside the numerous amendments that had been proposed by the states, and proceeded with a partial but legally meaningless ceremony of ratification. Many delegates expected the three remaining states – Delaware, New Jersey, and Maryland – to fall into line. These states balked at signing the Confederation because it failed to provide for the creation of a national domain in the west. By 1779 Delaware and New Jersey had swallowed their objections – though only under protest. But Maryland held out until February 1781, and the Articles did not take effect until 1 March 1781. By then the landed states had initiated the process of ceding their western land claims, which eventually led to the creation of a national domain northwest of the Ohio River. But by then, too, the war itself was almost over: the climactic victory at Yorktown was only months away. The Articles of Confederation thus proved largely irrelevant to the victory they were meant to secure.

More than that, the nearly three and a half years that had elapsed between the submission of the Articles to the states and the final act of ratification had revealed that many of the assumptions that had guided the framers of 1776–7 were flawed. The failure of the states to meet congressional requisitions for men, supplies, and taxes seemed to demonstrate that the Articles had placed too much confidence in the willingness and ability of the states to serve as the administrative agents of the union. Indeed, Congress had begun considering the need to secure amendments even before the Confederation took effect.

Some delegates were attracted to the idea of giving Congress "coercive" powers over the states. But how could a recalcitrant state be coerced to do its duty? and how could the states ever be expected to approve so drastic an increase in federal power? Rather than pursue so impractical a measure, most members instead favored asking the states to grant Congress independent sources of revenue. On 3 February 1781 – several weeks before the Articles were to take effect – Congress asked the states to grant it the power to collect a duty (or impost) on foreign goods imported in America.

This modestly drawn measure drew intense opposition in Rhode Island, which effectively blocked its adoption. But the problems the impost was meant to address did not disappear. Even with the war winding down in 1782, Congress needed revenues both to meet its current expenses and to service the enormous national debt incurred during a long and costly war. At the urging of Robert Morris, its newly appointed Superintendent of Finance, Congress spent the months between the summer of 1782 and the spring of 1783 struggling to frame a comprehensive revenue program. After a prolonged period of intense political maneuvering marked by rumors of an insurrection of unpaid soldiers and various threats from Superintendent Morris, Congress proposed (18 April 1783) two new amendments to the Confederation. One was a revised version of the impost; the other proposed altering the method for calculating each state's share of the national expenses from the impractical formula based on the value of improved lands to a simple apportionment on the basis of population (with slaves counted at the three-fifths ratio that the Federal Convention of 1787 would later adapt to the issue of representation).

Like the impost of 1781 – as well as two further amendments that Congress proposed a year later – these two measures failed to secure the unanimous approval of the states. With the struggle for independence successfully concluded, it quickly became apparent that the states no longer shared the same overriding sense of a common national interest that had carried them, though with great difficulty, through the war. It would take only a few years for many Americans to conclude that the Articles of Confederation no longer provided an adequate framework either for mediating conflicting interests or for carrying out national policy on those rare occasions when Congress proved capable of decision.

REFERENCES

1. Ford, Worthington C.: *Journals of the Continental Congress, 1774–1789.* 34 vols. (Washington, DC: US Government Printing Office, 1904–37): Vol. 9, 908.
2. Smith, Paul H.: *Letters of Delegates to Congress, 1774–1789,* 13 vols. to date (Washington, DC: US Government Printing Office, 1976–): Vol. 8, 435.
3. Ford, Vol. 9, 800–1.
4. For the complete text, see Ford, Vol. 9, 907–25.

FURTHER READING

Jensen, Merrill: *The Articles of Confederation: an Interpretation of the Social-Constitutional History of the American Revolution, 1774–1781* (Madison: University of Wisconsin Press, 1940).
——: *The New Nation: a History of the United States during the Confederation, 1781–1789* (New York: Alfred A. Knopf, 1950).
Onuf, Peter S.: *The Origins of the Federal Republic: Jurisdictional Controversies in the United States* (Philadelphia: University of Pennsylvania Press, 1983).
Rakove, Jack N.: *The Beginnings of National Politics: an Interpretive History of the Continental Congress* (New York: Alfred A. Knopf, 1979).

31

The War for Independence, to Saratoga

DON HIGGINBOTHAM

IN the winter of 1774–5, the British ministry, frustrated and angered by a decade of disturbance and controversy in the North American provinces, elected to respond with military force. To be sure, scarlet regiments had been sent to Boston in 1768 and again – in larger numbers – in 1774. But their presence in the Massachusetts capital had scarcely intimidated the so-called Whigs or patriots there, nor had those steps had a sobering effect on popular leaders in the other English-speaking seaboard colonies. The landing of 3,500 troops in Massachusetts in 1774, the combining of civil and military authority in the appointment of General Thomas Gage as successor to the departing Governor Thomas Hutchinson, and the passing of the Coercive Acts had instead resulted in the First Continental Congress and in a groundswell of American sympathy for the beleaguered Bostonians.

I. BRITAIN'S OPENING MILITARY GAMBIT: LEXINGTON AND CONCORD

If the ministry did not want an all-out war, it did instruct General Gage to engage in a major display of muscle; the Massachusetts politicians would surely be sobered by such an act. So it was, then, that Gage, hesitant to move on his own in such a tense atmosphere, dispatched a troop column on the night of 18 April to destroy the Massachusetts Provincial Congress's military stores at Concord. Recently formed Massachusetts minutemen companies responded to the challenge. Although the next morning the locals were dispersed at Lexington Green, Lieutenant Colonel Francis Smith's column found only a portion of the munitions that had been assembled at Concord. They also found, on their return journey to Boston, an aroused countryside as minute companies from surrounding communities subjected them to such a deadly rain of musketry that they were fortunate to reach the safety of the city, their casualties in all categories numbering approximately 275.

Rather than pulling back or giving pause, Britain sought a military solution to its decade-old political problem: the constitutional relationship between the metropolitan center and the colonial peripheries of empire. It did so without taking a long view of the implications. While the mailed fist approach never received a full airing in official quarters, it did trigger warnings of overwhelming costs, of French and Spanish intervention, and, as Lord Chatham put it, of the wreckage of both Britain and America. But instead of acknowledging concerns of the parliamentary opposition, the government only half-heartedly entertained ideas for halting the bloodshed before the American war became a full-scale international conflict.

These schemes need not long detain us. In 1776 Admiral Richard, Lord Howe, and his brother General William Howe were appointed joint commanders-in-chief in America and peace commissioners, but, as commissioners, they could merely listen to American grievances and inform the colonists that their views would receive a hearing in London *after* they put down their arms. The Howes' peace offer (such as it was) had no chance of success, and in fact it was only presented to America after the Declaration of Independence. The second British peace initiative also amounted to too little, too late. Cobbled together after Burgoyne's disaster at Saratoga, it essentially proposed to turn the clock back to 1763 in terms of British–American relations and to renounce Parliament's right to tax the colonists. Reaching America after the signing of the Franco-American alliance of 1778, it was as ill-timed as the previous olive branch.

2. THE MILITARY RESOURCES OF THE COLONISTS

Even so, the American cause did not rely solely on Britain's international difficulties. The colonists drew up military ideas and practices that had served them reasonably well in the century and a half before Lexington and Concord. The militia, seemingly a dying institution in Stuart England, became the colonists' mainstay of defense in the seventeenth century. Provincial publicists never tired of touting the virtues of the militia over professional or "standing armies." The sturdy yeomanry of Virginia or Massachusetts were infinitely superior to long-enlisted European soldiers who fought for pay and not for patriotism. John Adams averred that the militia was a cornerstone of New England society, along with the county court, the town meeting, and the Church. The Reverend Ebenezer Gay praised the universality of militia service. There were "no Exceptions . . . for the High, nor the Low; for the Rich, nor the Poor; for the Strong, nor the Weak; for the Old, nor the Young." If the militia bore the burden of defense, it still fell short of its admirers' claims. Normally the militia served as a body from which volunteers and draftees were obtained for more extended duty in reconstituted militia companies and regiments. As the years passed, people on the upper end of the social scale received exemptions, and those at the very bottom – "loose, idle, dissolute persons" – fell outside the system.

While the eighteenth-century militia continued to be a valuable instrument of social control at home – it put down riots and disorders in the colonial period and disarmed and tyrannized the loyalists in the Revolution – its place in the more sophisticated post-1688 imperial wars was taken by semi-professional forces, which were a hybrid between the militia and a standing army. The term applies to men who received a bounty in return for a year's enlistment and agreed to fight outside their own colonies and be governed by a more rigorous military code than applied to the militia. Their officers also saw themselves as a cut above their militia counterparts, whom they criticized for their ignorance and lack of leadership. Semi-professional officers not infrequently devoured European military treatises and hoped to learn first-hand from observing British regulars during the French wars of the mid-century.

Massachusetts and Connecticut in particular felt heavy demands for manpower in these struggles. Massachusetts provided the bulk of the 1745 New England expeditionary force that employed European siege tactics in the capture of the fortress of Louisburg on Cape Breton Island. So many Connecticut officers and men shouldered arms in the Seven Years' War that the province's military organization became an American likeness of a mercenary European army.

Washington, Virginia, and the Continental Army   The case of Washington and Virginia is especially instructive because of the former's subsequent role in the War of Independence. Washington had not yet reached the age of 24 when he became colonel of the Virginia Regiment in 1755, but he had read several military books, talked extensively to older Virginians who had held British commissions, and kept notes on British Army procedures he observed while an unofficial aide to General Edward Braddock before the latter's death in the Battle of the Monongahela. Despite innumerable obstacles during his three-year command, Washington made impressive strides in the training and disciplining of his regiment. He and his officers thought of themselves as professionals and petitioned British authorities to take their unit into the royal service. If they were rebuffed in these efforts, they nonetheless drew praise from Generals John Forbes and Robert Monckton.

Seventeen years later when the Second Continental Congress, meeting in the aftermath of Lexington and Concord, adopted the New England forces besieging General Gage in Boston and appointed Washington their commander-in-chief, the legislators were taking a logical and predictable step in the history of early American military institutions: from seventeenth-century militia, to eighteenth-century semi-professional forces, to professional army in 1775. In some respects this new Continental Army, as it was called, appeared to be an extension of a semi-professional colonial force of the Seven Years' War, for many of its officers had held commissions in the last imperial war, and its soldiers were enlisted for a year or less.

Although a second and smaller American army under Richard Montgomery and Benedict Arnold was driven out of Canada after initial successes, Washington's main American Army was not tested by its British counterpart in Boston – except in the bloody but inconclusive Battle of Bunker Hill (for illustration, *see* figure 48, p. 585), which occurred before the Virginian's arrival in the Bay colony. Those months from July of 1775 to March of 1776 were crucial in two ways: one, Washington demonstrated that an American army need not be feared by its own citizens; and second, he had time to bring order and system to his command as he watched the enemy from his well-entrenched positions overlooking the city. Finally, William Howe, Gage's successor, sailed away on 17 March, St. Patrick's Day, preferring to regroup, await reinforcements, and attack where the Americans seemed more vulnerable than in Massachusetts, the hotbed of American radicalism.

3. THE BRITISH CAMPAIGN OF 1776

The campaign of 1776 saw Britain take the offensive; but it is hardly accurate to say, as did earlier generations of historians, that she possessed the lion's share of the advantages. Problems of transportation, communication, and supply bulked large two hundred years ago. So did her lack of sufficient men under arms. Her generals and admirals were competent enough, though little more than that – Generals Gage, Howe, and Clinton were too cautious; Burgoyne and Cornwallis were too aggressive. Admiral Howe was hesitant and perhaps more interested in winning over the colonists by the carrot than by the stick; Sir Henry Clinton called Howe's naval successors – Gambier, Graves, and Arbuthnot – "old women"; they fumed and strutted and got along poorly with their army counterparts. The generals in America, who were members of Parliament with alliances to rival political factions, also distrusted each other.

The recruitment of Germans and loyalists With human resources decidedly limited in an age when the productive elements of society were excluded from shouldering arms, Britain turned to her time-honored tradition of buying military manpower. That undertaking always included looking to the German states. This traffic in human flesh, so roundly condemned by Enlightenment philosphers, brought 30,000 German troops from six principalities into the American war. Valuable though they were, their presence deeply embittered Americans and doubtless converted many fence-sitters to the idea of independence. But even greater animosities stemmed from Britain's recruitment of the loyalists, from her urging royalist-oriented colonists to spy, obstruct, and fight their fellow Americans. British authorities, as well as loyalist leaders such as Joseph Galloway, persisted for years in the notion that opposition to the Crown was the work of a small minority that intimidated the larger populace. Acknowledging that for the time being British forces were inadequate to throttle the rebellion in New England, the ministry sent a small fleet in the spring of 1776 to the coast of the Carolinas to tap this reputed source of fidelity. The outcome should have demonstrated the myth of ubiquitous loyalism: the rebels' destruction of a 1,400-man Tory contingent at Moore's Creek Bridge near Wilmington, North Carolina, and the repulse of the royal naval squadron at Charles Town, South Carolina, in June of 1776. Although illusions persisted, Britain undertook no new significant southern ventures for several years.

The middle colonies were the focus of British operations in 1776 and for some time thereafter. Lord George Germain, the Colonial Secretary and director of the war effort (instead of the non-assertive First Minister, Lord North), was an eternal optimist, but even he acknowledged that it would take a massive show of force to crush the rebellion in a single campaign. Certainly he expended abundant energy that year as the creaky machinery of Hanoverian government assembled huge quantities of supplies, dozens of vessels, and a formidable fighting force. In fact, Germain and company made their greatest effort in that year: raising and sending to America the most imposing military expedition in English history, a feat never again equaled in the war and, in relative terms, never repeated until the twentieth century.

The battle for New York City In August of 1776 the Howe brothers rode at anchor before New York City. Their armada, drawn mainly from England but also containing elements from the former garrison at Boston and from the abortive southern expedition, consisted of 73 warships carrying 13,000 seamen and several hundred transports bearing 32,000 troops. Their strategy was to take New York City, cut off New England from the other rebel colonies, and then crack the heart of the rebellion, which they were convinced was in the Puritan colonies. In the process, they hoped to draw Washington into a major battle that would bring a climactic triumph. In all of this Germain and the Howes were supposedly in agreement. But, as we have already indicated, the Howes were also peace commissioners, and the Admiral in particular seems to have hoped to persuade the rebels to lay down their arms before the above-mentioned scenario unwound. To what extent these desires influenced his conduct and carried over to his brother, the General, will probably never be known.

But we can say that the campaign opened on a high note for the British, a low note for the Americans, although it concluded as something of a draw. Washington was eager to defend New York City, as was the Continental Congress, not only because of its strategic importance but also because New York had been a divided colony and loyalism was still potent there. Given the various islands, bays, and rivers in the area,

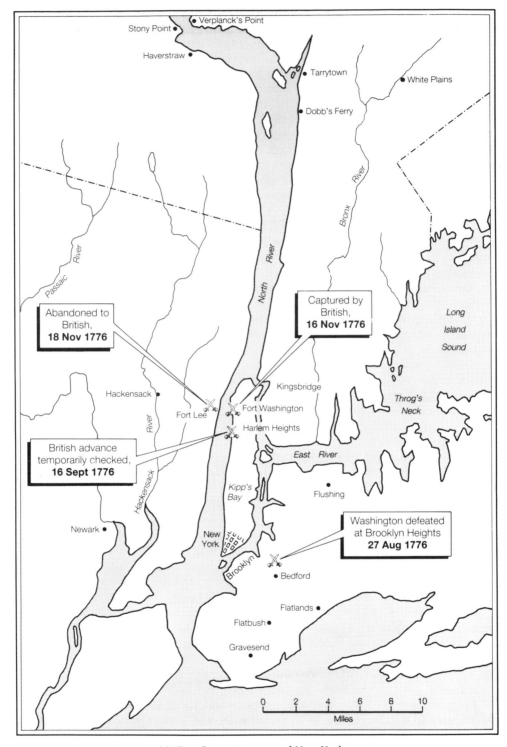

MAP 3 Campaigns around New York

Washington faced the danger of being isolated and cut off from retreat; but he became even bolder when he ferried the bulk of his militia-dominated army from Manhattan to Brooklyn on Long Island, where William Howe's army had assembled. Digging in on Brooklyn Heights, Washington hoped Howe would assault him frontally, with the kind of crimson carnage that had marked Bunker Hill. Instead, the British executed a skillful nocturnal flanking movement and hammered unsuspecting American units that had been posted in advance of the main line. American losses in all categories came to nearly 1,500 compared with Howe's fewer than 400. Howe, as was to be his custom, did not immediately press his advantage. With his back to the water, Washington subsequently under cover of darkness transported his remaining 9,000 men back to Manhattan.

Although Washington had reunited the two wings of his army on Manhattan, his situation remained extremely precarious. He risked the danger of a retreat northwards being cut off by a British landing at the far end of the island. General Howe's coming ashore at Kip's Bay on 15 September posed that very threat, but the Briton failed to drive swiftly across the island and Washington pulled back just in the nick of time. The next two months witnessed a series of minor battles and skirmishes at Harlem Heights, White Plains (on the mainland), and elsewhere as Howe continued his unsuccessful efforts to encircle Washington's army, which capitalized on a measure of luck and Howe's lethargic movements. But the Briton did overrun and capture the garrison of Fort Washington, which the American commander had unwisely left behind on Manhattan.

With the greater New York City area and its nearby islands securely in British hands, Washington fled across New Jersey and over the Delaware River, while Howe, dividing his forces, seized Newport, Rhode Island, and established outposts throughout the Jersies. For the moment, at least, the Revolution had reached its nadir. Those were the times, as Thomas Paine wrote in *The Crisis*, that "tried men's souls." Yet the year had not been a total loss for the Americans. The British had given up Boston, suffered the loss of a large loyalist body in North Carolina, and been repulsed at Charles Town. Moreover, a second British offensive that year directed by General Guy Carleton, who pressed southwards from Canada, encountered Colonel Benedict Arnold's small-ship flotilla on Lake Champlain. The Battle of Valcour Island saw Arnold's outgunned vessels get the better of Carleton, who now, with the approach of winter, retired northwards.

The Trenton–Princeton campaign   General Howe, now Sir William, had hardly earned his knighthood in the campaign of 1776, which, in fact, did not end with the calendar. For Washington launched his brilliantly unorthodox Trenton–Princeton winter campaign, which continued from Christmas through the New Year. Sensitive to the psychological need to end the campaign on an upbeat note, he once again took risks, but this time with positive results for his now-minuscule 3,000-man force. Howe, settled down to enjoy the New York social scene, had left his widely separated New Jersey garrisons ripe for the picking. After crossing back into that colony on Christmas night, Washington surprised the celebrating Hessians at Trenton, capturing or killing 1,000 of the Germans. He then returned briefly to the Pennsylvania side of the Delaware, called up militia reinforcements, and then reoccupied Trenton. Outmaneuvering Lord Cornwallis, who had hastened in pursuit of him, Washington dashed to Princeton, defeated its garrison, and found winter sanctuary in the mountains about Morristown.

Britain's lack of strategy   The campaign of 1776 revealed ambivalences and con-tradictions that plagued Britain's military effort throughout the War of Independence. Part of the problem lay in the fact that British generals were not trained in strategic thinking; indeed, the word strategy in its later sense had not come into being. Military men lacked a body of theoretical and historical doctrine from which to choose alternatives for practical application. That development came in the next century in the studies of Jomini and Clausewitz, who analyzed Napoleon's revolution in warfare. There were, however, as Ira Gruber has pointed out, implicit options in the military literature available to commanders of the time. There was the then prevailing phil-osophy of circumscribed war, associated with France's Marshall Saxe, with its stress on eschewing decisive engagements and exhausting the opponent by a variety of undertakings. At the same time, there was a tradition dating from antiquity, best exemplified by Caesar, stressing mobile, aggressive operations leading to the destruc-tion of the enemy in combat. Beginning with the Howe brothers in 1776, British chieftains never made a clear-cut decision in favor of one or the other, but rather tried one, then the other, and sometimes both in the same campaign. Furthermore, the relationship between the land war and the naval war remained muddled, and the navy's blockading operations were sporadic and rarely coordinated with the army's movements.

4. THE BRITISH CAMPAIGN OF 1777

The Howes had grown increasingly pessimistic about cracking the American rebellion in late 1776, and their state of mind was less than totally optimistic the following year. For a while, at least, they seemed to look to new approaches. If annihilating Washington's army would be difficult and overrunning the continent even more so, then another possibility would be a naval war in which the fleet strangled American commerce and the army captured port towns for use as naval bases. After advancing and then discarding a number of plans, Sir William decided to move against Phi-ladelphia, the rebel capital, a conquest that might well damage American morale but hardly prove fatal to the cause if Washington's army remained intact. Howe had little if any interest in the British force in Canada, previously commanded by Carleton but now headed by General John Burgoyne, who seemed to be all the things that Howe was not: confident, bold, and aggressive.

General Howe's victories at Brandywine Creek and Germantown   Amazingly, Colonial Secretary Germain sanctioned the campaign of 1777 without imposing a unifying concept. Scholarly opinion no longer holds that Howe had orders to advance up the Hudson for a union with Burgoyne. It may be that Burgoyne believed that Howe would at the very least clear the lower Hudson valley before heading for Philadelphia. But Germain did not instruct Howe to do so, nor did Burgoyne later act as if he needed Howe's assistance in conducting his own operations. Few in the highest positions in England or America evidently worried about how the Canadian Army might cope in the northern wilderness. Germain, however, had assumed that Howe would advance on Philadelphia by land and that he would keep in touch with Burgoyne. But Howe, though leaving garrisons at New York City and Newport, Rhode Island, took the bulk of his army – 13,000 men – to Philadelphia by sea, which for weeks isolated him from the outside world and allowed Washington to maneuver between Burgoyne and himself. One can only speculate as to Howe's motives. Certainly he disliked interior

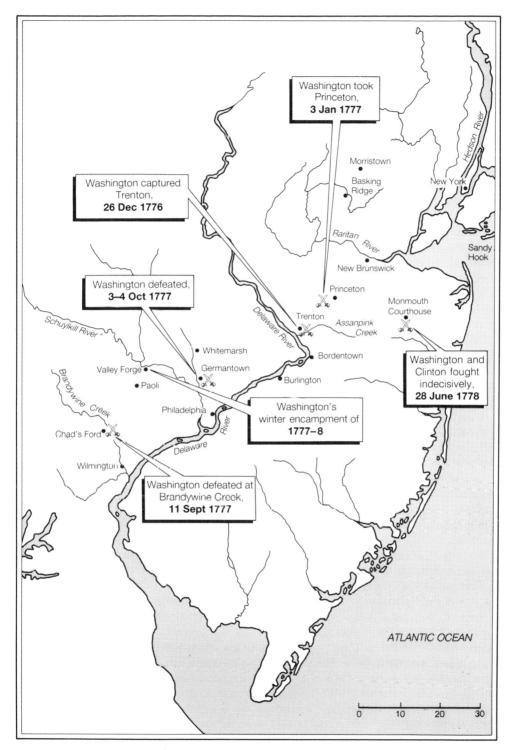

Washington took
Princeton,
3 Jan 1777

Morristown

Basking
Ridge

New York

Hudson River

Washington captured
Trenton,
26 Dec 1776

Raritan River

Sandy
Hook

New Brunswick

Washington defeated,
3–4 Oct 1777

Princeton

Monmouth
Courthouse

Schuylkill River

Delaware River

Trenton

Assanpink
Creek

Whitemarsh

Bordentown

Washington and
Clinton fought
indecisively,
28 June 1778

Valley Forge

Germantown

Brandywine Creek

Paoli

Burlington

Philadelphia

Washington's
winter encampment of
1777–8

Chad's Ford

Delaware River

Wilmington

Washington defeated at
Brandywine Creek,
11 Sept 1777

ATLANTIC OCEAN

0   10   20   30

MAP 4 Operations in New Jersey and Pennsylvania

campaigning, and his descent on the Quaker City by sea was consistent with his campaign of the year before and would extend the blockade down the coast, all of which must have found favor with his brother, the Admiral.

On 23 July 1777 the Howe brothers' expedition headed southwards, put in briefly at Delaware Bay, and then returned to sea, finally debarking its human cargo at the head of Chesapeake Bay, even farther from Philadelphia, now 57 miles away. Amazed at Sir William's desertion of Burgoyne, Washington endeavored to turn Howe back on 11 September, at Brandywine Creek; but the British general executed a skillful flanking movement, similar to his successful tactics on Long Island, and defeated Washington in a hard-fought contest, Sir William's casualties in all categories amounting to 500, half the number of Washington's.

The Virginian was hardly intimidated; after Howe finally reached Philadelphia, Washington, stalking nearby, again offered battle, attacking Howe's 9,000-man force quartered at Germantown on the night of 3 October. The American plan was probably too complicated, involving as it did four converging columns, and the outcome was indecisive. Each general's losses were approximately what they had been two weeks earlier at Brandywine. Yet Howe was paying a heavier price in manpower than Washington, who, after both Pennsylvania encounters, replenished his own depleted ranks. If Washington was game for another round, Sir William had no stomach for more costly bloodletting, convinced now that the war could not be won in 1777.

General Burgoyne's defeat at Saratoga   Meanwhile, Burgoyne's army from Canada got off to a good start, as was almost always true of British campaigns in the Revolution. Moving down Lake Champlain in June of 1777, with 7,000 men – Indian scouts, loyalist parties, British regulars, and German Brunswickers – he forced the American evacuation of Fort Ticonderoga. From that time on Burgoyne did few things right. He halted at Skenesborough after skirmishing with the American rearguard, in no hurry to press his advantage while the rebels were back on their heels. He gave General Philip Schuyler, the commander of the American Northern Department, time to plant obstructions in the already arduous pathway to the Hudson, with the result that the Canadian-based army needed 24 days to travel the next 23 miles. Burdened by excessive paraphernalia in rough country, Burgoyne was already in trouble when he learned that one of his diversionary parties in the Mohawk Valley had been halted by rebel irregulars and that a second probing contingent had been routed at Bennington, Vermont.

Crossing the Hudson, Burgoyne encountered a well-entrenched and revitalized American Northern Army, now commanded by General Horatio Gates, ably assisted by General Benedict Arnold and Colonel Daniel Morgan. Twice – on 19 September and 7 October – Burgoyne sent forward substantial columns which thrashed about in search of Gates's lines. Both times Gates dispatched regiments to claw at his opponent from advantageous wooded locations. Burgoyne's casualties in the first and second battles of Bemis Heights exceeded Gates's by roughly 1,200 to 470. Soon surrounded, and aware that the small British garrison remaining in New York City could hardly break through to his rescue, Burgoyne capitulated at the village of Saratoga on 17 October. A European army was scarcely equipped for wilderness warfare (the Howe brothers knew that), to say nothing of fighting a countryside in arms. And invariably, when the British plunged into the interior of the continent, that was what happened: people turned out in their militia units and bolstered American regular forces.

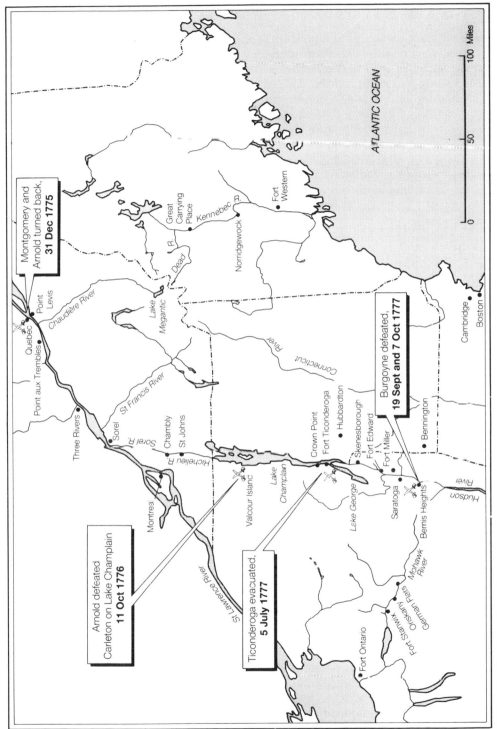

MAP 5 The Northern Campaigns

5. THE ADVANTAGES OF THE AMERICANS

It was no small advantage to Americans to be fighting on their own soil and to be more flexible in their military operations than their opponents. If they did not contemplate a massive guerrilla war, they nonetheless resorted advantageously at times to winter campaigning and night attacks, and they effectively employed backwoods riflemen, light infantry, and militia in harassing the flanks, interrupting communication and supply routes, and raiding isolated posts. Militia were no more useful in formal fixed-position warfare than they had been in the colonial period, but operating on the fringes and behind the lines they were often most effective; and never more so than in serving as a local constabulary or police force that disarmed and intimidated the loyalists. As James Simpson, a South Carolina loyalist, expressed it, the militia's greatest contribution to the rebel cause was in helping to erect and sustain civil governments, for it was "from their civil institutions that the rebels derive the whole of their strength."

The greatest burden, however, fell on Washington and his Continental Army, and it steadily improved. No longer do serious historians dismiss the Continental Army as an assortment of "ragtag and bobtail" that prevailed almost in spite of itself. Even in defeat, as at Long Island and Brandywine, it could fight surprisingly well, and it learned from its mistakes. To be sure, it shrank in size each winter, as it did during the dark months at Valley Forge following the campaign of 1777. But the spring months saw its ranks swell, sometimes dramatically. Drawing on the American semi-professional tradition from the colonial era, it became more professional with each passing year, with longer enlistments, larger bounties, stricter articles of war, and better training. Washington and his staff, with the support and assistance of Congress, fashioned a military instrument that showed remarkable staying power in a war that lasted eight and a half years. No small credit was owing to certain European professionals. Friedrich Wilhelm von Steuben standardized drill procedures and served as Washington's *de facto* chief-of-staff; and French volunteer officers formed a first-rate corps of engineers and introduced a scientific and technical tradition that would lead to the creation of the United States Military Academy and to the army's nineteenth-century role in the development of the West.

6. THE DISADVANTAGES OF THE BRITISH

If the strengths of the militia and Continentals were less clear in the spring of 1778 than they are in retrospect, it is nonetheless true that British leaders were increasingly frustrated by waging a war 3,000 miles from home against an armed population diffused over enormous stretches of territory. It was disheartening to seize somewhere along the way every single American urban center, including the capital city of Philadelphia, and have nothing to show for it other than the possession of real estate, for America had no vital strategic center. Thus far, too, British efforts to win over all the Indian tribes and drive American settlers out of the West had met with limited success. If the frontier war raged back and forth, with neither side able to assert firm dominance, it produced such colorful figures as Daniel Boone and George Rogers Clark of Kentucky for the Americans and such controversial individuals as Colonel Henry Hamilton, British commandant at Detroit, the alleged "Hair-Buyer."

Moreover, France threatened to turn the conflict into an international war. Already she had made available to the patriots aid in the form of arms, munitions, and clothing, funneled through Caron de Beaumarchais' fake "Hortalez and Company" (*see* Chapter 33, §1). She had also assisted the tiny Continental Navy and rebel privateers by clandestinely allowing them the use of her ports. Since under no circumstance could Americans contest the waves with mightly Britannia, French succor, then as well as in later years, made American sea raiders, and particularly the exploits of John Paul Jones, a nuisance and an embarrassment to England, causing insurance rates to skyrocket in London's mercantile circles. Emboldened further by British failures in 1777, the Bourbon kingdom concluded treaties of commerce and alliance with the United States on 6 February 1778, an action that soon led to France's entering the war on the side of the Americans in hopes of settling old scores with England. Consequently, Britain had to distribute her military and naval forces more thinly in the American theater in order to anticipate Gallic threats in Europe, the West Indies, India, and on the high seas.

7. THE INTERNATIONAL IMPACT

When Sir Henry Clinton, who succeeded William Howe as military commander-in-chief, evacuated Philadelphia with orders to concentrate his forces in New York City and dispatch units to the defense of the West Indies, Washington broke camp at Valley Forge and gave chase across New Jersey. Clinton's long baggage train extending over a dozen miles was tempting to the Continental commander who had been dogged by reversals in 1777. On 28 June American advance regiments, under General Charles Lee, caught up with Clinton's rearguard at Monmouth Courthouse. Becoming disorganized, Lee's troops fell back and were met by Washington, who arrived with the main army. The Continentals stood firm, exchanging volley for volley with some of Clinton's veteran regiments, which had been hastened back to Monmouth. In military terms, the outcome was indecisive, but it was a moral victory for Washington's

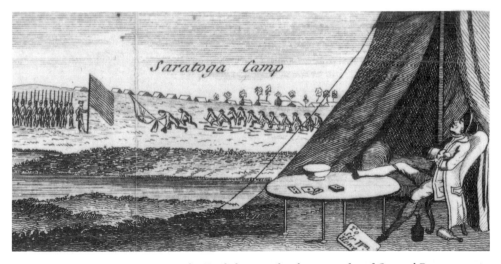

FIGURE 26 A cartoon expressing the English scorn for the surrender of General Burgoyne at Saratoga and for the inactivity of General Howe (seen here sleeping outside a tent) (from the "Westminster Magazine," June 1779).

soldiers, proof of how far they had come under the tutelage of Steuben at Valley Forge. While Clinton continued to New York City, Washington followed more slowly and encamped at White Plains, New York, close enough to watch his adversary. As the American commented, the two armies were juxtaposed in almost the same location they had occupied two years before. The unproductive meanderings of Howe (*see* figure 26) and Clinton elicited a bit of doggerel from the London *Evening Post*:

> Here we go up, up, up
> And here we go down, down, downy
> There we go *backwards* and *forwards*
> And here we go round, round, roundy.

FURTHER READING

Carp, E. Wayne: *To Starve the Army at Pleasure: Continental Army Administration and American Political Culture, 1775–1783* (Chapel Hill: University of North Carolina Press, 1984).

Gruber, Ira D.: "British strategy: the theory and practice of eighteenth-century warfare," *Reconsiderations on the Revolutionary War: Selected Essays*, ed. Don Higginbotham (Westport, Conn.: Greenwood Press, 1978), 83–103.

Higginbotham, Don: *The War of American Independence: Military Attitudes, Policies, and Practice, 1763–1789* (New York: Macmillan, 1971).

Royster, Charles: *A Revolutionary People at War: the Continental Army and American Character, 1775–1783* (Chapel Hill: University of North Carolina Press, 1979).

Shy, John: *A People Numerous and Armed: Reflections on the Military Struggle for American Independence* (New York: Oxford University Press, 1976).

Wright, Robert K.: *The Continental Army* (Washington, DC: Government Printing Office, 1983).

32

The War for Independence, after Saratoga

DON HIGGINBOTHAM

THE year 1778 brought home to Britain the new international character of the war (*see* Chapter 33, §3). The French Admiral the Comte d'Estaing appeared in American waters that summer and narrowly missed intercepting a convoy of British transports bound from Philadelphia to New York. The Frenchman suffered equally poor luck when a storm obliterated his favorable chances of defeating Admiral Howe off Narragansett Bay and sealing off the British garrison in Rhode Island. Even so, Britain had little to boast of after three years of campaigning. If she possessed Newport and New York City, she had evacuated Boston and Philadelphia, and later in 1778 she gave up Newport as well. For the next two and a half years Washington remained a short distance from New York City as the opposing sides watched each other and limited their activities to occasional raiding expeditions.

I. BRITAIN'S SOUTHERN STRATEGY

The war that began in New England and shifted in 1776 to the middle states now took on a southern complexion. Thus far unsuccessful in the North and short of manpower after France entered the fray, Britain adopted a southern strategy. The region below the Potomac had experienced little of the war since 1776, the year in which the British assault on Charles Town had been turned away and uprisings of loyalists in North Carolina and Cherokee in the back country had been crushed. Although the South had yet to be tested, Colonial Secretary Germain and his London colleagues believed reports that the region was overwhelmingly devoted to the Crown. That meant fewer troops would be needed than had been the case in the North. It also meant, to London planners, that royal regiments would not directly occupy every bit of territory gained from the rebels. Rather, they would "Americanize" the conflict: the loyalists would police and defend many areas, thus freeing the King's regulars for combat elsewhere.

In pushing the new strategy – pressed by loyalist exiles and royalist officials from the South – Germain ignored the advice of Sir William Howe, who, before returning to England, had warned the Colonial Secretary that it was hazardous to put great dependence on the King's friends anywhere in America. Nowhere were they so ubiquitous and dedicated that they could be counted on to hold districts previously overrun. Howe's concerns, of course, received scant attention at Whitehall, which likewise ignored the danger of dispersing Britain's military resources from New York to the Floridas, an arrangement that might well have encouraged the French Navy to return to American waters and cooperate with the rebels in picking off British bases.

But the southern plan seemed so simple and desirable that it was beguiling. Step by step the regulars–loyalists combination would roll up the lower South and then the upper South. Perhaps Britons believed so fervently in the southern strategy because they really had no alternative to winning the war after it had become an international conflict. Moreover, it was noted that the South was nearer the West Indies and therefore British forces in both theaters could coordinate their efforts. And certainly the South produced commodities of greater value to England's mercantile scheme of things than New England and the middle states. As one Briton put it, the war had "begun at the wrong end" of America.

2. THE CONQUEST OF GEORGIA AND SOUTH CAROLINA

Although the initial undertaking in the South resulted in the reduction of Georgia in the winter of 1778–9, the French naval danger reappeared in 1779 when d'Estaing and American forces laid siege to Savannah. But the admiral's concern over the approaching hurricane season led to a direct assault on the British positions, which resulted in heavy Franco-American losses, the sudden departure of d'Estaing, and an American withdrawal. Once again the British were lucky in their encounter with d'Estaing, and the French continued to be dogged by ill-fortune. The year 1779 had been curious in terms of implementing the new British strategy. Sir Henry Clinton, perhaps ambivalent about the southern approach and not entirely reconciled to giving up the idea of a climactic battle with Washington, had moved slowly to commit the preponderance of his resources to the South.

As Whitehall reiterated its wish to focus on the South, Clinton was at long last already moving. Soon after heavy reinforcements reached Georgia, Clinton, himself leading the advance, besieged Charles Town, South Carolina. The American commander, Benjamin Lincoln, a solid if unimaginative general, had initially bowed to the Carolinians' insistence that the city be defended; but later, fearing its destruction, they persuaded him to surrender his more than 5,500 men, presenting Clinton – on 12 May 1780 – with the biggest bag of American prisoners captured in the entire war. A second, hastily assembled American Southern Army under General Horatio Gates appeared in upper South Carolina in early August. Eschewing the prudence he had displayed against Burgoyne, Gates hastily advanced and stumbled upon a British column at Camden on 16 August. Gates's militia, holding one side of his main line, broke and fled, and Cornwallis soon swept the field.

With the stain of British conquest spread over Georgia and South Carolina, London officialdom predicted that North Carolina and Virginia would be back in the royal fold in short order. Yet late twentieth-century experience reminds us that pacification of the countryside is difficult. Guerrilla warfare often continues, and so it was in the American Revolution. Clinton, just after the fall of Charles Town and before his own return to New York, had issued a proclamation freeing prisoners of war from parole and restoring their full citizenship, *provided* they take an oath to the Crown and support British efforts to bring law and order to South Carolina. The proclamation was disastrous in two respects. First, it compelled former rebels, many of whom were now willing to sit out the war quietly, to take sides – to opt for outright loyalism or rebellion. Second, it was too tolerant for the hardline loyalists to accept. Bitter and hardened by their earlier misfortunes, furious with Clinton's leniency, loyalists so terrorized former Whigs that their behavior drove countless Carolinians and Georgians back into the field on the revolutionary side.

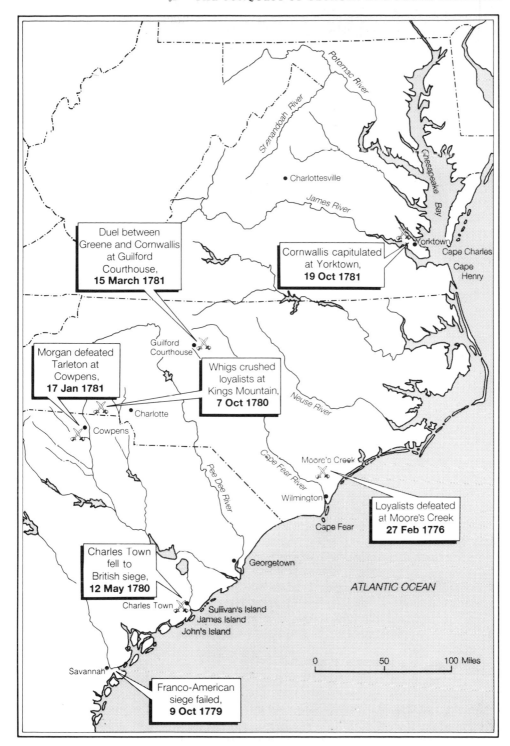

MAP 6 The Southern Campaigns

3. THE AMERICANS REGAIN LOST GROUND

If Clinton had helped exacerbate the problem of pacification, he did recognize that Lord Cornwallis, now in command in the South, should not launch a northward thrust before South Carolina was completely subdued. Cautious and methodical, Clinton was very different from the bold, aggressive Cornwallis, who wasted little time in launching an invasion of North Carolina. At Charlotte he learned of the destruction of his 1,000-man loyalist left wing, at the hands of far western frontiersmen, at Kings Mountain, just below the Carolinas' border. Even when successful, Cornwallis had trouble in grasping that the defeat of American armies did not mean American capitulation. For that matter, in a people's war Continental armies had a way of reappearing.

Still another small southern army entered South Carolina, commanded by General Nathanael Greene, Washington's ablest lieutenant and former quartermaster-general. The ex-Quaker from Rhode Island, a flexible, resourceful general, resolved to play the guerrilla role until he could augment his thin ranks. Dividing his army so that each division sat on the flanks of Cornwallis at Winnsboro, Greene took a position on the Pee Dee River, while General Daniel Morgan, with the other division, advanced southwestwards into the state, rallying guerrilla parties and checkmating the loyalists in his vicinity. When Cornwallis sent Banastre Tarleton's Tory Legion after Morgan, the Americans won a lopsided victory at the Cowpens on 17 January 1781. Tarleton lost more than 900 men as compared with Morgan's 72.

Now began a merry chase, with Cornwallis setting out after the retreating Morgan, and with Greene endeavoring to reunite with Morgan before Cornwallis overtook his subordinate. Linking up in central North Carolina, the Americans retired briefly into Virginia and then returned to challenge Cornwallis at Guilford Courthouse (near present-day Greensboro). Greene's reinforced army had a heavy numerical advantage; but Cornwallis had the veterans. The Briton also held the field, and Greene withdrew after inflicting heavy losses – more than 500 as against Greene's own 250. Cornwallis, his army no longer an effective fighting machine after Kings Mountain, Cowpens, and Guilford Courthouse, limped to Wilmington on the coast before proceeding to Virginia.

With Cornwallis's posts in South Carolina vulnerable, Greene returned to the Palmetto State. One by one the interior stations fell – until Lord Rawdon, the British commander there, pulled back his remaining units to the coast. Greene never won an open-field battle against either Cornwallis or Rawdon, but he outmaneuvered them and wore them to a frazzle. The war wound down to occasional raids and skirmishes as Greene's army kept Savannah and Charles Town under observation until the British evacuated those cities in 1782. A masterful strategist, Greene had made the most of his slender resources. He made the British play his game, ever on the move and never letting up to allow his adversaries to regroup. If guerrilla warfare was scarcely understood by professional soldiers in his day, he employed methods that have been the stock-in-trade of revolutionists in recent times.

Cornwallis, meanwhile, continued his meanderings in tidewater Virginia, his southern campaign having failed. He had not pacified the lower South before moving into North Carolina, and his efforts to Americanize the war had proved unsuccessful. Cornwallis, however, did have a curious theory about how to smother the flames of sedition in the lower South. In possession of North Carolina, he would then have the South Carolina guerrillas isolated and cut off from supply lines to the north. Then, failing in the Tarheel State, he claimed that he must overrun Virginia to complete the subjugation of North Carolina. Undoubtedly, he and other British leaders had exaggerated the strength of loyalism, but they had hardly given Americanization a meaningful test. As he had moved northwards, allegedly pacified areas erupted in brutal civil war between loyalists and Whigs. Such was the "bizarre chain of ideas and circumstances" that brought Cornwallis to Virginia, where he lacked a plan of operations and stood exposed to encirclement from land and sea on the tip of the Virginia peninsula.

4. THE BRITISH SURRENDER AT YORKTOWN

In the Old Dominion, Cornwallis had taken under his command British raiding parties led by the turncoat Benedict Arnold (who had gone over to the royal side in September 1780) and William Phillips. Following two months of indecisive campaigning, he retired to Yorktown on the coast and began erecting fortifications, all of which displeased his superior in New York, Sir Henry Clinton, who had never intended to make that state the center of operations in the South. If Cornwallis's thinking was muddled, Clinton erred in not explicitly ordering Cornwallis to get out of Virginia and to consolidate British gains in the lower South before undertaking new initiatives.

Just as Clinton realized that the Chesapeake region was vulnerable to French sea

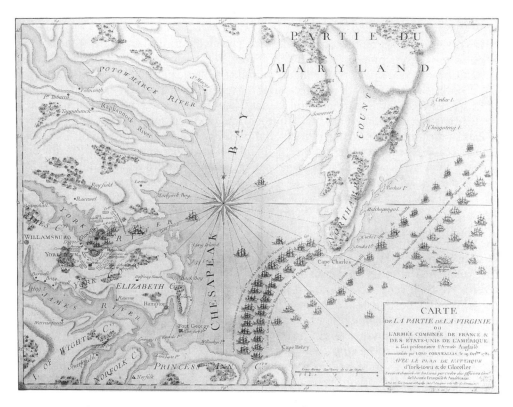

FIGURE 27 The Siege of Yorktown, 19 October 1781, showing naval action and the subsequent blockade of the bay by the French fleet

power, so too did the Franco-American allies find his Yorktown base an inviting target. There had been no major allied campaigning since d'Estaing's earlier failures; but since 1780 5,500 French troops under the Comte de Rochambeau had been stationed in Rhode Island, along with the Comte de Barras' French naval detachment at Newport. Washington, who had thought of Rochambeau's joining him in an attack on New York, proved that he was flexible and opportunistic when he received word that the French Admiral de Grasse was in the West Indies and crowding sail for Chesapeake Bay with 20 ships of the line and 3,000 soldiers. Washington and Rochambeau, on 17 August 1781, wrote to the admiral that they would hasten southwards to cooperate in snaring Cornwallis on the Virginia peninsula. As a small American force under La Fayette, operating in the Old Dominion, positioned itself to block Cornwallis's escape up the peninsula, de Grasse arrived in time to transport the regiments of Washington and La Fayette from Chesapeake Bay to the James River. With the appearance of de Barras' French squadron from Newport, the allies had completed a remarkable feat of coordination and synchronization, unprecedented in an era without modern, instantaneous means of communication (*see* figure 27).

Cornwallis's only hope now was the royal navy, which did not rise to the occasion, partly at least because the Cabinet in London had felt – after d'Estaing's setbacks – that any French naval push in support of the rebels could easily be scotched. Clinton in New York sent an outmanned naval expedition under Admiral Thomas Graves in a game effort to save Cornwallis. After a day of indecisive bombardments, Graves and de Grasse pulled apart, then jockeyed for position between 6 and 9 September, after which Graves returned to New York.

Cornwallis's time of reckoning was not far away as he drew his 8,000 men back to his entrenchments immediately before Yorktown. Although the allied force numbered 17,000, it was the artillery – a military arm that had grown increasingly significant in the eighteenth century – that hastened the British denouement. Nothing was spared as French gunners and General Henry Knox's American artillerymen pinpointed gun batteries, ships in the harbor, and troop encampments. On 17 October a British drummer and officer sounded the parley and waved a white flag. Two days later the articles of surrender were signed and British soldiers in new scarlet uniforms stacked their arms while their musicians appropriately played an old tune called *The World Turned Upside Down*.

5. THE EFFECTS OF WAR ON AMERICAN LIFE

The ultimate meaning of Yorktown for Britain was hardly transparent at the time to the Americans, who suffered from an acute case of war-weariness and internal discord after more than six years in arms. If the Crown's followers had their share of misery, so did the Revolutionists. There were massacres of civilians by loyalists and Indians in western New York, and there were destructive raids in Kentucky and other frontier areas, as well as along the coast. The fierce, partisan war in the southern back country took the lives of untold non-combatants on both sides. In the absence of men, in military service, women had to protect home and hearth; their letters displayed a growing knowledge of business and financial affairs, and men not infrequently responded by referring to "our farm" and no longer to "my farm." While the Revolution did not erase the differences between the work roles of men and women, these were certainly eroded.

The economy   The vicissitudes on the economic front seemed endless. Neither enlisted men nor officers turned a profit from their army duty. Both soldiers and civilians felt the pain of hardships stemming from mounting inflation and soaring prices. Such upward trends were probably inescapable in a country without a stable national currency and hardly any sizable manufactures. There was no alternative for Congress and the states but to emit vast quantities of paper currency, which, lacking specie backing, declined sharply in value. People on fixed salaries were particularly hard hit; for although wages increased they hardly kept pace with inflation. Planters and merchants not infrequently accused the other of exacerbating inflation. Although merchants may well have profited more than any other single component of the population, those engaged in privateering and importing military stores combined private gain with public service. Despite their complaints, some farmers may have benefited from inflation, since their obligations, taxes and debts did not necessarily increase at the rate of their produce. Some were successful – if not patriotic – in selling only a part of their crops to meet obligations and then held back the remainder in anticipation of still higher prices later.

In any case, the war profoundly disrupted the American domestic economy. The decline of external commerce, which had been the linchpin of the prewar economy, cut off patterns of exchange and weakened incentives normally motivating farmers and others to generate the surpluses so desperately needed by the Continental Army. Particularly harmful was the curtailment of trade with the West Indies and Southern Europe, which had brought to the colonies goods and occasionally cash. Some states appear to have suffered more than others. Connecticut, for example, bordered the early combat zones and for seven years felt the impact of Britain's occupation of New York City. Price inflation, currency devaluation, hoarding, and illicit commerce with the enemy in nearby New York all extracted their heavy toll on public morale, patriot loyalties, and governmental machinery. Despite the valiant efforts of state leaders, many citizens saw stringent taxation, price-fixing, and impressment as abridgements of privacy and personal liberty.

Civil–military relations   At the same time that home-front economic problems went from bad to worse, civil–military relations showed severe strains. That fact is hardly surprising given traditional Anglo-American reservations about standing armies and given the agonizingly protracted nature of the conflict. Throughout, Washington was expected to respect the home front, to be the servant of Congress, and to be sensitive to the concerns of state and local officialdom. These requirements placed on the army's conduct produced frustrations in the officer corps, as did the failures of Congress and the civilian sector to meet the Continentals' needs. Prominent generals such as Nathanael Greene and Charles Lee bluntly voiced their unhappiness, Lee excoriating the federal lawmakers for "having no military men in their body" and therefore "continually confounding themselves and everybody else in military matters."

In this tense atmosphere, punctuated by more battlefield defeats than victories and by stressful winter army encampments at Valley Forge and Morristown, dire rumors seemed permanently to threaten civil–military relations. There were widely circulated, albeit erroneous, reports towards the end of 1777 that Congress, displeased by Washington's twin setbacks at Brandywine and Germantown, would replace the commander-in-chief with Horatio Gates, the victor over Burgoyne. Washington himself believed that Generals Gates and Thomas Conway and a faction of congressmen sought his ouster. The episode, known as the Conway Cabal, amounted to little

315

if anything since Washington's detractors were few in number and unorganized. The truth was that Washington and his subordinates were overly sensitive owing to their military reverses, pitiable winter conditions, and unhappiness with Congress over pay and other benefits. Spring brought green foliage, new recruits, a healthier frame of mind at Valley Forge, and an end to the Conway Cabal.

Yet some Americans were uncomfortable with Washington, not because of either his successes or failures in battle but rather because he was praised excessively and sometimes in language reminiscent of kingship. John Adams fumed about the "stupid veneration" accorded the Virginian. The one attempt to encourage Washington to accept a crown took place some months after Yorktown when Colonel Lewis Nicola, an Irish-born Huguenot, wrote to the commander-in-chief to that effect. Washington, replying that Nicola's screed left him with "painful sensations," admitted that the army's legitimate needs had not always been met; but he sternly warned the colonel that he would work to obtain them only in what he called "a constitutional way."

The Newburgh Addresses and troop revolts   Small though the army was as the war wound down in 1782 and 1783, it nevertheless frightened some Americans as never before. The officers complained of their pay being in arrears, and they reminded Congress of its earlier promise in 1780 to award them half-pay for life as compensation for their extended services and sufferings. Rumors were rampant, including one that a segment of the army had lost faith in Washington for not having pressed harder for the military's demands. Discontent climaxed on 10 March 1783, at Washington's encampment at Newburgh, New York. There circulated that day the anonymous "Newburgh Addresses," penned by 24-year-old Major John Armstrong (*see also* Chapter 36, §2). Calling for a gathering of officers, they urged Washington's subordinates not "to be tame and unprovoked when injuries press down hard upon you."

The meaning of the addresses, especially the possibility of taking violent action, is subject to differing interpretations, as is the question of whether the leaders wished to include or exclude Washington from their subsequent measures of seeking relief. One view holds that the affair was "the only known instance of an attempted coup in American history." If so, it appears to have been almost completely limited to the younger officers. And it may well be that the whole affair was more an effort on the part of disgruntled public creditors and advocates of a stronger central government to use the army than it was any movement initiated within the military ranks. In any event, Washington himself seized the initiative, calling the officers together and persuading them to work through him and other legitimate channels to secure their just rewards. Washington was keenly aware that military tensions are inherent in free and open societies – for the precise reason that the military does not have a blank check in such societies – and he labored successfully to keep those tensions under control. He demonstrated that a professional army was not incompatible with civil liberty and constitutional government.

At the time, however, the army's fidelity to its civilian masters was not as clear as it is in retrospect, a statement that holds true for enlisted men as well as officers. While the congressmen also sought relief in 1783 for officers, in June that body faced a mutiny – the last of several – on the part of several hundred troops, who surrounded the Pennsylvania State House where Congress and the executive council of the state were in session. Boisterous from liquor, the soldiers demanded that their complaints be addressed at once. As the civilians inside steeled themselves and passed through the cordon of milling soldiers, the latter heaped verbal abuse upon the congressmen.

Word of the approach of loyal Continentals under General Robert Howe resulted in the mutineers' dispersing. Another crisis had been averted.

A professional army   Still, the overall record of the army, officers, and enlisted men is exceedingly impressive. In a war twice the length of the Civil War or World War II, it displayed staying power, the ability to survive. Its desertion rate, about 20 per cent, may seem high by present standards, but it was remarkably low compared with that of European armies of the day. It was never numerically more than a shadow of the more than 60,000 men that Congress had agreed to raise for the duration in 1776. Consequently, it had to resort to militia drafts, short-term enlistments, and, in time, to the bottom of the barrel of human resources. British deserters and prisoners of war found their way into the Continental ranks, as did men in bondage, both white indentured servants and Blacks. By 1778 the army was heavily sprinkled with slaves and free Negroes. The ideals of the Revolution, combined with the service of Blacks in the cause of freedom, brought a profound change in the legal status of Negroes above the Mason–Dixon line. If the Revolution failed to produce any significant alteration in the status of women in America, females nonetheless played a role with the Continental Army, not only in gathering clothing and other necessities but also by their presence in the camps. They performed valuable domestic duties, and some of them shouldered arms. Without the distaff side, admitted Washington, some of the best soldiers would have deserted.

This was the heterogeneous army that became an object of concern for British commanders, a source of intimidation for the loyalists, a rallying point for the militia, and a living, day-to-day symbol of the Revolution and of emerging American nationality. A scavenger for soldiers and supplies, Washington faced the additional challenge of wiring it together, making it fight and occasionally win – all without unduly antagonizing civilians and public officials. Yet he prevailed over these internal obstacles and the British foe alike.

6. BRITAIN'S DECISION TO END THE OFFENSIVE

Britain, to be sure, did not suffer total military defeat. Even after Yorktown, she held New York, Savannah, and Charles Town, and the King's Indian friends remained troublesome on the frontiers. Although George Rogers Clark had several years earlier launched a spectacular campaign in the Illinois country highlighted by the capture of Vincennes, and though General John Sullivan razed the homelands of the Iroquois in western New York, the tribesmen were sheltered and resupplied at Detroit and Niagara. Indeed, the international war seemed to be going in Britain's favor. In 1782 she struck back sharply at France and her ally Spain, which had entered the war in 1779. In April, Admiral George Rodney defeated Admiral de Grasse in the West Indies. Almost simultaneously in India, the French under the Balli de Suffren were repulsed by Admiral Sir William Hughes. Nor did the Bourbons fare better at Gibraltar, where Lord Howe's fleet and General George Eliot's determined resistance saved that rocky eminence for England.

British military resurgence, however, did not translate into a fresh burst of enthusiasm at home for continuing the conflict. The administration's majorities had steadily declined until a motion to renounce all attempts to regain America passed the House of Commons. North and Germain resigned their posts and the King formed a new government drawn largely from the opposition forces of the Marquis of Rockingham and the Earl of Shelburne, both of whom were committed to peace. To have continued the struggle against both the Bourbons and America could have meant imposing heavy taxes, regimenting the economy, and drawing productive citizens into the army and navy. Very few, least of all the King and his ministers, were willing to pay that price. They would not risk derailing their mercantile economy, nor would they chance arming citizens who might in turn demand a greater part in the political system in exchange for their service. No European monarchy in the period before the French Revolution would take that gamble.

Still, the failure to regain America was painful for both material and psychological reasons. Britain, like America in the 1960s, with its Vietnam involvement, suffered from a superpower mentality. For the leaders of a country that could boast of such a long winning tradition against its continental opponents, to accept military and naval failures and the possibility of anything short of total victory was extremely difficult. Moreover, there is another applicable Vietnam analogy: the North cabinet, as was true of the Lyndon Johnson administration nearly two centuries later, persisted in prosecuting a war as long as it did because of a foolish belief in the domino theory – for Britain this meant that the loss of the mainland colonies would lead to secessionist movements in Ireland, the West Indies, and elsewhere and to the collapse of its hegemony in international trade; for the Johnson team, it meant the fall to communism, one by one, of most Southeast Asian states.

7. THE CONSEQUENCES OF AMERICAN INDEPENDENCE

Britain   What were the consequences of the War of Independence for Europe and for the United States? Britain, notwithstanding the loss of America, remained supreme in the colonial and maritime field. Already she had begun to lay the basis for a "Second British Empire," whose vital center was the great subcontinent of India, and which led to new fields of commerce in the Pacific and the South China seas. And American trade soon fell back into its prewar channels with Britain, the most industrial nation of the time. Shelburne's generosity to the Crown's rebellious American subjects in the 1783 Treaty of Paris was owing in part to his desire to pry America away from France and to pull the colonies back into the imperial orbit. But for a variety of reasons, including the collapse of Shelburne's ministry and Britain's unwillingness to adopt American free trade ideas, Anglo-American relations did not show dramatic improvement for more than a century.

France   France in the long run gained little at Britain's expense. America was a restless satellite, scarcely willing to remain unequivocally in the diplomatic constellation of Versailles. Since the French alliance had been a marriage of convenience, America soon returned to a unilateral approach to foreign relations more in harmony with her world outlook.

In fact, the colonists might well have kept Britain from restoring royal control throughout America even without direct French military intervention. Once again America's late twentieth-century experience in Vietnam reminds us of the difficulties of waging distant wars against a mass insurgent movement. One view goes so far as to assert that France's entry into the conflict probably discredited moderates and appeasers in Parliament, saving the North ministry from collapse after Burgoyne's disaster and steeling the kingdom to fight with an infusion of new vigor.

What then was crucial about the French alliance? Simply put, it brought the war to an end before America unraveled; the country was showing signs of approaching such a condition with the collapse of the economy and the restlessness of the army. Without international pressures, Britain might have held on to several major cities and their environs, making American independence hardly meaningful, and leaving unresolved the ownership of the trans-Appalachian West, which, to the amazement of European diplomats, Britain ceded to America in 1783. Finally, an endless struggle – neither side capable of winning outright – might have wrenched the Revolution to the left, generating the guerrilla war American leaders had thus far avoided (except in the lower South) in order to preserve the fabric of American political and cultural life.

While the Revolutionists never turned to bush fighting as their principal means of resistance, some European officers were fascinated by certain unorthodox features of the war, especially in the South but at times elsewhere too, such as in the Burgoyne campaign, where partisan forces cooperated with the Continental Army in cutting off Burgoyne's communications and in sealing off his retreat. But any tactical lessons were learned mostly from small-unit engagements and woodland fighting, not from the major battles of the Continental Army, which usually dueled its British counterparts in the European manner. Because European *chasseurs* and *Jägers* were not unlike American guerrillas in some respects, as were partisan fighters in the Low Countries and the Balkans, American practices lent weight to evolving trends instead of creating new ones. By employing productive citizens (along with the lower echelons of humanity, of course), Americans did reject the concept of the soldier as necessarily set apart from his own countrymen, a creature without his stake in society. This use of the citizen as soldier did fire the European imagination, especially since it conformed to Enlightenment principles on the "natural" way to wage war. Here then was a political ideal as well: confidence in the individual as a trustworthy citizen. And it was chiefly in the political arena – not that of military strategy or tactics – that the American Revolution influenced the French Revolution; but the War of Independence also helped to precipitate the upheaval in the Bourbon monarchy, beginning in 1789, because of the huge debt France incurred in aiding the United States a short time earlier.

America   As for America, it required an extended period of peace in which to recover and complete its unfinished business, which meant getting the nation solidly on its feet. It needed to disband the army, deal with the public debt, organize the western lands, and grapple with the Articles of Confederation. Many felt that this first constitution of the nation, ratified in 1781, was inadequate without amendments or even more extensive alteration to meet the internal and external requirements of the United States.

Some of those needs would take years to resolve; but not the departure of the army, which melted back into civilian life from which it had come. There was real poignancy in Washington's farewells to the officers of the army and to Congress. The commander-in-chief met with his subordinates for a final time at Fraunces Tavern in New York City. After calling each man present to come forward – and "take my hand" – he was off to Annapolis, Maryland, where Congress was in session and where once again emotions surfaced. As he phrased it, he bade "an Affectionate farewell to this August body ... and take my leave of all the employments of public life."

Washington and certain other military men, as well as numerous congressmen and diplomats, emerged from the war as nationalists, and they worked for a stronger union, their efforts bringing the culmination of the Revolution in the writing and ratification of the Federal Constitution in 1787–8. That document also embraced the twin military traditions of the Revolution: it provided for a professional army and navy – *in time of peace* as well as in time of war – without constitutional limits on the size and length of service of those forces; and it recognized the continued role of state militias; but the latter, now for the first time, would in certain instances be subject to federal control. The nationalists' military plan had been enunciated as early as 1783 in Washington's "Sentiments on a Peace Establishment," an essay drafted at the request of Congress. Much of it was implemented in the 1790s, providing military institutions that survived with little change down to the beginning of the twentieth century. Such military power would never have been written into the new national parchment had Washington's Continental Army threatened the liberties of his countrymen. From the time that it took its modern form in late seventeenth-century England, the concept of civil control of the military had never been severely tested by the pressures of a divisive war that strained Britain to the breaking point. It was in America rather than in the mother country that such a test first took place, between 1775 and 1783.

FURTHER READING

Higginbotham, Don: *George Washington and the American Military Tradition* (Athens: University of Georgia Press, 1985).

Kohn, Richard H.: *Eagle and Sword: the Federalists and the Creation of the Military Establishment in America, 1783–1802* (New York: Free Press, 1975).

Mackesy, Piers: *The War for America, 1775–1783* (Cambridge, Mass.: Harvard University Press, 1964).

Royster, Charles: *Light-Horse Harry Lee and the Legacy of the American Revolution* (New York: Alfred A. Knopf, 1981).

Willcox, William B.: *Portrait of a General: Sir Henry Clinton in the War of Independence* (New York: Alfred A. Knopf, 1964).

33

Diplomacy of the Revolution, to 1783

JONATHAN R. DULL

T HE American Revolution was the first successful colonial war of independence. This unprecedented success was achieved against one of the greatest powers of Europe, a nation which indeed could claim to be the greatest naval and financial power in the world. It was not accomplished, however, by American efforts alone. The United States received the direct or indirect assistance of a number of European states which found it to their advantage to weaken Great Britain's position in the European balance of power or to procure territorial or commercial benefits at Britain's expense. The American Revolution thus had a diplomatic impact throughout Europe, an impact much more immediate than the gradual spread of its example to the other nations of the world.

The American Revolution posed in itself a question of diplomacy: were the American colonies an inseparable part of the British Empire or were they free to combine into an independent state with its own foreign policy? For Americans who came to believe the latter, the central diplomatic issue was that of procuring British recognition of their independence. This issue did not arise, however, until many months after the Battles of Lexington and Concord. The task of the Second Continental Congress, which convened only weeks after those battles, initially differed little from that of the First Continental Congress of 1774. That task was to secure from the British Crown redress of American grievances. Like its predecessor, this Congress followed the traditional method of petitioning the Crown, but it also coordinated the successful military blockade of Boston. The British Government offered an uncompromising answer to the Olive Branch Petition and to the news of the Battle of Bunker Hill. It declared America to be in rebellion, warned the other states of Europe not to intervene, and began to assemble an army large enough to crush the insurrection.

I. THE PERIOD OF LIMITED FRENCH AID

In November 1775 Congress learned that the Olive Branch Petition had been ignored and that Britain was planning to expand its military efforts. Its reaction was cautious and measured. It rejected a proposal to send an ambassador to France, instead establishing a committee of secret correspondence to communicate with America's friends "in Great Britain, Ireland, and other parts of the world." Other parts of the world, however, had already taken steps to communicate with America. A few weeks after its establishment the committee met secretly in Philadelphia with a foreign visitor, a young French nobleman named Julian-Alexandre Achard de Bonvouloir. He had been sent to America by the French Ambassador to Great Britain. Speaking "unofficially" for the French Government, Bonvouloir told the five committeemen that France had no designs on Canada, that she wished the Americans well, and that she would permit them to use her ports. In reply, the Americans asked for further assurances of French goodwill, in particular the use of two military engineers and the right to exchange in French ports American raw materials (such as tobacco) for war materiel.

It was thus the need for supplies of war, particularly gunpowder, which stimulated America's first contact with France. Already that need had produced an extensive private smuggling network reaching from France and the Netherlands to the American coast via the Dutch Caribbean island of St. Eustatius. This smuggling network was insufficient for the needs of the American Continental Army, however, and in March 1776 Congress decided to send a purchasing agent to France, a former congressional delegate from Connecticut named Silas Deane.

Bonvouloir's mission produced even more dramatic results in France. His report of the meetings with the Committee of Secret Correspondence provoked a major foreign policy debate within King Louis XVI's chief advisory body, the *conseil d'état*. The French Controller General (finance minister), Anne-Robert-Jacques Turgot, was reluctant to see France become involved in the American rebellion. He argued that the French monarchy's most urgent needs were those of reforming its budget and reducing its debts. He believed, moreover, that France would benefit from a British victory over the rebels, which would leave Britain to bear the expenses of a continued military occupation of America. The French foreign minister, Charles Gravier, Comte de Vergennes, argued, however, that the British economy and the British Navy were dependent on Britain's maintaining her monopoly of American trade and that hence the French Government should subsidize the American rebellion. Vergennes, whose central interest was not colonies but France's position in European affairs, believed that weakening Britain would improve France's own position in the European balance of power and increase her long-term security. In early May 1776 the King decided in favor of Vergennes and soon thereafter forced Turgot from the *conseil*. Providing a direct subsidy was too dangerous, so the French Government devised a stratagem to funnel military supplies to America. It loaned 1,000,000 *livres tournois* (about £40,000) to a trading company, which would purchase arms at reduced prices from government arsenals. The company would then sell the arms to the Americans on credit and would eventually be repaid in American tobacco. To head the company Vergennes chose a former secret agent of King Louis XV, the playwright PIERRE-AUGUSTIN CARON DE BEAUMARCHAIS. Beaumarchais named the new company Roderigue Hortalez & Co. France furthermore persuaded Spain, which was anxious to see Britain's troubles prolonged, to provide matching funds.

France's commitment to the American cause was less than absolute. The astute Vergennes may have realized that providing arms to the Americans was likely to lead eventually to war with Britain, but he was too prudent to alarm the naive young King Louis XVI, who was still concerned with domestic reforms and far from ready to contemplate a war. At the moment the question of hostilities was still academic. The French Navy would need almost two years to refill its arsenals and repair its ships before it could think of going to war. Vergennes left the question of finding funds for naval rearmament to his ally in the *conseil d'état* Naval Minister Antoine-Raymond-Gualbert-Gabriel de Sartine. It was Sartine's success in maneuvering the King into giving these funds which, as much as the activities of Roderigue Hortalez & Co., began France on the way to war.

The French policy of limiting her aid had the further advantage that it would

FIGURE 28 Benjamin Franklin, as American ambassador to the French Court, being fêted by Parisian society; Louis XVI and Marie Antoinette look on as a wreath of laurels is placed on his head (detail from engraving by W. O. Geller, *c.* 1830, after a painting by Baron Jolly).

prolong the American rebellion without alarming American public opinion, which was still mistrustful of Catholic states in general and France in particular. News of King Louis XVI's decision reached Congress about 15 September 1776, the date the British captured the city of New York. The military situation was so threatening it is hardly surprising Congress reacted enthusiastically to the promise of French assistance. It decided to establish a diplomatic mission at the French court and then elected three commissioners to fill it: Silas Deane, the purchasing agent already in Paris, Arthur Lee, a former colonial agent who was presently the London agent of the Committee of Secret Correspondence, and Benjamin Franklin, who was, with the possible exception of George Washington, America's best-known public figure. Franklin, a congressional delegate from Pennsylvania and member of the Committee of Secret Correspondence, had already undertaken two futile diplomatic missions on behalf of Congress. The first had been to Montreal during the last weeks of the American occupation; he was thus a witness to the first failure of American foreign policy, that of winning Canadian support for the Revolution. Secondly, on 11 September he and two colleagues met unsuccessfully with Admiral RICHARD HOWE, British naval commander and peace commissioner, who had hoped to arrange a reconciliation but lacked the power (and inclination) to recognize American independence. Franklin's election as commissioner to the French court proved vital to establishing the credibility of the American mission (*see* figure 28).

Franklin soon sailed to France, where in late December he joined his colleagues. Initially they were authorized to offer nothing more than American trade in exchange for France's signing a commercial treaty which would surely provoke Britain to war. As a result of the near collapse of Washington's army in December 1776 Congress amended the commissioners' instructions, permitting them to discuss with France joint military planning. It did not matter, however, since France was still unprepared for war and Vergennes dared not meet openly with the commissioners. He entrusted discussions with them to his under-secretary (*premier commis*) Conrad-Alexandre Gérard. Although Hortalez & Co. continued its vital shipments of war supplies, the commissioners were restricted to waiting for the French Government to recognize their existence. Their contacts with Gérard and Vergennes were often tense, particularly because of the use of French ports by American privateers, which threatened to provoke a premature war with Britain. Because the American mission was full of British spies (e.g., the commissioners' unofficial secretary Edward Bancroft), the French Government could not tell the commissioners about the French Navy's continued unreadiness for war. In the late summer of 1777 British threats forced the French to expel a squadron of American warships, leading to considerable bitterness. The British threats were probably hollow; determined to end the American rebellion quickly, the British Government stopped short of treating the French provocations as a cause of war.

2. THE TREATIES OF ALLIANCE AND OF AMITY AND COMMERCE

In spite of their frustrations, the commissioners wisely refrained from issuing ultimatums to the French Government. Their patience was rewarded on 4 December 1777 when a messenger from America brought news of Burgoyne's surrender at Saratoga. For Vergennes the timing of the news was opportune. French naval rearmament was finally almost complete and he had already begun to press the Spaniards about jointly intervening directly in the war. The news of Saratoga provided an argument he could use with both Spain and King Louis XVI (who was still reluctant about hostilities): unless the Americans were promised military assistance they might make a compromise peace with Britain and attack the French and Spanish West Indies. It is impossible to know with any certainty how genuine were Vergennes' fears, but on their face they seem illogical; why should the Americans abandon their claims to independence after just winning a major victory? The British Government, however, unwittingly bolstered Vergennes' arguments by sending a secret agent to meet with the commissioners. Nevertheless Vergennes' arguments failed to convince the astute Spanish Foreign Minister, José de Moñino y Redondo, conde de Floridablanca. Spain was happy to prolong Britain's difficulties – the governor of Spanish Louisiana, Bernardo de Gálvez, was particularly helpful in providing gunpowder to the Americans – but Spain had no interest in American independence. Floridablanca postponed any decision, however, until the treasure fleet from Mexico reached Spain. Vergennes was more successful in overcoming the scruples of King Louis XVI. News that the treasure fleet had been delayed at Havana meant there was little reason to postpone negotiations with the American commissioners. Vergennes feared that the Americans might balk at signing a treaty of military alliance as well as a commercial treaty, but the commissioners' only major objection was that the proposed treaty of alliance would not take effect until the start of hostilities. (The French wished this so they could choose when and where to commence war with Britain.) Once American suspicions on this point had been removed the negotiations went quickly. The treaties, both of them drafted by France, were signed on 6 February 1778. The Treaty of Amity and Commerce was exceptionally generous so as to win American support for the alliance. It gave the Americans most-favored-nation status and generally avoided extracting commercial advantages for France. The Treaty of Alliance was also highly beneficial to the United States. France rejected any claim to Canada (although not to the vitally important Newfoundland fishery), promised not to make peace until Britain recognized American independence, and guaranteed in perpetuity American "liberty, sovereignty and independence." Each party to the alliance guaranteed whatever territories might be conquered during the war by the other. A secret addendum to the treaty invited Spain to join the alliance. The terms of the treaties reflected the European-centered nature of France's war aims; Vergennes wished, above all, not for colonies or even trade, but rather to weaken Britain.

Copies of the treaties were sent to Philadelphia, where Congress immediately ratified them (4 May 1778). Two clauses in the commercial treaty dealing with export duties, which had been left to Congress's discretion, were deleted. The chief questions now facing France were those of breaking relations with Britain and of beginning hostilities. A few weeks of further discussion with Spain convinced Vergennes there was little point in delay. The British Government knew from its secret service of the existence of the treaties, but chose to ignore them. The French Government forced its hand by announcing on 13 March the Treaty of Amity and Commerce (although not the Treaty of Alliance). Britain had no choice but to recall its ambassador to the French court. France reciprocated and then publicly recognized the commissioners as diplomatic representatives of the United States and began openly preparing for war.

Britain now modified its campaign plans for the coming year by ordering the evacuation of Philadelphia, the concentration of British forces in New York, and the sending of a large detachment to attack the strategically important French Caribbean island of St. Lucia. All this, however, would require considerable time. France's plans called for seizing the initiative and exploiting the advantage of surprise. A dozen ships of the line (the large warships that were the primary basis of naval strength) would be sent from the Mediterranean naval base of Toulon directly to America in hopes of capturing New York and thereby ending the war in a single stroke. The French hoped that the British, fearing the squadron might be *en route* to the English Channel to support an invasion of Britain, would not be able to reinforce New York in time. The French squadron sailed from Toulon on 13 April. Aboard Admiral d'Estaing's flagship *Languedoc* was Gérard, who had been selected as France's first minister plenipotentiary to the United States. He was accompanied by Deane, recalled by Congress for his excessive generosity in distributing in France commissions in the Continental Army.

3. THE BEGINNING AND EXPANSION OF HOSTILITIES

D'Estaing had been ordered to commence hostilities when he arrived in America. For diplomatic reasons, however, France hoped hostilities would begin in Europe. It was important to her for Britain to appear the aggressor. War was soon expected in Central Europe between France's nominal ally Austria and the other great German power, Prussia. Austria had provoked the confrontation by bribing the new ruler of Bavaria into ceding considerable territory to her. Vergennes did not wish France to become involved in the dispute, particularly in support of Austria. The Austro-French treaty of alliance was defensive in nature; if either nation was attacked she could call on the other for assistance. If France could claim she was attacked by Britain she could call for Austrian assistance; if, as expected, Austria refused, France would have an excuse to remain neutral in the Austro-Prussian dispute. (This strategy worked; the subsequent Austro-Prussian war lasted only a few months before Russian threats to intervene on Prussia's behalf forced Austria to return most of her newly acquired territory.) Britain on her part wished to appear the victim of French intervention so she could call for help on the Netherlands under terms of *their* defensive alliance. Hostilities commenced on 17 June in a manner sufficiently ambiguous for both combatants to claim to be victims (and for both Austria and the Netherlands to evade any obligations): a French frigate encountered the British home fleet, became involved in a dispute over protocol, and ended by fighting a British counterpart for a number of hours. Both countries reacted to the incident by authorizing reprisals against the other's shipping; neither issued a formal declaration of war. Six weeks later a major fleet battle off the French coast ended any doubts the two countries had gone to war.

At approximately the same time, d'Estaing was vainly attempting to break through Admiral Howe's defensive line off New York. D'Estaing's failure to win a decisive victory changed the diplomatic and military situation. During the 1778 campaign Britain, still awaiting sailors from incoming overseas convoys, had been unable fully to man her fleet. By the opening of the 1779 campaigning season, however, the French Navy could expect to be outnumbered by about 90 ships of the line to 65. Its only hope of survival, let alone victory, lay with the 50 ships of the line of the Spanish Navy. Britain could purchase Spanish neutrality by offering her Gibraltar, but refused to do so, believing she could defeat both navies combined. France did not have the luxury of bargaining and had to offer whatever price Spain demanded for her participation in the war. The price was high. France had to agree to a risky joint invasion attempt on England itself, which Spain wished in order to end the war quickly and protect the Spanish colonial empire. France also had to promise to continue the war until Spain acquired Gibraltar and to help Spain achieve as many as possible of her other territorial objectives, such as the reconquest of Florida and the Mediterranean island of Minorca. Floridablanca delayed making an agreement until he was certain Britain would not meet his demand for Gibraltar, but it was finally signed at the Spanish palace of Aranjuez on 12 April 1779.

The entrance of Spain into the war (although not into a formal alliance with the United States) completed the transformation of the war into a European conflict; already the main theater of Western Hemisphere naval operations had shifted to the Caribbean. The agreement to continue the war until Spain acquired Gibraltar may not have been compatible with the Franco-American alliance's emphasis on American independence, but the disparity of naval resources left France no alternative. The issue of Gibraltar might bedevil any future peace negotiations, but France took immediate steps to forestall the United States further complicating matters. Through Gérard, Vergennes asked Congress to define its peace objectives. Vergennes had no interest in America beyond seeing her achieve her commercial and political independence, so he instructed Gérard to help moderate the congressional demands. His lobbying was partially successful; Congress insisted on the Mississippi as a western border (although Florida would be left to Spain to reconquer), but the delegates of New England were foiled from demanding a share of the Newfoundland fishery as a peace ultimatum.

Congress was also badly divided by news of dissension among its diplomatic representatives – charges by Arthur Lee against former commissioner Deane and a bitter dispute between Lee and Franklin, which the newly arrived commissioner John Adams (who replaced Deane) vainly attempted to mediate. Gérard's arrival in America caused the dissolution of the unwieldy American diplomatic arrangements in France. Protocol dictated that the United States accredit a minister plenipotentiary to the French court. Congress would also need to elect a peace commissioner for the time Britain was ready to begin negotiations. Furthermore Congress wished to send a diplomatic representative to Spain. The election of these representatives added to congressional bickering but a compromise was reached among the various political factions by which Franklin was elected as minister to France, Adams as peace commissioner, and President of Congress John Jay as minister to Spain.

Gérard's influence in Congress was less the product of his political skill than of America's growing dependence on France. (Gérard, who resigned his position for reasons of health at the end of the year, was actually less adept than was his successor, Anne-César, chevalier de la Luzerne.) This dependence was manifested by George Washington; in 1778 he had opposed asking French help in capturing Canada, but by late 1779, with the British having opened a new front in Georgia and South Carolina, he was willing to encourage the French to send an expeditionary force to the United States. Washington's message was conveyed to Vergennes by the general's former aide, the Marquis de La Fayette, who presently was serving with the French Army.

4. THE DECISIVE BRITISH DEFEAT IN NORTH AMERICA

Washington's change of attitude was welcome at the French court. As Vergennes had feared, the attempted invasion of England proved to be a fiasco. At the end of 1779 France convinced Spain the allies should shift their strategy. By using their superiority in ships and troops against all the points held by the overextended British they might wear them down until there was the opportunity for a decisive victory. The idea of an expeditionary force in North America fitted well with this strategy and King Louis XVI quickly approved the plan. On 2 May 1780 a force of 6,500 men under command of JEAN-BAPTISTE-DONATIEN DE VIMEUR, Comte de Rochambeau, sailed from France for Newport, Rhode Island. Rochambeau's army reached America safely. The British also failed to intercept critically important French and Spanish reinforcements for the West Indies. The British Navy had won a victory off Gibraltar in January 1779 which almost forced Spain out of the war, but it was unable to follow up the victory. The troops which reached America and the West Indies in 1780 were those which would win the decisive victories of 1781.

The major diplomatic development of 1780 occurred in Northern Europe. Since the beginning of the Revolution Britain had attempted to deprive America of war supplies by intercepting neutral shipping carrying them. In 1778 she also began intercepting supplies bound for France. She thereby became embroiled with Dutch and other neutral shippers, who considered naval materiel such as timber and masts to be legitimate cargo. On 28 February 1780 Empress Catherine II of Russia announced the formation of a League of Armed Neutrality to protect the rights of such neutral shippers. Her action stunned the British, who considered themselves particular friends of Russia and who had hoped for Catherine's support. During 1780 other neutrals such as Denmark and Sweden joined the League while Britain watched helplessly. Britain was not prepared, however, to see the Netherlands, the most important neutral shipper, also join. To preclude this, Britain on 20 December 1780 opened hostilities on them (thereby negating their eligibility). In so doing they added another 15 ships of the line to their enemies and opened the North Sea as another theater of operations for the overcommitted British Navy.

By the beginning of 1781 even the few ships of the Dutch Navy were critical because all the other combatants were strained to their limits. Spain had already almost dropped out of the war; without the Spanish Navy to put pressure on Gibraltar and to help threaten another invasion attempt on England, the British could detach enough ships from Europe to gain an overwhelming superiority in the Western Hemisphere. The American Navy was negligible – its only ship of the line was still under construction – but the Continental Army was vital to pinning down the British in New York and newly captured South Carolina. By now the Americans, their currency virtually worthless, were completely dependent on French financial help. Congress consequently became totally acquiescent to French wishes. John Adams, who had returned to France to await the summons to a peace conference, alienated Vergennes by his rudeness and ignorance of diplomatic protocol. At France's request Congress replaced him as peace negotiator by a five-member peace commission consisting of Adams, Franklin, Jay, the former President of Congress Henry Laurens, and Thomas Jefferson. It even instructed the peace commission to accept the advice of King Louis XVI when negotiations finally began. France was in as nearly desperate a condition. Money was available for the 1781 campaign, but should it fail Vergennes admitted he might have to reconsider his commitment to American independence, possibly through accepting Russian mediation.

Luckily for the United States it was the British who broke first. Britain failed to provide enough ships of the line for North America and the Comte de Grasse (commanding a French fleet which arrived from the West Indies), Rochambeau, and Washington trapped at Yorktown Britain's only remaining mobile striking force. Cornwallis's surrender on 17 October 1781 was only one in a string of British defeats from mid-1781 to early 1782 – the Spaniards captured West Florida and Minorca, de Grasse the Caribbean islands of Tobago, St. Christopher, and St. Eustatius – but it was the one which delivered a fatal blow to the government of Lord North and to Parliament's determination to suppress the American rebellion.

5. THE PEACE NEGOTIATIONS

Parliament's 27 February 1782 decision to end offensive war against the Americans doomed the existing government and on 20 March North resigned. He was succeeded by Charles Watson-Wentworth, Marquis of Rockingham. Rockingham's Colonial Secretary, William Petty, Earl of Shelburne, moved immediately to open negotiations with his old acquaintance Franklin, using as his agent an elderly Scottish merchant, Richard Oswald. Negotiations with France, however, were the responsibility of Rockingham's Foreign Secretary, Charles James Fox. Fox selected his own agent to meet with Vergennes, a young nobleman, Thomas Grenville. By early May both Grenville and Oswald had begun their negotiations in Paris.

By then the military situation was shifting. Freed from defending exposed outposts such as Minorca and Yorktown, the British Navy began a resurgence. Now it was the French Navy and its allies that were overextended, as was shown by the defeat and capture of de Grasse on 12 April 1782, while beginning an operation against Jamaica. This defeat at the Battle of the Saintes and other failures undermined Vergennes' confidence in the French Navy. France, moreover, was approaching the limits of its ability to borrow money and a major diplomatic crisis was developing in Eastern Europe (where a dispute over the Crimean peninsula seemed likely to lead to a general war between the Russians and the Turks). These factors made Vergennes anxious to conclude peace.

The British Government, however, was ill-prepared to exploit France's difficulties. Because of the divisions within the Rockingham Cabinet, Britain herself was vulnerable to the United States. Fox wished to take control of all the peace negotiations, hoping by the offer of independence to detach the Americans from the French alliance. Then Britain could, if she chose, crush France, Spain, and the Netherlands, extracting from them compensation for her loss of America. Shelburne's approach was totally different. He was reluctant to offer the Americans independence and hoped for some form of federal union with the former colonists; he did not share Fox's Francophobia and wished a general peace with all Britain's opponents. These differences presented enormous leverage to Franklin, temporarily the sole American negotiator. (Jay joined him in Paris on 22 June but fell ill from influenza, Adams was at The Hague negotiating a Dutch–American commercial treaty, Laurens was a prisoner in London, and Jefferson was still in the United States.) He could have chosen to deal with Grenville, but instead wisely chose to continue discussions with Oswald. Fox had overreached himself and on 30 June was repudiated by the rest of the Cabinet. By coincidence Rockingham died the next day and was succeeded as First Lord of the Treasury (and *de facto* Prime Minister) by Shelburne.

The peace negotiations now entered a new phase. Shelburne, like Vergennes, sincerely wished peace, but time was against him. The British military position was strengthening, Shelburne's support in Parliament was unreliable, and the King (and British public opinion) was wavering between wishing peace and wishing revenge on France and her European allies. Ironically Shelburne soon adapted Fox's negotiating strategy for his own purposes. He moved to divide his enemies by conceding the demands of the patient Franklin. The Americans could have not only British recognition of their independence, but also the territorial boundaries they wished (except for Canada). The threat of a separate American agreement could then be used to force a general peace, since such an agreement would free the garrisons of New York and Charles Town to attack the West Indies. First, however, the stalled negotiations with France must also be revived. Soon after the offer to Franklin, Shelburne sent word to Vergennes that he was ready to offer generous terms to all Britain's enemies. He used de Grasse, an honored prisoner of war, to carry the message.

Vergennes doubted Shelburne's sincerity, but decided to send a representative to England to sound him out. His under-secretary Joseph-Mathias Gérard de Rayneval (brother of Conrad-Alexandre Gérard) held a series of meetings in mid-September at Bowood, Shelburne's country estate. Shelburne repudiated the extravagant offers conveyed by de Grasse, but nevertheless managed to convince Rayneval that Britain was not only willing to make a reasonable peace with France, but would also help contain the Russian threat in Eastern Europe.

The mission to Bowood saved the Anglo-French negotiations; it also indirectly resolved a serious problem that had arisen in the American negotiations. John Jay, now recovered from his influenza, had joined Franklin and then, when his older colleague was stricken with a kidney stone, had taken over the negotiations. Jay distrusted Shelburne as much as did Vergennes, and hence demanded a confirmation of his intention to recognize American independence. For seven weeks the negotiations were stalled by a dispute over the wording of Oswald's commission to deal with the United States.

During these weeks the British crushed a Spanish attack on Gibraltar, thereby increasing the bellicosity of the British public and reducing Shelburne's freedom to make diplomatic concessions. Jay, however, was suspicious of Vergennes as well. When the American commissioner learned of Rayneval's mission to England he feared Britain and France were preparing their own settlement at the expense of the United States. He quickly accepted a compromise on the wording of Oswald's commission.

In October detailed discussions began in Paris on the substantive issues still separating Britain and the United States: the boundary between the United States and Canada, compensation for American loyalists who had lost their property, and the extent of American rights off Newfoundland and the other fisheries. During the discussions Jay was gradually joined by Franklin, Adams, and finally Laurens.

European negotiations meanwhile were proceeding in Paris among Alleyne Fitzherbert (Grenville's replacement), Vergennes, and Pedro Pablo Abarca de Bolea, conde de Aranda, the Spanish Ambassador to the court of France. France had agreed to surrender most of her conquests in order to speed the peace, but Spain refused to concede her demand for Gibraltar. Finally after another trip to England by Rayneval a complicated exchange of territories was arranged: Spain would receive Gibraltar but would return Minorca; in addition, Britain would receive the French Caribbean islands of Guadeloupe and Dominica, for which France would be compensated by the undeveloped Spanish colony of Santo Domingo (now the Dominican Republic).

6. THE AGREEMENTS

A few days later the arrangement collapsed. On 29 November the American and British negotiators (acting separately) signed a provisional agreement conceding British acknowledgment of American independence, generous borders for the United States, and even American participation in the Newfoundland and St. Lawrence fisheries. (For further discussion of the treaty's negotiation and its long-term consequences *see* Chapter 38.) In deference to the Franco-American alliance the agreement was made conditional upon a general peace being reached, but this was largely a sham. The war-weary American people were hardly likely to continue fighting in order to help France and Spain obtain their war objectives. The British hence would be free to use the New York and Charles Town garrisons against France and Spain; Jay, embittered by his treatment in Spain, even encouraged the British to attack the Spanish garrison of West Florida.

British public opinion was so shocked by the generous terms given the Americans that Shelburne claimed he could no longer count on parliamentary approval for the cession of Gibraltar. He withdrew his agreement to the exchange of territories and for several weeks peace was in doubt. A huge Franco-Spanish naval and military expedition was preparing to sail from Europe for another attempt on Jamaica (a potential exchange for Gibraltar). At Vergennes' request its commander, Admiral d'Estaing, explained to King Carlos III of Spain the obstacles to its success and was delaying its departure as long as possible, but once it sailed the chance of peace would disappear. At this desperate conjuncture the Spaniards finally relented; Aranda took the responsibility of conceding on Gibraltar in exchange for Spain's obtaining Minorca and all of Florida. Vergennes took upon himself the task of negotiating on behalf of the Netherlands, surrendering to Britain a small trading post in India in exchange for the vital Dutch port of Trincomalee in Ceylon. (The Dutch were not in a position to refuse the intervention since France was currently occupying the Dutch island of St. Eustatius and the Cape colony of southern Africa.) In a final compromise France agreed to a return to the *status quo ante bellum* in India and to return all its conquests in the West Indies except the small island of Tobago; Britain returned St. Lucia and agreed to improved French fishing rights off Newfoundland, the abolition of British rights to maintain a commissioner at Dunkirk (to prevent fortification of that famous privateering port), and French retention of Senegal. A general armistice as signed at

Versailles on 20 January 1783; the final treaty of 3 September 1783 merely confirmed the terms reached eight months earlier.

7. RESULTS OF THE WAR

The results of the war proved the wisdom of Turgot, who had predicted American independence would bring France no real benefit. Within a few years American trade with Britain had revived, while her trade with the rest of Europe languished. British prosperity revived and Britain soon regained her position in the European balance of power; France, crippled by debt, saw her influence in Europe continue to decline. The Dutch, the war's most unwilling combatants, were humiliated by their failures; their subsequent attempts to reform their political institutions were foiled by foreign intervention. Spain permanently regained Minorca as a result of the war, but her recovery of Florida was only temporary; within half a century all her possessions on the American continent were gone. Ironically the most important territorial gains were made by Russia; with the powers of Western Europe distracted by the American war she was able to gain the Crimea from the Turks. Within a few years of the war's end the great powers of Europe had largely forgotten America and had turned their attention to the problems and opportunities presented by the declining strength of the Poles and Turks. It would take another great revolution, that of 1789, to return France and Britain to the center of events.

FURTHER READING

Dull, Jonathan R.: *A Diplomatic History of the American Revolution* (New Haven, Conn., and London: Yale University Press, 1985).

——: *The French Navy and American Independence: a Study of Arms and Diplomacy, 1774–1787* (Princeton, NJ: Princeton University Press, 1975).

Harlow, Vincent T.: *The Founding of the Second British Empire, 1763–1793*, 2 vols. Vol. 1, *Discovery and Revolution* (London: Longmans, Green & Co., 1952).

Hoffman, Ronald, and Albert, Peter J. (eds.): *Peace and the Peacemakers: the Treaty of 1783* (Charlottesville: University Press of Virginia, 1986).

Hutson, James S.: *John Adams and the Diplomacy of the American Revolution* (Lexington: University Press of Kentucky, 1980).

Madariaga, Isabel de: *Britain, Russia, and the Armed Neutrality of 1780: Sir James Harris's Mission to St. Petersburg during the American Revolution* (New Haven, Conn.: Yale University Press, 1962).

Morris, Richard B.: *The Peacemakers: the Great Powers and American Independence* (New York, Evanston, Ill., and London: Harper & Row, 1965).

Scott, H. M.: *British Foreign Policy in the Age of the American Revolution* (Oxford: Oxford University Press, forthcoming).

Stinchcombe, William C.: *The American Revolution and the French Alliance* (Syracuse, NY: Syracuse University Press, 1969).

Stourzh, Gerald: *Benjamin Franklin and American Foreign Policy*, rev. ed. (Chicago and London: University of Chicago Press, 1969).

34

Confederation: state governments and their problems

EDWARD COUNTRYMAN

BETWEEN 1776 and 1787 the 14 newly independent states (including Vermont) were the scenes of exciting political innovation and of great political achievement. Yet those same states became the despair of the men whom most Americans regarded as the wisest and most experienced in the country. The states had good claim to call themselves genuinely sovereign, acknowledging no political superior. Yet they were part of a larger emerging nation, and there were points when their actions put the whole of American nationhood at risk. They made themselves the most democratic polities on earth. Yet by 1787 and 1788 enough Americans were unhappy with what they had achieved and what they stood for to accept the radically different vision of the future that the Federalists put forth. The states had won a revolutionary war but it seems that in the eyes of many of their own people they lost the peace that followed.

I. THE NEW POLITICAL MEN

The states were born in diversity, from passionate democratic experiment in Pennsylvania to sober institutional balance in Massachusetts. But beneath the differences among their constitutions lay a common set of developments and problems. In terms of political sociology one of the most important developments was the entry into the center of public life of men who might, at best, have watched from the periphery during the colonial era. People who had cut their political teeth in the Sons of Liberty during the years of resistance and in the committees and conventions of the independence crisis were now becoming assemblymen and state senators. Jackson Turner Main (1966) has called this process the "democratization" of the legislatures, leading to "government by the people."

This democratization had two primary sources. One was a simple enlargement of the opportunity to take part. Before independence, assembly elections were held at intervals that varied widely: annually in New England; roughly triennially in Virginia; far less often in New York. After it, they took place annually in every state but one. Under the old order some of the assemblies had been remarkably small: New Hampshire's had 34 members in 1765, New York's 28 in 1769, and New Jersey's 20 in the same year. But by the mid-1780s New Hampshire's lower house had 88 members, New York's had 65, and New Jersey's had 39. Large or small, the colonial institutions had been dominated by men of wealth and standing: "gentlemen of long-tailed families" in Virginia's House of Burgesses; lowland planters and Charles Town merchants in the South Carolina Commons House of Assembly; port-town merchants,

Harvard graduates, and the "river gods" of the Connecticut Valley in the Massachusetts General Court; the DeLanceys and Morrises and Livingstons and Van Rensselaers who ran public life in colonial New York; the Philadelphia merchant and Quaker elite in Pennsylvania.

The Revolution brought the withdrawal, whether voluntary or forced, of many of these men and groups. Some became neutrals or outright loyalists, such as Pennsylvania's Joseph Galloway and the New York political faction centered on the DeLancey family. The DeLanceys controlled their province from their victory in the assembly election of 1769 until the independence crisis. Then, effectively, they vanished. Others who chose the Revolution nonetheless lost their nerve and with it their ability to rule, most significantly the patriot wing of the old Pennsylvania elite. The panic with which such men as John Dickinson faced the moment of independence cost them their chance to shape their province's future, at least until they found their political footing again. Still others moved to a higher sphere, as generals, congressmen, and diplomats. Ultimately these included the Adams cousins of Massachusetts, New Yorkers as diverse as John Jay and Alexander McDougall, and George Washington himself. For these men the Revolution meant a leap from mere provincial prominence to national and even world fame.

In every province, both the newly created seats and the vacant places began to be filled by the new men of the Revolution. ABRAHAM YATES, a shoemaker turned lawyer turned politician, of Albany, New York, had been denied a seat in the colonial assembly when he sought one in 1761, thanks to the hostility of Sir William Johnson. Now, deeply hostile not only to loyalists such as Johnson's heirs but to all "high flyers," he graduated from the chairmanship of his city's revolutionary committee to a position of power in the state senate. His story was repeated hundreds of times, as artisans, freehold and even tenant farmers, and small-time professionals and traders became makers of high public policy. Some stayed a session or two and then returned to obscurity. Others, such as Yates, William Findley of Pennsylvania, and Abraham Clark of New Jersey, became men of considerable political consequence.

Massachusetts Numbers alone did not guarantee power, for in the upheaval of the mid-1770s the most basic and valuable political skill was the ability to organize. With it, a few might well take charge of many, as the case of Massachusetts shows. Based on the separate representation of each town, the state's assembly was huge, with a potential membership of more than 200. The farmers of the interior had the power to exercise absolute control in the lower house, but a number of factors kept them from doing so. One was simple inexperience. To these men parliamentary procedure and the correct mode of drafting bills were arcane mysteries, not skills to be taken for granted. A second was the inability, or unwillingness, of many of the interior towns to provide salaries and expenses. These were absolute necessities if a farmer or a village artisan or even a small-town lawyer was to go to Boston for an extended legislative session. A third was the reluctance of the men of the interior actually to act together politically: everything in their political culture told them that this was partisanship, and all of them knew that partisanship was fundamentally wrong.

The result was that the merchants and professionals of the seaboard counties, men such as Nathaniel Gorham of Boston and Jonathan Jackson of Newburyport, took effective control. They, too, were "new men," but they stepped into places vacated by the likes of Samuel Adams, not Joseph Galloway or James DeLancey. They did not share the political culture of the interior villagers, or even of the Boston crowd, and

333

they had no scruples about organizing privately in order to take public power. Until the aftermath of Shays's Rebellion, these men would run the commonwealth according to their view of its best interests.

New York Developments elsewhere were more complex. The young elite of New York's revolution – landholders such as ROBERT R. LIVINGSTON, GOUVERNEUR MORRIS, and Philip Schuyler, and professionals such as JOHN JAY and Egbert Benson – understood the importance of organization and coordination. In 1777, after they succeeded in writing and implementing a state constitution that was to their own taste, they reminisced to one another about the "well-planned delays, indefatigible industry and minute . . . attention to every favourable circumstance" that had enabled their "council of conspiracy" to achieve its institutional goals. They planned to dominate the new government as well and deployed themselves carefully: Schuyler (as they expected) to the governor's chair; Livingston and Jay to the high posts of Chancellor and Chief Justice; Benson, Morris, and a clutch of lesser Livingstons to the assembly. "They may chuse who they will," Schuyler smugly predicted during the first election, 'I will command them all."

But the governorship in fact went to GEORGE CLINTON, who would hold it until 1792. Like Schuyler he was a seasoned man of public affairs, having served with some prominence in the colonial assembly. But to the men who had so confidently expected to rule, "George the governor" (as one of their confidants dismissively described him) was a plebeian. His "family and circumstances" did "not entitle him to so distinguished a predominance." In the assembly Benson found himself not the *de facto* leader he had expected to be but rather obliged, thanks to his possession of the necessary technical skills, to draft bills for men whom he scorned and on behalf of causes that he loathed.

To repeat such accounts 14 times would be tedious. Each separate state had its own separate story. But from New Hampshire to Georgia the Revolution brought obscure men to prominence and responsibilities that none of them must ever have expected. Their presence was a gain, for it brought to the fore men of energy, commitment, and local sensitivity, if not of wide experience, deep learning, or "family and connections." But it also brought problems, as the many bungled pieces of legislation they passed and the partisanship they provoked would show.

2. LEGITIMIZING THE NEW STATE GOVERNMENTS

The new governments had to establish their own legitimacy, and the men in charge soon found that more was necessary to do it than simply proclaiming a constitution and calling an election. Anticipating trouble, the ever-astute John Adams wrote in 1776 of the need to "glide insensibly" from the old order to the new. But his desire was not fulfilled. Instead, during their earliest years the governments had to prove their ability to rule both to their supporters and to their enemies. In some states they nearly broke under the effort.

New York New York, Pennsylvania, Maryland, and South Carolina provide the clearest examples. New York entered independence as a mere fragment of the province that it had been. In August 1776 the British conquered the southern district, comprising Manhattan, Long Island, Staten Island, and the lower portion of Westchester County. They would remain until the end of 1783, and to large numbers of the district's people that was perfectly acceptable. A few months after the invasion, at the very beginning of 1777, what had been the New York counties of Cumberland and Gloucester, together with part of Charlotte (now Washington) County, broke free to establish Vermont. Geographically, the free New York that adopted a republican government in April 1777 was no more than a strip running along the Hudson and Mohawk valleys.

Had Continental troops and state militia not stopped the British Army under General John Burgoyne at Saratoga in October 1777 there would have been no state to be governed at all. Even after the major military threat was ended, profound instability remained. Although the state constitution was proclaimed in April, the legislature did not assemble until the autumn. It was scattered almost immediately, when a minor British expedition took and burned Kingston, the temporary capital, during the Saratoga crisis. The legislature did not actually begin permanent operations until early in 1778.

Moreover, it faced immense difficulty from its own "subjects." Popular loyalism was intense in the landlord-ridden counties along the east bank of the Hudson and in the Mohawk Valley. Among the patriots, the revolutionary committees of the independence crisis persisted. Despite the denunciation by the state constitution itself of the "many and great inconveniences" that attended "government by Congresses and Committees," they continued meeting until well into 1778. New York's state constitution was never an issue of serious debate, despite its relatively conservative institutions and despite its never being submitted for the popular ratification that the artisans of New York City had demanded as early as May 1776. But during the first years, the survival of the state government was by no means a certainty.

Pennsylvania   For Pennsylvania the problem was just the reverse. There the difficulty was not loyalists, or separatism, or, for the most part, the course of the war. It was the state's radical constitution, adopted in 1776 (*see* Chapter 29, §4). The document reflected the most democratic impulses of the Revolution, as its emulation by Vermont and the similar proposals that came forward in many other states show. But it also reflected the precise balance of Pennsylvania politics at the moment of independence. Pennsylvania's moderates acted swiftly to regain power, establishing their Republican Society and dedicating themselves to the abolition of a government that they believed to be the height of political folly. With leadership that included the jurist JAMES WILSON, the merchant and financier ROBERT MORRIS, the physician BENJAMIN RUSH, and the writer-politician JOHN DICKINSON, they were formidable, despite the abilities of Joseph Reed, Charles Willson Peale, and GEORGE BRYAN on the other "Constitutionalist" side.

The Constitutionalists enjoyed real popular support. But the Republicans appreciated the importance of their state's social complexity and its fundamentally commercial economy in a way the Constitutionalists never did. The state constitution never became an object of general veneration and respect, providing a framework within which disputes might be worked out. Instead, it became and remained the primary object of dispute itself. In 1790 a constitutional convention finally got rid of it, establishing an upper legislative house and a governorship to bring Pennsylvania into line with the dominant American model.

Maryland   Maryland's problems were akin to New York's, and almost as severe. The state never had to endure massive invasion or protracted warfare. But it did have

335

many militant loyalists, particularly on the eastern shore of Chesapeake Bay. Maryland loyalism drew on many roots. These included the economic difference between eastern-shore small farmers and the opulent tobacco planters who had written the state constitution and who dominated the new government, the dissent of Methodists and Baptists in a state dominated by Anglicans and newly enfranchised Catholics, and the possibility of an alliance between poor Whites and slaves. In Maryland, as in New York, the militia was unreliable, the courts could not be opened, and taxes were almost impossible to collect.

The situation was not helped by having a political system that was deliberately "closed." Maryland's planter elite lacked the social confidence of its Virginia counter-part. The Virginians boldly set up institutions that were almost as democratic in formal terms as Pennsylvania's, secure in the certainty that their own sort would continue to rule. But the Marylanders erected a "fortress of institutions" around themselves. They established high property qualifications for public office, the only assembly that was chosen for a term longer than a single year, and a system of electors that stood between the voters and the state senate. The document reflected the well-justified fear of the elite that it might lose control of the whole situation.

South Carolina   South Carolina's instability sprang from a combination of pre-independence tensions and the fortunes of war. Despite the homogeneity of low-country society – later referred to as the "harmony we were famous for" – the state's people entered independence with many conflicting interests and possibly with differ-ent ideas about its future. Like the great northern ports, Charles Town saw a rapid growth in political awareness among artisans during the independence crisis. As in Philadelphia or New York, these formed the core of the town's Sons of Liberty. Again as in the North, some of them found in the non-importation of the late 1760s a chance to advance their own prosperity, with no overseas rivals in the local market for the goods they made. For the town's merchants, who lived by overseas trade, and for artisans who served the long-distance economy, non-importation had a different meaning. The interior was even more split, with deep hostility between the planter-dominated lowlands and a back country where slavery and the plantation system had not yet taken full shape. It may or may not be the case that back-country people wanted a different social model; it is certainly the case that they thoroughly mistrusted the low-country gentlemen who ruled their province. When the lowland planter and jurist William Henry Drayton set out to rally the back country in 1775, he met indifference and resistance rather than support.

To this essential social instability was added a massive British invasion early in 1780. Sir Henry Clinton's forces quickly captured Charles Town and the low country, and the people who did not flee took the oaths of submission that the conquerors required. In an address to Clinton, a large number of Charlestonians and planters repudiated independence and the "rank democracy" to which it had led, calling it a "tyrannical domination, only to be found among the uncivilised part of mankind." Among the men who sought British protection were the former president RAWLINS LOWNDES, Colonel CHARLES PINCKNEY, and Henry Middleton, who had been president of the Continental Congress. In the interior, the invasion led to the most vicious warfare the Revolution saw, both between British and American and between patriot and loyalist. What was left of the revolutionary government fled the state.

New laws of taxation For three of these states, New York, Maryland, and South Carolina, the answer to the problem of legitimacy came in the form of dramatic demonstrations of responsiveness to public demands. In New York it happened in 1779, when the legislature totally reversed its previous policies on loyalism and taxation. Instead of simply controlling the "disaffected," the state would punish them: the Confiscation Act passed that autumn was only the first of a series of harsh laws that would eventually be long enough to fill a sizable volume. Instead of taxing as lightly as possible, the state would strike at the rich, allowing assessors to rate them according to "circumstances and other abilities to pay taxes, collectively considered." This mode of taxation was never elegant and by 1782 Alexander Hamilton had concluded that it was "radically vicious." But in a state where the rich had never had to pay before, it proved popular.

Even earlier, Charles Carroll of Carrollton had begun to argue "the wisdom of sacrifice" to his own kind in Maryland, insisting that they recognize the social need for taxing the rich and for issuing cheap paper currency. To his father, Charles Carroll of Annapolis, it surpassed "in iniquity all the acts of the British Parliament." But to the son all "great revolutions" brought "partial injustice and suffering" and these had to be endured. Better for the planter elite to lose some of its property than all of its power. In South Carolina the change came somewhat later. But by the revolution's end "the inhabitants" had adopted the egalitarian "mode of respectful Representation" when they addressed their legislators, instead of the "humble petitions" of an earlier day. They began assuming that "people who were no better than they but who happened to sit in the legislature would act" to do what the people wanted. To its historian Jerome Nadelhaft, "that was the revolution" there.

A governor of no "family and connections" in New York; an intensely democratic but deeply divisive institutional experiment in Pennsylvania; the elite's need to accept "the wisdom of sacrifice" in Maryland; the "snarls of invidious animals" in South Carolina: these were the political situations that the early state governments faced. There was no real question of "gliding insensibly" from the old order to the new. Instead, there was a pressing need for change.

3. THE NEW GOVERNMENTS AND THE ECONOMY

Beneath these questions of political sociology a deeper issue was also crystallizing, with equally long-range causes and consequences. This was the proper stance of the government in relation to the economy. Like the question of institutional responsiveness, it came to a head in the late 1770s, as the states tried to grapple with the runaway inflation that accompanied wartime shortage and the collapse of the Continental dollar. But in larger terms a major change in political economy was underway.

Throughout the colonial period the imperial, provincial, and local governments had operated on the principle that they had a duty as well as a right to intervene in the economy for "the public good." At the imperial level the whole crisis had been about establishing the nature and scope of the public good, and independence meant the definitive American rejection of Parliament's assertion that it could do so. At the provincial and local levels, intervention had usually been for the sake of controlling the market-place, with the goal of establishing a balance among the good name of local wares in the larger world and the direct interests of producers, traders, and consumers. Assizes of bread, laws against such market offences as "forestalling," "regrating', and "engrossing," and the regular use of embargoes to counter shortages were normal and accepted parts of economic life.

At the end of the 1770s, popular pressure for such intervention became intense, due to the unprecedented demands of a large-scale wartime economy and to the worst and most widespread inflation Americans had ever known. All over the northern states, particularly, people responded to the crisis in ways that both long-established custom and revolutionary experience legitimated. They rioted, taking goods they needed, and paying according to "just" prices that they set themselves. They treated "monopolisers" and "hoarders" just as they had learned to treat loyalists, ostracizing them, carting them about for public ridicule, and sometimes tarring and feathering them. They put pressure on the state governments for action, in the form of price-control legislation and embargoes. In 1779 they elected new popular committees and gave them the task of bringing the economy under control. As they did so, they were starting to repeat the steps that had brought down the old order, for these committees, like the revolutionary committees of 1774, 1775, and 1776, claimed a mandate to take direct action. A dual crisis faced the new governments. Both the working of the economy and their own fragile legitimacy were at stake.

For many Americans the long-standing belief in "corporatist" political economy was an article of faith, just as much as the newly founded belief in republicanism. Indeed, the two reinforced each other. In Gordon Wood's phrase (Wood, 1969), corporatism and classical republicanism were both "essentially anti-capitalistic" in their assertion of the primacy of the small community and of stasis over the individual and change. In Pennsylvania the Constitutionalist Society made acceptance of corporatist political economy a condition of membership during the 1779 crisis. But two new elements were now present, and both pointed towards a redefinition of the whole issue.

One was the sheer dimensions of the problem. The enormous economic dislocations of the war years were part of the birth pangs of a national economy that would be much more powerful and much more tightly integrated than the old economy of the British Empire had ever been. There had been wars and depressions and inflation and shortages before, but never over so large a scale or for reasons that were so thoroughly interlinked. Beneath economic corporatism, as most Americans understood it, was a working assumption that the local economic unit could and sometimes should isolate itself. The larger economy of the Atlantic world had always impinged on colonial life, but it usually had been possible to shut it out, at least for a while. The demands of the war could not be shut out. If the army was not to collapse, if the French were not to take the aid they were supplying and go home, and if the British were not to triumph, there had to be cooperation across community and state lines. In the new situation locally focused embargoes and price controls would be ineffectual at best and pernicious at worst.

The second element was ideological. Throughout the western world advanced thinkers were developing the idea that a free market was superior to any form of controlled economy. The trend found its supreme expression in Adam Smith's *The Wealth of Nations*, published the same year that independence was declared, but it had been taking shape for over a century. Now its American moment arrived, as men with an awareness of large-scale national need and of the new dimensions and possibilities of the market-place contemplated the economic mess that surrounded them and rejected the old solutions. Let the price "limitation" be "limited to the City of Albany" urged Egbert Benson of New York, writing to John Jay. Jay agreed. So did Pennsylvanians such as James Wilson and Robert Morris; so did the hard-headed men who had taken control of the revolution in Massachusetts. Nor was the new sense restricted to the elite, for so did Thomas Paine and so did the organized leather workers of Philadelphia.

The consequence was that during the late 1770s and the early and middle 1780s the state governments became arenas in which two economic ideologies contended. There could not have been any Americans who doubted the fundamental importance and even sanctity of private property. But the social nature of private property became the subject of intense dispute. In Massachusetts, liberal market-place values won handily; even before the adoption of the Constitution of 1780 the commonwealth adopted policies of hard money and high taxation. There would be no attempts at all to use public power to cushion the state's citizens against the larger demands of the economic world. There would be no cheap paper money that debtors could use to pay what they owed, or legal procedures that they could use to stave off their creditors.

But elsewhere the older beliefs remained strong and men who held them were still able to shape policy. Not really paradoxically, these tended to be precisely the obscure men whom the Revolution had brought to prominence. Paper money, stay laws, compulsory debt arbitration, laws that disadvantaged British and loyalist creditors, tender laws, and continuing attempts at embargoes and price controls were the result. As often as not, the legislation was ill-drawn and poorly thought out. In larger terms and in the long run it was bound to be ineffectual, for no amount of locally focused effort could stave off the growing power of the national and Atlantic economic spheres. But in the short run the effect was to aid profoundly in stabilizing the new political institutions. People with real grievances and real fears – of bankruptcy, of losing their farms, of the debtors' prison – came to the conclusion that the new state governments could be theirs to control and to use.

4. THE EMERGENCE OF PARTISANSHIP

By and large the new men of state politics did not enter public life as part of an organized attempt to seize power. Perhaps the only exceptions came in Pennsylvania and Vermont. In the first, the coalition of back-country Scotch-Irish Presbyterian farmers and Philadelphia artisan-radicals that created the state's constitution of 1776 began quickly to consolidate itself as the Constitutionalist Party. In the second the former Green Mountain Boys who had waged a decade-long guerrilla struggle against New York now had to create and lead a state.

But the effect of such men's entry was division. The patriots of 1776 created a remarkable political coalition, held together by a common view on the issue of independence. The great desire that year was for unity: even men who had been openly loyalist were welcomed back to the fold if they would make the necessary gestures of commitment to the revolutionary cause. The political foe was Britain and its minions, not Americans of differing backgrounds or beliefs or interests or political opinions. Inherently fragile, however, the unity of 1776 could not last. Although partisanship was a dirty word in virtually everyone's political vocabulary, it was the necessary outcome both of American social reality and of people's revolutionary experience.

One reason was the fact that the Revolution was teaching people to regard themselves in specific social terms as well as in terms of a new national identity. Men of power and wealth had always known that for political purposes they were merchants, planters, and landlords as well as Pennsylvanians or Virginians. They had begun to

339

show it in the late years of the old order by organizing groups such as New York's Chamber of Commerce. They had always known how to cooperate in their own interests, even when they were also thinking in terms larger than themselves. That was what had made them a ruling elite. But even they needed reminding about the facts of political life. In 1784 and 1785 Alexander Hamilton conducted a remarkable campaign aimed at convincing New York's aristocrats, who had fallen to squabbling among themselves, to forget their disputes and "endeavour to put men in the Legislature whose principles are not of the *levelling kind.*"

The novelty was the emergence of such political consciousness, assertiveness, and mutual cooperation among the lesser men who traditionally had been the ruled rather than the rulers. The two clearest cases are urban artisans and small farmers. Artisan consciousness had grown steadily during the years of resistance, from hesitant offers to cooperate with "our neighbours the merchants" for the sake of the grand cause to strident assertions that in "Questions of ... great Consequence, the Consent of the Majority of the Tradesmen, Farmers and other Freemen" was needed. By 1773 New York artisans were meeting "at Beer Houses" in order "to concert Measures"; the following year they purchased their own meeting place, naming it Liberty Hall. In Philadelphia even the privates in the militia developed their own consciousness, electing a committee to represent them, making their own political demands, and providing much of the driving force for the "corporatist" attempt to resolve the inflation crisis of 1779.

This did not lead immediately to partisanship in the modern sense. Except in Pennsylvania, where Constitutionalists and Republicans rapidly faced one another down, there were no recognized labels, no party organizations, no coordinated campaigns. But it did form the raw material from which partisanship could emerge. By and large the Revolutionaries expected that in the republican political order people would put citizenship ahead of self-interest, the public above the private. But definitions of citizenship and of what was genuinely public differed, as the inflation crisis showed. For many, perhaps most, Americans the "public" meant the small cohesive community, held together by custom and mutuality. For a growing number it meant the nation, whose immediate interest was keeping the army supplied. And for at least some it meant a large-scale commercial society, in which the maintenance of stable, predictable conditions of contract and exchange would be regarded as more important than the prevention of local and personal suffering.

New York   Within this context partisanship emerged in fits and starts. From its first session in 1777 until 1781, voting patterns in New York's legislature were essentially chaotic, with little predictability about how a man would vote or who his associates would be from one issue to the next. There was ample conflict but there was not yet structure. But in the fifth session (1782), predictability from one issue to another did begin to emerge. By the eighth session (1784–5), the assembly was splitting the same way on fully half of its roll-call votes, whatever the ostensible issue. Land policy; treatment of loyalists; taxation; the future of old institutions such as New York City's Trinity Church; paper currency: issue after issue provoked the same split. The fundamental question at stake was what kind of society independent New York would be.

During the war years men did try to manage elections. But these first efforts were haphazard, ill-coordinated, and local in focus. At the war's end there was still no generally accepted label for either of the developing sides. Writing of New York City's first free election, at the end of 1783, Robert R. Livingston described the efforts of "the tories . . . the violent Whigs . . . and those who wish to suppress all violences," but his reference was specific to the town, not general for the whole state. Historians have sometimes written of "Clintonians" and "Anti-Clintonians," but those terms are anachronistic. Only slowly did Governor George Clinton emerge as an openly partisan leader. As late as 1786 his name was at the head of an assembly ticket put forward by men who in fact wanted him out of office.

But the divisions of the mid-1780s did directly prefigure the split between Federalist and Anti-Federalist in the state in 1788. The only exception was that New York City's "late exiled Mechanics," who had been the "violent Whigs" of 1783, now joined the merchants and professionals – the former "tories" and their friends who had wished to "suppress all violences" – in favoring the Constitution. The frantic attempts at unity among all patriots of the independence period had given way to open expression of difference, open organization, and open political labels as well-recognized sides maneuvered in order to get power.

New York's experience of partisan development had much in common with that of its two major neighbors, Pennsylvania and Massachusetts. In all three, a coalition of farmers, artisans, and merchants came apart along its own internal lines of stress. In all three the fundamental issue was the shape of the republican future. In all three that issue lay behind debates on such seemingly diverse issues as debtor–creditor relations, loyalism, education, and land policy. In all three, as well, the issue of the government's stance *vis-à-vis* the demands of a mobilized citizenry had to be confronted. Finally, in all three the "radical" or "democratic" or "popular" position developed two poles. Artisans and farmers alike clung to a vision of a society of equal, productive men, which merchants and urban professionals did not share. Neither artisans nor farmers were enamored of the idea of a free market, at least as envisaged by a Robert Morris or an Alexander Hamilton. But in none of these states did they develop a strong alliance. In 1788 most artisans in New York City, Philadelphia, and Boston found that they had good reason to support the Constitution. Most farmers in the three states found equally good reason to oppose it.

Pennsylvania But in New York the course of partisan development worked to strengthen the state government. In Pennsylvania and Massachusetts, it did not. From the point of view of legitimating the new order, Pennsylvania's partisanship developed too quickly and cut too deep. It took almost half a decade for New York's independence coalition to split, another three years for genuinely coherent partisanship to solidify in the legislature, and two more for party labels and organization to appear. But in Pennsylvania the split came suddenly and was tied directly to the issue of independence. New York's conservatives – a Robert R. Livingston or a John Jay – may have been reluctant to make the leap, but they made it. They may have wanted leniency for Tories during the war and they may have been willing to work with them after it. But no one could have accused them of being loyalists themselves. Pennsylvanians such as Dickinson, however, were tainted in exactly that way, at least to the eyes of their patriot foes, thanks to their fatal attempt in 1776 to keep hesitating past the moment when hesitation was still possible. To the Constitutionalists, the Pennsylvania Republicans would always be crypto-loyalists.

The second problem in Pennsylvania was the very clarity of focus and intensity of organization that partisanship took from the beginning. With the constitution of 1776 as the main issue there was no room for temporizing; as on independence, one was either for or against. The Constitutionalists recognized this by their policy of requiring an oath of loyalty on the part of voters and office-holders, not simply to Pennsylvania's independence but to the constitution itself. With so sharp a division on so fundamental a question it is not surprising that both sides were fully organized by 1779, the year that New York's independence coalition first came under serious strain. In one sense the emergency of the Republican and Constitutionalist clubs so early was a measure of the vitality of Pennsylvania's political life. But in another it was a sign of forced hot-house growth, with the branches taking on weight and density before the stem had the strength to hold them up.

Massachusetts   In Massachusetts the problem was not the too-rapid development of partisanship but rather its stunting. The state's independence coalition was as tense in its internal relationships as it was passionate in its commitment against the British. When the countryside mobilized in response to the Coercive Acts, some villagers were fearful that the whole crisis stemmed from the desire of Boston merchants to secure a market for their surplus goods by cutting off external trade. Their fear sprang from a loyalist canard, spread by the Tory press of John Mein, but the charge struck a responsive chord in Puritan village culture. More than any other Americans, New England farmers clung to the ideal of a cooperative, communal society, and more than most they had always been able to live relatively free of the large commercial market-place. Their collective life, with its town meetings and its gathered churches, reinforced their sense that they could run their own affairs to suit themselves. Ordinary Bostonians shared some of this ethos, as their passionate attachment to town-meeting government demonstrates. But of necessity Boston was much more immersed in the world of commerce than most of the towns of the interior. Within Boston the tension between commerce and community reached right back to the founding. But in the aftermath of independence its men of commerce took firm control not only of the town but of the whole state.

Meanwhile Boston's mechanics fell politically silent. They would remain so until 1788, when they emerged under the leadership of Paul Revere as a strong pro-Constitution force. The farmers' whole ethos, in turn, told them that the proper way to organize themselves was in consensual groups, not in partisan formations. Throughout the Confederation years they gathered to voice their grievances, but their medium was the town meeting or the county convention. The delegates they sent to the legislature felt themselves bound by town-meeting instructions, but neither they nor their constitutents accepted the legitimacy of state-level cooperation in the manner that New Yorkers or Pennsylvanians did. In consequence, despite the state's adoption of policies that glaringly favored one social interest at the expense of another, the legislature did not become a focus of party development. Its members did not develop the kind of creative political dialogue with their constituents that the New Yorkers engendered or the Pennsylvania Constitutionalists had fondly expected. There was no state figure like New York's George Clinton, slowly taking on a partisan role on the "popular" side, or Pennsylvania's president Joseph Reed, known as a Constitutionalist and ably administering the state during the worst years of the war. Most people in Massachusetts accepted their state's constitution of 1780. But all over the interior there were men who found that, though it was easy enough to make their wishes known, there was no way to turn them into governmental action.

Shays's Rebellion   The result was Shays's Rebellion. This uprising of central and western Massachusetts farmers was not an isolated event, springing from causes peculiar to its own region. There were "combustibles in every state," and as David Szatmary (1980) shows, the rising itself was a New England-wide movement. Even in distant South Carolina, 1785 and 1786 saw debtors gathering to close courts and demand state laws to protect them from the effects of the postwar depression. But it was in Massachusetts that the issues and forces involved crystallized.

The problem was threefold. First, like most of America, Massachusetts found itself caught in a contracting network of debt that reached all the way to London. Second, in Massachusetts, unlike most other states, there was no structure of state laws to cushion debtors against creditors or, in an alternative reading, to protect virtuous patriots against the British and former loyalists. Third, there was no partisan structure able to channel popular demands to and through the institutions of the state government. The fundamental issue was the emerging power of an increasingly capitalist economy, with Boston looking towards the future and the towns trying to cling to the past. The new large situation required predictability and stability for the enforcement of contractual obligations, conditions that the Federal Constitution would in fact guarantee. But both long tradition and the history of the Revolution told the farmers they were correct to resist.

This is not the place to recount the story of either the uprising or its suppression (*see* Chapter 36, §4). The important point is the transformation in political practice that ensued. Although the farmers' amateur militia proved no match for the state's troops, and though the insurgents found themselves obliged to crawl before the triumphant state authorities, the interior finally realized the power of its numbers and organized to win the next election. John Hancock replaced James Bowdoin as governor. More towns than ever before elected representatives, 228 in all, and 60 per cent of the men they chose were new to the assembly. Even in the 40-member state senate, established specifically to protect property, 16 new faces appeared.

It might have heralded a genuinely radical alteration in the state's direction, but in fact it did not. The year was 1787, and both the rebellion in Massachusetts and the subsequent election served to convince the coalescing Federalist movement that radical change of another sort was in fact required. The real outcome of Shays's Rebellion came not in changes to the state's laws but in the near-victory of Massachusetts' Anti-Federalism in 1788. When the state's ratifying convention met, the two sides were almost evenly matched. This was a direct reflection of the political awakening of the interior, just as the strength of Anti-Federalism in the New York convention – which significantly met in Poughkeepsie rather than New York City – reflected that state's decade of partisan development.

As Gordon Wood has shown (1969), the major concern of the emerging Federalists was the states, not the Articles of Confederation. James Madison framed his "Vices of the Political System of the United States," the preparatory notes that he wrote before the Federal Convention, around the problem of controlling and limiting the state governments. Originally he wanted the central authority to have an absolute veto on state legislation. To the Federalists the state administrations were filled with "Characters too full of Local attachments and Views," men of "narrow souls" who pandered "to the vulgar and sordid notions of the populace." "The vile State governments are sources of pollution which will contaminate the American name for ages ... Smite them," wrote Henry Knox, who had commanded the expedition that smote the Shaysites, to Rufus King, sitting in the Philadelphia convention.

5. THE RATIFICATION OF THE CONSTITUTION

Enough ordinary white adult male Americans agreed, for one reason or another, to accept the Constitution and thus end the era of state autonomy. Some did it with reluctance and on the promise of the amendments that became the Bill of Rights. Others did it with enthusiasm, as the great ratification parades of the major towns showed. But even in 1788, at the Federalists' moment of triumph, the states and what they stood for still commanded wide support, so much that in the three key states of Virginia, Massachusetts, and New York ratification was a close-run thing. Had the Anti-Federalists won at the right moment in any of them, or even in strategically important New Hampshire, it might have been stopped completely and the states would have gone on as before.

Even in 1788, to many of their citizens – the term "subjects" had fallen out of use and the change is telling – the state governments were not "vile" but rather popular, responsive institutions, a vast improvement on what had gone before. This belief developed at an uneven pace, but the local story in each of the states grew from the large complexities of the Revolution. What took place in the states between 1776 and 1788 did not complete the Revolution; that was to be the Federalists' great achievement. But it did express in its complexity both the hopes and the experience of the many sorts of people who had joined in agreeing on independence but who thereafter found themselves disagreeing on where independence should lead and what it should mean.

FURTHER READING

Bogin, Ruth: *Abraham Clark and the Quest for Equality in the Revolutionary Era* (Rutherford, NJ: Fairleigh Dickinson University Press, 1982).

Brown, Richard D.: "Shays' rebellion and the ratification of the Federal Constitution in Massachusetts," *Beyond Confederation: Origins of the Constitution and American National Identity*, ed. Richard Beeman et al. (Chapel Hill: University of North Carolina Press, 1987), 113–127.

Countryman, Edward: *The American Revolution* (New York: Hill & Wang, 1985; Harmondsworth: Penguin, 1987).

——: *A People in Revolution: the American Revolution and Political Society in New York, 1760–1790* (Baltimore: Johns Hopkins University Press, 1981).

Main, Jackson Turner: "Government by the people: the American Revolution and the democratization of the legislatures," *William and Mary Quarterly*, 23 (1966), 391–406.

——: *Political Parties Before the Constitution* (Chapel Hill: University of North Carolina Press, 1973).

——: *The Sovereign States, 1775–1783* (New York: New Viewpoints, 1973).

Nadelhaft, Jerome J.: *The Disorders of War: the Revolution in South Carolina* (Orono: University of Maine Press, 1981).

——: " 'The snarls of invidious animals': the democratization of revolutionary South Carolina," *Sovereign States in an Age of Uncertainty*, ed. Ronald Hoffman and Peter J. Albert (Charlottesville: University Press of Virginia, 1981).

Patterson, Stephen E.: *Political Parties in Revolutionary Massachusetts* (Madison: University of Wisconsin Press, 1973).

——: "The roots of Massachusetts federalism: conservative politics and political culture before 1787," *Sovereign States in an Age of Uncertainty*, ed. Ronald Hoffman and Peter J. Albert (Charlottesville: University Press of Virginia), 31–61.

Pole, J. R.: *Political Representation in England and the Origins of the American Republic* (New York: St. Martin's Press, 1966; repr. Berkeley: University of California Press, 1971).

Ryerson, Richard Alan: "Republican theory and partisan reality in revolutionary Pennsylvania: toward a new view of the Constitutionalist Party," *Sovereign States in an Age of Uncertainty*, ed. Ronald Hoffman and Peter J. Albert (Charlottesville: University Press of Virginia, 1981), 95–133.

Szatmary, David: *Shays' Rebellion: the Making of an Agrarian Insurrection* (Amherst: University of Massachusetts Press, 1980).

Sydnor, Charles S.: *Gentlemen Freeholders: Political Practices in Washington's Virginia* (Chapel Hill: University of North Carolina Press, 1952).

Weir, Robert M.: "The harmony we were famous for: an interpretation of pre-revolutionary South Carolina Politics," *William and Mary Quarterly*, 26 (1969), 473–501.

Wood, Gordon S.: *The Creation of the American Republic, 1776–1787* (Chapel Hill: University of North Carolina Press, 1969).

——: "Interests and disinterestedness in the making of the Constitution," *Beyond Confederation: Origins of the Constitution and American National Identity*, ed. Richard Beeman et al. (Chapel Hill: University of North Carolina Press, 1987), 69–109.

Zemsky, Robert M.: *Merchants, Farmers and River Gods: an Essay on Eighteenth-Century American Politics* (Boston: Gambit, 1971).

35

The West: territory, states, and confederation

PETER S. ONUF

T
HE establishment of effective authority along the northern and western frontiers represented one of the leading challenges to the United States during and
after the Revolution. Reports of fabulously fertile frontier lands inspired a rage
for emigration, particularly in areas where land was overused and in short supply.
But the rapid expansion of settlement kept the frontiers in an uproar, stretching the
political capabilities of state and central governments to the limit and provoking
chronic conflict with the Indians. Meanwhile, frontiersmen invoked revolutionary
notions of popular sovereignty and self-determination as they sought increased representation in the state assemblies or recognition as new states. Separatist movements
were, in turn, symptomatic of pervasive jurisdictional confusion, the leading legacy
of British rule. State boundary claims in frontier areas were rarely clearly defined;
the claims of large, "landed" states, generally based on vague and often mutually
contradictory colonial charters, were particularly controversial. Not surprisingly, the
small, "landless" states were reluctant to recognize large state claims. How, they
asked, could a union of such unequal states survive? Beyond these political and
constitutional issues was the question of land titles. Jurisdictional confusion led to
conflict, sometimes violent, between rival groups of land speculators, settlers, and
their political allies and sponsors.

The American Congress thus confronted a daunting array of challenges in the West.
Before the Revolution, imperial officials focused their attention on the increasingly
rebellious coastal cities. Chaotic conditions on the frontiers were bound to set Americans squabbling among themselves, British commentators believed, and so serve the
counter-revolutionary cause. Congress, made up of delegations from states with
conflicting claims, was singularly ill-equipped to resolve jurisdictional disputes. As a
result, the western problem dominated congressional politics over the next few years,
absorbing more energy – to less apparent effect – than anything other than the
conduct of the war itself. Yet, paradoxically, congressional inaction helped keep
jurisdictional issues at bay during the war years, when any decisive action was bound
to be dangerously divisive.

With the coming of peace, the states moved with surprising rapidity to negotiate a
broad settlement of the western lands controversy. Legendary for its impotence in
other policy areas, Congress acted quickly and effectively to establish its authority
over the new national domain in the region north and west of the Ohio River. In three
short years (1784–7), Congress passed a series of ordinances for selling public lands
and exercising federal jurisdiction that established a framework for the future development of the national frontier and the expansion of the union. In 1776, the West
appeared to be a source of discord and conflict that jeopardized the common cause.

But the image of the West was dramatically different in 1787. In a "critical period" of deepening inter-sectional tension, the development of the national domain represented one of the few clear, substantial interests shared by all the states. Congress's western policy was predicated on a commitment to the union and on the belief that the new nation's future prosperity and power depended on frontier development.

I. CONGRESS AND THE WEST

Pressures from settlers and speculators for access to frontier lands mounted after Anglo-American victory over the French and their Indian allies in the American Seven Years' War. The Vandalia Company, a consortium of influential American and English investors, sought a Crown charter for a new colony in western Virginia. Other groups, such as Connecticut's Susquehannah Company, enjoyed the support of their colony governments. Claiming that Pennsylvania's Wyoming Valley fell within the limits of the Connecticut Charter of 1662, the Susquehanna Company sent hundreds of settlers into the contested region. New Hampshire's royal governor Benning Wentworth enriched himself and his associates by granting town charters in the northeastern counties of New York. Other speculators, including the Illinois and Wabash companies and a group headed by Judge Richard Henderson of North Carolina, sought royal confirmation for private purchases from Indian proprietors. Eager settlers, including large numbers of "squatters" as well as land company titleholders, pushed the frontiers of settlement into regions reserved to the Indians by the royal Proclamation of 7 October 1763. Americans generally saw the Proclamation as a temporary measure, designed to placate the Indians.

The result of all this frenetic activity was sporadic conflict between Whites and Indians, beginning with Pontiac's "rebellion" (1763), as well as jurisdictional controversy between colonies and chronic confusion about the imperial government's position on various title and boundary questions. Distracted by mounting resistance to British policy throughout the colonies, imperial authorities failed to articulate or implement a coherent western policy. The new American Congress inherited all of these unresolved problems: settlers continued to pour into contested areas; speculators turned first to the new state governments and then to Congress for confirmation of their grants and purchases; and the states themselves sought to extend their claims at each other's expense. How, under such circumstances, could the Americans hope to mount a united effort on behalf of their rights?

Congress's liabilities as putative successor to the imperial government were obvious to contemporaries. As colonists, Americans had acknowledged the ultimate authority of Privy Council to adjudicate inter-colonial conflicts. The colonists also recognized that private titles ultimately depended on royal sanction. In theory, the King was the original titleholder to all of British America, and he retained his title in frontier regions, except in proprietary or charter colonies. Not only did the King "own" all ungranted, public lands in the West, but the authority of Crown officials to manage relations with the natives and regulate the activities of Whites in the region was unquestioned.

In all these respects, Congress found itself at a relative disadvantage. The new states were reluctant to accord extensive powers to Congress, particularly where those powers – for instance, in determining boundaries – jeopardized their vital interests. After independence, representatives of the "landed" states with extended western claims insisted that the states, not Congress, succeeded to the Crown lands. The Articles of Confederation (drafted in 1777; ratified in 1781) gave Congress general powers over Indian affairs, but with crippling qualifications: Congress was to have "the sole and exclusive right" of "regulating the trade and managing all affairs with the Indians, not members of any of the States, provided that the legislative right of any State within its own limits be not infringed or violated." In other words, the Articles upheld the authority of the states to govern frontier areas within their own limits. And because all American territory fell within the limits of one state or the other, Congress's "sole and exclusive right" was at best prospective: Congress could not have a western policy until it gained title, by cession from the states, to frontier territory.

The Revolutionaries recognized that failure to resolve the western problem endangered the common cause. Under British rule, jurisdictional controversies were usually only of local significance, particularly to speculators and their client-settlers. Colony officials might have a personal stake in the outcome of these conflicts, but they generally did not engage the interest of the larger community. After independence, however, boundary and title questions took on a new importance to public-spirited citizens concerned with their states' prospects for future development as well as with the more immediate benefits of public land sales revenue. As a result, endemic local controversies merged into a larger, more fundamental debate over the organization of the union. Jurisdictional confusion on the frontiers thus constituted a double threat to the American cause. Title and boundary conflicts that had erupted into violence before independence – including the Green Mountain Boys' guerrilla war against New York in what would become Vermont, as well as violent conflict between Connecticut and Pennsylvania forces in the Wyoming Valley – fragmented the patriot coalition and offered obvious counter-revolutionary opportunities to the British. These controversies also raised basic questions about Congress's role in ascertaining and enforcing the states' respective territorial claims.

2. LANDED AND LANDLESS STATES

The great division among the states was between the large, landed states with their extensive western claims – Massachusetts, Connecticut, New York, Virginia, North Carolina, and Georgia – and the small, landless states. Led by Maryland, the landless states sought to curb landed state claims and establish Congress's title to the western lands. Small state delegates warned that, if their large neighbors monopolized frontier development, the resulting inequalities in population and power would destroy the union. Sales of western lands would provide the landed states an inexhaustible source of revenue, enabling them to lower taxes and so attract settlers from overpopulated and overburdened landless states. Not coincidentally, many influential politicians in landless Maryland and Pennsylvania were investors in the Indiana Company – successor to the Vandalia scheme – and other speculative ventures. Landed state leaders thus concluded that private interest, not legitimate political or constitutional concerns, explained the landless states' hostility to their claims. Virginians, whose extensive claims in the Kentucky District and in the vast region north and west of the Ohio River constituted the leading target of landless state machinations, vigorously defended the sanctity of charter boundaries. They insisted that Congress's role was to protect the rights of its members, from each other as well as against the common enemy.

The landless states first sought to set limits to large state western claims in the Articles of Confederation. Congress, they argued, was the logical successor to the

Crown's jurisdictional and property rights in the West. The problem with this formulation was that it made Congress an interested party in the western lands controversy, thus compromising its position as an impartial, superintending authority. The landed states successfully rebuffed this direct challenge to their claims, and the final draft of the Articles sent out to the state legislatures in 1777 guaranteed the states' territorial pretensions. By withholding their approval of the document, however, Maryland and other landless estates hoped to force territorial cessions from the claiming states. The Articles would be acceptable once the landed states had relinquished their western claims to Congress. In effect, the landless states acknowledged that national title would have to be built on state titles. Maryland kept up the pressure by refusing to ratify the Articles until 1781. Thereafter, the landless majority in Congress continued to campaign for unconditional cessions.

The protracted impasse over the western lands revealed a general awareness of the importance of the West for the future of the union. Because Congress could not act decisively without jeopardizing its authority, some sort of accommodation among the states was prerequisite. On 6 September 1780, Congress first called on the landed states for territorial cessions, thus establishing a framework for compromise. Congress further pledged, in a resolution of 10 October, that the western lands would be developed for the common benefit of the United States and that new states eventually would be formed in the national domain. Landed state leaders agreed, at least in principle, that Congress should exercise control over the western lands. As the central government's financial obligations mounted and successive efforts to establish a national impost failed, revenue from public land sales seemed increasingly critical to the survival of the union. Furthermore, jurisdictional confusion subverted congressional efforts to coordinate and direct military and diplomatic efforts on the frontiers. The radical defects of Congress's authority thus became conspicuous as general agreement on the broad outlines of western policy emerged.

The landed states responded to the call for cessions with a series of offers which were rejected by the landless majority in Congress. Most controversial was Virginia's cession of January 1781. Landless state delegates complained about the extensive region, including the Kentucky District, that Virginia withheld from its cession; furthermore, Virginia insisted on the invalidation of all private titles in the ceded territory that it had not sanctioned. But Congress could avoid these embarrassing conditions by accepting New York's unconditional cession (February 1780) of much of the same territory covered by the Virginia cession. New Yorkers sought to trade their western claims, based on its supposed "suzerainty" over the Iroquois, for congressional support of their claims in the New Hampshire Grants (Vermont). On 29 October 1782, after a delay of more than two and a half years, the small states finally mustered a majority in favor of accepting New York's offer.

Congress hoped to avoid considering the relative merits of overlapping state titles by gaining cession from all the states. But Congress's inability to establish a plausible title on the basis of New York's cession exposed the limitations of this policy. Whatever the merits of its charter claims, Virginia had been militarily and politically active in the region north and west of the Ohio River and therefore had concrete interests to protect. Suspicions of congressional motives had led the state's leaders to stipulate specific cession conditions, securing Virginia's interests and guaranteeing that the new national domain otherwise be dedicated to the common benefit of the entire union. To Virginians, rejection of their state's offer and acceptance of New York's revealed Congress's partiality for the interests of private "landmongers." Such machi-

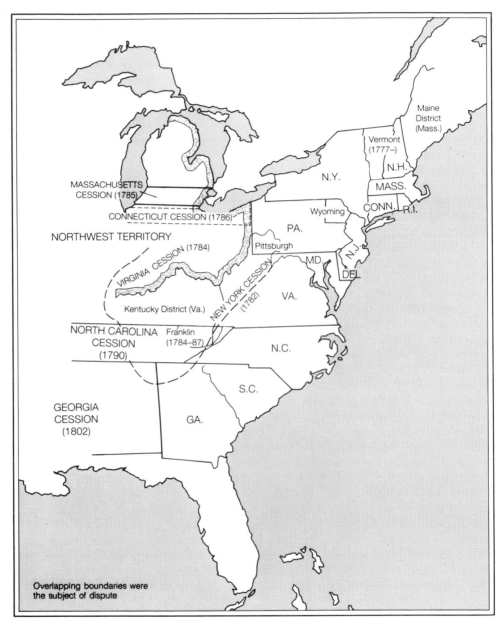

MAP 7 Western land cessions and new state movements

nations convinced the usually moderate James Madison that "the present Union will but little survive the present war."

Although completion of the New York cession proved a hollow victory for the landless states and their land company allies, it did set the stage for ultimate resolution of the western problem. Splitting the landed bloc and gaining control over Congress did not enable the small states to dictate policy to Virginia. To the contrary, small state delegates were increasingly hard pressed to explain why they found Virginia's conditions unacceptable. Meanwhile, American victory on the battlefield and rapid progress towards a definitive peace meant that western policy issues – treaty agreements with Indian nations, the distribution of military bounties, the sale of public lands, and the organization of new settlements – could not be evaded. Jurisdictional questions were no longer speculative or prospective. If the American states did not act quickly, the national government would never gain control over frontier development.

In the negotiations leading up to the completion of its cession in March 1784, Virginia enjoyed a decisive advantage: Congress could not organize or govern the Northwest Territory until Virginia relinquished its claims. At the same time, however, Virginians were more and more conscious of the difficulties and dangers of preserving their state's authority over such a vast region. With the onset of peace, traders, speculators, and squatters poured across the Ohio; meanwhile, Kentuckians complained of the inconveniences and inequities of Virginian rule. New state, separatist movements gained momentum in Kentucky and in southwestern Virginia as well as in the frontier regions of other large states; rumors of secret negotiations between disaffected elements and the Spanish and English spread rapidly. Responding to these developments, many Virginians became convinced that their state would be best served by sanctioning a new state in Kentucky and relinquishing jurisdiction over the trans-Ohio region to Congress. It was crucial in both cases to draw the various interested parties into binding agreements that would protect Virginian land titles and other essential interests.

The most controversial provision of Virginia's offer was its invalidation of unauthorized purchases by private land companies. Small state delegates ultimately realized, however, that their refusal to accommodate Virginia on this point jeopardized Congress's future rule in the West. Clearly, completion of the western land cessions would serve the interests of the landless states. The cessions would strengthen the union by helping to equalize the states and by guaranteeing that all of the states would share equally in the benefits of frontier development. Meanwhile, the ceding states – Virginia, Massachusetts (1785), and Connecticut (1786) – could be assured that the national domain would be administered according to the conditions and within the limits set forth in their cession acts.

3. WESTERN POLICY AND THE UNION

The furor over the western lands often obscured general agreement on the most desirable outcome: all parties agreed that Congress should develop and govern the new nation's vast hinterland. But could Congress be trusted to promote the national interest, or would it favor a particular group of states, or influential private interests? These, of course, were the same questions Americans asked about the proposed new national government in the ratification debates of 1787–8. The western lands controversy thus raised fundamental questions about the organization of the union under the Articles of Confederation. In effect, completion of the cessions amended the Articles, enlarging Congress's power by giving it direct jurisdiction over national territory while guaranteeing that that power would be exercised only for limited purposes.

Once the constitutional issues were resolved, congressmen had little trouble agreeing on the main lines of western policy. Congress had already committed itself to the eventual creation of new western states and to the development of the national domain

351

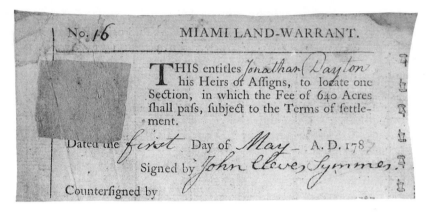

FIGURE 29 Land Warrant (1787) issued by Judge John Cleve Symmes to
Jonathan Dayton for whom Dayton, Ohio, was named. Symmes had grant of
land between the two Miami rivers, including present Dayton and Cincinnati.

for the "common benefit." Anticipating the rapid completion of the Virginia cession,
Congress thus named a committee headed by Thomas Jefferson to prepare an ordinance
for implementing those principles. The first territorial government ordinance, adopted
on 23 April 1784, a few weeks after the completion of the Virginia cession, articulated
the basic principles that subsequently governed American territorial policy. The
ordinance set forth boundaries for future states in unceded areas of western Virginia,
North Carolina, and Georgia, as well as for ten new states in the trans-Ohio region
recently ceded by Virginia. Settlers in the national domain were promised that, once
the free population of any one of these embryonic states had reached 20,000, they
would be entitled to "establish a permanent constitution and government for themselves." Then, when the number of "free inhabitants" in a new state equalled that of
the "least numerous of the thirteen Original states," it would be admitted to the union
"on an equal footing."

Meanwhile, another committee, also including Jefferson, sought to secure the
common benefit by establishing a system for the sale of public lands. But disagreement
over the cost of land, the size of parcels, and the relation between surveys and sales
led Congress to reject the first proposed land ordinance (on 30 April 1784). The major
contribution of the rejected ordinance was the grid survey system that was later
incorporated in the land ordinance adopted by Congress on 20 May 1785. Congressmen then agreed that surveys should precede sales, that federal lands should sell
for a minimum of a dollar an acre, and that townships (of six miles square) should be
sold alternately by individual lot (640 acres) and as a whole. Lands would be sold at
auctions in each of the original states.

Jefferson and his fellow policy-makers anticipated that the territorial government
and land ordinances would work together to govern the process of frontier settlement.
They thought the key to political and social order was the regular distribution of
property and the elimination of title conflicts that ordinarily produced so much conflict
on other frontiers. But efforts to implement the new system soon showed the need for
revisions. When the Seven Ranges, the first series of townships surveyed by United
States Geographer Thomas Hutchins and his surveyors, were brought to auction late
in 1787, only 72,934 acres were sold, producing a mere $117,108.22 in revenue.

Impatient to gain a quicker, more substantial return from the national domain, congressmen began to look more favorably on large-scale speculative enterprises, such as the Ohio Company, which promised to settle the region beyond the Seven Ranges with industrious and orderly New Englanders (*see* figure 29). In exchange for a substantial reduction in price – the company paid a total of $1,000,000 (in depreciated Continental securities) for 1,500,000 acres – the Ohio Associates agreed to assume responsibility for extending the survey system.

Congress had to offer more attractive terms for its lands, and so modify the 1785 ordinance, because of the need to compete for settlers with states with extensive public land reserves, such as New York and Massachusetts, as well as with British Canada. Yet the demand for Ohio lands, already well known for their productivity, was potentially great. In order to exploit that demand, however, Congress would not only have to sell its lands at competitive prices but would have to establish effective temporary government for the region. The experiences of federal surveyors and military garrisons on the Ohio showed the inadequacy of Congress's original western policy, embodied in the territorial government and land ordinances of 1784 and 1785. Federal lands would be worthless unless the illegal settlers who swarmed into the region were driven off, and bona fide purchasers were able to develop their property in peace.

The Northwest Ordinance, adopted on 13 July 1787, represented the culmination of protracted efforts to elaborate provisions for the temporary government of the national domain. The authors of the new ordinance did not abandon the commitment to create new and equal states set forth in the 1784 ordinance. But because the statehood promise was grounded in the prior cession "compact" between Virginia and the United States, the new territorial government committee felt free to draft an entirely new ordinance. Major changes included a reduction in the number of prospective new states from ten to between three and five and a new population threshold – 60,000 "free inhabitants" (a fixed rather than variable standard that would probably accelerate the admission of new states). But most crucial was the institution of direct congressional rule, to be gradually relinquished in successive stages. While the 1784 ordinance stipulated that settlers would establish their own temporary government, the 1787 document gave legislative as well as executive and judicial authority to the governor and three territorial judges – all federal appointees. Only when there were 5,000 free male inhabitants in the territory would a popularly elected assembly exercise any authority. In the event, self-government was long-delayed: the first assembly in the Northwest Territory was not convened until 1799.

What is most remarkable about this new, avowedly "colonial" system of territorial government was that it aroused so little controversy in Congress. At a time when inter-sectional tensions were running high and disunionist sentiment was on the rise, northerners and southerners in Congress agreed that a "high-toned" administration of the Northwest Territory was essential. The explanations for this consensus are straightforward. First, continuing rumblings on the frontiers – threats of Indian wars, separatist movements, foreign adventurism, and widespread defiance of state and federal officials by illegal settlers – underscored the immediate threat to the common interests of the states in Congress. Before the resolution of the western lands controversy, Maryland and other landless states had encouraged new state movements and other assaults on large state jurisdictional pretensions. Now, of course, the small states would not countenance any challenge to federal jurisdiction or property interests in the new national domain. Regardless of their distinctive interests on other questions, notably on the regulation of commerce or on the navigation of the Mississippi, congressmen agreed on the importance of public land sales as a source of desperately needed revenue.

Congressmen recognized that the institution of effective temporary government on the northwestern frontier represented a crucial test for the durability of the union. Awareness that the national domain was jeopardized by separatist movements, diplomatic intrigues, and Indian wars dictated a united front. For many policy-makers and commentators these prudential concerns were reinforced by the belief that the development of the West was the key to the nation's future prosperity and power. "If we make a right use of our natural advantages," an Independence Day orator promised in 1785, "we soon must be a truly great and happy people." But this "right use" was not foreordained. If Congress failed to act expeditiously, all would be lost. The value of the western lands, as a source of revenue and of economic growth, depended on attracting orderly, industrious commercial farmers to the region. The land ordinance would assure that new settlements would extend gradually and systematically from the old, thus facilitating the extension of trade routes and the establishment of civil authority. Restrained within defensible limits, these settlements would coexist peacefully with their Indian neighbors, so eliminating expensive and debilitating wars. The national frontier would thus be a valuable source of revenue, not a drain on the treasury. Most important, carefully regulated settlement was the best guarantee of continuing "union" between the East and the frontiers, a union based on complementary and common interests.

Prospective settlers could only be attracted to the Ohio country if their lives and estates were protected against the depredations of the "white savages" and "banditti" who infested it. Mannasseh Cutler, lobbyist for the Ohio Associates, carried this message to New York, where Congress was sitting, and helped spur final passage of the Northwest Ordinance. By establishing a strong territorial government, the Ordinance guaranteed the continuing federal presence that potential purchasers of federal lands demanded. Yet the compact articles of the Ordinance promised that the federal hold gradually would be relaxed as the new states grew towards social and political maturity. The most famous article, the sixth, was supposed to prohibit the future importation of slaves into the region; introduced at the final stages of deliberations, the slavery ban was probably a concession to the Yankee sensibilities of the Ohio Associates.

Every state delegation then represented in Congress voted for the Ordinance. This remarkable unanimity stands in contrast to congressional divisions during the western lands controversy and to contemporaneous sectional splits on other questions. Challenges to national authority in the Ohio country helped clarify the common interests of the eastern states in regulating frontier development. The overarching conflict was between western farmers and speculators who sought unlimited access to western lands and eastern policy-makers who were determined to restrain settlement and thereby foster development and strengthen the union. Congress's hostility to westerners was apparent both in its military actions against illegal settlers and in its efforts to attract easterners to the national domain. Western policy-makers hoped to restrain the dangerous centrifugal tendencies of uncontrolled settlement; they were convinced that the survival of the union depended on easternizing the West.

Congressional western policy was most notably successful in establishing a durable federal presence and protecting national property interests in the Northwest Territory. And by asserting its control over new state formation, Congress effectively discouraged the separatist agitation that kept frontier settlements in a turmoil in the mid-1780s. The immediate effect of congressional rule was to depoliticize the frontier and so reassure eastern congressmen that they would not be overwhelmed by delegates from poor, lightly populated western states. The drafting and implementation of the land and government ordinances thus created a framework for economic development and the expansion of the union that successfully addressed easterners' fears about losing population, wealth, and political power to the frontiers. Limited expansion would be integrative, drawing old and new states closer together by fostering common interests. Congress would exercise direct rule while these bonds remained weak and undeveloped, thus holding localistic tendencies in check.

Although congressional western policy established a broad framework for territorial expansion, its original scope necessarily was limited. As long as vast stretches of the American hinterland remained under state jurisdiction, the political aspirations of frontiersmen jeopardized national security and competition from state land offices undercut the value of federal lands. The new national government therefore sought to normalize frontier politics and extend the national domain. In 1790, North Carolina ceded its western claims to the United States; although the Southwest Territory added little to the national domain – most lands had already been transferred to private hands – the federal government extended its authority over an area that had been a hotbed of separatism and chronic conflict with the Indians. Shortly thereafter, in 1791 and 1792 respectively, the independent republic of Vermont and the Kentucky District of Virginia were admitted to the union.

The great achievement of western policy-makers was to secure the union of East and West during a period of political crisis and constitutional change. By resolving a divisive legacy of jurisdictional confusion on the frontiers, the American states were able to define their common interests more clearly.

FURTHER READING

Abernethy, Thomas Perkins: *Western Lands and the American Revolution* (New York, 1937; repr. New York: Russell & Russell, 1958).

Cayton, Andrew R. L.: *The Frontier Republic: Ideology and Politics in the Ohio Country, 1790–1825* (Kent, Ohio: Kent State University Press, 1986).

Jensen, Merrill: *The Articles of Confederation: an Interpretation of the Social-Constitutional History of the American Revolution, 1774–1781* (Madison: University of Wisconsin Press, 1940).

——: *The New Nation: a History of the United States During the Confederation, 1781–1789* (New York: Alfred A. Knopf, 1950).

Onuf, Peter S.: *The Origins of the Federal Republic: Jurisdictional Controversies in the United States, 1775–1787* (Philadelphia: University of Pennsylvania Press, 1983).

——: *Statehood and Union: a History of the Northwest Ordinance* (Bloomington: Indiana University Press, 1987).

Rakove, Jack N.: *The Beginnings of National Politics: an Interpretive History of the Continental Congress* (New York: Alfred A. Knopf, 1979).

Slaughter, Thomas P.: *The Whiskey Rebellion: Frontier Epilogue to the American Revolution* (New York: Oxford University Press, 1986).

36

Demobilization and national defense

E. WAYNE CARP

AS a result of the Continental Congress's inability to pay its soldiers, the demobilization of the Continental Army, a process spanning nearly two years from the American victory at Yorktown (1781) to the signing of the Paris Peace Treaty (1783), was an inglorious affair. It was punctuated by a revolt of the Pennsylvania Line and a potential *coup d'état* by nationalist army officers at army headquarters in Newburgh, New York. For the majority of enlisted men, moreover, demobilization was particularly bitter: they simply left camp and drifted home, unpaid and unheralded. Revolts and rumored coups renewed America's distaste for standing armies in peacetime. These ideological fears, coupled with the Confederation Congress's political and economic weaknesses, made the postwar establishment of permanent military institutions a difficult, piecemeal process. In 1784, Congress rejected George Washington's proposals for a small peacetime army and a national militia. But soon thereafter, forced to defend the frontier against the Indians, Congress authorized the First·American Regiment, a regular army of 700 men drawn from state militias, which would remain in service throughout the Confederation period. With little cooperation from the states, this small force proved unable to cope with foreign intrigue, Indian raids, and, most importantly, Shays's Rebellion. In 1787, the nation's leaders met in Philadelphia to remedy the weaknesses of the Articles of Confederation. Despite strong opposition from the Anti-Federalists, the Constitution significantly strengthened the nation's capacity to defend itself militarily. Nevertheless, it took several American defeats at the hands of the Northwest Indians (1790, 1791) before Congress created the Legion of the United States and finally accepted in principle a permanent peacetime regular army and reorganized the state militias under the Militia Act of 1792.

I. LOCALISM AND REAL WHIG IDEOLOGY

The demobilization of the Continental Army and the establishment of permanent military institutions must be understood within the context of colonial American political culture and the experience of the American Revolutionary War. Two aspects of colonial American political culture, localism and Real Whig ideology, particularly influenced the colonists' military beliefs and practices. The colonists' localistic perspective resulted largely from more than a half century of "salutary neglect" by British officialdom and the emergence in the colonies of a *de facto* system of self-government. During the imperial crisis of the 1760s and 1770s, Americans viewed Parliament's taxation and its claims of undivided sovereignty as threats not only to their liberty and property, but also to their traditional way of life.

The militia symbolized and reinforced Americans' attachments to their local communities. Springing up with the first English settlements, the militia was composed of part-time soldiers, existing primarily for local defense, who rarely ventured beyond their provincial borders or engaged in offensive war. During the eighteenth century, as settlement grew and population increased, the militia's fighting skills atrophied. Colonists ceased to depend on the militia for defense and instead relied on volunteers and draftees commanded by British regulars or Americans. Thus, although by mid-eighteenth century the militia had long ceased to be an effective shield against foreign or Indian attack except on the frontier, the colonists continued to believe that it was invincible when defending the local community.

The colonists' beliefs in Real Whig ideology, which led them to distrust professional standing armies, reinforced their faith in the militia. Real Whig anti-military sentiment was primarily a legacy of the English Civil War and Oliver Cromwell's Protectorate, during which the civilian government was replaced with what amounted to a military dictatorship. Throughout the seventeenth and eighteenth centuries, Real Whig political writers repeatedly warned that a standing army endangered English liberties, that professional soldiers were a source of social oppression, and that the very existence of a professional army was evidence of a corrupted people. Real Whig arguments against standing armies became deeply embodied in most colonial Americans' ideological world-view.

One of the greatest ironies of the American Revolution is that those aspects of the colonists' political culture most responsible for propelling Americans into revolt – their fear of concentrated power, their tradition of self-government, and their abhorrence of standing armies – made waging war, mobilizing manpower, and supplying the army almost impossible. By 1780, as a result of military defeats, manpower and supply shortages, public apathy, and financial chaos, the Revolution had nearly collapsed. The experience of fighting a war under a weak central government, uncooperative state legislatures, and repeated military defeats convinced many Revolutionaries, who considered themselves nationalists, of the necessity to strengthen Congress's powers. Although the Continental Army, now composed of seasoned regulars, eventually defeated the British at Yorktown with the aid of the French, most Americans congratulated themselves on their own and the militia's patriotic resistance against tyranny. The debate over America's national peacetime military establishment was shaped, but distorted, by the experience of fighting a war shackled by ideological fears of standing armies and a strong national government.

2. THE NEWBURGH ADDRESSES AND THE REVOLT OF THE PENNSYLVANIA LINE

In the midst of celebrating military victory over the British, the demobilization of the Continental Army reignited the nation's anti-military prejudices. A series of alarming events revolving around the issue of pay for officers and enlisted men appeared to pose a serious threat to civilian government. In particular, officers' demands for pensions escalated into a threat of a *coup d'état*. Historians still disagree on the exact details of the "Newburgh conspiracy," but the broad outlines are clear. In late 1782, as the approximately 10,000-man Continental Army unofficially began to demobilize at its final cantonment at Newburgh, New York, an impoverished and bitter officer corps feared that the army would disband before Congress made good its promise to fund their half-pay for life pensions. Congress viewed the officers' pension proposal as a European military affectation that America should avoid; the officers believed the

357

pensions were just recompense for their financial sacrifices during the war. In December 1782 a committee of three, representing the disgruntled officers, carried a petition to Congress offering to accept a commutation of half-pay for life to some equivalent lump-sum payment and warning of the "fatal effects" if denied. Extreme nationalists such as Alexander Hamilton, Robert Morris, and Gouverneur Morris, their plans for a strong central government thwarted, seized the opportunity presented by the potentially mutinous army to attempt to coerce reluctant congressmen to strengthen Congress's taxing power. Their effort failed, and amid a chorus of denunciation of officers' greed and fears that a half-pay settlement would corrupt America's republican society, Congress rejected a resolve to commute half-pay for life to six years' full payment, preferring that the state legislatures handle the problem of officers' pensions. When word reached camp of Congress's refusal to meet their demands, a second group of officers, encouraged by extreme nationalists and led by General Horatio Gates, issued the inflammatory Newburgh Addresses calling upon the army to refuse to disband if its grievances were not redressed. At an officers' meeting on 15 March 1783, Washington's dramatic appeal to the army's tradition of subordination to civil authority effectively dissipated the officers' enthusiasm for rebellion. A week later, tension was further defused when word arrived that Congress had voted the officers full pay for five years and enlisted men full pay for four months, although the source of funding was left to the future. Yet, as Richard H. Kohn has written, "the Newburgh conspiracy was the closest an American army has ever come to revolt or *coup d'état*" and the fears it raised among political leaders lingered long after the event (Kohn, 1975, p. 17).

In June 1783, a revolt by a segment of the Pennsylvania Line insured that America's heritage of distrusting standing armies would emerge from the war as strong as ever. Two months earlier, Washington had recommended that Congress grant three months' full pay to enlisted men who were no longer obeying their officers. But a financially bankrupt Congress refused to heed Washington's advice. Instead, in June Congress furloughed the soldiers to their homes, pending a discharge once the definitive treaty of peace had been signed, without any provision for settling their accounts or a word of appreciation. Outraged, 80 new recruits of the Pennsylvania Line marched from Lancaster to Philadelphia, joined several hundred other angry soldiers quartered in the city, and barricaded several members of Congress and the Executive Council of Pennsylvania in the State House demanding their pay before they went home. The revolt quickly petered out, however, when several congressmen walked out of the State House unharmed amid insults shouted by drunken soldiers. Alarmed, Congress moved from Philadelphia to Princeton, and Revolutionaries everywhere noted the army's threat to civil authority.

Meanwhile, the rest of the Continental Army troops decided not to wait for their pay and complied with the congressional furlough. By mid-June most of the disgruntled enlisted men had started for home, while 700 soldiers were retained for garrison duty. The Continental Army disbanded unhappily, amid threats of mutinies and coups.

3. WASHINGTON'S "SENTIMENTS ON A PEACE ESTABLISHMENT"

In the midst of the Continental Army's unruly demobilization, Congress was forced to consider what kind of permanent military organization to create, because the New York and Pennsylvania authorities requested military aid for negotiating Indian treaties and garrisoning British-occupied forts. In April 1783, in response to a congressional committee, Washington sent Congress his "Sentiments on a Peace Establishment," outlining his understanding of the nation's future military needs and American republicanism. Washington advocated a small permanent army of 2,631 men designed to protect the frontier and to serve as a nucleus for security in a general war. He also recommended that a national militia be established, consisting of a reserve force of all male citizens aged between 18 and 55 and a select group of young men aged 18 to 25 specially trained for military emergencies. Washington's "Sentiments," a product of wartime experience, represented the nationalists' new understanding of republicanism, which now emphasized military preparedness, a select militia, and a peacetime standing army to protect republican institutions from foreign invasion and domestic insurrection. The "Sentiments" became the basis for all subsequent discussion about the organization of the armed forces in the early Republic.

In the immediate postwar era, Washington's proposals never stood a chance of enactment because of the nation's financial weakness and Congress's traditional fears of a standing army in peacetime. On 2 June 1784, Congress ordered General Henry Knox, the ranking senior officer, to discharge all but 80 soldiers. Nevertheless, recognizing that Indian defense demanded a larger force, Congress the next day erected the first national peacetime military force in American history by recommending that several states furnish 700 men from their militias to serve one year. Although only Pennsylvania met its quota of soldiers, Congress had created the First American Regiment.

4. SHAYS'S REBELLION

Throughout the Confederation era (1781–9), America's military weakness was manifest, especially in coping with Indian threats in the Northwest and South and with British refusal to abandon their forts in the Northwest, as the Treaty of Paris stipulated. In addition, Congress looked on helplessly as Spain closed the Mississippi to all United States shipping and stirred up secessionist sentiment in the Southwest (*see* Chapter 38, §2). The low point in the Confederation Congress's military experience occurred in September 1786, when a former Revolutionary War officer, Daniel Shays, and 1,100 debt-ridden farmers marched to the Court of Common Pleas in Hampshire County, Massachusetts, to prevent the seizure of their property for the payment of debts and taxes. Eight hundred militiamen, called out by the Confederation Congress to defend the Court, refused to act because they sympathized with the rioters. Consequently, in October, Congress called upon the states for $530,000 in order to raise a special force of 1,340 men to crush the rebellion. Only Virginia responded. More than any other single event during the Confederation period, Shays's Rebellion revealed the inadequacy of Congress's military powers under the Articles of Confederation.

Most importantly, Shays's Rebellion galvanized the movement to revise the Articles of Confederation and led directly to the calling of the Constitutional Convention. When the delegates met in Philadelphia in May 1787, opponents of a strong central government, termed Anti-Federalists by their detractors, denounced the Constitution's military provisions using Real Whig arguments against standing armies. Anti-Federalists particularly feared giving the national government the power to tax and control of the military. They worried that the new government would use a professional army to collect unjust taxes and questioned whether the country needed a standing army when at peace. The Massachusetts delegate Elbridge

Gerry even suggested that the Constitution should limit the national army to 3,000 men. For the Anti-Federalists, the militia was sufficient for the nation's defense.

5. THE CONSTITUTION'S MILITARY PROVISIONS

The Federalists – nationalist supporters of the Constitution – defended the Constitution's military provisions by turning to the "lessons" of the Revolutionary War. They argued that, had the United States relied on citizen soldiers alone during the war, America would have lost its independence. Although the Federalists credited the Continental Army with America's military victory, they argued that a national military force, encompassing both regular and militia soldiers, was essential to the preservation of America's independence. Such a force, Federalists explained, would prevent the proliferation of standing armies within each state and thus forestall the Confederation's collapse into warring sections. They also argued that, because of America's geographic isolation, the nation required only a small military establishment to protect the frontier, seaports, and federal arsenals. Thus the Federalists directly confronted Anti-Federalists' fears of centralized military power by arguing that the Constitution's military provisions were necessary for the survival of America's republican institutions.

Compared with the Articles of Confederation, the Constitution's military clauses represented a significant triumph for the nationalists. The proposed Constitution gave Congress the exclusive right to declare war and raise and support both an army and a navy, with the sole proviso that no army appropriation should run longer than two years. The President was made commander-in-chief of the armed forces and authorized to appoint military officers with the advice and consent of the Senate. In its militia provisions, the Constitution also signified an advance over the Articles of Confederation. Congress was authorized to call out the state militia in order to enforce federal law, maintain civil order, and repel invasions; and to exert control over the organization, arming, and disciplining of the state units. Both clauses represented radical departures from the tradition of virtual independence which colonial and state militias had enjoyed.

Although the Constitution's military clauses represented a nationalistic triumph, other constitutional provisions undercut federal control of the military by creating a series of barriers against the possibility of military despotism. Control of the military was divided by vesting the executive branch, not Congress, with its command, although the commander-in-chief was in turn dependent on the Congress for military appropriations. The Constitution also divided military power between the federal government and the states. The states retained their militias and could be called into federal service only for limited purposes. The Second Amendment to the Constitution further guaranteed the existence of the state militias by mandating that "a well-regulated militia being necessary to the security of a free state, the right of the people to bear arms shall not be infringed." Many Anti-Federalists felt that the state militias would be a counterweight to any possible misuse of a national standing army.

6. THE LEGION OF THE UNITED STATES AND THE UNIFORM MILITIA ACT

The ratification of the Constitution had little immediate effect on the nation's military establishment. Rather, it laid the foundations upon which a stronger national power

360

might be built in the future. Congress initially rejected Secretary of War Henry Knox's proposal to increase the regular army from 840 to 2,033 men and to provide for a select militia similar to the one Washington proposed. But because Indian relations in the Northwest were fast deteriorating, Congress resolved in 1790 to increase the First American Regiment's strength to 1,216 men. In the wake of the crushing defeats that the Northwest Indians administered to the militia-dominated Regiment in 1790 and 1791, however (see chapter 40), Congress authorized for three years a reorganized, regular army of more than 5,000 men, dubbed the Legion of the United States. Significantly, after the defeat of the Northwest Indians by General Anthony Wayne at the Battle of Fallen Timbers (1794) and the signing of the Treaty of Grenville, Congress did not dismantle the Legion. Instead, in March 1796, Congress accepted the necessity of a small peacetime standing army to garrison frontier posts, coastal forts, and federal arsenals. The continuance of the Legion constituted a watershed in the creation of America's permanent military establishment: it was the beginning of the nation's acceptance in principal of a standing army in peacetime.

Problems with the Northwest Indians, as well as persistent anti-standing army ideology, also led Congress in 1792 to enact the Uniform Militia Act which, contrary to Knox's proposal for a select militia under federal control, provided for universal military training and delegated to the states the responsibility for enrolling all male citizens aged 18 to 45 for militia duty. Congress thus provided loopholes in the law to allow the states to evade compliance with federal guidelines. It failed to provide procedures for training the militia, to institute a system of inspection, or to impose penalties on either the states or individuals for non-compliance with its provisions. Historians have failed to agree on the merits of the Uniform Militia Act. Scholars such as John K. Mahon have denounced the Militia Act as a "virtual abdication by the federal government of all authority over the state militias" (Mahon, 1983, p. 56). On the other side, Russell Weigley, while admitting the Act's military deficiencies, praises it for preserving the tradition of a citizen soldiery. Henceforth, America's permanent military establishment would continue to build upon two foundations: the Regulars in the United States Army and the Militia Act of 1792.

FURTHER READING

Carp, E. Wayne: "The problem of national defense in the early republic," *The American Revolution: its Character and Limits*, ed. Jack P. Greene (New York: New York University Press, 1987), 14–50.

Cress, Lawrence Delbert: *Citizens in Arms: the Army and Militia in American Society to the War of 1812* (Chapel Hill: University of North Carolina Press, 1982).

Hatch, Louis Clinton: *The Administration of the American Revolution* (New York: Longmans, Green and Co., 1904).

Kohn, Richard H.: *Eagle and Sword: the Beginnings of the Military Establishment in America* (New York: Free Press, 1975).

Mahon, John K.: *History of the Militia and the National Guard* (New York and London: Macmillan, 1983).

Weigley, Russell F.: *History of the United States Army*, enlarged edn. (Bloomington: Indiana University Press, 1984).

37

Currency, taxation, and finance, 1775–1787

ROBERT A. BECKER

THE Revolution created a financial crisis in the rebelling colonies. Colonial taxes had been very light, but the rebels had to raise unprecedented sums to continue the war, creating in the process huge public debts in every state. At the same time, Congress issued a national currency and spent it, creating a national debt, although it had no independent taxing powers whatever. As both state and national governments struggled to raise enough to continue the war, and after it, to pay their war debts, fierce disputes arose about how best to do both. Despite all their difficulties, the new republics and the Continental Congress managed to raise enough through currency emissions, taxes, loans, and occasional confiscations to secure independence. In the postwar years, several of the states managed, as well, to reduce significantly their own and the nation's remaining debts. Out of their experience with wartime taxes and with the collapse of the Continental currency in the middle of the war, Americans drew conclusions about the nature (and worth) of their first constitution, the Articles of Confederation, and about the viability of the state-centered republican government it established, some concluding that it was best to locate fiscal and monetary authority in the states, which could respond quickly to local crises and needs, while others concluded that economic stability (and thus effective government) could be achieved only if those powers were located in a national government, far from the influence of popular majorities in the several states. Their experiences directly affected the movement for a new national government that ended in the Philadelphia Convention of 1787, and shaped the content of the Constitution it produced.

I. THE BEGINNINGS OF NATIONAL FINANCE

When the Second Continental Congress convened at Philadelphia in May 1775 the colonies were already at war, and by the end of June Congress began taking on the responsibilities of a government. It raised an army and declared the colonies collectively responsible for what was spent defending their common cause. How that money should be raised, however, posed a dilemma. Barring the question of what authority Congress had to tax anyone, there was the problem of whether a people brought to war in protest over British taxes could safely be asked to pay unprecedented American ones. Prudently choosing not to press the matter, Congress instead resorted to the colonial governments' customary way of raising money during crises, issuing paper currency – a practice "so ingrained in the colonists that nothing else was seriously considered" (Ferguson, 1961, p. 26).

The colonies had normally issued currency in two ways. Some had printed bills of credit and loaned them out, at interest, to individuals who put up land as security. This not only put the money into circulation quickly, it provided a reliable public

FIGURE 30 (a): A United States 50-dollar certificate (1778); (b): a Rhode Island 20-shilling bill (1786); (c): a military due bill, 1784

(a)

(b)

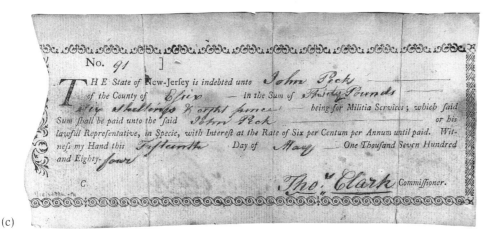

(c)

income (the interest payments) that kept taxes low. New York, for example, had £40,000 out on loan and made £1,350 a year from it until the Currency Act of 1764 ended the practice. Pennsylvania took in about £2,000 a year in interest from its loan office until 1768. Delaware normally paid all of its regular government expenses from interest on its bills of credit. But loan office revenues were slow to come in because the interest payments began only a year after the money was loaned out. More commonly, and especially during wars, the colonies had simply printed money and spent it while promising to collect future taxes to redeem it. Bills so issued were, in effect, tax anticipation notes.

In the critical months after Lexington and Concord, Congress busily printed money (creating a national currency; *see* figure 30a) and spent it (creating a national debt). It expected each rebelling colony, ultimately, to sink (i.e., to tax in and remove from circulation) a sum in proportion to its population. It could have left it up to each colony to emit its proportion of the money, but an irrefutably *national* currency had important advantages. Congress could create and spend it as rapidly as necessary without having to ask anyone's approval or to wait for the various provincial congresses to act. And such a currency would serve, in Gouverneur Morris's words, as a "bond of union to the Associated colonies" (Burnett, 1941, p. 81). In June 1775, Congress issued $2,000,000 in currency. In July it printed $1,000,000 more and then $3,000,000 more before the year's end. It prudently chose to delay redemption (i.e., the date on which it would ask the states to start taxing the money in) until 1779, thus also postponing the sensitive matter of deciding exactly how large a share of this new national debt each rebelling colony should shoulder.

That these measures were woefully inadequate soon became clear. As rebellion turned to revolution and the price of independence rose beyond what even the gloomiest reluctant rebel had imagined possible, Congress discovered that it had no choice but to "stuff ... the maw of the Revolution with paper money" (Ferguson, 1961, p. 29). By the end of 1776 there was $25,000,000 in Continental currency in circulation and more obviously on the way. With expenses running at about $1,000,000 a week in paper by mid-1778, Congress began printing currency in lots of five or ten million every few weeks. It had printed more than $241,000,000 by 1780 when it finally abandoned new emissions.

Table 1   Depreciation of Continental currency (currency required to purchase $1.00 specie)

	1777	1778	1779	1780	1781
January	1.25	4.00	8.00	42.50	100.00
April	2.00	6.00	16.00	60.00	167.50
July	3.00	4.00	19.00	62.50	
October	3.00	5.00	30.00	77.50	

Source: Ferguson, 1961, p. 32.

Inevitably, the currency depreciated (see table 1). By July 1777 Continental currency had lost two-thirds of its face value (that is, it took $3 Continental to purchase $1 specie). By January 1779 it took $8 Continental to buy $1 specie. By October it took $30. One year later it took $77. By April 1781 Continentals circulated at more than 167 to 1 against specie. To stem the decline (and the resulting upward spiral of prices), Congress called upon the states to fix prices, confiscate loyalist property, and begin taxing in specie and the Continental paper already issued. In November it asked the states for $5,000,000 to be sent to the common treasury in 1778. By the fall of 1779 it had requested $95,000,000, and it expected $135,000,000 in 1780. That did not include the $6,000,000 a year in Continental currency it had asked the states to retire from circulation (by taxes) every year beginning in 1779 (Ferguson, 1961, pp. 33–4). Some states began confiscating loyalist property, but the effect on the worth of Continental currency or on the cost of the war was negligible. (Jackson Turner

Main estimates that confiscated loyalist property amounted to less than 4 per cent of the worth of all property, real and personal, in the colonies [Main, 1973, p. 330]). Only taxation held real promise as a way of propping up the currency and managing the debt. But Congress had no power, in law or in fact, to tax or to compel the states to tax. Under the Articles of Confederation, "all charges of war and all other expenses that shall be incurred for the common defense or general welfare" were to be "defrayed out of a common treasury, which shall be supplied by the several states, in proportion to the value of all land within each state...." The resulting taxes could only be "laid and levied by the authority and direction of the legislatures of the several states ..." (Tansill, 1927, pp. 30–1). Congress, then, merely had the right to ask the states to tax on its behalf. In fact, its requisitions produced relatively little real income. E. J. Ferguson estimates, for example, that the $12,897,575 Congress had received by requisition by 1780 was worth only $776,000 in specie (Ferguson, 1961, p. 35).

Next to simply printing money and receiving state contributions, Congress's only significant source of revenue was loans. Benjamin Franklin and Silas Deane arranged a £1,000,000 loan from the French Farmers General in March 1777, secured by promised delivery of American tobacco to France. American envoys won a direct subsidy from France of 2,000,000 livres in 1777 and had secured 4,000,000 in loans and another 5,000,000 in supplies by 1779. Smaller Dutch and Spanish subsidies brought direct foreign aid for the Revolution by early 1781 to $2,213,000 in specie (Ferguson, 1961, pp. 34–42). Virtually all of it was spent in Europe on war supplies and its impact on the worth of the national currency was negligible.

Congress borrowed from Americans too. It opened a Continental Loan Office to sell bonds paying 4 per cent interest to the public. Congress was, in effect, asking buyers to bet on rebel victory in the war. Relatively few bonds sold. The interest was too low to be attractive (private loans paid from 8 to 18 per cent interest). And of course, if the war was lost, the bonds would be worthless, whereas private debts might still be collected through the postwar English courts. Congress raised the interest to 6 per cent in February 1777, and in September it offered to pay the interest in bills of exchange (in effect, in specie, or nearly so) drawn against French subsidies supplied to the Revolution's agents in France. Even so, only $3,330,000 worth sold by the time Congress withdrew the offer in March 1778. Thereafter, Continental bonds paid interest only in paper money, which depreciated at an appalling rate. Nevertheless, the bonds depreciated less and more slowly than Continental currency did. All told, the Loan Office disposed of about $60,000,000 in Loan Office Certificates (as they were known) before Congress closed it in 1781 (Ferguson, 1961, pp. 37–9).

Congress was also obligated for millions worth of military supply certificates, which were written by army quartermasters and other Continental supply officers to pay for goods seized and services coerced by the army, or voluntarily provided by patriots, and which did not, as a rule, pay interest. These were, in effect, merely congressional IOUs (as were the certificates issued to soldiers in lieu of pay) and the total was enormous. E. James Ferguson estimates $95,000,000 worth had been issued by late 1781 in only ten states (Ferguson, 1961, p. 63). As the Continental currency depreciated, the worth of the certificates depreciated too. By 1780, or even earlier, few accepted them unless coerced, and those who saw their property seized and paid for with quartermasters' certificates believed, with some justice, that their goods had simply been confiscated.

By late 1779 Continental currency depreciation was so out of hand, and Congress's efforts to support the national currency had had so little effect, that it stopped printing money and devised a plan to replace the existing Continental paper with a new, more valuable and less volatile national currency. In March 1780 Congress revalued the outstanding Continental currency at 40 to 1 (i.e., it declared each $40 in currency to be worth $1 in specie, which substantially overvalued the currency) and called on the states to tax in all of the old money over the next year. For every $40 in old money a state collected and destroyed, it would receive $2 in new Continental money, 60 per cent of which it could keep for its own purposes and 40 per cent of which Congress would spend. The new money's success depended on the taxing ability of states which were themselves facing financial crises similar to the one Congress faced, and had been since the opening days of the war.

2. FINANCING REVOLUTION IN THE STATES

As British authority collapsed in the early spring of 1775, the provisional revolutionary governments and colonial assemblies (where they continued to sit) began to raise money to fight a war they hoped would last only months. By mid-summer, however, these nascent rebel governments understood that they faced prolonged war. To pay for it, they turned to the same sources Congress relied on, borrowing money and emitting currency backed by promises of taxes at some conveniently distant date.

This was unavoidable, for the imposition of high taxes (and sometimes any taxes) threatened to undermine support for the Revolution. The New York Provincial Congress warned in the spring and summer of 1775 that any attempt to tax would provoke "popular disgust ... or opposition." Under the circumstances, it told Congress in May, collecting taxes was "clearly impossible" (NY Provincial Congress, 1842, Vol. 1, pp. 14, 92; Vol. 2, pp. 17–18). Delaware's cautious assembly, fearing wholesale desertions to the King's colors, flatly refused to tax. The provisional revolutionary governments of Virginia, North Carolina, and Georgia all issued paper and postponed taxing. The South Carolina Provincial Congress printed £1,870,000 in paper between June 1775 and March 1776 without collecting new taxes. Those few rebelling colonies which tried to tax early in the war ran into stiff public resistance. New Jersey, for example, had to resort to force and confiscations to collect even part of the £10,000 tax it levied in June 1775.

Another problem the new governments faced was the uncertainty of their own legitimacy. By what authority did they claim the right to tax anyone? Back-country settlers in New Hampshire, for example, insisted that the Revolution had placed them in a state of nature and thus they owed unquestioned obedience (and taxes) to no government, royal or rebel, until a new constitution was drafted and properly ratified. Others felt the same.

Issuing paper money while avoiding taxes also let the rebelling states put off deciding how much people should pay (see figure 30b). Once taxing began, the new states could not avoid the question of what constituted *just* taxation. Were the old colonial tax systems, thought by many to be discriminatory and oppressive, simply to be re-enacted by the new republics? Or would new, more equitable systems have to be devised? Resolving such questions would create divisions within the rebel legislatures that they could ill afford. Not taxing allowed these troublesome matters to be shunted aside and the various state governments to appear more united than in fact they were. Under the circumstances, fighting first and paying later made political sense.

Massachusetts's Provincial Congress issued £26,000 in paper in May 1775, £100,000 in August, and £75,000 more in December, with taxes to redeem some of it put off until the 1780s. New Hampshire issued £40,000 in 1776, with some of the sinking fund taxes delayed to the 1790s. Rhode Island issued money in September without bothering to name any sinking taxes at all. By the summer of 1776 New York had emitted £300,000 with virtually no funding in place. By the end of 1775 the several states had borrowed more than £1,000,000 from their own citizens and issued more than £3,000,000 in paper. By January 1778 the states had probably put in circulation £7,000,000 in paper of one sort or another (Main, 1973, pp. 224–5).

Most of this paper was made legal tender in hopes of forcing its acceptance by merchants and farmers. With money from various sources flooding the new states, with taxes to support it not yet levied or not effectively collected, with Continental and state supply officers bidding against each other for military supplies, and with bad news from the battlefields undermining confidence in the rebel cause, what resulted was unavoidable: prices soared and the state currencies depreciated. In trying to stem the collapse of their currencies, however, the states had an advantage the Congress lacked: they could tax, presuming they could muster the will to do so. Beginning in 1777, most of them did.

In that year, all the states save Delaware, New York, and Georgia began levying high taxes to reduce the amount of circulating paper, to raise money to supply the Continental Army and the state militias, and to meet, whenever possible, Congress's requisitions. To make these levies more palatable, many of the states substantially reformed their tax laws. Virginia, for example, eventually replaced a land tax that fell equally on every acre with an *ad valorem* land tax. Maryland enshrined the ability-to-pay principle in its new state constitution, which denounced poll taxes as "grievous and oppressive." Paupers aside, it insisted, "every ... person in the state ought to contribute his proportion of public taxes for the support of the government according to his actual worth in real or personal property ..." (Shipton, 1955, No. 14836).

The amounts levied were huge compared with the taxes colonists had been accustomed to paying. Rhode Island, for example, which normally operated its colonial government on £4,000 a year, levied taxes of £96,000 in 1777 and £94,000 in 1778, and had levied a total of nearly half a million in taxes by the end of 1779. Even allowing for inflation, these were wholly unprecedented levies. In a two-year period (1778 and 1779), Pennsylvania levied £5,000,000. In no year between 1763 and 1775 had colonial Pennsylvania raised more than £34,000 in taxes.

Complaints, evasion, and occasional rioting followed. And finally, state taxes failed either to shore up the Continental currency or to raise enough to keep paying and adequately supplying the Continental Army and state militias. New York, for example, managed to collect only about a third of all the taxes it levied from 1777 to 1781. By the summer of 1782 even so ardent a Continental nationalist as Alexander Hamilton had to concede that his fellow New Yorkers could not (rather than would not) pay all that Congress asked of them. By 1782 uncollected taxes in Pennsylvania alone totaled £3,300,000 in Continental currency, £84,700 in state currency, and £19,500 in specie. Loyalists often had to be forced to pay, which was difficult and at times impossible in states with large Tory populations. Even enthusiastic rebels often refused to pay specie taxes and insisted that they be permitted to pay any tax in Continental currency or any other government (state or national) note they had been forced to take in payment for confiscated goods or coerced service. They were reluctant to pay even Continental paper on time for, the longer they delayed, the more it depreciated and the cheaper the tax became. Most of what did come in, however, was Continental paper (now much devalued), much of which was burned, and therefore could not be used to pay for men and supplies. War crises forced some states to begin printing still more money even as Congress begged the states to stop and to bend all their efforts towards supporting the national currency. The same military crises forced commissary and quartermaster officers to continue issuing certificates in huge quantities. And rampaging inflation meant that, even when large sums were taxed in, they bought fewer and fewer supplies. By December 1780, therefore, it was clear that Congress's refunding plan had failed. By April 1781 it cost $150 Continental to buy $1 specie, and soon after it passed at $500 to $1 or more. By mid-1781 the national currency had collapsed and been abandoned by Congress and the public.

The Continental currency had, despite its chaotic end, served its purpose. It financed the first years of the Revolution when no other funds were readily available. From France, Benjamin Franklin delivered its eulogy:

> The general effect of the depreciation among the inhabitants of the states has been this, that it has operated as a *gradual tax* upon them, their business has been done and paid for by the paper money, and every man has paid his share of the tax according to the time he retained any of the money in his hands, and to the depreciation within that time. Thus it has proved a tax on money, a kind of property very difficult to be taxed in any other mode; and it has fallen more equally than many other taxes, as those people paid most, who being richest had most money passing through their hands (Franklin, 1819, p. 477).

Thus some $226,000,000 worth of what E. James Ferguson calls the "common debt" of the Revolution simply disappeared (Ferguson, 1961, p. 67). The debt represented by the Loan Office certificates, however (i.e., Continental bonds), Congress refused to abandon, establishing instead a scale of depreciation to reduce it to its specie value at the time it was contracted. Congress insisted that it alone remained obligated for both principle and interest. For those who hoped to increase the power of Congress in general and its fiscal authority in particular, the existence of an exclusively *national* debt was critical.

3. THE ATTEMPT TO REINVIGORATE CONGRESS

By 1781 Congress had already relinquished some of the powers of a sovereign national government to the states. It no longer issued a national currency and had stopped paying the army (an unquestionably national responsibility that several states began to assume instead; Congress would not resume responsibility for the army's pay until 1783). Some members of Congress who saw in the erosion of Congress's financial autonomy a threat to the union thought it essential to win for Congress financial independence and so to re-establish its sovereign authority as a national government.

Led by these Continental nationalists, in the first months of 1781 Congress asked the states for the power to collect a 5 per cent impost on all foreign goods imported into the United States. Under the Articles of Confederation, however, it could not be done without the unanimous consent of the states. Congress could only make its request and then wait for the states to act. It did act to reorganize the executive departments of the Confederation, replacing the often factious committees that oversaw finance, military, and diplomatic affairs with departments headed by single executive officers. To run the new Department of Finance, Congress chose ROBERT MORRIS, a prominent Philadelphia merchant and committed nationalist who sat in Congress from 1775 to 1778.

Morris took office in June 1780, shortly before Washington began his campaign against Cornwallis. He spent his first months juggling foreign loans, importuning merchants, harassing states to send the supplies they had promised, and pledging his own credit to arrange the supplies and transport needed to shift Washington's army from New York to Virginia.

Foreign loans and subsidies, particularly from France (nearly 4,000,000 in specie during his first year in office alone, more money than France had supplied in all the earlier years of the war combined [Ferguson, 1961, p. 126]) made Morris's early success possible. When news of Cornwallis's surrender reached Europe, Dutch inves-tors (who had sniffed skeptically at American loans earlier) became willing to lend large sums. Yorktown bought for the Continental nationalists the time they wanted to reorganize the national finances and to re-establish national credit so that the new nation might enter the postwar years (now evidently approaching) with an efficient national government that could establish a national currency, fund the national debt, and guarantee fiscal stability. Morris began by consolidating the national debt as a prelude to funding it. This involved two things: first, calling in all the still outstanding individual claims upon the Congress, reducing them to specie value in accord with a scale of depreciation, and exchanging them for new interest-bearing Continental notes (which debt Morris estimated would amount to $30,000,000); and second, once the war ended, settling accounts between the national government and the states by deciding how much each had spent in the common cause. During the war, Congress had issued currency, borrowed money at home and in Europe, and issued, through its agents, an untold number of notes and certificates of public debt (i.e., the com-missary and quartermasters' certificates, and others issued to soldiers in lieu of pay). So had the states. Congress needed to know the dollar value of each state's contributions (so it could credit them), and the amount it had sent to each state to conduct the war (so it could bill them). That herculean task was not completed until 1790, when Alexander Hamilton reported the totals to the new United States Congress (see table 2). Morris would have preferred that Congress simply take over and agree to pay all the states' Revolutionary War debts, but that implied an accretion of national authority that the states were, as yet, unwilling to brook.

Table 2 The total paid to and received from each state by Congress during the Revolutionary War (in $)

State	Paid to state	Received from state
New Hampshire	440,974	466,544
Massachusetts	1,245,737	3,167,020
Rhode Island	1,028,511	310,395
Connecticut	1,016,273	1,607,295
New York	822,803	1,545,889
New Jersey	366,729	512,916
Pennsylvania	2,087,276	2,629,410
Delaware	63,817	208,878
Maryland	609,617	945,537
Virginia	482,881	1,963,811
North Carolina	788,031	219,835
South Carolina	1,014,808	499,325
Georgia	679,412	122,744

Source: Nevins, 1924, p. 478.

Starting in 1782, Continental commissioners in each state began receiving claims against the government, verifying them, reducing them to what they had been worth in specie at the time they were incurred, and exchanging them for new interest-bearing Continental bonds. This consolidated national debt (which included the old Loan Office debt, plus the new consolidated quartermasters' certificates and soldiers' claims) totaled about $27,000,000 in specie. Morris proposed that Congress pay only the interest on the new, consolidated debt and "leave posterity to pay the principle" (Nettels, 1962, p. 33). He recommended national land, poll, and excise taxes and a national tariff on imported goods and urged the states to meet Congress's requisitions as rapidly as possible. To tide Congress over until the Articles were properly amended, Morris helped organize the Bank of North America, which made short-term loans to the government, and he issued notes, backed by his personal credit, to pay government bills. Finally, however, his plans to restore the nation's credit and Congress's authority depended on matters beyond his control – on the states' willingness to deliver to Congress substantial tax revenues (and especially specie) and to surrender the very autonomy over taxes they had contested with England in the Revolution. What they might have been willing to do during the crisis of war, facing defeat as an alternative, they were not willing to do once the war had evidently been won. By the end of 1782 the great financial problem facing the states was no longer how to finance a war of national survival, but how they might best retire the state and national Revolutionary War debts.

Morris had hoped that national creditors would pressure their state governments to grant Congress the power to tax, and, to that end, he suspended interest payments on the national debt in 1782. Instead, many began urging the states to take over payment of the national debt themselves, to assume responsibility for paying both the principle and interest owed to their own citizens. Some states had been paying at least part of the national debt since 1780, when Congress stopped paying the army. In 1782 Maryland offered to exchange state bonds paying 6 per cent interest for Continental notes held by its citizens. Other states did likewise. By the mid-1780s three states (Pennsylvania, Maryland, and New York) had thus converted more than $9,000,000 of Continental debt into state debt. To slow down the states' assumption of the national debt, Congress began in 1784 to pay the interest it owed not in specie (which it did not have), but in new certificates (called "indents" after the way they were oddly bordered on one side to discourage counterfeiting). They were simply another form of Congressional IOU, and, even though the states could tax them in and pay a portion of their requisitions to Congress with the indents, they were not popular with creditors and soon began to depreciate.

By 1786 it was also clear that all 13 states were unlikely ever to approve the still unratified impost plan, much less any wider taxing powers for Congress. In addition, the states were forwarding so little money to Congress that, while it could meet its day-to-day expenses, it had to default on payment of some of its European loans. By August 1786 the Board of Treasury (a committee which assumed control of the nation's finances when Morris resigned in 1785) had abandoned hope of enhancing Congress's powers and recommended that Congress simply distribute what remained of the federal debt among the states and allow each to retire its share as it saw fit. Congressional nationalists opposed the idea, for in their view formally abandoning the national debt to the states meant abandoning sovereignty to the states, which they were not yet prepared to do. Still, by 1786 Congress appeared increasingly moribund, the national debt was being converted piecemeal, by state action, into state debt, and the Continental nationalists' plans seemed to have collapsed along with the autonomy of the Congress on which they had pinned their hopes.

4. FUNDING THE DEBT: THE STATES

The states ended the war, as did Congress, with massive debts to pay. Virginia's public debt stood at £4,250,000 in 1784; Massachusetts's at about £1,500,000 in 1785. The state debts included money owed for supplies, their old depreciated war currencies, some of which still circulated, and debts owed to soldiers for back pay. The post-revolutionary states regularly allocated 50 to 90 per cent of their revenues to pay the interest they owed on their revolutionary debts. To raise it, and some principal, the states levied heavy new general taxes, and tried where possible to collect indirect taxes, such as imposts – the very revenues Congress wanted to appropriate for the national debt. The politics of postwar finance and taxation in every state was, then, a matter of vigorous and occasionally violent dispute.

The states handled their debt in various ways. Virginia, for example, reduced the outstanding debt to its depreciated value, (i.e., its postwar value in specie), calling in its still circulating war currency, and exchanging it (some at 1,000 to 1) for new interest-bearing state bonds. Similarly, it sank much of what it owed its soldiers by either accepting soldiers' certificates (issued in lieu of pay) for western lands, or by passing taxes payable in such certificates (see figure 30c). On the other hand, Massachusetts consolidated its debt not at its current postwar value, but at its value in specie at the time the debts were incurred. This left the state with a staggering specie debt (£1,600,000) which required high specie taxes to pay it. The legislature's refusal to relent on its deflationary debt policy in the midst of the postwar depression was in part responsible for the outbreak of rioting in western Massachusetts known as Shays's Rebellion (see Chapter 36, §4). Throughout the new republic, as taxes rose to sink the states' debts in the midst of deflation and depression, angry taxpayers began demanding relief – tax abatements and postponements, the right to pay in virtually any sort of outstanding state or federal notes or certificates, or to pay in commodities and produce. Most states (Massachusetts excepted) adopted extensive tax relief programs in the mid-1780s. Among the most popular demands of the protesters, and politically the most volatile, was the renewed emission of state legal-tender paper money which, harassed taxpayers believed, would make both taxes and private debts easier to pay.

In 1785 Pennsylvania's legislature responded with £150,000 in bills of credit. It reserved two-thirds of that to pay interest owed to Pennsylvanians on the state and national debt, and made the rest available as loans, backed by land as security. South Carolina emitted £100,000 to be lent out to landowners. North Carolina issued £100,000 in legal-tender paper. In 1786 New York printed £200,000, New Jersey emitted £100,000, Georgia £30,000, and Rhode Island £100,000. The states' experience with the new paper varied. Some issues were managed wisely, held their value, and provided relief to taxpayers and income to the state. Other issues, however, were so bitterly fought by creditors (who were often required by law to take them at face value, but who just as often flatly refused to accept the money except at a discount, if they would accept it at all) and so badly managed that they depreciated rapidly. Rhode Island's attempts to force its money into circulation became notorious and reinforced the continental nationalists' belief that the state legislatures were too prone to truckle to the mob, especially on money matters, and too likely to consult the public will rather than the public good. Under the Rhode Island currency law, debtors had to accept the paper at full face value for their debts (i.e., they could not demand a discount for taking it, even though it had lost 75 per cent of its specie value within a year of being issued). If a creditor refused to accept it, the debtor could deposit paper sufficient to clear his debt with a court and have it declared paid. The money was then forfeit to the state if the creditor still refused to take it. This not only helped wipe out much private debt in Rhode Island, it also helped sink the state's Revolutionary War debts, since those who refused to accept state paper in payment at its full face value saw the debts they held declared forfeit. In 1788, then, when it took $8 in Rhode Island currency to buy $1 in specie, public creditors were forced either to accept the paper (and thus accept only one-eighth of the specie value of what they were owed in full payment), or to refuse it and receive nothing. (Supporters of the plan countered that much of the debt had been bought up by speculators at ten cents on the dollar, so, even at eight to one, they were in effect getting a premium, not taking a loss.) By such methods, Rhode Island had substantially reduced its Revolutionary War debt by the 1790s.

All told, the states were remarkably successful in the postwar years in managing their war debts, servicing the national debt, and financing their operations, while providing practical relief to pressed debtors, public and private, who were cash poor in the depressed postwar economy. The "liquidated" domestic debt of Congress (i.e., the war debt owed to Americans that had been verified, reduced to its specie value at the time it was incurred, and converted to interest-bearing bonds) stood in 1787 at only £28,000,000. The republic's foreign war debt in 1788 was only £10,275,000 more (Jensen, 1950, p. 383).

The methods by which all this had been accomplished, however – devaluation of the debt, currency inflation, tax suspensions and abatements, and the impoverishment of Congress – served only to convince Morris, Hamilton, Madison, and other continental nationalists that the Articles of Confederation were fatally flawed, and that the Republic's prosperity (and its survival) depended upon a new constitutional order that would place national fiscal and monetary policy beyond the reach of popular whim and state legislators. In the aftermath of Shays's Rebellion, their hopes for change rode exclusively on the Federal Convention called to meet in Philadelphia the following summer. Their unhappiness with the Republic's experience in currency, finance, and taxation helped shape both the fiscal powers the new Constitution located firmly in federal hands and the clear limits it established on the monetary powers of the states.

FURTHER READING

Anderson, W. G.: *The Price of Liberty: the Public Debt of the Revolution* (Charlottesville: University Press of Virginia, 1983).

Becker, R. A.: *Revolution, Reform and the Politics of American Taxation* (Baton Rouge: Louisiana State University Press, 1980).

Burnett, E. C.: *The Continental Congress* (New York: Macmillan, 1941).

Ferguson, E. J.: *The Power of the Purse: a History of American Public Finance, 1776–1790* (Chapel Hill: University of North Carolina Press, 1961).

——: "The nationalists of 1781–1783 and the economic interpretation of the constitution," *Journal of American History*, 56 (1969), 241–61.

Franklin, B.: "Of the paper money of the United States of America," *The Posthumous and Other Writings of Benjamin Franklin*, ed. W. T. Franklin, 2 vols. (London: Henry Colburn, 1819), 473–9.

Jensen, M.: *The New Nation: a History of the United States During the Confederation, 1781–1789* (New York: Knopf, 1950).

Kaminski, J. P.: "Democracy run rampant," *The Human Dimensions of Nation Making: Essays on Colonial and Revolutionary America*, ed. J. K. Martin (Madison: State Historical Society of Wisconsin, 1976), 243–69.

Main, J. T.: *The Sovereign States* (New York: Watts, Franklin, 1973).

Nettels, C. P.: *The Emergence of a National Economy, 1775–1815* (New York: Holt, Reinhart and Winston, 1962).

Nevins, A.: *The American States During and After the Revolution, 1775–1789* (New York: Macmillan, 1924).

[New York Provincial Congress], *Journals of the Provincial Congress, Provincial Convention, Committee of Safety of the State of New York, 1775–1777*, 2 vols. (Albany: 1842).

Shipton, C. K. (ed.): *Early American Imprints, 1639–1800: a Microprint Compilation by the American Antiquarian Society* (Worcester, Mass.: American Antiquarian Society, 1955–).

Tansill, C. C. (ed.): *Documents Illustrating the Formation of the Union of the American States* (Washington, DC: US Government Printing Office, 1927).

Ver Steeg, C. L.: *Robert Morris, Revolutionary Financier* (Philadelphia: University of Pennsylvania Press, 1954).

373

38

Foreign relations, after 1783

JONATHAN R. DULL

THE 1783 Peace of Paris brought the United States recognition of her independence, the territorial boundaries she had claimed, and even continuation of American sharing of Britain's fishing grounds (*see* Chapter 33, §6). To the shock and disappointment of Americans, however, subsequent events demonstrated that the power of the United States was largely illusory. Great Britain excluded Americans from most trade with the British West Indies and refused to evacuate nine military posts within the borders of the United States. Spain closed the Mississippi River to American shipping and France largely disappointed the expectations of Americans who hoped she would break Britain's near monopoly of American markets. Even the Barbary States of northern Africa treated the United States with contempt. Congress found itself unable to compel the compliance of the individual American states that was necessary for a coherent national foreign policy; starved of revenue, unable to raise an army or navy, lacking even the means of commercial retaliation, Congress, indeed, was almost helpless in international affairs. This situation helped prompt the adoption of the Constitution, which was intended among other purposes to permit the United States to act more effectively in its relations with other nations. While the Constitution alleviated some problems, there were others which it could not solve. The United States was still economically backward and lacked the means to build a modern army and navy to rival those of the great powers of Europe. Protected by geography, America preserved her independence, but not until well after her industrial revolution did she become an international great power.

I. AMERICA'S GAINS FROM THE TREATY OF PARIS

The disappointments of the post-Revolutionary War years were all the more acute because of the exorbitant expectations raised by the 1783 peace treaty. Except for Florida (which she had not sought) all the territory between the Appalachians, the Great Lakes, and the Mississippi was accorded to her. Although establishing exact borders with Spanish Florida and British Canada would present unexpected difficulties, the United States had won a great diplomatic victory. The extent of this territory, however, was not a reflection of a dominant American military or legal claim to the area. Except for a few Spanish, British, and American military posts (and some scattered settlements in Kentucky and Tennessee), the area beyond the Appalachians was populated only by Indian tribes, whose rights were not considered during the peace negotiations. The fact that the entire area was accorded to the United States rather than to Spain or Britain should be attributed to the dynamics of the peace negotiations themselves rather than to a pre-existing superiority of American claims. The chief minister of Britain, William Petty, Earl of Shelburne, abandoned Britain's claims to the area as a negotiating tactic to split the United States from Britain's other enemies, France, Spain, and the Netherlands. This sacrifice, necessary if Shelburne were to achieve peace and the opportunity to implement domestic reforms, seems not to have been too painful for him. Shelburne apparently believed that Britain, which maintained control of the St. Lawrence, would still dominate the region economically by buying its produce and selling it British manufactures. Spain was a more serious rival; the peace commissioner John Jay feared that France would dictate a partition of the area between Spain and the United States. France, however, had no designs on Canada and hence little interest in the region. The French Foreign Minister, Charles Gravier, Comte de Vergennes, feared a deterioration of France's military situation and wished above all for a speedy peace; Spain had more pressing desires elsewhere, such as Gibraltar, Minorca, and Florida, and had little to offer in exchange for them. Thus, only the United States seriously pressed a claim to the area and, thanks to Shelburne's needs and the astuteness of the American peace commissioners, chiefly Franklin, was able to obtain it in the provisional agreement of 29 November 1782 and the final treaty of 3 September 1783.

Unfortunately for the United States, effective control of the West depended on military posts such as Niagara, Detroit, and Michilmackinac. The United States won these posts in the peace treaty but she could not force the British to evacuate them. Britain thus was able to hold them hostage to force American compliance with other articles in the peace treaty. The American peace commissioners (Franklin, Jay, John Adams, and Henry Laurens) had been forced to make last-minute concessions on two issues: payment of debts to British merchants and compensation to loyalists for confiscated property. On the former issue the commissioners made commitments which the individual American states failed to honor, giving the British a justifiable excuse not to evacuate the nine forts they still held. On the latter issue the commissioners promised to recommend to the individual states that they offer redress to the loyalists; when their promise proved meaningless, British public opinion was further alienated.

The peace treaty was also flawed by various imprecisions. One, already mentioned, was the lack of clarity in deliniating borders. Due largely to deficiencies in mapping, the border between the northeastern United States and Canada was drawn in a contradictory manner, engendering disputes that were not resolved until 1842. (A less significant error was also made about the northwestern corner of the United States.) Britain was also partially responsible for the ambiguity concerning the northern portion of her former colony of West Florida (which extended to the Mississippi River). The provisional treaty with the United States detached this area from Florida and awarded it to the United States, but a month later the British assigned all of Florida to Spain. The final treaties failed to resolve the issue, which became an object of negotiation between the United States and Spain. Article 3 of the treaty, which assigned the Americans limited rights to catch and dry fish from the Newfoundland and St. Lawrence fishing banks, also was ambiguous; disputes over fishing rights, although partially resolved in 1818, bedeviled relations between the United States and Great Britain for more than a century.

2. POSTWAR RELATIONS WITH BRITAIN, SPAIN, AND FRANCE

The key issue regarding the treaty, however, was not the precision of its language, but rather the spirit in which it was interpreted. Ironically the United States paid a price for its very success in the peace negotiations. Shelburne, who seems to have genuinely wished for good relations with the United States, undermined his parliamentary majority by the generous terms of peace with the United States and Britain's other opponents. Parliament stopped short of rejecting the peace agreement, but it drove Shelburne from office and refused his legislation permitting Americans to share in British trade. The coalition government of Lord North and Charles James Fox which succeeded Shelburne was far less friendly to America. The change in British attitudes was dramatically demonstrated by the 2 July 1783 Order in Council by which the Americans were largely denied commercial access to the British West Indies. Subsequent orders in council placed restrictions on American trade with Canada, Britain, and Ireland. By 1787–9, American trade with the West Indies was barely half what it had been in 1770–2 (although precision is impossible because of extensive smuggling). JOHN ADAMS, the American minister to the British court, tried unsuccessfully for three years to obtain redress. While British trade prospered, severe hardships were suffered by American shipbuilders, merchants, farmers, and fishermen.

The United States was subjected by Spain to further economic dislocations. The conditional peace agreement between Britain and the United States promised the Americans continued navigation of the Mississippi, but the subsequent Anglo-Spanish agreement on Florida left both banks of the lower river in Spanish possession. In 1784 Spain closed the lower river to American shipping. She then sent a diplomatic representative, Diego de Gardoqui, to negotiate the navigation and border issues with John Jay, the new American Secretary of State. Jay, despairing of reopening the river, suggested to Congress it forbear navigation of the river for 25 or 30 years in exchange for Spain's opening her European ports to American ships and goods; because of opposition from southern states he failed to obtain the necessary congressional authorization and the disputes were not resolved until the 1795 Pinckney Treaty.

The difficulties with Britain and Spain were made more difficult by the effective dissolution of America's alliance with France. The French monarchy, facing the threat of bankruptcy and attempting to preserve the diplomatic status quo in Europe, had little attention to spare for America. France did open certain West Indian ports to some American goods in 1784, but in general she greatly disappointed those such as the American Minister to France, Thomas Jefferson, who hoped French trade would help break America's dependence on Britain. French merchants lacked knowledge of American markets and did not have the credit resources to match those of British merchants. The United States signed commercial treaties with the Netherlands (1782), Sweden (1783), and Prussia (1785), but these too did little to break the British stranglehold; Great Britain continued to take nearly half of America's exports and to provide almost all her imports.

Perhaps the most embarrassing failure of American foreign policy resulted from the withdrawal of British naval protection for American merchant shipping in the Mediterranean. The sale of the few surviving American warships from the Revolutionary War left this shipping totally exposed to the privateers of the North African Barbary States. Agreement was reached with Morocco, but Algiers, Tripoli, and Tunis continued with impunity to capture American ships.

Congress had neither the military nor the commercial means to retaliate against any foreign opponent. It could not even control the 13 states of the American union. As already mentioned, the individual states embroiled Congress with Britain by blocking payment of debts to British merchants and compensation to former loyalists. Indeed, America virtually had 13 separate foreign policies, as particular states ratified the peace treaty individually, established their own trade policies, sought foreign loans, and negotiated independently with both Indian tribes and foreign states. The opposition of a single state was sufficient to block congressional attempts to raise a federal revenue; only the Dutch loans contracted in 1782 and 1784 kept the government from bankruptcy, and by 1787 hopes for further loans seemed dim. Without revenue Congress could not hope to raise a real army or to rebuild the navy; the latter disappeared totally and the former was too weak to prevent settlers from encroaching on Indian lands or to protect them from Indian retaliation. Disillusioned by Congress's inability to force the British to evacuate their posts, to open the Mississippi for their produce, or to defend them from Indian attack, frontiersmen in Kentucky and Tennessee began contacts with British and Spanish officials. Separatist movements arose in Vermont and even on the small island of Nantucket.

3. THE EFFECT OF THE CONSTITUTION ON AMERICAN FOREIGN RELATIONS

Economic hardship, threats to American unity, and a sense of national humiliation were factors in the summoning of the Constitutional Convention. They also influenced debate within the convention and provided reasons to support ratification of the Constitution. The new frame of government promised to alleviate some of the foreign policy difficulties of postwar America. It strengthened the executive, empowering the president to appoint the secretary of state, to draft treaties and, with congressional concurrence, to declare war. With its new ability to establish taxes, raise an army and navy, and regulate trade, the federal government acquired the means in theory to make itself respected abroad. Nevertheless, the Constitution could not rectify all the underlying weaknesses which relegated the United States to the ranks of the lesser international powers.

The central source of weakness was the American economy. The United States of the late eighteenth century was still an underdeveloped country by the standards of Western Europe. The American population, while growing rapidly, was still well below that of the European major powers (except for Prussia). America lacked the industrial development to compete with Britain even for American markets (with the exception of the largely self-sufficient and economically primitive frontier). Moreover, the United States was woefully short of banking and credit facilities. Like other economically subservient states, America served chiefly as a provider of raw materials (such as foodstuffs, tobacco, indigo and, increasingly, cotton) to more developed economies such as Britain's. Lacking a sufficient economic base, the United States could not create the huge and complex armies and navies by which the great powers of Europe enforced their will. The obstacles to such creations were administrative as well as material. During the Revolution the United States had found several generals of great ability – Washington, Knox, Greene – but it could not count on such continued good fortune. As the War of 1812 would demonstrate, it was not easy to find officers to raise, train, provision, and coordinate large bodies of troops (and fleets of ships). The United States was also handicapped by pervasive rivalries among the states and between sections of the country, East versus West as well as North versus South. This made it difficult to implement effective commercial, diplomatic, or military policies. Fortunately for America these weaknesses were counterbalanced by the security accorded by geography. Protected by the width of the Atlantic and the vastness of her size, America's survival was not really menaced, at least by outside forces. Other nations might harm the United States, but only her own disunity could destroy her. The greatest challenge to her unity lay 75 years in the future; once that was mastered the United States could resume her other great revolution, the Industrial Revolution, which would raise her first to the ranks of the great powers and then to their leadership.

FURTHER READING

Bemis, Samuel Flagg: *Pinckney's Treaty: America's Advantage from Europe's Distress*, rev. edn. (New Haven, Conn.: Yale University Press, 1960).

Kaplan, Lawrence S.: *Entangling Alliances with None: American Foreign Policy in the Age of Jefferson* (Kent, Ohio, and London: Kent State University Press, 1987).

Marks, Frederick W., III: *Independence on Trial: Foreign Affairs and the Making of the Constitution* (Baton Rouge: Louisiana State University Press, 1973).

Ritcheson, Charles R.: *Aftermath of Revolution: British Policy Towards the United States, 1783–1795* (Dallas: Southern Methodist University Press, 1969).

Whitaker, Arthur Preston: *The Spanish-American Frontier, 1783–1795: the Westward Movement and the Spanish Retreat in the Mississippi Valley* (Boston and New York: Houghton Mifflin, 1927).

Wright, J. Leitch: *British and the American Frontier, 1783–1815* (Athens: University of Georgia Press, 1975).

39

Slavery and anti-slavery

SYLVIA R. FREY

NEW World slavery had its origin in the vast area located between the lapping waters of the Atlantic Ocean on the south and the looming Kong Mountains on the north, the Volta River on the west, and the Niger River in the Gulf of Benin on the east. For nearly four centuries the three powerful and highly complex African civilizations of Benin, Dahomey, and Yoruba supplied slave labor to the West Indies and the Americas. Slavery had, in one form or another, existed from antiquity: in Plato's Athens, in Caesar's Rome, and in Christian Europe. Although slavery had long since died out in most of Western Europe, it remained at least a marginal institution in Spain and Portugal, and it existed in Africa itself, albeit in a relatively mild form. Despite differences from area to area, and even from tribe to tribe, the African system of slavery was deeply rooted in the general social and political structure. The majority of domestic slaves were debtors, whose enslavement was often payment for a bad debt; prisoners taken in war or kidnapped from other tribes; or criminals enslaved for antisocial crimes, such as adultery or theft. Most African slaves were regarded as valuable and useful people. More often than not, they were recognized as members of their owners' households. They enjoyed certain social rights, including marriage and rights of inheritance for their children, as well as protection against want or ill-use.

I. THE BEGINNINGS OF THE MODERN SLAVE TRADE

The year 1441 is generally accepted as the official beginning, so to speak, of the modern international slave trade, upon which New World slavery was based. In the first recorded skirmish between Europeans and Africans south of the Sahara, a young Portuguese explorer named Antam Goncalvez took 12 Africans captive and carried them to Lisbon as a gift for Prince Henry. In 1443–4 a second cargo followed. Thereafter a steady stream of Portuguese caravels descended on the surf-beaten African coast. The exploring navigators were soon followed by sea-traders, whose trading posts, called factories, spread with daunting speed southwards from the estuary of Senegal to Sierra Leone on the Guinea Coast. Within ten years after the trade was initiated Portugal was importing 1,000 Africans a year. The discovery of America by Columbus in 1492, Pedro Alvares Cabral's landing in Brazil eight years later, followed by Balboa's sighting of the Pacific Ocean altered drastically the nature of the slave trade.

Although European merchant adventurers had been making regular sea voyages round the western bulge of Africa and their fortified factories dotted the Guinea coast, the slave trade played only a small role in Europe's economic life. The planting of the first New World colony by Spain and the establishment in 1503 of the encomienda

FIGURE 31 A West African trading post (engraving from "La Galérie Agréable" by Pieter Van der Aa, 1729): an African is selling Africans to the French.

system led to a brief and tragic experiment with Indian slave labor. Ravaging disease decimated the Indian population and led to an acute labor shortage. The labor shortage, in turn, was exacerbated by the first Spanish shipment in 1515 of slave-produced sugar grown in the West Indies, which marked the beginning of Europe's transition to capitalism. To relieve the problem of labor supply, Charles V approved the importation of slaves directly from Africa. Three years later the first cargo arrived. Within 50 years of the discovery of America, the annual rate of direct shipment from Africa to Spanish colonial America was running at several thousand. The profits from the slave trade soon attracted competition from France and England. The spread of European settlement across the Atlantic created a new demand for slaves and brought the Dutch, the Danes, and the Swedes into the rapidly developing trade. The introduction of sugar into the French West Indies in 1640 precipitated an enormous expansion of the trade in the seventeenth century.

The establishment of the European slave trade provided the framework for the rise of organized slave raiding and warfare in the forest belt of sub-Saharan Africa, which in turn became the chief instruments to build up African trading empires (*see* figure 31). With muskets and gunpowder obtained through the European trade, chiefdoms (such as the once petty Akan state) began organized slave raiding and warfare on lesser states in the interior. Their success at controlling the trade and establishing markets promoted the rise in the eighteenth century of the Ashanti Union in what is now northern Ghana; of Oyo, the great center of the Yoruba people; of the Kingdom of Benin in the forests west of the Niger; and of the remarkable Fon Kingdom of

380

Dahomey, whose port Ouidah controlled the trade with the Europeans. The long-range impact of the slave trade on West Africa over four centuries has not been calculated. The transformation of formerly peaceful, peasant communities into militarized slave raiding states destroyed human and material resources which might have been diverted to more creative enterprises. The demographic consequences alone were staggering. Global estimates on the number of people exported from Africa across the Atlantic have been calculated at 11,698,000.

2. THE EARLY SLAVE TRADE IN AMERICA

For the Europeans and the Americans, however, the slave trade provided the basis for the development of capitalism. Slave labor on plantations and mines in the New World made possible the development of tropical and semi-tropical America and allowed the accumulation of capital necessary to exploit the mineral and agricultural resources of the New World colonies. The creation of the various slave regimes of the New World was immediately influenced by local economic forces. In the mainland colonies of British North America, the character of slavery was determined by the rise of staple crop agriculture and the plantation system. It was first introduced into the British mainland colonies in 1619, when a Dutch man-of-war deposited 20 Africans captured from a Spanish vessel bound for the West Indies on the sandy coast of Virginia. Claiming a need for food, the captain of the vessel offered to trade his human cargo for "victualle." His offer was accepted, thus inaugurating the nefarious traffic in human flesh. For many years afterwards, slavery existed without sanction of law, but perforce of custom. In 1661, however, the Virginia assembly, the oldest representative body in British America, approved a declaration that children should follow the condition of their mothers. By it, Virginia made slavery statutory and hereditary – an attitude which set it apart from all other slave systems in history. In 1670 the assembly approved another act declaring that "all servants not christians," who entered the colony "by shipping," should be "slaves for their lives," thus establishing perpetual chattel slavery.

The legal institutionalization of slavery in Virginia, followed a quarter century later by the development of comprehensive slave codes, ran parallel to several other developments, the most significant being the growth in the size of the black population and the rise of staple agriculture. For most of the seventeenth century, however, Blacks constituted only about 3 per cent of the Chesapeake population. The majority were imported from the West Indies. Most lived on small plantations of fewer than 11 slaves and were engaged in the small-scale production of tobacco. Between 1727 and 1769, however, 39,679 slaves were imported into Virginia, four-fifths of them from Africa. By 1770 slaves represented 40 per cent of the population of Virginia and 30 per cent of the population of Maryland.

A number of factors were responsible for the growth of slavery in the Chesapeake. First was the rapid rise of tobacco, the earliest experiments on which were carried out by John Rolfe in 1612. The royal prohibition on the production of tobacco in England and the higher cost of Spanish leaf created an expanding market for Chesapeake tobacco in England. The reorganization of the tobacco trade early in the eighteenth century by Scottish merchants, who landed huge contracts from the French tobacco monopoly, contributed to the explosive growth of the industry. The expanding market in turn produced a large demand for labor, which was temporarily satisfied by a flood of white emigrants from England. High mortality rates in the Chesapeake and rising real wages in England cut short that source of supply and contributed significantly to the demand for slave labor. Despite recurring depressions in the industry, expansion continued to the Revolution, and Chesapeake planters with access to capital were able to build up immense estates, their home plantations averaging 3,000 acres and 80 slaves.

In the meantime, a different type of plantation economy was developing along the low coastal plains of South Carolina, southern North Carolina, and Georgia. Black slavery in Carolina originated with the founding of the colony in 1670. The Fundamental Constitutions promised land grants to persons who brought slaves to the colony. Barbadians constituted one-third of the early settlers and many of them brought their slaves with them. The introduction of rice seed from Madagascar, and its successful cultivation on the low-lying islands and marshes and along the riverbanks, led to the development of a staple economy centered on the production of rice, the large-scale production of which coincided with the emergence in 1720 of a clear-cut black majority in the colony. In the 1740s a second staple crop, indigo, was introduced by Eliza Lucas on her father's plantation in Wapoo Creek. Although slavery was banned in Georgia until 1751, Carolina migrants quickly forged a plantation economy which closely resembled that of South Carolina. Situated between Virginia and South Carolina, the colony of North Carolina shared characteristics of each of her more prosperous neighbors. In the northern part, adjacent to Virginia, tobacco was grown; in a small area of the Cape Fear valley rice was cultivated. The mainstay of the colonial economy was, however, naval stores, most of which were produced in the southern part.

Plantation societies   Differences in the various plantation societies were the result of a combination of factors peculiar to each system. Chief among these were the different geographic and environmental conditions, the economics of production, the culture of the master class, and the provenance of the slave population. The older, more stable plantation society of the Chesapeake was characterized by a type of paternalism that expressed itself in distinctive patterns of management and labor organization. The strict regimentation required in tobacco cultivation led to a reliance on gang labor and on maximum surveillance and control. On small farm units of fewer than 20 slaves, where a majority of Chesapeake slaves resided, every step of the production cycle was supervised by the master. Slave drivers and foremen carried out some of these functions on larger units, but masters, eager to maximize production, tended to maintain centralized control. In some cases, though not in all, the paternalistic system resulted in improved material circumstances but relatively less individual freedom for the slave population.

An entirely different plantation ethos characterized the low-country plantation system. Whereas the majority of Chesapeake slaves lived with resident owners, low-country slaves often did not. Masters eager to escape the disease-ridden environment of the rice fields spent part of each year in Beaufort or Charles Town, leaving the supervision of daily plantation activities in the hands of overseers and black drivers. The grueling and unhealthy nature of the work involved in rice cultivation made the task system a more practical form of labor organization in the lower South. The relative lack of supervision and the slaves' freedom to engage in production for private use, once the individual work assignment was complete, resulted in greater autonomy for the low-country slave population and in a more exploitative mentality among the planter class.

The differences between one plantation society and another were also owing to the disparate origins, different patterns and rates of growth, and relative size of the slave populations of the various regions. By the eve of the American Revolution, more than 270,000 slaves lived in the colonies of Virginia and Maryland, approximately 66 per cent of them in the tidewater, the remainder in the developing piedmont. The early slave trade to the Chesapeake dealt mainly in slaves from the West Indies. Beginning in the 1680s slaves were imported directly from Africa, an estimated 90 per cent of them in English shipping. After 1769, however, the importation of African slaves declined dramatically owing to a combination of factors. The major factor was the changing demographic configuration. By and large, Virginians preferred Africans from the Niger Delta, perhaps because tobacco culture required less physical strength, and an estimated 37.7 per cent of all eighteenth-century imports were from the Bight of Biafra. Virginians cared less for slaves from Kongo-Angola, probably because the long voyage left the Africans weak, and only 15.7 per cent were from Angola. Until roughly 1740 the Chesapeake slave population was culturally diverse, disproportionately male, and widely dispersed throughout the region on small plantations. A more generally balanced sex ratio after 1740, together with improved nutrition and epidemiological conditions and greater family stability, made natural reproduction possible. The shift from tobacco to the less labor-intensive cultivation of wheat, beginning in the 1760s, produced a slave surplus, leading in 1778 to Virginia's prohibition of the slave trade, to the passage in 1782 of a law permitting manumission, and to a similar ban on importations adopted by Maryland in 1783. The slave surplus in Virginia also contributed to the practice of hiring slaves out and, in the post-revolutionary era, to the growth of the domestic slave trade between Virginia and the lower South. Both Maryland and Virginia supported the federal prohibition of 1807 on the external trade.

3. THE GROWTH OF THE SLAVE POPULATION

Although the low-country slave population had begun to grow naturally, its increase in the eighteenth century still depended on continual immigration. Shipping records indicate that between 1672 and 1775 nearly 90,000 black slaves entered the port of Charles Town, the largest and most dynamic of the five colonial ports engaged in the slave trade from Africa. Approximately half of the slaves transhipped from Charles Town were sent to Savannah or Sunbury in Georgia. North Carolina received the second largest number, and the remainder were sent to the other English colonies along the Atlantic coast, to European colonies in Florida, Mobile, and New Orleans, or to the West Indies and the Caribbean. South Carolina planters, who demonstrated an acute awareness of ethnicity, preferred slaves from the Guinea coast, Gambia, Sierra Leone, and Angola, because they were presumed to have characteristics suited to certain kinds of work. During the colonial period nearly 8,000 Africans from Gambia were sold into slavery in South Carolina. The second largest number of Africans brought to colonial South Carolina was from Angola. Between 1735 and 1740 Kongo-Angolans constituted 70 per cent of South Carolina's slave population, and they remained the dominant group throughout the century. Slaves from Sierra Leone constituted the third largest group in terms of total numbers. Up to 7,000 slaves per year were exported from Bance Island, a slave trading station at the mouth of the Sierra Leone River, which was operated by Richard Oswald of London. On the eve of the Revolution, South Carolina's slave population numbered 100,000, compared with

70,000 Whites. Predominantly young, male, and African, it was heavily concentrated in the low country, some 55,058 in the Charles Town district alone. Although South Carolina's southern neighbor Georgia was late in inaugurating slavery, its slave population had grown to 15,000, two-thirds of whom lived in the low country.

Influences of slavery on the plantation system   Although other variables enter into it, it is now increasingly recognized that the distinctive features of the low-country plantation system owe a great deal to the origins of the slave population. It is, for example, probable that the highly profitable rice plantation system of South Carolina and Georgia relied heavily on the technical knowledge of slaves from the "Rice Coast" of West Africa, where local farmers had been cultivating wet rice on the flood plains and dry rice on the hillsides for centuries before the Portuguese introduced different varieties of paddy rice from Asia in the sixteenth century. By the eighteenth century, West African farmers were using elaborate irrigation systems in the cultivation of wet rice. In addition to the technical expertise and labor patterns that they brought, it is also possible that "Rice Coast" slaves contributed to the technology of rice cultivation. Wooden mortars and pestles, used to process rice, and "fanners," the large winnowing baskets used to separate the grain and chaff which are still in use in Sierra Leone today, were perhaps introduced by West Africans, who may also have contributed to the system of sluices, banks, and ditches used in the cultivation of wet rice.

The low-country slave population also had a significant linguistic and cultural impact, particularly in the Sea Island Region, whose semi-tropical climate and disease environment led to the geographical and social isolation of the black population and permitted the development of an independent slave culture strongly influenced by African patterns. The preponderance of peoples from the Kongo-Angola area and from Gambia and Sierra Leone made possible the development of a distinctive language, which retained many elements of African languages. Known as Gullah, it contained thousands of African words and place names, which suggests the influence of several language patterns, including the Tshi (Gold Coast), KiKongo (Kongo-Angola), and Mande (Upper Guinea). Drawing upon African cultural patterns, low-country slaves re-created a world of aesthetic autonomy in music and dance, in stoneware and basketry, in wood sculpture and architecture, in style of worship, and in burial customs, much of which survives today.

Slavery in the North   Although slavery is traditionally associated with the southern colonies, it was an established institution in all of the 13 British mainland colonies, and several of the northern colonies were actively engaged in the slave trade. Important socio-economic differences distinguished the New England and middle colonies from the southern colonies, however, and guaranteed that slavery would remain a marginal institution. By contrast to the southern colonies, which made a rapid transition from subsistence to commercial agriculure, the New England economic system was, under the constraining influence of geography and religion, gradually transformed from household production to a commercialized economy. Although slavery existed, in Massachusetts as early as 1633, the slave population of New England never exceeded 16,000. The middle colonies developed a more varied economic life and relied upon a mix of white wage labor and slave labor. In parts of New York, where slavery was introduced as early as 1628, and in East Jersey, Blacks constituted up to 14 per cent of the population. Elsewhere they represented only a fractional minority of the total. Native-born, English speaking, the relatively small black populations of New England and the middle colonies enjoyed the benefits of education and church membership, thus making their integration into the community possible.

4. THE ANTI-SLAVERY MOVEMENT

Although it was a vital part of the labor system only in the South, slavery enjoyed almost universal acceptance. No systematic body of thought against it existed, while philosophical justifications for it were as old as the institution itself. From the classical and hellenistic period, Greek and Roman writers had constructed philosophical defenses for the overriding importance of property rights. Because slaves constituted a special form of property in classical antiquity, it was necessary to devise a rationalizing ideology for the specific problem of slavery. Greek and Roman writers constructed two main types of philosophical justification: the first, the theory of "natural slavery" suggested by Plato and fully developed by Aristotle, argued that certain people are slaves by nature and actually benefit by slavery; the second type represented slavery as the result of accident rather than nature, and denied that a "good" person could ever "really" be a slave at all. Orthodox Christian writers generally accepted the latter view. Early church fathers, such as St. Augustine, viewed slavery as evil in principle but accepted it as divinely ordained. New Testament writers advanced the idea of the equality of souls before God, but made no effort to prescribe a general code of morality with respect to economic or political behavior, under which rubric slavery fell. The result was that Christianity offered no unqualified denunciation of private property ownership or of slavery or kindred forms of unfree labor.

Religious Paradoxically the roots of anti-slavery sentiment were religious in origin. The first explicit religious condemnation of slavery in America was the 1688 Germantown petition of the Mennonites, a sect similar to the Quakers. The mildly worded Germantown Protest, which argued from the golden rule, went unheeded. It was soon followed, however, by more elaborate, distinctly religious anti-slavery literature, most of it written by Quakers such as George Keith, John Hepburn, Ralph Sandiford, and Benjamin Lay. At least one New England Puritan, Judge Samuel Sewell, was among the anti-slavery pioneers. Sewell's tract *The Selling of Joseph* (1701) attacked the Biblical arguments traditionally used to justify slavery and advanced the opinion that, as children of God, blacks had "equal Right unto Liberty," an original right which could not be forfeited either by consent or by captivity in war.

No practical results came of any of these early efforts until the evangelical upsurge known as the Great Awakening swept through New England and the middle colonies, beginning in the 1740s. The frenzy of religious revivalism associated with it reinvigorated the Quaker anti-slavery tradition and produced a flood of anti-slavery tracts, the most influential of which were written by Anthony Benezet and John Woolman. Benezet, a Quaker schoolmaster in the Friend's English School in Philadelphia, wrote nine tracts between the late 1750s and his death in 1784. The three which are considered most important are *A Short Account of That Part of Africa, Inhabited by the Negroes* (1762), *A Caution and Warning to Great Britain and her Colonies* (1766), and *Some Historical Account of Guinea* (1771). The practical issue of Benezet's tracts, which were directed at the suppression of the slave trade, were apparent on both sides of the Atlantic. His *Short Account* apparently influenced the great English barrister Granville Sharp, who in 1772 led the successful court battle to free James Somerset, a slave in

England. His *Historical Account* attracted the attention of Thomas Clarkson, who directed the successful fight to abolish the British slave trade in 1807. At Benezet's urging the prominent Philadelphia physician Benjamin Rush published his influential *An Address to the Inhabitants of the British Settlements in America, Upon Slave-Keeping* (1773). Although Benjamin Franklin's *Observations Concerning the Increase of Mankind* (1751) represented the first American attack on slavery from an economic and demographic perspective, Franklin too was influenced by the moral arguments of Benezet.

Woolman's efforts were directed at the Quaker community. For a quarter of a century Woolman traveled from Quaker meeting to meeting, trying to persuade his fellow Quakers to free their slaves. His extended tours of Maryland, Virginia, and North Carolina in 1746 and again in 1757 gave him first-hand experience with slavery and powerfully influenced his essay *Some Considerations on the Keeping of Negroes*, the first part of which appeared in 1754, the second in 1762. In it Woolman laid down the basic tenets of religious anti-slavery thought: the brotherhood of all God's children as partakers of the Inner Light; liberty as the gift of God to all his children; the entitlement of all God's children to "treatment according to the Golden Rule." Woolman's work had a notable impact among Quakers. In 1754 the Philadelphia Yearly approved a resolution written by him advising members of constituent meetings against purchasing slaves. In 1755 the Yearly advised monthly meetings to admonish any friend who persisted in the practice of buying slaves. In 1758 the Woolmanites scored a major victory with the adoption by the Yearly of the 1758 minute enjoining Friends to free their slaves or face discipline from the monthly meetings. The Philadelphia example spread through New England and New York, whose yearly meetings also approved minutes outlawing slavery. In New England, where the slave population was small and assimilable, and in Pennsylvania and New York, where Quaker influence was strong, slavery was practically abandoned by the Quakers before the Revolutionary War. Outside the Society of Friends, the religious movement did not produce important results until the revolutionary era, when the religious and moral movement began to converge with new political and economic ideas to produce a searing intellectual indictment of slavery.

Secular   The tradition of religious anti-slavery in New England and the middle colonies intersected with two independent but parallel systems of thought and culminated eventually in a powerful secular anti-slavery movement. The first developed out of the writings of John Locke, the seventeenth-century English philosopher whose ideas were formulated in opposition politics under Charles II. In their struggle with Britain over imperial policies, revolutionary leaders relied upon a popularized version of Lockean philosophy, which affirmed the existence of immutable laws of nature and the doctrine of natural rights, whose guiding values of liberty and equality found resonance in the religious principles of the spiritual equality of all God's children and liberty as His special gift to each of them equally. Although Locke himself had justified slavery, the French philosopher Montesquieu, in his *Spirit of the Laws* (1748), was the first to expound the theory that slavery was forbidden by natural law, an argument later vaguely made by Woolman and by Benezet, whose *A Caution and Warning...* quoted from the writings of Montesquieu. The rising tide of anti-slavery thought was supported by the publication in 1776 of Adam Smith's *Wealth of Nations*, whose utilitarian arguments that slavery was the "dearest of any" form of labor seemed to fit the economic realities of the late eighteenth century.

The three convergent, often interlocking, movements produced a fundamental intellectual reorientation, whose leading religious or moral, political and economic motifs raised questions about the obvious contradictions between society's professed values, religious and secular, and the existence of chattel slavery. Although most Americans drew back from the logic of their own arguments when it came to Blacks, the Boston Revolutionary James Otis did not. In *The Rights of the British Colonies Asserted and Proved* (1764), essentially an argument against the British writs of assistance, Otis bluntly asserted that "The Colonists are by the law of nature free born, as indeed all men are, white or black." During the controversy over the Stamp Act, anti-slavery literature began to proliferate. Produced by a diverse group of ministers, lawyers, merchants, and schoolteachers, it appealed to both religious sanctions and natural law. Among the anti-slavery advocates were Blacks themselves, including the poet Phillis Wheatley, whose work gained international recognition, and the one-time slave Caesar Sarter, whose essay on slavery appeared in the *Essex Journal*. "Freedom suits" brought by slaves against their masters in New England courts gave practical application to the ideas of anti-slavery writers, as did the wartime flight of thousands of slaves to the British Army.

5 . EMANCIPATION IN THE NORTH

The practical issue of the intellectual anti-slavery movement was a trend in the northern states towards gradual emancipation, the preliminary to which was the passage of slave-trade legislation. In 1766, the year of the repeal of the Stamp Act, Boston instructed its representatives to "move for a law, to prohibit the importation and purchasing of slaves for the future." A number of New England towns approved similar instructions, and in 1767 the General Court debated but declined to take action on several bills prohibiting or restricting the slave trade. In 1771 a prohibitory bill passed the House and Council, but Governor Thomas Hutchinson refused to sign it. Although Massachusetts did not succeed in prohibiting the slave trade until 1788, Pennsylvania (1773), Rhode Island (1774), and Connecticut (1774) all passed prohibitory acts, and the general Articles of Association adopted by the first Continental Congress in 1774 contained a slave-trade clause which pledged the Association "neither [to] import nor purchase any slave imported after the first day of December next," after which time it agreed "wholly [to] discontinue the slave trade" and "neither [to] be concerned in it ourselves" nor to "hire our vessels, nor sell our commodities or manufacturers to those who are concerned in it."

Efforts to remove restraints on manumission, which existed in many states, were the next steps on the road to emancipation. Encouraged by petitions from Quakers and local abolitionist societies, several northern states adopted measures to facilitate voluntary manumission. Delaware approved a measure permitting manumission by will or other instrument (1787), and similar acts were passed in New Jersey (1786, 1798), New York (1785, 1788), Kentucky (1798, 1800), and Tennessee (1801). Concern that the freedmen might become a public charge led most states to establish age limitations and impose restrictions, including the requirement that the manumittor provide some form of maintenance for freedmen. During the Revolutionary War years, all of the northern states except New York and New Jersey took steps to abolish slavery.

Actual emancipation in the northern states was achieved by a variety of means: direct legislative action, direct constitutional provision, and the judicial process as supplementary to the Constitution. Early attempts at legislative emancipation in New England and New Jersey failed, but in 1780 the Pennsylvania Assembly enacted the first gradual emancipation law in American history. In New York and New Jersey, where slavery was more deeply entrenched, gradual emancipation legislation was not adopted until 1799 and 1804 respectively, New Jersey being the last state to do so before the Civil War. Both states made emancipation contingent upon the inclusion of abandonment clauses, which permitted owners of negro children freed by the act to abandon them a year after birth, after which time they were considered paupers and therefore subject to be bound out to service by the overseers of the poor. Since the law did not prohibit overseers from binding out children to the very masters who had abandoned them, masters were entitled to receive reimbursement from the towns for the support of the children they had abandoned.

Although the doctrine of natural rights was the foundation upon which all states constructed their new state constitutions, only that of Vermont provided for the total prohibition of slavery. It, however, established the precedent for similar action in the new states formed from the Northwest Territory. In Massachusetts and New Hampshire emancipation was accomplished by constitutional provision supplemented by judicial action. After petition campaigns waged by slaves in both states failed to achieve legislative emancipation, slaves, aided by anti-slavery lawyers, began suing for freedom in the courts. In the 1781 case of *Brom and Bett v. John Ashley*, heard in the Inferior Court of Common Pleas, Great Barrington, Massachusetts, ELIZABETH FREEMAN, or "Bett," argued that the phrase in the new Massachusetts constitution of 1780 declaring all individuals were "born free and equal" applied to black as well as white Americans. Bett's claim to a share in the heritage of the Revolution established the precedent for a series of court decisions which effectively destroyed slavery in Massachusetts.

6. ENTRENCHMENT AND EXPANSION IN THE SOUTH

Although the northern record of emancipation was sullied by the general refusal to offer to freed Blacks full membership in the political community or to alter in any way their degraded social status, by a slow, often tortuous process, slavery was gradually abolished in all of the northern states. In the southern states it emerged from the Revolution as a firmly entrenched sectional institution, thus foreshadowing conflict at some remoter date. There are several reasons for these divergent developments, including the lack of economic dependence on slavery in the northern states, and the fact that the major intellectual tradition of religious radicalism reinforced by revolutionary ideology, which gave impetus to the anti-slavery movement in New England and the middle colonies, was largely absent in the South. The period of intense religious revivalism known as the First Great Awakening was also experienced in the South, but its geographic strength was limited to a few counties in Virginia's piedmont and the upper tidewater. Before the tradition of religious anti-slavery could become very deeply rooted, popular attention was preoccupied with the events of the imperial conflict.

White southerners also had a different conception of revolutionary ideology. Although they embraced the ideology of republicanism, which espoused the notions of liberty and equality, they had built a social order upon the contrary ideal of inequality. The ideal of equality, which captivated so many of their northern countrymen, held no allure for a people committed to slavery, for it was identified by them with racial anarchy and barbarism. From the white southern perspective, an ordered inequality was the best safeguard of harmony and peace. Unable to identify fully with the values of equality and liberty that were projected by the language of republicanism, white southerners fastened upon the rights of property as the focal point of their attachment to republican thought.

The experience of the Revolutionary War reinforced these ideas. Years of military occupation, continuous naval assaults, and bitter internecine warfare produced massive damage and overwhelming chaos in the South. British efforts to use slavery as a matter of tactics threatened to shatter social cohesion and to destroy the existing social order. The flight of thousands of slaves to the British Army or to sanctuaries in the developing Southwest and in Florida contributed to the devastation of southern plantation economies and to the severe depletion of the slave labor force. Faced with the disintegration of their society and the forfeiture of their material power, southerners emerged from the war, not persuaded to end slavery, but convinced that its restoration was the indispensable condition for the economic rehabilitation of the entire region.

The result was the further entrenchment of slavery everywhere in the South except Maryland, and its expansion westwards: into the southside and transmontane areas of Virginia and the back country of Georgia and South Carolina; across the Allegheny Mountains into Kentucky and Tennessee; and southwest to frontier plantations in Mississippi and Alabama. During and after the Revolution, Maryland's slave population grew slowly. A small state with no hinterland for expansion, in 1783 Maryland removed restraints on manumission, and by 1810 more than 20 per cent of the state's black population was free. By contrast, neighboring Virginia's slave population nearly doubled between 1755 and 1782, most of the growth owing to natural increase. Left by the transition from tobacco to wheat with a superfluity of slaves, tidewater planters resorted to the manumission, transfer, and sale of the surplus. In 1782 Virginia revised the slave code to permit individual manumission, and some 10,000 slaves were subsequently freed. During the 1790s and 1800s many times that number were taken into Kentucky and Tennessee by the hundreds of small, middling, and large planters fleeing the depression-ridden tidewater, or were marketed in slave-hungry Georgia and South Carolina. When that source of supply proved inadequate to meet the insatiable demand, planters from the lower South began importing slaves from Africa. Between 1783 and 1807 an estimated 100,000 Africans were imported into Savannah and Charleston to meet frontier demands in the back country. By 1790 Georgia's slave population was almost 30,000, nearly double the prewar figure. South Carolina, which lost an estimated one-quarter of its slave force during the war, imported almost 20,000 Africans before 1800, and between 1800 and 1807, when the slave trade was closed by federal law, another 39,075. The closing of the international trade accelerated the domestic trade, and between 1810 and 1820 approximately 137,000 slaves from the Chesapeake were marketed in Mississippi, Alabama, and the developing area west of the Mississippi River.

Unsuccessful anti-slavery movements   By the time the postwar anti-slavery movement was launched in the South, slavery was the pivotal institution of southern society. The catalyst for the short-lived crusade was the Second Great Awakening, which broke out on the banks of the James River in 1785 and erupted intermittently thereafter until 1820. Unorganized and generally confined to a handful of European evangelical leaders and northern itinerant preachers, the movement was inaugurated by Methodist conferences in 1780, 1783, and 1784, the last the Baltimore "Christmas" Conference, which directed members of the Society to manumit their slaves or face excommunication. When the English churchmen Thomas Coke, the first superintendent of the church in America, and Francis Asbury, ordained a superintendent by Coke, attempted to enforce the injunction among Virginia Methodists, they met with bitter hostility and open threats of violence. As a consequence, the so-called Slave Rule was suspended in 1785, barely six months after it was adopted. Coke and Asbury then launched a petition campaign for the general emancipation of Virginia slaves. Although a number of the great Virginians of the revolutionary generation, including Washington, Jefferson, Madison, and Mason, were philosophically opposed to slavery, none was willing publicly to support the anti-slavery movement. The petition campaign was rejected by the Virginia Assembly and stirred a pro-slavery attack. Methodist efforts to achieve gradual emancipation continued intermittently until 1808, when the denominational effort was abandoned in favor of spiritual salvation of the slave population of the South.

The congregational organization of the Baptist polity militated against an organizational anti-slavery effort. In Virginia, the center of southern Baptist strength, the Baptist General Committee of the state adopted a resolution drafted by John Leland, a Massachusetts native, condemning slavery, but it failed to win support in the associations. Advised by the Roanoke and Strawberry associations against further interference with the institution of slavery, the General Committee decided in 1793 to drop the divisive issue on the grounds that it was a matter more appropriately decided by the state. David Barrow, a native of Virginia, led a short-lived but significant anti-slavery movement in Kentucky. Finding no anti-slavery sentiment in the regular Baptist associations, Barrow formed the Licking-Locust Association, Friends of Humanity, and through it preached emancipationism. After Barrow's death in 1819 the movement rapidly disintegrated, however. Although Baptist churches in the lower South contained thousands of black members, there was no Baptist anti-slavery sentiment outside Virginia and Kentucky.

The American Revolution produced an ambiguous legacy. It created the illusion of a young nation united on the principles of liberty and equality, when in fact from the very inception there were invidious divisions along geographical, demographic, and ideological lines. Building upon the revolutionary ideal of political freedom, the "commercial" states of the North moved towards the gradual extinction of slavery. Driven by a different set of imperatives, the "plantation" states of the South entrenched and extended slavery, the very antithesis of freedom. The federal Constitution, which banned the slave trade after 1808 but implicitly recognized the existence of slavery, preserved the moral contradictions present in the situation and passed on to another generation the problem of creating the "more perfect union."

FURTHER READING

Berlin, Ira, and Hoffman, Ronald: *Slavery and Freedom in the Age of the American Revolution* (Charlottesville: Published for the United States Capitol Historial Society by the University Press of Virginia, 1983).

Bruns, Roger (ed.): *Am I Not a Man and a Brother: the Antislavery Crusade of Revolutionary America, 1688–1788* (New York: Chelsea House Publishers, 1977).

Curtin, Phillip D.: *The Atlantic Slave Trade: a Census* (Madison, Milwaukee and London: University of Wisconsin Press, 1969).

Essig, James D.: *The Bonds of Wickedness: American Evangelicals Against Slavery, 1770–1808* (Philadelphia: Temple University Press, *c.* 1982).

Kulikoff, Allan: "A 'prolifick' people: black population growth in the Chesapeake colonies, 1700–1790," *Southern Studies*, 16 (1977).

Littlefield, Daniel C.: *Rice and Slaves: Ethnicity and the Slave Trade in Colonial South Carolina* (Baton Rouge: Louisiana State University Press, 1981).

Locke, Mary Stoughton: *Anti-Slavery in America from the Introduction of African Slaves to the Prohibition of the Slave-Trade (1619–1808)* (Boston: Ginn, 1901).

McLeod, Duncan J.: *Slavery, Race and the American Revolution* (Cambridge: Cambridge University Press, 1974).

Morgan, Edmund. *American Slavery, American Freedom: the Ordeal of Colonial Virginia* (New York: W. W. Norton, 1975).

Pole, J. R.: "Slavery and Revolution: the conscience of the rich," *Paths to the American Past* (New York: Oxford University Press, 1979).

Wood, Peter H.: *Black Majority: Negroes in Colonial South Carolina, from 1670 through the Stono Rebellion* (New York: Alfred A. Knopf, 1974).

Zilversmit, Arthur: *The First Emancipation: the Abolition of Slavery in the North* (Chicago and London: University of Chicago Press, 1967).

40

Indians and the new republic

JAMES H. MERRELL

IT DID not bode well for relations between the new republic and its native neighbors that the only reference to American Indians in the Declaration of Independence was to "merciless Indian savages." Nor did it help that during the Revolutionary War most tribes sided with Great Britain. After the war ended in 1783 the new nation sought to punish the Indians for their loyalty to the King. The peace treaty with Britain gave the United States claim to all of the lands east of the Mississippi River, and the victorious Americans began trying to convince the Indians of the claim's validity. But native resistance soon compelled the federal government to adopt a more pacific approach. Beginning in the late 1780s the new nation was negotiating for Indian lands and promising money, supplies, and civilization in exchange. This policy, which lasted into the 1820s, was only slightly more successful. Opposition from frontier settlers, from the states, and from the Indians themselves combined with a lack of commitment to native rights at the national level to hamper the policy's effectiveness, helping to pave the way for the Indians' removal from the East after Andrew Jackson's election to the presidency in 1828.

I. THE INDIANS AND THE REVOLUTIONARY WAR

At the outbreak of the American Revolution there were perhaps 200,000 Indians living east of the Mississippi River, made up of 85 different nations. The vast majority of these nations planned to stay out of the conflict between England and her rebellious colonies. "We are unwilling to join on either side ..., for we love you both – old England and new," the Oneidas explained to the governor of Connecticut in March 1775, a month before the fighting began at Lexington and Concord (Graymont, 1972, p. 58). Initially both Britain and America, aware that Indian allies could be expensive and unpredictable, were inclined to respect the natives' wishes. But the temptation to recruit Indian warriors – and the fear that the other side would recruit them first – proved too great to resist. By the time Americans officially declared their independence in July 1776, both sides were seeking Indian allies.

Most Indians, forced to make a choice in order to continue receiving essential trade goods, ended up supporting the King. While abandoning neutrality was often a difficult and painful decision, choosing between Britain and America was not. The British had a history of trying to protect Indian land from encroachments; the Americans had a history of making those encroachments. The British had long supplied Indians with gifts, and continued to do so after 1776; the hard-pressed Americans were unable to match the Crown's largesse. In addition, the British Americans most influential among the natives, such as John Stuart in the South and Guy Johnson among the Iroquois, remained loyal to the King; the Americans had no one with their prestige. In the end, most of the Indians who did join the patriot cause were from small enclaves located amid the colonial settlements – such as the Mashpees on Cape Cod and the Catawbas in the Carolina piedmont – or, like the Oneidas, were heavily influenced by a pro-rebel missionary. Together all of these pro-American Indian allies were few compared to the estimated 13,000 native men who fought for the British.

North and South, during the war Americans felt the effects of Britain's successful recruiting among the Indians. In 1776, for example, Cherokee war parties struck all along the southern frontier, while in 1778 the Iroquois launched attacks on New York and Pennsylvania. In the Ohio River valley an alliance of Indian nations – including Delawares, Shawnees, Wyandots, and Miamis – used British supplies and sometimes British troops to maintain their control of the region. Many Indians who remained loyal to the Crown paid dearly, however. American forces struck back, invading the Cherokees' mountain homes in 1776 and 1780, in 1779 marching into the heart of Iroquoia under Major General John Sullivan, and in 1780 and 1782 attacking the Shawnees in the Ohio country.

2. THE TREATY OF PARIS AND THE THEORY OF CONQUEST

The Indians' suffering during the Revolutionary War continued in another form once peace was made in 1783, for in the Treaty of Paris that ended the conflict Britain ceded to the United States all of the lands east of the Mississippi River. Since none of the Indian nations living on those lands had surrendered to the Americans and no native diplomats were at the treaty negotiations, the news that the King had granted away all of their territory came as quite a shock to the natives. It was especially surprising because the Indians had scored some of their greatest victories of the war in 1782: the Iroquois were still attacking settlements in the Mohawk Valley, and farther west Indian loyalists defeated the Americans on the banks of Lake Erie and at Blue Licks in Kentucky. To Britain's native allies, it looked like the war was all but won; now the English had made a shameful peace, and the Indians were furious. At the British post at Niagara the Iroquois bluntly told the commander "that if it was really true that the English had basely betrayed them by pretending to give up their Country to the Americans without their Consent, or Consulting them, it was an Act of Cruelty and injustice that Christians only were capable of doing" (Calloway, 1987, pp. 10–11).

Nonetheless the deed was done, and the victorious Americans soon began trying to put the treaty's terms into effect. In the autumn of 1783 Congress sent commissioners into Indian country armed with a theory of conquest derived from the Treaty of Paris. By defeating Great Britain, the argument went, the United States had also defeated Britain's Indian allies, and was therefore entitled to all of the Indians' lands. Thus the American commissioners came not to buy Indian territory but to demonstrate the new nation's generosity by returning to the Indians some of what once had been theirs. "We claim the country by conquest," federal agents informed Delawares and Wyandots in 1785, "and are to give not to receive" (Downes, 1940, p. 294). When, in the following year, a Shawnee protested that "God gave us this country, ... it is all ours," he was advised to "stop persisting in your folly" (Horsman, 1967, p. 22).

Behind the commissioners' strong words lay the new nation's urgent need for more land. To federal officials the Indian territory promised rescue from bankruptcy: those

MAP 8 Approximate location of major Indian nations in 1780

acres would either be granted to veterans to fulfill the government's promises of land bounties to soldiers or sold outright to settlers and speculators to raise money. On paper the plan appeared to be working. Between October 1784 and January 1786 the United States all but dictated treaties to the Six Nations and the Shawnees, to a confederacy of western Indians including Wyandots, Delawares, Chippewas, and Ottawas, and in the South to the Cherokees, Choctaws, and Chickasaws. But appearances were deceiving. The Indians later repudiated these agreements, stating that those who had assented to the terms were under duress or else had no authority to sign. Reiterating their arguments against the conquest theory, native leaders swore to defend the boundaries they had established in treaties with Britain before the Revolution.

The Indians had the resources to back up their threats. The Spanish remained in Florida, the British (defying the Treaty of Paris) in the Old Northwest; both encouraged native resistance and sent supplies to further that resistance. Among the Indians were men such as the Mohawk JOSEPH BRANT and the Creek ALEXANDER McGILLIVRAY, men with the vision and the political skills in both native and European cultures needed for leadership. McGillivray, with Spanish support, unified the Creeks and turned the nation against the United States so effectively that federal representatives "could not get enough of them to come to a meeting to justify a peace treaty on any terms" (Jones, 1982, p. 154). Brant used his influence among both the British and the Indians to help forge a confederacy of northern nations that rejected any treaty made without the unanimous approval of every member of the confederacy.

Citizens of the new nation were undeterred by the work of the British and Spanish, Brant and McGillivray. Those near the frontier saw a vast expanse of territory that, to their minds, was not put to proper use, and during the 1780s settlers poured across Indian boundaries to occupy the north side of the Ohio River as well as new territory in Georgia and Tennessee. The Indians made good on their promise to defend their homelands. In the latter half of the 1780s native war parties drove out many of the invaders in the South while their counterparts along the Ohio River picked off boats loaded with new settlers bound for Indian country. Efforts by the United States to punish the natives for these attacks were disastrous failures. In October 1790 Indian defenders badly mauled General Josiah Harmar's army when it invaded western Ohio. A year later, not far away, they all but destroyed General Arthur St. Clair's forces near what is now Fort Wayne, Indiana. In a few hours half of the 1,400 militia and American regulars were killed or wounded and the survivors were fleeing in panic back to the Ohio.

These defeats only proved what some of the new nation's leaders had suspected all along. However attractive the conquest theory might be, it was only a theory, and the United States lacked the means to make it reality. A national army with fewer than 700 men in 1789 (when the Creeks alone had between 3,500 and 6,000 warriors) was not going to subdue the Indians, even with the help of the militia. Nor was it likely to force Spain to stop supplying the Creeks or compel Britain to abide by the Treaty of Paris and abandon the forts it still held in the Old Northwest.

3. THE POLICY OF NEGOTIATION

Clearly if the young nation was to expand it was going to have to find a better way to come to terms with its Indian neighbors. Beginning in the mid-1780s some federal officials began to lobby for a different approach. Most outspoken among them was Henry Knox. Knox had been a general in the war for independence; after 1785 he was Secretary of War under the Articles of Confederation and in George Washington's administration. As a military man, Knox knew that crushing Indian resistance was impossible. As a government official, he recognized that military operations were an

FIGURE 32 The peace made between General Anthony Wayne and the Indians at Fort Greenville in 1795 (painting attributed to one of Wayne's soldiers): the treaty was intended to protect Indian lands from further encroachment by settlers, but by 1805 had become worthless to the Indians.

expense the republic could ill afford. As a patriot, he was concerned that land grabs and skirmishes with the natives would be an everlasting stain on the republic's record. Finally, as a product of the Enlightenment, he believed that environment shaped a people's culture, and that a change in environment could help raise the Indian from "savagery" to "civilization." Drawing upon all of these sources, Knox argued that there was a better way to pacify the Indians and acquire their territory at the same time. Recognize the Indians' right to the soil, he urged. Negotiate for that land in good faith, and pay for any cessions made. Finally, repay the Indians not only with cash but also with teachers, preachers, plows, and other tools of civilization. Such a policy, he argued, would save money, bring honor to the republic, and still allow for the nation's expansion.

Others, including Washington and many members of Congress, shared Knox's views, and in the late 1780s the talk of conquest faded. In August 1787 Congress advocated dropping "a language of superiority and command" in favor of dealing "with the Indians more on a footing of equality, . . . and instead of attempting to give lands to the Indians to proceed on the principle of fairly purchasing of them" (Horsman, 1967, pp. 41–2). This less belligerent policy – which in fact was a return to British practice before 1776 – continued after a new federal government was established under the Constitution. The nation's new framework of government scarcely mentioned Indians – saying only that Congress has the power "to regulate commerce with foreign nations, and among the several States, and with the Indian tribes." Nonetheless, this provision, and the Constitution's treaty-making clause, empowered the federal government to pass a series of laws in the early 1790s establishing a national policy that respected Indian land rights, acquired those lands through treaties confirmed by the Senate, and promoted civilization among the natives (*see* figure 32).

The Indian policy formulated during the late 1780s and early 1790s was to remain in place for the next four decades, even though the Indians' military power steadily declined. For all of those 40 years, the policy met with stiff and sometimes violent opposition. Much of that resistance came from the frontier, where settlers did not share their national leaders' views on Indians. In 1800, for example, Arthur St. Clair, then governor of the Northwest Territory, reported that Indians regularly faced "injustice and wrongs of the most provoking character, for which I have never heard that any person was ever brought to justice" (Edmunds, 1983, p. 22). Despite federal treaties making peace, setting boundaries, and promising punishment of trespassers, the frontier folk would not be stopped. "We think that the United States do not want our lands," Cherokee leaders told federal officials; "but we know as well who do want them – the frontier people want them" (Horsman, 1967, p. 118).

The states contributed in their own way to resistance to federal policy. Before the Revolution each colony had enjoyed wide latitude in dealing with Indians, and after 1776 the states were reluctant to give up their traditional powers. The first federal constitution, the Articles of Confederation, had done little to encourage them. Article 9 gave Congress "the sole and exclusive right and power of ... regulating trade and managing all affairs, with the Indians, not members of any of the states, provided that the legislative right of any state within its own limits not be infringed or violated." Obviously this was open to interpretation, and the states took it to mean that they could deal with the Indians much as they always had. During the 1780s various states, on their own initiative, fought or negotiated with various native nations. In the autumn of 1784, for example, the Iroquois met representatives from New York, the United States, and Pennsylvania in turn. Indeed, of the 21 treaties Indians made between May 1783 and November 1786, only six were with the United States; seven were with individual states, two more were with the putative state of Franklin, the rest were either with Spain or with individuals. The Constitution, and the federal laws that followed, took power away from the states; nonetheless, some still made trouble. Besides complaining that Indian land cessions were not going fast enough, states such as Georgia encouraged settlers to violate treaties and cross boundary lines in an attempt to increase the pressure on the federal government to step up the pace of negotiations.

As if opposition from settlers and their state governments were not enough, the nation's efforts to implement its Indian policy also had to contend with Indian reluctance. While the United States plan of recognizing Indian rights to the soil was an improvement over the conquest theory, that new policy was accompanied by relentless pressure to sell land. Indians resented this pressure and, often, the civilization program that went with it. Native resentment took several forms after 1800. Among Senecas, Shawnees, and Creeks, nativistic prophets won large followings by urging a return to traditional values. In some nations – the Shawnees and Creeks especially – this nativism spilled over into open warfare during the War of 1812. The government's civilization program enjoyed more success elsewhere. Many Cherokees learned

English, converted to Christianity, established cotton plantations, and obeyed a law code modeled on those of their white neighbors. The problem was that even the Cherokees most willing to accommodate America's civilization plans were not willing to sell their nation's lands, at least not at the rate the United States demanded. In fact, these acculturated natives were economically, socially, politically, and educationally better equipped to resist the American advance. Thus whatever the response – violent resistance by nativists, a religious movement such as those headed by the Shawnee Prophet and the Seneca Handsome Lake, or accommodation – Indian opposition was as difficult to overcome as that of the settlers and the states.

Added to all of these opponents was one final problem: the doubts at the federal level, where the policy was formulated and implemented. The policy's sponsors faced two dilemmas. First, the government placed greater emphasis on western expansion than on fair treatment of the natives. If the two policies clashed, if tribes refused to retreat before the white advance, they were manipulated, even coerced, into signing treaties. The second problem was that policy makers were increasingly pessimistic about the Indians' prospects for civilization. Even Knox had known that the task of transforming Indians into white people would be difficult; as resistance continued and even mounted, Knox's successors in the federal government became convinced that it was not only difficult, it was impossible. With the election of the frontiersman and Indian fighter Andrew Jackson in 1828, the republic's treatment of Indians would change dramatically from the course charted after the Revolution.

FURTHER READING

Calloway, Colin G.: *Crown and Calumet: British–Indian Relations, 1783–1815* (Norman: University of Oklahoma Press, 1987).

Downes, Randolph C.: *Council Fires on the Upper Ohio: a Narrative of Indian Affairs in the Upper Ohio Valley until 1795* (Pittsburgh: University of Pittsburgh Press, 1940).

Edmunds, R. David: *The Shawnee Prophet* (Lincoln: University of Nebraska Press, 1983).

Graymont, Barbara: *The Iroquois in the American Revolution* (Syracuse, NY: Syracuse University Press, 1972).

Horsman, Reginald: *Expansion and American Indian Policy, 1783–1812* (East Lansing: Michigan State University Press, 1967).

Jones, Dorothy V.: *License for Empire: Colonialism by Treaty in Early America* (Chicago: University of Chicago Press, 1982).

Merrell, James H.: "Declarations of independence: Indian–white relations in the new nation," *The American Revolution: its Character and Limits*, ed. Jack P. Greene (New York and London: New York University Press, 1987), pp. 197–223.

Prucha, Francis Paul: *American Indian Policy in the Formative Years: the Indian Trade and Intercourse Acts, 1790–1834* (Cambridge, Mass., 1962), repr. (Lincoln: University of Nebraska Press, 1970).

Sheehan, Bernard W.: *Seeds of Extinction: Jeffersonian Philanthropy and the American Indian* (Chapel Hill: University of North Carolina Press, 1973).

41

The impact of the Revolution on the role, status, and experience of women

BETTY WOOD

WOMEN from all walks of life played a visible and significant part in the struggle for American independence. However, the female experience during the revolutionary era was diverse. Women's perceptions of, and reactions to, the revolutionary movement were shaped by their class and race, as well as by their gender. Although the Revolution prompted a reappraisal of women and their role in the new Republic, the lives of most women did not change dramatically during the first decade or so of American independence. In the short term the Revolution neither ended nor inaugurated a "Golden Age" for American women.

Contrary to the impression conveyed by successive generations of male historians, and that which still pervades the popular view of the American Revolution on both sides of the Atlantic, the female experience during the revolutionary era amounted to rather more than BETSY ROSS stitching her flag, PHILLIS WHEATLEY writing her poetry, and ABIGAIL ADAMS urging her husband John and his fellow delegates meeting in Philadelphia in 1776 to "Remember the Ladies."

Research dating from the 1970s, more often than not undertaken by female scholars, has largely succeeded in exploding the traditional assumptions, myths, and stereotypes which have permeated the historiography of the American Revolution ever since the late eighteenth century. In their place is rapidly emerging a far more subtle, comprehensive, and realistic assessment of the often very different perceptions and activities of American women during the momentous and turbulent years between 1763 and 1790. Although, everywhere on the mainland, they were denied the franchise, and hence effectively excluded from any formal participation in political life, women from all social classes contributed in various, and often quite tangible, ways to the shaping and timing of the decision for American independence. Moreover, by their efforts on the home front, but not necessarily only in the home, they also played by no means an insignificant part in ensuring the eventual achievement of that independence.

I. THE ROLE OF WOMEN IN PRE-REVOLUTIONARY AMERICA

The longer-term forces at work in the societies and economies of British North America which both encouraged and enabled women to participate in the revolutionary movement were of critical and continuing importance in shaping their status, their daily lives, and the esteem in which they were held both within their families and by the community at large. The complex demographic, social, economic, and cultural processes which ever since the late seventeenth century had interacted to bring about the ever-increasing modernization of American but especially of northern society were, and would remain, profoundly important in defining both the experiences and the perceptions of women. By the same token, they would also help to shape the ways in which women were perceived and perceived each other. The twin processes of urbanization and industrialization, the inexorable growth of market economies, were to exert an enduring and arguably in the longer term a rather more tangible influence on the lives of American women than either republican ideology or the transient events of the War for Independence.

In the South, which was not entirely immune from the process of modernization, the growth and institutionalization of black slavery after the late seventeenth century played a decisive and invidious part in shaping both the status and the daily lives of women. Race was of fundamental significance in delineating the range of interactions deemed possible and desirable between white and black women. White and black women alike, and indeed black men also, albeit in rather different ways, were to be the victims of the often ambiguous sexual attitudes and behavior of white men. By the mid-eighteenth century race was and, despite the challenge posed to the institution of slavery during the revolutionary era, would remain by far and away the most potent and divisive force in defining the experience and attitudes of all southern women.

Predictably, the revolutionary era was not marked by a uniform or unifying cluster of distinctively female ideas, perceptions, or patterns of behavior. Class, race, and place of residence, as well as gender, all contributed to the shaping of what were often dramatically different female experiences, to the definition of female ambitions and aspirations, and to the opening and closing of windows of opportunity for women. The lives of some women, black and white, were to be completely and permanently transformed as a result of the American Revolution; for others, and arguably for the majority of women, the 1780s meant simply a return to their "normal" roles and responsibilities.

For hundreds of white women, of all ages and from all walks of life, the decision for American independence meant only the shattering of the world they had known, an abrupt and often traumatic break with the past and an uncertain future. Although these women and girls may or may not have completely endorsed the loyalist sympathies of their husbands and fathers, for them the American revolution was to mean an often involuntary and permanent exile in England, Canada, or the Caribbean. For many black women too, the loyalist sympathies of their masters and mistresses could also mean their enforced removal from the mainland, often to the harsher slave regimes of Britain's sugar islands.

Women's exclusion from political life   To all intents and purposes, women were excluded from any formal participation in the political life of the mainland colonies. Politics and government, both at the local and increasingly at the inter-colonial level, were very much a male preserve. Indeed, even the most ardent feminist would be forced to concede that, in all its aspects, the formal political movement from resistance to revolution was dominated by men; that, in the final analysis, the decision for American independence was taken in and by exclusively male political forums. But this male dominance of the halls of government, which was not to change with the securing of independence, should not be allowed to obscure the significance of the fervor with which many American women embraced the patriot cause or the importance of their albeit, and necessarily, informal political contribution to that cause.

Women's work outside the household   Some scholars have regarded the colonial period, but more specifically perhaps the seventeenth century, as being something of a "Golden Age" for American women, and in some senses this was indeed the case. During the initial stages of settlement, in the labor-hungry communities of both North and South, the willingness of women to work at often quite arduous physical tasks outside the household, traditionally the preserve of men, often earned them the high esteem of their menfolk. Indeed, much the same held true in other "frontier" societies as settlement expanded through the colonial period. One might say that in these communities, because of their scarcity and the value of their labor, women enjoyed something approximating a social and economic, if not a political, equality with men, if only an equality of physical hardship and deprivation. In all probability it was a situation which by no means all women relished. However, it was an essentially temporary and expedient equality, born of necessity rather than indicative of a fundamental reassessment of the status and role of women, which would persist as these often precarious frontier communities were transformed into more settled and stable societies.

2. OLD WORLD PERCEPTIONS OF WOMEN

Predictably, these evolving societies relied heavily on the perceptions and definitions of the role and status of women that they had brought with them from the Old World. The colonists had no intention of jettisoning the social thought, roles, and relationships which underpinned English society. What they sought to create in the New World were their own versions, albeit sometimes highly idealized or anachronistic versions, of that society. Certain of the perceptions and definitions which informed the shaping of the societies established in seventeenth-century British America, not least those having to do with the appropriate legal status of women, were to be modified in and by the requirements imposed by the American environment. However, both in theory and in practice, the status and role of women everywhere in British North America bore more than a passing resemblance to the English model. Crossing the Atlantic did not produce a dramatic or permanent change in the status of women or, it might be added, in the attitude of most women towards their designated role in society. In some respects, and despite the consequences for women of the increasing modernization of colonial society, which arguably did more than anything else to confirm and reinforce gender distinctions, very little changed during the course of the colonial period, at least in the working lives of men and women.

The ideal colonial woman   The ideal and idealized colonial woman, the woman who would have been lauded by both John Winthrop and Thomas Jefferson, was one who fulfilled the role of obedient wife, fruitful mother, efficient home-maker and dutiful daughter. As in England, the woman's place was very definitely in the home, in the private as opposed to the public sphere. The patriarchal family, which everywhere on the mainland was regarded as being the all-essential cornerstone of an ordered and orderly society, was to be the center of the woman's world, the reason for her existence. A woman's importance lay in what she contributed as a wife and mother to the formation, stability, and continuing cohesion of the family unit. Her broader civic duty lay in the influence which she might bring to bear on shaping and perhaps modifying and moderating the opinions and attitudes of her husband and sons.

However, her husband was the undisputed head of the family, the ultimate decision maker, whose word was, if necessary, law.

Education   The often limited education, both formal and informal, of girls and young women was designed to fit them for the roles of wife, mother, and home-maker. Any form of higher education was effectively closed to women; men deemed it to be both unnecessary and beyond their intellectual capacity. Formal entry into most professions, with the exception of teaching, was an avenue closed to women. The expectation was that such work as they undertook should be within an essentially family oriented, domestic context.

Religion   In many respects it was religion which provided those women who wanted it with a recognized and legitimate entrée into the wider world. Of course, it was unthinkable to male divines, priests, and clergy that women should be accorded any formal ministerial recognition or responsibilities. Only in the Quaker communities, founded towards the end of the seventeenth century, did women enjoy anything like complete equality of religious participation and involvement. But so far as most other sects and denominations were concerned, religious activities did provide an appropriate sphere in which women might cultivate and apply what were widely regarded as being the quintessential female virtues of piety, humility, and charity.

Single women   In the final analysis, however, marriage and motherhood were regarded as a woman's main role and objective in life. The high incidence of marriage and remarriage as well as the high rate of natural increase in the mainland colonies certainly suggests that the majority of women conformed to this expectation of them, if only because to remain single was to invite sarcasm and ridicule. How many colonial marriages were happy must remain a matter for conjecture. Legal separations were possible and, if she were the injured party, the wife could expect continuing material support from her husband. Divorce was a virtually impossible option for either partner.

However, the only sure ways for a woman to gain a significant measure of, if not complete, control over her own destiny were arguably to remain single, be legally separated from her husband, or be widowed. True, she had to make her way and support herself in what was very much a man's world, and her social class as well as her gender could determine just how hard a struggle that might be. Yet in terms of her legal standing and status, and particularly in respect of her rights regarding the accumulation and disposal of property, she enjoyed various benefits which, in theory at any rate, were largely denied to married women.

In practice, however, both within and outside the domestic sphere, the status, esteem accorded, and daily lives of women in mid-eighteenth-century America did not always correspond precisely with the image and expectations of the "ideal woman." Within the home, the wife's input into decision making reflected the nature of her marriage, her husband's character, and his assessment of what she brought or contributed to the family. By no means all colonial husbands and fathers were petty tyrants who ruled their households with a rod of iron. On the contrary, many husbands regarded their wives as partners rather than as subordinate ornaments and acknowledged the contribution they had made to the family estate, as well as their competence to manage the same, by naming them as their executrices. Indeed, during their lifetimes many husbands had little hesitation in leaving their wives in charge of their affairs while they were away at war or on political or other business.

Working women   There is abundant evidence that colonial women in the middling and lower ranks of society retained an importance as economic producers. Many worked alongside their menfolk in the agricultural economies of the mainland and, in the towns, filled a range of skilled and semi-skilled occupations. The skills that women acquired by working with their fathers and husbands could stand them in good stead should they decide to remain single or if they were widowed. The competence of many colonial women was not in doubt and, it might be suggested, they both took pride in and drew inspiration from the recognition of this fact.

3. THE REVOLUTIONARY ERA

Women's awareness of political life   Never, since the days of Anne Hutchinson and Margaret Brent, had colonial women been disinterested, passive, and mute observers of the world around them. However, comparatively few women stepped so completely outside their assigned gender roles as did Anne Hutchinson to voice opinions and engage in public activities which explicitly challenged the exclusive authority traditionally claimed by men. Those who did were depicted as posing an unacceptable threat to the maintenance of an ordered and orderly patriarchal society and their deviant behavior was often ascribed to witchcraft or other sinister motives.

Most colonial women did not behave in such an assertive and, from the male standpoint, such a deeply threatening manner as had Anne Hutchinson during the 1630s. But this did not necessarily mean that, by the mid-eighteenth century, all women had unthinkingly and uncritically internalized the role of wife and mother. They did not totally lack the time, inclination, intellectual ability, and confidence to take cognizance of, and seek to plan an active part in defining, the rapidly changing world in which they lived and their designated place within that world.

Women in all social classes were not immune to, insulated from, or uninvolved in the political, religious, and social discourses taking place in the world in which they lived. To a great extent, however, their awareness of and participation in those discourses depended upon images and information presented to them by men. Most of the literature available for their consumption, be it in the form of newspapers, pamphlets, or books, had been produced by men for men. This did not necessarily mean that all women could, or wished to, read such materials; that those who did so absorbed uncritically the ideas and information they conveyed; or that women simply mimicked the attitudes of male authors as well as those of their husbands and fathers. What it did often mean, however, was that women were obliged to operate within an intellectual frame of reference largely devised by men.

Although denied a formal role, or even a formal voice, in the political lives of their societies, many colonial women took both a keen and an active interest in politics. Their political involvement, the options open to them, and their modes of behavior reflected both their station in life and, to a considerable degree, the stratagems devised and deemed appropriate for them by their menfolk. In the increasingly turbulent political life of the major port towns in the North, for example, women, probably drawn mainly from the lower orders of society, were visible and accepted members of the "urban crowd." It was by no means unknown for women to campaign quite openly for candidates in local elections. Thus white Georgians, male and female, do not seem to have been unduly surprised, and certainly were not scandalized, by the fact that in 1768 Mrs. Heriot Crooke and Mrs. James Mossman, the wives of two

403

FIGURE 33 The Society of Patriotic Ladies at Edenton, North Carolina, signing a document which reads: "We the Ladys of Edenton do hereby Solemnly Engage not to Conform to that Pernicious Custom of Drinking Tea, or that we the aforesaid Ladys will not promote ye wear of any Manufacture from England untill such time that all Acts which tend to Enslave this our Native Country shall be Repealed" (detail from engraving by ?Philip Dawe, 1775).

prominent planters, rode around the countryside campaigning on behalf of Sir Patrick Houstoun's candidacy for a seat in the Assembly.

As of the early 1760s, women in all walks of life lacked neither an interest in, nor an often intimate knowledge of, the political world in which they lived or the ways in which that world operated. They could and did assess for themselves the merits of the competing claims of British and American ideologues and politicians. Individually and collectively, women's voices were heard during the 1760s and 1770s – not for the first time, but on a scale hitherto unknown. Moreover, men were not always concerned to silence them. Indeed, colonial politicians saw women as invaluable, indeed as absolutely necessary, allies in the struggle they were waging against Great Britain, and quite explicitly solicited their support.

Patriot women Examples of the female commitment to the patriot cause, and the support given by women to that cause both before and during the War for Independence, are manifold. Among the best known is the Edenton resolution. In October 1774, 51 women from Edenton, North Carolina, signed a statement in which they declared their unwavering commitment to the patriot cause and their intent to do all that they could to further the same (*see* figure 33). Equally well known are the 36 women in Philadelphia who in 1780 launched what was to prove an immensely successful campaign to raise money to help equip American troops. Within a matter of weeks they managed to collect around $300,000.

In Edenton and Philadelphia, and elsewhere on the mainland also, some women were taking the initiative. But there was a very real sense in which women were participating in a political campaign devised and orchestrated by men. And those men had fairly explicit ideas about the most appropriate ways in which women could help them. During the 1760s and early 1770s male patriots freely acknowledged that the success of the most important weapon in their political armoury, the boycotting of British goods, depended upon the cooperation of women, upon their willingness to change their patterns of consumption. It is abundantly clear that many women in all social classes were willing to do precisely that. However, male patriots went on to suggest that women could express their support for the American cause not only by wearing homespun clothes but also by making them. It was in their homes, in an essentially domestic context, sitting at their wheels and looms, that women could most appropriately assist their menfolk. And, it must be said, that is precisely what many women from all walks of life did, often with great gusto and enthusiasm. Patriot men were concerned to ensure that the horizons of women did not extend very far beyond their wheels and looms.

Working women In a purely practical sense, the War for Independence, when it came, was to have essentially similar consequences for women as had all previous colonial wars. Out of necessity, women were required to fill various economic roles often closed to them in peacetime. As their fathers, husbands, sons, and brothers went off to fight, for whichever side, so many women found themselves left to run the family farm or business. For those who had worked alongside the men in their family, and in the process acquired invaluable knowledge and expertise, this might have been an unwelcome prospect, but was certainly not daunting. It was a rather different proposition for women whose husbands and fathers had effectively denied them any detailed knowledge of their business affairs. But in either case, the assumption was that when men returned from the war they would resume their usual role and responsibilities in the family. And more often than not that is exactly what did happen. But of course many men did not return from the war. For their wives this meant not only the trauma of bereavement but also the psychological and sometimes material problems of adjusting to widowhood.

Black women It would seem reasonable to suggest that, in the longer term at any rate, the War for Independence *per se* did not result in any significant or permanent changes in the status, roles and daily lives of most white women. However, the dislocations of war, especially in the southern theater, did offer possibilities of escape and flight to black women. An unknown number of slave women did run away, but their freedom was often to prove both precarious and temporary.

In some respects it was patriot ideology rather than the War for Independence *per se* which seemed to hold out the best prospect of freedom, if not complete equality, for black men and women, both in the North and in the South. To some degree, that prospect began to be realized during the 1770s and 1780s, albeit often gradually and grudgingly in the North and, through the device of private manumission, on a limited scale in parts of the South. In the South, however, most black men and women ended the revolutionary era as they had begun it: as chattel slaves. The accommodations and compromises made in Philadelphia in 1787 ruled out the possibility that this situation would change in the foreseeable future.

Many people, on both sides of the Atlantic, had pointed to the apparent inconsistency, if not hypocrisy, of a patriot ideology which demanded freedom, liberty, and equality for white Americans but which denied those self-same things to black Americans. But, with the notable exception of Thomas Paine, no patriot pamphleteer or politician suggested or even hinted that women too might legitimately claim full and equal participation in the political society which men were so busy defining and bringing into existence. Neither did American women make the same claim on their own behalf or, during the 1790s, enthusiastically applaud Mary Wollstonecraft when she did.

4. THE NEW REPUBLICAN WOMAN

Yet the social and political discourse of the revolutionary era did not, and arguably could not, totally avoid the question of women. In many respects, it was the greater visibility of women in the America of the 1760s and 1770s, the part which they were playing and ought to be playing in the revolutionary movement, that prompted an intense examination of various attitudes and assumptions which previously had been largely taken for granted by both sexes. During the 1780s, with the achievement of American independence, the debate focused on the attributes which made for the "ideal" republican woman, the role of women in the new republic, and how they might best be prepared for that role. The outcome of that debate, in which women participated and with which they by and large concurred, was to return women to the private, domestic sphere from which it seemed by their actions if not by their words they might be trying to escape.

The woman's view   The fact of the matter was, however, that the political upheavals and disruptions of the revolutionary era did not dramatically change the self-perception of American women, or at least of those middle- and upper-class women who committed their thoughts and opinions to paper. Both before, during, and after the War for Independence, these women were arguing vociferously not for a complete redefinition of their role and status which, amongst other things, would have accorded them complete political equality with men, but for the acknowledgment by men of the equal importance and value of the private sphere in which they operated and were content to continue operating. As Abigail Adams put it – and she was by no means atypical of women in her social class – "if man is Lord, women is *Lordess* – that is what I contend for." When she urged the delegates meeting in Philadelphia to "Remember the Ladies," she was not and probably would not have dreamed of suggesting that Jefferson amend the Declaration of Independence to read "All men and women are created equal." Rather, she was emphasizing the importance of and claiming an equality of status for the private sphere in which women operated. Abigail Adams, and women like her, subscribed to many of the same social attitudes, assumptions, and values as American men.

Marriage   Abigail Adams would not have dissented from the almost universally held view of the social and moral role, function, and importance of marriage and the family. Virtually every woman of her social class was truly appalled by Paine and Wollstonecraft's critiques of marriage and horrified by the way in which the latter practiced what she preached. The path suggested by Paine and Wollstonecraft pointed, or seemed to be pointing, to a complete breakdown of society – to social chaos, disorder, and anarchy. For women to step from the private to the public sphere, assuming that they had the time to combine the roles of wife, mother, and home-maker with the demands of a public career, would be one step along that infinitely dangerous path. In fact, the vehement denunciation by women such as Abigail Adams of state constitutions and election laws which, with the notable exception of those of New Jersey, explicitly denied women even the possibility of formal participation in political life, would have been more surprising and difficult to explain than their apparently placid acceptance of this state of affairs. Because of a dearth of first-hand written evidence, the perceptions of women further down the social scale are much more difficult to unravel.

Attributes of the republican woman   If one of the principal concerns and preoccupations of some upper- and middle-class women during the 1780s was with establishing the importance and equality of the private sphere, then another, and one which they shared with some men – most notably perhaps with Benjamin Rush – was defining the attributes of the "ideal" republican woman and determining how girls and women might best be prepared to fulfill their assigned role in the new Republic.

In some ways, the "ideal" republican woman shared many of the same attributes and was required to display many of the same virtues as the "ideal" Roman matron. Her civic duty lay in the benign, almost civilizing, influence which she exerted over her husband and sons in ensuring that they became wise, virtuous, just, and compassionate members of the body politic and, if called upon, good rulers.

Education   The "ideal" republican woman was not a frivolous, empty headed orna-ment. On the contrary, she was expected and required to be a competent partner who could engage in serious discourse on a wide range of matters with her husband and sons. The problem was, as Benjamin Rush, JUDITH SARGENT MURRAY, and others realized, that the traditional modes and methods of educating girls, when they were educated at all, scarcely fitted them for such an awesome responsibility. Girls had to be educated, and suitably educated, if they were ever to live up to the high expectations of the republican woman. The "ideal" republican woman had to know how to cook and manage an efficient household, but she also had to know something about those subjects which would be of interest and concern to her husband. In what was to be one of the more tangible benefits accruing to women as a direct result of the American Revolution, much greater attention than ever before came to be paid to the formal education of girls and, not least, to the devising of curricula more in keeping with those available to boys.

Comparatively few female lives, black or white, in North or South, town or country-side, remained completely untouched or unaffected by the ideas and events of the American Revolution. But although, because of their commitment and contribution to the revolutionary cause, white women came to be regarded in a rather more positive light during the 1780s and 1790s, these years did not witness a "revo-lutionary" change in the status, role, and daily lives of American women.

FURTHER READING

Depauw, Linda G.: *Founding Mothers: Women of America in the Revolutionary Era* (Boston: Houghton Mifflin, 1975).

Hoffman, Ronald, and Albert, Peter J. (eds.): *Women in the Age of the American Revolution* (Charlottesville: University Press of Virginia for the United States Capitol Historical Society, 1989).

Kerber, Linda K.: *Women of the Republic: Intellect and Ideology in Revolutionary America* (Chapel Hill: University of North Carolina Press for the Institute of Early American History and Culture, 1980).

Lewis, Jan: "The republican wife: virtue and seduction in the early republic," *William and Mary Quarterly*, 44 (1987), 689–721.

Norton, Mary Beth: *Liberty's Daughters: the Revolutionary Experience of American Women, 1750–1800* (Boston: Little, Brown, 1980).

Wilson, Joan Hoff: "The illusion of change: women and the American Revolution," *The American Revolution: Explorations in the History of American Radicalism*, ed. Alfred F. Young (Dekalb: Northern Illinois University Press, 1976), 383–445.

42

The impact of the Revolution on education

MELVIN YAZAWA

I. REVOLUTIONARY REPUBLICANISM

THE American Revolution was never simply a movement for colonial independence. Partly of necessity, but primarily by choice, independent Americans were to be citizens of a republic. And because Americans seemed to be so advantageously positioned to attempt an experiment in republicanism, having been conditioned by colonial practices and being able to draw upon an accumulation of past wisdom, the fate of the new nation was supposed to determine once and for all whether men were capable of governing themselves without the benefit of kings or lords. The revolutionary generation, as Robert Livingston declared in 1787, was thus never destined for a "humble peace and ignominious obscurity." If they succeeded in proving a republican system to be workable and durable, their success would be emulated elsewhere in the world and the realm of liberty would be extended; if they failed, their failure would establish the limits of human aspirations.

Revolutionary republicans confronted two major obstacles to success. First, in a republic, ordinary men must behave in an extraordinary fashion. For self-government to work, citizens must be willing to sacrifice their selfish interests for the good of the whole; otherwise, chaos reigns and the orderly rule of a monarch becomes a welcomed alternative. It was precisely this quality of "civic virtue" that was missing from past republican experiments and, consequently, led to their demise. Were Americans sufficiently virtuous? From the outset of the imperial crisis to 1776, the Revolutionaries were convinced of their moral superiority. Indeed, independence was necessary in large part because the Revolutionaries had come to consider Britain and the British people to be lost in corruption. Unless a speedy separation was effected, Americans could expect to be tainted with British vices. This heady notion was quickly dispelled once the fighting began in earnest.

Wartime experiences – flagging enthusiasm after 1776, declining enlistments, battlefield reverses, looting and the destruction of private property by revolutionary forces, and disciplinary problems among soldiers and civilians alike – understandably undermined all initial assumptions of moral superiority. Although some may have hoped that the end of the war and the enduring commitment to republicanism might effect a moral regeneration among Americans, they were soon disappointed. David Ramsay, the South Carolina physician and revolutionary historian, echoed a common complaint in 1785 when he lamented over the "declension of our public virtue." Liberty and independence, rather than encouraging sentiments of gratitude and sacrifice, had given rise to "Pride, Luxury, dissipation & a long train of unsuitable vices."

The second obstacle to the success of the revolutionary experiment in republicanism

409

was rooted in the circumstance and composition of the American population. The conventional wisdom of the eighteenth century recommended republican systems rather reluctantly, and then only for small states encompassing a homogeneous population. Was the new American nation too large? Were its people too diverse for republican self-rule? James Madison, of course, provided a measure of reassurance by reversing the logic of the conventional argument for small republics. Contrary to common belief, Madison said in *The Federalist* no. 10, stability was more likely to be achieved in a large republic than in a small one. In an extended republic comprising a vast array of competing interests the formation of an unjust combination constituting a majority of the whole was highly improbable. Separate factions would lack either a common motive or a convenient opportunity to form a self-interested majority capable of subverting minority rights. Civic action, under these circumstances, "could seldom take place on any other principles than those of justice and the general good." Underlying Madison's logic, however, was the assumption that the competing interests would, in the end, recognize the general good and make the private concessions necessary to secure it. Ultimately, then, as Madison acknowledged, disparate interests must be contained within a "practicable sphere."

The very nature of the obstacles suggested a solution. Education, properly conceived and executed, might remedy any defects in the American character. "Education," Thomas Jefferson explained, "engrafts a new man on the native stock, and improves what in nature was vicious and perverse into qualities of virtue and social worth." For the newly independent and infinitely diverse American people the establishment of a national system of education promised to be especially beneficial. In addition to engrafting qualities of virtue essential in a republic, a common education might forge an otherwise discordant conglomeration of factions into a harmonious whole. As Benjamin Rush, the prominent Philadelphia physician and signer of the Declaration of Independence, noted, education "will render the mass of the people more homogeneous and thereby fit them more easily for uniform and peaceable government."

2. REPUBLICAN EDUCATION

The American Revolutionaries said and wrote much about education in the new republic. Common themes, however, quickly emerged. First, they conceived of education broadly. Few writers were willing to confine their thoughts to the mechanics of reading, writing, and arithmetic. The vast majority instead viewed education as nothing less than the process by which the uninitiated were transformed into full participating members of society. Robert Coram, editor of the *Delaware Gazette*, offered a succinct definition of education in his 1791 plan for a national system of schools. Education, Coram said, entails the "instruction of youth in certain rules of conduct by which they will be enabled to support themselves when they come to age and to know the obligations they are under to that society of which they constitute a part."

Since 1776, "that society" was of course republican, and the "obligations" youths were expected eventually to assume were the obligations of self-governing citizenship. Accordingly, the second common theme of the revolutionary educational theorists emphasized the necessity of a system of education that would disseminate knowledge widely. If the dissemination of knowledge failed to keep up with the extension of political rights, then the bulk of the people would take on civic responsibilities for which they were poorly prepared and the American republic would likely experience a speedy decline. Educated citizens, on the other hand, might advance the common good and prolong the life of the republic. They would, in the first place, choose their rulers wisely and thereby reduce the chances of ambitious or venal men ever being entrusted with power. But even if magistrates, once elected, attempted to abuse their power, an informed and vigilant populace would quickly check such transgressions. Despots survived only by maintaining "a dark cloud of ignorance" over their subjects, declared Simeon Doggett, a New England Unitarian minister and former tutor at the College of Rhode Island (Brown). Therefore, "let general information and a just knowledge of the rights of man be diffused through the great bulk of the people in any nation, and it will not be in the power of all the combined despots on earth to enslave them."

Two additional considerations strengthened the case for an extensive system of education in the new republic. First, revolutionary writers tended to couple knowledge with virtue and liberty; ignorance with vice and tyranny. In the *Spirit of the Laws* (1748), Montesquieu made famous the idea that systems of government and education ultimately must coincide. Despotic states might ignore the principles of education (indeed they were well advised to do so), but democratic republics were dependent on the powers of education. Only through education might ordinary men be inspired to place public over private interest, a choice that was "ever arduous and painful" to make. Education thus exercised and extended the "crude wisdom which nature bestows," Samuel Harrison Smith observed. Smith, the Philadelphia journalist who later founded the Jeffersonian newspaper the *National Intelligencer*, argued that the "diffusion of knowledge actually produces some virtues, which without it would have no existence." Most important to the life of the republic, knowledge tended to inspire a "spirit of universal philanthropy" and to lift the "mind to an elevation infinitely superior to the sensation of individual regard." In short, education grafted a spirit of selflessness onto originally selfish stock.

A second consideration usually associated with the notion of the importance of disseminating knowledge widely focused on the nature and necessity of female education. The life of the republic was dependent on the moral character of its citizenry, and women as mothers were the chief guarantors of civic virtue within the family. It was commonly known, as Benjamin Rush remarked in 1786, that "*first impressions upon the mind are the most durable.*" And because the first impressions of children were ordinarily derived from their mothers, it was essential that women be qualified for this responsibility. In addition to the "usual branches" of domestic education, then, women needed to be "instructed in the principles of liberty and government." No plan of republican education would be complete if it ignored the women of the republic.

Republican systems of education, then, had to be inclusive. However, a system that embraced every part of the community would still be inadequate if it did not provide for the filtration of talent. Most revolutionary leaders assumed that the majority of men were unfit to manage the abstruse affairs of state. Natural aristocrats, an elite group defined by superior talents rather than inherited family position, were best able to protect the welfare of the whole. A third common theme in the literature on education thus described a graduated arrangement of increasingly restrictive institutions designed to single out the naturally superior. Jefferson offered the best summary discussion of this theme. In his *Notes on the State of Virginia*, he described an arrangement of local district schools, county grammar schools, and the College of William and Mary. At each level, the "best geniuses will be raked from the rubbish," Jefferson said. Other writers also commented on the utility of selective promotions. A graduated

FIGURE 34 The earliest view of Harvard College (engraving, 1726, after a drawing by William Burgis). Cricket was often played by Harvard boys in the field outside the gates.

system of education supposedly reflected the natural order of the world. God, it was commonly assumed, had distributed natural abilities in unequal portions; a republican system of education should complement this natural order. Samuel Knox, a Presbyterian minister and educator whose ideas were probably influenced by the writings of Jefferson, believed that a hierarchical arrangement geared for the advancement of "such as discovered the brightest genius" was in the best interest of America. Each level of institution might then be structured to accommodate a particular group of citizens whose natural abilities could carry them no further. In the end, every citizen would theoretically be prepared to assume his particular station in the republic.

Finally, because of the heightened political significance of education in the new nation, the Revolutionaries insisted that it must become a public responsibility. "Wisdom and knowledge, as well as virtue, diffused generally among the body of the people, being necessary for the preservation of their rights and liberties," declared the Massachusetts constitution of 1780, it is the "duty of legislatures and magistrates" to extend the "opportunities and advantages of education in the various parts of the country." The dissemination of knowledge was "so momentously important," said Samuel Harrison Smith, that it "must not be left to the negligence of individuals." In America, circumstances not only justified, they dictated the "establishment of a system which shall place under a control, independent of and superior to parental authority, the education of children." Robert Coram fully endorsed these sentiments. "Education should not be left to the caprice or negligence of parents, to chance," he cautioned. Independence and the commitment to republican government thus accelerated the trend, well underway by the middle of the eighteenth century, towards the enlargement of the civic responsibilities of the state (in caring for orphans and the poor, for example) and the diminution of the social space occupied by the family.

An obvious corollary of this final theme of public supervision over education was the insistence on the part of the revolutionary writers that the youth of America be educated within the borders of the new nation. To do otherwise would be shameful. The practice of sending students abroad was, as the Georgia legislature announced in 1785, "too humiliating an acknowledgement of the ignorance or inferiority of our own" institutions. Before the Revolution, such a practice was perhaps "an appropriate reflection of our servile station in the British Empire," Noah Webster said. But whatever propriety there existed "ceased with our political relation to Great Britain." To continue sending American youths abroad for an education was inconsistent with true independence. Furthermore, the benefits of education, especially in an extended republic as diverse as the American polity, were unavoidably tied to geography. The smooth functioning of countervailing factions within Madison's "practicable sphere" was dependent on the power of education to encourage self-interested men willingly to make the compromises necessary to secure the common good. In other words, each faction ultimately must be inspired by a love for the republic; otherwise, the array of competing interests would be productive only of anarchy and confusion. This love for the republic, or patriotism, was an affection that had to be consciously inculcated in the minds of youngsters. Webster prescribed a program of instruction that began with a kind of political catechism: "As soon as ... [the American child] opens his lips, he should rehearse the history of his own country; he should lisp the praise of liberty and of those illustrious heroes and statesmen who have wrought a revolution in her favor." The alternative to this sort of patriotic education on American soil was a foreign education that regrettably would give rise to an attachment to foreign governments or to principles foreign to America.

3. REPUBLICAN SCHOOLING

The Revolutionaries' insistence on the establishment of an American system of publicly supervised institutions of education that would promote the welfare and ensure the permanence of the republic manifested itself in a variety of ways. Indeed, given the importance of the subject, the novelty of the situation, and the tradition of localism that was rooted in the American colonial past, institutional multiplicity was perhaps all but inevitable.

The pace of activity in the realm of public education varied from state to state and between localities. The New England states, building on precedents and priorities set during the colonial period, led the way in the creation of institutions at the lower levels. Massachusetts, in particular, was inclined to codify its intention to educate its citizens. In addition to its 1780 constitution, which charged magistrates and legislators to promote institutions of learning, Massachusetts enacted a public schooling law in 1789. According to its provisions, towns comprising at least 50 families had to furnish six months of schooling during the year; towns of 200 families were required also to support a grammar school. There was little resistance to the 1789 law because, as Lawrence A. Cremin has observed (1980), it merely "codified the commonplace." Massachusetts towns and their inhabitants had, in the course of the last decades of the eighteenth century, grown accustomed to the idea of schooling and school-going.

Although Massachusetts was an early champion of public education, it made almost no attempts to subsume its various institutions under one administrative organization. Thus in 1837, when Horace Mann became secretary of the newly created Massachusetts board of education, he complained about the absence of a "common, superintending power" over the 3,000 public schools in the Commonwealth. Each school was "governed by its own habits, traditions, and local customs"; consequently, the various schools remained "strangers and aliens to each other."

Unlike Massachusetts, New York attempted early to effect a grand design for a system of integrated institutions. Beginning in 1784, New York officials sought to implement an administrative structure that would promote learning throughout the state and serve as a supervisory body for all of the state's various academic institutions. The initial legislation in 1784 established the University of the State of New York and lodged broad administrative powers in its board of regents. Unfortunately, the first board was dominated by King's College men and remained preoccupied with the affairs of that institution (renamed Columbia by the 1784 law). A revised law in 1787 restructured the university as a more representative and comprehensive organization for regulating the state's colleges and schools. Again, however, the university failed to operate as an administrative unit for the state. Not until 1812 did the legislature, acting on a report commissioned by Governor Daniel D. Tompkins, pass a law erecting an alternative to the system first described in 1784. The 1812 law appointed a superintendent of schools whose responsibilities included the management of a three-tiered organization comprising local districts, towns, and the state. As a result of the 1812 legislation, institutions chartered by the legislature existed alongside academies chartered by the regents of the university. Also, local districts set up high schools under their own auspices. In the early years of the republic, therefore, New York succeeded in developing institutions that disseminated knowledge more widely, but it failed to realize fully its design to bring all of these institutions under one uniform administration.

In the South, educational systems, especially at the lower levels, developed more slowly than they did elsewhere. Virginia often led the way, although not without setbacks of its own. The 1779 Bill for the More General Diffusion of Knowledge, drafted by Jefferson, called for a division of each county into units called "hundreds" and the creation of publicly supported elementary schools in each hundred as well as grammar schools in each county. The bill, Jefferson said, would prepare the people to "understand their rights, to maintain them, and to exercise with intelligence their parts in self-government." The measure came before the legislature in 1780, 1785, and 1786, but failed to pass. In 1796 the Virginia legislature did enact that portion of the bill that provided for the creation of elementary schools. However, the 1796 law let each local county court decide whether to institute the program. None did.

From the late eighteenth century through the 1840s, Virginians tried repeatedly to develop a comprehensive school system. In 1810 the legislature established an endowment for the "sole benefit of a school or schools, to be kept in each and every county." Although a modest endowment initially, the fund grew in 1816 when it became the repository of money owed to Virginia by the federal government. Unfortunately, competing factions, each with its own plan for the income generated by the fund, effectively stalled the implementation of any program of comprehensive schooling. Jefferson himself, in 1816–17, helped to defeat a measure sponsored by

Charles Fenton Mercer that would have created an integrated system of primary schools, academies, colleges, and a state university located in the Shenandoah Valley. Jefferson opposed the Mercer plan in part for partisan reasons – Mercer was a Federalist spokesman for western interests in the Virginia House of Delegates – and in part because he had advanced a plan of his own which called for the location of the state's university in his home county of Albemarle. Neither Mercer nor Jefferson was able to gain the votes necessary for implementing his program. The result was a substitute measure that allowed only the accommodation of the children of the poor in already existing elementary schools. A subsequent piece of legislation in 1829 made publicly supported schooling for the poor mandatory. Virginia, thus, had made advances in public schooling in the early years of the republic; however, only in the education of paupers did it achieve a degree of uniformity.

4. ASSESSMENT

What, ultimately, did the founding fathers achieve in the realm of education? There are at least two ways of addressing this question: first by examining the institutional changes that came in the wake of Independence and second by assessing the long-range impact of altered expectations among the bulk of the citizenry.

Some present-day critics of the revolutionary generation's commitment to education have noted that no statewide systems of public schooling were completed in the immediate postwar years. In short, the charge is that the deeds of the founding fathers failed to keep up with their words. Such criticism, however, ignores the flurry of activity in institution-building in the last quarter of the eighteenth century. Between 1775 and 1800, for example, academies flourished. At a time when the boundary between public and private schooling was still in the process of being defined, academies were not only the principal institutions of secondary education but were often supported through a combination of public taxes and private subscriptions. A quick count shows that Virginia chartered 20 academies during these years; Massachusetts, 17; New York, 19; Pennsylvania, 11; and Maryland, 7. Many more academies went unchartered; thus we know that in these states alone there were probably between 100 and 200 new institutions of secondary education after the Revolution.

At the level of higher education, the Revolutionaries' achievement was perhaps even more impressive. The life of the republic was dependent on the preparation of ordinary men and women for extraordinary responsibilities, but it was also dependent on the selection of men of superior virtue and talent for public offices. As Jefferson remarked, "that form of government is the best which provides the most effectually for a pure selection of ... natural aristoi into the offices of government." Colleges were, therefore, essential to the success of the republic because, by singling out the naturally gifted for special training, they facilitated the process of pure selection. Between 1783 and 1800, 16 new colleges opened that still exist today. At least five other colleges gained state charters but failed to survive the nineteenth century. In the immediate postwar years, then, the number of colleges operating in the new nation more than tripled.

As impressive as the numbers of new colleges founded was the trend towards publicly supported institutions. In the 1780s and 1790s, the state universities of Georgia, North Carolina, and Vermont received their charters. In addition, St. John's College (Maryland), Transylvania University (Kentucky), the College of Charleston, Williams College (Massachusetts), and Bowdoin College (Maine) either originated under state auspices or maintained a quasi-public character in spite of denominational affiliations. Indeed, it was this connection to the public realm that often determined the nature and pace of internal developments in the various institutions. For example, curricular changes – especially an increased emphasis on politics and modern history, English grammar, mathematics, moral philosophy, and natural sciences – reflected the perceived need for both "practical" and patriotic education in the new republic. Furthermore, the intrusion of outside concerns into college hallways altered the expectations of students and faculty alike. This publicly inspired alteration leads us to the second way of assessing the educational achievements of the founding fathers.

American colleges, understandably, had become increasingly politicized in the course of the Independence movement, and politicization did not end with the end of the war. On the contrary, colleges remained arenas of public controversy and were embroiled in the ongoing political struggles of the 1780s and 1790s. The debate over the federal Constitution, Hamiltonian finances, the French Revolution, the Jay Treaty, and other issues forced the various campuses to choose sides. By the end of the 1790s, New England colleges were recognizably Federalist while the College of William and Mary was decidedly Republican. In the long run, this sort of political identification impeded the development of unified statewide systems of public education. Thus Jefferson, it will be recalled, prevented the implementation of the Federalist Charles Fenton Mercer's comprehensive plan of 1816–17. Ironically, what present-day critics are wont to identify as evidence of disinterest on the part of the Revolutionaries is evidence of precisely the opposite. Because education was so important to them and because the stakes were so high – involving, they believed, the fate of the republic itself – competing factions among the founding fathers found it difficult in the extreme to establish comprehensive systems of education.

The founding fathers' emphasis on the importance of an educated citizenry also led to a fundamental change in the student population. Jefferson and others envisioned a change at the elementary and secondary levels of schooling; however, the transformation of the collegiate population was perhaps the most revealing demographic change in the early republic. Between the 1790s and the 1820s, collegiate populations became more heterogeneous in terms of social background, geographical origins, and age composition. In New England colleges, where the evidence is most complete, larger numbers of needy students began arriving on the various campuses. Yale, as one student observed in 1822, became a "strange medly" of the sons of "wealthy merchants and poor farmers ... of aristocratic planters and poor backwoodsmen." The change in the student population was even more dramatic at the newer colleges. Institutions founded in the last half of the eighteenth century and the early decades of the nineteenth century recruited the rural poor. By 1830 nearly 200 students, approximately 13 per cent of the total New England college population, were indigents. Older students entering the various colleges added to the heterogeneity of the student population. Again, changes were most immediately apparent on the newer campuses. Students entering college after the age of 21 constituted one-third of the combined populations of such colleges as Brown, Dartmouth, Williams, Bowdoin, Colby, Amherst, and the University of Vermont.

The medley of students entering American colleges during the early republic put an end to the colonial ideal of *in loco parentis*, the notion that colleges were carefully controlled communal environments in which college authorities acted as parental figures. Poorer students often lived with families in nearby towns or farms rather than in college residential halls. Furthermore, some colleges were forced to alter school routines to accommodate their students' seasonal patterns of work. Finally, mature men in their twenties when they entered college were unlikely to put up with campus rituals that made them errand boys of adolescent sophomores.

The Revolution thus had both an immediate and a long-range impact on American education. The Revolutionaries equated education with the dissemination of virtue and knowledge and, consequently, viewed its success as intricately intertwined with the success of the republic itself. Subsequent generations of Americans would modify the content as well as the rationale for comprehensive systems of education; however, the priorities set by the Revolutionaries remained influential. The idea that education was too important to be left entirely to private and parental influences, that institutions of learning be inclusive and patriotic, and that the bulk of the people be rendered safe for self-government through instruction continued to resonate in the thoughts of Americans in the nineteenth and twentieth centuries.

FURTHER READING

Allmendinger, David F., Jr.: *Paupers and Scholars: the Transformation of Student Life in Nineteenth-century New England* (New York: St. Martin's Press, 1975).

Cremin, Lawrence, A.: *American Education: the Colonial Experience, 1607–1783* (New York: Harper & Row, 1970).

——: *American Education: the National Experience, 1783–1876* (New York: Harper & Row, 1980).

Herbst, Jurgen: *From Crisis to Crisis: American College Government, 1636–1819* (Cambridge, Mass.: Harvard University Press, 1982).

Middlekauff, Robert: *Ancients and Axioms: Secondary Education in Eighteenth-century New England* (New Haven, Conn.: Yale University Press, 1963).

Miller, Howard: *The Revolutionary College: American Presbyterian Higher Education, 1707–1837* (New York: New York University Press, 1976).

Robson, David W.: *Educating Republicans: the College in the Era of the American Revolution, 1750–1800* (Westport, Conn.: Greenwood Press, 1985).

Yazawa, Melvin: *From Colonies to Commonwealth: Familial Ideology and the Beginnings of the American Republic* (Baltimore: Johns Hopkins University Press, 1985).

43

The impact of the Revolution on social problems: poverty, insanity, and crime

MELVIN YAZAWA

HOW revolutionary was the American Revolution? In the realm of politics and ideology, the impact of the Revolution was conspicuous. The switch from being loyal subjects of a king to being independent citizens of a republic entailed, we know, much more than simply a modification in the forms of rulership. But how much change did the Revolution produce in American society? Social evolution is an ongoing phenomenon; it becomes difficult to determine, therefore, which changes in society were due to the Revolution itself and which were due to evolutionary impulses that owed little if any of their impetus to the imperial crisis. In assessing the impact of the Revolution on social problems, we must begin with an understanding of long-range trends that preceded the mid-century crisis. Ultimately, as we shall see, changes in social and political perceptions were intimately intertwined.

I. POVERTY

The problems associated with poverty and providing for the poor did not sprout suddenly as a result of the Revolution. To be sure, the War of Independence exacerbated the conditions of the poor and may temporarily have added to the total number of needy in America. Wartime dislocations were unavoidable: seaport economies were disrupted, towns and communities occupied, the laboring poor burdened with military service, and destitute war widows left to care for dependent children. But the problem of poverty was more deeply rooted in the American past. Gradually, over the course of the eighteenth century, a growing class of poor inhabitants appeared in every colony.

Historians have identified at least two factors that contributed to the swelling of the ranks of the poor. First, the pressure of an ever-increasing population on a limited supply of land may have resulted in a declining standard of living for many third- and fourth-generation sons. After the first decades of the eighteenth century, especially in the older agricultural communities of New England, opportunities dwindled as successive generations typically held fewer and fewer acres of land per capita and brought even marginal lands into cultivation. The fact that there were growing concentrations of wealth at the top of the social pyramid and an emergence of larger numbers of paupers in these communities led the historian Kenneth A. Lockridge (1970) to suggest that American society was becoming "Europeanized." Second, between the Glorious Revolution and the 1760s, the colonists participated in a series of imperial wars that made military contractors and a few merchants wealthy but hurt those at the edges of poverty in America's urban centers. A recurrent cycle of heavy taxes to finance the wars, inflation, wartime boom and postwar depression characterized the experiences of the inhabitants of Boston, New York, and Philadelphia from King William's War (1689–99) to the Seven Years' War (1756–63). Increased numbers of fatherless and husbandless families, along with impoverished war veterans, added to the woes of these cities. By the 1760s a class of genuinely poor people made up between 10 and 20 per cent of the populations of these seaboard centers.

If the problems of poverty were not new by the time of the Revolution, neither were the solutions. In the seventeenth and first half of the eighteenth century, colonial authorities relied primarily on informal means of rendering assistance. For the most part, this meant that relatives of the needy took them into their homes. Private keepers shored up the system by boarding some of the poor and charging towns for their services. By the latter half of the eighteenth century, however, the trend towards institutionalization was apparent. In the principal urban centers first, publicly supported almshouses replaced the system of lodging the poor with kin or neighbors. Boston, where the problem of poverty appeared early, built its almshouse in 1685; Philadelphia and New York built theirs in 1732 and 1736 respectively. Rural communities followed suit in the late colonial and revolutionary years.

The timing of the switch from boarding out the poor to placing them in institutions varied, but the trend was unmistakable. There were two reasons for this transformation in the colonial poor-relief system. First, communal authorities found it increasingly difficult financially to cope with the growing numbers of impoverished inhabitants. Even with the proliferation of mutual-aid societies and the charitable contributions of such groups as the Society for the Propagation of the Gospel in New York and the Quakers in Pennsylvania, the cost of poor relief rose rapidly after mid-century. The boarding-out system was expensive and subject to overcharging by unscrupulous private keepers. Replacing it with publicly administered poorhouses, at the very least, might reduce the incidence of corruption by reducing the number of keepers who needed to be policed.

In addition to keeping costs down, institutionalization served a second purpose: it conveniently subjected the poor to efforts at rehabilitation. The colonial poor had always been easy targets of suspicion. Several colonies, beginning with Massachusetts in 1699, passed workhouse legislation aimed initially at dissuading "Rogues, Vagabonds, [and] Common Beggars" from entering their jurisdictions. As the number of needy rose and the cost of maintaining them increased, the distinction between the unfortunate poor and idle vagabonds became blurred. In Pennsylvania, for example, where the number of needy requiring assistance in the early 1760s so increased that the almshouse filled to overflowing with five or six beds stuffed into rooms ten or eleven feet square, the overseers of the poor petitioned the legislature to authorize the construction of a new almshouse and workhouse. The legislature responded in 1766 with the creation of a corporation of Contributors to the Relief and Employment of the Poor. The Contributors, most of whom were Quaker merchants, were to pay for the construction of a new "bettering house," but could count on funds from the provincial poor tax to help with operating expenses. The financial difficulties of the contributorship, which was forced to borrow over one-half of the £11,750 required to complete the building, coupled with stresses created in trying to accommodate approximately 360 persons admitted annually between 1768 and 1775, must have soured the dispositions of the new managers of the bettering house. It is also true, however, that they were philosophically inclined to view their charges as being sorely in need of personal reformation. Relief efforts outside the almshouse must be phased out, the managers argued, because they were utterly "inconsistent with and sub-versive of the Nature and Design" of the new institution. Relief must be offered in conjunction with rehabilitation. House rules, therefore, strictly supervised the hours of sleeping and waking, eating and working. In this way, the managers of the bettering house hoped, habits of industry might be inculcated among the internees to save them from perpetual poverty.

How did the American Revolution affect the poor and patterns of poor relief established in the colonial period? Although the Revolution did not significantly alter the social structure of America, some scholars have argued that the perceptions of the poor changed dramatically in this era. The historian Gary B. Nash (1979), in particular, contends that the urban poor of the 1760s and 1770s responded not only to the constitutional principles enunciated in revolutionary pamphlets, but also to the conditions of their lives. They adhered to a "popular ideology" that ultimately led them to consider the proper distribution of wealth in America. As a New Yorker asked in 1765, was it equitable "that 99, rather 999, should suffer for the Extravagance or Grandeur of one? Especially when it is considered that Men frequently owe their Wealth to the impoverishment of their Neighbours?" Nash's argument is suggestive and intriguing. Whether changing social and economic circumstances contributed to the politicization of the urban poor and provided the impetus for their participation in the Independence movement, however, remains a matter of considerable debate among historians. There is some evidence to suggest that the imperial crisis and the natural rights proclamations of the revolutionary leaders accentuated the resentments of the laboring poor and other "outsiders" and contributed to the decline of deference in the new nation. If the perceptions of the poor probably underwent some changes as a result of the Revolution, perceptions about the poor were also affected.

The movement towards institutionalizing the poor was not stalled by the Revolution. On the contrary, the republican doctrine of the Revolutionaries encompassed certain ideas about the poor that amplified the need for almshouses. For a republic to survive, all agreed, its citizens had to be virtuous. The classical definition of civic virtue stressed self-sacrifice for the good of the whole. The founding fathers, however, discovered that this definition was too constraining and too often contradicted by the reality of their own behavior. Consequently, in the 1780s and 1790s, their understanding of virtue placed a premium not on self-abnegation, but on industriousness. The good citizen was an active and diligent worker. "Idleness," which bred depravity and poverty, replaced "luxury" as the greatest threat to the welfare of the republic. The idea expressed earlier by the managers of the Pennsylvania "bettering house," that the poor required rehabilitation, was supported by ideological imperatives after the Rev-olution. The poor appeared blameworthy for their own impoverishment, especially in America where, it was commonly asserted, the natural abundance of the land returned a comfortable sufficiency with little exertion.

By the 1820s, when state legislatures began sponsoring systematic examinations of the dimensions of poverty within their borders, distrust of the poor seemed custom-ary. The prevalence of pauperism amidst the scarcity of the Old World was unavoidable and tragic, but its presence in America was mortifying. "In this country," investigators in New York reported, "the labour of three days will readily supply the wants of seven." Thus only the indolence and dissipation of the poor could account for their misery; in a country where "all the necessaries of life are so abundant and cheap ... there can be no danger of a meritorious individual being allowed to suffer." If the character of the poor accounted for the persistence of poverty, its reformation held

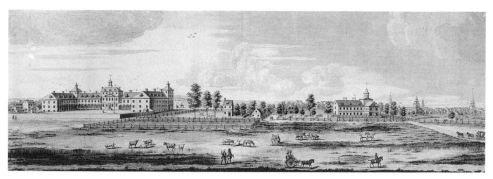

FIGURE 35 A general view of Philadelphia, showing the House of Employment and the Almshouse (left), built in 1767, and the Pennsylvania Hospital (right), opened in 1752 (engraving by J. Hulett after a drawing by Nicholas Garrison, 1767).

the key to eliminating poverty in the republic. Almshouses, similar to those established in the late colonial period, flourished between the 1810s and 1830s. And, much like the managers of the Pennsylvania "bettering house," the new almshouse planners aimed at inculcating habits of diligence and industry among the internees by strictly regulating their behavior. Order, regularity, discipline, constancy, obedience, and respect for authority were lessons to be learned through exacting routines. Well-regulated poorhouses, reformers believed, would finally put an end to the embarrassing anomaly of poverty in America.

2. INSANITY

In the half century before the Revolution, the American colonists' understanding of the nature and treatment of insanity underwent a fundamental transformation. First, providential or supernatural explanations gave way to natural ones. Rather than tracing the causes of insanity to sources outside human control, experts increasingly focused on human factors. And, in part because of the rise of an increasingly professional medical establishment, physicians came to replace ministers as the chief authorities on insanity. Eighteenth-century physicians were not always clear about what they meant by insanity, let alone what the symptoms of the various forms of derangement were, but they were quite definite about its causes. As a rule, they identified two sets of natural causes: predisposing and precipitating. Predisposing causes included such factors as heredity, climate, and systems of government. Precipitating causes were events or activities that immediately preceded and seemed to incite bouts of derangement; these included excessive love, grief, anger, fear, envy, and pride. Because madness was a disease with natural origins, there was room for optimism about its treatment. The worst effects of all predisposing and precipitating causes of insanity might be ameliorated by the application of medical remedies.

Having affixed a medical face to madness, most commentators suggested cures for the disease. To begin with, it seemed wise to remove the afflicted from the general population and to place them in secured settings. Confinement of the insane promised to accomplish two things at once: prevent the insane from injuring anyone and thus promote the peace and safety of the general public, and subject the insane to the sort of custodial care most conducive to effecting a cure and thus promote their own welfare. Unfortunately, good intentions were rarely enough. Confinement was ordinarily onerous and often cruel. It could hardly have been otherwise. Before 1752, when the Pennsylvania Hospital (*see* figure 35) admitted its first patients, the mentally ill were incarcerated in jails and almshouses. Without the benefit of trials and without formal commitment proceedings, the insane became inmates. Confinement was an end in itself.

Finally, treatment of the mentally ill increasingly became the responsibility of medical institutions. The history of the Pennsylvania Hospital illuminates the nature of the changes taking place in America. In the 1730s, Philadelphians began using their almshouse as a place of confinement for many of the city's most unruly cases of insanity. By mid-century, the almshouse was overcrowded and the Pennsylvania assembly was forced to grant a charter to a group of prominent philanthropists to establish a hospital whose mission would include the care and treatment of the insane. The founders of the Pennsylvania Hospital, Benjamin Franklin among them, hoped that the afflicted would benefit from the medical remedies afforded them: the insane might be cured of their malady if they were "subjected to proper management for their recovery." For the first time in American history, a public institution agreed to receive the mentally ill for curative treatment.

The early history of the Pennsylvania Hospital failed to support its founders' initial optimism. Insane patients lived in prisonlike basement cells and found their movements further restricted by leg chains, manacles, and "Mad shirts." Attending physicians usually focused their attention on the most recently admitted patients. Such neglect, however, may have been a blessing in disguise for the remaining inmates. Medical treatment tended to stress physical therapeutics. Preternatural excitement in the blood vessels of the brain needed to be relieved; consequently, bleeding, purges, emetics, and blistering were often prescribed for all forms of derangement.

In the late eighteenth century, psychologically oriented treatments came to complement, if not replace, these grimly heroic measures. By the time the new wing of the Pennsylvania Hospital – a west wing intended solely for the care of the insane – was completed in 1796, gentler prescriptions were in order. However, the "moral treatment" movement, which emphasized a humanitarian approach to patients' physical and emotional needs, was not a direct product of the American Revolution. Its inspiration, instead, came from across the Atlantic via the experiments of Philippe Pinel in France and William Tuke in England. Tuke, the founder of the asylum at York whose therapy included a mild regimen of entertainment, exercise, good food, and comfortable lodgings, was especially influential among American reformers.

How did the Revolution affect the perception and treatment of insanity in America? The Revolution reinforced and accelerated the movement towards asylum-building. The commitment to republicanism placed a premium on the civic competence of the individual citizen. Independent participation in the affairs of the republic required self-discipline and a rational understanding of self-interest. The insane, by any of the definitions offered by eighteenth-century physicians and informed laymen, were incapable of precisely this sort of rational calculation. Passions, which normally were under the control of the faculty of reason and therefore restrained in their operations, were excessive in the insane. The Revolution, unfortunately, seemed to have predisposed some people to bouts of passionate excess. At the very moment when self-control became essential to their political survival, Americans were in danger of losing it. The connection between political and biological health thus may have given a special poignancy to the challenge of insanity in America.

The revolutionary generation also subscribed eagerly to Enlightenment ideas of progress and the perfectibility of human nature. "This empire is commencing at a period when every species of knowledge, natural and moral, is arrived at a state of perfection, which the world never before saw," Timothy Dwight, patriot preacher and later Hartford Wit, boasted in 1776. Not surprisingly, eighteenth-century notions of curing the insane through the application of a therapeutic regimen struck a responsive chord among American reformers. Indeed, believing themselves to be blessed with superior knowledge and unburdened by the habits of the Old World, Americans expected to improve on all facets of the treatment of the insane.

The urgency of the situation, coupled with enlightened optimism, conspired to advance asylum building in the early republic. In 1776 only the Pennsylvania Hospital and the Eastern Lunatic Hospital at Williamsburg – the first public hospital built exclusively for the treatment of the insane – combined confinement with curative treatment. Between the end of the War of Independence and 1825, however, seven other states established provisions for hospitalizing the insane: New York, Maryland, Massachusetts, Kentucky, South Carolina, Ohio, and Connecticut. And in 1825, with the founding of the Western Lunatic Asylum at Staunton, Virginia became the first state with two public hospitals for the mentally ill.

All of these public and semi-public institutions followed similar internal routines. They adopted a variation of the "moral treatment" system Tuke implemented at the York Retreat in England. The Friends' Asylum (1817) in Pennsylvania, the Bloomingdale Asylum (1821) in New York, and the Hartford Retreat (1821) in Connecticut, in particular, attempted to employ Tuke's methods. The process of effecting a cure began with the removal of the afflicted from his familiar surroundings. As the indefatigable Philadelphia physician Benjamin Rush advised, the "first thing to be done ... is to remove the patient from his family and from the society of persons" to whom he had been accustomed. The patient would benefit from the immediate suspension of the precipitating causes of his distraction. Furthermore, once institutionalized, the patient came under the "complete government" of the attending physicians and received "remedies with ease, certainty and success." Moral treatment entailed exposure of the patients to a world of precise schedules, regular work routines, systematic procedures, and disciplined habits. In the end, it was hoped, such treatment would reduce psychological stress and promote mental health.

American asylums, however, even more than their European counterparts, continued to rely on medical therapeutics. American physicians held on longer to the theory that insanity was a somatic disease, that it was due to abnormalities or lesions in the brain. Reformers insisted that moral treatment be used in conjunction with physical prescriptions. Rush's influential *Medical Inquiries and Observations upon the Diseases of the Mind* (1812), the first serious American contribution to the study of mental illness, recapitulated many of the postulates of moral treatment. But Rush also prescribed copious bleeding ("from 20 to 40 ounces of blood may be taken at once") along with daily purges ("so as to excite an artificial diarrhea"), emetics (to "assist purges in exciting the alimentary canal"), and blistering (so that diseases "intrenched ... in the brain" may be "dislodged"). Rush's "tranquilizer," consisting of a sturdy chair with straps that kept a patient seated upright and immobile, was ideal for treatment involving the "application of cold water and ice to the head, and warm water to the feet." Tuke's vision of institutions where "everything is done to make the patients as comfortable as they can be" existed in an uneasy alliance with more heroic remedies in the asylums of the early republic. Nevertheless, the idea that insanity was a disease best treated in an expertly managed environment was part of the conventional wisdom of reform by the early decades of the nineteenth century.

3. CRIME

Crime, like poverty and insanity, was part of the fabric of colonial society. How did the Revolution affect this social problem? In order to answer this question we must differentiate between the incidence of crime itself and society's perceptions of criminal activity. The former deals with changes in crime rates over an extended period; the latter focuses on the impact of Independence on Americans' understanding of the obligations they were under in dealing with crime.

The calculation of crime rates is fraught with problems. Historians are limited by the sources at hand, and, where criminality is concerned, the sources are primarily in the form of court records. These are often incomplete, as in the case of Virginia, where trial court records for the years 1777–88 were lost during the Civil War. Even if complete runs of court proceedings were available, however, the historian would still have to move cautiously, because such records include only the accused who had successfully been apprehended and bound over for trial. Whether officially recorded crime accurately reflects actual levels of criminality is a puzzle that cannot be fully resolved. Furthermore, differences in societal and prosecutorial priorities almost surely account for differences in the rates of certain recorded crimes. For example, studies done of Massachusetts and Richmond, Virginia, in the early national period, conclude that rape "as a significant legal phenomenon simply did not exist" before 1800. It is unlikely that rape did not occur in these years; it is far more likely that victims did not seek redress through the court system. What happened in courts may thus have little to do with what happened in the larger society.

With these caveats in mind, historians have nevertheless traced long-range patterns in identifiable criminal behavior. Their findings suggest that, for most of the eighteenth century, crime rates remained quite stable. Because of regional variations and differences in judicial procedures, inter-colonial or inter-state comparisons are not very meaningful; however, within specific locales, changes over time are accounted for largely in terms of population growth. Crime rates increased as the population increased, and only occasionally, as in New York in the 1730s and 1760s, did crime rise faster than population.

Although official crime rates did not change dramatically over the course of the century, the kinds of crimes being prosecuted in some states did. In revolutionary Massachusetts, where the change is best documented, theft-related crimes replaced violations of the moral or religious order as the offenses most frequently prosecuted. Whereas, in the two decades before independence, only about 13 per cent of all prosecutions involved crimes against property, by the early decades of the nineteenth century that figure had risen to over 40 per cent. Meanwhile, prosecutions for crimes of morality dropped from over 50 per cent to about 7 per cent. The legal historian William E. Nelson contends that this change reflects the transforming power of the American Revolution. Concern over property rights, which after all had been instrumental in the colonists' protests against the actions of King and Parliament, superseded ethical and moral concerns. Even after independence, the revolutionary generation continued to equate protection of property with the preservation of liberty.

For Nelson, the Revolution marked a turning point, if not in overall crime rates then in the definition of crime in America. Other historians, however, have questioned the relationship between the Revolution and the transformation of criminality in Massachusetts. First, the shift from ethical considerations to the protection of property was well underway by the mid-eighteenth century. Prosecution of sexual misconduct peaked in the early 1730s and declined thereafter. Furthermore, authorities tended increasingly to focus on cases of illegitimacy in order to settle questions of child support rather than to express moral disapproval. The trend away from a definition of crime as sin thus preceded the imperial crisis. Second, increases in crimes against property possibly reflected changes in actual behavior resulting from long-term social and economic developments. An expanding commercial economy could conceivably have fostered an increase in burglary and larceny by separating places of employment from private residences and by making transactions more impersonal and stolen property more difficult to identify. Also, migration into and out of many Massachusetts towns experiencing commercial growth undermined the old order of the community and thereby weakened the efficacy of communal oversight. Finally, by the early nineteenth century, social stratification had contributed to a heightened sense of cohesiveness among the various economic and occupational classes. One result of this development may have been the use of judicial proceedings by the propertied to bolster their control over the poor and propertyless; at any rate, the latter groups were more often charged with and convicted for crimes against property.

If the impact of the Revolution on the prosecution of theft was somewhat oblique, its effect on the punishment of crime was direct. Influenced by the writings of Cesare Beccaria and Montesquieu, the Revolutionaries came to believe that they were obligated to apply the principles of the Enlightenment to criminal law in the new republic. From Montesquieu's *Spirit of the Laws*, published in 1748, they learned that "severity of punishments is fitter for despotic governments, whose principle is terror, than for ... a republic, whose spring is ... virtue." Indeed, because the "imagination grows accustomed" to habitual severity, harsh punishments eventually lose their ability to deter "great crime" and thus corrupt the very spirit of the republic. If severe punishments would not discourage crime, what would? Beccaria's *Essay on Crimes and Punishments* (1764) provided the answer. Certainty of punishment, not extreme harshness, was an effective deterrent. In an enlightened system of correction, every penalty must be proportioned to the offense committed and must be administered without exception.

In revolutionary America the application of these lessons is seen most clearly in the campaign to limit the use of capital punishment. William Bradford, the attorney-general of Pennsylvania, was a leader in the movement. In 1792 Bradford was distressed because he thought independent Americans were still operating under criminal codes imposed upon them by a "corrupted monarchy." The death penalty, in particular, was "an exotic plant and not the native growth of Pennsylvania," said Bradford. His fellow Pennsylvanian Benjamin Rush added that republics founded on "peaceful and benevolent" principles ought not to adhere to a system of punishment that was the "natural offspring of monarchical governments." In addition to such concerns over the propriety of the death penalty, republican reformers voiced a practical objection. Capital punishment was so contrary to humanity that juries might choose to acquit a criminal rather than to execute him. As a result, the system of punishment became unpredictable and the efficacy of all laws was undermined. Relying on variations of these arguments, late eighteenth- and early nineteenth-century reformers in Pennsylvania, New York, and Virginia successfully curtailed the number of offenses punishable by death in their respective states. And increasingly,

425

it appears, executions elsewhere were confined to murder convictions. Nineteenth-century Massachusetts laws, for example, allowed the death penalty for six crimes, including burglary and robbery. In the 1780s, 29 felons were executed; of these, 23 were guilty of burglary or robbery while four were convicted murderers. Over the next 30 years, a total of 17 persons were executed – 11 for murder, but only one for burglary. Laws may have remained the same, but the application of the laws reflected attitudinal changes initiated by the Revolution.

In place of capital punishment, American reformers suggested incarceration. If, as William Bradford said, the death penalty was an abomination in the "bosom of a youthful republic," imprisonment was an ideal alternative. First, it could be tailored to reflect the seriousness of each offense, thus ensuring that the principles of proportionality and certainty of punishment were honored. Second, and more immediately relevant, the inmates themselves would benefit from the experience. Prisons, like poorhouses and asylums, promised reformation. Criminals, perhaps even more than the insane, stood a good chance of being cured of their disorder while incarcerated.

The Revolutionaries' optimism concerning the rehabilitative powers of prisons was founded on their belief that the human mind was the seat not only of such intellectual faculties as memory and understanding, but of a "moral faculty." Relying heavily on the ideas championed by the philosophers of the Scottish Enlightenment, American reformers argued that the moral faculty regulated one's ethical posture. It followed that the moral faculties of criminals were deranged or diseased. The key to the reform impulse lay in the realization that a person's moral faculty was as responsive to physical causes as his physical being. In a properly structured institutional environment, every moral precept would be accompanied by a physical regimen. As the moral faculty healed, disorder would give way to order and vice would succumb to virtue.

Given the leadership roles assumed by Pennsylvanians such as Rush and Bradford, it is hardly surprising that the first penitentiary in the new republic was located in their state. The Walnut Street Jail, erected in 1773 and designated as a penitentiary-house by the Pennsylvania Assembly in 1789, successfully incorporated the basic principles of the reformers. In its heyday from 1790 to 1799, the Walnut Street Jail became the model for penal reform in the United States and Europe. Caleb Lownes, a Quaker merchant and an Inspector of the Jail in the 1790s, captured the spirit of its advocates when he chided those who thought prisoners deserved only to be "perpetually tormented and punished." The prisoner, Lownes said, "is a rational being of like feelings" with ourselves. "Mild regulations, strictly enjoined," and not severity, would advance the cause of rehabilitation. The "rules of the house" thus covered a wide spectrum of daily and weekly routines. From employment to leisure-time activities, from daily diet to divine worship, the inmates of the Walnut Street Jail found their lives closely monitored. Even personal hygiene was a matter of public supervision: prisoners "shall be shaved twice a week, their hair cut once a month, change their linen once a week, and regularly wash their face and hands every morning." Prisoners who distinguished themselves by strict attention to the rules could expect "rewards"; conversely, offenders would suffer "close, solitary confinement." Within the walls of the penitentiary, isolated from outside contact and subjected to "mild, yet firm measures," the criminal would be reclaimed by civil society.

After 1799 the Walnut Street Jail fell into disrepair. Persistent problems of overcrowding quickly rendered the "rules of the house" all but meaningless. By 1835, when the institution was finally abandoned, it was no longer in the forefront of penal reform. That honor belonged to New York's Auburn state prison, established in 1819, and to Philadelphia's Eastern State Penitentiary, which opened in 1829. Still, it is important to note that the precedent and practices set by the Walnut Street Jail were reflected in the designs and operations of these latter-day institutions.

The period from the 1820s to the 1840s was, we know, characterized by a ferment for reform. Among other things, Americans began wholeheartedly to embrace the almshouse, asylum, and penitentiary as solutions to the problems afflicting the poor, the insane, and the criminally inclined in society. Although the number of such institutions constructed in these years outpaced all earlier efforts, the enthusiasm for institutional solutions was not new. Nineteenth-century reformers drew their inspiration from an earlier generation of optimistic social planners. The impact of the Revolution on the social perceptions of Americans thus had a lasting influence on the policies of the republic.

FURTHER READING

Alexander, John K.: *Render Them Submissive: Responses to Poverty in Philadelphia, 1760–1800* (Amherst: University of Massachusetts Press, 1980).

Cray, Robert E., Jr.: *Paupers and Poor Relief in New York City and its Rural Environs, 1700–1830* (Philadelphia: Temple University Press, 1988).

Dain, Norman: *Concepts of Insanity in the United States, 1789–1865* (New Brunswick, NJ: Rutgers University Press, 1964).

Deutsch, Albert: *The Mentally Ill in America: a History of their Care and Treatment from Colonial Times* (Garden City, NY: Doubleday, Duran and Co., 1938).

Greenberg, Douglas: *Crime and Law Enforcement in the Colony of New York, 1681–1776* (Ithaca, NY: Cornell University Press, 1974).

Hindus, Michael Stephen: *Prison and Plantation: Crime, Justice, and Authority in Massachusetts and South Carolina, 1767–1878* (Chapel Hill: University of North Carolina Press, 1980).

Jimenez, Mary Ann: *Changing Faces of Madness: Early American Attitudes and Treatment of the Insane* (Hanover, NH: University Press of New England, 1987).

Lockridge, Kenneth A.: *A New England Town, the First Hundred Years: Dedham, Massachusetts, 1636–1736* (New York: W. W. Norton, 1970).

Nash, Gary B.: *The Urban Crucible: Social Change, Political Consciousness, and the Origins of the American Revolution* (Cambridge, Mass.: Harvard University Press, 1979).

Nelson, William E.: *Americanization of the Common Law: the Impact of Legal Change on Massachusetts Society, 1760–1830* (Cambridge, Mass.: Harvard University Press, 1975).

Rothman, David J.: *The Discovery of the Asylum: Social Order and Disorder in the New Republic* (Boston: Little, Brown and Co., 1971).

44

The impact of the Revolution on church and state

ROBERT M. CALHOON

HURCH–STATE relations in the American Revolution differed from state to state and region to region; at the same time, unifying forces within American religious life and more divisive tendencies implicit in American religious individualism cut across state and regional lines – paradoxically unifying the polity and attenuating the links between churches and politics. The ambiguous language of the First Amendment to the Constitution, conjoining a ban on established churches with the protection of the free exercise of religion, reflected that complex heritage. In the five southern colonies and in several New York counties, patriot regimes disestablished the Anglican Church; in Connecticut and Massachusetts they allowed the Congregational Church to retain its legal establishment; in the rest of the revolutionary states they protected freedom of conscience while largely restricting office-holding to Protestants.

I. VIRGINIA

Although the Virginia Declaration of Rights guaranteed freedom of conscience and the legislature substantially disestablished the Anglican Church in 1776, the "Bill for Exempting Dissenters from Contributing to the Support of the Church" left open the possibility of a general assessment of taxpayers for the support of Christian instruction. Assessment bills in 1779 and 1784 would have allowed individuals to designate their own churches as the recipients of their payments and would have placed all undesignated assessments in a pool for distribution to all Christian churches. An especially revealing document, the 1779 bill contained a cumbersome definition of a "Christian" church and stipulated that "no Person whatsoever shall speak any thing in their Religious Assemblies disrespectfully or Seditiously of the Government of this State."

Religious assessment became the central issue in the decade-long struggle over religious policy in Virginia. Led by staunch Anglicans in the aristocracy, by Tidewater Presbyterians, and – for complex, murky reasons – by Patrick Henry, the pro-assessment forces believed that "a general diffusion of Christian knowledge hath a natural tendency to correct the morals of men, restrain their vices, and preserve the peace of society" (Buckley, 1977, p. 186). In opposition, Jefferson, Madison, Shenandoah Valley Presbyterians, and the state's Baptist and Methodist evangelicals contended that religious practice was private and voluntary and that any government sponsorship of religious teaching, no matter how benign or even-handed, was fraught with potential mischief.

428

Although enactment of religious assessment seemed assured in 1785, Madison skillfully mobilized a coalition of evangelical and rationalist opponents of state-promulgated religious teaching. His "Memorial and Remonstrance against Religious Assessments" blended religious fears of assessment with philosophical beliefs in private judgment. Sensing that public sentiment was running in his favor, Madison sought a dramatic victory by proposing defeat of assessment through the vehicle of adopting Thomas Jefferson's Statute for Religious Freedom, drafted in 1779. When Jefferson's bill passed in December 1785 by a vote of 74 to 20, freedom of conscience and its inviolability from government influence became fundamental law in Virginia. Jefferson's statute reaffirmed the will of the people as the arbiter of issues of liberty and the extent of governmental power.

Madison saw religion and piety as useful means in the building of a functioning republican order. In the "Memorial and Remonstrance," therefore, he made philosophical arguments uphold the positive value of freedom of conscience, while pious sentiments evoked revulsion at the harm done by public enforcement of religion. The first of 15 numbered paragraphs in the document linked the whole issue of freedom and religion to Enlightenment experience. It quoted Article XVI of the Virginia Declaration of Rights (1776) that "the duty we owe to our Creator can be directed only by reason and conviction," and then paraphrased the language of Jefferson's proposed Statute on religious Liberty by asserting that "the opinions of men, depending [as they must] only on the evidence contemplated by their own minds, cannot follow the dictates of other men" (Jefferson's bill declared that "God hath created the mind free" and "altogether insusceptible of restraint"). From these presuppositions, and probably from Locke's *Letter on Toleration*, Madison drew two conclusions: first, that "homage" to the "Creator" preceded "both in order of time and in degree of obligation ... the claims of civil society" and, second, that "religion is wholly exempt from" the "cognizance" of "civil society." A person entering into a political compact "must always do it with a reservation of his duty to the ... universal sovereign."

Madison devoted the remainder of the "Memorial and Remonstrance" to a blending of the secular and spiritual concerns. While his arguments were eclectic, the rhetoric subtly mixed evangelical fears of secular impurity with rationalist aversion to encroachments on private judgment. He argued that the power to establish Christianity as the favored recipient of public financial support – adroitly equating assessment with establishment – enabled government to establish particular sects of Christians over others and to enforce conformity, praised the "primitive" Christianity that existed before the rise of ecclesiastical establishment, and, in the same breath, incorporated Jefferson's charge that established churches "beget habits of hypocrisy and meanness." He reminded his readers that the avowed purpose of assessment was the instilling of a particular kind of self-control – "correct the morals of men, restrain their vices, and preserve the peace of society" – by denouncing the use of "religion as an engine of civil policy." In a still more pointed reference to the religious implications of assessment, he questioned whether a public official could be a "competent judge of religious truth"; no evangelical reader of the awkward, and narrowly Anglican, five-part definition of a Christian church in the 1779 assessment bill could fail to find that formulation theologically offensive.

Equally distasteful to Baptists and Methodists was a well-meaning provision in the 1784 bill allowing sects without ministers – Mennonites and Quakers – to receive funds designated for them directly rather than through clergymen. Madison seized on this notion to illustrate the dangers of allowing legislators to make religious designations. "Are the Quakers and the Mennonists the only sects who think a compulsive support of their religions unnecessary and unwarrantable?" Madison demanded; "can their piety alone be entrusted with the care of public worship? Ought their religions to be endowed above all others with extraordinary privileges by which proselytes may be induced from all others?" Nothing of the kind was intended by the provisions of the 1784 bill, nor did Mennonite and Quaker practice involve the stealing of proselytes. Madison did not let these facts stand in the way of scoring the telling point that legislation hinging on matters of internal church polity inevitably would arouse destructive jealousies. Religion lay beyond the authority of the state, he declared, moving boldly in the direction of secular libertarianism, in the same way as did "all our fundamental rights" (Hutchinson, Vol. 8, 1973, pp. 299–304).

2. THE OTHER SOUTHERN STATES

In the other southern states, the disestablishment of the Church of England and the creation of some degree of public sanction for Protestant Christianity proceeded with less controversy than in Virginia. In South Carolina the 1776 Provincial Congress left Anglicanism established, and the following year dissenters led by the Congregationalist minister William Tennent asked for "equal and free religious privileges" for "all Protestants" (Curry, 1986, p. 148).

The 1778 constitution restricted office-holding to Protestants and allowed all churches which endorsed the existence and public worship of one God, rewards and punishment in an afterlife, the truth of Christianity and the Bible, and the obligation of all citizens to bear witness to the truth when asked by government to do so. These provisions satisfied Tennent. South Carolina in effect established Protestantism but provided no public support for the churches.

The 1776 North Carolina constitution restricted office-holding to those who did not deny the "truth of the Protestant religion" nor hold "religious principles incompatible with the freedom and safety of the state" (Calhoon, 1976, p. 69). This provision did not prevent the distinguished jurist William Gaston, a Roman Catholic, from accepting appointment to the state Supreme Court in 1833 on the grounds that he did affirm the truths of Protestant Christianity as well as others peculiar to Catholicism, nor did it deter the legislature from seating Jacob Henry, a Jew, in 1809 as the representative from Carteret County.

The Georgia constitution likewise limited office-holding to Protestants. It also adopted language on the financial support of religion which left open the possibility of use of public funds, by counties, for the support of Christian ministers, but the practice never went into effect, and the 1798 state constitution abolished it.

The Maryland constitution of 1776 promised religious liberty to all Christians, while declaring the worship of God, in the manner each individual "thinks most acceptable," a public duty. Adopting a law authorizing religious assessment in 1784, the legislature affirmed its power to "interpose in matters of religion as far as concerns the general peace and welfare of the community." The following year, newly elected anti-assessment legislators managed to defeat a bill putting religious assessment into effect; Marylanders, one lawmaker observed, had begun "to taste the sweets of religious liberty" (Curry, 1986, pp. 154–7).

3 · NEW ENGLAND

Congregationalists in Massachusetts and Connecticut, on the other hand, had tasted the sweets of organic community life in which a publicly supported church in each town upheld moral values on which the community rested. Where Virginia leaders of the Revolution divided into those supporting public maintenance of religion and those opposed to it, the leadership of the Revolution in these two states preserved an established Congregationalist Church. The Separate Baptists led by Isaac Backus, a sect which had arisen during the Great Awakening of the 1740s as a powerful evangelical rival of both New Light revivalist Congregationalists and Old Light traditionalists, represented the only opposition to the maintenance of the establishment in the Bay Colony. The audacious demands of some Baptists for abolition of church taxes during the revolutionary crisis of 1774 and the apolitical indifference of others to the patriot cause thereafter had tainted them with an undeserved reputation for Toryism, weakening their public voice in the debate over church and state in 1780.

The 1780 Massachusetts constitution contained two provisions on religion. Section Two stated paradoxically that it is the "duty" of each citizen to worship "the SUPREME BEING," but while also being free to do so according to "the dictates of his own conscience." Section Three reasoned that the dependence of order and government upon the "piety, religion, and morality" of the people justified and necessitated public support of ministers and teachers of religion and authorized the towns to provide such payments. Each citizen could specify which church his own taxes should support; so long as churches conducted themselves "peaceably," no one sect could be legally subordinated to another. John Adams had misgivings about Section Three, but he reluctantly supported it as an integral part of the new constitution, with which he was generally pleased. The only notable figure to oppose Section Three, Joseph Hawley of Northampton, privately regretted the "looseness and uncertainty of language" in the document and questioned whether the unalienable freedom of man, upheld in the constitution, did not take precedence over the strategy of preserving order through moral and religious suasion. But Hawley's objections were restricted to private correspondence and anonymous newspaper essays. In 1810, Theophilus Parsons, a member of the committee which drafted Section Three, offered in a state Supreme Court decision this convoluted but intriguing explanation of the intent of the framers: "the convention acted on the ground that the moral duties are essential to the welfare of a free state"; religious liberty might conflict with the right of the state to spend public funds for socially necessary purposes, such as the support of religious education, Parsons conceded, but the "protection of persons and property," engendered by religion, helped resolve the contradiction between freedom of conscience and the maintenance of public morality (McLoughlin, 1971, pp. 603, 604, 611).

Article Three not only sought to reconcile freedom of conscience with the inculcation of respect for property; it also sought to harmonize public maintenance of Congregationalist churches with sectarian equality. The final clause forbad "subordination of any one sect or denomination to another ... by law" (Curry, 1986, p. 174). Towns were free to apply public funds to the support of whichever ministry they chose; in Massachusetts the dominance of the Congregationalists invariably qualified the church for public support. Led by ISAAC BACKUS, Massachusetts Baptists contended that religion was a matter between God and each individual and that the state had no business paying support to any ministers. Backus, it should be noted, based this claim

431

on grounds very different from those taken by dissenters in Virginia. He conflated religious liberty and Christian liberty; the former was freedom from human interference in belief or worship, while the latter derived from the irresistible working of the Spirit in the lives of believers. Christian liberty, as Backus understood it, required that believers obey God exclusively and that the community become open to the conversion of all. The result of this uninhibited spirituality, Backus confidently predicted, would be the creation of the Christian republic. He therefore supported Sabbath observance laws, military chaplains, and exclusion of non-Protestants from office as desirable public policies.

Connecticut, the other state with a modified establishment of Congregationalists, avoided much of this controversy by simply adopting its colonial charter to serve as a state constitution by removing references to the King. As the Reverend Judah Champion explained in 1776,

> our civil liberties ... are nearly connected with ... our religious [liberties].... Our religious privileges are not inferior to our civil [duties].... None may impose for doctrine the commandments of men or force others to believe with them.... But if any, under pretense of conscience, sap the foundations of civil society, ... they are to be restrained by the civil arm. (Curry, 1986, pp. 178–9).

As in Massachusetts, Baptists in Connecticut opposed only the public payment of ministers and the humiliating requirement that members of other churches secure certificates of their financial support of their own church bodies. In several Connecticut towns the Congregationalists were a minority or were too poor to support an established church if Baptist, Quaker, or episcopal neighbors, or disaffected Congregationalists secured exemption from church taxes. In these cases the legislature repeatedly fashioned compromises, giving Congregationalists the power to tax all inhabitants who did not present exemption certificates and then in 1791 allowing dissenters to produce their own certificates rather than those issued by a dissenting minister or church official.

Colonial New Hampshire had a system of church–state relations modelled on that of Massachusetts. In towns with Presbyterian majorities, however, special laws created two tax-supported parishes in which Presbyterians alone gave certificates of tax exemption to town officials, thus signalling their status as dissenters. After independence, the state tried to compel Baptists to support Congregationalist ministers and, when controversy erupted, granted them specific exemptions. In some cases Baptists became the majority within a town, whereupon they simply exempted themselves. In New London a Baptist minister accepted the position as the town's paid clergyman, but under pressure from Isaac Backus relinquished it on the ground that it was "bondage to be supported by tax and compulsion" (Curry, 1986, p. 187).

Vermont's 1777 constitution required office-holders to be Protestants who believed in God and in the divine inspiration of the Old and New Testaments, and it allowed towns to support "ministers of the gospel" on petition of seven inhabitants and poll of two-thirds of the voters. The legislators assumed that most such publicly supported clergy would be Congregationalists, but significantly did not preclude other denominations. In 1785 Vermont required "every sect or denomination ... to keep up some form of religious worship," implicitly omitting any compulsory payment of support from the populace (Curry, 1986, pp. 188–9).

In both New Hampshire and Vermont, the Congregational establishment quietly atrophied after 1790. Baptists in Connecticut suffered under the hegemony of the

Congregationalist-dominated Federalist Party throughout the early national period, but when the party began to disintegrate after 1816 the Baptists became valuable members of the Republican coalition which came to power in 1817 and the following year revised the state's 1776 constitution (which was essentially the 1661 colonial charter with references to the King expunged). "The course which the Baptists and Methodists are pursuing" in the campaign for a new constitution, one Federalist observed, "is indeed extraordinary. The ground taken by these sectaries [i.e., adamant demands for complete separation of church and state] seems to preclude every argument that might be adduced in support of the principle on which our laws are founded" (McLoughlin, 1971, p. 1050). "The Federalists never did understand the practice of pressure politics by interest groups," William G. McLoughlin succinctly observed.

In Massachusetts as well, declining Federalist and ascendant Republican Party strength prepared the way for the overthrow of Congregational privileges, but here partisan conflict became intertwined with the split among Congregationalists over the doctrine of the Trinity and the validity of Unitarian rationalism. In town after town Unitarian majorities took over Congregationalist churches and with them public tax support. In the Dedham Case (1818–21), the courts upheld the power of a majority of church members over that of the ruling deacons to control church property and appoint ministers. During the 1820s, Massachusetts evangelicals stood aloof from the Republicans, but the latter shrewdly played on evangelical fears that "religion enforced by law leads to craft, fraud, deceit, treachery, hypocrisy, and every other evil thing" (McLoughlin, 1971, p. 1204) to gain control of the legislature in 1823. In 1824 the Republicans enacted a law simplifying the creation of self-incorporated religious bodies and easing requirement for dissenters seeking exemption from church taxes. When this law did nothing to help Trinitarian Congregationalists regain control of established churches under Unitarian control, the Trinitarian Congregationalists became disenchanted with the whole idea of public support for religion – paving the way for abolition of such support altogether in 1833.

4. NEW YORK, PENNSYLVANIA, AND RHODE ISLAND

New York, Pennsylvania, and Rhode Island were far more pluralistic than the Anglican-dissenter South or the Congregationalist-Baptist New England. Following Roger Williams's insistence on the inviolability of conscience, Rhode Island proscribed any public subsidy for churches, though the colony kept such a low profile in matters of church and state that few people in colonial America knew of this practice, and Williams himself slipped into obscurity after his death until rediscovered by Isaac Backus in the 1740s. Colonial Rhode Island did bar Jews from office-holding and during the Seven Years' War required Roman Catholics to take an oath of allegiance. After Independence Rhode Island was the only state other than Virginia to abolish all religious discrimination. During the colonial period, New York established tax support for Protestant churches in four southern counties without specifying the Anglican Church as the intended recipient of public support. In practice and public perception, this arrangement did establish the Church of England, a privilege fortified when in 1753 King's College – over bitter Presbyterian opposition – was created under modified Anglican control. In 1777 the legislature, without admitting that an establishment of religion had ever existed in New York, abolished any presumed claim to public support of episcopal churches, though it did impose a test oath on Catholics.

FIGURE 36 A view of the Moravian settlement at Bethlehem, Pennsylvania (painted and engraved by Paul Sandby after a sketch by Governor Thomas Pownall).

Pennsylvania developed the most complex and modern form of church–state relations. Quakers and German Pietists shared a total aversion to state interference in religion, and the unique positions of these two persuasions effectively separated church and state. However, German Reformed and Lutheran disputes over church property originally serving both German-speaking groups involved civil courts in colonial Pennsylvania in religious disputes:

> Religious liberty divorced theological conflicts from the state. The colony allowed trustees of religious groups to hold property; if there were schisms or dissension within a church, the courts decided the matter based upon property law, not ecclesiastical precedent. The state would not try to determine whether either of two feuding religious groups was legitimately entitled to claim the property as being truly Presbyterian, Baptist, Lutheran, or Reformed. (Frost, 1988, p. 330)

When the Ephrata Community (a Dunker enclave) practiced celibacy, some husbands of women who deserted their families to join the community sued for alienation of affections; Pennsylvania colonial courts refused to accept jurisdiction in the matter. The Moravian community at Bethlehem (*see* figure 36) became a self-governing entity in which communal property-owning stood outside of provincial law – a situation the Moravians and the colonial government secured by allowing Moravians to hold the key offices of justice of the peace and representative to the Assembly. After the War for Independence the Pennsylvania Quakers reconsidered their relationship to the political and social order, they abandoned their old stance as the one true church, and accepted the status of a Protestant denomination. The 1776 Pennsylvania constitution required legislators to affirm their belief in God and in the truth of the Old and New Testaments. Early legislation in the Commonwealth of Pennsylvania made blasphemy, profanity, drunkenness, and theater-going illegal. At the request of Jews, legislators' adherence to the New Testament was dropped. The 1790 constitution – which scrapped the radical democratic features of the 1776 document – followed on professedly moral grounds the earlier instrument on blasphemy and drunkenness and allowed non-discriminatory public support of religion.

5. THE FIRST AMENDMENT TO THE CONSTITUTION

The intention of the religious freedom provisions of the First Amendment must be determined from the terms of the amendment itself, the brief and somewhat cryptic debate in the First Congress, the context of church–state relations during the 1780s, and cross-currents of Federalist and Anti-Federalist thought which led to the adoption of a Bill of Rights. Stung by Anti-Federalist attacks over the absence of libertarian guarantees in the Constitution, Madison duly asked the House of Representatives to consider a bill of rights. In May 1789 he proposed that "the civil rights of none shall be abridged on account of religious belief or worship, nor shall any national religion be established, nor shall the full and equal rights of conscience be in any manner, or on any pretext, infringed" (Curry, 1986, p. 199). In August the House considered the issue. Elbridge Gerry wanted to proscribe imposition of "religious doctrines" rather than beliefs or worship – a reflection of historic Puritan aversion to Anglicanism. Roger Sherman thought the amendment unnecessary because Congress had no jurisdiction over religion. Daniel Carroll of Maryland preferred a simple ban on imposed articles of faith lest a more extensive guarantee arouse religious divisions within American society, to which Madison replied that the "necessary and proper" clause might well be interpreted as giving Congress a pretext to legislate on matters of religion. Both Peter Sylvester of New York and Benjamin Huntington of Connecticut feared the amendment would endanger religion itself, Sylvester referring darkly to the possible abolishing of religion and Huntington more pointing to the licentiousness he perceived existing in Rhode Island, where no public support of churches existed. Samuel Livermore of New Hampshire preferred a simple ban on laws "touching on religion or infringing the right of conscience" (Curry, 1986, p. 201). Ranging from religious support for civic virtue to rationalist libertarianism, these comments were representative of views on church and state in the period.

After two days of Select Committee discussion of the amendment, a new proposal emerged, reflecting Madison's views: "no state shall infringe the equal rights of conscience." Thomas Tucker of South Carolina objected prophetically that the probable target of the amendment would be states hauled into court by aggrieved sects, and Madison assured him that he did not want to disrupt the existing balance between state autonomy and the federal judiciary. Ironically, Tucker did not pursue the matter. On 21 August Fisher Ames of Massachusetts suggested that "Congress shall make no law establishing religion, or to prevent the free exercise thereof, or to infringe the rights of conscience." The Senate version changed this language to a prohibition on laws "establishing articles of faith or a mode of worship, of prohibiting the free exercise of religion." On 25 September the House proposed and the Senate accepted what became the terms of the First Amendment: "Congress shall make no law respecting the establishment of religion or prohibiting the free exercise thereof" (Curry, 1986, pp. 206–7).

The legislative record of these debates and votes is very sparse, but one crucial piece of evidence exists in the Senate journal. During a closed debate in that body, a proposal to allow non-discriminatory public support for religion was initially approved and then withdrawn, probably in anticipation of Madison's objections in the House. Here was a distinct echo of the assessment controversy in Virginia; the Senate retreat on this key point strongly supports the position taken by the Supreme Court in *Everson vs. New Jersey* (1947), which maintained in matters of public education a formal barrier between church and state.

FURTHER READING

Buckley, Thomas E.: *Church and State in Revolutionary Virginia, 1776–1787* (Charlottesville: University of Virginia Press, 1977).

Calhoon, Robert M.: *Religion and the American Revolution in North Carolina* (Raleigh: North Carolina Division of Archives and History, 1976).

Curry, Thomas J.: *The First Freedoms: Church and State in America to the Passage of the First Amendment* (New York: Oxford University Press, 1986).

Frost, J. William: "Pennsylvania Institutes Religious Liberty, 1682–1860," *Pennsylvania Magazine of History and Biography*, 110 (1988), 327–47.

Hutchinson, William T., et al. (eds.): *The Papers of James Madison* (Chicago: University of Chicago Press, 1962–).

McLoughlin, William G.: *New England Dissent, 1630–1833: the Baptists and the Separation of Church and State* (Cambridge, Mass.: Harvard University Press, 1971).

Pole, J. R.: *The Pursuit of Equality in American History* (Berkeley: University of California Press, 1978).

Wilson, John F. (ed.): *Church and State in America: a Bibliographical Guide: the Colonial and Early National Periods* (Westport, Conn.: Greenwood Press, 1986).

45

Legal reform and the Revolution

BRUCE H. MANN

TWO pictures of American law on the eve of the Revolution predominate. One is that it was not American at all, but English, "heavily burdened with the formalism of the strict law" (Pound, 1938, p. 6). The other is that it was rude and provincial, of "no more relevance to the law of our own industrialized society than the law of the Sioux or the Cheyennes" (Gilmore, 1977, p. 8). A more benign version of the second picture posits a rather placid legal system based on "ethical unity," "consensus," and "stability" (Nelson, 1975, p. 4). Both pictures identify the Revolution as the turning point, before which all was darkness or English, and after which all was modern and American. Neither picture attempts to explain how or why the Revolution should have been so pivotal. Instead, historians have simply assumed that the revolutionary consequences of the Revolution must have extended to law. That law did change in the revolutionary era is undeniable. Some of the changes had revolutionary overtones, especially in the laws of inheritance, slavery, and criminal punishment. Most, however, were evolutionary, reflecting processes that began before and continued after the Revolution, which itself interrupted or, sometimes, accelerated them, but did not transform them.

I. THE ANGLICIZATION OF AMERICAN LAW

To understand the impact of the Revolution on law, one must first have a sense of what law was like before the Revolution. This is not a simple task, because colonial law was not one legal system but several. The only certain generalization one can make is that neither of the pictures noted above is accurate. Legal historians long ago demonstrated that the law of Puritan New England was a blend of English practice and biblical precedent shaped by the demands of life in a physical and spiritual wilderness. As one moved southwards, the mixture of influences changed – Dutch antecedents in New York, Quaker sentiment in Pennsylvania, the accommodations required by slavery in the Chesapeake – but nowhere was the result either entirely English or rudely primitive. Instead, what one encounters everywhere are legal systems that developed to meet the needs of the societies they served, growing in complexity and sophistication as the societies of which they were a part did likewise. The direction of this development was inevitably English, partly because of the obvious imperial constraints, but also because lawyers in the common law tradition were creatures of habit, and habit for them was determined by English precedents.

By the eve of the Revolution, all of the colonies had developed economies that were, in varying degrees, commercial, with farmers, planters, and artisans linked together through market transactions mediated by merchants and traders. The major colonies all boasted commercial centers, where social stratification and the differentiation of

437

economic activity combined to create a new world of legal relations. This world was more modern and less personal than prevailed in the smaller, more communal settlements of the seventeenth century. It was characterized by the use of technical pleadings that reshaped cases into questions of law rather than disputes over fact, by the spread of credit instruments such as notes and bonds in which the form of the instrument mattered more than the substance of the transaction, and by the emergence of lawyers as a professional class.

The Revolution changed none of that. What it did do was to free American law from a necessary dependence on English precedent. Every state had to confront the question of what portions of English law remained in force or deserved to be re-enacted. The Revolution made that question a matter of conscious choice. Some reformers called on legislatures to seize the opportunity to create an American law that would capture the revolutionary essence of the new nation. Every legislature declined, however. Instead, the most common response was to enact general statements that British statutes and common law in force as of a certain date (1607 and 1776 were common choices) remained in force. This response did not mean that American law was to be English, but rather that the common law tradition had taken deep root in English North America and that any American innovations would be variations on a common law theme.

2. DEVELOPMENTS INFLUENCED BY REVOLUTIONARY SENTIMENT

To be sure, there were occasional statutory reforms that had clear links to revolutionary sentiment. By 1804, for example, every northern state had enacted legislation for the gradual emancipation of slaves. Thomas Paine made clear the connection of such laws with the Declaration of Independence in his preamble to the first one, the Pennsylvania Act for Emancipation in 1780. With less fanfare, but no less deliberately, by 1800 every northern state except Delaware had followed colonial Connecticut in permitting judicially granted full divorce, rather than allowing only legal separation, although in general the Revolution brought women little legal benefit. The strongest revolutionary rhetoric, however, accompanied not the status of persons, but changes in the laws of inheritance.

Reform of the laws of inheritance The model for inheritance reform was Virginia, where Thomas Jefferson championed a republican ideal for the transmission of wealth from one generation to the next. The guiding principle of Jefferson's ideal was the proposition " '*that the earth belongs in usufruct to the living*' ... the dead have neither powers nor rights over it" (Jefferson, 1950, vol. 15, p. 392). To this end, Virginia in 1776 abolished entails, a restricted form of property ownership designed to hinder successive generations from selling off family estates. Three years later Jefferson proposed abolishing primogeniture, by which the land of a father who died intestate passed to his eldest son to the exclusion of all other children, and replacing it with partible inheritance, by which all children would share the property equally. The Virginia assembly complied in 1785. For Jefferson, entail and primogeniture epitomized aristocratic control and hence were inappropriate in a republican society. Other states agreed. By the turn of the century nearly every state had abolished both devices, often with rhetorical flourishes that described the reforms as necessary "to promote that equality of property which is of the spirit and principle of a genuine republic" (North Carolina, 1804, vol. 1, ch. 22).

438

In truth, the reforms were largely symbolic. Many colonies before the Revolution applied partible inheritance rather than primogeniture anyway, albeit often with the gesture of a double portion for the eldest son. Moreover, when fathers disposed of their property by will, they rarely bestowed everything upon their eldest sons or entailed their estates. The symbolism, however, was no less powerful for being redundant. The reforms and the rhetoric that heralded them stood as clear renunciations of a feudal past in the name of a republican future.

Towards an American jurisprudence   Similar aspirations appeared in the early attempts to develop an American jurisprudence. When James Wilson, associate justice of the United States Supreme Court, delivered a course of lectures on law in the College of Philadelphia (now the University of Pennsylvania) in 1790–1, his inaugural lecture was a paean to American singularity. For Wilson, the principles of American law were not simply different from those of English law, but "materially *better*." He dedicated his lectures to laying the foundation for "a separate, an unbiased, and an independent law of education ... in the United States" (Wilson, 1896, vol. 1, pp. 14, 24). Similarly, the great James Kent, in his introductory law lecture at Columbia College in 1794, affirmed that "the rudiments of law ... ought accordingly to be drawn from our own history and constitutions" rather than from English law, much of which was "utterly subversive of an equality of rights; and totally incompatible with the liberal spirit of our American establishments" (Kent, 1903, pp. 333–4).

Despite such pronouncements, American jurisprudence was inevitably drawn to Sir William Blackstone's *Commentaries on the Laws of England* for guidance. Thomas Jefferson may have thought that the *Commentaries* had "done more towards the suppression of the liberties of man, than all the millions of men in arms of Bonaparte" (Jefferson, 1859, vol. 6, p. 335), but for hundreds of American lawyers Blackstone was the bible of the common law. Nearly 2,500 copies in various English or American editions were in circulation in the colonies by 1776, a number that rivaled sales in England, and its popularity continued to grow after the Revolution. In addition, numerous English legal treatises were imported, and many others appeared in American editions. Blackstone, however, remained the dominant influence on American legal thought. The *Commentaries* were clear, comprehensive, and oracular – qualities that, together with lawyers' resistance to change and their reverence for the common law, enabled Blackstone's conservatism to shape the early development of American law and assure that America would remain within the common law fold. The influence of English common law was also aided by the lack of an accessible American alternative. The first American treatise, Zephaniah Swift's *A System of the Laws of the State of Connecticut*, was not published until 1795–6. Moreover, the absence of published American case reports hindered the development of an American common law and made reliance on English precedents inevitable. Ephraim Kirby's volume of reports for Connecticut in 1789 began to address the need, but systematic case reporting did not flower until the opening years of the nineteenth century, by which time a foundation of English influence had been established.

Criminal law   At first blush, changes in criminal law and punishment at least appeared revolutionary. By one account, the focus of criminal law changed in the revolutionary era from the preservation of morality to the protection of property – that is, from a system preoccupied with moral and religious offenses to one that dealt primarily with economic offenses against persons and property. This, however, overstates the change.

Criminal prosecutions for the most common moral offenses of the colonial period, fornication and bastardy, did decline, but protection of property had always been a major concern of the criminal law. Moreover, the legal system had begun to assume a new attitude towards the enforcement of private morality well before the Revolution. Private immorality remained punishable, but secularization drained the prosecution of much of its religious content. By 1750, prosecutions for fornication existed largely to fix liability for the costs of rearing illegitimate children. The divergence of sin and crime that began before the Revolution continued after, with little aid or hindrance from the Revolution itself.

The nature of criminal punishment, as distinct from the crimes to be punished, was a different matter. There it is possible to see the influence of revolutionary ideology. Criminal punishments before the Revolution were notably sanguinary – whipping, ear-cropping, branding, and execution. To be sure, none of the mainland American colonies matched England in the widespread use of physical punishments, but they shared with England a retributive ideal of criminal punishment. Imprisonment existed largely for purposes of detention before trial or to confine debtors rather than to punish convicted criminals.

Two changes occurred after the Revolution. Several states moved to limit the number of capital crimes and to restrict or eliminate corporal punishment. In their place, imprisonment for specified terms of months or years became common. To some extent, the change represented ideas that had first been considered in the 1760s. An Italian theorist, Cesare Beccaria, gave the ideas theoretical currency in his *Essay on Crimes and Punishments*, in which he rejected the death penalty in favor of rational punishments based on certainty rather than severity. The new punishments were to deter rather than revenge. Also important, however, was the wartime perception of British barbarity. It is not at all clear that the British were any more barbaric than the Americans in dealing with criminals – a category that included traitors, as defined on both sides – but benevolence and humanity were important elements of the collective self-image of revolutionary Americans, who believed themselves to be more virtuous than their corrupt imperial masters. Whatever the reality, state criminal codes enacted after the Revolution sharply reduced the number of capital offenses. Virginia, for example, in 1796 abolished the death penalty for all crimes committed by free men and women with the exception of premeditated murder. Also after the Revolution, opposition to capital punishment itself appeared for the first time. Although their opposition was similar to that of European Enlightenment figures, writers such as Benjamin Rush of Philadelphia added a distinctly American flavor to the debate by arguing that capital punishment, together with other excessive punishments, was a hallmark of repressive monarchies and as such was antithetical to the principles of republican government.

The second change – the appearance of a new institution, the prison, to house convicted criminals – was required by the first. The familial or household organization of colonial almshouses and jails provided neither the discipline nor the security to make them suitable places for incarcerating criminals. The prisons and houses of correction built in the 1790s were not the full-fledged penitentiaries of the 1820s, but they were nonetheless a sharp departure from previous ideas of what to do with convicted criminals. Enlightenment ideas would doubtless have led to the same conclusion, but the Revolution added a republican vocabulary that made the changes seem, at least to their makers, uniquely American.

440

Debt and debtors   The Revolution did release forces that in turn had significant legal consequences, although it is difficult to describe the consequences themselves as revolutionary in origin. The most significant set of forces was related to the acquisition of vast unsettled lands in the trans-Appalachian West. The cession of state claims in the region to the federal government in the 1780s and the Northwest Ordinance of 1787 unleashed a frenzy of speculation as settlers and investors sought to tap the new source of national wealth. Land warrants and scrip issued to veterans by the states and the Continental Congress formed part of the medium of speculation as speculators bought up claims for a fraction of their face value and attempted to create monopolies of settlement in the most desirable regions. Not all of the speculative activity occurred on the western frontier. The Philadelphia merchants Robert Morris, John Nicholson, and James Greenleaf, for example, sunk – and lost – huge sums into the development of the new "federal city" on the banks of the Potomac, a project for which the mechanic's lien was invented to encourage builders to build on credit by giving them a security interest in the building. Whatever their geographic preference, speculators financed their acquisitions by issuing stock certificates and promissory notes, thereby drawing thousands of smaller investors into their schemes. When the land markets collapsed in the 1790s, the webs of indebtedness created by large speculators drew thousands of people into insolvency and debtor's prisons.

The resulting widespread economic distress coincided with changing attitudes towards debt and debtors. Most of the colonies had experimented with different forms of debtor relief in the decade or two before the Revolution. The most common experiment was with insolvency statutes, which enabled debtors to distribute their property among their creditors but did not relieve them of legal liability for their debts. Except in the tobacco colonies of the Chesapeake, the scale of individual indebtedness was relatively small. In those colonies, however, the level of planter indebtedness to British merchants ran so high – and expectations of paying it so low – that Chesapeake tobacco planters used the language of slavery and enslavement to describe their ties to their British creditors, a vocabulary that elided smoothly into the rhetoric of the Revolution itself.

Economic distress among farmers in the years immediately following the Revolution brought increasing pressure for debtor relief legislation. Shays's Rebellion in western Massachusetts in 1786–7, tenant unrest in upstate New York in 1786 and 1791, and the Whiskey Rebellion in western Pennsylvania in 1794, although not primarily debtor movements, all had overtones of frustration with mercantile creditor interests. Nowhere was this more prominent than in the success of the Shaysites in closing down local courts, thereby preventing creditors from using legal process to collect their debts. As long as debt remained largely a rural phenomenon, however, calls for debtor relief went unheeded. Only the large-scale economic collapse of the 1790s, when numerous prominent men found themselves imprisoned for debt or fugitives from their creditors, made the calls audible. The presence of once-wealthy and politically powerful merchants in the pool of insolvent debtors confounded the normal expectations of social and economic status and conferred a stronger urgency on the issue of debtors' relief. To a generation steeped in the rhetoric of revolution and nation-building, the ideological stakes were high.

The debate over national bankruptcy legislation, which would relieve debtors of continuing liability for their debts after their property had been distributed among their creditors, went to the heart of what the character of the new nation would be. What the Federalists envisioned as a commercial republic, in which the safety net of bankruptcy would allow entrepreneurs to soar without fear of lasting ruin, appeared to Republicans as an economy built on chance and speculation, where benefits bore no necessary relation to labors. Federalists such as Congressman James A. Bayard argued that a national bankruptcy act would support mercantile activity and that the prevailing attachment laws, which exempted land from seizure, were a reactionary principle in a commercial society. His Republican opponents feared that a national bankruptcy system would expose farmers to ruin and ultimately undermine the moral order of an agrarian republican society.

The law that emerged, the Bankruptcy Act of 1800, was a victory for the Federalists, albeit only a temporary one – it was repealed after three years. Its principal feature was that it was not available to all debtors, only to merchants and traders. This feature in particular makes the Act a fitting symbol for legal change in America in the revolutionary era, because it was drawn directly from the English bankruptcy act. The impact of the Revolution on law may not have been thoroughly revolutionary, but American law did change dramatically in the century from 1740 to 1840. The striking presence of the Revolution in the middle of that century made legal change a matter of choice and public debate, which may be revolutionary enough.

FURTHER READING

Friedman, Lawrence M.: *A History of American Law*, 2nd edn. (New York: Simon & Schuster, 1985).

Gilmore, Grant: *The Ages of American Law* (New Haven, Conn.: Yale University Press, 1977).

Horwitz, Morton J.: *The Transformation of American Law, 1780–1860* (Cambridge, Mass.: Harvard University Press, 1977).

Jefferson, Thomas: *The Writings of Thomas Jefferson*, ed. H. A. Washington (New York: Derby & Jackson, 1859).

——: *The Papers of Thomas Jefferson*, ed. Julian P. Boyd (Princeton, NJ: Princeton University Press, 1950–).

Kent, James: *An Introductory Lecture to a Course of Law Lectures* (New York: 1794); repr. *Columbia Law Review*, 3 (1903), 330–43.

Mann, Bruce H.: *Neighbors and Strangers: Law and Community in Early Connecticut* (Chapel Hill: University of North Carolina Press, 1987).

Nelson, William E.: *Americanization of the Common Law: the Impact of Legal Change on Massachusetts Society, 1760–1830* (Cambridge, Mass.: Harvard University Press, 1975).

North Carolina: *The Public Acts of the General Assembly of North Carolina*, ed. James Iredell (Raleigh: 1804).

Pound, Roscoe: *The Formative Era of American Law* (Boston: Little, Brown and Company, 1938).

Roeber, A. G.: *Faithful Magistrates and Republican Lawyers: Creators of Virginia Legal Culture, 1680–1810* (Chapel Hill: University of North Carolina Press, 1981).

Wilson, James: *The Works of James Wilson*, ed. James DeWitt Andrews (Chicago: Callaghan and Company, 1896).

46

Confederation: movement for a stronger union

MARK D. KAPLANOFF

IN order to endure, any constitution – even a written one – must allow orderly development in political practice and constitutional interpretation. Initially, it appeared that the Articles of Confederation provided a framework within which a successful process of evolution might have taken place. Together, though, the end of the Revolutionary War and the boldness of some attempts at altering the Articles ended the possibility of continued development; ultimately, in order to secure the "perpetual union" which the Articles promised, it was necessary to bypass them altogether.

I. FRUSTRATION AND THE NEW NATIONALISM

Even before the Articles of Confederation were finally ratified, problems were apparent and various expedients necessary. (The Articles were proposed by Congress to the states on 15 November 1777 and formally ratified on 1 March 1781; *see* Chapter 30). The nation had a war to fight, and Congress was increasingly hard pressed; in some areas it made significant innovations, but generally it simply muddled through. Congress gradually pushed ahead in creating a new administrative structure for the national government. In October 1777 Congress decided to create Boards of War, Treasury, and Admiralty, each with a professional administrative staff. Beginning in 1777 it established various bodies which heard admiralty appeals from state courts (which decided admiralty cases in the first instance); these were the first federal courts, and they exercised the first federal appellate jurisdiction. Besides structural innovations, there were also developments in constitutional theory. In September 1779 the President of Congress (John Jay) argued that a complete and lasting union had been formed in 1775–6 and that the nation already had enduring powers and responsibilities. By defining treason, requiring oaths of allegiance, and issuing passports and, implicitly, by the provisions in the Articles requiring inter-state comity, a doctrine of national citizenship began to emerge. Finally, as Congress struggled to secure cooperation from recalcitrant states, some congressmen (notably James Madison) began to argue that Congress under the Articles had all implied powers necessary to fulfil its obligations, including the power to coerce uncooperative states.

Yet scattered achievements should not mask the fact that Congress was unable to meet many of its responsibilities and was increasingly forced to rely on the states. Internal factionalism hindered the formulation of foreign policy. Proposals to reform national finances were stalled by political bickering, then ineffective when belatedly put into effect. Problems of supplying the army mounted. As early as the autumn of 1779, Congress began to transfer responsibility for provisioning the army to the states, but they were often unwilling or unable to respond. The result was bitter political

443

acrimony and real hardship for the army; however, men were kept in the field, diplomacy continued, and independence remained in prospect. In the circumstances an independent United States would not have had a powerful, elaborately structured national government, but it is likely that the union would have endured and a workable system of federalism might have evolved.

But circumstances did not permit the experiment; a fiscal crisis intervened. Starting in 1776, Congress had issued paper currency and other paper obligations which circulated as money (eventually amounting to more than $200,000,000), and the value of the paper soon began to plummet (*see* Chapter 37, §2). By 1778 inflation at Philadelphia reached levels in excess of 20 per cent a month, and nothing – not state taxation, local price-fixing movements, or national fiscal reform – was able to stabilize the value of the paper. With a limited stock of specie and a worthless currency, the army could not purchase supplies, commerce dried up, farmers refused to market their crops, and the cities were short of food. Something had to be done.

A small group of men perceived the crisis as an opportunity and began to formulate a comprehensive program for reform and national development – Philip Schuyler, James Duane, Gouverneur Morris, and Alexander Hamilton among the most active. All were friends and professional colleagues, all sat in Congress for New York at some time, all had ties with the army's general staff, all had family links to New York's landed and mercantile elite. The two youngest, Morris and Hamilton, had the boldest vision; impatient with America's present difficulties, they looked forward to a time when the United States would become a great empire. (The word itself, used by both Morris and Hamilton, distinguished their rhetoric from the austere republicanism of most of their contemporaries.) The genesis of their proposals could be found in private memoranda and correspondence as early as 1778. By 1780 their ideas were well developed, and Hamilton presented their vision in its fullest form in his "Continentalist" letters published (somewhat after their composition) in 1781–2.

These impatient nationalists drew many problems together – currency collapse, a powerless national government, congressional indecision – and proposed a wide-ranging scheme of reform. They called for a convention of the states empowered to create a new framework of government. National government should have full sovereignty except for states "internal police," it should have an explicit power to coerce states which did not comply with congressional requisitions, and it should also have independent sources of revenue – an impost (customs duties), a land tax, and an excise. They particularly wanted to create strong executive offices. These bold political proposals were, moreover, matched by a bold vision of political economy. First, they proposed to fund the national debt by converting all Continental paper money and paper obligations into long-term interest-bearing bonds with interest guaranteed by new national revenues. This would relieve Congress of the short-term need to repay its debts, secure the government's ability to borrow, cause public creditors to support the national government, and create a body of capital for productive investment. Additionally, a national bank (with part of its capital based on the new bonds) would facilitate treasury and commercial transactions, further increase the supply of capital, and allocate credit to the most productive sectors of the economy.

These men had a bold vision of "development economics" with the United States as an underdeveloped nation. Since the beginning of the century Britain had experimented with fiscal and economic reforms which ultimately created the machinery of a modern nation state and which promoted new capital markets, industrial development, and rapid economic growth. But it had been precisely this nexus of administrative and fiscal reform – when applied to the colonies – which had sparked the American Revolution. Most Revolutionaries had contrasted American simplicity with the degeneration and corruption which they saw developing in Britain; they sought to preserve a simpler, freer way of life, freed from the encroachments of a developing nation state or advanced fiscal and credit systems. Men like Hamilton disagreed; theirs was a nationalism of a new sort. Where others saw threat, they saw potential; for them, Britain was the model and independence merely the prelude to a great experiment in nation-building.

This "new nationalism" was too bold for its time, but it had a lasting importance. Morris and Duane hesitated about making their full program public. General Schuyler worked throughout 1780 for a convention of the states to refashion national government. In the autumn his proposals were supported by the New York legislature and a convention of delegates from New York and the New England states. But the boldness of the movement alienated even those congressmen committed to strengthening national government and, once submitted to Congress, the proposals were quietly forgotten. By early 1781 the convention movement had been superseded by Congress's own, more modest reform efforts. Yet an important beginning had been made. Over the following years suggestions of a national convention were often repeated; more importantly, visions of a great new nation became increasingly attractive amidst the commercial and political frustrations of the next few years. At America's two greatest urban and commercial centers the "new nationalists" themselves remained politically active and professionally successful, a small and committed group of men ready for other opportunities to initiate the great task of nation-building.

2. MORRIS, MADISON, CONGRESS, AND NEWBURGH

During the autumn and winter of 1780–1, Congress presented a threefold plan of reform. In September, it requested states with extensive unsettled territories in the West to cede part of their lands to the nation. On 3 February 1781 it proposed an amendment to the Articles empowering the national government to levy an impost of 5 per cent on imported goods. Four days later it created three executive departments, Finance, War, and Marine (a Department of Foreign Affairs had been established a month earlier), each under the control of a single officer. Together, these developments were limited efforts to address the familiar problems of finance and administration, not a fundamental attempt to reshape national government. Indeed Congress shied away from more sweeping reforms, particularly on the crucial question of nation–state relations. Several congressional committees addressed broad questions of amending the Articles of Confederation. The most detailed report (22 August 1781) proposed seven additional articles changing regulations about congressional quorums and voting and granting Congress powers to admit new states, to levy taxes, and to coerce states which did not comply with congressional requisitions. The report was forgotten after cursory discussion. The proposal most often mooted – some sort of coercive power over uncooperative states – was never formally voted upon. Even those members committed to strengthening national government realized that Congress's standing was not sufficient to win approval for such a fundamental addition to congressional authority.

Within the national government the initiative passed to the newly appointed Superintendent of Finance, Robert Morris. Not until Franklin Roosevelt would an American chief executive assume office at a time of such financial crisis and public

445

paralysis, and, as with Roosevelt, Morris's personality and personal proposals defined the terms of national political debate once he was in office. But in two important ways Morris's situation differed from that of Roosevelt. Firstly, Roosevelt devoted his career to politics; Morris was a merchant (in twentieth-century terms, a broker, investor, and arbitrageur), and he had a merchant's disdain for politics and politicians. Secondly, Morris did not command an organized political party, nor did he have the means to shape mass public opinion.

Morris's program provoked immediate and enduring controversy. Did he intend to go as far as the younger "new nationalists" (two of whom, Gouverneur Morris and Alexander Hamilton, were among his closest associates)? Morris himself never set out his ideals of constitutional development at any length. Contemporary critics accused him of seeking to establish an aristocratic regime based on favoritism and corruption. Historians have charged that he sought to create a strong nation state, dominated by conservative capitalists, and supportive of their interests. More recently, though, others have argued that Morris was hesitant about constitutional change and merely seeking a few limited new powers for national government. (For this point of view, with citations to earlier work on the other side, see Rakove, 1979, 298–307.) Whatever the constitutional implications, the specific economic proposals of the Morris program were enough to elicit deep opposition. He sought to balance national government's current income and expenditure, to secure new revenues for Congress, to consolidate all Congress's past financial obligations into a funded national debt, and to establish a national bank. It was a program designed not merely to win the war but to establish the basis of long-term economic development; however, only a handful of Americans at the time saw anything but threat in the adoption of such a British-style system of political economy.

Even Congress, where the defects of national government were most keenly felt, refused to accept much of Morris's program; Congress readily approved administrative reform, cost-cutting, and foreign subsidies but shied away from new and long-lasting commitments. In August 1781 Morris proposed new federal taxes – a land tax, a poll tax, and an excise; Congress never acted on the proposals. In February 1782 Morris made his first formal proposal to fund the Continental debt, a proposal repeated and developed in his detailed report on public credit on 27 July 1782. Even though French subsidies were reduced after the victory at Yorktown (19 October 1781) and the states showed decreasing inclination to comply with congressional demands, Congress disregarded Morris's proposals and continued to pass requisitions vainly hoping to meet current obligations while waiting for approval of the impost of 1781.

Ever impatient of politics and politicians, Morris began to recruit support from pressure groups outside Congress. The first to whom he turned was the Philadelphia financial community. Arguing that it would be invidious to pay some creditors and not others, Morris proposed in June 1782 that interest payments be suspended on most of the publicly held Continental debt. Meanwhile, he cooperated with a Philadelphia committee of public creditors which lobbied for new national revenues in order to fund the Continental debt. Congress continued to wait. In November, however, the Rhode Island legislature refused to ratify the impost proposal on the grounds that it threatened the principles of the Articles of Confederation. A congressional delegation set out in December to urge the state to change its mind but turned back when news arrived that Virginia had rescinded its earlier ratification. Meanwhile, the states continued to evade congressional requisitions, interest payments were suspended, and the Philadelphia creditors now sought aid from their state. Despite congressional

446

protests that the state was impinging upon national authority, Pennsylvania in December decided to service that part of the national debt owed to its citizens. Morris's own program had been rejected, his efforts had provoked a backlash which killed the earlier impost proposal, and his erstwhile allies now proposed the transfer of a national responsibility to the states.

Thereupon Morris turned to a second, more threatening interest group – the army. A peace treaty had not yet been concluded, the British still occupied several Atlantic ports (including New York City), and a large Continental force remained encamped at Newburgh, New York. Since 1781, moreover, Morris had suspended army pay (while continuing to pay administration officials), blaming the states' failure to meet congressional requisitions. In December 1782 a small group of officers petitioned Congress for immediate relief, stating that Congress could expect "at least a mutiny" if no action was taken.

Throughout the winter, the atmosphere of crisis increased. Congress consulted Morris, who replied that the army's demands could not be met without granting the government his recommended new powers of taxation. He also offered his resignation and began correspondence with dissatisfied officers at Newburgh. There were further protests at the camp and public threats of recourse to force. Fortunately, by mid-March two Virginians intervened. At a dramatic meeting at Newburgh on 15 March 1783 George Washington, the army's commander-in-chief, outfaced the hotheads who were threatening mutiny. Meanwhile, in Congress, James Madison had begun to fashion acceptable compromise proposals for national finance.

Was there a real threat of a coup? Certainly many had reason to play up the threat of mutiny. Afterwards there was persistent suspicion against some of the young officers and some of Morris's younger associates (particularly Gouverneur Morris), although Robert Morris himself generally escaped blame. It will probably never be possible to tell how far things might have gone; it is not the custom for people who dabble in treason to keep detailed records. Military unrest does have a way of getting out of hand, and democratic traditions – indeed any traditions – had not become well established in national politics. Fortunately, as things turned out, Newburgh helped to shape tradition, by defining lasting limits on military involvement in American politics.

Appropriately the architect of Congress's final response to the crisis of 1783 was James Madison – the nationalist in Congress with the greatest concern for con-stitutional propriety. Madison was a nationalist in the sense that he wanted to strengthen the national government and its authority, but he had different experi-ences, temperament, and ideals from the Morrisite nationalists. From his arrival in Congress in 1780, Madison worried that national government did not have sufficient powers, but he also fretted about the precise definition of the powers it had. During 1780 and 1781 he advocated an amendment to the Articles to give Congress coercive powers over states which failed to meet congressional directives, and he argued that Congress had implied powers under the Articles in order to fulfill the broad purposes of the Confederation. Later, he served on important committees which considered fiscal affairs and generally advocated measures proposed by Robert Morris, but there were always differences between Madison and the Morris group. Madison always saw the profits from the disposal of western lands as a potentially important financial asset for Congress. (Morris doubted that much money could readily be secured this way.) Madison questioned both the wisdom and constitutional propriety of chartering a bank and disliked plans for a long-term funded public debt. The Morrisites hoped to use fiscal policy to promote new forms of economic growth and the development of a powerful nation. Madison sought to confine national government to its appropriate limits, to limit advanced economic development, and to preserve an egalitarian, agrarian society.

In late February 1783 Madison began to work out a compromise. He proposed a three-part program: there was to be a revised and limited impost (lasting only 25 years, with the states responsible for collection). New taxes were to be enacted by the states dedicated to servicing the national debt. Finally, the method of allocating national expenses between the states was to be changed from the existing, unworkable scheme based on land values to a system based simply on population (with five slaves being counted as equivalent to three free men). After much debate and minor amendment the proposals were approved by Congress on 18 April 1783 and sent to the states. Significantly, Morris's strongest supporter in Congress, Alexander Hamilton, opposed the package on grounds that it did not go far enough.

The congressional program of April 1783 was the last attempt at comprehensive reform of government under the Articles of Confederation. After three years' debate it looked as if a workable compromise had been reached, yet the proposals themselves indicated how the ambit of possible reform had narrowed. Although the problems of national government had intensified, the final proposals were much less than Morris had advocated, less even than those considered by Congress before Morris had taken office. Since then a well-articulated opposition had arisen to increased central power, and Congress rightly realized that any proposal to strengthen national government would be met with suspicion. The heritage of Robert Morris's administration was an ambivalent one. He had succeeded in financing America's final military effort, and in the long run his efforts foreshadowed the Hamiltonian program of the 1790s, so important in setting up the new government under a new Constitution. In its immediate aftermath, however, Morris's administration acted as an inoculation; it inspired a vigorous and successful opposition to Congress's efforts to reform government under the Articles of Confederation.

3. CONGRESS IN PEACE AND DIFFICULTY

After 1783 the momentum of nationalism dissipated; Congress's problems did not. Morris finally left office in November 1784, and the most active nationalists had retired from Congress before that. The states responded slowly to the amendments to the Articles proposed in 1783, but by 1786 it became clear that the amendments had failed. Meanwhile, Congress had to grapple with familiar financial difficulties and also to confront new problems about the West and peacetime diplomacy. Only in the West was significant progress made, but even there policy was not properly implemented because of lack of resources. The men who took over the leadership of Congress after the spring of 1783 had an ideological commitment to maintaining the strict limits on government established under the Articles of Confederation. Successive difficulties persuaded even them that national government needed strengthening; by 1787 they spoke of the need for greater power in almost Morrisite terms, but they proposed nothing concrete. The standing of Congress had fallen so low that it could not even propose reforms necessary for its own preservation.

The West, the area of Congress's greatest conceptual achievement in these years, was also the source of immense practical frustration. As early as 1780 negotiations had begun between Congress and Virginia (the state with the largest claims to unoccupied lands in the West) about ceding an area in the West to Congress. Squabbling over terms delayed the final cession until 1 March 1784, after which Congress for the first time exercised authority over a national domain (*see* Chapter 35, §3). Under the Articles, Congress had no authority for domestic governance, but the area was now outside state jurisdiction, and Congress was able to act without challenge. In a series of measures beginning in 1784 and culminating with the Northwest Ordinance of 1787, Congress planned the orderly development of the national domain. Lands were to be surveyed systematically and sold to settlers on reasonable terms, but funds were lacking to implement the plan, and little money was ever raised from land sales.

Peacetime diplomacy also turned out to be fraught with difficulties (*see* Chapter 38). Americans had been able to secure a highly satisfactory treaty of peace with Britain in 1783. Afterwards, recalcitrant states did not abide by the terms of the peace treaty concerning restitution for confiscated loyalist property and the payment of debts owed to British nationals. In retaliation, Britain refused to vacate certain forts in the American West. An economic downturn and hostile British commercial policy caused Americans to seek new trading partners, and Congress's representatives sought to negotiate treaties of amity and commerce with most of the powers of Europe; with little to bargain with, they were generally unsuccessful. Spain, which controlled Louisiana, declared in 1784 that the free navigation of the Mississippi would no longer be allowed. In subsequent negotiations, the American representative sought to alter his instructions in order to concede western navigation in return for privileges in Atlantic commerce with Spain; the request provoked such bitterness that contemporaries spoke seriously of possible division of the union along sectional lines.

National finances also degenerated after 1783. Congress had to depend on the increasingly unworkable system of requisitions. By cutting expenses to the bone, Congress was able to maintain a balance between current receipts and expenditure for a couple of years, but beginning in 1786 the Continental treasury ran an ever-increasing deficit. Moreover, cost-cutting was achieved by measures which diminished national authority. During these years individual states began to service the Continental debt owed to their residents. Left with the foreign debt to deal with, Congress coped by suspending payments to France and Spain and trying to maintain its credit in Amsterdam, but by 1786 it appeared that it would be necessary to default on the Dutch loans as well. Congress was failing to meet its international obligations, even when reduced to a minimum, and on the point of losing its sole remaining dependable source of funds.

Although the fundamental problem in national government remained that of federalism – the proper relation of the nation and the states – the implications had become much more serious. The question was no longer of the role of the states within the union but the nature of the union itself. During the war Congress had coped, albeit sometimes by desperate expedients, with the "external" business of diplomacy, defense, and international borrowing; now this business simply could not be managed. Internally, the Articles envisaged an American "common market" in which the free inhabitants of any state could do business in every state on an equal footing, yet the various state fiscal systems often discriminated against non-residents. The "perpetual union" of the Articles was clearly not developing as planned.

In the circumstances it was surprising how little Congress proposed by way of reform; indeed, as problems mounted, Congress grew perceptibly more hesitant. In July 1783 the British Government ordered the closure of West Indian ports to American ships, and there were widespread demands for retaliation. On 30 April 1784 Congress proposed an amendment granting powers during 15 years to ban foreign ships from American ports and to restrict the trade of foreign merchants. The states were slow to reply, the commercial situation deteriorated, and merchants petitioned for more forceful measures. A year later a congressional committee proposed an amendment granting permanent power to regulate foreign and inter-state commerce and to impose import and export duties. (This was distinguished from the still-pending impost proposal of 1783 by handing over both the revenue from the duties and the responsibility for collecting them to the individual states.) Throughout the summer Congress intermittently debated the report, but it fell foul of North–South sectionalism and familiar fears about over-mighty central government, and no proposal was sent to the states.

By the spring of 1786 it was clear that all amendments already proposed were unlikely to succeed. Some congressmen sought to seize the initiative and make one last effort at comprehensive reform. In May, Charles Pinckney proposed that Congress appoint a grand committee to review national affairs and then issue a call for a national convention to consider the report; in August the committee recommended seven additional Articles. Six dealt with familiar problems of regulating trade, raising revenue, and securing observance of treaties and national laws; the seventh addressed the increasing difficulty of maintaining a quorum in Congress. The proposals considered in 1785 about trade regulation were reiterated. Financial penalties could be imposed on states late in meeting requisitions, and Congress was to be given the ultimate right to raise taxes in any persistently uncooperative state. Future revenue amendments would require the assent of only 11 states, and, in the most striking innovation, a federal court would be established with appellate jurisdiction over decisions of state courts on international law, foreign affairs, national revenue, and congressional trade regulation. These proposals did not fundamentally depart from the Articles as traditionally understood. Only one new federal power was proposed – the long-advocated one to regulate commerce. The states retained their role in implementing congressional policy, and non-compliance was to be dealt with not by coercion but by financial sanctions and judicial review. Although Congress took the unusual step of publicizing the committee proposals, debate was desultory, and they were never formally acted upon. A failure of nerve was apparent by late 1786. Efforts ceased even to secure the approval of earlier proposals. (All amendments formally proposed by Congress had achieved ratification by at least 11 states, and the 1784 request for power to pass navigation acts had been ratified by every state, although the varied forms of ratification needed reconciliation.) By default, the initiative in reforming national government passed outside Congress.

Why was it so difficult for Congress to secure amendments? The fate of the 1783 impost proposal illustrated the problems. Prominent congressmen privately hoped it would fail, warning that independent revenue for Congress would strengthen "aristocratical influence" and "establish" an arbitrary Government." Within the states amendment was hotly contested. Approval in the critical states of Massachusetts (1783) and Virginia (1784) was secured only by the influence of John Adams and George Washington respectively. In Connecticut feelings were particularly high against the commutation of army officers' pensions, and the impost was twice rejected before eventual approval in 1784. Rhode Island held out until 1785. Georgia, which generally showed little interest in national affairs, delayed ratification until 1786. When the impost was finally killed by squabbling between Congress and New York about the measure's implementation (the state insisted upon appointing local collectors of the impost), the outcome seemed almost the result of exhaustion.

Three lessons could be drawn from this unedifying story, and they applied to all congressional business after 1783. One set of difficulties was structural and procedural – the requirements of unanimity for amendment and high majorities for congressional decisions and quorums. A broader question was that of Congress's standing. Effective government was carried out by the states; little attention was paid to Congress by ordinary people or even by state legislatures. Finally, there was the problem of ideological resistance to central power. Constantly reiterated, Whiggish fears of taxes, aristocracy, and tyranny took on a reality of their own. By 1786 the minimum proposals necessary to make national government workable under the Articles were subject to fierce and principled resistance. The earlier opposition to Robert Morris had borne its poisoned fruit.

4. THE ROAD TO PHILADELPHIA

Although national government by the mid-1780s was no longer able to respond positively to its difficulties, there remained two areas of creative tension in national affairs. One was in the relationship between the states and the nation. Although the constitutional system of federalism under the Articles had proved unworkable, at another, deeper level the authority of the states and the nation had developed in a reciprocal fashion, and the creative interplay continued, albeit in different ways. On the eve of the Revolution, provincial assemblies had called the Continental Congress into being, and Congress, in turn, had given vital sanction to organization of the new state governments. Ten years later, as Congress foundered, it was constitutional development within the states which provided the model and state legislatures which provided the sanction for a successful movement to remake national government. Moreover, a perceived political crisis within the stages did much to strengthen the cause of national reform. The second area of tension was in the relationship between America and Britain. Americans could not easily shed their British heritage; inherited attitudes and ideas continued to shape their understanding of politics and of nationhood. It was, however, a more mundane connection with Britain which provided the specific opportunity to initiate reform. Britain remained America's most important trading partner, and (in terms of the long-term norms of American development) international trade had a particularly important role in the American economy. After the peace Americans experienced an extraordinary sharp and painful trade cycle. The resulting crisis sparked new popular support for strengthening national authority, exacerbated political problems within the states, and provided the catalyst for a successful movement to reconstruct national government.

Only twice have major wars been fought on American soil, and in both cases they precipitated enormous constitutional creativity and unprecedented political bitterness. Up to 1786 the creativity and the conflict were most apparent within the individual states. The most important legacy of this period was the development of a new American conception of constitutionalism. It was out of the varied experience of the 13 states during this decade that Americans came to understand how legitimate government should be instituted (a constitutional convention, popular ratification, and a constitution unalterable by the ordinary process of legislation) and how government should be structured (a bicameral legislature, a separate executive, and an independent judiciary). Likewise, this was a time of unprecedented rise in the level of governmental activity in the states, whether measured by the volume of legislation, levels of taxation and expenditure, or the number of cases before the courts. Finally, there was a marked broadening of participation in politics, both in theory and in practice. More men voted, representation was extended to areas previously denied, and formerly excluded interest groups demanded that their interests be attended to; although there were still limits on democracy, practice was gradually broadening expectations. Varied demands, of course, could not all be met, and the level of political contentiousness rose along with the increases in participation and governmental activity.

Political controversy was also shaped and exacerbated by the economic relationship with Britain. America was dependent on Britain for both markets and credit, and complex links of loans and transactions tied even the most isolated farming community to transatlantic markets. General participation in an economy based on agricultural exports and extensive credit did not mean, however, that all Americans shared, or thought that they shared, a common interest. In the seaports and the nearby developed hinterland the level of economic activity visibly depended upon international trade. In isolated farming areas the connection with international trade was less apparent, much less of what was produced was sent to market, and cash was scarce, but ultimately the backwoods economy was also tied into transatlantic exchange, even though in different ways than those from more developed areas. Moreover, the division between isolated rural areas and the more advanced ones was the fundamental division which shaped the politics within the states. Although there were not organized political parties in the modern sense, historians have identified a consistent pattern of cleavage in state politics between backwoods "localists" and "cosmopolitans" from the more developed areas. (The terms are defined and explored more fully in Main, 1973.) This political conflict was well established by mid-decade, but it was exacerbated by the postwar economic cycle. At the end of the war there was enormous pent-up demand for imports from Britain. There was no corresponding rise in demand for American exports; instead British policy actively sought to restrict American exports in order to encourage Canadian development. The result was a trade imbalance. By the end of 1784 a severe economic contraction was underway, and the impact on politics soon followed (see Chapter 57).

In 1785 and 1786 the dominant political questions within each state revolved around debt, and local controversy began to inspire a new conservative nationalism. The states had heavy public debts from the Revolution. Taxpayers were increasingly in arrears. Individuals were hard pressed to pay their private debts. Many demanded government action, but there was marked disagreement about what to do. Generally "cosmopolitans" favored enforcing existing contracts, levying taxes to pay public obligations in full, and embarking on government-sponsored schemes to promote commercial recovery. "Localists," on the other hand, advocated debtor relief, reduced taxes, and cutbacks in government activity. Whatever the results in individual states (and they varied widely), conservative "cosmopolitans" had reason for anxiety. If "localists" dominated the politics of a given state, conservatives were obviously dissatisfied; on the other hand, if "cosmopolitans" enacted a conservative fiscal program, it was likely to meet violent resistance. (Shays's Rebellion in Massachusetts during the winter of 1786–7 was merely the most widely publicized of many violent episodes.) By 1786 a number of influential men had begun to speculate that a strengthened national government with a broader sphere of authority might be an attractive alternative to state politics with its rancor and excess.

More immediately, retaliation was demanded against Britain's trade policy. During 1785 the press and public meetings discussed possible measures, including congressional regulation of commerce, state tariffs, and private boycotts of British goods. Soon it became clear that local action by itself would be unsatisfactory, as competing ports might take advantage of local tariffs or non-importation to win business away from rivals. For any policy of commercial retaliation to work, it had to work nation-wide, and the campaign increasingly focused on the effort to secure ratification of the 1785 proposal to give Congress power over trade. For the first time there was a broad-based popular movement advocating stronger national authority.

Ironically, the events which finally gave coherence and effectiveness to the impulses for reshaping national government began not in one of the great northern port cities but in Virginia. The unexpected location had profound importance, for it meant that the movement did not begin in the rarified world of the northern urban elite, nor was it initially shaped by contention and partisanship. Instead it began with the largest state in the union and the most respected man in America sensibly transacting a bit of down-to-earth business. Both Virginia and Maryland claimed authority over the navigation of the Potomac, and importers took advantage of the confusion to evade customs. In March 1784 James Madison suggested that the issues be resolved by commissioners appointed by the two states; this was accepted, and after some mishaps and delay the commissioners met at George Washington's home at Mount Vernon on 25 March 1785. The commissioners agreed on a wide variety of issues; they settled questions about navigation and naval jurisdiction and recommended that the two states coordinate their currencies, their customs duties, and their methods of dealing with protested bills of exchange. The commissioners carefully stipulated that navigation should be open to people of all states and wrote to the government of Pennsylvania (into whose territory it was hoped to extend the navigation of the Potomac) suggesting that Pennsylvania should cooperate with their recommendations. The Mount Vernon Conference had raised questions of national importance about commerce, currency, navigation, and debt, and, more significantly, it provided an example of effective inter-state cooperation.

The lesson was not lost on the most thoughtful nationalist in Virginia. Since leaving Congress, Madison had served in the Virginia legislature, where he was accepted as an authority on national affairs and where he sought to secure state ratification of the various amendments proposed to strengthen the Articles. When the commissioners' proposals were considered, Madison argued that they should be submitted to Congress under Article VI of the Confederation (which required congressional consent for any "treaty, confederation, or alliance" between states), but the legislature chose to ratify on its own. Madison then quietly pushed a proposal that Virginia invite all states to appoint commissioners to meet to discuss "such commercial regulations [as] may be necessary to their common interest and their permanent harmony." Considered on the final day of the legislative session, the motion passed with little fanfare, and other states were duly invited to send representatives to a meeting at Annapolis in September 1786.

Rather few states chose to do so. By any reasonable standard the Annapolis Convention was not a success, but it did provide a framework within which to work and a new definition of the scope of reform. Eight states responded favorably to Virginia's invitation, but for various reasons commissioners appeared from only five. The Convention met on only three days and chose not to make concrete recommendations. Instead, the commissioners invited the states to select representatives

453

for a further convention to assemble in Philadelphia in May 1787. But significant things were achieved. Firstly, urban and commercial nationalists from the mid-Atlantic states enlisted in the Virginia-based movement for reform. Secondly, they broadened the definition of possible objects. Those proposed by the Virginia legislature had been limited, and Madison in particular aspired to nothing more than congressional power to regulate trade. The New Jersey delegation, on the other hand, had broad authority to consider any matters necessary to the "common interest," and a delegate from Philadelphia recommended a general enquiry into the commercial laws of individual states. The major contribution, however, was made by Alexander Hamilton, a representative from New York. Hamilton had never abandoned his early advocacy of a national convention with plenipotentiary powers to change the Articles. Now he was able to graft his proposal onto the more modest Virginia scheme. As the draftsman of the Convention's address to the states (for which he has always been given credit), Hamilton proposed a wide brief for delegates to the Philadelphia Convention – "to devise such further provisions as shall appear to them necessary to render the constitution of the Federal Government adequate to the exigencies of the Union." The Convention's resolutions were then sent to Congress and the states.

During the next months things went the reformers' way. Congress was understandably cool and did not act until 21 February 1787, when it declared that it would be "expedient" to hold a convention "for the sole and express purpose of revising the Articles of Confederation." Already five states had acted on their own to name delegates, and in the end eight of the 12 states which sent delegates gave them authority to work under the sort of broad remit proposed at Annapolis rather than the narrower one recommended by Congress. Around the union distinguished men who had previously stood aloof from efforts at reforming national government were now willing to serve as delegates. Public opinion was also shifting. There was a sense of crisis as stalemate and sectional rancor continued in Congress and open rebellion broke out in Massachusetts. Among those in national politics, including even those who would later oppose the new Constitution, there was by 1787 a broad consensus for fundamental reform.

Meanwhile, Madison systematically studied history and political theory and considered the problems of state and national politics in order to determine the principles upon which American government should be based. His conclusions were enormously creative. In his most fundamental innovation he proposed that national government ought to operate directly upon the people (rather than acting through the intermediate agency of the states) and that it ought to receive its authority from the people (rather than from the states). This insight, first of all, allowed a new understanding of federalism. If the sovereign people delegated authority both to the national government and the states, the national government could be given power to act independently in its own sphere and also to impose certain restrictions on state activity. Although the specific mechanism which Madison envisaged – a federal negative on state laws – was rejected, limits on state authority imposed under the terms of the Federal Constitution have become a fundamental feature of American federalism. Secondly, the idea of deriving national authority from the people allowed Madison to abandon old notions of a confederation of states and to draw on the new American experience of constitutionalism in order to propose ways to create and structure national government. Its constitution should be drawn up by a convention and ratified by the people. Drawing upon traditional theories of mixed government as well as the practical experience of the states, Madison proposed a complex structure for national govern-

454

ment with an independent executive and judiciary enforcing the enactments of a bicameral legislature. The precise details which he proposed in the Virginia Plan (present at the beginning of the Philadelphia convention) were not accepted, and other nationalists disagreed not only about details but some of the principles behind them. Nonetheless Madison provided the agenda, and, once it was accepted, delegates at Philadelphia could discuss national government in familiar terms they had learned from constitution-making in the states.

When the Federal Convention assembled at Philadelphia in May 1787 the movement for a stronger national government was returning to its birthplace, but success was only ensured because the route had included a detour through Virginia. The high-toned nationalism of the "new nationalists" in 1779–81 and the Morrisites in 1781–3 had been both premature and ultimately unrealizable. Nationalism needed a broader constituency than a small arrogant urban elite. Time was needed not only to realize the full problems of the nation but also to draw upon the lessons of the states. This is what the Virginians contributed on the way to Philadelphia.

5. A MORE PERFECT UNION

From beginning to end, government under the Articles of Confederation was a creature of the Revolutionary War. The exigencies of wartime diplomacy prompted Congress to propose the Articles to the states, and military responsibility forced Congress to exercise broad authority. It was a time of constant crisis, myriad expedients, and ultimate victory. Victory, however, diminished Congress's responsibilities and made the need to strengthen national government less compelling. The threat of military intervention, whether real or fanciful, fueled a suspicion of central power which frustrated any attempts to reform the Articles. The business of the Revolution, however, was not finished, and Congress was unable to deal with pressing problems of finance and diplomacy within an unworkable constitutional system and after a precipitous loss of its own public standing.

Yet it was also the heritage of the war which made possible the resurrection and transfiguration of national government. It was the war which gave birth to American nationalism; for the first time, people of all states cooperated in a common cause, came to expect mutual rights and privileges, and began to share a sense of national identity. The problem, of course, was that Americans also paid allegiance to their individual states and that the states successfully carried out most of the necessary business of governing. Both in theory and practice it was difficult to work out how the states and the national government could coexist effectively. The very notion of federalism (formally defined as a political system in which two governments exercise jurisdiction over the same territory and neither has the power to destroy the other) was – and is – difficult to conceive. The practical problems of defining the sphere of national government and working out the boundaries of national and state power proved impossible to solve under the Articles of Confederation, yet the years of frustration highlighted the problems and forced some men to begin searching for new solutions. With a bold disregard of grammar and an even bolder optimism, the new Constitution of 1787 promised Americans "a more perfect Union"; it was only after the experience of the Articles that the promise could be made and later realized.

FURTHER READING

Burnett, E. C.: *The Continental Congress* (New York: Macmillan, 1941).

Ferguson, E. J.: *The Power of the Purse: a History of American Public Finance, 1776–1790* (Chapel Hill: University of North Carolina Press, 1961).

Jensen, M.: *The Articles of Confederation: an Interpretation of the Social-Constitutional History of the American Revolution, 1774–1781* (Madison: University of Wisconsin Press, 1940).

——: *The New Nation: a History of the United States during the Confederation, 1781–1789* (New York: Alfred A. Knopf, 1950).

Main, J. T.: *Political Parties Before the Constitution* (Chapel Hill: University of North Carolina Press, 1973).

Morris, R. B.: *The Forging of the Union, 1781–1789* (New York: Harper & Row, 1987).

Rakove, J. N.: *The Beginnings of National Politics: an Interpretive History of the Continental Congress* (New York: Alfred A. Knopf, 1979).

Wood, G. S.: *The Creation of the American Republic, 1776–1787* (Chapel Hill: University of North Carolina Press, 1969).

47

The Federal Convention and the Constitution

MARK D. KAPLANOFF

THE Federal Convention met at Philadelphia from 25 May to 17 September 1787; during that time 55 delegates from 12 states took part in drafting the Constitution, which remains (with amendments) the fundamental law of the United States. (Of the 13 original states Rhode Island did not participate.) The most basic question that historians have asked about the Constitution has been whether it should be seen as a counter-revolutionary effort to limit the internal effects of the American Revolution or a pragmatic attempt to secure its success after difficult times during the early and mid-1780s. In one particular version of this discussion scholars (drawing especially on the work of Charles A. Beard) have debated whether delegates sought to defend the interests of commercial and financial property-holders. Others, looking in detail at the dynamics of decision-making within the Convention, have emphasized the conflicts during the drafting process and the difficulties resolving them; writing in this vein, one early historian summed up the Constitution as "a bundle of compromises" (Farrand, 1904, p. 484). Three compromises in particular have been identified as the most important. In the Connecticut Compromise of early July small states secured equal representation for all states in the US Senate. The slave trade compromise of late August forbade federal interference with the foreign slave trade before 1808 and granted certain other guaranteees to southern planters. The compromise about the presidency in early September established the intricate method of electing the US President. Other historians, however, have correctly emphasized the shared experience and common goals which allowed the delegates to reach agreement on a radically new plan for national government.

I. BACKGROUND

Delegates, for the most part, had personal experience of national affairs and agreed that the powers of the national government needed substantially to be increased. Of the 55 delegates who attended, 42 had served in Continental Congresses or in Congress under the Articles of Confederation. Others had served in the Continental Army, several on its general staff. Delegates tended to be well-to-do lawyers, planters, and merchants. They were well educated (26 had graduated from college, nine from Princeton) and well prepared. JAMES MADISON of Virginia, who has deservedly been called the "Father of the Constitution," had served in Congress for many years and had long advocated strengthening the federal government; during the winter of 1786–7 he had made an intensive study of political theory in preparation for framing a new constitution. As early as 1781 Alexander Hamilton of New York had proposed a convention to draft a new framework for national government. Among other active

457

nationalist delegates at the Convention were GOUVERNEUR MORRIS and JAMES WILSON of Pennsylvania, RUFUS KING of Massachusetts, and Charles Pinckney of South Carolina; all were young, college-educated lawyers with experience in Congress. Although less active, Benjamin Franklin of Pennsylvania and George Washington of Virginia (who presided over the Convention) were the best-known Americans of their day, and their presence and quiet approval ultimately did much to strengthen the nationalists' cause. Among other prominent and active delegates were JOHN DICKINSON of Delaware, ROGER SHERMAN and Oliver Ellsworth of Connecticut, Elbridge Gerry of Massachusetts, and George Mason and Edmund Randolph of Virginia. Of these the first three were delegates from smaller states, initially critical but committed nationalists after the Connecticut Compromise; the second three were at first active supporters of a stronger national government but later refused to sign the Constitution. The one consistently active and articulate opponent of the nationalist view at the Convention was LUTHER MARTIN of Maryland, a lawyer and public official whose career and vision had remained firmly state-centered. Generally, though, few politicians with a localist orientation attended the Convention, and those there who held such views said little or chose to leave.

Circumstances outside the Convention also worked in favor of strengthening the national government. Under the Articles of Confederation, the federal government was unable to raise sufficient funds to pay its debts and expenses. It could not secure compliance by the states with international treaties, and sectional division within Congress thwarted diplomatic negotiations. Over the years various proposals had been made to grant the federal government an independent revenue, power over international and inter-state commerce, and even coercive powers over the states, yet all the proposals had failed. The severe contraction in international trade and credit in 1784–5 had led to widespread distress and had embittered the already strife-ridden politics within the individual states. Debtors struggled for relief, and in several states violence broke out, most frighteningly in Shays's Rebellion in Massachusetts. Many prominent men worried that the idealism of the Revolution was degenerating into selfish, unjust politics and internecine strife, and some began to see that strengthening the national government might work to curb the excesses of the states. General apprehension of crisis and the failure of earlier attempts at amending the Articles of Confederation allowed nationalists at Philadelphia to argue that the Convention provided the last chance for fundamental and necessary reform.

Arrangements within the Convention also favored the nationalists. They set the agenda at the beginning, and more cautious delegates never successfully forced the debate onto other ground. The secrecy in which the delegates debated allowed them to explore wide-ranging proposals. Yet the more avid nationalists did not railroad their proposals through; the rules and practices of the Convention facilitated consensus-building. After giving brief notice any delegate was allowed to reopen discussion on any point, and debates and votes were often repeated. Discussion was exhaustive, and delegates spoke freely. Although the rules allowed a decision by a simple majority (voting was by state, and each state had one vote), delegates were reluctant to conclude controversial business if voting remained closely divided.

Voting patterns reveal some of the results of these arrangements. More than 560 roll-call votes were recorded during the course of the Convention and statistical analysis shows that voting alignments can be divided into four chronological periods. Within each period there were two opposing blocs of states, and the times when voting alignments shifted coincided closely with the three major compromises. It was also

458

(a)

(b)

FIGURE 37 (a): Edmund Randolph portrayed by Constantine Brumidi as a member of Washington's first cabinet (begun *c.* 1859–60; one of a group of frescos and oil paintings on the walls of the president's room in the United States Capitol, Washington, DC); (b): portrait drawing of Elbridge Gerry by John Vanderlyn (1798)

significant that no state was always on the losing side; each state was part of a majority coalition during at least one period.

2. THE VIRGINIA AND NEW JERSEY PLANS

The Convention began its substantive business on 29 May when Edmund Randolph (*see* figure 37a) introduced the so-called Virginia Plan, a set of 15 brief resolutions sketching an entirely new model for a national government. Authorship has been universally ascribed to James Madison (probably with some collaboration by other Virginia delegates). Summarizing the audacious nature of the plan, one historian concluded that it "proposed, in effect, a sovereign parliament for America" (Murrin, 1987, p. 598). The new national government represented individual citizens (to a degree) and could act directly upon them. The national legislature would have power to pass laws "in all cases to which the separate states are incompetent, or in which the harmony of the United States may be interrupted by the exercise of individual

459

legislation," to "negative" state laws "contravening ... the articles of union," and to use force against recalcitrant states (Farrand, 1937, vol. 1, p. 21). The legislature was to have two houses, the lower house elected by the people, the upper elected by the lower. Each state was to be represented in each house in proportion either to taxes ("contributions") or to free population. There was to be a national judiciary and an executive elected by the legislature for an unspecified term and ineligible for re-election. A Council of Revision drawn from the executive and the judiciary was to exercise a veto on legislation. Generally, though, details of the structure and powers of the executive and judiciary were vague. Provision was also made for the admission of new states, for amendment, and for ratification by a popular convention or conventions.

For the next two weeks the Virginia Plan was virtually unchallenged. Although some delegates complained that the proposals exceeded their authority, on 30 May the Convention agreed to support a government *"national & supreme"* and proceeded to debate the individual resolutions of the plan. In the most important decision of these days it was voted on 6 June that state representation in the national legislature and the apportionment of internal taxes would be proportionate to the total free population plus three-fifths of the slave population, the so-called three-fifths clause. (This formula had first been proposed by Congress in 1783 as the basis for apportioning taxes among the states.) Other decisions fixed seven-year terms for the upper house of the legislature, three-year for the lower, with the upper house elected by state legislatures. Delegates decided that there should be a single executive serving a seven-year term. The Council of Revision was rejected and the executive given a veto subject to being overturned by a vote of two-thirds in each house of the legislature. The provision for coercing states was dropped. It was decided to create a national judiciary (which had not existed under the Articles of Confederation). Although the Convention was moving remarkable quickly, a note of caution was sounded as delegates from smaller states warned that they would never accept representation in both houses of the legislature proportional to state population.

The apparently easy momentum of the nationalists was halted on 14 June when William Paterson of New Jersey introduced an alternative "purely federal" plan. Jointly prepared by members of the New Jersey, Connecticut, New York, Maryland, and possibly Delaware delegations, the so-called New Jersey Plan proposed keeping a unicameral national legislature in which each state had one vote, but even this plan went significantly beyond the Articles of Confederation. The national government was to have new powers – power to raise money through customs duties and a stamp tax, power to regulate commerce, and power to compel delinquent states to honor financial requisitions. There was to be a plural executive (elected by Congress) and a national judiciary. Finally, in the most innovative provision, acts of Congress and treaties were to be "the supreme law of the respective states" and binding on state courts.

Debate over the New Jersey Plan was brief, and it was rejected decisively. Paterson and Luther Martin made theoretical arguments in its favor based on state sovereignty and also argued that public opinion was unprepared for more radical changes. Opponents replied that the Convention was free to propose anything and criticized the injustice of the plan and likely impotence of the government it proposed. On 19 June the Convention voted by seven states to three (with one divided) to abandon the proposals. Connecticut and Maryland, whose delegates had been involved in drafting the plan, were among the states who failed to support it. The plan and its fate vividly illustrated the dilemma of delegates from the smaller states. Many of them wished to make substantial enlargements in the powers and structure of the national government but only if they were guaranteed that their states would not be overwhelmed within it.

3. THE CONNECTICUT COMPROMISE AND FEDERALISM

For the next two weeks the Convention made little progress. Debate ranged over many issues, but the question of representation in the national legislature had to be resolved before others could be addressed. Representation proportional to population in both houses was supported by six well-populated or growing states (Massachusetts, Pennsylvania, Virginia, North Carolina, South Carolina, and Georgia) but opposed by five other states (Connecticut, New York, New Jersey, Delaware, and Maryland). Debate became increasingly acrimonious, supporters of proportional representation charged their opponents with narrow self-interest, delegates on the other side refused to yield, and some even threatened to withdraw.

The impasse was broken in early July. On 2 July there was a tie vote on representation. (The vote of Georgia was divided.) Immediately Roger Sherman of Connecticut proposed that the matter be referred to a committee, which was then chosen with one member from each state. None of the strongest advocates of representation proportional to population was included; large-state members were generally moderates while those from the other states were insistent on some equality of state representation. Three days later the chairman, Elbridge Gerry (*see* figure 37b), reported its proposal: states should have equal votes in the upper house while money bills should originate in the lower house and not be subject to amendment in the upper. (This has come to be called the Connecticut (or Great) Compromise; equal representation for states in the upper house had been first suggested by delegates from Connecticut and by John Dickinson of Delaware in early June and formally proposed by the Connecticut delegation after the defeat of the New Jersey Plan.) For two weeks the decision was delayed. (During this time the Convention approved the system of reapportioning congressional seats according to periodic censuses.) On 16 July the compromise was finally accepted with five states voting in favor, four against, and one divided. (Georgia now voted against compromise, but North Carolina voted in favor. Massachusetts's vote was divided. No delegates from New York or New Hampshire were present.)

The outcome was really a concession not a compromise. Georgia and North Carolina, which defected from the "large-state" bloc on crucial votes, were relatively unpopulated and undeveloped states, large states only in terms of anticipated growth. Elbridge Gerry, who chaired the committee and helped divide the vote of Massachusetts, was an older, conservative delegate never committed to the expansive nationalism of some of his younger colleagues. Generally, though, what lay behind the compromise was a sense of crisis and impasse; delegates from the smaller states would not cooperate without some concession. Many "large-state" delegates were unhappy (notably James Madison), and some went so far as to hold a meeting the next morning to try to concert a strategy to overturn the compromise, but they were unable to agree even among themselves, and the decision was not reconsidered in the Convention itself once the final vote was taken.

Afterwards, from 17 to 26 July, the Convention dealt with miscellaneous points before adjourning while a committee produced a draft constitution. The jurisdiction of the federal courts was extended and the negative on state laws rejected. This was

461

a significant retreat from the grant of broad and coercive powers to the national government over the states in the Virginia Plan. Along with the Connecticut compromise these decisions initiated the development of America's distinctive federalism – a system in which both the states and federal government maintain large areas of their own competence and federal courts act as arbiters of the limits of state and federal power.

4. NATIONALISM AND SECTIONALISM

The drafting committee (Committee of Detail) met on 26 July and reported on 6 August. Under the chairmanship of John Rutledge of South Carolina, it consisted of five members, among whom James Wilson was probably the most active. Beginning with the amended Virginia Plan and drawing upon the constitutions of the states (particularly Massachusetts and New York) and the Articles of Confederation, the committee produced a document closely resembling the final Constitution. Much was set out in detail which had only been sketched previously, including provisions for the internal organization of Congress, a definition of the jurisdiction of the courts, and a grant of powers to the President.

In two important ways the committee went beyond what the Convention had already decided; the draft set out a list of specific powers granted to the national government (along with a complementary list of powers denied to state governments), and it made the first detailed provisions for the executive and judiciary. The powers granted included – among others – powers to tax and to borrow money, to regulate foreign and inter-state commerce, to make war, and to establish inferior courts and criminal law in certain areas, along with the right to enact all laws "necessary and proper" to execute these or other powers vested in the federal government by the Constitution. Although the grant was broad-ranging, it was also significant that powers were specifically enumerated and limited. State governments were forbidden to engage in diplomatic relations (including relations with each other) or to wage wars of their own, and were also prohibited from coining money, issuing paper money "without the consent" of Congress, or laying duties on imports. For the first time the President was given independent powers in foreign and military affairs and also the right to recommend legislation. In the section on the judiciary, the draft provided for inferior federal courts (in addition to and subordinate to the Supreme Court) and gave a broad definition of the jurisdiction of federal courts. The conception of a sovereign legislature was giving way to a new vision of a separate legislature, executive, and judiciary, each with independent powers. The draft did not, however, set out the relationship between the three branches in the form finally approved; the President was still to be elected by Congress, the Senate had powers to make treaties, to make judicial and diplomatic appointments, and to act independently in settling disputes between states, and the Supreme Court was to try impeachments. The draft also contained other miscellaneous provisions that were later rejected – a fixed ratio of representation to population in apportioning the House of Representatives, a requirement for a three-quarters majority in Congress to override a veto and two-thirds to admit a new state, and a proposal for property qualifications for federal officers.

The draft also made three concessions to southern interests. This was most immediately a response to the demand by Charles Cotesworth Pinckney of South Carolina on 23 July for "some security to the Southern States agst. an emancipation of slaves, and taxes on exports." But an accommodation of southern interests was also fostered by the widespread recognition of the fundamental nature of the North–South division. The draft made three explicit concessions to the South: no tax or duty was to be laid upon exports, the slave trade ("the migration or importation of such persons as the several states shall think proper to admit") was neither to be taxed nor prohibited, and no navigation act was to be passed without a two-thirds majority in each house of Congress. (Southerners feared that measures to promote northern shipping might increase freight costs on their exports.)

During the next three weeks questions about slavery provoked bitter controversy. On 8 August northern delegates attacked slavery on both pragmatic and moral grounds and proposed taking no account of slaves in allocating congressional representation, but the three-fifths clause was reaffirmed by a vote of ten states to one (New Jersey). On 21–2 August critics of slavery were joined by the largest slaveholder in the Convention, George Mason, who bemoaned slavery and attacked the slave trade in particular. South Carolinians replied by impugning the motives of Virginians (who, they claimed, would profit if the closure of the foreign slave trade increased the value of their existing holdings) and defending slavery on grounds of economics and morality. They were joined by northerners (notably Roger Sherman and Oliver Ellsworth from Connecticut) who did not wish to upset a delicate sectional balance. The matter was referred to a committee which reported its proposals on 24 August. Congress could not stop the slave trade until 1800 (but could impose a limited tax upon it), the prohibition on export duties was reiterated, but the requirement of a two-thirds majority for navigation acts was abandoned. There was desultory debate up until 29 August, and delegates from South Carolina were able to secure an additional eight years for the slave trade (until 1808) and a new clause (copied from the Northwest Ordinance) requiring states to return fugitive slaves apprehended within their borders. On the only significant roll-call vote (to extend the time during which the slave trade was protected), the three states of the Deep South (Georgia, South Carolina, and North Carolina) were joined by the New England states (New Hampshire, Massachusetts, and Connecticut) and Maryland.

Of the three major "compromises" in the Convention, the slave trade compromise provides the clearest example of give-and-take between readily identifiable interest groups. The multiplicity of issues raised and the inter-regional nature of the alliances made it possible to do business. So too did the desire – expressed even by the most violent speakers for and against slavery – to strike a bargain. Although it took time to work out the details, the broad outlines of a possible compromise had been apparent from the start, and the final terms were accepted with little difficulty.

Certainly questions relating to slavery were among the most vexatious at the Convention, but the overall importance of slavery in the formation of the Constitution should not be overestimated. Representatives of no other sectional interest (and there were several which had previously provoked bitter quarrels in national politics) made such strident and persistent demands, but business was done when it had to be, and the issue did not dominate the proceedings of the Convention nor intrude much into the text of the Constitution. As one historian has pointed out, "It would have been impossible to establish a national government in the eighteenth century without recognizing slavery in some way" (Ohline, 1971, p. 582). The provisions in the Constitution which dealt directly with slavery were the three-fifths clause (with consequences for congressional apportionment, for taxation and, in the final draft, for the election of the President), the protection of the slave trade, and the fugitive slave clause. (Some historians have also seen concern to protect slavery in provisions about citizenship and domestic violence and a few other miscellaneous clauses, but it is unlikely that slavery was a primary consideration in drafting these other articles.) More significantly the word "slave" was deliberately not used in the text, it being thought wrong, in Madison's words of 25 August, "to admit in the Constitution the idea that there could be property in men." The omission was revealing both of the moral issue and the difficulty that participants had in confronting it. The Constitution neither strengthened nor undermined slavery; faced with a fundamental moral problem, the delegates chose ultimately to avert their gaze.

5. THE PRESIDENCY

By the end of August the most important unresolved issues related to the presidency. From the beginning it had been clear that the executive would pose particular difficulties for the Convention. Americans of the revolutionary generation were deeply suspicious of executive power and had no obvious models for a national executive. Prior Congresses had tried various ways of delegating executive power, but none had been notably successful and almost no reference was made to them at the Convention. Constitutions of the individual states contained a bewildering variety of provisions about state executives. Finally, as the rest of the draft Constitution evolved, interest groups emerged with stakes in specific proposals about the executive.

Nevertheless, there was always a small group committed to a strong and energetic presidency, most notably James Wilson, Gouverneur Morris, and Alexander Hamilton. All had been associated with Robert Morris during the difficult years when he managed national finances (*see* Chapter 37, §3), and they had concluded that the United States needed a much more effective administration. They also had theories about the necessity of energetic government and strong leadership in nation-building. (Even though they often cooperated with men like Madison, there was an important distinction between their "executive" nationalism and the more "parliamentary" vision of the Virginia Plan.) Throughout the Convention these men fought to have the president elected independently of the legislature, to give him a veto, and to grant him considerable powers of his own. These delegates were always a minority, but they achieved a surprising amount, and their achievements can be attributed to tenacity and exceptional skill in parliamentary maneuver.

It was determining the method of electing the president (along with the closely related issues of length of term and the possibility of re-eligibility) that caused particular difficulty throughout the Convention. The initial decision of 29 May that the executive be chosen by the legislature for a seven-year term with no possibility of re-election was opposed by a small group who advocated popular election (principally James Wilson and other "executive" nationalists) and by others who wished to give state governments a role in the election. Questions were raised whether election by the legislature would undermine the executive's independence, whether a long term would make him too powerful, and whether ineligibility for re-election would destroy an incentive for good behavior. Later on, practical questions of interest intruded as well; small states opposed allocating votes on population alone, the South insisted upon taking some account of slaves (hence opposing popular election), and peripheral states worried about a body of electors assembling at a central place.

The result was continuing dissatisfaction. Time and again the delegates returned to the problems of election, term, and re-eligibility in a situation that one historian has compared to "three-dimensional chess" (Roche, 1961, p. 810). Various proposals suggested that the president be elected by electors chosen by state legislatures; by state governors or electors chosen by them; by the national legislature choosing among nominees made by the people; by the national legislature in the first instance with re-election by electors chosen by state legislatures; even by a group of national legislators chosen by lot. None of these suggestions found much support. Terms were proposed ranging from two years to life ("during good behavior"), and ineligibility and re-eligibility were canvassed again and again. In mid-July a proposal by Oliver Ellsworth for an electoral college briefly commanded majority support but foundered on fears by larger states about the allocation of electors. Although unable to settle on an alternative, delegates were increasingly worried by objections to legislative election, and their anxieties and divisions were skillfully exploited by James Wilson and Gouverneur Morris. The final break came late in August. Playing on small-state apprehensions that the votes of the Senate would be swamped in legislative election by joint ballot of both houses, Gouverneur Morris moved election by electors once again, and several consequent motions resulted in tie votes. The deadlock was apparent, and on 31 August the Convention referred the question of presidential election to the "Committee on Postponed Matters" appointed that day.

This committee (chaired by David Brearly and including both Madison and Gouverneur Morris) proposed an acceptable, if inelegant, solution on 4 September. The president was to serve for a four-year term with no limit on re-eligibility. He was to be elected by electors voting in their respective states (which reassured states at the periphery). Each state could choose its electors as its legislature directed (leaving open the possibility of popular participation), and each state was entitled to a number of electors equal to the state's combined representation in both houses of Congress. (This took account of free population and of the slaves of the South but gave less populous states a small bonus from their representation in the Senate.) If no candidate received a majority, election would be made by the Senate (a further sop to the small states). This last point alone proved unacceptable. Delegates feared concentrating too much power in the Senate, and on 6 September the proposal was amended so that inconclusive contests would be settled by the House of Representatives, "the members from each State having one vote." At last the system of presidential election was complete.

The question of the president's powers was neither addressed at such length nor settled so clearly. The Virginia Plan contained the potentially broad grant of "the executive rights vested in Congress by the Confederation," but after objections in early June executive authority was reduced to powers to execute the laws and to appoint to some offices. (The Senate, it was proposed, would appoint most high officers.) This was the situation until the Committee of Detail reported in early August. In a passage almost certainly drafted by James Wilson and closely modeled on the New York state constitution (which established the strongest executive in the 13 states), the report gave substantial independent powers to the president. He was to be commander-in-chief of the armed forces. He was authorized to carry on diplomacy (although the Senate was still empowered to make treaties). He had a role to play in legislation with power to recommend measures to Congress and to exercise a veto, although it could be overturned by a vote of two-thirds in each house of Congress.

The proposed powers provoked surprisingly little discussion or opposition; as business continued, the Convention even increased presidential powers. Instead of creating a council of state which might have circumscribed the president's freedom to act in administrative affairs, the brief provisions about the heads of executive departments seem to envision them in a subordinate role. The president was authorized to make

465

treaties and to appoint judges and ambassadors with the "advice and consent" of the Senate. (The meaning of the phrase was unclear at the time, but in practice the initiative passed to the president (see Rakove, 1984).) Moreover, in the final text there was a contrast between the grant of legislative powers "herein specified" to Congress and the grant of executive powers without qualification to the president. It was later argued (by some former delegates among others) that the Constitution grants the president executive powers broadly understood of which the specific ones mentioned are merely examples.

In the presidency the Convention created an office with considerable independence and potential. The president had independent powers and a source of election independent of Congress. Drafting left room for the expansion of presidential authority by usage and interpretation. Yet the executive's role was not completely separated from that of the legislature or judiciary. As they fitted the executive into the new structure of government, delegates were beginning to work according to the evolving theory of "checks and balances." The older doctrine of "separation of powers" sought to isolate completely independent roles for legislature, executive, and judiciary (*see* Chapter 76, §4). The framers of the Constitution did seek to give each of the three branches of government a role of its own but also to commingle their activities to a degree, in order that the business of government would be carried on with deliberation and restraint and also so that any branch that tried to exceed its legitimate powers could be curbed by the others.

6. OTHER BUSINESS; OTHER VIEWS

The judiciary was the branch of government to which the Convention paid least attention. In the initial discussion of the Virginia Plan the proposal for a national judiciary was easily accepted, but it was decided not to have federal courts inferior to the Supreme Court. In practice this would have left most of the adjudication of federal law to state courts, and this was explicitly proposed in the New Jersey Plan. Indeed this would have been the effect of the first version of the eventual "supremacy clause," which was proposed on 17 July by the most ardent supporter of states rights at the Convention, Luther Martin, as an alternative to a federal negative on state laws. His proposal that federal laws and treaties should be "the supreme law of the individual states" and the courts of the states "bound thereby in their decisions, any thing in the respective laws of the individual states to the contrary notwithstanding" was accepted unanimously. As things then stood, this meant that state courts would have decided questions of federal law bound by state rules of procedure and state constitutions; subsequent development altered things completely. On 18 July the Convention decided to provide for inferior federal courts. Later on, Martin's proposal itself was amended to make state constitutions (as well as laws) subordinate to the federal Constitution (as well as to federal laws and treaties). Still, details about the judiciary were so sketchy in the Constitution that the work was only truly completed by the Judiciary Act of 1789 (principally written by the former delegate Oliver Ellsworth). This Act not only defined the structure of federal courts and their particular jurisdiction but established an appellate jurisdiction whereby federal courts could review state court decisions that assertedly conflicted with the federal Constitution or laws. In this final refinement of American federalism, federal courts adjudicated federal laws, state courts adjudicated state laws, but federal courts had the final say in resolving conflicts between state and national authority.

The courts were not, however, given a final say in determining the limits of federal authority; the Constitution is notably silent on judicial review – the principle that the courts are the final interpreters of the Constitution with the power to void unconstitutional acts by other branches of government – although it has become a fundamental feature of American constitutional law. Some delegates did make incidental remarks assuming that the courts would exercise some sort of review, but others rejected it unequivocally, and it is probable that a majority of delegates who thought about the question would have maintained that each branch of government had the authority to interpret the Constitution for itself but not to bind other branches. On the other hand, the supremacy clause did make the most forceful statement of judicial authority in any American constitution to date, the doctrine of judicial review was already developing in American courts, and it was later possible to argue that it was implied in the Constitution. Certainly historians continue to disagree about the delegates' intentions and about the general understanding of judicial review at the time. (For good statements of conflicting points of view, see Rossum, 1987, pp. 232–9 and McCaughey, 1989, pp. 491–7.)

Likewise significant in the development of constitutional law were the prohibitions on state governments. The Committee on Detail in early August proposed the first specific restraints, which were designed to keep states from meddling in military affairs, diplomacy, or international trade. Also included was a prohibition on states (without the consent of Congress) emitting bills of credit or making anything but specie legal tender in payment of debts. These restrictions on economic regulation were debated and extended in late August (although the debates were brief and rather confused) and strengthened further by the final drafting committee. The final text of the Constitution also prohibited states passing any "ex post facto Law, or Law impairing the Obligation of Contracts" – the so-called contract clause. These limits on the powers of state governments to regulate domestic economic affairs have attracted much attention from historians who have argued that the Constitution was designed to protect property rights, but the principal concern of the delegates was probably to secure an orderly and uniform system of interstate commerce, an American "common market." It is also true that people in 1787–8 (including delegates to the Convention) were uncertain about the precise significance of these provisions, and for many years afterwards the restrictions seem to have had little practical effect (see Boyd, 1987). They were important not because they immediately increased the exercise of federal power but because they opened the way for increases in the future.

Meanwhile, during August, the Convention had gone through the draft Constitution making several important changes and additions which were later incorporated in the final document. Rejecting a fixed ratio of representatives to population, delegates established a small House of Representatives that need not grow too large in the future. The Convention declined to fix property qualifications for federal office-holding or suffrage in federal elections; voting in federal elections was to be open to all who voted for state legislatures, which left precise suffrage requirements up to the individual states. Delegates decided that the Constitution should go into effect when ratified by popular conventions in nine states. (This echoed the condition in the Articles of Confederation requiring consent of nine states on important questions but avoided the requirement under the Articles for unanimous consent of the states for amendment.) When the question of western lands arose, delegates chose not to sanction extending federal control over any territory already under the jurisdiction of one of the existing states, but they did give the federal government authority over territory

467

outside state boundaries and also provided for the easy admission of new states into the Union.

As the debate went on, a few delegates were becoming increasingly alienated, including three – Mason, Gerry, and Randolph – who had played prominent and constructive roles earlier in the Convention. Unlike other unsatisfied delegates, who simply departed, these three continued active until the end. Harking back to older, revolutionary suspicions of power and corruption, they expressed worries that the central government would be too strong, that the liberties of the people were threatened, and, to a lesser extent, that the independence of the states was at risk. They also felt that the interests of their own regions were not properly protected. Throughout August they lodged continuous objections to the powers of the president and the Senate and the possibility of collusion between them. They proposed detailed restrictions on federal military power and expressed strong anxieties about the small number of people necessary to make treaties and to regulate trade. Although some of Mason, Gerry, and Randolph's specific proposals were accepted, by the end of the month each had made it clear that he might not accept the Convention's final proposals, and Mason had called for a second convention. Early in September Mason proposed the creation of a small council of state drawn from different regions of the country in order to check the president's power and to safeguard regional interests. On 12 September Gerry and Mason proposed adding a bill of rights to the Constitution.

This proposal illustrated the often positive nature of Mason, Gerry, and Randolph's opposition. Their political instincts were sound and their suggestion constructive. The decision not to include a bill of rights (taken with little discussion and by a unanimous vote) was undoubtedly a liability during the ratification debate. The first ten amendments to the Constitution (drafted by James Madison) promptly added one (*see* Chapter 28, §3), and it did not weaken the new government; instead it helped to secure the long-term acceptance of the Constitution and played a fundamental role in the later development of American constitutionalism. Even if they were critical of many details, Mason, Gerry, and Randolph did want a stronger national government substantially like the one proposed; ultimately their opposition led not to the rejection of the Constitution but to its modification and completion.

Meanwhile, in the first weeks of September, the Convention moved to put the finishing touches on the proposed Constitution. The Committee on Postponed Matters proposed an acceptable method of impeachment in which the House of Representatives would vote an indictment (impeachment) and the Senate would act as a court to try the officer impeached. James Madison proposed a workable process of amendment whereby amendments could be proposed by either two-thirds of Congress or two-thirds of the state legislatures and then he accepted when ratified by three-quarters of the states. On 8 September the Convention appointed a five-member Committee of Style to draft the final text of the Constitution; it included Madison and Hamilton, but it is generally conceded that Gouverneur Morris was the principal draftsman. The committee's report was debated from 12 to 15 September and accepted with only minor changes. On 16 September, after the three remaining opponents restated their objections, the amended document was accepted by a unanimous vote of the states present. The next day, with Washington presiding and Benjamin Franklin delivering a brief valedictory, the engrossed Constitution was read and signed, and the Convention adjourned to await the decisions of the state ratifying conventions.

7. CONCLUSION: THE CONSTITUTION

Writing shortly after the Convention (in *The Federalist*, no. 45), James Madison gave his judgment of what the Constitution had achieved: "The changes which it proposes, consist much less in an addition of NEW POWERS to the Union, than in the invigoration of its ORIGINAL POWERS," an invigoration accomplished by constructing "a more effectual mode of administering them." This comment by "the Father of the Constitution" suggests how best to judge the document. The change in the demarcation of power was not great; the federal government was given limited new powers (principally long-advocated ones over trade and revenue), and limited restrictions were imposed on state governments. On the other hand, there was a marked change in the structure of government (and thereby in the potential to exercise federal power more effectively). The article on the legislature created a government which represented the people and made laws which acted directly upon them. The next article instituted a federal executive endowed with broad competence. The provisions on the judiciary and the law not only made the Constitution supreme law but ensured that it could be pleaded as ordinary law in every court in the land. The states had a role to play in federal government and broad areas of their own authority, but they also had to obey the law.

Even if the results were a departure from recent practice, this did not mean that they departed from revolutionary principles or recent experience. The American Revolution had sought to preserve liberty and the rule of law. In the heady days of 1775–6 the struggle had been carried on by mass action and the assertion of local rights. During the long years of war and troubled peace, action by crowds and committees proved cumbersome and often intrusive on private rights; in a series of practical experiments in constitutionalism, more structured governments had been established in the states with greater legitimacy but more carefully limited powers. Nationalism too was a product of Revolution, and the army and Congress were America's first national institutions. In 1775 boycotting British trade had seemed not only a good political tactic but an assertion of America's sturdy self-reliance; economic setbacks over the next decade demonstrated Americans' dependence on world trade and the need for effective commercial policy. This was the background against which the delegates acted and against which their achievement can be judged. The Constitution created an American common market, an effective national government, a workable scheme of federalism, an embryonic system of constitutionalism limiting both state and national authority, and a scheme of representation open-ended enough to evolve towards representative democracy.

This did not mean that the framers thought that they had settled all possible specific questions about the nature and limits of governmental authority in the United States. Later, in *The Federalist*, no. 48, Madison himself sadly acknowledged that "mere parchment barriers" could never be relied on completely to prevent abuses of power. What the framers sought to create was quite literally a framework, a set of rules within which a continuing process of evolution and definition could take place. Their greatest achievement at the time was to find workable solutions to problems which had arisen during the Revolution and its aftermath; their greatest legacy was to create a system sufficiently open-ended to allow their successors to solve other problems as they arose in the future.

FURTHER READING

Beard, C. A.: *An Economic Interpretation of the Constitution of the United States* (New York: 1913); repr. (New York: Free Press, 1986).

Boyd, S. R.: "The contract clause and the evolution of American federalism, 1789–1815," *William and Mary Quarterly*, 44 (1987), 529–48.

Farrand, M.: "Compromises of the Constitution," *American Historical Review*, 9 (1904), 479–89.

——: *The Framing of the Constitution of the United States* (New Haven, Conn., and London: 1913); repr. (New Haven and London: Yale University Press, 1962).

Farrand, M. (ed.): *The Records of the Federal Convention of 1787*, rev. edn., 4 vols. (New Haven, Conn.: Yale University Press, 1937; London: Oxford University Press, 1937); repr., 5 vols. (New Haven and London: Yale University Press, 1987). Vol. 5, *Supplement to Max Farrand's The Records of the Federal Convention of 1787*, ed. J. H. Hutson.

Finkelman, P.: "Slavery and the constitutional convention: making a covenant with death," *Beyond Confederation: Origins of the Constitution and American National Identity*, ed. R. Beeman, S. Botein and E. C. Carter (Chapel Hill and London: University of North Carolina Press, 1987).

Jillson, C. C.: "Constitution-making: alignment and realignment in the federal convention of 1787," *American Political Science Review*, 75 (1981), 598–612.

Levy, L. W., and Mahoney, D. J. (eds.): *The Framing and Ratification of the Constitution* (New York: Macmillan, 1987; London: Collier Macmillan, 1987).

McCaughey, E.: "*Marbury* v. *Madison*: have we missed the real meaning?," *Presidential Studies Quarterly*, 19 (1989), 491–528.

Murrin, J. M.: "Gordon S. Wood and the search for liberal America," *William and Mary Quarterly*, 44 (1987), 597–601.

Ohline, H. A.: "Republicanism and slavery: origins of the three-fifths clause in the United States Constitution," *William and Mary Quarterly*, 28 (1971), 563–84.

Rakove, J. N.: "Solving a constitutional puzzle: the treatymaking clause as a case study," *Perspectives in American History*, 1 (1984), 233–81.

Riker, W. H.: "The heresthetics of constitution-making: the presidency in 1787, with comments on determinism and rational choice," *American Political Science Review*, 78 (1984), 1–16.

Roche, J. P.: "The founding fathers: a reform caucus in action," *American Political Science Review*, 55 (1961), 799–816.

Rossiter, C.: *1787: the Grand Convention* (New York: Macmillan, 1966; London: Collier Macmillan, 1966).

Rossum, R. A.: "The courts and the judicial power," *The Framing and Ratification of the Constitution* (New York: Macmillan, 1987; London: Collier Macmillan, 1987), 222–41.

48

The debate over ratification of the Constitution

MURRAY DRY

WHEN the Federal Convention adjourned on 17 September 1787, it sent the completed Constitution to Congress with a resolution that "the preceding Constitution be laid before the United States in Congress assembled, and ... afterwards be submitted to a Convention of Delegates, chosen in each State by the People thereof, under the Recommendation of its Legislature, for their Assent and Ratification" (Farrand, 1937, vol. 1, p. 665). Thus began a remarkably full, candid, and thoughtful popular deliberation on the future of republican government in America. It took place in the newspapers, with the most important essays receiving wide circulation in different states, in pamphlets, and, ultimately, in the several state ratification conventions, whose members were either chosen by the state legislatures or elected directly by the people. The Constitution's acceptance was assured on 26 July 1788, when New York became the eleventh state to ratify, and by the time Rhode Island ratified the Constitution, on 29 May 1790, more than 1,900 convention votes had been cast: 1,157 for the Constitution, 761 against (see table 1).

Notwithstanding each state's distinctive interests and personalities, one can with justification speak about the ratification debate in general terms. Both Federalist

Table 1 Ratification of the Constitution: dates and votes by state convention

State	Date	Vote
Delaware	7 December 1787	30–0
Pennsylvania	12 December 1787	46–23
New Jersey	18 December 1787	38–0
Georgia	2 January 1788	26–0
Connecticut	9 January 1788	128–40
Massachusetts	6 February 1788	187–168
Maryland	21 April 1788	63–11
South Carolina	23 May 1788	149–73
New Hampshire	21 June 1788	57–47[a]
Virginia	26 June 1788	89–79
New York	26 July 1788	30–27
North Carolina	1 August 1788	84–184
	21 November 1789	194–77[b]
Rhode Island	29 May 1790	34–32[c]
Total		1,157–761

Sources: Elliot, 1891, except for [a]: Walker, 1888, pp. 42–3, 45; [b]: Trenholme, 1932, p. 238; and [c]: Kaminski, 1989, pp. 385, 390, note 55.

supporters of the Constitution and Anti-Federalist critics appealed to the principles of the American Revolution, swore their dedication to the union, and claimed to be acting on true federal and republican principles. The purpose of this essay is to explain the ratification debate in light of these grounds of agreement. Part 1 reviews the major decisions of the federal convention, introduces the major protagonists, and describes each party's approach to the debate and manner of framing the issue; part 2 examines the deepest ground of disagreement between the Federalists and Anti-Federalists, the nature of republican government; part 3 discusses the most important constitutional applications of that disagreement over republican government, those involving federalism and the separation of powers; part 4 considers the argument over the absence of a bill of rights; and the conclusion considers the significance of the ratification debate for the principles of the American Revolution as well as subsequent constitutional development in America.

I. POINTS OF DEPARTURE

The work of the Federal Convention and the "non-signers"   The framers of the Constitution decided to establish a genuine government for the union, rather than to attempt to strengthen a mere congress whose powers depended on the good will of the states. They also compromised on legislative apportionment, with equality in the Senate, to satisfy the small states, and on slavery and commercial regulation of navigation, to satisfy sectional concerns of North and South. The first decision accounts for the departures and opposition of the framers John Lansing and Robert Yates of New York and LUTHER MARTIN and John Francis Mercer of Maryland, and the sectional compromises account, in large part, for the non-signing of George Mason and Edmund Randolph of Virginia and Elbridge Gerry of Massachusetts. (Mason and Randolph also opposed the unitary executive, all three feared the power of the Senate, and Mason called for a bill of rights.) Randolph wrote a public letter explaining his refusal to sign and urging a second convention. Then, under James Madison's influence, he supported the Constitution in the Virginia convention, explaining his shift in terms of the needs of union, the fact that nine states had already ratified, and Massachusetts's proposal for recommendatory amendments (Elliot, 1891, vol. 3, pp. 25–6).

Identifying the protagonists and their writings   The major ratification debates took place in Pennsylvania (November–December 1787), Massachusetts (January–February 1788), Virginia (June 1788), and New York (June–July 1788). In Pennsylvania, James Wilson was the major spokesman for the Constitution, and he was assisted by BENJAMIN RUSH and Thomas McKean. William Findley, John Smilie, and Robert Whitehall opposed ratification. In Massachusetts, no prominent Anti-Federalists were among the convention delegates, although Gerry was present to answer questions in writing. The major Federalists were RUFUS KING, Nathaniel Gorham, and Fisher Ames. In addition, John Hancock and Samuel Adams played a major role in the recommendatory amendments proposal (Gillespie, 1989, pp. 141–61). In Virgina, the debate was largely between the Anti-Federalist PATRICK HENRY and JAMES MADISON, the "Father of the Constitution." Henry was assisted by Mason, William Grayson, and James Monroe. Madison was assisted by Randolph, Edmund Pendleton, Arthur Lee, George and Wilson Nicholas, and John Marshall. In New York, the debate was largely between ALEXANDER HAMILTON, in support of the Constitution, and MELANCTON SMITH, who recommended significant amendments but then voted to ratify. Hamilton was assisted by Robert Livingston and John Jay, Smith by Lansing.

When we turn to the major writings of the Federalists and Anti-Federalists, we encounter numerous pseudonyms. That is because the eighteenth-century practice was to emphasize the argument rather than the authority of the individual. The Federalists had the advantage, however: everyone knew that George Washington and Benjamin Franklin supported the Constitution, and the authors of the famous *Federalist Papers*, Alexander Hamilton, James Madison, and John Jay, who wrote under the pseudonym "Publius," were identified soon after publication. Likewise, Oliver Ellsworth was soon identified as the author of the "Landholder" essays, John Jay was known as the author of a pamphlet by "A Citizen of New York" in support of the Constitution, and two of James Wilson's most important speeches were published in pamphlet form (Ford, 1892, p. 137; Ford, 1888, pp. 67, 155; McMaster and Stone, 1888, pp. 217–31). The case is different with the Anti-Federalists. "Centinel," the major Pennsylvania Anti-Federal writer, was probably George Bryan, but his son, Samuel, also claimed authorship. "Agrippa," the major Massachusetts Anti-Federalist, appears to have been James Winthrop. It is unclear, however, whether New York's "Cato" was Governor George Clinton, and the evidence is only circumstantial for identifying the Maryland "Farmer" as John Francis Mercer. Not even the authors of the two best and most important Anti-Federal writings, the *Letters from the Federal Farmer* and the *Essays of Brutus*, long thought to be Richard Henry Lee and Robert Yates respectively, can be identified with certainty (Storing, 1981, intros. to 2.7, 4.6, 2.6, 5.1, 2.8, 2.9; Wood, 1974).

Two approaches to the ratification debate   Both parties to the debate expressed support for a candid examination of the Constitution and both identified good government with individual liberty (Storing, 1981, 2.9.2, 2.9.24, and Cooke, 1961, 1, 10, and 51). There was only partial agreement on the urgency of the situation, however. According to Publius, which name Hamilton chose after Publius Valerius, surnamed Publicola, a Roman consul in the first year of the Republic, "the crisis, at which we are arrived," may well determine "whether societies of men are really capable or not, of establishing good government from reflection and choice, or whether they are forever destined to depend, for their political constitutions, on accident and force" (Cooke, 1961, 1, p. 3). While both the Federal Farmer and Brutus referred to the country's critical situation (Storing, 1981, 2.8.1, 2.8.3, and 2.9.2), they thought there was plenty of time and the people should not be rushed. "Remember," Brutus wrote, "when the people once part with power, they can seldom or never resume it again but by force" (Storing, 1981, 2.9.3). But Patrick Henry refused to accept the critical period argument: "Sir, it is the fortune of a free people not to be intimidated by imaginary dangers. Fear is the passion of slaves. Our political and natural hemisphere[s] are now equally tranquil" (Elliot, 1891, vol. 3, p. 140).

Likewise, each side connected the debate over the Constitution to the principles of the Revolution differently. An Anti-Federalist from Massachusetts, writing as "A Republican Federalist," saw little difference between Great Britain and Congress.

> The revolution which separated the United States from Great-Britain was not more important to the liberties of America, than that which will result from the adoption of the new system. The *former* freed us from a *foreign subjugation*, and there is too much reason to apprehend, that the *latter* will reduce us to a *federal domination*. (Storing, 1981, 4.13.13)

473

In the New York convention, Thomas Treadwell decried the absence of a bill of rights as "depart[ing] widely from the principles and political faith of '76, when the spirit of liberty ran high, and danger put a curb on ambition" (Elliot, 1891, vol. 2, p. 401).

On the other side, Hamilton, also in the New York convention, suggested that, while an "extreme spirit of jealousy" was "natural" "[i]n the commencement of a revolution which received its birth from the usurpations of tyranny," it had become "predominant and excessive" (Elliot, 1891, vol. 2, p. 301; see also Cooke, 1961, 1, p. 5). And John Marshall, in a speech supporting the Constitution in the Virginia convention, emphasized the difference between Congress and Parliament (Elliot, 1891, vol. 3, pp. 225–6).

2. TWO VIEWS OF REPUBLICAN GOVERNMENT

The above remarks suggest that the Federalists and Anti-Federalists understood the requirements of republican government differently. The Anti-Federal position is presented first, because it was the deepest ground of the critics' opposition to the Constitution and the Federalists were forced to respond to it.

The Anti-Federalist conception emphasized persuasion over coercion and drew on two sources, Montesquieu's discussion of republics and the constitutional controversy which led to the American Revolution. From Montesquieu, they argued that only a small territory and homogeneous population could support republican government; otherwise "the public good is sacrificed to a thousand views ... and depends on accidents" (Storing, 1981, 2.9.11). From the Revolution, they argued that two essential ingredients of republican government, a substantial representation and jury trial, were not secure. A full and equal representation "is that which possesses the same interests, feelings, opinions, and views the people themselves would were they all assembled," it required regulation so that "every order of men in the community, according to the common course of elections, can have a share in [government]," including "professional men, merchants, traders, farmers, mechanics etc" (Storing, 1981, 2.8.15). The jury trial concern was twofold; article three provided for jury trial in all criminal cases, save impeachment, but it also provided for appellate review, by the Supreme Court, of all cases "in law and fact." That Congress could make exceptions to this was no guarantee that it would. And no jury trial was provided for in civil cases.

The Anti-Federalist "small republic" position differs from each of its sources. Montesquieu's argument about the public good went together with more restrictions on individual freedom than the Anti-Federalists, in general, supported. George Mason's proposal for a sumptuary law, to discourage consumption, is an illustrative exception to the rule (Farrand, 1937, vol. 2, pp. 344, 606). Likewise, the emphasis on representation moved away from Montesquieu's republic, where no such substitute for civic participation is mentioned. Except for "A Maryland Farmer," who proposed the direct government of the citizens with the Swiss cantons as his model, the Anti-Federalists took representation for granted. As for the revolutionary argument concerning "no taxation without representation," the application was imperfect, since in that case, unlike the one presented by the Constitution, no American had a vote for any representative in Parliament. The Anti-Federalists meant that the proposed federal representation was inadequate.

To explain what he meant by a substantial representation, the Federal Farmer argued that, while there was no constitutional aristocracy in America, there was a natural aristocracy, in contrast to a natural democracy; the former class consisted of governors, members of Congress, state senators, the principal officers of Congress, the superior judges, the "most eminent professional men," and the wealthy; the latter included "in general the yeomanry, the subordinate officers, civil and military, the fishermen, mechanics and traders, many of the merchants and professional men" (Storing, 1981, 2.8.97). The elective principle produces a substantial representation of the natural democracy, or the middling class, in the state governments; but in the federal government under the Constitution, election is bound to produce a largely if not exclusively aristocratic body.

The Federalist conception of republican government emphasized election as the means to an effective administration of government. The most extensive formulations came from a speech by James Wilson, on 24 November 1787 in the Pennsylvania Convention, which was subsequently published in pamphlet form, and from the *Federalist Papers*.

Wilson argued that representation was the key to America's superiority over both ancient governments and the British Constitution:

> the world has left to America the glory and happiness of forming a government where representation shall at once supply the basis and the cement of the superstructure. For representation, Sir, is the true chain between the people and those to whom they entrust the administration of the government; and though it may consist of many links, its strength and brightness never should be impaired. (McMaster and Stone, 1888, pp. 222, 223)

Wilson concluded by suggesting that the different "links" between the people and their representatives provided for the best possible government. "In its principles, Sir, it is purely democratical; varying indeed, in its form, in order to admit all the advantages, and to exclude all the disadvantages which are incidental to the known and established constitutions of government" (McMaster and Stone, 1888, pp. 230–1).

While Madison employed the term "republic" to distinguish direct from representative democracy, he also emphasized election as the essential and defining character of such a government (Cooke, 1961, 39, p. 251). Moreover, Madison's argument in *The Federalist*, no. 10 (*see* figure 38), reveals how election over the extended sphere improves republican government by refining it. The founder's task is to control the effects of faction, of interested and/or passionate action which violates the rights of citizens and/or the permanent and aggregate interests of the community. Since the majority principle was strong in America, it would control a minority faction; the real problem consisted in the majority faction, which threatened majority tyranny. Assuming that people will tend to give their suffrage to those who are able, election, in contrast to lottery, will result in the selection of the more able, and to a greater extent in a large, diverse constituency, where the competition will be keener for the relatively fewer seats. This could be called the "refinement" view of representation, in contrast to the Anti-Federal emphasis on "reflection." In addition, if the larger constituencies are also made up of more diverse economic interests, and Madison assumed they would be in America, then the candidates will have to moderate their views to gain a majority, just as the elected representatives will have to do the same thing in order to form legislative majorities.

Hamilton provided a more direct reply to the Anti-Federal argument concerning the class character of representation in *The Federalist* and in the New York convention. First, he claimed that "the idea of an actual representation of all classes of the people

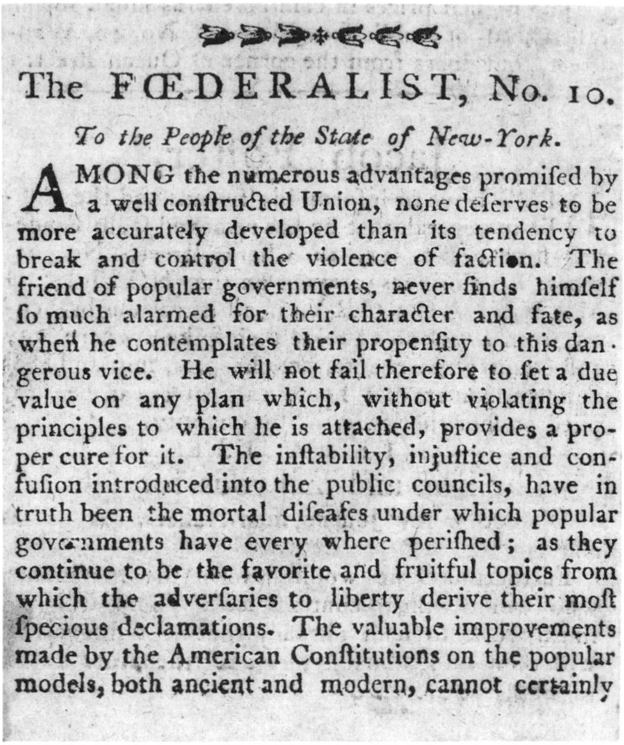

> ❧❧❧✦❦❦❦
>
> ## The FŒDERALIST, No. 10.
>
> *To the People of the State of New-York.*
>
> AMONG the numerous advantages promised by a well constructed Union, none deserves to be more accurately developed than its tendency to break and control the violence of faction. The friend of popular governments, never finds himself so much alarmed for their character and fate, as when he contemplates their propensity to this dan· gerous vice. He will not fail therefore to set a due value on any plan which, without violating the principles to which he is attached, provides a proper cure for it. The instability, injustice and confusion introduced into the public councils, have in truth been the mortal diseases under which popular governments have every where perished; as they continue to be the favorite and fruitful topics from which the adversaries to liberty derive their most specious declamations. The valuable improvements made by the American Constitutions on the popular models, both ancient and modern, cannot certainly

FIGURE 38 A detail from "The Federalist," no. 10, which first appeared in the "New-York Packet" on 23 November 1787. Madison's essay is now regarded as perhaps the greatest single American contribution to political theory.

by persons of each class is altogether visionary," since as long as people are free to choose, those in certain professions will defer to those in others. Hamilton argued that there were three key classes, or interests, in American society – the commercial, the landed, and the learned professions. As the merchant is the natural representative of the mechanics and manufacturers, so the large landholder is, especially on matters involving taxes, the natural representative of the small landholder; and the men of the learned professions, lawyers especially, will have the confidence of all parts of society (Cooke 1961, 35, pp. 219–20).

The Anti-Federalists challenged the alleged harmony of interests between large and small landholders, and they did not all share Hamilton's confidence in men of the learned professions. In the Massachusetts convention, Amos Singletary said:

> These lawyers, and men of learning, and moneyed men, that talk so finely, and gloss over matters so smoothly, to make us poor illiterate people swallow down the pill, expect to get into Congress themselves; they expect to be the managers of this Constitution, and get all the power and all the money into their own hands, and then they will swallow up all us little folks, like the great Leviathan. (Elliot, 1891, vol. 2, p. 102)

Such distrust was the basis of the Anti-Federal concern that a government too far removed from the people could not keep their confidence.

The fullest exchange on the character of representation in the new government took place between Smith and Hamilton in the New York convention. After defining natural aristocracy in terms of birth, education, talents, and wealth, as the Federal Farmer did, Smith made two claims on behalf of the middling class, or yeomanry.

476

First, they were by habit and necessity "more temperate, of better morals, and of less ambition, than the great." Second, they were "the best possible security to liberty," "because the interests of both the rich and the poor are involved in that of the middling class. No burden can be laid on the poor but what will sensibly affect the middling class" (Elliot, 1891, pp. 246–8).

Smith's argument was fully consistent with free choice, as long as the number of representatives was substantial enough for the yeomanry (or middling class) to get elected, and it was sound should that class embody the entire community. It also combined the Anti-Federal focus on civic virtue with the need to rely on representation.

In reply, Hamilton advanced two unusual and provocative arguments. First, "as riches increase and accumulate in few hands ..., virtue will be ... considered as only a graceful appendage of wealth, and the tendency of things will be to depart from the republican standard" (Elliot, 1891, vol. 2, p. 256). This hinted at a new republican form, where inequality of condition would flourish; perhaps that is why Hamilton sometimes used the term representative government (Elliot, 1891, vol. 2, p. 353). Then, he went after Smith's celebration of the middling class.

> It is a harsh doctrine that men grow wicked in proportion as they improve and enlighten their minds. Experience has by no means justified us in the supposition that there is more virtue in one class of men than in another. Look through the rich and the poor of the community, the learned and the ignorant. Where does virtue predominate? The difference indeed consists, not in the quantity, but kind, of vices which are incident to various classes; and here the advantage of character belongs to the wealthy. Their vices are probably more favorable to the prosperity of the state than those of the indigent, and partake less of moral depravity. (Elliot, vol. 2, p. 257)

What Hamilton saw as a division between the few and the many, Smith saw as a tripartite division, with an agricultural middle class holding the balance of power. Hamilton said inequality was inevitable if individual liberty was secured (Madison says the same in *The Federalist*, no. 10) and, if forced to choose, he opted for the public benefits of the vices of the few wealthy. Smith did not regard substantial inequality as inevitable and found the frugal yeoman as the representative of the public good.

Another element to Anti-Federal republicanism concerned the importance of religion as a source of character formation and a common set of beliefs. For example, in the Massachusetts convention, Charles Turner argued that "without the prevalence of *Christian piety, and morals,* the best republican Constitution can never save us from slavery and ruin." If the Constitution was to be ratified, he hoped the legislature would recommend to the several states that laws be passed providing for religious education.

> May *religion,* with sanctity of morals[,] prevail and *increase,* that the patriotic civilian and ruler may have the *sublime, parental* satisfaction of *eagerly* embracing every opportunity of mitigating the rigours of government, in proportion to that increase of morality which may render the people more capable of being *a law unto themselves.* (Storing, 1981, 4.18.2)

Others, including the Federal Farmer, criticized the Constitution's lack of any qualifications for office, aside from age, citizenship, and residency: "It can be no objection to the elected, that they are Christians, Pagans, Mohametans [*sic*], or Jews; that they are of any colour, rich or poor, convict or not. Hence, many men may be elected who cannot be electors" (Storing, 1981, 2.8.150). Herbert Storing has pointed out that the "Anti-Federalist position was not so much that government ought to foster religion as that the consolidating Constitution threatened the healthy religious situation as it then existed in the states" (Storing, 1981, vol. 1, p. 23).

The Federalists, who emphasized the checking of ambition by ambition, assumed the requisite amount of civic virtue (Cooke, 51, 55, pp. 349, 378).

This disagreement over the nature of republican government has been described in two different ways: as a social conflict between the many and the few, in which the Anti-Federalists spoke for the "radical Whig tradition of mistrust of governmental authority," while the Federalists "meant to restore and to prolong the traditional kind of elitist influence in politics that social developments, especially since the Revolution, were undermining" (Wood, 1969, pp. 520, 513); and as a political disagreement over whether republican government based on the principles of individual liberty and consent could succeed over an extended territory and population (Storing, 1981, vol. 1, pp. 5–6, 71–5). One difficulty with the former interpretation, however, is that the Constitution the Federalists were defending contained no property qualification for any offices, and it was generally known that the suffrage requirements, which were left to the states, would become more popular (Farrand, 1937, vol. 1, p. 49).

3. THE CONSTITUTIONAL STRUCTURE AND POWERS: FEDERALISM AND THE SEPARATION OF POWERS

We turn now to an examination of the most important constitutional issues: federalism and separation of powers.

Federalism   The federalism topics involve disputes over terminology (who were the true federalists?), over the preamble and the legality of the proposed Constitution, and over several provisions of Article I.

The Anti-Federalists charged that the supporters' appropriation of the name Federalists was an act of larceny, since they were the true federalists (Storing, 1981, vol. 1, pp. 8, 80). This issue was complicated by the ambiguity of usage during the Confederation period and the subsequent change in meanings as a result of the Constitution and the ratification debate. During the Confederation period, "federal" referred to measures designed to support and strengthen Congress. At the same time, the federal principle meant that the states were primary, not the union, and hence it was appropriate for the state legislatures to control the unicameral Congress, through election, recall, and federal reliance on state requisitions of men and money. As supporters of a measure to strengthen the authority of the union, the Constitution, the Federalists had a claim on their name; on the other hand, the opponents argued that the measures proposed were so strong as to go beyond the federal principle.

Both sides revised their views in light of the Constitution. The Federalists used the compromise over legislative apportionment and other provisions recognizing the states to argue that the Constitution was "partly federal, partly national." Most of the Anti-Federalists, on the other hand, moved away from the standard view of federalism, since they agreed that the Articles of Confederation were inadequate, precisely because requisitions, previously understood as the essence of a federal system, did not work, and they preferred to revise the proposed Constitution (Dry, 1989, pp. 65–9).

The debate over the preamble and the proposed mode of ratification of the Constitution shows how the terminological dispute was connected to a substantive issue. For example, when the preamble came under discussion in the Virginia Convention, Patrick Henry dramatically objected:

478

My political curiosity, exclusive of my anxious solicitude for the public welfare, leads me to ask who authorized them to speak the language of *We the People*, instead of *We the States*. States are the characteristic, and the soul of a confederation. If the states be not the agents of this compact, it must be one great, consolidated, national government, of the people of all the states. (Elliot, 1891, vol. 3, p. 22)

With Congress's limited instructions to the Federal Convention, to meet "for the sole and express purpose of revising the Articles of Confederation" in mind, Henry and other Anti-Federalists questioned the legality of the Federal Convention's work (Storing, 1981, vol. 1, pp. 12–14). The standard answer to this objection was that the Constitution was but a proposal until ratified by the people through specifically chosen conventions (see Wilson in McMaster and Stone, 1888, 219–20). But this reply was not sufficient to legitimate the ratification provision, which violated the Articles of Confederation in two ways: the ratification of nine states, rather than all 13, was sufficient to bring the Constitution into being, and the state legislatures were bypassed for the conventions. Luther Martin pressed this objection in the Federal Convention and again in his *Genuine Information* (Storing, 1981, 2.14.114). The fullest defense, alluded to in the Federal Convention by Hamilton and spelled out by Madison in *The Federalist*, no. 40, was that the mode of ratification was an exercise of the people's right to form and re-form governments, i.e., to revolution (Farrand, 1937, vol. 1, p. 283; Cooke, 1961, p. 265). Beyond the legal point, the Federalists, especially Madison, argued that a popular form of ratification, that is, through state conventions rather than state legislatures, was necessary to assure the supremacy of the new federal government (Farrand, 1937, vol. 1, pp. 122–3).

Due to the importance of federalism for the ratification debate, the major state ratification conventions focused their attention on provisions in Article I, to which we now turn. Topics of discussion included representation, the two- and six-year terms of office for the House and Senate, the "time, place, and manner" clause, and the extent of the legislative powers.

The concern about the possible misuse of the "time, place, and manner" clause reflects the extent of distrust more than any solid argument; Congress had to be able to provide for its own elections if a recalcitrant state (i.e., Rhode Island) refused to do so. The rotation and recall argument, which was not made in connection with the popularly elected house of representatives, reflects the traditional notion of federalism. If, as the Federalists claimed, the Senate was the branch of government representing the states, the state governments should be able to control their senators. But many were satisfied with the key elements of the compromise, according to which the states did elect their senators and were guaranteed their equal representation (Constitution, Article V). The argument for an increase in representation, which Smith and many other Anti-Federalists made, ultimately gets directed at a reduction in federal legislative powers. That is because no reasonable increase in federal representation could match the extent of representation in the states.

Hence the major Anti-Federal argument for constitutional change was for a redistribution of the powers of government, as between the nation and the states, to reflect the distribution of representation. Their most important proposals concerned restrictions on the federal powers to tax and to raise armies; the former should be limited to the power to tax foreign imports, and the latter should not extend to a general power to raise armies in time of peace, unless two-thirds of both houses support it (Storing, 2.9.126). Thus they attempted to reply to Hamilton's great challenge, expressed in *The Federalist*, no. 23, that one not embrace the contradiction of, on the one hand, supporting union and entrusting certain national objectives to the federal government, and, on the other hand, refusing to grant ample powers for the attainment of those objectives (Cooke, 1961, p. 151). To the question of how one could foresee the extent of the powers necessary for raising and supporting armies, Brutus assumed that the power would be granted when truly needed, and he also argued that the object of government in the United States was not only to "preserve the general government, and provide for the common defence and general welfare of the union," but also to support the state governments (Storing, 1981, 2.9.80). Seven state conventions proposed limits on the federal tax power, to the import, with requisitions as the backup provision; five state conventions proposed restrictions on standing armies; and four state conventions proposed a limitation on the powers to those "expressly" delegated (see table 2, p. 482).

The separation of powers   The separation of powers objections involved the powers of the Senate, the re-eligibility of the executive and the absence of a council of appointment, and the judiciary.

The Anti-Federalists' position on the separation of powers reflected their judgment that the threat to republican government came from a concentration of power in the hands of the few. Patrick Henry, Centinel, and A Maryland Farmer argued that the proposed Constitution was an unsuccessful hybrid of the pure separation of powers, which to them meant legislative supremacy, and mixed government, which required a hereditary monarch and nobility. Since the materials for a mixed government were not present in America, the only sound choice was to construct a government with a simple structure, where the middling class would predominate in the legislature and the legislature would be the supreme branch of government (Storing, 1981, vol. 1, pp. 53–63).

The most common Anti-Federalist criticism of the Senate, in addition to the absence of rotation and recall, discussed above, concerned that body's participation in the appointment and treaty-making powers. The Anti-Federalists preferred a council of appointment, elected by the legislature, as many of the state constitutions provided, and many preferred that treaties be approved by both houses.

The Anti-Federalist assessment of the executive was surprisingly moderate, in light of their apprehension about consolidated government. While Mason and Randolph opposed unity in the Federal Convention, neither made this point in expressing his objections after the federal convention adjourned, and there was general acceptance of a unitary executive, except, of course, for the council of appointment. The Anti-Federalists did oppose re-eligibility, however, which Hamilton and other Federalists regarded as an essential inducement to channeling ambition into constitutionally constructive action, good behavior. Most Anti-Federalists accepted the qualified veto also (Dry, 1987, pp. 285–7).

As for the judiciary, Brutus's prescient account anticipated the full development of both judicial review and federal judicial power (Storing, 1981, 2.9.130–196). By extending the judicial power to all cases in law and equity arising under the Constitution, Article III permitted the courts "to give the constitution a legal construction." That plus the equity jurisdiction gave the courts the power "to explain the constitution according to the reasoning spirit of it, without being confined to the words or letter." Hence, "the real effect of this system of government will ... be brought home to the feelings of the people through the medium of the judicial power" (Storing, 1981, 2.9.30).

Brutus argued that the courts should not be permitted to interpret the Constitution against acts of Congress, or, alternatively, if they were to have that power, they should be responsible to the electorate. He also thought that lower federal courts were unnecessary, as the states could provide the courts of first resort (Storing, 1981, 2.9.169, 183).

The fullest Federalist account of the separation of powers in the Constitution came from the *Federalist Papers*. To defend the Constitution's assignment of powers to the different branches of government, Madison argued that, rightly understood, which meant on the basis of Montesquieu's example of England and the state constitutions, the doctrine of the separation of powers was fully compatible with some sharing or overlapping of powers among the different branches, that it did not require a pure separation of kinds of power into distinct branches. It is an impressive argument.

To appreciate how the Anti-Federalists could object, it is necessary to recall that the most famous authors of the doctrine, Locke and Montesquieu, supported constitutional monarchy. Might not the republican form of government affect which branch receives the appointment power, the treaty-making power, and the direction of foreign affairs generally? And what about the number of individuals assigned to each branch? James Wilson, for example, shared the Anti-Federal concern that the Senate might have too much power (McMaster and Stone, 1888, pp. 326–7).

Hamilton's account of the judiciary in the *Federalist Papers* was in direct response to Brutus's essays. A comparison of *The Federalist*, no. 51, where the separation of powers doctrine was presented in terms of ambition checking ambition, with *The Federalist*, no. 78, where the judiciary was first discussed and its good behavior tenure was defended, yields the following tension. In the former Madison asserted that "the interest of the man must be connected with the constitutional rights of the place," and in the latter Hamilton maintained that a written constitution required, for its protection, a learned judiciary, insulated from popular control, whose "proper and peculiar province" was "the interpretation of the laws." The judiciary provided a distinctive function, and judges were expected to interpret the laws with learning and disinterestedness (Stoner, 1987, pp. 208–16).

Brutus agreed about the distinctiveness of the courts, but he thought the judiciary should not have the power to construe the Constitution. For Hamilton, the judges acted as the people's representatives in government by upholding the Constitution, which the people, through their popular ratification conventions, have laid down as their frame of government and fundamental law. The written Constitution plus an independent judiciary produces what is known as judicial review, the doctrine that a law contrary to the "manifest tenor" of the Constitution is void, or the Constitution has no legal standing (Cooke, 1961, 78, pp. 524–5).

The question whether or not to have lower federal courts with full jurisdiction over all cases in law and equity arising under the Constitution concerned federalism again. Brutus's proposal to rely on state courts to adjudicate federal questions was inconsistent with the new form of federalism, but it must be acknowledged that he predicted what came to be called "loose construction."

4. THE BILL OF RIGHTS: AN ANTI-FEDERALIST VICTORY, OF SORTS

The most common Anti-Federal argument against the Constitution concerned the absence of a bill of rights, and, in a certain sense, it was their only successful position.

The Constitution would not have been ratified without the promise, first made in the Massachusetts Convention and subsequently accepted, that recommendatory amendments accompanying a vote for unconditional ratification would be considered by Congress (Rutland, 1983, pp. 143–9). An examination of the arguments for and against the need for a bill of rights shows the Anti-Federalists to have had the stronger argument.

The main Federalist arguments in defense of the Constitution without a bill of rights

Table 2 Major amendments proposed by the Anti-Federalists, state by state

	Pa	Ma	Md	SC	NH	Va	NY	NC	RI
Jury trial in civil cases	<u>×</u>	×	×		×	×	×	×	×
Jury trial in criminal cases with no appeal on matters of fact			×						
No interference in state election laws unless the state fails to provide for elections	<u>×</u>	×	<u>×</u>	×	×	×	×	×	×
State control of its militia	<u>×</u>		<u>×</u>			×	×	×	×
Strict separation of powers	<u>×</u>					×		×	×
Non-supremacy of treaties	<u>×</u>							×	
Restriction of jurisdiction of federal courts	<u>×</u>	×	×		×	×	×	×	×
Limitation of powers to those "expressly" or "clearly" delegated		×	×	×	×		×		
No direct taxation unless the import tax is insufficient and/or requisitions fail		×	<u>×</u>	×	×	×	×	×	×
No congressionally authorized monopolies		×			×		×		×
Special two-thirds congressional majority required for navigation acts						×		×	
Restrictions on a standing army			<u>×</u>		×	×	×	×	×
Limitation on presidential re-eligibility						×	×	×	
Limitation on Senate re-eligibility							×		
State recall of senators							×		×
Oath not to violate state constitutions							×		
Provision for freedom of speech and/or press	<u>×</u>		×			×	×		
Provision for freedom of religion and/or rights of conscience			<u>×</u>		×		×		×

Sources: Schwartz, 1980, pp. 658–60, 712–13, 732–5, 756–7, 760–1, 840–5, 911–18; and Elliot, 1891, Vol. 1, pp. 334–7, Vol. 4, p. 249.
Note: <u>×</u> indicates that the proposed amendment was defeated; all others were passed.

were: first, the entire Constitution, as it provides for a well-framed government with power checking power and offices filled by election, is a bill of rights; second, there is an internal bill of rights, especially in Article 1, sections 9 and 10; and third, unlike the state governments, the federal government is one of enumerated powers, and hence what is not enumerated is not given, and the state bills of rights remain in force (McMaster and Stone, 1888, pp. 143–4, 252–4; Cooke, 1961, 84). The Anti-Federal responses, in reverse order, were: first, the clear supremacy of the federal Constitution and the extensiveness of the powers granted call into question any reliance on the state bills of rights on the one hand, or the implied restrictions on powers on the other; second, to the extent that one might rely on the principle of implied restrictions on powers, the very fact that certain restrictions are noted suggests, if anything, that what is not expressly reserved is granted; and third, the general argument about a well-constructed government points back to the discussions of federalism and republican government (Storing, 1981, 2.9.22–33; vol. 1, pp. 64–70).

An examination of the major Anti-Federal proposals for amendments reveals the significance of the federalism issue as well as the differences between most of their proposals and what eventually resulted in the first ten amendments (table 2).

In one sense, however, the Anti-Federalist demand for a bill of rights derived from their understanding of republican government. That goes back to the importance of mild government and the educational value of proclaiming the rights and keeping the people aware of them. As the Federal Farmer put it, "If a nation means its systems, religious or political, shall have duration, it ought to recognize the leading principles of them in the front page of every family book" (Storing, 1981, 2.8.196). The affirmation of rights against the government does reflect Anti-Federal constitutionalism. Unlike several state bills of rights, however, the rights enumerated in the Bill of Rights are largely individual rather than collective. Consequently, the civic education that the Bill of Rights has provided has been primarily to support individual rights rather than obligations to the community.

5. CONCLUSION

The ratification of the Constitution (*see* figure 39) established the American frame of government and thereby completed the American Revolution, since the principles of the Revolution looked up to collective self-government in the service of individual liberty, the natural rights of life, liberty, and the pursuit of happiness. Consideration of the arguments on the merits, as presented in the ratification conventions and in the fullest and most thoughtful writings on the Constitution, yields the conclusion that the Federalists won because they had the better argument (Storing, 1981, vol. 1, p. 71). The Anti-Federal critics were in part the victims of their own candid patriotism; they wanted to secure the blessings of liberty, and they acknowledged that this required a genuine government, rather than modified Articles of Confederation. Hence, they never could answer Hamilton's charge that they were attempting to reconcile contradictions by agreeing to the proper objects of a national government but refusing to grant the necessary powers, i.e., the powers to tax and raise armies without limit (Cooke, 1961, 23, p. 151). To assume that there were limits to the resources that might be necessary to wage war or enforce treaties, or to assume that the states could be relied on to supply what was needed in an emergency, was to overlook the lessons of the confederation period.

The Anti-Federalists nonetheless deserve to be considered junior partners to the

Federalists in the crowning achievement of the American founding. First, they were thoughtful critics of a new form of republican government, one that emphasized effective administration and relied primarily on self-interest rather than love of country. Future generations of Americans have found it useful to be reminded of the limits of this largely successful "low but solid" approach to free government. Second, the Anti-Federalists' call for a bill of rights did succeed, even if it was not all that they had in mind. Third, on important constitutional issues, federalism and the separation of powers, Anti-Federalist arguments survived ratification, albeit with modification. This is especially true with federalism, where advocates of both the strict construction of federal legislative powers and the states'-rights view of the union attempted to achieve the Anti-Federal objective of a balance between the nation and the states. Examples of the strict construction view include the opposition of Madison and Jefferson to the establishment of a national bank, in 1790, under the implied powers doctrine; examples of the states'-rights view include Madison's and Jefferson's opposition to the Alien and Sedition Acts of 1798, John Calhoun's nullification argument in the 1850s, and the secessionist argument at the outset of the Civil War. As for the separation of powers, two disputes can be connected to the ratification debate: the ongoing debate, since Washington's Neutrality Declaration in 1793, over the scope of executive power in war and foreign affairs, and the more recent division between supporters of the Bill of Rights, which includes the judicial power of enforcing rights against the government, and supporters of the Constitution, meaning primarily the

FIGURE 39 A series of allegories appeared in "The Massachusetts Centinel" from 16 January to 2 August 1788 showing the progress towards the ratification of the Constitution. The last of the series shows New York in place; North Carolina is swinging up, helped by a hand reaching from a cloud, and the crumbled pillar representing Rhode Island has a sign reading "The foundation good – it may yet be saved."

separation of powers and checks and balances among the political branches of government. This division departs somewhat from the ratification debate, as each side favors strong national government; the partisans of the Bill of Rights resemble the Anti-Federalists in their distrust of government, but not in their reliance on a strong federal judiciary to protect individual rights.

Finally, the contemporary disagreement about liberalism and republicanism, or individual rights versus communal, or communitarian, concerns (Sandel, 1984, pp. 1–11), can be related to the ratification debate over republican government. The contemporary communitarian position is not necessarily against big government, however, and the Anti-Federalist "small republic" position acknowledged the primacy of individual liberty.

484

FURTHER READING

Beeman, Richard, Botein, Stephen and Carter, Edward C. II (eds.): *Beyond Confederation: Origins of the Constitution and American National Identity* (Chapel Hill: University of North Carolina Press, 1987).

Cooke, Jacob (ed.): *The Federalist* (Cleveland and New York: World Publishing Co., 1961) [Internal citations refer to an essay number and, where appropriate, a page number as well; since the essay numbers are standard in all full editions, and the differences in the text are insignificant, any full edition of *The Federalist* may be consulted].

Dry, Murray: "The Anti-Federalists and the Constitution," *Principles of the Constitutional Order*, ed. Robert L. Utley Jr. (Lanham, Md.: University Press of America, 1989), 63–88.

——: "The case against ratification: Anti-Federal constitutional thought," *The Framing and Ratification of the Constitution*, ed. Leonard W. Levy and Dennis J. Mahoney (New York: Macmillan, 1987), 271–91.

Elliot, Jonathan: *The Debates of the State Conventions on the Adoption of the Federal Constitution, as Recommended by the General Convention at Philadelphia in 1787*, 3rd edn. (Philadelphia: Lippincott, 1891).

Farrand, Max (ed.): *The Records of the Federal Convention*, rev. edn. in 4 vols. (New Haven, Conn.: Yale University Press, 1937).

Ford, Paul Leicester (ed.): *Essays on the Constitution of the United States* (Brooklyn, NY: 1892); repr. (New York: Burt Franklin, 1970).

——: *Pamphlets on the Constitution of the United States, Published During its Discussion by the People, 1787–1788* (Brooklyn, NY: 1888); repr. (New York: Burt Franklin, 1971).

Gillespie, Michael: "Massachusetts," *Ratifying the Constitution*, ed. Michael Gillespie and Michael Liensch (Lawrence: University of Kansas Press, 1989), 138–67.

Gillespie, Michael, and Liensch, Michael (eds.): *Ratifying the Constitution* (Lawrence: University of Kansas Press, 1989).

Jensen, Merrill, Kaminski, John P., and Saladino, Gaspare J., et al. (eds.): *The Documentary History of the Ratification of the Constitution*, 8 vols. to date (Madison: State Historical Society of Wisconsin, 1976–).

Kaminski, John P.: "Rhode Island," *Ratifying the Constitution*, ed. Michael Gillespie and Michael Liensch (Lawrence: University of Kansas Press, 1989), 368–90.

Kesler, Charles (ed.): *Saving the Revolution: the Federalist Papers and the American Founding* (New York: Free Press, 1987).

Levy, Leonard W., and Mahoney, Dennis J. (eds.): *The Framing and Ratification of the Constitution* (New York: Macmillan, 1987).

McMaster, John Bach, and Stone, Frederick D.: *Pennsylvania and the Federal Constitution* (Philadelphia: Pennsylvania Historical Society, 1888).

Main, Jackson Turner: *The Antifederalists: Critics of the Constitution* (Chapel Hill: University of North Carolina Press, 1960).

Rutland, Robert Allen: *The Ordeal of the Constitution: the Anti-Federalists and the Ratification Struggle of 1787–1788* (Norman: University of Oklahoma Press, 1966).

——: *The Birth of the Bill of Rights: 1776–1791*, rev. edn. (Boston: Northeastern University Press, 1983).

Sandel, Michael (ed.): *Liberalism and its Critics* (New York: New York University Press, 1984).

Schwartz, Bernard: *The Roots of the Bill of Rights*, 5 vols. (New York: Chelsea House Publishers, 1980).

Stoner, James: "Constitutionalism and judging in the *Federalist*," *Saving the Revolution: the Federalist Papers and the American Founding*, ed. Charles Kesler (New York: Free Press, 1987), 203–18.

Storing, Herbert J.: "The 'other' Federalist papers: a preliminary sketch," *Political Science Reviewer*, 6 (1976), 215–47.

——: *The Complete Anti-Federalist*, 7 vols. (Chicago: University of Chicago Press, 1981); first

485

vol. separately pubd as *What the Anti-Federalists Were For!* [Internal references refer to the volume, entry number, and paragraph].

Trenholme, Louise Irby: *The Ratification of the Federal Constitution in North Carolina* (New York: Columbia University Press, 1932).

Walker, Joseph B.: *A History of the New Hampshire Convention* (Boston: Supples and Hurd, 1888).

Wood, Gordon S.: *Creation of the American Republic, 1776–1787* (Chapel Hill: University of North Carolina Press, 1969).

——: "The Authorship of *The Letters from the Federal Farmer*," *William and Mary Quarterly*, 31 (1974), 299–308.

PART 4

EXTERNAL EFFECTS OF THE REVOLUTION

49

Great Britain in the aftermath of the American Revolution

IAN R. CHRISTIE

THE series of setbacks and defeats encountered by the British in the American War of Independence – the surrender of Burgoyne's army at Saratoga, the subsequent intervention of France and Spain, the capture of Cornwallis's army at Yorktown – followed by the acknowledgment of the secession of the 13 North American colonies, created serious political tensions within Great Britain, and generated a sense of despondency about the country's future. Among the members of the political class, from the King downwards, the fear spread that its position as a leading great power had been destroyed, and that French world ascendancy was unavoidable. Very few far-sighted people – though there were a few – foresaw that the political independence of America would strike no serious blow at the natural economic interdependence of the two English-speaking communities. Even fewer foresaw the remarkable recovery of British power within a few years of the signing of a humiliating peace. In the immediate period of wartime and postwar crisis recriminations over the responsibility for disaster created bitter tensions among the politicians, and the repercussions spread widely among an informed public in the middling ranks of society. From the beginning of 1780 till the summer of 1784 the domestic political atmosphere was one of constant strain, until at last, with the war over and the process of repair and reconstruction begun, the natural conservative stability of the nation reasserted itself.

I. BRITAIN AND EUROPE

French statesmen believed in 1783 that they had successfully cut Great Britain down to size, and for the time being at least the country's pretensions to rank as a great power had been seriously checked. With the winning of independence by the Americans the Crown had lost a quarter of its subjects and a good deal more than a quarter of the economic resources, including shipping and seamen, which contributed to the sinews of war. In strategic terms the balance had been tilted adversely both in the New and in the Old World. American mainland bases which had provided a back-up for the defense of the West Indian portion of the British Empire had gone, and the return of East and West Florida to Spain enhanced that nation's military and naval position in the Caribbean. The situation of the British in the West Indies was also weakened by the cession of Tobago and St. Lucia, while in the Mediterranean the return of Minorca to Spain deprived the nation of an important naval base, the loss of which was to be signally felt at the beginning of the next round of wars against the Bourbon powers. Although in North America the British still retained possession of Newfoundland,

Canada, and the maritime provinces of Nova Scotia and New Brunswick, these represented little in the way of strength, and it was by no means clear whether Canada, in particular, might be a liability rather than an asset, a pawn in American hands readily open to invasion if ever the Americans saw fit to join any combination of Britain's enemies.

From the diplomatic viewpoint the war appeared to have clinched, to the advantage of France, the growing alienation of the British from one of their traditional allies – the United Provinces – which had already begun to show itself during the Seven Years' War. And by a cautious avoidance of any aggressive move against Hanover the French had managed to humiliate Britain without creating east of the Rhine any apprehensions about the balance of power which might have attracted European states towards the British camp. The general attitude in Europe immediately after the war was that Britain had become a negligible quantity in the scales of power, no longer alliance-worthy – a country which might be ignored in the considerations of European power politics.

Nevertheless, as events were soon to show, the situation was far from irretrievable. The British Isles still remained a formidable base for naval power, as its rulers well understood, and the impetus of the wartime naval construction program was determinedly prolonged into the years of peace. Whatever the losses in the West, the British position in the East had not been adversely affected. French pressures and pretensions had been beaten off, and, if anything, the British hold on India had been consolidated, carrying with it both present and future commercial advantage. The Dutch rivals in this area had been worsted and humiliated, being obliged by the peace terms to abandon their Indian trading base at Negapatam and to concede British demands for freedom of navigation in the Spice Islands. The great ships of the British East India Company still brought in their lucrative cargoes from Canton. Britain's freedom in the sea lanes was still secure in East and in West, and, within three or four years after being written off as of no account, British governments were once again exerting their weight in Europe, combatting French pretensions, and entering into the diplomatic combinations with Holland and Prussia which made up the Triple Alliance system of 1788. Behind this modest recovery on the international stage lay a saga of internal political recovery, administrative and financial modernization, and economic advance.

2. DOMESTIC POLITICAL DIFFICULTIES

Defeat in America temporarily disrupted the normal pattern of British domestic politics. Up till 1779 the ministry headed by Lord North appeared stable internally and assured of general support within Parliament and out-of-doors. The Declaration of Independence had appeared to vindicate the Cassandra-like prophecies of ministers, that from the start the colonial protests about Parliament's powers had been leading up to a repudiation of imperial control; and many of the men who had previously sympathized with the colonists and had signed petitions in their favor were alienated from them by the Declaration. The government at first received wide support for its policy of preserving imperial unity by force of arms, and it was not until defeat at Saratoga had shown up the limitations of British military power, and till France and Spain had become involved in support of the Americans, that disillusionment began to spread.

At one level this was manifested by dissensions within the ministry ostensibly over

Ireland (*see* Chapter 51). During much of 1779 the administration seemed in a parlous state. The Earl of Suffolk, Secretary of State for the Northern Department, was incapacitated and died in office. Through much of the year Lord North appeared to be on the verge of a nervous breakdown and unable to take steps either to secure the appointment of a successor or to deal with the pressures upon him from the Southern Secretary and the President of the Council to take decisive measures to resolve Irish grievances. Eventually these two ministers resigned, and the administration was reconstituted with two new secretaries of state. Thereafter it was to soldier on with a narrower political base until the virtual withdrawal of parliamentary confidence in March 1782 in the wake of the second major British military defeat at the hands of the colonists at Yorktown.

At another level discontent found a focus in the county association movement launched by Christopher Wyvill at York in December 1779. This public agitation, organized initially by the local gentry, and keyed to securing support from the upper and middling classes of society, began as a campaign to reduce taxation by curbing what was believed to be governmental corruption and extravagance, regarded as the mainstay of a misguided and inefficient administration in Parliament. As a protest by hard-pressed tax-payers it initially attracted wide support, and the leaders of opposition in Parliament soon sought to exploit it and fill their sails with the fair wind of public opinion. In response to widespread petitioning by the associators the Opposition brought forth its program of legislation against placemen, contractors, and electors who held posts in the revenue services. The government managed to beat off this attack in Parliament; and in the face of temporary military successes in South Carolina and a conservative reaction against the attempt by Wyvill to bring forward a measure securing more frequent general elections, the popular movement had lost steam by the summer. It proved impossible to resuscitate it to any extent the following year and, in the event, it played no part in the bringing down of the government in the early months of 1782.

3. THE RESIGNATION OF LORD NORTH

The resignation of Lord North and his colleagues in March 1782 was due entirely to a withdrawal of parliamentary confidence. There is little doubt that North himself welcomed it as a release from an intolerable situation. For although he and most of the ministers were now convinced that the country would have to cut its losses in America, the King, whose chosen servants they were, remained obstinately determined beyond the eleventh hour to try to salvage something out of the wreck by military means. So long as George III remained adamantly opposed to any peace recognizing American independence, North could not make the about-turn on policy which would have enabled him to retain support in Parliament: although the existing majority remained on the whole well-disposed towards him, its members could see no alternative to deserting the ministry in divisions in the House of Commons if the war was to be brought to an end. Finally, in mid-March 1782, it was the privately expressed intention of some independent country gentlemen, whose defection would be decisive, to do just that, which enabled North to wring out of the King a reluctant permission to announce his resignation.

This move destroyed altogether for the time being the normal pattern of eighteenth-century politics, whereby a group of ministers of the monarch's choice stood secure in the support of safe majorities in the two Houses of Parliament, while opposition politicians unavailingly sought to undermine their reputations with the public and make their situations untenable, but could rarely achieve more than the occasional rejection of an unpopular government measure. Now George III found himself obliged to recruit a new administration from politicians nearly all of whom for one reason or another had incurred his disapproval or dislike – in most instances because of incompatibility of views on the American question. Not only this, but he was obliged to acquiesce in a ministerial commitment to make peace on the basis of American independence, which he thought ruinous to the kingdom for whose fate and prosperity he as monarch bore responsibility. Also he was constrained to accept a program of administrative reform which involved ministerial and, in some degree, parliamentary interference with the running of executive government which he felt to be his particular constitutional responsibility. To his mind the pretensions of the main opposition party, led by the Marquis of Rockingham, to a lion's share of leading positions in the new administration reflected the behaviour of "faction," which on principle he disapproved.

Such was the turmoil into which defeat in America had thrown the state of politics that the King's early attempts to restore what might be considered from his point of view a state of normality proved distinctly unhappy in their results. During the three months' duration of the administration nominally headed at the Treasury by Rockingham (not a single speech by whom in the House of Lords is reported for that period) George III systematically tried to shore up the situation as co-premier of the Home Secretary, the Earl of Shelburne. Not only did he find Shelburne more congenial to work with, but he was aware that Shelburne, like his former political mentor, William Pitt, Earl of Chatham, was averse from seeing parliamentary encroachments upon the royal prerogative, symbolized both by the Rockinghamites' claim to hold office whether the King liked it or no and by their program of "economical reform." The royal stance led naturally in July 1782 to the appointment of Shelburne as First Lord of the Treasury on the death of Rockingham, a move which exacerbated inter-party jealousies and resulted in the withdrawal from office of Charles James Fox and other leaders of the Rockingham connection.

4. THE FOX–NORTH COALITION AND THE EAST INDIA LEGISLATION

This political maneuvering on the King's part was doomed to failure since the balance of forces in the Commons made it unviable. In the Parliament which had been elected in 1780 Shelburne and his friends commanded only exiguous personal support, insufficient in combination with the court and administration party to ensure safe majorities in parliamentary divisions. The Rockinghamite party remained a formidable force; but so also did North and his considerable following, and Shelburne was in no situation to pay the sort of political price for support that North might have found acceptable. The decision of North and Fox to join forces in February 1783 meant irretrievable disaster for Shelburne in the House of Commons. Shelburne was particularly vulnerable because on him fell the primary responsibility for negotiating a peace which many politicians believed gave too much away unnecessarily in America to the United States and in particular failed to secure any guarantee for loyalists of reinstatement in their lands or of compensation in respect of property confiscated or destroyed. In February 1783 votes of censure on the peace terms in the Commons spelled the necessity for resignation to Shelburne just as, a year before, the imminent

492

FIGURE 40 A coat of arms explaining the Coalition Government: Lord North (left) and Charles James Fox hold the arms of the new government which pins George III to the ground. In the upper left quarter of the crest is an American flag held by North in a field with Edmund Burke pulling the lion's teeth and a paper designated Reform Bill; in the lower right quarter Britannia is depicted upside down with an olive branch in her hand – referring to the frustrated reunion with America.

threat of the passage of a vote of no-confidence had spelled the end for Lord North.

After stubbornly resisting the inevitable through an inter-ministerium of some six weeks, George III had no alternative but to bow to the situation and admit the leaders of the Fox–North coalition to office (*see* figure 40). Even more than the events of March 1782 he felt this to be an inadmissible invasion of his prerogative of selecting ministers. Oppressed with the feeling that, with the royal functions reduced to a nullity, he could no longer effectively serve the country in his royal role, for a brief space he seriously contemplated abdication. At this point, perhaps, came the peak in the graph of the distortions introduced into British politics by the American winning of independence. In the end wiser counsels prevailed. From politicians who had no sympathy with either North or Fox came hints that perhaps in due course a situation which the King – and not the King alone – regarded as a gross violation of the constitution might be set to rights.

Ultimately, the return to a traditional pattern of politics, and the vindication of the royal prerogative, followed with surprising speed, within less than a year. This process of readjustment was greatly facilitated involuntarily by the leaders of the Fox–North coalition themselves. A thorough overhaul of the relationships between the royal administration and the role of the East India Company as the governing authority in large parts of the Indian sub-continent was long overdue. The coalition ministry was bound to tackle this problem. But it did so in such a way as to make itself both unpopular and highly vulnerable. The measures foreshadowed in its proposed East

493

India legislation of December 1783 entailed invasions of chartered rights which had not been fully negotiated and agreed (and probably would not have been agreed) by all concerned. In particular, the intended conferment of powers to make appointments in India upon a body of parliamentary commissioners nominated by the coalition appeared to place in the hands of the coalition parties a vast reservoir of patronage carrying political influence far greater than the royal patronage recently curbed by the Rockingham administration's economical reform legislation of 1782. Some zealous constitutional reformers, Wyvill among them, felt that all power in the state would be transferred from the royal administration to Charles Fox as the dominant personality in the coalition, and ludicrous charges were made against him of aspiring to usurp control of the state like another Cromwell.

5. THE ESTABLISHMENT IN OFFICE OF PITT

The affairs of the nascent British Empire in the East thus contributed to bring an end to the distortions in British politics set up by the American achievement of independence. In December 1783 the way was clear for the King to turn the tables on the coalition, for royal influence to sway the votes of the House of Lords against Fox's East India Bill, and for the coalition ministers to be dismissed and a new administration recruited from non-coalition politicians headed by the youthful William Pitt.

In the early weeks of 1784, although the small Fox–North majority in the Commons created difficulties for Pitt, a massive display of public opinion in the form of addresses and petitions revealed widespread support for the King's action. This show of public opinion was confirmed by the general election of April 1784. Not only were some of North's closest supporters displaced in a number of nomination boroughs where he had arranged seats for them in 1780, but many Foxites lost their elections in open constituencies after acrimonious public political debates in which a general distrust of the coalition was clearly evident. In the new Parliament Pitt had an assured majority. Thus, within two years of the end of the American war politics had returned to their accustomed channel. So, in the longer term the consequences of the American Revolution for British politics were minimal. Tensions which might have been if not dangerous at least debilitating had been eliminated. King and ministers were again at one. The government was once again clearly the King's government, conducted by ministers of the King's choice, as it had been in the 1770s. Parliamentary support for the ministry was assured. Opposition was once again reduced to a powerless rump in Parliament, capable of creating occasional embarrassment for ministers – as it was to do in respect of Pitt's proposed Irish legislation in 1785 – but not of effectively challenging their tenure of office and power. One innovation indeed there was. To hold a general election only three and a half years after the previous one was unprecedented in the Hanoverian period, and the part played by the elections of 1784 in the resolution of the political crisis of the previous 12 months gave an enhanced importance to the role of public opinion in political affairs. This apart, the political machine during the administration of the younger Pitt continued to function much as it had done under the 12-year leadership of Lord North.

6. INDUSTRIALIZATION AND FINANCIAL REFORM

The restoration of political stability was undoubtedly one important factor in British recovery after the loss of the American colonies. Two other factors in particular deserve mention. One – industrialization – owed little or nothing to the influence of the American Revolution, save insofar as war stimulated demand for military and naval clothing and weaponry. But the expansion in metallurgy and the truly dramatic increase in textile production, with consequent stimulus to export and import trade, soon made up any deficiencies in the nation's economy that might have been expected to arise from the loss of the American war. The lift-off of the cotton industry in the years after the war was phenomenal and is easily discernible from the customs figures for imports of cotton wool: in 1780 rather under 7 million lbs., in 1785 more than 15 million, and in 1790 doubling to more than 30 million. There is ample evidence over this period for a wide diffusion of modest prosperity in the form of higher earnings among large sections of the working people as well as among small businessmen. Canal-building, road-construction, the beginnings of the erection of factories, and the growth of industrial villages were all facets of the development of an indispensable infrastructure for industrialization, forming a basis for national power and prosperity hardly conceivable in the war-disaster years of 1781–2.

The other factor of recovery – administrative and financial reform – was much more directly a product of the American crisis, for in part it was engendered by the pressures created by the war. One of North's most successful counter-strokes to the parliamentary Opposition's campaign against alleged extravagance and corruption at the beginning of 1780 was to secure parliamentary approval for the establishment of a statutory commission of inquiry into the public accounts, rather than an opposition-sponsored parliamentary committee of inquiry which would have devoted its energies to political point-scoring. The commission voted into being in 1780 carried out over several years a thorough examination of the procedures of the revenue and spending departments, and laid an indispensable foundation for reforms undertaken after 1784 by the younger Pitt in the administration of the revenue and the control of expenditure.

North himself, before his resignation, had begun to experiment with a broadening of the basis of taxation, introducing an inhabited-house duty and a tax on male servants in 1778. After 1784 Pitt's attempts to extend the catchment area of taxation still further were not always successful, but he achieved considerable success in combatting loss of revenue through smuggling by the reduction of the various customs duties, particularly on tea and wines. More effective in achieving efficiency in the collection of revenues was his reapportionment of responsibility for this among the various existing agencies. Regularity in administration was imposed by a new treasury commission of audit. Simplicity in government accounting was achieved by the creation of the consolidated fund, and the public credit was enormously strengthened by Pitt's reorganization of the sinking fund. Much of all this financial reform was based on the reports of North's commission, which continued its work up to 1787, and can therefore be seen as a direct effect of the American crisis. It was of particular significance that under the impact and strain of unsuccessful war the political and administrative machinery of Great Britain should so effectively stand up to the task of self-examination and reform, effectively contributing to the achievement of national recovery. In this, above all, the contrast between Britain and France was particularly marked. Indeed, it is not too much to say that the work of the commission on the public accounts marked the divide between the *ancien-régime* system of financial administration the country had inherited from the Middle Ages and a modern, efficient administrative machine based on some degree of cost efficiency and eliminating, at least to some extent, surviving inefficient and sinecure offices. Although many reforms

495

remained to be achieved, Britain emerged from the American crisis with a financial system much superior to that with which it had entered it.

In sum, restored political stability, a relatively effective financial system, and a thriving industrializing economy all combined within a very few years of the American Revolution to re-establish national self-confidence and the sinews of power in Great Britain.

FURTHER READING

Binney, J. E. D.: *British Public Finance and Administration, 1774–1792* (Oxford: Clarendon Press, 1958).

Butterfield, Sir Herbert: *George III, Lord North, and the People, 1779–1780* (London: Bell and Sons, 1949).

Cannon, John: *The Fox–North Coalition: Crisis of the Constitution, 1782–4* (Cambridge: Cambridge University Press, 1969).

Christie, Ian R.: *The End of North's Ministry, 1780–1782* (London: Macmillan, 1958).

——: *Wars and Revolutions: Britain, 1760–1815* (London: Edward Arnold; Cambridge, Mass.: Harvard University Press, 1982), chapters 6–8 and chapter bibliographies.

——: *Stress and Stability in Late Eighteenth-Century Britain: Reflections on the British Avoidance of Revolution* (Oxford and New York: Oxford University Press, 1984), chapters 3 and 5.

Ehrman, John: *The Younger Pitt: the Years of Acclaim* (London: Constable, 1969).

Watson, J. Steven: *The Reign of George III, 1760–1815* (Oxford: Clarendon Press, 1960), chapters 9–11.

50

The American Revolution and Canada

G. A. RAWLYK

THE residents of the British colonies north of New York and Massachusetts – present-day Canada – refused to join the American Revolution. And their rejection of American republicanism, a rejection shaped by a counter-revolutionary conservatism, was significantly strengthened in the 1780s with the arrival of almost 50,000 loyalists. Many of the leading loyalists were determined to build north of the United States a deferential, ordered and British society, characterized by what the British North America Act of 1867 – the Act creating Canada – referred to as Peace, Order and Good Government.

When the American War of Independence broke out, there were approximately 130,000 European inhabitants in what is now Canada: 90,000 in Quebec, 20,000 in Nova Scotia (which in 1776 also included present-day New Brunswick), 1,000 in the Ile-St.-Jean (later to be called Prince Edward Island), and some 15,000 permanent residents of Newfoundland. The inhabitants of the two latter island colonies were never seriously tempted to join the Revolution. They were effectively shielded from American republicanism because of their powerful British orientation and the isolated nature of their primitive settlements, and also by the British Navy. On the other hand, especially in 1775 and 1776, many Nova Scotia and Quebec residents felt themselves under considerable pressure to join the American patriots in their attempt to shatter the existing framework of the British North American colonial system. Instead of triggering a major, indigenous pro-American political outburst in Nova Scotia, however, the revolutionary crisis helped to precipitate one of the most important social movements in Nova Scotia history – the widespread religious revival known as the Great Awakening. The Revolution also ensured that the conservative bias of the political culture of the region would be firmly entrenched.

In the inland colony of Quebec, even though the Yankee liberators were turned back and the revolutionary ideology was rejected, the Revolution helped to intensify certain existing class and racial tensions in the colony. However, it is clear that the timely passage of the Quebec Act in 1774 and the basic fear of change helped to secure the loyalty of the vast majority of inhabitants – especially the French-speaking *Canadien* majority.

I. NOVA SCOTIA

In 1776, of an estimated total Nova Scotia population of 20,000, only a little more than one-half was of New England origin – settlers who had arrived during the previous 15 years. Nova Scotia in 1776, therefore, was not a homogeneous New England colony. Rather, it was little more than a political expression for a number of widely scattered and isolated communities stretching from Pictou on Northumberland Strait to the Acadian villages on Cape Breton Island, to Canso and then to Halifax and Yarmouth, and along the Bay of Fundy coast to Maugerville on the St. John River and the tiny outpost of Passamaquoddy on the St. Croix.

During the revolutionary decade, there were at least two distinct Nova Scotias – Halifax and the outsettlements. The actual influence of the capital was largely restricted to the Bedford Basin region. Petty political squabbling, graft and corruption, economic and social stagnation seemed to characterize Halifax life in the pre-revolutionary years.

The Nova Scotia "Yankees" Apart from Yorkshire and Scots-Irish residing in the Chignecto–Minas Bay region, the Highland Scots of Pictou, and the German-speaking Protestants of Lunenburg, the outsettlements were dominated by the Nova Scotia "Yankees." These inhabitants of the coastal strip of the southern half of peninsular Nova Scotia and of the valley of the St. John River had strong cultural and economic ties with their former homeland. They also were suspicious of the small clique of Halifax merchants who controlled the legislative and executive functions of government and who attempted to impose centralized control over the isolated townships. Consequently, when the revolutionary crisis engulfed North America, the Halifax authorities, not without reason, expected the Yankees to flock to the American side. Only in the vicinity of the two western frontier settlements of Maugerville and Cumberland, however, was there any indigenous revolutionary activity.

In the western region of Nova Scotia there were four phases in the collective response to revolution on the part of a large number of inhabitants – most of whom were recently arrived New Englanders. There was, before 1775, a prevailing apathy concerning the political and economic questions that were disturbing New Englanders. The Nova Scotia Yankees, by emigrating in the early 1760s, had missed a critical decade in the ideological development of the New England colonies. And consequently, most of them were incapable of comprehending the arguments used during the immediate pre-Revolution period. In a sense then, their political thinking had congealed before the Stamp Act crisis. The second phase occurred in late 1775 and early 1776. During these months, the government's militia policy precipitated a crisis which, together with the underlying sympathy for family and friends in New England, was used by politically aware leaders to bring the local revolutionary movement into public view. There followed a period of a number of months when the leaders attempted to broaden the base of support, in the Chignecto by bringing in an invading force from Maine and by intimidation, and in Maugerville by persuasion. Then, in 1777, most of the remaining settlers quickly reverted to their British allegiance.

Most other Nova Scotians, even though they probably never passed beyond the earliest phase of the Maugerville–Chignecto reaction to the Revolution, still must have shared the basic vacillation and confusion of that reaction. In a very real sense the essence of Nova Scotia's response to the Revolution was that of acute confusion. The activities of American privateers merely added to the existing chaos. Almost every Nova Scotia settlement, with the exception of Halifax, was ravaged by American privateersmen. Here indeed was a strange way to make American converts of Nova Scotians!

It is too simplistic, however, to conclude that the New England privateering raids drove the wavering Nova Scotia "Yankees" into the welcoming arms of the mother country. Some of the well-to-do merchants, who bore the brunt of the expeditions, probably did move in this direction. But the majority of Yankee inhabitants, who had little of any value to lose to freebooters, certainly did not. These men must have been able to distinguish clearly between the rapacious privateersmen and the people and governments of the independent states. Moreover, the ordinary Nova Scotia inhabitants had as much to fear from the press-gangs as from the privateers.

As in Newfoundland and St. John's Island, the Revolution brought to Nova Scotia a sudden burst of economic prosperity. Halifax, as always during periods of war, sucked in huge sums of money for military purposes; some of this money made its way to the outsettlements, as did revenue from the considerable illicit trade carried on with the Americans. This commercial activity, however, did little to neutralize the general feeling of uneasiness, fear, and puzzlement concerning the war. Until local leaders were able to make some sense out of the confusing contemporary situation, the Nova Scotians were bound to have remained in a troubled frame of mind, as they desperately searched for a new sense of identity to replace their disintegrating dual loyalty to both Old and New England.

Henry Alline and the religious revival Henry Alline was one Nova Scotian who was able to perceive a special purpose for his fellow colonists in the midst of the confused revolutionary situation. He was the charismatic leader of the intense religious revival which swept the colony during the war period. The Great Awakening of Nova Scotia may be viewed as an attempt by many inhabitants to appropriate a sense of identity. Religious enthusism in this context, a social movement of profound consequence in the Nova Scotia situation, was symptomatic of a collective identity crisis as well as a searching for an acceptable and meaningful ideology. Resolution of the crisis came not only when the individuals were absorbed into what they felt was a dynamic fellowship of true believers, but also when they accepted Alline's analysis of contemporary events and his conviction that their colony was the centre of a crucial cosmic struggle.

Alline was born in Newport, Rhode Island, in 1748, and in 1760 moved with his parents to Falmouth in the Minas Basin region of Nova Scotia. Like most young people in the settlement, he was brought up in a pious Christian atmosphere. His morbid sense of introspection and the pressure he was under to commit himself one way or another in the revolutionary struggle helped to precipitate a psychic crisis and conversion in 1775. As Alline observed in his famous *Journal*:

> my whole soul seemed to be melted down with love; the burden of guilt and condemnation was gone, darkness was expelled, my heart humbled and filled with gratitude, and my will turned of choice after the infinite God ... my whole soul seemed filled with the divine being ... my whole soul was filled with love, and ravished with a divine ecstasy beyond any doubts or fears ... for I enjoyed a heaven on earth, and it seemed as if I were wrapped up in God (1806, p. 34).

Under a compulsion to have others share with him this intense religious experience, Alline resolved to preach his evangelistic message to his fellow Nova Scotians.

Eventually Alline visited almost every settlement in Nova Scotia; and only Halifax, Chester, and Lunenberg were unaffected by the revival he largely articulated into existence. Almost single-handed, Alline was able to draw the isolated communities together and to impose upon them a feeling of unity. They each were sharing a common experience; he was providing them with answers to disconcerting and puzzling contemporary questions. For Alline, the Nova Scotia revival was an event of world significance. The social, economic, and political backwater that was Nova Scotia was the new center of the Christian world. He thus was attempting to thrust them into the middle of the world stage.

In his sermons, preached as he criss-crossed the colony, Alline developed the theme that the Nova Scotia Yankees, in particular, had a special predestined role to play in bringing about the millennium. It must have required special effort for the preacher to convince Nova Scotians of their world role. But Alline, striking deep into the Puritan New England tradition that viewed self-abnegation and frugality as virtues, contended that the relative backwardness and isolation of the colony had removed the inhabitants from the prevailing corrupting influences of New England and Britain. As a result, Nova Scotia was in an ideal position to lead the world back to God.

The implication of the conjunction of events, of civil war in New England and an outpouring of the Holy Spirit in Nova Scotia, was obvious to Alline and the hundreds who flocked to hear him. God was passing New England's historical role of Christian leadership to Nova Scotia. With two powerful Protestant nations furiously battling one another, the whole course of events since the Reformation seemed to be ending in a meaningless tangle. In the world view of those New Englanders fighting for the revolutionary cause, Old England was corrupt and the Americans were engaged in a righteous and noble cause. There was therefore some meaning for hostilities. But to Alline the totally evil civil war had no such meaning. Rather, along with all the other signs of the times, it could only indicate one thing, that the entire Christian world, apart from Nova Scotia, was abandoning the way of God.

What was regarded as the tragic backsliding of New England had presented Nova Scotia with an opportunity to put things right. Alline was determined that the new City upon a Hill would lead the world back to the pristine purity of the Christian faith. By permeating his Evangelical preaching with this mission-oriented rhetoric, he provided his audience with a new collective identity based upon their belief that they were indeed a people with a unique history, a distinct identity, and a special destiny. This, in a profound sense, was Nova Scotia's response to the American Revolution.

2. QUEBEC

The American invasion   Governor Guy Carleton, who had returned to Quebec in the late summer of 1774, was certain that the Quebec Act would bring both contentment and unflinching loyalty to his colony. He was so confident of the accuracy of his analysis of the situation that he permitted two of his regiments, in the autumn of 1774, to be sent to reinforce General Gage's beleaguered army in Boston. This decision left Carleton with fewer than 1,000 regulars.

By early autumn of 1775, Washington and the Continental Congress had reversed themselves and decided that it was now essential for the Americans to strike quickly and boldly at the colony of Quebec. There were at least three major reasons for such a decision. First, it was felt that, with fewer than 1,000 British regulars in the colony and with many of the inhabitants seemingly disaffected, the time was propitious for such an invasion. Second, there was a widespread conviction in the Continental Congress that Quebec had to be captured in 1775 in order to prevent a powerful British offensive from the north in the spring of the following year and also to discourage possible Indian raids. Finally, there was, without question, a strong expansionist desire – a desire to absorb the considerable economic potential of the St. Lawrence–Great Lakes system.

Despite the fact that the American army was still poorly organized, by September 1775 a two-pronged offensive was directed against Quebec. One 2,000-man column, under the command of Richard Montgomery, moved up the Lake Champlain–Richelieu River, while the other, consisting of 1,100 troops under Benedict Arnold, traveled by way of the Kennebec River wilderness route. On 3 December the two prongs converged at the capital of the colony, Quebec. Relatively few *Canadiens* had rushed either to the side of the invaders or to support Carleton. Most had, instead, stuck to their farms and sold supplies, for hard cash, to anyone – American or British. There was a kind of pragmatic neutralism underlying the response of most habitants to the American invasion.

Confronted by the extraordinary weakness of the British military presence and by early decisive American successes, it is not surprising that many *Canadiens* preferred to remain neutral. American propaganda and British military weakness were, without question, critical factors in the development of this pragmatic neutrality as was the profound fear of change which characterized the *Canadien* mentality. There were, moreover, important economic considerations motivating them. The period from 1770 to 1778 was one of unusually good harvests and French-Canadian farmers were eager to reap the rewards of their food fortune. Under the French regime, during the frequent periods of war, they had been compelled to make significant sacrifices, only to see various speculators enriching themselves at the expense of the colony. In the early years of the Revolution the war-weary *Canadiens* were determined to share in the profits of warfare and to watch from the sidelines the bloody battle between the groups of Englishmen.

After the Americans failed in an assault on Quebec city during the night of 30–31 December 1775, however their position in the colony gradually eroded. They completely destroyed their credibility as enlightened liberators when they began to terrorize the countryside and to offer the despised paper money for provisions. The outbreak of smallpox, and the spread of desertion among the invading forces, their lack of discipline and effective leadership, and finally the arrival in early June 1776 of a British fleet carrying thousands of reinforcements all resulted in an American withdrawal from the colony on 2 July – just two days before the issuing of the Declaration of Independence.

During the following year, 1777, the British at Quebec tried to gain the initiative against the Americans by sending a force of 7,000 regulars against Albany, New York. Lieutenant-General John Burgoyne's army, however, met a disastrous end, a humiliating surrender, at Saratoga in October. It is impossible to be certain as to how Burgoyne's capture affected the thinking of the Quebec residents. What may be ascertained, however, is that in 1778, when France entered hostilities on the side of the Americans, the colony was again thrown into a state of confusion and turmoil.

The putative French invasion and the arrival of the loyalists This was the general situation that faced a new governor of Quebec, General Frederick Haldimand, who arrived in late June (Carleton, knighted after his successful defence of Quebec city, had subsequently fallen out with the imperial authorities). When rumors about an imminent French invasion led on land by the Marquis de La Fayette and supported

FIGURE 41 A loyalist encampment at Johnston (now Cornwall) on the St. Lawrence River (watercolour by James Peachey, 1784)

from the sea by Admiral D'Estaing began to sweep the colony in 1778 and 1779, not only the ordinary French-Canadian farmers were excited and pleased but many *Canadien* seigneurs and priests as well. An intense pro-French sympathy cut across class lines in sharp contrast to the lack of a unified response to the earlier American invasion.

The very real possibility of a return to French rule had apparently tapped the large reservoir of ethnic pride lying near the surface of the collective consciousness of many French Canadians. They wished to have the *fleur-de-lis* of France once again waving over Quebec territory. Since many American leaders had little desire to see France re-established on their northern borders, it was decided in the autumn of 1780 to postpone indefinitely a joint Franco-American assault on Quebec. By this time, after two years of waiting, the early exhilaration of those ardent pro-French supporters was being replaced by a growing incredulity and bitterness as they realized that there was no substance to the rumors about an imminent French invasion. For the rest of the war – in fact until peace was concluded in 1783 – Quebec remained securely in British hands. The colony had, during the American Revolution, come to possess a distinctive constitutional and legal structure which *Canadiens* began to view as theirs by right: a bulwark to their own separate identity within North America and the British Empire.

More than 35,000 loyalists eventually made their way in the early 1780s to Nova Scotia and more than 10,000 to Quebec (*see* figure 41). Their arrival compelled the British authorities to create three new colonies in British North America: Upper Canada, which is present-day Ontario, New Brunswick, and Cape Breton Island. The loyalists obviously strengthened the pro-British and anti-American bias of what remained of British North America – for they, like most Nova Scotians and residents of Quebec, had rejected the American Revolution and a great deal that it represented.

FURTHER READING

Alline, H.: *The Life and Journal of the Rev. Mr. Henry Alline* (Boston: Gilbert & Dean, 1806).
Brebner, J. B.: *The Neutral Yankees of Nova Scotia: a Marginal Colony During the American Revolutionary Years* (New York: Columbia University Press, 1937).
Neatby, H.: *Quebec, 1760–1791* (Toronto: McClelland & Stewart, 1966).

Ouellet, F, F.: *Histoire economique et social du Quebec, 1760–1850* (Montreal: Fides, 1966); trans. Institute of Canadian Studies, *Economic and Social History of Quebec 1760–1850* (Toronto: Gage, 1980).

Stewart, G. and Rawlyk, G. A.: *A People Highly Favoured of God: the Nova Scotia Yankees and the American Revolution* (Toronto: Macmillan, 1972).

51

The American Revolution and Ireland

MAURICE J. BRIC

BEFORE 1776, a shared constitutional status and political discourse bound Ireland and the sibling colonies of British North America. Discursive themes were essentially shaped by reference to the imperial matrix in London. Accordingly, Irish patriots believed that American writers such as John Dickinson and James Wilson were developing themes first set forth by William Molyneux (1656–98) and Jonathan Swift (1667–1745). By the 1770s, the cause of America was the cause of Ireland.

Both Molyneux (in the 1690s) and Swift (in the 1720s) had established the outlines of a patriotic agenda that incorporated each side of the British Atlantic world: the independence of local legislatures, freedom of trade, and political reform. As the pre-eminent vehicle for this agenda, the American Revolution could hardly be denounced by the members of the Irish Parliament without their admitting that the British Parliament had the right to tax the Irish. Accordingly, while commemorative dinners, addresses and parades celebrated the assertion of the "liberties of America," patriotic leaders and clubs in Ireland kept in close contact with their American colleagues in order to ensure that, as the (Dublin) *Freeman's Journal* put it on 18 February 1766, British policy in America was not "part of a plan of Humiliation nearer home."

Irish newspapers also published a stream of reports on the background to and the movement towards American independence. These reports were drawn from a variety of sources, including the legislative assemblies, contemporary American publications and newspapers, and the debates and resolutions of various revolutionary groups.

Relatively few pamphlets on the American Revolution were published in Ireland. Although these, together with newspaper essays, affected the Lord Lieutenant in 1779 "with more terror than 10,000 soldiers," the fact is that they largely ignored the ideological themes of the Revolution for the narrower political capital of condemning what Benjamin Franklin termed "the heavy yoke of tyranny" in Ireland itself. Therefore the celebrated *Letter to the Town of Boston*, penned by the Irish patriot leader Charles Lucas (1713–71) in 1770, ignored the great constitutional concerns of the day and largely confined itself to berating the "base, perfidious, vindictive, rapacious Ministers" of the British Government. Similarly, proposals made in America by Franklin for a "consolidating union" between Ireland, Britain, and the colonies, and in England by William Pulteney to set up a "general Parliament, to take care of the general interests of the whole" were misunderstood or ignored by Irish patriots.

I. THE IMMEDIATE REACTION IN IRELAND TO THE REVOLUTION

For all the rhetorical protestations of fellowship, patriotic Irish reaction to the American Revolution was less pro-American than anti-government and this may account for the Revolution's minimal impact on contemporary Ireland. At parliamentary level, the Irish were more interested in the internal and organizational character of their own parliament than in its ideological basis, and the American Revolution did not alter this.

To a large extent also, the influence of the American Revolution on Ireland was determined, and ultimately limited, by that sense of domestic insecurity that had long molded the development of eighteenth-century Irish politics. This was highlighted by the announced participation of France (June 1778) and (a year later) Spain in the Anglo-American conflict. These declarations constituted the ultimate threat to the interlocking system of established networks, ties, and traditions that bound Ireland and Britain.

Accordingly, while the Irish Parliament expressed its "abhorrence" of the developing Revolutionary War, Henry Grattan (1746–1820) and his patriot colleagues drew a fine line between their view of the Anglo-American war and a potential threat from Catholic France. Their loyalty to the British Crown in the face of a foreign enemy was always unconditional.

Outside Parliament, the loyalty of even the island's most vocal pro-American group, the Irish Presbyterians, was also never in doubt. Should "necessity" call them forth to oppose "the jealous enemies" of their ancient liberties and religion, wrote one of their ministers, William Steele Dickson, "we are ready to approve ourselves the steady friends of the constitution." Well might the Lord Lieutenant conclude that the notion of a French war had "not only altered the language but the disposition" of the Revolutionaries' strongest supporters in Ireland.

2. THE POLITICAL SITUATION IN LATE EIGHTEENTH-CENTURY IRELAND

These reactions to the development of the American Revolution reflected not only traditional fears but also the shifting alignments of late eighteenth-century Irish politics. These had been complicated by the residency of the Lord Lieutenant (from 1767) and by the presumed threat to a Protestant ascendancy based on land from a rising Catholic and Protestant bourgeoisie based on commerce and the professions.

Both the socio-economic and the political status of the Catholic leadership was greatly undermined by the Penal Laws. These laws, the majority of which were passed between 1695 and 1704, effectively placed everybody outside the Established (Anglican) Church in a legal limbo. However, because the laws contained loopholes on the acquisition of commercial wealth, a new Catholic middle class emerged. Not only did this emerging group challenge what was left of the traditionally landed leadership but it actively sought some sort of accommodation with the Hanoverian Succession. Through the Test Act of 1774, the abjuration of both the temporal and the deposing powers of the Papacy, the renunciation of loyalty to the exiled Stuart dynasty, and the proclamation of loyalty to George III set the scene for the repeal of many of the Penal Laws.

The quest not only to change old attitudes to the Stuarts but to prove Catholic loyalty to George III shaped the reactions of Ireland's Catholics to the American Revolution. In February 1779, Dr. John Troy, bishop of Ossory (1776–86), condemned the Americans as "rebels" and called on all Catholics to "be loyal." A year earlier, on the French declaration of war, six Catholic peers and 300 other lay leaders expressed both their "abhorrence at the unnatural rebellion" in America and their loyalty to

505

George III. However, as with the political emphasis of the patriots, this was less a protest against the American Revolution *per se* than one to the administration that Catholic Ireland could be "trusted" with liberation from the Penal Laws.

As an aspect of negotiations on repeal of the Penal Laws, most Catholic leaders agreed with this emphasis and shared in the contemporary reassessment of their traditional affinity towards France. However, although it was a strategy that was politically pragmatic, it also smothered differences between the older Catholic peerage and the newer bourgeois "intruders" as to who would lead Irish Catholicism into the nineteenth century. By and large, the aristocratic Catholic leaders of the 1770s had had relatively little emotional or personal attachment to America. For many Catholic merchants, however, Europe had been replaced by America in their affections as a result of their involvement in transatlantic commerce. Especially in the southern ports of Ireland, these merchants were affected by the embargo of February 1776 which forbade the export of provisions (except corn) to all countries other than Great Britain and the loyal colonies.

3. THE AMERICAN EXAMPLE INSPIRES MOVES TOWARDS IRISH LIBERTY

The embargo inspired a number of resolutions and petitions. In June 1776, for example, a petition to George III from the merchants of Cork linked the "ruination" of their American trade to a call for the dismissal of Lord North, while several other cities and counties resolved not to import British goods. Such protests inevitably invited comparisons with revolutionary America. British Whigs warned North that Ireland might "go the way of" America, as rumors circulated that Franklin, then American minister to France, had been empowered "to treat with Ireland on commerce and matters of mutual interest and support."

In April 1778 a British parliamentary committee sought to prevent what it saw as the further dismemberment of the British Empire and recommended the suspension of Ireland's trade restrictions. But protectionist resentment in Britain undermined these parliamentary moves, and consequently the non-importation movement blossomed during late 1778 and 1779. The "armed associations" of Irish patriotism, the Volunteers, grew to an estimated 40,000 by the end of 1779, while within the blossoming non-importation movement, both inside and outside the Irish Parliament, the slogans of revolutionary America found a rhetorical home in Volunteer resolutions and reviews.

In November 1779 Dublin mobs protested against government policy and decorated the cannons outside the Irish Parliament with the legend "a free trade or else." Although the effects of the embargo on Irish commerce are unclear, opposition to it enlivened the patriot movement and, in Edmund Burke's words, changed "a mere question of commerce into a question of state." Indeed, with rumors that the French were mounting an invasion of Ireland, some saw the free trade movement as an aspect of the second front that the French had opened in mid-1778.

In the face of the protests in Ireland, North was obliged to introduce "free trade" measures in December 1779 and February 1780. While these concessions were welcomed in Ireland, they "ought not," as John Adams reported to Congress, "to be considered as anything more than a great beginning" of a patriotic campaign to redress constitutional disabilities as well.

These disabilities were enshrined, first, in Poynings's Law (1495), which stipulated

506

that bills had to be initiated in the English Privy Council and that, consequently, the Irish Parliament could only consent to (or reject) bills and, second, in the so-called Declaratory Act, which proclaimed the right of the British Parliament to legislate for Ireland. In April 1780 Grattan observed that "a country enlightened as Ireland, chartered as Ireland, armed as Ireland, and injured as Ireland, will be satisfied with nothing less than liberty." For the next two years the Lord Lieutenant, the Earl of Carlisle (1780–4), and his chief secretary William Eden, who had earlier sought to negotiate with the American rebels, now sought to conciliate the Irish patriots.

Such experience of the realities of American patriotism as well as the quickening pace of Volunteer activity in Ireland convinced the Administration of Ireland that it had no alternative but to advise the repeal of the Declaratory Act and the alteration of Poynings's Law. Although the concessions of 1782 were limited, they were sufficient to ensure that the revolutionary American path would not be taken by Irish patriots. The British Government felt assured of their ultimate loyalty, and, although its responses to both "free trade" and legislative independence were influenced by events in America, Carlisle accurately concluded that Irish and American patriotism were following divergent courses.

Carlisle believed that Irish patriots less understood the American Revolution than related it to their own domestic situation. Thus, although Irish responses to the Revolution revealed the effects of a wide range of ideological, personal, religious, and regional factors, in the last analysis they were pragmatic. The American Revolution revealed and, to some extent, inspired changes in the Irish polity in a crucial period of its development.

FURTHER READING

Bric, Maurice J.: "Ireland and the Broadening of the Late Eighteenth-Century Philadelphia Polity" (Ph.D. dissertation, Johns Hopkins University, 1990).

——: "The Irish and the 'New Politics' in America," *The Irish in America: Emigration, Assimilation, and Impact*, ed. P. J. Drudy (Cambridge: Cambridge University Press, 1985).

Doyle, David Noel: *Ireland, Irishmen and Revolutionary America* (Cork: Mercier Press, 1981).

Edwards, Owen Dudley: "The American Image of Ireland: a Study of its Early Phases," *Perspectives in American History*, 4 (1970), 199–284.

Johnston, Edith Mary: *Ireland in the Eighteenth Century* (Dublin: Gill & Macmillan, 1974).

Kraus, Michael: "America and the Irish Revolutionary Movement in the Eighteenth Century," *The Era of the American Revolution*, ed. Richard B. Morris (New York: Harper & Row, 1939).

McDowell, R. B.: *Irish Public Opinion, 1760–1800* (London: Faber & Faber, 1943).

——: *Ireland in the Age of Imperialism and Revolution, 1760–1801* (Oxford: Oxford University Press, 1979).

O'Connell, Maurice: *Irish Politics and Social Conflict in the Age of the American Revolution* (Philadelphia: University of Pennsylvania Press, 1965).

52

The American Revolution and the sugar colonies, 1775–1783

SELWYN H. H. CARRINGTON

I. PRE-WAR RELATIONS – INTERDEPENDENCE

IT IS generally held that, without the unrestricted access to American markets, the plantation system of the British West Indies would not have developed so fully and the importance of the sugar colonies to British economic growth during the eighteenth century would have been far less significant. In fact, the insecurity of their artificial economy was not apparent to the majority of planters and merchants because their unrestricted commercial system functioned smoothly until the dispute between Britain and America erupted. Yet there were signs that any attempt at interference with this commercial relationship was fraught with disastrous implications for the survival of the plantation system.

In the commerce that developed, not only did the Americans supply the planters with a variety of foodstuffs and lumber and consume large portions of their rum and minor products, but they were also the mainstay of the carrying trade between the continent and the West Indies (Edwards, 1794, p. 399). These vessels were mainly brigs, schooners, and snows, ranging from 30 to 90 tons, and were well-suited to the transportation of bulky commodities (Bell, 1917, p. 278) "over shallows and Bars," often off-loading their goods in creeks and small bays which were unsuited to large merchantmen.[1]

American monopoly of inter-colonial shipping had posed serious threats to British shipping interests. The economist Josiah Tucker wrote that the Americans were poised to engross not only that branch of the trade but also the carrying trade between Britain and the West Indies. John Adams was equally aware of British opposition, and is credited with the epigram "The Americans were spreading too much canvass on the seas and their wings needed clipping."[2] It was, however, Lord Sheffield who cited American competition as justification for excluding the United States from the West Indian carrying trade in the post-1783 period. He wrote:

> The American shipping, by various means, were monopolizing this business; they used to give their lumber at half price to those who would load their vessels with sugar. They were encouraged, and sent away loaded in a few weeks, while our ships were often obliged to come away half loaded. One consequence was that British sugar ships were gradually lessening in number, every man concerned in ... withdrawing himself as fast as he could. (Sheffield, 1784, p. 163)

Taken together, America and the West Indies comprised the major trading block in an area encompassing Canada, the Spanish mainland, and the Caribbean. Furthermore, Britain could not compete with the Americans, whose products were

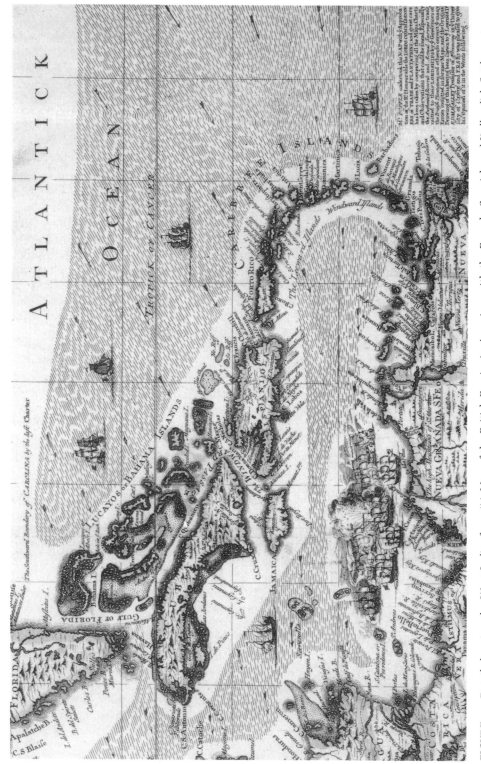

FIGURE 42 Detail showing the West Indies from "A Map of the British Empire in America, with the French, Spanish and Follandish Settlements adjacent thereto" (Henry Popple, 1733, reprinted ?1750)

cheaper and much more geared to a slave economy. Any interference with American–West Indian commercial relations threatened the pre-eminent position of the West Indies as the center of the British imperial economic system. The Earl of Dartmouth expressed most clearly the hopes and fears of many: "The State of Affairs in North America and particularly in the New England Colonies is become very serious. It is to be hoped however that nothing will happen to obstruct the Commerce that for mutual interest ought to be cherished on both sides."[3]

2. THE WAR AND WEST INDIAN TRADE

The outbreak of fighting between Britain and the American colonies had deep and lasting consequences for the sugar colonies. Previous eighteenth-century wars had been mere annoyances and had posed no serious threat to the plantation system. Colonial shipping was protected by a strong Royal Navy; freight and insurance rates remained low; the slave trade, although affected, met the needs of the planters and merchant classes; and of course food and lumber reached the islands in large enough quantities. In fact, historians have observed that on these occasions colonial commerce "prospered more than in times of peace" (Pares, 1963, p. 471; Sheridan, 1973, p. 266). During the American war, however, West Indian trade with the United States was first affected by two Restraining Acts passed early in 1775, and was later terminated by the Prohibitory Act of 1776. Thereafter emerged a number of crises which contributed to the retardation and subsequent decline of the sugar economy.

The Prohibitory Act terminated all commercial intercourse between the West Indies and the rebellious colonies. Canada, Nova Scotia, and Newfoundland were expected to fill the vacuum. However, certain provisos exempted categories of American vessels from capture, and also allowed British merchants to trade with loyal colonies of those areas under the control of British forces. These loopholes worked to the benefit of American merchants and their West Indian sympathizers,[4] and led to an extensive illegal trade in arms, ammunition, and some plantation supplies with the rebels (Ford, 1904: 11, pp. 257–9; Setser, 1937, p. 11).

After 1776 the planters faced severe shortages of all categories of foodstuffs, lumber, and other plantation supplies. As a corollary, prices increased significantly, and the general conditions of the sugar plantations were aptly described by John Pinney, an attorney and planter of Nevis, "You have no idea of the distressed and unhappy state of this country."[5]

In order to prevent devastation to life and property, many planters tinkered with the plantation system by attempting self-sufficiency through the production of local food. Overall, the gains were minimal, while the losses in sugar production from labor shortages were quite marked. The very nature of the monocultural sugar plantation system made even this temporary alternative unworkable, and for survival the planters embarked on a frantic search for external sources of food and lumber. Jamaica introduced a bounty system which facilitated the importation of American supplies through the foreign free ports; the Antiguan Assembly passed a bill for this purpose but the latter was rejected by the Council. Barbados did nothing in this area, believing that market conditions would have a greater impact. Some governors, however, such as William Mathew Burt of the Leeward Islands, supported the importation of foreign goods, but this was rejected by the Colonial Office as an infringement of British commercial policy (Carrington, 1987, pp. 828–9).

The cessation of American–West Indian commerce initiated a "redirection of trade" which saw the expansion of business between the sugar colonies and the United Kingdom. Agents from Scottish and other merchant-houses were sent out to secure new business and to direct the trade on a commission basis. However, there were several disadvantages to the planters: insurance costs spiralled as there was need for special clauses to allow vessels to ply among the islands; American privateers had a devastating effect on the trade and inter-island shipping; the quantity of supplies were inadequate, and spoilage further reduced it. Furthermore, related factors such as increased demand for Scottish and Irish herrings, high freight insurance, lighterage, commission, and other charges pushed the costs of food for the slaves beyond the ability of planters to pay and maintain profits. In order to lessen the hardships to West Indian planters, Parliament allowed the export of food to the islands and removed all restrictions on Irish–West Indian trade between 1778 and 1780. Larger quantities of beef, pork, and herrings reached the islands, but it is doubtful that this quality of food was given to the slaves.[6]

Commercial gains to the West Indies were negligible. Ireland imported minimal tropical products and the value of her imports declined substantially between 1778 and 1783, while Irish exports to the West Indies increased. The imports of West Indian products into Scotland increased initially to fill the vacuum created by the loss of the tobacco trade (Sheridan, 1976, p. 618). But this development was short-lived, and, as the Scottish economy went into recession and large quantities of West Indian products rotted in warehouses, Houston and Company's letters to its agents reflect the general situation: "We have resolved to restrict trade to the West Indies."[7] It then stopped the practice of taking sugar estates for mortgages, and it resolved that nothing could induce the company "to go deeper into the West Indian trade."[8]

Throughout most of the war, the main source of food for West Indian slaves was the neighboring foreign islands, which continued to receive unlimited quantities of American products. Hence the British sugar colonies were hit by continuing food shortages with tragic results. Deaths from malnutrition among the slaves reached several thousands in the Leeward Islands and Jamaica. An estimated 5,000 slaves perished in Barbados between 1780 and 1781; the slave population declined from 78,874 in 1774 to 63,248 in 1781, and in 1784 it was given as 61,808. Faced with heavy losses, some planters re-emigrated to England, as exemplified by Pinney's letter to his uncle. "I want to contract my concerns here and fix a fund in England – not solely to depend upon estates subject to every calamity" (Pares, 1950, pp. 93–4).[9]

Thus the loss of the American source of foodstuffs and plantation supplies led to two major problems. First, the decrease in the labor force through heavy losses among the slave population, especially since the slave trade had declined markedly as a result of the war; and then, as a corollary, there was a decline in the quantity of West Indian products exported to Britain. Despite this, there was an inadequate number of ships to transport Caribbean products to Britain for several reasons. The most significant were a large number of merchantmen was requisitioned for war services; the prohibition of American–West Indian commerce removed an extremely large portion of British shipping; a large portion of merchant vessels captured by American privateers was not replaced because of high labor costs and the shortage and high costs of material.

In addition to the economic woes which resulted from the American war, there was a significant psychological blow. The Revolution had virtually broken the spirit of numerous planters, who lost the resilience so characteristic of this group in the eighteenth century. Furthermore, the loss of direct trade with America had another ominous consequence. It forced the merchants and planters to depend on the foreign islands for their American supplies, thus creating an extensive illegal trade between United States and West Indian merchants in foreign colonial ports – a situation which continued in the post-1783 period, despite the tightening of British mercantilist policies. The West Indian sugar economy also went into a decline from which it never truly recovered.

3. AMERICAN PRIVATEERING: ITS CONSEQUENCES

Privateering was a traditional wartime activity of the colonists. Yet, although previously it had only minimal effect on colonial trade, efforts were made by Britain to regulate the activity of enemy privateers (Bemis, 1935, p. 55). In all previous wars the Admiralty contended mainly with French privateers and was able to estimate their number and to restrict their movements by employing an effective convoy system.[10] On the contrary, during the American war, the Admiralty was unable to estimate the numbers and strength of rebel privateers which infested the secluded creeks and small bays around the Caribbean islands. The latter thus successfully blockaded colonial ports, captured merchant vessels, and seriously threatened British colonial commerce as well as the security of the islands (Davis, 1962, p. 332). American privateers fulfilled two extremely important functions: they became a weapon in America's fight for independence, and they were an important means of transporting arms and munitions of war and tropical products to the continent.

In order to fulfill the first function, the privateers attacked West Indian shipping as the vessels made their way unprotected from Barbados through the network of foreign and British islands to Jamaica. Cruisers were normally employed to protect the trade but, in order to do so, the strength of the naval force along the American coast would have had to be weakened.

Many of the American privateers found protection in the ports of the foreign governments, where there were hundreds of United States supporters as well as agents of Congress and some states. Some of the most famous were William Bingham and Richard Harrison, representatives for Virginia and Maryland, at Martinique (Brown 1937, pp. 54–9); Stephen Ceronio at Cape Francois in St. Domingue; and Abraham van Bibber and Samuel Curson at St. Eustatius. Many pursued their private enterprises with the help of resident Americans or British merchants. They secured British registers for American privateers and other vessels to be used if stopped by ships of the Royal Navy. For example, John Spear of Antigua received cargoes of provisions and lumber from his father, William Spear of Baltimore, through the services of Abraham van Bibber, without paying commission. John agreed to provide Abraham with British manufactures, gunpowder, arms, and registers for rebel vessels.

The Edenton merchant William Savage, in transacting a business deal with John Crohon and Company of St. Eustatius, advised the firm to secure the support of the British West Indians, without which it would fail. Likewise, Isaac Gouverneur, the agent for Braxton, Willing and Morris of Philadelphia, also received invaluable support from William Mactier (McTair) of St. Kitts. In Jamaica, Joseph and Eliphalet Fitch, formerly of Boston, provided American rebel vessels with invaluable information about the movement of British warships. These activities enabled the privateers to evade capture and to distress British shipping.

From July 1776, all vessels belonging to British subjects, except those owned by the Bermudians and Bahamians, were subject to capture (Maclay, 1924, p. 69).

Congress as well as many states joined private individuals in sending small navies of warships and privateers on expeditions in the Caribbean (Paullin, 1906, pp. 441–9; 452–3). During these voyages they captured hundreds of West Indian ships laden with rum, molasses, sugar, indigo, and other tropical products. On occasions, continental warships fought battles with ships of the Royal Navy. The success of the *Alfred* (Captain Elisha Hinman) is a classic example; on a trip to the Caribbean in 1777 it captured the *Druid* (Captain Cateret Bourchier). This incident sparked complaints about Lord Howe's handling of the fleet in America, and the lack of protection for the West Indian trade.

The privateers and continental warships also made physical attacks on the islands. A few cases would illustrate their successes. In May 1777 part of the crew of the *Oliver Cromwell* landed at Sandy Point, Tobago (a plaque marks this incursion). Several months later a party of American rebels landed at Bloody Bay in the same island and carried off the gunpowder. Early in 1779 another village, Charlotteville, was successfully attacked.[11] Dominica was also besieged by privateers, and in the case of Barbados, the *Johnson* of a mere eight guns terrorized coastal estates and the colony's trade (Schomburgk, 1848, pp. 335–6). The village of Moryeau in Grenada was burnt and American vessels carried off the gunpowder.

The successful harassment of the islands and their trade served the American war effort well. The British Government had to withdraw parts of the navy blockading the coast to protect the islands, thus enabling American privateers to sail unmolested to the United States with the necessities of war. These attacks by rebel privateers added immensely to the planters' struggle for survival, and at times may even have influenced their opposition to British imperial rule (Carrington, 1988, pp. 84–101).

4. AMERICAN WAR: ITS POLITICAL AND CONSTITUTIONAL IMPACT

One of the more interesting but relatively unexplored areas is the impact of the American Revolution on political and constitutional development in the West Indies. Like many in the United States, several colonists in the islands believed in the emerging ideology of the "Rights of Man," and for most of the second half of the eighteenth century West Indians, too, struggled to control such areas as taxation, the appropriation and expenditure of public money, the upholding of the rights and privileges of their Assembly, the control of all local appointments which they previously held, the usurpation of greater portions of the executive power, the prevention of the unwarranted removal of judges and other local officers, and the forcing of Parliament to abolish those parts of its commercial laws antithetical to colonial trade. In fact, the American concept of "no taxation without representation" originated in Barbados in 1651, when the Assembly denied the British Parliament the right to legislate for the island, since "legislation without representation was a violation of the rights of Englishmen." In Jamaica in 1680, the Assembly successfully established its right to legislate in all domestic matters (Schuyler, 1929, pp. 103–16; Williams, 1970, pp. 179–80; cf. Boyd, 1974, p. 548; Goveia, 1956, pp. 56–7), and finally it was a Grenadian planter who filed a suit in England that led to Lord Mansfield's famous ruling in 1774 in *Campbell vs. Hall*.

In his litigation against William Hall, a Collector of the Customs, Alexander Campbell argued that the Crown had surrendered its right to tax the colonies when local legislatures were established. In this historical and celebrated decision, Lord Mansfield upheld the contention that "Royal Orders" could not supersede the laws and were unenforceable in the colonies without authorization of the local legislatures. This ruling came at the height of the dispute between Britain and her colonies in America, and the colonists welcomed it as supporting their struggle against subjugation by the British Parliament.

Hence many of the constitutional claims of the period did not originate with the American war, although influenced by it, but were well known and discussed throughout the islands. The 1774 "Petition and Memorial" to King George III in support of the Americans in their dispute with Parliament was a restatement of the Jamaican Assembly's constitutional position in an earlier petition in 1766, when it was involved in the protracted Oliphant Case controversy. Other pro-American addresses came from Tobago, from the Assembly of Grenada and the Grenadines, and from the Council of St. Vincent. The Assembly of Barbados, while not overtly pro-American, established a fund for the people of Boston and despatched a petition to the King critical of British policy.

Not only did the assemblies forward petitions and other documents establishing the principles on which the Americans were fighting for their freedom; many West Indians openly spoke in favor of rebellion and even drank to the American struggle as the "Immortal Honour of Incountering death in every form rather than submit to slavery," which they equated with a submission to British authority. In Jamaica, support for the Americans abated after an abortive slave rebellion in 1776 among the house slaves who were imbued with the "spirit of Dear Liberty,"[12] who were emulating the planters' avowed stance, and who themselves wished to gain their freedom. The political and constitutional crises which occurred in Jamaica, Barbados, Grenada, St. Vincent, and the Leeward Islands from 1774 to 1783 were primarily influenced by the pro-republican ideology of a large number of the inhabitants, as well as an accelerated effort on the part of many assemblies to gain power over the executive branch, since they viewed Britain's attempt to subdue the colonists by force as a threat to their own political existence.

There thus developed a struggle for power centered around four traditional areas – the control of internal taxation and the disbursement of the public revenue; the composition and proceedings of the assemblies which embodied their right to appoint their own officers and to have a greater say in the executive decision-making process; the control of the local militia and the islands' defenses; and, in general, a stricter observance of basic parliamentary privileges.

One of the first areas of the prerogative to be attacked was defense, including the governors' total control of the forts, fortifications, public works, martial law, and the control of the militia during this period. In Jamaica in 1778 the Assembly took control of the area by naming all its members and the entire Council to join the Governor as Commissioners for Forts, Fortifications and Public Buildings. His function was now one of making recommendations only. In Barbados, St. Vincent, Antigua, St. Kitts, and Grenada, the assemblies assumed control of public works, including forts and fortifications, by their insistence on examining public accounts before payments were authorized; all works to be paid out of the public purse had to be vetted by the assemblies before the governors could undertake them.

Another area of grave concern in the islands was the declaration of martial law, the calling out and drilling of the militia. There were always complaints of governors' misuse of this prerogative; but there is little doubt that the war in America motivated the West Indian assemblies to seek greater control over martial law and the militia.

After a protracted dispute, in 1779 the legislature of Jamaica passed an Act establishing the Assembly, the Council and the Governor of the Council of War. This thus gave the Assembly control of the milita and martial law. While the Barbados Assembly did not take the same path, it refused to pass a militia bill over the consequences of which it would have no control. It thus told both governors Edward Hay and James Cuninghame that it was "most unwilling ... in times too ... propitious to the claims of civil liberty in the Colonies than ever, to renounce a principle of attachment so Honorable to Society, and enforce Obedience to a power congenial with the Habits of despotic sway."[13] Repeated calls for a militia act met with no success in St. Vincent. In those islands where the assemblies passed legislation to regulate the militia they were useless. Most contained no articles of war, penalties for desertion were unenforceable, and a majority of the inhabitants refused to cooperate.

The Americans had included the unwarranted removal of judges as one of its main complaints against the King in their "Declaration of the Rights of Man." Since 1751 the Jamaica Assembly had sought to give security of tenure of office to judges in the island by legislation which was allowed "to lie on the table" in England. The dismissal of four judges in 1778 led to a prolonged constitutional crisis until January 1781, when the Judges Act was passed giving tenure *quamdiu se bene gesserint* (also expressed as *ad vitam aut culpam* – privilege to be held during good behavior). After 1783 the Act was incorporated into the Governor's Instructions. In Barbados the question was also debated and was cited as a grievance by the Assembly. Although it did not pass legislation as in the case of Jamaica, its opposition to unjustified removals was recognized. There is therefore little doubt that the upheaval caused by the American war had enabled the judges in most islands to hold their places *quamdiu se bene gesserint*, and not *durante bene placito* (during the pleasure of the grantor) as before the war (Carrington, 1988, pp. 128–61).

5. CONCLUSION: A SUMMARY

The impact of the American War of Independence on the economy of the West Indies is fairly well known. The war had caused severe hardships, and the islands went into a state of economic decline from which only minimal recovery was made as late as the 1790s. The political and constitutional impact is less well known. It is quite clear that the American Revolution had found support among a large sector of the inhabitants who shared the political and constitutional ideology of the Americans, as demonstrated in the writings of Edward Long and Bryan Edwards, as well as in the celebrated victory for the Grenada planters in Lord Mansfield's ruling in *Campbell vs. Hall* in 1774 and in the continuous persecution of some governors, as in the case of Valentine Morris of St. Vincent from 1775 to the island's capture in 1779.

It was during this period of crisis in the British Empire that the assemblies vociferously made their claims of co-equality with the British House of Commons. In addition, they refused to raise taxes; they restricted the governors' powers in every facet of political life; they usurped executive power and they persecuted all colonial officials opposed to their tactics and/or ideology. This opposition formed part of a wider movement which was manifested in the American War of Independence. All the governors who served in the West Indies during this period complained of the rise of a "republican spirit," which to the planters meant the retention of power in their hands. Valentine Morris of St. Vincent, John Dalling of Jamaica, Edward Hay and James Cuninghame of Barbados, and Lord George Macartney of Grenada shared

William Mathew Burt's observation of the state of politics in the Leeward Islands: "Others in this part of the world have caught the infection from America and deeply tinged with the principles of Republicanism, attempt bringing all to a level."[14]

Horatio Nelson reached a similar conclusion (Nicolas, 1845, 1: p. 114), as did Sir Guy Carleton, former Governor of Canada and Commander-in-Chief of British forces in America during the war, who strongly opposed free trade between the West Indies and the United States. He wrote: "It is not in the Revolted provinces alone that a Republican spirit is to be found, but the tint has ... spread to other parts of America and to the West Indies."[15] During the American war, therefore, the colonial system was indeed severely tested and, although the islands remained "loyal" to Britain, the planters in their political and constitutional disputes, arising at times out of their declining economic conditions, sought to establish the common ideology of the "Rights of Man," and they severely tested the imperial ties.

REFERENCES

1. Minutes of the Committee of the Privy Council (1784). B.T. 5/1 fo. 27d. Edward Long: "History of Jamaica," Vol. 1. British Museum: Add. MS 12, 404, 402d. See also Carrington, Selwyn H. H.: *The British West Indies During the American Revolution*, and Hewitts, M. J.: "The West Indies in the American Revolution," D.Phil. Thesis, Oxford University, 1936.

2. Josiah Tucker: "The State of the Nation in 1777, compared with the State of the Nation in the famous year of conquest and Glory of 1759" (1777). Bristol Public Library: Jefferies Collection of MSS. Vol. VII, fo. 87. I wish to thank the late Professor Julian P. Boyd for supplying the anecdote.

3. The Earl of Dartmouth to Edward Payne, 5 October 1774. C.O. 152/54.

4. Merchants of Grenada to Lord Macartney, 3 June 1977. Adm. 1/310, fo. 123; James Young to Philip Stephens, 12 June 1777. *Ibid.*, fos. 114–114d; Clark Gayton to John Dalling in Journal of the Assembly of Jamaica, 31 October 1777. C.O. 140/59; Macartney to Sir William Howe, 16 November 1778. C.O. 101/21, fo. 198.

5. John Pinney to William Croker, June 1778. Letter Book 4, p. 220.

6. Houston and Company to James Smith, 1 October 1776. Houston Papers: H.L.S. MS. 8,793, p. 55; Houston and Company to John Constable, 7 February 1777. *Ibid.*, p. 170; Houston and Company to Lewis Chavel & Co., 13 October 1777. *Ibid.*, p. 39. "Invoice of Fifty Barrels Herrings ... on Account and Risque of William Bryan Ese. of Jamaica," 17 September 1777. Chisholme Papers: N.L.S. MS. 188:75, fo. 34.

7. Houston & Company to Turner & Paul, 27 May 1777. N.L.S. MS. 8,793, p.325.

8. Houston & Co. to Samuel Cary, 9 April 1778. N.L.S. MS. 8,793, p. 428.

9. Cf. Pinney to Simon Pretor, 12 June 1777. Pinney Papers. Letter Book 2, p. 114.

10. R. P. Crowhurst: "British Oceanic Convoys in the Seven Years War, 1756–1763," Ph.D. Thesis, University of London, 1970.

11. Peter Campbell to Lord Macartney, 6 July 1777. C.O. 101/20, fo. 211d; "Memorial of the Proprietors ... in Tobago" to Lord George Germain (1777). *Ibid.*, fo. 242; cf. 28 May 1778. C.O. 101/21, fo. 150; Extract of a letter from Lieutenant Oswald Clark, 18 January 1779. C.O. 101/23, fos. 78–78d; cf. Macartney to Germain, 28 January 1779. *Ibid.*, fos. 76–76d.

12. R. Lindsay to Dr. Robert Robertson, 6 August 1776. Robertson–MacDonald Papers. N.L.S. MS. 3,942, fos. 260d–261.

13. Journal of the Assembly of Barbados, 1 October 1776. C.O. 31/39.

14. William Mathew Burt to Germain, 25 October 1780. C.O. 152/60, fo. 258.

15. "Minutes of the Committee of the Privy Council for Trade," 16 March 1784. B.T. 5/1, fo. 14d.

FURTHER READING

Bell, Herbert C.: "The West Indian trade before the American Revolution," *American Historical Review*, 22 (1917).

Bemis, Samuel Flagg: *The Diplomacy of the American Revolution* (New York: American Historical Association, 1935).

Boyd, Julian P.: "Jefferson's expression of the American mind," *Virginia Quarterly Review*, 50, 4 (1974).

Brown, Margaret L.: "William Bingham: agent of the Continental Congress in Martinique," *Pennsylvania Magazine of History and Biography*, 61 (1937).

Carrington, Selwyn H. H.: "The American Revolution and the British West Indies' Economy," *Journal of Interdisciplinary History*, 17, 4 (1987), 823–50.

——: *The British West Indies During the American Revolution* (Holland: Royal Institute of Linguistics and Anthropology/Foris Publications, 1988).

Davis, Ralph: *The Rise of the English Shipping Industry in the Seventeenth and Eighteenth Centuries* (London: Macmillan, 1962).

Edwards, Bryan: *The History, Civil and Commercial, of the British Colonies in the West Indies*, 2 vols. (London: Stockdale, 1794).

Ford, Worthington Chauncery (ed.): *Journals of the Continental Congress, 1774–1789* (Washington: 1904).

Goveia, Elsa V.: *A Study of the Historiography of the British West Indies to the End of the Nineteenth Century* (Mexico: 1956).

Maclay, Edgar Stanton: *A History of American Privateers* (London: Appleton, 1924).

Nicolas, Sir Charles Harris (ed.) *The Despatches and Letters of Admiral Lord Viscount Nelson*, 7 vols. (London: 1845–6).

Pares, Richard: *A West India Fortune* (London: Longmans and Green, 1950).

——: *War and Trade in the West Indies, 1739–1763* (London: Cass, 1963).

Paullin, Charles Oscar: *The Navy of the American Revolution: its Administration, its policy and its Achievements* (Cleveland: Burrows, 1906).

Schomburgk, R. H.: *The History of Barbados* (London: 1848).

Schuyler, Robert L.: *Parliament and the British Empire: Some Constitutional Controversies Concerning Imperial Legislative Jurisdiction* (New York: Columbia University Press, 1929).

Setser, Vernon G.: *The Commercial Reciprocity Policy of the United States, 1774–1829* (Philadelphia: University of Pennsylvania Press, 1937).

Sheffield, John: *Observations on the Commerce of the American States* (Dublin: 1784).

Sheridan, Richard: *Sugar and Slavery: an Economic History of the British West Indies, 1623–1775* (Baltimore: Johns Hopkins University Press, 1973).

——: "The crisis of slave subsistence in the British West Indies during and after the American Revolution," *William and Mary Quarterly*, 33 (1976).

Williams, Eric Eustace: *From Columbus to Castro: the History of the Caribbean, 1492–1969* (London: Deutsch, 1970).

53

The effects of the American Revolution on France and its empire

DAVID P. GEGGUS

THE American Revolution gave *ancien régime* France its last foreign policy success, a very popular war that brought revenge for the humiliations of 1756–63, but at a cost many historians have considered disastrous. Within five years of the war's end the French Government was bankrupted and forced to embark on revolutionary reorganization that within another five years brought the abolition of the aristocracy, the overthrow of the monarchy, and the start of another, far more costly, war against almost the whole of Europe. Both the financial and ideological impact on France of its participation in the War of Independence are controversial. The American and French revolutions were similarly engendered by wider movements in the Western world, which led governments to extend their fiscal demands at the same time that libertarian and egalitarian ideas gained currency. Moreover, the French Revolution was an event of much greater magnitude and expressed deep-rooted domestic tensions. Even so, the American Revolution probably hastened the outbreak of the great upheaval in France and helped shape its early years.

I. THE FRENCH GOVERNMENT

From the very end of the Seven Years' War in 1763, the French Government began preparing for a new conflict with Britain that would avenge its disastrous losses. As early as 1775, the foreign minister, Charles Gravier, Comte de Vergennes, recognized that the crisis in North America might bring such an opportunity. Despite opposition from the finance minister Turgot and the reluctance of the young Louis XVI to support a revolt against a legitimate sovereign, Vergennes obtained permission in May 1776 secretly to assist the rebel colonists. PIERRE-AUGUSTIN CARON DE BEAUMARCHAIS was engaged as an intermediary, and the departure of volunteers for America was tacitly countenanced. Although Vergennes feared the impact of "so terrible an eruption" (Manceron, 1978, p. 153) on France's own colonies, his ministry instructed the pro-government press to publicize the patriot cause, and even founded a newspaper, *Les Affaires de l'Angleterre et de l'Amérique*, for this purpose.

France declared war in June 1778, four months after concluding treaties of alliance and trade with the confederated colonies. The decision actively to intervene resulted not from Franklin's persuasive diplomacy, but from the assurance brought by the victory at Saratoga that the rebellion would not collapse. The government's aims were limited. England was to be weakened by the loss of the 13 colonies, and France, it was hoped, would benefit commercially. To La Fayette's dismay, Versailles displayed no desire to reconquer French Canada. A continued British presence in North America was considered necessary to limit the power of the emergent new state, whose future alliance was not seriously valued. American brusqueness during the peace negotiations, and the failure of French merchants after 1783 to make inroads into the North American market, helped maintain the French Government in its aristocratic coolness towards the United States (*see* Chapters 33 and 38).

2. PUBLIC OPINION

In their struggle against bigotry and injustice at home, social commentators such as Voltaire had since the 1730s depicted British North America as a land of prosperity and religious toleration, popularizing the image of "the virtuous Quaker" free of Old World corruption. However, before the Stamp Act crisis, Frenchmen knew and cared little about the 13 colonies. Benjamin Franklin's defense of the colonies before Parliament, and his subsequent visit to Paris in 1767 at the invitation of the French Government, set in motion a current of pro-Americanism that would not diminish for 25 years.

French interest in North America was therefore already growing when the events of 1776 sent a wave of emotional enthusiasm through France, expressed in poetry, plays, and novels, banquets, new fashions, new books about America, and translations of old ones. Aristocratic young men, eager to fight the traditional foe, took ship for the New World to offer their military services. In salons, colleges, and academies, reading clubs and masonic lodges, the meaning of the Revolution was avidly discussed. The periodical press, expanding fast in these years, carried not only frequent war reports, but also the writings of colonial patriots and the acts and resolutions of their legislatures. The state constitutions and bills of rights were published in French at least five times between 1777 and 1786, and, like the Declaration of Independence, were deliberately ignored by the government censor.

Interest in the Revolution was also promoted by the increase of personal contacts, hitherto rare, between Americans and Frenchmen. When most well-to-do French persons still wore powdered wigs, plain-dressed American sea-captains, merchants, and diplomats created a vivid impression. Benjamin Franklin, who was regarded as the personification of New World virtue and simplicity, became a household name after his return in 1776, and his picture appeared on all manner of every-day items. Both Franklin (for illustration, *see* figure 28, p. 323) and John Paul Jones (*see* figure 43) were received at court, sculpted by Houdon, and admitted into the new masonic lodge of the Nine Sisters. Other members included the future revolutionaries Brissot, Sieyès, Danton, Pétion, Condorcet, and Camille Desmoulins. Franklin played a major role in the propagation of occult masonry, and his and George Washington's membership facilitated French identification with the patriot cause. A different type of contact came through the 8,000 French soldiers who served in the United States and returned home to recount their experiences. Peace brought the establishment of a regular packet service between the two countries, and the flood of publications continued through the 1780s.

Two levels of public opinion may be distinguished. The most popular form, a vague pro-Americanism, was rooted in a jingoistic Anglophobia that generated enthusiasm for the insurgents because they were enemies of the British. Among the politically conscious, those who were pro-reform and anti-autocratic saw the American Revolution as a vindication of their own ideas and an inspiration for their own struggle against royal absolutism and social injustice. In the 1780 edition of the Abbé Raynal's

FIGURE 43 A bronze medallion portraying John Paul Jones (by Augustin Dupré after a bust by Jean Antoine Houdon, 1789)

very influential *History of the two Indies*, Diderot inserted two chapters on North America, which, while justifying the colonists' rebellion, covertly attacked the foundations of *ancien régime* France and caused the book to be banned.

> There is no form of government with the prerogative of being immutable; no political authority which, created yesterday or a thousand years ago, cannot be abrogated in ten years or tomorrow; no power, however respectable or sacred, that is authorized to regard the state as its property. (Raynal, [1780] 1981, p. 325)

Both these trends in opinion were reinforced by the fashionable literary image of the noble savage and his colonial counterpart, the noble frontiersman. The resulting vision of America was frequently an idealized distortion that depicted an undifferentiated nation of hard-working, godly farmers who lived in harmony, free of jealousy, greed, and intolerance. This "American mirage" reflected French preoccupations with social privilege, corruption, and despotism as much as transatlantic realities. This is well illustrated by the French edition of St. Jean de Crèvecoeur's *Letters of an American Farmer*, which became more sentimental and propagandist in its revised translation (*see* CREVECOEUR, MICHEL-GUILLAUME JEAN DE). Americans in France, such as Franklin, Jefferson, and Philip Mazzei, attempted to promote a more realistic image. However, first-hand experience was no guarantee of accuracy; the radical journalist Jacques-Pierre Brissot, founder of the "Société Gallo-Américaine," visited the United States in 1788, but proved one of the fiercest defenders of the American myth. Myth or not, he declared, it served a purpose.

Rather than introducing new ideas, the American Revolution catalyzed trends already present in *ancien régime* France. As early as the 1750s, Frenchmen began to claim they were living in a dynamic new era of change, and the liberal, egalitarian, assumptions of the Enlightenment had become commonplace long before the War of

Independence. By the 1760s even aristocratic opponents of the Crown were using words such as "nation," "constitution," and "citizen." By 1776 the phrase "imprescriptible and inalienable rights" was already in use. The very fact that the ideology of the American Revolution was not novel, and spoke to existing aspirations, helps explain the enthusiasm that greeted it. It also renders it extremely difficult to assess America's impact on the development of French opinion.

For the youthful La Fayette, one can say his conversion to the cause of moderate constitutionalism was directly owing to his pursuit of military honors. And his fellow officer the Comte de Ségur later reminisced, "I was far from being the only one whose heart palpitated at the sound of the growing awakening of liberty, seeking to shake off the yoke of arbitrary power" (Cobban, 1963, p. 122). On the other hand, Condorcet and Brissot, two of the most influential "Americanists," had both read Rousseau before reading the Declaration of Independence. Beaumarchais had written the anti-aristocratic *Marriage of Figaro* before being won over to the cause of the insurgents, though he could not get it published until the 1780s. The Marquis de Chastellux, who published in 1786 a popular account of his wartime experience in Rochambeau's army, had already praised American society in his *De la félicité publique* in 1772. This serves as a reminder that much of what the French found admirable in North America, such as religious toleration, the absence of institutionalized privilege, and freedom of speech, was not a product of the Revolution at all.

What was stunningly unique about the events in America was that they put into action what hitherto Frenchmen had merely discussed as abstract propositions. Contemporaries familiar with the concept of a social contract felt they were witnessing, as if in the primeval past, the birth of a new society. For a nation completely lacking a political life, America provided a practical demonstration of successful and sweeping political reform. That this was achieved without considerable bloodshed or persecution brought a new respectability to the idea of revolutionary change, and inspired belief in a new era of progress. Governments truly could be made accountable to their subjects.

The spectacle of European ideas being applied across the ocean also reinforced their claim to be considered as universal truths. The physiocrat and former minister Turgot opposed on financial grounds France's assisting the rebel colonists, but in 1778 he wrote to Joseph Price that they were the hope of the human race and perhaps would provide a model for it. Even the royal censor, the Abbé Genty, declared in a prize essay: "The independence of the Anglo-Americans is the event most likely to accelerate the revolution which must bring happiness on earth. In the bosom of this new republic are true treasures that will enrich the world" (Mornet, 1933, p. 396–7).

Although difficult to prove, contemplation of the American dream must have increased the dissatisfaction of at least those already dissatisfied with the *Ancien Régime* in France. One may surmise from the events of the 1780s that the focusing of national attention on the American Revolution made French opinion more impatient of despotic authority and social inequality, and more ready to consider radical reform and republicanism as workable options for some societies. The theory of enlightened despotism no longer found champions among intellectuals. And the role in limiting royal power claimed for the aristocracy, in theory by Montesquieu and in practice by the *parlements* (the chief law courts), was less readily accepted.

Here several qualifications need to be introduced. There is no evidence that any French soldier returned from America a convinced revolutionary. Indeed the word would not be coined, by Mirabeau, until 1789, and some claim that the modern concept of revolution came not from the Atlantic world or the Enlightenment but from German Illuminism. Similarly, contemporary interest in republican democracy was also fueled in the 1780s by a growing fascination with Ancient Greek and Roman culture. This helped increase the popularity of Rousseau as a political thinker and diminish that of Montesquieu. It also reduced the reputation of the British Constitution. *Anglomanes* thus gave ground to more democratic *Américanistes* in the postwar years for reasons besides the triumph of the United States. Nevertheless, despite having participated through their wartime alliance in the overthrow of a legitimate sovereign, the French gave no sign of seeking a republic themselves when their own revolution began. One might add that the exhilarating sense of living in a new age of progress also owed as much to the Enlightenment as to the American Revolution, which it pre-dated. It was as the Enlightenment in action that the Revolution was hailed in Condorcet's *De l'influence de la Révolution d'Amérique sur l'Europe* (1786), which was the period's most powerful statement of the idea of progress. In his later history of the world, Condorcet depicted the Revolution as a great event, a harbinger of the French Revolution, but even so, only one link in the chain stretching from Descartes to the foundation of the French republic, which constituted the ninth age of history.

Another problem in assessing America's impact on France is that it did not provide a clear-cut example. While most states had two-chamber assemblies, and few yet had elected governors, it was the constitution of Pennsylvania that gained greatest praise from commentators such as Turgot, Condorcet, and Brissot. Although favoring a very restricted franchise, they saw little good in the separation of powers, and thought the federal constitution made the presidency too powerful. Not only John Adams but also Thomas Jefferson seemed somewhat conservative in the company of such men, whom they met as ambassadors in Europe. Ironically, one way the Revolution undermined the position of the French aristocracy was by the creation of the hereditary order for veteran officers, the Order of Cincinnatus. Perceived as an incipient nobility, this created uproar among admirers of America, led by the Comte de Mirabeau, and engendered a heated debate on the evils of aristocracy. It should be said, however, that the controversy was secretly initiated by Franklin.

In addition to such critical analysis by the friends of America, there were some overtly hostile currents in French thought. The theory of American degeneracy, derived from Buffon and applied to the New World's Caucasian inhabitants by De Pauw, was also a product of these years, though it could make little headway given the physical presence in Paris of Franklin and Jefferson. Many aristocrats who crossed the Atlantic did not like what they found there, and came back critics of American society. And royalists and conservatives naturally were happy to predict disaster for the new republic. French attitudes towards the 13 former colonies nonetheless remained overwhelmingly favorable down through the early years of the French Revolution.

3. FRENCH FINANCES

The chaotic system of French Government accounting made it very difficult even for the king's ministers to know the government's true financial position. For this reason the financial impact on France of intervention in North America is a rather murky subject. Historians have often claimed that the price of American independence was the French Revolution, since it began with the financial crisis of 1786. Jacques Necker, the finance minister from 1777 to 1781, is generally blamed for funding the war solely with loans at very high interest, and for covering up their impact in his published accounts. Recent research shows that Necker's loans were not as expensive as once thought. Moreover, although the war cost France more than 1,000 million livres, and Necker's loans totalled more than 500 million, his peacetime successors also borrowed very heavily. The apparent miracle of financing a war without recourse to taxation certainly impeded the postwar implementation of much-needed tax reform. However, the war was far from solely responsible for the bankruptcy of 1788.

4. THE FRENCH REVOLUTION

When assessing the American impact on the French Revolution, the same problems arise as with the development of French opinion in the preceding decade. Driven forward by internal forces, the French Revolution could probably have unfolded in much the same way had the United States never existed. However, in the influence of certain individuals, perhaps in some constitutional forms and reforms, one may see the imprint of American example. The onset of the Revolution and the hostility of foreign powers undoubtedly made Frenchmen feel closer to the United States, and the active involvement of Americans such as John Paul Jones, JOEL BARLOW, and THOMAS PAINE helped intensify pro-American sentiment during the early years of the Revolution. The death of Franklin, for example, made a profound impact on all levels of Parisian society.

The concepts of a constitutional convention, a written constitution, and a declaration of rights, in the forms they were best known in France, can be called American concepts. The Estates-General were called in France shortly after the United States had ratified its own federal constitution. State constitutions and bills of rights had been meticulously analyzed in France for more than a decade. Although the Estates-General was a medieval body, it was commonly expected that it would provide France with a constitution. This it began to do, on transforming itself into a National Constituent Assembly in June 1789. Its Declaration of the Rights of Man bore close resemblance to the Virginia Declaration of Rights, though it was more self-consciously universalist. La Fayette, advised by Jefferson, and Mounier, another admirer of the United States, had a major share in writing the document.

Potentially the most direct link between the American and French revolutions is provided by the peasant soldiers who served in Rochambeau's army. On campaign in North America, they witnessed first-hand the life of prosperous small farmers, who knew nothing of the seigneurial exactions and high taxes that burdened rural France. The regions in which the soldiers were most heavily recruited were also those that experienced the worst rioting in 1789 against the relics of the feudal regime in the countryside. It is tempting to imagine that these veterans returned to their villages with broadened horizons, and encouraged their neighbors to be less accepting of existing inequalities. However, it is not known how many troops had returned by 1789 to the districts they had originally left. It is possible simply that the poorest rural areas produced most popular discontent and most recruits for the army.

In the debates of September 1789 on the form of the new constitution the opposing parties both appealed to American example. The supporters of bicameralism and a strong executive were resoundingly defeated. Although their plan conformed most closely to American precedent, and had the backing of Jefferson, they were known as *Anglomanes* or *Monarchiens*. Those favoring a single-chamber legislature and a temporary royal veto included the leading *Américanistes*, Brissot and Condorcet, though their chief spokesman, the Abbé Sieyès displayed little interest in American affairs. American influence on the question is thus difficult to assign. John Adams, curiously, approved of the outcome. He recognized that, under a balanced government, the progress of reform would have been jeopardized owing to the existence of an hereditary monarch and aristocracy in France.

Of the French officers who participated in the War of Independence, only a handful were prominent in the French Revolution. The Marquis de La Fayette, seconded by Charles de Lameth, played a major role in breaking down barriers between the aristocracy and Third Estate in the period 1787–9. As head of the Paris National Guard, however, he became more notable for attempting to restrain rather than further the course of the Revolution. The Comte de Custine became a general in the army of the Republic, but was executed for treason. Mention could also be made of Du Châtelet, a journalistic collaborator of Condorcet.

Condorcet and Brissot proved to be very influential figures during the years of 1789–92, both as journalists and politicians. Their ideas prevailed in many key controversies, such as over the Declaration of the Rights of Man, the form of the constitution, the abolition of privilege, and the declaration of war in 1792. However, although they had been enthusiastic interpreters of America, their ideas notably evolved in response to domestic pressures during the course of the French Revolution. This is particularly true of their republicanism. Condorcet had as early as 1774 denounced kings as the dupes of priests, and in 1786 had declared a republic to be the best form of government. However, not till the King fled Paris in June 1791, proving himself an enemy of the Revolution, did Condorcet call for a French republic. Brissot also proved a reluctant republican. Nevertheless, he did make frequent references to American precedent when rousing public opinion to support a war against the hostile monarchies of Europe. "With few soldiers [the Americans] won numerous battles against the superior forces of the English, and it was because their cause was just" (Gidney, 1930, p. 123).

With the triumph of moderate constitutionalism in 1789 the symbolic importance to France of the United States declined. It was among the supporters of constitutional monarchy that the American myth had most appeal, and as the Revolution moved to the left the United States found fewer admirers. Brissot attempted to reverse this trend, when he published in April 1791 his *Nouveau voyage dans les Etats-Unis de l'Amérique septentrionale*. He acknowledged that, having won their own liberty, the French did not need any lessons from the Americans in that area. However, for the secret of preserving that liberty the United States remained an important object of study. By forcing France into war in 1792, Brissot was paradoxically to be largely responsible that this lesson was never learned.

5. THE FRENCH COLONIES

The impact of the American Revolution on France's colonial empire was felt most perceptibly in the Caribbean colony of Saint Domingue (modern Haiti), which was the world's major producer of sugar and coffee. With a population in 1789 of 60,000 Whites and free coloreds and a half million slaves, its 8,000 plantations made it one of the wealthiest European colonies. It accounted for some two-fifths of French overseas trade and had been the engine of France's great commercial expansion during the eighteenth century. Saint Domingue experienced its own complex and extremely destructive revolution simultaneous with the revolution in France. Beginning in 1788 as a movement of wealthy planters for greater colonial autonomy, it resulted in the expulsion of all Whites and the creation of the independent state of Haiti in 1804. Although the American Revolution was not of critical importance in the causation of this upheaval, it does seem to have played a multi-faceted role in raising tensions within the colony on the eve of the revolution that would destroy it.

Unlike their British counterparts and neighbors, French colonists lacked any system of representative government. They also suffered more severely from metropolitan laws of trade. These forced them to pay high prices for imports and denied them access to the foreign markets where most of their produce was eventually sold to the sole profit of French merchants. France's Caribbean colonies, therefore, had more substantive reasons for rebellion than any British possessions, and indeed since 1770 Raynal and other French writers had predicted eventual colonial secession. However, vulnerability to slave revolts, to naval blockade, and to foreign invasion made West Indian islands (whose wealthiest proprietors resided in France) particularly dependent on their mother countries for protection. This considerably reduced the relevance to them of the example of the American Revolution. Dissident planters in Saint Domingue tended to be Anglophiles who looked to a British takeover rather than independence. Perhaps for this reason the struggle of the 13 colonies excited among them no obvious sympathy for the insurgents.

Nevertheless, the desire for self-government had a long history in Saint Domingue and it was notably strengthened by the War of Independence. Aside from its (apparently slight) ideological impact, the American Revolution gave Saint Domingue a tempting taste of free trade. When France intervened in the conflict, colonial administrators (liberally interpreting the Franco-American trade treaty) opened the colony's ports to Yankee traders, who supplied its needs more cheaply than could French merchants. These commercial contacts were continued in restricted form after the war through a new system of free ports, which were visited in the late 1780s by more than 600 American vessels per year, chiefly from Massachusetts and Philadelphia. Numerous American merchants established themselves at Cap Français and Port au Prince, and by 1790 Saint Domingue was absorbing 10 per cent of United States exports. The free-port trade, however, was heavily taxed and subjected to frustrating prohibitions. It also provoked a retaliatory increase in freight charges by resentful French merchants. In addition, smuggling was curtailed by new measures reminiscent of British action in North America 20 years before.

Such conflicts of interest encouraged planters to think of themselves as "Americans" rather than Frenchmen. When prominent colonists established a scientific society at Cap Français in 1784 they called it "Le Cercle des Philadelphes." Among the many adepts of occult freemasonry who were members was Bacon de la Chevalerie, who had links with the Nine Sisters' Lodge in Paris and who five years later became the first revolutionary leader in Saint Domingue. Ironically, friction between colony and metropole reached its height at a time when both the Minister of Marine (La Luzerne) and the Colonial Intendant (Barbé de Marbois) were former diplomats who had served in Philadelphia during the war.

The abolition of slavery in northern states such as Massachusetts, where freed Blacks migrated to the seaports, must have been discussed in Saint Domingue by visiting American seamen, but it is not known how this affected the slaves. The American Revolution certainly had more direct impact on the colony's free colored community, which formed a sort of middle class of mixed racial descent and was victimized by an entrenched system of discrimination. In 1779 a special regiment of free coloreds was raised and, along with a battalion of Whites, sent to Georgia to fight alongside the rebel colonists at Savannah. The regiment's muster roll reads like a list of future revolutionaries. Besides the future King Henry Christophe, it included many of the leaders who, in the 1790s, would direct the struggle for civil rights and then free colored domination in Saint Domingue. Such men returned from Georgia with military experience and a new sense of their own importance. For the first time they cautiously began to pressure an intransigent government to dismantle the system of racial inequality.

Autonomist and secessionist attitudes among Saint Domingue Whites, and aspirations for freedom and equality among its non-Whites, also developed in response to the appearance in Paris in 1788 of an anti-slavery society called the "Amis des Noirs." Founded by Brissot, its members included Condorcet, Mirabeau, and La Fayette. The question here is to what extent the movement was inspired by the American Revolution. Anti-slavery thought in France certainly long pre-dated the revolt of the 13 colonies, and Condorcet was an abolitionist by 1776. In La Fayette's case, it was apparently his experiences in North America that converted him, for on his return he immediately began an experiment with freed slaves in France's Guiana colony. Other veterans, however, reported that North American slaves were relatively well-treated. Neither Washington nor Jefferson chose to encourage the movement. The key figure was Brissot. His interest in anti-slavery and the initial proposal for an abolition society, which was founded before his trip to the United States, came from his Quaker friends in London. Even so, he subsequently made ample use of American evidence to buttress his arguments about the safety of abolishing the slave trade, the superiority of free labor, and the ability of Blacks. With the outbreak of the French Revolution, the "Amis des Noirs" became active supporters of the free coloreds and the principal bugaboo of the white colonists.

In these ways the American Revolution helped prepare the ground for the Haitian Revolution. Whether the Whites' desires for autonomy, the free coloreds' for equality, or the slaves' for freedom would of themselves have led to rebellion is a matter of speculation. However, it was clearly the French Revolution that precipitated Saint Domingue's destruction. Weakening the traditional sources of authority in the colonies, it not only enflamed social and political aspirations but also undermined the institutions that had held them in check. Initiating a decade of turmoil in Saint Domingue, it thus brought into existence the New World's second independent state.

FURTHER READING

Cobban, A.: *A History of Modern France*, 3 vols. Vol 1, *Old Régime and Revolution, 1715–1799*, 3rd edn. (Harmondsworth: Penguin, 1963).

Debbasch, Y.: *Couleur et liberté* (Color and liberty) (Paris: 1967).

Echeverria, D.: *Mirage in the West: a History of the French Image of American Society to 1815* (New York: Octagon Books, 1966).

Fay, B.: *L'esprit révolutionnaire en France et aux Etats-Unis à la fin du XVIIIe siècle* (Paris: Champion, 1924); trans. R. Guthrie, *The Revolutionary Spirit in France and America* (New York: Harcourt, Brace, 1927).

Frostin, C.: *Les révoltes blanches à Saint-Domingue aux viie et xviiie siècles* (White revolts in Saint Domingue during the seventeenth and eighteenth centuries) (Paris: L'Ecole, 1975).

Gidney, L.: *L'influence des Etats-Unis d'Amérique sur Brissot, Condorcet et Mme Roland* (The influence of the United States on Brissot, Condorcet, and Mme Roland) (Paris: Rieder, 1930).

Harris, R. D.: *Necker, Reform Statesman of the Ancien Régime* (Berkeley: University of California Press, 1979).

McDonald, F.: "The relation of French peasant veterans of the American Revolution to the fall of feudalism in France," *Agricultural History*, 25 (1951), 151–61.

Manceron, C.: *The Wind from America, 1778–1781* (New York: Alfred Knopf, 1978).

Mornet, D.: *Les origines intellectuelles de la Révolution française (1715–1787)* (Intellectual origins of the French Revolution) (Paris: Armand Colin, 1933).

Palmer, R.R.: *The Age of the Democratic Revolution: a Political History of Europe and America, 1760–1800*, 2 vols. Vol. 1, *The Challenge* (Princeton: Princeton University Press, 1959).

Raynal, G.T.: *Histoire philosophique et politique des deux Indes* (Paris: 1780); repr., ed. Y. Bénot (Paris: Maspéro 1981)

54

The impact of the American Revolution on Spain and Portugal and their empires

KENNETH MAXWELL

I. INTRODUCTION

HISTORY writing since the second world war has tended to de-emphasize the role of individuals, institutions and events and, instead, has sought to plot the longer-term trends in economic development, to delineate social and economic structures and to track shifts in mentalities. Topics such as the impact of the American Revolution on the territories of the other European colonial powers to its south have been, as a consequence, much neglected. Although much has been achieved by this emphasis, and conjunctural economic analysis and an understanding of the social complexity of the Americas is essential to any understanding of the reception of the North American Revolution in Latin America, it has also led to the almost total exclusion of detailed examinations of elites or institutions, and above all of intellectual life and politics, all areas in which the impact of the North American model was, of course, most influential among Latin Americans of the late colonial period. Hence today we tend to know more about slaves than their masters; more about the forced Indian labor drafts of upper Peru (contemporary Bolivia) than the attitudes of Peruvian merchants and bureaucrats in Lima; more about Mexican silver production than the political role of mining entrepreneurs. As to intellectual history, the most recent work on the enlightenment in Latin America – a decisive framework for explaining what was and what was not taken from the North American example by the Latin American elites of the period – is 20 years old, and the best account remains the collection of essays edited by Arthur Whitaker in the early 1940s (twice reissued in the early 1960s, but long since out of print). A third problem is related to context. That is, we have a division of historical output concerning Latin America into two broad categories, one which might be called the vertical dimension, the other the horizontal. The vertical dimension is a form of history writing confined by the geographical limits of what became after independence national entities. National histories inevitably stress originality and uniqueness rather than any common colonial background, and are sometimes hostile to a point of view that would place the new nations that emerged in Latin America within an international or a comparative framework, or even within a colonial or neo-colonial context. The horizontal dimension is of course the comparative one – but this is also something we lack for Latin America. The *Cambridge History of Latin America* (Cambridge, 1984–), for example, is almost totally devoid of comparative analysis, especially in its colonial and early national volumes, a factor emphasized by the ease with which the original volumes are now being subdivided and reissued as what are essentially national histories. And a final caveat: according to the latest textbook in the field, *Early Latin America* by Stuart B. Schwartz and James Lockhart (Cambridge, 1983), this topic is not very important at all. To them the Latin American revolutions (and, by implication, the American Revolution, which they mention twice in a text of 480 pages) were no revolutions at all, and national independence a shadow thing at best. As they put it, "It has been said often and truly that the division between colonial and national periods is an artificial one especially in the social, economic, and cultural domains where so much current scholarly interest lies."

This is not the view of radical comparativists such as Susan Deans and Edward Countryman ("Independence and Revolution in the Americas," *Radical History*, 27 (May 1983), 144–72). For them independence, that is, political emancipation from Europe, was a critical transition which at the very least requires an inquiry into the place of Latin America within the process of industrial, political and social transformation that flowed from the circum-Atlantic upheavals of the late eighteenth century, of which the American Revolution was, of course, the most dramatic colonial manifestation. The question they raise is one raised some time ago by Stanley and Barbara Stein (1970); that is, why at independence did the histories of South and North America diverge so dramatically, or, to put the question in Immanuel Wallerstein's terms, how was it that North America moved from the periphery to the core of the world system, while Latin America remained peripheral? Brazilian historians such as Fernando Novais and Emilia Viotti da Costa have also been concerned to place the late eighteenth and early nineteenth-century experience of Brazil within the context of a crisis of the old regime and the old colonial system in the face of the Atlantic and industrial revolutions. Less work of this nature has been undertaken on Spanish America, although Tulio Halperin has long focused on the economic and political complexities of the independence period, both in the La Plata region and more broadly in Spanish America (*Reforma y disolución de los impérios Ibéricos, 1750–1850* [Madrid: Alianza, 1985]). Nancy Farriss in her book on the Maya sees the impact of the reformist proto-liberal policies of the Spanish Bourbons as marking the critical divide in the history of Meso-America. Much of the new economic history of late colonial Mexico is seeking some explanation for the paradox of coexisting boom and rising social tensions within the most important of Spain's colonial holdings in the Western Hemisphere. But the important point about these disagreements is to emphasize that the issue of the significance of the impact of the American Revolution on developments in Latin America is not one which should be assumed, but which requires justification.

Above all, we are here talking about process, or rather about three discrete processes. One involves ideas in their social context. For Latin America and the Iberian powers Spain under Carlos III (1759–88) and for Portugal during the long predominance of the Marques de Pombal (1750–77), led to major reform in the management of colonial affairs that in some instances served to pre-empt and in others to mitigate the impact of the American Revolution. Secondly, there is the issue of revolution as example and as potentiality, involving the creative articulation of new institutional mechanisms of government. In both Brazil during the late 1780s and Spanish America in the aftermath of the wars of independence, the North American constitutional as well as the federal model proved attractive. Thirdly, we are dealing with colonial opposition to metropolitan powers; that is, the pre-eminent lesson of the North American example was the successful waging of a war of independence. It is in this aspect, of course, that the ambiguity of the Iberian and Ibero-American role is most apparent, since

Spain in particular was an important component of the European alliance that helped the North Americans escape from British rule. And many would-be Latin American nationalists saw Britain as a potential ally against Spain. Process, therefore, is an element in the period because we are dealing with a complex interaction involving the impact of the Enlightenment as well as the coincidental experimentation with new state institutional forms (confederation, federalism, constitution-making, bills of rights, etc.), as well as a process of decolonization. All imply a delinking and a reformulation of previously set patterns; an upsetting, changing and resetting of the context within which collectivities define themselves.

There are two major paradigms for examining the impact of the North Atlantic democratic revolutions in Latin America. First, there is the Robert Palmer–Jacques Godechot vision of an Atlantic-based transformation, an essentially political and institutional view which sees mutual influence in political theory, constitutional experimentation and the politics of democratic incorporation. In this view the Enlightenment is a positive, benign and causative influence, essentially a progressive force.

A second view is a more economistic view – partly Marxian but also capable of incorporating much of classical liberalism – that is, it is a view that sees a general crisis of the old colonial system which effects the British Empire in the 1770s and the Spanish and Portuguese in the early nineteenth century, all of which flows from the shift from commercial to industrial capitalism. In this view the intellectual contribution is minimal. The revolutions in America, both North and South, represent a shift from formal to informal domination, with the newly industrializing states of Europe – especially Britain – replacing the decaying bureaucratic and mercantilist empires of Spain and Portugal.

2. BRAZIL

How do Brazil and Spanish America fit into this picture? The case of Brazil is especially interesting since, given the Atlantic focus of its trade, its large slave population and its close links via Lisbon to the British-dominated commercial system of the North Atlantic, its local elites were closely attuned to the events surrounding the struggle between Britain and its North American colonies.

The economic characteristics of the eighteenth-century Portuguese-Atlantic system were first, the pre-eminence of colonial, mainly Brazilian, staples. Second, the growth, decline and revival of manufacturing industry in Portugal was inversely proportional to the rise and fall of gold production in the Brazilian interior. That is to say, Portuguese domestic manufacturing thrived before 1700, and again after 1777, but languished during the golden age. This had major implications for Portuguese foreign and colonial policy. Portugal also remained throughout the eighteenth century a chronic grain importer – from Northern Europe at the beginning of the century and from North America, especially Virginia and the Carolinas, towards the end. This fact during the 1780s and 1790s had a major impact on the attitudes of the new North American republic, marked especially in the person of Thomas Jefferson, towards proto-nationalist republican movements in Brazil. These attitudes were ambivalent at best when Virginia's trade with Portugal was placed in the balance against support for nationalist movements of uncertain origin in Portugal's vast South American territories.

Finally, the eighteenth-century Luso-Atlantic world was characterized by the struggle between France and England, a struggle which increasingly compromised Portugal. Lisbon tried to accommodate both, but by its very Atlantic nature, and because of the central economic role of Brazil within the Luso-Atlantic commercial system, Portugal was tied inextricably to Britain and, though it always sought to remain neutral and retain thereby the prosperous entrepot function of Lisbon for the export of colonial products, it was very rarely able to maintain neutrality long. It was this need for external political and military support in Europe which was of course at the core of the commercial concessions Portugal had made to England in the 1640s, and which Brazil for similar reasons would be obliged to concede again in Britain in 1810. It was the French seizure of Lisbon in 1807 which forced the effective political and economic emancipation of Brazil in 1808 by neutralizing the power of those in Portugal opposed to recognition of Brazil's central political role, collapsing thereby the structure of the Luso-Atlantic system as it had existed since the 1660s and replacing Lisbon as the required intermediary by direct access between the rest of Europe and the Brazilian ports.

The role of Brazil in Portuguese calculations and diplomacy, economic and institutional, thus held much higher priority than did the colonial weight of North America in British calculations. Preoccupation with the development of the Portuguese Atlantic empire on the one hand, and with Portugal's diminished stature and apparent backwardness on the other, permeated the Portuguese intellectual milieu of the age.

Portuguese policy under the Marquês de Pombal   The most dramatic reformulation of Portugal's policy towards Brazil occurred during the long period of rule by the Marquês de Pombal. Pombal himself took much from classic mercantilist theory and practice in his policy-making, both from its British and its French or Colbertian origins, but the use of the term mercantilism to describe Pombal's policy is not entirely appropriate. Mercantilism, when defined narrowly, describes a policy whereby trade is regulated, taxed and subsidized by the state to promote an influx of gold and silver. The objective of such state intervention is aimed more broadly at achieving a favorable balance of trade.

Pombal's policy was at once more limited and more focused than this. Its objective was to use mercantilist techniques – monopoly companies, regulation, taxation and subsidies – to facilitate capital accumulation by individual national merchants. This aid to individual Portuguese capitalists had wider objectives and consequences because it was part and parcel of a scheme to fortify the nation's bargaining power within the international commercial system.

The problem for an enlightened Iberian economic nationalist, which is perhaps a more accurate way to describe Pombal, was not so much to encourage the influx of precious metals; this was rarely a problem for Iberian economic policy-makers given the fact that Spain and Portugal and their empires were the principal source of the world's bullion supply in this period – gold from Brazil and silver from Peru and Mexico. The dilemma was precisely the opposite, that is, policy-making needed to devise measures to retain capital within their own economic system and at the same time to multiply the positive and diminish the negative economic impact of being producers of precious metals. The theory and practice of mercantilism was, after all, the creation of bullion-poor Northwestern Europe. The application of the theory and practice of mercantilism in the bullion-rich Iberian peninsula was bound to be partial because the end of the policy was fundamentally different from that sought by mercantilism's progenitors. The Iberians aimed to retain bullion, the Northwest Europeans aimed to attract it.

Pombal's methods reflected, in fact, the peculiarities of Portugal's position within the Luso-American system, and the particular impact on Portuguese entrepreneurship of the Brazilian gold boom between 1700 and 1760. Essentially, the all-powerful minister placed the power of the state decisively on one side of the conflict that had developed between Portuguese entrepreneurs as a consequence of the gold boom. He chose the large established merchants over their smaller competitiors because he saw the small merchants as mere creatures or commission agents of the foreigners. With support from the state he hoped the large Portuguese merchants in time would be able to challenge the foreigners at their own game. His economic policy was a logical one in view of Portugal's position within the eighteenth-century international trading system. It protected mutually beneficial trade (such as the Portuguese wine trade) but it also sought to develop a powerful national class of businessmen with the capital resources and the business skills to compete in the international as well as in the Portuguese domestic market with their foreign, especially British, competitors. It was not an easy policy to pursue, at least overtly, because it was essential to achieve this outcome without bringing into question the political and military support the treaties with Britain guaranteed and which was essential if Spanish ambitions were to be kept at bay.

At the same time in Brazil, in striking contrast to the Bourbon reformers in Spanish America, Pombal sought to incorporate and coopt the Brazilian oligarchy. Portugal was after all a small country with a large empire. It did not possess the resources of a Britain or a France. It did not have the military capabilities or the economic resources to force Brazil into a subservient role. Indeed, as Pombal had watched the British attempt to repress the rebellious colonists in English-speaking North America during the 1770s, he was fortified in his belief that conciliation was a more effective weapon against colonial uprisings than military force.

Portugal's colonial policy under Pombal in effect served to diffuse tensions within the colonial nexus by preventing any polarization along colonial versus metropolitan lines. The intervention of the Pombaline state had almost always been sectoral; that is, it had swung state support behind one side in a series of pre-existing conflicts which themselves bridged the metropolitan–colonial divide. Hence Pombal supported the large entrepreneurs against their smaller competitors; he had aided the Church and educational reformers such as the Oratorians while destroying the Jesuits and their colleges; he had crushed powerful elements among the old aristocracy while encouraging the access of businessmen to noble status. The benefits as well as the displeasure of the Pombaline state, in other words, helped and hindered both Brazilian and Portuguese, forging in fact a series of alliances across the Atlantic as well as counter-alliances which linked Portuguese and Brazilian interests at a variety of levels. Some of these results of policy were unintentional; but the conciliatory aspect of Pombal's policy towards powerful Brazilian interests was entirely explicit.

The fundamental problem for Portugal, however, arose from the logic of the Brazil-based Atlantic system within which Pombal had operated. In the final analysis, Brazil would inevitably become the dominant partner within the Portuguese-speaking empire. If the political constraints, which had governed the whole period from the 1660s to the end of the eighteenth century, also changed, that is, if for example Great Britain no longer saw it as in her own interest to protect Portugal from her continental neighbors, then the British might opt for a direct relationship with the colony rather than with mother country. Since the whole basis of Portugal's prosperity had been built on the manipulation of colonial monopolies, cash-crop exports, colonial markets and colonial gold, such a rupture would bring fundamental change, and would close an epoch.

The Minas Conspiracy of 1789   Nevertheless, despite, and in many respects as a result of, these structural conditions of Portugal's relationship with Brazil, the American Revolution had an immediate and very explicit impact in the most important province of late colonial Brazil, Minas Gerais. The starting-point here is an economic one. As the gold boom faded in the late eighteenth century, the diverse pressures arising from the growth of import-substituting industries in both the metropolis and Brazil after Pombal's fall from office in 1777 challenged the conciliatory basis of his system. With the rise of manufacturing came the rise in influence of powerful new lobbies on both sides of the Atlantic. By the 1780s, the Portuguese Government was faced with a choice, Either the maxims of the classic mercantilist tradition had to be abandoned, or they had to be more strictly observed, In other words, Brazil had to return to a more classically colonial status or the issue had to be confronted as to how and when Brazil's central status in the economic system was to be consolidated by a recognition of its potential political role.

The problem with the traditional view of metropolitan–colonial relationships espoused by Melo e Castro, Pombal's successor in colonial policy-making, and the manufacturing interests which stood behind him, was that broader changes within the international economic and political system were making the whole rationale of their fiercely neo-mercantilist position increasingly anachronistic. In England the Industrial Revolution was underway, which was to transform over the next 30 years the competitive position of the British textile industry in international markets. In addition, the lessons the British were to learn from the loss of their North American colonies led to a policy which would seek direct access to South American markets, even at the expense of the old privileged trading relationships in Europe. Moreover, the tensions within the Luso-Brazilian system itself threatened to become serious. The interests of the local oligarchies in Brazil had been woven so closely into the structure of administration that, in some regions, especially those less linked to the cash-crop export sector, such as the interior captaincy of the Minas Gerais, and where changing economic conditions were leading to a strong desire for economic autonomy, many now saw their self-interests at variance with those of the imperial policy-makers in Lisbon.

The intellectual climate in Brazil had changed too. Especially important was the fact that the international context had been transformed by the successful revolt of the British colonies in North America, an event which had profound impact on many educated Brazilians. The hardening of colonial policy particularly with respect to the collection of tax arrears and the suppression of colonial enterprises – especially manufacturing – led in 1789 to the Minas Conspiracy, where important members of the oligarchy in Minas Gerais prepared to move in armed rebellion against the Portuguese Crown and establish an independent and republican government. Their plot was betrayed and failed, but it shocked the system profoundly.

The Minas Conspiracy was a complex, tragic affair; yet because of its timing, 1789, it provides a unique perspective on the intellectual climate in one part of Latin America in the period between the American and French revolutions. Its failure, in fact, is the reason we know so much about the conspirators – their lives, their ideas, their assets. Once the conspiracy was denounced and its instigators imprisoned, they were interrogated, their properties were confiscated and their words were remembered, recorded and used against them by the agents of the Portuguese Crown. For the historian this provides a treasure trove because it is one of those rare occasions where ideas, reading patterns and concrete proposals can be seen quite explicitly in the context of a proposed rebellion. The task of the leading intellectuals of the region, men such as Gonzaga, a magistrate, Claudio Manuel da Costa, a lawyer, and Luis Vieira, a priest, had been to formulate the laws and constitution of the new state and provide the ideological justification for the break with Portugal. All three men were well informed of events in Europe, two of them educated there. They all possessed good libraries; that of Vieira contained more than 600 volumes. Books and information often reached them more rapidly than official dispatches passed through the cumbersome bureaucracy from Lisbon to the captaincy's governor. Vieira's cosmopolitan collection of books contained Robertson's *Histoire de l'Amerique*, the *Encyclopédie*, as well as the works of Bielfeld, Voltaire and Condillac. Claudio Manuel da Costa was reputed to have translated Adam Smith's *Wealth of Nations*. And circulating among the conspirators was a copy of the *Loix constitutives des Etats-Unis de l'Amerique* (1778), which contained the Articles of Confederation and the constitutions of Pennsylvania, New Jersey, Delaware, Maryland, Virginia, the Carolinas and Massachusetts. They possessed constitutional commentaries by Raynal and Mably, and Raynal's lengthy discussion of the history of Brazil in his *Histoire philosophique et politique* was much debated. Gonzaga had long been interested in jurisprudence. His famous *Cartas chilenas*, a satirical poem set ostensively in Chile, was in fact an attack aimed very directly at the governor of Minas and his cronies. Luis Vieira had often argued against Portugal's right to dominion in America, and was a warm admirer of the North Americans' struggle for independence. The conspirators had in fact in 1787 established a secret contact with the United States via Thomas Jefferson while he was Ambassador to France, a meeting about which Jefferson had informed the committee of secret correspondence of the Continental Congress. Jefferson himself was ambivalent – Virginia grain was exported to Portugal.

Although the program of the conspiracy reflected the specific and immediate compulsions which had thoroughly alienated the leading citizens of Minas Gerais from the Portuguese Crown and forced along the path of revolution, and tax arrears and threatened tax levies were important stimulants to rebellion in Minas as in North America, it also reflected the presence among their ranks of those able and distinguished magistrates, lawyers and clerics who had been forced into a reassessment of the colonial relationship by other motives, and who drew their inspiration from the example of North America, the constitutions of the American states and the works of the Abbé Raynal.

From the fragments of information that exist, an outline of their proposals can be rediscovered. The system of the government was to be republican. Restrictions and monopolies were to be abolished. Manufactories were to be established and the exploitation of iron ore deposits encouraged. A gunpowder factory would be set up. Freedom was to be granted to native-born slaves and mulattos. A university would be founded in Vila Rica. All women who produced a certain number of children were to receive a prize at the expense of the state. There was to be no standing army. All citizens were instead to bear arms and when necessary to serve in a national militia. Parliaments were to be established in each town, subordinate to a supreme parliament in the capital. For the first three years Gonzaga would rule – after which time there would be annual elections. No distinctions or restrictions of dress would be tolerated, and the elite would be obliged to wear locally manufactured products. All debtors to the royal treasury would be pardoned.

Strong tones of economic nationalism were present in the discourse of the plotters. The sentiment was most explicit in the statements of Tiradentes, a junior military officer of the Minas Dragoons and the only victim of the plot, whose hanging and quartering by the Portuguese later made him one of republican Brazil's national heroes. He praised the beauty and natural resources of Minas as being the best in the world in words reminiscent of the Abbé Raynal's. Free, and a republic like British America, Brazil could be even greater, he claimed, because it was better endowed by nature. With the establishment of manufactories, Tiradentes said, there would be no need to import commodities from abroad. Brazil was a land which had within itself all that was needed; no other country was required for its sustenance. The reason for the country's poverty despite all these riches, he said, was "because Europe, like a sponge, was sucking all the substance, sending out every three years governors, bringing with them a gang that they called servants, who after devouring the honor, finances, and offices that should have belonged to the natives returned happily to Portugal bloated with riches." Colonel Gomes, another conspirator, claimed that the merchants of Rio de Janeiro were behind the uprising to make an English America. "The Abby Raynal had been a writer of great vision," one of the conspirators observed, "for he had prognosticated the uprising of North America, and the captaincy of Minas Gerais was now in the same circumstances."

The conspiracy in Minas Gerais moreover had occurred at a special moment in time. The plot was concerted before the French Revolution. But the arrest, the trial and the sentencing of those involved (*see* figure 44) coincided with growing revolutionary turmoil in Europe. The chronological relationship of the Minas Conspiracy to the French Revolution is of critical importance. The Minas oligarchs had believed they could control and manipulate the popular will. Remarkably they had spoken of freeing Brazilian-born slaves. They had taken as their example the American Revolution, where political readjustments in their view had taken place without social upheaval. But the example of the American patriots had not prepared them for the spectacular repercussions of the French Revolution in the Americas. The revolt of the slaves on the French sugar island of Saint Domingue (Haiti) during 1792 brought an awful awakening to those slave owners who had talked naively of republics and revolt and ignored the social and racial consequences of their words.

The Bahian plot of 1798   In the climate of opinion that followed the Saint Domingue revolt, the discovery of plans for an armed uprising by the mulatto artisans of Bahia during 1798 had a very special impact; the plans demonstrated what thinking Whites had already begun to realize: that ideas of social equality propagated within a society where a mere third of the population was white risked being interpreted in racial terms. The Bahian affair revealed the politicization of levels of society barely concerned in the Minas Conspiracy. The middle-aged lawyers, magistrates and clerics in Minas Gerais (most of them opulent, members of racially exclusive brotherhoods and slave owners) contrasted markedly with the young mulatto artisans, soldiers, sharecroppers and salaried school-teachers implicated in the Bahian plot. Embittered and anticlerical, the Bahian mulattos were as opposed to rich Brazilians as to Portuguese dominion. They welcomed social turmoil, proposed an overthrow of existing structures, and sought an egalitarian and democratic society where differences of race would be no impediment to employment and social mobility. The pardo [mulatto] tailor João de Deos, one of the leaders who at the time of his arrest possessed eight children and no more than 80 reis, proclaimed that "All [Brazilians] would become Frenchmen, in

FIGURE 44 A copy of the sentence passed against the leaders of the uprising at Minas Gerais (Rio de Janeiro, 18 April 1792)

order to live in equality and abundance.... They would destroy the public officials, attack the monasteries, open the port ... and reduce all to an entire revolution, so that all might be rich and taken out of poverty, and that the differences between white and brown would be extinguished, and that all without discrimination would be admitted to positions and occupations."

It was obviously not the North American patriots that provided the example for João de Deos and his colleagues. They also sought to raise up public opinion. Handwritten manifestos appeared throughout Bahia on 12 August 1798. Addressed to the "Republican Bahian People" in the name of the "supreme tribunal of Bahian democracy," the manifestos called for the extermination of the "detestable metropolitan yoke of Portugal." Clergy who preached against popular liberty were threatened. "All citizens, especially mulattoes and blacks," were told that "all are equal, there will be no differences, there will be freedom, equality and fraternity." There was no equivocation over slavery: "all black and brown slaves are to be free so that there will be no slavery whatsoever." The government would be "democratic, free and independent." "The happy time of our liberty is about to arrive, the time when all will be brothers, the time when all will be equal."

As in the case of Minas nine years previously, the Bahian artisans were caught red-handed. The appearance of the manifestos in Bahia, the demand for liberty, equality and fraternity, and the racial composition of the conspiratorial conclave, however, provoked a reaction out of all proportion to the incidents themselves. The arrested conspirators were all hanged and quartered or transported to be abandoned on the coast of Africa. Since 1792, slave owners throughout the Americas had barely hidden their concern that the revolution in the Caribbean might prove contagious. For slave owners in Brazil, at least, the words of the Bahian mulattos made the contagion of Saint Domingue a concrete reality.

Portuguese steps to accommodate tensions in Brazil   With republicanism discredited by the abortive uprising in Minas Gerais and later association with social and racial turmoil, there was room for metropolitan initiatives. And, for the white minority in Portuguese America, the failure of the elitist movement in Minas Gerais during 1789 and the threat from below revealed by the Bahian artisans in 1798 provided two powerful incentives for comprise with the metropolis. Psychologically, the situation was propitious for accommodation.

The recognition of this fact by influential members of the Portuguese Government during the 1790s had profound impact on the future development of Brazil. It was at this point that a group of skillful and enlightened ministers took over the reins of government in Lisbon. One Luis Pinto de Sousa Coutinho became Portugal's foreign minister. He was a man with first-hand knowledge of Brazilian conditions, having distinguished himself as governor of Mato Grosso (1769–72) before being appointed as ambassador to the Court of St. James. In Britain he had provided William Robertson with information on South America for Robertson's famous history, a service he had also provided for the Abbé Raynal some years earlier. Once back in Lisbon, Luis Pinto made contact with Brazilian intellectuals. On 31 May 1790 he sent two of the more promising young Brazilians to Paris to take courses in physics and mineralogy. Afterwards the scholars were to visit the mines of Saxony, Bohemia and Hungary, and to return to Portugal by way of Scandinavia and Great Britain.

The leader of the expedition, Manuel Ferreira da Camara, had close links with those caught up in the events of Minas Gerais. His elder brother was implicated on several occasions during the judicial inquiry into the conspiracy, and had fled from Minas by way of the backlands to Bahia. Luis Pinto's extension of the powerful protection of his office to these young Brazilian scholars during the critical year of 1790, and his remarkable act of faith in sponsoring the visit to the center of European social and political upheaval, can be considered quite remarkable.

The reasoning behind these actions was explained by another leader of this group of enlightened ministers, D. Rodrigo de Sousa Coutinho. In 1779 Rodrigo had visited Paris, where he met the Abbé Raynal. He told Raynal that the population and resources of France would have made her insupportable to the rest of Europe were it not for the disorder of her financial administration. Raynal replied that "Providence had given France the forces but refused her good sense. France would indeed be terrible if her natural power was matched by a just and wise administration." Writing to his sister, Rodrigo later wondered: "What would be better for Europe, to be a factory of the English or a slave of France? The only thing that can console us is the almost total impossibility of France reforming her system of government." Reform of course came through revolution, and France's power was projected over Europe by the regime of Napoleon Bonaparte, and it was just as formidable as Rodrigo has suspected it could be.

Rodrigo attributed the collapse of the French monarchy to its fiscal situation. His opposition to monopolies and the contracting of revenues and his fervent support of an efficient and solvent financial administration grew from his belief that intelligent reform was essential if Portugal were to avoid a similar collapse. The revolution in France, he believed, should accelerate reform in Portugal, not delay it. To achieve sound fiscal policies, Rodrigo recommended "wise and enlightened reforms, executed by intelligent men, capable of forming well organized systems, the utility of which would be recognized by all." His optimism epitomized that of the Enlightenment itself. In 1801 Rodrigo went so far as to propose the establishment of the monarchy in Brazil, a compromise that promised political change without social disintegration. The task of formulating these plans was largely turned over to the young Brazilians whose European educational expedition the government had sponsored.

The recognition of the central place of Brazil in the Luso-Brazilian commercial system, and the open espousal in 1801 of the need to move the court to Brazil, was of course strenuously opposed by powerful vested interests in Portugal. Portuguese neutrality during the revolutionary wars in Europe brought great prosperity. The opulent Portuguese merchant industrialists were well aware that this wealth arose from the control of the re-export of colonial staples such as cotton, sugar, tobacco and hides, not to mention the retention of captive markets in Brazil for their manufactured goods. The ideas of making Brazil the center of the Portuguese Empire had also become a position acceptable to the British. In 1803 the British envoy in Lisbon, Robert Fitzgerald, was already advising London that "the British property within [Portugal itself] forms no object of great national importance – especially when in the opposite balance are viewed the innumerable advantages to be derived from an open and unrestricted trade with the Brazils." The project became a reality nonetheless when in 1807 Napoleonic troops crossed the frontier from Spain and moved rapidly on Lisbon. It is vital to emphasize, however, that the decision of the Portuguese court to move to Brazil was not a panic measure. Napoleon's invasion of 1807 in fact served to neutralize opposition to the move. The Portuguese fleet was ready – treasure, archives and the apparatus of a bureaucracy loaded for the retreat across the Atlantic. And, as we have seen, the process of the last two decades of the eighteenth century in Brazil had made many previously skeptical Brazilians receptive to the idea of a new world monarchy. D. João, the Prince Regent, arrived in Rio de Janeiro in 1808 after a brief stay in Bahia, not as an exile but as the head of a functioning national state. 1808 may therefore be viewed as a real watershed in both Brazilian and Portuguese history.

3. SPAIN

The example of the American Revolution was particularly important in Brazil for reasons that lay in the coincidence of its anti-colonial message with severe tension between Lisbon and a major segment of the local elite in the one area in the Portuguese territories in the Americas with the capacity to articulate as well as make effective an independent state, possessing as it did in the 1780s adequate revenues, military forces, administrative experience and a close attention to international developments. That it failed despite all these elements is an indication of how difficult the achievement of colonial independence would be in Ibero-America.

The circumstances in the core regions of Spanish America were even less propitious. The impact of the American Revolution would here be confined to the peripheries.

Very little impact can be discerned in the two great core regions of Spanish dominion, Peru and Mexico. In many respects, the North Americans, in terms of trade, influence and contacts, followed the sea-lanes, and their role was most significant within the Caribbean and along the coastlines, where they had long been involved in the transatlantic complex as purveyors of codfish, sugar, slaves, grain, tobacco and, most recently, cotton. But here it was the North American commercial role within the Atlantic commercial systems as a whole that was decisive. The grain trade, in particular, found ready customers in the Iberian peninsula among the colonial overlords of South and Central America. And trade more than republican ideology would be the watchword in the United States' dealings with both Spain and Portugal. These powers, Spain in particular, had aided in very substantial ways the attainment of American independence: it was a connection which made for some caution when it came to aiding and abetting revolutionaries to the South, at least until the Napoleonic period, when for all effective purposes the United States gained direct access to Spanish American ports (smuggling had already long existed) and Spain to all intents and purposes lost direct administrative control of its empire in America owing to British control of the sea-lanes.

But, for other reasons, the ground in Spanish America was not fertile for the American model. The eighteenth century had seen three major processes at work. First, the old monopolistic trading connection of Atlantic convoys of protected ships sailing on a regular pattern between the Caribbean and monopoly port of Seville (later Cadiz) had been superseded by a *de facto* diversification of trade. Some of this diversification was illegal – but like the trade through Jamaica, where the North Americans were actively involved, this had become a substantial contribution to overall Atlantic commerce. Spain had also eventually permitted other Spanish ports into Atlantic commerce, gradually ending the Cadiz monopoly between 1765 and 1789, as well as given formal administrative recognition to the peripheral coastal regions away from the old Highland Indian populated core areas (where Spain's major bases in the Western hemisphere had been since the time of the Conquest). Thus, while Lima and Mexico City remained important, new regions, such as the Rio de la Plata, Caracas and Cuba, also developed. These previous backwaters – good for provisions but producing very little else – all became major exporters in the late eighteenth century – Buenos Aires, an exporter of salt beef, silver, hides and grains; Caracas for cacao and hides; Cuba, especially after the revolt in Haiti, a major center for sugar and slaves. Second, from mid-century on, Spain had attempted to implement a series of major administrative, mercantile and fiscal reforms aimed at the enhancement of the power of the metropolis through the more efficient exploitation of its colonies. As in Portugal, there had been growing awareness in Spain that its role as a great power was severely undermined by the failure to adapt to modern conditions; which in eighteenth-century terms meant using the power of the state to increase revenues and impose a more centralized administrative system. This preoccupation with national regeneration was in the forefront of the minds of several high government officials. Jose de Carvajal, for example, foreign minister from 1746 to 1759, saw Spanish America as the means for Spain to recuperate its position in Europe if the recourses could be more effectively utilized. The 1743 proposal of Jose de Campillo, minister of finance, in which he called for a "New System for the American Economy" (Nuevo Sistema de Gobierno Económico para la América), encapsulated the intention to turn to the empire as a market for Spanish manufactures and as a source of raw materials. Campillo wished to see a system of general inspectors (visitas generales),

the creation of intendancies, and the introduction of "free trade" into colonial administration. The intendant system had been previously adopted in Spain itself and
established a system of provincial governors with a mixture of military, financial
and judicial authority directly responsible to Madrid. It was, however, the Bourbon
monarch Carlos III (1759–88) whose reign became associated with the implementation of a series of far-reaching new governmental measures for the administration
of the vast Spanish territories in the New World. The urgency of these reforms became
more than ever evident after the seizure of Havana by the British in 1762 during the
Seven Years' War.

The administration of colonial territories under Carlos III   The Spanish Bourbon reforms
took place against the background of demographic and economic recovery in much
of Spanish America, and much controversy exists among historians as to the cause
and effect of reform and prosperity. It is generally agreed, however, that the impact
of the new governmental measures varied considerably from region to region. One
immediate consequence was that tensions were aggravated between European Spaniards and the old Latin American white creole oligarchies which had for several
centuries, it should be remembered, found a political niche within local administrations
throughout the Americas. The Bourbon reforms, especially the intendant system, were
therefore first introduced in the regions where the old creole oligarchies were less
formidable; Cuba after 1764 and the Rio de la Plata after 1776. Only in 1784 was
the system initiated in Peru and in 1786 in Mexico. Spain's involvement in the war
of North American independence also had the effect of bringing major new fiscal
demands. The articulation of the new systems owed much to the reforming visitor
general of New Spain (Mexico), José de Galvez (1765–71), who later became long-
term secretary for the Indies (1776–87). His objective in Mexico had encompassed
the establishment of a tobacco monopoly (to raise revenue), the reorganization and
raising of the sales tax (the Alcabala), the stimulation of silver production (by lowering
the price of mercury) and the expulsion of the Jesuit order.

Thirdly, this ferment of innovation and the reaction to it revealed just how complex
Spanish American colonial society had become by the late eighteenth century and
how difficult it would be in Spanish America either for a clear regional focus for proto-
nationalistic sentiment to emerge, or for the creation of a cohesive social base to
support any rebellion against Spain. Internal social, racial and caste divisions permeated colonial society, and it was very difficult anywhere in Spanish America for
European Spaniards living in the colonies, creole magistrates, soldiers and local
businessmen to come together in even the embryonic nationalist movement which
had made the idea of an independent Minas Gerais on the North American model so
pertinent in Brazil in 1788–9.

Social unrest and incipient nationalism   Movements of social protest did, of course,
emerge in Spanish America and with much more violence, bloodshed and disruption
than ever occurred in Brazil. But those movements were limited in their ideological
content. They did not make the leap from protest against bad government to an attack
on the rule of Spain in America. The most significant of these movements of protest
and rebellion, the Comunero rebellion in New Granada (present-day Colombia and
Venezuela) in 1781 and the Tupac Amaru rebellion in upper Peru (present-day
Bolivia) in 1780–1, never projected themselves into an anti-colonial struggle, and
both, especially the latter, served to terrify the creole elites and make them acutely

aware of the risk of race and ethnic violence implicit in the complexity of Spanish America's social makeup.

Given the heterogenity of Spanish America in the late eighteenth century, the uneven impact of imperial reform, the diversification of the economic system and its reorientation towards the Atlantic trading system in the new peripheral growth areas such as Venezuela and the Rio de la Plata, as well as the limited anti-colonial sentiment apparent in the rebellions of the 1780s, incipient nationalism was, when it emerged, more a characteristic of disgruntled elites than of the masses. The latter were on the whole more preoccupied with immediate inequalities and exploitation than with intra-imperial injustices, and felt more actually the oppression of the local oligarchies than of the Crown in Madrid. The rebels in both upper Peru and Venezuela in fact had looked to the Crown for redress of grievances. The notion of independence from Spain, of a colonial emancipation from Europe, was hence confined to a very small number of the white creole elite and developed after the putative popular revolts of the early 1780s had been repressed. These aspirations also were of a reformist rather than a revolutionary nature, and, while the institutional model of the new North American nation was often an inspiration, in terms of overseas contacts and hope of assistance it was England to which they looked rather than to the United States.

A Spanish version of the proclamations of the Continental Congress was in the hands of the Venezuelan conspirators of 1797 (the conspiracy of Manuel Guel and Jose Maria España) who hoped to establish an independent republic on the North American model. And by the turn of the century works by John Adams, Washington and Jefferson were circulating in both Mexico and South America. Key leaders of the independence movement, most notably Francisco de Miranda, visited the United States, as did Simon Bolivar, who admired Washington, though he was not uncritical of the North American system. Miranda in particular summed up the complex reaction to the events of 1776 in North America and 1789 in France. "We have before our eyes two great examples," he wrote in 1799, "the American and the French Revolutions: let us prudently imitate the first and carefully shun the second." After the revolt in French Saint Domingue, as in Brazil, property owners throughout Spanish America became even more cautious, especially if that property included African slaves. "I confess that as much as I desire the liberty and independence of the New World," Miranda observed, "I fear anarchy and revolution even more." This attitude was to be the legacy of the revolutionary period, and it meant that the United States model after the turn of the century would be viewed as one which matched social conservatism with political independence from Spain.

4. CONCLUSIONS

In summary, then, in the case of Portugal and Brazil, the basic argument has been that during the period between 1750 and 1808 it had become very evident that the impact of the American Revolution in Brazil, which was a powerful influence before 1789, was nonetheless diluted and eventually rejected by the mid-1790s. This rejection was partly owing to the failure of the attempt in Brazil during early 1789 to set up an independent state modeled on the United States, but it was due also to the counter-influences of the French Revolution and most particularly the manifestation of the French Revolution in the Americas, the great slave revolt in the French Antilles.

The white Brazilian elite, slave owners and those opposed to slavery alike, found by the 1790s that republicanism and democracy were concepts too dangerous for experimentation within a society half-slave, and where Blacks outnumbered Whites two to one. The consequence was that those who avidly and approvingly followed the events in North America before 1790 turned away from the North American model, and, encouraged by the Portuguese metropolitan government, which had learned its own lessons from the revolt of the 13 colonies, embraced monarchy in the interests of preserving the status quo against racial and social upheaval. A similar interaction between the chronology of revolutions and elite attitudes took place in all the American states and ex-colonies where slavery was entrenched.

The Haitian revolt also had a critical impact on the attitudes of the governments of Spain, France and Britain towards America, in the latter case being a principal cause of the profound shift in policy with respect to colonial rebellions in the Western Hemisphere, making them all much more cautious.

In mainland Spanish America, independence followed from external more than internal events: the collapse of the Bourbon monarchy in Spain itself in the face of the Napoleonic onslaught in 1808. Unlike in Portugal, where the French invasion brought about a denouement to the dilemmas of the metropolitan colonial relationship with the removal of the Portuguese court to Brazil and the *de facto* (later *de jure*) establishment of Rio de Janeiro as the seat of a new world monarchy, in Spain the invasion in effect cut Spanish America loose of the old metropolis for a critical six years between 1808 and 1814, with major consequences for Spanish American unity and stability. The successor Spanish American republics often took shape within the new boundaries imposed by the eighteenth-century reformers, but they all faced massive problems of internal social cohesion and economic and administrative dis-locations. The conflicting pressure arising from unequal economic growth within the Spanish Empire in America, the ambiguities of an administrative reform which was in part an attempt to respond to those changes, as well as the several social, ethnic and racial tensions which permeated the social makeup of Spanish America had all served to limit the development of a broad-based anti-colonial sentiment before 1808, and fragmented the social bases of support for a nationalistic project on the North American model, limiting thereby in the potential impact of the North American example. Again, as in the lowland tropical areas of the Western Hemisphere, the example of Haiti reinforced the fears arising from the bloody uprisings in Upper Peru in the early 1780s. Those who saw the American model as relevant tended after 1800 to see it as the conservative option. Latin Americans were interested in the United States as a model for nation-building; federalism, for example, proved attractive to many. But, for an effective partnership, they more often looked to Great Britain and to trade: espousing "liberalism" in the sense of access to world commerce rather than liberalism in the sense of democracy.

For Latin America, especially for the areas where plantation economies and African slavery predominated, it is essential, therefore, to look at the relationship between the three revolutions of the late eighteenth century, the American, the French, and the Haitian, and for Spanish America to look to the vicissitudes of the eighteenth-century experience with reform and rebellion. From the perspective of the Americas at the time, the great slave revolt of 1792 in French Saint Domingue was a second "American" revolution that seemed no less important than the first. It brought to the forefront of elite consciousness fears and tensions inherent to plantation systems throughout the New World. Within the empires of Spain and Portugal the Haitian revolt served to stimulate both a reapproximation between local oligarchs and the more progressive elements within the metropolitan governments as in the Portuguese-speaking empire, and as in Spanish America made it inevitable that the independence movements when eventually they came would always find questions of race, class and social stability close to the surface. Whereas in the 1780s would-be Latin American revolutionaries had found inspiration in George Washington, by the 1790s they recoiled in fear before the example of Toussaint L'Ouverture.

FURTHER READING

Afonso, Ruy: *A Primeira revolução social brasileira* (1798) (São Paulo, 1942).

Alden, Dauril: "The Marques of Pombal and the American Revolution," *The Americas*, 17, 4 (1961), 369–82.

Aldridge, O. A. (ed.): *The Ibero-American Enlightenment* (Urbana, Il, 1971).

Barbier, Jacques A.: *Reform and Politics in Bourbon Chile, 1755–1790* (Ottawa, 1980).

Brading, D. H.: *Miners and Merchants in Bourbon Mexico* (Cambridge: Cambridge University Press, 1973).

Fisher, H. E. S.: *The Portugal Trade: a Study of Anglo-Portuguese Commerce, 1700–1770* (London, 1971).

Fisher, J. R.: *Government and Society in Colonial Peru* (London: Athlone, 1970).

Godinho, Vitorino Magalhães: *Prix et monnaies au Portugal, 1750–1850* (Paris, 1955).

Gonzalez, António Garcia-Baquero: *Cadiz y el Atlántico (1717–1778)*, 2 vols. (Seville, 1976).

Herr, Richard, *The Eighteenth Century Revolution in Spain* (Princeton, NJ: Princeton University Press, 1988).

Jacobson, Nils, and Puhle, Hans-Jürgen (eds.): *The Economics of Mexico and Peru During the Late Colonial Period, 1700–1810* (Berlin: Colloquium Verlag, 1986).

Liss, Peggy K.: *Atlantic Empires: the Networks of Trade and Revolution, 1713–1826* (Baltimore: Johns Hopkins University Press, 1983).

Lynch, John: *Spanish Colonial Administration, 1782–1810* (London, 1958)

——: *The Spanish American Revolutions, 1808–1826* (London, 1975).

Mattoso, Satia Queiros: "Conjoncture et société au Brasil à la fin du XVIII siècle, prix et salaires et à la vielle de la revolution des alfaiates, Bahia, 1798," *Cahiers des Ameriques Latins*, 5 (1970), 33–53.

Maxwell, Kenneth R.: *Conflicts and Conspiracies: Brazil and Portugal, 1750–1808* (New York: Cambridge University Press, 1973).

Mota, Carlos Guilherme: *Atitudes de inovação no Brasil, 1789–1801* (Lisbon: 1972).

Novais, Fernando: *Portugal e Brasil na crise do antigo sistema colonial (1777–1808)* (São Paulo, 1978).

Palmer, R. R.: *The Age of Democratic Revolution*, 2 vols. (Princeton, NJ: Princeton University Press, 1959, 1964).

Phelan, John Leddy: *The People and the King: the Communero Revolution in Colombia, 1781* (Madison, 1978).

Stein, Stanley J., and Stein, Barbara H.: *The Colonial Heritage of Latin America* (New York: Oxford University Press, 1970).

Whitaker, A. P. (ed.): *Latin America and the Enlightenment* (Ithaca, NY: Cornell University Press, 1961).

——: *The United States and the Independence of Latin America* (Baltimore: Johns Hopkins University Press, 1941).

55

The influence of the American Revolution in the Netherlands

JAN WILLEM SCHULTE NORDHOLT

THE Dutch Republic, officially called the Republic of the Seven United Netherlands, was an oligarchy, where the power was in the hands of a small elite of regents and a Stadtholder, who were, however, divided among themselves. The great majority of the Dutch people had no influence at all in government. Not surprisingly, therefore, the rebellion of the Americans against their British King George III was received with mixed feelings. The conservative circles around the Stadtholder, Prince William V, who was himself a cousin of George III, were strongly opposed to the Americans, but they found a great deal of sympathy among the burghers who were hankering after a voice in the government. The example of the American Revolution led to an intensification of the party strife between, on the one hand, the court, most of the regents, and the clergy of the Established (Dutch Reformed) Church, supported by the lower classes, and, on the other, the anti-Orangist regents, the *petit bourgeoisie*, and the dissenters, who formed a coalition, which was soon to assume the noble name of Patriots.

I. DUTCH RELATIONS WITH THE BRITISH AND THE AMERICANS

From the very beginning there were difficulties. Since the early seventeenth century there had been a Scottish brigade stationed in the Netherlands, and in times of war England could request the use of these troops. This is what George III immediately did in 1775, but in the Republic this sending of the soldiers to support the King against his own subjects met with strong opposition. It was argued that after all England was not at war, but was being confronted with an internal uprising. In essence this resistance was the first protest of the Patriots against the pro-British policy of the Stadtholder. It was headed by a nobleman, a deputy of the States of the Province of Overijssel, Johan Derk van der Capellen tot de Poll, who soon developed into the great leader of the pro-American party. The Dutch Government preferred to remain neutral in the conflict between England and its colonies. One of the reasons was that there was a great deal of money to be earned under the circumstances. Via the island of St. Eustatius in the Caribbean (*see* figure 45) an enormous contraband trade of weapons and munition for the American rebels got under way.

The Americans, on their part, were looking to the Netherlands for financial and diplomatic support. At the suggestion of Benjamin Franklin, Congress had in 1776 appointed an agent in The Hague, the first official representative of America in a foreign country. This was a Swiss intellectual, Charles Guillaume Frédéric Dumas. Dumas was the rare example of a pure enthusiast, who fervently believed in the

FIGURE 45 A general view of the Dutch island of St. Eustatius, showing the two volcanic peaks and the principal settlement of Oranjestad; the island prospered as a supply base for the colonies during the Revolution (tea smuggled from St. Eustatius helped keep prices low in places such as Boston), but declined with the British occupation of 1781 (from "Atlante dell' America," Livorno ..., 1777).

American cause. He was all ardor and hence not very suited for a diplomatic role; his influence was limited and he was not able to accomplish much of significance. Curiously enough, the first secret Dutch–American treaty, between the city of Amsterdam and the American agent William Lee, which was concluded at Aix-la-Chapelle in 1778, was negotiated without his knowledge. But Dumas did play an important role when in 1779 John Paul Jones sailed his fleet into the roads of Texel. It was he who organized the support for Jones. And it was he who with his propaganda paved the way for John Adams. Some years earlier he had invited Benjamin Franklin to come to Holland and he had promised that he would be his John the Baptist. Now he could accomplish that role for John Adams.

With the arrival of John Adams in the Republic in the summer of 1780, Dutch–American relations entered a new phase. Adams came to Holland with the goal of obtaining loans from the Amsterdam bankers, but he soon realized that an official recognition of the American Republic by the Dutch Government was an important condition for the achievement of his goal. He first settled in Amsterdam, where he tried to gain the support of the Patriot leaders. He also made attempts to influence the press, and for that purpose he made friends with important Dutch journalists such as Johan Luzac, editor of the *Gazette de Leyde*, a French-language paper which was being read all over Europe. In Amsterdam he supported a French writer, Antoine Marie Cérisier, and induced him to start the publishing of another paper, *Le Politique Hollandais*, again in French. Impatient as he was, Adams could not wait for the moment when it would please the Dutch Government to receive him. Against the advice of Franklin he decided on his own impetuous so-called militia diplomacy. He drew up a "Memorial to their High Mightinesses the States General of the United Netherlands," which he not only presented at The Hague but also had translated and printed in Dutch, English, and French. The document, which was written in fervid language, appealed to the supposed exact similarity between the two countries, which had both fought a revolution against a foreign king, had the same Protestant religion, the same love of freedom, and the same spirit of commerce and free enterprise. He therefore pleaded for speedy recognition.

2. WAR BETWEEN BRITAIN AND THE NETHERLANDS

In the meantime Adams's efforts had been made considerably easier by the fact that in December 1780 war had broken out between Great Britain and the Netherlands. In September 1780 the British had arrested the new American envoy to the Netherlands, Henry Laurens, on the open sea when he was on his way to Holland, and among his papers they had found the text of the secret treaty of Aix-la-Chapelle. This gave them the long-wanted excuse to declare war on the Dutch Republic and make an end to the smuggling of arms to the American rebels. Their first act of war was the conquest of the island of St. Eustatius and the complete destruction of all the Dutch warehouses there. The Dutch suffered heavy losses during the war: many of their ships were captured and their entire trade was paralyzed. In spite of the fact that a naval battle at the Dogger Bank in the summer of 1781 remained undecided, Britain still maintained her position as the ruler of the seas.

The war caused a good deal of commotion in the Republic and the protest against weak government policy was increasing rapidly. The Stadtholder was singled out for blame for the unhappy state of affairs. In September 1781 an anonymous pamphlet entitled *To the People of the Netherlands*, which was strongly anti-Orangist and which demanded greater popular influence, proved to be enormously successful. It was written, as it turned out much later, by Johan Derk van der Capellen. But Van der Capellen worked not only in secret. He openly called on the people to arm themselves as the Americans had done. At the same time he appealed to the burghers to exert their influence by presenting petitions to the government. This very moderate form of democracy was practiced for the first time in the winter of 1781–2, when in many cities petitions, called requests, were drafted demanding the recognition of the American Republic. Expectations were running high indeed, especially after the capitulation of Yorktown. America was regarded as an inexhaustible new market.

3. THE INFLUENCE OF JOHN ADAMS AND THE AMERICAN CONSTITUTION ON DUTCH POLITICAL THOUGHT

The American cause became very popular. In February 1782 the States of Friesland were the first to acknowledge the United States. The other provinces soon followed suit and on 19 April 1782 recognition was extended by the States General, the highest sovereign of the Republic. So John Adams became the first American envoy in the Netherlands. Through the mediation of Dumas, who served as his *chargé d'affaires*, he had by then already bought a house in The Hague, which thus became the first American embassy building on foreign soil. Moreover, in October 1782 a Treaty of Amity and Commerce between the Dutch and American Republics was signed. This was soon to be followed by the coveted loans from the Amsterdam bankers, which in the course of the next few years were to reach the amount of 30 million guilders. These loans formed the financial foundation of the United States.

After the peace treaty of Paris, Adams was appointed as minister to the court of St. James (1785), but he also continued in his post in The Hague. In 1788, in the company of Thomas Jefferson, who was then American minister in Paris, he paid his last visit to the Amsterdam bankers and departed for America. He had been completely successful in achieving his objectives in the Netherlands.

But John Adams did not only change the political relations between Holland and the United States. He was also very much concerned with ideas. His ideological influence on the political thinking of the Patriots was considerable. It was owing to his efforts that a collection of all the constitutions of the 13 American states and of the Articles of Confederation was published in Dutch translation. Dutch reformers who had for a long time been struggling with the problems of a federal state were very interested in the American solutions to that problem. In 1784 the young Rutger Jan Schimmelpenninck, who was later to become one of the most important leaders of the Batavian Republic, wrote a dissertation on *A Well Organized Popular Government*, in which he closely followed the model of the Constitution of Massachusetts, written by John Adams.

But in constitutional matters things never got beyond the planning stage. Nothing ever came of all the beautiful proposals for constitutional reform which were drafted by the Patriots during the years 1782 to 1787. In the latter year all their hopes were completely frustrated: through the intervention of England and Prussia the semi-civil war which had been raging between the Orangists and the Patriots suddenly came to an end. With this counter-revolution the authority of the Stadtholder was reinstated and the Patriots were forced to flee to France. America had also lost its popularity; in The Hague there was even an anti-American riot in front of the embassy, where Dumas was living at the time. It was, in all probability, another "first" – the first "Yankee-go-home" manifestation in the world.

It is perhaps pure coincidence, unless we accept that all these events were part of the same struggle towards a democratic revolution, that in that same year the new Constitution was drafted in Philadelphia. However, in spite of the internal turmoil, the American Constitution attracted considerable attention and admiration among the intellectuals in the Netherlands. Johan Luzac published it first in his *Gazette de Leyde* and soon the Dutch papers followed suit and gave at least abstracts from it. A scholar, Gerhard Dumbar, wrote a three-part volume explaining the new Constitution to the Dutch people (*The Old and New Constitutions of the United States, explained in their Foundations from the best Sources*, Amsterdam, 1793–6). But it was not only the Patriots who expressed their admiration. The Constitution also appealed to conservatives. The brilliant young statesman Gijsbert Karel van Hogendorp, who had visited the new nation in 1783–4 and been very disappointed by the (in his opinion) far too loose structure of the American republic, was now of the opinion that with the Constitution, by introducing a safeguard against too much popular influence, America had found the ideal balance between order and freedom.

But the American example could nevertheless not serve as a model for the Dutch. First the counter-revolution of 1787 restored the *Ancien Régime* of the Stadtholder and made all reforms impossible. Then, in 1795, the old government was indeed dismantled, but now the French model became the dominant one. In 1795 the revolutionary armies of the French republic occupied the Netherlands and put an end to the old Dutch Republic. The Stadtholder escaped to England, and the Patriots, who had fled eight years earlier, returned in triumph and founded the Batavian Republic. Now the achievements of the French Revolution, such as equality before the law, the abolition of the Established Church, and other similar reforms were carried through. An elected General Assembly set to work to draft a constitution. During the endless debates that followed, America was not forgotten, but by now it was the conservatives who put their trust in the American example. The radical reformers referred to the French model. They wanted to abolish federalism entirely and therefore called themselves Unitarists. The more conservative members, on the other hand, pleaded for the preservation of the old provinces and consequently called themselves Federalists, with a clear reference to America. It is true that there was a certain irony in this use of the same word. In America federalism stood for unity, in the Netherlands for variety. Yet American and Dutch Federalists had much in common: they were both rather conservative and afraid of too much democracy, and hence supporters of a mixed form of government and a separation of powers.

But no discussion could disguise the indisputable fact that the French model was compellingly close, the American far away. The Batavian Republic was increasingly becoming a satellite of France and was experiencing various *coups d'état*, where the French examples, more or less radical according to the situation in France itself, served as a model. America was disappearing behind the horizon.

After the so-called French era (1795–1813), independence was restored in the Netherlands. The son of the last Stadtholder returned as King William I. A constitution was drafted by Van Hogendorp. In this document the American influence is of little significance. It is true that, to a certain extent, Van Hogendorp sought to retain the provincial differences, but he did so without following the American model. Dutch provinces do not have anything like the same power as American states. National unity was the dominating force in the new Kingdom of the Netherlands. America remained an example from afar, which does not mean that John Adams was not right in proclaiming that there were (and are) many common values between the two countries.

FURTHER READING

Edler, Friedrich: *The Dutch Republic and the American Revolution* (Baltimore, 1911).

Foley, Mary Briant: "The Triumph of Militia Diplomacy: John Adams in the Netherlands, 1780–82," Ph.D. dissertation, Loyola University, Chicago, 1968.

Hutson, James S.: *John Adams and the Diplomacy of the American Revolution* (Lexington, Ky., 1980).

Morison, Samuel E.: *John Paul Jones: a Sailor's Biography* (Boston, 1959).

Riker, William H.: "Dutch and American federalism," *Journal of the History of Ideas*, 18 (1957), 495–521.

Schulte Nordholt, Jan Willem: "The Example of the Dutch Republic for American Federalism," *Federalism, History and Significance of a Form of Government* (The Hague, 1980), 65–77.

——: *The Dutch Republic and American Independence* (Chapel Hill, London, 1982).

Van Wijk, F. W.: *De Republiek en Amerika* (Leiden, 1921).

Van Winter, Pieter Jan: *Het Aandeel van den Amsterdamschen Handel aan den Opbouw van het Amerikaanche Gemeenebest*, 2 vols. (The Hague, 1927–30); trans. as *American Finance and Dutch Investment, 1780–1805, with an Epilogue to 1840* (New York, 1977).

56

The influence of the American Revolution in Russia

HANS ROGGER

SOVIET historians describe the American "bourgeois" revolution as above all a war for national independence. That view prevailed also in the government of Catherine II (1762–96) and among those of her subjects who could follow public affairs. This is one reason for the tolerant, even benign, official and non-official reactions to American events. Others were their remoteness from Russia and the opportunities they presented to her diplomacy and trade.

I. OFFICIAL RELATIONS

Although relations between Russia and Britain were friendly, the request George III made in 1775 for 20,000 Russian troops to be sent to America was refused by Catherine and her advisers. They had just put down the Pugachev rebellion and ended a long war with Turkey, and were not averse to seeing Britain embroiled in a distant conflict which the Empress might arbitrate with benefit to her prestige and influence. It was a conflict, moreover, for which the intransigence of the English was blamed and which they were not believed certain to win. "Patient neutrality" was the course adopted while awaiting the outcome of the war and profiting from the increase in trade it brought.

In 1780, patient neutrality turned into "armed neutrality." Supported by other states whose vessels the British had seized, Russia declared that neutral ships might freely sail to belligerents' ports; that enemy goods in neutral ships, except war contraband, were not subject to seizure; and that a blockade had to be enforced rather than merely proclaimed. Russia's defense of neutral shipping was a boon to the fledgling republic and greeted as such by its leaders, who in the same year appointed the first American diplomat to St. Petersburg. Francis Dana was to "engage Her Imperial Majesty to favour and support the sovereignty and independence of these United States" (Bashkina, 1980, p. 98).

During his stay (1781–3), Dana was neither received nor recognized in his official capacity. To avoid antagonizing England and to keep open the possibility of her mediation, Catherine observed "strict impartiality." When Britain recognized the independence of the United States, Russian representatives abroad were allowed to deal with them as with other republics. Although full and formal relations did not begin until 1809, quasi-official, commercial, and private contacts increased in the 1780s and became cordial during the next two decades.

2. POPULAR OPINION

Despite the Empress's distaste for their act of rebellion, the colonists enjoyed the sympathy of many, perhaps most, educated Russians. Catherine's son, the Grand Duke Paul, in 1781 praised the Americans for their "internal force and virtue" (Griffiths, 1969, p. 22), reflecting the general view that they were moderate and reasonable men whom English ineptness and arrogance had goaded into disaffection. Russians' opinions of the new nation's struggle, laws, and institutions were shaped by foreign writers and journals, by one Russian book and several translated volumes, and increasingly by their own press, which was for the most part favorable to the Americans.

This was especially true of one of the country's two newspapers, the *Moscow Gazette*. For Nikolai Novikov, its publisher and a leading figure of the Russian Enlightenment, the foundation of the American republic was as much a moral as a political act, and Franklin was a kindred spirit in the fight against the vices of courts and aristocrats. Posterity, the newspaper predicted, would revere him as a divinity; as electricity had transformed physics, events in the colonies would transform all of politics. Washington was declared to be greater than other patriots and liberators, for he had founded a nation that would "become a refuge for the liberty which luxury and depravity had driven from Europe" (Bolkhovitinov, 1976, p. 159). John Adams was praised for his republican simplicity of dress and bearing, the fervor of his republican convictions, and the eloquence with which these were expressed.

In his *Journey from Petersburg to Moscow* (1790), Aleksandr Radishchev, Russia's first radical, voiced boldly the revolutionary implications of the war. More than a national conflict, it was a popular rising against the abuses of arbitrary government, part of the fight for the freedom and dignity of all men which the Americans had waged willingly and won by their own efforts. Theirs was not an army of ignorant conscripts or mercenaries, but a host of free men who were inspired, like their leader, by the love of liberty. They had preserved that precious gift, proclaiming freedom of the press and civil liberty. Not even slavery, which Novikov too condemned, extinguished for Radishchev America's achievement; few Russians after him spoke of it with such passion.

Frightened by the French Revolution, Catherine suppressed the *Journey* and exiled its author. Yet, in a time of reaction, America appeared as the one nation where liberty and law survived. Demanding these for Russia, the officers who staged the ill-fated rebellion of December 1825 looked to a revolution that had avoided terror and despotism to erect a constitutional federation in which the rights of citizens were secure and the powers of government restrained. America showed that a state need not be cruel to be strong or rulers tyrannical to be obeyed. The Decembrists' failure and growing awareness of America's defects – crass commercialism, corrupt politicians, fickle electorates – dimmed the bright image of the young republic. But its chief features endured: the public and private virtues of its founders, the laws and institutions created by them.

America's youth would always be the period of greatest attractiveness to Russians; radical or conservative antipathy never displaced totally their original, largely liberal, image of the United States. But, like liberalism itself, it made no permanent conquest of the Russian mind, although democrats and socialists did on occasion invoke the principles and achievements of the Revolution as models or a source of hope.

FURTHER READING

Bashkina, N. N. et al. (eds.): *The United States and Russia: the Beginning of Relations, 1765–1815* (Washington: Government Printing Office, 1980).

Bolkhovitinov, N. N.: *Stanovlenie russko-amerikanskikh otnoshenii 1775–1815* (Moscow: Nauka, 1966); trans. Elena Levin, *The Beginnings of Russian-American Relations, 1775–1815* (Cambridge, Mass., and London: Harvard University Press, 1975).

⸻ : *Rossiia i voina SShA za nezavisimost' 1775–1783* (Moscow: Mysl', 1976); trans. C. Jay Smith, *Russia and the American Revolution* (Tallahassee, Fla: Diplomatic Press, 1976).

Griffiths, D. M.: 'Nikita Panin, Russian diplomacy, and the American Revolution,' *Slavic Review*, 28 (1969), 1–24.

Hecht, David: *Russian Radicals Look to America* (Cambridge, Mass.: Harvard University Press, 1947).

Laserson, M. M.: *The American Impact on Russia, 1784–1917* (New York: Macmillan, 1950).

Rogger, Hans: "How the Soviets see us," *Shared Destiny: Fifty Years of Soviet-American Relations*, ed. Mark Garrison and Abbott Gleason (Boston: Beacon Press, 1985), 107–45.

PART 5

INTERNAL DEVELOPMENTS AFTER THE REVOLUTION

57

Social and economic developments after the Revolution

STUART BRUCHEY

with a section on demographic aspects by JIM POTTER

THE American Revolution, unlike its French and Russian counterparts, was essentially a political movement of protest against a distant central government's interference in the local affairs of a people long accustomed to govern themselves. For this reason it was not accompanied by deep and widespread social upheaval. Contrary to the views of older scholars, the Revolution did not erase loyalist "colonial aristocrats" from American society. Although it is perhaps true that a "majority of the old aristocracy" emigrated from eastern Massachusetts, most respected families in the central and western parts of the state chose the Whig side and remained dominant in local affairs after independence. Few outstanding persons can be identified in the Tory emigration from New Hampshire, a state in which, except for the region around Portsmouth, society was not highly stratified. The elite in Connecticut tended to be loyal to the Crown, but at least half the Tories never left that state. Perhaps the majority of the prominent merchants of New York and Philadelphia were loyalist, or at least neutralist, but many stayed on in those centers of trade. In Maryland one group of planters, lawyers, and merchants struggled against another group of the same composition, with the plain people taking little part in the conflict. In the back country of North Carolina, though, the plain people were most stubbornly loyalist. Probably Virginians came closest to unanimity in the patriot cause. At any rate, loyalist claims for British compensation after the Revolution numbered only 13 persons born in Virginia.

I. LAND AND INHERITANCE

Similarly, no wholesale redistribution of landed property appears to have taken place either during the Revolution or as a result of it. A far lesser degree of democratization of land-ownership than earlier scholars supposed followed upon the breakup of large landed estates and their sale in smaller parcels. Although some of the land in the southern counties of New York seized by the revolutionary government of that state went to former tenants and other landless persons, the bulk of it was bought by wealthy patriots. The same seems to have been true in Maryland, western Massachusetts, New Hampshire, and the Carolinas. Even in Pennsylvania, where the largest estate of all – the 21.5 million acres of the Penn family – was confiscated, the legislature "confirmed, ratified, and established for ever" the private manors of the Penns, amounting to more than 500,000 acres. Furthermore, the abolition of primogeniture and entail, to which

Jefferson himself attached great significance, appears to have represented more a sweeping up of dead letters than a substantive legal reform (*see* Chapter 45, §2). Neither operated to any important degree in Virginia, where most estates were not entailed and could be freely alienated. Primogeniture was mandatory only if a property owner died intestate, but most Virginia planters made wills. Furthermore, the conclusion that no radical change of custom in devising estates took place in Virginia as a result of abolishing primogeniture and entail may well apply to other colonies. Certainly in New England the estate of an intestate parent was distributed equally to all the children from the beginning of settlement, and subsequent legislation merely confirmed this custom of partible descent, saving a double share for the eldest son. Pennsylvania adopted similar legislation in 1693.

Nevertheless, the Revolution appears to have exerted some effect. Not only was primogeniture outlawed in Georgia (1777), North Carolina (1784), Virginia (1785), Maryland and New York (1786), South Carolina (1791), and Rhode Island (1798), but in this same period New England and Pennsylvania dispensed with the Mosaic double portion for the eldest son, providing by statute for an equal division among all the children. Whether or not large investments made by absentee land-owners for the sake of income from leases and rentals, especially during the generation after 1725, deserve recognition as a form of "mercenary feudalism," to which the Revolution was required to put an end, is a question worthy of additional thought and research.

2. THE EMERGENCE OF A *NOUVEAU RICHE*

In contrast, changes in the ownership of more liquid assets appear to have been significant. No less an authority than Alexander Hamilton claimed that the Revolution had "destroyed a large proportion of the monied and mercantile capital of the country, and of personal property generally." Loss and destruction may have been especially severe in the port cities of New York and Philadelphia. "You can have no idea," a New York correspondent wrote to John Jay, "of the sufferings of many who from affluence are reduced to the most abject poverty." In Philadelphia, Peletiah Webster testified to "the most pernicious shift of property," to "the many thousands of fortunes which are ruined."

But the war created as well as destroyed liquid wealth. Wealth was created by new opportunities in trade, privateering, and land speculation. Those who came into possession of it emerged as a *nouveau riche* class which was to rise in the nineteenth century to challenge the long social dominance of an older entrenched elite.

As early as 1777 it seemed to Robert Treat Paine of Boston that the "course of the war has thrown property into channels, where before it never was, and has increased little streams to overflowing rivers." From the same city James Bowdoin wrote in 1783: "When you come you will scarcely see any other than new faces . . . the change which in that respect has happened within the few years since the revolution is as remarkable as the revolution itself." "I sometimes almost lament that the Aristocracy in 1783 was suppressed," Stephen Higginson wrote four years later.

And so it went in city after city. In Charleston, David Ramsay asserted that new, bold traders had replaced the old and "rapidly advanced their own interests." "The men that had no money hardly, is now got the money," Dr. Joseph Orne said of society in Salem, Massachusetts, adding that they were called "the new Fangled Gentlemen." "Those who five years ago were the 'meaner people'," declared an embittered loyalist,

Samuel Curwen, "are now, by a strange revolution, become almost the only men of power, riches and influence."

In 1965 David Hackett Fischer observed that late eighteenth- and early nineteenth-century Americans "who analyzed the structure of their society sometimes divided it into two groups – the better sort and the meaner sort, the respectable and the ambitious." The distinction, he continued, was "not simply between wealth and poverty, but between attainment and aspiration, between those who had and those who hungered. The most hungry, the most ambitious, the most 'mean' from an elitist perspective were men who had much and wanted more – men who wished to add respectability to riches, or riches to popular influence." The domestic economy was to move to a higher growth path in the second third of the nineteenth century, when the numbers of the "meaner sort" were swelled by fortunes won in the wars of the French Revolution and Napoleon and in the cultivation and export of cotton.

3. ECONOMIC CONFUSION AND THE BEGINNINGS OF A POSTWAR POLICY

It was in the area of legal and institutional change that the Revolution was to exert its most significant and enduring effects on the American economy. Three underlying factors were involved in this change. The first was postwar insecurity of property rights; the second, the need to remove the power to regulate inter-state and foreign commerce from the states and place it in the central government; the third, to grant that government the power to tax.

Threats to property rights after the Revolution took the form both of social upheaval and of state laws enacted in an effort to cope with grievous economic problems. Not only urban communities but also farm families buying and selling on markets were affected by these problems. Although the important trade with England continued after the war on terms highly favorable to the United States – with tobacco, lumber, potash, pearlash, tar, pitch, pig iron, and bar iron, for example, being admitted either duty free or at tariff rates giving Americans a clear advantage over other countries in the competition for the British market – the important islands of the British West Indies were shut to American vessels. New Englanders dependent on these island markets for the sale of their lumber, livestock, and other provisions were especially hard hit by the exclusion. One South Carolinian visitor to the region in the mid-1780s reported that Boston was "going fast to decay" and that the "ruin'd wharves of New-Port imply a melancholy truth," namely, that the "Northern and Eastern states are ruined [by the war] they were so anxious to bring about." American ships had once dominated the trade with the islands, and while (because smuggling took place) official figures do not fairly measure the effect of their postwar exclusion, they reveal a decline in American exports by nearly one-half between 1771–3 and 1793.

Influence of British policy Englishmen were by no means unanimously agreed on this policy. Indeed, the Prime Minister himself, William Pitt, had offered a bill in Parliament calling for the continued admission of American vessels. Unhappily, his bill encountered opposition stirred by the publication in 1783 of Lord Sheffield's influential pamphlet *Observations on the Commerce of the American States*, which argued that England's "great national object is to raise as many sailors and as much shipping as possible." Parliament should endeavor to divert the whole Anglo-American trade to British ships.

557

Sheffield also pointed out that the new American states lacked leverage in commercial bargaining with other countries. Their first constitution, the Articles of Confederation, adopted in 1781, had explicitly declared each state to be sovereign, free, and independent (Article 2), and had withheld from the central government the power to pass laws regulating commerce. With individual states seeking commercial advantage over other states by lowering their tariff and tonnage duties, and with the Continental Congress powerless to stipulate uniform rates throughout the union, the fledgling republic could offer neither inducement nor threat to the nations of Europe whose trade it sought on favorable terms.

The perceptive Alexander Hamilton saw the situation clearly. "Suppose, for instance," he wrote in 1787, "we had a government in America, capable of excluding Great-Britain (with whom we have at present no treaty of commerce) from all our ports, what would be the probable operation of this step upon her politics? Would it not enable us to negotiate with the fairest prospect of success for commercial privileges of the most valuable and extensive kind in the dominions of that kingdom?" But Lord Sheffield was no less clear-eyed. America had no such government. "No treaty can be made with the American States that can be binding on the whole of them." "It will not be an easy matter," he concluded, "to bring the American States to act as a nation; they are not to be feared as such by us." Pitt's bill was lost.

The deflationary impact of reduced exports and heavy imports The impact of British policy was by no means confined to the direct trade between the United States and the islands. One way in which merchants had been accustomed for many years to pay for their imports of goods from England was to order their ship captains to proceed from the islands to England with West Indian products and bills of exchange received from the sales of their outgoing cargoes. Such indirect remittances lessened the need to pay for an excess of imports over exports by shipping gold or silver to the mother country. After the war the burden on specie exports became very heavy, especially because American merchants had responded to a long pent-up wartime demand by ordering huge quantities of British goods. The loss of both specie and West Indian markets combined to exert strong downward pressure on prices, making the decade after 1782 a period of severe deflation.

Prices of American exports fell in relation to those of imported goods, the terms of trade declining each year between 1784 and 1789 from an index of 112 in the former year to 88 in the latter. The resultant burden of debt was especially onerous in Massachusetts, where taxes which Hamilton said were the highest in the nation, together with the execution of court orders for the sale of property of delinquent taxpayers, created grave social tensions. Debtors importuned legislators to issue paper money to ease their tax payments and other obligations. Creditors, on the other hand, objected to being paid in paper that was worth less than specie.

To some extent the scenario was enacted in other states as well. When the paper money forces won out in seven states – with four of the states declaring the bills legal tender in private payments – alarmed creditors and other property owners sought to defend their interests. In Rhode Island, for example, merchants refused to accept paper, some of them closed their stores, and would-be buyers resorted to force and rioting, with farmers pledging to withhold produce from townsmen refusing to accept paper at par with specie. In 1786 armed attacks on creditors and tax collectors took place in Maryland, and a large band of armed men imprisoned the legislature in New Hampshire. That same year unrest in Massachusetts culminated in Shays's Rebellion, the well-known affair in which a Revolutionary War captain led a group of farmers into revolt against the government of the state (*see* Chapter 36, §4).

In these circumstances, aggravated the more by state laws postponing the collection of debts or providing for their payment in installments or in commodities rather than in money, it is not surprising to find a growing concern over the insecurity of property rights. That concern began to dominate the criminal law of Massachusetts in the 1780s, especially after the end of the war, when the number of cases of prosecution for theft and similar offenses more than tripled those of the war years. In Middlesex County alone there were four prosecutions for rioting and five for attacks on tax collectors between 1780 and 1785, and in the western counties attempts were made to prevent the courts from sitting and to rescue prisoners. A recent study of the legal history of Massachusetts concludes that postwar violence "undoubtedly heightened the fear of social breakdown and disorder in the state."

4. ECONOMIC DISORDER AND THE SECURITY OF PROPERTY

Contemporaries saw clearly the connection between the commercial, political, and social situations and between these and the security of property. "Another unhappy effect of a continuance of the present anarchy of commerce," James Madison wrote in March 1786, "will be a continuance of the unfavorable balance on it, which, by draining us of our metals, furnishes pretexts for the pernicious substitution of paper money, for indulgences to debtors, for postponement of taxes. In fact, most of our political evils may be traced to our commercial ones." Madison vigorously defended a constitutional revision which would transfer the power of coining money from the states to the federal government and forbid the states from emitting bills of credit (paper money). "A rage for paper money, or for any other improper or wicked object," he wrote in *The Federalist*, no. 10, "will be less apt to pervade the whole body of the Union than a particular member of it." The "Monied Interest will oppose the plan of Government," Gouverneur Morris said, "if paper emissions be not prohibited."

Years later Chief Justice John Marshall of the United States Supreme Court testified to the influence of the unsettled conditions of the 1780s on the inclusion of the contract clause. It was "the prevailing evil of the times," he wrote in *Ogden v. Saunders* (1827), "which produced this clause in the constitution." Marshall defined the evil in terms of "the practice of emitting paper money, of making property which was useless to the creditor a discharge of his debt and changing the time of payment by authorizing distant installments." "The power of changing the relative situation of debtor and creditor, of interfering with contracts," he added, "[was used] to such an excess by the state legislatures as to break in upon the ordinary intercourse of society, and destroy all confidence between man and man." Had he then been alive, Hamilton would have agreed, for in the era of the Constitutional Convention, and later as well, he expressed the conviction that the "relaxed conduct of the State Governments [had] undermined the foundations of Property and credit."

The concern of the founding fathers with the insecurity of property rights is easily explained. It is not that they were crass materialists, but rather that they were Lockeans. No philosopher exerted upon their values a stronger influence than John Locke, and to Locke the security of one's material wealth was intimately linked with one's freedom. Indeed, he defined "property" broadly to embrace one's life, liberty, and estate. The framers appear to have conceived property more narrowly, synonymously with estate, but the association with liberty was inseparable. "Property must be secured," John Adams wrote, "or liberty [cannot] exist." Hamilton saw it the same way: "Adieu to the security of property[,] adieu to the security of liberty."

Because the framers were endeavoring to erect and defend a structure of fundamental law, it is the more understandable that they should have emphasized fundamental relationships rooted in the law of nature and described for them so clearly by Locke. One of the most basic was the relationship between property and liberty, and, since legislative majorities in the states had threatened that relationship, the framers decided that an increase in federal power was essential to its preservation. As a close student of American constitutional development, Edward S. Corwin, once observed, "the problem of providing adequate safeguards for private rights and adequate powers for a national government were one and the same problem." The Constitution of 1787 met the problem head-on by granting the federal level of government sufficient power to restrain the activities of the states in the crucial area of property rights. According to the Constitution (Article 1, Section 10), the states were forbidden to emit bills of credit (paper money), to coin money, to make anything but gold and silver a tender in payment of debt, or to pass any law impairing the obligation of contract.

The regulation of commerce   By granting to Congress the "power to regulate commerce with foreign nations, and among the several states, and with the Indian tribes" (Article 1, Section 8), the Constitution restrained the activities of the states in these areas as well. A state could no longer set its tariffs and tonnage duties below those of other states in its effort to attract foreign vessels and their cargoes to its ports. Foreign powers could no longer play off one state against another; duties enacted by Congress were uniform in all the ports of the nation, and this enabled the government to negotiate favorable commercial treaties with a number of European governments, including even England, in 1794.

Even more importantly, control of inter-state commerce by the national government prevented the states from erecting tax and other kinds of walls around their boundaries in order to protect their local industries and products from competition with goods made in other states or imported from abroad. The importance of federal control of inter-state commerce to the development of the American economy cannot be overemphasized. In essence, the inter-state commerce power laid the foundation for a national market, for the American common market of the nineteenth and twentieth centuries. Such was the strength of local interests, however, that eternal vigilance on the part of the Supreme Court of the United States was required to keep that foundation from erosion. Even after Chief Justice John Marshall struck down as unconstitutional a legislative attempt by New York to infringe upon the commerce power (*Gibbons v. Ogden*, 1824), it was necessary for the Court to speak again and again in the later nineteenth century, most notably in *Welton v. Missouri* (1876), *Webber v. Virginia* (1880), and *Minnesota v. Barber* (1890). By preventing the states from circumscribing the dimensions of the national market the Court lent powerful assistance to the rise of American industry and to the nation's economic growth.

5. ECONOMIC CONSEQUENCES AND PRE-REVOLUTIONARY TRENDS

Let us summarize the case thus far for the significance of the American Revolution from the point of view of subsequent change in the American economy and society. Had there been no Revolution there would have been no war-incurred debt or need for federal taxing power to pay interest on that debt, owed both to foreign powers and to Americans themselves. There would have been no loss of the British West Indies to American shipping, no massively irregular imports in 1783, no "post-war" deflation, no widespread threats to the security of property rights in the form of responses by state legislatures to the deflation and its accompanying heavy burden of indebtedness. There would have been no need to call a constitutional convention in 1786 and hence no Constitution of 1787 providing for a Supreme Court to defend and protect national power from infringement by the states. Does this mean that if the independence movement had not formed all would have gone on as before, with the American colonies continuing to develop as a prosperous member of the British Empire, serving the latter's mercantilist purposes as source of industrial and other raw materials and market for products made in Britain?

Certainly the Americans did not view the Acts of trade and navigation as onerous: coinciding as they did with the natural conditions of trade, most colonial importing and exporting was conducted within the framework of British law. But what of the restrictions on colonial manufacturing imposed by the Woolens Act (1799), the Hat Act (1732) and the Iron Act (1750)?

Restraints on the colonial economy   Surely this legislation was representative of long-standing British policy to discourage manufacturing development in America. Vetoing a Pennsylvania statute in 1706, the Board of Trade remarked, "It cannot be expected that encouragement should be given by law to the making of any manufactures made in England in the plantations, it being against the advantage of England." On the eve of the Revolution itself Benjamin Franklin learned at first hand how adamant the British had become on the subject of manufactures. Just before leaving England in 1775, Franklin was drawn into informal negotiations with men closely connected to the ministry and asked to write out a set of propositions he believed would lead to permanent union. One of them was that all acts restraining manufactures be repealed. This proposition, Franklin relates, "they apprehend would meet with difficulty. They said, that restraining manufacturers in the colonies was a favorite here; and therefore they wish'd that article to be omitted, as the proposing it would alarm and hinder perhaps the considering and granting others of more importance." Can it be shown, then, that British legislation hindered the development of a more diversified American economy?

Almost certainly the answer is no, and the reason is that scarcities of capital, labor, and technological knowledge militated against the growth of manufacturing. These, rather than hostile laws, were the decisive counters. This is not to deny the existence of urban craft shops, of the domestic industry of rural households, of the manufacture of clothing, utensils, nails, furniture, and other products. One finds evidence of these things almost throughout the colonial period, as well as of shipbuilding, lumber and flour milling, and other mill industries employing water power. Manufacturers used tools belonging to age-old craft traditions rather than machinery, and in general enterprises were small in scale. They were neighborhood industries, widely dispersed rather than geographically concentrated, local manufactures protected by high transport costs from the competition of distant producers. Furthermore, they were technologically backward. Most of the water wheels were undershot and utilized only a fraction of the water power applied to them. There was so little understanding of power transmission that it was generally necessary to employ a separate wheel for each piece of machinery. These characteristics endured until shortly before the

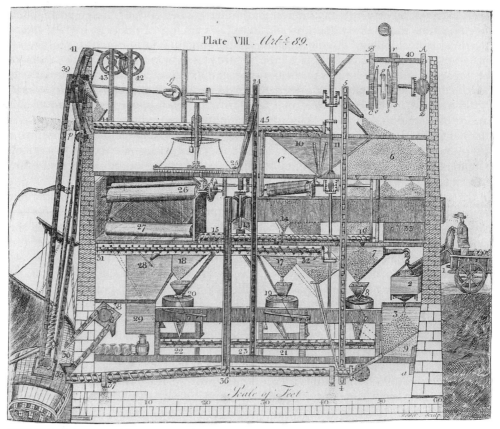

FIGURE 46 In 1791 Oliver Evans of Wilmington, Delaware, devised a flour mill operated entirely by water power: the grain is emptied by the waggoner into the scale pan (right, figure 1) and the process ends with the flour being loaded into barrels (left, figure 29) (from "The Young Mill-wright and Miller's Guide," 1795).

Revolution. Even in England the great inventions that gave the nation its industrial eminence were not successfully applied to manufactures until about the same time. About the year 1790 manufacturing everywhere broke free from ancient technical constraints, and processes of production were revolutionized (*see* figure 46). In sum, it is highly doubtful that manufacturing would have developed in the colonies even if British hostility had been replaced by encouragement. The "factor balance" would have remained decisive, just as it did in the early decades after the achievement of independence.

The power to form corporations   What of the power to form corporations (incorporated joint stock companies) – a legal device *par excellence* for assembling large pools of investment capital? Were colonial legislatures free to do so? And did the Revolution have any effect on incorporation in the United States? To begin with we must note that Parliament in 1741 extended the Bubble Act of 1720 to the colonies. The Act prohibited the erection of corporations without legal authority from Parliament or Crown. Now, one eminent authority, Joseph S. Davis, believes that the significance of the extension may easily be exaggerated. Although acknowledging that the act "may possibly have hindered the development of colonial joint stock companies, corporate or unincorporate," he finds no evidence that it was of any significance in the colonies after 1750. Davis contends that it is not British opposition but primarily the relatively undeveloped nature of the economy that explains the paucity of business corporations formed in the colonial period. Businesses were generally small scale and local in character. No large supplies of capital or labor were seeking employment, and those which were found outlets in unincorporated joint stock companies – legally part-nerships – which sometimes reached surprising size in mining, land speculation, and other areas of late colonial enterprise. Had capitalists sought incorporation, they would generally have found few legal obstacles in the way. Not only Parliament and Crown, but also colonial proprietors, governors, and legislatures possessed "within limits which were not always clear but which were for the most part wide, the right to erect corporations for operation in America."

Nevertheless, it does not follow that the mushroom growth of corporations in the early national period was unrelated to political change. During the entire colonial period only a half-dozen business corporations have been traced, two in the seventeenth century and four in the eighteenth. In contrast, more than 300 business corporations received charters from state governments during the 11-year period between 1789 and 1800. And during the first decade of the nineteenth century, the corporation law of at least one state (Massachusetts) witnessed the triumph of the doctrine of limited liability, a triumph which must certainly have encouraged both the security of investment and the transferability of property. To ascribe the startling growth in the number of business corporations to a greater degree of economic and social maturity in the post-revolutionary period is not persuasive. Can that much maturity have come in so short a time? A distinct political element is present and deserves recognition.

Most colonial corporations were erected by charters granted by royal governors in the name of the Crown, although usually with the consent of the provincial councils. That is to say, the sovereign was recognized as the source of legal authority, with parliamentary approval required after 1688 in the case of a grant of exclusive or monopoly privilege. In both royal and proprietary colonies the legal right of the assembly to incorporate was subject to the negative of the governor or of higher English authority. The Revolution brought an important change in this situation. Because of the fiction that the Revolution had been fought to free the colonists from the exactions of the Crown, a revulsion against executive authority became manifest in the early state constitutions, as well as in the Articles of Confederation. The power to incorporate, in sum, shifted from the executive to the legislative arm, where it was more sensitively responsive to community pressures on government to aid in the provision of community services. With the Revolution came a new view of the role of legislation in the legal system, a shift to the belief that law rested not on its conformity with past law and principle but rather on the power of a legislative majority.

More than two-thirds of those 300 corporations were organized to finance the costs of constructing inland navigation, turnpikes, and bridges. Even if it is true that the British authorities would not have hesitated to approve colonial requests for incorporation in general, is it not likely they would have frowned on the purposes served by most of these corporations? Given the values of the imperial system, can British governments have been expected to encourage wholesale movements of population to the West and the development of manufactures in the inland communities resulting therefrom? The Board of Trade was well aware of the connection between the two, for in a paper laid before it in 1768, manufacturing was viewed clearly as "a consequence which, experience shows, has constantly attended, in a greater or less degree, every inland settlement."

6. THE BREAKING OF THE IMPERIAL PATTERN

British opposition to colonial manufacturing, then, and to the development of infra-structure to inland areas that would encourage manufacturing, lay, as Franklin discovered in 1775, at the heart of imperial policy with respect to the American colonies. A growing, diversified, more mature colonial economy would provide sinews of strength which might challenge the subordinate colonial role in the empire. Indeed, despite the legislative efforts of the mother country to restrain that development, so much wealth had already been accumulated in commerce and agriculture by 1763 that the social and political elite which the wealth had brought into being was poised to challenge the post-1763 abridgement of its economic freedom. As Silas Deane said in a letter of June 1781 to Robert Morris: "The Parliamentary regulations and restrictions on our commerce were a principal cause of the unhappy contest between the two countries, and we were impatient under them because we were apprehensive, that they were part of a system to enslave us entirely." It was fear of this larger "system" that roused the colonists.

Therefore, even if we acknowledge the primacy of the "factor balance" in manu-facturing development and the role of the private sector in bringing it about, it does not follow that action on the part of government is irrelevant to economic change. To see this we need only ask whether manufacturing growth would have been restrained by legal discouragement after the factor balance began to shift in its favor. Suppose the colonies had remained within the British Empire: would continuation of a policy of discouragement have inhibited the development of manufacturing? There are some who would say that the question is not a historical one, that it is hypothetical or counterfactual in nature and ought not to be asked. In truth, however, the intertwined filaments of a causal web can be separated in no other way. It may be granted that our answers to such questions are neither true nor false. At best, they represent historical judgments, not historical facts. What makes for uncertainty is the possibility of change in other important elements of a situation. It is possible, for example, that the British Empire would have given way to the British Commonwealth before in fact it did, in which case an industrialized United States might have continued its political connection as partner rather than tutelary. But that is not likely. The Revolution itself played an important role in a gradually evolving view of the need to restructure Britain's relationship with its dependencies. Had the Revolution not occurred, imperial change might have been much longer in coming. Till then, to express the thought in words written by Alexander Hamilton in February 1775, "Those things we manufacture among ourselves, may be disallowed. We should then be compelled to take the manufactures of Great-Britain, upon her own conditions." History is fact chosen and explained by judging men and women. In my own opinion the breaking of the imperial connection was a necessary condition, although by no means a sufficient one, for the emergence of a modern industrial economy in America.

Demographic aspects of the Revolution and its aftermath

JIM POTTER

1. POPULATION GROWTH

The first census of the United States, taken in 1790, may be regarded as an important, albeit indirect, consequence of the American Revolution. It followed from Article 3, Section 2, of the Constitution of 1787, which apportioned membership of the House of Representatives and direct taxes according to the population of each state "by adding to the whole number of free persons ... three-fifths of all other persons [i.e., slaves]." This census, predating the first British census by 11 years and only the second national census in the modern world, when considered with the 124 counts held in the colonies between 1623 and 1775, enables the reconstruction of a picture of the American population at the time of the Revolution.

The main feature to emerge is the extreme rapidity of population growth during that period, with the total almost doubling (as T. R. Malthus observed a few years later) in the generation before the first census. Between 1770 and 1790 the white population increased by almost one and a half million, reaching 3.1 million in the latter year. The one decade after the Declaration of Independence saw an increase of just under three-quarters of a million. This rapid growth occurred despite the war-induced diseases (estimated to have killed ten times more people than the fighting) and the emigration of loyalists. Moreover, most of the later increase is attributable to natural growth, since the important contribution of immigration, both before and after these decades, was cut off by the European wars. Indeed, it was in the closing decades of the eighteenth century that the natural growth rate of the American population was higher than at any other time.

2. AGE STRUCTURE AND ITS IMPLICATIONS

Rapid natural population growth implied a preponderance of young people, and this had both political and economic implications. The census of 1790 confirmed the impression created by earlier colonial counts that the median age of the white male population was 16 years. In 1790, therefore, almost half the 3.1 million white Americans had been born after the Declaration of Independence; in 1800 two in three had been born after the Declaration. Already in the 1790s the expression "We Americans" was in common use. One might confidently estimate that by the time of Jefferson's inauguration not more than one American in four could possibly have had any recollection of colonial status. Thus the demographic features of the revolutionary period strongly reinforced the creation of a national identity.

Economically, such a youthful age structure implied large families (an average of four surviving children, making a household of six individuals), with a correspondingly heavy burden on those in the most productive age group. The resultant shortage of labor, both on farm and later in factory, on which many colonial and subsequent observers commented, was in part at least a consequence of the demographic structure.

It was above all the huge productivity of American agriculture, increasingly facilitated after the Revolution by the availability of new land, that permitted rapid population growth to occur. The War of Independence itself (and the health problems in the growing towns highlighted in the yellow fever outbreaks in Philadelphia and

New York in the 1790s) focused attention on medical ignorance, the inadequacies of existing hospitals, the butcheries that passed under the name of surgery, even the bitter animosities among medical practitioners. Nevertheless, recent studies relating to diet, stature, and life expectancy indicate that, now that the initial tribulations of early colonial settlement had been overcome, the population was (by all contemporary standards) extremely healthy and endowed with a large capacity for work.

For many decades of the late colonial period the modal age of marriage for women was 20 or 21 years and the incidence of infant mortality much lower than in contemporary Europe. It was almost certainly the quite rapid growth of a small number of urban centers after the Revolution that brought about the first reduction in the natural growth rate owing to later marriage and higher infant mortality.

3. POPULATION REDISTRIBUTION

The colonial period saw a gradual dispersal of the white population, reducing the earlier apparent concentration in the most populous colonies. By 1790 the three major regions, New England, the middle states, and the South Atlantic, each had just under one-third of the total white population. Over half the population was now to be found outside the formerly predominant areas of Pennsylvania, Virginia, Massachusetts, and Connecticut. As well as regional differences in the rate of natural growth and in the incidence of immigration, internal mobility played an increasing part in the redistribution progress. Movement occurred between the older settlements but also to the new lands at the frontiers – north, south, and more and more to the west. By the time of the Revolutionary War, most regions of early settlement had become emigration areas, with an accompanying transference of ways of life, attitudes, and religion to the reception areas. For an important clue to these movements we can turn once again to the first census. Whereas the United States as a whole had a male surplus in 1790 (as continued to be the case until 1940), Connecticut and Massachusetts both had small female surpluses, indicating the movement away of males.

The westward movement of population in particular, taking to the frontier a preponderance of men between 20 and 30 years, was accelerating during the period of the Revolution as the earlier constraints against territorial expansion were for the most part removed. Although Dr. Thomas Walker had discovered the Cumberland Gap through the Alleghenies from western Virginia into Kentucky in 1750, westward migration had for a time been inhibited by hostile Indians, the British Proclamation of 1763 (a very important cause of the Revolution), and the Quebec Act of 1774. The period of the Revolutionary War saw the Grand Opening of the Western Frontier, and already by 1783 the Wilderness Road had taken many thousands of settlers through the Cumberland Gap. The first census reported 100,000 people in Kentucky and Tennessee, mostly migrants of the previous ten years. By the time of the 1800 census, around 15,000 were recorded as far west as the Mississippi Territory and Indiana.

Characteristically, western settlements were initially predominantly male and adult. After a decade or more, however, a second phase occurred: family size, and therefore eventual natural growth, became larger than in the older areas. By 1800 the states with the greatest percentage of children were those whose main settlement had been under way during the two preceding decades. Tennessee and Kentucky had the highest proportion of children under nine years but the lowest proportion of persons between 16 and 45 years (though still an above average male surplus between those ages).

566

4. THE BLACK POPULATION

Another feature of population structure at the time of the Revolution is that the percentage of Blacks in the total population was at its highest ever, at about 21 per cent. The black population, almost entirely slave, was of course heavily concentrated in the South. In 1780 over half the population of South Carolina and about 40 per cent of that of Virginia was black, in contrast with that of New England at only 2 per cent. The first census showed a slave population of almost 700,000, of whom 90 per cent were in the South Atlantic states. Fifteen thousand slaves were already recorded in Kentucky and the Southwest territory.

5. CONCLUSION

Apart from the loss of life attributable to the Revolutionary War, and the migration of loyalists, it is not possible to regard any of these population changes as consequences of the war. Nevertheless, as has been argued above, very important changes were occurring during the revolutionary period, and a picture of America during this time would be incomplete without inclusion of the demographic detail.

FURTHER READING

Bailyn, Bernard: *Ideological Origins of the American Revolution* (Princeton, NJ: Princeton University Press, 1967).

Bruchey, Stuart: *Enterprise: the Dynamic Economy of a Free People* (Cambridge, Mass.: Harvard University Press, 1990).

Clark, Victor S.: *History of Manufacturing in the United States, 1607–1860*, 3 vols. (Washington, DC: Carnegie Institute, 1929), I.

Corwin, Edward S.: "The progress of constitutional theory between the Declaration of Independence and the meeting of the Philadelphia Convention," *American Constitutional History: Essays by Edward S. Corwin*, ed. Alpheus T. Mason and Gerald Garvey (New York: Harper & Row, 1964).

Davis, Joseph S.: *Essays in the Earlier History of American Corporations*, 2 vols. (Cambridge, Mass.: Harvard University Press, 1917), II.

East, Robert A.: *Business Enterprise in the American Revolutionary Era* (New York: Columbia University Press, 1933).

Ferguson, E. James: *The Power of the Purse* (Chapel Hill: University of North Carolina Press, 1961).

Ferguson, E. James (ed.): *The Papers of Robert Morris, 1781–1784* (Pittsburgh: University of Pittsburgh Press, 1973).

Fischer, David Hackett: *The Revolution of American Conservatism: the Federalist Party in the Era of Jeffersonian Democracy* (New York: Harper & Row, 1965).

Gilbert, Felix (ed.): "Letters of Francis Kinloch to Thomas Boone, 1782–1786," *Journal of Southern History*, 8 [1942].

Greene, Jack P.: "An uneasy connection: an analysis of the preconditions of the American Revolution," *Essays on the American Revolution*, ed. Stephen G. Kurtz and James H. Hutson (Chapel Hill: University of North Carolina Press, 1973), esp. pp. 35–45.

——: "The social origins of the American Revolution: an evaluation and interpretation," *Political Science Quarterly*, 88 (1973), 3–19.

Holroyd, John (Lord Sheffield): *Observations on the Commerce of the American States* (London, 1783).

Jones, Alice Hanson: *The Wealth of a Nation to Be* (New York: Columbia University Press, 1980).

Madison, James: *Letters and Other Writings of James Madison*, 4 vols. (Philadelphia: J. P. Lippincott, 1867).

Nelson, William E.: *Americanization of the Common Law: the Impact of Legal Change on Massachusetts Society, 1760–1830* (Cambridge, Mass.: Harvard University Press, 1975).

Nettels, Curtis P.: *Emergence of a National Economy, 1775–1815* (New York: Holt, Rinehart, and Winston, 1962).

Syrett, Harold C. (ed.): *The Papers of Alexander Hamilton*, 26 vols. (New York: Columbia University Press, 1961–73).

FURTHER READING (demographic aspects)

Cassedy, J. H.: *Demography in Early America: Beginnings of the Statistical Mind* (Cambridge, Mass.: Harvard University Press, 1969).

Greene, E. B. and Harrington, V. D.: *American Population Before the Federal Census of 1790* (New York: 1932).

Potter, J.: "Demographic development and family structure," *Colonial British-America*, ed. J. P. Greene and J. R. Pole (Baltimore and London: Johns Hopkins University Press, 1984).

Wells, R. V.: *The Population of the British Colonies in America before 1776* (Princeton, NJ: Princeton University Press, 1975).

58

The religious consequences of the Revolution

ROBERT M. CALHOON

THE most immediate effect of religion on the newly independent American republic was ideological. Moderate Calvinism helped knit together into a coherent civic creed the two main divergent strands of revolutionary thought. The older of these was *contractual*, derived from the Puritans and from John Locke. It justified revolution as the righteous response to the British tyranny which had violated the compact between the sovereign and the people. The newer one – also popularized and emphasized by Calvinist clergymen – was *republicanism*, originating in Cicero's Rome, resurrected by Renaissance civic humanists, adopted by English opposition theorists in the 1720s and 1730s and by Scottish moral philosophers two decades later, and thence transmitted to America in books and pamphlets as well as through the minds of publicists who crossed the Atlantic. Republicanism intermingled readily with Old Testament notions of a sinful people who had a Lockean covenant with a stern but loving Creator. Republicanism was communal and pessimistic; secularized Lockean Calvinism was optimistic and individualistic. Preachers, infusing both traditions with Biblical images, were particularly adept at combining and harmonizing these dark and light elements in patriot political consciousness.

I. LOCKEAN CALVINISM AND REPUBLICANISM

New England Congregationalists New England Congregationist sermons of the pre-revolutionary period enunciated the classic American reformulation of Locke. "Once it was acknowledged," in these pulpits, "that rulers were more likely to violate the common interest than were subjects," it was "reasonable to endow the people with a right to frame a constitution 'as the standing measure of the proceedings of government' for their own protection and to solicit their ruler's consent to it" (Buel, 1964, pp. 170–1). This discovery of divinely sanctioned fundamental law was profoundly conservative in the sense that it obligated subjects to be dutiful, watchful, and conscientious about public affairs, but also radical in its assumption that sinfulness concentrated within the bowels of government was far more immoral, destructive, and obnoxious to the Lord of the universe than the isolated misdeeds of individuals. The contract meant that, to counter the misdeeds of a ruler, the people had to act in concert with dignity, eloquent rhetoric, and personal self-sacrifice in order to vindicate the cause of liberty and the legitimate interests of the community.

As the struggle for liberty shifted from resistance to revolution a mutually constraining compact came under severe stress; accordingly New England clergymen took the lead in using millennial rhetoric and radical English opposition thought to express a darker and more desperate vision: images such as "the great whore of

Babylon" from Revelation, as well as older notions of New England as the chronically sinning children of Israel who continually tested the patience of a loving but stern father, introduced just the note of terror into revolutionary politics that republicans such as Cicero or Machiavelli considered necessary to summon men to the common defense of liberty. Linking Lockean contractualism and the republican apprehension together most securely was the old idea of a Puritan ethic – a calling from God to every believer to consider salvation, talent, ambition, productivity, and family responsibilities as gifts of God to be employed with discipline and thrift. Revolutionary clergymen readily applied the Puritan ethic to politics, considering liberty itself a gift held in trust. Sacrifice in the public cause then became a purging, purifying experience which expelled dangerous poisons of selfishness, complacency, and political myopia from the human spirit and replaced them with life-giving qualities of zeal, energy, and sagacity. "We boast of liberty, and value ourselves much on being free, when at the same time we have been taken captive by Satan at his pleasure," explained one Massachusetts preacher in 1774: "This is a much more shocking absurdity than it would be for a man confined in a dungeon to boast that he is at liberty because he is not called on, in providence, to go into the field and labour," to which another added, "it is an indispensable duty, my brethren, which we owe to God and our country, to rouse up and bestir ourselves, being animated with a noble zeal for the sacred cause of liberty" (Stout, 1986, pp. 297–8).

North Carolina Presbyterians Combining Lockean obligation and republican zeal, David Caldwell, a Presbyterian minister in piedmont North Carolina, blamed tyranny on human slothfulness – political inactivity, unreflectiveness, apathy, and stupid concern with personal comfort – and he assigned to the spirit of God the task of redeeming the slothful and filling the human frame with activity, poise, and libertarian consciousness. The political and social implications of these tendencies in human nature, for Caldwell, were ominous. Throughout history "sloth" as a state of mind and body and as a moral condition had tempted rulers to exercise tyrannical power. The slothful were people who seemed, to arrogant and unreflective rulers, to be fit objects of unbridled governmental coercion. The "ignorance, disregard of moral obligation, and supreme love of ease" of the groveling sluggard corresponded exactly with a tyrant's appetite and cynicism. Not only did the slothful encourage and facilitate oppression, their own "shame" and "sinking spirits," their own pitiful compliance and submission became self-made chains of slavery. The miraculous way in which God might intervene to preserve colonial liberty, Caldwell declared, would occur only as the Holy Spirit penetrated the encrustations of habit and lethargy and converted the soul, the conscience, the moral sense within the human frame into something graceful and swift and responsive (Calhoon, 1988, pp. 94–5).

The stresses of war strained this compound of Lockean and republican religious thought about politics. The savage irregular warfare in North Carolina during 1781 prompted Samuel McCorkle, a Presbyterian minister from Rowan County, North Carolina, to warn that "a plundering Whig is worse than a non-plundering Tory." "It is in your interest to join with the [latter], if disposed to join you, [and] to support and execute the laws upon the [former], if indisposed to repent or restore," he instructed North Carolina leaders in a sermon on "The Crime and Curse of Plundering." McCorkle equated plundering of helpless Tories with the looting of "silver and ... gold and vessels of brass and iron" by an Israelite soldier named Achan in the Book of Joshua, which "kindled ... the anger of the Lord against the children of

FIGURE 47 (a): the First Church of Christ, Congregational, at Farmington, Connecticut, built in 1771; (b) the African Episcopal Church of St. Thomas, Philadelphia (lithograph by W. L. Breton, 1829)

(a)

(b)

Israel." McCorkle's argument, in fine republican pessimism, held that individual enterprise and enrichment did energize society but also had a corrosive influence. No one had a right to injure the public good in the pursuit of private gain, and in war the line between rational self-interest and besotted greed and vengeance became perilously thin (Calhoon, 1988, p. 80).

Chaplains in the Continental Army   Another vivid measure of the stress between Lockean duty and republican heroism appeared in the service of chaplains to the Continental Army. Abiel Leonard, minister of the Congregationalist church in Woodstock, Connecticut, joined Washington's army in early 1776. "He engaged early in the army and has been indefatigable in the duties of his station," observed General Nathanael Greene; "in a word he has done every thing in his power both in and out of the line of duty to promote the good of the service." A year later Leonard was sick and worried about the health and well-being of his family. On the way back from furlough, Washington reprimanded him for overstaying his leave. That night, while staying in a tavern and deeply depressed, he slit his throat with a razor. "The cut is so near his chin that the tongue is wounded and he cannot speak, but writes ... [and has] expressed a great desire to get well." Leonard died 18 days later. Those who knew Leonard and his ability to inspire the troops attributed his wound to a "fit of lunacy, ... how soon may reason be unsealed." Religious zeal functioned imperfectly as a remedy to the psychological toll taken by life in the army (Royster, 1979, pp. 173–4).

2. NATIONALISM: JOHN WITHERSPOON AND JAMES MADISON

With the successful winning of independence, Lockean and republican influences continued to inform American religious experience in two major ways. Nationalists such as John Witherspoon of the College of New Jersey at Princeton, and his student, James Madison, drew on both Lockean and republican traditions for guidance in political realism and a vision of the future of the republic based on both Enlightenment and Calvinist concepts of human nature. Localists and democrats, on the other hand, suspicious of concentrations of power and of hierarchies in society, used the same ideas to promote egalitarianism and anti-institutionalism.

Witherspoon's republicanism was a mixture of Calvinist doctrines of depravity and civic humanist notions about virtue. To enable them to understand evil, Witherspoon told his students that God had "implanted" in human beings "conscience, enlightened by reason, [by] experience, and [by] every way ... we ... learn the will of our Maker." This formulation was the very conception of human nature that Witherspoon had condemned time and again in Scotland as leader of the orthodox wing of the Presbyterian Church of Scotland opposing the influence of Scottish moral philosophers, especially Francis Hutcheson. In 1758 he scornfully dismissed Enlightenment Christianity in Scotland as "a pliant and fashionable scheme of religion, a fine theory of virtue and morality" (Calhoon, 1988, p. 81).

Witherspoon's theological reorientation, following his installation as President of Princeton in 1768, has perplexed historians more than it did his contemporaries. American Presbyterians knew little of the ecclesiastical wars in Scotland, and the Trustees of the College of New Jersey were attracted to Witherspoon more for his reputed erudition and eloquence than for his orthodoxy. Once in America he sought to revitalize the finances and academic stature of the college by nurturing a new consensus among American Presbyterians based on Scottish moral philosophy as well as self-conscious piety.

Madison's analysis of constitutionalism easily adopted the framework Witherspoon had taught him at Princeton 17 years earlier. Witherspoon's didactic "virtue/vice" and "ethics/politics" polarities were, to start with, spacious and subtle enough to provide Madison a framework for an elegant, persuasive political theory. The creative tension in Witherspoon's concept of virtue and vice was his paradoxical treatment of human action as an expression of virtue and yet the dependence of such action on divine grace. Whether or not he resolved his paradox by assigning the moral sense a critical role in the work of redemption, or merely trusted that, in America, Providence would enhance the potency of virtue among sinful men, Witherspoon certainly did envision a symbiotic tie between vice and virtue which would fashion a secularized Calvinism that filled a real need in early national political culture.

Madison made the most of this discovery. "As long as the connection subsists between his reason and his self-love," he predicted, "[man's] opinions and his passions will have a reciprocal influence on each other," with passions "attach[ing] themselves" in dangerous ways to rational thought. "The first object of government" was to protect society from destructive jealousies over material inequality especially fomented by organized groups or factions united by a common sense of deprivation. "The latent causes of faction," Madison concluded, "are sown in the nature of man." Thence arose disputes over religion and politics, rivalries between the followers of different leaders, the influence of demagogues, and the persistence of "frivolous and fanciful" dissatisfactions. "But the most common and durable source of faction has been the various and unequal distribution of property" – debtors and creditors, "landed," "manufacturing," "mercantile," and "monied" interests. These political actors, left to their own devices, would "clog the administration" of government and "convulse the society."

Madison saw the solution in the ideological materials with which Americans were already familiar – and in human nature and social reality itself. He sought to remove the most prominent of the conditions: provinciality, isolation, and localized conflict, which encouraged "men of factious tempers, of local prejudices, or of sinister designs" to "obtain the suffrages and betray the interests of the people." "An extensive republic" would enlarge the pool of talented, public-spirited candidates for office and focus public attention on issues of the common weal. Admittedly, Madison adroitly conceded, the creation of a spacious republic carried with it the risk of "render[ing] the representative too little acquainted with all" the "local circumstances and lesser interests" of his constituents. But, turning this difficulty to his own advantage, Madison reminded his readers that these were the very circumstances that encouraged narrowly self-interested behaviour and made legislators "too little fit to comprehend and pursue great and national objects." Intrinsic to human society, according to Madison's formulation, was a kind of latent, moral inertia that could be overcome only by a quickened pace of moral stimulation and intellectual challenge (Calhoon, 1988, pp. 85–6). Jefferson's Virginia Statute for Religious Liberty was adopted by the legislature fortuitously in 1786 when support flagged for a clumsy but superficially popular plan for public subsidization of ministerial salaries. Madison seized this opportunity to discredit as well as defeat this "religious assessment" plan by arguing brilliantly that even non-sectarian governmental inculcation of religion would debase the human spirit and subvert the public good.

3. RELIGIOUS EDUCATIONAL PHILOSOPHY: BENJAMIN RUSH AND HENRY ALLASON

While eschewing direct public entanglement in religion, republicans employed religious teachings as well as Enlightenment philosophical arguments to construct an educational philosophy appropriate to the needs of the new nation. It taught, according to Benjamin Rush, that each "pupil ... does not belong to himself but ... is public property" (Yazawa, 1985, p. 143).

Rush believed that evangelical Christianity was a natural re-enforcement of republicanism and the only means of containing "the irregular and compulsive impulses of the human heart" which weaned individuals away from devotion to the common weal. The cause of liberty could have lasting meaning, he warned, only if it was a prelude to "the *salvation of all mankind*":

> Republican forms of government are the best repositories of the Gospel: I therefore suppose they are intended as preludes to a glorious manifestation of its power and influence upon the hearts of men. The language of these free and equal governments seems to be like that of John the Baptist of old, "Prepare aye the way of the Lord – make his paths strait."

If Christian discipleship was an antidote to the individualism of egocentric desires flying off in all directions, then, in Rush's thinking, infusing civic virtue with the "power" of "the gospel" would create a disciplined, sustainable experiment in republican government. Personal service to the community – especially moral leadership inspired by worship – would fill individuals with premonitions of immortality and assure them of fame beyond the grave. "How delightful to a good man should be the thoughts of surviving himself," he told Elhanan Winchester, who had just published a funeral sermon about John Wesley and a volume on prophesy:

> your works however much neglected or opposed now will be precious to those generations which are to follow us.... The persons who are to exist a hundred years hence are as much our fellow creatures as ... are our contemporaries. It only requires more grace to love them than the persons whom we see ... every day; but in proportion as we attain to this supreme act of love, we approach nearer the source of all love.

That kind of ardent service of fellow souls yet unborn was, for Rush, the essence of republican self-denial.

Christianity in a republic appealed to Rush, not only as a way of fixing ambition on the spiritual well-being of others but also as the only reliable way of deepening personal consciousness and effecting a reformation of the deepest roots of behavior. By fusing republican notions about equality and virtue to Christian habits of introspection and humility, Rush developed a theory about education and discipline. "Solitude," he insisted, was the only appropriate form of discipline in a republic:

> Too much cannot be said in favor of SOLITUDE as a means of reformation, which should be the *only* end of *all* punishment. Men are wicked only from not *thinking*. O! that they would *consider*, is the language of inspiration. A wheelbarrow, a shipping post, nay even a gibbet, are all light punishments compared with letting a man's conscience loose upon him in solitude. Company, conversation, and even business are the opiates of the Spirit of God in the human heart. For this reason, a bad man should be left for some time without anything to employ his hands in his confinement. Every *thought* should recoil wholly upon *himself*.

The process by which solitude turned an individual "wholly upon himself" was for Rush the essence of pious individualism (Rush, 1951, pp. 511–12, 611–12).

574

One evangelical schoolmaster found the process of inculcating virtue to be an especially compelling calling. "In order to be virtuous," Henry Allason, a self-educated Methodist teacher in Maryland, reminded himself in 1807, "a man must resist his propensities, inclinations, and tastes, and maintain an incessant conflict with himself" that is between the guidance of the "heart" and the demands of "ambition" and public expectation. Learning to work through such experiences, Allason believed, required teachers who could "preside" over a schoolroom: "men well recommended, not given to intrigue and hence to loss of virtue. We should not ask if he is a wit, a bright man, a philosopher, but is he fond of children, does he frequent the unfortunate rather than the great?" Such a teacher would remember that the only punishment appropriate in a republican culture was exclusion of an offender from the company of other students, an "exile" proportionate to the seriousness of the offense and administered in a manner respectful of the student's personal dignity.

Tying these standards and assumptions together was Allason's belief that

> nothing is durable, virtue alone excepted. Personal beauty passes quickly away, fortune inspires extravagant inclinations, grandeur fatigues, reputation is uncertain, talents, nay genius itself are liable to be impaired. But virtue is ever beautiful, ever diversified, ever equal, and ever vigorous because it is resigned to all events, to privations as well as to enjoyments, to death as to life, happy ... [am I] if I have been able to contribute ... toward redressing some of the evils which oppress my country and to open some new prospect of felicity.

Education for a republican like Allason was decidedly more public and shared than personal and private; happiness and virtue could only be known in civic activity. Allason felt this ideal constantly slipping away, retrievable only by recurrence to first principles of self-discipline and comradeship with others. To be a republican was to seize the day and live out a credo of public service and unselfishness before evanescent favorable circumstances evaporated (Calhoon, 1988, pp. 124–5).

4. NEW EVANGELICAL SECTS

In contrast with Enlightenment evangelicals such as Witherspoon and Madison, who conceived of constitutions and political discourse as instruments of "conflict resolution," the many Anti-Federalist Baptists and Methodists, and some Presbyterians, opposed ratification of the Constitution. They valued instead "conflict management" as an ongoing function of churches and communities in which elites did not achieve predominance and irrepressible democratic impulses did not dissipate in the quest for national stability. Lemuel Burkitt, a Separate-Baptist minister in Hertford County, addressed large, spirited crowds during the ratification struggle in North Carolina. His "peroration did not address religious liberty, the constitutional issue historians have characteristically associated with religious dissenters in the South.... Instead he raised an issue associated with the Harringtonian [republican] tradition of Anglo-American political thought, namely the dangers of a standing army and centralization of power" (Marini, 1990). This kind of localized, community rooted, communal evangelicalism swept away Congregationalism in northern New England during the revolutionary era, as Freewill Baptists, Shakers, and Universalists created hundreds of new churches. Influenced in part by the revivals in Nova Scotia led by Henry Alline, these radical sects on the outer edges of revolutionary New England developed in their worship and especially in their hymnody a "language of the soul" which was sensuous, personal, otherworldly, and didactic (Marini, 1982, pp. 156–71).

A less visible and more precarious variety of marginal evangelical churches were black churches in Wilmington, Charleston, Savannah, and elsewhere in the South. William Meredith, a Methodist missionary from the West Indies, settled in Wilmington in 1795, preached to Blacks, and organized an all-black congregation which built its own meeting-house. There Blacks conducted their own services for nearly 15 years until the arrival of the white Methodist minister William Capers, whose parishioners appropriated the "negro meeting-house" (Hinks, 1989, p. 34). Andrew Bryan, a slave owned by Whitefield's convert Jonathan Bryan, began preaching to Savannah Blacks in 1782. Fearful of slaves being taken away by the departing British, patriot officials in Savannah ordered him whipped, but "would freely suffer death for the cause of Jesus Christ" (Raboteau, 1978, p. 141), a willingness to endure punishment like that of the apostles in the book of Acts which shamed officials into releasing him.

The spread of evangelical Christianity among slaves and free Blacks in Virginia, the Carolinas, and Georgia after the Revolution sent unmistakable tremors throughout the region. A slave scare – fear of imminent servile uprising – in eastern North Carolina in 1802 took place in the very localities where biracial conversions and baptisms occurred during the revivals of 1801. The abortive black uprising in Charleston in 1822, led by Denmark Vesey, drew its ideology and inspiration from Christian millennialism. Probably influenced by Vesey, the first full-scale indictment of slavery written by an American Black, David Walker's *Appeal to the Coloured Citizens of the World* (1829), proceeded from the assumption that "the day of our redemption from abject wretchedness draweth near when we shall be enabled ... to stretch forth our hand to the LORD our GOD, but there must be a willingness on our part for GOD to do these things for us!" (Hinks, 1989, p. 1).

Ultimately the most far-reaching religious consequences of the Revolution came between the 1820s and the 1850s, when evangelical zeal, a millennial sense of being a chosen people, and the new cultural milieu of romanticism combined to undergird a wide-ranging set of movements known as romantic reform. Some of the artistic and intellectual leaders for abolitionism, women's rights, public education, temperance, and the rights of Indians became Unitarians – those former Congregationalists who rejected orthodox theology – and their off-shoot the Transcendentalists, who sought to infuse rational religion with spiritual joy. But the rank and file of romantic reform movements came from evangelical churches and channeled the optimistic, Arminian, and millennial expectancy of religious revivalism in the early nineteenth century into a crusade to purify American society. James G. Birney, a Princeton graduate practicing law in Alabama in 1817, experienced conversion at a revival meeting. His first response to that religious experience was to become a lawyer for Indians being forced from their ancestral lands, and in 1832 he became an agent of the American Colonization Society. Disappointed in the response of other slave-owners to colonization, he moved to Kentucky and then to Ohio, where he edited abolitionist newspapers. In 1837 he became Secretary of the American Anti-Slavery Society and in 1840 and 1844 an anti-slavery candidate for President. New England missionaries to the Cherokees waged a long and losing struggle in the courts to protect that tribe from removal from Georgia to reservations west of the Mississippi. The more pervasive impact of Christianity on American Indians, however, was the Jeffersonian conviction, rooted in a deistic view of creation and ethics, that Indians could be civilized and thereby converted into yeoman farmers – a vision which ironically paved the way for the destruction of Indian civilization by the relentless expansion to the West of yeoman farmers of European descent.

FURTHER READING

Buel, Richard: "Democracy and the American Revolution: a frame of reference," *William and Mary Quarterly*, 21 (1964), 165–90.

Calhoon, Robert M.: *Evangelicals and Conservatives in the Early South, 1740–1861* (Columbia: University of South Carolina Press, 1988).

Hatch, Nathan O.: *The Sacred Cause of Liberty: Republican Thought and the Millennium in Revolutionary New England* (New Haven: Yale University Press, 1977).

Hinks, Peter J.: "'We Must and Shall be Free': David Walker, Evangelicalism and Antebellum Black Resistance," Ph.D. dissertation, Yale University, forthcoming.

Isaac, Rhys: *The Transformation of Virginia, 1740–1790* (Chapel Hill: University of North Carolina Press, 1982).

Marini, Stephen A.: *Radical Sects of Revolutionary New England* (Cambridge, Mass.: Harvard University Press, 1982).

——: "Religion, Politics, and Ratification," *Religion in a Revolutionary Age*, ed. Ronald Hoffman and Peter J. Alberts (Charlottesville: University of Virginia Press, forthcoming).

Raboteau, Albert J.: *Slave Religion: the "Invisible Institution" in the Antebellum South* (New York: Oxford University Press, 1978).

Royster, Charles: *A Revolutionary People at War: the Continental Army and American Character, 1775–1783* (Chapel Hill: University of North Carolina Press, 1979).

Rush, Benjamin: *Letters of Benjamin Rush*, ed. Lyman H. Butterfield (Princeton, NJ: Princeton University Press, 1951).

Stout, Harry S.: *The New England Soul: Preaching and Religious Culture in Colonial New England* (New York: Oxford University Press, 1986).

Yazawa, Melvin: *From Colonies to Commonwealth: Familial Ideology and the Beginnings of the American Republic* (Baltimore: Johns Hopkins University Press, 1985).

577

59

The cultural effects of the Revolution

NORMAN S. GRABO

HE strongest cultural impact of the American Revolution was on the verbal
arts – poetry, fiction, theater, and the popular press. But even there the result
was not a drastic change from how things had been before the Revolution.
Rather the war and the resulting shifts in social governance seem to have accelerated
a general movement towards a distinct cultural identity that had been under way
since the 1750s. The war released great pent-up energies that were determinedly self-
reflective and patriotic and at the same time fiercely determined to meet the marks
set by English and European civilization. The sciences – particularly medicine –
struggled to find a professional identity and quality without achieving any spectacular
advances. At the same time American painting soared in sophistication and
accomplishment, but it would be hard to say that either sluggishness in the sciences
or the brilliance of painting owed much directly to the Revolution. What the culture
of letters showed, however, was that the Revolution confirmed already dawning hopes
and inspired great visions of a practical glory in the future. It forced a potent ethnic
mix to embark on a long voyage of self-definition.

I. CULTURAL DIVERSITY

When Rip Van Winkle woke up – having slept right through the Revolution – nothing
had changed, except the color of George's coat on the tavern sign, from red to blue.
Looking back in his *Travels* from about the same vantage point as Washington Irving
(1820), Timothy Dwight, the President of Yale, generally agreed: the basic revolution
in American culture had occurred in the late 1750s when Americans played their
little part in the worldwide conflict known as the Seven Years' War. Massive influxes
of both British and French soldiery brought with them new tastes, habits, and manners.
They brought as well new literary works and criticism, new standards in painting,
new music, theater, and, most important, new ideas.

Boys born in the early 1750s were in college when revolutionary anxiety was
growing intense – at Harvard, Yale, Princeton, Dartmouth, Pennsylvania, Columbia,
and Rhode Island. All Christian and ministerial to begin with, these cultural instruments provided in the 1770s increasing numbers of boys with a systematic exposure
to Enlightenment attitudes developing both in France and Britain. America's future
ministers, lawyers and judges, statesmen and politicians, teachers, scientists, and
tradesmen were being groomed for a world that had not been visible to their fathers.

More important as instruments of cultural expression were the many newspapers
(since 1690) and magazines (since 1740) that sprang up and died as rapidly as weeds.
Couriers, post-boys, and gazettes flourished and failed quickly. But they could be found

in any port city, and, although they were pitched at relatively local subscribers, their uniform pretensions to intellectual authority give a sense of standardized provincial manners, customs, diversions, and concerns that may be somewhat misleading. Published weekly, twice weekly, and monthly, they were generally divided into sections – a period intelligencer (covering international events from Europe to China), an encyclopedia essay, the serialization of a history or travel account, an Addisonian essay, and sometimes a poetical miscellany, but almost always some kind of serious "entertainment," usually on the first page. Newspapers also printed port news dates of arrival and departure, occasionally notice of goods – and noticed merchandise for sale – fabrics or ribbons, anvils, slaves, land, and livestock. In exceptionally diverse and sophisticated Charles Town, the *South Carolina Gazette* outdid most in its announcements of concerts, theatrical performances, dance and music lessons, even the manufacture and repair of musical instruments.

When the British occupied Charles Town under General Henry Clinton, it seemed through all the colonies as if their most elegant and charming cultural center had been violated. Finally persuaded to an alliance with the Revolutionaries, France's first effort was to harry the occupiers of Charles Town, which was in many respects a French spa, even to its prominent use of the French language. The complete dominance of English in the popular press masks what must have been a powerful multiplicity of tongues and accents. The sounds of Africa, Europe, the Mediterranean, and the West Indies enriched the coastal air as much as did the spices and aromas of various ethnic cuisines. Provost William Smith of the College of Pennsylvania discussed modern educational theory in elegant English with a strong overlay of Aberdeen Scots, and the enormously successful publisher Mathew Carey kept the lilt of his native Irish alive, no doubt tinged with his years as an apprentice printer in Paris, long after his postwar emigration to Philadelphia. We tend to forget that passionate conversations about religion and politics, as well as family matters, were as likely to be thought through and spoken in vigorous German, French, Dutch, Yoruba, Gullah, Spanish, Swedish, or Farsi before they assumed the public voice of written English, a form of apparently benign oppression that went unchallenged by the Revolution.

In the wake of warfare, as young American idealists welcomed peace, some saw this linguistic diversity as the inheritance of Babel. They yearned for, even prophesied, a world where nationalism would be transcended by an international language identical with reason and based on the morality of nature. They never specified what language that would be.

The college generation of the early 1770s was only eight to 12 years old when the British Admiralty tightened trade restrictions. A young boy such as Philip Freneau, whose father sailed trading vessels between New York, Philadelphia, Haiti, Jamaica, and Charles Town, would surely not have known or cared about British restrictions on colonial trade and manufacture. But he would have heard his father's complaints about the difficulty of making a living at sea – the high costs of insurance and the heavy risk capital, to say nothing of the dangers, and then the additional taxes! He would have heard them in salty French. There must have been a deep anger and sullenness – one rarely articulated or preserved, and therefore difficult to prove – in those boys. Whether they came from the sea or from ministerial households, villages or farms, they seem to have come of age with a great sense of material deprivation, and a sullen hostility to arbitrary authority. Even their best suits were made abroad – not because foreign clothing was better (although it was), but because remote administrators in England would not permit the manufacture of finished goods in America.

Timber, fish, bread and grain, mineral ores, indigo, and other raw materials found a long way around to American use.

2. POETRY AND THEORY OF THE ARTS

By 1770 the boys were voicing their unrest in a curiously formal way. Commencement Day became an occasion for producing celebratory orations and poems, addressed to parents, trustees, and invited dignitaries, prominent citizens and public officials. Poems on the "Rising glory of America" began to spring up on these occasions, visionary poems not content with self-congratulation, but full of visions of a future that did not include colonial limitations. Typically these poems – such as the best known by PHILIP FRENEAU (1752–1832) and his friend Hugh Henry Brackenridge (1748–1816) at Princeton – progressed through a series of set themes: firstly the discovery of the Americas, secondly the present accomplishments of Americans in science and the useful arts, thirdly future expansion westward across the continent, fourthly commerce as the chief instrument of civilization, and lastly the future pre-eminence of America in the fine arts. These subtle anticipations of American "Manifest Destiny" built on the economic imperialism of an unrestricted commerce had so little basis in experience that they must be seen as expressing the fantasies of an oppressed mentality.

Such poems were often courteously printed, either in newspapers or separately, setting the manner for later Federalist-inspired Forefathers' Day and Fourth of July occasions well into the nineteenth century. Especially at Yale the genre took on considerable force. John Trumbull (1750–1831), who apparently began the mode, gave it up after some satirical turns. But his friend Timothy Dwight (1752–1817), who would later become an eminent President of Yale (1795–1817), emphasized the new opportunity opened by the Revolution in his allegory of Joshua's epic revolt in *The Conquest of Canaan* (published in 1785, and dedicated to Washington as the new Joshua, but actually written during the war). Joshua's vision shows an America at the last stage before the apocalyptic destruction of the world and a new millennial order.

Dwight's student JOEL BARLOW (1754–1812) found the allegorical equivalent of George Washington not in Joshua or elsewhere in the Bible, but in Christopher Columbus and the original lawgiver of Peru, the Incan Manco Capac, who had to fight and destroy in order to bring about a social order designed for the happiness of mankind. Barlow's *The Vision of Columbus* was published in 1787 – the year of the Constitutional Convention in Philadelphia – though much of it had been written during the war. It shows again that in periods of crisis, when American writers tried to define exactly who they were, they looked back to Hispanic discoveries and to the civilizations of Aztec Mexico and Incan Peru, acknowledging in a rudimentary way a revolutionary consciousness of the importance of Hispanic elements in the American experience.

Young collegians were as likely to think themselves "Sons of Columbus" as "Sons of Liberty," plowing what Walt Whitman would call one hundred years later a watery "Passage to India." Such grandiose ideas flourished especially at Yale, which throughout the 1770s turned to the serious study of Lord Kames's eye-opening *Elements of Criticism* (1762). Kames taught Americans that the fine arts were more than entertainment or recreative diversions, that they were significant expressions of human nature, especially of human passions. Since the will is itself but a mode of passion, to control the images by which it operates can deeply affect personal choices in areas of ethics and morality, of course (as Jonathan Edwards had been urging since the 1740s), but also in social and political behavior. No prince, said Kames, can wisely ignore the role of the fine arts in furthering political order, and a generation of Americans came out of the Revolution believing that no republic could ignore that role either.

Kames almost completely secularized American thinking about the arts. For him the Bible was essentially a collection of literary images from whose congruity and propriety one's sentiments might usefully be refined. Art whether architecture, gardening, or literature (and especially theater) – depended upon the suitability of images to their referents in nature. Thus a Kamesean analysis of the political situation in America might argue that King George had failed to produce an image of proper government in the colonies. The incongruities between right principles and actual policy were so great as to be ludicrous. Merely to describe them would be to write satire, which punishes by ridicule and laughter. On the other hand, Kames's notions of suitability and propriety were so fussy as to encourage in young and only moderately talented poets the most grand and pompous trash. The sublime visionary poems, for example, all derive from Virgil's *Aeneid*, somewhat pneumatically pumped up by the Miltonic overtones of *Paradise Lost*. How could American resistance not be compared to the glory and grandeur of ancient Greece and Rome? Here were the new Columbuses, like Adam on the verge of a great new era.

At a more general level something of the same lesson was being acquired through popular fiction. English novels, especially by Richardson and Defoe, circulated widely in America after 1744, subtly insinuating sentimental notions of family duties. Like *Robinson Crusoe*, whose hero's anxious years of isolation are framed by the parable of the prodigal son, novels reinforced a sense of mutual pious duties between parents and children. Children owed proper respect and obedience to their parents. But parents had certain special obligations towards the welfare of their children as well which, if not observed, justified breaking the family ties. In short, reading Americans had had a long indoctrination into the grounds of justifiable revolt. How deep that psychological preparation was may be questionable, but there was certainly, on one hand, an audience alert to British appeals to its wayward and ungrateful colonial children, and, on the other, to the revolutionary accusations against British cruel and irresponsible parenthood in documents such as Thomas Jefferson's Declaration of Independence and Thomas Paine's *Common Sense* and *The Crisis*.

Kames argued that the end of study of the fine arts was the formation of taste, that somewhat mysterious capacity to distinguish the good from the bad. At some level taste became indistinguishable from a Moral Sense, which, presumed to be universal, lay beyond the reach of nationalist politics. This leads to the irony, then, of cultural elitists joining the cause of nationalist reformation on the grounds of a theory quite inimical to their actions. This irony was compounded by the fact that once the Continental Army had taken the field it became the chief institution to patronize promising men of "genius," as they were then called. Men of literary talents especially found appointments as brigade chaplains. Timothy Dwight, Joel Barlow, Hugh Brackenridge, and the dramatist Royall Tyler were among the most prominent of the young literary men who found time for writing in the army.

While some writers shared Freneau's bitterness at the war's disruption of artistic ambitions – "An age employed in edging steel / Can no poetic raptures feel" – others, such as Dwight and Barlow, saw warfare itself as ennobling. For both, war is the mother of fame, honor, glory, and bravery. They perceive events through highly posed martial gestures. These are presumed to realize the noblest potentialities of human nature. Dwight, for example, sought to represent manners that "might belong to the amiable and virtuous, of every age: such as elevated without design, refined without ceremony, elegant without fashion, and agreeable, because they are ornamented with sincerity, dignity, and religion, not because they are polished by art and education." In a poem conspicuously dedicated to General Washington, this description was quickly applied to the revolutionary hero, and is a fair representation of most portraits, painted as well as verbal, of revolutionary leaders both during and after the war.

More than Dwight, Barlow was a painterly poet, casting subjects into scenic tableaux, making word paintings of one patriotic hero after another, or of whole gatherings of heroes arranged as in a pageant (for example, his description of the Philadelphia debate leading to the Declaration of Independence). The poem attempts to stop the action of the present, to freeze it at those points when every gesture, every bit of color and costume, is laden with significance.

But whereas a superior poet like Freneau found himself overwhelmed by the torrent of immediate details, actors, and events, Dwight and Barlow controlled the Revolution by containing it within an overarching design. For Dwight that design was the millennium that would follow the apocalypse of Revelation. For Barlow, too, the Revolution was an intermediary step towards a millennium, but one achieved by natural causes. It would take the shape of one world of free international commerce, a congress of united nations, adoption of a single language, and a patriotism defined by universal principles of morality rather than national boundaries. In both views the Revolution was celebrated for its necessary but temporary character, and the fledgling United States was seen rather as a means to some providential design than as an end in itself. This could yet be a spur to very practical social activity: Barlow envisioned a system of canals tied to the natural watercourses that would penetrate inland America and finally enable commerce to move easily and cheaply from coast to coast. His young friend the inventor Robert Fulton enthusiastically joined in that vision.

3. SCIENCE AND MEDICINE

Perhaps the end of Barlow's vision of combined poetry and engineering helped spur the scientific expedition of Meriwether Lewis and William Clark, not merely into the interior, but all the way to the Pacific (1804–6). The primitive character of that adventure tells much about the state of post-revolutionary science in America. Following the Newtonian view of a mechanistic universe susceptible to rational principles, Americans tended to study the factual edges – Cotton Mather, hybridization of corn; John Winthrop IV, earthquakes; Franklin, electricity – using the Royal Society of London as the most eminent medium for sharing information and speculations. But the war ravaged most scientific activity, closing institutions, destroying books, and scattering the curious.

Indeed, science still seemed to be a branch of polite literature before the turn of the century, something one talked about with other intellectually disposed young men at one's boarding house or convivial club, where attorneys, clergymen, physicians, and merchants mingled. Physics, chemistry, agronomy, botany, zoology, geography, and geology all stood in need of data, of agreed upon morphologies, and of basic theory. Medicine represents the disarray of science at that time, the disastrous yellow fever plague that struck Philadelphia in the summer of 1793 providing a test case (*see* Chapter 61, §4). No one had the slightest knowledge of the nature or causes of diseases such as smallpox, diphtheria, or yellow fever. Hospitals were quickly overcrowded and badly managed. Those who could, fled, including inadequately educated medical practitioners. Hospitalization was a death sentence for thousands.

The mayhem was no less than it had been during the war, where disease destroyed more human life, on both sides, than did fighting (*see* Chapter 61, §2). Dr. BENJAMIN RUSH, a signer of the Declaration of Independence, Surgeon General to the Continental Army, the most distinguished leader in medical education at the time, and a worldwide model for compassionate treatment of the mentally deranged, was helpless before the onslaught of the annual plague. Like other natural philosophers, Rush had no workable pathology, no genetics, no germ theory, no simple tools like thermometers, no statistics or applicable mathematics, and no workable chemistry with which even to understand, let alone battle this and other diseases.

Deluged equally with an overload of data and speculation, Americans joined in efforts – usually local in character – to form professional societies and journals to share and preserve their interests. These led inevitably to hospital administrative reforms, better sanitation, emphasis on preventive medicine, and higher standards for research, education, and certification. New Jersey had a medical society by 1766; after the war similar associations arose in Massachusetts (1781), New Hampshire (1791), Connecticut (1792), and Delaware (1789). With Mitchill's and Smith's *American Medical Repository* (started in 1797), at least the groundwork was laid for professionalizing that branch of science. Other disciplines were undergoing the same kind of development: agriculture with the New Jersey Society for the Promotion of Agriculture, Commerce, and Art (1781); astronomy – perhaps the leading American science of the period under DAVID RITTENHOUSE – in the rejuvenated American Philosophical Society (originally begun in 1743–4); law in several state bar organizations; and sociology under the Virginia Constitutional Society (1784) and other societies designed to apply scientific principles and procedures to questions of social and political behavior.

The spirit of science even found a significant place in religion, where skepticism first floated a deistic religion of nature or rational religion, in works such as Thomas Paine's *The Age of Reason* (1794–6) and Ethan Allen's *Reason the Only Oracle of Man* (1784). Condemned by some such as Dwight as simple atheism and "infidelity," this use of science led eventually – through the influence of young intellectuals such as gathered in Boston as the Anthology Society, with its institutional embodiment in the Boston Athenaeum – to the scientific examination of the Bible and the development of Germanic principles of criticism as expressed in their *Monthly Anthology* (1803–11).

4. MANNERS AND THE STAGE

The revolution also reinforced the long-lived American advocacy of plainness in speech, dress, buildings, and manners – obviously making a virtue of necessity. But it was more than that, for it was a studied plainness, as it had been for Puritan preachers in the early seventeenth century. The most dramatic examples are probably the radical appeals of Thomas Paine in *The Crisis* (1776) and *Common Sense* (1776), and *The Federalist Papers* (1787–8) by John Jay, James Madison, and Alexander Hamilton. All were calls to a dangerous commitment in desperate circumstances; all equally show the possibility of passionate resolve tied to rational constraint, clear thinking, and arresting simplicity. Radical reformers took pains not to appear lunatic.

Benjamin Franklin especially epitomized affected Yankee simplicity during his many years as an American agent in France, where courtiers and philosophers found him more charming and agreeable than did many of his American associates back home. With comic exaggeration, that character found his way onto the stage in plays such as the appropriately titled *The Contrast* (1787), by Royall Tyler (1757–1826), in the character of simple but honest Jonathan, the absolute foil to Chesterfieldian British manners.

What we might call amateur theater dates in America from 1598 in El Paso, Texas, with the Oñate expedition, and presumably was not unusual in taverns in earliest Virginia. The more sophisticated French in Nova Scotia wrote original masques as early as Marc Lescarbot's *Neptune's Triumph* in 1607. But as a professional art form it did not exist until Lewis Hallam's American Company appeared to tour the coastal cities in 1752. Military regiments enacted Addison's *Cato* (1713) – a tragedy of patriotic self-sacrifice set in colonial Africa, and trotted out throughout the century whenever lessons in patriotism required reinvigorating. During the war *Cato* emerged again, and on both sides. Although theater was outlawed by the Continental Congress, it went on, sometimes attended by General Washington himself, with Philip Freneau, the future ardent Anti-Federalist, willingly writing a prologue for one performance honoring the present general.

From *The Group* (1775), by Mercy Warren (1728–1814), the "old lady" who wrung praise even from strong Federalist/Tory critics, to *André* (1798), by William Dunlap (1766–1839), the Revolution provided subjects for stirring and vivacious images that did not fail to move deep political passions. Honoring the much admired Major André was acceptable, but, when in the play the rebellious friend Captain Bland passionately denounced the declared execution of the hero/spy by pulling the regimental cockade from his hat and throwing it to the floor, the audience rose up in angry repudiation, and the scene had to be rewritten before the play could find approval. We might surmise, then, that the chief impact of the Revolution on the theater was to provide images of acceptable political and social behavior, and thus to break down local resistances to theater, although it would take another century before a respectable drama would take its place in American cultural life.

5. MUSIC AND PAINTING

When the exalted images and sentences of the serious poets were put upon the stage in costume and gesture they tended towards bombast, melodrama, or operatic hyperbole. There was a good deal of music in the plays of the time, beginning with a ballad opera called *The Disappointment* (1767), featuring a black dandy called Raccoon, the invention either of Colonel Thomas Forrest or Andrew Barton. This was a great age of English vocal music, when British quarterlies regularly reviewed currently published music for home performance. Tunes were often traditional, with new words set to fit the current occasion or dramatic situation. And although Francis Hopkinson (1737–91), who first came to public attention as a college student in Pennsylvania in the 1750s, was both composer and lyrist, his words (preserved in anthologies) have outlasted his melodies. We have thus tended to lose the robust reality of rousing music sung in camps, in taverns, in homes, in social clubs and singing schools, and in political meetings, as well as on the stage.

Instrumental music, essentially non-referential, seems to have been unaffected by the Revolution in any direct way. The outstanding Andrew Law (1749–1821) stood

FIGURE 48 "The Death of General Warren at the Battle of Bunker's Hill," 17 June 1775 (painting by John Trumbull, 1786): Colonel Israel Putnam is portrayed on the far left, and the British generals Sir William Howe and Sir Henry Clinton are brandishing swords in the center background.

out among choral tunesmiths of the time such as Oliver Holden (1765–1844), William Selby (?1738–1798), Benjamin Carr (1768–1831), Rayner Taylor (1747–1825), and dozens of others who set music to psalms, hymns, anthems, and show songs, all within an English or European tradition, regardless of the politics or the theology of the words they set. The eccentric self-taught Boston tanner and composer William Billings (1746–1800), himself an ardent Revolutionary whose "Chester" was a patriotic fifist's delight during the war, had declared his own independence from Anglo-European musical decorums as early as 1770, however. But his quirky – some say grotesque or primitive – effects strike one as only accidentally connected with the politics of the time. Military bands doubtless introduced symphonic music for the first time to many Americans.

Somewhat more surprising, perhaps, is the absence of revolutionary influence in American painting. Unlike music, the field of painting seemed suddenly overwhelmed with talent. Benjamin West (1738–1820), John Singleton Copley (1738–1815), Gilbert Stuart (1755–1828), John Trumbull (1756–1843), Charles Willson Peale (1741–1827), whose Baltimore museum (1814) became the first public museum in the country, and a score of other talented and ambitious painters found their way in the 1760s and 1770s to England, especially to Study at West's atelier in London after 1764. They exhibited portraits and historical paintings in Europe as well, to considerable and well-deserved acclaim. On both sides of the ocean there were prominent and wealthy clients to capture on canvas and, as the Revolution threw up new heroes, soldiers, statesmen, and ambassadors, plenty of subjects (*see* figure 48). But

585

again, except for changes in costume, whatever advances came along in this art were owed to influences other than the Revolution.

The most distinctively American style during that time was the primitivism or naive style of Paul Revere (1735–1818) or Winthrop Chandler (1747–90), with its roots clearly in the tradition of puritan limners of the preceding century. During the American Revolution, English and European artists were more likely to be fascinated by Winckelmann's post-1755 exacavations of Pompeii, with their new revelations of ancient dress, furniture, buildings, and other designs, study of which would technically affect historical paintings. Some of this was carried by Americans into paintings recording stirring moments in the conflict – as Trumbull's *The Battle of Bunker's Hill* – but even the patriotic subject often seems an occasion for the display of technical virtuosity rather than a deeply felt display of change in the social and political world. In any event, American painters equaled British painters in the age of Reynolds and Gainsborough too quickly and too easily, and gained almost too ready acceptance for there to be a visual correspondence to the political turmoil.

6. HISTORY AND THE NOVEL

Even in the verbal arts, where the Revolution was articulated most consciously – in law and rhetoric, the press and theater, and poetry and fiction, one must conclude that the primary impact of the Revolution on cultural activity was its energizing divisiveness. It drove a deep wedge, first between revolutionaries and loyalists, and later between democrats and Federalists. These divisions required on each side clarity of self-definition and fierce assertions of equality of accomplishment. Hostilities between America and England released great cultural energies, and with them great fears. Hector St. John Crèvecoeur's *Letters from an American Farmer* (1782) depict with great vivacity the nightmare terror of revolution, its apparent enforcement of barbaric and savage inclinations in all peoples. In contrast, Thomas Jefferson's *Notes on Virginia* (1785) sought to display elegantly that in climate and natural phenomena America was the equal of any place in creation. The Connecticut Wits elaborately exhibited a self-destructive America plummeting headlong towards anarchy in their *American Antiquities* (1787–8), while at the same time the *Federalist Papers* demonstrated an American capacity for political philosophy unmatched in the modern world. Snarling Freneau, the "smutty link-boy to the muses," hammered away viciously at the aristocratic pretentions of the Federalists, while the Federalist Joseph Dennie (1768–1812) argued annoyingly and alliteratively against the Jeffersonian democrats in his great periodical *The Port Folio* (1801).

That this vituperative and often quite unfocused spirit of debate was actually moving in positive and definitive directions may be seen in the establishment of several new colleges; the beginnings of local historical societies, with the radical printer Isaiah Thomas's American Antiquarian Society at Worcester (1812); and with self-reflective publications such as Jeremy Belknap's *History of New Hampshire* (1784, 1791, 1792), Jedediah Morse's *American Geography* (1789); and Noah Webster's *An American Dictionary of the English Language* (1828, on work begun in the 1780s). Such reactions to the Revolution would carry their cultural consequences through the 1790s and into the nineteenth century.

By 1789, when *The Power of Sympathy*, by William Hill Brown (?1765–93), initiated the American novel, Americans, especially young women, were already addicted to reading fiction – all imported. They thrilled to threats of seduction, rape, abandonment,

586

yielding to the blandishment of irresponsible rakes (often British officers), and hoping for rescue by an honorable American – the pattern brilliantly caught in the immensely popular *Charlotte Temple* (1794), by Susannah Rowson (1762–1824). Snappish editorials and thundering sermons could not stem the habit. Brown even incorporates anti-novel warnings within his novel – a feature that constituted a common amusement in the form. Tabitha Tenney (1762–1837) made that joke the central feature of her satirical misadventures of Dorcasina Sheldon in *Female Quixotism* (1801).

Most such work, like the scandalous *The Coquette* (1797), by Hannah Foster (1759–1840), were strongly didactic and sentimental, and pretended to be true historical tales. Even in their frequently epistolary form they trumpet their British origins, and revolutionary reflections tend to be quite incidental. The case is different, however, with Hugh Henry Brackenridge, whose career took him first into teaching, then law, and then frontier politics in Pittsburgh. His massive *Modern Chivalry* (1792, 1793, 1797, 1815), like Tenney's *Quixotism*, turns to Cervantes as a model, but then accretes into an almost formless Menippean satire on everything happening in America since the Revolution – the impossibilities of the Articles of Confederation, hopeless tax collecting, pretentious universities and learned societies, elections run on rum, slavery and race relationships, greed and power hunger, property qualifications for the franchise, dancing, and presidential levees. These are strung in a series of alternating essays, sketches, anecdotes, jokes, and adventures involving the learned rationalist Captain Farrago and his disaster-prone companion, the bog-trotter Teague O'Regan.

More complex are the gothic romances of Charles Brockden Brown (1770–1810), especially *Wieland* (1798), *Arthur Mervyn* (1799, 1800), *Ormond* (1799), and *Edgar Huntly* (1799). Rife with images of irrational terror, benighted fanaticism, misled revolutionary idealism, psychic disorders, and insanity, Brown's novels imply a post-revolutionary America deeply anxious about its existence in the political wilderness of modern democracy. Still reeling from the terrible aftermath of the French Revolution, these intense tales may easily be seen as allegorical cautions against too great a trust in human reason, high hopes, and Columbian symbolism.

Brown and Brackenridge are – each in his way – penetrating critics of the Revolution, without succumbing to the fierce factionalism that captured other powerful voices such as Joseph Dennie and Philip Freneau. They announce the possibility that will be realized in the impresario character of others – the great Philadelphia publisher MATHEW CAREY and the poet, playwright, theatrical manager, biographer, historian, and painter William Dunlap (also of Philadelphia and New York). Figures of no mean cultural influence themselves, they energized and enabled others to give voice, music, color, myths, memories, and form to the violence of independence.

FURTHER READING

Buell, Lawrence: *New England Literary Culture: From Revolution through Renaissance* (Cambridge: Cambridge University Press, 1986).

Davis, R. B.: *Intellectual Life in the Colonial South, 1585–1763*, 3 vols. (Knoxville: University of Kentucky Press, 1978).

Greene, Jack P.: *Pursuits of Happiness: the Social Development of Early Modern British Colonies and the Formation of American Culture* (Chapel Hill: University of North Carolina Press, 1988).

Greene, Jack P. and Pole, J. R. (eds.): *Colonial British America: Essays in the New History of the Early Modern Era* (Baltimore: Johns Hopkins University Press, 1984).

Nye, Russel B.: *The Cultural Life of the New Nation, 1776–1830* (New York: Harper & Row, 1960).

Silverman, Kenneth: *A Cultural History of the American Revolution: Painting, Music, Literature, and the Theatre in the Colonies and the United States from the Treaty of Paris to the Inauguration of George Washington, 1763–1789* (New York: Thomas Y. Crowell Company, 1976).

60

The effects of the Revolution on language

JOHN ALGEO

T HE Revolution created a new national variety of English as well as a new nation. Although American English became a distinct entity almost as soon as the first settlers from Britain arrived in the New World, its status as an institutionalized or standard variety of the language had to await the Revolution and subsequent efforts to create a culturally, as well as politically, independent society. Today, American is spoken by more persons than any other variety of the language; consequently British and other varieties of English around the globe are massively influenced by it and thus by the linguistic consequences of the Revolution.

Those consequences appear in both the system of the language and attitudes towards it. A language system consists of words, spoken or written, related to each other by grammar and used by its speakers to interact. But a language also involves the attitudes of its speakers towards the world and the language itself. The effects of the Revolution can be seen in all these aspects: the system of words, pronunciations, spellings, grammar, and meanings, but also strikingly in the attitudes of speakers of American English.

I. SETTLEMENT

The American colonies were settled from many regions of the motherland. The diverse cultural traditions of seventeenth- and eighteenth-century Britain were exported with concentrations in various colonies: the Puritans from the eastern counties to New England, the Cavaliers and their indentured servants from southern England to Virginia, the Quakers from northern England to the Delaware valley, and the Scots and Scots-Irish to the Appalachian range and elsewhere in South Carolina and Georgia. Those groups brought with them their ways of talking English along with other cultural features that have survived as identifiable strains even in present-day national life (Fischer, 1989). Alongside the four major strains, other regional cultures were Dutch in the Hudson valley; African and West Indian in coastal South Carolina and Georgia; Highland Scots in the Carolinas; Swedish, German, French, and others elsewhere.

If we knew a great deal more than we do about language varieties in the British Isles from the end of the sixteenth century, when the first colonists learned their English, through the time of the Revolution, we could trace the roots of American English with more confidence than in fact is possible. Unfortunately, the English of England during American colonial days is the least well described of all its historical periods. The detailed study of English in America during the same period is even less satisfactory. Consequently much of what can be said about the earliest linguistic relationships between Britain and America must remain a matter of likely generalities rather than documented fact.

The lack of certainty about origins extends also to subvarieties of American English, such as the speechways of the early Africans in the American colonies and hence of their present-day descendants. Concerning the genesis of Black English, as these speechways have been called, there are two major theories, neither of which has enough factual support to silence the other, but each of which enjoys outspoken support from its adherents.

One theory is that the African slaves, originating from many different tribes, came to America without a significant common language. On the plantations, they learned English from the overseers, and thus Black English is a variety of provincial British English with an admixture of African elements and other modifications springing from the manner and circumstances in which it was acquired.

The other theory is that many African slaves came to America already knowing a pidgin with English elements in it – a pidgin being a simplified speechway combining features from two or more languages and used for communication among people who normally speak different languages. On the plantations, the pidgin was the only way many of the slaves could communicate among themselves, and it had the added advantage of shutting out the slave master. So it was used as the primary language of the slaves; that is, it became a creole. As time passed, this creole accepted increasingly many features from standard English, thus becoming more like it.

According to the first of these theories, Black English began as a subdialect of southern American English, to which African elements were added. In the second, it began as a creole, a non-English language, which has assimilated to English. The historical facts are not adequate for choosing confidently between the two theories, so present-day views of Black English and its history are governed largely by political or other affective responses. The genesis of Black English lies in pre-revolutionary days, but the nature of that genesis is obscure. What is clear is that Black English is one of the strains from which American English has drawn.

Like the African forced immigrants and their speech, the social groups from Old England who settled in various colonies, bringing with them the speechways of the homeland, had an influence that has survived in present-day American dialects. The New England colonies extended their influence westwards, as the present-day Northern dialect region. The Delaware valley colonies likewise extended westwards as the North Midland dialect region. The colonies from Viriginia southwards became the Southern or Coastal Southern dialect region along the Atlantic and Gulf coasts. And the southern Appalachian settlements expanded westwards to the Ozarks and beyond as the South Midland or Mountain Southern dialect region. The persistence of colonial settlement patterns in twentieth-century dialect regions is notable.

2. COLONIAL HOMOGENIZATION AND DIFFERENTIATION

In addition to the cultural differences of colonial America and their persistence, however, a complementary tendency to homogenization is equally notable. The language of the colonies and the early nation seemed to contemporary observers to be remarkably uniform, foreshadowing the rise of American English as an identifiable, relatively homogeneous variety. As John Witherspoon, a Scots Presbyterian minister who became President of Princeton University, put it in 1781:

The vulgar in America speak much better than the vulgar in Great-Britain, for a very obvious reason, viz. that being much more unsettled, and moving frequently from place to place, they are not so liable to local peculiarities either in accent or phraseology. There is a greater difference in dialect between one county and another in Britain, than there is between one state and another in America. (Mathews, 1931, p. 16)

The pressure towards a colonial speech more uniform than that of the mother country can be seen also in Australia, New Zealand, South Africa, and of course Canada. This colonial homogenization is a consequece of the fact that colonists who speak different motherland dialects adapt to one another, with a resulting partial loss of differentiating features and the appearance of a more uniform variety of the language. It is often claimed that colonial varieties of speech are more conservative than the language of the mother country; it is, however, difficult to measure degrees of innovation versus conservatism in pronunciation, vocabulary, and grammar, so the reality of "colonial lag" (as it is called) is disputed. The existence of colonial homogenization, on the other hand, is easier to document and to explain.

Although the colonists brought their English speechways with them, certain forces operated from the beginning to make English in America different from that in Britain: language drift, the new physical and social environment, and contacts with other languages.

There is an inevitable drift in the history of languages by which small changes are continually introduced. Within a relatively homogenous speech community whose members are in frequent contact with each other, innovations will either be spread quickly to most members of the community or be suppressed. Thus, although the language of the community changes, it does so uniformly, thus maintaining its identity.

When one speech community is divided from another, however, so that their members interact less frequently or in restricted ways, each community will drift in its own direction. If two communities are divided for an extended period, the result will be distinct dialects of the common language, or eventually even separate languages.

The Atlantic Ocean was an effective barrier to easy communication, guaranteeing that over time the language of the colonies and that of the motherland would drift apart. And so they did, eventually creating distinct British and American varieties of English. Since the colonists, however distant they might be from each other, were more likely to interact directly with each other than with persons still in the British Isles, they tended to grow linguistically more alike and less like those in Britain. Hence the phenomenon of colonial homogenization.

The natural tendency of a language to change is reinforced when its speakers encounter new circumstances of life. In that case, the vocabulary especially is rapidly modified, by using old words in new ways (as *creek* for a stream rather than an estuary), by making new words from old words or word-parts (as *scrub oak* for a type of tree), or by borrowing words from other languages (as *squash* from Algonquian or *cookie* from Dutch). Exposure to new experiences is a powerful motive for language innovation. The colonists met new topography, climate, flora, fauna, and humanity. They found themselves in new social groupings. The result was an adaptation of their language to the new circumstances in which they used it.

The English colonists were not alone in the New World, the Amerindians who held the land before them were still there. So were colonists and entrepreneurs from other European nations: Dutch, Swedes, French, Germans, and, to the south, Spaniards. Shortly they were joined by Africans, many brought immediately from the Caribbean.

As English-speaking colonists interacted with those peoples, they were influenced by them.

3. ATTITUDES TO AMERICAN ENGLISH

As a result of the factors of drift, environmental pressure, and foreign contacts, the English of the American colonies began to differentiate at once from that of the homeland and to acquire a character and system of its own. Changes in the English of America were noticed early. In 1735 one traveler in Georgia, Francis Moore, observing the location of the town of Savannah, complained, "... the bank of the river (which they in barbarous English call a bluff) is steep ..." (Mathews, 1931, p.13).

Most of the early comments were complaints. Any change in language has always tended to be seen as degeneration by those who have not yet participated in the change. That tendency was especially strong in the eighteenth century, when "ascertaining, correcting, and polishing" the language, before "fixing" it to prevent further change, were taken as self-evidently desirable aims. Thus American and British English began the process of mutual differentiation with the first permanent English settlement in 1607. But Americans and Britons alike tended to regard the features differentiating the two varieties as flaws in American.

Despite Witherspoon's complimentary view that the vulgar in America speak much better than their counterparts in the old country, his examples of Americanisms consisted of American provincialisms, vulgarisms, common or personal blunders, cant phrases, and other departures from the standard of England. The Revolution contributed to the actual differentiation of the two varieties, as any major political and social event will, for example, by ending old political institutions and creating new ones to which the vocabulary had to adjust. However, the major linguistic effect of the Revolution was not on the language system, but rather on linguistic attitudes. And that change in attitude came about only gradually.

Long after the Revolution, many Americans continued to look to London for their linguistic model. John Pickering, in his *Vocabulary or Collection of Words and Phrases Which Have Been Supposed to Be Peculiar to the United States of America* (1816), confessed that

> none of our countrymen, not even those, who are the most zealous in supporting what they imagine to be the honour of the *American* character, will contend, that we have not in some instances departed from the standard of the language. (Mathews, 1931, p. 67)

The standard, for Pickering and many others, was still that "spoken and written in England at the present day." But the intoxicating sense of new nationhood brought others to the conclusion that political independence was imperfect without cultural independence as well. That conclusion revalued the differences distinguishing American from British and reformed attitudes towards the language.

The quest for cultural independence led to a promotion of American letters and of the American version of the English language. The political patriotism that underlay the Revolution was matched by linguistic patriotism on the part of an anonymous American writing in 1774:

> The English language has been greatly improved in Britain within a century, but its highest perfection, with every other branch of human knowledge, is perhaps reserved for this Land of light and freedom. As the people through this extensive country will speak English, their

592

advantages for polishing their language will be great, and vastly superior to what the people in England ever enjoyed. (Mathews, 1931, p. 40)

Among the founding fathers, John Adams held similar views, based upon his assumption that, since a republic requires eloquence for advancement to its public offices, its language will be of "the greatest purity, copiousness, and perfection." Although Adams's crystal ball may have been clouded with respect to the linguistic effects of political rhetoric, it was clear enough about the future of the English language when in 1780 he wrote to the President of Congress:

> English is destined to be in the next and succeeding centuries more generally the language of the world than Latin was in the last or French is in the present age. The reason of this is obvious, because the increasing population in America, and their universal connection and correspondence with all nations will, aided by the influence of England in the world, whether great or small, force their language into general use, in spite of all the obstacles that may be thrown in their way, if any such there should be. (Mathews, 1931, p. 42)

The most notable figure in promoting American English was Noah Webster, who may be accounted a Founding Father of American English, if not of the republic. Today Webster is remembered chiefly as the embodiment of American lexicography, the creator of "Webster's Dictionary," which in the popular mind is less a particular book than an archetypal one. He is also associated with the "Blue-backed speller" and spelling reform. Both those activities were related to Webster's advocacy of "Federal English" as the language of the new nation (Baron, 1982).

Ironically, Webster's dictionary was not particularly American in content and his influence on American spelling was not innovative, but regulatory. As Thomas Pyles has remarked, Webster's

> use of American writings [as illustrations in his *American Dictionary*] is actually the principal justification for the use of *American* in the title, for despite all his high-sounding talk about an American language, Webster really had little conception of the differences between American and British English in his day. (Pyles, 1952, p. 120)

Similarly, it is often assumed that characteristically American spellings were invented by Noah Webster. He was very influential in popularizing certain spellings in America, but he did not originate them. Rather, from the competing variety of a less orthographically rigid age, he chose already existing options such as *center, color,* and *check* on such grounds as simplicity, analogy, or etymology. British practice settled on different options: *centre, colour, cheque.*

As important as Webster's role in American lexicography and orthography was, perhaps his greatest contribution was promoting a sense of pride in distinctively American language variants. As Pyles put it,

> Webster was certainly one of the most influential commentators upon language who ever lived. More than any other single person, he shaped the course of American English, for he supplied us with the schooolmaster's authority which we needed for self-confidence. (Pyles, 1952, p. 123)

That is, Webster's contribution was less to the ways Americans use English than to the attitudes they have towards their own usage.

4. LATER DEVELOPMENTS

Webster did not, however, settle the question of the identity of American English as a distinct standard. Overt arguments and covert preferences contended through the nineteenth century and into the early decades of the twentieth. Second only to Webster as an influence on attitudes towards American English was H. L. Mencken, the Baltimore journalist and social critic whose anti-British and pro-German sentiments made it expedient for him to turn to a subject less explosive than international politics during World War I. Consequently in 1919 he published his polemical work *The American Language*, which went through four editions and two supplements before it was abridged and updated by Raven I. McDavid, Jr., in 1963.

In the first edition of his book, Mencken's thesis was that British and American English were two streams whose divergence since the Revolution was becoming so great that they were well on their way to being separate languages, hence his title. Mencken supported this thesis partly through an elaborate joke by which he compared a formal, prim British style with a highly colloquial, slangy, or folksy American one.

Mencken's thesis was attacked by George Philip Krapp in his more sober but also less entertaining response, *The English Language in America* (1925), the title of which also announces its thesis. But Mencken himself recognized that his thesis had been wrong and therefore modified it to argue that in fact the two streams were converging. However, since the American stream was many times larger than the British and, in Mencken's view, a great deal more vital, he predicted the increasing Americanization of British English, foreseeing much the same future as had John Adams a century and a half earlier.

Language development is a slow process. The structural differences between present-day American and British English are minor (Algeo, 1988); vocabulary differences are greater. Both are the consequence of impulses set in motion by the colonization of America. The attitudes that recognize American as the major national variety of the English language alongside British spring from and still echo the Revolution.

FURTHER READING

Algeo, John: "British and American Grammatical Differences," *International Journal of Lexicography*, 1 (1988), 1–31.
Baron, Dennis E.: *Grammar and Good Taste: Reforming the American Language* (New Haven, Conn.: Yale University Press, 1982).
Fischer, D. H.: *Albion's Seed: Four British Folkways in America* (New York: Oxford University Press, 1989).
Krapp, George Philip: *The English Language in America*, 2 vols. (1925), repr. (New York: Ungar, 1960).
Mathews, M. M.: *The Beginnings of American English* (1931), repr. (Chicago: University of Chicago Press, 1963).
Mathews, M. M. (ed.): *A Dictionary of Americanisms on Historical Principles* (Chicago: University of Chicago Press, 1951).
Mencken, H. L.: *The American Language* (1919, 1921, 1923, 1936, 1945, 1951), abridged and augmented by Raven I. McDavid, Jr. (New York: Knopf, 1963).
Pyles, Thomas: *Words and Ways of American English* (New York: Random House, 1952).

61

Medicine before and after the Revolution

MARY E. FISSELL

FOR MUCH of the eighteenth century, medicine in America strongly resembled its counterpart in Britain. While regional differences in health and medical provision were marked, most inhabitants of the 13 colonies experienced health care organized on British models. During the Revolution, military medicine was severely hampered by lack of organization and sufficient funds. The Revolution intensified and accelerated some changes in the professional structures of medicine, but little substantial innovation can be traced to the war. Nor did medicine notably alter patterns of mortality in this period.

I. HEALERS AND HEALING

As in the mother country, health care was provided by a wide range of practitioners. For most Americans, self-medication or domestic medicine was a first line of defense. Books such as William Buchan's *Domestic Medicine* (1769) or S. A. Tissot's *Advice to the People* (first English edition 1765) were imported from England and reprinted in the colonies. In the late eighteenth century medicine chests for the home were commercially produced and sold widely. These often contained fairly orthodox remedies, and may have helped to make domestic practice more equivalent to health care provided by full-time practitioners. Many patent remedies were bought and sold over the counter; these were often old British standbys such as Bateman's Drops or Dover's Powders, fundamentals of domestic and professional practice alike. What little is known about popular healing suggests that, like its British equivalent, it depended upon a congeries of beliefs deriving from Galenic theory and magical ideas.

The line between home healing and that provided by a "professional" was vague; many practiced medicine with little training and on a part-time basis. Even for trained practitioners, medicine was often a part-time, even casual, occupation. For example, Joseph Pynchon, a leading mid-century Boston practitioner, had started his career in his spare time while serving in the General Court. On the elite level, men of learning might be very knowledgeable about medicine. For example, Benjamin Franklin was sometimes referred to as a medical man because of his invention of bifocals and research on electricity, although he did not train as a physician. So, too, those few who received a college education often acquired some medical knowledge; the University of Virginia provided medical education to all its undergraduates until 1830.

The distinctions between physicians, surgeons, and apothecaries typical of London medicine rarely applied in the colonies. In part this was due to the lack of physicians – few MDs emigrated and few colonists could afford a European training. But even the few physicians in large cities often compounded and sold drugs, a practice which their English brethren could not have countenanced. By the late eighteenth century a few

FIGURE 49 A portrait of Benjamin Rush by Charles Willson Peale (1783 or 1786)

American cities were beginning to afford opportunities for genteel medical practice. But, as in the mother country, the typical practitioner was a surgeon-apothecary, the ancestor of the general practitioner.

These medical men were trained either through apprenticeship or were self-taught. Apprenticeship, although sometimes denigrated by later graduates of medical schools, provided a fairly cheap and often effective means of one-to-one instruction. In rural areas where practitioners traveled many miles on horseback to see patients (almost all medical care took place within the patient's home) the apprentice provided valuable assistance.

Midwifery was very much a female pursuit – again, often a part-time one. Childbirth was an occasion for women to join together in support, and most births were attended and managed by a group of the mother's friends and relatives in addition to the midwife. By 1800 this pattern had altered for urban wealthy women, who began to rely upon male midwives, usually surgeons. These men, such as Dr. William Shippen of Philadelphia, took a more interventionist approach to labor and delivery, using opium, bloodletting, and forceps.

For much of the century, American therapeutics were transplanted British ones,

596

with the addition of a few Native American remedies like sassafras. Many therapeutic agents were intended to rid the body of noxious humors, so patients expected and experienced bleeding, purging, blistering, and vomiting. Historians have characterized American medical practice as pragmatic, free from the overly theoretical debates and speculative systems which afflicted learned European medicine of the period.

But in the last decades of the century, patients began to undergo what is referred to as "heroic" medicine, so-called because of its dramatic and severely debilitating effects, caused by intensive bleeding and purging. Some of the responsibility for this therapeutic style must be given to Benjamin Rush (*see* figure 49), the Philadelphia physician and educator whose name became a byword for bloodletting. Rush advocated a medical system which was the direct descendant of those described by his Edinburgh teachers William Cullen and John Brown. Where Cullen and Brown emphasized that the body in illness was either under- or over-stimulated, Rush thought he had found a unitary cause of disease in morbid excitement. William Cobbett remarked that Rush's medicine was one of those great discoveries made from time to time for the depopulation of the earth, but Cobbett's sarcasm did not dent Rush's reputation as an outstanding medical man or diminish the popularity of heroic medicine.

2. MEDICINE IN THE REVOLUTION

Unlike many other wars, the American Revolutionary War did not promote medical innovations or lead to the restructuring of the profession. Throughout the war, medical provision for the military was hampered by two serious problems: the lack of trained and equipped surgeons, and organizational difficulties which were worsened by political squabbles among the top ranks. Both contributed to the large numbers of deaths from disease; typical estimates suggest that, for each soldier killed by the enemy, nine died from disease.

Most of the ailments which struck the American forces were those familiar to any eighteenth-century military operation: dysentery, smallpox, venereal disease, and camp fevers (probably typhus and typhoid). Malaria also plagued the troops, especially as campaigns moved south. Smallpox was especially severe in the early years of the war, and in New England, where inoculation had sometimes been banned. After the first two years of war smallpox became less significant, since by then many troops had either succumbed or been inoculated. Similarly, as discipline became better in the forces, the standards of camp hygiene improved, and dysentery and diarrhea declined. However, the Americans always suffered more from enteric diseases than did the British, who were better-disciplined and equipped with surgeons who could draw upon considerable experience in military hygiene and medicine.

The problems of medical organization were basically those of integrating various provincial units, creating a functioning hierarchy, and ensuring adequate funding – none of which was fully resolved. In February 1775 the Provincial Congress of Massachusetts appointed Drs. Benjamin Church and Joseph Warren to oversee the medical needs of the local militia. A few months later the Massachusetts Committee on Public Safety found that regimental surgeons were not always adequately trained.

Such conflicts between regimental surgeons (usually political appointments) and centralized authority were often repeated throughout the war. In May 1775 the Continental Congress created an Army Medical Department and named Benjamin Church its first Director-General. The department's difficulties in integrating regimental surgeons were exacerbated by lack of funds; the Continental Congress and

Washington himself failed to appreciate the costs of medical care. Regimental surgeons, for example, initially did not receive medical supplies from the department and were chronically lacking in essentials such as bandages and blankets. It was not until January 1779 that the Continental Congress finally allocated monies for medical supplies for the regimental surgeons.

Church's career was terminated when a treasonable letter from him to a British officer was intercepted. In October 1775 Dr. John Morgan, a Philadelphia physician and founder of the first American medical school, was appointed in Church's stead. Unfortunately, the choice of Morgan seems to have led to a series of notable conflicts between leading Philadelphia medical men serving in various military capacities. Morgan attempted to institute a system of examinations for hospital mates and regimental surgeons and mates, and to standardize medical military discipline. But he continued to face substantial organizational difficulties and limited funds, problems exacerbated by his inability to avoid political wrangling. Morgan's old rival Dr. William Shippen, Jr., was put in charge of the Flying Camp in New Jersey and then, in October 1776, appointed to oversee army medicine west of the Hudson. Morgan and Shippen feuded over supplies and authority, with Shippen complaining directly to the Congress about outbreaks of illness in the winter campaigns of 1776–7. Then Morgan attempted to court-martial Dr. Samuel Stringer, who oversaw army medicine in northern New York State, for misconduct. But in January 1777 the Congress fired both Morgan and Stringer.

To Morgan's chagrin, Shippen was appointed Director-General in his stead. Under Shippen's guidance, Congress adopted a plan in April 1777 to increase the pay of medical personnel and to organize the department into four regions. Drs. Jonathan Potts, Isaac Foster, and Benjamin Rush headed the northern, eastern, and middle divisions, while Dr. William Rickman enjoyed greater autonomy as director of the southern region. As a result, a direct chain of command was set up from regimental surgeon to director and regional hospitals were inaugurated, although organizational difficulties did not disappear as a result.

The dispute between Morgan and Shippen took on a new dimension when Benjamin Rush accused Shippen of war profiteering. Congress relieved the Director-General of the responsibility of supplying hospitals in February 1778, but the problems with Shippen's administration were not resolved and Rush kept up his attacks. In June 1779 Morgan made a formal accusation of misconduct to Congress. Shippen stood trial in early 1780, faced with charges of peculation, neglect of patients, and financial mismanagement. In July he was discharged from arrest, having been acquitted on four of the five counts. But neither his name nor reputation was cleared, and in January 1781 Shippen resigned. His replacement, Dr. John Cochran, completed the reorganization of the medical department by subsuming all four regions under his direct control. But he continued to have problems ensuring that the medical department had sufficient funds – in the spring of 1781 he noted that one hospital had been forced to permit ambulatory patients to beg for food. By avoiding the political in-fighting which characterized the administrations of his predecessors, Cochran continued in office until the signing of the peace treaty.

3. PROFESSIONAL STRUCTURES

Although most medical practitioners continued to be self-taught or apprenticeship-trained, the medical professions in large cities became stratified in the last three decades of the century. New institutions, such as hospitals and medical schools, reflected and accelerated this trend. But local medical cultures remained strong; for instance, the patterns of development in Boston and Philadelphia were markedly different.

The first hospital in the 13 colonies was founded in Philadelphia in 1751, and the consequences of its foundation shaped Philadelphia medicine into the next century. As in some provincial British cities, the hospital assumed an educational function; apprentices walked the wards and were given lectures by the hospital staff. The new institution was a voluntary one, run by a lay board, and staffed by medical men who were not paid for their attendance. Philadelphia already had an almshouse where inhabitants received medical care from a paid staff, and this quickly became a stepping-stone for younger medical men ultimately hoping to attain a prestigious hospital post.

In 1765 John Morgan took Philadelphia medical education a step further with the foundation of a medical school. During the Revolution the school closed (many of its staff were directly involved in the war), but despite political wrangling medical lectures were resumed after the war. In 1786 a dispensary was added to the roster of the city's medical charities. The College of Physicians, founded in the following year, was an elite and prestigious group of medical men elected to their posts.

Boston's medical societies, on the other hand, were similar to the first state medical society in America, that of New Jersey (founded 1766). Such societies were intended to regulate practice, not honor leading medical men. The Boston Medical Society (founded 1781) examined and licensed practitioners. The society also established an influential fee-bill which dictated fees for various medical services, in effect creating a medical cartel of fixed prices.

Post-revolutionary Boston's medical life was characterized by the founding of learned institutions, often of an elitist nature, such as the Medical Society, the Boston Athenaeum, and the Historical Society. Medical lectures had been given by John Warren to army surgeons during the war, and in 1782 the Harvard corporation appointed three professors of medicine. Some have seen these foundations as a wave of American institution-building, intended to replace or repudiate British models. Others have argued that Boston was just catching up with Philadelphia.

Both cities continued to develop distinctive medical cultures. For example, Philadelphia medicine was strongly influenced by the Edinburgh medical school; many more Philadelphians than Bostonians trained in Edinburgh. Philadelphians were used to walking the wards, receiving extensive clinical instruction, and being offered the opportunity for anatomy and dissection. But Bostonians lacked hospital training until the medical school moved to Boston in 1810, and, when they did go abroad, they tended to choose London. Reciprocally, Edinburgh offered Philadelphians theoretical models of medicine as well as many personal connections. No doubt students' choices were also shaped by their parents' purses; Bostonians often had commercial links with London rather than Edinburgh, making the metropolis a practical option.

Despite the establishment of additional medical schools, including Kings in New York City (1768) and Dartmouth in New Hampshire (1800), medical training continued on traditional lines in many parts of the country. One of the Pennsylvania medical school's first graduates, for example, trained more than 50 apprentices during his career. So, too, domestic medicine and patent remedies continued to flourish; professional structures did not immediately alter patterns of health care.

4. HEALTH

Nor can it be said that medical initiatives dramatically altered patterns of mortality in the new nation. At the time of the Revolution, at least three different patterns of mortality characterized the colonies.

New arrivals to the Chesapeake and southern colonies could expect about a year of "seasoning," in which they were vulnerable to very high mortality from such unfamiliar diseases as *falciparum* malaria (British colonists knew only the milder *vivax* form) and yellow fever, as well as familiar ailments like dysentery and typhoid. But even those who weathered this severe initial period still experienced much higher mortality than in the mid-Atlantic and New England colonies, although those who lived inland, away from salt water, fared somewhat better. Black slaves who survived their passage were somewhat better equipped than white settlers to withstand malaria and yellow fever, but were particularly prey to respiratory ailments, worms, and dietary deficiencies.

In contrast, contemporaries noted the healthiness of rural New England, which did not experience the southern pattern of sharp annual peaks in mortality. However, towns and villages did undergo severe mortality crises caused by epidemics of diphtheria, smallpox, dysentery, and fevers. Ironically, the very healthiness of rural New England – its lack of endemic disease, its salubrious environment, and its relatively small numbers of new immigrants – made for occasional severe epidemics.

Towns and cities in the mid-Atlantic and New England colonies fell somewhere between the two extremes of rural New England and the South. Ports were host to endemic disease as well as epidemics. Smallpox remained one of the most dreaded epidemic diseases, recurring every few decades despite the availability of inoculation. At the end of the century smallpox was rivaled by yellow fever, which killed 10 per cent of Philadelphia's population in the epidemic of 1793. In major cities endemic diseases of poverty had also become significant killers – consumption, for example, was often the leading cause of death in large cities by the turn of the century.

The one notable contribution post-revolutionary medicine made to eradicating disease was the introduction of vaccination for smallpox. This was safer than inoculation, since it involved infection with cowpox, a milder ailment than the smallpox it protected against. In 1799 Dr. Benjamin Waterhouse, the professor of the theory and practice of medicine at Harvard, received a copy of Edward Jenner's pamphlet which described vaccination. Waterhouse published an account of vaccination in a Boston newspaper, and over the next three years obtained vaccine material from England and carried out tests to show that vaccination protected against smallpox.

FURTHER READING

Bell, W.: *John Morgan, Continental Doctor* (Philadelphia: University of Pennsylvania Press, 1965).

Cash, P., Christianson, E. H., and Estes, J. W. (eds.): *Medicine in Colonial Massachusetts* (Boston: Colonial Society of Massachusetts, 1980).

Dobson, M.: "Mortality gradients and disease exchanges: comparisons from old England and colonial America," *Social History of Medicine*, 2 (1989), 259–97.

Shryock, R.: *Medicine and Society in America, 1660–1860* (Ithaca: Cornell University Press, 1962).

62

The construction of gender in a republican world

RUTH H. BLOCH

R EFERENCES to gender continuously intruded into American revolutionary discourse, for notions of civic morality were repeatedly encoded in language describing ideal masculine and feminine traits. Between the 1760s and 1790s, moreover, dominant ideals of masculinity and femininity were subtly transformed. What had earlier been an essentially male standard of public virtue gradually gave way to a conception of social morality as largely depending on female influence. Ideas about the proper arena in which to perform civic obligations concurrently shifted away from the military and government towards the private institutions of the church and the family. A new view of appropriate relationships within the family served to elevate the status of wives and mothers, whose very femininity was now often perceived as indispensable to the maintenance of republican virtue.

How much these underlying changes in conceptions of gender were specifically due to the events of the Revolution is a debatable question. A similar upgrading of the roles of wife and mother occurred, for example, among the English bourgeoisie during the same general period. In its broadest sense, this reconstruction of gender relations can be associated with the long-term development of the commercial economy and the ascendancy of a pre-Romantic culture of sentimentalism as much as with the American Revolution itself. Across the Atlantic world the ascendant commercial middle classes increasingly celebrated the value of private domestic life, and the emotionalism previously held against women came to be viewed in a positive light.

In America, however, the Revolution did cast these general, transatlantic changes in a specifically republican and national framework. Both the history of female participation in the patriot cause and the growth of female education in the early republic pushed towards a more generous assessment of women's capabilities (*see* Chapter 41, §§ 3 and 4). Since gender symbolism permeated revolutionary debate, moreover, critical changes in republican ideology hinged in part on the revision of gender definitions. The shift from a masculine to a feminine conception of virtue simultaneously reflected a new understanding of gender relations and a new understanding of republicanism itself.

Unlike other concepts associated with American revolutionary ideology – such as liberty, equality, property, happiness – gender was not, however, considered by eighteenth-century Americans themselves to be a revolutionary issue. Republican ideology contained no explicit call for the reconstruction of popular understandings of masculinity and femininity. Whatever tensions and changes occurred in gender relations during the American Revolution were barely noticed by contemporaries. For the most part even those who commented explicitly on such matters as marriage and female education assumed the continuance of a legal and political system that institutionalized female subordination and relegated men and women to fundamentally different social roles.

I. THE MASCULINE CONCEPT OF POWER

The main intellectual sources of early revolutionary ideology, Lockean liberalism and classical republicanism, both assumed the dependency and invisibility of women. According to each of these traditions, citizenship was based on a combination of property-holding and military service. For both, the fundamental contest for power within states was a male drama including in its cast of characters free property-holders, noblemen, and kings. Opposition to absolute despotism was justified in the interest of preserving the liberty and independence of a citizenry that was composed of self-reliant, rights-holding, and arms-bearing men (*see* Chapter 73, §2).

Frequently such a conflict between tyrant and subject was described in familial terms. Royalists had long employed the metaphor of paternal authority to legitimate monarchical rule. A king, argued James I, can be compared with "Fathers of families; for a King is trewly *Parens patriae*, the politique father of his people" (McIlwain, 1918, p. 307). In his anti-patriarchal argument against Filmer, Locke had redefined citizenship as a contractual agreement analogous to marriage. Yet both marriage and the subordination of women still remained, in his view, outside politics. The invention of the state was an exclusively masculine act.

In the early revolutionary movement, American patriot ideology drew heavily from both liberal and classical republican thought in its formulations of the imperial conflict. The metaphor of England as the "mother country" had in traditional royalist fashion long pointed to the familial obligations and loyalties inherent in the imperial system. Initially American patriots expressed themselves in these conventional terms in the hope of achieving peaceful reconciliation. As James Otis phrased his appeal in response to the Revenue Act of 1764, "few if any instances can be given where colonies have been disposed to forsake or disobey a tender mother" (Otis, [1764] 1965, p. 448). As the struggle with Britain intensified, however, the image of the imperial mother quickly turned from tender to cruel. In 1765 John Adams likened mother Britain to the monstrous Lady Macbeth, who would have "plucked her nipple from the [infant's] boneless gums,/And dashed the brains out" (Adams, 1850–6, 3: p. 464). The tyrannical lust for power represented a violation of the feminine maternal principle earlier associated with benign imperial rule. Power itself was typically symbolized as aggressively masculine, embodied above all in the supposedly ruthless and self-interested machinations of the King's notorious ministers.

The King himself was usually spared such negative characterizations until the mid-1770s. Until then, protestations of loyalty still typically sought to distance expressions of filial love for the father from the outrage expressed towards his ministers. Yet after the battles of Concord and Lexington, the image of George III as a heartless father emerged with a vengeance. "We swore allegiance to him as a *King*, not as a *Tyrant*," a patriot newspaper angrily declared in 1775, "as a *Father*, not as a *Murderer*" (*Boston Gazette*, 17 July 1775). Crystallizing this growing anti-patriarchal sentiment, Thomas Paine's *Common Sense* characterized George III as "the royal Brute of Britain." As Paine elaborated the familiar familial analogy, America was best understood not as a dependent child but as an adolescent son coming of age. King George figured in his pamphlet as a "wretch, that with the pretended title FATHER OF HIS PEOPLE can unfeelingly hear of their slaughter, and composedly sleep with their blood upon his soul" (Paine, [1776] 1976, p. 92).

2. THE FEMININE CONCEPT OF LIBERTY

If the image of tyrannical power was aggressively male, the image of its symbolic opposite, liberty, was passively female (for illustration, *see* figure 50, p. 611). Particularly in the early years of the revolutionary movement, liberty was commonly depicted as delicate and vulnerable, susceptible to brutal acts of violence suggestive of rape. Cartoons and other graphic portrayals of the imperial struggle often presented America as a chaste virgin. The portrait of America as an Indian princess uncorrupted by European civilization was a common variation on this theme. Another popular feminine image of America was drawn from the Book of Revelation – that of the unprotected woman in the wilderness encountering the wrath of the antichristian dragon. Taken together, these various patriotic representations of women highlighted the fragility of American liberty in the face of British power.

3. THE MILITANT IDEAL OF MASCULINE VIRTUE

The symbolic dualism of active male power and passive female virtue was particularly pronounced during the period of resistance in the 1760s and early 1770s. As the patriot movement progressed from resistance to rebellion, however, an alternative masculine ideal of virtue rose to the fore. Paine's influential view of America as an adolescent boy chafing against unjust parental restrictions merged in the mid-1770s with a patriotic ideal of youthful male heroism. In accord with fundamental assumptions of classical republicanism, the language of republicanism in the opening years of the war glorified the physical courage and valiant self-sacrifice of male citizen-soldiers. Military service offered young men the promise of public glory and fame. At the height of the military vogue, a toast on the first anniversary of American Independence made the underlying exclusion of women from this militant conception of citizenship particularly clear, declaring, "May only those Americans enjoy freedom who are ready to die for its defence" (Royster, 1979, p. 32).

Ironically, women were in fact present in the American Army as camp followers. Far from being valorized for their participation, however, they only embarrassed the military leadership. A suggestive woodcut of a woman posed with a gun occasionally appeared in publications of the 1770s, but this image of female militancy predated the conflict with Britain and the stories it was chosen to illustrate had no connection to the American Revolutionary War. Only later would the disguised woman soldier DEBORAH SAMPSON GANNETT become the popular heroine of American folklore. The term "manly" became itself nearly synonymous with public virtue in revolutionary discourse. "Effeminacy," on the contrary, signified laziness, cowardliness, and corruption. "Idleness is the mother or nurse of almost every vice," explained the college president John Witherspoon in a patriotic sermon predicting the victory of American troops over "those effeminate and delicate soldiers, who are nursed in the lap of self-indulgence" (Witherspoon, 1776, pp. 56–7).

This ideological association of femininity with laziness and luxury left little room for a republican ideal of woman analogous to that of the militant republican man. Women received recognition as patriots only rarely in the 1760s and 1770s, and then primarily for acts of stoic self-denial in support of the cause. They were praised for abstaining from extravagant imported goods and for laboring to produce homespun yarn, both as individuals and occasionally as "Daughters of Liberty." Women who worked hard and spurned luxury could thus be perceived as renouncing "effeminacy" and as conforming in a limited way to the essentially masculine ideal of republican virtue. A patriotic speech delivered by a young college graduate in 1780 praised the "ladies" for "their admiration of military virtue" and "their generous contributions to relieve the wants of the defenders of their country" (Kerber, 1980, p. 106). Women were similarly valorized in revolutionary propaganda for eagerly sending their men into battle. Young single women ostensibly favored the amorous attentions of courageous soldiers, for, in the words of a patriotic poem of 1778, *"Love hates a coward's impotent embrace"* (Royster, 1979, p. 30). One Philadelphia newspaper publicized the fighting words of a New Jersey matron to her soldier grandsons, "Let me beg of you ... that if you fall, it may be like men" (Kerber, 1989, p. 21). At the height of the military fervor, the feminine conception of liberty as passive and in need of protection thus merged with the otherwise highly masculine version of heroic republican virtue.

4. A LESS COMBATIVE IDEAL: FAMILY LIFE

The symbolic elevation of the male soldier proved, however, short-lived. In the face of growing anxieties about corruption and social disorder both during and after the war, American Revolutionaries needed to establish a less combative ideal of republican citizenship consistent with peace and stability. Widespread political disillusionment in the 1780s undercut earlier millennial expectations of social perfection. Americans lost their earlier confidence that liberty would be preserved if it depended for its survival on the self-sacrificial virtue of the people.

The ideological transformation that underlay the United States Constitution redefined the relationship of men to the state. No longer urged into direct public service, ordinary citizens could, argued the authors of the *Federalist Papers*, indirectly contribute to the greater public good by exercising their freedom to pursue separate and competing interests. The state would protect itself against the destruction forces of selfish factionalism through an election system designed to filter out the most local and particular interests and a structure of government based on the institutional mechanisms of checks and balances. The active display of public virtue, still expected among civic leaders, was no longer required of the majority of republican men.

Not that the revolutionary generation altogether abandoned its hopes for a virtuous society. The virtue that had earlier been associated with the collective, public life gradually became redefined as a private, individual characteristic. Instead of being demonstrated in political activism and public service, it became chiefly manifest in the personal relationships of friendship and family.

This shift away from the earlier valorization of public virtue corresponded to a change in the representation of gender within republican ideology. The increased emphasis on the virtues of private life focused greater amounts of attention on emotional relationships between women and men. Just as the patriarchal family had long stood for royalists as a natural justification of monarchical government, so American Revolutionaries devised their own republican understandings of courtship and marriage. Novels and magazines of the 1780s and 1790s excoriated parents for arranging mercenary marriages detrimental to their children's happiness. Couples were to marry out of neither self-interest nor lust but affectionate friendship. The marital relationship was idealized as voluntary and equal, a metaphor for the relationship between citizens in a republic. And the future of the nation depended on the capacity for mutual love that was best learned in marriage. "That MAN who resolves to live without WOMAN, or that WOMAN who resolves to live without MAN, are ENEMIES TO THE COMMUNITY in which they dwell," pronounced a piece on the "Genius of Liberty" printed in 1798 (Lewis, 1987, p. 709).

5. THE NEW CIVIC ROLE OF WOMEN

Yet the egalitarian values expressed in this republican conception of marriage reflected no commitment to the political or social equality of women and men. Unlike French revolutionary women, who insisted on bearing arms and forming their own republican societies, American women never claimed universal rights for themselves. Instead of appealing to the ideal of universal equality, the primary justification for female self-assertion was made on the grounds of gender difference. The feminine qualities of sympathy, delicacy, and piety would, according to this view, soften the sensibilities of otherwise overly aggressive and self-interested men. One anonymous tract of 1787 entitled *Women Invited to War* called American women to a collective religious crusade against postwar corruption and greed. Women were increasingly accorded recognition for a new civic role, that of requiring proper republican behavior of male suitors, husbands, and sons. As a Columbia College orator expounded upon the public import-ance of this private influence, "Yes, ye fair, the reformation of the world is in your power" (*New York Magazine*, May 1795, p. 298).

These new ideals of femininity found repeated expression in the growing body of literature in the early republic devoted to female education. Male leaders such as Benjamin Rush began to insist that American women needed greater knowledge in order to inculcate proper republican manners and morals in their husbands and children. Not only men but educated and articulate women, ranging from the sen-timental novelist Hannah Foster to the political polemicist and historian Mercy Otis Warren, contributed to the delineation of the roles of republican wife and mother. Even JUDITH SARGENT MURRAY, who came the closest to anticipating Mary Woll-stonecraft in her insistence upon women's innate rational capacities, never rejected the centrality of marriage and motherhood.

While differing from the modern idea of social and political equality, a feminine principle thus entered into conceptions of the relationship between civil society and the republican polity. This was a new development in the history of American political thought, one anticipated by neither classical republican nor classical liberal theory. Women were now increasingly represented as a crucial part of the republican moral order even as they remained outside the institutions of government. The expanded definition of female civil obligations also enhanced women's domestic status, chal-lenging, if by no means eliminating, older hierarchies within the family. In the new symbolic order, the republican wife and mother can be seen as the counterpart to the image of the benevolently paternal Founding Fathers. Moral guides rather than imperious rulers, these new models of political authority replaced the earlier patri-archal ideal of monarchy while retaining the analogy between the family and state. In the course of reformulating this analogy, gender relations had been significantly redefined.

These ideological changes never overcame strict limitations in the appropriate roles for republican women, however. The more elevated notion of the civic value of personal domestic relationships gave rise to a still more deeply gendered definition of public and private spheres. The Revolution provided no impetus to re-evaluate the context of male economic and political power that rendered women ultimately dependent for all their newfound authority within the home. The idealization of domestic relationships encouraged the privatization of morality, a process which indirectly sanctioned men's pursuit of self-interest in the public domain. The republican construction of gender – built on the premise that female virtue could counteract male selfishness – at once increased the public value attributed to women and widened the symbolic polarity between feminine dependency and masculine autonomy within subsequent American culture.

FURTHER READING

Adams, John: *The Works of John Adams*, ed. C. F. Adams (Boston, 1850–6).

Bloch, Ruth H.: "The gendered meanings of virtue in revolutionary America," *Signs: Journal of Women in Culture and Society*, 13 (1987), 37–58.

Kerber, Linda K., *Women of the Republic: Intellect and Ideology in Revolutionary America* (Chapel Hill: University of North Carolina Press, 1980).

——: "'History can do it no justice': women and the reinterpretation of the American Revolution," *Women in the Age of the American Revolution*, ed. Ronald Hoffman and Peter J. Albert (Charlottesville: University Press of Virginia, 1989).

Kerber, Linda K., et al.: "Beyond roles, beyond spheres: thinking about gender in the early republic," *William and Mary Quarterly*, 46 (1989), 565–85.

Lewis, Jan: "The republican wife: virtue and seduction in the early republic," *William and Mary Quarterly*, 44 (1987), 690–721.

McIlwain, Charles: *The Political Works of James I* (Cambridge: Cambridge University Press, 1918).

Paine, Thomas: *Common Sense* (Philadelphia, 1776); repr., ed. Isaac Kramnick (New York: Penguin, 1976).

Otis, James: *The Rights of the British Colonies Asserted and Proved* (1764), in *Pamphlets of the American Revolution*, ed. Bernard Bailyn (Cambridge, Mass.: Harvard University Press, 1965).

Royster, Charles: *A Revolutionary People at War* (Chapel Hill: University of North Carolina Press, 1979).

Smith-Rosenberg, Carroll: "Domesticating 'virtue': coquettes and revolutionaries in young America," *Literature and the Body: Essays on Populations and Persons*, ed. Elaine Scarry (Baltimore: John Hopkins University Press, 1988), 160–84.

Witherspoon, John: *The Dominion of Providence* (Philadelphia, 1776).

PART 6
CONCEPTS

63

Liberty

ELISE MARIENSTRAS

"THE history of our country is the history of liberty," wrote the poet and diplomat Joel Barlow in 1810. Indeed, liberty was the key word of the Revolution. The figure of liberty was drawn, painted, and embroidered. Trees of liberty were planted. Poems, ballads, and sermons were written in celebration of liberty. Liberty was cited as one of the "unalienable rights" in the Declaration of Independence, and was the main right to be protected by the First Ten Amendments to the Constitution.

However, from the beginning of the conflict with the mother country in the early 1760s, to the Declaration of Independence in 1776, and through the adoption of the Bill of Rights 15 years later, the meaning of liberty changed as it was understood differently. Liberty is one of the concepts whose significance is most flexible, being discussed in different languages at different times according to the political philosophy of the men who speak of it. At the time of the Revolution, three different meanings at least were attached to the word "liberty": the most conservative trend among the revolutionary leaders – the "reluctant revolutionaries" such as John Jay – understood liberty in a rather limited fashion; the moderate or Whig wing – people such as John Adams – insisted on its links with order and property; the radicals – artisans, small farmers, and spokesmen such as Thomas Paine viewed liberty as a principle and as a natural right which justified an individual's stand if he happened to oppose authority.

Moreover, one must take into account the diverse conceptions of liberty inherent in the traditions in which American views and practices of liberty were grounded. The British colonists had been nurtured on the old English contradiction between the idea of royal prerogative and the freedom of subjects. Two revolutions centering merely around this issue were won in the seventeenth century. The colonists were well aware of that history. They were also heirs to a Western tradition which started, as J. G. A. Pocock terms it, at the "Machiavellian moment" in sixteenth-century Florence, where philosophers enunciated the basic principles of a *res publica* (Pocock, 1975). The paramount principle was the collective or republican notion of liberty, for which the citizens would be ready to sacrifice their lives. According to that conception, individual freedom was to be second to collective liberty. Later, at the time of the Enlightenment, political writers hesitated between these two conceptions. So did the American founding fathers and the people: within two decades they shifted from one conception to the other.

I. THE FIRST PHASE OF THE REVOLUTION: "LIBERTY AGAINST TYRANNY"

At the beginning of the colonial crisis, in the 1760s and early 1770s, the American revolutionary leaders merely relied on their own experience and rights as Englishmen.

They rested these rights on the theories of liberty underlying the British common law and its effects on the juridical system. They opposed the conservative, "court" party conception of the Tories in England and of those colonists such as Jonathan Boucher or Peter Oliver, who were to become "loyalists" and who envisaged liberty as resulting from a "mixed" government in which the different parts of the nation, represented by the King, the Lords, and the Commons, were balanced against one another and where tradition and history were the best safeguards of public freedom. Thomas Hutchinson, Governor of Massachusetts, even denied to the colonies the privilege of enjoying in full the free system of government that was in force in Britain. "Massachusettensis" (Daniel Leonard), the opponent of John Adams, wrote that the Revolution, then within sight, would sacrifice "real liberty to licentiousness" (Massachusettensis [1775] 1972, Letter III). According to the British Tories and the colonial loyalists, liberty was always relative. It was granted by the government within the limits that were necessary to the maintenance of law and order.

In contrast, the "Country" party writers were merely influenced by John Locke's *Second Treatise of Government* or, in the first period of their resistance to the Navigation Acts, by Trenchard's and Gordon's *Cato's Letters* (1721). Like the early eighteenth-century radical writers, they affirmed that liberty was a fragile good, constantly threatened by the tendency of the rulers to abuse their powers and to use their military forces as potential weapons against the freedom of the governed. Like Trenchard and Gordon, they contended that liberty was the concern of the governed only, and that it rested on the will of the people to put checks on the rulers' power.

They also diverged from the conservative writers on the definition of the source of liberty. Whereas the latter limited freedom to what was granted to the governed by the rulers, early Whig leaders insisted on the "natural" origins of freedom, born, as John Locke had explained, out of the state of nature, and further preserved by the people when they entered a compact to form a civil society. Civil liberty is, according to Lockean thought, the continuation of natural liberty, limited only by the interests of the other members of the society. Liberty cannot be granted: it is a common and universal good, to which all men in society are entitled and which they can voluntarily diminish only by a preliminary compact.

Therefore, following James Otis's *Rights of the British Colonies, Asserted and Proved* – a pamphlet written to deny the right of Parliament to levy a tax on sugar (1764) – the early revolutionary leaders stressed their rights to British constitutional freedom, and at the same time their right to natural "truth, equity, and justice."

As the conflict with Britain developed with the Stamp Act crisis, the colonists found it more and more necessary to distinguish their own rights from the traditional rights of the British people. Richard Bland, for instance, wrote in 1769:

> I have observed before that, when subjects are deprived of their civil rights, or are dissatisfied with the place they hold in the community, they have a natural right to quit the society of which they are members and to retire in another country. Now when men exercise these rights and withdraw themselves from their country, they recover their natural freedom and independence. (Bland, 1769, p. 12)

Eight years later, in a pamphlet originally meant as Virginia's instructions to its delegation to the Continental Congress, Thomas Jefferson argued that emigration from Britain was at the root of the rights of American British colonists. In this tract, Jefferson elaborated on Richard Bland's and James Wilson's theories of the right to freedom of emigration and on emigration as the source of a new liberty. Indeed, the colonists had left England as free British subjects. Their emigration had made them free, even though they still paid allegiance to the King. Denying the right of the King to ultimate proprietorship of their lands in America, Jefferson presented American freedom as a step towards greater liberty. *A Summary View of the Rights of British America* (Williamsburg, [1774]) is a strong plea in favor of liberty as an individual right, and primarily as a right to property of land in freehold. By having come to a new country and entered there into a new compact, the British emigrants had applied their exertion to acquire new lands, to reclaim them, and to plant on them.

Thus, as the Navigation Acts and constitutional conflict went on, the colonists started to give liberty a broader meaning. Besides, while, until the eve of independence, liberty was seen mainly as a right to be defended *against* encroachments by the British executive and legislative power, it then took a new, more active sense. It became the cornerstone of the republic.

2. THE DECISIVE STEP OF THE REVOLUTION: REPUBLICAN LIBERTY

When the Second Continental Congress decided, in July 1776, that separation from the mother country had become incvitable, its members would have been embarrassed to continue defining their right to freedom merely on the basis of the British Constitution and of their rights as Englishmen. The "self-evident" rights enumerated in the Declaration of Independence were basically natural and universal. As independent

FIGURE 50 "Liberty Displaying the Arts and Sciences" (painting by Samuel Jennings, 1792): the artist clearly envisages that Africans will be liberated in the new American republic.

citizens, the former Sons of Liberty, the minutemen and the continental privates, the pamphleteers and the members of the Continental Congress henceforth considered themselves as the true protectors of liberty. A new nation was born; sovereignty had changed hands from the King in Parliament to the People; it then devolved onto the several states of the Confederation. In the contest between proponents of a strong central government and supporters of the sovereignty of the states, the latter associated liberty with popular local control. But, for all the Revolutionaries, liberty was to be the guiding principle for the creation of the republic. The American citizens thus started to see it as formative of the character and culture of the American people (*see* figure 50). From being British, liberty became American.

A fourfold definition of American liberty was now at hand: it was a liberty inscribed in geography and space; it was a liberty created by the American citizens; it was the cause of all mankind; and it would be the basic principle of the new civil society.

Firstly, the new nation rested its liberty on such principles as Thomas Jefferson, Richard Bland, and Benjamin Franklin had described before independence: Americans were at a great distance from Europe. An ocean – as Jefferson and Washington would later argue in their "non entangling alliances" theories – was a natural and providential barrier against oppression from the outside world. And the enormous potential resources of a vast continent were enough to make the young republic independent from another country, and individuals free from economic exploitation. In *Common Sense* (1776), Thomas Paine used the cosmic metaphor of stars and planets to demonstrate that it was contrary to the laws of nature to make a continent the satellite of a small island. On this matter, Paine did not repeat Franklin's and John Adams's prophecies that, one day, "America would become the center of empire" and that "America, an immense territory, favored by nature ... will ... be able to shake off any shackles that may be imposed upon her and perhaps place them upon the imposers" (Van Doren, 1947, p. 256).

Instead, Paine and many others gave liberty a second meaning: American liberty would be the outset of a great human future. From America, it would expand over the whole planet. "Liberty is the spirit and genius, not only of the gospel, but of the whole of that revelation, we have first and last, received from God," wrote John Mellen (Mellen, 1795, p. 9). For the American Revolutionaries, liberty played the main part in revolutionary religious and civil millennialism.

Ironically, in the late 1770s, liberty took a third meaning which was more nationalistic than universal. American Revolutionaries described liberty as being particular to those emigrants who fled European tyrannical powers, thrived in the New World, and retained their ancient love for liberty. From then on, the American nation would ever be described as the land of liberty; liberalism would be conceived as the main component of the United States system of government as well as its main ideology.

The fourth and principal feature of liberty as it was conceived and glorified in the years following the Revolution was republicanism. Far from being new to the former colonists, the tradition of the "commonwealthman" inherited from the British revolutions was revived and strengthened in the new revolutionary era. Maxims like those written by Benjamin Rush to his wife in 1776 were common: "The new era will be characterized by freedom ... without licentiousness, government without tyranny, and religion without superstition ..." (Butterfield, 1951, I: p. 99).

Yet the Revolutionaries continued to fear abuse of power from the government. In the new republic, however, the most threatening danger for liberty might be an excess of freedom, a misunderstanding of the true meaning of liberty, and above all the constant possibility of a failing of civic virtue. One of the keywords of this era was "republican virtue," a quality without which civil liberty would be a vain term. Now, the revolutionary leaders were facing a situation where the tyrant could be the people themselves or their representatives. Sermons as well as speeches, patriotic poems, and dramas stressed the importance of preserving republican liberty, even at the expense of individual freedom. "A citizen owes everything to the Commonwealth," wrote Samuel Adams to Caleb Davis in 1781 (Cushing, 1904–8, IV: p. 255). And Benjamin Rush was even more radical when writing "Every man in a republic is public property" (Wood, 1969, p. 61). These assertions did not lead to a negation of the principle of individual liberty. On the contrary, during the decade following the Declaration of Independence, liberty was even more cherished than before. It only changed from a negative, defensive concept to a positive, dynamic one. Liberty was to be the cornerstone of a republic in which the sovereign people would never, as Josiah Quincy put it, be "interested to injure themselves" (Wood, id.) Their liberties depended on the collective freedom of the body politic. The solution rested on the construction of a commonwealth which would provide at once public freedom and citizens' participation in political power.

3. LIBERTY AND LIBERTIES IN THE FEDERATION

The abstract concept of liberty such as the early Revolutionaries had thought of was mostly inspired by the ancient republics, small enough to allow the citizens to put direct checks on the government. The ideal republic was a small one, inhabited by a limited number of citizens. In America, however, the space was almost limitless, and the population was growing fast. Each state was already larger than Athens had been, and in order to survive the states needed to unite into a great republic. How could liberty be protected when the citizens could not govern by themselves, but were to trust representatives? Those who were to be known as Anti-Federalists vested the protection of liberty in the several states. States' rights against a national government's tendency to encroach on civil liberties became, in the 1780s, the principal concern of the American republicans. Only in the states would property, individual safety, and freedom of expression, religion, and self-defense be guaranteed and protected.

Indeed, with the establishment of new governments in the several states, constitutions were adopted which provided for the preservation of freedom through a balance of powers. Everywhere, bills of rights were adopted, more or less copied after the Virginia Bill of Rights of 1776. Besides, liberty gradually ceased to be spelled in the singular and became plural, often replaced by the wording "freedom of" with a limited sense.

Indeed, when the Constitutional Convention met in Philadelphia in March 1787, many of the delegates were more concerned with the menace "anarchy" or "popular licentiousness" presented to property than by an ideal of republican collective liberty. The principle of the safety of individual property seemed threatened by the recent Shays's rebellion or by the abolitionists aggressively opposing slavery. From 1787 on a tension developed between republicanism and liberalism. Both ideologies cared for liberty. Neither required a commitment to egalitarianism. But each conceived of liberty and social order in different terms.

Although the Federalists conceded some provisions which limited the power of the federal government and guaranteed habeas corpus, they did not explicitly provide for rights to specific liberties in the Constitution. The checks and balances system of government and the federal organization of the Union were considered by the authors of the *Federalist Papers* as sufficient safeguards against abuse of authority. The spirit of 1776 was over. With institutionalization, republican ideology and its rigid moral demands were henceforth relegated to mere rhetoric. From then on liberty was generally conceived as the sum of individual rights, and the public good was envisioned as the satisfaction of individual self-interest.

Above all, liberty came to be identified with the protection of private property. Although the Bill of Rights also guaranteed freedom of the press, of opinion, of expression, and of religion, property of one's own body and one's goods became the liberties most often fought for. But physical and civil liberty were still not enjoyed by everyone. The Constitution had not banned slavery.

Some of the Revolutionaries, politicians or clergymen, continued to envision a republic where liberty could be enjoyed by all men. For those who were not content with mere rhetoric on liberty but who exalted the new nation as destined to embody a secularized New Jerusalem, chattel slavery appeared as a thorn in the body of the republic, and as a sin to be condemned: "The new Jerusalem is free in a more exalted sense than the church on earth," wrote James Dana in a thundering sermon against the slave trade (Dana, 1791).

But although the slave trade was eventually banned by Congress in 1808, the institution of chattel slavery would endure for almost one century after the colonists had fought against what they termed the British policy of "enslaving" them. Until the Civil War slave-holders and abolitionists would debate over the compatibility of slavery and the principles embodied in the Declaration of Independence and the Bill of Rights. New England and the mid-Atlantic states did not wait long to free their slaves. But for most of the southerners chattel slavery was not incompatible with a republic founded upon individual freedom. Neither did women or Indians have access to complete liberty as it was granted to white men. For a long time the concept of liberty was to remain limited.

From the revolutionary period, however, American citizens had gained much in the matter of freedom. Liberty, fragile as it would always be, now rested on a Constitution and a Bill of Rights which could always be referred to when freedom was at risk. The Virginia Statute of Religious Liberty of 1786 became a landmark in the new freedom of religion. The Establishment clause and the Free Exercise clause, included in the First Amendment, provided once and for all for the separation of Church and State and for equal protection of all faiths and opinions. The First Ten Amendments to the Constitution had been conceived as fundamental safeguards for the citizens against any abuse of power. By enumerating the different fields of liberty, they also achieved the transformation of what had been a rather abstract concept into a series of concrete liberties whose embodiment and enlargement were always possible. Later on, disinherited individuals or groups would struggle in order to carry out into the social, economical, and political spheres the promises which had been inscribed in the fundamental documents.

FURTHER READING

Bailyn, Bernard: *The Ideological Origins of the American Revolution* (Cambridge, Mass.: Harvard University Press, 1967).

Bland, Richard: *An Enquiry into the Rights of the British Colonies* (Williamsburg, 1769); repr. in *A Collection of Tracts*, 4 vols. (London, 1773).

Butterfield, L. H. (ed.): *Letters of Benjamin Rush*, 2 vols. (Princeton, NJ: Princeton University Press, 1951).

Cushing, Henry A. (ed.): *The Writings of Samuel Adams*, 4 vols. (New York: G. P. Putnam's Sons, 1904–8).

Dana, James: *The African Slave Trade: a Discourse Delivered Before the Connecticut Society for the Promotion of Freedom by the Pastor of the First Congregational Church in Said City* (New Haven, 1791).

Kammen, Michael: *Spheres of Liberty: Changing Perceptions of Liberty in the American Culture* (Madison: University of Wisconsin Press, 1986).

Massachusettensis [Leonard, Daniel]: *To the Inhabitants of the Province of Massachusetts Bay* (Boston, 1775); repr. in *The American Colonial Crisis*, ed. James Mason (New York: Harper and Row, 1972).

Mellen, John: *The Great and Happy Doctrine of Liberty* (Boston, 1795).

Otis, James: *Rights of the British Colonies, Asserted and Proved* (Boston, 1764).

Pocock, J. G. A.: *The Machiavellian Moment: Florentine Political Thought and the Atlantic Political Tradition* (Princeton, NJ: Princeton University Press, 1975).

Reid, Phillip: *The Concept of Liberty in the Age of the American Revolution* (Chicago: University of Chicago Press, 1988).

Trenchard, John, and Gordon, Thomas: *Cato's Letters* (London, 1721).

Van Doren, Carl (ed.): *Letters and Papers of Benjamin Franklin and Richard Jackson* (Philadelphia: American Philosophical Society, 1947).

Wood, Gordon: *The Creation of the American Republic, 1776–1787* (Chapel Hill: University of North Carolina Press, 1969).

64

Equality

J. R. POLE

THE United States was almost certainly the first country to base its existence on an abstract principle of social relations. The Continental Congress adopted the statement that "all men are created equal" as the fundamental moral precept of the Declaration of Independence. Americans also believed in other principles, notably liberty. But equality is prior to and more fundamental than liberty in the canon of American principles: for if all men, or all persons, are equal *in rights*, then all must be equal in their right to liberty; no single American can have a greater right, or a right to more liberty, than any other.

But equality is also a relative value. Colonial society was in many respects more wide open than was generally the case in Europe. But it was also a slave society, and in other areas property-owners depended considerably on indentured service. There was a more conscious claim to equality of status than in European nations, but there were also enormous disparities: disparities of wealth, and disparities of associated social status and political power.

Personal ambition played a forceful part in the hopes and expectations of innumerable colonials, and ambition is not an inherently egalitarian type of motivation. The abstract principle of equality would have seemed an unlikely candidate for the central role it was soon to attain in formal American ideology.

I. EQUALITY OF STATUS

Yet, in spite of these discouragements, many reports from the 1760s and 1770s indicating a restless drive for economic opportunity and social recognition among the more subordinate classes of the population carried messages reflecting a demand for equality. After the repeal of the Stamp Act, Anne Grant, the daughter of a great proprietor in Albany County, New York, recorded a little sardonically that her father's visitors "from Hampshire or Connecticut," recent settlers in the neighborhood, "came in without knocking; sat down without invitation; and lighted their pipe without ceremony; then talked of buying land; and finally, began a discourse of politics, which would have done honor to Praise-God Barebones, or any of the members of his parliament." In Massachusetts, a few months after the Stamp Act riots, Thomas Cushing wrote anxiously to Thoms Hutchinson, Lieutenant-Governor and Chief Justice of the province, "A Spirit of Levillism Seems to go Through the Country, and very little distinction between the highest and lowest in Office." In Philadelphia, a Church of England cleric observed soon afterwards that "the poorest labourer on the shore of the Delaware thinks himself entitled to deliver his opinions in matters of religion and politics with as much freedom as the gentleman and the scholar." Even in Virginia the newly rising religious sect of Separate Baptists was carrying a message of brother-hood and sisterhood that challenged the supremacy of the Established Church – and this was perceived as a threat to supremacy in society as well as religion.

2. COLLECTIVE AND INDIVIDUAL EQUALITY

Thus, although colonial America produced very little egalitarian political theory, there was an undertow of sometimes violent social demand. Americans were increasingly sensitive to questions of equality in two broadly defined areas. The first was the collective level: as British subjects, Americans were fully entitled to all the privileges and protections that Britons enjoyed at home under the common law. But there was conspicuous contrast of treatment. In Massachusetts in 1761 the Superior Court authorized customs officers to use writs of assistance, which permitted them to enter private premises; but only two years later the Court of Common Pleas in London declared that general warrants – whose effects were closely similar – were illegal. When Charles Townshend as Chancellor of the Exchequer introduced his Tariff Act in 1767 he specifically included a power to use writs of assistance in the colonies. The English cases had been widely reported in the colonial newspapers, which brought home the difference of treatment under the common law. This issue was an important theme in John Dickinson's *Letters from a Farmer in Pennsylvania*, published in late 1767 and 1768.

Parliamentary taxation without representation was a still more glaring dem-onstration of the same point: it was an offense against their lawful rights as British subjects; but at the emotional level it was no less serious as an offense against their dignity and self-respect. In other more personal ways British superiority wounded colonial sentiments. Probably none of these was more significant for the future than the painful susceptibility of the young Virginia militia colonel George Washington, who badly wanted a commission from the King. Washington failed in this aspiration and deeply resented being out-ranked by commissioned officers junior to him.

This collective theme culminated in the Declaration of Independence, with the assertion that the time had come for "one people" to assume its equal station among the nations. But Thomas Jefferson, in his *Summary View of the Rights of British America*, had already written two years earlier that *every individual* American was the equal of *every individual* in Britain, thus bringing together the collective and the individual themes of equality. And in many sectors of colonial society the individual theme was more prominent and immediate than the still latent issue of national status.

3. THE EQUALIZING PROCESS OF REVOLUTION

It is doubtful, however, whether this theme would have been able to gain effective political leverage if the quarrel with Britain had not taken place when it did. After momentary upsurges of protest, ordinary colonists tended generally to accept the posture of deference to their superiors just as their counterparts did in Britain; men of old family, of large estates or property, of law and learning seldom had much difficulty in reasserting their traditional sway over the minds of the less educated – and less organized – men in humbler walks of life. The revolutionary upheaval unsettled these habits of mind, however. The suffrage was already widespread, extend-ing to nearly all small freeholders and many urban artisans, and the sheer necessities of revolutionary organization called for the creation of numerous local committees, which brought thousands of local people into active, if limited, political power. The leaders of society could not ignore these men, who played a crucial role in enforcing such measures as the non-importation agreements. The Revolution, among many other things, was a process of widespread popular political mobilization. It was an equalizing process.

4. THE VARIOUS CATEGORIES OF EQUALITY

But even equality could not mean the same thing for everybody. Considered at the individual level, equality broke down into a variety of segments, which are susceptible to separate analysis.

Equality before the law   The cardinal enlightenment principle was that of equality before the law, which was a matter of very general agreement in America. (Such anomalies as benefit of clergy, which actually saved many individuals from execution, were gradually abolished.) The exceptions to this generalization fell, not along lines of social or economic class, but of gender and race. Women occupied a separate sector of society, in which their role was not less important than men's but was theoretically sheltered behind the legal privileges of the male sex. Not all women felt that this theory worked to their advantage or protection, and many women took part in local economic life and had access to the courts when their interests were affected. But they had no direct access to the political process. Married women were held to be inferior to their husbands in law, and lost control of their property on marriage. (A wife who murdered her husband was guilty of petit treason, and liable to be burned to death, not hanged.) Slaves had no legal rights and no normal access to the legal system, although there were some striking exceptions. For some years after the Revolution, the courts of Virginia and Maryland were surprisingly sympathetic to claims to freedom based on oral evidence and memory given by other slaves.

Political equality   At the level of political rights, equality was becoming an active principle of participation both in elections and in committees. But political rights were generally held to be associated with property, both in the right of suffrage and in the equally important matter of the distribution of representatives. The idea that individuals might have an equal right to vote simply *as individuals* was not sufficiently established to form a political program. Individual political equality did make an advance in the revolutionary process, but it did so in alliance with the interests of high concentrations of property. Thus in Boston, which had been badly under-represented before the Revolution, the men of property wanted more representation, and they acquired it on the basis of Boston's population being much larger than that of other towns. Boston's representation in the Assembly at once went up from four to 12. This principle was very gradually generalized. By the time of the Federal Constitution, one-man, one-vote in equal electoral districts was an accepted principle.

Religious equality   The demand for religious equality was sectarian before it was individual. The challenge of the Separate Baptists in several colonies and the claims of other minority sects put intense pressure on the prevailing religious establishments. Jefferson's famous Statute for Religious Freedom eventually prevailed in Virginia in 1786, and laid the groundwork for the First Amendment to the United States Constitution – also, like the Virginia Statute, introduced by Madison. This established the formal neutrality of the Federal Government in all matters of religion, leaving the states to follow their own preferences.

Equality of opportunity Glimmerings of the idea of equality of opportunity were perceived in demands for access to economic privileges before the Revolution; they grew in number and confidence after the war. Hamilton, writing *Federalist*, no. 36, expressed the conviction that America could, and under the Constitution would, give opportunities to all who deserved them: "There are strong minds in every walk of life that will rise superior to the disadvantages of situation, and will command the tribute due to their merit, not only from the classes to which they particularly belong, but from society in general. The door ought to be equally open to all ...."

Equality of esteem Pervading all these can be discerned a passionate demand for equality of esteem. The Revolution spurred people in many downtrodden walks of life, including white women, free Blacks, and slaves, to become conscious of their moral worth. Political and legal institutions did not fully respond to these demands; America remained in many respects an unequal society, but even so it was a society that had to respond to demands based on these concepts.

5. THE LANGUAGE OF THE REPUBLIC

When the United States Constitution was formulated it forbade titles of nobility and permitted no inherited political or ecclesiastical privileges. New inequalities constantly crept into the society – inequalities of opportunity and esteem, sometimes even in law and politics, based on race and ethnicity, religion and class.

But the Revolution had put a weapon in the hands of the oppressed. It was more than a set of laws: it was a language. Under British rule, the language of both political and social relations was essentially paternalistic. The language of politics assumed the subordination of the people to the King, of the colonies to the parent country, of wives and children to the father and husband, of the people to their rulers. The language of the Republic assumed equality in at least the political if not in all of the social sides of these relations. The struggles for equality could in future be fought out in the language of the Republic.

FURTHER READING

Becker, Carl L.: *The Declaration of Independence* (New York: Vintage Books, 1959).

Davis, David Brion: *The Problem of Slavery in Western Culture* (Ithaca, NY: Cornell University Press, 1966).

Epstein, David E.: *The Political Theory of The Federalist* (Chicago: University of Chicago Press, 1984).

Lakoff, Sanford A.: *Equality in Political Philosophy* (Cambridge, Mass: Harvard University Press, 1964).

Pole, J. R.: *The Pursuit of Equality in American History* (Berkeley: University of California Press, 1978).

White, Morton: *The Political Philosophy of the American Revolution* (New York: Oxford University Press, 1978).

Wood, Gordon S.: *The Creation of the American Republic* (Chapel Hill: University of North Carolina Press for the Institute of Early American History and Culture, 1969).

65

Property

ALAN FREEMAN AND ELIZABETH MENSCH

> This land is my land,
> this land ain't your land.
> I gotta shotgun
> and you ain't got one.
> If you don't get off,
> I'll blow your head off.
> This land is
> PRIVATE PROPERTY.
>
> Anon.

T HE concept of property serves to define one's simultaneous relationship to others and to resources. Historically, the key American resource has been land. The bit of schoolyard doggerel quoted above captures, in an appropriately aggressive way, the concept of property that has been dominant in American culture since the early nineteenth century: exclusive, possessive, and individualistic, a personal right of territorial sovereignty.

With their characteristic tendency to universalize themselves, Americans take for granted that "property" has always meant a liberal, privatized, protected right. Yet the message of history is contingency. A quick visit to America's past reveals that the modern concept of property did not triumph until after the Constitution of 1787. During the long colonial period property acquired a variety of meanings utterly at odds with the modern, liberal definition. The Revolution then triggered a period of rhetorical excess and lively enthusiasm that threatened to subject property to the leveling passions of a free and democratic people. Against that background, the architects of the Constitution built an institutional and conceptual web to secure property from the whims of the masses.

I. THE COLONIAL PERIOD

Widely read in the colonies were the Whig articles of Gordon and Trenchard, first published in England in the 1720s. They proclaimed that

> And as Happiness is the Effect of Independency, and Independency is the Effect of Property; so certain Property is the Effect of Liberty alone, and can only be secured by the Laws of Liberty. (Mensch, 1982, p. 641)

Similarly Sir William Blackstone, whose famous *Commentaries on the Laws of England* appeared in the colonies in 1771–2, proclaimed that "There is nothing which so generally strikes the imagination, and engages the affections of mankind, as the right of property" (Blackstone, 1766, p. 2). Americans on the eve of their Revolution could readily agree on their shared affection for property, so long as the rhetoric was sufficiently vague to obscure significant differences.

Those differences had emerged with the earliest settlements, and often reflected particular regional needs or prior English experience. Land might serve as a basis for community organization, a source of subsistence, a resource for the production of revenue, a commodity exchangeable for speculation, or a power base for a carefully structured social/political hierarchy. These functions often overlapped and collided with one another. Although the cumbersome and intricate English common law of property was available to every colony, but regional selectivity led to lack of uniformity in application.

In New England, property, while privately owned, was subordinate to community organization. Under the "township" model developed in Massachusetts, the founding fathers of each new township held both political authority and title to the land, and land was distributed in proportion to the wealth or status of the original heads of household. The founders also controlled undistributed land, subjecting newcomers to strict social authority – not usually resented by a people communally committed to their "Bible commonwealth." That commitment led New Englanders to reject feudal incidents, such as quit-rents. Their "General Lauues and Libertyes" of 1648 (Massachusetts) provided that

> all our Lands and Heritages shall be free from all Fines and Licenses upon alienations, and from all Hariots, Wardships; Liveries, Primerseizens, year, day and wast, Escheats and forfeitures, upon the death of Parents or Ancesters, be they natural, unnatural, casual or judicial and that for ever.

Notably, they also rejected primogeniture.

In the South property ownership contemplated more individual initiative and resourcefulness. In Virginia, by the 1620s the leaders were "tough, unsentimental, quick-tempered, crudely ambitious men concerned with profits and increased land-holding, not the grace of life" (Bailyn, 1977, p. 44). The result was a system of large tobacco plantations dependent for labor first on English indentured servants and later on black slaves. With expansion, vast tracts of undeveloped land were acquired through paper transactions without any care in survey or description. Meanwhile, actual settlers gradually began to occupy those same tracts of land. Inevitable was the resulting conflict between property as subsistence and livelihood, and property as asset exchangeable for speculation. On the eve of the Revolution it was apparent that the fiction of pure "title by occupancy," so fondly embraced by English common law, could not survive the strain, but neither could the elaborate claims of paper title wholly unrelated to possession and use.

Close to the feudal tradition of property as carefully structured hierarchy were the huge land grants that established Pennsylvania, the Carolinas, Maryland, and much of provincial New York. For example, from the time of its founding by the Dutch, New York had been characterized by land grants of hundreds of thousands of acres. Conferred on a few political favorites, those vast grants were conceived by royal governors as a way of maintaining a hierarchically structured, Crown-centered political and religious authority, especially as against rampant sectarian diversity. Many grant proprietors were given the authority to conduct manor courts and name ministers, as well as to collect rents. While often not exercised, such authority was understood as a natural extension of the Crown's own unitary prerogative authority over provincial law, religion, and land. Provincial grantees also soon recognized their grants' potential as a source of capital accumulation. Thus Robert Livingston argued that proprietors of large grants could, by extracting rents from tenants, "oblige their Tenants to . . . raise more than they consume" (McAnnear, 1940, p. 88). This would provide proprietors with the capital required for investment in mills, where wheat could be efficiently processed and also concentrated in the hands of a few landlord merchants for investment on the world market.

In marked contrast, many New York communities, especially separatist townships on Long Island, developed a roughly egalitarian model. Land was often distributed in lots based on family size, and grants were subject to condition of settlement: absentee land-owning led to forfeiture, and contracts to sell unimproved land could be voided. The goal was that none should use land for purely speculative profit or to gain power over others. This model was closely associated with the most direct forms of participatory democracy, along with sectarian religious enthusiasm: the ultimate goal of property arrangements was the "enlargement of the Kingdom of Christ in the Congregational way and all other means of comfort in subordination thereunto" (Mensch, 1982, p. 650).

Implicit in this New York contrast was a conflict over theories of both property and political participation. Building on both the civic humanist tradition and the "yeoman farmer" imagery of England, most eighteenth-century political theorists assumed that only a freeholder could exercise sufficient independence to support responsible and autonomous political judgment. In the colonies, as in England, the propertyless were regarded as too dependent and morally unfit for political participation. In seventeenth-century Virginia, for example, all freemen had been permitted to vote until declining mortality rates gave rise to a sizable class of servants and ex-servants, a "giddy multitude," a propertyless "rabble" (Fredrickson, 1981, p. 62). In 1670 Virginians adopted a property qualification for suffrage, as had every colony but one by the time of the Revolution.

Conversely, at the other extreme were the assertions of radical democracy unleashed during the English Civil War, captured by the pervasive claim "the voice of the People is the voice of God." That position could lead to redistribution of property to achieve equality and an independent electorate. The influential English republican theorist James Harrington taught that a stable commonwealth depended upon the people's owning at least three-quarters of the land, or the "over-balance." Ownership of the over-balance by the few rather than the many necessitated an "agrarian" law to correct the balance through redistribution. Such a scheme was consistent with the experience of colonists from areas like Long Island, where an egalitarian distribution of property was specifically intended to ensure democracy.

One solution to the assumed link between property and politics was simply to rely on the vast land resources in the New World to enable settlers to become land-holders through industry and effort, and thereby to join the political community. This approach led to conflict when actual settlers struggled to preserve their claims against huge land-owners, whose paper titles derived from mysterious "sovereigns" and their grantees. To recognize titles based on occupancy and use collided with property as exchangeable commodity, necessary to the development of commerce and trade. Furthermore, to reject the Crown as legitimate source of title placed a dangerous power in the people themselves. John Locke's natural law theories were an effort to challenge Crown prerogative without yielding to the most radical claims of the people, providing an important model for post-revolutionary notions of property. Notably, however, Locke's own views were not unambiguously liberal and modern. Much in the natural law tradition he invoked supported communitarian visions of property, being premised on the assumption that God originally gave land to all men in common and that only sin led to private entitlement. Locke was concerned with theology and virtue, not just property rights, and even retained doubts about the legitimacy of excessive accumulation. Nor was he prepared to repudiate aristocracy altogether in the quest for possessive individualism. Indeed, Locke himself joined a failed North Carolina settlement scheme which linked land-ownership to political status in an elaborate balance between aristocracy and democracy (*see also* Chapter 9, §1).

2. THE REVOLUTION AND ITS AFTERMATH

In the immediate post-revolutionary period Americans sought to build a true republic. That meant not merely eliminating English domination, but reordering politics and social relations towards the realization of virtue. Many post-revolutionary theorists, influenced by Harrington, assumed that property was therefore properly subject to political control. At the end of the war an anonymous pamphleteer in South Carolina quoted *Cato's Letters* approvingly: "Men in moderate circumstances, are most virtuous. An equality of estate, will give an equality of power; and equality of power is a natural commonwealth" (McDonald, 1985, p. 89). Some gentlemen of large "estate" were surprisingly willing to put theory into practice. Thomas Jefferson, for example, proposed that Virginia distribute 50 acres of land to all citizens (a category limited, of course, to white males) willing to farm, for the sake of ensuring an independent electorate; and he proposed a Harringtonian agrarian law to limit holdings.

More alarming to the elite intelligentsia was the eager embrace of republican theory by those whom genteel society could never consider gentlemen. "When the pot boils the scum will rise," James Otis had warned, and his prediction came true with a vengeance (Wood, 1969, p. 476). Those elected to state legislatures were often of low social standing; nor did they seem the "natural aristocrats" who could be expected to lead a virtuous republic. As one complaint stated, men fit only to "patch a shoe" suddenly felt qualified to "patch the state" (Wood, 1969, p. 477).

State legislators were bent on instituting property reform: the only question was whether that reform would result in a broad program of mandatory republican equality. In the years just before the war lawyers had given renewed emphasis to feudal forms – engaging, for example, in solemn discussion of feudal incidents of tenure such as knight service. Post-revolutionary state legislators, however, quickly abolished all forms perceived locally as feudal. Their clear preference for allodial, rather than tenurial, land-holding represented rejection of feudal hierarchy and Crown privilege. Similarly, the fee tail was almost universally scorned. An Act of 1776 in Virginia abolished entail because it did "injury to the morals of youth" (McDonald, 1985, p. 12) and discouraged trade and improvement of land.

Elites feared that this zeal to reform would not be confined to archaic relics of a feudal past, but would threaten all legally acquired inequality. Most at risk were the large estates based on "paper title" and the speculative investment they made possible. Montesquieu had written of the importance of regulating contracting in a republic, to preserve equality and the virtues of "frugality" and "simplicity." Sparta, often touted as a model of civic virtue, had forbidden trade and mandated equality of land-holding. In that spirit of "simplicity" most states passed laws to control spending,

623

especially for luxuries, and many state constitutions required such laws. The Massachusetts Bill of Rights, for instance, announced that principles of "piety, justice, moderation, temperance, industry and frugality" were necessary to preserve "liberty," so that the people had a "right" to require observation of those principles in legislation (McDonald, 1985, p. 90).

Even more extreme was the wholesale expropriation of loyalist estates which quickly followed the war. Estimates indicate that the value of property confiscated by state bills of attainder amounted to more than $20 million, almost a tenth of the value of all improved real estate. This breaking up of "dangerous monopolies of land" was often accompanied by demagoguery, and led to speculative gain for insiders. Still, most states mandated resale into small parcels to promote republican independence. Given that legislative zeal, many feared a general levelling of property. While wholesale redistribution of all large holdings never became the norm, and the fever for confiscation had abated by 1787, other legislation further underscored the leveling potential of democracy. Debt relief was common; so was the printing of paper money. Regulation of prices and wages was routine, and many people advocated abolition of monopolies and corporations as vestiges of Crown privilege. Such pervasive legislative control over wealth suggested that the nightmare version of republicanism could easily become reality: to subordinate property to the requirements of democracy meant not the triumph of reason and virtue, but mob rule.

The challenge of the 1780s was to develop a notion of property that would stem majoritarian excesses, without appealing to now-despised aristocratic institutions. Throughout the colonies the notion of ownership "right" had been rooted in a conception of title as derived from the Crown. The post-revolutionary survival of that right required conceptual transformation. While the vagaries of natural law theory and the technicalities of the common law tradition provided useful reference points, their quite various interpretations in the colonies left no uniform law or practice, and no coherent theory of property right.

That such a right was developed is a tribute to the sophistication of the framers and to the Supreme Court Justices who later enunciated Federalist theory. Even before the Constitutional Convention, future Federalists, especially in New York, had become adept at protecting large property holdings from democratic excess. Alexander Hamilton, invoking both natural and common law, had successfully argued in court against enforcement of an anti-Tory Trespass Act. In an atmosphere of frenzied confiscation, Hamilton's victory was a firm stroke against Tory-baiting. It also provided an important (albeit ambiguous) precedent for judicial review by interposing "law" between property and democratic legislation, without appeal to Crown grant rights.

Similarly, in a striking symbolic success, New York's political elite protected a huge land grant to a despised institution, Trinity Church in Manhattan. Trinity, whose advisors included Hamilton and John Jay, had a long, inglorious history: her holdings were based on a flimsy Crown grant from a corrupt royal governor who had established her in order to impose Anglicanism on a resentful, dissenting populace. During the war most of her officers remained staunchly and arrogantly loyalist. Calls for confiscation of her land arose immediately after patriot victory, and early state proceedings were directed towards that end. Yet the politically adroit elite in New York severed Trinity's link to Anglicanism's Crown-based ecclesiastical structure and then quelled the call for confiscation by petitioning for a fresh title premised on the church's newly assumed identity as private right-holder, as both religious body and owner of property.

Such victories against the confiscatory spirit were not simply crass protection of established interests; nor were they mere retreat to feudalism. Instead, they represented a modern, Humean conception of republicanism. Hume, whose work influenced both Hamilton and Madison, explicitly rejected republicanism as realization of Spartan simplicity and equality (*see* Chapter 9, §6). A polity like Sparta, Hume argued, was "violent and contrary to the more natural and usual course of things ... [for it] aggrandizes the public by the poverty of individuals" (Stourzh, 1970, pp. 71–2). The less circumspect Hobbes declared outright, "the *wealth* and *riches* of all the particular members, are the *strength* of the commonwealth" (Stourzh, 1970, p. 73).

Hamilton became the frankest spokesman for the "modern policy," as it came to be called. The goal was to encourage the "natural" appetite for personal gain by protecting private wealth, for private wealth would ultimately lead to national prosperity. Inevitably, as Hamilton honestly acknowledged, the classical goal of republican virtue would have to surrender to the modern, enlightened goal of commercial development. Hamilton thus reminded the delegates to the Federal Convention, "the difference of property is already great amongst us. Commerce and industry will still increase the disparity. Your government must meet this state of things ..." As he stated at the New York Ratifying Convention, "as riches increase and accumulate in a few hands; as luxury prevails in society; virtue will be in a greater degree considered as only a graceful appendage of wealth, and the tendency of things will be to depart from the republican standard" (Stourzh, 1970, pp. 70–1).

Thus Federalists were delicately poised on the threshhold of modernity. They had rejected not only feudalism, but also the classic conception of republican virtue which depended upon "frugality" and equality. The dilemma was to formulate a conceptual scheme for protecting property which was not outrageously antithetical to republican principles, yet would effectively interpose a wedge between democratic people (public) and economic advantage (private). Their stroke of genius was to propose that the people themselves were the architects of that wedge.

The new conception of property as private right reached its fruition through the Constitution of 1787, which supplied the one ingredient previously missing – an authoritative source. Emerging property theory in the 1780s had still been uncomfortably dependent upon natural law to insulate property from legislative interference. The new Constitution provided a crucial text in the form of the "contract clause" ("No State shall ... pass any ... Law impairing the Obligation of Contracts ..."). That text, combined with the theory of judicial review articulated by Hamilton in *The Federalist*, no. 78, provided the basis for an inviolable right of property, derived from the republican people themselves, but protected from their majoritarian excess by their own constitutionally structured judiciary.

The famous case of *Fletcher v. Peck* (1810) offered a dramatic opportunity for the realization of this new theory of property rights. In January 1795 the Georgia legislature, through outright bribery led by one of its United States senators, had corruptly deeded more than 35 million acres of its western lands (including all of the present state of Mississippi) to speculators. A year later a new legislature, elected to end corruption, voted to repeal the grant. The case would not be decided by the Supreme Court until 1810. Yet in 1796, within a month of the repeal legislation, Hamilton wrote a legal opinion arguing that Georgia had no power to repeal the corrupt grant. Hamilton contended that "every grant from one to another, whether the grantor be a state or an individual, is virtually a contract that the grantee shall hold and enjoy the thing granted against the grantor, and his representatives." He therefore

FIGURE 51 "The Residence of David Twining, 1787" (painting by David Hicks, 1845–8): Hicks lived on this Quaker farm during the Revolution.

concluded, "taking the terms of the constitution in their large sense," that the revocation by Georgia was in violation of the contract clause of the Constitution (Magrath, 1966, p. 150).

Chief Justice Marshall's famous opinion in *Fletcher v. Peck* followed Hamilton's reasoning and reached the same conclusion. Marshall offered a deft blend of natural law and English common law (the *bona fide* purchaser doctrine), yet relied ultimately, as did Hamilton, on the *constitutional text.* That the source of title was the sovereign state (and corruptly so) made no difference, as Trinity's tainted source of title had also made no difference. In the new world of private right-holders all are equally secure against the interference of the state.

The genius of the solution is its relationship to Hamilton's theory of judicial review. The ultimate source of sovereignty is the people. In theory, the people acted directly as a body when ratifying the Constitution ('We the people ...'). Yet the Constitution, as a legal text, can be authoritatively interpreted only by those trained in the "artificial reason" of the law. Thus the people, by adopting the Constitution, effected a Hobbesian covenant, even a political transubstantiation: they relocated their sovereignty in an intricate web of institutional arrangements whose meaning now belonged to a judicial priesthood. In so doing they surrendered forever their active democratic control over property rights.

That the Constitution's solemn role was the careful protection of property was not lost on influential members of the emerging American judiciary. John Marshall made that clear during his more than 30 years as Chief Justice. As the almost equally famous Justice Joseph Story put it in 1829, upon his inauguration as Dane Professor of Law at Harvard: "[T]he lawyer's most glorious and not infrequently perilous" duty was to guard the "sacred rights of property" from the "rapacity" of the majority. Only the "solitary citadel" of justice stood between property and mob rule. It was the lawyer's noble task to man that citadel, whatever the cost. "What sacrifice could be more pure than in such a cause? What martyrdom more worthy to be canonized in our hearts?" (Story, 1829).

FURTHER READING

Appleby, J.: "Republicanism in old and new contexts," *William and Mary Quarterly*, 43 (1986), 20–34.

Bailyn, B.: "Shaping the republic," in Bailyn, B, Davis, D. B., Donald, D. H., Thomas, J. L., Wiebe, R. H., and Wood, G. S.: *The Great Republic: a History of the American People* (Lexington, Mass.: D. C. Heath, 1977), 1–227.

Banning, L.:"Jeffersonian ideology revisited: liberal and classical ideas in the new American republic," *William and Mary Quarterly*, 43 (1986), 3–19.

Blackstone, W.: *Commentaries on the Laws of England*, 4 vols. Vol. 2, *Book the Second* (Oxford: 1766), repr. (London: Dawsons, 1966).

Cunliffe, M.: "Property," *Encyclopedia of American Political History*, ed. J. Greene (New York: Charles Scribner's Sons, 1984), Vol. 2, pp. 1018–30.

Dunn, J.: "From applied theology to social analysis: the break between John Locke and the Scottish Enlightenment,"*Wealth and Virtue: the Shaping of Political Economy in the Scottish Enlightenment*, ed. I. Hont and M. Ignatieff (Cambridge: Cambridge University Press, 1983).

Fredrickson, G.: *White Supremacy: a Comparative Study in American and South African History* (New York and London: Oxford University Press, 1981).

Kloppenberg, J. T.: "The virtues of liberalism: Christianity, republicanism, and ethics in early American political discourse," *Journal of American History*, 74 (1987), 9–33.

McAnnear: "Mr. Robert R. Livingston's reasons against a land tax," *Journal of Political Economy*, 48 (1940), 63.

McDonald, F.: *Novus Ordo Seclorum: the Intellectual Origins of the Constitution* (Lawrence: University Press of Kansas, 1985).

Magrath, C. P.: *Yazoo: Law and Politics in the New Republic: the Case of Fletcher v. Peck* (Providence, RI: Brown University Press, 1966).

Mensch, E.: "The colonial origins of liberal property rights," *Buffalo Law Review*, 31 (1982), 635–735.

——: "Religion, revival, and the ruling class: a critical history of Trinity Church," *Buffalo Law Review*, 36 (1988), 427–571.

Mensch, E., and Freeman, A.: "A republican agenda for Hobbesian America?," *Florida Law Review*, 41 (1989), 581–622.

Minogue, K. R.: "The concept of property and its contemporary significance," *Nomos*, 22 (*Property*) (1980), 3–27.

Morgan, E.: *Inventing the People: the Rise of Popular Sovereignty in England and America* (New York and London: W. W. Norton, 1988).

Pocock, J. G. A. (ed.): *The Political Works of James Harrington* (Cambridge: Cambridge University Press, 1977).

——: *Virtue, Commerce, and History* (Cambridge: Cambridge University Press, 1985).

Story, J.: *Discourse upon the Inauguration of the Author as Dane Professor of Law*, 1829; unpubd, Cornell Law School Collection.

Stourzh, G.: *Alexander Hamilton and the Idea of Republican Government* (Stanford, Calif.: Stanford University Press, 1970).

Wood, G. S.: *The Creation of the American Republic, 1776–1787* (Chapel Hill: University of North Carolina Press, 1969).

66

The rule of law

JOHN P. REID

T HE concept of the rule of law during the second half of the eighteenth century
is not easily defined as it meant one thing in North America and had for some
decades been taking on a quite different definition in Great Britain. In Great
Britain its scope and theory was narrowing from what it had been – or what its
exponents had tried to make it mean – in Stuart times. Put in historical perspective,
the definition of the rule of law in Great Britain had been changing from what it still
means in the twentieth-century United States to what it would mean in ninteenth-
and twentieth-century Great Britain. Put in terms of eighteenth-century common-law
jurisprudence, the concept of the rule of law in Great Britain was coming to mean
adherence to the command of the legislature and ceasing to mean adherence to
"right" over "power"[1]

I. CONTRASTING CONCEPTS OF THE RULE OF LAW

As an ideal, the concept of the rule of law in eighteenth-century Great Britain was a
support for liberty as liberty was then defined – as a restraint on governmental power,
especially arbitrary power, and less, as we would think of it, as liberating the individual.
One fundamental element of liberty was the certainty of law, and the certainty of law
was established, in part, by the rule of law. "Free Government is the protecting the
People in their Liberties by stated Rules," Thomas Gordon had pointed out earlier in
the century. "Only the Checks put upon Magistrates make Nations free," his colleague
John Trenchard agreed, "and only the want of such Checks makes them Slaves."[2] In
the American colonies the concept was summed up by the Connecticut clergymen
Jared Eliot. "Blessed be God. . . . We live under a Legal Government," he said, explaining
that by "Legal" he meant "Limited." "It is a Corner-Stone in our Political Building,
That no mans Life, Limb, Name *or Estate, shall be taken away but by his Peers and by the
known Laws of the Land.*"[3] What distinguished "Law and Freedom from Violence and
Slavery," Edmund Burke added, "is, that the property vested in the Subject by a
known Law – and forfeited by no delinquency defined by a known [law] could [not]
be taken away from him by any power or authority whatsoever."[4]

At its strongest, the rule of law was a general principle that government and
governed alike are subject to due process. In popular expression, the concept of the
rule of law defined government as "The empire of laws, and not of men,"[5] or
the circumscribing of power by "some settled Rule or Order of Operation."[6] In the
seventeenth century the ideal of the rule of law had obtained constitutional primacy
because the power it circumscribed was monarchy. "[I]t is one of the Fundamentals
of Law," the prosecutor of Charles I had asserted, "that the King is not above the

Law, but the Law [is] above the King."[7] Charles could be criminally charged because a prince disobeying the law was a "rebel."[8] "King Charles," an eighteenth-century writer explained, "either could not, or would not distinguish, between the executive power, which our constitution has lodged in the crown, and the supreme power, which our constitution hath lodged in the law of the land, and no where else."[9] When these words were written in 1771, "law of the land" may have meant something quite different in Great Britain than in the colonies. It is most unlikely that a majority of Britons at that time thought of "law of the land" or "rule of law" as expressing fundamental or immutable law, rather than merely positive law. The Crown might still be subject to the rule of law, but in Great Britain "law" in this sense was coming to mean what Parliament declared. It was that change in the concept of "law" – whether we call it fundamental, immutable, or constitutional – that American Whigs resisted.

2. BRITISH LAW DEFINED AS STATUTE

Although theory was changing and it is difficult to tell just when certain principles became dominant, it seems safe to assert that, by the age of the American Revolution in Great Britain, the rule of law no longer included the notion of the sovereignty of law over the ruler. It may even be that the rule of law had become procedural only, not substantive, holding that government actions must conform to legislative command while that command could change at legislative will. In other words, the rule of law now restrained power from violating liberty largely by limiting the definition of liberty to the legislatively permitted. "An *English* individual," a writer who thought American resistance in 1775 was legal explained, "cannot, by the supreme authority, be deprived of liberty, unless by virtue of some law, which his representative has had a part in framing."[10] The word "law" in this context had shrunk from meaning "right" to meaning "statute." It was enough that laws be promulgated and certain for the rule of law to serve the liberty of the individual. "To assert an absolute exemption from imprisonment in all cases." Blackstone protested, "is inconsistent with every idea of law . . .: but the glory of the English law consists in clearly defining the times, the causes, and the extent, when, wherefore, and to what degree, the imprisonment of the subject may be lawful."[11]

As understood in Great Britain, therefore, the principle of the rule of law may not have restrained parliamentary power so much as guided it. Certainty of procedure was perhaps its most basic and most universally recognized element, and meant, in John Locke's words, "to govern by *promulgated establish'd Laws*, not to be varied in particular Cases."[12] Almost as well known, although in eighteenth-century Great Britain as likely to be breached as to be honored, were the elements that punishment should not be *ex post facto* and property should not be taken without compensation. Another aspect of the rule of law was protection of legal rights. "[T]he very Essence of Government," as an anonymous commentator on revolutionary principles pointed out, "consists in making and executing Stated Rules, for the determining of all Civil Differences, and in doing all other Acts that tend to secure the Subjects against all Enemies Foreign and Domestick, in the quiet Possession of their legal Rights."[13] The most salient expression of the rule of law in eighteenth-century Great Britain, however, the one that American Whigs most likely thought of first when asked if Great Britain was ruled by the rule of law, was the principle of equal application. "Laws, in a Free State," it was said, should be equally applied. "[T]he Peer should possess no privilege destructive to the Commoner; the Layman obtain no Favour which is denied the Priest; nor the Necessitious excluded from the Justice which is granted to the Wealthy," or, in the words of Locke, there was but "one Rule for Rich and Poor, for the Favourite at Court, and the Country Man at Plough."[14]

3. AMERICANS AND ARBITRARY POWER

In the American colonies the concept of the rule of law was more English than contemporary British, that is, it was closer to the constitutional values of seventeenth-century England than to the newer constitutional understanding of eighteenth-century Great Britain. For Americans, the rule of law primarily meant to be free of arbitrary power. To understand what colonial Whigs meant by the rule of law, therefore, it is necessary to define what they (and eighteenth-century Britons) meant by arbitrary power, and to do that we must rid ourselves of twentieth-century thoughts about arbitrariness having something to do with despotism, tyranny, or cruel government. It may today, but that was not the legal definition in the eighteenth century. Then it was not the harshness, the brutality, or the certainty of the exercise of power that made government arbitrary. It was, rather, the possession of power unchecked. Tyrannical power was abuse of power, arbitrary power was power without restraint.

In eighteenth-century parlance on both sides of the Atlantic, arbitrary was the difference between liberty and slavery, right and power, constitutional and unconstitutional. To the eighteenth-century American legal mind, knowing what was arbitrary delineated the concept of the rule of law. "For it is certain," Jared Eliot reminded Connecticut's law-makers in 1738, *"That to the Constitution of every Government, Absolute Sovereignty must lodge somewhere.* So that according to this Maxim, Every Government must be Arbitrary and Despotick. The difference seems to be here: Arbitrary Despotick Government, is, When this Sovereign Power is directed by the Passions, Ignorance & Lust of them that Rule. And a Legal Government, is, When this Arbitrary & Sovereign Power puts it self under Restraints, and lays it self under Limitations."[15] It was, Viscount Bolingbroke had said, a matter of power and not of the type and structure of government. Whether power was vested in a single monarch, in "the *principal Persons of the Community,* or in the *whole Body of the People,*" was immaterial. What matters is whether power is without control. "Such Governments are Governments of *arbitrary Will,*" he concluded.[16]

Just as the eighteenth-century concept of arbitrariness should not be confused with cruelness or terror, for it could be benevolent, mild, and materially beneficial, so it should not be confounded with absoluteness. "[E]ven *absolute Power,*" John Locke pointed out, "where it is necessary, is *not Arbitrary* by being absolute, but is still limited by that reason, and confined to those ends, which required it in some Cases to be absolute," such as martial discipline which vests an army officer with power to order a trooper to die but cannot "command that Soldier to give him one penny of his Money."[17] Law was the distinction. If the officer acted within the parameters of the law, his absolute orders were not arbitrary. That element – law or the rule of law – was all important to eighteenth-century constitutional thought. For "court whigs", Reed Browning has pointed out – and also, it should be added, for most educated Britons and Americans – there were "but two types of government: arbitrary and lawful,"[18] or, as John Arbuthnott explained in 1733, "what is not legal is arbitrary."[19]

4. THE BRITISH AND PARLIAMENT

For the British of the age of the American Revolution this meaning of "legal" had changed as the constitutional principle emerged that Parliament could not be arbitrary in law. English constitutional history, especially the history of the Glorious Revolution, taught Britons that Parliament was the institutionalization of liberty, and, as a consequence, law that was the command of Parliament was the law of liberty. The Glorious Revolution had established the principle of parliamentary supremacy over the Crown. Once Parliament attempted to extend that supremacy by claiming parliamentary sovereignty over the law and the constitution, the American theory of the rule of law could not survive in the British constitutional world. The fact that the concept of the rule of law, for so long understood to be a barrier constraining the power of the Crown on behalf of liberty, would not be extended to restrain parliamentary power, sums up much of the American Revolution's constitutional controversy. Legal theory in Britain was drawing apart from legal theory in the colonies primarily on the issue of constitutional restraint on legislative authority. The difference was summarized by a pamphlet published in Philadelphia the year of the Declaration of Independence. "No country can be called *free* which is governed by an absolute power," the pamphleteer contended; "and it matters not whether it be an absolute royal power or an absolute legislative power, as the consequence will be the same to the people."[20] British lawyers may have been reluctant to do so, but soon they would acknowledge an absolute power in Parliament.

Americans may not have appreciated how deep the gulf had become. The realization that some Britons now equated law, liberty, and constitutionalism with parliamentary legislation could have staggered American constitutionalists had the fact sunk into their legal consciousness. They would never break free of the fundamentals of anti-Stuart constitutionalism in which power unrestrained was not legal. They could not see what difference it made for arbitrary decision to be legislative rather than monarchical. "There cannot be a more dangerous doctrine in a state, than to admit that the legislative power has a right to alter the constitution," another Philadelphian wrote, also in 1776. "For as the constitution limits the authority of the legislature; if the legislature can alter the constitution, they can give themselves what bounds they please."[21] It is not an exaggeration to suggest that the legal aspects of the American Revolution could be told inder the title *In Defense of the Rule of Law*.

REFERENCES

1. For the eighteenth-century dichotomy between "right" and "power" in jurisprudential theory, *see* John Phillip Reid: "In the taught tradition: the meaning of law in Massachusetts-Bay two hundred years ago," *Suffolk University Law Review*, 15 (summer 1980), 947–61.

2. Gordon: Letter of 20 January 1721, *Cato's Letters: or, Essays on Liberty, Civil and Religious, And other Important Subjects. In Four Volumes*, 6th edn. (London, 1755), 2: 249; Trenchard: Letter of 9 February 1722, *ibid.*, 4: 81.

3. Jared Eliot: *Give Cesar his Due. Or, the Obligation that Subjects are under to their Civil Rulers, as was shewed in a Sermon Preach'd before the General Assembly of the Colony of Connecticut at Hartford, May the 11th, 1738. The Day for the Election of the Honourable the Governour, the Deputy-Governour, and the Worshipful Assistants* (New London, Connecticut, 1738), 36.

4. Speech of Edmund Burke, Commons Debates, 26 May 1767, *The Writings and Speeches of Edmund Burke*, ed. Paul Langford (Oxford: Clarendon Press, 1981), 2: 65.

5. [Charles Inglis:] *The True Interest of America Impartially Stated, in Certain Strictures on a Pamphlet Intitled Common Sense*, 2nd edn. (Philadelphia, 1776), 12.

6. Anon.: *The Fatal Consequences of the Want of System in the Conduct of Public Affairs* (London, 1757), 2. 1722, *ibid.*, 4: 81.

7. John Cook: *King Charl[e]s his Case, an Appeal to all Rational Men, Concerning his Tryal at the High Court of Justice. Being for the most part that which was intended to have been delivered at the Bar, if the King had Pleaded to the Charge, and put himself upon a fair Tryal* (London, 1649), 6.

8. *Boston Evening-Post* (25 March 1771), p. 2, col. 1. *See also New York Evening-Post* (7 December 1747), repr. *Boston Evening-Post* (28 December 1747), p. 1, col. 2.

9. Anon.: *An Historical Essay on the English Constitution: Or, an impartial Inquiry into the Elective Power of the People, from the first Establishment of the Saxons in the Kingdom. Wherein the Right of Parliament, to Tax our distant Provinces, is explained, and justified, upon such constitutional Principles as will afford an equal Security to the Colonists, as to their Brethren at Home* (London, 1771), 80.

10. Anon.: *Resistance no Rebellion: In Answer to Doctor Johnson's Taxation no Tyranny* (London, 1775), 14.

11. William Blackstone: *Commentaries on the Laws of England* (Oxford, 1765–9), 3: 133.

12. John Locke: *Two Treatises of Government: a Critical Edition with an Introduction and Apparatus Criticus*, ed. Peter Laslett, 2nd edn. (Cambridge: 1967), Book 2, Sec. 142.

13. Anon.: *The Revolution and Anti-Revolution Principles Stated and Compar'd, the Constitution Explain'd and Vindicated, and the Justice and Necessity of Excluding the Pretender, Maintain'd against the Book Entituled Hereditary Right of the Crown of England Asserted* (London, 1714), 15.

14. [John Shebbeare:] *A Second Letter to the People of England on Foreign Subsidies, Subsidary Armies, and their Consequences to this Nation*, 4th edn. (London, 1756), 17; John Locke, *supra* note 12, Book 2, Sec. 142.

15. Jared Eliot: *supra* note 3, 36 footnote.

16. [Henry Saint John, Viscount Bolingbroke:] *A Dissertation upon Parties; In Several Letters to Caleb D'Anvers, Esq.*, 2nd edn. (London, 1735), 159.

17. John Locke: *supra* note 12, book 2, Sec. 139.

18. Reed Browning: *Political and Constitutional Ideas of the Court Whigs* (Baton Rouge: Louisiana State University Press, 1982), 196.

19. *The Freeholder's Political Catechism. Written by Dr. [John] Arbuthnot* ([London], 1769), 9.

20. Anon.: *Four Letters on Interesting Subjects* (Philadelphia, 1776), 19.

21. Demophilus: *The Genuine Principles of the Ancient Saxon, or English Constitution Carefully collected from the best Authorities: With some Observations, on their peculiar fitness, for the United Colonies in general, and Pennsylvania in particular* (Philadelphia, 1776), 35.

FURTHER READING

Reid, John Phillip: "In legitimate strips: the concept of 'arbitrary,' the supremacy of Parliament, and the coming of the American Revolution," *Hofstra Law Review*, 5 (spring 1977), 459–99.

———: *The Concept of Liberty in the Age of the American Revolution* (Chicago: University of Chicago Press, 1988).

Thompson, E. P.: *Whigs and Hunters: the Origin of the Black Act* (1975).

67

Consent

DONALD S. LUTZ

AMERICANS justified their break with Britain on the grounds that they should be subject only to laws to which they had consented. The Declaration of Independence is deservedly famous for stating a robust doctrine of consent, and for reflecting the importance of the concept for American political thought. The American notion of consent was partly derived from English common law, but between 1620 and 1776 the colonists developed a perspective that varied considerably from the one held in Britain. The process was not one of consciously modifying an existing theory. Rather, the colonists first developed institutions that met their needs and strongly held values, and then they appropriated from European thinkers theories that supported what they were already doing. By 1776 Americans had a fully articulated theory of consent undergirding a set of well-established consent-based institutions. An important feature of American consent theory by this time was the assumption of popular sovereignty, an idea that had never taken hold in Britain. Between 1776 and 1787 theory and institutions evolved in the direction of a more active, direct, and continuous notion of consent. The United States Constitution successfully combined effective government with institutions of consent at the national level, although an ambiguity in consent theory remained for Americans to resolve.

I. THE MAGNA CARTA AND COLONIAL CHARTERS

Consent as a political concept in England is usually traced back to the Magna Carta signed in 1215 AD. King John had been forced by his barons to agree to a number of articles limiting the power of the monarch, including one that held the king could not tax the barons without their consent. Over time the meetings for obtaining consent evolved into Parliament, a body of representatives elected by men of property. Although Magna Carta was an agreement between the aristocracy and the king, the wording of the tax provision was very general and supported the conclusion that no man should be taxed without his consent. As a result of Magna Carta, therefore, the English linked consent with taxation, considered an elected legislature the primary consent-giving institution, and in the long-run viewed consent as being relevant to any property owner whether a member of the aristocracy or not.

The link between Magna Carta and the American Revolution was the colonial charter. All charters, beginning with Queen Elizabeth's Letters Patent to Sir Humphrey Gilbert (1578), contained two critical provisions. First, English colonists brought with them the rights of Englishmen, which meant the common law. Magna Carta had for several hundred years been printed as the first common law statute, and thus Englishmen brought with them the right not to be taxed without their consent, and the implied right to representation in an elected legislature as the means for giving consent. The second key provision in colonial charters was to make explicit the implied right to an elected legislature. Colonists were allowed to erect their own local governments, as long as the laws they passed were not contrary to the laws of England.

However, important differences in their circumstances led the colonists to develop a markedly different set of institutions to those found in Britain. The right to vote in England had been defined by statute since 1430 to require the ownership of enough property to earn 40 shillings in rent per year, which usually amounted to about 50 acres. The distribution of land by the late eighteenth century produced a regularly voting electorate of about 5 or 6 per cent of adult males. In America, where land was cheap and plentiful, and with no prior claims of ownership by the aristocracy and gentry to contest, a similar 50-acre requirement enfranchised most white adult males. Thus, even though American statutes generally required about the same amount of property in order to vote, the electorate in America was about ten times the percentage of the male population as it was in England.

Forced to rely upon themselves for survival, the colonists produced a considerable number of foundation documents designed to elicit cooperation from everyone. The Mayflower Compact (1620), the Pilgrim Code of Law (1636), the Fundamental Orders of Connecticut (1639), and the Rhode Island Acts and Orders (1647) are some early examples. The last three effectively functioned as to what we now call constitutions.

These documents had several important characteristics in common, one of which was that they were signed by all adult males. The signatures showed that consent for the political institutions created by each document was being given by the people as a whole. The American view thus required popular consent, and implied popular sovereignty, before there was a political theory justifying either. In New England Thomas Hooker and Roger Williams wrote tracts during the 1630s and 1640s which argued for popular consent based on religious principles derived from a dissenting Protestant reading of the Bible. Religious reasoning was important for explaining the emergence of documents founded upon popular consent in New England before anywhere else, but similar documents were eventually written throughout the colonies.

Colonial documents of political foundation thus rested upon *de facto* popular consent. These documents made an elective legislature the central consent-giving body, as was the case in Britain, but then tied the legislature to popular consent through annual elections by a broadly defined electorate. All of this happened before James Harrington, Thomas Hobbes, Algernon Sidney, JOHN LOCKE, or CHARLES-LOUIS DE SECONDAT, Baron de Montesquieu, wrote their influential tracts on consent. Eventually, the theories of these Europeans were appropriated to justify and underwrite what had already been developed institutionally in the colonies.

2. COMPETING THEORIES OF CONSENT

When the British Parliament levied a series of taxes in the Stamp Act (1765) and the Townshend Acts (1767) to defray expenses from the recent war with France, the colonists objected. Benjamin Franklin testified before Parliament that the colonists did not object to paying their fair share for a war that was fought, in part, to protect them, but they were only willing to pay taxes levied by legislatures elected through their own consent. Since the colonists were not represented in Parliament, any tax levied by it upon the colonies was taxation without their consent. The colonists also argued that they were operating under charters from the king, and these charters granted them the right to create their own legislatures and elect their own representatives.

The argument made little sense to most Britons, since the vast majority of British subjects could not vote yet were considered represented in Parliament. It was a matter of more than numbers. The British by this date saw Parliament as sovereign, whereas the Americans saw the people as sovereign. The argument was rooted at least as much in divergent interests – British mercantilism versus colonial aspirations for economic development, for instance – as it was about constitutional principles. But their differing views on consent inclined the Americans to make a case they found to be reasonable and compelling given their experiences, while at the same time inclining the British to defend a position reasonable and compelling from their experiences. Efforts at conciliation often foundered upon conflicting habits of thought, and the mental blinders they produced, as much as on an inability or unwillingness to compromise on concrete political or economic issues. The American Revolution thus resulted, at least in part, from competing theories of consent.

3. "PASSIVE" AND "ACTIVE" CONSENT: LOCKE AND SIDNEY

John Locke's *Two Treatises of Civil Government* (1690) had an ironic place in the dispute. By British standards Locke was too insistent upon Parliament's dependence on the consent of the majority, and therefore he was largely ignored by British commentators in the late eighteenth century. By American standards Locke did not impute enough of a role to majority consent, but he was widely cited by Americans in a manner that attributed to him a more radical theory than he actually defended. In fact, the position argued by the Americans was more congruent with Algernon Sidney's theory in *Discourses Concerning Government* (1698), although largely by accident rather than through conscious borrowing.

Both Sidney and Locke saw civil society as resting upon a compact in which each individual consents to be bound by the will of the majority. Whatever form of government the majority establishes is thereby presumed to rest upon the consent of all. In other words, the original compact has two parts or two aspects. The first part is a unanimous agreement to be bound by the majority, and the second is the agreement by the majority to a particular form of government. This much Sidney, Locke, and the Americans had in common.

However, Locke's theory of consent is weaker than that advocated by Sidney and the Americans for two reasons. First of all, Locke argues that, when a person comes of age, that person gives his tacit consent to the compact by not leaving the country or resisting the government, and by taking advantage of the laws, especially those protecting property. In such a fashion, says Locke, most of us pass without noticing into civil society. Second, Locke has little to say about consent beyond its role in the original compact. He does not argue for the necessity of elections or any other instrument of continuing consent. This is not enough for Sidney. He denies that tacit consent is meaningful. Every person must willingly and consciously give his consent. Furthermore, government must rest on continuously recurring consent, otherwise the notion of consent is vitiated.

The differences in these two theories of consent can be put another way. For Sidney, the unanimous consent upon which the civil society rests in the first place should be an actual event which all newcomers must re-enact. Americans had already developed

636

the concept of a written constitution signed by all relevant people, or by representatives elected for that express purpose. Newcomers could be added to the civil society by taking an oath to uphold it. This is how Algernon Sidney would have it done, and it might be termed an "active" theory of consent.

Locke, on the other hand, had a "passive" version. As long as one did not specifically object, or act in a manner so as to indicate rejection, consent was assumed. Political theorists frequently refer to Locke's approach as the "acquiescence model." In effect, Locke's theory was that a government had the consent of the people to exist and to act until those people said "no." Sidney's theory was that the government did not have the consent of the people either to exist or to act until the people explicitly said "yes."

We can state the two theories of consent in a more formal manner. Sidney's active, direct, and continuous consent refers to a situation where the right of one man to act in a certain way is conditional upon another man's having expressed the wish that he act that way. Locke's passive, indirect, discontinuous consent involves always acting in a manner that the doer knows, or is assumed to know, will not prevent another from acting. Not only is Locke's notion of consent passive, note that two men need not even meet in order for one to consent to the other's acting – hence such consent is indirect. In Sidney's version there must be some form of direct interaction, and the interaction must take place either continuously or with some frequency.

4. PARLIAMENTARY AND POPULAR SOVEREIGNTY

One can see, then, that the institution of annual elections reflects Sidney's theory, while Locke would not require such frequency – he never argued for it. Further, Sidney would expect the legislature to mirror the people at large, and he would also expect the people to send demands or instructions to their representatives, instructions which would be heeded. Locke, on the other hand, would expect representatives to deliberate for the common good more or less free from popular instructions, but subject to removal if a majority protested. American consent theory strained toward Sidney's active, direct, continuous approach, although there were a number of Americans who professed Locke's acquiescence version as well. Regardless of the differences, Americans had a strong tendency to believe that government must originate in the consent of the people; whether in Locke's sense or Sidney's sense did not matter. The British, on the other hand, did not think in terms of popular sovereignty. After the Glorious Revolution of 1688, Parliament was held to have ultimate power, and the British developed the legal fiction of the "king in Parliament" to define British sovereignty. Americans had by 1776 come to view parliamentary sovereignty as incompatible with popular sovereignty.

Americans were concerned not only with how to structure the act of consent upon which government rested, but also with who should give consent, on what range of issues, and through what processes or procedures. The broadest-known existing electorate became even broader. Efforts were made to tie legislatures more closely to the consent of the majority. Annual elections were already in use in every state, but some went further. For example, Pennsylvania required that before a bill become a law it had to be passed a second time by next year's legislature, with the people being able to question members of the legislature during the intervening election. Most interesting is what happened to the framing and ratification process for constitutions themselves.

FIGURE 52 "The Political Cartoon, for the Year 1775": George III and Lord Bute are led towards a ravine in a carriage driven by Lord Mansfield and drawn by two horses named Pride and Obstinacy who are trampling on the Constitution and the Magna Carta. While Lords Chatham and Camden try to stop the carriage, a group of English clergymen, Lord North among them, look on with approval. On the left some Scotsmen make plans at a table; on the right a Member of Parliament offers bribes to the crowd; America, the city across the sea, burns (from the "Westminster Magazine," May 1775).

Britain had no written constitution, yet it was assumed by Americans that government had to rest upon such consent-giving instruments. However, it had been a century or more since those now known as Americans had engaged in constitution writing, and at first the method for consenting to a new constitution did not completely match the theory. The first six state constitutions were written and adopted by state legislatures, although in each case the legislature met in special session as a convention. Even with the legislatures tied to a broadly defined electorate through annual elections this did not seem congruent with popular consent in a direct sense. In August 1776, three months after the Declaration of Independence, Delaware became the first state to elect a special body to write a state constitution, followed in 1777 by New York, whose legislature felt that "the right of framing, creating or new modeling civil government is, and ought to be in the people." Such practice became standard after this, although not until the Massachusetts document in 1780 and the second New Hampshire constitution in 1784 was the document also submitted to the people for approval in a popular referendum. These two changes made the practice of consent theory completely congruent with popular sovereignty. The American commitment to popular consent along the lines described by Algernon Sidney thus moved them to invent new constitutional methods for coherently and consistently expressing this conviction.

5. THE DECLARATION OF INDEPENDENCE

Consent tended to become so active, direct, and continuous after 1776 that some, such as James Madison, feared American institutions would be undermined by the very consent theory upon which they were built. Madison and other Federalists were able to design a national Constitution which combined effective government with consent-giving institutions at the national level.

The Declaration of Independence is the document in which the American people consent to the creation of a civil society known as the United States of America. It proclaims itself to be a unanimous declaration in the title, and the list of signatures at the end is the familiar American method going back to the Mayflower Compact (1620) of consenting to the creation of a civil society through one's own signature or the signature of an elected representative. The United States Constitution is the agreement creating a form of government. We have here, then, the documentary expression of the double compact advocated by both Locke and Sidney, but implemented in the active sense preferred by Sidney. Both agreements, however, reflect an ambiguity in the American notion of consent.

The Declaration does not address a situation where individual Americans are in a state of nature. Each lives under an already operating government based upon his consent at the colony level. Rather, it is a situation where "it becomes necessary for one people to dissolve the Political Bands which have connected them with another." The people are acting, not a collection of individuals. Most of the document is a list of abuses which Americans had suffered as a people at the hands of the English. Communitarianism, not individualism, permeates the list of abuses. The phrase "all men are created equal" thus has a double meaning with respect to consent. Liberty and equality pertain to individuals in the state of nature, but are focused upon the community in civil society. The American people are equal to the English people precisely because both peoples are composed of individuals who would be equal in the state of nature with the same ability to give or withhold consent. Put most directly, the Declaration enunciates the basic American view that consent is given individually because consent rests on all individuals, but the agreement collects the individual acts of consent to create the consent of the people, an entity in itself.

The important question then becomes, does the Declaration of Independence rest upon the consent of all Americans directly, or upon their consent collected as members of a state? In the second instance consent would be direct from individual to state, but indirect from individual to nation, so that the agreement is really between the states as collective entities. The evidence in both the Declaration and the Constitution is contradictory. The central position of federalism in the Constitution, whereby a person is simultaneously a citizen of a state and the United States, clearly implies that we should read the two founding documents as being based upon the simultaneous consent of both individual Americans and collections of individuals in the states. This paradox, or ambiguity, in American consent theory guaranteed that the concept of consent would continue to play a central role in future American politics.

FURTHER READING

Franklin, Julian S.: *John Locke and the Theory of Sovereignty* (Cambridge: Cambridge University Press, 1978).
Lutz, Donald S.: *Popular Consent and Popular Control: Whig Political Theory in the Early State Constitutions* (Baton Rouge: Louisiana State University Press, 1980).

Morgan, Edmund S.: *Inventing the People: the Rise of Popular Sovereignty in England and America* (New York: W. W. Norton, 1988).

Parsons, Theophilus: *The Essex Result* (Newburyport, Mass.: 1778); repr. in *The Popular Sources of Authority*, ed. Oscar Handlin and Mary Handlin (Cambridge, Mass.: Harvard University Press, 1966), 324–65.

Partridge, P. H.: *Consent and Consensus* (New York: Praeger Publishers, 1971).

Plamenatz, J. P.: *Consent, Freedom, and Political Obligation*, 2nd edn. (Oxford: Oxford University Press, 1968).

Pole, J. R.: *Political Representation in England and the Origins of the American Republic* (Berkeley: University of California Press, 1971).

68

Happiness

JAN LEWIS

THE term "happiness" is a key word in the revolutionary vocabulary because American patriots often asserted its assurance as the object of government and its pursuit as one of mankind's inalienable rights. Both of these usages of the concept have been immortalized in the second paragraph of the Declaration of Independence, although the precise meaning attached to the word as well as the possible sources for Thomas Jefferson's phrasing have long been contested by scholars. It is worth quoting this section of the Declaration in its entirety, for it establishes the context for understanding the meaning of happiness not only to the revolutionary generation, but also to all those who have debated it since then:

> We hold these truths to be self-evident, that all men are created equal, that they are endowed by their Creator with certain unalienable Rights, that among these are Life, Liberty and the pursuit of Happiness. – That to secure these rights, Governments are instituted among Men, deriving their just powers from the consent of the governed, – That whenever any Form of Government, becomes destructive of these ends, it is the Right of the People to alter or to abolish it, and to institute new Government, laying its foundation on such principles and organizing powers in such form, as to them shall seem most likely to effect their Safety and Happiness. (Becker, 1969, p. 186).

Jefferson had used the term happiness a third time in his rough draft of the Declaration, in the penultimate paragraph, when, after rehearsing the Revolutionaries' grievances against their "British brethren," he observed that "the road to happiness and to glory is open to us too; we will climb apart from them" (Becker, 1969, p. 169). Although this section was dropped from the version adopted and signed in Philadelphia, there is no record that either of the other uses of "happiness" was questioned or debated. Therefore we may conclude that the meaning of the concept was either so clear and commonly understood that no comment was required, or that its connotation was so vague and ambiguous that each could attach to it his own definition.

Not until almost half a century had passed would the sources – and hence the intent – of the happiness passages be questioned. Then, John Adams pointed to James Otis's pamphlet *The Rights of the British Colonies Asserted and Proved* (Boston, 1764) as the model, and Richard Henry Lee to John Locke's *Two Treatises of Government* (1690). Both Adams and Lee were correct, at least to the extent that both the philosophy and phrasing of the Declaration, including the happiness passages, were strikingly similar to those of works known to have circulated in the colonies in the years before 1776. Jefferson himself disclaimed originality, saying in a letter to Lee (8 May 1825) that the Declaration was "intended to be an expression of the American mind . . . all its authority rests on the harmonizing sentiments of the day" (Koch and Peden, 1944, p. 719) – not only Locke, but Aristotle, Cicero, Sidney, and others (*see* Chapter 28). Most of those who have interpreted the meaning of happiness in the Declaration since have followed Lee's lead and found in Locke the most important key to Jefferson's intent. Recently, scholars who believe that revolutionary theorists drew as much, if not more, from Scottish Enlightenment thinkers have argued that happiness was a social more than an individualist concept (*see* Chapter 9, §§1 and 6).

I. THE INFLUENCE OF LOCKE: PROPERTY AS A CONDITION OF HAPPINESS

The case for Locke's influence – stated perhaps most forcefully by Carl Becker, who wrote in *The Declaration of Independence* (1922) that "Jefferson copied Locke" – rests upon the similarity of reasoning and rhetoric both. The entire document, and especially the first paragraph of the Declaration, may be read as a restatement of Locke's doctrines of natural rights, the compact theory of government, and the right to resist tyranny. It has been argued that Jefferson merely substituted the rhetorically more felicitous "pursuit of happiness" for Locke's characteristic invocation of "property," and that consequently "the pursuit of happiness" should be translated as "property." Locke, incidentally, never used the precise phrase "life, liberty, and property," but instead spoke of "life, liberty, and estate" and "lives, liberties, and fortunes" (Locke, 1690, pp. 387, 420), and intended the term "property" to embrace all three elements of that which he believed a man possessed by natural right (p. 414). Nonetheless, the term "life, liberty, and property" had been used in important revolutionary documents, so there is good authority for interpreting "happiness" as "property." The Declaration of Colonial Rights and Grievances, adopted by the First Continental Congress on 1 October 1774, asserted that the colonists were "entitled to life, liberty and property" (Morris, 1970, p. 132), and James Otis in *The Rights of the British Colonies Asserted and Proved* (1764) said that government was designed "above all things to provide for the security, the quiet, and happy enjoyment of life, liberty, and property" (Otis, in Schlesinger, 1964, p. 326). The Virginia Declaration of Rights (June 1776), written by George Mason, noted that

> all men are created equally free and independent, and have certain inherent natural rights, of which they cannot, by any compact, deprive or divest their posterity; among which are the enjoyment of life and liberty, with the means of acquiring and possessing property, and pursuing and obtaining happiness and safety. (Mason, in Jones, 1953, p. 12).

Jefferson's debt to Mason and, if not as directly, Locke is clear. That "happiness" might mean "property" was one of "the harmonizing sentiments of the day."

To say that the philosophy of the Declaration was Lockean and that happiness ought to be translated as property is to underscore the individualistic and contractarian aspects of revolutionary thought. Such an interpretation suggests that the purpose of government is to protect the individual and to secure his rights and possessions. Indeed, Locke wrote that "the great and chief end of men's uniting into commonwealths, and putting themselves under government, is the preservation of their property" (Locke, 1690, p. 412). The common good entailed the protection of the individual and his property. The Lockean reading of the meaning of happiness likewise implies that human happiness proceeds from the individual's enjoyment, improvement, and use of his possessions. It is well known that Jefferson and other Revolutionaries believed that property was prerequisite to individual independence, and hence citizenship, so that a Lockean interpretation of happiness need not be read as narrowly economic or necessarily proto-capitalist. At the time of the Revolution, most American political writers believed that their society was uniquely egalitarian, that property was held or was available to virtually all white men, and that, as James Madison later recalled, "a provision for the rights of persons was supposed to include of itself those of property" (Madison, in Wood, 1969, p. 412). Protecting property and preserving liberty were virtually identical, or, as Locke had seen it, the one included the other.

2. THE EIGHTEENTH-CENTURY USE OF THE TERM

Interpreting "happiness" as "property" is therefore consistent with the tenets of republicanism (*see* Chapter 73, §1). Nonetheless, some of the scholars who have illuminated the republican dimension to revolutionary thought have found the Lockean reading of the meaning of happiness deficient. They note that Jefferson had abundant opportunity to use the word "property" in the Declaration, but clearly chose not to. Moreover, Jefferson recommended that the Marquis de La Fayette excise the inalienable right of property (*propriété*) from the draft of the Declaration of Human Rights that he wrote for France in 1788 (Willis, 1978, p. 230). Perhaps Jefferson had reasons other than felicity of style for naming the pursuit of happiness, but not property, as an unalienable right.

Those who have questioned the Lockean, individualist interpretation of "happiness" have observed that the term was in wide use among eighteenth-century political and moral theorists, so that, when Jefferson chose it, he intended it to evoke the meanings associated with happiness rather than those attached to property. When theorists used the term, they usually differentiated between a social and an individual happiness. The distinction is most clear in John Adams's *Thoughts on Government* (1776), where it is noted that "upon this point all speculative politicians will agree, that the happiness of society is the end of government, as all divines and moral philosophers will agree that the happiness of the individual is the end of man" (Adams, 1851). Like Adams, most political writers concerned themselves primarily with the social construction of happiness. Josiah Quincy, Jr., in his *Observations on the Act of Parliament Commonly Called the Boston Port-Bill* (1774), claimed that the object of government was "the greatest happiness of the greatest number" (Quincy, in Schlesinger, 1964, p. 326), while Richard Henry Lee hoped, a month after the signing of the Declaration, that "by a wise and just confederation, the happiness of America will be secured" (Lee, 1911). Three years later, in his *Bill for the More General Diffusion of Knowledge*, Jefferson himself suggested that a system of public education would be "expedient for promoting public happiness" (Jefferson, 1779). It was this public or social happiness that Jefferson seemed to have in mind when he wrote, in the Declaration, that it is the right of the people to create, alter, or abolish government in order "to effect their safety and happiness."

3. WILSON, BURLAMAQUI, AND HUTCHESON: PUBLIC HAPPINESS

When revolutionary theorists spoke of the happiness of society, they seemed to intend more than the sum total of individual happinesses. Even if it is granted that the phrase "the pursuit of happiness" derives from Locke and means the right of the individual to be secure in his property, there is considerable evidence that revolutionary thinkers understood something different by public happiness. The meaning of this term is suggested by one of the other works commonly supposed to be a source for the Declaration. Jefferson copied portions of James Wilson's *Considerations on the Nature and Extent of the Legislative Authority of the British Parliament* (1774) into his *Commonplace Book* although, curiously, not this passage, which bears a striking resemblance to the second paragraph of the Declaration:

> All men are, by nature, equal and free: no one has a right to any authority over another without his consent: all lawful government is founded in the consent of those who are subject to it: such consent was given with a view to ensure and to increase the happiness of the governed, above what they would enjoy in an independent and unconnected state of nature. The consequence is that the happiness of the society is the first law of every government. (Wilson, in Becker, 1969, p. 108)

As Jefferson would later do, Wilson invoked both the Lockean social compact theory of government and the public conceptualization of happiness.

Wilson cited as his source the Swiss jurist Jean Jacques Burlamaqui, who held that God, "by creating us, proposed our preservation, perfection, and happiness" (Burlamaqui, 1807). Burlamaqui believed, consequently, that individuals had an obligation to pursue their happiness, and that this duty preceded any actions by men themselves. The pursuit of happiness, then, was a "primitive" right, whereas property – and the consequent right to protect it – was "adventitious," proceeding from men's efforts to satisfy their wants. Jefferson's enumeration of the pursuit of happiness as one of mankind's unalienable rights, then, is consistent with the views expressed in Burlamaqui's *Principles of Natural and Politic Law*, a French edition of which he purchased in 1769 (White, 1978, p. 37).

Another of Burlamaqui's modifications of Locke is relevant to an understanding of the meaning of "happiness." Like Locke, Burlamaqui rejected the notion of innate ideas, but, while Locke believed that moral truths could be discerned by reason, Burlamaqui attempted to reconcile Locke's rationalism with the doctrines of the Scottish Enlightenment philosopher Francis Hutcheson, who held that men were born with an innate moral sense. According to Morton White, Burlamaqui believed that both reason and the moral sense were inherent, that both lead to the truth, and that "reason verifies what the moral sense first brings to our attention" (White, 1978, p. 111). At the time he wrote the Declaration, Jefferson seems to have followed Burlamaqui in subscribing to both a Lockean rationalism and a Scottish Enlightenment sensationalism, and, like Burlamaqui, he generally gave priority to reason, which verified, clarified, and developed the impressions conveyed by the moral sense.

This understanding of Jefferson's epistemology may clarify his use of the term "happiness," for Garry Wills has recently argued that Jefferson's intellectual debt was primarily to the Scottish Enlightenment philosophers, particularly Hutcheson, and that, consequently, we should look to Hutcheson for an understanding of "happiness." Hutcheson believed that it is benevolence that is the source of happiness, for we become happy "when we reflect upon our having done virtuous actions." Because "the surest way to promote ... private happiness [is] to do publicly useful actions," happiness might be attained only in society. And it followed that "the action is best which procures the greatest happiness of the greatest numbers" and that "the general happiness is the supreme end of all political union" (Hutcheson, 1755, 1726). American revolutionary theorists who echoed Hutcheson were not utilitarians, for they grounded happiness in a "self-evident" truth, perceived by an intuitive reason or an innate moral sense, rather than in social usefulness. Nor were they individualists, for they held that happiness derived not from the gratification of self-interest, but from doing good for others.

4. FROM COMMUNALISM TO INDIVIDUALISM

At the time the Declaration was written, both the Lockean and Hutchesonian definitions of "happiness" were in use among American revolutionary theorists. Whether by accident or intent, when Jefferson harmonized the "sentiments of the day," he invoked both the individualist and the social meanings of the term. Yet at the time he wrote, there was no apparent inconsistency, for few saw any necessary conflict between the rights of the individual and the welfare of the entire society. Just as Jefferson believed he could harmonize the sentiments of the day, so most revolutionary thinkers believed that a properly working government could harmonize the interests of its citizens, securing simultaneously and reciprocally the happiness of the individual and the society.

Over the course of the Revolution, this inherently unstable consensus on the meaning of happiness would fracture. The factious and self-interested actions of the American people themselves convinced Madison, among others, that the individual pursuing his own happiness might undermine that of the society at large; it appeared evident that the interests of the individual and the society were not identical. Indeed, it is not clear that the American people, as distinguished from revolutionary ideologues, conceptualized happiness in public terms. Jack P. Greene has suggested that the conditions of settlement of the colonies so enhanced individual autonomy that, by the time of the Revolution, at least, the pursuit of happiness meant, essentially, personal independence – the ability to provide for oneself and one's family and be free from the intrusions of government or society (Greene, 1988). Such a notion of independence was, of course, profoundly individualistic and essentially Lockean in its conceptualization. To be sure, historians have debated precisely when the balance in America was tipped from communalism to individualism, but it is generally agreed that the spread of an individualist practice of happiness was one of the underlying social causes of the Revolution, and that the Revolution itself only exacerbated that trend (*see* Chapter 6, §§2, 3, and 4). Whatever its intent, the Declaration's phrase "pursuit of happiness" seemed to legitimate the individualistic strivings of the American people.

In the decades after the Revolution, American men and women would come to define happiness almost exclusively in private, personal terms. If happiness retained its Lockean association with property and, consequently, material well-being, it also acquired an emotional connotation, as men and women came to expect that they should find happiness at home, in the intimate relationships of the family. In this sense, the history of the concept "happiness" is similar to that of "virtue," a related term, and one equally significant in the revolutionary vocabulary. As Ruth H. Bloch has demonstrated, the term "virtue" had two meanings: public virtue referred to the willingness of the individual to sacrifice his self-interest for the public good, while private virtue suggested a number of personal qualities, such as piety and frugality (Bloch, 1987). In the decades after the Revolution, "virtue" was stripped of its public meaning, so that it eventually came to be associated almost entirely with admirable personal characteristics, especially those of women (*see* Chapter 63, §§4 and 5). Although the meaning of happiness was never feminized in the same way, it also lost its public connotations, so that, ultimately, most Americans would define and pursue it in private and personal ways. It was left for later generations to rediscover the more complex understanding of happiness that was embraced by Jefferson and his colleagues in the revolutionary endeavor.

FURTHER READING

Adams, John: "Thoughts on Government," *Works of John Adams*, ed. C.F. Adams (Boston, 1851), IV, 193; repr. in White, 1978, 233.

Becker, Carl L.: *The Declaration of Independence: A Study in the History of Political Ideas* (1922); 3rd edn. (New York: Alfred A. Knopf, 1969).

Bloch, Ruth H.: "The gendered meanings of virtue in revolutionary America," *Signs: Journal of Women in Culture and Society*, 13 (1987), 37–58.

Burlamaqui, Jean Jacques: *Principles of Natural and Political Law*, trans. Thomas Nugent (Cambridge, Mass.: 1807), Part II, Chapter IV, Section VI; repr. in White (1978), 162.

Ganter, Herbert Lawrence: "Jefferson's 'pursuit of happiness' and some forgotten men," *William and Mary Quarterly*, 16 (1936), 422–34, 558–85.

Greene, Jack P.: *Pursuits of Happiness: the Social Development of Early Modern British Colonies and the Formation of American Culture* (Chapel Hill: University of North Carolina Press, 1988).

Hamowy, Ronald: "Jefferson and the Scottish Enlightenment: a critique of Garry Wills's *Inventing America: Jefferson's Declaration of Independence*," *William and Mary Quarterly*, 36 (1979), 503–23.

Hutcheson, Francis: *An Inquiry into the Original of our Ideas of Beauty and Virtue*, 2nd edn. (1726), 177; repr. in Margaret Canovan: "The un-Benthamite utilitarianism of Joseph Priestly," *Journal of the History of Ideas*, 45 (1984), 436.

——: *A System of Moral Philosophy*, Vol. II (1755); repr. in Wills, 1978, 252.

Jefferson, Thomas: *Bill for the More General Diffusion of Knowledge* (1779), in *The Papers of Thomas Jefferson*, ed. Julian Boyd (Princeton, 1950), II, 526–33; repr. In David M. Post: "Jeffersonian revisions of Locke: education, property-rights, and liberty," *Journal of the History of Ideas*, 47 (1986), 153.

Koch, Adrienne, and Peden, William: *The Life and Selected Writings of Thomas Jefferson* (New York: Modern Library, 1944).

Lee, Richard Henry: *The Letters of Richard Henry Lee*, ed. James C. Ballagh (New York: Macmillan, 1911), I, 211; repr. in Ganter (1936), 585.

Locke, John: *Works*, 10 vols. Vol. 5, *Two Treatises of Government* (1690) (London: Thomas Tegg, 1823), repr. (Germany: Scientia Verlag Allen, 1963).

Madison, James: "Observations on Jefferson's Draft of a Constitution for Virginia" (1788), *The Papers of Thomas Jefferson*, ed. Julian Boyd (Princeton, 1950), VI, 310; also repr. in Gordon S. Wood: *The Creation of the American Republic, 1776–1787* (Chapel Hill: University of North Carolina Press, 1969), 410.

Mason, George, *Virginia Declaration of Rights* (1776), in Kate Mason Rowland, *The Life of George Mason* (New York and London: 1892), Appendix X, I, 434; also in Howard Mumford Jones: *The Pursuit of Happiness* (Ithaca: Cornell University Press, 1953; repr. 1966), 12.

Morris, Richard B. (ed.): *The American Revolution, 1763–1783* (New York: Harper and Row, 1970).

Otis, James: *The Rights of the British Colonies Asserted and Proved* (Boston: 1764), in *Some Political Writings*, ed. Charles F. Mullett (University of Missouri Studies, 4, 1929), 309; also repr. in Arthur M. Schlesinger: "The lost meaning of 'the pursuit of happiness'," *William and Mary Quarterly*, 21 (1964), 326.

Quincy, Josiah: "Observations on the Act of Parliament commonly called the Boston Port-Bill," *Memoir of the Life of Josiah Quincy, Junior, of Massachusetts, 1774–1775*, 2nd edn. (Boston: 1874), 323; also repr. in Arthur M. Schlesinger: "The lost meaning of 'the pursuit of happiness'," *William and Mary Quarterly*, 21 (1964), 326.

White, Morton: *The Philosophy of the American Revolution* (New York: Oxford University Press, 1978).

Wills, Garry: *Inventing America: Jefferson's Declaration of Independence* (New York: Doubleday, 1978).

Wilson, James, *Considerations on the Nature and Extent of the Legislative Authority of the British Parliament* (1774), repr. in Becker, 1969, 108.

69

Suffrage and representation

ROSEMARIE ZAGARRI

BEGINNING in 1962, the United States Supreme Court embarked on a series of decisions which mandated that all state legislatures be apportioned according to the principle of "one person, one vote." This principle actually embodies two distinct concepts: the idea that each person is entitled to the vote and the notion that each person's vote should be worth the same as every other person's. The former is achieved through universal adult suffrage; the latter through numerical apportionment, which makes representation in the legislature proportionate to population. The idea of "one person, one vote" first appeared during the American Revolution. In the years thereafter it gained a permanent place in both the state and the federal governments. However, it took almost two centuries for these principles to be fully realized in practice.

I. CONCEPTS OF REPRESENTATION IN THE REVOLUTIONARY ERA

Representation was at the center of the American controversy with Great Britain. As the colonies developed, each one established a system of representative government, modeled on Parliament, in which the lower house of the assembly was popularly elected. The colonists believed that only their colonial assemblies – their elected representatives – had the right to tax them. Before the Sugar and Stamp Acts of 1764 and 1765, Parliament had never attempted to tax the colonists. Previous Acts had been designed to regulate trade or to provide for the defense of the colonies. In the wake of the budget crisis following the Seven Years' War, however, Parliament tried for the first time to pass laws for the explicit purpose of generating revenue – in other words, to tax the colonists without their consent.

In the debate over the Stamp Act, it became clear that concepts of representation in England and the colonies had diverged. Defenders of the Stamp Act in Britain promoted an idea known as "virtual' representation. Parliament, they said, legislated for the good of the entire realm. Although Americans did not send representatives to the House of Commons, their interests were known and taken into account there. The colonists, they argued, were as well represented as any non-elector in England. The Americans, however, insisted that only their elected representatives could tax them. They rejected virtual representation and the comparison with non-electors in England. Because of the large distance separating England and America, Members of Parliament could not have a direct knowledge of the colonists' situation or interests. They claimed that even those who could not vote in England could personally convey their needs or express their displeasure to Members of Parliament. Even more important, in England representatives were subject to the same laws as the people. This was not

648

the case with America. Representatives in the House of Commons could impose harsh taxes on the colonies without ever feeling the effects themselves or seeing the consequences before their eyes. To tolerate the Stamp Act, it was said, would mean to permit the possibility of an unending string of ever more burdensome taxes.

The Stamp Act crisis forced Americans to define their understanding of representation, an understanding which they expanded upon in the subsequent debates leading up to the Revolution. Close ties should exist between the constituents and their legislators. The people should know and be known by their representatives – personally, if possible. The legislature should reflect precisely the interests and wishes of those that elected them. The representatives should legislate as the people would, were they all able to be present. Unless the people's desires conflicted with the common good, they should promote the interests of their local constituency above all others. This notion of representation, though adequate for governing the colonies, effectively limited the compass of republican government to a small area.

2. REPRESENTATION IN THE STATES

As Americans focused their attention on representation issues, they began to realize that the structure of representation in their own governments was inadequate and, in many cases, unjust. In all the colonies before the Revolution, the corporate method of apportioning representatives prevailed. Under this system the legislature determined how many representatives communities, such as counties, towns, or parishes, would be allowed to send. In some colonies each community sent the same number of representatives to the legislature. In Virginia, for example, each county was entitled to send two delegates to the House of Burgesses, while in Connecticut each town received two representatives in the lower house. In other colonies the apportionment was more arbitrary and left to the whim of the legislators. In South Carolina the assembly seemed to have no method at all for determining the number of representatives assigned to each parish. They wanted to preserve the power of the older, more established regions by giving them the preponderance of representatives. No colony conducted regular censuses before the Revolution, and no colony systematically based its representation on population.

Inequalities under the corporate system of apportionment had grown increasingly apparent by the eve of the American Revolution. Since the legislators controlled the distribution of representatives, they wanted to prevent the diminution of their own power. They had a stake in preserving the status quo. As a result, they often refused to grant representation to new communities or failed to give extra representatives to more populous areas. Because the regions closest to the coast were the most long-settled, the legislatures tended to be dominated by easterners. By 1775, for example, Pennsylvania's three eastern counties had 26 delegates, while eight western counties, containing more than half the population, had only 15. As larger numbers of settlers moved into the interior, more people either had no representatives or so few that they had no real power in the assembly. Even before the Revolution, some colonists began to protest against inequities in their own legislatures.

The Revolutionaries' emphasis on equality and natural rights reinforced the importance of making every elector's vote equal to every other elector's. Under the corporate system of representation this was not the case. When a county of 2,000 inhabitants received the same number of representatives as a county with 10,000, the vote of a person in the county with 2,000 was worth more and had more influence on the

649

outcome of the election. Moreover, under the corporate system the majority of people might not have the majority of votes in the assembly. If communities rather than individuals were the basic unit of representation, then a majority of communities containing less than half the population might have more representatives than communities that had more people, as demonstrated in the example of Pennsylvania given above.

During the Revolution most of the states wrote new constitutions which altered the structures of their governments. Some states took this opportunity to correct problems in their method of apportioning representatives. First of all, many states took apportionment out of the hands of the legislators and made it a part of their constitutions. By describing the method of distributing representatives in the document which formed the fundamental law of the state, apportionment would be less likely to be manipulated to the advantage of certain legislators and regions at the expense of others.

Then the states faced even more difficult problems: overcoming the resistance of an entrenched elite in the legislature and finding a new system of apportionment to replace corporate representation. In Massachusetts, for example, large numbers of people in the seaboard towns cooperated with the great commercial and shipping interests there to overcome the opposition of legislators to a new system based on numbers of people, or on property owned, or on some combination of these factors. In other states increasingly numerous westerners also placed pressure on the assemblies. In any case, the method Americans most often turned to was proportional, or numerical, representation. Under this system the number of representatives was made proportionate to the population. In other words, a ratio was established between the people and their representatives – for example, one legislator for every 30,000 inhabitants. This method assumed that the individual rather than the community formed the basic unit of representation. Communities – counties, towns, parishes, or specially created legislative districts – received representation in proportion to their strength in numbers. Political units with more people received more representatives; those with fewer people received fewer representatives. Numerical representation would insure that the majority would rule.

In their first state constitutions, Pennsylvania, New York, Massachusetts, and New Hampshire quickly implemented some form of numerical representation in the lower houses of their state legislatures. In 1789 Georgia followed suit. Both South Carolina and New Jersey acknowledged the principle of numerical representation in their early constitutions, but South Carolina did not actually institute the system until 1808 and New Jersey not until 1844. The Northwest Ordinance of 1787 prescribed the method for the new states carved out of the Ohio Territory. All but two of the 20 states entering the Union between 1789 and 1860 provided for numerical representation in at least one house of their legislatures.

In the wake of the Revolution, then, most states did accept the notion of numerical representation in some form. Some states only used the method in one house. Some states used a combination of property and population in determining representation. Most states defined the represented population as something less than the total number of inhabitants. The Massachusetts and Pennsylvania constitutions, for example, counted only taxable inhabitants; the Georgia constitution, like the United States Constitution, included all Whites but only three-fifths of all Blacks. Nevertheless, the principle and practice of numerical apportionment was well established. In the last decades of the nineteenth century, however, an intense rivalry developed between rural areas and the increasingly populous cities. State legislatures, dominated by rural interests, began to deviate substantially from the norm of numerical representation. Inequities had become so common and so severe that the Supreme Court, beginning in 1962 with *Baker v. Carr*, issued a series of decisions designed to compel states to maintain proportional representation in both houses of their legislatures as well as in their congressional districts. The Court imposed from above a standard that had emerged from below in the revolutionary era.

3. REPRESENTATION FOR THE NATION

At the federal level, the most important decision concerning representation occurred at the Constitutional Convention in Philadelphia during the summer of 1787. Delegates from the larger states – states which either had large populations or expected to have large populations in the near future – argued for numerical representation in both houses of the national legislature. Representatives from the smaller states insisted that the states deserved to be represented as states – in other words, as corporate entities – in at least one house. This split represented the most serious threat to the success of the Philadelphia convention. Neither side wanted to back down; both sides claimed that they were correct. In fact, the smaller states did have the long colonial tradition of corporate representation on their side. The large states, however, had the greater fairness of the numerical system to support their position. After debating the issue for over one and a half months, a compromise was reached. The Great Compromise (sometimes called the Connecticut Compromise) included, among other things, provisions which made representation proportionate to population in the lower house of the national legislature and equal for each state in the upper house. It also included a clause requiring a decennial census for the purpose of keeping representation in the lower house commensurate with population. The convention's resolution of this vexing question, then, produced a system that combined both new and old concepts of representation.

Concepts of representation were also central in the debate over the ratification of the United States Constitution. The opponents of the Constitution, the Anti-Federalists, maintained that it was impossible to establish a republic in an area as large as the United States. Following Montesquieu, they claimed that republics could exist only in small territories having homogeneous populations. A large republic was bound, they said, to degenerate into despotism or split into many warring factions. They criticized the proposed system of representation because it lacked the personal intimacy of representation at the state level. The Congress, they said, had too few members to represent such a numerous, diverse population. Only wealthy, prominent – and unrepresentative – individuals would be elected to federal office. As a result, the federal representation would be detached and unresponsive to the needs and wishes of the constituents.

The Federalist supporters of the Constitution responded by proposing a new concept of representation. In *The Federalist* no. 10 James Madison gave the classical formulation of this theory. Madison argued that representative government was not only possible, but preferable, in a large territory. Factious majorities, seeking to promote their own selfish interests, represented the gravest threat to the stability of the country; these could not be stopped by normal democratic processes. In the United States, however, the population was so diverse and so spread out over a vast area that it would be impossible for factious majorities to form.

Even more important, however, was Madison's distinction between a democracy and a republic. A democracy, he said, was a form of government in which all the electors must meet personally to vote on every issue. A republic, on the other hand, was a form in which the people elect representatives to conduct the public business for them. The process of election would help filter out corrupt and untrustworthy candidates and raise to office those who were worthy of the public trust. The wisest and the most virtuous would prevail. Federal representation was of a different stripe from that in the states. Congressmen need not have personal knowledge of nor personal contact with their constituents. They would govern in the national interest, removed from the particularistic concerns of the states. The Federalists, then, formulated a new concept of representation better suited to American circumstances. Ironically, the Federalists' theory bore more than a passing resemblance to the discredited concept of virtual representation that many Americans had so vigorously opposed.

4 . SUFFRAGE

The Revolution also catalyzed sentiment in favor of expanding the franchise by reducing or abolishing property qualifications for voting. The colonies had followed the practice in England of requiring electors to own a certain amount of wealth or property before being allowed to cast a ballot. In England, the standard was possession of a 40-shilling freehold; that is, to own land worth 40 shillings per year in rental value or income. Because of the scarcity of land in England, this represented a substantial sum and prevented the majority of Englishmen from voting. In seventeenth-century elections in England, no more than one-fifth of the adult male population could vote. Although some colonies, such as Rhode Island and eighteenth-century Massachusetts, adopted the 40-shilling rule, many set their own requirements in terms of acreage. North Carolina and Georgia, for example, insisted that the voter own 50 acres of land; Virginia required the voter to own 100 acres of vacant land or 25 acres of improved land. Other colonies had variations on these basic requirements, which changed somewhat over time.

An elaborate rationale existed to justify the need for property qualifications for voting. It was believed that only property owners had a real stake in society, a permanent interest in the government's future. They were the ones on whom taxes fell most heavily. Only they had the independence to vote for the best candidate; poorer individuals might sell their votes or be susceptible to bribery.

Yet the property qualification for voting had a far different effect in the colonies than in England. Because land was cheap and abundant in America, most men owned property. As a result, the vast majority of white males were eligible to vote; whether they exercised this privilege was another matter. Although the numbers varied over time and from colony to colony, it is believed that from 50 to 80 per cent of the white male population could vote in colony-wide elections before the Revolution. Furthermore, colonists with little or no property were often allowed to vote for the town or county officials even when they could not vote for delegates to the legislative assembly. Unlike in England, then, the property qualifications for voting did not prove to be a highly restrictive barrier to political participation in the colonies.

Nevertheless, property qualifications for voting came under attack during the revolutionary era. There had been some pressure in the late colonial period to reduce or abolish property qualifications. News that radicals in Britain such as Joseph Priestly and James Burgh were demanding liberalization of the franchise strengthened American commitment to the cause. After 1767, however, Britain refused to allow any colony to alter the structure of its government and so no changes were made. The revolutionary crisis intensified demands. Once the fighting began, some soldiers realized that, although they were expected to die for their country, they could not vote for their elected officials. The protests against taxation without representation led naturally to objections to representation without suffrage.

As was the case with apportionment, the writing of the new state constitutions provided the opportunity for states to reform injustices in their electoral system. Pennsylvania, North Carolina, New Hampshire, New Jersey, Maryland, and New York all reduced the property qualifications for voting during the Revolution. Some states, such as New York and North Carolina, instituted lower property qualifications for those voting for members of the lower house and higher qualifications for those voting for the upper house. Pennsylvania established the most generous rule, extending the franchise to all adult white male taxpayers. (Vermont, which was at this time not a part of the Union, was even more liberal. In 1777 it gave the franchise to all adult males who would take the Freeman's Oath, thus becoming the first place to establish universal manhood suffrage.) Over the next several decades, more and more states followed Pennsylvania's lead. By 1824 the right to vote had become independent of property ownership and taxpaying. Nearly all adult white males were allowed to vote, except in Rhode Island, Virginia, and Louisiana, which still retained more restrictive requirements.

Other changes in the revolutionary era also broadened the franchise. In three states – New York, Pennsylvania, and North Carolina – free Blacks were permitted to vote on the same terms as Whites. No state specifically granted the vote to women. However, due to an ambiguity in the New Jersey constitution of 1776, women did vote there, until a law was passed in 1807 closing the loophole. All of the changes at the state level were crucial, because the United States Constitution did not prescribe national qualifications for the franchise; that was left up to the individual states.

Many years had to pass before truly universal adult suffrage prevailed in the United States. The Fifteenth Amendment, passed in 1870, gave the vote to Blacks. The Nineteenth Amendment, passed in 1920, recognized the right of women to exercise the franchise. Yet, without the impetus for reform stimulated by the American Revolution, these changes may not have occurred at all.

FURTHER READING

Dinkin, Robert J.: *Voting in Revolutionary America: a Study of Elections in the Original Thirteen States, 1776–1789* (Westport, Conn.: Greenwood Press, 1982).
Pitkin, Hanna F.: *The Concept of Representation* (Berkeley: University of California Press, 1967).
Pole, J. R.: *Political Representation in England and the Origins of the American Republic* (1966) (Berkeley, University of California Press, 1971).
Reid, J. P.: *The Concept of Representation in the Age of the American Revolution* (Chicago: University of Chicago Press, 1989).
Williamson, Chilton: *American Suffrage: From Property to Democracy, 1760–1860* (Princeton, NJ: Princeton University Press, 1960).
Zagarri, Rosemarie: *The Politics of Size: Representation in the United States, 1776–1850* (Ithaca: Cornell University Press, 1987).

70

Republicanism

ROBERT E. SHALHOPE

IMMEDIATELY upon declaring their independence from the British monarchy
in 1776, Americans committed themselves to establishing republican forms of
government. They set about drafting constitutions within their newly formed
states that would confirm the legitimate authority of the people. Intent upon creating
a republican political system within their new nation, Americans actually created
much more – a republican society. Even before the end of the Revolution, republicanism had become a cultural system that permeated every facet of American life –
a pervasive ideology that would affect the behavior and thought of Americans for
years to come.

I. JOHN LOCKE AND THE EIGHTEENTH-CENTURY "COMMONWEALTHMEN"

In their effort to present a cogent intellectual defense against the actions of Parliament
following the end of the Seven Years' War (1763), Americans drew upon a wide
variety of sources – classical antiquity, the English common law, and Enlightenment
rationalism. While most of these served an illustrative rather than a determinative
role in their thought, the work of John Locke (1632–1704) stood out as a major
exception. Indeed, by the 1760s, his belief that the people retained the right to rebel
against unlawful or oppressive authorities had become entrenched in the consciousness of articulate and inarticulate colonists alike. Locke's principles and his
ideas regarding the social contract could be employed to highlight the resistant rather
than the submissive side of the traditional protection–allegiance covenant between
king and people. For many colonists, then, Locke helped smooth the way towards
resistance without a radical departure from a familiar, traditional ideology. His ideas
became the essential and familiar conduit for changed colonial beliefs.

While Lockean principles underlay the colonial perception of the relationship
between rulers and the ruled, a group of English writers – eighteenth-century trans-
mitters of the radical social and political thought of the Civil War and Commonwealth
era – provided the colonists with a theory of politics that simultaneously explained
why the British behaved as they did in the post-1763 years and provided the ideological
basis for an American response. From the 1720s onwards, men such as John Trenchard, Thomas Gordon, Robert Viscount Molesworth, RICHARD PRICE, and James
Burgh offered Americans a cohesive set of ideas that fused classical thought, common
law theories, and Enlightenment principles into a coherent whole and which provided
both clarity and direction to the colonial opposition. Under the intense pressure of
events after 1763, the ideas of these men became integrated into a comprehensive

and forceful image of politics and society that penetrated widely and deeply throughout colonial culture to form the essential substructure of American republicanism.

The writings of these eighteenth-century 'commonwealthmen' emerged from a bitter hostility towards social, economic, and political forces transforming English society after the Glorious Revolution of 1688. These men perceived their society as degenerate and diseased, corrupted by vice and luxury and materialistic, commercial values. Behind this perception lay a political critique: excessive governmental power was spawning the decadence and decay eating away at the very foundations of English society and was rapidly carrying the nation towards the fate of ancient Rome.

While such ideas gained little popularity within English society, they became increasingly popular and influential in the American colonies. This body of opposition thought literally permeated colonial culture throughout the 1760s and 1770s. There the imposition of new colonial legislation after 1763 raised troubling questions, questions for which English radical and opposition writers seemed to provide particularly reasonable and uniquely relevant answers. Within this context, a comprehensive theory of politics emerged throughout the American colonies that made sense of the bewildering changes of the mid-eighteenth century for a great many diverse sorts of Americans.

2. POWER AND LIBERTY

This theory of politics focused on the role of power – defined as the control or domination of some men over others within American lives. For Americans, the disposition of power lurked behind every political event; it was the ultimate explanation for whatever political behavior they observed. Power became omnipresent in public affairs and always aggressively expanded beyond its just and safe limits. It was this aggressiveness that so troubled provincial writers because, in their minds, justice, equity, and liberty always fell victim to the inordinate demands of power. As a consequence, they saw the public world separated into two innately antagonistic spheres: power and liberty. The first, constantly and brutally assertive, must always be opposed, while the second, delicately innocent and passive, required a ceaseless and vigilant defense. From this basic insight colonial authors drew a central, all-important conclusion: the preservation of liberty relied entirely upon the moral strength and vigilance of the people. Only they could maintain effective restraints on those who wielded power.

Such a perspective led many colonists to see a pattern to the new British actions, a pattern whose meaning became unmistakably clear in light of Americans' understanding of opposition literature. Britain was succumbing to the all-too-familiar tendencies seen throughout history for nations to degenerate with age, to fall prey to the madness and corruption of power. Viewed in this manner, the actions taken by the British represented not merely mistaken or ill-advised behavior, but a deliberate attack upon liberty in Britain that was spreading its poison to the American colonies through unconstitutional taxes, an invasion of placemen, a purposeful weakening of the colonial judiciary, plural office-holding, an undermining of the prerogatives of the provincial assemblies, and the presence of a standing army. If unchecked, such a plot could destroy the sacred British Constitution and with it all the protection for individual liberties.

The belief that they faced a ministerial conspiracy against liberty transformed the meaning of resistance, in the minds of many colonists, from a constitutional quarrel over the power of Parliament to govern them to a world-regenerative creed. In their minds, the lamp of liberty burned brightly only in the American provinces. Not to resist the British would be treasonable to themselves and to posterity. Out of these beliefs emerged the American perception of republicanism as the great moral force within their culture and throughout the western world.

A belief in the regenerative quality of their resistance meant, for many Americans, that the Revolution was more than just a political revolt; it represented the creation of a fresh world, a republican world. Consequently, republicanism stood for more than simply the substitution of an elective system for a monarchy. It infused the political break from Britain with a moral fervor and an idealism linked inextricably with the very character of American society. The sacrifice of individual interests to a greater common good comprised both the essence of republicanism and the idealistic goal of the Revolution. Thus, the Revolution represented more than a rejection of British corruption. It required a reformation within provincial societies as well, a reformation defined in republican terms. For most Americans, republicanism expressed a longing for a communal attempt to control the bewildering and selfish impulses generated by the emergence of a capitalistic market economy in their midst. Emphasizing a morality of social cohesion, these people hoped to create an organic state joining individual citizens together into an indissoluble union of harmony and benevolence: a true republic. Theirs was a noble, though fragile, ideal because republics, by definition, depend entirely upon the character and spirit of their citizens. Unique among all polities, republics necessitate an absence of selfishness and luxury; their very existence rests upon virtue – the willingness of citizens to place the common good above their private desires. The presence or absence of virtue, therefore, determines whether or not a society remains republican. For Americans, the moral character of their society formed the prime measure of the success or failure of their revolution: republicanism blended indistinguishably with political revolution and moral regeneration.

On the eve of the Revolution, then, Americans embraced a distinctive set of political, social, and ethical attitudes that united them against the British. Assuming that history revealed a continual struggle between the spheres of liberty and power, American Revolutionaries quickly formed a consensus in which the concept of republicanism epitomized the new social and political world they believed they were creating. Preserving a republican polity meant protecting liberty from ceaseless aggressions of power. In addition, since Americans believed that what made republics great or what ultimately destroyed them was not force of arms but the character and spirit of the people, public virtue became the essential prerequisite for good government. A people practicing frugality, industry, temperance, and simplicity constituted sound republican stock, while those who wallowed in luxury were corrupt and would corrupt others. Since furthering the public good – the exclusive purpose of republican government – required the constant sacrifice of individual interests to the greater needs of the whole, the people, conceived of as a homogeneous body (especially when set against their rulers) became the great determinant of whether a republic lived or died. Thus, republicanism meant maintaining public and private virtue, internal unity, social solidarity, and vigilance against the corruptions of power. United in this frame of mind, Americans set out to gain their independence and to establish a new republic.

3. REPUBLICANISM AND LIBERALISM

While the bulk of Americans espoused republican ideas in their struggle against the British, these ideas did not bear the same meaning for everyone involved. Indeed, it soon became apparent that republicanism represented a general consensus solely because it rested on such vague premises. Few things were certain: Americans believed that republicanism meant the elimination of an aristocracy and a monarchy as well as the absence of inherited authority and unearned privilege. Beyond this, agreement vanished – what form a republican government should assume and, more importantly, what constituted a republican society remained unclear. With the passage of time, it became apparent that republicanism and revolution carried different meanings in various regions of the country and even different meanings for distinct groups within the same locale. Some people enthusiastically accepted the New World market relations, while others remained deeply anti-capitalistic. Some wanted to retain a communal society based on social hierarchy, others desired an open, competitive society without regard for rank or status, while still others preferred a simple, homogeneous society of relative equality held together by deep corporate bonds. These disparate desires emerged as discrete fragments of two cultural impulses – republicanism and liberalism – coursing through the lives of late eighteenth-century Americans. At times, the two appeared to run parallel to one another, at others they seemed in direct conflict, and quite often they melded into a nearly indistinguishable whole. In many ways, republicanism – a familiar ideology permeating all walks of life – shaped Americans' minds; it offered them a self-image that provided meaning and identity to their lives. Liberalism – as yet an unarticulated behavioral pattern more than a sharply delineated mode of thought – unconsciously shaped their day-to-day activity.

Most Americans clung to a harmonious, corporate view of themselves and their society even while behaving in a materialistic, utilitarian manner in their daily lives. Thus, while rapidly transforming their society in an open, competitive, modern direction, Americans idealized communal harmony and a virtuous social order. Republicanism condemned the values of a burgeoning capitalistic economy and placed a premium upon an ordered, disciplined personal liberty restricted by the civic obligations dictated by public virtue. In this sense, republicanism formalized or ritualized a mode of thought that ran counter to the flow of history; it idealized the traditional values of a world rapidly fading rather than the market conditions and liberal capitalistic mentality swiftly emerging in the late eighteenth century. And yet the confrontation with the British in the 1760s and the 1770s instilled new vigor into traditional republican values by stigmatizing the institutions, values, and attitudes of a mother country posed on the verge of the industrial revolution. Consequently, the Revolution sanctified virtue (defined as the subordination of self to the greater good of the community), corporate harmony, unity, and equality at the very moment when those values had already become anachronistic.

This resulted in ambivalence, inconsistencies, and ironic incongruities. Americans wrestled with changes that transformed their society while continuing to idealize an essentially premodern set of values. Economic, social, and political changes began to alter institutions and modes of behavior in fundamental and dramatic ways. More and more isolated agrarian villages began to be tied into larger commercial networks; opportunities abounded that revealed the unlimited potential for human freedom; and the bonds holding together families, churches, and communities eroded and in many

657

cases simply fell away. Americans found themselves caught up in confusing ambiguities arising from a tension between old values and new modes of behavior. And yet the conflict between traditional republican values and newly emerging liberal behavior patterns never became so clearcut as to set one specific set of ideas in direct opposition to another. Indeed, this tension seethed as fiercely within single individuals and groups as it did between competing elements within American society. As a result, Americans could, and did, believe simultaneously in corporate needs and individual rights. They never had a sense of having to choose between two starkly contrasting traditions – republicanism and liberalism. Instead, they domesticated classical republicanism to fit their contemporary needs; they unselfconsciously amalgamated inherited assumptions with their liberal actions.

4. REPUBLICAN INTERPRETATION OF THE WAR

The tension between republican ideology and liberal behavior patterns carried throughout the Revolution. And yet the war itself, or rather its victory, prompted most Americans to view their efforts in republican terms and to enshrine these values in the meaning of the war. Most Americans entered the Revolution with the millennial expectation of creating a new republican society comprised of virtuous citizens free of Old World corruption. The Revolution carried the promise of regeneration with a desperate insistency born of the doubts and uncertainties arising from transformations already affecting the colonial societies. During the course of the war, however, American behavior had manifested disturbing and disappointing signs of European vice: sectional, factional, and personal rivalries emerged; public officials and governmental contractors indulged in widespread graft and corruption; farmers demanded usurious prices for their crops, while merchants displayed similar greed in selling their trade goods; many individuals engaged in a lucrative trade with the enemy; and others strove desperately to avoid military service. The techniques employed to win the war also raised grave questions about the republican character of Americans: the continental government found itself forced to conscript citizens, to confiscate property, and to engage the mysterious and very likely corrupt financial and administrative talents of shrewd and ambitious individuals. Worst of all, the militia – the backbone of a republican society – proved ineffective; only the creation of a regular army with rigorously disciplined soldiers and self-seeking ambitious officers saved the cause.

Despite these experiences, Americans chose to believe that their victory represented a confirmation of their moral strengths, a testament to their republican ideals. In 1783 they celebrated public virtue, not its failure. To preserve their millennial vision of the future, Americans could not recognize the reality of the many questionable expedients employed to win the war. Concerned about their failures and anxious about their bequest to posterity, the revolutionary generation redefined its experiences and made them as virtuous and as heroic as they ought to have been. Thus, victory – gained by the fallible, partial, and selfish efforts of many Americans – allowed an entire generation to ignore these unpleasant realities and to claim that it had remained true to the republican standards of 1775. They offered those standards and the image of a unified, virtuous republican citizenry to future generations. To celebrate the victory was to celebrate the regenerative character of the revolutionary movement. The young nation's triumph validated a unique national character based upon the predominance of republican virtue. The language of the revolutionary victors belied their experiences during the war just as republican language had belied the experiences of Americans for several decades before the outbreak of the Revolution. Republican ideals expressed a reaction against tendencies actually dominant in colonial society, not their political fulfillment. Classical republicanism expressed seemingly anachronistic ideas at the very moment when the circumstances of the American Revolution transformed them into a national ideology.

5. POST-REVOLUTIONARY REPUBLICANISM

By the end of the eighteenth century, the American commitment to republicanism had grown even stronger than it had been in 1776. Republicanism existed as a social fact, a cultural system whose tenets permeated American society. Throughout the decades following the outbreak of the Revolution America had indeed become republican, but hardly in the manner intended by its early leaders. During this time economic and demographic changes taking place at an unparalleled rate began to work fundamental transformations within the new nation. Geographic expansion spawned incredible mobility, and great numbers of Americans became involved in the market economy and strived to gain all the advantages they could from their new-found social and economic autonomy.

Revolutionary republicanism, rather than constraining these activities, seemed to encourage them and to afford them legitimacy. The emphasis placed upon equality in revolutionary rhetoric stimulated great numbers of previously deferential men to question all forms of authority and to challenge distinctions of every sort. Rather than generating an increased commitment to order, harmony, and virtue, republicanism appeared to be fostering an acquisitive individualism heedless of the common good or the benevolent leadership of a natural elite. Post-revolutionary America, instead of becoming the New World embodiment of transcendent classical values, appeared increasingly materialistic, utilitarian, and licentious: austerity gave way to prosperity; virtue appeared more and more to connote the individual pursuit of wealth through hard work rather than an unselfish devotion to the collective good. No longer a simple, ordered community under the benign leadership of a natural elite, America seemed instead to be moving towards a materialistic and utilitarian nation increasingly responsive to the desires of ordinary, obscure individuals.

The rapid democratization and vulgarization that took place in American society throughout the last decades of the eighteenth century helped create a far more open and liberal society than had been anticipated by most revolutionary leaders. Indeed, the transformations taking place within American society throughout these years were so complex and indeliberate, so much a mixture of day-to-day responses to a rapidly changing socio-economic environment, that most Americans were unaware of the direction such changes were taking them and their society. Their commitment to republicanism allowed them to continue to imagine themselves as members of a virtuous, harmonious organic society long after the social foundations of such a society had eroded. The fact that republican language became increasingly disembodied from the changing cultural context made self-awareness all that much more difficult. The presence of an ideology as powerful as republicanism fostered an unconscious tendency among the dominant majority of Americans to make reality amenable to ideas, and ideas to reality, so as to create an integral world view credible enough to foster a collective as well as an individual sense of identity and security. Adherence to republican ideals helped to ease the strains present within late eighteenth-century American society. It allowed groups and individuals to dissociate themselves, their institutions, and their society from harmful and evil actions. It allowed – even impelled – men to view themselves as committed to the harmony, order, and communal well-being of a republican society while actively creating an aggressive, individualistic, liberal, and materialistic one. Ironically, then, republicanism provided the fertile seedbed within which the individualistic liberalism of the nineteenth century took root.

FURTHER READING

Appleby, Joyce: *Capitalism and a New Social Order: the Republican Vision of the 1790s* (New York and London: New York University Press, 1984).

Bailyn, Bernard: *The Ideological Origins of the American Revolution* (Cambridge, Mass.: Harvard University Press, 1967).

Kloppenberg, James T.: "The virtues of liberalism: Christianity, republicanism and ethics in early American political discourse," *Journal of American History*, 74 (1987), 9–33.

Robbins, Caroline: *The Eighteenth-Century Commonwealthman: Studies in the Transmission, Development, and Circumstances of English Liberal Thought from the Restoration of Charles II Until the War with the Thirteen Colonies* (Cambridge, Mass.: Harvard University Press, 1959).

Shalhope, Robert E.: "Toward a republican synthesis: the emergence of an understanding of republicanism in American historiography," *William and Mary Quarterly*, 29 (1972), 49–80.

——: "Republicanism and early American historiography," *William and Mary Quarterly*, 39 (1982), 334–56.

Watts, Steven: *The Republic Reborn: War and the Making of Liberal America, 1790–1820* (Baltimore: Johns Hopkins University Press, 1987).

Wood, Gordon: *The Creation of the American Republic, 1776–1787* (Chapel Hill: University of North Carolina Press, 1969).

71

Sovereignty

PETER S. ONUF

DEFINING and locating sovereignty, the ultimate authority in a political community, represented a major conceptual and practical challenge to the American Revolutionaries. The idea that there had to be a single, absolute power to decide and command contradicted the colonists' experience in the empire; furthermore, the distribution of power between states and central governments guaranteed that any effort to locate such a power would fail. In the decade preceding independence, American patriots organized resistance to parliamentary claims to sovereignty over the colonies, thus reinforcing the colonists' traditional hostility to centralized authority. But independence did not resolve the problem of sovereignty: the Revolutionaries now had to construct a political order that would gain recognition from foreign powers and command the allegiance of American citizens. The success of the Revolution did not depend on the establishment of a supreme, sovereign law-making authority, but the new regime did have to achieve legitimacy, both at home and abroad.

As the institutional embodiment of the "common cause," the Continental Congress succeeded to many functions of the British Crown, particularly in managing foreign policy and in promoting the states' collective interests. As a result, Congress naturally laid claim to the aura of legitimacy traditionally surrounding royal government. The transfer of authority from Crown to Congress did not, however, resolve the sovereignty question, but instead brought to the fore fundamental tensions and contradictions in British constitutionalism. First, the Revolutionaries deconstructed the orthodox British notion of sovereignty, denying that the authority of the Crown merged with that of the other branches in Parliament. Americans proclaimed their loyalty to a king whose personal "sovereignty" or prerogative – considered apart from his role in Parliament – was constitutionally limited. Congress, by succeeding to this authority, might thus be considered "sovereign," but only in a sense that contemporaneous British commentators would have considered anachronistic.

The American situation was further complicated by the Revolutionaries' determination to preserve the political integrity of colony-states with legislative and taxing authority within their respective jurisdictions. The Revolutionaries thus faced the daunting tasks of locating effective authority *among* as well as *within* their newly constituted governments. They had to establish procedures for adjudicating the kinds of jurisdictional conflicts which the successful assertion of parliamentary sovereignty would, by definition, have eliminated.

I. PARLIAMENTARY SOVEREIGNTY

The Revolutionaries' protracted efforts to establish an effective and legitimate new political order represented an answer to the British idea of parliamentary sovereignty set forth by WILLIAM BLACKSTONE in his influential *Commentaries on the Laws of England* (1765-9). Parliament "hath sovereign and uncontrollable authority in making, confirming, enlarging, restraining, abrogating, repealing, reviving and expounding of laws," he wrote, "this being the place where that absolute despotic power, which must in all governments reside somewhere, is entrusted by the constitution of these kingdoms" (Greene, 1967, p. 87). Blackstone thus formulated the modern conception of sovereignty, against which American constitutional claims now appear reactionary and anachronistic. But the colonists could plausibly argue that the sovereignty asserted by Parliament represented a dangerous innovation in British constitutionalism, particularly when extended to the empire as a whole. Defenders of parliamentary supremacy saw that body as the palladium of British liberty, and so could not imagine that its "absolute despotic power" jeopardized the integrity of the British Constitution or the sanctity of British rights. In the constitutional struggles of the previous century Parliament had successfully curbed royal prerogative, the greatest threat to the constitution. But British consitutionalists remained "fearful of resurgent monarchy," wrote the legal historian John Phillip Reid, and therefore "insisted that parliamentary sovereignty must not be diluted by the slightest iota" (Reid, 1987, p. 262). As a result, even Britons who sympathized with the American cause were appalled by the colonists' apparent willingness to jeopardize their rights by renouncing parliamentary protection and inviting the Crown to play a larger role in imperial governance.

Because of the enormous discrepancy between parliamentary claims to sovereignty and actual conditions in the empire, the Americans were well situated to see potentially dangerous contradictions in the new constitutional orthodoxy. Parliamentary sovereignty over the colonies might have seemed a logical and necessary extension of its sovereignty in Britain, but colonists could assert that Parliament had, in fact, never played a significant role in governing the empire. By contrast, the King's presence was pervasive and his authority was generally revered; Crown appointees constituted the "government" in each colony as well as the governing apparatus of the imperial state.

Colonial protests against innovations in British policy centered on the issue of representation. Americans questioned the central premise of the new orthodoxy, that the King-in-Parliament "represented" – was in some sense identical with – the British state and, by extension, the imperial state. Reasonably enough, colonial polemicists such as DANIEL DULANY denied that any colonist "is or can be *actually* or *virtually* represented by the British *House of Commons*" (Bailyn, 1965, pp. 618–19). The administration's argument for "virtual" representation, based on the analogy between the colonies and various unrepresented municipalities in Britain, illuminated the defective premises of parliamentary pretensions. "To what purpose," wondered James Otis, "is it to ring everlasting changes ... on the cases of Manchester, Birmingham, and Sheffield, who return no members? If those by now so considerable places are not represented, they ought to be" (quoted in Bailyn, 1967, p. 169). The plausibility of the claim that Parliament legitimately exercised "despotic' authority depended on a willingness to embrace the fiction that that body was truly representative. Therefore, the logic of the idea of sovereignty itself – not an anachronistic attachment to "premodern" constitutional forms – drove Americans to resist parliamentary pretensions.

The radical idea that the British Government was an artificial, despotic, unrepresentative encumbrance on the British people as well as on the American colonists was most fully developed by Thomas Paine in *Common Sense*. The British Constitution, wrote Paine, consisted of the "base remains of two ancient tyrannies" – "the remains of monarchical tyranny in the person of the king" and "the remains of aristocratical tyranny in the persons of the peers" – "compounded with some new republican materials" in the House of Commons (Greene, 1967, p. 272). Paine thus questioned the legitimacy of the respective branches: William the Conqueror, for instance, was a "French bastard" and "a very paltry rascally original" for the modern monarchy (Greene, 1967, p. 275). But more significant than these sensational thrusts was the assumption Paine shared with many of his American readers that the "compounding" of the branches in the orthodox conception of King-in-Parliament was fundamentally illegitimate. Neo-Harringtonian critics of the Whig ascendancy had long since warned that the constitutional independence of the Commons was jeopardized by the King's influence and patronage. "These means of subversion are known collectively as corruption," wrote J. G. A. Pocock, "and if ever Parliament or those who elect them – for corruption may occur at this point too – should be wholly corrupt, then there will be an end of independence and liberty" (Pocock, 1973, p. 125). Even before the onset of the imperial crisis, colonists tended to view the British Constitution from this dissenting perspective. After 1763, repeated encroachments on American rights appeared to justify the pessimistic conclusion that the historic balance of powers in the British Government no longer operated effectively to protect constitutional liberties. The result was a growing disparity between British and American perspectives on the character of the imperial state and the scope of parliamentary authority. For orthodox Whigs, cooperation among the branches and the assertion of parliamentary sovereignty signified the final perfection of British constitutionalism; for Americans, the despotic power of a corrupt Parliament was neither sovereign nor constitutional.

2. POPULAR SOVEREIGNTY

The colonists based their claims to English rights on an idealized conception of the "ancient constitution." But the debate over representation also forced Americans to grapple with the distinctively modern dilemma of political legitimacy. As the Revolutionaries rejected imperial rule, they recognized the importance of connecting the emerging governmental infrastructure with the larger political community. The fiction of parliamentary sovereignty may have been exploded, but patriot leaders had to construct a more plausible fiction of their own. The ultimate solution was to invoke the idea of "popular sovereignty," a notion deeply imbedded in British constitutionalism and most succinctly expressed by the great contract theorists. But who were the "sovereign" people in 1776? Divided by political, ethnic, and religious differences, Americans did not speak with a single voice or express a single, sovereign will. The belated, controversial decision for independence clearly revealed America's disunited state. Ironically, it was only *after* independence had been achieved and the new states had consolidated their authority that the notion of a sovereign American people began to make sense. Before the Revolutionaries could invoke the sovereignty of the people they had to construct a regime in which the people could believe. Not surprisingly, they borrowed heavily from the old imperial order.

In the final, crucial phase of the imperial crisis, when the Americans explicitly rejected Parliament's jurisdiction, they insisted that their allegiance to the King provided the only constitutional foundation for imperial rule. "Our allegiance to his majesty," John Adams wrote in his *Novanglus* letters (1775), "is not due by virtue of any act of a British parliament, but by our own charter and province laws." George III, it followed, was "king of the Massachusetts, king of Rhode Island, king of Connecticut, &c." (Mason, 1972, p. 208). Of course, the sovereignty of such a king bore little resemblance to the sovereignty claimed by Parliament; royal prerogative was constitutionally limited and did not include "despotic" law-making powers. From the colonial perspective, the apotheosis of royal authority did not represent a reversion to divine right absolutism, but rather a final, desperate effort to guarantee colonial rights within the imperial framework.

3. CONGRESS

The American conception of the imperial constitution flowed logically from the colonial assemblies' aggressive claims to local legislative supremacy and control over taxation. But American legislators did not seek to exercise the full range of sovereign powers and their protestations of loyalty to the Crown were genuine. The assemblies played an increasingly equivocal and tentative role as the final break approached, precisely because of a pervasive sense of the insufficiency of their legitimate powers. During this period, according to Jerrilyn Marston, Americans were "loathe to destroy the precious constitutional balance by removing the symbol of political authority, the king" (Marston, 1987, p. 33). Meanwhile, Congress took the lead in organizing the inter-colonial resistance movement and began to exercise a broad range of sovereign powers; perhaps most crucially, colonists agreed that Congress should speak for all the colonies in representing American grievances to the King and in seeking some sort of constitutional accommodation. George III's unwillingness to deal with Congress, a body with no constitutional standing, and his determination to uphold parliamentary authority precluded any settlement, hastened the movement for independence, and facilitated the transfer of legitimate authority to Congress.

Because Congress thus stood in the place of the King, the colonies were able to make the transition to independent statehood with relative ease. After sanctioning various *ad hoc* arrangements in specific colonies, in May 1776 Congress urged revolutionaries to form new governments "where no government sufficient to the exigencies of their affairs" had yet been established (Greene, 1967, p. 283). The question of which came first – the new states or the new national government – is a perennial favorite among constitutional historians, but can never be resolved. Clearly, the different levels of government drew legitimacy from each other and the interdependence of local and central authorities was well established before independence. As a result, the revolutionary leadership institutionalized a broad distribution of powers in the new regime that was fundamentally incompatible with a Blackstonian definition of sovereignty. On one hand, the state governments extended their jurisdictions and gained legitimacy through the process of constitution-writing. At the same time, however, the exigencies of warfare and diplomacy reinforced the importance of Congress's role as successor to the Crown's executive powers while illuminating its defects as a national legislature.

The great paradox of early American constitutional development was that Congress should exercise so many attributes of sovereignty without any constitutional sanction. The Articles of Confederation were sent out to the states in 1777 but did not gain unanimous approval and go into effect until 1781. The contrast between Congress and the state governments is striking: at first, the states hesitated to act without congressional authorization; thereafter, constitutional revision in the states increasingly depended on explicit popular approval. But the idea that the legitimacy of congressional authority should be grounded directly in the sovereign people did not take hold until reformers pushed for a new federal Constitution in 1787. Nor did the state legislatures play a crucial part in legitimizing Congress; if anything, the declining prestige and growing ineffectiveness of Congress during the period when the Articles were in effect (1781–9) suggests the opposite conclusion.

Both the original impulse towards confederation and the ratification of the Articles reflected strategic and diplomatic imperatives. Congressmen needed to convince skeptical foreign powers that they were empowered to enter into engagements on behalf of the American people. Many congressmen were also persuaded of the necessity for resolving outstanding differences among the states and providing for the authoritative determination of future conflicts. In neither case, however, did congressmen assume that their authority rested solely or primarily on the states' ratification of a continental constitution. More plausibly, confederation would be a means of binding the states not to interfere with Congress as it exercised sovereign powers it already legitimately enjoyed. But, once the confederation was finally completed, the results were disappointing to nationalist-minded politicians. With victory soon in hand, the need for a national sovereignty no longer seemed compelling. The focus of confederation politics thus shifted towards the kind of inter-state and inter-sectional conflicts that the need for wartime cooperation had held in check. As a result, the Articles functioned less as a national charter than as a treaty of alliance among semi-sovereign states.

4. FEDERAL UNION

Dissatisfaction with the Articles reflected growing ambiguity about the functions of Congress and the legitimacy of its authority. Critics complained that the central government was constitutionally incapable of fulfilling its mandate and that the state governments were all too eager to fill the resulting power vacuum. During the "critical" period before the meeting of the Constitutional Convention in the summer of 1787, frustrated nationalists began to argue that only a king could effectively exercise national sovereignty. But the founders contrived a radically different solution to the crisis of legitimate authority. Concluding that the monarchical model was inadequate to the exigencies of national government, the founders sought to construct a true national legislature as well as an efficient and powerful executive. Because the reconstituted union would itself be a kind of state – and not simply a league of states – the founders recognized the need to ground its authority in popular consent. The federal union was like a "pyramid," proclaimed the Pennsylvanian James Wilson, and therefore must rest on as "broad a basis as possible" (Onuf, 1983, pp. 202–3).

The idea of popular sovereignty had a long history in Anglo-American thought and practice. But the legitimacy of the central government had never before depended on the consent of the people. The genius of the founders was not only to borrow constitutional forms from the states, but to establish their authority on the same foundation. Thus, implementation of the new system depended on its ratification by specially elected state conventions, not by the state governments; members of the lower house of the new congress were to be popularly elected. It would be a mistake, however, to exaggerate either the extent of popular power or the importance of

665

FIGURE 53 The first Great
Seal of the United States
(1782), designed by Charles
Thomson and drawn by
William Barton. The device
was adopted on 20 June
1782 and put into force
by Washington's inaug-
uration in 1789.

popular consent in the new federal union. The states continued to play a crucial role
in the national government through representation in the senate, and the popular
will was only indirectly expressed in choosing the new national executive. As a result,
Anti-Federalists had little difficulty in showing that the proposed system was not truly
popular or representative by state constitutional standards. But such criticism was
beside the point. The Federalists simply had to establish that the state governments
did not "represent" the American people exclusively. If the states were not sovereign
in this sense, the principle of popular sovereignty did not therefore necessarily preclude
the expansion of national power.

By directly appealing to the sovereign people, the Federalists hoped to discredit the
states' pretensions to sovereignty. "The people of America have mistaken the meaning
of the word *sovereignty*," Benjamin Rush wrote in 1786: "hence each state pretends
to be sovereign. In Europe it is applied only to those states which possess the power
of making war and peace" (Onuf, 1983, pp. 7–8). The Federalists pursued this line of
argument in the ratification debates, suggesting that Congress's "imbecility" under
the Articles and the tendency for the states to fill the resulting power vacuum would
destroy the union. The danger was that the states would then assume all the attributes
of sovereignty, thus jeopardizing their republican constitutions. Implicit in these
dire predictions was a conception of national sovereignty derived from the imperial
executive and subsequently exercised more or less effectively by Congress – despite
inter-state and inter-sectional jealousies and notwithstanding constitutional obstacles
incorporated in the Articles of Confederation.

Yet, just as the Federalists' appropriation of the idea of popular sovereignty helped
neutralize the resistance of sovereign states, the establishment of a national constitutional order helped mitigate fears that perfecting the union meant a return to
despotic, monarchical rule. The crisis of legitimate authority during America's "critical

666

period" reflected pervasive confusion about the source and scope of authority at all levels of American government. If the states were not truly "sovereign" – and could not be so without destroying the union – the putatively sovereign Congress was not the government of a true state, and therefore could not command the loyalty and resources of the American people. But the federal Constitution enabled Americans to transcend the antagonism among the states and between the states and Congress that had been institutionalized in the Articles of Confederation.

The Federalists persuasively argued that Americans did not have to choose between state governments resting on popular consent and a strong national government wielding a sovereign, superintending authority somehow derived from the old imperial regime. But neither the states nor Congress should be considered "sovereign," insisted supporters of the new regime. The recent history of state constitutional development emphasized the distinction between the sovereign people – the constituent power – and their governments. Federalists exploited this crucial distinction as they sought to legitimize the radical expansion of federal power. According to their conception of popular sovereignty, Americans should be able to distinguish between the source of legitimate authority and the various governments charged with its exercise.

The paradoxical result of dissociating legitimate authority from its institutional forms was that all American governments gained in legitimacy. As Nathaniel Chipman of Vermont wrote, shortly after the new government was established: "solely an impression of the efficiency of the federal government, favored perhaps, by its national magnitude and importance, added, at the instant of organization, a degree of energy to the state governments, and put an end to those factions and turbulent commotions, which made some of them tremble for their political existence" (Onuf, 1983, p. 273). Simply, the Americans had achieved – or were under the "impression" that they had achieved – the integration between governmental authority and political community on which modern conceptions of sovereignty are premised.

FURTHER READING

Bailyn, B.: *Pamphlets of the American Revolution, 1750–1765* (Cambridge, Mass.: Harvard University Press, 1965).

——: *The Ideological Origins of the American Revolution* (Cambridge, Mass.: Harvard University Press, 1967).

Greene, J.P. (ed.): *Colonies to Nation, 1763–1789: a Documentary History of the American Revolution* (New York: McGraw-Hill, 1967).

Marston, J.: *King and Congress: the Transfer of Political Legitimacy, 1774–1776* (Princeton, NJ: Princeton University Press, 1987).

Mason, B. (ed.): *The American Colonial Crisis: the Daniel Leonard–John Adams Letters to the Press, 1774–1775* (New York: Harper & Row, 1972).

Morgan, E.S.: *Inventing the People: the Rise of Popular Sovereignty in England and America* (New York: W.W. Norton, 1988).

Onuf, P.S.: *The Origins of the Federal Republic: Jurisdictional Controversies in the United States, 1775–1787* (Philadelphia: University of Pennsylvania Press, 1983).

——: "State sovereignty and the making of the constitution," *Conceptual Change and the Constitution*, ed. T. Ball and J.G.A. Pocock (Lawrence: University Press of Kansas, 1988), pp. 78–98.

Pocock, J.G.A.: "Machiavelli, Harrington, and English political ideologies in the eighteenth century," *Politics, Language and Time: Essays on Political Thought and History* (New York: Atheneum, 1973), pp. 104–47.

Pole, J. R.: *The Gift of Government: Political Responsibility from the English Restoration to American Independence* (Athens: University of Georgia Press, 1983).

Reid, J. P.: *Constitutional History of American Revolution: the Authority to Tax* (Madison: University of Wisconsin Press, 1987).

Wood, G. S.: *The Creation of the American Republic, 1776–1787* (Chapel Hill: University of North Carolina Press, 1969).

72

Nationality and citizenship

ELISE MARIENSTRAS

A T THE end of the eighteenth century it was generally agreed that the new-born United States did not resemble any other known nation. There was no uniform language. No common history was shared by the inhabitants. Few people yet had family graves with ancestors buried in what would become the national territory. The new state did not aim to restore the legitimacy of an earlier nation-state. Until the very moment of the Declaration of Independence the colonists had been the subjects of the British Crown, which means that they had been members of the British nation (Pole, 1973, p. 3). When they severed their allegiance to the King, the Revolutionaries broke at the same moment their ties to British nationality and their identity as British subjects. They were suddenly compelled to define themselves anew.

Significantly, at the time of the Revolution and for a few decades longer, the former colonists debated over the name of the new nation. Some, including the poet Joel Barlow, preferred "Columbia," in which he found a resonance of his own nationalist epic "The Dream of Columbia" (Barlow, 1807). "America" seemed improper to many, since it referred to a continent rather than to a nation within its borders. Eventually the new nation was named "United States," a political term and not, like Spain, England, or France, a word derived from the name of a people. Moreover, some of the political and intellectual leaders regretted, as did Jedidiah Morse in 1792, that, although she had become formally independent, America was still dependent on Great Britain for her manners, her laws, and her education (Morse, 1792, p. 212). Morse argued for keeping the young men at home instead of sending them to study in England. Noah Webster, the "Schoolmaster to America," as his biographer called him (Warfel, 1936), contemplated a reformation of the English language which would at once "naturalize" the English tongue into American (Webster, 1783). These are some of the indications of the difficulty of defining the United States as a nation. Historians have tried to handle this issue by assigning to the American nation a special character derived from the circumstances of its birth, or its environment, or a particular turn of the American mind. They have echoed the perplexities assailing the American Revolutionaries who had to invent a new kind of citizenship as well as a new nationality.

Many questions arose as soon as the Americans ceased to consider themselves British and settled down to the task of building a nation. Since the 1750s the colonists had assumed three kinds of identity, calling themselves indifferently British-Americans, British subjects, or by the adjective derived from the name of their province. After independence they were left with two identities, not being sure which, the national or the provincial, should prevail. When they became 13 "independent states" the colonies had yet to find what would be the cement of a united body, and how to transform former subjects into citizens of a nation-state as well as of a particular provincial state. The problems that arose were of a cultural, an institutional, and a political nature.

I. A PROBLEMATIC NATION

The Declaration of Independence, by which the revolutionary leaders officially proclaimed that the colonists no longer belonged to the British Empire, did not hint at the issue of nationality. The colonists' right to secede from Great Britain was said to be based upon universal natural rights rather than upon particular national rights. And the last paragraph of the Declaration referred only to the political and international powers of the new independent states without mentioning that they now constituted a nation.

Indeed, in the late 1770s and afterwards, the founding fathers were so doubtful about the existence of the nation that they, as it were, suppressed the word from the official language and replaced it by the word "Union," which is still more often used than "nation." For instance, in 1787–8 the promoters of the Constitutional Convention changed the name by which they were known from "Nationalists" to "Federalists." The terms "nation" and "nationalist" held negative implications for people who feared the tyranny of a strong, centralized government. In order to win the ratification elections over the Anti-Federalists, James Madison and Alexander Hamilton wrote, in *The Federalist Papers*, that the new government would be partly national, partly federal.

This does not mean that only the Federalists desired to establish a nation. The Anti-Federalists merely objected to a national government which would invade individual liberties. The Federalists believed in the necessity of a strong federal state, fit to protect property and national prosperity. But Federalists and Republicans shared a fundamental creed: the necessity to preserve the Union, that is, the nation.

The question which then arose was: to what extent did ordinary people share this sense of unity, of national identity? Did the colonists, as some historians argue (Merritt, 1966), begin to be conscious of being different from their English "brothers" in 1763, after the Seven Years' War? Or had they, on the contrary, become more and more Anglicized in the second half of the eighteenth century, importing more and more European goods, copying more frequently English manners and culture, and even reviving such old English traditions as feudal tenancy, which had then almost disappeared from England (Murrin, 1987)?

Indeed, during the colonial era the 13 coastal colonies, although they enjoyed a large degree of autonomy, were offshoots of the British nation. The empire was conceived as nothing other than a geographical extension of the kingdom. *Jus sanguinis* applied to all inhabitants on condition that they were freemen and Christians. No matter where they resided, or whence they came, all members of the empire were supposed to be inheritors of the same past, of the same traditions, of the same destiny. As they maintained when they rebelled, the colonists were entitled to the rights and liberties of every British subject. On the eve of the American Revolution they were thus privileged British subjects, and they were proud of their nationality.

One must, however, take into account the particularities of the British Americans, and firstly, that they or their ancestors had emigrated from Europe, were confronting a new environment, and were meeting men whose races and cultures were different from those of any European people. Moreover, coming from different parts of Europe, Euro-Americans did not share a common past. They did not eat the same foods, speak the same languages, or belong to the same churches (Morse, 1792). By dealing with the Indians who stood in the path they were ready to conquer or with the imported Africans, whom they deemed inferior to themselves, the colonists had innovated – they had lived through experiences unknown in Europe. They had been "creolized" (Breen, 1984, pp. 195–232).

Did they cease for this reason to be British? Until 1776 the colonists continued to pay their allegiance to the King. They claimed to be loyal British subjects and, moreover, affectionate and obedient "children" of the mother country – a patriarchal metaphor which Thomas Paine vigorously repudiated in *Common Sense*, but which nevertheless was frequently used in the post-revolutionary United States as a way of depicting the ties between the citizens and the nation or the nation's "father," George Washington.

Changing allegiance from England to the United States took, in the words of the leaders, but a short time. John Adams later wrote that the Revolution was in the hearts of the people long before it came to their minds (Adams, 1818). Yet, the transformation which changed the British colonists into American citizens was a slow process. Before independence, members of the elite tried to resist it. They kept close relations with the mother country. Although they had a very different way of life from that of their counterparts living in England, they thought of themselves as sharing in the English culture. During the Revolution some of them chose to stay loyal to the King, and left America when the war broke. The case of the loyalists, who continued their allegiance to the Crown and returned to the mother country or fled to Canada while keeping a strong affection for the country where they were born or where they had lived, is a good, though paradoxical, indicator of the complex meaning of the American sense of national identity.

2. AMERICAN NATIONALITY AS A COLLECTIVE AND INDIVIDUAL SENSE OF BELONGING

The American nation was so new in kind that the revolutionary leaders had to "invent" a new way of attaching the people's sense of identity to it. Members of the American elite, who had initiated the rebellion against the Crown, had no difficulty in shifting their allegiance from Great Britain to the new nation. But the plain people, who were devoid of political power, were not used to mixing their private and public identities. The idea of a national community was foreign to most of them. They had been used to separating in their minds the concept of a state which had been embodied by a distant king and the only real community they knew, which was the local one.

Although they had a strong symbolic sense of British nationality, they were much more involved in their local affiliations. They had a physical knowledge of the limits of their county and province; they had walked through their fields to the next town and church, and participated in local institutions and politics. Now they had to lodge their collective and their personal identity in the same place, a place, however, which was to be apprehended differently at both levels. The problem faced by the early national-era leaders was to help fuse the former colonists' personal sense of belonging into a collective, national attachment to the new nation. This was a process which was to take many years and which would never be completely achieved. Mental dimensions of space, of time, of kinship were to be enlarged. The diversity of the

671

peoples and of the different states had to be overcome and a sense of national unity built through the creation of institutions, the invention of rituals, and the working together of all the parts of the nation in order to achieve a common goal.

The new nation had to be created in the minds of the people as well as in the juridical realm and on the battlefield. The former colonists were induced to think of the United States not only as a federation of 13 governments, but as a newborn being, made of several million people, promised to a brilliant future, and endowed with the mission to protect and spread liberty all over the world – a mission, according to John Adams, inherited from the early Puritans or, as argued by others such as Thomas Jefferson, from the Saxon ancestors. With the help of what historians have come to name "civil religion," with which the clergy, the political leaders, and the intellectuals concurred, the new nation was to be an "imagined community" (Anderson, 1983, Bellah, 1967).

FIGURE 54 The Easton Flag, an early version of the "Stars and Stripes": there were numerous variations in the design of the American flag, dating officially from 14 June 1777; it was originally a marine flag used by John Paul Jones.

Civil religion provided at once an ideological content to citizenship and a fervent spirit of patriotism. As soon as independence was proclaimed, patriotism relied on ideology more than upon traditional national feelings. By shifting the nature of the cause they were struggling for, from a customary conflict between national foes to the modern ideological antagonism of liberty against tyranny, the patriot leaders laid the first basis for a national identity and character. Civil religion thus became the means by which every member of the nation was to be united in a common creed. With the help of new symbols and rituals, the farmer and the mechanic, from their limited view of a close community, were brought to envision the national destiny. The national flag (*see* figure 54), iconograpic representations of Liberty, Fourth of July processions, festivals and celebrations such as George Washington's birthday, days of fasting ordered by Congress – all involved the citizens in new, "invented" traditions which would become part of a common national culture.

3. FORGING AN AMERICAN CITIZEN

There was still another condition to the durability of the nation. The American citizen himself had to forget his ancient being and be transformed into a "new man." "The principle of patriotism," wrote Benjamin Rush, "stands in need of the reinforcement of prejudices in favor of our country, and it is well known that our strongest prejudices are formed in the first one and twenty years of our lives" (Rush, 1786). This is the reason why some of the most eminent of the early national leaders devoted so much attention to education. The republican citizen's virtue was to be inculcated from early childhood. Early national-era textbooks, initiated by Noah Webster's *Spelling Book*, were meant as instruments of civic education. Indeed, the schoolteacher was to be the first, if modest, builder of American citizenship.

However, the legal status and definition of citizenship remained ambiguous for a long time. It was not until after the Civil War that a general and national definition of the American citizen appeared in the Fourteenth Amendment to the Constitution.

Indeed, the question of citizenship arose as soon as the colonists denounced their allegiance to the King, even before independence was proclaimed: in January 1776 New Hampshire adopted a new constitution, and was soon followed by South Carolina, which, in March 1776, required all its officers to swear an oath "to support, maintain, and defend" the provisional constitution (Kettner, 1978, p. 175). All at once, the traditional oath of allegiance to the King was dropped from the rebellious documents, as if allegiance had simply shifted from the monarch to the new independent and sovereign states.

In so doing, local assemblies, conventions, or committees acted as representatives of all the inhabitants, or at least of the majority of them. The loyalists, or the people who disagreed with the majority decisions, were at first considered as a minority who had to comply with the general will. But war, cases of plotting, espionage, and counterfeiting forced the states and the Continental Congress to separate more clearly the people who agreed with the new policies from those who stayed loyal to the King. Thus, in a pragmatic manner, the states and the Continental Congress took the first steps towards defining the status of the inhabitants. On 24 June 1776 Congress resolved that

> all persons residing within any of the United Colonies, and deriving their protection from the laws of the same, owe allegiance to the said laws, and are members of such colony; ... [and] that all persons, members of, or owing allegiance to any of the United Colonies ... who shall levy war against any of the said colonies ..., or be adherents to the king of Great Britain ... are guilty of treason against such colony. (*Journals of the Continental Congress*, V, pp. 475–6)

A few days later, the Declaration of Independence repeated in other words the assertion that, in the same manner as allegiance to the King had been tied to his duty of protection, so was citizenship in the new states dependent upon a contract which provided for state protection to the citizens in return for their allegiance to the republican government.

Thus citizenship was defined through allegiance, as it used to be in the British Empire. But now that the people had become sovereign, citizenship came to be considered as contractual and volitionary. A further step was taken when, after the treaty of peace in 1783, questions of debts, confiscation, or inheritance required that a distinction be made between what the British tradition called "the natural" subjects of the King, who were named "real subjects" in the diplomatic documents, and the citizens of the United States. Originally, most Americans had been "natural" subjects. Again, the notion of volitionary personal allegiance was used to distinguish citizens from aliens. However, the status of the *"ante-nati"* was not definitely solved, and it was debated with reference to *Calvin's case*, which Sir Edward Coke had reported in 1607, when, the kingdoms of Scotland and England being united under the same king, the nationality of Scottish subjects became an issue. Two centuries later the arguments of Sir Edward Coke were recalled, proving that the question of nationality and citizenship, as new as it presented itself in the United States, also carried on the old British tradition.

More easy to solve than such legal cases, the process of naturalization provided citizenship to those aliens who were ready to swear their loyalty to the revolutionary United States. After some confusion about which, of the separate states or the Union, would be entitled to determine the rules of naturalization, the Federal Constitution of 1787 determined a national standard of naturalization through laws voted by Congress. Several Acts were adopted, in 1795, in 1798, and in 1802, the last one becoming the main legal document on citizenship up to the Civil War. Significantly, these naturalization laws differed mainly about the time of residence which was required from the applicant to be granted American nationality. From two years to 14, it was eventually settled at five years, considered enough for those imbued with "foreign principles" to assimilate the habits, values, and mode of thought necessary for responsible participation in a self-governing republican community (Kettner, 1978, p. 219). For, although citizenship was primarily considered a matter of personal election, the political community did not open its doors to everyone without qualification. The Federal Constitution, as well as the states, reserved citizenship to white freemen, implicitly excluding Blacks, even though they were free, and Indians who belonged to tribes, then considered as foreign nations. Citizenship was not extended to Blacks before 1868 or to Indians before 1924. White women also, while they could be treated as citizens in economic matters, were not entitled to all the privileges of citizenship before 1919.

For those who were admitted as citizens, citizenship, however, was an ambivalent concept and reality. The Constitution did not solve the indetermination of citizenship which had come out of the Revolution. The Articles of Confederation had paved the way for a dual citizenship. Article IV of this first American constitution had stated that "the free inhabitants of each of [the] states ... shall be entitled to all privileges and immunities of free citizens in the several states." There was some debate about the meaning of the phrase "free inhabitants," but it is clear from further documents that, implicitly, the American people were considered at once citizens of their own state and citizens of the United States. A dual citizenship was created, which resembled only in shape the former dual subjectship of the colonists.

The Constitution of 1787, while presenting the concept of citizenship indirectly through naturalization, also made clear that the American inhabitants were citizens both of their state of residence and of the United States as a whole. However, the discussions that arose between Federalists and Republicans about the "implied powers" of Congress involved the idea that a common citizenship in a national political community conflicted with the sovereignty of the states. Political implications of citizenship were referred to only in the articles dealing with eligibility to the highest federal positions. But qualifications for the main political right of the citizen, that of suffrage, were left to each state to decide upon.

Gradually, a vertical integration from the several states to the Union was attempted.

The Federalists, particularly, insisted on the necessity of homogenizing the citizens in order for the union to endure (Washington, Vol. 27, p. 50). Once again, it would be left to the Union victory in the Civil War, and its aftermath in Reconstruction, to ensure the prevalence of national citizenship over that of the states, and once and for all to confront directly the question of individual citizenship with all the duties and rights attached to it.

FURTHER READING

Adams, John: "To Hezekiah Niles," 13 February 1818, *The Works of John Adams*, 10 vols., ed. C. F. Adams (Boston: Little, Brown & Co., 1856), Vol. 10, p. 285.

Anderson, Benedict: *Imagined Communities: Reflections on the Origin and Spread of Nationalism* (London: Verso, New Left Books, 1983).

Barlow, Joel: *The Columbiad: a Poem* (Philadelphia, 1807).

Bellah, Robert N.: "Civil Religion in America," *Daedalus*, 96 (1967), 1–21.

Breen, Timothy: "Creative adaptations: peoples and cultures," *Colonial British America*, ed. J. P. Greene and J. R. Pole (Baltimore and London: Johns Hopkins University Press, 1984).

Kettner, James H.: *The Development of American Citizenship, 1608–1870* (Chapel Hill: University of North Carolina Press, 1978).

Marienstras, Elise: *Nous le peuple: les origines du nationalisme americain* (Paris: Editions Gallimard, 1988).

Merritt, Richard: *Symbols of American Community, 1735–1775* (New Haven, CT: Yale University Press, 1966).

Morse, Jedidiah: *The American Geography* (Philadelphia, 1792).

Murrin, John M.: " 'A roof without walls': the dilemma of American national identity," *Beyond Confederation: Origins of the Constitution and American National Identity* (Chapel Hill: University of North Carolina Press, 1987). 333–48.

Pole, Jack R.: *Foundations of American Independence, 1763–1815* (London, 1972); repr. (London and Glasgow; Fontana, 1973).

Rush, Benjamin: *Thoughts upon the Mode of Education Proper in a Republic* (Philadelphia, 1786).

Savelle, Max: "Nationalism and other loyalties in the American revolution," *American Historical Review*, 67 (1962), 901–23.

Warfel, Henry R.: *Noah Webster, Schoolmaster to America* (New York, 1936; repr. 1966).

Washington, George: *The Writings of George Washington*, ed. J. C. Fitzpatrick (Washington, DC: Government Printing Office, 1931–44).

Webster, Noah: *The American Spelling Book* (Boston, 1783).

73

The separation of powers

MAURICE J. C. VILE

O F ALL the decisions taken at the Constitutional Convention in Philadelphia, the decision to build the new system of government on the basis of the doctrine of the separation of powers had the most far-reaching effect. It not only distinguished the American system sharply from the British system, against which the Founding Fathers were reacting, but it also meant that the future development of the American polity was to be very different from that of nearly every other democracy that was to evolve during the nineteenth and twentieth centuries, for the latter were to choose parliamentary government as the pattern for their constitutional arrangements.

I. THE CONCEPT OF THE SEPARATION OF POWERS AND THE ENGLISH CIVIL WAR

The concept of separating the exercise of the legislative and executive functions, and entrusting them to different branches of government, had its roots in Greek political thought, was echoed by Cicero, and was developed by Marsilius of Padua in the fourteenth century and embodied in the institutions of the Venetian Republic. The transformation of these ancient and medieval concepts into a modern form which could reasonably be labeled the doctrine of the separation of powers, took place, however, during the English Civil War, and attained its most clear and precise expression during the Protectorate. The battle between King and Parliament served to sharpen the distinctions made between the functions of government which had previously characterized the accepted constitutional theory, the mixture of monarchy, aristocracy, and democracy – King, Lords, and Commons. At the extreme, the opponents of the royal power argued with Milton that the King should have no function in the making of the law, but should be concerned solely with its execution. With the execution of the King and the abolition of the House of Lords, the need was clear for a new constitution of government, and in 1653 the *Instrument of Government*, although never implemented, provided the first written constitution of modern times. The *Instrument* entrusted the legislative power to Parliament, giving the Protector only a suspensive veto of 20 days, and in Article II confided the "exercise of the chief magistracy and the administration of the government" to the Lord Protector. The defense of the *Instrument*, *A True State of the Case of the Commonwealth*, published in 1654 and probably written by Marchamont Nedham, set out the necessity for the separation of the executive and legislative powers if corruption and tyranny were to be avoided. Nedham's second work, *The Excellencie of a Free State* (1656), reiterated that "A fifth Errour in Policy hath been this, viz. a permitting of the Legislative and

676

Executive Powers of a State, to vest in one and the same hands and persons." According to John Adams, Nedham's work was well known in colonial America. Indeed, the momentous events taking place in England had their impact in the colonies, and in Massachusetts in 1679 the Elders of the Church asserted that the Charter of the Company of Massachusetts Bay had set up a "distribution of differing interest of power and privilege between the magistrates and freemen, and the distinct exercise of legislative and executive power."

2. EIGHTEENTH-CENTURY CONSTITUTIONAL THEORISTS

The ideas which were evolved in England in the mid-seventeenth century were further developed by Locke, Montesquieu, and Blackstone, in a much less extreme form, one which was adapted to the restored monarchy and the mixed and balanced constitution of post-revolutionary England, and which fitted well with the forms of government then established in the American colonies themselves. The separation of powers remained an essential element in the constitution of a free state, but the branches of government must have the ability to prevent the abuse of power by the others. Montesquieu summed up his view thus: "Here, then, is the fundamental constitution of the government we are treating of. The legislative body being composed of two parts, they check one another by the mutual privilege of rejecting. They are both restrained by the executive power, as the executive is by the legislative." The eighteenth-century constitutional theorists also abandoned the twofold division of the functions of government into legislation and execution which had largely characterized the preceding century, and asserted the importance of a separate judicial function of government, and, following the Bill of Rights, the independence of the judges. However, with the increasing tension between the American colonies and the mother country in the 1770s, Americans increasingly used the separation of powers to attack the structure and operation of British government, and as a consequence to criticize also the structure of colonial governments. The role of the Governor's Council, which had a finger in every pie, was attacked as an affront to the separation of powers. James Otis, in 1764, mounted a passionate attack upon the appointment of Lieutenant-Governor Hutchinson as Chief Justice of Massachusetts, and demands were made for the exclusion of members of the judiciary from the colonial legislature. Above all, the exercise by the colonial governors of the royal prerogative was under attack, in particular the exercise of the veto power, which was actively used to disallow bills passed by colonial legislatures, long after the sovereign had, in Jefferson's words, "modestly declined the exercise of this power in that part of his empire called Great Britain." "Demophilus," and other pamphleteers in revolutionary Pennsylvania, demanded that the role of the Governor must be "solely executive," the same demand that the radicals had made during the English revolution.

As in mid-seventeenth century England, the more radical the attack upon the established institutions, the more extreme the demands for the implementation of a thoroughgoing separation of powers. The authority of Montesquieu was invoked on all sides, but the great philosopher's emphasis upon the importance of checks and balances was appealed to only by Tories and by the more conservative elements, whose voices were not very audible amidst the revolutionary fervor of 1775. The radicals in Pennsylvania and in the New Hampshire Grants, later to become the state of Vermont, would have nothing of mixed and balanced government. In the words of the historian Samuel Williams of Vermont, in the "American system of government

677

... the security of the people is derived not from the nice ideal application of checks, ballances, and mechanical powers, among the different parts of the government, but from the responsibility, and dependence of each part of the government, upon the people." In other words the branches of government should be separate from each other, and each answerable directly to the people, not to the other branches. The direct and only check upon each branch of government is, therefore, the electorate, leading to demands for the election not only of legislators and of the head of the executive, but of judges also. Thus began a major strand of American constitutional thought which is still important today, particularly in the sphere of state government.

3. THE DRAFTING OF STATE CONSTITUTIONS

In the revolutionary atmosphere of 1776, the separation of powers was the only respectable ideological basis for the drafting of constitutions for the newly declared states in order to replace their redundant colonial charters. A clear statement of the doctrine came in the preamble to the Constitution of Virginia of June 1776:

> The legislative, executive and judiciary departments shall be separate and distinct, so that neither exercise the powers properly belonging to the other: nor shall any person exercise the powers of more than one of them at the same time, except that the justices of the county courts shall be eligible to either House of Assembly.

All the elements of the doctrine are here – separate branches of government exercising different functions, and a prohibition upon membership of more than one branch at any one time. The last of these characteristics of the doctrine has had the greatest influence on shaping the distinctively American political scene, making "cabinet government" impossible, breaking the link between executive and legislature, and making it possible for legislators to maintain their independence of action without destroying the stability of the executive.

The constitutions of Pennsylvania, Virginia, and of four other states written in 1776 and early 1777 reflected the revolutionary doctrine that power was delegated by the people to the several branches of government. In these constitutions the effort was made to remove all vestiges of prerogative powers; the only exception that was made was to give to some governors the power of pardon or reprieve. No veto power was wielded by the governors of these states. The Constitution of Virginia provided that the governor "shall not, under any pretence, exercise any power or prerogative, by virtue of any law, statute or custom of England." Jefferson later wrote that the Constitution of Virginia was designed to remove all discretionary power from the executive, indeed that no power could be exercised which was not clearly embodied in legislation. The only concession to the theory of checks and balances, associated as it was with notions of monarchy and aristocracy, was the adoption of bicameral legislatures in all but two of these states. Pennsylvania, engaged in an internal upheaval as well as in revolution against Britain, enacted the most radical constitution, providing for a unicameral assembly, a directly-elected plural executive, the Supreme Executive Council, and a Council of Censors with the duty of enquiring every seven years "whether the legislative and executive branches of government have performed their duty as guardians of the people, or assumed to themselves, or exercised other or greater powers than they are intitled to by the constitution."

The constitution for the new state of Vermont, written in 1777, adopted the same radical pattern as that of Pennsylvania, but the other early state constitutions, such as those of Virginia, Georgia, and Maryland, retained some semblances of the theory of the balanced constitution, in particular bicameralism. However, a reaction very soon set in against what was seen as the effects of extreme democracy, and against the extreme form of the doctrine of the separation of powers, a reaction which was to gain momentum, and to become a vital factor in shaping the Constitution of the United States. The idea that the separation of powers, standing alone as the theoretical basis of a constitutional structure, was an adequate protection against the abuse of power by governments very quickly came under attack. State legislatures began to meddle in all the aspects of government, including the exercise of the judicial power. As Jefferson wrote in his *Notes on the State of Virginia*, published in 1781, the constitution of that state had separated the powers of government, but because "no barrier was provided between the separate powers" the legislature, merely by casting its decisions in the form of legislation, could interfere in those aspects of government which were properly the preserve of the executive and judicial branches. Thus, Jefferson asserted, "all the powers of government, legislative, executive and judiciary, result to the legislative body." Americans learned, as their English forebears had learned during the rule of the Long Parliament, that legislatures can be as tyrannical as kings or governors.

Even in 1777 the Constitution of New York recognized the need for a system of government with greater checks to the exercise of legislative power, but it was in the debates leading to the adoption of the Constitution of Massachusetts in 1780 that the problem of reconciling the separation of powers with the need to provide effective checks to the abuse of power by any of the branches of government was squarely faced. The *Essex Result*, the views of the people of Essex County on the shape of the proposed state constitution, drafted by Theophilus Parsons, clearly set out what was to be the American solution to the problem of ensuring freedom from the exercise of excessive power by government. The *Result* did not in any way recede from a belief in the importance of the separation of powers, but it emphasized that this in itself was not enough. "Each branch is to be independent, and further, to be so balanced, and be able to exert such checks upon the others, as will preserve it from a dependence on, or a union with them." This was exactly the position taken by Madison in the Constitutional Convention in Philadelphia:

> If a constitutional discrimination of the departments on paper were a sufficient security to each against encroachments of the others, all further provisions would indeed be superfluous. But experience had taught us a distrust of that security; and that it is necessary to introduce such a balance of powers and interests, as will guarantee the provisions on paper.

4. THE FEDERAL CONSTITUTION

Although the Federal Constitution represented a movement back towards the principles of the balanced constitution of mid-eighteenth-century Britain, the final result was very different from that model. The Convention specifically rejected the British system of parliamentary government and the role of the Cabinet in that system. JAMES IREDELL noted that in England "everybody knows that the whole movement of their government ... [is] directed by their *Cabinet Council*, composed entirely of the principal officers of the great departments," which was, in the view of George Mason, "the worst and most dangerous of all ingredients for such a council in a free country." Resisting the proposal that the President be elected by the legislature, Gouverneur

Morris said that in England "the *real* King . . . is the Minister. . . . Our President will be the British Minister, yet we are about to make him appointable by the Legislature." Along with the rejection of the idea of government by a cabinet went the complete exclusion of office-holders from membership of the legislature, a motion which was accepted by the Convention without opposition. Thus the personnel of the legislative and executive branches were to be completely separate, with the exception of the role of the Vice-President as presiding officer of the Senate. The former prerogatives of the Crown were dealt with by dividing them and distributing them between the President and the Congress – a qualified veto power for the President which can be overturned by the Congress, the presidential appointing power subject to Senate confirmation, and the negotiation of treaties by the President subject to ratification by the Senate. Only the power of pardon remained unscathed from the former powers of the King.

The role of the Supreme Court and the judiciary in this combination of the separation of powers and checks and balances was less clear. A major difference between the *Instrument of Government* of 1653 and the Federal Constitution over a century later was the firm establishment in the latter of a separate and powerful judicial branch; but neither the extent of the power of the judiciary to check the other branches, nor a clear prohibition on dual membership, was provided by the Constitution. There is evidence in the revolutionary period of the development of the idea of judicial review of legislation, of the power of the courts to declare legislature decisions unconstitutional and therefore void. JAMES WILSON argued that case before the Pennsylvania ratifying convention, and Alexander Hamilton in *The Federalist*, no. 78, justified the exercise of judicial power over Acts of Congress. However, it is not until the Supreme Court itself asserted this power that it could clearly be seen to be a consequence of the doctrine of checks and balances which Madison enunciated so clearly in *The Federalist*, no. 47: "Unless these departments be so far connected and blended, as to give to each a constitutional control over the others, the degree of separation which the maxim requires, as essential to a free government, can never in practice be duly maintained."

The acceptance by the Convention of the separation of powers modified by the old theory of checks and balances was not, however, the end of the debate. John Adams, in his *Defence of the Constitutions of the United States* (1787–8), had urged upon the American people the desirability of a return to the old form of mixed government, and, although the Convention did not by any means accept the ideas there set out, Adams's work became the stalking-horse of those who opposed what they saw as monarchical and aristocratic elements in the new constitution. The doctrine of the separation of powers became the most coherent theoretical basis of the Anti-Federalists' attack upon what they saw as, in the words of Nathaniel Chipman in *Sketches of the Principles of Government* (1793), "a confusion of powers," a perpetual war of one part against the others, a situation incompatible with republican government. Jefferson himself, in his later years, returned to the idea that each of the three branches of government should be directly accountable to the people and not to each other, and the great exponent of Jeffersonian Republicanism, John Taylor of Caroline, in his major work, *An Inquiry into the Principles and Policy of the Government of the United States* (1814), presented a coherent and thoroughgoing analysis based upon the separation of powers, rejecting totally the remnants of mixed government to be found in the Federal Constitution. John Taylor drew upon the tradition of radical thought stretching back to the work of Marchamont Nedham during the Protectorate in order to put forward an extreme version of the separation of powers as the basis for a free system of government, but, at the level of the Federal Government at any rate, the triumph of the Federalists was complete, and the American version of a separation of the legislative, executive, and judicial branches of government, in which each could check the others and yet retain its own independence, became the foundation of a uniquely democratic system.

FURTHER READING

Gwyn, W. B.: *The Meaning of the Separation of Powers* (New Orleans: Tulane University Press, 1965).
Levy, L. W.: *Original Intent and the Framers' Constitution* (New York: Macmillan, 1988).
Vile, M. J. C.: *Constitution and the Separation of Powers* (Oxford: Clarendon Press, 1967).

74

Rights

RONALD HAMOWY

A NUMBER of legal theorists have observed that the conception of universal rights with which the late eighteenth century was most comfortable had its origins in the Reformation. From this religious schism emerged the notion that the primary function of the state is to provide the structural arrangements within which each of us might freely choose the path to our own salvation. This conception of the proper limits of government is particularly prominent in Puritan thought as it developed in England in the seventeenth century. The perception of the character of government there put forward, which differs markedly from the political notions of Plato and Aristotle, precludes the state from attempting to create a virtuous society and from acting as the instrument by which individual men rise to goodness. Since fundamental differences in religious beliefs are inconsistent with a universally acceptable notion of what a good and virtuous society is, any social order prepared to tolerate differing conceptions of religious truth cannot have as one of its ends the establishment of a moral community. It follows that governments are devised for far more limited purposes, specifically that they have their origin in the desire to establish the minimum amount of social control compatible with individual freedom and with individual choice of religious practice and belief.

I. THE EIGHTEENTH-CENTURY CONCEPTION OF NATURAL RIGHTS

Two developments during the course of the seventeenth century were pivotal in shaping the conception of rights embraced by the American colonists immediately before the Revolution. The first of these was that English legal theory began to adapt the older notion of legal privilege, historically attached to specific groups or classes within society or to Englishmen alone, to the idea of rights that were applicable to all men. This transmutation began to emerge in the constitutional controversies of the first half of the seventeenth century, where the rights asserted against the Crown were still couched in terms of the traditional privileges and liberties of Englishmen but where a suggestion of some more general, universal notion of rights begins to appear. Thus, while the Petition of Right (1628), which was largely the work of Sir Edward Coke, speaks of a series of specific "rights and liberties" to which Englishmen are heir, the document adumbrates the notion that there exists a fundamental law that forever protects the subject from certain political intrusions. The conception of an original, underlying law, superior to any act of government, irrespective of which branch, from which certain rights are derivable, appears most clearly in Coke's dictum on the role of the common law in *Dr. Bonham's Case* (1610), where he notes that "in many cases, the common law will control acts of parliament, and sometimes adjudge them to be utterly void; for when an act of parliament is against common right and reason, or repugnant, or impossible to be performed, the common law will control it and adjudge such act to be void."

At the same time that the English were extending the notion of rights to encompass something broader than the traditional privileges accorded certain groups, Continental legal philosophers were in the process of elaborating a modern theory of natural law which provided the framework for the eighteenth-century conception of natural rights. The writings of Hugo Grotius and Samuel Pufendorf, especially, were enormously influential in providing the philosophical groundwork upon which seventeenth- and eighteenth-century politics and law rested. The natural-law jurists were successful in relocating the foundations of natural law from the dictates of God and the postulates of religion to reason itself. The existence of a set of universal principles governing man's conduct could, it was henceforth argued, be established by an appeal to common reason, independent of any religious truth. There exist certain principles of law and justice, the natural-law jurists argued, that are immutable and discoverable by reason, under which all societies ought to organize themselves. These principles transcend all differences of time and place and are not artificial but rest upon our common nature as human beings. To the extent that these principles give rise to certain rights, these rights are ours by virtue of our humanity and are neither devised nor bestowed upon us by the conventional arrangements of men. They precede the establishment of a political community and do not follow from it. Indeed, the political community itself is a product of the association of individual wills who freely contract to enter civil society for particular prudential reasons.

2. JOHN LOCKE AND ALGERNON SIDNEY

While the natural-law school of Grotius and Pufendorf had emancipated natural law from religious dogma and had located the origins of political institutions in voluntary contract, it was not until the publication of John Locke's *Two Treatises of Government* in 1690 that a systematic theory of universal, inalienable rights appears. The main outlines of Locke's doctrine are clear and unambiguous: all men are by nature free and independent beings, originally constrained solely by the law of nature, i.e., the rule of right reason; the state of nature into which men are originally born, while not a pre-social one, is a pre-political one; while pre-political, mankind's original state is not lawless inasmuch as the law of nature dictates that no man may harm another in his life, health, liberty, or possessions; it further follows from the law of nature that men may be restrained from invading others' rights and may be punished by others for doing so; governments are established solely for the purpose of better protecting the rights with which all men are naturally endowed; the power to protect one's life, liberty, and estate against injury and to judge of and punish those who offend against them can be surrendered to the civil magistrate only by individual consent; once a government acts beyond its trust, the preservation of the lives, liberties, and estates of its subjects, it ceases being legitimate and may no longer command the allegiance of the people. At that point revolution is lawful. The whole Lockean schema is predicated on the primacy of man's right to property, under whose rubric Locke understood man's rights to life, liberty, and estate. These rights, with which all men are born, are thus inherent and inviolable. Grounded in the law of nature itself, they are invulnerable to legislative action and provide to each individual a private sphere

683

totally immune to social control. Indeed, the very legitimacy of any government stands or falls upon whether these rights are respected.

Locke, of course, was not alone in advocating a theory of indefeasible natural rights the protection of which was the end of government. Similar sentiments appear in Algernon Sidney's *Discourses on Government*, which first appeared in print in 1698, some 15 years after Sidney's execution for treason. Sidney writes of men's "natural liberty," of the "common rights of mankind" which proceed from the laws of nature, and of the fact that "government is not instituted for the good of the governor, but of the governed." But what emerges with greatest clarity from the pages of the *Discourses* is a ringing defense of the right of the people to rebel against a tyrannical government. The writings of both Locke and Sidney were of immense importance in shaping radical thought in England at the end of the seventeenth century, particularly in providing the theoretical justification for resistance to Stuart oppression. It is therefore not surprising that the works of these two authors should have been embraced with such warmth by the American Revolutionaries in their struggles with the British Government. They are cited over and over again in the political literature that issued forth in such quantity in the period immediately before the Revolution and their conclusions on the nature of law and government were almost universally accepted by educated Americans.

3. THE ENGLISH BILL OF RIGHTS

Radical Whig doctrine, of which Locke's political theory was the most compelling and thorough statement, served as the ideological underpinning of the English Revolution of 1688–9, by which Prince William of Orange and his wife Mary, daughter of James II, were offered the crown of England. On 11 December 1688, James II had fled his kingdom, having flung the Great Seal, the symbol of constitutional authority, into the Thames. Since James's only Parliament had been dissolved the previous summer, his flight plunged the nation into a constitutional crisis which was resolved only by the creation of an extra-legal convention, which first met on 22 January 1689. The convention, whose debates were dominated by the radical Whigs, was successful in linking the settlement of the throne with a declaration of rights, in which the political prerogatives of the Crown were sharply restricted and in which the Whig conception of the proper relationship between king and Parliament was set forth. While William and Mary agreed to abide by the rights set forth in the declaration, the document did not have the force of law until enacted as a statute by the Convention Parliament some ten months later. The Bill of Rights, as the statute came to be known, is properly regarded as one of the fundamental charters of English liberty and was often invoked in the colonial argument against arbitrary government. Among its provisions are that "excessive bail ought not to be required, nor excessive fines imposed, nor cruel and unusual punishments inflicted" and that "grants and promises of fines and forfeitures of particular persons before conviction are illegal and void." But of greater importance to the colonists in their conflict with Britain was the Bill's provision that laws made or suspended without the consent of Parliament (i.e., the representatives of the people) are illegal. Since, in the minds of the American Revolutionaries, the Parliament of Great Britain no more represented the people of the colonies than did the General Assembly of New York represent the people of Virginia, it followed that laws enacted by the British Parliament – and without the consent of the colonies – that were aimed at regulating the affairs of her American colonies were void.

684

The Bill of Rights does not speak to the theoretical foundations of the rights it specifies except to describe them as "the true, ancient, and indubitable rights and liberties of the people of this kingdom." But there is ample historical evidence to support the conclusion that most members of the Convention were intimately familiar with and, in many instances, embraced the principles of natural law and natural rights as they were to be spelled out in Locke's *Treatises*. A large number of political tracts were published in London during the fall and winter of 1688-9, written by radical Whigs and advancing the notion that all political power was ultimately based on a contract between subject and ruler, that the powers of government were limited by the terms of the contract that established it, that this consisted in securing the rights and liberties of the people, and that, should the terms of this contract be violated, the people were free to dissolve the government and to choose a new one. The Bill of Rights is perfectly consistent with this view in seeking to restrict the prerogatives of the king and to shift the axis of political power from the king to Parliament.

4. AMERICAN COLONIAL CLAIMS TO NATURAL RIGHTS

The absence of any theoretical preamble to most of the colonial charters and the fact that the protections that they afforded were couched in terms of the traditional prerogatives accorded Englishmen might also suggest that their authors did not embrace a conception of rights derivable from nature. But this is to mistake the purpose of these charters, which was to provide a frame of government for each of the colonies. To the extent that they set limits to the powers of the colonial governments, it is to be expected that these charters would concern themselves primarily with the procedural protections accorded the colonists as Englishmen living overseas. Even the Fundamental Constitution of Carolina (1669), which provides that "no person whatsoever shall disturb, molest, or persecute another for his speculative opinions in religion, or his way of worship," a protection that goes far beyond any then existing in England, does not suggest whence this right derives. It is only because its author is John Locke that we know that its source is in the law of nature itself. Indeed, many of the protections mentioned in the various charters at the least suggest that they are included by virtue of the colonists' humanity and were derived from God or nature, and not from the state. Even with respect to the provisions that dealt with the specific powers granted the various colonial governments, it is apparent that the rights that were subject to legislative construction, such as the right to property, could be circumscribed only under the strictest conditions. Thus, the Massachusetts Body of Liberties, enacted in 1641, specified that "no man's goods or estate shall be taken away from him nor any way damaged under color of law or countenance of authority unless it be by virtue or equity of some express law of the country warranting the same, established by a General Court and sufficiently published, or in case of the defect of a law in any particular case by the word of God."

There is a body of scholarly opinion that contends that the claims made by the American colonists in their controversies with Great Britain were consistently framed in the language of English rights and that arguments based on the authority of natural law were irrelevant to the debate. For example, John Phillip Reid writes that "the revolutionary controversy was concerned with positive constitutional rights, not abstract natural rights," and that "at every important occasion when the American whig leadership gathered to claim rights and state grievances, nature was rejected as the sole authority for rights." But even Reid's somewhat extravagant assertions concede that the colonists did in fact often appeal to the law of nature as an alternative authority for the rights they asserted. Nor does there seem much doubt, despite Reid's reservations, that, as open rebellion with Great Britain approached, the colonists increasingly resorted to arguments based not on the prerogatives peculiar to Englishmen but rather on man's natural rights. Indeed, Reid himself offers several examples in which the colonial position is couched in terms that are unambiguously grounded on the law of nature. Thus, among the resolutions of the freeholders of Granville County in 1774 is the following: "Resolved, That those absolute rights we are entitled to as men, by the immutable Laws of Nature, are antecedent to all social and relative duties whatsoever." And the Boston Declaration of 1772, which invokes the "eternal and immutable laws of God and nature" and whose introductory comments read like a précis of Locke's *Treatises of Government*, provides that "among the natural rights of the colonists are these: first, a right to life; secondly, to liberty; thirdly, to property; together with the right to support and defend them in the best manner they can." And, with particular reference to the protections afforded Americans by the several colonial charters, James Otis observed: "Should the charter privileges of the Colonists be disregarded or revoked, there are natural, inherent, and inseparable rights as men and citizens that would remain."

Regardless of how firmly and how frequently the American colonists might have based their earlier claims against Great Britain on their rights as Englishmen, there is no doubt that, as open rebellion approached, the nature of their demands shifted to claims grounded on natural rights. Nor can there be any doubt that the prevailing political orthodoxy, particularly among Americans, was Lockean. Whether the colonists' debt was directly to Locke or to other writers of lesser rank, such as Emmerich de Vattel or Jean Jacques Burlamaqui, who, among others, both treated the first principles of government in a manner similar to that found in the *Treatises*, is not terribly important. The fact is that the conception of rights as deriving from the law of nature and the notion that political authority was, by virtue of its essential qualities, severely circumscribed, were commonplaces with which few educated colonists would take issue. And these conclusions were, in the minds of all Americans, ultimately attributable to Locke.

5. STATE CONSTITUTIONS AND THE DECLARATION OF INDEPENDENCE

The language of the Declaration of Independence is evidence of the pervasiveness of the Lockean notion of rights among the colonists. There is no reason to question Jefferson's claim, when writing some years later about the political principles contained in the Declaration, that, "with respect to our rights, and the acts of the British government contravening those rights, there was but one opinion on this side of the water; all American whigs thought alike on these subjects." The truth of Jefferson's assertion is vouchsafed by the fact that several states, as part of their new constitutions, enacted declarations of rights explicitly couched in Lockean language by the end of 1776. The first of these, Virginia's Declaration of Rights, was drafted by George Mason and antedated the Declaration of Independence by well over a month. Indeed, given the similarity of language between the two documents, there is good reason to believe that Jefferson had a copy of the Virginia Declaration before him when composing the Declaration of Independence. Article I of Mason's Declaration reads: "All men are by nature equally free and independent, and have certain inherent rights, of which,

686

when they entered into a state of society, they cannot by any compact, deprive or divest their posterity; namely, the enjoyment of life and liberty, with the means of acquiring and possessing property and pursuing and obtaining happiness and safety." The language of Pennsylvania's Declaration of Rights is almost identical: "All men are born equally free and independent, and have certain natural, inherent and inalienable rights, amongst which are, the enjoying and defending life and liberty, acquiring, possessing and protecting property, and pursuing and obtaining happiness and safety."

The conception of rights embraced by the American revolutionary theorists conceived of them as eternal and immutable, as antedating the establishment of all political authority, and as belonging to all men by virtue of their humanity alone. Since their exercise does not conflict with others' rights, this conception logically entails the strictest limits on the actions of government, a notion that shaped much of early American political philosophy. The gradual erosion of this understanding of rights and its replacement with the view that individual rights are, by their nature, conflicting and that their exercise requires that others be impelled to act in certain ways entails a very different conception of government, one in which the political authority is required to intervene actively, both to mediate between the rights of citizens and to provide the means whereby certain rights can be realized. It is important, when examining the notion of rights within the context of the American Revolution, that this second, more modern, and somewhat vulgar conception is not confused with the way the eighteenth century understood the term, as so often happens. Fortunately, this newer notion of rights has not totally supplanted its eighteenth-century rival, which still serves to animate citizens against the arbitrary incursions of a despotic government. We all owe a great deal to seventeenth- and eighteenth-century political theory and particularly to radical Whig thought for providing a theory of rights and of government consistent with individual autonomy and freedom. While so many of the insights that the eighteenth century has furnished us have been abandoned, we still remain indebted for a conception of rights that places the individual above the state and that makes the ultimate test of government whether those rights are protected.

FURTHER READING

Bailyn, Bernard: *The Ideological Origins of the American Revolution* (Cambridge, Mass.: Belknap Press of Harvard University Press, 1967).

Corwin, Edwin S.: *The "Higher Law" Background of American Constitutional Law* (Ithaca, NY: Cornell University Press, 1955).

Gierke, Otto: *Natural Law and the Theory of Society, 1500 to 1800*, trans. Ernest Barker (Cambridge: Cambridge University Press, 1950).

Reid, John Phillip: *Constitutional History of the American Revolution: the Authority of Rights* (Madison: University of Wisconsin Press, 1986).

Rossiter, Clinton: *Seedtime of the Republic: the Origin of the American Tradition of Political Liberty* (New York: Harcourt, Brace, 1953).

Tuck, Richard: *Natural Rights Theories: Their Origin and Development* (Cambridge: Cambridge University Press, 1979).

75

Virtue

JAMES T. KLOPPENBERG

VIRTUE was ubiquitous in eighteenth-century American discourse. An all-purpose term of approbation, virtue had different, and occasionally incompatible, meanings in different contexts. When Montesquieu distinguished between three sorts of virtue – Christian, political, and moral – in *The Spirit of the Laws*, he was only confirming what contemporaries already knew. While the categories of religion, politics, and ethics may have been separable in principle, however, in linguistic practice they were usually blurred. Understanding the range of meanings associated with virtue in revolutionary America requires distinguishing among these different vocabularies and understanding how they changed from 1763 to 1800.

I. CHRISTIAN IDEAS OF VIRTUE

Virtue lay at the heart of Christian doctrine. While Aquinas followed Aristotle in conceiving of the intellectual and moral virtues as a mean between defects and excesses, he placed primary emphasis on the infused theological virtues of faith, hope, and especially charity, which had no counterpart in ancient philosophy. The Christian ideal of universal benevolence translated into a wide variety of philosophical and political outlooks in America, ranging from the rationalism of Charles Chauncy and Jonathan Mayhew to the Augustinian rigor of Jonathan Edwards, and from the covenant tradition of Puritan New England, which became especially raucous during the Great Awakening, to the far less participatory mainstream Anglicanism of the South. But religion in America remained vibrant throughout the eighteenth century, and representatives of various traditions proclaimed resistance to all forms of oppression, real or imaginary (*see* Chapter 7). In his sermon *A Discourse Concerning Unlimited Submission*, delivered in Boston in January 1750, Mayhew warned that "a spirit of domination is always to be guarded against, both in church and state." Virtue required vigilance against "the slavish doctrine of passive obedience and nonresistance" (Bonomi, 1986, p. 196). In a variety of ways, the Protestant inclination to interpret experience in terms of a providential plan shaped Americans' attitudes towards their privileged but fragile status as God's chosen people.

Christian ideas of virtue were sufficiently ambiguous to suggest contradictory implications for public life. The awakening might involve challenging all forms of authority or merely reconstituting it on a purified foundation. The recurring emphasis on man's depravity might signal the distance America had fallen from its lofty aspirations, or it might reflect the chosen community's dogged faithfulness to its original ideals. The commitment to God might require selfless obedience to duty, or it might require the individual's liberation from all merely earthly forms of authority.

FIGURE 55 The frontispiece from Montesquieu's "Le Temple de Gnide" (1772): Montesquieu is surrounded by allegorical figures and copies of his works (engraving by N. Le Mire).

Different religious communities interpreted virtue in different ways, and their recognition of those disagreements only made their competing claims more strident.

2. REPUBLICAN IDEAS OF VIRTUE

The classical republican tradition likewise contained various conceptions of virtue. The political ideas of Cicero and Seneca were no more identical than were those of Plato and Aristotle, and the political writings of seventeenth-century English republicans such as John Milton and Algernon Sidney further complicated the notion of

689

civic virtue. Although any generalization about republicanism is perilous, given the breadth of the tradition, American republicans tended to rely on independent citizens to protect fragile civic virtue against the threat of corruption represented by the extension of executive power. The republican ideal of community, in which individuals defined their interests according to their perception of the common good, figured prominently in the political literature produced in America, particularly between the end of the Seven Years' War and the ratification of the Constitution.

Yet just as the Christian ideal of virtue was both central and ambiguous, so the republican ideal of the virtuous citizen was fuzzy. Greek and Roman republicans feared rather than welcomed change. They preferred cities to the countryside, hierarchy to equality, Spartan simplicity to economic prosperity, and military conquest to domestic tranquility. Machiavelli, a more proximate source of republican ideas, elevated the will to combat fortune above the individual's responsibility to adhere to the moral law. The quest for glory was essential to the Renaissance conception of *virtù*. Force and fraud were but part of the standard repertoire of statesmanship, and aspirations to greatness outweighed calculations of justice. As a weapon wielded against perceived corruption, the republican tradition exerted a powerful appeal in America, but Americans who cherished progress, democracy, commerce, and peace felt compelled to reject as much of the republican tradition as they endorsed.

3. EIGHTEENTH-CENTURY MORAL PHILOSOPHY

Moral philosophy provided a third tradition of discourse on virtue. Understanding these ideas is complicated by the controversies swirling around the ethics of John Locke and Scottish common sense realists such as Francis Hutcheson, Adam Ferguson, Thomas Reid, and Dugald Stewart. Locke's writings were perhaps more widely cited in America than those of any other thinker. Recent interpretations of his work emphasize the importance of seeing Locke on his own terms rather than as the progenitor of a tradition of "possessive individualism." His concept of individual liberty dissolves if it is removed from the context of divinely established natural law, which encumbers the freedom of individuals at every turn with the powerful commands of duty. Locke's belief in a natural law discernible by reason led him to condemn the unregulated pursuit of self-interest that Thomas Hobbes considered natural and that later writers who celebrated a market economy sanctioned. As Locke wrote to Edward Clarke in April 1687, "He that has not a mastery over his inclinations, he that knows not how to resist the importunity of present pleasure, or pain, for the sake of what, reason tells him, is fit to be done, wants the true principle of Virtue, and industry; and is in danger never to be good for anything" (Dunn, 1985, p. 194). For Locke, as for his American readers, freedom could be exercised virtuously only within the boundaries of natural law discerned by reason.

Scottish moral philosophy appealed to Americans because it offered an ostensibly empirical ethics that did not require invocations of authority yet conformed to conventional Christian conceptions of virtue. The idea of a moral sense that was just as much a part of man as his physical senses proved irresistible in the age of Locke's psychology and Newton's physics. For a culture still strongly committed to traditional religious values, yet searching for alternative ways of justifying these commitments, Scottish common sense realists offered both novelty and reassurance. Different Scots appealed to different Americans, since the Scots' explanations ranged from those grounding the moral sense on feelings, with Hutcheson, to those who grounded it on rational intuition, with Reid. All of these Scottish moralists, however, shared a commitment to the accountability of the individual to the community, and that commitment appealed to Americans as much as did their comforting theories of knowledge.

4. AMERICAN VIRTUE IN PRACTICE, 1763-90

Although religious, republican, and ethical conceptions of virtue were hardly identical, and in some of their forms quite clearly incompatible, Americans after 1763 imaginatively braided them together. As Gordon Wood has explained, "The traditional covenant theology of Puritanism combined with the political science of the eighteenth century into an imperatively persuasive argument for revolution. Liberal rationalist sensibility blended with Calvinist Christian love to create an essentially common emphasis on the usefulness and goodness of devotion to the general welfare of the community. Religion and republicanism would work hand in hand to create frugality, honesty, self-denial, and benevolence among the people." To use the revealing phrase of Samuel Adams, through revolution America would become "the *Christian* Sparta" (Wood, 1969, p. 118), an amalgamation of Christian benevolence, classical republicanism, and selfless devotion to moral duty.

During the War for Independence, these feelings intensified. When militia men and Continental regulars held their ground against British soldiers, they fortified their courage by pledging to uphold their virtue rather than break and run. Facing a particularly stark conflict between self-interest and duty, they expressed their commitment in the vocabularies of virtue (Middlekauff, 1984, pp. 330-1). Women who sustained the revolutionary struggle in a variety of ways likewise learned to think of themselves as virtuous citizens, and some challenged men to extend to them the privileges they had earned as a result of their devotion to the cause of liberty (*see* Chapter 41, §4).

Virtue, at least until the achievement of independence, functioned as a fighting word, a challenge boldly hurled against corruption. During the period from 1783 to 1787, virtue no longer meant simply resistance to government and authority. As the bracing experience of war gave way to confederation and disarray, some Americans began to doubt their ability to preserve their new nation. The Reverend Asa Briggs of Vermont warned in his election sermon of 1786, "Political virtue may serve as a support for a while, but it is not a lasting principle." Virtue, Briggs and others insisted, can only rest on piety (Bloch, 1990, p. 55). Such sentiments found expression in the authorization for public support of religious education and worship in the Massachusetts Constitution of 1780. The Virginia Statute for Religious Freedom of 1786, which challenged the public's authority to dictate belief, was something of an anomaly.

It is possible to interpret the Constitutional Convention as an attempt to create institutions embodying the virtue of a republican citizenry, or as an admission that, since civic virtue is impossible, the aim of politics is merely to harness the effects of vice. Alternatively, the debates on the ratification of the Constitution can be understood to illustrate the persistence of the competing clusters of religious, republican, and ethical ideas about virtue circulating before the revolution. Neither Federalists nor Anti-Federalists fit neatly into the categories of liberalism or republicanism. Spokesmen for both groups expressed ideas drawn from the vocabularies of Christianity, classical republicanism, and Lockean or Scottish common sense philosophy, and both veiled considerations of self-interest with proclamations of their own virtue and their

691

opponents' corruption. In a characteristic formulation, the Yale President Timothy Dwight insisted that a virtuous republic must rest on the pillars of "Piety to God, Good-will to mankind, and the effectual Government of ourselves" (Hatch, 1977, p. 109).

Adams, Madison, and Jefferson   Neither John Adams, James Madison, nor Thomas Jefferson, arguably the most important theorists of the revolutionary generation, fit comfortably within any of these categories. While his early enthusiasm for more popular government gave way to distrust in the wake of Shays's Rebellion and the French Revolution, Adams continued throughout his career to invoke both the Puritan convenantal and classical republican traditions in his writings. Reflecting on his plan for the Massachusetts Constitution, he described it as "Locke, Sidney, and Rousseau and deMably reduced to practice" (Adams, 1850–6, IV, p. 216), an apt characterization of the mixture of ideas that seemed so natural to the founders and so unsettles twentieth-century critics.

Likewise Madison, who so soberly described the pervasiveness of self-interest in *The Federalist*, no. 10, slipped easily into the languages of republicanism and Scottish moral philosophy in no. 55:

> As there is a degree of depravity in mankind which requires a certain degree of circumspection and distrust: So there are other qualities in human nature, which justify a certain portion of esteem and confidence. Republican government presupposes the existence of these qualities in a higher degree than any other form. Were the pictures which have been drawn by the political jealousy of some among us, faithful likenesses of the human character, the inference would be that there is not sufficient virtue among men for self government; and that nothing less than the chains of despotism can restrain them from destroying and devouring one another. (Madison, Hamilton, and Jay, 1961, p. 378)

Madison was a realist but not a cynic, and he realized that the separation of powers was a necessary but not sufficient condition to insure what he sometimes termed "the common good of the society."

Jefferson too was guardedly optimistic about the harmonious interaction of self-interested individuals only because he believed their inner moral gyroscopes would prevent them from oppressing one another. Jefferson defined self-interest as Locke's virtue rather than Hobbes's possessive individualism. In a letter to Benjamin Rush written in 1803, Jefferson criticized as "defective" ancient republican philosophers' overly narrow conception of those who fall "within the circle of benevolence." The advance of Christian over classical conceptions of virtue, according to Jefferson, lay precisely in the universality of Christian charity, which extends "not only to kindred and friends, to neighbors and countrymen," as does republican duty, "but to all mankind, gathering all into one family, under the bonds of love, charity, peace, common wants and common aims." Finally, in his meditation on the "foundation of morality in man," Jefferson distinguished benevolence from egotism. "Self-love, therefore, is no part of morality," he wrote to Thomas Law. "It is the sole antagonist of virtue, leading us constantly by our propensities to self-gratification in violation of our moral duties to others.... nature hath implanted in our breasts a love of others, a sense of duty to them, a moral instinct, in short, which prompts us irresistibly to feel and to succor their distresses." Jefferson acknowledged the importance of civic virtue, and he insisted on the importance of individual rights, but he never surrendered his devotion to the Christian ideal of universal benevolence as "the most perfect and sublime" conception of ethics (Jefferson, 1984, pp. 1124–5, 1136–7).

5. THE DECLINE OF VIRTUE

References to virtue continued to be widespread in American political discourse through the 1790s, but the accelerating development of the contradictory religious, political, and economic tendencies that began to appear in those years of rapid change gradually destroyed the bonds that might have linked an optimistic and egalitarian republicanism to an ethically attuned and democratically alert liberalism. The latent inconsistencies within these traditions became manifest when the crises that temporarily fused them together were resolved and social and economic change upset their equilibrium. Benjamin Franklin wrote that "only a virtuous people are capable of freedom" (Franklin, 1905–7, IX, p. 80). The American record after the 1790s suggests that a free people may be incapable of virtue. During the early nineteenth century the meaning of virtue lost its earlier religious, civic, and ethical significance and became a label for bourgeois propriety or feminine purity. When independence lost its identification with benevolence, when self-interest was no longer conceived in relation to the egalitarian standard Jefferson upheld – in his theory if not in his practice – then freedom itself, especially the freedom to compete in the race for riches without the restraint of natural law, ironically became an obstacle in the way of justice, a poor substitute for the earlier Christian, republican, and moral conceptions of virtue.

FURTHER READING

Adams, John: *The Works of John Adams*, 10 vols., ed. Charles Francis Adams (Boston, 1850–6).

Bloch, Ruth: "Religion and ideological change in the American Revolution," in *Religion and American Politics*, ed. Mark A. Noll (New York: Oxford University Press, 1990), 44–61.

Bonomi, Patricia: *Under the Cope of Heaven: Religion, Society and Politics in Colonial America* (New York: Oxford University Press, 1986).

Dunn, John: *Rethinking Modern Political Theory* (Cambridge: Cambridge University Press, 1985).

Franklin, Benjamin: *The Writings of Benjamin Franklin*, 10 vols., ed. Albert H. Smyth (New York, 1905–7).

Hatch, Nathan: *The Sacred Cause of Liberty: Republican Thought and the Millennium in Revolutionary New England* (New Haven, Conn.: Yale University Press, 1977).

Jefferson, Thomas: *Writings*, ed. Merrill D. Peterson (New York: Library of America, 1984).

Madison, James, Hamilton, Alexander and Jay, John: *The Federalist*, ed. Jacob E. Cooke (Middletown, Conn.: Wesleyan University Press, 1961).

Midlekauff, Robert: "Why men fought in the American Revolution," in *Saints and Revolutionaries: Essays on Early American History*, ed. David D. Hall et al. (New York: W. W. Norton, 1984), 318–31.

Wood, Gordon: *The Creation of the American Republic, 1776–1787* (Chapel Hill: University of North Carolina Press, 1969).

PART 7
BIOGRAPHIES

Biographies

Adams, Abigail (*b*. Weymouth, Mass., 11 November 1744; *d*. 28 October 1818). Wife and home-maker. The daughter of the Reverend William Smith, a Congregationalist Minister, and his wife Elizabeth Quincy, she received no formal schooling, but was educated at home. She met John Adams when she was 15, and married him five years later. The marriage, which lasted 54 years, inaugurated one of the most famous of all American dynasties.

Adams's enduring reputation stems from rather more than the by no means inconsequential fact that she was the wife of one president of the United States and the mother of another. She was not a published author during her own lifetime. However, her private correspondence, especially with her husband (who was absent from Massachusetts for lengthy periods on political business), but also with an extensive network of friends, comprises a compelling testimony of female life and expectations during the revolutionary era. Although her household and family was in many respects the center of Adams's world, her letters, which were published by her grandson Charles Francis Adams in 1840, reveal an intelligent woman with an astute political awareness as well as one with a keen sense of social and racial justice. She was, for example, vehemently opposed to the institution of chattel slavery.

Like several other women of her social rank and circle, including her cousin Mercy Otis Warren, Adams was deeply concerned with the possible significance and implications of the American Revolution for the status and

FIGURE 56 Portrait (by an unidentified artist) traditionally said to be that of Abigail Adams

rights of women. Yet her oft-quoted remark to her husband in 1776 that he and his male colleagues meeting in Philadelphia ought to "Remember the Ladies" should not be construed, and was certainly not intended, as a radical demand for the full and equal participation of women in political society. Her main concern was that men should recognize the importance, and above all concede the equality, of the private, domestic sphere occupied by women. Like Judith Sargent Murray, she was adamant that girls should receive a formal education, similar to that available to boys in the middling and upper ranks of American society, which would prepare them

697

for their vitally important duties and obligations as republican women (*see* Chapter 41, §4).

To a considerable degree, the contours and contents of Adams's life were defined by her husband's political career. That career physically separated them for lengthy periods during the 1760s and 1770s, but gave them five years together in Europe in the 1780s. It was only in 1801, when John had completed his service as Vice President and then President of the United States, that they retired to a more settled family life in their native Massachusetts.

FURTHER READING

Adams, Charles Francis (ed.): *Letters of Mrs. Adams, the Wife of John Adams*, 4th edn. (Boston: Wilkins Carter, 1848).
Butterfield, L. H., et al. (ed.): *The Adams Family Correspondence*, 4 vols. (Cambridge, Mass.: Harvard University Press, 1963–73).

BETTY WOOD

Adams, John (*b*. Braintree [now Quincy], Mass., 31 October 1735; *d*. Quincy, 4 July 1826). Lawyer, writer, and diplomat, second President of the United States. Adams was the workhorse of the American Revolution. He was willing to put himself in the background at the First Continental Congress in order to move the southern colonies towards support for militarily besieged Massachusetts. At the Second Congress he was convinced earlier than most that separation from Great Britain was inevitable. Concluding early in 1776 that independence was theoretically a *fait accompli*, he fought doggedly on the floor of Congress for a formal declaration of the fact. He served long and hard both in the Congress and as a diplomat in Europe.

Like most opponents of the British revenue measures who called themselves Whigs, Adams consistently hoped for conciliation with the mother country from the Writs of Assistance Case in 1761, which he attended as a young lawyer, to the battles of Lexington and Concord in 1775. These battles, together with the logic of his disputatious writings, finally turned him into a radical in spite of himself. He was first active against the Stamp Act in 1765, denouncing it in his newspaper series *A Dissertation on the Canon and the Feudal Law* and by preparing the Braintree Instructions – a statement of opposition intended for the use of his town's representative to the provincial legislature.

Adams's most important act before independence was his principled, successful court defense of the Boston Massacre soldiers who fired into a crowd in 1770. His most important writings were his *Novanglus* essays of 1775 and *Thoughts on Government* in 1776. In the former he argued the illegality of the British revenue Acts on the grounds that Parliament was limited to regulating external trade only for the colonies. The American Whig party, he insisted, wished above all to preserve the British Constitution; it was the current British Parliament that threatened order with its unconstitutional "innovations." *Thoughts on Government*, written in January 1776 when Adams was already convinced of the necessity for independence, recommended republican legislative and executive forms for adoption by state governments at a time when it seemed that the southern states might establish aristocratic or even monarchical governments.

At the Continental Congress Adams served on some 90 committees, 25 of which he headed. His labors on one of these, the Board of War and Ordnance, rendered him a virtual one-man war department. (He also served in the Massachusetts Provincial Congress.) Both Benjamin Rush and John Jay called him "the first man in the House"; other delegates referred to him as "the Atlas of Independence." On 1 July 1776, his greatest moment in politics, he delivered the crucial speech supporting a resolution of Independence, which he regarded as more important than the written declaration (on the committee for drafting which he served with Thomas Jefferson).

Adams's years of diplomacy from 1778 until signing the peace treaty with England in 1783, were less satisfying. He was forced to serve alongside Benjamin Franklin, who was lionized by the French, and whom he came to dislike for his inefficiency and neglect of consular business. But Adams did succeed in securing from the Netherlands both recognition of the new United States and badly needed loans for its war effort (see Chapter 55, §3). And while he was at home briefly in 1779 he drafted the Constitution of Massachusetts, which served as a model for other states and for the Federal Constitution.

Adams remained in Europe as a diplomat after the peace, now as a representative of the United States of America. He served as Ambassador to the Court of St. James from 1785 to 1788, and had the satisfaction of being presented to George III. While Ambassador he attempted to influence the Constitutional Convention through his argument for bicameralism in *A Defence of the Constitutions* (1787–8). Soon afterwards he returned home to serve as Vice President under Washington, and then as President. After only one term he was defeated by Jefferson in the election of 1800.

For illustration, *see* FRANKLIN, BENJAMIN.

FURTHER READING

Chinard, Gilbert: *Honest John Adams* (Boston: Little, Brown and Company, 1933).
Haraszti, Zoltán: *John Adams and the Prophets of Progress* (New York: Grosset and Dunlap, 1964).
Howe, John R., Jr.: *The Changing Political Thought of John Adams* (Princeton, NJ: Princeton University Press, 1966).
Shaw, Peter: *The Character of John Adams* (Chapel Hill: University of North Carolina Press, 1976).
Smith, Page: *John Adams*, 2 vols; (Garden City, NY: Doubleday, 1962).

PETER SHAW

Adams, Samuel (*b*. Boston, 27 September 1722; *d*. Boston, 2 October 1803). Statesman. Samuel Adams's real role in the 1760s and 1770s is impossible to know, as either he destroyed most of his papers or they were lost after his death. But contemporary observers both friendly and hostile agree that Adams was crucial in moving the town of Boston, and by extension the American colonies, from resistance to revolution in the critical decade preceding the War for Independence (*see* Chapter 19, §2).

Adams served as a tax collector in Boston from 1756 to 1765. His leniency provoked a town-meeting investigation which found him over £10,000 in arrears, but also probably endeared him to the inhabitants, who sent him to the House of Representatives to replace Oxenbridge Thacher on the latter's death in 1765. Serving as the House's clerk until 1780, Adams played a key role in drafting the assembly's protests and in organizing popular resistance in Boston against British measures. His writings are most distinguished by his simultaneous devotion to John Locke's doctrine that government respect man's natural rights, to Calvinist virtue and piety (he hoped America would be a "Christian Sparta"), and to the idea that British officials both in Massachusetts and at home had plotted to reduce America to slavery. Adams belonged to the Loyal Nine, North End Caucus, and Sons of Liberty, and won fame for his behind-the-scenes politicking in addition to his effective printed propaganda. He was instrumental in drafting the Circular Letter of 1768 which called for the Massachusetts Convention that protested against the arrival of British troops (*see* Chapter 13, §5). He led the Bostonians in successfully demanding the troops' removal following the Massacre of 5 March 1770; he may well have played a role in forming the crowd which provoked the soldiers to fire.

Adams created the first Committee of Correspondence in Boston in 1772 to keep alive the spirit of resistance during a quiet period. He capped his leadership in 1773 by arranging for the publication of letters written by governors Francis Bernard and Thomas Hutchinson which argued for a reduction in colonial liberty, and also by chairing the Boston Town Meeting which adjourned to hold the Boston Tea Party. Probably these two activities, combined with his reputation as the soul of Boston's resistance, led to his exemption, along with John Hancock, from a general amnesty offered by Britain in 1774.

Although Adams made his most substantial contributions in Boston before 1774, he continued to influence events thereafter. As a member of the Continental Congress from 1774 to 1780, he joined with Virginia's Arthur Lee in attacking Benjamin Franklin for corruption and favored a loosely knit confederation. He returned to Massachusetts in 1780 and served on the three-man committee which wrote the state constitution. Adams penned the address that was sent out to the towns, which had turned down a proposed constitution two years earlier, urging that they adopt the 1780 document. He therefore supported increased property qualifications for suffrage and a State Senate which explicitly represented property. Despite his identification with the Boston crowd and "lower orders," Adams's republicanism incorporated the belief that society's fate was best entrusted to those who possessed at least moderate fortune.

Adams's prominence continued in the late 1780s and beyond. He played a critical role, as a state senator, in persuading the General Court to proclaim Daniel Shays and his followers as rebels, and sought to punish them harshly, an unpopular stance which probably cost him the congressional election of 1788. He was Lieutenant-Governor of Massachusetts from 1789 to 1793 and Governor from 1793 to 1797. Adams initially opposed the United States Constitution, but was persuaded by Federalist-orchestrated demonstrations in Boston to grant it his reluctant consent. In his last years he affiliated with the Jeffersonian Republicans, which limited his influence in a predominantly Federalist state.

For illustration, *see* LEE, RICHARD HENRY.

FURTHER READING

Maier, Pauline: "A New Englander as revolutionary: Samuel Adams," *The Old Revolutionaries: Political Lives in the Age of Samuel Adams* (New York: Knopf, 1980), 3–50.

Miller, John C.: *Sam Adams: Pioneer in Propaganda* (Boston: Little, Brown, 1936).

Seccombe, Matthew: "From Revolution to Republic: the Later Political Career of Samuel Adams" (Ph.D. diss. Yale University, 1978).

Shipton, Clifford K.: "Samuel Adams," *Sibley's Harvard Graduates*, X: *1736–40* (Boston: Massachusetts Historical Society, 1958), 420–65.

Williams, William Appleman: "Samuel Adams: Calvinist, mercantilist, revolutionary," *Studies on the Left*, 1 (1960), 47–57.

WILLIAM PENCAK

Allen, Ethan (*b.* Litchfield, Conn., 21 January 1738; *d.* Burlington, Vt., 12 February 1789). Soldier, politician, and writer. After his father's death in 1755 Allen became head of the family household, served briefly in the Seven Years' War, farmed, speculated in land, and invested in mining. By 1770 he was involved in a cause for which he became best known: statehood or independence for Vermont.

During the Revolutionary War Allen fought to wrest the colonies from Britain's control and free Vermont from competing claims by New York, New Hampshire, and Massachusetts. He helped seize Fort Ticonderoga from the British (10 May 1775) and then participated in the invasion of Canada, during which he was captured. Exchanged after a two-year imprisonment, Allen worked to maintain the Republic of Vermont's self-proclaimed independence. When failure appeared imminent, he unsuccessfully negotiated with Sir Frederick Haldimand to return Vermont to the British Empire in exchange for guaranteeing the state's existence. Allen's actions have been called treasonous since he held commissions in the Continental Army and Vermont militia.

After the war Allen continued to push for acceptance of Vermont's statehood. It became one of the United States in 1791, two years after Allen's death. A leading American deist and author of *Reason the Only Oracle of Man*, Allen was controversial in matters both political and religious.

FURTHER READING

Jellison, Charles A.: *Ethan Allen: Frontier Rebel* (Syracuse, NY: Syracuse University Press, 1969).

J. MARK THOMPSON

Amherst, Jeffery [1st Baron Amherst] (*b.* Riverhead, Kent, 29 January 1717; *d.* Montreal, Kent, 3 August 1797). Commander-in-Chief of the British Army in North America and Britain. Amherst made his reputation leading British forces to victory in the Seven Years' War. After commanding an expedition that captured the French base at Louisburg on Cape Breton in 1758, he became Commander-in-Chief in North America. He devoted the ensuing campaigns to a cautious but successful conquest of Canada. In 1759, while James Wolfe took Quebec, Amherst pushed the French from Lake Champlain; in 1760 he trapped the remaining French forces at Montreal, captured them, and brought Canada under British control. He resigned his command in 1763.

He took a far more passive role in the American Revolution. Having refused repeatedly to command against the colonists, he became Commander-in-Chief in Britain and a member of the Cabinet only after France entered the war in 1778, remaining in office until 1782. But Amherst had little influence on policy. Unable to persuade his colleagues to rely on a naval blockade to end the rebellion in America, he devoted himself to military administration and the defense of the British Isles.

FURTHER READING

Long, J. C.: *Lord Jeffery Amherst: a Soldier of the King* (New York: Macmillan, 1933).

IRA D. GRUBER

Arnold, Benedict (*b.* Norwich, Conn., 14 January 1741; *d.* London, 12 June 1801). General. Arnold spent his early years as a successful merchant in New Haven. As captain of militia, he led his company to Boston after the battles at Lexington and Concord in April 1775.

Quarrelsome, vain, and ultimately traitorous, Arnold nevertheless provided valuable service to the patriot cause in the early years. Along with Ethan Allen, he forced the capitulation of Fort Ticonderoga in May 1775, and the following winter he led one of two columns converging on Quebec. In October 1776, as a brigadier general in the Continental Army, he halted Guy Carleton's descent from Canada at the Battle of Valcour Island. Promoted to major general, he played an important part in the American victory at Saratoga. Thereafter, his career took a dramatic downward turn.

Arnold felt pressured by growing debt following his second marriage (to the young Peggy Shippen), unfairly criticized by political opponents, and unappreciated by his fellow Americans. Probably for these reasons, he secretly negotiated through Major John André to surrender West Point to Sir Henry Clinton in return for a royal military commission and substantial financial remuneration. When the plan was uncovered he fled to enemy lines and was made a brigadier general in command of a loyalist legion.

Following the war Arnold established himself as a merchant shipper in England, where he died in relative obscurity.

FURTHER READING

Wallace, Willard M.: *Traitorous Hero: the Life and Fortunes of Benedict Arnold* (New York: Harper, 1954).

J. MARK THOMPSON

Asbury, Francis (*b.* Hamstead Bridge, England, 20 August 1745; *d.* Spotsylvania, Va., 31 March 1816). Itinerant minister, superintendent, and bishop of the American Methodist Church. Dispatched to the American colonies in 1771, Asbury was the sole disciple of John Wesley to remain throughout the course of the Revolution. Because Methodists initially avoided a break with the established Anglican Church and because Wesley opposed the American cause, Asbury was considered suspect by patriots. A thorough pragmatist, however, he gradually adjusted himself to the Americans – although he apparently never renounced his British citizenship – and managed to mitigate opposition to himself and fellow Methodists.

By 1784 Asbury had consolidated his leadership and was named co-superintendent (later, bishop) of the new, independent American Methodist Church. His emphasis on religious enthusiasm and revivalism, carried out by a group of itinerant preachers tightly controlled by an authoritarian church structure, helped Methodism gain converts in the postwar years, particularly in the South and West. By 1816 chuch membership had grown to 214,000 from 5,000 in 1776.

FURTHER READING

Baker, Frank: *From Wesley to Asbury* (Durham, NC: Duke University Press, 1976).
Rudolph, L. C.: *Francis Asbury* (Nashville, Tenn.: Abingdon Press, 1966).

STEPHEN A. YOUNG

Bache, Sarah Franklin (*b.* Philadelphia, 11 September 1743; *d.* Philadelphia, 5 October 1808). Wife, home-maker, and wartime relief worker. The youngest child of Benjamin and Deborah Franklin, she married Richard Bache in 1767. The marriage eventually produced eight children and, by her own admission, her main preoccupation during her first decade of married life was with her family. In 1780, however, she joined the fund-raising committee of Philadelphia women organized by Esther De Berdt Reed to further the patriot war effort. Upon Reed's death Bache assumed the main responsibility for continuing a campaign which raised more than $300,000 for Washington's army. After the war her family once again became the main focus of her life.

FURTHER READING

Ellet, Elizabeth F.: *The Women of the American Revolution*, Vol. 1 (New York: Baker and Scribner, 1848), 332–48.

BETTY WOOD

Backus, Isaac (*b.* Norwich, Conn., 9 January 1724; *d.* Middleborough, Mass., 20 November 1806). Baptist minister and advocate of religious liberty. A child of the Great Awakening, Backus experienced a personal religious conversion while plowing a Connecticut field in 1741. That event, coming a year after George Whitefield's first tour of New England and combined with a family history of questioning the Puritan establishment, set Backus on a life devoted to furthering the cause of evangelical pietism and opposing New England's traditional church–state alliance. Eventually it led to his formulation in the early 1770s of a theory of separate civil and ecclesiastical governments. Backus was an eloquent spokesman for the persecuted Baptists of New England, and in 1774 he led a deputation to Philadelphia to present their grievances to the Continental Congress. For many more years he wrote very extensively on Baptist sectarian interests, theology, and church history.

Unlike Jefferson and Madison, who carried out the successful disestablishment of the Anglican Church in Virginia in 1785 while operating under the principles of rationalism, Backus argued that doing the same to New England's Congregationalist churches would lead to a truly Christian state, in which government could create a climate conducive to spreading God's word.

FURTHER READING

Grenz, Stanley: *Isaac Backus: Puritan and Baptist* (Macon, Ga.: Mercer University Press, 1983).
McLoughlin, William G.: *Isaac Backus and the American Pietistic Tradition* (Boston: Little, Brown and Co., 1967).

STEPHEN A. YOUNG

Banneker, Benjamin (*b.* Maryland, 9 November 1731; *d.* Ellicott's Mills, Md., 9 October 1806). Astronomer. He was born into Maryland's free black community and received enough education at home and from a Quaker school to develop his gift for mathematics into a lifelong avocation. He farmed on land his parents left him near modern-day

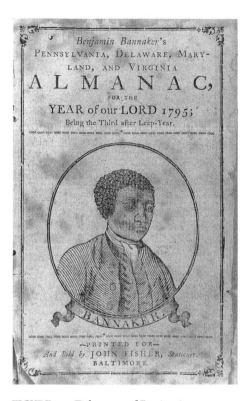

FIGURE 57 Title page of Benjamin Banneker's "Almanac" (woodcut engraving, 1795)

Ellicott City, devoting what spare time he had to independent study and correspondence with other scientists and mathematicians. He demonstrated his ingenuity in 1770 by building a clock that chimed all the hours, the first of its kind made in America. His reputation was such by 1791 that he joined his neighbor Andrew Ellicott as a member of the commission to survey the boundaries of the national capital. Another Ellicott lent him several books on astronomy, in which subject Banneker immersed himself, becoming expert enough to publish his own almanac in 1792 (*see* figure 57). He put out a new edition for every subsequent year until his death. The almanac supplements the astronomical tables with Banneker's and others' writings on pacifism, Christian love, and the abolition of the slave trade. In such proposals as that for a "Peace-Office" to supplement the exist-

ing War Office, he showed that he had learned more than arithmetic from the Quakers.

FURTHER READING

Allen, W. W., and Murray, D. A. P.: *Banneker, the Afro-American Astronomer* (Washington, DC, 1921); repr. (Freeport, NY: Books for Libraries Press, 1971).
Patterson, L.: *Benjamin Banneker: Genius of Early America* (Nashville: Abingdon, 1978).

THOMAS COLE

Barlow, Joel (*b*. Redding, Conn., 24 March 1754; *d*. Zarnowiec, Poland, 24 December 1812). Poet, pamphleteer and diplomat. His two most ambitious poetical efforts, *The Vision of Columbus* (1787) and its revised and expanded version *The Columbiad* (1807), proclaimed his faith in the destined greatness of the American nation and in the principles of liberty. He served as a chaplain to the Continental Army in 1780. In 1788 he left for France on private business but became caught up in revolutionary politics. His writings from this period shocked his former friends and associates but earned him an honorary citizenship from the French government. In 1796 he agreed to become the American Consul to Algiers, where he obtained the release of Americans taken prisoner at sea. He wrote to President Adams advising reconciliation with France and criticizing anti-French elements in the United States, which letter completed his alienation from the Connecticut elite. Ironically, his most famous poem, "The Hasty-Pudding" (1793), expresses the yearning of a Yankee in France for his native land. Barlow returned to America in 1804. President Madison asked him to undertake negotiations with Napoleon, but he died on his way to meet the Emperor in retreat from Russia.

FURTHER READING

Bernstein, J.: *Joel Barlow* (New York: Rutledge Books, 1985).
Douty, E. M.: *Hasty Pudding and Barbary Pirates* (Philadelphia: Westminster Press, 1975).

THOMAS COLE

Barré, Isaac (*b.* Dublin, 15 October 1726; *d.* London, 20 July 1802). British soldier and politician. Barré served in Canada in 1759, and from 1761 sat in Parliament on the interest of the Earl of Shelburne, with whom he acted as one of the Chatham group. Briefed by correspondence with American acquaintances, he kept Parliament informed of colonial opinion. He opposed the Stamp Act, supported the moves for its repeal, and followed Pitt's line in criticizing the Declaratory Act of 1766. He held minor office from 1766 to 1768, but then followed Pitt, now Earl of Chatham, into opposition. In 1769 Barré forecast the loss of the colonies if the government persisted in trying to tax them in Parliament. In 1774, like Chatham, he sought to preserve British supremacy over the colonies and supported the Boston Port Bill, but he opposed the government's other coercive legislation and also the Quebec Act. He criticized the attempt to recover control of the colonies by military force as a mistaken policy and one bound ultimately to fail, since America could not be held without the goodwill of the population; and he constantly attacked North's administration on the grounds of corruption and inefficient conduct of the American war. His name is linked with that of John Wilkes in the name of the Pennsylvania city of Wilkesbarre.

FURTHER READING

Brown, Peter: "Colonel Barré," *The Chathamites* (London: Macmillan; New York: St. Martin's Press, 1967).

IAN R. CHRISTIE

Beaumarchais, Pierre-Augustin Caron de (*b.* Paris, 24 January 1732; *d.* Paris, 18 May 1799). French playwright and satirist. He is today best known as a playwright, but it was his talent for espionage that brought him the patronage of such important figures as Gabriel de Sartine, head of the Paris police and later French Naval Minister, and Charles Gravier, Comte de Vergennes, the French Foreign Minister. While in London in 1775

to pay off a disgruntled former member of King Louis XV's secret diplomatic service, Beaumarchais met the American ex-colonial agent Arthur Lee. Soon thereafter he began urging King Louis XVI to support the American rebellion. His letters probably were not of great significance in themselves, but Vergennes, engaged in the same cause, apparently found them useful. When the King finally agreed to aid the Americans, the French Government advanced Beaumarchais 1,000,000 *livres tournois* (about £40,000) to establish a trading company to sell them arms (*see* Chapter 33, §1). Beaumarchais' company, which he named Roderigue Hortalez & Company, chartered more than half a dozen ships which brought critical war supplies to America. Beaumarchais continued his activities after France entered the war in 1778, but faced increasing financial difficulties; some of his ships were captured and the Americans, wrongly believing the supplies were actually meant to be gifts from the French Government, refused to reimburse him. This engendered litigation which lasted until 1835, when Congress finally compensated Beaumarchais' heirs.

FURTHER READING

Morton, Brian N., and Spinelli, Donald C.: *Beaumarchais: a Biography* (Ann Arbor, Mich.: Olivia and Hill, 1988).

JONATHAN R. DULL

Bernard, Sir Francis (bapt. Brightwell, Berks., 12 July 1712; *d.* Aylesbury, Bucks., 16 June 1779). Governor of Massachusetts. He was governor of New Jersey from 1758 to 1760, then was appointed governor of Massachusetts, where his initial popularity was undermined by his commitment to upholding imperial policy and authority. Critical of the British Government's fiscal policy, he urged reduction or abolition of the duties set in the Plantation Act of 1764, suggested a system of colonially voted taxation with quotas fixed by Parliament, and condemned the Stamp Act as inexpedient, but he showed lack of tact in opposing challenges to parliamentary authority at Boston. By 1766 he was at loggerheads with the legislature and powerless to enforce unpopular laws in the province. In February 1768 the assembly ignored Bernard's protests in its decision to send a circular letter to other colonies calling for cooperation in resisting the Townshend Duties. On his representation royal troops were sent to Boston to maintain order, creating a new level of tension between Britain and the colonies, and he urged the inclusion of colonial representatives in Parliament as the only way of avoiding a separation. After some of his letters were stolen and printed at Boston the assembly sent official complaints against him to London. Bernard was recalled but given a baronetcy, and replaced as governor in 1770.

IAN R. CHRISTIE

Blackstone, Sir **William** (*b.* London, 10 July 1723; *d.* Wallingford, Berks. [now Oxon.], 14 February 1780). English legal theorist. Blackstone's reputation in England and America rests chiefly on his *Commentaries on the Laws of England* (1765–9), which played an important part in shaping American thinking on political sovereignty and the common law.

The son of a London tradesman, Blackstone entered successively Pembroke College, Oxford (1738), and the Middle Temple (1741) and was called to the bar in 1746. He eventually rose to the highest ranks of his profession, assuming the Vinerian Professorship of Law at Oxford (1758–66), sitting in Parliament (1761–70), acting as Solicitor General to the Queen (1763–70), and serving as a Justice of the Court of Common Pleas (1770–80).

The *Commentaries*, which grew out of Blackstone's lectures at Oxford, were an immediate success on both sides of the Atlantic. As Sir William Jones wrote the year after his death, Blackstone successfully distilled the complex cases and statutes comprising the common law into "a general map of the law," making it available to a wider lay public. The

Commentaries served as the cornerstone of legal education in the United States throughout the nineteenth century, with a textbook edition being issued as recently as the close of the Second World War.

FURTHER READING

Boorstin, D. J.: *The Mysterious Science of the Law* (Cambridge, Mass.: Harvard University Press, 1941).

Stourzh, G.: "William Blackstone: teacher of revolution," *Jahrbuch für Amerikastudien* (Heidelburg: Carl Winter Universitätsverlag, 1970), 184–200.

ELIGA H. GOULD

Bland, Richard (*b.* Virginia, 6 May 1710; *d.* Williamsburg, Va., 26 October 1776). Pamphleteer and politician. Bland was a leader in the Virginia House of Burgesses and its revolutionary successors from 1742 until 1776. He was a member of the Continental Congress (1774–5), Virginia's Committee of Correspondence (1773–5), and its Committee of Safety (1775–6). An early advocate of colonial rights, he helped pen the burgesses' remonstrances against Dinwiddie's Pistole Fee, the Stamp Act, and the Townshend Act. Bland published tracts of his own as well. His *Modest and True State of the Case* (1753) censured Lieutenant-Governor Robert Dinwiddie's attempt to attach a fee of one pistole to all land grants. When the Privy Council disallowed Virginia's Two-Penny Act because it lacked a suspending clause, he argued in *A Letter to the Clergy of Virginia* (1760) and *The Colonel Dismounted* (1764) that colonists had a right to legislate for themselves. Finally Bland's *An Inquiry into the Rights of the British Colonies* (1766), a response to the Stamp Act, spoke out against taxation without representation.

From a prominent family, with an education from William and Mary and perhaps the University of Edinburgh, Bland had a reputation for scholarship, especially regarding Virginia history. He was married three times – to Anne Poythress, Martha Macon, and Elizabeth Blair.

FURTHER READING

Rossiter, C.: "Richard Bland: the whig in America," *William and Mary Quarterly*, 10 (1953), 33–79.

MARY GWALTNEY VAZ

Bowdoin, James (*b.* Boston, 7 August 1726; *d.* Boston, 6 November 1790). Governor of Massachusetts and first President of the American Academy of Arts and Sciences. Born the son of a wealthy Boston merchant, Bowdoin graduated from Harvard in 1745. He was first elected to the Massachusetts General Court in 1753, and four years later was appointed to the colony's council. As a delegate to the Albany Congress of 1754 Bowdoin supported Benjamin Franklin's plan for colonial union. He was suspected by some of only lukewarm endorsement of the colonists's position during most of the 1760s, but by 1768 he openly supported the colonists and was associated with the Sons of Liberty. He served on the executive council of the provincial assembly from 1775 to 1777, and presided over the Massachusetts constitutional convention of 1779. Bowdoin was elected Governor of Massachusetts in 1785, and in 1786 suppressed an insurrection of indebted farmers in what became known as Shays's Rebellion.

FURTHER READING

Shipton, Clifford K.: *Sibley's Harvard Graduates*, Vol. 11 (Boston: Massachusetts Historical Society, 1960).

KURT W. NAGEL

Brant, Joseph [Thayendanegea] (*b.* New York State, *c.* 1742; *d.* Ontario, 24 November 1807). Principal leader and warrior of the Mohawk Iroquois both in the United States and Canada. Once called the "most ferocious being" ever born, Brant emerged as a Mohawk leader during the American Revolution. His influential family included his sister Mary, who was the companion of the British Indian Superintendent William Johnson. Under Johnson's patronage Brant

FIGURE 58 Joseph Brant as portrayed by George Romney (1776)

was educated by missionaries among the Iroquois and by Eleazer Wheelock in Lebanon, Connecticut. Ordered home by his sister at the outbreak of Pontiac's Rebellion, Brant spent the next decade living quietly, using his bilingual abilities as an interpreter for visiting missionaries; by 1774 he began serving likewise for the British Indian Department. In the company of William Johnson's successor, Guy Johnson, he went in 1775–6 to London, where he was presented at court, dined with Boswell, and sat for his portrait by Romney (*see* figure 58). After returning in 1776, Brant and his warriors resisted American invasions of their homelands and supported loyalist partisans. A skillful leader, but never a butcher, he earned the gratitude of General Frederick Haldimand, who aided the faithful Mohawks in finding Ontario lands. From 1785 until his death, the man whom Daniel Claus described as "sober, quiet, and good natured" dominated the politics, economics, and religious life of the Canadian Mohawks.

FURTHER READING

Graymont, Barbara: *The Iroquois in the American Revolution* (Syracuse, NY: Syracuse University Press, 1972).

Kelsay, Isabel T.: *Joseph Brant, 1743–1807: Man of Two Worlds* (Syracuse, NY: Syracuse University Press, 1984).

O'Donnell, James H., III.: "Joseph Brant," *American Indian Leaders: Studies in Diversity*, ed. R. David Edmunds (Lincoln: University of Nebraska Press, 1980), 21–40.

Stone, William L.: *Life of Joseph Brant-Thayendanegea*, 2 vols. (New York: A.V. Blake, 1838).

JAMES H. O'DONNELL III

Brant, Mary [Konwatsi'tsiaienni] (*b. c.* 1736; *d.* 16 April 1796). Reputedly descended from powerful Mohawk Chiefs, Brant was an important political figure among the matrilineal Iroquois of northern New York. Her influence was enhanced by her long-term common-law relationship from 1759 until his death in 1774 with Sir William Johnson, Superintendent of Indian Affairs. During the Revolution Brant's assistance to refugee loyalists and her passing of crucial information to the British before the Battle of Oriskany made her a target for patriot harassment. Forced to relocate to Cayuga, because of her status as head of a society of Six Nation matrons she played a key role there in keeping the Indians loyal to the British. "One word from her," noted the Indian Agent Daniel Claus, "is more taken Notice of ... than a thousand from any White Man ..." Consequently, the British prevailed on her to move first to Niagara and then to Carleton Island, where she interceded diplomatically on their behalf with her people. Following the war, in recognition of her services she was built a home at Kingston and given the largest government pension ever granted to an Indian.

FURTHER READING

Graymont, Barbara: "Konwatsi'tsiaienni," *Dictionary of Canadian Biography*, Vol. 7: *1836–1850* (Toronto: University of Toronto Press, 1988), 416–18.

KATHERINE M. J. MCKENNA

Bryan, George (*b.* Dublin, 11 August 1731; *d.* Philadelphia, 27 January 1791). Jurist and statesman. Bryan arrived in America in 1752. A leader of Philadelphia's Scots–Irish Presbyterian faction, he served in the state assembly in 1764, supporting proprietary interests, and sat as judge in the orphans' court and court of common pleas. He sat on the committee to instruct Pennsylvania's delegates to the Stamp Act Congress (1765), then was chosen as a delegate. He was appointed naval officer of the port of Philadelphia in 1776. Although not a member of the convention, Bryan is credited as the major force in the drafting of Pennsylvania's radical 1776 constitution. He was elected to the Supreme Executive Council of Pennsylvania and in March 1777 was chosen as its vice-president; he held this office until October 1779, serving as acting president for seven months. In 1779 Bryan served on the commission to settle the boundary dispute with Virginia and was elected to the state assembly, where he led the Constitutionalist party. He is credited as the author of Pennsylvania's gradual emancipation act. In April 1780 he was named to the state supreme court and sat on this bench until his death. He was also elected to the Council of Censors (1784). Bryan was opposed to the Constitution, and after ratification was a member of the Harrisburg convention of irreconcilables, which met to demand a new constitutional convention (September 1788).

FURTHER READING

Konkle, B. A.: *George Bryan and the Constitution of Pennsylvania, 1731–1791* (Philadelphia: W. J. Campbell, 1922).

GRANT E. MABIE

Burgoyne, John (*b.* ?Hackney, Middx., 4 February 1722; *d.* London, 3 August 1792). British general, politician, and dramatist. Burgoyne was in Boston for the battle of Bunker Hill but without command. He returned to Britain and in 1776 was sent with reinforcements for Sir Guy Carleton and helped clear Quebec of American forces. He

FIGURE 59 General John Burgoyne: portrait by Sir Joshua Reynolds (1766)

returned home late that year, but in 1777 came back to command the army instructed to enter New York from Canada and link up with Sir William Howe at Albany. Defeated by American forces under Horatio Gates at Saratoga, he and his army were taken prisoner. He was released on parole in 1778 and sailed to England, where he took up his seat in Parliament and thereafter opposed the war.

Burgoyne remains a figure of controversy. His nickname of "Gentleman Johnny" implies that he was a military dilettante, and so he was often considered, but the modern consensus is that he was a very competent and even innovative commander. The main controversy concerns the extent of his responsibility for the defeat at Saratoga, a defeat which most historians see as the turning point of the war. One school holds that he was the victim of bad planning by and lack of cooperation from Lord George Germain and Howe, who failed to support him during the campaign and blamed him for its failure afterwards. The other school holds that Burgoyne was the primary author of his own failure. It points out that in the

campaign plan, which he drew up himself, only minimal help from Howe was expected, and suggests that he pressed on with the campaign, even when he knew that it must end in defeat, because to turn back would ruin his reputation, and he felt he could blame the disaster on Germaine's "inflexible" orders to proceed to Albany.

FURTHER READING

Billias, George Athan: "John Burgoyne: ambitious general," *George Washington's Opponents: British Generals and Admirals in the American Revolution* (New York: William Morrow, 1969), 142–92.

Burgoyne [John], Lieutenant-General: *A State of the Expedition from Canada as Laid Before the House of Commons by Lieutenant-General Burgoyne* (London, 1780).

Glover, Michael: *General Burgoyne in Canada and America: Scapegoat for a System* (London: Gordon and Cremonesi, 1976).

Willcox, William B: "Too many cooks: British planning before Saratoga," *Journal of British Studies*, 2 (November 1962), 56–90.

R. ARTHUR BOWLER

Burke, Aedanus (*b.* Co. Galway, Ireland, 16 June 1743; *d.* 30 March 1802). Lawyer. Dividing his career between politics and the judiciary, Burke (who studied for the priesthood) mingled republican ideology and Christian theology into his own creed for the new political state. In a grand jury charge in 1778 he praised South Carolina's new constitution for eliminating "unnatural distinctions between nobleman and commons." He strongly opposed the 1782 Confiscation Act as lacking the forgiveness necessary for reconciliation of patriots and loyalists into "one harmonious democratic-republican society" (*An Address to the Freeman of South Carolina*, Philadelphia, 1783). In the same year he published an attack on the aristocratic implications of the Society of the Cincinnati (*Considerations on the Order of the Cincinnati*, Charleston, 1783), which turned public opinion against it. He opposed the United States Constitution at the state ratification convention (1788), where (fearing a monarchy) he moved a resolution to limit the presidency to one term. A district from the largely Anti-Federalist upcountry elected him to the House of Representatives of the First Congress (1789–91), where he continued the fight to limit government's power. He supported the Bill of Rights Amendments and a strong state militia for national defense, while opposing the excise tax and the United States Bank.

At the level of state service, Burke was Associate Judge of South Carolina's Court of Common Pleas and General Sessions in 1778, and Chancellor of the Court of Equity in 1799. He served in the General Assembly from St. Philip and St. Michael's parishes (Charles Town) from 1779 to 1788. With Justices John Faucheraud Grimké and Henry Pendleton, he wrote a digest and revision of South Carolina law, which was not adopted, but which influenced the state constitution of 1790.

FURTHER READING

Meleney, John C.: The Public Life of Aedanus Burke: Revolutionary Republican in Post-Revolutionary South Carolina (Columbia: University of South Carolina Press, 1989).

REBECCA STARR

Burke, Edmund (b. Dublin, 12 January 1729; d. Beaconsfield, Bucks., 9 July 1797). British statesman and philosopher. Engaged by Rockingham in July 1765 as his private secretary at the Treasury (see figure 21, p. 241), Burke thereafter adhered to Rockingham's party and held minor office in 1782 and 1783. So long as possible he sought to uphold the supremacy of Parliament over the colonies, but realized this could only be on terms the colonists would accept. In two great speeches, on American taxation in 1774 and on conciliation in 1775, he advocated a relationship foreshadowing British imperial development in the late nineteenth century, whereby, in effect, parliamentary sovereignty over the colonies would be exercised only with their consent, for purposes which they recognized were indisputably of common interest. Burke deplored the outbreak of the American War,

and after Saratoga believed any attempt to hold on to America by force would be doomed to failure. In 1780–2 he was a leading advocate of "economical reform" and piloted through the Commons the Establishment Act abolishing a number of offices tenable with a seat in the Commons. In the 1790s he campaigned in speeches and writing against the French Revolution which to him, unlike the American Revolution, betokened a total breakdown of the rule of law. Burke wrote lengthy works on philosophy, notably on the origins of the sense of beauty, and was a parliamentary speaker of extraordinary eloquence.

FURTHER READING

Ayling, Stanley: Edmund Burke: his Life and Opinions (London: John Murray, 1983).
Cone, Carl B.: Burke and the Nature of Politics, Vol. 1 (Lexington: Kentucky University Press, 1957).

IAN R. CHRISTIE

Burke, Thomas (b. Ireland, 1747; d. 2 December 1783). Lawyer and Governor of North Carolina. Dubbed "the Disturber" (he was one of only two delegates to be censured by a vote of Congress), Burke had a tumultuous career in North Carolina and Confederation politics. He began his political life as a delegate from Orange County to North Carolina's Provincial Congress, and held 15 committee assignments in the two years from 1774 to 1776. His advocacy of such principles as popular sovereignty, separation of church and state, separation of powers, and annual elections helped ensure their inclusion in the state constitution of 1776. Burke represented North Carolina in the Continental Congress (apart from a brief period in 1778) from late 1776 to June 1781. Throughout, he was a sharp critic of the Congress's secrecy proceedings and any use of military power that infringed civilians' rights. He was responsible for the final form of Article II (later the basis of the Tenth Amendment to the Federal Constitution) guaranteeing to each state all powers not explicitly delegated to Congress.

Burke was elected governor in June 1781, and the following September he and his council were captured in a Tory raid on Hillsborough; after imprisonment and parole he returned to his official duties in North Carolina. During his shortened tenure as governor he organized the supply of patriot troops and secured a policy change from the Continental Army to prevent unwarranted seizure of civilian supplies.

FURTHER READING

Rakove, Jack N.: *The Beginnings of National Politics: an Interpretative History of the Continental Congress* (Baltimore and London: Johns Hopkins University Press, 1979), 164–76, 314.
Watterson, John Sayle: *Thomas Burke, Restless Revolutionary* (Washington, DC: University Press of America, 1980).

REBECCA STARR

Camden. *See* PRATT, CHARLES.

Campbell, John [4th Earl of Loudoun] (*b.* 5 May 1705; *d.* Loudoun Castle, Scotland, 27 April 1782). Commander-in-Chief of British forces in North America. Loudoun created the army that won the Seven Years' War. He assumed command in North America in 1756, hoping to persuade the colonists to pay for and wage the war under his direction, but he found them preoccupied with rights and profits. They refused to raise men for service in the regular army or under British officers; they provided quarters, fuel, and food only grudgingly; and they charged exorbitantly for supplies and labor. Loudoun soon understood that to win the war the British would have to rely mainly on regular forces – forces raised in England, supported by English taxes, supplied by English contractors, and trained for service in American conditions. But he was unable to assemble such an army in time to use it effectively. Obstructed both by the British Government and by colonial assemblies, and delayed by foul winds, he failed to mount any offensive in 1757 and was promptly recalled. However, he did leave behind a regular army that was prepared to conquer Canada.

FURTHER READING

Pargellis, Stanley M.: *Lord Loudoun in North America* (New Haven, Conn.: Yale University Press, 1933).

IRA D. GRUBER

Carey, Mathew (*b.* Dublin, 28 January 1760; *d.* Philadelphia, 16 September 1839). Writer and publisher. As a young printer in Ireland he twice ran foul of the British authorities for defending the rights of Roman Catholics. On the first occasion he exiled himself to Paris for a year, meeting both Benjamin Franklin and General La Fayette while there. He arrived in Philadelphia in 1784 after his second flight from British law, and struggled for a time as a publisher and bookseller before attaining prosperity in the 1790s. He was the first American journalist to report legislative debates in his newspaper. He wrote one bestselling pamphlet on the yellow fever epidemic of 1793 in Philadelphia and many others on questions of public policy, promoting African colonization and public education, among other schemes, and even returning to Irish history for a defense of the Catholic role in the uprising of 1641. He devoted his greatest and most sustained effort, however, to advocating the protection of American manufacturing. He argued against free trade both practically, with calculations and tables of figures, and theoretically, by challenging Adam Smith's principles of political economy. He submitted "Irrefragable Facts Against Plausible Arguments," as one of his titles ran, to convince the southern states that their long-term interests also lay in a protected domestic market.

FURTHER READING

Bradsher, E. L.: *Mathew Carey: Editor, Author, and Publisher* (New York, 1912); repr. (New York: AMS Press, 1982).

Rowe, K. W.: *Mathew Carey: a Study in American Economic Development* (Baltimore, 1933); repr. (New York: AMS Press, 1982).

THOMAS COLE

Carleton, Sir Guy [Baron Dorchester] (*b.* Strabane, Co. Tyrone, 3 September 1724; *d.* Maidenhead, Berks., 10 November 1808). British general and administrator. He was governor and commander-in-chief in Quebec from 1766 to 1778, and as such was largely responsible for keeping that colony out of the Revolution. Appointed commander of the British Army in America in May 1782, he organized its withdrawal the following year. In 1786 he was created Baron Dorchester and again appointed Governor of Quebec, a post he held until 1796.

As Governor of Quebec, Carleton was largely responsible for the passage of the Quebec Act (1774). Although that Act helped to inflame American opposition to Britain, Carleton believed that it would ensure the loyalty of the French Canadians, so when fighting broke out in Massachusetts he dispatched most of his Regulars to Boston. In the event, few French Canadians were interested in fighting in Britain's cause, and when American forces invaded the province in late 1775 Carleton was quickly besieged in Quebec City. His defence of the city earned him a knighthood, but his failure to destroy the American Army in Canada and occupy Fort Ticonderoga the following summer when he received reinforcements from Britain brought criticism which led to his resignation. He returned to Britain in 1778.

In 1782 Carleton succeeded Sir Henry Clinton as commander in America. He was also commissioned to attempt a reconciliation with the rebels, but when that failed he had little to do but supervise the British evacuation. He became sympathetic to the plight of the American loyalists at this time, and arranged for their evacuation to Britain's Caribbean islands and Nova Scotia and Quebec and persuaded the governors there to grant them land. As Governor of Quebec after 1786 he continued to be solicitous towards the loyalists' interests.

FURTHER READING

Browne, G. P.: "Carleton, Guy, 1st Baron Dorchester," *Dictionary of Canadian Biography* (Toronto: University of Toronto Press, 1983), Vol. 5, 141–55.

Burt, Alfred L.: *The Old Province of Quebec, 1760–1791* (Minneapolis: University of Minnesota Press, 1933).

Reynolds, P. R.: *Guy Carleton: a Biography* (Toronto: Gage, 1980).

Smith, P. H.: "Sir Guy Carleton: soldier-statesman," *George Washington's Opponents: British Generals and Admirals in the American Revolution*, ed. G. A. Billias (New York: William Morrow, 1969), 103–41.

R. ARTHUR BOWLER

Carroll, Charles, of Carrollton (*b.* Annapolis, Md., 19 September 1737; *d.* Baltimore, 14 November 1832). Planter, businessman, and politician. Carroll served in the Maryland and national governments for 27 years, beginning as a member of the provincial Committee of Correspondence in 1774 and the Council of Safety in 1775. Early in 1776 the Second Continental Congress appointed him one of four commissioners to persuade the Canadians to join the Revolution. Elected to Congress upon his return from Canada, Carroll signed the Declaration of Independence (the only Roman Catholic to do so) and remained in Congress until 1778 (*see* figure 68). A member of the Maryland senate (1777–1801), he also represented his state in the United States Senate (1789–92).

DANIEL DULANY, JR., precipitated Carroll's political career in 1773 by defending in print (as "Antilon") Governor Robert Eden's imposition by proclamation of high fees for governmental services. Calling himself "First Citizen," Carroll replied, and in the ensuing debate he emerged as a popular leader. Fearful by 1776 of the democratic forces unleashed by the Revolution, Carroll led in writing a conservative state constitution that promoted stability and order, and in 1788 he supported the federal constitution for similar reasons.

Carroll's father guided him through 16 years of study in Europe to make him a worthy heir to one of the largest fortunes in the 13 colonies. The training succeeded, and Carroll substantially expanded his family's wealth during his lifetime. He is perhaps best remembered, however, as the last living signer of the Declaration of Independence.

FURTHER READING

Hoffman, Ronald: *A Spirit of Dissension: Economics, Politics and the Revolution in Maryland* (Baltimore: Johns Hopkins University Press, 1973).

Van Devanter, Ann C. (comp.): *"Anywhere so Long as There Be Freedom": Charles Carroll of Carrollton, his Family and his Maryland* (Baltimore: Baltimore Musuem of Art, 1975).

RONALD HOFFMAN

Chase, Samuel (*b.* Somerset Co., Md., 17 April 1741; *d.* Washington, DC, 19 June 1811). Lawyer and politician. Chase sat in the Maryland lower house (1765–6, 1768–71, 1773–7, and 1777–88) and served on Maryland's Committee of Correspondence (1773–5). He represented the colony in the Continental Congress (1774–8) and in 1776 was a member of the congressional mission to persuade the Canadians to join in the revolt. He was also a delegate to Maryland's Constitutional Ratification Convention in 1788 and served as a judge of the state's General Court from 1791 to 1796. He was appointed an Associate Justice of the Supreme Court of the United States in 1796, a position he held until his death.

Chase began his political career in 1763 by advocating local reform in Annapolis. He entered the general assembly's lower house in 1765, having combined popular support from artisans and mechanics with backing from the powerful Dulany family. His championship of radical resistance to the Stamp Act cost him the support of the Dulanys, but Chase's outspoken opposition to both Parliament and Maryland's proprietory govern-

ment increased his political influence, and in 1776 he was one of the Maryland signers of the Declaration of Independence. Often accused of demagogy, Chase worked carefully during the war to advance his interests while adopting those policies Maryland's elite leaders deemed necessary for preventing anarchy.

A frequently controversial figure, Chase was not returned to Congress in 1778 because of his attempts to use privileged information to corner the flour market. As a Supreme Court justice, he was impeached by Congress in 1804, but acquitted by the Senate.

FURTHER READING

Hawe, James, Beirne, Francis F., Beirne, Rosamond R., and Jett, R. Samuel: *Stormy Patriot: the Life of Samuel Chase* (Baltimore: Maryland Historical Society, 1980).

Hoffman, Ronald: *A Spirit of Dissension: Economics, Politics, and the Revolution in Maryland* (Baltimore: Johns Hopkins University Press, 1973).

RONALD HOFFMAN

Chatham. *See* PITT, WILLIAM.

Clark, George Rogers (*b.* nr Charlottesville, Va., 19 November 1752; *d.* nr Louisville, Ky., 13 February 1818). General. Born into a family of farmers of Scottish descent, he received little formal education as a child and eventually pursued a career as a surveyor.

During the Revolutionary War Clark worked tirelessly to protect Kentucky and frontier settlements from British incursions. In 1777 he proposed and the Virginia legislature accepted a plan to uproot British control in the West. The government directed Lieutenant-Colonel Clark to capture enemy posts in the Illinois country and, if possible, Detroit as well. In July 1778, without firing a single shot, Clark's small force seized Kaskaskia and Vincennes. The British regained Vincennes, but Clark returned on 25 February 1779 and captured the fort along with its commander, Henry Hamilton. Promoted to brigadier general in 1781, he led a final expedition against the pro-British Shawnee. With little material and financial assistance, Clark helped the United States gain the upper hand in the western war.

Clark's reputation declined in the postwar years. In 1786 he led an unauthorized and unsuccessful expedition against the Wabash, and during the 1790s volunteered to assist France's seizure of Louisiana. Late in life Clark suffered from alcoholism and debilitating strokes that whittled away his mental and physical health.

FURTHER READING

Harrison, J. H.: *George Rogers Clark and the War in the West* (Lexington: University of Kentucky Press, 1976).

J. MARK THOMPSON

Clinton, George (*b.* Little Britain, NY, 26 July 1739; *d.* Washington, 20 April 1812). Governor of New York and Vice President of the United States. Clinton studied law with William Smith of New York City and returned home to Ulster County to practice. He began his political career and his leadership of the patriot cause when he was elected to the Provincial Assembly in 1768. Clinton attended the Second Continental Congress, and accepted a command as brigadier general in the New York militia in 1775. In June 1777 he was elected Governor of the state. John Jay commented that Clinton's background "did not entitle him to so distinguished a pre-eminence," but the voters disagreed and elected him for six consecutive terms. Clinton led a powerful political organization, and his determined opposition to a strong national government posed a huge challenge to the state's Federalists during the campaign to ratify the United States Constitution. Historians disagree over whether he wrote the series of Anti-Federalist letters signed "Cato" that appeared in the *New York Journal* from October 1787 to April 1788. Clinton has also been credited occasionally with the letters of "Brutus," which appeared

in the same newspaper, and with the writings of "A Republican." As president of the state's ratifying convention, he narrowly failed to hold a majority against the Constitution. He continued to serve as Governor until 1795, when New York politics fell temporarily under Federalist control. In 1800 Clinton was returned to the governor's office as part of a Republican victory. In 1804 and again in 1808 he was elected Vice President of the United States, an office he held until his death.

For illustration, *see* LEE, RICHARD HENRY.

FURTHER READING

DePauw, Linda Grant: *The Eleventh Pillar: New York State and the Federal Constitution* (Ithaca, NY: Cornell University Press, 1966).
Spaulding, Ernest Wilder: *His Excellency George Clinton, Critic of the Constitution* (New York: Macmillan, 1938).

ELIZABETH P. MCCAUGHEY

Clinton, Sir Henry (*b.* 16 April 1730; *d.* London, 23 December 1795). Commander-in-Chief of the British Army in North America. Clinton was an able tactician and strategist, but he lacked the confidence to be a successful commander in the War for Independence. As third in command to Thomas Gage in 1775 and second to Sir William Howe from November 1775 to May 1778, Clinton was too insecure to press his ideas on his superiors. Once he succeeded Howe, he did well enough on the defensive, evacuating Philadelphia and securing New York and Rhode Island in 1778; he also took Charles Town by a long, prudent siege in 1780. Yet, having fewer troops and opportunities than Howe and being unsure of himself, Clinton failed to bring the Continental Army to action along the Hudson (1779–80) and to cooperate with the British Navy in attacking the French at Rhode Island (1780–1). Nor could he impose his strategy for a gradual reconquest of the South on his energetic second, Charles, Earl Cornwallis (1780–1) or save Cornwallis at Yorktown in

October 1781. He resigned his command in 1782 and returned to England.

For illustration, *see* figure 48, p. 585.

FURTHER READING

Willcox, William B.: *Portrait of a General: Sir Henry Clinton in the War of Independence* (New York: Alfred A. Knopf, 1964).

IRA D. GRUBER

Corbin, Margaret Cochran (*b.* Pennsylvania, 12 November 1751; *d.* Pennsylvania, *c.* 1800). Revolutionary soldier. Corbin was one of the many eighteenth-century women who followed their menfolk to war. What makes her experience somewhat exceptional is that she is known to have fought, and been seriously wounded, in the War for Independence. When her husband John, a private, was killed in 1776 at Fort Washington she took his place in the patriot lines. Subsequently her heroism earned her a pension from the government of Pennsylvania. Nothing is known of her activities after the war.

FURTHER READING

Hall, Edward H.: *Margaret Corbin: Heroine of the Battle of Fort Washington, 16 November 1776* (New York: American Scenic and Historic Preservation Society, 1932).

BETTY WOOD

Cornwallis, Charles [1st Marquis and 2nd Earl Cornwallis] (*b.* London, 31 December 1738; *d.* Ghazipore, India, 1805). British general. He decided early upon a military career and studied his profession on the Continent. During the Seven Years' War he fought with distinction, rising to regimental command. Although mildly opposed to Britain's American policies he nonetheless volunteered to fight against the Americans when the Revolution erupted. Commissioned a major general, he served under generals Howe and Clinton. His chance to exercise

FIGURE 60 Charles Cornwallis: painting by John Singleton Copley (*c.* 1794–5)

independent command came when Clinton left him in charge of British forces in the South after the American surrender of Charles Town, South Carolina, in early 1780. Although he won victories in the open field against the Americans, he never understood the nature of American guerrilla warfare. That misunderstanding eventually led him to Virginia and surrender at Yorktown. Of the senior generals who served in America, Cornwallis alone escaped blame for the loss of the colonies. After Yorktown he enjoyed a distinguished career, particularly as governor-general of British India.

FURTHER READING

Gruber, Ira D.: *The Howe Brothers and the American Revolution* (New York: Atheneum, 1972).
Willcox, William B.: *Portrait of a General: Sir Henry Clinton in the War of Independence* (New York: Alfred A. Knopf, 1964).

FRANKLIN B. WICKWIRE

Crèvecoeur, Michel-Guillaume Jean de [J. Hector St. John] (*b.* Caen, France, 31 January

1735; *d.* Sarcelles, France, 12 November 1813). Essayist. He came to the New World as a soldier with the French, but stayed on to wander and eventually settle in British America. On the basis of his experiences between 1769 and 1780, when he, his American wife, and their children resided in Orange County, New York, Crèvecoeur wrote *Letters from an American Farmer* (1782). Further writings were found and published in 1925 as *Sketches of Eighteenth Century Life*; he published under the Anglicized name of J. Hector St. John and in his adopted language of English. Crèvecoeur offered descriptions of farm life and work as well as travel reports from various colonies, and praised the freedom and opportunity of America, especially recommending it for immigrants. He depicted himself as a Pennsylvania farmer in these supposed first-hand accounts, perhaps because the religious and ethnic diversity of that colony and its broad distribution of land-ownership captured better what he valued about America than did the patchwork of manors in colonial New York. He defined the American as a "new man," who had liberated himself from European ideas of rank, nationality, and religious affiliation.

FURTHER READING

Philbrick, T.: *St. John De Crèvecoeur* (New York: Twayne Publishers, 1970).

THOMAS COLE

Dartmouth. *See* LEGGE, WILLIAM.

Deane, Silas (*b.* Groton, Conn., 24 December 1737; *d.* at sea, 23 September 1789). Statesman and diplomat. Deane graduated from Yale in 1758, and became a successful attorney and merchant. In 1772 he was elected to the Connecticut Assembly, and two years later was named one of Connecticut's delegates to the Continental Congress. He was sent to France by that body in 1776 as America's first foreign representative. He was later joined by Benjamin Franklin and Arthur Lee.

The three diplomats succeeded in signing treaties with France in 1778, but were less successful in their other task of obtaining supplies and competent foreign officers for the American Army. Much of the blame for these failures fell upon Deane. He had promised American commissions to scores of incompetent European officers and, at best, confused public accounts with his own. Recalled by Congress, he was unable to provide sufficient accounts for his public expenditures. In an attempt to exonerate himself he returned to Europe in 1781. The British captured and published his letters to friends urging them to accept reconciliation with Britain. Disgraced as a traitor, Deane died aboard ship in the English Channel.

FURTHER READING

Dexter, F. B.: *Yale Biographies and Annals, 1745–1763* (New York: Henry Holt, 1896).
James, C. H: *Silas Deane: Patriot or Traitor* (East Lansing: Michigan State University Press, 1975).

KURT W. NAGEL

Dickinson, John (*b.* Talbot Co., Md., 2 November 1732; *d.* Wilmington, Del., 14 February 1808). Political leader. Dickinson has been called the "Penman of the American Revolution." His writings, both official and personal, were frequent and notable. Born in Maryland and brought up in Delaware, he was the son of Samuel and Mary Cadwalader Dickinson. By 1757, after studying at London's Middle Temple, he enjoyed a lucrative legal practice in Philadelphia. Immersed in history and law, politics soon involved him.

As an active member of the Pennsylvania Assembly, he attended the Stamp Act Congress where, though not a member of the committee, his suggested resolutions were adopted with few changes. When the Townshend Acts replaced the Stamp Act, Dickinson protested in 12 anonymous letters to the Philadelphia *Chronicle* entitled *Letters from a Farmer in Pennsylvania* (*see* figure 61 and Chapter 13. §5). These dealt with the vicissitudes of liberty in England's history and cau-

FIGURE 61 John Dickinson with a copy of the Magna Carta and his "Farmer's Letters" (engraving by James Smither, 1768)

tioned the colonies about the dangers of parliamentary taxation. Reprinted throughout the colonies, Dickinson's advice henceforth was sought by colonial leaders as British restrictions increased.

Dickinson also took an active role as a delegate to the First Continental Congress. In the early years of protest he had been regarded as a radical, yet cautioned that the "cause of liberty should not be sullied by turbulence and tumult." More moderate, he sought redress by formal petitions to the King. Later, seemingly more conservative, he was more forthright, as in his corrective additions to the *Declaration on the Causes and Necessity of Taking up Arms*. Moreover, he became colonel of the First Battalion of Associators of Philadelphia.

By 1776 petitions proved ineffective. Independence was called for. Dickinson doggedly argued against such a course, pointing out that the colonies lacked both a binding union and a necessary foreign alliance. Appointed to a committee to prepare a document for Confederation, he was largely responsible for the resultant draft of Articles, which were national in character but much watered down in subsequent congressional passage. When the vote for independence was set, Dickinson was aware the tide had run against him. He did not take his seat, thus permitting the Pennsylania delegation to vote favorably with one voice. That same day he prepared to lead his battalion to northern New Jersey, there to face embarking British soldiers.

After returning from military duties Dickinson retired to his Delaware estate with his wife and two daughters, and in 1779 Delaware returned him to the Congress. Two years later he was elected governor. But Dickinson hoped to regain political favor in Pennsylvania, and in 1783 he became that state's president.

When in 1788 Virginia proposed the Annapolis convention to amend the weakened Articles of Confederation, Dickinson, a member of the Delaware delegation, became chairman. The call for a Federal Convention in Philadelphia followed. Dickinson again represented Delaware. His voice was heard declaring, "Experience must be our only guide. Reason may mislead us." With determination he sought to protect the interests of small states in matters of representation. When the Federal Constitution was proposed for ratification Dickinson took up his pen and, once again, wrote a series of letters, published as *Letters of Fabius*, setting forth reasons to support it.

In 1801 Dickinson's writings were collected and published in two volumes, testimony to his political thought and his enduring position in the American struggle for independence.

FURTHER READING

Dickinson, John: *The Political Writings of John Dickinson, Esq.*, Vol. 1 (Wilmington, Del., 1801).

Flower, Milton E.: *John Dickinson: Conservative Revolutionary* (Charlottesville: University of Virginia Press, 1983).

Ford, Paul Leicester (ed.): *The Writings of John Dickinson*, Vol. I, *Political Writings, 1764–1774* (Philadelphia, 1895).

Jacobson, Davie L.: *John Dickinson and the Revolution in Pennsylvania, 1764–1776* (Berkley, Calif., 1965).

Stillé, Charles J.: *The Life and Times of John Dickinson* (Philadelphia, 1891).

MILTON E. FLOWER

Draper, Margaret Green (*b. c.*1730; *d.* England, 1807). Publisher. Born into a Boston newspaper family, she also married a publisher, Richard Draper, in 1750. Following Richard's death in June 1774, she took over production of the *Massachusetts Gazette and Boston Newsletter* with his partner John Boyle. They soon parted ways, possibly over his patriot sympathies. Draper ran the newspaper alone for several months before joining up with the loyalist John Howe. They continued to produce the only paper published during the siege of Boston until the evacuation in 1776, ending the 72-year tradition of Boston's oldest newspaper. Draper left behind much valuable property and £2,100-worth of printing materials when she fled, first to Nova Scotia and then to London. There she lived out her days in exile with her daughter on a government pension of £100 per year granted in recognition of her loyalty and severe losses.

FURTHER READING

Dictionary of American Biography, Vol. 7 (New York: Charles Scribner's Sons, 1931), 442–3.
Loyalist Claims, Audit Office 12, p. 105.

KATHERINE M. J. MCKENNA

Duane, James (*b.* New York, 6 February 1733; *d.* Duanesburg, NY, 1 February 1797). Lawyer and Mayor of New York City. Duane began his legal training in the law office of James Alexander, without any prior college education. He was admitted to the bar in 1747 and rose rapidly to prominence in his profession. During the Anglo-American crisis he frequently took a middle course, for example, speaking out against the violence of the Stamp Act riots in New York. In 1774 he was appointed to the Committee of Fifty-one and, despite protests from radical patriots, he was sent to the First Continental Congress. There he defended Joseph Galloway's Plan of Union (*see* GALLOWAY, JOSEPH), though he also supported the non-importation agreement. He served in the New York Provincial Congress, the Second Continental Congress, the New York Committee of Sixty to carry out the non-importation "Association," and the Committee of One Hundred. In the Continental Congress he served on several important committees dealing with financial affairs, Indian relations, and the drafting of the Articles of Confederation. Because of his moderate stands and his long association with Trinity Church and King's College, he was accused of loyalism, but was immediately and publicly defended by such patriots as John Jay and Alexander McDougall. As Mayor of New York City from 1784 to 1789 Duane led the rebuilding of the city after the British occupation. At the Poughkeepsie ratifying convention in 1788 he was an ardent defender of the new Federal Constitution. In 1789 President Washington appointed him the first federal judge of the district of New York, and Duane sat on that bench until his retirement in 1794.

FURTHER READING

Alexander, Edward P.: *A Revolutionary Conservative: James Duane of New York* (New York: Columbia University Press, 1938).

ELIZABETH P. MCCAUGHEY

Dulany, Daniel, Jr. (*b.* Annapolis, Md., 28 June 1722; *d.* Baltimore, 17 March 1797). Lawyer and politician. Born into a prominent Annapolis family, Dulany sat in Maryland's lower house (1751–4) and upper house (1757–63, 1765–6, 1768–71, 1773–4), and received proprietary appointments as Maryland's commissary general (1754–6, 1759–61) and commissioner for the sale of proprietary manors (1766–71). Most important were his positions as a member of the council (1757–76) and as Maryland's secretary (1761–76), which gave him extensive wealth and power.

After attending Eton and Clare College, Cambridge, and studying law at London's

Middle Temple, Dulany actively practised law in Maryland from 1747 to 1763. He wrote *Considerations on the Propriety of Imposing Taxes* (1765), which demolished the concept of "virtual representation" but repudiated radical resistance to the Stamp Act. Although a business partner with the Carroll family, Dulany, using the pseudonym "Antilon," became involved in 1773 in a notable exchange of public letters with CHARLES CARROLL of Carrollton, who wrote as "First Citizen." The issue, known as the "fee controversy," related primarily to the extent of the proprietary government's authority. Bested by Carroll in the debate, Dulany continued to support the proprietary government to which he and his family owed their power and wealth, but with the coming of the Revolution his influence waned. While officially neutral, Dulany was known to have loyalist sympathies, and his family lost about one-half of its property to patriot confiscations after 1780.

FURTHER READING

Hoffman, Ronald: *A Spirit of Dissension: Economics, Politics, and the Revolution in Maryland* (Baltimore: Johns Hopkins University Press, 1973).
Land, Aubrey C.: *The Dulanys of Maryland: a Biographical Study of Daniel Dulany the Elder (1685–1753) and Daniel Dulany the Younger (1722–1797)* (Baltimore: Johns Hopkins University Press, 1955).

RONALD HOFFMAN

Dunk, George Montagu [2nd Earl of Halifax] (*b.* 6 October 1716; *d.* 8 June 1771). British statesman. He held minor court office in the 1740s, and then, as Head of the Board of Trade (1748–61), actively promoted colonial commerce and the extension of political control and mercantilist regulation within the empire. He was Lord-Lieutenant of Ireland (1761–3), First Lord of the Admiralty (January–October 1762), and Secretary of State (Northern, 1762–3; Southern, 1763–5). In the last of these posts he implemented the policies embodied in the Proclamation of 1763 setting up new colonies and imposing a check on westward migration, and he assisted in the preparation of Grenville's measures of colonial taxation. To reinforce imperial control on the frontier he promoted the formation of the Indian department, and he favored the establishment of colonial civil lists to strengthen the position of the governors. As a friend and ministerial colleague he may have influenced the views on colonial questions of Lord Hillsborough. In 1766 he was one of 33 peers who protested against the repeal of the Stamp Act. As a stop-gap in the offices of Lord Privy Seal and Secretary of State (1770–1), however, he was ill and inactive.

FURTHER READING

Basye, A. H.: *The Lords Commissioners of Trade and Plantations* (New Haven, Conn.: Yale Historical Publications), Miscellany 14, pp. 32–104, 133–6.

IAN R. CHRISTIE

Dunmore. *See* MURRAY, JOHN.

Fauquier, Francis (*b. c.* 1704; *d.* Williamsburg, Va., 3 March 1768). Lieutenant-Governor of Virginia. Fauquier was the son of a businessman, a director from 1751 of the South Sea Company, and a writer on fiscal questions. Since the governorship was held as a sinecure, he was the effective head of the royal administration. From 1758 until his death he displayed dexterity and pliability in his relations with the Virginia legislature and at times, in order to secure cordial cooperation, tacitly ignored instructions from London. About the beginning of 1760, in reply to forecasts from Pitt of parliamentary taxation of the colonies for defence, he warned Pitt that such a step would cause trouble. In 1765 he sanctioned the clearance of ships supplied with certificates that stamp duties could not be charged for lack of the stamps. But the passage of the Virginia Resolutions against the Stamp Act provoked him into dissolving the assembly and it was not summoned again till November 1766, its official involvement with the Stamp Act Congress being thus prevented. His relations with the colonists were also soured by his official stand against unauthorized westward migration across the Proclamation Line into Indian lands.

IAN R. CHRISTIE

Franklin, Benjamin (*b.* Boston, 17 January 1706; *d.* Philadelphia, 17 April 1790). Statesman and scientist. The oldest Revolutionary, Benjamin Franklin was the fifteenth of 17 children of a pious Puritan who made soap and candles. He signed the Declaration of Independence in 1776 (aged 70), served as joint commissioner (elected 26 September 1776) to France and later as sole minister plenipotentiary (elected 14 September 1778), and, with John Jay and John Adams, negotiated the Treaty of Paris in 1782. Only Franklin signed all three fundamental documents of American nationhood: the Declaration of Independence, the Treaty of Paris, and the United States Constitution.

On Sunday, 6 October 1723, Franklin (aged 17) arrived in Philadelphia, where he gradually became a successful printer and publisher. He retired in 1748 (aged 42) to devote himself to civic activities, science, literature, and politics. He became the foremost scientist of the mid-eighteenth century, winning (30 November 1753) the Copley medal of the Royal Society of London for his electrical studies. As a result of his scientific achievements, he was given honorary Masters' degrees by Harvard (25 July 1753), Yale (12 September 1753), William and Mary (20 April 1756), and Cambridge (6 July 1758), as well as an LLD from the University of St. Andrews (12 February 1759) and a DCL from Oxford (30 April 1762). He was elected a Fellow of the Royal Society of London on 29 April 1756 and a foreign member of the French Royal Academy of Science in August 1772.

Beginning with the publication of his bitter hoax *Rattlesnakes for Felons* (9 May 1751), proposing that America send rattlesnakes to Britain in exchange for its criminals transported to America, Franklin was America's primary propagandist. His Albany Plan of Union (10 July 1754) was the most famous proposal for a union of the American colonies during the colonial period. He was elected to the Pennsylvania Assembly on 9 May 1751, and accepted its nomination as agent to Britain on 3 February 1757. There he wrote a constant stream of American propaganda. His effective testimony in the House of Commons against the Stamp Act (13 February 1766) contributed to its repeal and established him as America's pre-eminent representative. By 1771 he had also been elected the representative of New Jersey, Georgia, and Massachusetts. The colonists generally perceived Franklin's humiliating excoriation by Solicitor-General Alexander Wedderburn before the Privy Council (29 January 1774) as Britain's reply to the Boston Tea Party (16 December 1773). Franklin had been made America's scapegoat.

After arriving back in Philadelphia (5 May 1775) Franklin served in the Second Continental Congress until he was sent to France. During the Revolutionary War he borrowed funds for the colonies from France, issued letters of marque for American privateers, managed the interests of the United States Navy overseas, negotiated for humane treatment of American prisoners of war, financed numerous individual Americans who escaped from Britain, oversaw the purchase and shipping of arms and other materiel for the United States Army, coordinated and often wrote American propaganda for English and European distribution, and cultivated friendly relations with the French Foreign Minister Vergennes and such influential French statesmen as Anne Robert Jacques Turgot and the Duc de La Rochefoucauld. Franklin was the most essential and successful American diplomat of all time.

In 1782 Lord Rockingham became Prime Minister of Britain and initiated American peace talks. Richard Oswald began the negotiations with Benjamin Franklin. The preliminary peace treaty, dated 30 November

FIGURE 62 "The American Peace Commissioners (Treaty of 1782)" (left to right): John Jay, John Adams, Benjamin Franklin, William Temple Franklin (secretary) and Henry Laurens (unfinished painting by Benjamin West, 1783–4)

1782, was signed by Franklin, Jay, Adams, and Henry Laurens for the United States (*see* figure 62). In 1785 Jefferson replaced Franklin in France. Franklin returned to Philadelphia (14 September 1785) and was elected to the Supreme Executive Council of Pennsylvania (11 October 1785). As its president, he was, in effect, Governor of Pennsylvania (1785–8). Active in the Constitutional Convention, Franklin made the closing speech (17 September 1787), which became the most frequently reprinted propaganda in favor of the adoption of the Constitution. His last public writing (23 March 1790) brilliantly satirized slavery.

FURTHER READING

Labaree, Leonard W. et al. (eds.): *The Papers of Benjamin Franklin*, 26 vols. (New Haven, Conn.: Yale University Press, 1959–).
Lemay, J. A. Leo (ed.): *Benjamin Franklin: Writings* (New York: Library of America, 1987).
Van Doren, Carl: *Benjamin Franklin* (New York: Viking, 1938).

Wright, Esmond: *Franklin of Philadelphia* (Cambridge, Mass.: Harvard University Press, 1986).

J. A. LEO LEMAY

Freeman, Elizabeth [Bett; Mumbet] (*d.* Massachusetts, 1792). Born a slave, she was in her later years a beloved servant of the Sedgwick family of western Massachusetts. Freeman (affectionately known as "Mumbet") is known to history because she was a plaintiff in a suit in 1781, *Brom and Bett v. Ashley*, whereby two slaves successfully sued for freedom. This suit, contemporaneous with the better-known Quok Walker suit, helped to establish formal recognition of the end of slavery in Massachusetts. Moreover, it attracted talented legal minds, inasmuch as the attorneys for the plaintiffs were Theodore Sedgwick and Tapping Reeve.

Although little is known about Brom, we know more about Freeman because two members of the Sedgwick family subsequently wrote about her. She was a slave in the household of Colonel John Ashley, one of the leading citizens of Berkshire County. According to Catherine Sedgwick, she decided to sue for freedom after hearing about the ideas in the Declaration of Independence. On the other hand, the leading modern student of the case, Arthur Zilversmit, thinks that the case was probably arranged to test the constitutionality of slavery in Massachusetts. In any event, the case did have an important impact in that, by deciding not to appeal, Colonel Ashley tacitly accepted the abolition of slavery (*see also* Chapter 39, §5).

FURTHER READING

Zilversmit, Arthur: "Quok Walker, Mumbet, and the abolition of slavery in Massachusetts," *William and Mary Quarterly*, 25 (1968), 614–24.

GLENNA MATTHEWS

Freneau, Philip (*b.* New York, 2 January 1752; *d.* Monmouth Co., NJ, 19 December 1832). Poet. He was born into a wealthy New York merchant family of Huguenot origins, and distinguished himself as a poet and patriot from his days at Princeton (BA, 1771), where "The Rising Glory of America," of which he was co-author, was read at commencement. He supported himself by editing and contributing to newspapers in New Jersey and Pennsylvania and by periodically shipping out to sea. All experience provided grist to his poetic mill, and, in addition to poems denouncing British tyranny, he wrote of the sea and nature and of hardships aboard "The British Prison Ship," where he had languished for two months. He argued also for an American literature that would eschew British models. Engaged in 1791 by the Secretary of State Thomas Jefferson as a translator, he proved of service to the liberal wing of President Washington's administration by publishing an anti-Hamiltonian newspaper, the *National Gazette*. Its attacks brought a reference to him as "that rascal Freneau" from Washington, who demanded his dismissal of Jefferson. Out of the national scene, Freneau resumed literary, journalistic, and maritime activities.

FURTHER READING

Bowden, M. W.: *Philip Freneau* (Boston: Twayne, 1976).
Marsh, P. M.: *Philip Freneau: Poet and Journalist* (Minneapolis: Dillon Press, 1968)

THOMAS COLE

Gadsden, Christopher (*b.* Charles Town, 16 February 1724; *d.* 28 August 1805). Merchant. He became the leader for independence in South Carolina. In 1764 his special election from St. Paul's Parish struck the first spark of revolution when Governor Thomas Boone refused to seat him. The Commons House held that only it could control its membership, and in the ensuing struggle Boone was recalled. The next year Gadsden was one of the colony's three delegates to the Stamp Act Congress. His temperament and conduct appealed to the city's politically self-conscious mechanics, and from 1768 onwards they elected him to the House and as their spokesman for the Sons of Liberty. Because many were forced to swear allegiance to Great Britain in order to work during Charles Town's occupation, Gadsden opposed the 1782 Confiscation Act as bearing unfairly on them.

Gadsden served in the Commons House of Assembly from 1757 to 1775 and was a member of both provincial congresses (1775–6) and the First Continental Congress (1774–6). Here he succeeded in negotiating a compromise between the Congress and South Carolina's delegation when a dispute over exempting rice from the boycott threatened to break up the Congress. At home he returned to his House seat (1776–8), but was forced out when conservative rivals maneuvered his election to the state's vice presidency (1778–9). Imprisoned for ten months during Charles Town's occupation, he declined the office of governor made by the 1782 Jacksonborough Assembly on grounds of age and ill-health. Except for serving one more term in the House (1783–4), as a delegate to the 1788 ratification convention for the United States Constitution, which he favored, and as an Adams elector in 1800, Gadsden retired from politics.

FURTHER READING

Edgar, Walter B., and Bailey, N. Louise (eds.): *Biographical Directory of the South Carolina House of Representatives*, Vol. 2: *1692–1775* (Columbia: University of South Carolina Press, 1974).
Godbold, E. Stanley, and Woody, Robert H.: *Christopher Gadsden and the American Revolution* (Knoxville: University of Tennessee Press, 1983).

REBECCA STARR

Gage, Thomas (*b. c.* 1720; *d.* London, 2 April 1787). British general. He served as military governor of Montreal (1760–3), Commander-in-Chief of the British Army in North America (1763–75), and Governor of Massachusetts (1774–5). As Commander-in-Chief in America on the eve of the Revolution, Gage was a staunch but ineffectual supporter of imperial government. Like most British officers, he believed that the authority of the King and Paliament should be supreme in America – that the colonists should be made to pay taxes levied by Parliament to support imperial administration and defense. When the colonists opposed the Stamp Tax (1765) and the Townshend Duties (1767), Gage recommended using the army to intimidate the colonists or, that failing, to crush them. Yet he also sought to prevent clashes between soldiers and civilians, and he was unwilling to use or even deploy troops without instructions from civil authorities. In 1775, when Gage was at last ordered to use force, he was unable to do so effectively. His troops suffered heavy casualties in the battles of Lexington and Concord and of Bunker Hill; his army was blockaded in Boston; and he was recalled.

FURTHER READING

Alden, John R.: *General Gage in America* (Baton Rouge: Louisiana State University Press, 1948).

IRA D. GRUBER

Galloway, Grace Crowden (*d.* ?Philadelphia, 1782). Wife and home-maker. She was the daughter of one eminent man and the wife of another. Her father, Lawrence Crowden, was one of the wealthiest men in Pennsylvania; her husband, Joseph Galloway, was the author of the "Galloway Plan" which sought to effect a political reconciliation, and in the process a redefinition of the relationship, between Britain and the mainland colonies.

When her husband left for England in 1778 to pursue the doomed cause of peace, Galloway remained in Philadelphia to try and safeguard the family's interests. As her journal amply demonstrates, she enthusiastically endorsed the loyalist cause. She was ever contemptuous of the patriots, and the more so after they confiscated the Galloway's family home in Philadelphia. An increasingly bitter woman who never became reconciled to the prospect of American Independence, she died in 1782, shortly before her worst fears for the future were realized.

FURTHER READING

Werner, R. C. (ed.): "Diary of Grace Crowden Galloway," *Pennsylvania Magazine of History and Biography*, 55 (1931), 32–94; 58 (1934), 152–89.

BETTY WOOD

Galloway, Joseph (*b.* West River, Md., *c.* 1731; *d.* Watford, Herts., 29 August 1803). Lawyer and statesman. Galloway was born into a prominent mercantile and landowning family with large estates in Pennsylvania and Maryland. After studying law in Philadelphia and earning a reputation for excellence at the bar, he began his political career in 1756, when he was elected to the Pennsylvania Assembly. Galloway was a prominent spokesman for his colony in the Anglo-American crisis, as Speaker of the Pennsylvania Assembly (1766–75), chairman of the assembly's committee to correspond with the colony's London agents, and a delegate to the First Continental Congress (1774). He firmly believed that the crisis was constitutional and could be remedied by devising a new imperial government under a written constitution. In his own plan of union, Galloway called for a Grand Council, to which all the colonies would elect representatives, and a President General appointed by the King to serve during good behavior. Although the colonies would govern themselves on internal matters, any imperial regulations would require the consent of the Grand Council, the President General, and the British Parliament. When the First Continental Congress refused to endorse Galloway's plan, he abandoned the patriot cause and published his convictions in a statement of Whig-loyalism entitled *A Candid Examination of the Mutual Claims of Great Britain and the Colonies* (New York, 1775). Galloway warned that the Congress had abandoned the search for compromise and taken the "high road of sedition." He abhorred the "lawless power" that patriot leaders had seized to suppress free speech and press. When the British occupied Philadelphia Galloway was appointed Civil Administrator by General Howe (*see* Chapter 25, §4), but in 1778 Continental forces captured the city, and Galloway fled to England. His estate in America was confiscated, his petition to return to Pennsylvania after the Revolution was denied, and Galloway remained in exile for the last 25 years of his life.

FURTHER READING

Ferling, John E.: *The Loyalist Mind: Joseph Galloway and the American Revolution* (University Park: Pennsylvania State University Press, 1977).

Norton, Mary Beth: *The British Americans: the Loyalist Exiles in England, 1774–1789* (Boston: Little, Brown & Co., 1972).

ELIZABETH P. McCAUGHEY

Gannett, Deborah Sampson (*b.* Massachusetts, 17 December 1760; *d.* Massachusetts, 29 April 1827). Revolutionary soldier. In 1782 she disguised herself as a man and enlisted in the 4th Massachusetts Regiment under the name of Robert Shurtleff,

or Shirtleff. After fighting with that regiment for a year, and being wounded whilst on active service, her identity was discovered and she was discharged from the army. She subsequently received war pensions from both Congress and the Massachusetts government. After the war she married John Gannett, a Massachusetts farmer.

FURTHER READING

Vinton, J. A.: Introduction to *An Account of the Experiences of Deborah Sampson, afterwards Mrs. Benjamin Gannett, who served as a soldier in the Revolutionary Army under the name of Robert Shirtliff* (Boston: Wiggin and Lunt, 1866); repr. (New York: Arno Press, 1972).

BETTY WOOD

Gates, Horatio (*b.* Maldon, Essex, April 1727/8; *d.* New York, 10 April 1806). General. Gates first went to America while serving in the British Army. He gained valuable military experience in Nova Scotia and along the frontier from Virginia to New York before retiring in May 1765. He moved to Virginia in 1772 and three years later found himself fighting the army he had formerly served.

In June 1775 Congress commissioned Gates adjutant general of the Continental Army and in 1777, after much confusion and debate, commander of the Northern Department. In both roles he proved himself an able organizer and administrator. On 27 November 1777, after his defeat of Burgoyne at Saratoga and with his reputation rising, Congress placed Gates at the head of the Board of War. For much of his remaining career, however, the general was at the center of controversy. The decline of his reputation was in part owing to his disastrous defeat at the battle of Camden, two months after he took command of the Southern Department. But it also resulted from his alleged attempts to supersede George Washington as Commander-in-Chief. Although his role in the Conway Cabal (1777–8) and the Newburgh Conspiracy (1783) has never been established, Gates's contemporaries and historians have been suspicious and critical of him.

During his last years Gates settled into relative obscurity, playing only a minor role as a Republican party leader during the early national period. He died in New York, where he had lived comfortably off the wealth of his second wife, Mary Vallance Gates.

FURTHER READING

Nelson, Paul David: *General Horatio Gates: a Biography* (Baton Rouge: Louisiana State University Press, 1976).

J. MARK THOMPSON

George III (*b*. London, 4 June 1738; *d*. Windsor, Berks., 29 January 1820). As sovereign, George III bore ultimate formal responsibility for the American revolutionary crisis, but not real personal responsibility, for the policy which led to it was formulated by ministers and supported by Parliament. While at times influencing policy, the King by no means dictated it. Often he had no particular views on the policy to be adopted and relied on ministers to formulate it. In 1762–3 he, like his ministers, was concerned about imperial defense in anticipation of a Bourbon war of revenge, and concurred in provision by parliamentary taxation of the colonies to pay for it. When Parliament's power was challenged he was adamant about upholding it, seeing American Independence as the inevitable alternative. A critical view of an abrasive approach to the colonies seems apparent in his attitude towards Grenville after 1765 and to Hillsborough in 1772. In 1769 he vetoed hard-line proposals submitted by Hillsborough, but that same year he advocated maintaining Townshend's tea duty as a symbol of Parliament's power over the colonies, and so concurred in setting the fuse for the Boston Tea Party and the crisis of 1774–5. He approved the coercive policy of 1774–5 and the use of force leading to the American War, partly from a conviction that the secession of the colonies would spell the end of Britain as a great power.

FIGURE 63 George III in his coronation robes: painting by Allan Ramsay (*c*. 1767)

FURTHER READING

Brooke, John: *King George III* (London: Constable, 1972), 162–77.
Thomas, P. D. G.: "George III and the American Revolution," *History*, 70, 228 (1985), 16–31.

IAN R. CHRISTIE

Germain, Lord George [formerly Sackville] (*b*. London, 26 January 1716; *d*. Stoneland Lodge, Sussex, 26 August 1785). British army officer and politician. After early political experience in Ireland he was disgraced for his conduct at the battle of Minden (1759) and only re-established himself politically in the mid-1760s. A convinced supporter of parliamentary supremacy within the empire, he joined Grenville in opposing repeal of the Stamp Act. His convictions drew him into support of Lord North's coercive legislation in 1774, and he advocated changes in the government of Massachusetts even more extensive than those proposed by the British Government. By early 1775 he was deeply involved in discussions of colonial policy and in November became Colonial Secretary; till 1779 he was also ex-officio First Lord of Trade. Germain was an energetic director of military measures in America, and his policy was based throughout on the mistaken assumption that widespread loyalism among the colonists would prevail if given regular military support. Like other ministers, he underestimated the extent of American disaffection, and he lacked the dominating personality needed to coordinate military and naval policy. Opposing independence to the last, he resigned in February 1782 when it was clear the war was being abandoned, and was created Viscount Sackville.

FURTHER READING

Brown, Gerald Saxon: *The American Secretary: the Colonial Policy of Lord George Germain, 1775–1778* (Ann Arbor: University of Michigan Press, 1963).

IAN R. CHRISTIE

Gerry, Elbridge (*b.* Marblehead, Mass., 17 July 1744; *d.* Washington, DC, 23 November 1814). Merchant, Governor of Massachusetts, and Vice President of the United States. He participated in both the creation and the development of the American republic from the 1770s until his death. Gerry (pronounced with a hard G) graduated from Harvard in 1762, and entered his father's shipping business. In 1772 he was elected to both the General Court of Massachusetts and the committee of correspondence. As a member of the second Continental Congress he signed both the Declaration of Independence and the Articles of Confederation. He served in Congress throughout most of the war, and, while remaining suspicious of militarism, made the securing of war supplies his special interest. Gerry was elected to the Massachusetts Assembly in 1786 and sent to the Constitutional Convention a year later.

He refused to sign the Constitution and opposed its ratification. Nonetheless, in 1789 he was elected to Congress, where he was a supporter of Hamilton's economic policies, and was a member of the delegation sent to France during the XYZ affair. Gerry was elected Governor of Massachusetts in 1810. While governor he became famous as the original "gerrymanderer" for his partisan redistricting of the state. In 1812 he was elected Vice President.

For illustration, *see* figure 37b, p. 459.

FURTHER READING

Billias, George A.: *Elbridge Gerry: Founding Father and Republican Statesman* (New York: McGraw Hill, 1976).

KURT W. NAGEL

Goddard, Mary Katherine (*b.* Connecticut, 16 June 1738; *d.* Baltimore, 12 August 1816). Printer. She learned the art of printing from her parents, who published a newspaper in Rhode Island. During the late 1760s she assisted her brother in producing the *Pennsylvania Chronicle* and in 1774 assumed the sole responsibility for editing and publishing the *Maryland Journal*. In 1775 she became one of the comparatively few colonial women to hold public office when she was appointed to the position of postmaster of Baltimore, a position which she held for the next 14 years. But Goddard is better known for the fact that it was her press that produced the first printed copy of the Declaration of Independence to include the names of all the signers. She continued to work as a printer and bookseller until her death.

FURTHER READING

Wroth, Lawrence C.: *A History of Printing in Colonial Maryland, 1686–1776* (Baltimore: Typothetae, 1922).

BETTY WOOD

Gordon, William (*b.* Hitchin, Herts., 1728; *d.* Ipswich, Suffolk, 19 October 1807). Minister and historian. In 1770 he left England and followed his political sympathies to the American colonies, where he thought to find the rights of Englishmen defended with greater zeal than at home. He decided ultimately on the role of observer and chronicler for himself, for the importance of the American Revolution seemed too great not to preserve for posterity. In researching, Gordon traveled throughout the United States and gained access to private papers. With the conclusion of the war, he believed the time had come to tell his story, though he chose to go to England to compose and publish it for fear of adverse American reaction to the opinions it expressed. So "impartial" a history as he projected threatened to bring down libel suits even in England, he was warned. No copy of Gordon's original manuscript has survived, but the *History of the Rise, Progress and Establishment of the Independence of the United States of America* as it appeared in 1789 has been exposed as a largely plagiarized work. Gordon relied on the wartime reports of the *Annual Register*, a yearly review of books and events to which Edmund Burke was the chief contributor.

FURTHER READING

Libby, O. G.: in *Annual Report of the American Historical Society for the Year 1899*, Vol. I, pp. 367–88.

THOMAS COLE

Grasse-Rouville, François-Joseph-Paul de [Comte de Grasse] (*b.* 13 February 1722; *d.* 11 January 1788). French naval commander. He was the veteran officer who commanded the French fleet at the decisive victory at Yorktown in October 1782. He served in the navy from childhood, fought in the wars of 1740–8 and 1755–63, and participated as a squadron commander (*chef d'escadre*) during the 1779 and 1780 campaigns in the West Indies and North America. In March 1781 he took a fleet to the Caribbean, where he assumed command. When the hurricane season began he brought 27 of his 28 ships of the line to Chesapeake Bay,

where he joined the Franco-American Army which had trapped Cornwallis at Yorktown. His British counterpart, lacking de Grasse's strategic insight, sent only 14 of his 20 ships of the line to reinforce the half dozen at New York. On 5 September, at the Battle of Virginia Capes, de Grasse beat off a British relief force, which then retired to New York to await reinforcements. Only a handful arrived – the British home fleet was outnumbered by the fleets of France, Spain, and the Netherlands – and Cornwallis surrendered before relief could reach him. De Grasse then returned to the West Indies, where he was defeated at the Battle of the Saintes (12 April 1783). De Grasse was sent as a prisoner of war to England, where in August he was used by the British Government to convey to France a key diplomatic message (*see* Chapter 33, §5).

FURTHER READING

Dull, Jonathan R.: *The French Navy and American Independence: a Study of Arms and Diplomacy, 1774–1787* (Princeton, NJ: Princeton University Press, 1975).

JONATHAN R. DULL

Gravier, Charles [Comte de Vergennes] (*b.* Dijon, 29 December 1719; *d.* 13 February 1787). French diplomat. He served as the French Foreign Minister for the last 13 years of his life. Gravier entered the diplomatic service in 1739. During his service as ambassador in Constantinople (1755–68) and Stockholm (1771–4) he sought to counter Russian expansionism. At the same time he was a member of the "Secret du Roi," the secret diplomatic service founded by King Louis XV to elect a French king of Poland. While in Sweden he observed the support given Russia by Great Britain. Deeply disturbed by the partition of Poland by Austria, Prussia, and Russia in 1772, he devoted himself as Foreign Minister to restoring France's influence in European diplomacy. The American Revolution presented him the opportunity to strike at Great Britain while the Russians were still exhausted from recent hostilities against the Turks and Poles (*see* Chapter 33, §1). French success in helping America achieve her independence proved hollow, however, since this failed to weaken Britain. Vergennes' last years were spent trying to preserve the peace and diplomatic stability of Europe, to which end France even signed commercial treaties with Britain and Russia. He died just before the convocation of the Assembly of Notables, summoned by King Louis XVI to deal with the monarchy's fiscal crisis, which had arisen in large part from the huge debts France incurred during the War for American Independence.

FURTHER READING

Murphy, Orville T.: *Charles Gravier, Comte de Vergennes: French Diplomacy in the Age of Revolution, 1719–1787* (Albany: State University of New York Press, 1982).

JONATHAN R. DULL

Green, Anne Catherine Hoof (*b. c.* 1720; *d.* ?Maryland, 23 March 1775). Printer. Little is known of her life before her marriage in 1738 to Jonas Green, a printer, who in 1745 began to publish the *Maryland Gazette* and was also appointed to the post of printer for the Province of Maryland. It was probably as a result of working with her husband that Green acquired the skills that enabled her to work as a printer and publisher after his death in the mid-1760s. Such was her reputation that she inherited her husband's position as the official printer for the Province of Maryland. An enthusiastic patriot, she ensured that the American cause received a frequent airing in the pages of the *Maryland Gazette*.

FURTHER READING

Wroth, Lawrence C.: *A History of Printing in Colonial Maryland, 1686–1776* (Baltimore: Typothetae, 1922).

BETTY WOOD

Greene, Nathanael (*b.* Warwick, RI, 27 July 1742; *d.* Savannah, Ga., 19 June 1786). General. In June 1775, at the age of 32,

Greene became the youngest general in the Continental Army. Appointed a major general in 1776, he commanded brigades in several important battles in 1776–7, served as Quartermaster General from 1778 to 1780, and commanded the Southern Department in 1780–3. He was the only one of Washington's generals to serve throughout the war.

Nothing in Greene's background suggested a military career. Born into a Quaker family, he was apprenticed at an early age as an anchorsmith and merchant in the family business. Without formal schooling, he was an omnivorous reader and became a fluent writer.

In May 1775 the Rhode Island Assembly appointed him commander of the Rhode Island Army of Observation at the siege of Boston. His appointment remains a mystery, for he was without experience in military and civil affairs (contrary to information provided by biographers, he was not a member of the Rhode Island Assembly). In the two months before he was commissioned a brigadier general in the Continental Army, he demonstrated a remarkable aptitude for military leadership. To Washington and fellow officers, Greene revealed a keen, retentive mind, a large measure of common sense, a capacity for organization, and a genius for comprehending and assimilating the geography and topography of the country – an aptitude that helped him as a principal advisor to Washington on strategy.

In battle he proved to be a courageous, cool-headed, and resourceful commander, winning the respect and loyalty of colleagues and subordinates. At the battle of Trenton in 1776 – a turning point in the war – he led a victorious column. He won more laurels, if not victories, at Brandywine and Germantown in 1777. In March 1778 he reluctantly accepted the difficult and thankless post of Quartermaster General, and in the next two years he improved the supply system despite the continuous depreciation of the currency. Although he found the post financially rewarding, widespread criticism of the department's expenditures made him long for the "glory" of the line. In defiance of Congress he left the post in July 1780.

In October, following two disastrous defeats of the Continental Army in the South, Washington named Greene Commander of the Southern Department. When he arrived in the South, the British controlled Georgia and South Carolina and were poised to overrun North Carolina. A year later they controlled only two seaports. Although Greene never won a clear-cut tactical victory – "We rise," he said, "get beat, rise, and fight again" – he struck repeatedly at the British Army, eroding its popular support, with an ill-equpped, half-starved force, often numbering fewer than 2,000 men. This remarkable turnaround was the product of Greene's strategic brilliance and his ability to win the hearts and minds of the people. His achievement assured him a place in the pantheon of revolutionary heroes.

FURTHER READING

Showman, Richard K. et al. (eds.): *The Papers of General Nathanael Greene*, 5 vols. (Chapel Hill: University of North Carolina Press, 1976–).
Thayer, Theodore: *Nathanael Greene: Strategist of the American Revolution* (New York: Twayne Publishers, 1960).

RICHARD K. SHOWMAN

Grenville, George (*b.* 14 October 1712; *d.* London, 13 November 1770). British statesman. He held various junior offices under George II, and served briefly as Secretary of State and as Head of the Admiralty (1762–3), but became notorious for his policy of colonial trade regulation and taxation while First Lord of the Treasury (April 1763–July 1765). Embodied in the Revenue Act of 1764 and the Stamp Act of 1765, reinforced by new stringent regulations to ensure that revenue officers effectively discharged their duties and were backed up by the courts, this policy was the fulfillment of intentions under discussion in government circles from 1762, if not earlier, intended to transfer to the colonists part of the expense of the increased defense

forces which it was generally agreed would have to be maintained in America and the West Indies in the aftermath of the Seven Years' War to provide protection in case of a Franco-Spanish war of revenge (*see* Chapter 11). Not this policy but mutual failure of confidence between George III and Grenville caused the latter's resignation in 1765. The main preoccupation of Grenville's last years, spent in political opposition, was the defense of his American policies and an insistence that Parliament's authority over the colonies should be maintained.

FURTHER READING

Lawson, Philip: *George Grenville: a Political Life* (Oxford: Clarendon Press, 1984).

IAN R. CHRISTIE

Hale, Nathan (*b.* Coventry, Conn., 6 June 1755; *d.* Long Island, NY, 22 September 1776). Soldier. A young officer in the Continental Army hanged as a spy, he served as an idealized martyr hero for the Revolution. Hale graduated from Yale in 1773. Until the outbreak of war in 1775 he worked as a schoolteacher in East Haddam and New London, Connecticut. Commissioned a lieutenant in a Connecticut regiment in 1775, he saw action at the siege of Boston. He was promoted to captain on 1 January 1776 and selected for service in Lieutenant-Colonel Thomas Knowlton's company of rangers. After Washington's defeat on Long Island (27 August 1776) Hale was sent back behind the enemy lines on Long Island to gather information, but while attempting to return to the American Army he was captured. The next day Hale was hanged as a spy without a court martial. On the scaffold he reportedly paraphrased a line from Addison's *Cato*, "I only regret that I have but one life to lose for my country." In one of the darkest moments of the Revolution, after the defeats and near destruction of Washington's army around New York, Hale's example provided a much needed moral victory for the American war effort.

FURTHER READING

Dexter, F. B.: *Yale Biographies and Annals, 1763–1778* (New York: Henry Holt, 1896).

KURT W. NAGEL

Halifax. *See* DUNK, GEORGE MONTAGU.

Hamilton, Alexander (*b.* Nevis, West Indies, 11 January 1757; *d.* Weehawken, NJ, 12 July 1804). Statesman and lawyer. Hamilton entered King's College in New York (now Columbia University) in 1773. He wrote patriotic pamphlets in 1774–5 and joined the army in 1776, becoming Washington's secretary and aide-de-camp in 1777. He quickly demonstrated his administrative ability and began to formulate bold proposals for reform. His anonymous "Continentalist" letters of 1781–2 advocated a more powerful national government and a far-reaching program of economic development (*see also* Chapter 46, §1).

After returning to civilian life, Hamilton established a law practice but continued to work for a stronger national government. He served in Congress in 1782–3 and col-

laborated eagerly with Robert Morris in efforts to secure independent federal revenues. At the New York bar, Hamilton argued that national treaties could override state laws. At the Annapolis Convention (1786), he drafted the broad terms of reference in the call for the Federal Convention at Philadelphia. A delegate from New York at the Philadelphia Convention, Hamilton consistently advocated a high-toned government (even praising monarchy) but was only intermittently active. His most important role in establishing the Constitution was in the ratification struggle. He planned *The Federalist* and wrote the major part of the work himself. At the New York ratifying convention in June 1788 he maneuvered skillfully to secure ratification despite an initially hostile majority.

In 1789 Washington appointed Hamilton Secretary of the Treasury. His Report on Public Credit (1790) successfully proposed that the revolutionary debt (including debts of the states) be converted into long-term interest-bearing bonds. He also made successful proposals for a national bank and an excise, and his Report on Manufactures (1792) proposed tariffs, which were adopted, although its other proposals were not. An admirer of Britain and dependent on revenues from British trade for the operation of his fiscal system, Hamilton advocated conciliatory measures in disputes with the mother country, a policy leading to the unpopular Jay Treaty of 1794. These policies provoked bitter opposition, to which Hamilton responded pugnaciously. When criticized for exceeding constitutional limits, he advanced a sweeping interpretation of the implied powers of the federal government. When the excise provoked the Whiskey Rebellion (1794), Hamilton accompanied the punitive force dispatched to western Pennsylvania. More fundamental was the quarrel with Madison and Thomas Jefferson which spread into the press and then into federal and state elections; in these contests Hamilton acted as a leading partisan on the Federalist side.

In 1795 Hamilton retired to his lucrative

FIGURE 64 A portrait of Alexander Hamilton by John Trumbull (1806)

law practice in New York but continued to dabble in public affairs. When war with France threatened in 1798, he secured a commission as second in command of the army. In both 1796 and 1800 he plotted against the election of John Adams, the Federalist candidate, and sought to influence members of Adams's cabinet behind the President's back. In the election of 1800, however, Hamilton finally campaigned effectively for the Federalists in New York and threw his influence against the scheme to secure the election of Aaron Burr in the electoral college. The continuing animosity led Burr to challenge Hamilton to a fatal duel in July 1804 which left the latter mortally wounded.

Few men have accomplished so much in a short life; few have been so persistently misunderstood. The administrative and fiscal system which Hamilton instituted was vital to the success of government under the new Constitution and to the prosperity of the 1790s, although a manufacturing economy and broadly empowered federal government did not develop as he envisaged. In his ideas, Hamilton should not be dismissed simply as a reactionary elitist. Certainly he can justly be criticized: he was impatient of the niceties of democratic politics and constitutionalism, and he often exhibited the strident assertiveness of the *arriviste*. He had, however, a broad and progressive vision of national development. If an elite was important, it was not an elite of existing, entrenched interests; he hoped to create a new dynamic leadership committed to new forms of economic development and to building strong political institutions. The people, he thought, could not initiate such developments, but their cooperation was essential, and they always had the right to judge their leaders. It was government itself which played the greatest role in Hamilton's thinking; effective government was the key to building a great nation, not only in public policy but by fostering private economic development and shaping national character. Hamilton's vision resembled that of many twentieth-century leaders of newly independent post-colonial countries, and if American national development took a different course from the way he envisioned, he nonetheless did much to establish the framework within which successful development could take place.

FURTHER READING

Cooke, J.E.: *Alexander Hamilton* (New York: Scribner's, 1982).
McDonald, F.: *Alexander Hamilton: a Biography* (New York: Norton, 1979).
Mitchell, B.: *Alexander Hamilton*, 2 vols. (New York: Macmillan, 1957–62).
Stourzh, G.: *Alexander Hamilton and the Idea of Republican Government* (Stanford, Calif.: Stanford University Press, 1970).

MARK D. KAPLANOFF

Hamilton, Henry (b. Ireland, 1734; d. Dominica, 1796). British soldier and career official. After 20 years in the British Army in North America (1755–75) Hamilton sold his captain's half-pay commission and accepted the lieutenant-governorship of Detroit. Because his responsibilities included not only civil and some military authority, but also diplomatic and trade relations with the Indians, such as providing native auxiliaries with supplies in war time, his American adversaries labeled him the "Hair Buyer General." Although records indicate he ransomed hundreds of captives, he also issued rations to raiders who surrendered scalps. Consequently, when his defense of the British West against invading Virginians under George Rogers Clark failed in 1779, Hamilton was forced to surrender at Vincennes. Clark locked Hamilton in irons and triumphantly marched his manacled prisoner cross-country to Williamsburg. Governor Thomas Jefferson ordered Hamilton held in the mephitic town jail and "excluded all converse"; Jefferson's grounds were "National Retaliation" for all those reportedly butchered by Hamilton's savage allies. Only after months of protest from British and American officials (including Washington) was Hamilton freed. Four years as lieutenant-governor of faction-ridden Quebec were followed by a term as governor of Bermuda, where the new capital was named for him. His last appointment was as governor of Dominica.

FURTHER READING

Barnhart, John D.: *Henry Hamilton and George Rogers Clark in the American Revolution with the Unpublished Journal of Lieut. Gov. Henry Hamilton* (Crawfordsville, Ind.: R. E. Banta, 1951).

Jaebker, Orville J.: "Henry Hamilton: British Soldier and Colonial Governor" (Ph.D. dissertation, Indiana University, 1954).

O'Donnell, James H. III: " 'National Retaliation': Thomas Jefferson's Brief for the Imprisonment of Henry Hamilton," *Selected Papers from the 1985 and 1986 George Rogers Clark Trans-Appalachian Frontier History Conferences*, ed. Robert J. Holden (Vincennes, Ind.: Eastern National Park & Monument Association and Vincennes University, 1988).

Sheehan, Bernard: " 'The Famous Hair Buyer General': Henry Hamilton, George Rogers Clark, and the American Indian," *Indiana Magazine of History*, 79 (1983), 1–28.

JAMES H. O'DONNELL III

Hancock, John (*b.* Braintree, Mass., 23 January 1737; *d.* Quincy, Mass., 8 October 1793). President of the Continental Congress and Governor of Massachusetts. He was a leader of both the revolutionary movement and the struggle for ratification of the Constitution of 1787. Born the son of a poor minister, Hancock was adopted by an uncle, one of the wealthiest merchants in Boston. After graduating from Harvard in 1754 he took over his uncle's business at the age of 27. As British regulatory policy caused increasing friction with colonial merchants in the 1760s he turned to politics. The personal animosity between Hancock and British customs officials only increased his prestige. He was first elected to the General Court in 1769, and was the president of the Provincial Congress from 1774 to 1775. Hancock was a delegate to the second Continental Congress, and served as its president between 1775 and 1777. As president he was the first member to sign the Declaration of Independence,

FIGURE 65 John Hancock: painting by John Singleton Copley (1765)

which he did with such a flourish that his name has become synonymous with the flamboyant signature. Hancock attended the Massachusetts constitutional convention, and was elected the state's first governor. He served in this office from 1780 to 1785 and again from 1789 until 1793. As president of the state's ratifying convention Hancock was instrumental in gaining Massachusetts's acceptance of the Constitution in 1788.

FURTHER READING

Allan, H. S.: *John Hancock: Patriot in Purple* (New York: Macmillan, 1948).

KURT W. NAGEL

Henry, Patrick (*b.* Hanover Co., Va., 29 May 1736; *d.* Virginia, 6 June 1799). Lawyer and statesman. His father, John Henry, had emigrated from Aberdeen, Scotland, six years before Patrick's birth and, through hard work, timely land speculation, and an advantageous marriage, had become a moderately wealthy land-owner, colonel in the county militia, justice of the Hanover County Court and vestryman of his local Anglican parish.

Patrick Henry's formal education was negligible, but after failing in several attempts both at farming and at operating a general store he entered upon an informal course of study in the law. After an extraordinarily brief period of unsupervised legal study (estimates range from six weeks to three or four months), he was examined and admitted to the bar in Williamsburg in 1760. Although like most Virginia lawyers he was deficient in his technical knowledge of the law, he possessed superb skills of argumentation. Unlike many of his revolutionary counterparts in the state, who used their legal training only as an ornament to their other economic and political activities, Henry was an active attorney; he managed 1,185 cases in his first three years of practice, and continued to make a respectable income as a lawyer throughout his lifetime.

Henry's legal and political career began precisely at that moment when relations between the American colonies and the British Imperial Government in London were beginning to deteriorate. His first important legal case, the Parson's Cause Controversy, involved the defense of the rights of Virginia taxpayers against the claims of the Anglican clergy, and his entrance into the Virginia House of Burgesses in May 1765 coincided with the passage of the Stamp Act by the British Parliament. From the time of his celebrated denunciation of the Stamp Act until the Declaration of Independence in 1776, Henry led the militant opposition to British policy in Virginia. His legendary "give me liberty or give me death" speech in March 1775, though its authenticity has been difficult to corroborate, has, along with Lincoln's Gettysburg Address, become the most oft-recited piece of oratory in American history. Whatever the precise wording of that speech, all of his contemporaries agreed that Henry was a riveting orator (for illustration, see figure 20). His style marked an important break with the classical tradition. Most previous political oratory in America had placed a premium on formal learning and on allusion to classical texts; Henry's style, by contrast, was that of the evangelical preacher, relying on biblical texts and allusions, appealing, so his critics claimed, to passion rather than reason. In this sense, though he never articulated an explicitly democratic political philosophy, Henry was one of America's first popular politicians.

Henry was, at every point in his public career, a "Virginia" patriot, with loyalties to his colony and then his independent state, and not to the abstraction of an "American" nation. Although he served in the First Continental Congress in 1774, all of his public service from that time forward was on behalf of the state of Virginia; he was elected the independent state's first governor, serving five terms in all in that post. He also fulfilled several terms in the Virginia state legislature, declining offers to serve in the Continental Congress, the United States Senate, as Chief Justice of the United States Supreme Court, and Secretary of State during the Federalist administrations of Washington and Adams.

Henry's most conspicuous post-revolutionary service was as an opponent of the proposed United States Constitution in 1787-8. He declined election as a delegate from Virginia to the Philadelphia Convention in 1787, but later came to regret the way in which the delegates in Philadelphia had exceeded their instructions and devised what he believed to be a "consolidated government" in which "our rights and liberties are endangered and the sovereignty of the States will be relinquished" (Henry, 1891, Vol. III, pp. 400-1). Henry's extended critique of the proposed Constitution in the Virginia Ratifying Convention of 1788 is one of the clearest and most thoroughgoing articulations of an eighteenth-century states' rights position in existence.

In the latter part of the 1790s, partly out of a personal animus against Jefferson and partly because of his fears about disorder in society at large, Henry began to side with the Federalist party and to criticize the opposition of Jefferson, Madison, and the emerging Republican party towards Federalist policy. The Federalists persuaded him to come out of retirement to serve in the Virginia Legislature in 1799, but he died before he could take his seat.

FURTHER READING

Beeman, Richard R.: *Patrick Henry: a Biography* (New York: McGraw-Hill, 1975).
Henry, William Wirt: *Patrick Henry; Life, Correspondence, Speeches*, 3 vols. (1891).
Mayer, Charles: *Son of Thunder: Patrick Henry and the American Revolution* (New York: Watts, 1986).
Meade, Robert D.: *Patrick Henry*, 2 vols. (Philadelphia: Lippincott, 1957–69).

RICHARD R. BEEMAN

Higginson, Mehetabel Robie (*b.* Salem, Mass., 1727; *d.* 1818). She was the wife of the country lawyer John Higginson, who left her a widow about 1758. An independent, intelligent and opinionated woman, she early took a political stand in favor of loyalty to the King. With unusual foresight, she resolved to leave her homeland before the revolutionary conflict could worsen, and sailed for Halifax, Nova Scotia, in May 1775. There she waited out the war in unhappy exile until she was able to return to Massachusetts in May 1783. Her timely departure and the influence of patriot friends such as Timothy Pickering enabled her to regain possession of the property she had rented and put into storage. Nevertheless, she had to endure some initial resistance to her return, principally from a local "Reverend Doctor" who was in the habit of denouncing her from the pulpit on Sunday evenings. Her return to Salem was finally accepted, however, and for many years she and her daughter ran a very successful boarding school for young ladies.

FURTHER READING

"Letters of Jonathan Sewell," *Proceedings of the Massachusetts Historical Society*, 10 (1895–6), 418–20.
Robie-Sewell Papers, Pickering Papers, Massachusetts Historical Society.
Sewell Papers, National Archives of Canada.

KATHERINE M. J. MCKENNA

Hill, Wills [1st Earl of Hillsborough] (*b.* Fairford, Glos., 30 May 1718; *d.* Hillsborough, Co. Down, Ireland, 7 October 1793). British statesman. Baron Harwich in the British peerage and created Earl of Hillsborough (Ireland) in 1751, he held minor office under George II. He became concerned with colonial affairs as Head of the Board of Trade (1763–5, August–December 1766; also ex-officio, 1768–72), and as Secretary of State for the Colonies (1768–72). His general policy was shaped by the narrow view that fisheries, production of naval stores, and the supply of timber and provisions to the West Indies were the principal advantages of the North American colonies. Fostering these meant developing coastal areas: inland colonies would be of no benefit and also very difficult to control. Consequently he opposed the project for a new colony of Vandalia in the Ohio valley. Committed to the maintenance of parliamentary supremacy over the colonies, he reacted strongly to Massachusetts's defiance of the Townshend Acts, and his dispatch of troops to Boston to maintain order set the scene for the Boston Massacre. In 1769–70 Hillsborough advocated modification of the Massachusetts charter. Resigning in 1772 over the Vandalia question, he was created an earl in the British peerage. He opposed American Independence and served as Secretary of State (Southern Department) (1779–82). He was created Marquis of Downshire (Ireland) in 1789.

IAN R. CHRISTIE

Hopkins, Esek (*b.* nr Providence, RI, 26 April 1718; *d.* Scituate, RI, 26 February 1802). Commander of the US Fleet. In 1738 he began a long career at sea and eventually became a seasoned merchant captain and privateer. When the Revolutionary War began Congress organized an American Navy. The Navy Committee, which included Esek's older brother Stephen, assigned commissions more according to political and familial considerations than to skill and experience. The delegates named Hopkins commander of the Continental fleet and his eldest son, John Burroughs Hopkins, one of its captains.

Congress gave Commodore Hopkins the difficult, if not unrealistic, task of clearing the American coast of British raiders. Instead, he successfully plundered British supply bases in the Bahamas, but, in doing so, he alienated southerners in need of naval assistance. On 16 August 1776 Congress officially censured Hopkins for disobeying orders. On his return from the Bahamas, four of Hopkins's ships were outgunned by a lone enemy vessel and, by the end of 1776, the British fleet had bottled up his flotilla in Narragansett Bay. With even his own officers against him, in March 1777 Congress suspended Hopkins for incompetence. The following January his removal became permanent.

Most historians agree that Hopkins was neither solely responsible for the navy's problems nor capable of overcoming them.

FURTHER READING

Field, Edward: *Esek Hopkins* (Providence, 1898).

J. MARK THOMPSON

Hopkins, Stephen (*b.* Scituate, RI, 7 March 1707; *d.* Providence, RI, 13 July 1785). Statesman and jurist. He was a leader of the colonial resistance to British policy in Rhode Island. Hopkins was first elected to the Rhode Island assembly at the age of 25 and served regularly for the next 45 years. In 1739 he became chief justice of the court of common pleas, and in 1751 was elected to the Rhode Island superior court. He was a delegate to the Albany Congress of 1754, and there supported Benjamin Franklin's plan for colonial union. For most of the period between 1755 and 1768 Hopkins served as Governor of Rhode Island. As the conflict with the British Parliament deepened during the 1760s Hopkins played an active part, founding a newspaper in 1762 and writing a pamphlet, *The Rights of the Colonies Examined*, in 1765. Serving on the superior court in 1772 he prevented the arrest of the colonists who had

burned the British revenue cutter *Gaspée*. Hopkins was a member of the Continental Congress from 1774 until 1776, and signed the Declaration of Independence. His failing health kept him out of public life after 1776.

FURTHER READING

Foster, William E.: "Stephen Hopkins," *Rhode Island Historical Tracts*, 19 (Providence, 1884).

KURT W. NAGEL

Howe, Richard [4th Viscount Howe] (*b.* London, 19 March 1726; *d.* London, 5 August 1799). Commander-in-Chief of the British Navy in North America and peace commissioner. Howe assumed command in July 1776, determined to promote a negotiated settlement of the American rebellion. He may well have persuaded his brother WILLIAM HOWE, who commanded the British Army, to forego chances for a decisive battle at New York. He clearly did delay imposing a naval blockade, made repeated overtures to Congress, and urged the captains of his ships to "cultivate all amicable correspondence" with the colonists. These measures not only failed to produce a negotiated peace but helped the rebellion to survive and gain strength. While Howe resorted increasingly to force in 1777, the British Government reproved him for being too lenient. He decided to resign. Before he could do so, France entered the war, and he was forced to remain in America through the summer of 1778 to parry a French fleet under Admiral d'Estaing. Howe did not serve again until 1782–3 when, as Commander-in-Chief of the Channel fleet, he relieved and saved Gibraltar for Britain.

FURTHER READING

Gruber, Ira D.: *The Howe Brothers and the American Revolution* (New York: Atheneum, 1972).

IRA D. GRUBER

FIGURE 66 A portrait of General Sir William Howe (unknown artist, 1780)

Howe, Sir **William** [5th Viscount Howe] (*b.* 10 August 1729; *d.* Plymouth, 12 July 1814). Commander-in-Chief of the British Army in North America. Although he was commander of the British Army from 1775 to 1778, at a time when the rebels were inexperienced and without the support of French fleets and armies, Howe never found a way to end the rebellion. He went to New York in June 1776 to precipitate a decisive battle with the Continental Army. But after seeing rebel defenses and talking with his brother, RICHARD HOWE, he adopted a strategy that promised fewer casualties and a better chance of a negotiated settlement. Thus he maneuvered the rebels out of Long Island, Manhattan, and much of New Jersey. This prudent strategy foundered when his detachments were surprised at Trenton and Princeton. In the campaign of 1777 he oscillated between destroying the Continental Army and recovering territory. He sought a climactic battle in New Jersey; embarked for a gradual reconquest of Pennslyvania; and, while securing Philadelphia, tried again for decisive engagements at Brandywine and White-

marsh. Having failed to end the rebellion and coming under criticism for his leniency towards rebels and neglect of John Burgoyne, Howe resigned his command.

For further illustration, *see* figure 48, p. 585.

FURTHER READING

Gruber, Ira D.: *The Howe Brothers and the American Revolution* (New York: Atheneum, 1972).

IRA D. GRUBER

Hume, David (*b.* Edinburgh, 26 April 1711; *d.* Edinburgh, 25 August 1776). Philosopher. He contributed to the development of the British colonies as a historian and as a political philosopher. *The History of England* (3 vols., 1754–62) debunked some myths about the ancient liberties of Englishmen but nevertheless found a wide readership in America. Hume wrote from the assumption that self-interest, rather than reason or virtue or even vice, was the principal motivating force behind human actions. The cumulative effect of innumerable self-interested decisions accomplished more towards the perfection of government or the improvement of society than any one historical actor could. For Hume, the liberty necessary for the continued progress of British society was threatened not so much by a potentially tyrannical government as by ideologues who rejected anything they called "innovation." Hume hoped that, through the study of history, an understanding of human nature might be achieved that would make possible a "science" of politics, which would bring government into perfect conformity with people's natural inclinations. James Madison was especially influenced by Hume in his defense of the new federal system represented by the Constitution of the United States.

FURTHER READING

Colbourn, H. T.: *The Lamp of Experience: Whig History and the Intellectual Origins of the American Revolution* (Chapel Hill: University of North Carolina Press, 1965).

Forbes, D.: *Hume's Philosophical Politics* (Cambridge and New York: Cambridge University Press, 1975).

THOMAS COLE

Hutchinson, Thomas (*b.* Boston, 9 September 1711; *d.* Croydon, Surrey, 3 June 1780). Lawyer and Governor of Massachusetts. He brought a well-trained, cautious mind to the problems of Massachusetts as an elected representative (1737–49) and royal official, and also as the colony's historian. He believed that in the constitutional relationship between the mother country and the colonies each party should be free to pursue its own interests, though in a test of supremacy England and specifically Parliament should be able to decide for the whole, or the colonies' subordination within the empire would become meaningless. Hutchinson paid dearly for this scruple in August 1765, when Boston mobs burned his house as they vented their fury at the Stamp Act on the wealthy merchant and multiple office-holder (at the time he was a member of the Council and Lieutenant Governor). As the last royal governor of Massachusetts (1771–4; *see* figure 1b, p. 13), Hutchinson again served as a lightning rod for discontents with England. Opponents portrayed him as a traitor to his native country for having joined in an alleged general scheme to enslave the American colonists. He withdrew his family to England after the implementation of the Coercive Acts, there to complete his *History of the Colony of Massachusetts-Bay*.

FURTHER READING

Bailyn, B.: *The Ordeal of Thomas Hutchinson* (Cambridge: Belknap Press of the Harvard University Press, 1974).
Pencak, W.: *America's Burke: the Mind of Thomas Hutchinson* (Washington, DC: University Press of America, 1982).

THOMAS COLE

Iredell, James (*b.* Lewes, Sussex, 5 October 1751; *d.* 20 October 1799). Lawyer, Attorney General of North Carolina, and Justice of the Supreme Court. Iredell's greatest contribution to the revolutionary period came through his constitutional thought, especially in the relationship of legislative power to the Constitution. In *An Address to the Public* (1786), with reference to North Carolina's Constitution of 1776, Iredell wrote, "I have no doubt but that the power of the Assembly is limited and defined by the Constitution. It is the creature of the Constitution." In the North Carolina case *Bayard v. Singleton* (1786–7), which was argued before the Federal Constitution, Iredell formulated the first justification for judicial review, antedating Hamilton's defense in *The Federalist*, no. 78, and long before John Marshall's reasoning in *Marbury v. Madison*.

Iredell's publication *Answers to Mr. Mason's Objections to the New Constitution Recommended by the Late Convention at Philadelphia* (1788) brought him the attention of leading Federalists. On 10 February 1790 President Washington appointed him, at the age of 39, the sixth Justice of the Supreme Court, and its youngest member. His dissenting opinion in *Chisholm v. Georgia* asserts the divided sovereignty concept denied by the Court's nationalist majority, but held by most Americans at the time, as a resolution designed to counteract the *Chisholm* decision introduced the following day in the House of Representatives shows. The resolution became the forerunner of the Eleventh Amendment.

Iredell wrote on political topics from 1773, developing a pro-American constitutional argument in *To the Inhabitants of Great Britain* (1774). He opposed independence, but, after the break, assisted in redrafting the laws appropriate to North Carolina's new status. He was chosen as one of the state's three judges in November 1777, and served as its attorney general from 1779 to 1781.

FURTHER READING

Higginbotham, Don (ed.): *The Papers of James Iredell, 1776–1783*, 2 vols. (Raleigh: North Carolina Archives, 1976–).

Israel, Fred L.: "James Iredell," *The Justices of the United States Supreme Court, 1789–1969: Their Lives and Major Opinions*, ed. Leon Friedman and Fred L. Israel (New York: R. R. Bowker, 1969), Vol. I, 121–33.

Stourzh, Gerald: "The American Revolution, modern constitutionalism, and the protection of human rights," *Truth and Tragedy: a Tribute to Hans J. Morganthau*, ed. Kenneth Thompson et al. (Washington, DC: New Republick Book Company, 1977), 170–2.

——: *Fundamental Laws and Individual Rights in the 18th Century Constitution*, Bicentennial Essay Number 5 (Claremont, Calif.: Claremont Institute for the Study of Statesmanship and Political Philosophy, 1984), 22–3.

REBECCA STARR

Jay, John (*b.* New York, 12 December 1745; *d.* Bedford, NY, 14 May 1829). Jurist, diplomat, and President of the Continental Congress. Jay was educated at King's (Columbia) College (AB, 1764; MA, 1767), and was admitted to the New York bar (1768) after a four-year clerkship in the law office of Benjamin Kissam. In addition to law practice, he served as clerk of the New York–New Jersey Boundary Commission (1769–70).

Drawn into the politics of revolutionary New York, Jay stood for caution and compromise in dealings with Britain; in both the Continental Congresses and subsequently in the New York Provincial Congress, he worked against the movement for independence until after the Declaration of Independence was issued. Accepting the inevitable he became active in the committee work of the Provincial Congress, especially the Committee for the Detecting of Conspiracies and the committee appointed to report a proposed constitution for New York State. A member of the Constitutional Convention, Jay helped draft the final version of the 1777 Constitution and then was elected the first Chief Justice of the Supreme Court of New York State (3 May 1777).

He served as President of Continental Congress during a difficult time of diplomatic crisis, land disputes between the states, and military uncertainty (10 December 1778–29 September 1779). In the wake of a power struggle over diplomatic assignments, he succeeded Arthur Lee as Minister to Spain, serving until 21 May 1782, when he and his family left to join the American Peace Commission already assembled at Paris. Jay's efforts at Madrid were frustrated by his insistence that Spain recognize American independence and Spanish demands that the United States renounce claim to free navigation of the Mississippi River.

After a difficult overland trip Jay took up his duties as Peace Commissioner (23 June 1782; for illustration, *see* FRANKLIN, BENJAMIN), joining Benjamin Franklin and John Adams who were already negotiating with the British Commissioner, Richard Oswald. Jay took exception to Oswald's commission, construing it to be a tacit denial of American independence. While negotiations stalled, secret contacts between Britain, France, and Spain increased Jay's suspicion of the motives of his country's allies. Once the British Cabinet agreed to recognize independence in the text of a treaty, the American commissioners commenced bilateral negotiations which led to a preliminary treaty (30 November 1782). Among other things, the treaty ceded to the United States the vast territory west of the Appalachian mountains and east of the Mississippi.

Returning home after the exchange of definitive treaty ratifications, Jay was appointed Secretary for Foreign Affairs on 21 December 1784. He served in that capacity until the inception of the new government under the Federal Constitution, and was then appointed the first Chief Justice of the United States (26 September 1789). Serving as minister to Britain while retaining his commission as Chief Justice, Jay negotiated the controversial 1794 treaty that bears his name, and returned to the United States in 1795. He then resigned his post as Chief Justice (29 June 1795) and became Governor of New York. Elected to a second term in 1798, he retired in 1801 to his country estate at Bedford.

FURTHER READING

Monaghan, Frank: *John Jay: Defender of Liberty* (New York: Bobbs-Merrill, 1935).

Morris, Richard B.: *The Peacemakers* (New York: Harper & Row, 1965).

———: *John Jay: the Making of a Revolutionary: Unpublished Papers, 1745–1780* (New York: Harper & Row, 1975).

———: *John Jay: the Winning of the Peace: Unpublished Papers, 1780–1784* (New York: Harper & Row, 1980).

HERBERT A. JOHNSON

Jefferson, Thomas (*b.* Shadwell, Va., 13 April 1743; *d.* Monticello, Va., 4 July 1826). Statesman, third President of the United States. In 1776, at the age of 33, Jefferson served on the committee which drafted a declaration of independence for the representatives of the American colonies gathered in the Second Continental Congress. Fifty years later on the day of its adoption, 4 July, he died at his beloved Monticello. In between those dates, Jefferson served his country as minister to France (1785–9), Secretary of State (1789–93), Vice President (1797–1801), and President 1801–9); and his native state of Virginia as Governor (1779–81), delegate to the Continental Congress (1783–4), and founder of the University of Virginia.

In many ways the model of a democratic statesman, Jefferson has achieved his unique place in American culture because he exemplifies the revolutionary ideals which bind the nation together, ideals expressed in Jefferson's phrase that "all men are created equal and endowed by their creator with certain unalienable rights." That he was himself a slave-owner underscored the ambivalence his generation brought to the ideal of equality, but in no way diminished its power to endow the new United States with high moral purpose.

The journalist William Duane called Jefferson "the best rubber-off of dust he had ever met." This iconoclastic streak informed Jefferson's public life at every turn. The earth, he said, belonged to the living and to the living also belonged the task of living inquisitive and productive lives. To promote this

FIGURE 67 Thomas Jefferson: portrait by Cornelius Tiebout (1801)

end, Jefferson reworked the laws of Virginia after Independence. He was responsible for putting the seminal ideas that went into the Northwest Ordinance on the public agenda. In his voluminous correspondence he detailed the links between Enlightenment reform goals and the American experiment.

Although the conflict between the North and the South led historians to depict Jefferson as an advocate of states rights, he was a much more ambitious and successful national leader than state politician. His record as a wartime governor of Virginia was marred by an investigation of his official conduct and his comprehensive educational plans were never adopted. He did, however, secure the Bill for Establishing Religious Freedom in Virginia in 1786. In this he worked closely with James Madison, whose friendship and collaboration played a major role in Jefferson's life.

In Jefferson's day Virginia was the center of the nationalist sentiments that transformed the loose coalition of states in 1776 into the expansive, continental nation of the nineteenth century. From Virginia came the initiative to replace the Articles of Confederation with a stronger national government; four of the first five presidents under the new United States Constitution were Virginians. When Jefferson became alarmed at the elitist policies of the Treasury Secretary Alexander Hamilton, he organized the first national political movement. Popular in spirit and composition, the Jeffersonian opposition laid the foundation for all subsequent political parties. Jefferson's electoral victory in 1800 gave a functional meaning to the political philosophy enunciated in the Declaration of Independence.

Although his most stunning acts were the Louisiana Purchase and the Embargo, the long-term effects of his presidency came from his strict construction of the Constitution, his repayment of the revolutionary debt and his contraction of the size and activity of the federal bureaucracy. As President, Jefferson demonstrated that his nationalism was undergirded by a profound commitment to limited government.

Jefferson was not a man of contradictions so much as a person with rarely paired virtues. A true visionary, he possessed the skills of a first-class administrator. He was deeply influenced by the civilized traditions of Europe's enlightened elite, and he expended his political efforts on ordinary men. A talented amateur in botany, paleontology, music, linguistics, and architecture, Jefferson was a consummate professional in law, legislation, and party politics. While he was wide-ranging in both practical and philosophical interests, he also had the tenacity to follow a project through decades to completion. Despite these virtues and his truly remarkable capacity to imagine a social order that had never existed, Jefferson remained deeply committed to the superiority of the white race,

the male sex, and the civilized heritage of Europe. Ordinary white men were the beneficiaries of his liberating reforms; Blacks, women and Indians did not engage the play of his imagination.

Jefferson shares with George Washington and Abraham Lincoln the honor of a memorial in the national capital. His optimism, practical intelligence, and stirring endorsements of freedom have sustained the American commitment to natural rights, even as his own life demonstrated the difficulties inherent in this creed. Jefferson himself remained a divided man on the critical issue of slavery. After he left the White House, he turned his attention to education, working against the infirmities of age to secure a liberal foundation for his University of Virginia. Genuinely fearful for the future of the United States, he never lost hope in the value of human effort or the life of the mind. In contemporary America, Jefferson serves as the exemplar for both of the dominant political traditions, the one that emphasizes limited government as well as the one that teaches that the privileged few must yield to the needs of the ordinary many.

FURTHER READING

Cunningham, Noble, Jr.: *In Pursuit of Reason: the Life of Thomas Jefferson* (Baton Rouge: Louisiana University Press, 1987).

Miller, Charles A.: *Jefferson and Nature* (Baltimore: Johns Hopkins University Press, 1988).

Peterson, M.: *Thomas Jefferson and the New Nation* (New York: Oxford University Press, 1970).

JOYCE APPLEBY

Johnson, Joseph (*b.* 1751; *d. c.* 1776) Christian Mohegan Indian. Johnson had plans to found an autonomous Indian agricultural community in New York as a refuge for Christian Indians of southern New England. To this purpose, he accepted commissions from American authorities to counsel neutrality to the Iroquois lest they and their New England brethren be distracted from pursuit of their separate interests.

In the 1770s Johnson returned to the Mohegan community in Connecticut to become one of its foremost preachers during this painful period of adaptation to an expanding colonial population. In 1774 he negotiated with the Oneidas for land on which to establish a new town for the Mohegans and the remnants of other New England tribes. Johnson believed that Indians must convert to Christianity and practice intensive agriculture in order to hold on to their lands. "Brothertown" was to be model for the western tribes. "Now," he told the Oneidas, "we begin to look around ... and we perceive that we are strip[p]ed indeed, having nothing to help ourselves, and thus our English Brethren leaves us and laugh" (McCallum, 1932, p. 161). To further his goal, Johnson accepted commissions from the New York authorities and from the New Hampshire House to help keep the Iroquois neutral. Ironically New Hampshire instructed him to tell the Indians that the English intended "to strip the Inhabitants of the Colonies of their native Rights & privileges," and seize "the produce of our Lands" (McCallum, 1932, p. 195). George Washington also wrote to Johnson urging him to this mission.

Johnson died as this work began, and thus he was not forced to witness the dismemberment of the Iroquois Confederacy, or the terrible toll which Mohegan enlistment in American armies took on the Connecticut tribe. But his goal of founding an Indian farming community was realized by his followers after the Revolution.

FURTHER READING

McCallum, James D. (ed.): *The Letters of Eleazer Wheelock's Indians* (Hanover, NH: Dartmouth College, 1932).

DAVID W. CONROY

Johnson, Sir **William** (*b*. Co. Meath, Ireland, 1715; *d*. Johnson Hall, NY, 12 July 1774). British Indian Superintendent for the Northern Department and "Colonel of the Six Nations." Merchant, land speculator, colonial politician, soldier, diplomat, and imperial official, he dominated the Mohawk Valley and influenced colonial Indian affairs for more than three decades. After emigrating from Ireland in 1738, the ambitious Johnson soon managed his uncle Peter Warren's New York estates and his own Indian trade and frontier land investments. From the baronial Johnson Hall, Johnson carved such a niche on the frontier that the Iroquois named him Warraghiyagey, "he who does big business". During the Seven Years' War circumstances elevated him to command victorious forces at both Crown Point and Niagara. Rewarded with £5,000 and a baronetcy, the new Sir William Johnson was commissioned "Colonel of the Six Nations"; eventually he was named British Indian Superintendent for the Northern Department. In those offices he addressed colonial assemblies, imperial offices, and Indian councils from 1756 to 1774, always seeking the dominance of the Iroquois Confederacy (and to no lesser degree his own) over frontier issues from the Ohio country to New England. Although his ambition exceeded his actual achievements, his role as premier negotiator for Iroquois affairs and interpreter of royal Indian policy was unequaled. It was fitting that he died in the midst of an Indian conference at his home.

FURTHER READING

Flexner, James T.: *Mohawk Baronet, Sir William Johnson of New York* (New York: Harper & Brothers, 1959).
Hamilton, Milton W.: *Sir William Johnson: Colonial American, 1715–63* (Port Washington, NY: Kennikat Press, 1976).

JAMES H. O'DONNELL III

Jones, John Paul [Paul, John] (*b*. Kirkcudbrightshire, Scotland, 6 July 1747; *d*. Paris, 18 July 1792). Naval commander. With his long seafaring career beginning at the age of 12, John Paul rose from apprentice to merchant captain by early adulthood. Twice he was accused of murdering his own men, a neglectful ship's carpenter and a mutinous crewman. He was cleared of the first charge but chose not to risk trial for the second one. Instead he fled to America, assuming the surname Jones to conceal his identity.

Once the Revolutionary War began, Congress commissioned Jones a first lieutenant aboard the *Alfred*. Then, as captain and commander of the *Providence*, he quickly distinguished himself by capturing 16 prizes in a single cruise. Jones's greatest achievements came in European waters. In April 1778, aboard the *Ranger*, he ventured bodly into the Irish Sea, carrying out Congress's order to interdict shipping and raid enemy ports. The following year, in September, he engaged in a spectacular naval duel with Captain Richard Pearson's HMS *Serapis*. Jones's ship, the *Bonhomme Richard*, sank, but not before Pearson had surrendered the *Serapis*.

Although he was vain, ambitious, and contentious, Jones's courage and exploits earned him deserved praise. In the postwar years he served in the Russian Navy before retiring permanently in France. In 1905, after an extensive search, his remains were discovered and returned to the United States.

For illustration, *see* figure 43, p. 520.

FURTHER READING

Morison, Samuel Eliot: *John Paul Jones: a Sailor's Biography* (Boston: Little, Brown and Co., 1959).

J. MARK THOMPSON

Kalb, Johann [Baron de] (*b.* Hüttendorf, Bavaria, 29 June 1721; *d.* Camden, SC, 19 August 1780). General. Kalb began his military career at the age of 16 in a French infantry regiment. He acquired wealth by marriage and noble status simply by his own declaration; evidently, he found it easier to rise through the French ranks if he held a title. He was one of many foreign officers to provide devoted service and a degree of military professionalism to the Continental Army.

In late 1776 Brigadier General de Kalb received French permission to volunteer his services to the American cause. After considerable haggling Congress commissioned him a major general in the Continental Army on 15 September 1777. The following year de Kalb was chosen second in command of the proposed, but aborted, invasion of Canada. Again he received an important assignment, the relief of Charles Town, but the city fell to the British before the arrival of his reinforcements. He subsequently joined Horatio Gates in the Southern Department. At the Battle of Camden, of 16 August 1780, the enemy routed Gates's army. De Kalb's Continentals fought valiantly but were eventually driven back. During the fray de Kalb received numerous wounds, from which he died days later.

FURTHER READING

Zucker, Adolf E.: *General de Kalb: Lafayette's Mentor* (Chapel Hill: University of North Carolina Press, 1966).

J. MARK THOMPSON

King, Rufus (*b.* Scarboro, Mass. [now Maine], 24 March 1755; *d.* New York, 29 April 1827). Lawyer and politician. The oldest son of a successful merchant, King graduated from Harvard in 1777 and studied law with Theophilus Parsons before opening a law practice in Newburyport, Massachusetts. He began his political career as Newburyport's delegate to the Massachusetts General Court in 1783–5. As a member of the Continental Congress (1784–6), King witnessed daily the inadequacies and embarrassments of government under the Articles of Confederation, and he ardently supported the movement for a more powerful central government. At the Constitutional Convention he admonished the other delegates not to be restrained by the "phantom of state sovereignty." Yet King would not capitulate to the demands of the small states or the South for the sake of union. He demanded proportional representation in Congress, which was to the benefit of Massachusetts, and he led the resistance to the Committee of Detail's concessions to the

South. On 8 August 1787 he told the Convention that the Committee's report was full of "inequality and unreasonableness." He "never could agree" to allow slaves to "be imported without limitation & then be represented in the National Legislature." King campaigned vigorously for ratification at the Massachusetts convention. Soon afterwards he married into a New York family, and he served for a number of years as a Senator from his new state (1789–96, 1813–24). A firm Federalist, King defended the Jay Treaty and succeeded Thomas Pinckney as minister plenipotentiary to Great Britain in 1796. In 1804, and again in 1808, he was an unsuccessful candidate for Vice President of the United States. He was an outspoken critic of the War of 1812 and of slavery during his years in the Senate, where he served until two years before his death.

FURTHER READING

Ernst, Robert: *Rufus King: American Federalist* (Chapel Hill: University of North Carolina Press, 1968).

ELIZABETH P. MCCAUGHEY

Knox, Henry (*b.* Boston, 25 July 1750; *d.* Thomaston, Maine, 25 October 1806). General. As a bookseller in Boston, he pored over military treatises, trained in the local militia, and observed the practices and procedures of British Redcoats stationed in the colony. When the Revolutionary War began few Americans were more knowledgeable about military science than Henry Knox. Despite his lack of battlefield experience, Congress appointed him, on 17 November 1775, a colonel in charge of the Continental Artillery.

Knox transformed the virtually nonexistent artillery into one of the most proficient and professional branches of the Continental Army, drawing upon European precedent and American military experience. At Trenton and Princeton, Brandywine, Germantown, and Monmouth, Knox's mobile artillery kept pace with and supported the infantry. At Boston and Yorktown, the American gunners showed their ability to perform the art of siege warfare. Knox's achievements prompted Congress in March 1782 to make him a major general, retroactive to November 1781.

During the war Knox witnessed the ill-effects of uncooperative state governments and an impotent Congress. Consequently, as a staunch Federalist and Secretary of War from 1785 until his retirement in 1794, he worked to create a strong national government and an effective military establishment. His subsequent years were spent with his wife, Lucy Flucker Knox, in pursuit of private interests in Thomaston, Maine.

FURTHER READING

Callahan, North: *Henry Knox: General Washington's General* (New York: Rinehart, 1958).

J. MARK THOMPSON

Knox, William (*b.* Monaghan, Ireland, 1732; *d.* Ealing, Middx., 25 August 1810). British pamphleteer. Knox gained first-hand knowledge of America while serving as Provost-Marshal of Georgia (1757–61), and acquired estates there and in Jamaica. Back in London he served as agent for Georgia (1761–8) and for East Florida (1763–70). In 1763 he recommended the creation of a colonial aristocracy, the inclusion of colonial representatives in Parliament, and constitutional reforms to strengthen the colonial executives *vis-à-vis* the assemblies. He opposed Grenville's Stamp Act as too burdensome but by publicly defending in print Parliament's authority to tax the colonies offended the Georgia Assembly, which withdrew his agency. In 1768 in another pamphlet he advocated colonial self-taxation according to quotas fixed by Parliament (and also more liberal trade regulations), an idea taken up in Chatham's and North's conciliatory propositions of 1775. As under-secretary in the Colonial Department (1770–82) he established a considerable influence over policy. He unwaveringly supported the principle of parliamentary supremacy, insisting on the unity of the empire as a single political community. In 1780 he proposed the formation of a loyalist colony in Maine, and his thinking lay behind the establishment of New Brunswick as such a colony in 1784.

FURTHER READING

Bellot, Leland J.: *William Knox: the Life and Thought of an Eighteenth-Century Imperialist* (Austin: University of Texas Press, 1977).

IAN R. CHRISTIE

Kosciuszko, Thaddeus [Tadeusz Andrzej Bonawentura] (*b.* Mereczowszczyzna, Poland, 12 February 1746; *d.* Soleure, Switzerland, 15 October 1817). Polish soldier and military engineer. Kosciuszko was born into a family of noble status but modest means. He received considerable education, including studies at the Royal Military School in Warsaw and at the school of artillery and engineering in Mezieres, France. A stalled military career and a floundering love affair drove him from Poland to France and eventually to North America. In August 1776 he arrived in Philadelphia and by October had earned a commission as colonel of engineers in the Continental Army.

Kosciuszko was one of Washington's most successful foreign officers, contributing much needed professionalism to the adolescent American Army. He oversaw the construction of numerous river and land fortifications, including West Point – the linchpin of the Hudson River defenses. He also provided valuable service in the field. During the campaign of 1777 he masterfully covered the Northern Army's retreat and then selected the field of battle where Burgoyne's forces were subsequently defeated. He distinguished himself in the Southern Department as well, although he has been criticized for his role at the siege of Ninety-Six.

After the American War of Independence Kosciuszko returned to his homeland and led a short-lived Polish uprising.

FURTHER READING

Haiman, Miecislaus: *Kosciuszko in the American Revolution* (Boston: Gregg Press, 1972).

J. MARK THOMPSON

La Fayette. *See* MOTIER, MARIE JOSEPH PAUL YVES ROCH GILBERT.

Laurens, Henry (*b.* Charles Town, 24 February 1724; *d.* 8 December 1792). Merchant, planter, and diplomat, President of the First Continental Congress. Laurens's leadership and administrative ability secured a smooth transition from colonial to revolutionary government for South Carolina. His most significant service to the revolutionary movement, however, came through his leadership of the Continental Congress during its most critical period. Elected President (1 November 1777) barely three months after taking his seat (22 July 1777), Laurens supported General George Washington through several political plots to remove him from his command. But, more importantly, his tenure saw the French Alliance secured and the Articles of Confederation signed.

As President of South Carolina's First Provincial Congress (1775) and President of the Council of Safety in the Second Provincial Congress (1775–6), Laurens was chief executive of the state's patriot faction. He assisted in drafting the state's temporary constitution (1776), then handed the new government to his successor, President John Rutledge, and served as its vice president until his election to the Continental Congress.

In 1779 Laurens resigned the presidency to negotiate an alliance with Holland. His ship was captured *en route*, and Laurens was imprisoned in the Tower for 15 months. After his exchange for Lord Cornwallis, he joined the American Peace Commission in Paris (for illustration, *see* FRANKLIN, BENJAMIN), serving additionally for the next two and a half years as an unofficial "minister" to Great Britain. He signed the preliminary draft but, being absent, not the definitive peace treaty.

After his return to South Carolina in 1785, except to serve as a delegate to the state's ratification convention for the Federal Constitution (1788), Laurens retired from public life.

FURTHER READING

Chestnutt, David R. et al. (eds.): *The Papers of Henry Laurens*, 11 vols. to date (Columbia: University of South Carolina Press, 1968–86).

Edgar, Walter B., and Bailey, N. Louise: *Biographical Directory of the South Carolina House of Representatives*, Vol. 2: *The Commons House of Assembly, 1692–1775* (Columbia: University of South Carolina Press, 1974).

Wallace, David Duncan: *The Life of Henry Laurens, with a Sketch of the Life of Lieutenant-Colonel John Laurens* (New York: Knickerbocker Press, 1915).

REBECCA STARR

Lee, Ann (*b*. Manchester, England, 29 February 1736; *d*. Watervliet, NY, 8 September 1784). Mystic. In 1758 she identified with a small band of "Shaking Quakers," soon moving to a position of leadership that resulted in her being honored as "Mother Ann." Meeting with little success in England, she determined with a handful of followers to head for America, where a brighter future (she had been assured in a vision) awaited her and the group now called Shakers. After arriving in New York in 1774, she created the first of 11 communities in Watervliet (near Albany) in the year that the colonies declared their independence.

Lee's own unhappy marital experience, with four children dying in infancy, helped convince her that carnal lust was the root of all evil, not only in personal life but in social and political realms as well. It also convinced her that life's burdens were not born equally by males and females and that Christianity itself had exaggerated the exclusive masculinity of the deity as well as of the clergy. Mother Ann, in contrast, saw herself as a Second Incarnation, honoring this time the female principle; she also stressed a strict egalitarianism between the sexes. And, because of the evil associated with "living in the flesh," she ruled that celibacy represented the only pure religious life.

Lee abjured all violence and the taking up of arms, a position that during the Revolution brought more critical attention to the small group. But an emphasis on millennial themes (the group's proper name is the United Society of Believers in Christ's Second Appearing) brought in many new members from those caught up in revivalist and revolutionary fervor. By the 1790s Shakers had grown so rapidly in New York that the Congregationalist and geographer Jedidiah Morse, who was offended by their ecstatic worship no less than by their novel beliefs, predicted – wrongly – that "their interest is now fast declining."

FURTHER READING

Andrews, Edward Deming: *The People Called Shakers: a Search for the Perfect Society*, rev. edn. (New York: Dover, 1963).

EDWIN S. GAUSTAD

Lee, Arthur (*b*. Stratford Hall, Westmoreland Co., Va., 21 December 1740; *d*. Middlesex Co., Va., 12 December 1792). Pamphleteer and diplomat. Lee published numerous revolutionary tracts and letters in Virginia and London, writing his most important pamphlet, *An Appeal*, in 1774. While living in England after 1768, he associated with numerous British luminaries. As the imperial crisis heightened, Lee provided timely information to America's leaders and Congress's Committee of Secret Correspondence, while submitting petitions on behalf of colonial interests. He was deputy agent for Massachusetts beginning in 1770 and sole agent after 1775. Named to Congress's commission to France in 1776, he also made diplomatic visits to Spain and Prussia. With fellow commissioners Benjamin Franklin and Silas Deane, he concluded America's treaty with France in 1778, but dissension among the commissioners led to a major split in Congress and the recalls of Deane in 1777 and Lee in 1779. Lee entered the Virginia Assembly and Congress in 1781, negotiated treaties with the Indians in 1784 and 1785, and served on the Board of Treasury from 1785 to 1789.

The brother of Richard Henry Lee, Arthur received an English education at Eton and a medical degree from the University of Edinburgh. After studying at Lincoln's Inn and the Middle Temple he was admitted to the English bar. He was involved in a wide range of intellectual pursuits, was a fellow of the Royal Society of London, and took a special interest in botany.

FURTHER READING

Kammen, M. G.: *A Rope of Sand: the Colonial Agents, British Politics, and the American Revolution* (Ithaca, NY: Cornell University Press, 1968).
Potts, L. W.: *Arthur Lee: a Virtuous Revolutionary* (Baton Rouge: Louisiana State University Press, 1981).

MARY GWALTNEY VAZ

Lee, Charles (*b.* Chester, England, 26 January 1731/2; *d.* Philadelphia, 2 October 1782). General. Lee's father, a British officer, purchased a royal commission for him when he was 14, and over the next 30 years he saw extensive duty on both sides of the Atlantic, including service in the British and Polish armies. When he returned to North America in 1774, Lee's political ideals and military record attracted patriot leaders. On 17 June 1775 Congress appointed the veteran a major general in the Continental Army, subordinate only to George Washington and Artemas Ward.

During the Revolutionary War's first year Lee ably commanded the left wing of the army besieging Boston and organized southern defenses at Charles Town. He also stirred considerable controversy. Haughty, volatile (his Indian name was "Boiling Water"), and eccentric, Lee seemed more at ease with his retinue of dogs than with his comrades in arms. He criticized and ignored George Washington during the disastrous fall campaign of 1776 and grew doubtful of American success. After being captured on 13 December 1776, Lee spent 16 months in British custody pondering the mishandled war and even negotiating for peace. He returned to American lines and assumed command at the Battle of Monmouth, after which he was court-martialled for his performance on the field. Possibly a victim of political circumstances and certainly of his own indiscretions, Lee was given a one year suspension for disobedience, misbehavior, and disrespect. On 10 January 1780 Congress dismissed him permanently from the Continental Army.

Although endowed with considerable talent, Lee was too mercurial to deal with the complex demands of revolutionary military leadership.

FURTHER READING

Alden, John R.: *General Charles Lee: Traitor or Patriot?* (Baton Rouge: Louisiana State University Press, 1951).

J. MARK THOMPSON

Lee, Richard Henry (*b.* Stratford Hall, Westmoreland Co., Va., 20 January 1732; *d.* Chantilly, Westmoreland Co., Va., 19 June 1794). Statesman. Lee was a radical voice in pre-revolutionary Virginia, and served as a burgess for Westmoreland County (1758–75), a member of the Virginia conventions (1774–6), a delegate to Congress (1774–9; 1784–7), president of that body (1784–5), a member of the Virginia House of Delegates (1780–4), and a United States Senator (1789–92). He helped prepare the burgesses' remonstrances to the Stamp Act in 1764 and led the Westmoreland Association, which enforced a boycott of the stamps. After fighting to separate the offices of Speaker of the House and Treasurer in 1766, he urged the creation of committees of correspondence in 1768 and served on the one finally established in 1773. He helped organize a day of "Fasting, Humiliation, and Prayer" in 1774 after Boston's port closing. Active in Congress, Lee drafted key memorials and helped prosecute the war. Most importantly, in June 1776 he moved that the colonies declare themselves independent. Declining

FIGURE 68 A detail from "The Declaration of Independence" by John Trumbull (begun in 1786 but not completed until the 1820s) showing (from left) Richard Henry Lee, Samuel Adams, George Clinton, Arthur Middleton, Thomas Heyward, Charles Carroll of Carrollton, and Robert Morris.

election to the Constitutional Convention of 1787, he fought against the unamended document and probably published the anti-ratification pamphlet *Letters from the Federal Farmer* (1787).

The son of Councilor Thomas Lee of Stratford Hall and brother of Arthur Lee, he was educated in Wakefield, England. He was married twice, to Anne Aylett and to Anne Pinckard.

FURTHER READING

Chitwood, O. P.: *Richard Henry Lee: Statesman of the Revolution* (Morgantown: West Virginia University Library, 1967).
Lee, R. H.: *The Letters of Richard Henry Lee*, ed. J. C. Ballagh, 2 vols. (New York: Macmillan, 1911).

MARY GWALTNEY VAZ

Legge, William [2nd Earl of Dartmouth] (*b.* London, 20 June 1731; *d.* Blackheath, Kent, 15 July 1801). British politician, evangelical, and philanthropist. The step-brother of Lord North, he was First Lord of Trade (1765–6 and, ex-officio, 1772–5), Secretary of State for the Colonies (1772–5), and Lord Privy Seal (1775–82). A firm upholder of parliamentary supremacy over the colonies and therefore of the Declaratory Act, he concurred with the repeal of the Stamp Act as unduly burdensome and became erroneously credited by the colonists with sympathy for their constitutional claims. North's advancement to high office drew Dartmouth away from his political association with Rockingham, and he accepted office in 1772 to support North against the Bedford party in the Cabinet. He favored the Vandalia colony project and adopted a cautious moderate policy over the *Gaspée* affair. He deplored Thomas Hutchinson's confrontation with the Massachusetts Assembly over the issue of independence but upheld him against the assembly's complaints. After the Boston Tea Party he sought with partial success to moderate government policy but fully supported the Port Act and the Charter Act. In indirect confidential overtures with Franklin (winter 1774–5) he offered commercial concessions but would not compromise parliamentary supremacy, and he approved the scheme embodied in North's conciliatory propositions. He supported the use of force in 1775 but, being temperamentally unsuited to conduct a war, transferred to the office of Lord Privy Seal with a seat in the Cabinet. He continued to give largely passive support till North's fall in 1782.

FURTHER READING

Bargar, B. D.: *Lord Dartmouth and the American Revolution* (Columbia: University of South Carolina Press, 1965).

IAN R. CHRISTIE

Livingston, Robert R. (*b.* New York, 27 November 1746; *d.* Clermont, NY, 26 February 1813). Lawyer, diplomat, and cultural leader. Livingston was born into a politically prominent family and became perhaps its most important member. He graduated from King's College in 1756 and studied law with his cousin, the Triumvirate essayist William Livingston, and later with the noted jurist and fellow Triumvirate writer William Smith, Jr. Robert Livingston gained admission to the bar in 1770 and formed a partnership with John Jay. In 1775 he was elected to the Continental Congress, where he served for several terms (1775–6, 1779–81, 1784–5). In 1776 he regarded independence as eventually inevitable, though not yet timely, but as a member of the New York delegation to Congress he lacked the authorization to cast a vote for or against independence. He supported the revolutionary cause, and served on the committee that drafted the first constitution for New York state in 1777.

In 1781 Congress created the department of foreign affairs and appointed Livingston as secretary, where he served for two years and succeeded greatly in providing information on European affairs, recruiting personnel, and establishing routine diplomatic practices. In 1788, at the New York state ratifying convention in Poughkeepsie, Livingston was an outspoken advocate of the new constitution. Once the new federal government was established, he disapproved of Alexander Hamilton's financial policies and supported the Republican cause in New York state. In 1795 he took the lead in opposing the Jay Treaty and, writing as "Cato," published an *Examination of the Treaty of Amity, Commerce, and Navigation, Between the United States and Great Britain.* That year Livingston also ran unsuccessfully against Jay for the post of Governor of New York.

In 1801 Livingston was named minister to France, where he accomplished one of the greatest diplomatic negotiations in American history, the purchase of Louisiana. He retired from public life in 1804, and turned his interests to science and agriculture, subjects he explored in extensive correspondence with Washington, Jefferson, and European acquaintances. He was the founder and first president of the American Academy of Fine Arts. Late in his life he lent technical and financial support for the development of steamboats, and attempted to maintain a monopoly of steam navigation on New York waterways. That monopoly was struck down by the United States Supreme Court in *Gibbons v. Ogden* (1824).

FURTHER READING

Dangerfield, George: *Chancellor Robert R. Livingston of New York, 1746–1813* (New York: Harcourt, Brace, 1960).

ELIZABETH P. MCCAUGHLEY

Livingston, William(, Jr.) (*b.* Albany, NY, 30 November 1723; *d.* Elizabethtown, NJ, 25 July 1790). Lawyer, political essayist, and Governor of New Jersey. He was born into the wealthy, politically important Livingston family, and, following his three older brothers, graduated from Yale in 1741. He studied law with James Alexander and William Smith, Sr., and undertook a digest of the laws of New York in partnership with William Smith, Jr., which was published in 1752 and, in fuller form, in 1762. Livingston distinguished himself as a glib political writer in 1752 when he, John Morin Scott, and William Smith, Jr., wrote as the Triumvirate, attacking the plan for King's College in the pages of the weekly *Independent Reflector* and in the "Watch Tower" column of the *New York Mercury.* Livingston's "Watch Tower" essays assailed the movement for an Anglican episcopacy in America and accused the rival DeLancey political faction of favoring the Anglican cause. From 1758 until 1768, when he was unseated by the Delanceys, Livingston enjoyed immense political influence in the New York Assembly. In 1768 he moved to New Jersey. He hoped to retire, but he was chosen to speak for New Jersey at the First and Second Continental Congresses. After Independence he became the state's first governor and served for 14 years during war and the postwar reconstruction (1776–90). He firmly supported the movement for a stronger national government. Although he was a secondary figure at the Constitutional Convention, his influence was critical in winning New Jersey's quick and unanimous ratification of the new Constitution.

FURTHER READING

Dillon, Dothothy R.: *The New York Triumvirate: a Study of the Legal and Political Careers of*

William Livingston, John Morin Scott, William Smith, Jr. (New York: Columbia University Press, 1949).

ELIZABETH P. MCCAUGHEY

Locke, John (*b.* Wrington, Somerset, 29 August 1632; *d.* Oates, Essex, 28 October 1704). English philosopher. Renowned during the eighteenth century as England's foremost philosopher, Locke is perhaps best remembered in America for the *Two Treatises of Government* (1690), which figured prominently in the debates that culminated in the Declaration of Independence.

The son of a Somerset attorney who fought for Parliament during the English Civil War, Locke attended successively Westminster College and Christ Church, Oxford. After briefly considering the church and diplomacy, he settled on a career in medicine. In 1666 he met the future first Earl of Shaftesbury, who acted as his patron until his death in 1683. As a member of Shaftesbury's household, Locke was active in American affairs, drafting a clause in the South Carolina Charter (1669) guaranteeing religious freedom and serving as Secretary to the Council of Trade (1673–5).

Following Shaftesbury's disgrace, Locke withdrew from public life and in 1683 fled to the Netherlands. During this period he wrote the *Two Treatises* and *An Essay Concerning Human Understanding* (1690), both of which remained unpublished till after the Glorious Revolution. The *Second Treatise*, with its insistence on society's right to dissolve government, can be read as a revolutionary document, and as such helped shape the thought of Thomas Jefferson and the Declaration of Independence. Locke's *Letter on Toleration* (1689) was also important in America, influencing the ideas of Jefferson and James Madison on religious freedom.

For illustration, *see* figure 8, p. 85.

FURTHER READING

Ashcraft, R.: *Revolutionary Politics and Locke's Two Treatises on Government* (Princeton, NJ: Princeton University Press, 1986).

Dunn, J.: *The Political Thought of John Locke* (Cambridge: Cambridge University Press, 1969).

ELIGA H. GOULD

Loudoun. *See* CAMPBELL, JOHN.

Lowndes, Rawlins (*b.* St. Kitts, ?1721; *d.* 24 August 1800). President of South Carolina. A consistent conservative, Lowndes presented the only recorded lengthy and coherent set of counter-arguments made in South Carolina to the proposed Federal Constitution. He believed it would permit an interference in internal state affairs similar to that experienced at the hands of the British, an interference which Lowndes opposed from any quarter. In a House speech he ended by declaring he wanted his epitaph to read: "Here lies the man who opposed the Constitution, because it was ruinous to the liberty of America."

Lowndes was elected to every session of colonial legislature between 1749 and 1775, and was twice chosen Speaker (1763–5, 1772–5). He refused to qualify for the Twenty-eighth Royal Assembly (1768) because he believed the Massachusetts Circular Letter received by that session was an abridgement of internal self-government. While associate justice of the Court of Common Pleas in 1766 he refused to enforce the use of stamped paper.

As a member of both Provincial Congresses (1775–6), both Councils of Safety (1775–6), and the First (1775) and Second (1775–6) General Assemblies, Lowndes was one of the elite who guided the colony's revolutionary government. With ten others he formulated South Carolina's temporary constitution (1776). He disapproved of the more liberal constitution of 1778, but upon the resignation of President John Rutledge, who refused to sign it, he accepted election to the office and signed the constitution into law. He was South Carolina's last president (1778–9), as his successor took the title governor.

After the Revolution, Lowndes represented

St. Philip and St. Michael parishes from 1787 to 1790.

FURTHER READING

Vipermann, Carl J.: *The Rise of Rawlins Lowndes, 1721–1800,* Tricentennial Studies, No. 13 (Columbia: University of South Carolina Press, 1978).

REBECCA STARR

Macaulay(-Graham), Catherine Sawbridge (*b.* Wye, Kent, 2 April 1731; *d.* Binfield, Berks., 22 June 1791). Republican historian, pamphleteer, and controversialist. Born into a wealthy Whig family, Macaulay pursued a private education emphasizing Roman history, from which she derived an intense enthusiasm for the concept of liberty. In June 1760 she married George Macaulay, a physician, and three years later she published the first volume of her *History of England.* Widely hailed as a significant, able rebuttal to Hume's Tory history, Macaulay's republican account cast her immediately into the limelight. Samuel Johnson, in a famous incident of 1763, offered an insult by pretending to be converted to her principles.

With the death of her husband in 1766, Macaulay entered more fully into British society while continuing to research her history. Noted as much for her striking beauty and love of fashion as for her views, she was a target of both harsh criticism and adoration. Three more volumes of the *History* appeared by 1768, but the rush of events led Macaulay to address more current issues. In a pamphlet written against Hobbesian philosophy in 1769 she attacked the necessity and inevitability of monarchy, while being careful not to reject it outright. Her proposals for a balanced democratic system, including manhood suffrage, rotation in office, and land distribution, received wide respect among republicans and joined the pool of ideas from which the Americans would draw their principles of government. An attack on Burke the following year proved instrumental in illustrating the differences between radical and moderate opposition, which (as Burke

had hoped) aided the Rockinghamites a good deal more than the republicans. The fifth volume of the *History* appeared in 1771.

Macaulay left London for Bath in 1774, and published the following year an address condemning the administration's American policies, though it seems she found a wider audience in America than in Britain. In 1777 she met Franklin in Paris. She was remarried, in 1778, to William Graham, a surgeon's mate 26 years her junior. Although her American friends and correspondents, such as John Adams and Mercy Warren, were charitable, British society was aghast, and her popularity quickly dissipated. By 1783 the three final volumes of the *History* appeared. After the war the Macaulay-Grahams traveled to America and visited the Warrens and Washingtons. In a continuing correspondence with Washington, Macaulay-Graham proved an interested and sympathetic adviser, for which the former expressed more than usual appreciation. She was politically too democratic for patriots like John Adams, yet her taste for fashion and tradition led her to reject the American virtue of simplicity. She supported the Constitutional Convention of 1787, but soon lost faith in America and turned to France for the fountain of democracy, attacking Burke's *Reflections.* Her final pamphlet, *Letters on Education* (1790), advocated the same sports and education for boys and girls.

FURTHER READING

Donnelly, L. M.: "The Celebrated Mrs. Macaulay," *William and Mary Quarterly,* 7 (1949), 173–207.
Schnorrenberg, B. B.: "The brood hen of faction: Mrs. Macaulay and radical politics, 1765–1775," *Albion,* 11 (1979), 33–45.

GRANT E. MABIE

McCauley, Mary Ludwig Hays (*b. c.* 1754; *d.* Pennsylvania, 22 January 1832). Revolutionary soldier. The daughter of German migrants, she married John Hays in 1769. When her husband enlisted in the Pennsylvania armed forces she went to war with him.

Both were at the battle of Monmouth, and it was as a result of carrying water to the patriot troops that Hays earned the nickname of "Molly Pitcher." For her wartime services she was awarded a pension by the government of Pennsylvania. In the early 1790s, after the death of John Hays, she married John McCauley. She lived in Pennsylvania until her death.

FURTHER READING

Perrine, William D.: *Molly Pitcher of Monmouth County, New Jersey, and Captain Molly of Fort Washington, New York* (n.p., 1937).

BETTY WOOD

McCrea, Jane (*b.* New Jersey, *c.* 1752; *d.* New York state, 27 July 1777). Revolutionary heroine. Her enduring reputation stems from the manner of her death rather than from the achievements of her life. In 1777, at the time of Burgoyne's march from Canada into New York, she lived in the upper Hudson River valley. Before she could escape to the patriot lines she was shot and scalped, apparently by Burgoyne's Indian allies. Both during and after the War for Independence McCrea was depicted as a martyr to the American cause. Her death, but more especially the way in which she met her death, served to rally support for the patriots.

FURTHER READING

Hilliard-D'Auberteuil, M. R.: *Miss McCrea, 1784: a Novel of the American Revolution* (Gainesville, Fla.: Scholars' Facsimiles and Reprints, 1958).

BETTY WOOD

MacDonald, Flora (*b.* South Uist, Scotland, 1722; *d.* Isle of Skye, Scotland, 4 March 1790). Flora MacDonald became famous for aiding the escape of the Young Pretender, Charles Edward Stuart, from searching British troops following the battle of Culloden in 1746. In 1750 she married Allan Mac-Donald of Kingsburgh, Isle of Skye.

Economic changes in the highlands fol-

lowing The '45 led to large-scale emigration and the MacDonalds joined this movement in 1774. They purchased a plantation in Anson (now Montgomery) County in the North Carolina back country, where large numbers of Highland Scots had already settled. Here Flora's reputation and their relative wealth quickly made them community leaders. When the Revolutionary War came the Mac-Donalds remained loyal and used their influence to pursuade others to follow the same course. Flora probably helped her husband to raise a company for the ill-fated army of Highlanders defeated at Moore's Creek Bridge on 28 February 1776. Allan was captured there and Flora remained alone and harrassed on the plantation until it was confiscated in 1777. She was then allowed to go to New York where her husband, now exchanged, had obtained a commission in a British regiment. After two years there and at a garrison in Windsor, Nova Scotia, Flora returned to Scotland in 1780.

FURTHER READING

DeMond, Robert: *The Loyalists in North Carolina during the Revolution* (Durham, NC: 1960).

MacDonald, Allan Reginald: *The Truth About Flora MacDonald* (Inverness: 1938).

MacLean, J. P.: *Flora MacDonald in America* (Lumberton, NC: 1909).

Meyer, Duane: *The Highland Scots of North Carolina, 1732–1776* (Chapel Hill: University of North Carolina Press, 1961).

Vining, Elizabeth Gray: *Flora: a Biography* (Philadelphia and New York: 1966).

R. ARTHUR BOWLER

McDougall, Alexander (*b.* Scotland, 1732; *d.* 9 June 1786). Popular leader, pamphleteer, and general. McDougall went to America with his parents in 1738. After settling briefly in northern New York the family moved to New York City, where his father worked as a milkman. McDougall went to sea, became a small merchant, and joined the Sons of Liberty. His 1769 pamphlet *To the Betrayed Inhabitants of the City and Colony of New York* caused his imprisonment by the provincial assembly and won him fame as the "Wilkes of America." He was a leading figure in New York City during the independence crisis, presiding at mass meetings and serving on city committees and in provincial congresses. He became a colonel and eventually a major general in the Continental Army, and succeeded Benedict Arnold in command of West Point. McDougall led the delegation that discontented officers sent to Congress in 1782 to secure pay that they were owed. He represented his state in the Continental Congress for two terms and his city in the State Senate for one. He also became president of both the Bank of New York and the Society of the Cincinnati in his state.

FURTHER READING

Champagne, Roger J.: *Alexander McDougall and the American Revolution in New York* (Schenectady, NY: Union College Press, 1975).

EDWARD COUNTRYMAN

McGillivray, Alexander (b. c. 1759; d. Pensacola, Fl., 17 February 1793). Principal Chief of the Creek Indians. McGillivray was of mixed blood, and came into prominence during the American Revolution. The connections of his father, Lachlan McGillivray, in the Indian trade allowed the young man to move between the worlds of Savannah and the Creek towns. From this bicultural experience he acquired enough spoken and written English to obtain the job as Assistant Commissary for the British Southern Indian Department at Little Tallassee. After 1777, using influence acquired through his mother's clan connections, he led bands of Upper Creek warriors east towards the Georgia frontier and south to support the British defending Pensacola. When the Spanish attackers were repulsed at Pensacola in 1780, McGillivray's forest soldiers were credited with turning the tide. Nineteenth-century allegations of cowardice cannot be substantiated; their likely source was Louis Milfort's self-serving *Memoirs*. The zenith of McGillivray's power came after he was

chosen Upper Creek "Head Warrior" in 1783. For the next decade he played off tribal factions, Spanish authorities, American representatives, Georgia speculators, and his own partners in Panton, Leslie, and Company against one another to preserve Creek autonomy. McGillivray was the power on the southern frontier until his death, and his absence left a leadership vacuum never filled.

FURTHER READING

Caughey, John W.: *McGillivray of the Creeks* (Norman: University of Oklahoma Press, 1938).
Coker, William S., and Watson, Thomas D.: *Indian Traders of the Spanish Borderlands: Panton, Leslie & Company and John Forbes & Company, 1783–1847* (Gainesville: University Presses of Florida; Pensacola: University of West Florida Press, 1986).
Green, Michael: "Alexander McGillivray," *American Indian Leaders: Studies in Diversity*, ed. R. David Edmunds (Lincoln: University of Nebraska Press, 1980), 41–63.
O'Donnell, James H., III: "Alexander McGillivray: training for leadership, 1777–1783," *Georgia Historical Quarterly*, 49 (1965), 172–86.

JAMES H. O'DONNELL III

McGinn, Sarah Cass (b. Tryon Co., NY, 1717). As a child she was befriended by the Iroquois, who considered her to be as one of their own. She married Captain Timothy McGinn but was widowed in 1755. Because her family were loyalists their property was confiscated early during the Revolution and McGinn was detained for a time at Fort Eaton. There she was repeatedly interrogated, and was offered 12 shillings York currency per day and a guard of 15 men if she would agree to work to enlist the Indians in the patriot cause. Contemptuously refusing, McGinn escaped in 1777 to join the British forces besieging Fort Stanwix. When the siege failed, Sir John Johnson sent her to live among the Cayugas to hold them firm in British alliance; she was located first at Cayuga (1777–8) and later at Niagara and Carleton Island (near present-day Kingston, Ontario; 1783). After the British defeat at Saratoga, the American General Schuyler sent a belt of wampum to the Six Nations warning them to make their peace with Congress. McGinn stopped the belt from traveling further and persuaded the Indians to spread a more favorable account of British fortunes. Iroquois matrons customarily exerted extensive influence in war and diplomacy, enabling McGinn to make her voice heard in tribal councils. Thus she helped to induce the Cayugas and Senecas to continue their devastating raids on the frontier. In retaliation an American army invaded the Six Nations in 1779, and destroyed most of their towns. McGinn had chosen not just to remain loyal, but to pursue a political agenda with a spirit and at a level closed to women in colonial society.

FURTHER READING

Graymont, Barbara: *The Iroquois in the American Revolution* (Syracuse, NY: Syracuse University Press, 1972).
Haldimand Papers, National Archives of Canada, Vol. 21, pp. 774, 787, 876.
Loyalist Claims, Audit Office 12, Vol. 27, pp. 302–3.

DAVID W. CONROY,
KATHERINE M. J. McKENNA

Madison, James (*b.* King George County, Va., 16 March 1751; *d.* Orange County, Va., 28 June 1836). Statesman, fourth President of the United States. He grew up on the family plantation at Montpelier, Orange County, Virginia, and was educated by private tutors and at the College of New Jersey (now Princeton), where he earned the bachelor's degree in 1771. After a short period of postgraduate study he returned to Virginia, uncertain about his career path.

Events took command of Madison's life. In 1774 he was appalled by the persecution of Protestant dissenters in his home county and, though he expressed aversion to living as a slave-owner, he found in public life opportunities to strike at religious persecution but no chance to end slavery. His frail physique caused Madison to eschew military service

when the break with England came in 1775, but a year later he was elected to the Virginia Convention, which cut the ties to England as it created one of the first state constitutions and bills of rights. In debates for the latter proposal, Madison's suggested change of "toleration" of religion to "free exercise" of worship had far-reaching effects (*see* Chapter 44, §1).

Madison lost the contest to serve in the state legislature but his abilities were recognized when he was placed on the state executive council, where he first encountered Thomas Jefferson. Their lifelong friendship grew to historic dimensions, with the two Virginians destined to form the Republican (Democratic) political party and serve both as secretary of state and chief executive. In the Continental Congress from 1780 to 1783, Madison played a key role in shaping western policy and became painfully aware of the financial distress caused by the inadequate Articles of Confederation.

Back in Virginia, Madison returned to the state legislature and began pressing for a strengthened national government to meet the problems in postwar society. More than any other leader, he pushed for a convention that would either revise the Articles of Confederation or strike out in a new direction. Joined by Alexander Hamilton at the Annapolis Convention of 1786, Madison used that abortive meeting as a springboard and gained Washington's promise to attend a national meeting in Philadelphia in May 1787. There he helped draft a plan which was submitted to the delegates and became, in effect, a working blueprint for the Constitution that was finished in September 1787. Most of Madison's ideas for giving more power to the national government – a bicameral legislature, separate executive and judicial branches, and a responsible revenue system – were accepted by his peers.

The struggle to ratify the Constitution then engaged Madison's talents as a practical politician. From his New York base he assisted Hamilton in writing the letters of "Publius" (later published as *The Federalist*) and coor-

FIGURE 69 James Madison as Jefferson's Secretary of State: portrait by Gilbert Stuart (1805–7)

dinated pro-Constititution efforts in key states (*see* Chapter 72, §3). He was forced to return to Virginia to lead the fight for ratification there, and in debate was pitted against the powerful Anti-Federalist Patrick Henry. Madison was reluctant to concede that a bill of rights should have been included in the original Constitution, but he now promised to work for such a list of guaranteed civil rights. Having been elected to the First Congress he kept his pledge and was the principal author of the ten amendments finally ratified in December 1791 and known as the American Bill of Rights.

After serving in Congress from 1789 to 1797, and breaking with Hamilton over fiscal policy and other issues, Madison intended to retire from public life and took his wife, Dolley, back to Montpelier. Jefferson's election as president in 1801 ended Madison's retirement as he became secretary of state (*see* figure 69), and for the next eight years the two labored to guide their prosperous young nation as a rising neutral amidst a world in conflict. Caught between Britain's Orders in Council

and Napoleon's Continental System, they considered war with either France or Britain, or both, and ultimately settled on a strict neutrality evoked by a severe embargo. Madison became president in 1809, when the embargo was dropped in favor of a Non-intercourse Act that sought recognition of American rights on the high seas. A ruse by Napoleon led Madison into a diplomatic venture that ended with his war message to Congress in June 1812. A divided Congress voted for war, but the ensuing conflict brought little credit to American arms. The tiny American Navy was no match for the Royal Navy, but managed a few important victories on the Great Lakes. The land battles were a mixture of confusion and despair, and only Jackson's victory at New Orleans (fought shortly after the peace treaty had been signed at Ghent) gave a lift to American morale.

The treaty left territorial lines as they existed before the war and settled few of the outstanding issues. Nonetheless, Madison's final years as president came during a renewed sense of American nationhood. At this time Madison favored a national bank, internal improvements at federal expense, and an enlarged military force – all programs contrary to original Republican policy. In the 19 years of his retirement he spoke out against the disunion sentiments of irresponsible slavery advocates and prepared his 1787 Convention notes for posthumous publication. He was buried at the Montpelier family cemetery.

FURTHER READING

Adair, Douglas (ed.): "James Madison's Autobiography," *William and Mary Quarterly*, 2 (1945), 191–209.
Brant, Irving: *James Madison* (Indianapolis: Bobbs-Merrill, 1941–61).
Hutchinson, William T. et al.: *The Papers of James Madison*, 15 vols. to date (Chicago and Charlottesville, Va.: University of Chicago Press, University Press of Virginia, 1962–).
Ketcham, Ralph: *James Madison: a Biography* (New York: Macmillan, 1971).
Koch, Adrienne: *Jefferson and Madison: the Great Collaboration* (New York: Alfred A. Knopf, 1950).

Peterson, Merrill: *James Madison: a Biography in his Own Words* (New York: Newsweek Books, 1974).

Rutland, Robert A.: *James Madison: the Founding Father* (New York: Macmillan, 1987).

Schultz, Harold S.: *James Madison* (New York: Twayne, 1970).

Stagg, John A. C.: *Mr. Madison's War* (Princeton, NJ: Princeton University Press, 1983).

ROBERT A. RUTLAND

Marion, Francis (*b.* Berkeley Co., SC, *c.* 1732; *d.* Berkeley Co., 27 February 1795). General. The grandson of Huguenot immigrants, he was brought up in the sparsely populated Berkeley County, South Carolina. Although he longed for a seafaring career, he contented himself as a prosperous farmer near Eutaw Springs.

During the War of Independence Marion served in both state and federal forces, eventually attaining the rank of colonel in the Continental Line and brigadier general in the South Carolina milita. He spent the early years of the conflict training troops or performing garrison duty. Not until 1780, when the focus of war moved southwards and Great Britain invaded the lower states, did Marion earn his greatest fame. Thereafter, his skill as a guerrilla strategist coupled with his intimate knowledge of the local terrain earned him the sobriquet "Swamp Fox" and enabled him to rack up impressive battlefield victories. Furthermore, in contrast to other partisan leaders, Marion demonstrated a greater willingness and ability to coordinate his activities with those of Nathanael Greene's Continental forces. Despite severe shortages of men and materiel, Marion disrupted enemy supply lines, struck at British forces, and terrorized the loyalist population.

After the war Marion married Mary Videau, rebuilt his war-torn farm ("Pond Bluff"), and served in the South Carolina Senate.

FURTHER READING

Rankin, Hugh F.: *Francis Marion: the Swamp Fox* (New York: Thomas Y. Crowell, 1973).

J. MARK THOMPSON

Martin, Luther (*b.* New Brunswick, NJ, 20 February 1748; *d.* New York, 8 July 1826). Lawyer. Martin served as Maryland's Attorney General (1778–1805) and as a delegate to the federal Constitutional Convention (1787). When his law practice, one of the busiest in Maryland, was interrupted by the beginning of the Revolution, he became a member of the Somerset County Committee of Observation and wrote and distributed patriot literature to loyalist strongholds on the Eastern Shore. Thereafter, he contributed to the Revolution primarily by prosecuting Tories in his capacity as Attorney General.

At the Constitutional Convention, Martin became the leading spokesman for the states' rights position. Dissatisfied with the final document, he refused to sign the Constitution, arguing that the federal government should merely support sovereign state governments and that a truly federal government would include no proportional legislative representation.

Martin continued his voluminous law practice during the early decades of the nineteenth century. His successful defense of Samuel Chase in his 1804 impeachment trial secured his old ally's Supreme Court seat, and in 1807 Martin was one of the lawyers who defended Aaron Burr in his trial for treason. In poor health, partially attributable to alcoholism, Martin lived on Burr's charity from 1820 until his death.

FURTHER READING

Clarkson, Paul S., and Jett, R. Samuel: *Luther Martin of Maryland* (Baltimore: Johns Hopkins University Press, 1970).

Papenfuse, Edward C., Day, Alan F., Jordan, David W., and Stiverson, Gregory A. (eds.): *A Biographical Dictionary of the Maryland Legislature, 1635–1789*, 2 vols. (Baltimore: Johns Hopkins University Press, 1979, 1985); Vol. 2, 577–8.

RONALD HOFFMAN

Mason, George (*b.* Doeg's [now Mason's] Neck, Stafford [now Fairfax] Co., Va., 11 December 1725; *d.* Doeg's Neck, 7 October

1792). Writer and statesman. He served on his colony's committee of safety from 1775 to 1776. He was a member of the Virginia Convention (later Assembly) from 1775 until 1780 and a delegate to the Constitutional Convention in 1787. Ever reluctant to assume public office, his most important contributions to the Revolution came from his pen. The tracts and resolutions he wrote or helped write included a proposal for resistance to the Stamp Act published in 1765; a response to the Declaratory Act penned to a committee of London Merchants in 1766; the non-importation resolutions adopted by Virginia's leaders in 1769; an examination of Virginia's charter written in 1773; and the defenses of colonial rights and demands for unity known as the Fairfax Resolves (1774). His most significant work was his early draft of Virginia's first constitution and declaration of rights (1776), the latter becoming the model for the federal bill of rights.

Privately educated and from a prominent family, Mason was the archetypal Virginia gentleman, serving locally as vestryman and justice and speculating in land via the Ohio Company, of which he was treasurer. He married Ann Eilbeck in 1750 and Sarah Brent in 1780.

For illustration, *see* figure 24, p. 273.

FURTHER READING

Miller, H. H.: *George Mason, Gentleman Revolutionary* (Chapel Hill: University of North Carolina Press, 1975).
Rowland, K. M.: *The Life of George Mason, 1725–1792* (New York: Putnam, 1892).

MARY GWALTNEY VAZ

Montesquieu. *See* SECONDAT, CHARLES-LOUIS DE.

Montgomery, Richard (*b.* Swards, nr Feltrim, Ireland, 2 December 1738; *d.* Quebec, 31 December 1775). General. On 21 September 1756, after his education at St. Andrews and Trinity College, Dublin, Montgomery became an ensign in the British Army and saw considerable action in the New World: at Ticonderoga, Crown Point, Montreal, Martinique, and Havana. Although he reached the rank of captain, bleak prospects in the peacetime army led him to resign his commission and migrate to New York. He arrived in 1772, purchased a farm at King's Bridge, married the daughter of the wealthy and powerful Robert R. Livingston, and quickly established himself as a popular gentleman farmer. The War of Independence, however, disrupted his promising future.

In June 1775 Congress appointed Montgomery a brigadier general in the Continental Army and second in command for the invasion of Canada. The expedition initially floundered and the commander, Philip Schuyler, fell ill. Montgomery took charge in September 1775, reorganized his ragtag force, and proceeded into Canada. He seized the posts at Chambly, St. Johns, and Montreal before linking up with Benedict Arnold's troops outside Quebec. His bedraggled Americans assaulted the city on the snowy night of 31 December. Montgomery was killed early in the fray and the attack ended in confusion and disaster. In 1818 his remains were transferred from Quebec to St. Paul's Church, New York.

FURTHER READING

Smith, Justin H.: *Our Struggle for the Fourteenth Colony: Canada and the American Revolution* (New York: G. P. Putnam's Sons, 1907).

J. MARK THOMPSON

Morgan, Daniel (*b.* ? New Jersey, *c.* 1735; *d.* Wichester, Va., 6 July 1802). Soldier and frontiersman. Morgan was born to Welsh immigrant farmers and grew up alongside the Pennsylvania–New Jersey border. By 1753, however, the young frontiersman had settled in Winchester, Virginia. Despite an early partiality for drinking, gambling, and brawling, he became a respected land-owner after his commonlaw marriage to Abigail Curry.

When the Revolutionary War began, Morgan's previous military experience – as a teamster during the Seven Years' War and militia captain in Lord Dunmore's War – qualified him to command a Virginia rifle company in the new Continental Army. In this capacity and throughout the war he repeatedly proved himself to be a devoted and capable officer especially adept at guerrilla operations. He demonstrated unflinching bravery and determination during the ill-fated invasion of Canada in 1775. In the Saratoga campaign of 1777 he provided exceptional leadership on the battlefield, and his men effectively harassed and demoralized the enemy. Morgan's most renowned victory came in South Carolina. At the Battle of Cowpens (17 January 1781) his troops defeated Banastre Tarleton's Tory Legion in what scholars commonly cite as a classic example of the double envelopment. Soon thereafter a severe case of sciatica forced him into early retirement.

During the early national period Morgan became a staunch Federalist and was elected, in 1797, to a single term in the House of Representatives.

FURTHER READING

Higginbotham, Don: *Daniel Morgan: Revolutionary Rifleman* (Chapel Hill: University of North Carolina Press, 1961).

J. MARK THOMPSON

Morris, Gouverneur (*b.* Morrisania, NY, 31 January 1752; *d.* Morrisania, 6 November 1816). Lawyer and diplomat. Of aristocratic background, Morris argued for reconciliation in New York's provincial congress in May 1775, and was voted out of office. After being re-elected in January 1776, however, he supported rebellion. In the state constitutional convention he won religious toleration and a single governorship for New York. In Congress (January 1778–December 1779) he addressed financial, military, and diplomatic affairs. Morris lost office on account of his Tory family connections and moved to Philadelphia, where he wrote a series of articles against the Carlisle Commission and on finance under the pseudonym "An American." Soon after a leg amputation he was appointed assistant to Robert Morris in

FIGURE 70
Robert Morris, superintendent of finance (right), and his deputy, Gouverneur Morris: portrait by Charles Willson Peale (1783)

the Finance Office (July 1781; *see* figure 70). Together, the Morrises worked tirelessly for a financially united America, but they became out of touch with political and economic conditions in the new nation and began to lose favor. In 1782 Gouverneur helped negotiate a prisoner exchange and worked with Robert on the Report on the Public Credit. The Morrises opposed an early peace, fearing the death of their program. Continental experience and loyalties proved vital to Morris in the Constitutional Convention; elected by Pennsylvania, he went as an American. The most frequent participant in debate, he argued for a strong, centralized government of the well-born. As a member of the Style Committee he is credited with writing "We, the People of the United States." He declined an invitation to contribute to the *Federalist Papers*. As Minister to France (1792–4) Morris tried to smuggle the King out of Paris, and was dismissed at the request of the French. From 1800 to 1803 he served in Congress as a Federalist, but lost his seat in a Jeffersonian landslide. He spoke against the War of 1812, and approved of the Hartford Convention.

FURTHER READING

Kline, M.: *Gouverneur Morris and the New Nation, 1775–1788* (New York: Arno Press, 1978).

GRANT E. MABIE

Morris, Robert (*b.* Liverpool, 31 January 1734; *d.* Philadelphia, 8 May 1806). Merchant and financier. He was a leading figure in the Continental Congress (*see* figure 68), and was known as the Financier of the American Revolution. Among the key positions to which he was appointed were Superintendent of Finance (27 June 1781; *see* figure 70) and Agent of Marine (7 September), both of which he held until his resignation on 1 November 1784. As Congress's financier he immediately put his personal resources into the campaign that ended in the surrender of Lord Cornwallis at Yorktown in 1781, terminating large-scale warfare. Until the disbandment

of the American Army in 1783, as James Madison later phrased it, Morris "with $5,000,000 [mainly proceeds of French and Dutch loans and Pennsylvania cash resources put into his hands by the state] carried on the war to more effect, paid and clothed a large army and rendered more services than his predecessors in office had done for 4 times the amount." He founded the Bank of North America (1781), which was a commercial operation in Philadelphia and the first of its kind in the country; it was chartered by Congress and funded partly by private subscription but mainly by means of a French loan at Morris's disposal.

As the urgencies of war diminished, policies of the economic statesman he wished to be were Morris's chief concern. He was imbued with a vision of the United States as rising to "Power, Consequence and Grandeur." Measures he undertook helped to sustain the degree of unity which the states achieved during the war. He systematically led Congress towards committing the country to stronger central government and material interests that would cause wealth to flow "into those hands which could render it most productive." Reaching back for the principles of the British Whig program, he anticipated Hamiltonian finance in detail.

The son of an English merchant who had settled in rural Maryland, Morris was apprenticed to a prominent mercantile house in Philadelphia, rising to full partnership in the firm of Willing and Morris. He actively sided with the colonists in disputes with Britain, and in 1775 entered Congress as a Pennsylvania delegate. He voted against the Declaration of Independence but retained his post and signed it. His functions were practical rather than dogmatic. As chairman of the Secret Committee of Trade, he managed most procurement abroad, mingling conscientious public service with private trade, which was usually conducted in the name of Willing and Morris – an accepted procedure in those days. His commercial ties extended from America to Europe and the West Indies. When Congress was driven out of Philadelphia by

British occupation, Morris for a time managed its affairs. He left Congress in 1778, partly as a result of involvement in the Silas Deane–Arthur Lee controversy, which plagued Congress for several years.

He accepted the appointment as Superintendent of Finance on conditions he laid down, including his dismissal of anybody who improperly handled public money. Aided by his highly gifted assistant Gouverneur Morris (no relation), he tried to institute reforms. Congress lacked the fundamental power of taxation. Morris and the Nationalists gathering behind the measures he sponsored wanted national taxes that would support the central government and pay its debts. Auxiliary to this he initiated steps that were taken by Congress to assume revolutionary debts as a federal rather than a state obligation, the prospect being that a national debt resting on national taxation and the self-interest of creditors would, as it had in Britain, determine loyalty and foster economic growth. Frustrated, however, in the closing months of war by the refusal of two states to ratify the impost, a duty on imports proposed as a national tax, Morris and a coterie of Nationalists tried to forge an alliance between creditors and the unpaid army in order to present an ultimatum to the country. In imagery if not in elemental substance, the scheme evoked recollection of the crisis that precipitated the Second Civil War between Parliament and the Model Army during the Puritan Revolution. But George Washington was not an Oliver Cromwell, and the "Newburgh Affair" quickly disintegrated.

Morris's influence declined after demobilization of the army. He continued to serve in the Pennsylvania legislature (1775–9, 1780–1, 1785–6) and inconspicuously in the Constitutional Convention (1787). When government under the Constitution took shape, he was superseded in finance by Alexander Hamilton, always a protégé of President George Washington. He was in the United States Senate from 1789 to 1795 and played a role in the historic exchange of federal assumption of state debts for the location of the permanent capitol at Washington, DC. His chief business affairs passed from dispensing congressional payments to a big tobacco contract with the French Farmers General in the mid-1780s; a collaborative but unsuccessful plan to buy the American debt owed to France and sell it to Dutch investors; through unfathomable speculation in government and state debts in America; and, finally, to colossal purchases of western lands. Although he had settled and paid accounts left over from the Revolution, he went bankrupt for a large amount of money and spent three years in debtor's prison. He was released in 1801.

FURTHER READING

Ferguson, E. James: *The Power of the Purse: a History of American Public Finance, 1776–1790* (Chapel Hill: University of North Carolina Press, 1961).

Ferguson, E. James, and Catanzariti, John (eds.): *The Papers of Robert Morris*, 7 vols. to date (Pittsburgh: University of Pittsburgh Press, 1973–).

Oberholtzer, Ellis Paxson: *Robert Morris, Patriot and Financier* (New York: B. Franklin, 1903).

Ver Steeg, Clarence L.: *Robert Morris, Revolutionary Financier* (New York: Octagon, 1976).

E. JAMES FERGUSON

Morse, Jedidiah (*b.* Woodstock, Conn., 23 August 1761; *d.* New Haven, Conn., 9 June 1826). Minister, geographer, and historian. He lived almost all his life in New England, but through travel and research informed himself about all the known world and sought to educate others through his writings. His first published work, *Geography Made Easy*, appeared in 1784 when he was still a divinity student at Yale and went through 25 editions in his lifetime. It gave prose summaries of the land, people, and customs of different parts of the world for use in schools or within families. Morse worked by compiling facts, attempting to provide Americans with all they needed to know about the world and especially about their own continent, which he believed existing geographical textbooks neglected. A similar patriotic zeal showed in his efforts to make known the history of the revolutionary era. His histories of America and New England combined discussion of the natural environment and the aboriginal inhabitants with detailed annals of the Revolution and war, culled from available sources. In the pulpit, Morse preached against Unitarianism, seeking to uphold the Calvinist orthodoxy of New England Congregationalism. In the 1790s he took a staunchly Federalist stand against the "French influence" in the United States.

FURTHER READING

Morse, J. K.: *Jedidiah Morse: a Champion of New England Orthodoxy* (New York: Columbia University Press, 1939).

Philips, J. W.: *Jedidiah Morse and New England Congregationalism* (New Brunswick: Rutgers University Press, 1983).

THOMAS COLE

Motier, Marie Joseph Paul Yves Roch Gilbert [Marquis de La Fayette] (*b.* Chavagnac, France, 6 September 1757; *d.* Paris, 20 May 1834). French general. Motier inherited considerable wealth and a title, that of the Marquis de La Fayette, following the death of his parents. Unattracted to court life, he became ambitious for a military career. The peacetime army offered little chance of promotion, however, and so he turned to the American Revolutionary Continental Army. Congress, though suspicious of foreign adventurers, appreciated La Fayette's apparent enthusiasm for republican principles and offer to serve without pay. On 31 July 1777 it commissioned the 19-year-old Frenchman a major general, but without a salary or command.

La Fayette quickly gained the confidence of his fellow officers, especially George Washington. At the Battle of Brandywine, on 11 September 1777, and the skirmish at Gloucester two months later, he displayed impressive leadership and courage. Washington and

Congress thereafter entrusted him with the command of a division and then a proposed invasion of Canada. In January 1779 La Fayette traveled to France as a lobbyist for the American cause. After returning in April 1780, he served in Virginia, where he helped trap Lord Cornwallis's army at Yorktown.

Back in his homeland, La Fayette called for reforms and continued to lobby on behalf of the United States. During the French Revolution he lost his freedom and his fortune while spending several years in foreign exile and prison. He returned to France in 1799 and settled in La Grange.

FURTHER READING

Gottschalk, Louis: *Lafayette and the Close of the American Revolution* (Chicago: University of Chicago Press, 1942).

——: *Lafayette Joins the American Army* (Chicago: University of Chicago Press, 1937).

J. MARK THOMPSON

Murray, John [4th Earl of Dunmore] (*b.* 1730; *d.* Ramsgate, Kent, 25 May 1809). Governor of Virginia. A representative peer of Scotland (1761–74, 1776–90), he allied himself with the Bedford party. As governor of New York (1769–70) and of Virginia (1770–6; for illustration, *see* figure 1, p. 13) he stoutly upheld their territorial boundaries against claims by other colonies. In a frontier war in 1774 he sought to impose a mild rather than a draconian peace settlement on the local Indians. The imperial crisis brought friction with the Virginia Assembly. He dissolved it after a brief session in 1773, when it appointed a committee of correspondence to concert action with other colonies against the mother country, and again in 1774, when it voted to support Boston over the Port Act. In April 1775 Dunmore provoked a storm by transferring some of the colony's gunpowder to a warship. In May by proclamation he forbade the assembling of a convention. In June he convened the assembly to consider North's conciliatory propositions but, faced with riots, removed the seat of government to a warship, provoking the burgesses to

759

declare he had abdicated and to constitute themselves a convention. During the winter he vainly attempted to re-establish his authority by military force, and after a final failure in July 1776 he returned to England. Dunmore is particularly remembered in America for offering freedom to the slaves of the Virginian planters who would desert their masters and join the British cause – an offer which was widely accepted and caused furious resentment among the slave-owning classes.

IAN R. CHRISTIE

Murray, Judith Sargent (*b*. Gloucester, Mass., 1 May 1751; *d*. Natchez, Miss., 6 July 1820). Writer. She became one of the best-known, and most influential, female writers of her age. The daughter of a wealthy mercantile family, she was educated at home, like so many other girls of her social rank. In 1769 she married John Stevens, a trader. She began writing verse soon after her marriage, but by the late 1780s was being hailed as an essayist rather than as a poet.

From 1779, when she wrote her first essay, her principal concern was with the status and rights of women and, more specifically, with their role in the new republic. This was the theme of her first published work, *Desultory Thoughts upon the Utility of Encouraging a Degree of Self-Complacency, Especially in Female Bosoms* (1784), and of many of the pieces which she wrote for the *Massachusetts Magazine* during the early 1790s under the heading "The Gleaner." Writing under the pseudonym "Constantia," Murray argued vigorously that women were the intellectual and mental equals of men; that they were capable of receiving, and of right ought to receive, formal education similar to that available to men; and that such an education, which could be provided by establishing female academies, was essential if women were satisfactorily to fulfill their roles as republican women (*see also* Chapter 41, §4). The ideal republican woman would not only be "sensible and informed" but, should she

so need or desire, also be perfectly capable of achieving her economic independence.

In 1788, after the death of her first husband, Judith married John Murray, the founder of the Universalist Church in America. It was to be her writing, and especially her collected essays, *The Gleaner*, published in 1798, that largely supported the couple and their surviving child. In 1815, after her husband's death, Murray moved from Massachusetts to Natchez, Mississippi, to live with her daughter. She was buried there in 1820.

FURTHER READING

Field, Vena B.: *Constantia: a Study of the Life and Works of Judith Sargent Murray* (Orono: University of Maine Press, 1931).

BETTY WOOD

North, Frederick [Lord North] (*b*. London, 13 April 1732; *d*. London, 5 August 1792). British statesman. He was a Lord of the Treasury (1759–65), Joint Paymaster-General

FIGURE 71 Frederick Lord North: portrait by Pollard (1780)

(1766–7), Chancellor of the Exchequer (1767–82), and First Lord of the Treasury (Premier) (1770–82). North opposed repeal of the Stamp Act in 1766, and took over Townshend's policies of colonial taxation and fiscal administration at the exchequer in 1767. His repeal of all the Townshend taxes except that on tea in 1770 implemented a Cabinet decision of 1769. He was primarily responsible for steering the coercive legislation of 1774 through the House of Commons, as likewise the restraining Acts of 1775. After Lexington and Concord he remained a respected ministerial spokesman in the Commons, but as a leader of administration he was wholly a failure, incapable of ensuring that the activities of departmental ministers concerned with war operations were properly coordinated or of himself providing any firm unified direction. In 1778 he proposed conciliatory offers to the colonies which, if made in 1775, might have averted the war and American Independence. He resigned in March 1782 when faced with an imminent vote of no confidence in the Commons. He succeeded his father as 2nd Earl of Guilford in 1790.

FURTHER READING

Thomas, P. D. G.: *Lord North* (London: Allen Lane, 1976).

IAN R. CHRISTIE

Otis, James (*b.* West Barnstaple, Mass., 5 February 1725; *d.* Andover, Mass., 23 May 1783). Jurist and pamphleteer. He was one of the foremost early leaders of the colonial cause before the Revolution, but his career was prematurely ended by bouts of insanity. The son of an eminent jurist, Otis graduated from Harvard in 1743, and was admitted to the bar five years later. By 1760 he had become the King's advocate general of the vice-admiralty court in Boston. He resigned that post in 1761 in order to appear for Boston merchants in their case against the use of writs of assistance – used to enforce the Sugar Act of 1733. That same year he

was elected to the General Court, and continued to serve regularly in that body for the rest of his life. As the imperial crisis developed he wrote influential pamphlets such as *A Vindication of the Conduct of the House of Representatives of the Province of Massachusetts Bay* (1762), *Rights of the British Colonies Asserted and Proved* (1764), and *A Vindication of the British Colonies, against the Aspersions of the Halifax Gentleman* (1765). Otis became active in the Sons of Liberty and attended the Stamp Act Congress of 1765. While opposing British policy he did admit the supremacy of Parliament, and gradually became more moderate through the 1760s. After being struck on the head by a customs agent in 1769 he became increasingly insane, and, taking no part in the Revolution, was struck by lightning and killed in 1783.

FURTHER READING

Brennan, E. E.: "James Otis: recreant and patriot," *New England Quarterly*, 12 (1939).
Shipton, Clifford K.: *Sibley's Harvard Graduates*, Vol 11 (Boston: Massachusetts Historical Society, 1960).
Tudor, William: *The Life of James Otis* (Boston, 1823).

KURT W. NAGEL

Paine, Thomas (*b.* Thetford, Norfolk, 29 January 1737; *d.* New Rochelle, NY, 8 June 1809). Radical writer. He was the first public advocate of American independence. Born in England of a Quaker father and an Episcopalian mother, Paine spent the first 37 years of his life in obscurity. He was trained in his father's profession as a staymaker, but followed other professions, though most without success. He was married twice; his first marriage ended with the death of his wife, the second in a separation. In November 1774 he left England for America with a letter of introduction from Benjamin Franklin, whom he had met in London earlier that year.

In America, Paine edited the *Pennsylvania Magazine* and became acquainted with several leading republican thinkers. With the

FIGURE 72 Thomas Paine: engraving by W. Sharp after the painting by George Romney

appearance of *Common Sense* (*see* Chapter 26), he became very well known throughout the colonies and in England. During the Revolution he served in the Continental Army, most notably as an aide to General Nathanael Greene, and wrote a series of 16 essays, known as *The American Crisis*. In 1779 he became embroiled in the Silas Deane affair concerning allegations of Deane's private arms-dealing in France. In publicly denouncing Deane, Paine revealed the secret negotiations with the French on behalf of the American cause, and he was dismissed as Secretary to the Committee for Foreign Affairs. He then sent $500 to George Washington to help supply the American Army. In 1786, as an associate of the wealthy Philadelphia financier and merchant Robert Morris, Paine defended the Bank of the United States. Paine also designed an iron bridge, which he hoped would span the Schuylkill River, and in 1787 he returned to England seeking financial backers for his enterprise.

Paine renewed his political reputation in *Rights of Man*, which appeared in two parts in 1791 and 1792, when he responded to Burke's attack on the French Revolution. Paine's work was condemned in England and he was outlawed, so he moved to France, where he remained for the next ten years. Although he never learned to read or speak French, Paine participated in French politics. He helped draft a new constitution, which was not adopted, and he was also one of two foreigners to serve on the National Convention. In 1793 Paine was incarcerated in the Luxembourg Prison. He later wrote that he feared execution. After the Terror, James Monroe, the American Ambassador to France, secured his release. In 1796 Paine publicly denounced the Washington administration for failing to help him.

Shortly before his arrest he completed the first part of *The Age of Reason*, his celebrated attack on revealed religion; part two was completed after his release. This work led to accusations that he was an atheist. In 1797 he wrote his last major work, *Agrarian Justice*, which advocated a heredity tax on land to ameliorate poverty. When he returned to America in 1802, Paine was ignored. At his death in 1809 he was interred on his farm at New Rochelle, New York, which Congress had given him for his service during the Revolution. Ten years later the radical reformer William Cobbett, who wanted to return Paine's bones to England for a memorial burial, exhumed his remains but subsequently lost them.

FURTHER READING

Conway, M. D.: *The Life of Thomas Paine*, 2 vols. (New York: G. P. Putnam's, 1892).

Foner, P. (ed.): *The Writings of Thomas Paine*, 2 vols. (New York: Citadel Press, 1945).

Hawke, D. F.: *Paine* (New York: Harper and Row, 1974).

Kramnick, I. and Foot, M. (ed.): *The Thomas Paine Reader* (Harmondsworth: Penguin, 1987).

Williamson, A.: *Thomas Paine: His Life, Work and Times* (London: George Allen and Unwin, 1973).

JACK FRUCHTMAN, JR.

Parsons, Theophilus (*b.* Byfield, Mass., 24 February 1750; *d.* Boston, 30 October 1813). Jurist. One of the foremost American jurists in the eighteenth century, he was also a leader of the revolutionary cause in Massachusetts. Parsons graduated from Harvard in 1769, and after studying law he was admitted to the bar five years later. He practiced law in Falmouth, in what is now Maine, and later in Newburyport, Massachusetts. In 1779 he served as a member of the Massachusetts state constitutional convention, and nine years later worked for the ratification of the federal Constitution of 1787 at the Massachusetts ratifying convention. During this period Parsons was a member of what became known as the Essex Junto, a group within Massachusetts supporting strong executive government and property rights. Parsons served in the Massachusetts legislature from 1787 until 1791, and again in 1805. He was named chief justice of the state supreme court in 1806.

FURTHER READING

Cook, F.G.: "Theophilus Parsons," *Great American Lawyers*, Vol. 2, ed. W.D. Lewis (Philadelphia: J.C. Winston, 1907).

KURT W.NAGEL

Paterson, William (*b.* Co. Antrim, Ireland, 24 December 1745; *d.* 9 September 1806). Lawyer and jurist. Paterson attended the College of New Jersey (Bachelor of Arts, 1763; Master of Arts, 1766), then studied law as a clerk from 1764 to 1768 and was admitted to practice in 1769. He was a member of the New Jersey Provincial Congress (1775–6), a delegate to the state constitutional convention (1776), a State Senator (1776–7), and New Jersey Attorney-General (1776–83). As a delegate to the Federal Constitutional Convention of 1787, he introduced the "New Jersey Plan" which led to the creation of the Senate. He signed the Constitution and supported its adoption.

Paterson served in the United States Senate as a Federalist from 1789 to 1790, during which time he was co-author of the Judiciary Act of 1789. He was elected Governor of New Jersey on 30 October 1790 and held that office until 1793. As Governor, he compiled the *Laws of the State of New Jersey* and rewrote the rules of the common law and chancery courts. On 30 March 1793 he was appointed an Associate Justice of the United States Supreme Court, where he strictly enforced the Sedition Law of 1798 and refused to rule the repeal of the Judiciary Act of 1801 unconstitutional. Paterson served on the Court until his death.

CRAIG EVAN KLAFTER

Peale, Charles Willson (*b.* Queen Anne Co., Md., 15 April 1741; *d.* Philadelphia, 22 February 1827). Painter. He launched on a career of portrait painting only after he failed in the trade to which he had been apprenticed, saddle-making. Like other craftsmen, he sought the patronage of the wealthy and traveled to New England and Virginia in search of fresh markets. Through his connections with the colonial elite he received a letter of introduction to Benjamin West, the

FIGURE 73 "The Artist in his Museum": self-portrait by Charles Willson Peale (1822)

American expatriate painter then enjoying great success in London. Peale studied under West for two years, returning to find his services in demand throughout the colonies (for examples of his work, *see* figures 25, 49, 70, and 74). He had moved to Philadelphia by 1776, where some of the delegates to the Continental Congress sat for him. Peale served in the city militia until the evacuation of Philadelphia by the British in 1778, and painted portraits of revolutionary officers, including Washington. The great general and president became Peale's favorite and most famous subject. After the war Peale turned his gallery into an exhibition hall for natural curiosities (*see* figure 73) and devoted himself increasingly to amateur scientific pursuits. His collection was overseen by two of his sons, Titian and Rubens Peale, who kept up their father's interests, as did two others, Raphael and Rembrandt, who were painters.

FURTHER READING

Sellers, C. C.: *Charles Willson Peale* (Philadelphia: 1947); repr. (New York: Scribner, 1969).

THOMAS COLE

Pendleton, Edmund (*b.* Caroline Co., Va., 9 September 1721; *d.* Richmond, Va., 26 October 1803). Jurist and statesman. A justice of Caroline County (1751–77) and a burgess (1752–75), Pendleton was a firm supporter of independence, but a social and religious conservative who fought to retain Virginia's existing institutions. He was active in the House, serving on committees which framed remonstrances against the Stamp Act (1764) and the Townshend Duties (1768). In 1774 he worked to establish non-importation of British goods. On the Committee of Correspondence (1773–4), he also served in the Virginia conventions and the House of Delegates (1774–7), presiding after 1775. In 1776 Pendleton drafted Virginia's resolutions for a declaration of independence in Congress and was appointed to the committee to revise Virginia's laws. He was also a member of the Continental Congress (1774–5), president of the Committee of Safety (1775–6), judge of Virginia's High Court of Chancery (1778–9), and judge of Virginia's Supreme Court of Appeals (1779–1803). In 1788 he fought to ratify the Constitution while presiding over Virginia's convention.

Trained by Benjamin Robinson in the clerk's office of Caroline County, Pendleton developed an extensive legal practice early in his career and became a member of the Loyal Land Company. He was named John Robinson's executor in 1766 and thus shouldered the monumental task of settling the estate (*see* ROBINSON, JOHN). Pendleton married Elizabeth Roy in 1741 and Sarah Pollard in 1745.

FURTHER READING

Hilldrup, R. L.: *The Life and Times of Edmund Pendleton* (Chapel Hill: University of North Carolina Press, 1939).

Mays, D. J.: *Edmund Pendleton, 1721–1803: a Biography*, 2 vols. (Cambridge, Mass.: Harvard University Press, 1952).

MARY GWALTNEY VAZ

Petty, William [2nd Earl of Shelburne] (*b.* Dublin, 2 May 1737; *d.* London, 7 May 1805). British statesman. A follower of Chatham, he was First Lord of Trade (April–September 1763), Secretary of State, Southern Department (1766–8), Home Secretary (March–July 1782), and First Lord of the Treasury (July 1782–April 1783). He unsuccessfully explored schemes for raising an American revenue by quitrents and, isolated in the Cabinet after Chatham's breakdown of 1767, could do nothing to check Townshend's revenue policy, of which he disapproved. The creation of a separate colonial department in December 1767 removed from his hands the control of American affairs. In opposition from 1768 he approved the Boston Port Act but not the other punitive legislation of 1774. Shelburne opposed the American War but hoped for a peace that would preserve some connection between Britain and America, an issue dividing him from

Rockingham. In 1782 he accepted that independence must be conceded, and he personally conducted much of the negotiation leading to the Treaty of Paris of 1783. Accusations of yielding too much in America and failing to protect the interests of the loyalists led to votes of censure in the Commons and to his resignation in February 1783. This ended his active career. He was created Marquis of Lansdowne in December 1784.

FURTHER READING

Norris, John: *Shelburne and Reform* (London: Macmillan; New York: St. Martin's Press, 1963).

IAN R. CHRISTIE

Pickens, Andrew (*b.* Paxton Township, Pennsylvania, 19 September 1739; *d.* Oconee Co., SC, 11 August 1817). Militia officer. By 1752 his family had migrated from Pennsylvania to Virginia, North Carolina, and ultimately South Carolina, where they settled along Waxhaw Creek. Pickens prospered, becoming a successful farmer, militia captain, and justice of the peace by the eve of the Revolutionary War.

The War of Independence was both a colonial rebellion and an internecine struggle. Pickens joined patriot forces in 1775 and proceeded to fight the British as well as intimidate their loyalist and Indian supporters. His exploits came to a temporary end after his capture and parole in 1780. He honored this imposed neutrality until Tories burned his plantation and thus, according to Pickens, rendered the agreement void. Soon afterwards he joined Daniel Morgan for the American victory at Cowpens in January 1781. For the remainder of the war Pickens coordinated efforts with Nathanael Greene to wrest control of South Carolina from British hands. He also helped end hostilities along the frontier by leading punitive expeditions against the Cherokee Indians.

After the war's conclusion Pickens became active in Indian affairs as well as state and federal politics.

FURTHER READING

Ferguson, Clyde R.: "General Andrew Pickens" (diss., Duke University, 1960).

J.MARK THOMPSON

Pinckney, Charles(, Jr.) (*b.* 26 October 1757; *d.* 29 October 1824). Diplomat and Governor of South Carolina. Pinckney's role in the revolution in American government came in two ways: through his work at the Constitutional Convention at Philadelphia, by structuring a republican plan of government that would protect domestic slavery; and, in South Carolina, by bringing government into the Jeffersonian stream of republican thought.

His political career began in the revolutionary midstream, with his election to Third (1779–80) and Fifth through Seventh (1784, 1785, 1787–8) General Assemblies. Concurrently, he served as South Carolina's delegate to the Confederation Congress (1784–7). The difficulties in collecting assessments and the necessity to restore sound credit for overseas commerce convinced him of the need for a stronger central government. He was elected a delegate to the Constitutional Convention at Philadelphia, and presented his own plan for a federal union on 29 May 1787, the same day that the Virginia plan was brought forward. The plan was sent to the committee on detail, and was subsequently misplaced, so its exact content has become the subject of much debate. Later research indicates that 31 to 32 provisions from his plan appear in the finished constitution. Back in South Carolina, he supported it strongly both in the House of Representatives and at the state ratifying convention in 1788.

During the final decade of the century Pinckney was three times elected South Carolina's governor (1789–90, 1791–2, and 1796–8), and presided over the creation of a new state constitution (1790) modeled to fit with the federal instrument he had helped formulate. He also served three more terms in the House (1792–7) before receiving an appointment to fill an unexpired term as

765

United States Senator (1798). He was subsequently re-elected to the Senate, where he led the Democrat-Republican party.

By 1790 Pinckney's 1780s republicanism no longer fitted the Federalist mold. He opposed Jay's Treaty at the national level, and, espousing Thomas Jefferson's republican philosophy, became the advocate for reforms at home. In 1800 he managed Jefferson's campaign in South Carolina, which finally and fully estranged him from his relations, one of whom, Charles Cotesworth Pinckney, was the Federalist candidate for vice president. Rewarded with the post of Minister Plenipotentiary to Spain (1801–5), he secured American rights of deposit at New Orleans.

Back in South Carolina, Pinckney was returned to the House four more times between 1805 and 1813 (overall he was elected to 14 General Assemblies between 1779 and 1813), and was chosen on 9 December 1806 for his fourth gubernatorial term. In 1808 he supported a constitutional amendment that reapportioned representation in the legislature on the basis of population. The change gave a majority in the House to the ideologically more republican-minded upcountry, and also helped end the deep sectional divisions that had existed since before the Revolution. Pinckney withdrew from politics from 1814, only to be urged out in a Republican effort to defeat the Federalists in their low-country stronghold. He won a bitter contest for the United States House of Representatives seat from Charleston (1819–21), where his old republicanism found new expression in opposition to the Missouri Compromise. In fervent speeches from the floor of the House, Pinckney articulated the philosophy that would characterize the southern position from 1821 to 1860. One scholar has credited Charles Pinckney as the founder of the so-called Carolina Political Tradition, a republicanism formed in the world as it was in the 1780s, in which slavery was still the norm, a republicanism that was only defeated through the violence of war.

FURTHER READING

Bailey, N. Louise, and Cooper, Elizabeth Ivey (eds.): *Biographical Directory of the South Carolina House of Representatives*, Vol. 3: *1775–1790* (Columbia: University of South Carolina Press, 1981).

Kaplanoff, Mark D.: "Charles Pinckney and the American republican tradition," *Intellectual Life in Antebellum Charleston*, ed. Michael O'Brien and David Moltke-Hansen (Knoxville: University of Tennessee Press, 1986).

"Sketch of Pinckney's plan for a constitution," *American Historical Review*, 9 (1904), 735–47.

REBECCA STARR

Pinckney, Charles Cotesworth (*b.* Charles Town, 14 February 1746; *d.* 16 August 1825). Lawyer and diplomat. Pinckney combined a solid legal mind and political astuteness with a distinguished military career to form a figure who could bridge between state and national politics. During military service he was a colonel in the First South Carolina Regiment, commanded Fort Moultrie, and served as aide-de-camp to General George Washington. He was commissioned a brigadier-general by brevet in 1783. In national politics Pinckney was a delegate to the federal Constitutional Convention at Philadelphia and to the 1788 state ratification convention. During the House debates preceding the convention, he presented the chief arguments in response to the Anti-Federalist spokesman Rawlins Lowndes. In state politics he served 13 terms in the lower house of the colonial and state legislatures between 1769 and 1790.

President Washington, who trusted him, offered Pinckney successively the command of the army (1791) and the posts of Associate Justice of the Supreme Court (1791), Secretary of War (1794), Secretary of State (1795), and Minister to France (1796). He declined all but the last. In 1797 President John Adams sent him to France on a mission which became known as the XYZ affair. It was he who, when approached for a bribe by Hottinguer (X), cried "It is NO! NO! Not a sixpence!" Later popularized to "Millions for

Defense, but not a one cent for tribute," it made Pinckney a Federalist party hero.

Pinckney was the Federalist party's candidate for vice president in the 1800 election and for president in 1804 and 1807. He retired from state politics after completing his South Carolina Senate term in 1802.

FURTHER READING

Pinckney, Elise (ed.): *The Letterbook of Eliza Lucas Pinckney, 1739–1762* (Chapel Hill: University of North Carolina Press, 1972).

Zahniser, Marvin R.: *Charles Cotesworth Pinckney, Founding Father* (Chapel Hill: University of North Carolina Press for the Institute for Early American History and Culture at Williamsburg, 1967).

REBECCA STARR

Pinckney, Eliza Lucas (*b.* West Indies, 28 December ?1722; *d.* 26 May 1793). Experimental agriculturalist. Her experiments with indigo culture established that crop as South Carolina's second largest export during the colonial period. The Lucas family came to South Carolina in 1738. The next year, at the outbreak of the War of Jenkin's Ear, her father was recalled to his military post in Antigua, and the 16-year-old Eliza took over the management of the family's three plantations.

The need of the South Carolina planters for a wartime cash crop to replace rice inspired George Lucas to send his daughter seeds of several West Indian crops. In 1740 Eliza focused her experiments on indigo as the most promising. During the next three years of experimental planting, she also collaborated with specialists sent out by her father to perfect the dye extraction process and to adapt vat construction to local materials. In 1744 Pinckney produced "17 pounds of very good indigo," the equal of the best French product according to experienced London dealers, among whom it excited much interest. She distributed much of the 1744 seed crop among her neighbors, and by 1747 South Carolina's indigo production stood at 135,000 pounds, a figure that soon exceeded one million pounds. Pinckney also experimented with flax, hemp, and silk culture. Great hopes were held for the last, but it proved unprofitable.

Pinckney read widely, and, perhaps influenced by John Locke, adopted the most modern child-rearing methods; she had special toys constructed so her children might "play themselves into learning." She shaped her sons' English education in letters that have both historic and literary value, and passed on her public-spiritedness and her love of botany to both of them. In addition to becoming prominent Federalist leaders, Charles Cotesworth Pinckney was an early planter of sea-island cotton, while Thomas Pinckney patronized the development of the van Hassel dike system, which converted useless salt marshes into valuable rice lands.

FURTHER READING

Smith, Elise Pinckney (ed.): *The Letterbook of Eliza Lucas Pinckney, 1739–1762*, with an introduction by Walter Muir Whitsell (Chapel Hill: University of North Carolina Press, 1972).

Ravenel, Harriott Horry: *Eliza Pinckney* (New York: Charles Scribner's Sons, 1896).

REBECCA STARR

Pitt, William [1st Earl of Chatham] (*b.* London, 15 November 1708; *d.* Hayes, nr Bromley, Kent, 11 May 1778). British statesman. He attained great prominence through opposition rhetoric in the House of Commons and earned the sobriquet of the "Great Commoner." As Secretary of State he was largely responsible for the conduct of the Seven Years' War, and consequently was very influential in both parliamentary and public opinion after leaving office. In early 1763 he supported plans for a large army to be stationed in America for imperial defense but, perhaps owing to mental breakdown, took no part in the next two years' discussions about the finance to support it. He figured prominently in early 1766 as a vehement supporter of repeal of the Stamp Act, but on the muddled and constitutionally untenable ground that

Parliament could not lawfully impose internal taxes on the colonies though it had a perfect right to impose external taxes (customs duties); these latter, however, Pitt condemned as inexpedient. Appointed premier in July 1766 and created Earl of Chatham, he gave no clear leads on American policy before, early in 1767, he suffered a mental breakdown; but Charles Townshend's planning of further customs duties was not contrary to his constitutional principles. On recovering his health he resigned in October 1768. In 1775 the House of Lords rejected his "Provisional Act" for pacifying the colonies under which Parliament, while retaining general sovereign authority in America, would have specifically abandoned all taxing powers. He ended his life condemning policies of taxation and war, but nevertheless insisted American Independence should not be conceded. *See also* Chapter 3, §11.

FURTHER READING

Ayling, Stanley: *The Elder Pitt, Earl of Chatham* (London: Collins, 1976).
Christie, Ian R.: "William Pitt and American taxation: a problem of parliamentary reporting," *Studies in Burke and his Time*, 17 (1976), 167–79.
——: "The Earl of Chatham and American taxation, 1774–1775," *The Eighteenth Century*, 20 (1979), 246–59.
Tunstall, Brian: *William Pitt, Earl of Chatham* (London: Hodder and Stoughton, 1938).

IAN R. CHRISTIE

Pontiac (*b. c.* 1720; *d.* Cahokia, Ill., 20 April 1769). Ottawa war leader. He is traditionally credited with the leadership of the Indian war against the British in North America between 1763 and 1765. At the close of the Seven Years' War, native American peoples from Niagara to Michilimackinac were disturbed by the French withdrawal and the contempt displayed by the victorious British. According to traditional accounts, Pontiac organized the tribes against the expansion of the land-hungry British. Devising a series of clever stratagems, the forest soldiers quickly seized a number of frontier posts. The garrison at Detroit, however, managed to repulse the attack and avoid trickery. Confronted with failure and increasingly reluctant allies as the months passed, Pontiac ultimately abandoned the siege and agreed to peace. While he was present at Detroit, Pontiac should be seen in context as one of the several leaders from Ottawa, Chippewa, Delaware, Seneca, Potawatomi, Huron, Erie, Miami, Wea, and Shawnee villages. Inspiration came too from Neolin, the Delaware prophet, who urged that the "dogs clothed in red" be driven away. The struggle named after Pontiac was, more correctly, one of many periods of resistance in a 40-year defense (1755–95) of tribal autonomy. Judged against the broader backdrop, Pontiac can be removed from the prominence given him by Francis Parkman (1909). He was killed ignominiously by a Peoria Indian.

FURTHER READING

Jennings, Francis: *Empire of Fortune: Crowns, Colonies & Tribes in the Seven Years' War in America* (New York: W. W. Norton, 1988).
Parkman, Francis: *The Conspiracy of Pontiac and the Indian War after the Conquest of Canada* (1851); rev edn., 2 vols. (Boston: Little, Brown, 1909).
Peckman, Howard H.: *Pontiac and the Indian Uprising* (1947); 2nd edn. (Chicago: University of Chicago Press, 1961).
Wallace, Anthony F. C.: *The Death and Rebirth of the Seneca: the History and Culture of the Great Iroquois Nation, their Destruction and Demoralization, and their Cultural Revival at the Hands of the Indian Visionary, Handsome Lake* (New York: Alfred A. Knof, 1970).

JAMES H. O'DONNELL III

Pownall, Thomas (*b.* ?Saltfleetby, Lincolnshire, 4 September 1722; *d.* Bath, 25 February 1805). Governor of Massachusetts. He was a clerk at the Board of Trade (1743–54) and private secretary to the Governor of New York (1753–4) before serving as Governor of Massachusetts (1757–9; for illustration, *see* figure 1, p. 13); he was also appointed Governor of South Carolina in 1760, but declined the post. As spectator at the Albany Congress (1754) and through involvement in attempts to coordinate colonial defense efforts (1755 and 1757–9), he was deeply impressed with the need to reorganize and unify the empire, and publicized his views in his treatise *The Administration of the Colonies* (1764 and several later editions). He stressed the need for radical structural reform based on consensus and advocated the representation of the colonies in Parliament before any assumption by Parliament of an authority to tax them. In Parliament (1767–80) he upheld colonial claims to "no taxation without representation." Anxious to preserve imperial unity, in 1774–5 Pownall supported the Boston Port Act (though not the rest of the "Intolerable" Acts), the Restraining Acts, and North's conciliatory propositions; but from December 1777 he regarded America as irretrievably lost and pressed for an ending of the war on the basis of independence.

FURTHER READING

Schutz, John A.: *Thomas Pownall, British Defender of American Liberty: a Study of Anglo-American Relations in the Eighteenth Century* (Glendale, Calif.: 1951).

IAN R. CHRISTIE

Pratt, Sir Charles [1st Baron Camden] (bapt. London, 21 March 1714; d. London, 18 April 1794). British politician. While at Eton he contracted a life-long friendship with William Pitt, to whom he was to owe his professional and political advancement. He was Attorney-General to the Prince of Wales (George III) (1756–7); Attorney-General (1757–62); Lord Chief Justice of the Common Pleas (1761–6); Lord Chancellor (1766–70); and Lord President (1782–3; 1784–94). As Lord Chief Justice of the Common Pleas he handed down the celebrated vindication of English rights in the general warrants cases, which form the basis of the Fourth Amendment of the United States Constitution. In the House of Lords in 1766 Camden seconded Pitt's campaign against the Stamp Act and also opposed the Declaratory Act. After Chatham

fell ill in 1767 Camden was isolated and out of sympathy with the Cabinet majority which favored taxation of the colonies, but he remained in office after Chatham resigned and only withdrew, on grounds of domestic policy, early in 1770. In 1775 he supported Chatham's "Provisional Act" for conciliation with the colonies, going further than Chatham in vehemently maintaining that Parliament had no constitutional right to tax the colonies, and he introduced an abortive Bill for the repeal of the Quebec Act of 1774. After 1775 he strongly opposed the American War. He was created Baron Camden in 1761 and Earl Camden in 1786. Several American towns and counties bear his name.

FURTHER READING

Eeles, Henry S.: *Lord Chancellor Camden and his Family* (London: Philip Allan, 1934).

IAN R. CHRISTIE

Price, Richard (b. Tynton, Glamorganshire, 23 February 1723; d. Hackney, Middx., 19 March 1791). Pamphleteer. A Presbyterian clergyman in England and an author on various subjects, Price wrote in defense of the rights of the American colonies. He argued that Parliament could not impose any measures on the colonies that the British Constitution would not permit it to impose on the citizens of Great Britain. An exertion of arbitrary power anywhere in England or its possessions threatened the rights of all subjects. He accepted the colonists' right to declare independence as their last resort in the attempt to preserve their liberties. In early 1776 he published *Observations on the Nature of Civil Liberty*, which went through 20 editions in London, 12 in the first year alone. It enjoyed a wide readership in America as well, where Price numbered Thomas Jefferson, John Adams, George Washington, and Benjamin Franklin among his correspondents. He published some *Additional Observations* in 1777, pleading for an end to hostilities, and offered advice to the United States in *Observations on the American Rev-*

olution (1784). In this last pamphlet he urged Americans to guarantee the rights of free speech and to hasten the abolition of slavery, so that their country might become "a refuge to the world."

FURTHER READING

Cone, C. B.: *Torchbearer of Freedom: the Influence of Richard Price on Eighteenth Century Thought* (Lexington: University of Kentucky Press, 1952).
Hudson, W. D.: *Reason and Right* (London: Macmillan, 1970; San Francisco: Freeman Cooper, 1970).
Peach, B.: *Richard Price and the Ethical Foundations of the American Revolution* (Durham, NC: Duke University Press, 1979).

THOMAS COLE

Pulaski, Casimir [Kazimierz] (*b.* Winiary, Poland, 3 March 1747; *d.* nr Savannah, October 1779). Polish general. Pulaski was the oldest son of a Polish Count, and, like his father, fought to extricate Poland from foreign domination. By 1772, however, he was forced to flee his homeland, eventually taking refuge in France. While in Paris he met Silas Deane and Benjamin Franklin, who, impressed by his military skills, sent him with funds and a recommendation to America in 1777.

George Washington lamented the weakness of the Continental cavalry and hoped a foreign veteran could bolster this branch of the American Army. Consequently he recommended and Congress appointed Pulaski "Commander of Horse" with the rank of brigadier general. The Pole trained troops and established a riding school, but proved to be fractious, reluctant to follow orders, and unwilling to assume subordinate roles. On 28 March 1778 he resigned his post and took command of an independent legion. Complaining of inactivity while stationed along the Delaware River, Congress sent him to the Southern Department. On 9 October 1779 Pulaski was mortally wounded while charging enemy lines in the battle for Savannah. He died days later while aboard the *Wasp*.

FURTHER READING

Manning, Clarence A.: *Soldier of Liberty: Casimir Pulaski* (New York: Philosophical Library, 1945).

J. MARK THOMPSON

Putnam, Israel (*b.* Salem Village [now Danvers], Mass., 7 January 1718; *d.* Brooklyn, Conn., 29 May 1790). General. Putnam was the twelfth child of a prosperous farming family. In Pomfret, Connecticut, he established himself as a farmer and local leader, a position bolstered by his second marriage in 1767 to the wealthy widow Deborah Avery Gardiner. In June 1775 Congress commissioned Putnam one of four major generals in the Continental Army, based on his prominence in Connecticut society but also his significant military experience.

During the Seven Years' War Putnam had distinguished himself as one of Rogers' Rangers, served under Jeffery Amherst in the Albany campaign, narrowly escaped execution by Indians, and survived a shipwreck off the coast of Cuba. By the war's end Lieutenant-Colonel Putnam was widely hailed for his fierce bravery and skill as a scout, guerrilla warrior, and regimental leader.

Putnam's Revolutionary War service won him far fewer plaudits. He commanded during the first year the center of the American line during the Boston seige and later a critical position during the disastrous Battle of Long Island. By early 1777 George Washington doubted Putnam's abilities as a field commander. He placed him in charge of the Hudson Highlands but removed him after the loss of forts Clinton and Montgomery. Thereafter Putnam was given relatively unimportant assignments until a stroke ended his military career in December 1779.

For illustration, *see* figure 48, p. 585.

FURTHER READING

Niven, John: *Connecticut Hero: Israel Putnam* (Hartford: American Revolution Bicentennial Commission of Connecticut, 1977).

J. MARK THOMPSON

Ramsay, David (*b.* Lancaster Co., Pa., 2 April 1749; *d.* Charleston, 8 May 1815). Physician and historian. Ramsay left Pennsylvania, where he had studied medicine under Benjamin Rush, to practice in Charles Town, South Carolina, in 1773. During the War for Independence he served as a physician in the Continental Army in addition to fulfilling legislative duties (he was a member of the South Carolina State House of Representatives, 1776–81, a delegate to the Continental Congress, 1782–5, and a South Carolina State Senator, 1792–8). In the wake of independence, in common with many other Americans, Ramsay believed that the future of the republic depended on the understanding and virtue of the people themselves. A memorial of the struggles to achieve independence would help keep patriotism alive, and Ramsay participated in a broad cultural impulse when he set out to promote this end first on the local and then on the national level with *History of the Revolution of South Carolina* (1785) and *History of the American Revolution* (1789). These works were highly regarded in their time but have since fallen in critical esteem on account of Ramsay's extensive use of passages plagiarized from the *Annual Register*, the same source used by William Gordon. Ramsay relied on it even when writing about his home state, but he also included some eye-witness accounts of his own.

FURTHER READING

Cohen, L.: *The Revolutionary Histories* (Ithaca and London: Cornell University Press, 1980).
Libby, O. G.: "Ramsay as plagiarist," *American Historical Review*, 7 (July 1902), 697–703.

THOMAS COLE

Randolph, Edmund (*b.* Williamsburg, Va., 10 August 1753; *d.* Frederick Co., Va., 12 September 1813). Lawyer and statesman. He began his public career after serving briefly as Washington's aide-de-camp in 1775. He was a delegate to the Virginia Convention in 1776, Attorney-General of Virginia from 1776 to 1786, a member of Congress in 1779 and from 1781 until 1782, and Governor of Virginia from 1786 to 1788. A delegate to the Annapolis Convention of 1786, he also attended the Constitutional Convention of 1787, where he presented the Virginia Plan and participated vigorously in the debates. Although he could not sign the document in its final form, his support for the Constitution in the Virginia ratifying convention of 1788 helped assure its acceptance. While in the state legislature (1788–9), he helped revise Virginia's laws and then served as Washington's Attorney-General (1790–4) and his Secretary of State (1794–5). Damaging references contained in a captured letter written by the French minister forced his resignation from the latter post. Randolph's publication *A Vindication of Mr. Randolph's Resignation* was his attempt to clear his name.

After attending the College of William and Mary, Randolph studied law under his father John Randolph, the loyalist Attorney-General who returned to England in 1775. His uncle was Peyton Randolph, first president of the Continental Congress, while his father-in-law was the prominent Robert Carter Nicholas. The income from Randolph's life-long private practice, although substantial, never equaled the debts which constantly plagued him.

For illustration, *see* figure 37a, p. 459.

FURTHER READING

Conway, M. D.: *Omitted Chapters of History Disclosed in the Life and Papers of Edmund Randolph* (New York: Putnam, 1889).
Reardon, J. J.: *Edmund Randolph: a Biography* (New York: Macmillan, 1974).

MARY GWALTNEY VAZ

Randolph, Peyton (*b.* Williamsburg, Va., 1721; *d.* Philadelphia, 22 October 1775). Lawyer and politician. Attorney-General from 1748 until 1766 and a member of the House of Burgesses from 1748 until 1775, Randolph was active in the assembly's most important committees. In 1754 he traveled to London as special agent to fight against Lieutenant Governor Robert Dinwiddie's demand of a pistole fee for every land patent. During the Stamp Act crisis of 1764 he served on the committee to address the King and memorialize Parliament. After John Robinson's death in 1766, Randolph presided over Virginia's leaders, serving as Speaker of the House of Burgesses, moderator of its extra-legal sessions, and, from 1774, president of the Virginia Convention. He also became chairman of the Committee of Correspondence in 1773 and the first president of the Continental Congress in 1774. Randolph was a symbol of continuity between the colonial and revolutionary regimes, and his moderate voice lent credibility to the bodies over which he presided.

Randolph was trained at the College of William and Mary and the Middle Temple of London's Inns of Court. His father Sir John Randolph had been Speaker and Treasurer, while his loyalist brother John was Attorney-General when he left for England in 1775. His wife Elizabeth was a member of the prominent Harrison clan.

FURTHER READING

Reardon, J. J.: *Peyton Randolph, 1721–1775: One Who Presided* (Durham, NC: Carolina Academic Press, 1982).

MARY GWALTNEY VAZ

Reed, Esther De Berdt (*b*. London, 22 October 1746; *d*. Philadelphia, 30 January 1780). Wife, home-maker, and wartime relief worker. The daughter of a merchant, she moved to Philadelphia in 1770 upon her marriage to Joseph Reed, a New Jersey lawyer and patriot, and subsequently President of Pennsylvania. An ardent supporter of the American cause, Reed played a leading role in organizing, and chairing, a committee of women in Philadelphia who devoted themselves to raising money and materials for Washington's troops. She died, apparently of dysentery, in 1780.

FURTHER READING

Reed, William B.: *The Life of Esther De Berdt, Afterwards Esther Reed, of Pennsylvania* (Phi-

ladelphia: C. Sherman, 1853); repr. (New York: Arno Press, 1971).

BETTY WOOD

Reed, Joseph (*b*. Trenton, NJ, 27 August 1741; *d*. Philadelphia, 5 March 1785). Lawyer, soldier and statesman. After serving as deputy secretary for his native New Jersey (1767–9), Reed and his English wife settled in Philadelphia, where he set up legal practice. He soon began a one-sided correspondence with Lord Dartmouth, presenting the "colonial attitude." In 1774 he was appointed to the Philadelphia Committee of Correspondence, and in January 1775 was named president of the second Provincial Congress. A "reluctant revolutionary," Reed moved slowly towards independence. After Lexington and Concord he was appointed lieutenant-colonel of the Pennsylvania Associated Militia, then chosen as Washington's military secretary. The general missed Reed's service after he left for Congress, and in June 1776 made him an adjutant-general. It was Reed who decided not to accept an address from Admiral Howe to "George Washington, Esquire." His advice proved sound and valuable, particularly in the surprise attacks on Trenton and the night march on Princeton. He led troops at Brandywine, Germantown, and Monmouth. He declined both the command of the Cavalry and the chief justiceship of Pennsylvania, and did not take his seat in Congress until the military season ended. From 1778 to 1781 Reed served as president of the Supreme Executive Council. A member of the Carlisle Commission attempted to bribe him to urge conciliation, and he made the affair public news. Although he was nominated for a seat on the state supreme court in 1782, he was deemed too political a choice. The "Brutus" letter, attacking Reed's patriotism, led to a heated newspaper conflict. Re-elected to Congress in 1784 in spite of his wishes, he died before his term would have begun.

FURTHER READING

Roche, J. F.: *Joseph Reed: a Moderate in the Amer-*

ican Revolution (New York: Columbia University Press, 1957).

GRANT E. MABIE

Revere, Paul (*b*. Boston, 1 January 1735; *d*. Boston, 10 May 1818). Silversmith and engraver. He was active in the revolutionary movement in Boston, and is best remembered for his midnight ride to Lexington. Revere spent his youth learning the silver trade of his father. He took over his father's shop in 1754, and was soon one of the leading artisans of Boston. After the passage of the Stamp Act in 1765 he joined several revolutionary clubs, and used his skills to engrave cartoons for these organizations (for examples, *see* figures 8 and 11). Revere was a leader of the Sons of Liberty, took part in the famous Tea Party of 1773, rode as a courier for the Massachusetts committee of correspondence, and printed money for the provincial congress. He is most famous for his ride, immortalized by Henry Wadsworth Longfellow, to warn the colonists that the British were marching to confiscate the munitions stored at Concord on the night of 18–19 April 1775. During the Revolutionary War Revere founded a powder mill in Canton, Massachusetts, and served as a militia officer on unsuccessful expeditions to Rhode Island and Penobscot. Revere's businesses prospered after the war, and he established the first copper rolling mill in America in 1790.

FURTHER READING

Forbes, Esther: *Paul Revere and the World he Lived in* (repr. Boston: Houghton, 1962).

KURT W. NAGEL

Riedesel [Massow], **Frederika Charlotte Louise von** (*b*. Brandenburg-an-der Havel, Prussia, 11 July 1746; *d*. Prussia, 1808). Diarist. The daughter of a Prussian General, in 1762 she married Friedrich Riedesel, Baron Eisenbach, who later commanded the Brunswick forces who served with the British during the War for Independence. She joined her husband in North America in 1777. Following the British defeat at Saratoga, which the Baroness witnessed, the von Riedesels were sent to Virginia as paroled prisoners of war. There they rented accommodation from Thomas Jefferson, with whom they soon became on friendly terms. In 1780 von Riedesel was exchanged for the captured American General Ben Phillips. After further service in New York and Canada, the von Riedesels returned to Europe in 1783.

Baroness von Riedesel's journal of her experience in North America, which covers the years between 1776 and 1783, was first published in English in 1827. Although she was by no means an unbiased observer, her descriptions and assessments, be they of individuals, social behavior, political attitudes, or military matters, are always perceptive, often witty, and occasionally caustic.

FURTHER READING

Brown, Marvin L.: *Baroness von Riedesel and the American Revolution: Journal and Correspondence of a Tour of Duty, 1776–1783* (Chapel Hill: University of North Carolina Press for the Institute of Early American History and Culture, 1965).

BETTY WOOD

Rittenhouse, David (*b*. Germantown, Pa., 8 April 1732; *d*. Philadelphia, 26 June 1796). Scientist and astronomer. He was the most renowned observational astronomer in colonial British America and symbolized the participation of that part of the world in the intellectual activity of the Enlightenment. In his youth in rural Pennsylvania he had demonstrated a gift for mathematics and great mechanical ability, and earned his living by surveying and clock-making. His construction in 1767 of an "orrery," a movable mechanical model of the solar system, gained him wide recognition and the admiration of Thomas Jefferson in particular. The transit of Venus in 1769 gave astronomers world wide the chance to compare readings and arrive at a value for the solar parallax. Rittenhouse made his own instruments for observing the phenomenon, and the accuracy of his findings when compared with European readings made a good estimate possible. From this pinnacle of scientific achievement he continued to make contributions in mathematics and all branches of physics. He served in the government of Pennsylvania during the war and was named the first director of the Mint in 1792. Upon the death of Benjamin Franklin, the members of the American Philosophical Society elected him president, which post he held until his death five years later.

FURTHER READING

Hindle, B.: *David Rittenhouse* (Princeton: 1964); repr. (New York: Arno Press, 1980).

THOMAS COLE

Robinson, John (*b*. Virginia, 3 February 1704; *d*. King and Queen Co., Va., 11 May 1766). Politician. After entering the Virginia House of Burgesses in 1727, he became Treasurer of the Colony and Speaker of the House in 1738, positions he held until his death despite Board of Trade instructions to separate the offices. Challenging Virginia's Lieutenant Governor Robert Dinwiddie in 1754 during the Pistole Fee controversy, he paid Peyton Randolph for lobbying in London against a fee on land patents instituted by the governor. Robinson was challenged himself after 1758 by Richard Henry Lee, but deflected charges of corruption in the treasury until his unexpected death in 1766, when investigations revealed a shortfall of as much as £100,000. Robinson had lent expired currency to members of the colony's most prominent families. In the scandal's aftermath, the offices of Speaker and Treasurer were separated as Virginians began to question their own virtue. The whole affair underscored for the next decade's revolutionary leaders their belief that concentrated power led to corruption.

The son of Councilor John Robinson and a nephew of the Bishop of London John Robinson, he was educated at the College of William and Mary. Robinson's third wife Susanna was the daughter of Colonel John Chiswell, whose murder of a Scottish merchant contributed to the uproar of 1766.

FURTHER READING

Ernst, J. A.: "The Robinson scandal redivivus: money, debts, and politics in revolutionary Virginia," *Virginia Magazine of History and Biography*, 77 (1967), 146–73.
Greene, J. P.: *The Quest for Power* (Chapel Hill: Institute of Early American History and Culture, 1963).
Kennedy, J. P. (ed.): *The Journal of the House of Burgesses of Virginia, 1766–69* (Richmond, Va.: Colonial Press, E. Waddey, 1906).

MARY GWALTNEY VAZ

Rochambeau. *See* VIMEUR, JEAN-BAPTISTE-DONATIEN DE.

Ross, Betsy [Elizabeth Griscom] (*b*. Philadelphia, 1 January 1752; *d*. Philadelphia, 30 January 1836). Seamstress. She was one of the best-known women of the revolutionary era, but her enduring fame rests more on legend than on established historical fact. She worked as a seamstress and in the upholstery business established by her husband John, whom she married in 1773. Legend has it that she was approached by George Washington in 1776 and asked to produce a flag that would symbolize the patriot cause. Accordingly, or so the story goes, she devised the stars and stripes motif. Although she was employed by the Continental Congress to make flags and colors of various kinds, there is no evidence that Ross had a hand in either the design or the manufacture of the American flag.

FURTHER READING

Thompson, Roy: *Betsy Ross: Last of Philadelphia's Free Quakers* (Fort Washington, Pa.: Bicentennial Press, 1972).

BETTY WOOD

Rush, Benjamin (*b*. Byberry, Pa., 24 December 1745; *d*. Philadelphia, 19 April 1813). Physician. America's first professor of chemistry, at the College of Philadelphia, and a member of the American Philosophical Society, Rush wrote many articles on colonial affairs and the abolition of slavery. He suggested the title to Paine's *Common Sense*, and arranged for its first printing. A strong spokesman for independence, he was elected to Congress and signed the Declaration of Independence. He served on medical committees, and chaired the committee on intelligence. His opposition to Pennsylvania's constitution ended his legislative career. As surgeon-general (1777) and then physician-general of the Continental Army he tended the wounded at many battles. Impugning the abilities of Washington and others, Rush associated with the Conway Cabal and was forced to resign. After returning to private practice and the college, Rush engaged in educational and other reforms, while continuing to squabble over medical, military, and political affairs. He joined the fight for a new federal constitution, making sure Franklin was sent as a delegate for Pennsylvania and writing many pieces for the press. As a member of the state ratifying convention, he led the movement for adoption of the Constitution. He then pushed for a new state constitution. Rush became a renowned teacher to a whole generation of American doctors. His standard method of treatment, which relied heavily on bleeding, aroused intense controversy; he relentlessly pursued the search for a single-cause explanation of disease, and displayed notable courage during the Philadelphia yellow fever epidemic of 1793. He was named by John Adams as Treasurer of the Mint, a post he held from 1797 to 1813.

For illustration, *see* figure 49, p. 596.

FURTHER READING

Hawke, D.F.: *Benjamin Rush: Revolutionary Gadfly* (Indianapolis: Bobbs-Merrill, 1971).

GRANT E. MABIE

Rutledge, Edward (*b.* Christ Church Parish, SC, 23 October 1749; *d.* 23 January 1800). Lawyer and Governor of South Carolina. As a member of South Carolina's delegation to the First Continental Congress, Rutledge worked for methods to achieve redress for colonial grievances that would not preclude reconciliation with Great Britain. By the Second Continental Congress he became convinced that independence was necessary, and helped persuade other members of the delegation to yield to its declaration. Serving until 1777, he was active on various committees, including those for defense and claims and the first Board of War (1776).

Concurrently with his work in Congress, Rutledge served in the First (1775) and Second (1775–6) Provincial Congresses and the Second Council of Safety (1775), and then represented Charles Town (St. Philip and St. Michael) in the First (1776), Second (1776–8), and Third (1779–80) General Assemblies. After the Revolution he sat for Charleston in the House from 1782 to 1795 and in the Senate from 1796 to 1799. Known for his efficiency, Rutledge accomplished much of his program within the committee structure. His abilities (in 1792 he was chairman of 19 committees) caught President Washington's eye, who in 1794 offered him an associate judgeship on the Supreme Court, but Rutledge declined. The Rutledge–Pinckney political alliance (Edward and his brother John Rutledge, Charles Pinckney and Rutledge's law partner Charles Cotesworth Pinckney) effectively managed South Carolina politics for a decade, including the successful ratification of the Federal Constitution. Rutledge was serving as the state's governor (1798–1800) when he collapsed and died.

FURTHER READING

Edgar, Walter B., and Bailey, N. Louise (eds.): *Biographical Directory of the South Carolina House of Representatives*, Vol. 2: *The Commons House of Assembly, 1692–1775* (Columbia: University of South Carolina Press, 1974).

REBECCA STARR

Rutledge, John (*b.* Charles Town, September 1739; *d.* 18 July 1800). Lawyer and jurist, and President and Governor of South Carolina. Rutledge's chief contribution to the

Revolution came through his legal skill in drafting its critical documents. He entered the colonial rights struggle with an indictment of Governor Thomas Boone, written when he was chairman of the South Carolina Commons House committee on elections and privileges (1762) during the Christopher Gadsden election controversy. A delegate to the Stamp Act Congress (1765), Rutledge was chairman of the committee on detail that drafted Congress's petition to Parliament. As a member of the First and Second Continental Congresses, and also of the Council of Safety, South Carolina's executive body, he worked for reconciliation with Great Britain, helping to write South Carolina's temporary constitution of 1776 in those terms, and accepting the office of president under its formula. He vetoed the radically revised constitution of 1778, and then resigned in protest. Despite his disapproval, he accepted the legislature's election to the governor's chair in 1779, which compensated him with broad powers to execute the office. As a delegate to the Constitutional Convention at Philadelphia, he worked for a document that would apportion representation on the basis of wealth and protect domestic slavery. Although he did not achieve all of his goals, his chairmanship of the committee on detail permitted some drafting latitude, and, as a delegate to the state ratification convention (1788), he worked for its adoption.

Rutledge was appointed an Associate Justice to the United States Supreme Court in 1789, an office he resigned to become South Carolina's first Chief Justice (1791). On 1 July 1795 President George Washington appointed him Chief Justice of the United States Supreme Court, but the Senate refused confirmation after his impolitic attack on the Jay Treaty.

His state service included continuous service in the ten royal assemblies (1761–75), two Provincial Congresses (1775–6), and eight general assemblies (1776–90) that formed South Carolina's unbroken legislative government between 1761 and 1790.

FURTHER READING

Edgar, Walter B., and Bailey, N. Louise (eds.): *Biographical Directory of the South Carolina House of Representatives*, Vol. 2: *The Commons House of Assembly, 1692–1775* (Columbia: University of South Carolina Press, 1977).

REBECCA STARR

St. Clair, Arthur (*b. ?* Thurso, Scotland, 23 March 1736; *d.* Westmoreland Co., Pa., 31 August 1818). General. Little is known about him until he purchased, on 13 May 1757, a commission in the Royal Americans and served in Canada. In 1760 he married the niece of Governor James Bowdoin, Phoebe Bayard, and settled in the Ligonier Valley of Pennsylvania sometime after his military retirement in 1762.

The Revolutionary War catapulted St. Clair to greater prominence. He began as a colonel in the Pennsylvania militia, but, in January 1776 Congress appointed him a colonel in the Continental Army. By February 1777 he had earned the rank of major general for his service in the Northern Department and at Trenton and Princeton. Then, as commander on Lake Champlain, he bore the responsibility and stigma of surrendering Ticonderoga in July 1777. His reputation suffered despite exoneration by a military court. He subsequently commanded troops of the Pennsylvania Line, presided over West Point, and served as an aide to George Washington.

St. Clair suffered another controversial loss in the early national period. On 4 November 1791 a united Indian force routed his military expedition along the upper Wabash River. From 1787 to 1802 St. Clair served as governor of the Northwest Territory.

FURTHER READING

Smith, William H.: *The Life and Public Services of Arthur St. Clair* (1882); repr. (New York: Da Capo Press, 1971).

J. MARK THOMPSON

Schuyler, Philip John (*b.* Albany, NY, 10 November 1733; *d.* Albany, 18 November 1804). General. Schuyler was born into one of New York's oldest and most prominent Dutch families and tied to others by his marriage to Catherine van Rennselaer. After receiving an extensive classical education he became active in colonial politics. During the Seven Years' War he demonstrated his abilities as a logistician and administrator, skills that served him well in the Revolutionary War. On 19 June 1775 Congress appointed Schuyler a major general because of his political influence and military experience.

As commander of the Northern Department, Schuyler usually found himself involved in controversy. Critics, primarily New Englanders, complained of his arrogance, blamed him for the failure of the Canada expedition (1775), and hoped to replace him with Horatio Gates, who in fact superseded Schuyler as commander of the Northern Army after the loss of Ticonderoga in 1777. Despite his being cleared of responsibility, Schuyler's reputation suffered. Even so, he contributed significantly to Benedict Arnold's strategic victory at Valcour Island (1776), to General John Burgoyne's early setbacks in the 1777 campaign, and to the material support of the American Army throughout the war.

On 19 April 1779 Schuyler retired from the army but remained active in the war effort, Indian affairs, and the political arena. The following year his daughter Elizabeth married Alexander Hamilton.

FURTHER READING

Gerlach, Don R.: *Proud Patriot: Philip Schuyler and the War of Independence, 1775–1783* (Syracuse, NY: Syracuse University Press, 1987).

J. MARK THOMPSON

Seabury, Samuel (*b*. Groton, Conn., 30 November 1729; *d*. New London, Conn., 25 February 1796). Anglican clergyman, prominent loyalist pamphleteer, and first bishop of the Protestant Episcopal Church. Seabury was the son of a Congregational clergyman who converted to Anglicanism a year after the boy's birth. He studied at Yale College, where he earned a BA, and at the University of Edinburgh, where he qualified in medicine, and was ordained to the Anglican priesthood in 1753. He served as a priest and practiced medicine in New Jersey and New York, and advocated the creation of an American episcopacy. Together with other Anglican clergymen he helped write a series of loyalist essays called "A Whip for the American Whig" in 1768 and 1769. He acquired his major political fame during the final crisis, writing pro-British statements as "A. W. Farmer." These essays provoked the young Alexander Hamilton to produce his first political writing. The Revolutionaries confined Seabury briefly at the end of 1775, and he joined the British forces after the invasion of New York City the following summer. He received an honorary doctorate from Oxford University in 1777, was elected Bishop of Connecticut in 1783, and was consecrated the following year in Scotland. Thereafter he avoided all political involvement.

FURTHER READING

Bridenbaugh, Carl: *Mitre and Sceptre: Transatlantic Faiths, Ideas, Personalities and Politics, 1689–1775* (New York: Oxford University Press, 1962).
Woolverton, John Frederick: *Colonial Anglicanism in North America* (Detroit: Wayne State University Press, 1984).

EDWARD COUNTRYMAN

Sears, Isaac (*b*. West Brewer, Mass., 1 July 1730; *d*. Canton, China, 28 October 1786). Sailor and revolutionary mob leader. As a child, Sears moved with his family to Norwich, Connecticut, where he trained as a sailor. At the age of 22 he commanded a sloop trading between New York and Canada. He was a privateer during the Seven Years' War, and acquired a reputation for bravery that made him a leader of sailors and working men on the New York waterfront. During the Anglo-American crisis Sears headed nearly every incidence of mob violence in New York City, and he became widely hailed as "King

Sears." He served on many of the colony's patriotic committees and in the first Provincial Congress. He was a conspicuous leader of the New York Sons of Liberty, who turned back British tea in 1774, and a member of the Committee of Fifty-one. After the news of the battles at Lexington and Concord reached New York, Sears and his followers were largely in control of New York City, routing loyalists and seizing arms from the Customs House. During the years 1777–83, when the British occupied New York, Sears moved to Boston and engaged in privateering for the patriot cause. After the peace he returned to New York and won election to the state assembly. On a trip to Canton in 1786 he was struck with disease and died.

FURTHER READING

Teeter, Dwight L.: "King Sears, the mob and freedom of the press in New York, 1765–1776," *Journalism Quarterly*, 45 (1964, 539–44.

ELIZABETH P. MCCAUGHEY

Secondat, Charles-Louis de [Baron de la Brède et de Montesquieu] (*b*. Château La Brède, nr Bordeaux, 18 January 1689; *d*. Paris, 10 February 1755). Philosopher and jurist. Montesquieu's philosophical works were widely read in America, and the *Spirit of the Laws*, first translated into English in 1750, expressed ideas that applied to the post-independence task of agreeing upon a form of government. He deduced principles from studying the variety of laws in human society. He argued that a republican government could not maintain authority over a large territory, which point confirmed the Anti-Federalists in their belief that power was safest vested in the individual states. Their opponents turned to his observations of complex, extended polities (Montesquieu had chosen England as his example). A well-designed system of government could ensure the liberties of the people by balancing the interests of competing groups. Montesquieu's greatest legacy to American government lay in specifying the nature of such a design. The

framers of the Constitution endeavored to put into practice his recommendations on the separation of powers (*see* Chapter 73, §2). Montesquieu believed that a division of government into independent legislative, executive, and judicial branches would provide against the tyranny of one faction over the others or or one segment of society over the others.

For illustration, *see* figure 55, p. 689.

FURTHER READING

Spurlin, P. M.: *Montesquieu in America, 1760–1801* (Baton Rouge: Louisiana State University Press, 1940).

THOMAS COLE

Sedgwick, Theodore (*b*. West Hartford, Conn., 9 May 1746; *d*. Boston, 24 January 1813). Statesman, jurist, and early proponent of abolition. The son of a storekeeper, Sedgwick attended but was expelled from Yale, although he was later granted a degree in 1772. He studied law and was admitted to the bar in 1766. Being cautious and of a conservative nature he opposed Independence as late as May 1776. During that year he became the military secretary to General John Thomas. He served in the Massachusetts Assembly throughout the 1780s and was a member of the Continental Congress from 1785 to 1788. He was a delegate to the Massachusetts ratifying convention and supported the new Constitution. A Federalist, Sedwick was a Massachusetts congressman from 1789 until 1796, a United States Senator for three years between 1796 and 1799, and ended his legislative career as Speaker of the House from 1799 to 1801. The following year he became a Massachusetts supreme court justice. He remained in that office until his death.

FURTHER READING

Welch, Richard E.: *Theodore Sedgwick, Federalist: a Political Portrait* (Middletown, Conn.: Wesleyan University Press, 1965).

KURT W. NAGEL

Shelburne. *See* PETTY, WILLIAM.

Sherman, Roger (*b.* Newton, Mass., 19 April 1721; *d.* New Haven, Conn., 23 July 1793). Lawyer and statesman. The son of a farmer and shoemaker, Sherman had a brief elementary education. In 1745 he became county surveyor and in 1754 he was admitted to the bar. He was both elected to the legislature and made a justice of the peace in 1755. Moderately opposed to the British regulations of the 1760s, Sherman served as the head of the New Haven committee of correspondence. He was elected to the Connecticut council in 1766. In that same year he was elected to the superior court, where he served between 1766 and 1767 and between 1773 and 1788. Sherman was a delegate to the Continental Congress for most of the period from 1774 to 1784, and was a member of the committee which drafted the Declaration of Independence. At the Constitutional Convention of 1787 he presented the Connecticut compromise, which proposed a legislature of two houses, one based upon proportional representation, the other upon equal representation among the states. He fought for ratification of the Constitution and served as a Congressman from 1789 to 1791 and as a Senator from 1791 to his death.

FURTHER READING

Collier, Christopher: *Roger Sherman's Connecticut, Yankee Politics and the American Revolution* (Middletown, Conn.: Wesleyan University Press, 1971).

KURT W. NAGEL

Smith, Adam (*b.* Kirkcaldy, Scotland, 5 June 1723; *d.* Edinburgh, 17 July 1790). Economist and philosopher. Smith's great work, *An Inquiry into the Nature and Causes of the Wealth of Nations* (1776) spoke to American readers both as a work of political economy and as an effort in philosophical history. On the former score, Smith devoted a chapter to the growth of colonies in which he placed modern colonization in a historical context, analyzed the rapid improvement of the British plantations, and warned against regulating and restricting their trade, which measures colonists had already found grounds to oppose on principle. In addition, Smith's model of the progress of human societies allowed Americans to view their country as something other than a bastion of civic virtue that they were obliged to preserve. He believed that peoples naturally progressed from one mode of subsistence to another, and gradually acquired a higher standard of living and a more elaborate culture as they advanced. No single wisdom guided this process, but rather the momentum of many individual acts drove the whole society inevitably towards betterment. Faith in progress creates a different national character from that based on fear of corruption, and Smith helped Americans re-examine their ideas after independence.

FURTHER READING

Winch, D.: *Adam Smith's Politics: an Essay in Historiographic Revision* (Cambridge and New York: Cambridge University Press, 1978).

THOMAS COLE

Smith, Melancton (*b.* Jamaica, NY, 7 May 1744; *d.* New York, 29 July 1798). Merchant and politician. Smith began his career as a storekeeper in Dutchess County. After rising to the rank of major in the state's militia during the Revolution, serving on a state commission to detect loyalist activities, and acting as high sheriff of Dutchess County, he moved to New York City in 1785 to establish a lucrative mercantile business and law practice and serve in the Continental Congress (1785–8). In *An Address to the People of the State of New-York*, signed "A Plebeian," which appeared in the spring of 1788, he told New Yorkers they had "just cause to distrust" the Federalists who were urging "the adoption of a bad constitution, under the delusive expectation" that a Bill of Rights would be added later. Smith pointed to history, which afforded "no examples of persons once possessed of power, resigning it willingly." At the

New York State ratifying convention, which convened in Poughkeepsie in June 1788, Smith articulated the most important Anti-Federalist grievances, including the notion that the proposed House of Representatives was too small to provide a "true picture of the people." Only a more numerous body would make it possible to elect men of the middling sort, who would have an "acquaintance with the common concerns and occupations of the people." Although Smith was one of the first Anti-Federalists to speak out for unconditional ratification once news reached Poughkeepsie that the requisite nine states had already ratified, he participated in Governor George Clinton's unsuccessful effort the following year to bring about a second constitutional convention.

FURTHER READING

DePauw, Linda Grant: *The Eleventh Pillar: New York State and the Federal Constitution* (Ithaca, NY: Cornell University Press, 1966).
Kaminski, John P. (ed.): "New York: the reluctant pillar," *The Reluctant Pillar: New York and the Adoption of the Federal Constitution*, ed. Stephen Schechter (Troy, NY: Russell Sage College, 1985), 55–111.

ELIZABETH P. MCCAUGHEY

Smith, William (*b.* nr Aberdeen, 7 September 1727; *d.* Philadelphia, 14 May 1803). Provost of the College of Philadelphia. Smith emigrated from Scotland to America in 1751. He expanded the Academy of Philadelphia into a college, and became its provost in 1755. He was a leading supporter of proprietary interests and favored the creation of an American bishopric, perhaps hoping to get the job. Such views, and an unpopular call for limited suffrage and liberties for Germans, led to a conviction for sedition and libel against the assembly, though the Privy Council overturned the decision. Smith served as rector of Trinity Church in Oxford, Pennsylvania, from 1766 to 1777, and was a member of the American Philosophical Society. He opposed the Stamp Act, sat on the Committee of Correspondence (1774), and

preached a patriotic sermon in 1775 widely reprinted on both sides of the Atlantic. But he opposed independence, writing a strong attack on Paine's *Common Sense*. In eight letters signed "Cato" (1776), Smith called for reason and conciliation, and spoke against Pennsylvania Independents and their drive for political revolution through a new state constitution. The letters drew heated responses, and Smith was apprehended as General Howe advanced on the city. His charter for the college was abolished, and he migrated to Maryland. In 1782 he established Washington College, and sat as its president. He regained the provostship at Philadelphia in 1789, but was dismissed again when the college merged with the university of the state. He remained a celebrated speaker, and delivered an oration on the death of Franklin.

FURTHER READING

Gegenheimer, A. F.:*William Smith: Educator and Churchman, 1727–1803* (Philadelphia: University of Pennsylvania Press, 1943).

GRANT E. MABIE

Smith, William(, Jr.) (*b.* New York, 25 June 1728; *d.* Quebec, 3 December 1795). Lawyer, politician, and historian. Smith graduated from Yale College in 1745 and studied law in his father's office along with William Livingston, with whom he later formed a partnership. At the request of the New York Assembly, Smith and Livingston compiled and published the first digest of the colony's statutes in 1752. Livingston and Smith also joined with John Morin Scott as a literary Triumvirate in 1752 to write and publish the weekly *Independent Reflector*, which assailed the plans to establish King's College with an Anglican-dominated board of trustees and warned of the pernicious dangers of an American episcopacy. Smith made his reputation as a historian when he published *The History of the Province of New York, from the First Discovery of the Year 1732* (London, 1757). In 1763 he began his career as a Crown office-holder when he became Chief Justice of the colony, and in 1767 he succeeded his father as a member of the Governor's Council. Smith believed that no reconciliation between Great Britain and the American colonies was possible within the existing British constitutional system, and in his "Thoughts upon the Dispute between Great Britain and her Colonies" (1765–7) he looked towards the establishment of an American Parliament, chosen by the colonies and invested with the power of taxation in order to meet the Crown's requests for an American revenue. Smith believed that both the Americans and the British had failed to pursue reconciliation, and in 1777 he refused to take an oath of loyalty to the newly independent state of New York. Smith fled New York City with the British forces in 1783 and remained in England until 1786, when he sailed to Canada to serve as Chief Justice of Quebec.

FURTHER READING

Calhoon, Robert M. (ed.): "William Smith Jr.'s alternative to the American Revolution," *William and Mary Quarterly*, 22 (1965), 105–18.
Upton, L. S. F.: *The Loyal Whig: William Smith of New York and Quebec* (Toronto: University of Toronto Press, 1969).

ELIZABETH P. MCCAUGHEY

Steuben, Friedrich Wilhelm Ludolf Gerhard Augustin [Baron von] (*b*. Magdeburg, Prussia, 17 September 1730; *d*. nr Remsen, NY, 28 November 1794). Prussian general. Steuben was born in the Prussian fortress where his father was an officer of engineers. At the age of 17 he too joined the Prussian Army and served as an infantry officer, a corps staff officer, and an aide to Frederick the Great. In 1764, after leaving the military for political reasons, Steuben became chamberlain of a petty German court. The American Revolution possibly rescued him from debt and obscurity.

While in Paris in 1777 Steuben tendered his services to Benjamin Franklin, who then sent the Prussian veteran – possessed of inflated credentials – to America. On 14 January 1778 Congress accepted Steuben's offer to serve as a volunteer without rank and ordered him to Valley Forge. In May he became inspector general of the Continental Army with the rank of major general. Steuben trained first a "model company" and then the entire army according to a unique system of drill based on European practices but modified to American circumstances. On 29 March 1779 Congress authorized publication of Steuben's *Regulations for the Order and Discipline of the Troops of the United States*, commonly known as the Blue Book. Although Steuben served the patriot cause in various capacities, his most important contribution to American victory was to give the army a much greater degree of professionalism.

After retiring in 1784 Steuben spent his last years in New York.

FURTHER READING

Palmer, John M.: *General von Steuben* (1937); repr. (Port Washington: Kennikat Press, 1966).

J. MARK THOMPSON

Stevens, John (*b*. New York, 1749; *d*. Hoboken, NJ, 6 March 1838). Engineer and inventor. He began a career in New Jersey politics, married, and built an estate on the west bank of the Hudson before becoming captivated by the idea of steam-powered transportation. Schooling himself at the age of 40, he was soon able to draw up designs for improved boilers and engines. He hoped to establish a steamboat ferry service between New York and New Jersey but had built only a working prototype when Robert Fulton's steamboat *Clermont* completed its epoch-making round-trip from New York to Albany in 1807. Stevens and his partners engaged in fruitless legal battles with Fulton, to whom the New York legislature had granted a monopoly for the use of the Hudson River. Stevens had the satisfaction, however, of seeing his own boat ply between Philadelphia and Trenton as part of a regular service. Thereafter he turned his attention to steam-powered travel over land by rail, and persuaded both the New Jersey and Pennsylvania legislatures to authorize railroad companies, one of which finished a line from Philadelphia to Columbia, Pennsylania. An experimental locomotive that ran over a circular track on his Hoboken estate was the first such vehicle built in America.

FURTHER READING

Gregg, D.: "John Stevens, general entrepreneur, 1749–1838," *Men in Business: Essays on the History of Entrepreneurship*, ed. W. Miller (Cambridge, Mass.: Harvard University Press, 1952), 120–52.
Turnbull, A. D.: *John Stevens: an American Record* (New York: Century, 1928).

THOMAS COLE

Stiles, Ezra (*b.* North Haven, Conn., 15 December 1727; *d.* New Haven, Conn., 12 May 1795). Congregationalist minister, historian, and President of Yale University. A minister and educator of unbridled intellectual curiosity, Stiles was a traditional New England Calvinist who grew to embrace distinctly non-traditional views of both church and society. While he sympathized with the waning faction that clung to the Puritan church–state establishment, he was sensitive to and supported the awakening religious sentiment engendered by the Great Awakening. As a result, he adopted an ecumenism that placed him above – or at least apart from – his squabbling ecclesiastical contemporaries. That ecumenism led him not only to advocate the separation of church and state but to embrace other republican principles as well.

After some hesitation early on, Stiles wholeheartedly supported the Revolution, arguing that popular elections and a wide franchise, as well as separation of church and state, would lead the new nation to true freedom. As Yale's seventh president (1778–95), he managed to lead the college successfully through the war years, and by 1784 had increased enrollment to record numbers.

FURTHER READING

Morgan, Edmund S.: *The Gentle Puritan: a Life of Ezra Stiles, 1727–1795* (New Haven, CT: Yale University Press, 1962).

STEPHEN A. YOUNG

Stockton, Annis Boudinot (*b.* Darby, Pa., 1736; *d.* 1801). Wife, home-maker, and poet. She was both the wife and the mother-in-law of signers of the Declaration of Independence. In 1755 she married Richard Stockton, a lawyer and sometime Chief Justice of New Jersey. Their daughter Julia married Benjamin Rush. In 1776 Richard Stockton was captured by the British and swore an oath agreeing to take no further part in the War for Independence. Annis Boudinot Stockton's main contribution to the patriot war effort was as a poet, with such titles as "Addresses to General Washington in the Year 1777 after the Battles of Trenton and Princeton" and "The Vision: an Ode inscribed to General Washington" (1789).

FURTHER READING

Butterfield, L. H.: "Annis and the General: Mrs. Stockton's Poetic Eulogies of George Washington," *Princeton University Library Chronicle*, 9 (November 1945), 19–29.

BETTY WOOD

Stuart, John (*b.* Inverness, Scotland, 25 September 1718; *d.* Pensacola, Fl., 21 March 1779). British Indian Superintendent for the Southern Department. Stuart was one of numerous Scots who migrated to South Carolina; he failed as a merchant, but ultimately gained prosperity as a British colonial official. By 1756 he was captain of a provincial company defending Fort Loudoun in the Cherokee country. His gift for Indian negotiations saved his life after the fall of the fort; six years later it won him appointment as British Indian Superintendent for the Southern Department. Unlike the Northern Superintendent, Stuart did not live among the Indians, but from his Charles Town mansion he corresponded with deputies in the Cherokee, Creek, Choctaw, and Chickasaw nations and with other civil and military authorities. From time to time he traveled to frontier assemblies at Augusta or Mobile to dispense the King's gifts and play the forest diplomat. Forced to flee revolutionary South Carolina in 1775, he took refuge first at St. Augustine. After moving to Pensacola he attempted to carry on, but astronomical wartime costs, competition from American representatives, tribal factionalism, failure of warriors to aid British expeditions, conflicts with military officers and royal governors, and communication difficulties rendered him ineffective. Only death saved him the embarrassment of Germain's division and reduction of the Indian department.

FURTHER READING

Alden, John R.: *John Stuart and the Southern Colonial Frontier: a Study of Indian Relations, War, Trade, and Land Problems in the Southern Wilderness, 1754–75* (1944); repr. (Ann Arbor: University of Michigan Press, 1944; New York: Gordian Press, 1966).
O'Donnell, James H., III: *Southern Indians in the American Revolution* (Knoxville: University of Tennessee Press, 1973).

JAMES H. O'DONNELL III

Sullivan, John (*b.* Somersworth, NH, 17 February 1740; *d.* Durham, NH, 23 January 1795). General. After spending his early years in Maine he returned to New Hampshire, practiced law, and actively supported the patriot cause in the American Revolution. In June 1775 Congress commissioned this former militia officer one Continental Army's original brigadier generals. The following summer it promoted him to major general.

Sullivan commanded troops in many of the major revolutionary battles and campaigns. He performed adequately, if not admirably, at Trenton, Princeton, and Newport as well as during the expedition against the Iroquois in 1779. Nevertheless, he was the object of unrelenting criticism on account of his fiery temper, quarrelsome nature, and modest military talent. Because of his failures at Three Rivers, Staten Island, Brandywine, and Germantown, and because of his intemperate outbursts, Sullivan's opponents repeatedly called for his dismissal. When he tendered his resignation in November 1779, claiming ill-health, Congress accepted it.

After the war Sullivan remained active in New Hampshire politics, serving as the state's governor from 1785 to 1790. His brother James was a prominent Massachusetts legislator and jurist and his son George became a New Hampshire congressman.

FURTHER READING

Whittemore, Charles P.: *A General of the Revolution: John Sullivan of New Hampshire* (New York: Columbia University Press, 1961).

J. MARK THOMPSON

Sumter, Thomas (*b.* nr Charlottesville, Va., 14 July 1734; *d.* South Mount Plantation, nr Stateburg, SC, 1 June 1832). General. He served in the Virginia militia (1756—62), and was a captain of the South Carolina Rangers (1775–6), Commandant of the 6th South Carolina Continental Regiment (1776–8), and Brigadier General of the South Carolina militia (1780–2). He was also a delegate to the First and Second South Carolina Provincial congresses (1775 6) and served in the South Carolina legislature (1782–9), as a member of the United States Congress (1789–93, 1797–1801), and as a United States Senator (1801–10). Sumter was the most prominent figure to refuse to submit to British occupation in May 1780 and was elected general by those who had opened guerrilla resistance. Both winning and losing early battles, he revealed a talent for keeping men in the field; in October Governor John Rutledge named him Brigadier General in command of all state militiamen. He was almost destroyed by Banastre Tarleton at Fishing Creek (18 August 1780), but returned the favor at Blackstocks (20 November 1780), where he was badly wounded. Reluctant to subordinate himself to a Continental Army commander, he eventually shared military leadership of the revolt with two other partisan leaders, Francis Marion and Andrew Pickens. Because of his pugnacity Sumter was known as the "Gamecock"; he gained notoriety for "Sumter's Law," which authorized raising ten-month regulars and paying them with slaves and other booty.

FURTHER READING

Bass, Robert D.: *Gamecock: the Life and Campaigns of General Thomas Sumter* (New York: Holt, Rinehart, and Winston, 1961).
Ferguson, Clyde R.: "Carolina and Georgia patriot and loyalist militia in action, 1778–83," *The Southern Experience in the American Revolution*, ed. Jeffrey Crow and Larry Tise (Chapel Hill: University of North Carolina Press, 1978), 174–99.
Gregorie, Anne K.: *Thomas Sumter* (Columbia, SC: R. L. Bryan, 1931).

CLYDE R. FERGUSON

Tarleton, Sir Banastre (*b.* Liverpool, 21 August 1754; *d.* Leintwardine, Salop., 25 January 1833). British soldier. After entering the army in 1775 he volunteered for America and served actively under Clinton and Howe, rising to lieutenant colonel, commander of the British Legion, by 1779. Fame (or infamy) reached him as the leader of the British cavalry in the Charles Town expedition of 1780 and of Cornwallis's light troops in the southern campaign thereafter. Although a dashing officer who often defeated and sometimes routed his foes, Tarleton also acquired the reputation of a ruthless killer who refused quarter to beaten opponents. He led the British forces at the battle of Cowpens in January 1781 and lost decisively to Daniel Morgan. That defeat cost Cornwallis more than 800 men killed, wounded or captured, and nearly ruined his North Carolina strategy. Tarleton remained with Cornwallis during the Virginia campaign. He was paroled to England in 1782. Although he continued to serve in the regular army and reached the rank of general, Tarleton never held an important combat command after the Revolution.

FURTHER READING

Bass, Robert D.: *The Green Dragoon* (New York: Holt, 1957).
Higgins, W. Robert (ed.): *The Revolutionary War in the South: Power, Conflict, and Leadership* (Durham, NC: Duke University Press, 1979).

FRANKLIN B. WICKWIRE

Thomson, Charles (*b.* Maghera, Co. Derry, 29 November 1729; *d.* Lower Merion, Montgomery Co., Pa., 16 August 1824). Merchant and politician. Thomson arrived in America at the age of ten. A schoolmaster and Latin teacher, he acted as secretary in various Indian treaties in the 1750s, and was respected by all parties. He became a prominent (if not particularly successful) merchant and manufacturer, and was a leader of Philadelphia's Sons of Liberty. His efforts in the non-importation movement put him at the forefront of the city's factions of merchants, mechanics, and tradesmen in 1770. Non-importation was a particularly divisive issue for merchants, and Thomson clearly sided with radicals against Tory merchants. In 1774 he was elected to the Committee of Correspondence. Called "the Sam Adams of Philadelphia," his selection in the early days of the First Continental Congress as secretary to that body was a major victory for the radicals. He held the post throughout the existence of the Continental Congress, making his name highly recognized on both sides of the Atlantic. Joining Benjamin Rush and others, he pushed for a new state constitution. Thomson was given the honor of notifying Washington of his election to the presidency. Piqued by the realization that he was to have no part in the inaugural or in the new Congress, he resigned in July 1789. Although he was asked to write the inside story of the Continental Congress, Thomson steadfastly refused to divulge any of its secrets. In his later years he published several religious translations.

FURTHER READING

Zimmerman, J. J.: "Charles Thomson, 'The Sam Adams of Philadelphia'," *Mississippi Valley Historical Review*, 45 (1958), 464–77.

GRANT E. MABIE

Townshend, Charles (*b.* 27 August 1725; *d.* London, 4 September 1767). British statesman. He first became familiar with colonial affairs while serving on the Board of Trade (1749–54), and thus early became convinced of the need to free colonial governors from the financial controls exerted by their assemblies. His tenure of various offices between 1754 and 1763 did not involve him in colonial business, and his seven weeks as President of the Board of Trade in 1763 attested only his interest in securing an American revenue from the molasses duties. In 1765 he spoke in Parliament in support of the Stamp Act. In 1766, holding office under Rockingham, he voted for its repeal, and he also helped to shape the Declaratory Act. As Chatham's Chancellor of the Exchequer (1766–7) Townshend pursued what had discernably also been a Rockinghamite policy – the exaction of further revenues from the colonies by way of parliamentary customs duties (*see* Chapter 13). Consistently with his views expressed in 1753, he linked the taxes imposed in his Revenue Act of 1767 with a provision that these be used to provide civil lists for colonial governors. He also initiated the American Board of Customs, intended to improve efficiency in revenue-collection.

FURTHER READING

Namier, Sir Lewis, and Brooke, John: *Charles Townshend* (London: Macmillan; New York: St. Martin's Press, 1964)

IAN R. CHRISTIE

Vergennes. *See* GRAVIER, CHARLES.

Vimeur, Jean-Baptiste-Donatien de [Comte de Rochambeau] (*b.* Vendôme, France, 1 July 1725; *d.* 10 May 1807). French general. He was the commander of the French expeditionary force in the United States from 1780 to 1782. A professional soldier, Rochambau entered the French Army in 1742 and served with distinction in the War of Austrian Succession and the Seven Years' War. Early in 1780 he was promoted to the rank of *lieutenant-général* and given command of a corps of 5,000 men. The expedition sailed from Brest on 2 May and dropped anchor off Newport, Rhode Island, on 11 July. This venture was a risky one, since the Americans had not asked for French troops and might not welcome them; then, too, Rochambeau was subordinate to the far less experienced Washington. The success of the expedition in both diplomatic and military terms was in no small way attributable to Rochambeau's patience, level-headedness, and solid competence; the Yorktown campaign was a notable achievement in military cooperation. Rochambeau played a minor political role in the early phase of the French Revolution, becoming Marshal in 1791. He retired from the army in 1792. He was briefly imprisoned during the Terror.

FURTHER READING

Bonsal, Stephen: *When the French Were Here* (Garden City, NY: Doubleday, Doran and Co., 1945).
Kennett, Lee: *The French Forces in America* (Westport, Conn.: Greenwood Press, 1977).
Whitridge, Arnold: *Rochambeau* (New York: Macmillan, 1965).

LEE KENNETT

Ward, Artemas (*b.* Shrewsbury, Mass., 26 November 1727; *d.* Shrewsbury, 28 October 1800). General. Ward graduated from Harvard College in 1748 and thereafter served at various capacities in provincial and local government. In the Seven Years' War he demonstrated his administrative skill as a colonel of militia. He actively opposed royal authority during the growing rift with Great Britain and, once fighting began, he was named a general and commander-in-chief of Massachusetts forces. During the first months of the conflict he became the *de facto* leader of the army besieging Boston.

Ward did not distinguish himself during the War of Independence. In the organization of the Continental Army Congress passed over him and chose George Washington as its overall commander. However, since Massachusetts supplied the bulk of men and since Ward had been in charge at Boston, he became the highest ranking major general. If not graciously, Ward at least peacefully accepted the arrangement. In April 1776, after the British evacuated Boston, he offered his resignation, but remained at the head of the Eastern Department until 20 March 1777 when William Heath succeeded him.

After his military service Ward remained active in state and federal politics.

FURTHER READING

Martyn, Charles: *The Life of Artemas Ward* (New York: A. Ward, 1921).

J. MARK THOMPSON

Warren, Joseph (*b*. Roxbury, Mass., 11 June 1741; *d*. Charleston, Mass., 17 June 1775). Physician and politician. A leader of the opposition in Massachusetts to British policies towards the colonists, he died a hero's death at Bunker Hill. After graduating from Harvard in 1759 Warren studied medicine and began a private practice. With the passage of the Stamp Act in 1765 he became active in politics, and was soon an associate of Samuel Adams and John Hancock. He was elected a member of the Boston committee of correspondence in 1772. Two years later he presented what became known as the Suffolk Resolves to the Suffolk county convention. The Suffolk Resolves, protesting against the Intolerable Acts, were later adopted and endorsed by the First Continental Congress. It was Warren, a member of the Massachusetts committee of safety, who sent Paul Revere to Lexington and Concord on the night of 18–19 April 1775. With the outbreak of the war Warren was elected president of the Massachusetts Provincial Assembly, and in June 1775 he was named a major general of the provincial militia. Three days later he was

killed fighting the British at Bunker Hill (for illustration, *see* figure 48, p. 585), the first hero to enter the pantheon of the Revolution.

FURTHER READING

Cary, John: *Joseph Warren: Physician, Politician, Patriot* (Urbana: University of Illinois Press, 1961).

KURT W. NAGEL

Warren, Mercy Otis (*b*. Barnstable, Mass., 14 September 1728; *d*. Plymouth, Mass., 19 October 1814). Poet, dramatist, and historian. She discovered her literary calling during the final years of colonial rule. The struggles, as she saw them, of a virtuous people to resist enslavement shaped her political consciousness irrevocably. Her writings from later periods showed the same fervor as had her remonstrations against the British and their tools in colonial government.

Warren was a member, both by birth and by marriage, of leading patriot families. This perspective served her well when she came to compose the *History of the Rise, Progress, and Termination of the American Revolution* (3 vols., 1805), though it also imparted its biases. The enmity that had set in between her brother, James Otis, and Thomas Hutchinson was echoed in all her work. In her historical and political writings she invoked Hutchinson's name as the epitome of tyranny. In her first two dramatic efforts, *The Adulateur* (1773) and *The Group* (1775), he appeared as the despotic governor Rapatio.

Warren retained a tendency towards characterization in polar moral absolutes in her later work. Writing under the pseudonym "A Columbian Patriot" in 1788, she offered "Observations on the new Constitution," in which she invoked all the sacrifices of the late revolution in order to persuade Americans not to entrust their hard-won liberties to the proposed federal government. A mistrust of undefined and potentially abused power underlay her philosophy, together with the belief that maintaining public virtue was the only security against it. Fears that the rising generation was losing its moral compass in a rush to acquire wealth led her to gather together the materials for a history of the revolution. Recording the deeds of the founders might inspire respect for the principles that activated them, and implant the desire to emulate their watchfulness against tyranny in the reader who was ignorant or heedless of their achievements.

Although she adopted an unusually active public role for a woman of her time, Warren did not address questions of women's rights in her published work. In her plays the action is dominated by men and she speaks of liberty generally through masculine metaphors, often as a gift passed on from father to son. It would seem that she believed that men were destined to be the actors in great events, but also that women could influence their husbands, brothers, and fathers to make virtuous choices. Warren played that role herself in her own times, and gave the last word of *The Group* to a "Lady" who foretells the bloodshed to come, as well as the eventual triumph of liberty. Her character's oracular wisdom remains as ironic commentary in contrast to the declarations of male characters of how they will unsheathe their swords for liberty. She must rely on others to insure the outcome of events in which she is so interested.

FURTHER READING

Cohen, L.: "Explaining the Revolution: ideology and ethics in Mercy Otis Warren's historical theory," *William and Mary Quarterly*, 37 (1980), 200–18.

Hutcheson, M. M.: "Mercy Otis Warren, 1728–1814," *William and Mary Quarterly*, 10 (1953), 378–402.

THOMAS COLE

Washington, George (*b.* Westmoreland Co., Va., 22 Feburary 1732; *d.* Fairfax Co., Va., 14 December 1799). Commander-in-Chief of the Continental Army and First President of the United States. Energetic and determined, Washington ultimately succeeded at every major task he undertook. Undeterred by his

FIGURE 74 George Washington in the uniform of a colonel in the Virginia Militia: portrait by Charles Willson Peale (1772)

marginal status in the Virginia planter aristocracy, he sought public and private advancement, boosted by his ties with the influential Fairfax family. He volunteered for important military service in the Seven Years' War, including the Braddock campaign of 1755, where his sterling performance made him something of a colonial hero and earned him the notice of George II. Washington later became commander of the colony's frontier defenses. This difficult, often frustrating assignment helped prepare him for his crucial role in the War of Independence. So, too, did his years after 1758 as the manager of a large plantation and as a member of the provincial legislature.

Highly critical of Britain's post-1763 imperial policies, Washington advocated vigorous resistance as a member of the Continental Congress, which, after Lexington and Concord, appointed him Commander-in-Chief of the Continental Army. During the years 1775–8 his immediate forces, usually poorly supplied, faced the brunt of Britain's effort to subdue the rebellion: first at the siege of Boston, later at New York City (1776), and afterwards in New Jersey and Pennsylvania. Although they lost battles at Long Island, Brandywine, and Germantown, his troops usually fought reasonably well and inflicted heavy casualties; and his brilliant, albeit small, strokes at Trenton and Princeton in the winter of 1776–7 stoked American morale at the Revolution's low point. The summer of 1778, following the Valley Forge winter, found Washington's army growing in numbers and in professionalism, which was reflected in its strong showing against the British at Monmouth, New Jersey.

With the war now a stalemate in the North, Washington remained encamped near the enemy in New York until French offers of cooperation led him to campaign in the South. Racing to Virginia, he besieged the main British Army in that region and dug in on the Yorktown peninsula, while the French Admiral François de Grasse cut off the British escape route. After Lord Cornwallis's surrender on 19 October 1781, Washington struggled to hold his army together until he resigned his commission in 1783, following the treaty of peace.

A nationalist and an advocate of a stronger American union, Washington presided over the Constitutional Convention of 1787 and two years later accepted the presidency, serving two terms which saw him work to make the new American federalism successful and keep the nation out of the European wars of the French Revolution. Thereafter he retired to his estate, Mount Vernon.

Washington was an ideal leader of a democratic revolution. Persistent and dogged, he never knew when he was beaten. If he prudently sheltered his resources, he was hardly a Fabius. Hot-headed and impatient in his youth, he learned the virtue of patience. He was unfailingly deferential to Congress and respectful of state and local authority. He set invaluable precedents for the future of civil–military relations in America, to say nothing of similar precedents for the executive branch after 1789. Unlike countless revolutionaries

since his day, he never saw himself as the Revolution. Instead, because of his conduct and his character, he became the most meaningful symbol of the Revolution.

FURTHER READING

Cunliffe, Marcus: *George Washington: Man and Monument* (Boston: Little, Brown, 1958).

Freeman, Douglas S.: *George Washington: a Biography*, 7 vols. (New York: Charles Scribner's Sons, 1948–1957).

Higginbotham, Don: *George Washington and the American Military Tradition* (Athens, Ga.: University of Georgia Press, 1985).

DON HIGGINBOTHAM

Wayne, Anthony (b. Easttown [now Waynesboro], Pa., 1 January 1745; d. Presque Isle, Pa., 15 December 1796). General. After an incomplete education and a brief career surveying Wayne followed his father into the tanning trade. By 1774 he had acquired the family business and become a prominent leader in the local revolutionary movement.

The War of Independence provided Wayne with an opportunity to focus his interests and display his talents. If he was insensitive in family matters and inept at business, he excelled on the field of battle. An excellent administrator, motivator of men, and field commander, he was fearless in combat, but more cautious and deliberate than his epithet ("Mad Anthony") suggests. Although embarrassed by the losses at Paoli's Massacre and the confusion at Germantown, Wayne drew praise for his roles in the battles of Three Rivers, Brandywine, Monmouth, and Stony Point. In 1783 Congress breveted him a major general.

As a civilian after the war, Wayne experienced financial problems and political setbacks before Congress named him commander of a newly authorized army. His well-trained legion defeated a united Indian force at the Battle of Fallen Timbers (20 August 1794), thus finally pacifying the Old Northwest and bolstering the new nation's military prestige.

For illustration, *see* figure 32, p. 396.

FURTHER READING

Nelson, Paul David: *Anthony Wayne: Soldier of the Early Republic* (Bloomington: Indiana University Press, 1985).

J. MARK THOMPSON

Webster, Noah (*b.* Hartford, Conn., 16 October 1758; *d.* New Haven, Conn., 28 May 1843). Lexicographer. He supported himself at first as a schoolteacher and published *A Grammatical Institute of the English Language* (1783) to remedy the deficiencies of standard textbooks. In the original, and in subsequent revised editions with various titles, Webster sought to make actual American usage the new standard for correct speech and writing, and his works reached a wide readership. His additional plan to reform American spelling according to phonetic principles won little acceptance, and his textbooks stayed with traditional orthography. As a consequence of his literary success, Webster became interested in copyright. He traveled around the country, meeting the political leaders of the time and convincing them of the necessity of protecting authors' work. This activity led him into a career of journalism and political advocacy in the 1780s and 1790s. He was an early supporter of the Constitution and a Federalist under the administrations of Washington and Adams. After the turn of the century he devoted himself exclusively to the completion of his *magnum opus*, published in 1828 as *An American Dictionary of the English Language*. Its entries included non-literary as well as peculiarly American words and meanings, and it became instantly authoritative.

FURTHER READING

Moss, R. J.: *Noah Webster* (New York: Twayne Publishers, 1984).
Rollins, R. M.: *The Long Journey of Noah Webster* (Philadelphia: University of Pennsylvania Press, 1980).
Webster, N.: *Autobiography of Noah Webster: from the Letters and Essays, Memoir and Diary*,

ed. R. Rollins (Columbia: University of South Carolina Press, 1989).

THOMAS COLE

Webster, Peletiah (*b.* Lebanon, Conn., 24 November 1726; *d.* Philadelphia, 2 September 1795) Political economist. The scion of an old Connecticut family, he shared a common ancestor with Noah Webster. In 1755 he left the ministry, for which he had been trained at Yale, to become a merchant in Philadelphia. His new life eventually allowed him to pursue studious interests once again. Beginning in 1776, and over the next 15 years, he published under pseudonyms 25 essays on questions raised by the political and financial pressures of the war years and early nationhood. He advocated taxation rather than loans to support the Continental Army, opposed paper money, and argued for the necessity of a stronger federal government. He also claimed to have considered not only specific questions of policy but also the first principles behind them, thereby adopting a more scientific approach. These works were collected and published under his own name as *Political Essays on the Nature and Operation of Money, Public Finances, and Other Subjects* (Philadelphia, 1791). In the preface to this volume Webster gave a brief sketch of his life, without mentioning that he had suffered confiscation of goods and two brief periods of imprisonment under the British.

FURTHER READING

Corwin, E. S.: "The Peletiah Webster myth," *The Doctrine of Judicial Review, its Legal and Historical Basis, and Other Essays* (Princeton, NJ: Princeton University Press, 1914).

THOMAS COLE

Wheatley, Phillis (*b.* West Africa, 1754; *d.* 5 December 1784). Poet. Brought to America and sold in the Boston slave market at the age of six or seven, Wheatley was destined to become the most famous African-American woman of her generation. Her owners, John and Susannah Wheatley, intended to train her as a domestic but, significantly, decided to educate her at home with their own children. It soon became evident that she was a gifted child. To their credit, the Wheatleys did all they could to satisfy her thirst for knowledge and, in particular, to foster her literary talent. By the time she was 20 Wheatley was an internationally renowned poet. She wrote her first poem, "To the University of Cambridge," in 1767, and three years later her verse commemorating George Whitefield's death was published. Thanks to John Wheatley, a collection of her work entitled *Poems on Various Subjects, Religious and Moral* was published by the London printer Archibald Bell in 1773 (*see* figure 75).

With her work appearing in print as far afield as Philadelphia, New York, and London, Boston's black poet soon became something of a celebrity on both sides of the Atlantic. In the early 1770s she visited London, where she enjoyed the patronage of the eminent English philanthropist the Countess of Huntingdon.

By 1773 Wheatley had become an important weapon in the armory of the anti-slavery movement. In his *Address to the Inhabitants of the British Colonies in America, Upon Slave Keeping* (1773), Benjamin Rush cited her poetry as incontrovertible proof that Africans were not, by nature, mentally and intellectually inferior to Europeans. This assertion prompted Thomas Jefferson's tart remark that "the compositions published under her name are below the dignity of criticism." Other commentators, in Europe and America, sprang to her defense and, in the process, helped to establish her enduring reputation as a poet. For fairly obvious reasons, her advocates did not dwell too long on the content of her verse. A devout Christian and a staunch supporter of the patriot cause, she did not deploy the tenets of Christianity in a poetry demanding the secular liberation of Blacks. On the contrary, a central theme of her work was the profound gratitude she felt for having been transported from the spiritual "darkness" of Africa to the Christian "light" of North America.

In 1778 Wheatley married John Peters, a black lawyer. Two of their three children died at an early age.

FIGURE 75 Phillis Wheatley as portrayed on the frontispiece to her "Poems on Various Subjects, Religious and Moral" (engraving after Scipio Moorhead, 1773)

FURTHER READING

Mason, J. D. (ed.): *The Poems of Phillis Wheatley* (Chapel Hill: University of North Carolina Press, 1966).

BETTY WOOD

Wilkes, John (*b.* London, 28 October 1725; *d.* London, 26 December 1797). British politician. For many years a Member of Parliament for Middlesex, Wilkes was an alderman of London (from 1769), Sheriff (1771–2), Lord Mayor (1774–5), and City Chamberlain (from 1779). When he was prosecuted and found guilty of seditious libel for his attacks on the government in no. 45 of the *North Briton*, printers of colonial newspapers publicized his case (1763–4). On his return to London in 1768, which was followed by his sentencing and imprisonment for this offense and then his exclusion from the House of Commons after being three times elected for Middlesex, the colonists more widely identified his defiance of authority with their own resistance to what they saw as arbitrary exercise of taxing authority by Parliament. They sent congratulatory addresses to him, and the South Carolina Assembly voted £1,500 towards the payment of his debts. Wilkes corresponded with the Sons of Liberty at Boston. His name became a toast at patriot meetings and was adopted for place-names, and colonists named their children after him. As Lord Mayor he took a lead in organizing representations to the King against the American policy of North's administration. In Parliament he championed the colonists' defense of the principle of "no taxation without representation," and between 1775 and 1780 he delivered ten set speeches against the American war and in favor of peace.

FURTHER READING

Bleackley, Horace: *Life of John Wilkes* (London and New York: John Lane, 1917).
Trench, Charles Chenevix: *Portrait of a Patriot: a Biography of John Wilkes* (Edinburgh and London: Blackwood, 1962).

IAN R. CHRISTIE

Wilson, James (*b.* Fife, Scotland, 14 September 1742; *d.* Edenton, NC, 21 August 1798). Lawyer, pamphleteer, financier, and constitutional and legal theorist. After emigrating from Scotland in 1765, Wilson settled in Pennsylvania and emerged as a central figure in the public life both of that state and of America. Although reserved and scholarly, he was also ambitious for fame and wealth. Ambition early led him to western Pennsylvania to pursue a legal career, begun after study in Philadelphia under the illustrious lawyer John Dickinson. Before long Wilson's own growing professional eminence helped launch his career in politics.

In 1774 he published a widely noticed pamphlet he had written in 1768, his *Considerations on the Nature and Extent of the Legislative Authority of the British Parliament.* During the mid-1770s he served in the Continental Congress. Tending to the position of a moderate rather than a radical Whig, in 1776 he initially counseled delay against the rising sentiment for independence. Although he signed the Declaration, his evolving general reputation as a conservative, together with his opposition to the 1776 Pennsylvania Constitution, slowed his progress in national politics for a time. He then focused on developing a prominent law practice in Philadelphia, where he became an effective – and controversial – defender of indicted Tories. He also began aligning himself with the interest of the financier Robert Morris, and he became increasingly invested in land speculation.

Critical of weak government under the Articles of Confederation, he used his pen – and his place in Congress in 1783 and 1785–6 – to urge stabilizing measures, such as the chartering of a national bank and provisions for a national revenue.

His nationalism eventually brought him to the climax of his public career: his achievements in helping to frame and secure the Federal Constitution. At the 1787 Convention he played a part second only to Madison's. There, and during the Pennsylvania ratification campaign, he contributed at least as much as any other founder to promoting several of the distinctive features of American constitutionalism, especially the theory of the separation of powers, the importance of the presidency, and, above all, the fundamental principle of the sovereignty of the people.

In 1790 he successfully led a movement to replace the 1776 Pennsylvania Constitution with a document that showed his hand as framer even more than the new Federal Constitution did. After 1790, however, Wilson's public life was characterized by disappointments. He aspired to become Chief Justice of the first United States Supreme Court, only to be named an Associate Justice.

The extensive *Lectures on Law* he delivered as professor at the College of Philadelphia in the early 1790s went unfinished and neglected. Even his notable accomplishments on the bench were few, mostly because he was distracted by personal financial problems that finally grew so serious they drove him into hiding. Mentally and physically broken, he died in disgrace and virtually in exile.

FURTHER READING

Conrad, Stephen A.: "Metaphor and imagination in James Wilson's theory of federal union," *Law & Social Inquiry*, 13 (1988), 1–70.
McCloskey, Robert Green (ed.): *The Works of James Wilson*, 2 vols. (Cambridge, Mass.: Belknap Press of Harvard University Press, 1967).
Smith, Charles Page: *James Wilson: Founding Father, 1742–1798* (Chapel Hill: University of North Carolina Press, 1956).

STEPHEN A. CONRAD

Witherspoon, John (*b.* Yester, nr Haddington, Scotland, 5 February 1723; *d.* nr Princeton, NJ, 15 November 1794). President of the College of New Jersey. As a Presbyterian minister in Scotland, Witherspoon maintained a strict Calvinist orthodoxy against accommodations with humanism, and defended the rights of congregations to choose their own ministers. He carried his stern morality and belief in popular rights to the New World when in 1768 he assumed the presidency of the College of New Jersey, where he was James Madison's teacher. Once there he reinvigorated both the college and American Presbyterianism in general by uniting the factions formed in reaction to the Great Awakening and preaching and fund-raising on the college's behalf throughout the mainland colonies. Princeton became a hotbed of radical, anti-English thought during the pre-revolutionary period and Witherspoon personally attempted to lead the cautious New Jersey elite towards rebellion. He arrived at the Continental Congress in Philadelphia in 1776 just in time to speak in favor of the motion for independence and sign the Declaration. He was a member of the New Jersey State Legislature (1783, 1789) and the New Jersey ratifying convention (1787). In his writings and educational influence, he left an intellectual legacy of vigorous advocacy of causes without regard for the niceties of scholarship.

FURTHER READING

Collins, V. L.: *President Witherspoon* (New York: Arno Press, 1969).
Stohlman, M. L. L.: *John Witherspoon* (Philadelphia: Westminster Press, 1976).

THOMAS COLE

Wythe, George (*b.* Elizabeth City Co., Va., 1726; *d.* Richmond, Va., 8 June 1806). Jurist. As a member of the House of Burgesses (1754–5, 1758–68) Wythe helped articulate the political theory behind Virginia's resistance to parliamentary authority in the matter of the Stamp Act. He maintained that the colonial legislature was coordinate with rather than subordinate to Parliament and that Virginia owed allegiance and obedience to the Crown alone, though not all his fellow Burgesses could accept these ideas unreservedly in 1765. He was a member with Edmund Pendleton and Thomas Jefferson of the committee set up to revise the laws of Virginia. He held the post of Chancellor in the state judiciary (1778–1806) and in 1782 made one of the earliest enunciations of the right of the judicial branch to pass judgment on the constitutionality of legislative acts, the doctrine of judicial review (*Commonwealth v. Caton*). As a jurist he stood in the shadow only of Pendleton, who sat on the appellate court and had occasion to reverse some of Wythe's decisions. Wythe also taught law at the College of William and Mary, the first such professorship in the United States, and counted the young Jefferson among his students.

FURTHER READING

Blackburn, J.: *George Wythe of Williamsburg* (New York: Harper and Row, 1975).

Clarkin, W.: *Serene Patriot: a Life of George Wythe* (Albany: Alan Publications, 1970).

THOMAS COLE

Yates, Abraham (*b.* Albany, NY, 23 August 1724; *d.* Albany, 30 June 1796). Laywer, pamphleteer, and politician. He began his political career as sheriff of Albany from 1754 to 1759 and served many terms on the Albany Common Council between 1754 and 1773. During the Anglo-American crisis he chaired the Albany committee of correspondence (1774–6) and was elected to New York's revolutionary congresses (1775–7). He then served as a state senator (1777–90). Yates led the state congressional committee that drafted New York's first constitution and the committee that put the state constitution into operation. Throughout the 1780s he wrote pamphlets and newspaper articles opposing every attempt to strengthen the powers of the Confederation government. In a series of essays signed "Sidney" appearing in the *Albany Gazette* in the winter of 1788, Yates branded the Constitutional Convention's work as an illegitimate usurpation of authority and insisted that the nation's credit could be restored, its dignity in foreign affairs upheld, and its trade regulated without erecting a powerful central government. He probably also wrote the addresses signed "Sydney" which appeared in the *New York Journal and Daily Patriotic Register* in June 1788. Linda Grant DePauw has suggested Yates as the Anti-Federalist author "Cato," but other historians have attributed Cato's essays to George Clinton. From 1790 until his death in 1796 Yates served as major of Albany.

FURTHER READING

DePauw, Linda Grant: *The Eleventh Pillar: New York State and the Federal Constitution* (Ithaca, NY: Cornell University Press, 1966).
Kaminski, John P.: "New York: the reluctant pillar," *The Reluctant Pillar, New York and the Adoption of the Federal Constitution,* ed. Stephen L. Schechter (Troy, NY: Russell Sage College, 1985), 55–111.

ELIZABETH P. MCCAUGHEY

Young, Thomas (*b.* Ulster Co., NY, 1731; *d.* Philadelphia, 24 June 1777). Physician and politician. Young typified the men of humble origins who rose to prominence during the revolutionary crisis itself. Like James Warren and Benjamin Rush, Young was a physician; unlike them, he outraged even zealous patriots both by his extravagant rhetoric and blatant deism. Born of immigrant tenant farmers, Young acquired early in life a hatred for hierarchy: no sooner did he come to prominence in Albany's Sons of Liberty in 1766 than he left for Boston. He frequently contrasted his adopted city's democracy with a New York dominated by great families (*see* Chapter 19, §2). In Boston, he belonged to the North End Caucus Committee of Correspondence (the closest thing to public office he ever held), and played a key role in enforcing the non-importation agreements. He left Boston for Philadelphia in 1775 after a near-fatal assault on his person by two British officers. There, he associated with the radical faction and advised in overthrowing the provincial assembly and writing the new constitution guaranteeing universal white manhood suffrage. However, Young's vigorous defense of Vermont's right to self-determination led to censure by a Congress anxious not to offend powerful New York. Young had become acquainted with Ethan Allen in the 1750s; the two had collaborated in writing the deist manifesto *Reason: the Oracle of Man*. Young died suddenly of fever while serving as a hospital physician in Philadelphia, leaving a poverty-stricken wife and six children.

FURTHER READING

Hawke, David Freeman: "Dr. Thomas Young – 'eternal fisher in troubled waters': notes for a biography," *New-York Historical Society Quarterly,* 44 (1970), 6–29.
Maier, Pauline: "Dr. Thomas Young and the radicalism of science and reason," *The Old Revolutionaries: Political Lives in the Age of Samuel Adams* (New York: Knopf, 1980), 101–38.

WILLIAM PENCAK

Chronology

COMPILED BY STEVEN J. SARSON

POLITICAL AND LEGAL EVENTS	MILITARY CAMPAIGNS, CIVIL ORDER, AND WESTERN SETTLEMENT	SOCIAL, CULTURAL, ECONOMIC, SCIENTIFIC, AND RELIGIOUS DEVELOPMENTS
1688–99	1688–99	1688–99
1688, Dec 11. Glorious Revolution in England culminates when James II flees; Parliament declares him in abdication, and enthrones William and Mary.		**1688.** Germantown Petition by Pennsylvania Mennonites represents early condemnation of slavery.
1689, Feb 13. Convention adopts Declaration of Rights, later legislated as Bill of Rights. **April 18.** Glorious Revolution in America begins with overthrow of Dominion of New England by "Declaration of Gentlemen, Merchants and Inhabitants of Boston." Other New England colonies follow. Leisler's Rebellion topples Andros in New York. John Coode's Protestant Association overthrows Lord Baltimore and converts Maryland to a royal colony for 25 years. Other colonies declare William and Mary King and Queen more peacefully. Many colonies receive new charters. **Oct.** First appearance of John Locke's (anonymous) *Two Treatises of Civil Government*, which later influenced American revolutionary thought. Also influential was Algernon Sidney's *Discourses Concerning Government* (1699).	**1689, May 12.** William III enters England into Grand Alliance and War of the League of Augsburg (King William's War) against Louis XIV of France. French and Indians fight British in America, especially New England, New York, and the West Indies, making this the first of four major wars for empire.	**1689.** Founding of America's first public school, the William Penn Charter School, which charges tuition only to those able to pay.
		1690, Feb 3. To pay soldiers serving in Quebec, Massachusetts becomes first colony to issue paper money.

		1691. New Massachusetts Charter grants "liberty of conscience" to all Protestant Christians. Severe laws enacted against blasphemy and atheism (Oct 1697). Maryland establishes the Church of England (1692), rescinding Toleration Act of 1649. Catholics and Quakers object. Board of Trade rejects in 1696 but accedes in 1702.
		1692, March. Children in Salem, Massachusetts, claim to have been bewitched, auguring famous Witch Hunt and trials.
		April. Thomas Neale receives patent for post office in America.
		1693, Feb 8. Charter granted to College of William and Mary. Building begins in 1695, and is completed in 1702.
1694, Dec 19. Triennial Act ensures elections in England every three years.		**1694.** Building of Annapolis, planned town and new capitol of Maryland. Virginia follows with Williamsburg in 1699.
Dec 28. Death of Mary. William III remains King.		
1695, April 12. Expiration of Licensing Act ends state censorship in England.		
1696, May 15. Navigation Acts create Board of Trade and Admiralty Courts with jurisdiction over all colonial affairs, including appointment of officials and review of legislation. Board power decreases owing to takeover of colonial gubernatorial appointment by Secretary of State, Southern Department (1703).		**1696, May 15.** Act of Trade (Navigation Acts) excludes foreign shipping from colonies and enumerates goods required to be re-exported through England rather than exported directly to foreign countries. Adds rice, molasses, naval stores (1705–6), copper, beaver and other furs (1721).
	1697, Sept 30. Treaty of Ryswick ends King William's War with status quo ante bellum in Europe and America.	
	1698, March 20. Pierre Le Moyne d'Iberville enters mouth of Mississippi and begins French settlement of Louisiana territory (purchased by Jefferson 106 years later). New Orleans founded in 1718.	
		1699, March 8. Rev. Thomas Bray founds Society for Promoting Christian Knowledge in London to spread Christianity in "superstitious lands." Bray travels to America on missionary work (Dec 16).

		June 29. Massachusetts passes America's first workhouse legislation. **Dec 1.** Woolens Act forbids export of wool manufactures across colonial borders.
1700–9	1700–9	1700–9
		1700–1. Imports from all colonies equal 20% of all imports to Britain. 10% of British manufactures are exported to colonies. Colonial population approximately 275,000.
		1700, June 16. Bray founds Society for the Propagation of the Gospel (SPG), and helps establish America's first publicly funded library in Charles Town, South Carolina. Massachusetts expels Catholics (17 June). North Carolina Vestry Act establishes Church of England (15 Dec 1701), disallowed by proprietors but re-enacted in 1705 and 1715.
		June 24. Publication of Samuel Sewell's early anti-slavery tract, *The Selling of Joseph*. Other writings of the decade include Cotton Mather's *Magnalia Christi Americana* (1702); Robert Beverley's *The History and Present State of Virginia* (1705); and Ebenezer Cook's *The Sot-Weed Factor* (1708).
1701, Nov 8. William Penn grants Charter of Privileges to Pennsylvania.		**1701, Oct 16.** Dissatisfied with liberalism at Harvard, Congregationalists establish a "Collegiate School" at Killingsworth, Connecticut. Later moved to New Haven and renamed Yale (1745).
1702. In the opinion of the Counsel to the Board of Trade, common law extends to the colonies. **March 8.** Death of William III. Accession of Queen Anne. **April 26.** New Jersey Proprietors surrender authority to Crown.	**1702, May 4.** Grand Alliance declares War of Spanish Succession (Queen Anne's War) on France. Early British gains include capture of St. Christopher and Carolinian razing of St. Augustine, Spanish Florida. **July 24.** Antoine de la Mothe Cadillac establishes French settlement at Detroit.	
	1704, Feb 29. French and Indians massacre 50 settlers at Deerfield, western Massachusetts. Haverhill suffers same fate (30 Aug 1708).	**1704, April 24.** Founding of first successful colonial newspaper, the *Boston News-Letter*.

796

1706, March. Board of Trade increases power by introducing suspending clause requiring Crown approval before implementation of certain types of colonial legislation.		
1707, March 6. Anne signs Act of Union joining England and Scotland.		
		1709, Sept 3. Carolina proprietors grant 13,500 acres to sponsors of German and Swiss emigrants.
1710–19	**1710–19**	**1710–19**
	1710, Oct. British capture Port Royal and Acadia from France, but fail to capture Quebec.	
	1711, Sept 22. Tuscarora War begins between Indians and encroaching North Carolina settlers. War ends with whites capturing Ft. Nohuck (23 March 1713). Tuscaroras migrate north and join Iroquois Nations.	
1712, May 9. Division of Carolinas into separate colonies.		**1712, Aug 1.** Pennsylvania Assembly levies £20 duty on every imported slave. Board of Trade vetoes this attempt to stem slave trade and vetoes others in 1715 and 1719.
	1713, April 11. Treaty of Utrecht precludes Bourbon succession in Spain. Britain gains Newfoundland, Nova Scotia, Hudson Bay, Nevis, and St. Kitts.	**1713, April 11.** After Treaty of Utrecht, British Government begins encouraging foreign emigration to colonies.
1714, Aug 1. Death of Anne. Accession of George I and the Hanoverian line. **Aug.** Revival of Privy Council Committee on Colonial Affairs increases imperial bureaucracy and decreases Board of Trade power.		
	1715, April 15. Yamasee War begins between Indians and encroaching South Carolina settlers. Peace of January 1716 largely ends Indian threat to South Carolinians. Proprietors' disinterest in war leaves settlers bitter.	
1716, May. Septennial Act, promoted by Whigs worried about Jacobites, party struggle, and securing control over Hanoverians, increases life of Parliament to seven years.		
1717, July 13. Appointment of		

Martin Bladen to Board of Trade, a key figure for 30 years. **1719. May 11.** Earl of Westmoreland appointed President of Board of Trade. **Nov.** Commons House seizes power from Proprietors and converts South Carolina into a royal colony.		**1718, Feb.** American ships allowed into West Indies. Encourages vigorous sugar trade and rum manufacture, especially in New England. **1719, Dec. 14.** Founding of the *Boston Gazette*.
	1 7 2 0 – 9	1 7 2 0 – 9
1720, Nov. Trenchard and Gordon begin publishing *Cato's Letters* in response to South Sea Bubble crisis. Used by Americans to criticize Navigation Laws. **1721, April 1.** Walpole's administration begins years of metropolitan "salutary neglect" of colonial affairs. **1724, April 6.** Duke of Newcastle begins benign 24-year tenure as Secretary of State, Southern Department.	 **1724, Aug 14.** Dummer's/Lovewell's War begins between New Englanders and French-backed Abenaki Indians. Settlers win decisive Battle of Fryeburg, Maine (9 May 1725), but sporadic fighting continues until Abenaki recognize British authority in 1729.	**1721, April.** Smallpox epidemic breaks out in Boston. 6,045 out of a population of 10,597 contract the disease before epidemic ends (spring 1722). Dr. Zabdiel Boylston begins inoculation treatment (26 June 1721) and calculates that of 286 persons inoculated only 6 (2.1%) die, while of those 5,759 not inoculated 844 (12.8%) die. Despite the approval of the clergy, popular objections to inoculation remain vehement. Cotton Mather's son and two slaves stoned by mob. **1723, April.** William Price, influenced by Wren's Georgian style, begins building Boston's famous "Old North Church" C of E. It was from this steeple that a lantern was hung in 1775 to signal Paul Revere of British tactics. **Oct.** German Baptists in Germantown, Pennsylvania, found first Dunkard Church in America.

1727, **June 21.** Death of George I. Accession of George II.	1727, **Feb.** Beginning of indecisive 13-month Anglo-Spanish War.	1727, **Oct.** Benjamin Franklin begins great public career with establishment of the Junto, an enlightenment benevolent society. In October 1728 he publishes "Articles of Belief and Acts of Religion," espousing reason as basis of faith, and next year purchases the *Pennsylvania Gazette* as an oracle for his secular and religious beliefs.
		1728. New York city Jews build America's first synagogue.
1730–9	**1730–9**	**1730–9**
		1730, **May.** Virginia passes Tobacco Inspection Act favoring larger producers of better quality leaves. Maryland later follows, with resulting tobacco cutting riots in both colonies.
		1731, **May 7.** Parliament allows direct export of some colonial products to Ireland.
1732, **June 20.** Charter and parliamentary subsidies granted to Edward Oglethorpe and trustees for establishment of the colony of Georgia.	1732, **June 20.** Colony of Georgia established with slavery prohibition and parliamentary subsidies to encourage white settlement, partly in hope of securing South Carolina from dangers of slave revolt and attack from Spanish Florida.	1732. Franklin founds Library Company of Philadelphia, the world's first circulating library. In December 1733 he begins publishing *Poor Richard's Almanack*.
1733, **March.** Walpole faces political difficulties over excise crisis.		1733, **March.** Walpole's attempt to increase government finance by replacing tobacco and wine duties with inland duties results in excise crisis.
		May 17. Parliament passes Molasses Act establishing 6d per gallon duty on American imports of the product from the West Indies. Largely avoided by bribes to customs officers.
1734, **Oct.** John Peter Zenger, publisher of *New York Weekly Journal,* acquitted of libel charge; landmark case in the history of freedom of speech.		1734, **Dec.** Series of emotional conversions brought about by evangelist Jonathan Edwards marks beginning of Great Awakening. Edwards publishes theory and method of converting in his *Personal Narrative* (1739). English Methodist John Wesley begins tour (Feb 1736), and George Whitefield follows (Aug 1739).
		1735, **Feb.** First Moravian community established at Savannah, Georgia.

		1736, Aug 6. William Parks begins publishing the *Virginia Gazette.*
1737, May 25. Thomas Hutchinson begins political career with election to Massachusetts House of Representatives.		**1737, March 17.** Boston sees first celebration of St. Patrick's Day not held solely in church.
June 27. Lord Monson begins benign term as President of Board of Trade.		
	1739, Sept 9. First of three slave revolts in South Carolina in one year. 21 whites and 44 blacks perish.	
	Oct 23. War of Jenkins's Ear inspired by Captain Robert Jenkins's report to Parliament that Spanish customs officers had cut off his ear for suspected smuggling.	

1740–9	1740–9	1740–9
1740, Nov 10. Publication of Proprietor William Stephens's roseate *A State of the Province of Georgia.* Patrick Tailfer et al. make vitriolic response in *A True and Historical Narrative of the Colony of Georgia* (1741).	**1740, Jan.** James Oglethorpe invades Spanish Florida but fails to capture St. Augustine.	**1740.** Eliza Lucas Pinckney experiments with crops, primarily indigo, to supplement South Carolina's rice staple. British Government establishes 6d per pound bounty on indigo in 1748.
	Dec. War of Jenkins's Ear subsumed by War of Austrian Succession (King George's War) against France and Spain.	**Feb 15.** Naturalization Act empowers colonies to naturalize foreign Protestants resident for seven or more years.
		March 25. Wesley and Whitefield promote building of Bethesda Orphanage in Savannah. Whitefield embarks on tour of New England (1740); Edwards publishes *Some Thoughts Concerning the Present Revival of Religion in New England* and is criticized in Charles Chauncey's *Enthusiasms Described and Cautioned Against* (1742).
		Sept 8. Nine directors sign articles forming a Land Bank in Massachusetts (credits secured by land) in response to lack of adequate medium of exchange. Legalized by JPs (4 Dec) amid intense controversy.
	1741, Dec. "Negro Conspiracy" panic in New York City. Savage punishments.	**1741, March.** Parliament extends Bubble Act to colonies, prohibiting formation of corporations without parliamentary consent. Many colonists, including Samuel Adams's father, lose property in resulting Massachusetts Land Bank dissolution.

1742, Feb 2. Walpole driven from office, the first Prime Minister to resign over defeats in the House of Commons.	**1742, July 7.** Spanish attack on Georgia repelled at Bloody Swamp.	**1742, Sept 24.** Boston's Faneuil Hall opens to public. Work begins on another famous building, Carpenters Hall in Philadelphia, where the Continental Congress would sit.
		1743, May. Franklin founds the American Philosophical Society. Also co-founds the Academy of Philadelphia (Nov 1749), later renamed University of Pennsylvania. College of New Jersey, later renamed Princeton University, founded by Presbyterians (Oct 1746).
1744, Nov 23. Pelhamites petition George II to force Cartaret to resign, but William Pitt's exclusion from new ministry forces Henry Pelham to resign (Jan 1746). 1747 elections return Pelhamites to large Commons majority and restore stability to British politics.	**1744, March 15.** France officially declares war on England.	
	1745, June 16. New Englanders capture French Ft. Louisburg, Cape Breton Island. **July.** Charles Edward Stuart lands in Scotland. Jacobite Uprising peaks with invasion of England (Nov–Dec). Last casualties recorded at Clifton (18 Dec) after which Jacobites disperse and Stuart flees. **Sept 19.** Trespass arrest of Samuel Baldwin of Newark precipitates ten years of sporadic land riots in New Jersey. **Nov 29.** French and Indians burn Saratoga, New York.	**1745, Jan 17.** Jonas Green founds the *Maryland Gazette*.
1746, May 28. Thomas Hutchinson begins two years as Speaker of Massachusetts House. Becomes Member of Council in May 1749.		**1746, March.** John Woolman begins tour of Upper South colonies persuading fellow Quakers to free slaves.
	1747, May. George II grants 500,000 acres to Ohio Company of Virginia. Virginia Council grants 800,000 acres to Loyal Company (12 July 1748). Both companies send agents to survey in the early 1750s. French dispatch Jean Baptiste le Moyne de Bienville to make claims and establish forts in the Ohio Valley.	**1747, Dec.** First appearance of Jared Eliot's scientific agriculture theories in *An Essay on Field Husbandry*.
1748, Oct. Publication of Montesquieu's *Spirit of the Laws*, which influenced later American constitutional thought.	**1748, Oct 18.** Treaty of Aix-la-Chapelle ends French claim to Austria. American gains returned to France. In 1749 Britain	

Nov 5. Earl of Halifax appointed President of Board of Trade, and Duke of Bedford Secretary of State, Southern Department. Appointment of these activists reflects increased metropolitan concern over growing importance of provinces and with political and social disorders therein. Halifax secures increased Board of Trade power through greater scrutiny over colonial legislation, power of gubernatorial appointment and oversight, and the establishment of a packet-boat system for greater communication within the empire (1755). Activism temporarily halts, however, with war (1754–63).	establishes Nova Scotia with parliamentary subsidies as full colony and buffer zone.	
		1749, Jan 10. Georgia trustees relinquish ban on slavery. **March.** Parliament rejects Board of Trade bill to ban colonial paper money which enabled colonists to pay creditors (often British) in depreciated currency.
1 7 5 0 – 9	1 7 5 0 – 9	1 7 5 0 – 9
1750, Jan. Jonathan Mayhew delivers famous sermon in Boston, *A Discourse Concerning Unlimited Submission,* advocating virtue as a defense against tyranny. **1751, May 9.** Benjamin Franklin elected to Pennsylvania House of Assembly.		**1750, June 24.** Iron Act forbids inter-colonial iron trade but allows duty-free imports to Britain. Currency Act bans issuing of paper money in New England as of 25 September 1751. **1751.** Bishop Thomas Sherlock pushes Parliament for suffragan bishops in America. **May 9.** Franklin publishes "Rattlesnakes for Felons," satirically offering rattlesnakes in exchange for convicts transported to America. Wins Copley Medal of the Royal Society of London for his electrical studies (23 Nov 1753). Another scientific achievement was the first clock made entirely in America (1754), built by Benjamin Bannecker, a Maryland free black. Great writings of the decade include Franklin's *Observations Concerning the Increase of Mankind* (1751); Samuel Johnson's *Elementa Philosophica* (1752); Edwards's *Freedom of Will* (1754); William Smith Jr.'s *The History of the Province of New York* (1757).

1752, April 22. Lt. Governor Dinwiddie of Virginia attempts to levy fee on land grants. Resulting Pistole Fee Controversy reveals disagreement over nature of property rights between Crown and colonists.

June 25. Georgia trustees surrender authority to Crown.

1754, March 6. Death of Pelham inspires George II to complain, "I shall now have no more peace." Duke of Newcastle becomes Prime Minister.

1752, June. French attack Pickawillany trading post (at present-day Erie, Pennsylvania) and erect Ft. Presque Isle.

1753, March–April. French erect Fts. Le Boeuf and Verango.

Oct 31. Governor Dinwiddie of Virginia dispatches George Washington to demand French withdrawal from Ohio territory. Refusal reported in January 1754.

1754, Feb. Dinwiddie orders construction of fort at forks of Ohio River but French seize the site and erect Ft. Duquesne. Washington skirmishes with French at Great Meadows and erects Ft. Necessity (28 May).

June 19. Representatives of Iroquois Nations, New York, Pennsylvania, Maryland, and New England colonies meet for Albany Congress to discuss defense against French. Endorses Franklin's Plan of Union but it is rejected by colonies.

July 3. Washington forced to withdraw from Ft. Necessity, leaving French in control of the Ohio Valley. Marks beginning of series of British defeats.

1755, July 9. William Braddock defeated at Battle of the Wilderness and killed in retreat at Monongahela.

Sept 8. William Johnson defeats French in Battle of Lake George.

1752, Aug. Liberty Bell, a gift from England celebrating Pennsylvania's 50 years under Charter of Privileges, arrives in Philadelphia. Found to be cracked, it is twice recast before being hung in the State House (now Independence Hall). Tolled in celebration of Stamp Act repeal and Independence, its career as a symbol of liberty continued with the antislavery movement. It was cracked on 8 June 1835 while being rung to commemorate the death of Chief Justice Marshall and has remained in this condition ever since.

Sept 5. Lewis Hallam's American Company opens tour with performance of *The Merchant of Venice* in Williamsburg: start of professional theater in America.

1754, Aug. Encouraged by Woolman's *Some Considerations on the Keeping of Negroes* (1754), the Philadelphia Yearly resolves against Quakers buying slaves. Yearly of September 1755 advises monthly meetings to admonish Friends who continue to buy slaves. New York and New England Quakers follow. Woolman again tours the Upper South speaking to Quakers against slavery (1757).

Oct 31. Founding of Kings College of New York, later renamed Columbia University.

Nov. Scottish philosopher David Hume begins publishing three-volume *The History of England*. Completed in 1762.

	Sept–Oct. British expel Acadians from Nova Scotia.	
1756, June 29. Newcastle appoints Pitt Secretary of State, forming a coalition government with Pitt controlling foreign affairs. **Sept.** Thomas Pownall replaces William Shirley as Governor of Massachusetts. Hutchinson appointed Lt. Governor.	**1756, Jan 16.** Britain enters alliance with Prussia. France allies with Austria (1 May). **Feb 17.** William Johnson appointed to new post of Indian Superintendent for the Northern District, Edmond Atkin for the Southern District. **May 15.** Declarations mark the official beginning of the Seven Years' War (French and Indian War) after three years of fighting. **June 28.** French capture Minorca.	
1757, Feb 3. Pennsylvania elects Franklin agent to England. Franklin also appointed to represent New Jersey, Maryland, and Georgia.	**1757, Aug 9.** French capture Ft. William Henry.	
1758, Sept 14. Virginia Assembly passes Two Penny Act, permitting payment of obligations to clergy in tobacco at 2d per pound. Clergy seeks royal disallowance, and metropolitan authorities object to lack of suspending clause. Law finally disallowed by Privy Council.	**1758, July 8.** French capture Ticonderoga, but Pitt's new war policy meets success with capture of Louisburg (26 July), Ft. Frontenac (27 Aug), Ft. Duquesne (renamed Pittsburg) and Ticonderoga (25 Nov). **1759.** British capture Ft. Niagara (25 July), Lake Champlain (26 July), and Quebec (except Montreal, 18 Sept).	
1760	**1760**	**1760**
June 3. Thomas Pownall becomes Governor of South Carolina. Replaced in Massachusetts by Francis Bernard. Bernard appoints Hutchinson Chief Justice (10 Nov). **Aug.** New York Governor Cadwallader Colden causes controversy by not granting "good behavior" tenure to new Chief Justice, Benjamin Pratt. Board of Trade reiterates this policy, evoking similar controversies in New Jersey and both Carolinas in the early 1760s. Colden provokes further judicial controversy by overriding jury decision (Oct 1764). **Oct 25.** Death of George II. Accession of George III.	**Aug 8–9.** Cherokees capture Ft. Loudon, Tennessee, and massacre British retreating to Ft. Prince George. **Sept 8.** French surrender Montreal. Thomas Gage becomes Military Governor of Quebec. British capture Detroit (29 Nov). **Dec.** Frontier governors instructed to deny land grants in Indian territories.	

1761	1761	1761
Feb. Massachusetts Writs of Assistance case; court rules in favor of allowing customs officials to search private homes. Controversy results in James Otis's resignation from admiralty court and publication of his *Vindication of the Conduct of the House of Representatives*. The *Boston Gazette* also establishes itself as a major patriot advocate. **March 21.** Lord Sandys appointed President of Board of Trade. **May 25.** Lord Bute appointed Secretary of State, Northern Department. **Oct 5.** Pitt resigns over conduct of war. Replaced by Halifax as Secretary of State. Halifax also receives Northern Department post in 1762.	**Oct 8.** Death of Indian Superintendent (Southern District) Edmond Atkin. Replaced by John Stuart.	
1762	**1762**	**1762**
May 26. Resignation of Newcastle. Beginning of Bute ministry. **May.** Bernard and Council spend £72 of Massachusetts public funds fighting French privateers. Legislators object to this violation of their right to oversee appropriations. **Sept.** South Carolina Governor Thomas Boone sparks election controversy and political deadlock by refusing to seat Christopher Gadsden in the Commons House of Assembly.	**Jan.** Britain declares war on Spain. **Feb.** British begin attacking French West Indies. **Nov 13.** France cedes Louisiana to Spain in secret Treaty of Fontainebleau.	St. Cecilia Society, America's first music society and a gathering place for the elite, established in Charles Town.
1763	**1763**	**1763**
March 1. Charles Townshend appointed President of Board of Trade. Replaced by Lords Shelburne (April) and then Hillsborough (May). **April 8.** Resignation of Bute. Beginning of Grenville ministry. **April 23.** John Wilkes attacks the government in issue no. 45 of *The North Briton*. Grenville has Wilkes and 49 associates arrested under general warrant. Obtaining *Habeas Corpus*, Wilkes is acquitted through MPs' freedom from conviction for libel. Colonial newspapers	**Feb 10.** Peace of Paris. Britain gains Quebec, Florida, and all North America east of the Mississippi. Military presence of 15 regiments remain under Gage, based in New York. Cost of maintenance estimated at £225,000. Lord Bute suggests colonists should pay. **May 7–Nov 28.** Pontiac's Uprising. Johnson and Stuart estimate Indian population at 10,000. Congress of Augusta (5–10 Nov) is first of eight pre-Revolution southern Indian treaties.	**April.** Customs Board investigation of colonial tax evasion reveals annual revenue from American customs at £1,800. Suggests revitalization of Molasses Act (1733). Parliament passes "An Act for the further Improvement of His Majesties Revenue of Customs" (19 April) for inspection of ships below 50 tons, encouraging seizures, and preventing smuggling. Publication of first volume of Catherine Sawbridge Macaulay's *History of England*. Publication of Rev. East

sympathize with Wilkes and begin criticizing prospective sugar tax.	**June.** Establishment of Mississippi Company, which begins petitioning for western lands. **Oct 7.** Royal Proclamation Line forbids settlement west of line marked by Alleghenies. **Dec 13–27.** Paxton Boys massacre peaceful Conestoga Indians and march on Philadelphia.	Apthorp's *Considerations of the SPG.* Answered by Jonathan Mayhew's *Observations on the Charter*, opening controversy on the establishment of an American episcopacy.
1764	**1764**	**1764**
April 5. American Duties Act creates new Vice Admiralty Court in Halifax, Nova Scotia. Publications against the Act include Otis's *Rights of the British Colonists Asserted and Proved.* Thomas Pownall recommends more effective policy from metropolitan viewpoint in *The Administration of the Colonies.* **June 13.** To combat British policy the Massachusetts House establishes the first committee of correspondence. **Dec.** John Olyphant of Jamaica refuses to pay libel damages awarded against him, invoking "parliamentary privilege" principle. Governor Lyttelton has Olyphant arrested. House of Assembly frees him and arrests plaintiffs for seizing his property. Controversy paralyzes Jamaican politics for three years.	**Feb 13.** Disgruntled westerners deliver *A Remonstrance from the Pennsylvania Frontier* to their governor and assembly. **July 10.** Board of Trade issues "Plan of '64" for cooperation with Indians. Johnson secures first of 11 pre-Revolution northern Indian treaties.	**April 5.** American Duties/Sugar Act replaces Molasses Act with 3d per gallon duty, extends number of goods enumerated under Navigation Acts (all goods enumerated by 1767), and makes duties and fines payable in sterling. Currency Act (19 April) extends prohibition of paper money to colonies south of New York; all paper money in circulation withdrawn. **Aug.** Boston merchants agree on non-importation to counter Sugar Act. Mechanics join agreement (Sept) and other colonies follow. Publication of Richard Peters's *Thoughts on the Present State of the Church of England in America,* arguing for institution of four suffragan bishops in America. Provokes Archbishops Secker and Drummond to petition for colonial episcopacy.
1765	**1765**	**1765**
March 22. Parliamentary opposition to Stamp Act is led by William Pitt in the Commons and Earl Camden in the Lords. **April.** Samuel Adams resigns as Boston tax collector in response to Stamp Act and is subsequently elected to House of Representatives. Publications against the Act include Otis's *Vindication of the British Colonies*; John Adams's *Dissertation on Canon and Feudal Law.* The Virginian Patrick Henry makes famous "Treason Speech" and Burgesses pass the Virginia Resolutions (29 May). Sons of Liberty organize various colonies. **June 8.** Massachusetts General Court sends Circular to other	**March 24.** Mutiny/Quartering Act obliges colonists to provide barracks and supplies for British soldiers. **Aug 14.** Bostonians hang Stamp Collector Andrew Oliver in effigy from Liberty Tree and burn his house. Oliver resigns (15 Aug). Hutchinson's house also burned (26 Aug). Such acts, though condemned by Sons of Liberty, render Stamp Act unenforceable in most colonies.	**March 22.** Parliament passes Stamp Act to be effective 1 November. Attempts compromise by exempting ships under 20 tons from detailed documentation and allows direct importation of colonial iron and lumber to Ireland. **Oct 28.** New York agreement on non-importation. Other colonies follow. Colonists continue to conduct business without stamps after 1 November.

colonies promoting Stamp Act Congress. **July 10.** Resignation of Grenville. Beginning of Rockingham ministry. **Oct 7–25.** Stamp Act Congress, attended by eight colonies, meets in New York. Ratifies John Dickinson's "Declaration of Rights and Grievances" (19 Oct).		
1766	**1766**	**1766**
March 18. Repeal of Stamp Act. Indemnity Act prevents prosecution of non-compliants. But Declaratory Act asserts Parliament's right to legislate for colonies "in all cases whatsoever." Sons of Liberty disband. **May.** Death of John Robinson reveals corruption in Virginia gentry, provoking reforms which include separation of offices of Speaker and Treasurer. Tension highest with Robinson's father-in-law, John Chiswell, illegally bailed on a murder charge (June). **July.** Resignation of Rockingham. Beginning of Pitt ministry. Shelburne appointed Secretary of State. Mental health of Pitt (now Earl of Chatham) deteriorates, Charles Townshend becomes *de facto* Prime Minister by September. Lord North becomes Chancellor of the Exchequer. **Dec 18.** Robert Nugent appointed President of Board of Trade.	**Jan.** Second Quartering Act billets troops on unoccupied dwellings and taverns. New York refuses to comply. Soldiers and citizens brawl in New York streets (10–11 Aug). **May.** New York city crowd destroys opulent new Chapel St. Theater. Discontented tenants revolt in Hudson Valley. Settlers occupy Monongahela Valley of Pennsylvania without Indian consent or purchase. Ohio Company speculates in region of Pittsburgh. Illinois Company petitions for 1.2 million acres in Mississippi Valley.	**Jan 17.** Petitions of British merchants affected by boycotts reach Parliament. Franklin testifies to Parliament that the Stamp Act is an "internal tax" and that Parliament is restricted to levying "external taxes" (13 Feb). Parliament repeals (18 March). **Sept.** Charles Townshend begins devising external taxes for America. **Oct.** Anglican convocation in New Jersey petitions Archbishop of Canterbury and Bishops of London and Oxford for American bishoprics. **Nov 1.** American Trade Act reduces duty on molasses to 1d per gallon and creates two freeports in the Caribbean.
1767	**1767**	**1767**
June 29. Townshend Acts create duty collection and enforcement agency, Board of Customs Commissioners, based in Boston. Sons of Liberty reorganize in various colonies. **Sept 4.** Death of Townshend. Prime Ministerial duties fall to Duke of Grafton. **Nov 5.** Customs officials arrive in Boston. John Dickinson begins publishing *Letters from a Farmer in Pennsylvania* (dated Nov 5; published Nov 30).	**May.** Disorders against Townshend Acts include attack on British sea captain by gentry-led Charles Town mob. Another such attack (Sept) is led by Mayor of Norfolk, Virginia. **June 6.** New York Assembly finally appropriates money for quartering, but petitions Parliament to repeal. **June 29.** Parliament passes New York Restraining Act nullifying a provisioning act of 1766. Not enforced, however, because of 6 June compliance.	**Feb 27.** Parliament, despite Townshend's opposition, forces reduction of British land tax. **March 16.** Massachusetts House votes to prohibit slave trade. After four years in committee stage, however, Hutchinson vetoes. **April 23.** Staging of Thomas Godfrey's *The Prince of Parthia* is first performance of a play written by an American. Other achievements include publication of *To the University of Cambridge*, a poem by African-born slave Phillis Wheatley, and construction of

Dec 30. Massachusetts General Court adopts Samuel Adams's Circular Letter condemning Townshend Acts.		America's first planetarium by David Rittenhouse. June 29. Parliament passes Townshend Duties, tariffs on goods imported to America, believing colonists would accept "external" taxes. Oct. Second Anglican Convocation in New Jersey. Pamphlet war begins between Thomas Chandler and Charles Chauncey. Dec 31. Non-importation agreements within and among various colonies commence.
1 7 6 8	1 7 6 8	1 7 6 8
Jan 20. Hillsborough appointed Secretary of new Colonial Department. Feb 11. Adams's Circular Letter appears. March. Creation of new Vice Admiralty Courts in Boston, Philadelphia, and Charles Town. April 21. Hillsborough instructs Bernard to order Massachusetts General Court to rescind Circular Letter and other Governors to dissolve assemblies before countenancing it. July 12. Soame Jenyns appointed President of Board of Trade. July 18. *Boston Gazette* publishes "The Liberty Song." Sept 22. Massachusetts Convention meets to discuss Townshend Acts. Oct. Chatham, now recovered and horrified at government policy in his absence, resigns. Makes Grafton Prime Minister in name as well as practice.	March 7. Board of Trade *Report on the Western Problem* rejects idea of inland colonies, yet Grand Ohio Company petitions for 2.4 million acres for a western proprietary colony (1769). June 10. Seizure of John Hancock's sloop causes "Liberty Riot." Bostonians attack Customs Commissioners who withdraw to Castle William (11 June) and request military aid (15 June). Oct 1. Gage's troops arrive in Boston to restore order.	March. *New York Gazette* publishes "The American Whig," a Presbyterian attack on episcopalianism. Samuel Seabury and others respond with "A Whip for the American Whig."
1 7 6 9	1 7 6 9	1 7 6 9
Feb 9. Parliament revives Statute of Henry VIII for juryless trials of provincials in London. May 16. George Washington presents George Mason's Virginia Resolves to the Burgesses, who pass them. Massachusetts voters oust rescinders and return supporters of the Circular Letter, including John Hancock. Aug 1. On departure of Bernard, Hutchinson becomes Governor of Massachusetts.	Oct 9. Regulators petition North Carolina Assembly against eastern economic and political domination.	Jan 26. MP Isaac Barré predicts revolt of colonists if Parliament persists in taxation policy. May 17. Prorogued Burgesses meet in Williamsburg tavern and adopt the Virginia Association, a non-importation organization. June 3. In Norriton, Philadelphia, William Smith, John Lukens, David Rittenhouse, and John Sellers of the American Philosophical Society participate in international scientific observation of the Transit of Venus over the sun's disk.

Dec. South Carolina Commons votes £1,500 to pay debts of John Wilkes, arrested and expelled from Parliament after his election and re-election to the seat for Middlesex.		Dec. Cabinet decides to repeal all Townshend Duties except that on tea.
1770	1770	1770
Jan 31. Resignation of Grafton. Beginning of North ministry. **March.** On Hillsborough's instruction Hutchinson moves Massachusetts General Court to Cambridge. Inspires controversy over metropolitan alteration of colonial custom. Irish patriot Charles Lucas pens *Letter to the Town of Boston* opposing such attacks by the British ministry. Samuel Adams mounts campaign of opposition to British military presence. **April 12.** Repeal of Townshend Acts does not include the principle of making governors and magistrates independent of assemblies and answerable to Crown. **April 14.** British officials threaten treasurer of South Carolina with severe penalties if any public funds are appropriated without executive approval. Wilkes Fund Controversy paralyzes South Carolina politics until independence. **Nov.** Maryland Governor Robert Eden's Proclamation setting scale of government officers' fees inspires three-year controversy. Charles Carroll of Carrollton ("First Citizen") establishes himself as patriot leader by opposing Eden.	**Jan 19.** Confrontations between soldiers and New York citizens culminate in Battle of Golden Hill. **March 5.** Similar confrontations result in King Street Riot (Boston Massacre) in which five die. **Dec 4.** Verdict in Boston Massacre case acquits six soldiers and finds two guilty of manslaughter. Offenders branded on the thumb.	**March 5.** Parliament debates repeal of Duties. Townshend Acts, except tea duty and Board of Customs Commissioners, repealed on 12 April. **Nov 26.** Thomas Jefferson takes residence in small brick house at Monticello. Building of the mansion began the previous fall. Other achievements include Wheatley's verse commemorating the death of George Whitefield; Bannecker's clock that chimed all hours, the first of its kind in America; and Benjamin Rush's publication of the first American chemistry textbook, *A Syllabus of a Course of Lectures on Chemistry*, and his appointment as America's first Professor of Chemistry at the College of Philadelphia.
1771	1771	1771
Sept. Samuel Adams, concerned about quiescence, proposes network of corresponding societies to instruct and arouse the public. Boston Town Meeting forms Committee of Correspondence. Other towns follow.	**Jan 15.** Johnson ("Bloody") Act makes Regulator movement treasonable in North Carolina. Governor Tryon crushes Regulators at Alamance Creek, near Hillsborough (16 May).	**Jan.** Non-importation ends and trade returns to normal. **May.** "The Rising Glory of America" is read at Princeton commencement, attended by its co-author, Philip Freneau. **June 4.** Beginning of nine-month convention of clergy in Virginia to discuss the episcopal question.

1772	1772	1772
May. Elbridge Gerry elected to Massachusetts House and Boston Committee of Correspondence. **June 13.** Hutchinson announces he would now receive salary from Crown. General Court expresses resentment at gubernatorial escape from accountability to legislature. **Aug.** Hillsborough resigns as Colonial Secretary in opposition to projected colony of Vandalia in Ohio region. Replaced by Earl of Dartmouth. **Nov.** Boston Committee of Correspondence endorses Samuel Adams's *A State of the Rights of the Colonists* and other writings.	**June 10.** *Gaspée* Incident. Rhode Islanders burn Royal Navy schooner. Judge Stephen Hopkins prevents arrest of offenders.	Imports from colonies equal 36% of all imports to Britain. 37% of all British manufactures are exported to the colonies. Colonial population reaches almost 2.5 million.

1773	1773	1773
Sept. North Carolina Assembly devises new superior court law ignoring royal prohibition of laws for confiscating non-residents' property in debt suits. Controversy paralyzes North Carolina legislature and court system until independence. **Oct 16.** Mass meeting in Philadelphia condemns Tea Act. Virginians and Bostonians call on colonists to form inter-colonial correspondence committees. **Dec.** Samuel Adams secures publication of letters by Bernard and Hutchinson advocating reduction of colonial liberties.	**Dec 16.** Boston Tea Party. Sons of Liberty, disguised as Indians, board the *Dartmouth, Eleanor,* and *Beaver* and dump 90,000 lb of East India tea into the harbor. Similar incidents occur in other colonies.	**Jan 12.** Establishment in Charles Town of America's first museum. Walnut St. Jail in Philadelphia opens, the first American penitentiary. **Feb.** Pennsylvania legislature finally succeeds in killing the slave trade with £20 duty per head. Wheatley publishes *Poems on Various Subjects, Religious and Moral.* Rush cites Wheatley as evidence that Africans are not inferior to Europeans in *An Address to the Inhabitants of the British Settlements in America, Upon Slave-Keeping.* Mercy Otis Warren writes *The Adulateur,* portraying Hutchinson as "Rapatio." **May 10.** Tea Act gives monopoly to East India Company by granting tax concessions so it could sell at low prices to Americans. **June 15.** Parliament modifies Currency Act to allow issue of paper money through loan offices to pay public debts. **July 14.** First Annual Conference of American Methodists held in Philadelphia.

1774	1774	1774
Jan 29. Solicitor General Alexander Wedderburn humiliates Franklin before Privy Council over release of Hutchinson–Bernard letters and	**July 12.** Death of Indian Superintendent (Northern District) William Johnson. Replaced by his nephew Guy Johnson.	**March.** Barré reminds Parliament of vast importance of American commerce to Britain.

Boston Tea Party. Parliament passes Coercive or Intolerable Acts comprising Boston Port Act (31 March) closing the port; Massachusetts Government Act (20 May) providing that the King appoint Council members and town meetings occur only annually and discuss only local matters; Administration of Justice Act (20 May) providing for trials of provincials in other colonies or in England away from sympathetic juries; Quartering Act (2 June) billeting troops on unoccupied buildings. In addition, the Quebec Act (22 June) transfers jurisdiction of western lands to the Canadian Catholic colony governed by French civil law with no jury trials or elected assembly.

May 13. Gage arrives in Boston to replace Hutchinson as Military Governor.

May 17. Rhode Island issues the first call for a "Grand Congress."

June 17. Massachusetts calls for Continental Congress. All colonies except Georgia begin electing delegates. Gage dissolves Massachusetts General Court. Representatives meet illegally in Concord and invite the Pre-Government Act Council to resume business as if still under the 1691 Charter. Other colonial legislatures similarly ignore prorogations and dissolutions. Joseph Warren presents "Suffolk Resolves" (9 Sept) calling for non-importation, though most colonies prefer to await actions by Continental Congress. Opposition publications include Thomas Jefferson's *Summary View of the Rights of British America.* Jamaica sends "Petition and Memorial" to George III supporting Massachusetts. Other island governors report a "republican spirit." In Parliament itself Chatham, Wilkes, Edmund Burke, and Isaac Barré maintain vocal dissent.

Sept 5. First Continental Congress meets in Philadelphia. Warns Massachusetts to avoid aggression but promises aid if attacked. Rejects

May–Aug. Crowds close Massachusetts court houses in response to Coercive Acts and force judges to resign in public ceremonies.

Sept 1. Boston-based British troops seize cannon and powder from stores in Cambridge and Charles Town.

Oct 7. Massachusetts Congress names John Hancock to head Committee of Safety authorized to call out militia. Calls on localities to drill militia (Feb 1775).

Dec 14. Warned by Paul Revere of plan to garrison Portsmouth, New Hampshire, a band led by John Sullivan peacefully overawes guards at Ft. William and Mary and carries off arms and powder.

March 8. Massachusetts Assembly attempts to prohibit slave trade but is prorogued next day.

June 5. Solemn League and Covenant, drawn up by Boston Committee of Correspondence, binds subscribers to end trade in and consumption of British imports as of 1 October.

Oct 20. Congress recommends that colonies discourage horse racing, cock fighting, gambling, theater, and other "expensive diversions and entertainments." Evidence shows that such activities continued.

Oct 24. Congress forms the Continental Association, a non-importation organization, taking effect on 1 December. Enforced locally by Committees of Inspection.

Joseph Galloway's "Plan of Union" for an American Congress sharing power with Parliament (28 Sept). Adopts "Declaration and Resolves" against Intolerable Acts and taxation without representation (14 Oct). Adopts Continental Association for non-importation and authorizes local Committees of Inspection to enforce embargo if demands not met within one year (18 Oct). Adjourns (26 Oct), resolving to reconvene next May.

Oct 7. Massachusetts House, meeting in Salem, declares itself a Provincial Congress.

Dec. Pamphlet controversy between John Adams, writing as "Novanglus" and the Tory Daniel Leonard, as "Massachusettensis," who argues for Crown sovereignty whereby liberty is granted at pleasure. Adams replies that sovereignty is grounded in consent and Parliament's power is limited to regulating external trade.

1775	1775	1775
Jan 20. House of Lords rejects Chatham's conciliatory Provisional Bill whereby Parliament would remain sovereign in America but renounce taxation power. Parliament declares Massachusetts in a state of rebellion (9 Feb) but endorses North's conciliation plan whereby Parliament would forsake all but external taxes on colonies that taxed themselves (27 Feb). Rejects Burke's conciliation bill entailing acceptance of Continental Congress demands (22 March). **March 21.** Franklin departs England for America. Arrives in Philadelphia 5 May. **March 23.** Patrick Henry predicts fighting in New England in famous "Liberty or Death" speech. **May 10.** Second Continental Congress meets in Philadelphia. Resolves to put colonies in a state of defense (15 May). **May 16.** Provincial Congress of Massachusetts, after its prospective constitution is rejected by voters in America's first referendum,	**April 14.** Gage receives letter from Dartmouth commanding forceful implementation of Coercive Acts but refusing request for 20,000 troops to restore order. Dartmouth still believes trouble caused by a few rabble rousers. **April 18–19.** "Midnight Ride" of Paul Revere warns rural patriots that "the British are coming" to seize defense supplies. **April 19.** Battles of Lexington and Concord. Patriots harass Redcoat retreat to Boston. Massachusetts Congress mobilizes 13,600 soldiers. Neighboring colonies form militia groups to march on Boston. **May 10.** Ethan Allen and Benedict Arnold capture Ft. Ticonderoga and Crown Point. **May 25.** Generals Sir William Howe, Sir Henry Clinton, and John Burgoyne arrive to assist Gage. **May 26.** Congress resolves on state of defense, petitions Canadians to join resistance (29 May), forms Continental Army (15 June) of which George Washington takes	**Feb.** Massachusetts Congress appoints Drs. Benjamin Church and Joseph Warren to oversee medical needs of local militia. Committee of Safety later finds surgeons inadequately trained. Congress further shows increased professionalization of medicine through creation of Army Medical Department (May), although it suffered from inadequate funds and feuding administrators. Benjamin Church appointed first Surgeon General of Continental Army (25 July). **Feb 22.** "American Manufactory of Woolens, Linens and Cottons" established as America's first joint stock company. Shares sold on subscription at £10 each. **March 30.** Parliament passes "New England Trade and Fisheries Act" banning trade with West Indies but restoring it with Britain. Extended to Pennsylvania, New Jersey, Maryland, Virginia, and South Carolina (13 April).

suggests that Congress write a model constitution.

May 31. Mecklenburg County (North Carolina) Resolutions void all laws and commissions emanating from London.

June 9. Congress recommends Provincial Congress of Massachusetts elect its own executive Council in place of Crown appointees imposed by the Government Act. Massachusetts elects a 28-member alternative council and declares the 1691 Charter a temporary constitution (29 June).

July 6. Congress establishes Post Office with Franklin as Post Master General. Adopts "Olive Branch Petition" to George III explaining necessity of defensive measures, blaming corrupt ministers, and requesting the King to end armed conflict (8 July). Postpones decision on Franklin's Plan for Union and proposals for opening commerce and seeking political alliance with foreign nations (21 July). Rejects North's conciliation plan (31 July). Adjourns (2 Aug).

Aug 23. George III rejects the "Olive Branch."

Sept 12. Congress reconvenes, now with representatives from Georgia, the last mainland colony to send delegates. Recommends that colonies write new constitutions.

Nov. Dartmouth resigns as Colonial Secretary. Replaced by Lord George Germain, Viscount Sackville.

Nov 4. New Jersey Assembly declares reports of colonists' seeking independence groundless.

Nov 16. Burke makes famous conciliation speech proposing "Motion for a Bill to Compose American Troubles," advancing a parliamentary supremacy controlled by self-denying ordinance. No such bill is passed.

Dec 6. Congress disavows allegiance to Parliament but admits sovereignty of Crown.

Dec 21. New Hampshire Provincial Congress meets to draft new constitution.

command (3 July), decides to invade Canada and issues £2,000 in paper money for expenses (22 June), and issues John Dickinson's "Declaration of the Causes and Necessity of Taking up Arms" (6 July).

June 12. Gage imposes martial law, declares Americans in treason, and offers pardon to all those who surrender (except John Hancock and John Adams).

June 17. British capture Bunker Hill but take heavy losses in frontal assault.

Aug 23. George III proclaims the colonies in "open and avowed rebellion," declaring, "The die is now cast. The colonies must either submit or triumph." North issues "A Proclamation for Suppressing Armed Rebellion."

Sept 25. Americans invade Canada, reaching Montreal (13 Dec), where Ethan Allen is captured and held for war's duration. Forced to retreat (31 Dec).

Oct 10. Howe succeeds Gage as British Commander-in-Chief.

Nov 7. Governor Dunmore declares martial law in Virginia, offers freedom to slaves who fight patriot masters (17 Nov), and wins Battle of Great Bridge (11 Dec).

Nov 10. Congress raises two marine battalions, forms navy (28 Nov), of which Esek Hopkins takes command (22 Dec).

Nov 29. Congress forms secret committee to communicate with America's friends. Meets Bonvouloir, who assures French goodwill, use of ports, and neutrality in Canada. Sends Silas Deane to purchase war supplies (3 March 1776).

April 15. Franklin and Rush establish *The Society for the Relief of Free Negroes Unlawfully Held in Bondage.*

May. Massachusetts illegally prints £26,000 paper money. South Carolina prints £1,870,000 (June). Fearing taxes, both emissions funded by borrowing to be redeemed through taxes in the indefinite future. Congress issues £2,000,000 (22 June) and another £4,000,000 by year's end, delaying redemption until 1779.

Oct. 51 women in Edenton, North Carolina, sign pledge to support patriot cause, illustrating the importance of women in the Revolution. Thomas Paine writes article in *Pennsylvania Magazine* espousing women's rights. Other important writings are Warren's *The Group*, again featuring Hutchinson as "Rapatio"; John Trumbull's satire on American Tories, *M'Fingal*; and Samuel Seabury's loyalist *Letters of a Westchester Farmer*.

Dec 22. Parliament passes Prohibitory Act on trade with colonies and declares them beyond Crown protection.		

1776	*1776*	*1776*
Jan 5. New Hampshire becomes first colony to write new constitution. **Jan 10.** Publication of Thomas Paine's republican *Common Sense*; John Adams's "Thoughts on Government"; and (anon) *The People the Best Governors*. In England Richard Price publishes *Observations on the Nature of Civil Liberty* and *Additional Observations* (1777), advocating free states bound to the empire by affection and interest. **Jan 11.** Maryland instructs delegates to Congress not to consent to independence. Massachusetts, however, replaces delegate Thomas Cushing with Elbridge Gerry, making for a small majority in favor of independence by February. South Carolina adopts new constitution erecting the first independently operating government in America (26 March). North Carolina becomes first colony to instruct delegates in Congress to vote for independence, if in concert with others (12 April). Georgia adopts interim constitution (15 April). Pennsylvania election gives victory to opponents of independence (1 May). Rhode Island adopts interim constitution and repudiates allegiance to Crown (4 May). **May 10.** Congress adopts John Adams's motion calling on colonies to form their own governments and adds preamble (15 May) that all executive departments of government under Crown authority be suppressed. **May 11.** North Carolina adopts provisional constitution. Virginia instructs delegates to vote for independence (15 May). **May 27.** Virginia and North Carolina motions for independence laid before Congress. Richard Henry Lee proposes independence (7 June). Some delegations threaten to	**Jan 1.** British warship bombards Norfolk, Virginia. **Jan.** Britain secures treaties with several German states to provide 20,000 mercenary troops for American War. **Feb 28.** Back-country Scots Highlander loyalists routed at Moore's Creek Bridge, North Carolina. **March 5.** Americans capture Dorchester Heights and besiege Boston, forcing British evacuation (17 March). **May 2.** Louis XVI permits French foreign minister Comte Vergennes to lend Americans £40,000 through an arms trading company. **June 7.** Americans retreating from Canada defeated at Three Rivers. **June 27.** Thomas Hickey hanged for conspiring to deliver Washington to the British, the first American soldier executed by military court. **June 28.** British fail to take Charles Town and abandon the South for two years. Cherokees attack Carolina rebels but no other southern tribe joins. Johnson fails to secure military support of Iroquois for British. **July 2.** Howe lands on Staten Island with 10,000 troops. **July 12.** Admiral Richard Howe arrives off New York coast with British Navy. Esek Hopkins defeated at Nassau (March), trapped in Narragansett Bay (Aug), dismissed by Congress (2 Jan 1777). **Aug 27.** Washington, defeated at Long Island, retreats to Manhattan. Captured patriot Nathan Hale achieves martyrdom by proclaiming "I only regret that I have but one life to lose for my country" at his execution. Sullivan captured and sent to Congress as peace envoy. **Sept 11.** Staten Island Peace Conference breaks down over American refusal to rescind Declaration of Independence.	**March 9.** Publication of Adam Smith's *The Wealth of Nations*. **April 6.** Congress resolves to open American ports to all nations except Britain and its dominions and temporarily closes slave trade. **July 3.** Publication of John Leacock's satire of pre-revolutionary politics. *The Fall of British Tyranny*. In addition to *Book of the American Chronicles of the Times* (1774–5), this makes Leacock a leading satirist of his day. Charles Willson Peale, after studying in London under American painter Benjamin West, returns to Philadelphia and begins a brilliant career in portraiture. Before the Revolution many American artists moved to the metropolis; Peale begins a partial migration back. Legend has it that at this time Washington requested Philadelphia seamstress Betsy Ross to produce an American flag. Ross was commissioned by Congress to make various flags but it is not certain she designed or manufactured the stars and stripes. **Oct.** Jefferson's law against entails passes the Virginia legislature. Other colonies follow suit. These acts often merely ban a practice long in decline. Virginia also considers "Bill for Exempting Dissenters from Contributing to the Support of the Church." Begins ten-year struggle over the question of religious liberty. **Nov.** Henry Alline begins itinerant preaching in Nova Scotia. That colony, confused over the revolutionary crisis, undergoes a social-religious great awakening. **Dec 5.** Phi Beta Kappa founded at College of William and Mary as a social fraternity. **Dec.** $25,000,000 Continental paper money is in circulation.

walk out. Congress postpones voting until 1 July but authorizes a committee headed by Thomas Jefferson to draft Declaration of Independence (10 June) and appoints 13-member committee (one from each delegation) headed by John Dickinson to draft Articles of Confederation (12 June).

June 12. Virginia Convention passes 16 resolutions comprising Declaration of Rights. Adopts new constitution (29 June).

June 19. Government of Pennsylvania overthrown by Committee of Safety. New Pennsylvania Conference discards allegiance to Crown (24 June) and authorizes convention to meet on 8 July and draft constitution. New Jersey adopts new constitution. Grants women's suffrage until revised in 1807 (2 July).

June 24. Congress declares loyalist property open to seizure and recommends confiscation acts (27 Nov 1777).

July 2. Congress votes in favor of Lee's resolution. Unanimous except for New York delegates' abstention (not yet authorized to vote for independence). With a few alterations Congress accepts Jefferson's Declaration of Independence (4 July). Read publicly in Philadelphia (8 July) and to Washington's troops in New York (9 July). New York authorizes independence (9 July) and Congress adds the word "unanimous" to the Declaration's preamble (15 July). Engrossed copy of Declaration signed (2 Aug). Congress replaces title "United Colonies" with "United States" (9 Sept).

July 12. Committee presents draft Articles of Confederation to Congress. Issues of state representation, expense apportionment, and western lands prevent agreement.

Sept 20. Delaware writes new constitution. Pennsylvania ratifies its Declaration of Rights and new constitution, the most radical to date (28 Sept). Maryland adopts Declaration of Rights (3 Nov) and new constitution (8 Nov).

Congress sends Franklin and Arthur Lee to assist Deane as diplomatic commissioners to France (26 Sept).

Sept 15. William Howe captures New York City and invades New Jersey.

Oct 11. Sir Guy Carleton defeats Benedict Arnold at Valcor Island. American lake fleet destroyed at Split Rock (13 Oct).

Oct 28. Howe defeats Washington at White Plains.

Nov 16–18. Lord Cornwallis captures Fts. Washington and Lee, taking 2,000 prisoners.

Dec 11. Pursued by Howe, Washington crosses the Delaware. His third in command, Charles Lee, is captured (13 Dec) and held for 16 months.

Dec 26. Washington defeats Howe at Trenton and captures 1,000 Hessian troops.

Nov. Rockinghamites formally secede from Parliament in protest against colonial policy. **Dec 19.** *Philadelphia Journal* publishes first of Paine's Revolutionary War pamphlets, *The American Crisis*, written while serving with Nathanael Greene.		
1777	**1777**	**1777**
Jan 16. Vermont secedes from New York. Its July constitution goes further than that of Pennsylvania by establishing universal manhood suffrage and abolishing slavery. Georgia adopts new constitution (4 Feb). New York follows (20 April). **April 21.** Congress returns to Articles of Confederation and immediately passes Thomas Burke's (North Carolina) amendment guaranteeing sovereignty of individual states. **Sept 11.** Delaware adopts Declaration of Rights. **Oct 7.** Congress endorses one state, one vote principle of Articles. Agrees that expenses of national government be settled according to the amount of surveyed land in each state. Creates Boards of War, Admiralty, and Treasury (14 Oct). Approves the 13 Articles of Confederation, having somewhat diluted Dickinson's original nationalist outlook, and issues them to the states for approval (15 Nov). **Dec 14.** North Carolina adopts new constitution and Declaration of Rights (17 Dec).	**Jan 3.** Washington defeats Howe at Princeton. Howe retreats to New York. **July.** British capture Mt. Defiance (2 July) and Ticonderoga (6 July). Barry St. Leger marches south to join Burgoyne at Albany. His combined British–Indian forces attack Oneida Indians and destroy Iroquois unity. **July 23.** Howe advances on Pennsylvania with force of 15,000. Defeats Washington at Brandywine (11 Sept), captures Philadelphia (26 Sept) and Germantown (4 Oct). Congress flees Philadelphia for Lancaster, then York, Pennsylvania (19–30 Sept). **Aug 4.** Congress replaces Philip John Schuyler with Horatio Gates as Commander of Northern Army. **Sept 19.** Burgoyne defeats Daniel Morgan at first Battle of Bemis Heights, New York, but is defeated by Arnold at the second (7 Oct) and retreats to Saratoga. **Sept 25.** Thomas Conway writes letters to Congress and to Gates criticizing certain commanders, including Washington. Washington rebukes Conway, forcing Gates to disavow connection with "Conway Cabal." **Oct 17.** Gates attacks Burgoyne and secures important victory at Saratoga. Convention of Saratoga transports Burgoyne and 5,700 troops back to England. **Dec 18.** Washington settles army at Valley Forge for the winter.	**June 14.** Congress resolves on stars and stripes flag design. **July.** Vermont establishes the first constitution forbidding slavery. **July.** Congress finds that Continental currency has lost two-thirds of face value. Loan office sells certificates of various kinds, raising $60,000,000 before its closure in 1781. Delaware, New York, and New Jersey raise taxes to decrease the amount of circulating paper. **Nov.** Congress asks states to raise $5,000,000 for the common treasury.
1778	**1778**	**1778**
March 19. South Carolina adopts new constitution. Massachusetts voters reject proposed constitution in second referendum.	**Feb 6.** By Treaty of Amity and Commerce, France promises no peace until Britain recognizes American independence. France	**Jan.** By this time state currency emissions exceed £7,000,000. By mid-year Congress is printing $5–10,000,000 every few weeks.

May 11. Death of Chatham.
June. Ten states had either ratified the Articles of Confederation or were preparing to do so. Expecting Delaware, New Jersey, and Maryland to follow, Congress proceeds with French negotiations as if under the Articles.

announces treaty terms, confers full diplomatic status on American commissioners, and appoints Conrad Alexandre Gerard Ambassador to the US (13 March). Britain recalls its Ambassador to France. Congress replaces Deane, too generous with commissions and suspected of private arms dealings, with John Adams and appoints Franklin Minister to France and John Jay Minister to Spain (31 March). Ratifies treaty (4 May).
Feb 17. Parliament appoints Earl of Carlisle to Peace Commission in America. Congress rejects negotiations with Carlisle and declares no terms short of British withdrawal and recognition of independence acceptable (22 April).
April 13. Admiral d'Estaing and French fleet leave Toulon, arriving off New York on 11 July. John Paul Jones illustrates revival of American sea forces by attacking English port of Whitehaven and defeating the *Drake* in the Irish Sea (23 April).
May 8. Clinton replaces Howe as British Commander-in-Chief.
June 18. Clinton evacuates Philadelphia to protect New York.
June 28. Charles Lee engages Clinton at Monmouth. Washington saves Lee from total defeat and retreats to take position at White Plains above New York City. Lee court martialed and dismissed for ineptitude.
July 3. Loyalist and Indian forces massacre settlers in Wyoming Valley, Pennsylvania. George Rogers Clark captures Kaskasia (4 July) and battles to maintain American dominance in the West.
Aug 29. D'Estaing and Sullivan fail in joint offensive on Newport, Rhode Island.
Oct 3. Carlisle's *Manifesto and Proclamation* threatens destruction if Americans do not submit to peace. Returns to England (27 Nov).
Nov 11. British and Indians inflict Cherry Valley (New York) Massacre.
Dec 29. Lord Germain's new southern strategy bears fruit with British capture of Savannah.

March 6. New South Carolina constitution is first of many to restrict office-holding to Protestant Christians.
Dec. Jefferson's "Bill for the More General Diffusion of Knowledge" passes House but fails in Virginia Senate. A bill of 1796 establishes public elementary schools in each hundred, as Jefferson hoped, but fails to establish grammar schools in each county.

817

1779	1779	1779
April. People of Massachusetts vote for the first popularly elected Constitutional Convention in American history. Meets on 1 September. **June 1.** Thomas Jefferson elected Governor of Virginia. **Sept 13.** John Jay, President of Congress, issues circular letter to states praising a lasting union and the idea of American nationhood. Reflects a "new nationalism" promoted by Jay and others, notably James Madison. **Oct 22.** New York, having already seized much loyalist property, institutionalizes the practice with a Confiscation Act. All states follow suit within three years. **Nov 15.** Earl of Carlisle appointed President of Board of Trade. **Dec.** Christopher Wyvill of Yorkshire launches County Association movement against high taxes, corruption, and for a new triennial act. This, in addition to Wilkes and parliamentary opposition, reflects growing political disaffection in Britain in mid-war years.	**Jan 29.** Georgia campaign continues with British capture of Augusta. Andrew Pickens defeats loyalists at Kettle Creek (14 Feb) but loses heavily at Brier Creek (3 March). D'Estaing begins siege of Savannah (23 April). Benjamin Lincoln defeated at Stono Ferry (19 June). **Feb 3.** William Moultrie repels British at Port Royal, South Carolina. **Feb 25.** George Rogers Clark captures Vincennes. **March 29.** Congress approves Baron von Steuben's "Blue Book" army regulations. **April 12.** Franco-Spanish Treaty of Aranjuez recruits Spanish aid in American War in exchange for French aid in regaining Gibraltar and Minorca. Spain declares war on Britain (21 June). **May 10.** British capture and burn Portsmouth and Norfolk, Virginia. **July 15.** Americans capture Stony Point, New York, and Paulus Hook, New Jersey (19 Aug). **Sept 23.** John Paul Jones's *Bonhomme Richard* defeats *Serapis* and *Countess of Scarborough* off the east coast of England. **Oct 11.** Clinton evacuates Rhode Island to concentrate on New York and the South. **Oct 28.** Suffering heavy losses, d'Estaing withdraws from Savannah.	**Jan 14.** Continental currency deemed worth only one-eighth of face value. **Nov 17.** Currency depreciated to almost one-fortieth of face value. Congress requests $95,000,000 from the states rising to $180,000,000 next year. Asks states to retire $6,000,000 per annum of Continental currency and discontinues printing paper money with more than $241,000,000 already in circulation.
1780	1780	1780
March 20. New referendum approves Massachusetts constitution. Takes effect 25 October. **Oct.** Hartford Convention (New England states and New York) agrees on need for stronger central government. Alexander Hamilton and Gouverneur Morris write "Continentalist Letters" to that effect. **Dec 12.** Lord Grantham appointed President of Board of Trade.	**Feb 28.** Catherine II of Russia abandons "patient neutrality" policy and forms League of Armed Neutrality with Denmark, Sweden, Prussia, Austria, and Sicily. Congress sends Francis Dana to St. Petersburg (19 Dec) but he is ignored. **May 2.** Comte de Rochambeau's army leaves Brest, arriving off Rhode Island on 11 July. Postponement of Franco-American invasion of Canada alienates *Canadiens*.	**March 1.** Pennsylvania Act for Emancipation, drawn up by Thomas Paine, is the first Act for gradual abolition of slavery in America. Slaves' children born after the Act were to serve to age 28. Other northern states follow through the end of the century, usually emancipating slaves born after a certain date at age 25 or 28. **May 4.** American Academy of Arts and Sciences chartered at Boston. **May 20.** J. Hector St. John de Crèvecoeur sells manuscript of *Letters from an American Farmer* to

	May 12. Clinton captures Charles Town and 5,500 patriots. Provokes bitterness by offering freedom in exchange for oaths of allegiance. Dispatches Cornwallis to complete pacification of South Carolina and Georgia and to invade the Upper South. May 25. Two Connecticut regiments mutiny over rations and pay. Curbed by Pennsylvanians. June 13. Congress commissions Gates to command new Southern Army. Defeated by Cornwallis at Camden, South Carolina (16 Aug). Tory Banastre Tarleton defeats Thomas Sumter at Fishing Creek (18 Aug). Cornwallis invades North Carolina (8 Sept). Sept 6. Congress calls on landed states to cede western lands. Promises national domain would be used to benefit all states and that new states would be formed out of ceded lands (10 Oct). Sept 25. Revealed as a traitor, Benedict Arnold flees to the British, who reward him with money and military command. Oct 7. Nathanael Greene defeats Patrick Ferguson's Tennessee Loyalists, shielding Cornwallis's flank, at Kings Mountain, North Carolina. Cornwallis retreats to Winnsboro, South Carolina. Greene, appointed to command Southern Army (14 Oct), begins using tactics of guerrilla warfare. Sumter avenges Tarleton at Blackstocks (20 Nov). Dec 20. British capture Henry Laurens *en route* to Netherlands, discover secret Treaty of Aix-la-Chapelle, and, to prevent Dutch joining League of Armed Neutrality, declare war. British defeat Dutch warships supplying American arms from St. Eustatius.	Davies and Davis of London. Published early in 1782. Oct. Continental currency depreciated to one-seventy-seventh of face value. 36 Philadelphia women launch campaign to equip American troops, collecting around $300,000 in Continental dollars in two weeks.
1781	1781	1781
Feb 3. Congress unsuccessfully asks states to amend Articles of Confederation so it can raise 5% impost on foreign goods imported to America. Creates three new executive departments; Finance, War, and Marine (7 Feb).	Jan 1. 2,400 unpaid Pennsylvania soldiers march on Philadelphia protesting against new recruits receiving $25 commissions. Washington dispatches Robert Howe to quell mutiny. Jan 2. Landless state majority in	Feb 3. Having revalued currency at 100 to 1, Congress asks states to grant it power to collect duty on imports to America. States refuse, fearing excessive central power. By April currency is worth 167 to 1. It collapses in the summer, giving

Feb 27. Maryland ratifies Articles of Confederation, the last state to do so. Articles take full effect 1 March. **Aug 22.** Congressional Committee report proposes seven amendments to Articles to increase central government power, though never voted on or presented to the states. **Aug 22.** Elizabeth Freeman ("Bett") wins freedom in case of *Brom and Bett v. Ashley.* Establishing that the 1780 Massachusetts constitutional principle declaring all individuals "born free and equal" applied to blacks as well as whites, the case provides for the judicial dismantling of slavery in the state. It also illustrates the considerable power of courts (judicial review had first been established in New Jersey in 1780). Similar cases won in other northern states in the 1780s.

Congress rejects Virginia's conditional cession of western lands, demanding the whole Kentucky territory and validation of land titles not validated by Virginia. **Jan 17.** Daniel Morgan defeats Tarleton heavily at Cowpens, North Carolina. Other American successes are Henry Lee's harassment of Carolina loyalists and James Craig's occupation of Wilmington. David Fanning's loyalists begin guerrilla retaliation. Greene marches into South Carolina and suffers series of defeats but captures some small British posts (April–July). **March 15.** Cornwallis loses one-fourth of his forces at Guilford, North Carolina. Marches on Virginia, almost capturing Governor Jefferson and his assembly at Charlottesville (4 June). Occupies Yorktown (1 Aug). **April 2.** John Barry defeats British ships *Mars* and *Minerva.* French Admiral de Grasse captures Tobago and St. Christopher, and embarks for Chesapeake on 14 April. Receives correspondence of 21 May from Washington and Rochambeau to attack the British in Virginia. **June 11.** Congress names John Adams, Franklin, Jay, Jefferson, and Laurens to peace commission to England. **Sept 8.** Arnold burns New London, Connecticut, and captures Ft. Griswold. Greene defeated at Eutaw Springs, South Carolina (9 Sept). **Sept 10.** De Grasse drives British off the Virginia Capes, leaving Cornwallis without naval support. Washington and Rochambeau combine forces of 16,800 at Williamsburg (28 Sept) and besiege Yorktown (9 Oct), forcing Cornwallis's decisive surrender (18 Oct).

rise to the phrase "not worth a continental." **May 14.** Robert Morris appointed Superintendent of Finance. Proposes federal land, poll, and excise taxes, and a national bank (21 May). Congress approves national bank to make short-term loans to Congress and pay interest on national debt (26 May). Charters Bank of North America based in Philadelphia with capitalization of $400,000 (31 Dec).

1782	1782	1782
March 20. North resigns to avoid further votes of no confidence. Beginning of Rockingham/Shelburne ministry. **July 11.** Parliament abolishes Board of Trade.	**Feb 27.** Hearing of Yorktown surrender, Parliament votes to discontinue offensive operations in America. New Shelburne administration (20 March) opens informal peace talks in Paris (12	**May.** Virginia manumission law results in eventual emancipation of 10,000 slaves. **June 11.** John Adams secures loan of $2,000,000 from the Netherlands. Dutch aid confirmed

July 31. Death of Rockingham. Shelburne continues as Prime Minister with support of George III but without safe parliamentary majority.

April). Formal negotiations begin 27 September.

April 4. Carleton succeeds Clinton as British Commander-in-Chief and begins organizing withdrawal. Evacuates Charleston and Savannah (9 May).

April 12. British capture de Grasse at Battle of the Saintes, near Jamaica.

April 19. Netherlands becomes first nation formally to recognize the American republic.

Oct 19. Congress accepts New York's cession of western lands (also claimed by Virginia).

Nov 29. Richard Oswald signs provisional agreement with Franklin, Jay, and Laurens. Recognizes American independence, cedes all lands between Great Lakes and Mississippi River, and permits continued American participation in British fisheries. Agreement conditional on treaty with France. Vergennes, surprised at British generosity, criticizes US commissioners for not consulting him (15 Dec). Franklin's tactful reply (17 Dec) prevents discord.

and extended by Treaty of Amity and Commerce (8 Oct).

June 20. Congress adopts Great Seal of the United States.

July 27. Robert Morris presents Report on Public Credit recommending suspension of interest payments on national debt and Congress taking responsibility for state debts which it could redeem through taxation. Rejected for fear of excessive central power. National debt assessed at $27,000,000 specie.

Nov 22. Harvard appoints three professors of medicine to new medical school. Promoted by Nathan Smith, who went on to found medical schools at Dartmouth (1797), Yale (1810), Bowdoin (1820), and Vermont (1822).

1783	1783	1783

Feb 24. Concerned over Shelburne's generosity to Americans, Fox and North join forces to provoke his resignation. Fox and North become Secretaries of State in a coalition government with Duke of Portland as figurehead Prime Minister.

April 26. 7,000 loyalists leave New York, the last of the 100,000 to flee to Canada or Europe from test acts, loyalty oaths, disfranchisement, discriminatory taxes, confiscation, and expulsion.

Oct 31. New Hampshire Convention adopts new constitution. Takes effect June 1784.

Nov 17. Fox's East India Bill, attempting to usurp power in eastern empire from Crown to Parliament, is defeated amid controversy. Fox resigns and is replaced by King's favorite, William

Jan 20. Armistice in Europe established at near status quo ante bellum, pending formal Anglo-French treaty.

March 10. Army discontent over pay reaches climax with John Armstrong's "Newburgh Addresses," calling fellow officers to action, and "lash remonstrances" speech criticizing Congress. Washington calms the situation by personally calling for patience and obedience to civil authority (15 March). In Philadelphia Mutiny (17 June), soldiers surround the Pennsylvania State House where Congress is sitting. Peacefully dispersed on 24 June. Congress moves to Princeton, then Annapolis.

April 11. Congress proclaims cessation of war. Ratifies provisional treaty (15 April), begins

April 3. Treaty of Amity and Commerce with Sweden. Lord Sheffield's "Observations on the Commerce of the American States" advocates diverting Anglo-American commerce to British vessels and excluding American ships from West Indies. Influences defeat of Pitt's call to allow continued American trade in the islands.

April 18. Congress proposes two amendments to Articles: one giving it power to raise import duties, the other replacing the system of expense apportionment among the states based on land values with one based on population (including three-fifths of all slaves). Both are rejected.

May 13. Formation of the Society of Cincinnati with membership restricted to Revolutionary War

Pitt the younger. Fox–North retain Commons majority and defeat Pitt ministry 16 times in six months.

furloughing army (26 May).
May 2. Washington submits "Sentiments on a Peace Establishment": a blueprint for a republican militia and civil control thereof.
Sept 23. Treaty of Paris confirms provisional treaty and armistice.
Nov 25. British troops evacuate New York.
Dec 23. Washington resigns commission.

veterans and their first-born sons. Washington is first president, Hamilton second. Criticized for being aristocratic. Less aristocratic and more ethnic is the Society for the Friendly Sons of St. Patrick of Irish veterans in New York City.
May 30. Benjamin Towne establishes the first daily newspaper in the US, the *Pennsylvania Evening Post*. Noah Webster publishes *A Grammatical Institute of the English Language*, and begins work on his *American Dictionary* (1828).

1784	1784	1784
March 8. Pitt institutes Committee of Council on Trade and Plantations to replace defunct Board of Trade. **March 25.** Dissolution of Parliament. The subsequent elections give large parliamentary majority to Pitt, who forms a ministry of King's favorites. Relative calm returns to British politics which, combined with financial reforms, an industrializing economy, and continued primacy in trade with America, restores confidence and power of British nation within a short time.	**Jan 14.** Congress ratifies Treaty of Paris. **April 23.** Having finally received unconditional cession of Virginia western lands, Congress considers the first territorial ordinance. Though rejected over size of parcels to be distributed and apportionment of costs among the states (30 April), it provides precedents for methods of state admittance and the grid system. Other states follow Virginia in ceding land. **June 2.** Congress orders Henry Knox to discharge all but 80 soldiers of Continental Army. Rejects Washington's proposal for a small peace-time army but establishes the First American Regiment, 700 men from state militias, to defend the frontier. **Oct.** US begins dictating treaties to Indians, often quickly repudiated because made under duress or because of white settler encroachment.	**May 28.** Robert Morris resigns. Replaced by Treasury Board of Samuel Osgood, Walter Livingston, and Arthur Lee. **July 2.** British Order in Council denies American access to West Indies and later Canada, Ireland, and Britain. **July 6.** Richard Price publishes *Observations on the American Revolution*, dedicated to "the Free and United States of America." American achievements include Jeremy Belknap's *History of New Hampshire*; Jedediah Morse's *Geography Made Easy*; Rush's *Enquiry into the Effects of Spirituous Liquors*; and Judith Sargent Murray's "Desultory Thoughts upon the Utility of Encouraging a Degree of Self Complacency, Especially in Female Bosoms." **Aug 30.** John Greene lands the *Empress of China* at Canton, opening lucrative American China trade. **Nov 14.** Samuel Seabury consecrated as America's first Episcopal Bishop. **Dec.** Baltimore "Christmas Conference" organizes American Methodist Church. Francis Asbury is co-superintendent and first Bishop. Church instructs members to manumit slaves. Next year, however, Virginia Methodists suspend the "Slave Rule," beginning schism between northern and southern churches.

1785	1785	1785
Jan 24. Congress appoints James Monroe to lead a committee to draft an appeal to the states to give Congress power to secure treaties with foreign nations. No action taken. **July 11.** Massachusetts Assembly passes resolution favoring nationalistic revision of Articles of Confederation. Delegates to Congress fail to present it. **Nov.** Alexander Hamilton in New York, Benjamin Rush in Pennsylvania, and Aedanus Burke in North Carolina begin campaigns to restore rights and property to loyalists.	**Feb 24.** Congress replaces Franklin with Jefferson as Minister to France and appoints John Adams Minister to Britain. Adams formally demands British withdrawal from US soil in accordance with Treaty of Paris (30 Nov). British reply (28 Feb 1786) holds that presence in northern forts will be maintained until Americans fulfill obligations to British creditors and loyalists. **March 8.** Congress appoints Knox Secretary of War. Begins more pacific Indian policy, creating the first reservations next year.	**March.** Establishment of The Philadelphia Society for Promoting Agriculture, America's first purely agricultural society. Innovations in transportation include institution of the first regular stage routes between Philadelphia, New York City, Albany, and Boston. John Fitch begins pioneering work on steamboats. **March 25.** Mt. Vernon Conference promotes free navigation of rivers by states and coordination between states on matters of currency, duties, and debt funding. Most states ban export of goods on British ships. Pennsylvania deals with debt problem by issuing $150,000 in bills of credit. Other states follow. Even where debts are effectively managed, tension between debtors and creditors exists over currency depreciation and taxes. Jefferson proposes national coinage system (6 July), put into effect on 8 August 1786. Many begin to favor greater central government power over the economy. **May 10.** Publication of Jefferson's *Notes on Virginia.* Other publications include David Ramsay's *History of the Revolution in South Carolina;* Timothy Dwight's *The Conquest of Canaan,* lionizing Washington; and Macpherson's *Philadelphia Directory,* the first of its kind in America. **May 20.** Congress sets aside section 16 of each western reserve township for public schools. **Sept 10.** Treaty of Amity and Commerce with Prussia.
1786	1786	1786
June 26. Congress discusses Charles Pinckney's motion for reorganizing government. **Aug 7.** Congress proposes several amendments pertaining to power over commerce with foreign nations and between states, and power to requisition money from the states. Superseded by Constitutional Convention. **Sept 11.** Annapolis Convention	**Aug.** Depression and high taxes provoke indebted farmers in western Massachusetts to revolt. Only Virginia responds to Congress's call for money and men to end Shays's Rebellion. In other states debtor-farmers demand state laws for protection, close courts to prevent debt and tax collection, and attack tax collectors and even legislators. These economic difficulties and	**Jan 16.** Passage of Jefferson's Virginia Statute for Religious Freedom. **Jan 21.** At Madison's instigation, Virginia legislators invite all states to discuss economic and commercial problems at a conference in Annapolis. Depression reaches lowest point in summer, and when US defaults on interest payments to Spain, France,

meets. Delegates agree to a more ambitious convention meeting in Philadelphia in May 1787 to consider provisions "to render the constitution of the Federal Government adequate to the exigencies of the Union" (Hamilton).

problems of internal security highlight inadequacy of government under the Articles of Confederation and increase demands for stronger national government.

and the Netherlands (Aug) more become persuaded of need for governmental reform.
June 28. In exchange for gifts worth $10,000 the Emperor of Morocco agrees to end privateering on American ships by Mediterranean Barbary pirates.

1787	1787	1787
Feb 21. Congress approves Convention to revise Articles. **May 25.** 55 delegates to Constitutional Convention (from all states except Rhode Island) meet in Philadelphia. Edmund Randolph introduces the Virginia Plan, probably written by James Madison (29 May). Small state delegates disapprove of representation in federal government according to population. William Patterson introduces "purely federal" New Jersey Plan (14 June) proposing increases in federal power, especially to tax foreign and inter-state commerce, *within* the framework of the Articles. To ensure fair representation of small states it proposes one vote per state in federal legislature. Rejected in favor of entirely new national government (19 June). "Connecticut Compromise" (16 July) proposes bicameral legislature with equal state representation in the upper house and representation according to population in the lower, with money bills decided in lower house. Three-fifths of slaves would be counted in representative apportionment in the lower house. **July 19–26.** Convention draws up 23 "fundamental resolutions," forming a rough draft of a Constitution, and appoints Committee of Detail to draft final document. Begins debating draft (6 Aug). Attack on slavery and three-fifths clause roundly defeated (8 Aug). Two-year term for congressmen agreed (8 Aug). Six-year term for senators agreed (9 Aug). Power of Congress to regulate foreign, inter-state, and Indian commerce agreed (16 Aug). Congress forbidden from banning	**July 13.** Congress adopts Northwest Ordinance dictating that until a population of 5,000 was reached each area would be ruled by a federal governor. Thereafter a territory could elect an assembly, and when population reached 60,000 free inhabitants it could apply for statehood. Jefferson inserts clause banning slavery in these territories.	**Jan 1.** Publication of Joel Barlow's *Vision of Columbus,* comparing Washington to the discoverer of America. Also published that year were Rush's *Thoughts upon Female Education* and (anon) *Women Invited to War,* espousing a civic republican role for women in fighting government corruption. Established that year were the Pennsylvania Society for the Encouragement of Manufactures and Useful Arts and the first American cotton mill, at Beverly, Massachusetts, by John Cabot and Joshua Fisher. **May.** Founding of the British Anti-slavery Society.

African slave trade until 1808 and clause requiring states to return fugitive slaves passed (29 Aug).

Aug 31. Committee of Postponed Matters appointed to consider the presidency. Convention agrees on four-year term for president, electoral college representation for states equal to total representation in Congress, and House of Representatives to vote in the event of a tie (6 Sept). Many aspects of judicial power and balance of power between governmental branches and state and federal government remain ambiguous. Five-member Committee of Style appointed to make final draft (8 Sept).

Sept 12. Worried about excessive federal and executive power, Elbridge Gerry and George Mason propose a "Bill of Rights." Madison promises one at the first opportunity.

Sept 12–15. Debate over final draft. Unanimously accepted, with a few minor changes, by delegates of 12 states in attendance (16 Sept). To become operative when approved by nine states.

Sept 17. Convention adjourns. Franklin's closing speech becomes the most reprinted propaganda in favor of adoption. Other Federalist writings include *The Federalist Papers* by Hamilton, Madison, and Jay. Anti-Federalist literature includes Richard Henry Lee's *Letters from the Federal Farmer*, and "Cato's Letters," probably by George Clinton, in the *New York Journal*.

Dec 7. Delaware becomes the first state to ratify the Federal Constitution. Followed by Pennsylvania (12 Dec) and New Jersey (18 Dec).

1788	1788	1788
Jan 2. Georgia ratifies. Followed by Connecticut (9 Jan) and Massachusetts (6 Feb) proposing nine amendments. In a referendum in which Federalists refuse to participate, Rhode Island rejects the	**April.** John Adams resigns as Minister to Britain, still unable to secure withdrawal of soldiers from northwestern US territories. Other disappointing elements of Treaty of Paris were exclusion of Americans	**Feb 19.** Founding in Paris of French abolition society *Les Amis des Noirs*. Bankruptcy of French Government occurs, contributed to by the 1 billion livres spent on the American War between 1777 and 1783.

Constitution (24 March). Maryland (28 April) and South Carolina (23 May) ratify.

June 21. New Hampshire, proposing 12 amendments, becomes the ninth state to ratify, meaning the Constitution could go into effect. Virginia ratifies, proposing 20 amendments (25 June). North Carolina decides to withhold ratification until a bill of rights is incorporated (21 July). New York ratifies (26 July).

Sept 13. Congress names New York as site of new government. Fixes date of elections and meeting of First Congress. Last major act of Confederation Government is acceptance of cession by Maryland of ten square miles for future Federal District of Columbia (23 Dec).

from northern fisheries and West Indian trade by Britain and preclusion from Mississippi trade by Spain. Britain disappointed by inability to secure payment of creditors and compensation to loyalists; France at being unable to break British monopoly of American trade; and Indians at British surrender of western lands to the US.

Contributes to French Revolution of 1789.

1789	1789	1789

Jan 7. Presidential electors named by state legislatures. Congressional elections held and Electoral College casts ballots (4 Feb). First Congress convenes (4 March), though quorum not achieved until 1 April in the House and 5 April in the Senate. Senate declares Washington elected President with 69 votes and John Adams Vice President with 34 (6 April). Washington begins tour from Mt. Vernon to New York (16 April), inaugurated (30 April).

May. Georgia becomes first of many states to rewrite constitutions in early national period.

Aug 7. Knox appointed first War Secretary, Hamilton first Treasury Secretary (2 Sept), Samuel Osgood first Post Master General (22 Sept), Jefferson first Secretary of State (26 Sept), in Washington's first cabinet.

Sept 24. Judiciary Act establishes federal court system. John Jay appointed first Chief Justice.

Sept 25. Congress proposes 12 amendments, a "Bill of Rights," to encourage remaining states to adopt the Constitution.

Nov 21. North Carolina ratifies.

April 11. John Fenno founds Federalist *Gazette of the United States*. Important publications include William Gordon and David Ramsay's histories of the Revolution, both later revealed to have been plagiarized from wartime reports of the *Annual Register*; Webster's *Dissertation on the English Language*; and the first American novel, William Hill Brown's *The Power of Sympathy*.

1790	1790	1790
May 29. Rhode Island, last of the original 13 states, ratifies.		**March 23.** Franklin's last public writing satirizes slavery and asks Congress to abolish it. Franklin dies on 17 April.
1791		
Dec 15. Adopted by three-quarters of the states, the First Ten Amendments to the Constitution, known as the Bill of Rights, go into effect.		

Index

COMPILED BY MEG DAVIES

Note: The various Acts of Congress and of Parliament are grouped together under *Acts of Congress* and *Acts of Parliament*; battles of the War of Independence are grouped under *battles*, except for those of Concord, Lexington, Saratoga and Yorktown, which are indexed in detail in the appropriate place. Page references in *italics* indicate maps, tables and illustrations, while those in **bold** type are to the individual biographies on pages 697–793. The index uses the following abbreviations: Col. = Colonel; Gen. = General; Gov. = Governor; Lt.-Gov. = Lieutenant-Governor.

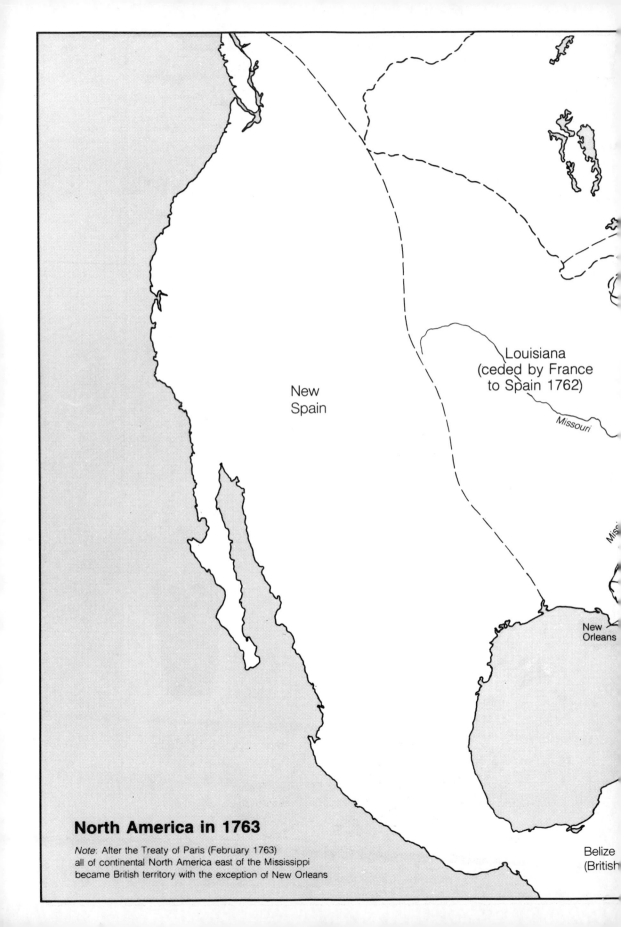

New
Spain

Louisiana
(ceded by France
to Spain 1762)

Missouri

Miss

Mis

New
Orleans

North America in 1763

Note: After the Treaty of Paris (February 1763)
all of continental North America east of the Mississippi
became British territory with the exception of New Orleans

Belize
(British

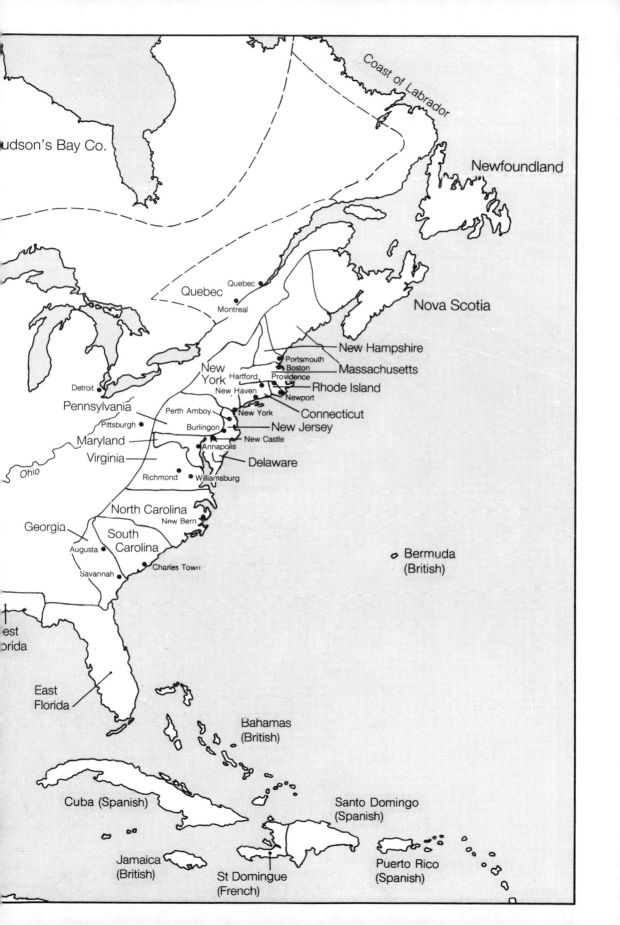

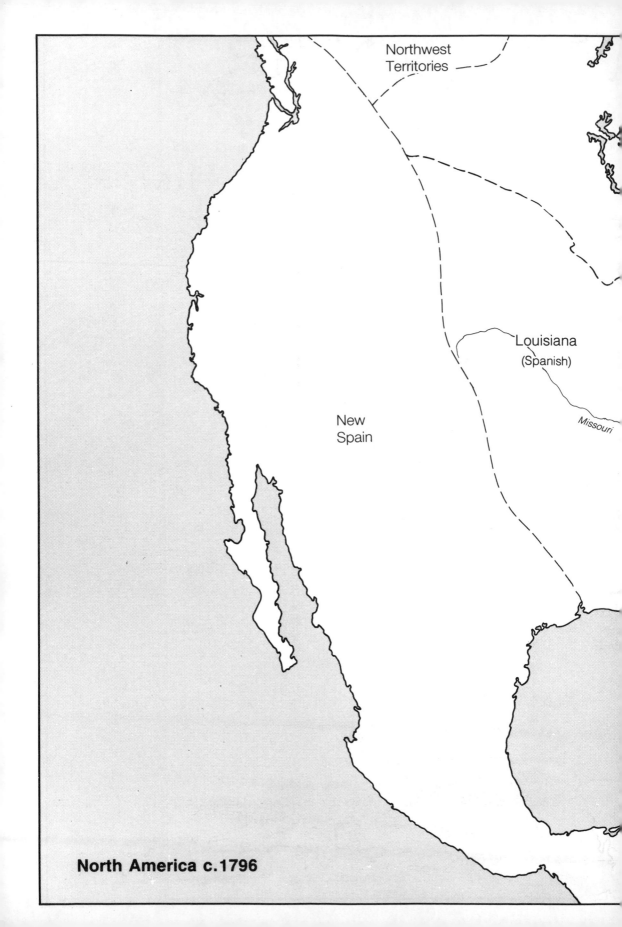

Northwest
Territories

Louisiana
(Spanish)

Missouri

New
Spain

North America c.1796

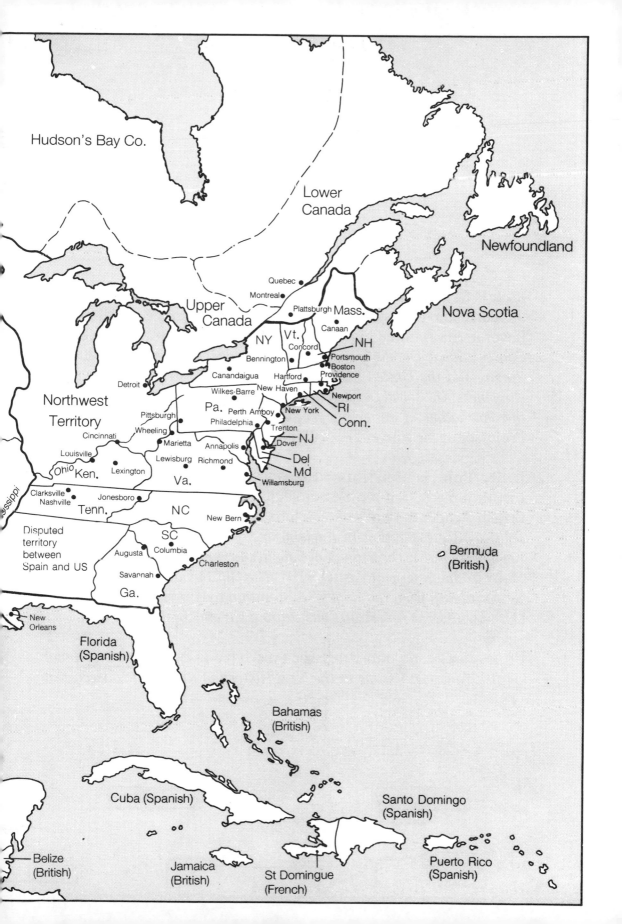

Hudson's Bay Co.

Lower Canada

Newfoundland

Quebec

Montreal

Upper Canada

Plattsburgh   Mass.

Canaan

Nova Scotia

NY   Vt.

Concord

NH

Bennington

Portsmouth

Detroit

Canandaigua   Hartford   Boston   Providence

Wilkes-Barre   New Haven

Northwest Territory

Pa.   Perth Amboy   New York   Newport   RI

Pittsburgh   Philadelphia   Conn.

Wheeling   Trenton   NJ

Cincinnati

Marietta   Annapolis   Dover   Del

Louisville   Lewisburg   Richmond   Md

Ohio   Ken.   Lexington   Va.   Williamsburg

Clarksville   Jonesboro

Nashville   Tenn.   NC

New Bern

Bermuda (British)

Disputed territory between Spain and US

SC   Columbia

Augusta   Charleston

Savannah

Ga.

New Orleans

Florida (Spanish)

Bahamas (British)

Cuba (Spanish)

Santo Domingo (Spanish)

Belize (British)

Jamaica (British)

St Domingue (French)

Puerto Rico (Spanish)

Editors

Jack P. Greene is the author and editor of many books and articles on early modern colonial British America and the American Revolution. Among his recent books are *Peripheries and Center: Constitutional Development in the Extended Polities of the British Empire and the United States, 1607–1788* (1986) and *Pursuits of Happiness: The Social Development of Early Modern British Colonies and the Formation of American Culture* (1988). He is Distinguished Professor at the University of California, Irvine.

J. R. Pole is Emeritus Professor of American History and Institutions, St Catherine's College, Oxford, and a Fellow of the British Academy. Books of which he is the author or editor include *Political Representation in England and the Origins of the American Republic* (1966), *The Pursuit of Equality in American History* (1978), *Paths to the American Past* (1979), *The Gift of Government: Political Responsibility from the English Restoration to American Independence* (1983), and *The American Constitution: For and Against* (1987).

Professor Greene and Professor Pole have also co-edited *Colonial British America: Essays in the New History of the Early Modern Era* (1984).